Seymour Chwast
Graphic Designer
Page 158

Mary Wilshire
Illustrator
Page 394

David Seidman
Comics Editor
Page 546

1988 Artist's Market

Please Note:

The Artist's Market welcomes new listings. If you are a user of freelance design and illustration and would like to be considered for a listing in the next edition, contact the editor by March 1, 1988.

The *Artist's Market* also welcomes submissions of artwork for possible inclusion in the next edition. The policy for submissions is as follows:

(1) artwork must be submitted by a freelance artist or a market who uses freelance work;

(2) the artwork must have been published by one of the markets listed in the book.

If you have material to submit which fits these guidelines, send it to: Editor, Artist's Market, 1507 Dana Ave., Cincinnati, OH 45207.

Distributed in Canada by Prentice Hall of Canada Ltd., 1870 Birchmount Road, Scarborough, Ontario M1P 2J7.

Managing Editor, Market Books Department: Constance J. Achabal

International Standard Serial Number 0161-0546

International Standard Book Number 0-89879-275-4

1988

Artist's Market

Where & How to Publish Your Graphic Art

Edited by
Susan Conner

Assisted by
Mary Tonnies

Cincinnati, Ohio

The Markets

Contents

Appendix

From the Editor

There is a message threading through the 2,500 listings in the *1988 Artist's Market*. The message is that, no matter where you live, there are thousands of opportunities waiting for you in the freelance art market. By submitting your artwork through the mail, you have access to markets not only in your backyard but across the country. With *Artist's Market* at hand, you have no boundaries as a freelance artist.

This fourteenth edition of *Artist's Market* includes more opportunities than ever. As the most comprehensive directory of freelance graphic art opportunities, this edition is the largest yet with 608 pages. Even though our cover says 550 new markets, by press time we had over 700 new listings, each marked with an asterisk (*) so you can locate them easily. We have also updated the listings that appeared last year—there are 54 company name changes, 257 address/phone changes, 217 contact person changes, 246 listings whose art needs have changed and 277 changes in the pay rate.

But *Artist's Market* is more than just a directory of names and addresses. This is a sourcebook containing names of contact persons and their needs, requirements and "inside" information such as tips on a company's current needs. There are also over 65 illustrations which have been sold by freelance artists from all over the country to companies all over the country. Detailed captions explain what made each piece of work successful.

The articles at the front of the book introduce you to the many job areas open to freelance illustrators and designers and give you some fundamental advice on the business of art. "Freelance Opportunities in the Graphic Arts" gives you an overview of the type of markets seeking freelance help and how to approach them. The question of how much to charge for your services as a freelancer is answered in "Fee Setting Basics from Freelance Artists."

Whether you are a beginner or an established professional, you will benefit from the insights given by our 11 Close-up interviews. Such prominent artists and art directors as Seymour Chwast, Stavros Cosmopulos and Eleanor Ettinger provide valuable tips on making initial contacts, presenting your portfolio and establishing a niche in the marketplace.

The Markets section presents a variety of listings suited to many skills. The introductions to these sections give you an overview of each market area and its requirements. You will also find the names of publications that provide either market news or additonal names and addresses of art buyers (but no marketing information). The addresses of these publications are found in the Artists Resource List at the back of the book.

The last section of the book, the Business of Freelancing, guides you through the essentials of handling initial presentations, portfolios, contracts, taxes, recordkeeping and mailing procedures. Refer to the Glossary to find the definition of a term you may not know.

The *Artist's Market* is a tool, providing practical advice and inspiration which can either launch your career or enrich your current endeavors. Now it's up to you to take advantage of these opportunities. I look forward to hearing your successes.

Susan Conner

• *Listings are based on editorial questionnaires and interviews. They are not advertisements (markets do not pay for their listings) nor are listings endorsed by the* Artist's Market *editor.*

• *Listings are verified prior to the publication of this book. If a listing has not changed from last year, then the editor has told us that his needs have not changed—and the previous information still accurately reflects what he buys.*

• *Remember, information in the listings is as current as possible, but art directors come and go; companies and publications move; and art needs fluctuate between the publication of this directory and when you use it.*

• *When looking for a specific market, check the index. A market might not be listed for one of these reasons: 1) It doesn't solicit freelance material, 2) It has gone out of business, 3) It requests not to be listed, 4) It did not respond to our questionnaire, 5) It doesn't pay for art (we have, however, included some nonpaying listings because we feel the final printed artwork could be valuable to the artist's portfolio, 6) We have received complaints about it and it hasn't answered our inquiries satisfactorily.*

• Artist's Market *reserves the right to exclude any listing that does not meet its requirements.*

Using Your Artist's Market

Markets in this book are organized according to their professional category, such as book publishers or magazines. However, artists find that their talents apply to many categories. The following chart will help you locate the markets that are seeking your specialty:

	Advertising agencies	Architectural firms	Art/design studios	Art publishers	Audiovisual firms	Associations & institutions	Book publishers	Businesses	Clip art firms	Fashion	Greeting card companies	Interior design firms	Landscape design firms	Magazines	Newspapers & newsletters	Performing arts	Public relations firms	Record companies	Syndicates
Airbrush artists	●		●				●			●				●					
Animators					●	●		●											
Audiovisual artists	●		●		●	●		●									●	●	
Calligraphers	●					●	●	●	●	●	●			●	●				●
Cartoonists	●					●		●	●		●			●	●				●
Chartists	●	●	●		●														
Filmmakers					●	●		●									●		
Fine artists				●			●		●		●	●		●	●	●			●
Game designers								●			●								
Interior designers		●										●							
Layout artists	●	●			●	●		●		●						●	●	●	
Map makers	●	●	●		●														
Mechanical artists	●	●			●	●		●		●						●	●	●	
Medical illustrators	●				●	●	●							●	●				
Model makers		●	●					●											
Package designers	●		●					●		●									
Poster designers			●	●		●		●		●	●					●	●	●	
Renderers		●			●							●	●						
Retouchers	●		●		●					●							●		
Scientific illustrators	●					●	●							●	●				
Typographers	●		●		●				●									●	

Interpreting the market listings

Listings include information on whom to contact, what type of work is needed, how artists are used, payment method and amount. Note the features illustrated by this sample listing:

contact information	**(1) *BERKMAN & DANIELS MARKETING & COMMUNICATIONS**, 1717 Kettner Blvd., San Diego CA 92111. **(2)** Creative Director: David R. Evans.
description	**(3) (4)** Full-service marketing communications firm that handles advertising and public relations. Clients: real estate, health care, entertainment, financial. Client list provided with an SASE.
type of work	**Needs: (5)** Works with 20 freelance artists/year. **(6)** Assigns 30 jobs/year. Uses artists for design, illustration, brochures, consumer and trade magazine ads, P-O-P displays, mechanicals, retouching, animation, posters and lettering.
how to contact	**First Contact & Terms: (7)** Send query letter with brochure showing art style or resume, tear sheets, photocopies, slides and photographs. **(8)** Samples are filed. Samples not filed are not returned.
reporting time	**(9)** Reports back only if interested.
portfolio information	**(10)** Call or write to schedule an appointment to show a portfolio, **(11)** which should include roughs, original/final art, Photostats, tear sheets, final reproduction/product and photographs.
payment	**(12)** Pays for design by the hour, $50. Pays for illustration by the project, "medium to high-end type fees." **(13)** Considers client's budget, turnaround time and rights purchased when establishing payment.
rights purchased	**(14)** Negotiates rights purchased; rights purchased vary according to project.
	Tips: (15) "We are not a proving ground for budding artists. We look at established artists who appreciate reproduction-quality work. Don't make excuses for work. Be organized and ready before presenting a portfolio. If you don't want me to see something, don't have it in the book."

(1) An asterisk (*) preceding a listing means it is new to this edition. **(2)** Names of contact persons are given in most listings. If not, address your work to the art director or person most appropriate for that field. **(3)** Dates indicating when the market was established are given in this area of the listings only if they are 1986, 1987, 1988. This indicates the firm or publication is new and possibly more open to freelance artists. The risk is sometimes greater when dealing with new companies. So far as we know, all are reputable but some are unable to compete with larger, older companies. Many do survive, however, and become very successful. **(4)** Editorial descriptions and client lists appear to help you slant your work toward that specific business. **(5)** The number or percentage of jobs assigned to freelance artists or the number of artists a market uses gives you an idea of the size of the market. **(6)** Many firms work on assignment only. Do not expect them to buy the art you send as samples. When your style fills a current need, they will contact you. **(7)** If a market instructs you to query, please query. Do not send samples unless that is what they want you to do. **(8)** Many art directors keep samples on file for future reference. If you want your samples returned, include a self-addressed, stamped envelope (SASE) in your mailing package. Include an International Reply Coupon (IRC) if you are mailing to a foreign market. **(9)** Reporting times vary, and some—such as this listing—will only contact you if interested in your work. **(10)** Markets want you to either mail portfolio materials or present them in person. Note whether to call or write for an appointment to show your portfolio. **(11)** The type of samples you include in your portfolio reflect your understanding of the market; inappropriate samples signify a lack of market research. When an art director specifies, as this one does, that you should include final reproduction/product in your presentation, do so. **(12)** Payment terms. **(13)** Markets often negotiate payment terms. Therefore, they do not specify the amount of payment but list the factors they consider when establishing payment. **(14)** Note what rights the market purchases. If several types of rights are listed, it usually means the firm will negotiate. But not always. Be certain you and the art buyer understand exactly what rights you are selling. **(15)** Read the tips added to many of the listings. They give you personalized advice or a view of general market information.

Freelance Opportunities in the Graphic Arts

by Bebe Raupe

Twenty-five years ago, if you told your parents you wanted to be an artist, it meant you were going to eke out a living in that musty garret referred to in all the literature about starving artists. Your parents had reason for concern, but you had few options if you wanted to make a living in art.

Today, though, careers abound in the burgeoning communications world for every sort of visual aptitude and skill. There are thousands of opportunities to use your inspirations, skills and perception as a visual person in graphic arts.

The watercolorist, for example, can turn his brush to freelance book illustration or try to interest a greeting card company in his art style. A realistic figure painter might do ads for a local clothing store or department chain, and find such satisfaction in this work that selling portraits becomes secondary. This sort of crossover—and even changeover—is very common.

Although it requires intelligent handling and an organized approach to get those first assignments, an artist is really only limited by his lack of awareness, by not exploring the avenues that are open in his own backyard—the real estate firm that needs graphics for a new condominium offering, the company that just went public and will need an annual report, the newspaper that is changing its look and needs illustrators for the weekend feature section and so forth. Once you have succeeded at the local level, venture forth and explore the needs of other institutions and firms at the county and state level, and expand from there. (You will find local, state and national contacts in the *Artist's Market* listings.)

Most freelancers will tell you that "breaking in" is difficult and likely to be low-paying at first. Luck plays a part in the game, but word-of-mouth and self-promotion both play a tremendous part in building the artist's freelance business. "The more often your work is seen, the more jobs present themselves," say most artists.

Unlike most other professions, formal credentials usually aren't needed to enter freelance relationships. Demonstrable skills as seen in your portfolio with finished art, drawings and comps (on ideas you'd like to create, and on small jobs you have done) open doors. This is not to say, however, that the knowledge and polish obtained from a post-secondary art education aren't a decided plus. It would be ridiculous to attempt scientific illustration, for example, without a solid background in natural history. Nonetheless, evidence of appropriate ability and art style is by far the most important factor used by art directors in deciding to contract work to an artist.

The growing market

Over the next decade, the number of art-related jobs is expected to grow at a rate equal to that of the general economy, according to the Bureau of Labor Statistics (BLS). Producers of goods, information and services will increasingly stress visual appeal. And self-employed artists will fulfill nearly half of that need, the BLS estimates, through freelance assignments.

Publishers, advertising agencies, retailers, manufacturers, media outlets and the government are said to employ roughly 180,000 artists in some capacity at the present time. However, this sort of data is hard to pin down because many small firms don't answer the BLS or are not queried, and the tally is probably somewhat *under* the real figure.

Bebe Raupe *is a Cincinnati, Ohio-based writer and contributing editor to* The Artist's Magazine, *where this article originally appeared.*

Artists and designers today work freelance or on staff in every type of enterprise, from private industry to government agencies to educational institutions. You would be hard-pressed to find a company or institution in your hometown that doesn't produce a brochure, some ads, signage and so forth. Go to your bookstore or library to find any of the art director's/designer's source books or competition annuals to get a feel for the type of artistic and creative work being produced for clients.

In the most recent Art Directors Club of New York annual (one of the best and most recommended), for example, award-winning works from close to 1,800 clients from all over the country are represented. Artists actually submitted close to 20,000 entries for their clients. And this is only one show out of perhaps 50 major and minor competitions this whole exciting field is involved with. Consider that for every piece submitted, artists worked on many others they didn't think up to snuff to win a creative award—but they were paid for their work.

Earning a living is where I started this piece, and it's important to mention that illustrators and designers are making a good deal more than "just a living." Nationwide staff incomes range from $10,000 to $12,000 annually to start, and many salaries go well over $100,000. A successful freelancer's income is probably commensurate to that.

Getting started

Because formal entry requirements are few, competition for these positions, whether full-time or freelance, is keen. Until a freelance artist establishes a reputation or a steady clientele, he is going to live from assignment to assignment. And to rise above the throng, keeping your portfolio up to date and giving it proper organization geared toward the work you intend doing are imperatives. Perhaps it's an obvious point, but it's one that should be stated: If you want to design logos for television stations, then you must show the television art director some samples of logos.

The following is a breakdown of different categories of freelance work in only some of the illustration, art and design fields. It's a miniguide to show you precisely what these jobs involve, the necessary requirements and background you'll need. You should be able to get going with some of the tips and opinions from art professionals who do this work and love it.

Illustration

Without a doubt, illustration offers the most commercial freelance opportunities. Years ago, most working illustrators served on staff jobs in art studios; but today, 99 per cent go the freelance route. Within this widely diversified specialty lies the chance to beautify books, interpret magazine or newspaper articles, draw for greeting card companies, illustrate posters, create art for catalogs and brochures and depict products in ads and billboards. Where else might your artwork appear? Film strips, audiovisual aids, manufacturers' catalogs, political cartoons and packaging.

Simply put, an illustration is artwork that communicates the ideas, tone and mood imparted by the printed words it accompanies. Illustration is not fine art for two basic reasons: one, it is created on assignment to solve a problem, usually according to strict specifications; two, it is created for reproduction.

Before embarking on the freelance path, you must decide whether you want to create editorial illustrations to illuminate substantive text; advertising illustrations, which sell a product or service; or fashion or other modes of illustration. Award-winning artist Murray Tinkelman, who teaches undergraduate and graduate illustration courses at Syracuse University, offers the view that in today's visually sophisticated world, "the only real difference between editorial and advertising art is that you get paid a great deal more for advertising, but they're very similar in terms of style."

It is true that attitudes about illustration are very open today, but not all styles will find their niche. Nor can you be comforted by the fact that advertisers and publishers need so many dif-

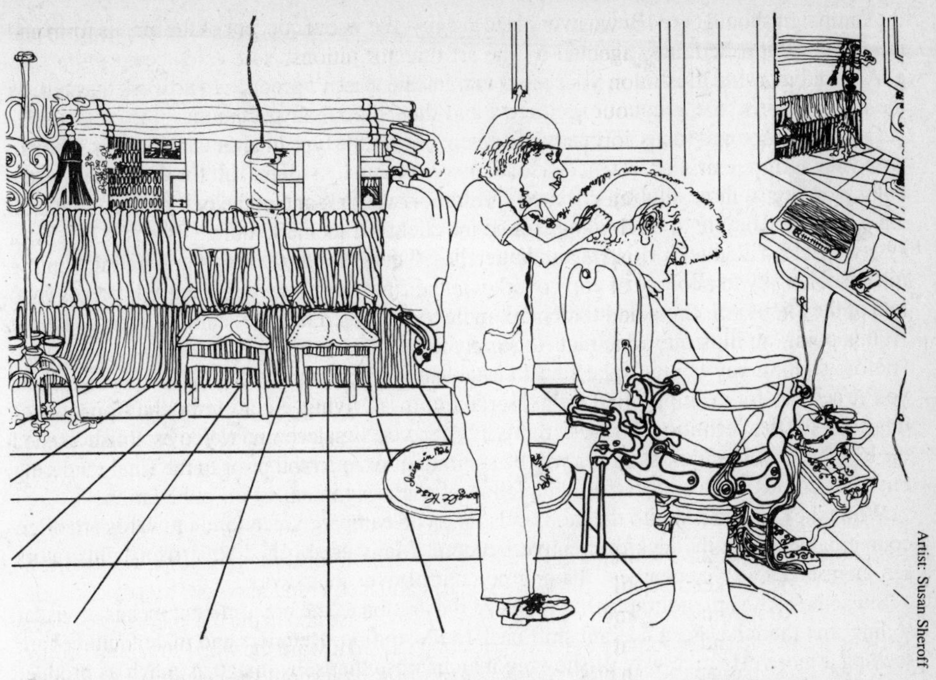

Artist: Susan Sheroff

Susan Sheroff of Farmington, Connecticut, walked into a Greenwich Village barbershop to get change for a meter. "I looked around and asked the barbers if I could sketch them and they agreed." Sheroff eventually entered this pen-and-ink drawing in a competition sponsored by the American National Bank and won a merit award. The shop used the drawing afterward as a promotion piece. The drawing resulted in a greater exposure for Sheroff, which brought new clients.

ferent forms of artwork that no single artist can do them all. Advertising, for example, is a fertile area, but the diversity and competition among clients encourage specialization; so someone will gain a reputation as an airbrush artist excellent with car renditions and another artist will be used solely for his light, cartoony approach in ads and articles, even though he can do other illustrations just as capably. If your best work is pen and ink, this medium limitation may turn into your specialty. Another illustrator may be chosen almost exclusively for his watercolor technique.

While beginners would not be advised to venture out of their regional areas when first building their clientele, the possibilities are expanding for work of all kinds for illustrators in every city. You don't have to live in New York, Los Angeles or Chicago anymore to work as an illustrator or get major clients, Tinkelman says. Since most artists live somewhere outside these three industry and art centers, that's good news. "The business of illustration has changed dramatically over the last five years," according to Tinkelman, because of the development of overnight and same-day delivery services. The illustrator can now work with clients far away and still meet urgent deadlines.

Advertising illustration

Unlike 30 years ago when "product renderers" dominated advertising, today's illustrator must be able to create art that evokes some viewer emotion toward the product. That emotion—be it an automobile's status or the sex appeal of a shampoo—will be determined by the advertising agency and the client. The account executive at a larger advertising agency serves as the liaison between the client and the art director, and it is he who orchestrates the direction the campaign should take. But at every size agency, the visual concept of the art, its form and mood are established and assigned by the art director himself.

As an advertising illustrator, your job is to translate these concepts into artwork that fulfills the art director's, the account executive's and their client's expectations.

Once the tenor and focus of an advertisement are set, the art director can get very specific with your assignment. For instance, a toddler-wear campaign might call for you to do a watercolor painting of three chubby-cheeked children—two girls and one boy—dressed in the client's clothes. They're to be dancing around the client's trademark mule, "Amos," in a fantasy-style field, filled with flowers and butterflies. The upper third of this horizontal painting must be blue sky to allow for a copy overlay in the final ad. You would be given proofs (photos) of the client's clothing and trademark mule to use as a reference, as well as an ad layout. At this point, an illustrator contracts to supply the needed artwork by the agency's deadline. (Before signing any contract, be sure to establish with the art director what specific rights you're selling, for example, first rights, serial rights, all rights, etc. Refer to the Appendix of this book for the definitions of these rights.) When you sign a contract, you establish a schedule by which preliminary sketches will be submitted for approval prior to the final rendering. Payment comes upon successful completion of the assignment or on publication.

While the pay can run into the thousands for an ad campaign, economic rewards are often counterbalanced by the lack of creative freedom. Many established advertising illustrators see themselves as "mechanics" having no control over their work.

Since the 1950s, photography has replaced illustration as the predominant means of visual selling, but there has been a slight shift back to illustration. Retailers and manufacturers are seeking a more effective way of showing merchandise that sells image as much as product. Since the idea behind this form of illustration is to show the product to its advantage, retailers and manufacturers seek illustrators who work in a realistic style.

Although illustrated newspaper ads (chiefly pencil sketches or pen-and-ink renderings) have remained a bastion for illustrators, the number is decreasing every year. On the other hand, direct-mail catalogs have gained increased favor among retailers.

The need for advertising illustration exists nationwide. Any city with one or more newspapers should have an advertising agency or major department store you might approach. Even if your hometown lacks opportunities, keep in mind that overnight mail services and telex machines enable artists to work for major companies and yet live anywhere in the country.

Artist: Barbara Kelley

This pencil drawing is one of a series assigned to illustrator Barbara Kelley of Brooklyn, New York, by Stan Grimes of Flynn & Sabatino of Miamisburg, Ohio. The art director remembered Kelley's unique pencil technique from an ad in the Wall Street Journal and from her promotion page in a creative sourcebook. Kelley worked from thumbnails and completed the project "in a professional and timely manner," according to Grimes, who bought all rights. Kelly now uses the piece in her portfolio.

Artist: Anni Matsick

Illustrator/designer Anni Matsick of State College, Pennsylvania, created this lighthearted pen-and-ink illustration to accompany a poem called "Pickles from My Pockets" in* Clubhouse. *Her instructions for the piece were, "Make it fun!" She binds this piece together with several illustrations of a similar nature and mails them to children's publications as a portfolio.

Editorial illustration

While advertising may be financially rewarding, the majority of freelancers interviewed prefer editorial illustration's aesthetic returns. The artistic latitude more than compensates for the lower pay in their view. Unlike advertising's structured confines, you alone visually interpret a story, following some basic direction from the magazine's art director—such as the illustration's premise, dimension and size, the mood and tone he's after, the medium he prefers, the color limitations and the basic editorial environment in which the story and art will appear.

Opportunities are expanding annually, say experts, thanks to the proliferation of new special-interest magazines. Some 400 new magazines are born each year, while newspapers—attempting to woo readers away from television—are increasingly emphasizing visual appeal. Sunday supplement magazines, which normally publish fifty-two times a year, have constant illustration needs.

If editorial work is your goal, again you have to determine what market your style best suits. Periodicals look for some degree of specialization in an artist's style, something that distinctly smacks of "a man's magazine" or "a health article," for example—something that projects their publication's inherent attitude.

Should your work be more generic, review illustrations used in magazines or newspapers you'd like to work with, emulating techniques and compositions that bring your work closer along their lines. To familiarize yourself with the very best being published, consult the *Art Director's Annual*, the *Illustrators Annual* and *Communication Arts* and *Print* magazines.

The medium you work in can also determine your market. Pen-and-ink drawings, for example, as well as other black-and-white art, are more suited to newspapers than magazines. But newspapers are running much more color work these days, and on occasion, magazines will say that black and white is just what they're after, especially for small art. Payment, preferred mediums and time allocations will vary with every assignment, according to Bill Nelson, who has done illustrations for *TV Guide*, *Time* and *Esquire*, among others.

Once you've targeted publications "in sync" with your style, send their art directors a portfolio—either 35mm slides or 4x5-inch transparencies. Never send originals, since you might not see them again. If you have published work, include tear sheets. "A clean and neat presentation is a must," advises Nelson, "as are business cards. Even if you're just starting out, you should have them."

If you are not within visiting distance, when you get an assignment, the art director will express-mail or telecopy the illustration's layout and specifications to you along with a copy of the manuscript. Sometimes an art director will want something very specific; in those cases, you'll be fulfilling "the human pencil" function many advertising artists perform.

More than likely, however, he'll want you to visually define the article, and then send him preliminary sketches. Once these have been reviewed and one chosen, this sketch (with corrections and suggestions) will be sent back to you for final rendering. This process can stretch out over weeks with a monthly magazine, or it can be compressed into a few days if you're working for a newspaper or a weekly magazine.

Before you begin, however, Nelson believes key details must be negotiated: how much you'll be paid, how long you'll have, and that you retain ownership of all rights and the original artwork.

Payment comes either upon successful completion of the assignment or upon publication and can vary widely according to your market. *The Washington Post Magazine*, for example, pays up to $1,500 for a cover, while *Time* pays $3,500. Obviously, smaller publications pay less, and many times the fee is set in advance.

Book illustration

Book illustration represents much of today's best American art, largely because of the form's permanence and the artistic latitude given freelancers. Recent changes in publishing, however, make it imperative that illustrators conduct themselves as savvy business people since, as one artist put it, "the art end may be glorious, but the business end is ruthless."

Income tax revisions now deny publishers a write-off for books in storage: therefore, every book published today has a shorter shelf life than it would have had seven years ago. As a result, fewer titles are being published each year (50,000 in 1986). In turn, book illustration opportunities are shrinking as publishers are less inclined to take chances on commercially unproven artists.

An artist may earn a fee outright or enter into a royalty agreement. But royalty earnings seem to be dwindling, according to top book people, as books spend less time on the shelves. Yet in today's world of media tie-ins, that same artist could more than recoup royalty losses if his original book renderings were later converted into a film, a videotape or, in the case of children's books, a television cartoon treatment.

To ensure maximum returns, a freelance artist must anticipate such possibilities upfront during contract negotiations. While business complexities can seem overwhelming, this doesn't mean artists with agents are the only ones who can profitably enter the book publishing arena. Veteran illustrators Leo and Diane Dillon have worked together successfully for 30

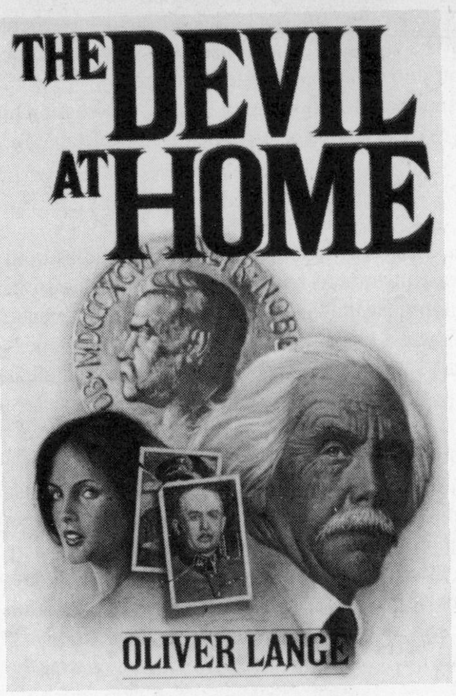

Artist: George Angelini

This jacket illustration by George Angelini of Ossony, New York, was assigned by Paul Scalenghe, art director of Stein & Day Publishers, for a mass market paperback. Scalenghe had worked with Angelini on many projects because of the artist's "great quality, his ability to meet deadlines and being right on target with the illustration." Angelini first read the manuscript, drew a few sketches and comps which Scalenghe reviewed, then completed this oil painting. Angelini received $1,500 for the hardcover rights and $750 for a buyout.

years, chiefly without commercial representation. While they've tried agents, the Dillons found they could garner assignments and handle contracts just as well themselves, with the help of an attorney recommended by the Graphic Artists Guild (for more information, contact The Guild at 30 E. 20th St., New York NY 10003). Much of their "agentless" success can be attributed to this legal consultation; an attorney's assistance—both in reviewing a contract and helping negotiate terms—is essential, the Dillons stress, in order to protect your full rights.

When they began as book illustrators, following stints as advertising and editorial artists, the Dillons compiled a list of publishers using art compatible with their style, then they personally approached the art director of each. The key to a successful book illustration portfolio "is to show (art directors) the format they want to see," says Diane. If you want to do covers, then devise an appropriate illustration and present it in final form, with type set over it—"make it look like a real cover would look." If you aspire to children's picture books, convince the art director you can show action and story progression by preparing a series of three or four finished illustrations, then present them on pages allowing space for text.

Book illustrating isn't the "way to get rich quick," says Leo. The artist on a royalty contract is paid an advance against royalties—which range generally from $1,500 to $10,000—with half paid when the contract is signed, the remainder when the job's complete. Once a book earns back its costs, an artist may receive more royalties, perhaps as much as 10 per cent of the profits, paid in a lump sum every six months. Unfortunately, most books don't hold the promise of this long-range return.

Depending upon how much time an illustration takes, the pay can seem paltry to the number of hours invested. If you've contracted to do 10 illustrations for $750, for instance, and your style requires four days from the initial sketch to the finished rendering, you'd only make $4.69 an hour. But if your style allows two or three completed illustrations a day, you would earn your advance in less than a week.

On a per rendering basis, covers tend to pay better than full book illustrations—anywhere from $450 to $3,000. However, since a cover is a sales device, publishers usually have specific ideas they want followed; therefore, you don't have completely free reign.

Consider the intricacy of your style when undertaking a book assignment, advise the Dillons, since "it can be a long time between halves of an advance." A style that's profitable for covers might not pay off for picture books.

Fashion illustration

A hybrid of advertising and editorial art, fashion illustration comfortably straddles both worlds. Forty years ago, Americans saw fashion illustrations more often than any other form, but, as with all visual sales techniques, photography dealt it a near fatal blow. Now, because of the fashion illustrator's aesthetic approach, there's a resurgence in illustration as retailers and manufacturers struggle to capture the consumer's eye with something unusual and exciting.

Working for a store's advertising department, doing layouts and sketches, is a good way to break into this field. Fred Brenner, an illustrator for 37 years (and who headed the Parsons School of Design's fashion seminar program), estimates that 90 per cent of all fashion illustrations are done for retail advertisers, either inhouse or by freelancers who have knowledge of a store's specific needs. Another good entry job, he says, is with a matrix service which sends drawings of current fashion out every two weeks to stores that can't afford to send buyers to New York. Freelance opportunities also exist in editorial illustration, which calls for interpretative work. Illustrations accompanying articles in trade magazines such as *Women's Wear Daily* and in lifestyle consumer magazines such as *Vogue* and *Gentlemen's Quarterly* feature this approach, which depicts trends.

Generally speaking, fashion illustration pays better than any other form of commercial art, Brenner says; experienced artists may produce four or five figures a day, for which they're paid $150 to $300 each. The competition is brutal, with perhaps only 5,000 fashion illustrators nationwide earning "good money."

If you want to freelance, submit your portfolio to the store's executive in charge of advertising or the art director of a fashion magazine. On-the-job fashion background is needed before embarking as a freelancer.

With experience, it's feasible to do fashion illustration at home, working from an ad layout and the garment (or a photograph of it). Keep in mind, however, that once your style becomes associated with one store, you usually cannot work for any other since your style has become its "look."

Design

While illustrators craft renderings for reproduction, the designer plans the printed page, blending illustrations into an overall design with headlines, body copy, art and/or photography and other elements—creating an integrated whole. The basis of all design is this establishment of order, of making a harmonious design out of disparate parts.

The definition and responsibilities of designers are broad-ranging and even vary from company to company. One designer might be asked to design an entire exhibit of products for a supermarket or for a sales meeting. Groups of designers, for example, were assigned to the Los Angeles Olympics; the Olympic logo (basic visual statement) was worked into myriads of materials, from the stadium floor signs to outside banners to signs for telephones, to publications and stamps. Corporate designers take on the job of corporate image programs for large, modern businesses. ITT, Xerox and IBM, for instance, have led the way for a revolution in corporate image in business, and thousands of designers have been the beneficiaries of such programs in firms of all sizes.

How specific your talents must be depends of course, on the kind of graphic designer you

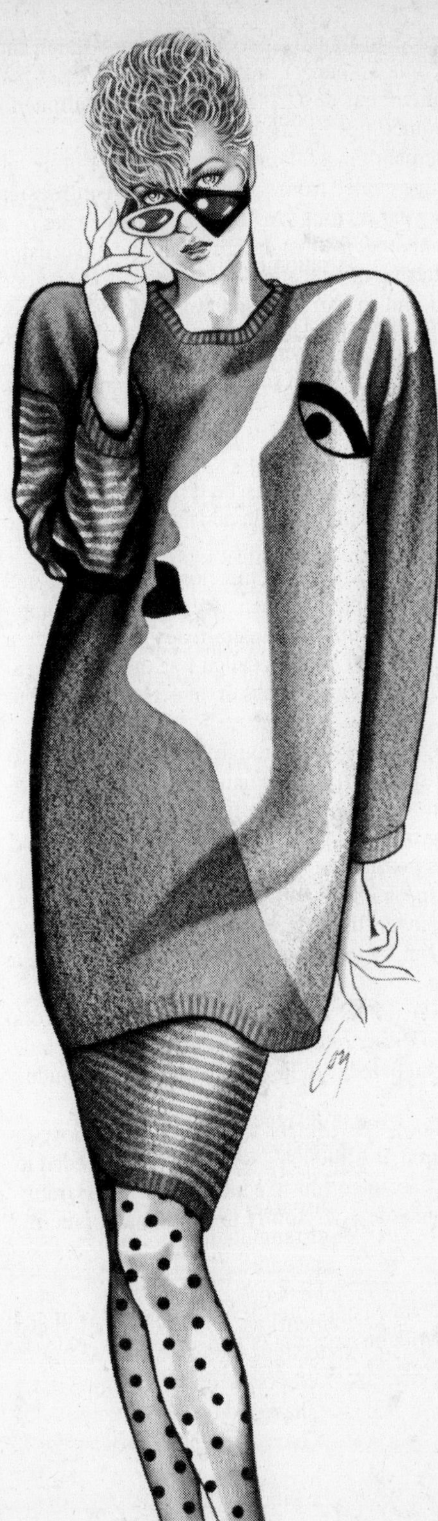

Fashion illustrator Lori Van Overbeke of Racine, Wisconsin, created this newspaper advertisement for Chapman's II, a specialty fashion store. She used pencil, wash and ink to create the piece, in which she wanted to convey "a definite statement on fashion reflecting the store's image and reputation." She first learned about the store at a retailer's advertising convention and then researched their advertising in the Milwaukee Journal, *where the ad ran. Lori was paid $125 for the drawing.*

become. Some designers are excellent, for instance, in annual report and brochure design and are conversant with printers and production people on papers, inks, printing processes and binding materials. Others are weak in these areas but design large spaces or multimedia events. Sometimes the designer specializes; sometimes he doesn't.

Because graphic design is very technical—demanding a full understanding of printing mechanics at one end of the spectrum, and knowledge gained from courses in advertising design at the other—assignments call for either a two-year or four-year art school certificate or a bachelor or fine arts degree from a college or university. Most design firms and advertising agencies also expect their people to have a smattering of education—to have read a few good books, to be able to speak the King's English and to carry oneself well. Maverick types have—and always will—make their way into the field, but lack of education is a real handicap. Many beginners lucky enough to be hired for their raw talents are directed by their supervisors to go to night school to take the missing advertising or design courses.

Mechanical jobs

Many graphic designers begin as mechanical artists, the people who turn the art director's layout into camera-ready art. This entry-level work often proves invaluable because you do and observe so much.

The mechanical artist might order copy to be typeset in the art director's chosen size and style and secure halftones of illustrations and photographs. He then assembles these components according to the dummy layout and pastes them up into camera-ready form, which a lithographer will photograph to make a printing plate. If color is called for, the mechanical artist indicates its position on the layout using either tissue overlays or an acetate film photomask.

Working as a mechanical artist provides designers with a thorough background in reproduction processes, says Irv Swillinger, assistant director/production head of South-Western Publishing in Cincinnati, Ohio. "You learn that there are many ways to achieve the same end," he says, "as well as which ways are the easiest and the least expensive. To be a good designer, you have to know the ins and outs of production."

Meeting deadlines is a prerequisite for doing mechanicals, although the time you have to complete a layout depends largely upon your employer. If you work for a book publisher, you might have several weeks to assemble a project, but for an ad agency, you might only have a few hours.

Some rudimentary knowledge of printing production is also important. Swillinger recommends International Paper's *Pocket Pal* as a good, basic reference. And as the printing business becomes further computerized, "a working knowledge of laser scanning and computers would be a tremendous asset," he says.

"Most mechanical artists come right out of school," Swillinger adds, "hoping to move into a design position after a year or two in production." Although a portfolio is not needed to secure this work, Swillinger suggests presenting "six or so finished mechanicals, preferably ones you've done for a real job, ones that demonstrate your ability to be neat and precise."

A final note

Now it's up to you to unlock the door to the freelance opportunities that exist for your specialty and interests. Find the markets for your artwork on a regular or part-time basis. All you need is tenacity, talent and, quite often, tact to reap the rewards of freelancing.

Fee-Setting Basics for Freelance Artists

by Kate Kelly

"How much should I charge?"

No other question plagues freelancers the way this one does—and small wonder. Setting a fee is a very difficult part of running a business because no two bidding situations are alike. One day you may be up for a job against your toughest competitor; another time you may be bidding for work where you have related, but not direct, experience; on another occasion you may be talking to a client who keeps changing his mind on the project.

All these variables make each pricing situation different and create doubts. What's more, it's sometimes difficult to learn from your mistakes. How do you find out if you lost the job because you asked too much money? And how do you apply what you've learned to future pricing situations? Setting a price on your services is a tough area, but the following guidelines will help.

Establish an hourly rate

No matter what your field or specialty, you need to develop an hourly rate. Though you may ultimately decide to quote a per project, per page, or per illustration price, knowing what your time is worth on an hourly basis is key to setting your fees.

To get started, you need to know what you would earn if you were doing similar work in a staff position. Perhaps you've been working on staff, or know someone who does, and that will give you a typical annual staff salary for your type of work. Now take the annual salary and divide it by 52 (the number of weeks in a year) to get the weekly rate of pay. Next, divide that figure by 40 (the number of hours in a week) to determine the hourly rate for this type of job. Finally take this figure and multiply it by 2.5 in order to determine what a freelancer needs to charge in order to make ends meet. Here is the formula in shorter form:

1. Annual salary ÷ 52 weeks/year = weekly rate
2. Weekly rate ÷ 40 hours/week = hourly pay
3. Hourly pay x 2.5 = hourly rate

Why the 2.5 multiple? The self-employed need a way to compensate for indirect costs including overhead such as rent, business insurance, social security and "down" time—hours devoted to marketing and administration. Profit, of course, must also be a part of this. Direct costs such as stats, mechanicals, typesetting, printing, travel expenses and messengers are generally passed directly to the client, but be sure to clarify beforehand what expenses each client will pay.

Compare your rate

Now that you have a possible hourly figure (the number derived in 3), you need to determine whether or not it is a competitive price. You need to get some idea of what others with similar experience are charging. Many freelancers belong to professional organizations where guidelines are given or where informal discussions at group meetings give you an idea of what is being charged. If you have current clients or know people who hire freelance help,

Kate Kelly *is the author of "How to Set Your Fees and Get Them." She also instructs a course on the subject at the New School, New York City.*

you can also ask what they have paid in the past. Once you know how you compare with the market rate, then you can decide where you want to position yourself. If you have been in the field for several years and have a steady clientele, then you may want to charge on the high side of the market rate. If you are just getting started, then you will probably decide to bill on the low side. Clients may start with you because you are affordable, and you can build up to a higher rate later on.

Presenting your fee

While every freelancer needs an hourly rate from which to estimate prices, many find that clients react poorly to being presented only with this information. Why? The answer lies partly in the fact that your hourly figure (which of course includes your overhead) may sound high to a staff person who may try to quickly compute his own hourly worth (forgetting about your overhead). In addition, the hourly rate also provides the client with no idea what his total costs will be. The company is left wondering, "Well, I wonder how many hours it takes to design an annual report?" Some companies already have a system for price presentation—perhaps per page, per illustration, or per project, and of course, you will want to present your price in a way that is standard for the company.

Whatever the system, or however you choose to present your fee, the price you quote will still be based on your hourly rate. For example, the designer who bids per project (for the overall job), must have a good idea how long it will take to design a logo for a client. If a designer's hourly rate is $40 per hour, and it will take an estimated 15 hours to develop a series of choices for the client and to refine the design that is chosen, then $600 ($40 times 15 hours) will be the price quoted.

Time estimates must obviously be as accurate as possible in order to come up with a fair price, so you need to become proficient at estimating how long a certain type of job will take. Many freelancers find that by noting hours spent on each job in their calendar or on individual job sheets they can learn how much time to allow for certain types of work. If you use the calendar method, you need to total the hours worked at the end of the month. You can tabulate job sheets at the end of each job.

Early considerations

Before you talk money with a client, you'll want to have a clear mind and focus on several things. First of all, never open a negotiation without having seen exactly what the client is talking about. While an in-person meeting is best, distance sometimes makes this difficult, so have them mail you any relevant material (previous ad campaigns, old brochures, last year's annual report, etc.)

Secondly, consider the nature of the people with whom you'll be working. Do they have a clear idea of what they want, or are they the type who will know what they want only after you design what they *thought* they wanted, but now don't want anymore . . . These factors must be considered, because they will make a big difference in how efficient you can be.

What is the job worth to the client?

Ask about the budget. If you can determine what the budget is for a job, then it gives you an overall picture of the project. The artwork for a brochure may be just one small part of the total project, but by learning what the overall budget is, you can determine whether the company is investing heavily in the project, or whether they intend to do a quick-and-easy job on it. Clients often won't reveal budget figures, but if they do, you're way ahead of the game.

You'll also want to evaluate how important the project is to them. If the president requested a specific brochure be created, you're in luck. If the director is trying to get approval for an ad campaign he's discussing with you, then you may be in trouble. You can treat a project more seriously if you know that the company is fully committed and also charge more if it's high priority.

You'll also want to understand how your work is going to be used. With a brochure, ask how many are to be printed, for whom is it intended and for how long do they anticipate using it. With editorial work, you can check on the publication's frequency and circulation. In advertising, you should know where the ad will appear, what size it will be and what circulation is expected over the life of the ad.

What should cost extra

For any business owner, there are certain requests or constraints which merit extra pay. For the self-employed artist, these likely include:

Tight deadlines and holidays. Often the reason an outsider is called to supplement the staff is because the staff is unavailable or overburdened. If you'll be working over a holiday or if the deadline is very tight, you may want to charge more.

The pain-in-the-neck factor. Some people are very difficult to work for. They want the project "yesterday" and keep calling to check on you, or they can't make up their mind what they want. Build in the extra time this takes so you don't feel taken advantage of in the end.

Travel time. If you're working through the mail or if the office is relatively close and you visit the offices only once or twice to pick up information, then travel time is not a major factor. However, if you must go there frequently and you're spending 30 minutes or more in transit, then many freelancers incorporate travel time into their project fee. After all, it is time when you can't work for someone else.

How much are the extras worth? It depends. Sometimes you'll feel that your competition is so tight that you can't afford to bill for more than your straight work time. However, if you aren't desperate for the job or if you know that for some reason they are very likely to select you over the competition, then build in something extra to compensate for your extra efforts. With the pain-in-the-neck factor, it's as simple as estimating how much extra time it will take you to work with them. For a tight deadline or working over a holiday, you might add $2 or $5 to your hourly rate, and charge them a premium by multiplying your hours by the higher hourly rate. Excessive travel time, of course, can be billed for actual time spent.

What rights do you sell?

While rights may not be a major consideration for the graphic artist who designs an annual report which by nature has limited usage, rights can be quite important in other areas where there may be additional income through resale later on.

Ideally, it is best to sell first rights only, and the price you charge will vary according to the exposure the work is getting. For example, an illustrator for a local advertisement will command less money than when he does the art for a national campaign. And should a company decide to take a local campaign national, the illustrator should receive additional compensation.

When a client wants the right to use the work in more than one way, some freelancers have success with selling one-year unlimited nonexclusive rights. This means that the artist can use the art in noncompetitive situations and will be able to show the piece in portfolio review.

However, sometimes the client wants a buy-out of the rights, in which case you'll want to negotiate for two things. First, they should pay more for all rights than for one-time rights (how much depends on what you think the market will bear and how much income you think you'll lose by not maintaining the rights—maybe nothing for a highly specialized item; maybe a lot for an illustration which has a timeless quality). Also, be certain that what you sell in a buy-out is all *reproduction rights*. That still leaves you with the original artwork and the right to display or feature it in your portfolio.

Coming up with a final figure

Once you have all this information in mind, you should be able to come up with a fair estimate of a price for the job. If you intend to give them a project rate, then simply multiply the number of hours it should take you (factoring in extra time for a difficult client, extended travel time, or a high priority project) by your hourly rate and that will give you the project rate. If you plan to charge per illustration, you simply figure the number of hours each item will take you and quote them a figure based on your hours spent times your hourly rate.

Negotiating

In any negotiation, each side needs to feel as though they won a concession in order for it to work out satisfactorily.

If you especially want a specific job (because you need the money, the credit, or an entry into the company), then you'll probably want to put in a conservative bid with the hope that you get the job. Under those circumstances, you'll also be more flexible when the client requests certain concessions.

However, if you've got a good amount of work and don't especially need the job, negotiate a bit high. One negotiating strategy is to ask for a little more than you really want, so that you can give something (a slight drop in price) without losing anything you need to make the job worthwhile. If they pay your higher price, that's terrific. If not, you didn't lose anything you needed to compensate you for the job.

Now (just to get the bad news over first), let's suppose you're not hired for this particular job. You can still profit from the experience by trying to find out what went wrong. Sometimes freelancers assume they lost a job because of the fee they asked, when in reality, the project was shelved or the budget for it was pulled. At the time you learn you didn't get the job, ask what their plans are. If they are working with another artist, see if the client will tell you if the ultimate decision was a price-based one. (Maybe the artist they hired was the nephew of the president.) And remember, too, they still may come back to you. If you're good and you gave them a fair price, they may soon learn there's a reason to pay fair money for good work.

But now let's assume you got the job. Ideally, you should get the first installment of your fee upfront. Then put all you have agreed to (what the job is, what you are to do, what the client is to provide, what expenses are to be paid, when the job is to be completed and when payments are due) in a letter of agreement which you should preferably originate and send to the client to have it signed and returned to you. Then get started!

The Markets

Advertising, Audiovisual & Public Relations Firms

Change has always been a constant in the advertising industry. However, the number of changes that took place in the last year occurred at a pace unknown in the past. The advertising community watched the merger of agency after agency; these unions were necessary to handle the complex and growing requirements of corporate clients.

Because of mergers, the parameters of advertising agencies, audiovisual companies and public relations firms have changed. It used to be that most agencies were full-service, that is, they provided all possible services to create public awareness of a client's products or services—art direction, marketing and media buying (purchasing ad space in publications). Then there was the trend towards specialization, with advertising agencies using independent public relations firms and art/design studios instead of inhouse staff. Now major agencies are buying companies which offer special services so they can again function as full-service agencies. Therefore, artists who have worked with public relations firms in the past probably will find themselves working with a firm who is a subsidiary of an advertising agency or an advertising agency itself.

Another major change, one that affects artists, is the switch from photography to illustration in advertising. Art directors have turned to illustration to recapture an audience saturated with photography. Last year there was an estimated 20 to 30 percent increase in the use of illustration in advertising.

In the wake of all the changes that have taken place, audiovisual firms have become indispensible to the corporate world for the development of slide presentations for employee education, project proposals and progress reports. Audiovisual materials include slide-tape, multi-image (two or more projector shows), multimedia (slide/film/video productions), film, videotape and computer graphics (which are used in preparing charts, graphs and diagrams).

Freelance artists are used by advertising, audiovisual and public relations firms on a regular basis or only when the workload is too heavy for inhouse staff. Since many have reduced or eliminated their staffs, their reliance on freelancers has increased. Usually art directors are faced with a short deadline and require a quick turnaround time. Thus they look for artists with flexibility, speed and a knowledge of print production. Because of the time factor, many art directors prefer to deal with local (within driving distance) artists who can be at hand to make last-minute changes. However, technological advances in long-distance communications now allow instantaneous exchanges.

Since this is a field of visual presentation, you must present yourself professionally—whether it is in person or through the mail. Your portfolio should display your best work in an easy-to-view manner. Gear it as much as possible to the agency's clients or type of clients. If you are mailing the portfolio, call the art director so he can expect to receive your package. Past experience with an ad agency, audiovisual firm or public relations firm is an asset in proving to an art director that you can handle the job. Mention other advertising campaigns you have participated in, noting the extent of your involvement, the client, the art director and your price range. Include roughs, thumbnails and comprehensives that demonstrate your working process from concept to finished work. Audiovisual artists should present 35mm slides, and video artists should submit disks containing examples of their work.

Once the interview is over, be sure to offer 'leave-behinds'—a resume, samples, brochure or business card—so that your style, name and address are available. The art director will contact you when an assignment arises that he feels fits your style.

Names and addresses (but no marketing information) of additional firms can be obtained from the *Standard Directory of Advertising Agencies*, the *Audio Video Market Place*, the *Literary Market Place*, *O'Dwyers Directory of Public Relations Firms* and the *Madison Avenue Handbook*. Read the weeklies *Advertising Age* and *Adweek* to keep current on the changes in the advertising field.

Alabama

J.H. LEWIS ADVERTISING AGENCY INC., Box 3202, Mobile AL 36652. (205)438-2507. Senior Vice President/Creative Director: Larry D. Norris. Ad agency. Clients: retail, manufacturers, health care and direct mail. Buys 15 illustrations/year.

Needs: Works with illustrators and designers. Uses artists for mechanicals and layout for ads, annual reports, billboards, catalogs, letterheads, packaging, P-O-P displays, posters, TV and trademarks.

First Contact & Terms: Prefers southern artists. Query. SASE. Reports in 5 days. No originals returned to artist at job's completion. Payment by hour: $40-80, layout; $30-50, mechanicals. Pays promised fee for unused assigned work.

SPOTTSWOOD VIDEO/FILM STUDIO, 2520 Old Shell Rd., Mobile AL 36607. (205)478-9387. Contact: Manning W. Spottswood. AV/film/TV producer. Clients: industry, education, government and advertising. Produces mainly public relations and industrial films and tapes.

Needs: Assigns 5-15 jobs/year. Artists "must live close by and have experience." Uses approximately 1 illustrator/month. Works on assignment only. Uses artists for illustrations, maps, charts, decorations, set design, etc.

First Contact & Terms: Send resume or arrange interview by mail. Reports only if interested. Pays for design by the hour, $25 minimum; by the project, $150 minimum. Considers complexity of project, client's budget, skill and experience of artist, geographic scope of finished project, turnaround time, rights purchased and quality of work when establishing payment.

Tips: "We are very small and go from project to project—most of them very small."

Arizona

FARNAM COMPANIES, INC., Box 34820, Phoenix AZ 85067-4820. (602)285-1660. Creative Director: Trish Spencer. Inhouse advertising agency—Charles Duff Agency—for animal health products firm. Client sells through distributors to feed stores, tack shops, co-ops, pet stores, horse and cattle industry.

Needs: Works with 3-10 freelance artists/year. Works on assignment only. Uses artists for illustrations for brochures, labels and ads. Especially looks for realism, skill in drawing animals and quick turnaround.

First Contact & Terms: Send query letter with resume and tear sheets to be kept on file. Prefers any type of samples "which clearly show quality and detail of work." Samples not filed are returned only if requested. Reports back only if interested. To show a portfolio, mail original/final art, final reproduction/product and tear sheets. Pays for illustrations by the project, $100 minimum. Considers client's budget, skill and experience of artist, and geographic scope for the finished product when establishing payment. Rights purchased vary according to project.
Tips: "Mail us samples of work. They should be of animals (horses, dogs, cats, cattle and small animals) with rates and time estimates if possible."

FILMS FOR CHRIST ASSOCIATION, 2628 W. Birchwood Circle, Mesa AZ 85202. Contact: Paul S. Taylor. Motion picture producer. Audience: educational, religious and media. Produces motion pictures and videos.
Needs: Works with 1-5 illustrators/year. Works on assignment only. Uses artists for books, catalogs, and motion pictures. Also uses artists for animation, slide illustrations and ads.
First Contact & Terms: Query with resume and samples (photocopies, slides, tear sheets or snapshots). Prefers slides as samples. Samples returned by SASE. Reports in 1 month. Provide brochure/flyer, resume and tear sheets to be kept on file for future assignments. No originals returned to artist at job's completion. Considers complexity of project, and skill and experience of artist when establishing payment.

GILBERT ADVERTISING, LTD., Suite 102, 3216 N. 3rd St., Box 15710, Phoenix AZ 85060. Creative Director: T.R. Gilbert. Specializes in corporate identity; newspaper and magazine ads; brochures, catalogs and catalog sheets; and direct mail programs. Clients: primarily small firms in manufacturing and commercial services.
Needs: Works with 10-20 freelance artists/year. Artists "must be willing to sell all rights to reproduction of artwork for established or agreed-upon fee. We do not deal through artist's agents." Works on assignment only. Uses artists for advertising, brochures, catalogs, mechanicals, retouching, direct mail packages, charts/graphs, AV presentations, lettering and logos.
First Contact & Terms: Send query letter with brochure, resume, business card, slides, photostats, photocopies, photographic prints, and/or tear sheets to be kept on file. Do *not* send original work. Samples not kept on file are returned by SASE. Reports only if interested. Pays for design by the project, $100-1,000 average; for b&w illustration by the project, $50-400 average; for color illustration by the project, $500-2,500 average. Considers complexity of project and client's budget when establishing payment.

PAUL S. KARR PRODUCTIONS, 2949 W. Indian School Rd., Box 11711, Phoenix AZ 85017. (602)266-4198. Contact: Paul Karr. Utah Division: 1024 N. 250 East, Box 1254, Orem UT 84057. (801)226-8209. Contact: Michael Karr. Film producer. Clients: industrial, business, educational, TV and cable.
Needs: Occasionally works with freelance filmmakers in motion picture and video projects. Works on assignment only.
First Contact & Terms: Advise of experience and abilities.
Tips: "If you know about motion pictures or are serious about breaking into the field, there are three avenues: 1) have relatives in the business; 2) be at the right place at the right time; or, 3) take upon yourself the marketing of your idea, or develop a film idea for a sponsor who will finance the project. Go to a film or video production company, such as ourself, and tell them you have a client and the money. They will be delighted to work with you on making the film. Work, and approve the various phases as it is being made. Have your name listed as the producer on the credits. With the knowledge and track record you have gained you will be able to present yourself and your abilities to others in the film business and to sponsors."

***MEDIA PEOPLE, INC.**, 6736 E. Avalon Dr., Scottsdale AZ 85251. (602)941-8701. Executive Producer/Director: Janyce Brisch-Kanaba. Audiovisual firm. "Media People, Inc. specializes in corporate communications. We assist corporations in producing creative marketing, sales and public relations projects. An area of our expertise is the production and distribution of broadcast and cable network television programming."

The asterisk before a listing indicates that the listing is new in this edition. New markets are often the most receptive to freelance submissions.

Needs: Works with 25 freelance artists/year. Assigns 100 jobs/year. Uses artists for design, illustration, animation and logos.
First Contact & Terms: Send brochure and slides. Samples are filed. Reports back within months. Write to schedule an appointment to show a portfolio or mail photostats. Pays for design by the hour, $30-50. Pays for illustration by the hour, $20-40. Considers complexity of project, client's budget and rights purchased when establishing payment.

PHILLIPS-RAMSEY, 829 N. 1st Ave., Phoenix AZ 85003. (602)252-2565. Senior Art Director: David Robb. Ad agency. Clients: savings and loan, racetrack, hotel, restaurant, high-tech, public utility, consumer goods, medical, home builders. Client list provided for SASE.
Needs: Works on assignment only. Uses artists for illustration, photography and production.
First Contact & Terms: Send brochure to be kept on file. Reports only if interested. Pays by the project. Considers complexity of the project, client's budget, geographic scope for the finished product, turnaround time and rights purchased when establishing payment. Buys all rights; "Our agency only works on a buy-out basis."

THE PRODUCERS, INC., 1095 E. Indian School Rd., Phoenix AZ 85014. (602)279-7767. President: Judi Victor. Ad agency and audiovisual firm. Clients: developers, financial industry, computer industry, retailers, restaurants, builders and government.
Needs: Works with 20-25 freelance artists/year. Uses artists for layout and design, illustration, photography, videography, airbrush, cartooning, animation and calligraphy. "Expediency, accuracy, creativity and ability to work with type and design simultaneously are especially important."
First Contact & Terms: Send query letter with brochure and samples to be kept on file. Samples not filed are returned. Reports within 2 weeks. Write for appointment to show portfolio, which should include tear sheets, comps, photostats or actual material (brochures, etc.) Pays by the hour. Considers complexity of the project, client's budget, skill and experience of artist and turnaround time when establishing payment. Buys all rights.
Tips: "Always write first, then follow up with a call for an appointment. Send samples if you feel it will help give you the edge over the many other artists we interview constantly."

JOANNE RALSTON & ASSOCIATES, INC., 3003 N. Central, Phoenix AZ 85012. (602)264-2930. Vice President: Marilyn Hinkins. PR firm. Clients: financial institutions; real estate developers/homebuilders; industrial, electronics, manufacturing firms; hospital; resort hotels.
Needs: Works with freelance illustrators and designers. Uses artists for brochures/flyers. Selects freelancers based on needs, cost, quality and ability to meet deadlines.
First Contact & Terms: Send flyers/brochures and ads to be kept on file. No originals returned to artist at job's completion. Request an appointment to show a portfolio. Negotiates payment based on client's budget, amount of creativity required from artist, where work will appear, artist's previous experience/reputation and ability to meet deadlines.

Arkansas

ADI ADVERTISING/PUBLIC RELATIONS, Box 2299, Ft. Smith AR 72902. President: Asa Douglas. Ad agency/PR. Clients: retail, personal service, small manufacturing, political.
Needs: Assigns 150-200 freelance jobs/year. Regional artists only, within two-days mail time. Works on assignment only. Works with 2-3 freelance illustrators and 5-10 freelance designers/month. Uses artists for consumer and trade magazines, billboards, brochures, catalogs, newspapers, stationery, signage and posters.
First Contact & Terms: Send brochure showing art style. Samples not kept on file are returned by SASE. Reports only if interested. Write to schedule an appointment to show portfolio, which should include roughs, original/final art, final reproduction/product and photographs. Pays for design by the hour, $10-100; pays for illustration by the hour, $25-300. Considers complexity of project, client's budget, skill and experience of artist and rights purchased when establishing payment. Buys all rights.
Tips: "Creative needs are satisfied with unusual, often unknown, ideas. There is a need for creative thinking on paper that can be added to a complete campaign. Show complete scope of your ability to work from production through design."

MANGAN RAINS GINNAVEN HOLCOMB, 911 Savers Federal Bldg., Little Rock AR 72201. Contact: Steve Mangan. Ad agency. Clients: recreation, financial, consumer, industrial, real estate.
Needs: Works with 5 designers and 5 illustrators/month. Assigns 50 jobs and buys 50 illustrations/year. Uses artists for consumer magazines, stationery design, direct mail, brochures/flyers, trade magazines and newspapers. Also uses artists for illustrations for print materials.

First Contact & Terms: Query with brochure, flyer and business card to be kept on file. SASE. Reports in 2 weeks. Call or write to schedule an appointment to show a portfolio, which should include final reproduction/product. Pays for design by the hour, $42 minimum; all fees negotiated.

California

ATARI CORP., 1196 Borregas Ave., Sunnyvale CA 94086. Director of Creative Services: M. Stevens. Computer and games manufacturer.
Needs: Works with 6 or more freelance artists/year. Local artists only. Works on assignment only. Uses freelance artists for design, illustrations, brochures, catalog, books, mechanicals, retouching, posters, press releases, motion pictures, charts/graphs and advertisements. "Artist must be talented in his or her field and must be deadline oriented."
First Contact & Terms: Send query letter with brochure showing art style and tear sheets. Reports only if interested. Pays for design by the hour, $200-2,000. Pays for illustration by the hour, $200-2,500. Considers complexity of project and client's budget when establishing payment. Buys all rights.
Tips: Looks for "generally fine detail. Subject matter depends upon the project. Software can cover space games, adventure games, fairy tales." A common mistake freelancers make in presenting a portfolio is "lack of subject variety."

***VICTORIA BASLER & ASSOCIATES**, 48 S. Raymond Ave., Pasadena CA 91105. (818)793-3015. Managing Director: Eva Marie Thompson. Ad agency. "We are a full-service advertising agency providing collateral, brochures, print, radio and television production and media. We also have public relations and marketing departments." Clients: car rental, fashion, banks, computers, medical, nonprofit organizations. Client list provided upon request.
Needs: Works with 10-20 freelance artists/year. Assigns 10 jobs/year. Prefers local artists. Works on assignment only. Uses artists for design, illustration, brochures, catalogs, newspapers, consumer and trade magazines, mechanicals, retouching, billboards, posters, lettering and advertisements.
First Contact & Terms: Send query letter with resume. Samples are filed, "or if artist wishes," returned by SASE. Reports back within 2 weeks. Write to schedule an appointment to show a portfolio. Pays for design by the hour, $10-20. Pays for illustration by the project, $50 minimum. Considers complexity of project, client's budget, turnaround time and skill and experience of artist when establishing payment. Rights purchased vary according to project.
Tips: "Save time by not calling first, but simply writing a letter and/or resume to agency. When freelance artists call, we have our receptionist request a letter/resume."

***MICHAEL BAYBAK AND COMPANY, INC.**, 9033 Wilshire Blvd., Penthouse, Beverly Hills CA 90211. (213)276-4660. Vice President-Advertising: George Duggan. Ag agency and public relations firm. "We are a public relations and advertising/marketing firm specializing in financial media and clients. We produce corporate information brochures, annual reports, etc. Clients: financial arena clients—money managers, newsletter writers, investment advisors and public companies.
Needs: Works with 3 freelance artists/year. Assigns 8-10 jobs/year. Prefers local artists. Works on assignment only. Uses artists for design, brochures, mechanicals, retouching, direct mail packages, logos and charts/graphs.
First Contact & Terms: Send query letter with brochure or resume and photographs. Samples are filed. Samples not filed are returned only if requested. Reports back within 30 days. Write to schedule an appointment to show a portfolio, which should include photographs. Pays for design by the hour, $10-20; by the project, $100-1,500. Pays for illustrations by the hour, $30-120; by the project, $100-1,500. Considers client's budget, turnaround time and skill and experience of artist when establishing payment. Rights purchased vary according to project.

BEAR ADVERTISING, 1424 N. Highland, Hollywood CA 90028. (213)466-6464. President: Richard Bear. Clients: fast food enterprises, sporting goods firms and industrial. Assigns 50-100 jobs/year.
Needs: Works with 1-2 illustrators and 2 designers/month. Local artists only. Uses artists for illustrations for annual reports, design of direct mail brochures, mechanicals and sign design.
First Contact & Terms: Call for interview. No originals returned. Negotiates pay.

***ALEON BENNETT & ASSOC.**, Suite 212, 13455 Ventura Blvd., Van Nuys CA 91423. President: Aleon Bennett. Public relations firm.
Needs: Works with 2 freelance artists/year. Works on assignment only. Uses freelance artists for press releases and advertisements.
First Contact & Terms: Send query letter. Samples are not filed. Samples not filed are not returned. Does not report back.

***BERKMAN & DANIELS MARKETING & COMMUNICATIONS**, 1717 Kettner Blvd., San Diego CA 92111. Creative Director: David R. Evans. Full-service marketing communications firm that handles advertising and public relations. Clients: real estate, health care, entertainment, financial. Client list provided with a SASE.
Needs: Works with 20 freelance artists/year. Assigns 30 jobs/year. Uses artists for design, illustration, brochures, consumer and trade magazine ads, P-O-P displays, mechanicals, retouching, animation, posters and lettering.
First Contact & Terms: Send query letter with brochure showing art style or resume, tear sheets, photostats, photocopies, slides and photographs. Samples are filed. Samples not filed are not returned. Reports back to the artist only if interested. Call or write to schedule an appointment to show a portfolio, which should include roughs, original/final art, photostats, tear sheets, final reproduction/product and photographs. Pays for design by the hour, $50. Pays for illustration by the project, "medium to high-end type fees." Considers client's budget, turnaround time and rights purchased when establishing payment. Negotiates rights purchased; rights purchased vary according to project.
Tips: "We are not a proving ground for budding artists. We look at established artists who appreciate reproduction quality work. Don't make excuses for work. Be organized and ready before presenting a portfolio. If you don't want me to see something don't have it in the book."

RALPH BING ADVERTISING CO., 16109 Selva Dr., San Diego CA 92128. (619)487-7444. President: Ralph S. Bing. Ad agency. Clients: industrial (metals, steel warehousing, mechanical devices, glass, packaging, stamping tags and labels), political, automotive, food and entertainment.
Needs: Local artists only. Works on assignment only. Uses artists for consumer and trade magazines, brochures, layouts, keylines, illustrations and finished art for newspapers, magazines, direct mail and TV.
First Contact & Terms: "Call first; arrange an appointment if there is an existing need; bring easy-to-present portfolio. Provide portfolio of photocopies and tear sheets, and client reference as evidence of quality and/or versatility." Reports only if interested. No original work returned to artist at job's completion. Pays by the hour, $5-50 average; by the project, $10 minimum. Considers complexity of project and client's budget when establishing payment.

***COAKLEY HEAGERTY**, 122 Saratoga, Santa Clara CA 95051. (408)249-6242. Art Director: Bob Peterson. Full-service ad agency. Clients: consumer, high-tech, banking/financial, insurance, automotive, real estate, public service. Client list provided upon request.
Needs: Works with 100 freelance artists/year. Assigns 500 jobs/year. Works on assignment only. Uses freelance artists for illustration, retouching, animation, lettering, logos and charts/graphs.
First Contact & Terms: Send query letter with brochure showing art style or resume, slides and photographs. Samples are filed. Samples not filed are returned by SASE. Does not report back. Call to schedule an appointment to show a portfolio. Pays for illustration by the project, $600-5,000. Considers complexity of project, client's budget, skill and experience of artist and rights purchased when establishing payment. Rights purchased vary according to project.

***COPY GROUP ADVERTISING**, Box 315, Encino CA 91316. Contact: Len Miller. Clients: resorts, travel spots, vacation areas and direct mail.
Needs: Uses artists for cartoons, illustrations, spot drawings and humorous sketches. "Artists with experience in book publishing, advertising and greeting cards would probably have the skills we're looking for."
First Contact & Terms: Send a small sampling of material for review. Prefers photocopies as samples; *do not send original work.* Reports in 3 days.

CUNDALL/WHITEHEAD/ADVERTISING INC., 3000 Bridgeway, Sausalito CA 94965. (415)332-3625. Contact: Alan Cundall. Ad agency.
Needs: Works with 6 designers/month. Uses artists for consumer magazines, stationery design, direct mail, slide shows, brochures/flyers, trade magazines and newspapers. Also uses artists for layout, paste-up and type spec.
First Contact & Terms: Send query letter and resume to be kept on file for future assignments. No originals returned to artist at job's completion. Pays for design by the hour, $35 minimum. Considers budget and complexity of project when establishing payment.
Tips: "Seek the counsel of a top agency art director as to the merits of your portfolio before seeing other agencies. Send resume and letter. We are besieged by 6 calls a week to see portfolios. We can't." Looks for "originality, versatility, ability to do direct mail and willingness to do grungy, all-type mechanicals, too."

DIMON & ASSOCIATES, Box 6489, Burbank CA 91510. (818)845-3748. Art Director: Bobbie Polizzi. Ad agency/printing firm. Serves clients in industry, finance, computers, electronics, health

care and pharmaceuticals.
First Contact & Terms: Send query letter with tear sheets, original art and photocopies. SASE. Provide brochure, flyer, business card, resume and tear sheets to be kept on file for future assignments. Considers complexity of project, turnaround time, client's budget, and skill and experience of artist when establishing payment.

DJC & ASSOCIATES, 6117 Florin Rd., Sacramento CA 95823. (916)421-6310. Owner: Donna Cicogni. Ad agency. Assigns 120 jobs/year.
Needs: Works with 1 illustrator/month. Local artists only. Works on assignment only. Uses artists for consumer and trade magazines, stationery design, direct mail, TV, brochures/flyers and newspapers.
First Contact & Terms: Send query letter with brochure showing art style or resume and samples. Samples not kept on file are returned by SASE. Reports in 1 week. Call to schedule an appointment to show a portfolio which should include original/final art, final reproduction/product, etc. No originals returned to artist at job's completion. Negotiates pay.

ESTEY, HOOVER ADVERTISING AND P.R., INC., Suite 225, 3300 Irvine Ave., Newport Beach CA 92660. (714)549-8651. Creative Director: Art Silver. Clients: consumer, financial, real estate, industrial and medical.
Needs: Works on assignment only. Wants highly talented professional illustrators, but will consider serious "up and coming" talent. Uses freelance artists for ads, magazine, newspaper, TV, AV, brochures, catalogs, posters, annual reports, storyboards. Likes "thinking, contributing illustration."
First Contact & Terms: Call for appointment or send "head sheet"—not originals. Reports only if interested. Prefers to see original material and published samples; will expect costs and price at time of viewing. Pays $50-5,000/project, net 30 days, or ongoing. Considers complexity of project, client's budget, skill and experience of artist, geographic scope of finished project and deadline when establishing payment.

***EXPANDING IMAGES**, B-105, 14 Hughes, Irvine CA 92718. (714)770-2342. President: Robert Denison. Audiovisual firm. Clients: mixed.
Needs: Works with 6 freelance artists/year. Uses artists for graphics, photography, illustration and design.
First Contact & Terms: Works on assignment only. Send samples to be kept on file. Prefers tear sheets as samples. Samples not filed are returned by SASE only if requested. Reports only if interested. Pays by the project. Considers client's budget and skill and experience of artist when establishing payment. Buys all rights.

GOAL PRODUCTIONS, 2027 N. Lake Ave., Alta Dena CA 91001. (213)797-7668. Executive Producer: Jack Oswald. Film/TV producer. Serves clients in marketing, industry and education. Produces motion pictures, videotapes, slidefilms and filmstrips.
Needs: Assigns 0-10 jobs/year. Artists "must be experienced and have reference from a first hand associate." Uses 1 animator/month and 1 designer/year. Works on assignment only. Uses artists for "productions that our basic staff of five or six cannot handle. Usually sound or camera assistants or grips."
First Contact & Terms: Send resume or query letter and arrange interview by mail. Send samples "only on request." Samples returned by SASE if not kept on file. Reports in 1 month. Payment varies with each client's budget. Original artwork returned to artist "depending on the contract we are working on." Negotiates rights.

HANNA-BARBERA PRODUCTIONS INC., 3400 Cahuenga Blvd., Hollywood CA 90068. (213)851-5000. Producer: Harry Love. TV/motion picture producer. Clients: TV networks. Produces animation and motion pictures.
Needs: Uses artists for animation and related artwork as needed. Uses mostly local artists.
First Contact & Terms: Provide resume to be kept on file for future assignments.

***DEKE HOULGATE ENTERPRISES**, Box 7000-371, Redondo Beach CA 90277. (213)540-5001. Owner: Deke Houlgate. "Our main specialty is publicity; sports promotion, automotive industry provide most clientele. We do very little brochure or sales promotion work." Clients: sports and event promotion companies, automotive and specialty products. Client list provided with a SASE.
Needs: Works with 2 freelance/artists/year. Assigns 6-12 jobs/year. Uses artists for design, illustration, magazines, retouching and press releases.
First Contact & Terms: Send query letter with brochure. Samples are sometimes filed. Samples not filed are returned by SASE. Reports back within 2 weeks. Write to schedule an appointment to show a portfolio. Pays artist's own rate. "I don't negotiate. Either budget covers artist's rate, or we can't use." Considers client's budget when establishing payment. Rights purchased vary according to project.

HUBBERT ADVERTISING AND PUBLIC RELATIONS CO., INC, 3198-M Airport Loop, Costa Mesa CA 92626. Senior Art Director: Chris Klopp. Ad agency. Clients: real estate and miscellaneous (all product, service).
Needs: Works with 5-10 freelance artists/year. Local artists only (southern California). Uses artists for line art/paste-up, advertising collateral illustration, b&w and 4-color; and layout comps. Especially seeks professionalism (marker skills); efficiency (clean); and deadline awareness (fast turnaround).
First Contact & Terms: Send query letter with resume and samples to be kept on file. Accepts any kind of copy that is readable as samples. Samples not filed are returned by SASE. Reports back only if interested. Write for appointment to show portfolio. Pays by the hour, $10-35 average. Pays in 60 days. Considers complexity of the project, client's budget and turnaround time when establishing payment. Rights purchased vary according to project.

WARREN MILLER ENTERPRISES, 505 Pier Ave., Hermosa Beach CA 90254. (213)376-2494. Owner: Warren Miller. Produces sports documentaries, commercials, television format films and video cassettes for home use.
Needs: Works with 1 ad illustrator and 1 advertising designer/year. Works on assignment only. Uses artists for direct mail brochures, magazine ads and posters.
First Contact & Terms: Send query letter with samples (original sports illustration—skiing, sailing, windsurfing, etc.) or write for interview. Reports within 2 weeks. Buys nonexclusive rights. Samples returned by SASE. Provide resume to be kept on file for future assignments. "We pay by the project and since they range from brochures to full color film posters, it is impossible to give a fair range. Some of these are complicated; some already laid out and need only finished art." Considers complexity of project and skill and experience of artist when establishing payment.
Tips: There is "less 'standard' work and a trend toward contemporary, avant-garde art in our area of business. We prefer to work with artists who have done sports illustrations and recreation-oriented art, but we respond to great talent. Please send some kinds of samples and background information on assignments."

***MOOSE COMMUNICATIONS**, Box 5188, Bear Valley CA 95223. (209)753-6210. Producer: Doreen Nagle. Audiovisual firm. "We are a full-service media firm specializing in film and video production for training aids, promotional features, TV, sales aids, marketing, home distribution. We are also experienced in print and radio media. We serve all types of clients who need our services."
Needs: Works with 5 freelance artists/year. Assigns 12 jobs/year. Uses artists for design, illustration, brochures, consumer and trade magazines, P-O-P displays, retouching, animation, direct mail packages, press releases, motion pictures, lettering, logos, charts/graphs and advertisements.
First Contact & Terms: Send query letter with resume, tear sheets, Photostats, photocopies, slides and photographs. Samples are filed. Samples not filed are returned by SASE. Reports back within 2 weeks only if interested. Write to schedule an appointment to show a portfolio or mail "any samples." Pays for design and illustration by the hour, $50 minimum; by the project, $150 minimum; by the day, $300 minimum. Considers complexity of project, client's budget, skill and experience of artist, how work will be used and rights purchased when establishing payment. Rights purchased vary according to project.
Tips: Artists need "professionalism, understanding of video production process."

***ON-Q PRODUCTIONS, INC.**, 618 E. Gutierrez St., Santa Barbara CA 93103. President: Vincent Quaranta. Audiovisual firm. "We are producers of multi-projector slide presentations. We produce computer-generated slides for business presentations." Clients: banks, ad agencies, R&D firms and hospitals.
Needs: Works with 10 freelance artists/year. Assigns 50 jobs/year. Uses artists for illustration, retouching, animation and lettering.
First Contact & Terms: Send query letter with brochure or resume, and slides. Samples are filed. Samples not filed are returned by SASE. Reports back only if interested. Write to schedule an appointment to show a portfolio, which should include original/final art and slides. Pays for design by the hour, $20 minimum, or by the project, $100 minimum. Pays for illustration by the hour, $20 minimum or by the project, $100 minimum. Considers complexity of project, client's budget, turnaround time and skill and experience of artist when establishing payment.
Tips: "Artist must be *experienced* in computer graphics and on the board. The most common mistake freelancers make are "poor presentation of a portfolio (small pieces fall out, scratches on cover acetate) and they do not know how to price out a job."

PALKO ADVERTISING, INC., Suite 207, 2075 Palos Verdes Dr. N., Lomita CA 90717. (213)530-6800. Account Services: Judy Kolosvary. Ad agency. Clients: business-to-business, retail and high-tech.
Needs: Uses artists for layout, illustration, paste-up, mechanicals, copywriting and P-O-P displays.

Produces ads, brochures and collateral material.
First Contact & Terms: Prefers local artists. Send query letter with brochure, resume, business card and samples to be kept on file. Write for appointment to show portfolio. Accepts tear sheets, photographs, photocopies, printed material or slides as samples. Samples not filed returned only if requested. Reports back only if interested. Pays for design by the hour, $15-30. Pays for illustration by the hour, $15-30, or by the project, $50-1,500. Negotiates rights purchased.

***PLANSKY HIGH PUBLIC RELATIONS**, Murphy Sq., #210, 111 W. Evelyn Ave., Sunnyvale CA 94086. (408)773-8000. Account Manager: Marina Donovan. Public relations firm. "We are a full-service public relations firm, specializing in high-tech and business services clients." Client list provided upon request.
Needs: Works with 10 freelance artists/year. Assigns 10 jobs/year. Works on assignment only. Uses artists for design, illustration, brochures, press releases and logos.
First Contact & Terms: Send query letter with brochure or resume, tear sheets, Photostats, photocopies, slides and photographs. Samples are filed. Samples not filed are not returned. Reports back to the artists only if interested. Write to schedule an appointment to show a portfolio. Pays for design and illustration by the project, $35. Considers complexity of project and client's budget when establishing payment. Rights purchased vary according to project.
Tips: "Send samples of your best work."

***THE RUSS REID CO.**, Suite 600, 2 N. Lake Ave., Pasadena CA 91101. (818)449-6100. Contact: Art Director. Ad agency. Clients: nonprofit organizations; client list provided upon request.
Needs: Uses freelance artists for trade magazines, direct mail, brochures, posters and newspapers.
First Contact & Terms: Arrange interview to show portfolio. Works on assignment basis only. Negotiates payment according to client's budget; "whether by the hour, project or day depends on job."

ROUNDTABLE FILMS, 113 N. San Vicente Blvd., Beverly Hills CA 90211. Advertising Manager: Mark Sherman. Audiovisual firm. Clients: Fortune 100 companies.
Needs: Works with 10-20 freelance artists/year. Prefers local artists. Works on assignment only. Uses artists for design, illustrations, brochures, catalog, books, magazines, newspapers, P-O-P displays, mechanicals, retouching, animation, direct mail packages, motion pictures, logos and advertisements. Artists should have "creativity, good listening skills, realistic idea of their worth in regard to what the market will bear."
First Contact & Terms: Send query letter with samples. Samples not filed are returned only if requested. Reports back within 10 days. Call or write to schedule an appointment to show portfolio, which should include thumbnails, roughs, original/final art and final reproduction/product. Pays for design by the hour, $35; by the project, $100; by the day, $240. Considers complexity of project, client's budget, skill and experience of artist, how work will be used and turnaround time when establishing payment. Rights purchased vary according to project.
Tips: "Show me how you will help me succeed in my job; help the company generate sales; and do it cost efficiently. Anyone that can prove those three facts will usually go to work for me."

RICHARD SIEDLECKI DIRECT MARKETING,Suite C-170, 2674 E. Main St. Ventura CA 93003-2899. (805)658-7000. Direct Marketing Consultant: Richard Siedlecki. Consulting agency. Clients: industrial, publishers, associations, air freight, consumer mail order firms, and financial. Client list provided for SASE.
Needs: Assigns 15 freelance jobs/year. Works with 2 freelance designers/month. Works on assignment only. Uses artists for consumer and trade magazines, direct mail packages, brochures, catalogs and newspapers.
First Contact & Terms: Artists should be "experienced in direct response marketing." Send query letter with brochure, resume and business card to be kept on file. Reports only if interested. Pays by the hour, $25 minimum; by the project, $250 minimum. Considers complexity of project and client's budget when establishing payment. "All work automatically becomes the property of our client."
Tips: Artists "must understand (and be able to apply) direct mail/direct response marketing methods to all projects: space ads, direct mail, brochures, catalogs."

VIDEO RESOURCES, Box 18642, Irvine CA 92713. (714)261-7266. Producer: Brad Hagen. Audiovisual firm. Clients: automotive, banks, restaurants, computer, transportation and energy.
Needs: Works with 8 freelance artists/year. Southern California artists only with minimum 5 years of experience. Works on assignment only. Uses artists for graphics, package comps, animation, etc.
First Contact & Terms: Send query letter with brochure showing art style or resume, business card, Photostats and tear sheets to be kept on file. Samples not filed are returned by SASE. Considers complexity of the project and client's budget when establishing payment. Buys all rights.

WANK, WILLIAMS & NEYLAN, 401 Burgess Dr., Menlo Park CA 94025. (415)323-3183. Art Director: Alvin Joe. Ad agency. Clients: restaurants, public transit, financial and industrial accounts, including electronics.

Needs: Works with 10 illustrators/month. Local artists primarily. Uses freelance artists for billboards, trade magazines, direct mail, P-O-P displays, brochures, catalogs, posters, signage, newspapers and AV presentations.

First Contact & Terms: Query with resume of credits. Works on assignment only. Payment depends on individual job.

***DANA WHITE PRODUCTIONS, INC.**, 2623 29th St., Santa Monica CA 90405. (213)450-9101. Owner/Producer: Dana C. White. Audiovisual firm. "We are a full-service audiovisual production company, providing multi-image and slide-tape, video and audio presentations for training, marketing, awards, historical, and public relations uses. We have complete inhouse production resources, including slidemaking, soundtrack production, photography, and A/V multi-image programming." Clients: "We serve major industry, such as GTE, Occidental Petroleum; medical, such as Oral Health Services, Whittier Hospital, Florida Hospital; schools, such as University of Southern California, Pepperdine University, and Clairbourne School; and public service efforts, such as fund-raising."

Needs: Works with 4-6 freelance artists/year. Assigns 12-20 jobs/year. Prefers artists local to greater LA, "with timely turnaround, ability to keep elements in accurate registration, neatness, design quality, imagination and price." Uses artists for design, illustration, retouching, animation, lettering and charts/graphs.

First Contact & Terms: Send query letter with brochure or tear sheets, Photostats, photocopies, slides and photographs. Samples are filed. Samples not filed are returned only if requested. Reports back within 14 days only if interested. Call or write to schedule an appointment to show a portfolio. Payment negotiable by job.

GLORIA ZIGNER & ASSOCIATES INC., 328 N. Newport Blvd., Newport Beach CA 92663. (714)645-6300. President: Gloria Zigner. Advertising/PR firm. Clients: hotels, insurance companies, hospitals, restaurants, financial institutions, manufacturers, electronic companies, corporate identities, builders and developers. Buys 12-24 illustrations/year.

Needs: Works with 2-3 illustrators and 2-3 designers/month. Uses artists for billboards, P-O-P displays, consumer magazines, stationery design, multimedia kits, direct mail, brochures/flyers, trade magazines and newspapers. Also uses artists for design, color separations, layout, lettering, paste-up and type spec.

First Contact & Terms: Local artists only. Write for interview. Reports only if interested. Provide brochure, flyer, business card, resume and tear sheets to be kept on file for future assignments. No originals returned at job's completion. Pays promised fee for unused assigned work.

Los Angeles

N.W. AYER, INC.,888 S. Figueroa, Los Angeles CA 90017. (213)486-7400. President/Creative Director: John Littlewood. Creative Supervisor: Bob Bowen. Art Directors: Lora Avery and Jacqueline Christie. Assistant Art Director: Bianca Juarez. Ad agency. List of clients provided upon request.

Needs: Uses 1-2 illustrators/month. Uses artists for billboards, P-O-P displays, consumer magazines, direct mail, television, slide sets, brochures/flyers, trade magazines, and newspapers.

First Contact & Terms: "People interested should research what type of clients N.W. Ayer has in such references as *Advertising Agency Register* and in the Red Book." Provide tear sheets, original art or photocopies to be kept on file for future assignments. Pays for design by the project, $200-2,000. Pays for illustration by the project, $250-3,500. Negotiates payment based on client's budget and amount of creativity required from artist. No originals returned at job's completion.

BANNING CO., Suite 210, 11818 Wilshire Blvd., Los Angeles CA 90025. (213)477-8517. Art Director: Bill Reynolds. Ad agency. Serves a variety of clients.

Needs: Works with 2 comp artists and 2-3 designers per month. Works on assignment only. Uses designers for P-O-P displays, consumer and trade magazines, stationery design, direct mail, brochures/flyers and newspapers.

First Contact & Terms: Call for interview. Prefers slides as samples. Samples returned by SASE. Reports within 2-3 weeks. Provide business card and brochure to be kept on file for future assignments. No originals returned at job's completion. All pay is based on job. Considers complexity of project, client's budget, turnaround time and rights purchased when establishing payment.

Tips: "This is a business first; art folks need some business skills—not just artistic ones. Have patience and confidence."

BOSUSTOW VIDEO, 2207 Colby Ave., West Los Angeles CA 90064-1504. Contact: Tee Bosustow. Video production firm. Clients: broadcast series, feature films, corporate, media promotion and home video.
Needs: Works with varying number of freelance artists depending on projects. Local artists only. Works on assignment only. Uses artists for titles, maps, graphs and other information illustrations.
First Contact & Terms: Hires per job; no staff artists. Send brochure showing art style and resume only to be kept on file. Do not send samples; required only for interview. Samples not filed are returned by SASE. Reports only if interested. Pays by the project, $50-500 average. Considers complexity of project, skill and experience of artist, client's budget and turnaround time when establishing payment. Usually buys all rights; varies according to project.

***BROYLES GARAMELLA KAVANAUGH & ASSOCIATES**, 8226 Sunset Blvd., Los Angeles CA 90046. (213)650-9888. Senior Art Directors: Tracy Weston, Jeff Price. Ad agency specializing in entertainment, marketing, advertising, design, lifestyle/leisure products.
Needs: Works with 15 freelance artists/year. Assigns 50 jobs/year. Works on assignment only. Uses freelance artists for design, illustration, brochures, catalogs, consumer and trade magazines, P-O-P displays, mechanicals, animation, billboards, posters, direct mail packages, motion pictures, lettering, logos and advertisements.
First Contact & Terms: Send query letter with tear sheets, or "telephone." Samples are filed. Reports back only if interested and project requires specific artist style." Call to schedule an appointment to show a portfolio, which should include thumbnails, roughs, Photostats and tear sheets. Pays for design by the hour, $15 minimum. Pays for illustration by the project, $800 minimum. Payment is negotiable. Considers complexity of project and turnaround time when establishing payment. Buys all rights.

***DYER/KAHN, INC.**, 5550 Wilshire Blvd., Los Angeles CA 90036. (213)937-4100. Creative Directors: Clive Piercy, Bill Murphy. Ad agency and audiovisual firm. "We are a multi-media design studio providing advertising, sales materials, P-O-P displays and corporate identity for a variety of clients, including film and record companies, real estate developers, fashion and restaurants."
Needs: Works with 10-15 freelance artists/year. Prefers local artists. Uses artists for design, illustration, brochures, catalogs, books, newspapers, consumer and trade magazines, P-O-P displays, mechanicals, retouching, animation, billboards, posters, direct mail packages, press releases, motion pictures, lettering, logos, charts/graphs and advertisements.
First Contact & Terms: Send a resume. Samples are filed. Reports back only if interested. Drop-off policy (Thursday 9-9:30 a.m.). Payment "varies project by project." Considers complexity of project, client's budget and turnaround time when establishing payment.
Tips: "Use drop-off policy. If an AD is available he/she will see you. If not, work will be looked at by noon and ready for pick-up."

***DYR**, 4751 Wilshire Blvd., Los Angeles CA 90010. (213)930-5000. Manager of Creative Services: Michelle Nelson. "We are a general service ad agency." Clients: hotels, motorcycles, ATVs, food, pens, lighters. Client list provided upon request.
Needs: Works with 200 freelance artists/year. Assigns 200 jobs/year. Works on assignment only. Uses freelance artists for design, illustration, brochures, catalogs, P-O-P displays, mechanicals, retouching, billboards, posters, direct mail packages, lettering, logos, charts/graphs and advertisements.
First Contact & Terms: Send query letter with brochure showing art style or resume, tear sheets, Photostats, photocopies, slides and photographs. Samples are filed. Does not report back. Write to schedule an appointment to show a portfolio, which should include Photostats, photographs, color, slides and video disks. Pays for design by the day, $300-600. Pays for illustration by the hour, $50-65; by the day, $300-400. Considers complexity of project, client's budget, turnaround time, skill and experience of artist, how work will be used and rights purchased when establishing payment. Negotiates rights purchased; rights purchased vary according to project.

GUMPERTZ/BENTLEY/FRIED, 5900 Wilshire Blvd., Los Angeles CA 90036. (213)931-6301. Executive Art Director: John Johnson. Ad agency. Clients: stockbrokers, banks, food companies and visitors' bureaus.
Needs: Works with 3-4 illustrators and photographers/month. Uses artists for illustration. Negotiates pay.
First Contact & Needs: Call to arrange interview to show portfolio.

THE HALSTED ORGANIZATION, 3519 West Sixth St., Los Angeles CA 90020. (213)386-8356. Art Director: Damon G. Shay. Ad agency, public relations and marketing firm. Clients: manufacturers, medical/dental, sporting goods and general consumer. Client list provided upon request.
Needs: Works with 15-20 freelance artists/year. Prefers local artists with own studio. Will consider all.

Uses artists for design, illustrations, brochures, mechanicals, retouching, posters, direct mail package, press releases, lettering and logos. Looks for "clean work, type spec ability is rewarded, photo retouch is great,"

First Contact & Terms: Send query letter with brochure showing art style or resume and tear sheets, photostats, photocopies, slides and photographs. Samples not filed are returned only if requested. Reports back within 10 days. Call to schedule an appointment to show a portfolio, which should include roughs, original/final art, tear sheets and b&w. Pays for design by the hour,$12.50-50; by the project, $120-no limit; by the day, $90-no limit. Pays for illustration by the hour, 12.50-50; by the project, $100-no limit; by the day 90-no limit. Considers complexity of project, turnaround time and client's budget, rights purchased when establishing payment. Buys one-time rights or reprint rights; rights vary according to project.

Tips: "Be enthusiastic, look professional and have a concise and varied portfolio. Smile."

PAUL MUCHNICK CO., 5818 Venice Blvd., Los Angeles CA 90019. (213)934-7986. Art/Creative Director: Paul Muchnick. Ad agency. Serves clients in mail order, giftwares, publishing, housewares and general consumer products.

Needs: Local artists only. Uses artists for layout, paste-up, brochures/flyers and retouching for newspapers, magazines and direct mail.

First Contact & Terms: Call for interview. No originals returned to artist at job's completion.

NATIONAL ADVERTISING AND MARKETING ENTERPRISES, (N.A.M.E.), 1352 S. Flower St., Los Angeles CA 90015. Contact: J. A. Gatlin.

Needs: Works on assignment only. Uses artists for graphic design, letterheads and direct mail brochures.

First Contact & Terms: Send query letter with tear sheet, Photostats and photographs. Samples not returned. Sometimes buys previously published work. Reports in 4 weeks. To show a portfolio, mail appropriate materials. Pays by the hour, $15-40.

Tips: "Submit repros of art, not originals."

RAPP & COLLINS/USA/LOS ANGELES, 5900 Wilshire Blvd., Los Angeles CA 90036. (213)936-9600. Vice President/Creative Director: Michael Goodwin. Ad agency. Clients: banking, food, fashion, etc. Client list provided upon request.

Needs: Uses artists for design, photography, illustration, comps and mechanicals. "Direct response experience required for design, comp and mechanical assignments."

First Contact & Terms: Send photographs or tear sheets to be kept on file. Samples not filed are returned only if requested. Reports only if interested. Call for appointment to show portfolio. Considers complexity of the project, client's budget, skill and experience of artist, geographic scope for the finished product, turnaround time and rights purchased when establishing payment. Buys first rights.

RUBIN POSTAER & ASSOCIATES, (formerly Needham, Harper Worldwide, Inc.), Suite 900, 11601 Wilshire Blvd., Los Angeles CA 90025. (213)208-5000. Manager, Art Services: Annie Ross. Ad agency. Serves clients in automobile, heavy equipment baking, savings and loan.

Needs: Works with about 4 freelance illustrators/month. Uses freelancers for all media.

First Contact & Terms: Contact manager of art services for appointment to show portfolio. Selection based on portfolio review. Negotiates payment.

Tips: Wants to see variety of techniques.

***SPUNGBUGGY WORKS, INC.**, 948 N. Fairfax, Los Angeles CA 90046. (213)657-8070. President: Herb Stott. Animation Producer: Kris Weber. Live Action Producer: David Persoff. AV/TV producer. Serves clients in advertising. Produces live, animation and combination materials for TV commercials.

Needs: Uses artists for design, animation, background art, ink and paint and special effects animation.

First Contact & Terms: Prefers Los Angeles-based artists with previous work experience. Send resume and samples (Photostats or brochures preferred). Drop-in applicants will not be seen. Samples not returned. Provide resume and brochure/flyer to be kept on file for possible future assignments. Works on assignment only. Reports "only if job arises for particular artist." Pays by the project. Amount of payment is negotiated with the individual artist and varies with each client's budget. No originals returned to artist following publication. Buys all rights.

Tips: "Knowledge of art and design as applied to animation is important. Letters addressed to 'Dear Sir' don't make a good impression on female management. If the name doesn't reveal gender use a general reference such as 'Dear Casting Director' or some unassuming opening."

San Francisco

ARNOLD & ASSOCIATES PRODUCTIONS, 2159 Powell St., San Francisco CA 94133. (415)989-3490. President: John Arnold. Audiovisual and video firm. Clients: general.
Needs: Works with 30 freelance artists/year. Prefers local artists (in San Francisco and Los Angeles), award-winning and experienced. "We're an established, national firm." Works on assignment only. Uses artists for multimedia, slide show and staging production.
First Contact & Terms: Send query letter with brochure, tear sheets, slides and photographs to be kept on file. Call to schedule an appointment to show a portfolio, which should include final reproduction/product, color and photographs. Pays for design by the hour, $15-50; by the project, $500-3,500. Pays for illustration by the project, $500-4,000. Considers complexity of the project, client's budget and skill and experience of artists when establishing payment.

CHARTMASTERS, 201 Filbert St., San Francisco CA 94133. (415)421-6591. Art Manager: Robert Burnett. Audiovisual firm.
Needs: Works with 5-6 freelance artists/year. Artists must sign W-2 form and work on premises as temporary employee." Uses artists for designs, illustrations, mechanicals, animation and chart/graphs. Experience in 35mm slide production, presentation and multi-image shows essential.
First Contact & Terms: Send resume and slides. Samples not filed are returned. Reports back only if interested. Call or write to schedule an appointment to show a portfolio. Pays for design by the hour, $10-18. Considers complexity of project and skill and experience of artist when establishing payment. Rights purchased vary according to project.

***DASHER COMMUNICATIONS**, 605 Third St., San Francisco CA 94107. (415)543-7864. Executive Producer: Jennifer Kauffman. Associate Producer: Mark Yellen. Estab. 1985. Audiovisual firm specializing in multi-image, video, major sales meeting, print and collateral materials. Clients: financial, real estate, corporations and PR groups.
Needs: Works with 50 freelance artists/year. Assigns 100 jobs/year. Prefers talented, national, experienced artists. Works on assignment only. Uses artists for design, illustration, brochures, animation, motion pictures and charts/graphs.
First Contact & Terms: Send resume. Samples are filed. Samples not filed are returned only if requested. Reports back within 1 month. Call to schedule an appointment to show a portfolio, which should include roughs, slides and video disks. Pays for design and illustration by the hour, $15-60.

FURMAN FILMS, 3466 21st St., San Francisco CA 94110. (415)824-8500. Producer: Will Furman. Audiovisual and motion picture production firm. Clients: variety of corporate clients, and agricultural co-ops.
Needs: Works with 5 freelance artists/year. Uses artists for paste-up, design, maps, illustrations, signs and type spec. Especially important are speed, accuracy, knowledge of film/video media, and flexibility in working hours.
First Contact & Terms: Works on assignment only. Send query letter with resume and business card to be kept on file; write for appointment to show portfolio. "Information is kept on file and interviews done when need arises for freelance assistance." Prefers Photostats, photographs or tear sheets as samples. Samples returned by SASE. Reports only if interested. Pays by the hour, $8-20 average; pays by the project, $100-250 average. Considers complexity of the project, client's budget, skill and experience of artist, turnaround time and rights purchased when establishing payment. Buys all rights or variable rights according to project; negotiates rights purchased.

HEAPING TEASPOON ANIMATION, 4002 19th St., San Francisco CA 94114. (415)626-1893. Owner: Chuck Eyler. Audiovisual firm. Clients: ad agencies, other production firms and local businesses.
Needs: Works with 5 freelance artists/year. Uses artists for design, mechanicals, animation and motion pictures. "Artists should have good pencil line quality and inbetweening experience."
First Contact & Terms: Send query letter with brochure showing art style or resume, tear sheets, photocopies and renderings/designs. Samples not filed are returned by a SASE. Reports back within 3 months with SASE and only if interested. Call or write to schedule an appointment to show a portfolio, which should include thumbnails, roughs, original/final art and video reels. Pays for design by the hour, $10-90; for illustration by the hour, $8-20. Considers complexity of project, client's budget and skill and experience of artist when establishing payment. Rights purchased vary according to project.

JOVART STUDIOS, Box 2404, San Francisco CA 94126. Art Director: Jorge Morales. Audiovisual firm. Clients: corporations.

Needs: Works with 5 freelance artists/year. Works on assignment only. Uses artists for design, illustrations, brochures, catalog, mechanicals, logos and charts/graphs.
First Contact & Terms: Send query letter with resume. Samples not filed are returned by SASE. Reports only if interested. Write to schedule an appointment to show a portfolio, which should include final reproduction/product. Pays for design by the hour, $10 minimum. Considers complexity of project and client's budget when establishing payment. Rights purchased vary according to project.
Tips: "We cannot answer every query, but we use freelancers occasionally and resumes will be kept on file but not necessarily acknowledged."

KETCHUM COMMUNICATIONS, 55 Union St., San Francisco CA 94111-1217. (415)781-9480. Executive Creative Director: Kenneth Dudwick. Ad agency. Serves clients in food and athletic footwear.
Needs: Uses freelancers for consumer and trade magazines, newspapers, print ads and TV.
First Contact & Terms: Call for appointment to show portfolio. Selection based on portfolio review, mailers from freelancers and contact by reps. Negotiates payment based on client's budget, amount of creativity required from artist and where work will appear.
Tips: Wants to see in portfolio whatever best illustrates freelancer's style. Include past work used by other ad agencies and tear sheets of published art.

LOWE MARSCHALK, (formerly Dailey & Associates), 574 Pacific, San Francisco CA 94133. (415)981-2250. Creative Director: John McDaniels. Ad agency. Clients: primarily travel, wine and food.
Needs: Works with 3-4 freelance illustrators and 2 freelance designers/month. Uses freelancers for billboards, consumer and trade magazines, direct mail, brochures/flyers, newspapers, P-O-P displays, stationery design and TV.
First Contact & Terms: Call for appointment to show portfolio. Selection based on past association and review of portfolios. Negotiates payment based on usage and where work will appear.
Tips: Wants to see features that demonstrate freelancer's originality and competency.

***HAL RINEY & PARTNERS, INC.**, 735 Battery, San Francisco CA 94111. (415)981-0950. Contact: Jerry Andelin. Ad agency. Serves cients in beverages, baseball team, brewery, computers, confections, insurance, restaurants, winery, and assorted packaged goods accounts.
Needs: Works with 5-6 freelance illustrators/month. Uses freelancers in all media.
First Contact & Terms: Call one of the art directors for appointment to show portfolio. Selection based on portfolio review. Negotiates payment based on client's budget, amount of creativity required from artist and where work will appear.
Tips: Wants to see a comprehensive rundown in portfolio on what a person does best—"what he's selling"—and enough variety to illustrate freelancer's individual style(s).

EDGAR S. SPIZEL ADVERTISING INC., 1782 Pacific Ave., San Francisco CA 94109. (415)474-5735. President: Edgar S. Spizel. AV producer. Clients: "Consumer-oriented from department stores to symphony orchestras, supermarkets, financial institutions, radio, TV stations, political organizations, hotels and real estate firms." Works a great deal with major sports stars and TV personalities.
Needs: Uses artists for posters, ad illustrations, brochures and mechanicals.
First Contact & Terms: Send query letter with tear sheets. Reports within 3 weeks. Provide material to be kept on file for future assignments. No originals returned at job's completion. Negotiates pay.

UNDERCOVER GRAPHICS, Suite 1-C, 20 San Antonio Pl., San Francisco CA 94133. (415)626-0123. Creative Director: L.A. Paul. AV producer. Clients: musical groups, producers, record companies and book publishers.
Needs: Works with 2-3 illustrators and 2-3 designers/month. Uses artists for billboards, P-O-P displays, corporate identity, multimedia kits, direct mail, TV, brochures/flyers, album covers and books.
First Contact & Terms: Send query letter with brochure or resume, tear sheets, slides, photographs and/or photocopies. Samples returned by SASE. Provide brochures, tear sheets, slides, business card and/or resume to be kept on file for future assignments. Reports in 4 weeks only if interested. To show a portfolio, mail roughs, original/final art, tear sheets and photographs. Originals returned to artist at job's completion. Pays $250-5,000, comprehensive layout and production; $10-25/hour, creative services; $25-500, illustrations. Considers complexity of project, client's budget, skill and experience of artist and rights purchased when establishing payment. Pays original fee as agreed for unused assigned illustrations.
Tips: Artists interested in working with us should "be creative and persistent. Be different. Set yourself apart from other artists by work that's noticeably outstanding. Don't be content with mediocrity or just 'getting by' or even the 'standards of the profession.' *Be avant-garde*."

Colorado

ALPINE FILM PRODUCTIONS, 1623 Race St., Denver CO 80206. (303)393-1189. Producer: Dee B. Dubin. Audiovisual firm. Clients: advertising firms, corporations and variety of businesses. Client list provided upon request.
Needs: Works with 100 freelance artists/year. Works on assignment only. Uses artists for design, brochure, animation and motion pictures.
First Contact & Terms: Send query letter with brochure showing art style or resume. Samples not filed are returned only if requested. Reports only if interested. To show a portfolio, mail appropriate materials plus tear sheets. Pays for design by the project. Considers client's budget, how work will be used and rights purchased when establishing payment. Rights purchased vary according to project. Pays for design by the project, $50-10,000. Pays for illustration by the project, $50 minimum.
Tips: "We are primarily a film production company, but we do use a lot of freelance artists (including film crew personnel), and some graphic and design artists." Mail information and follow up with phone call..

BROYLES ALLEBAUGH & DAVIS, INC., 31 Denver Technological Center, 8231 E. Prentice Ave., Englewood CO 80111. (303)770-2000. Executive Art Director: Kent Eggleston. Ad agency. Clients: industrial, high-tech, financial, travel and consumer clients; client list provided upon request.
Needs: Works with 12 illustrators/year; occasionally uses freelance designers. Works on assignment only. Uses freelance artists for consumer and trade magazines, direct mail, P-O-P displays, brochures, catalogs, posters, newspapers, TV and AV presentations.
First Contact & Terms: Send business card, brochure/flyer, samples and tear sheets to be kept on file. Samples returned by SASE if requested. Reports only if interested. Arrange interview to show portfolio or contact through artist's agent. Prefers slides or printed pieces as samples. Negotiates payment according to project. Considers complexity of project, client's budget, skill and experience of artist, geographic scope of finished project, turnaround time and rights purchased when establishing payment.

COLLE & MCVOY ADVERTISING AGENCY, INC., 6900 East Belleview Ave., Englewood CO 80111. (303)771-7700. Associate Creative Director: Celia Sheneman. Ad agency. Clients: newspaper, banks, resorts, various high-tech, hospital and amusement park.
Needs: Works with 6-8 freelance artists/year. Prefers local artists, but open to experienced "lancers" outside Denver. Very interested in Boulder. Uses artists for design, illustrations, brochures, catalog, magazines, newspapers, P-O-P displays, mechanicals, retouching, animation, billboards, posters, direct mail packages, logos, charts/graphs, advertisements and radio.
First Contact & Terms: Send query letter with brochure showing art style or resume and tear sheets, Photostats, photocopies, slides, photographs and "whatever they want to show." Samples not filed are returned only if requested. Reports only if interested. Call or write to schedule an appointment to show a portfolio, which should include thumbnails, roughs, original/final art, final reproduction/product, color, tear sheets, photographs, b&w and "whatever they want to show." Pays for design and illustration by the project, $150 minimum. Rights purchased vary according to project.
Tips: "We look forward to new styles and techniques for black-and-white work. We're more interested in an individual's style than what he/she has done. Also, we rely on the artist's conceptual ability, because we feel the artist must have that freedom."

KINETIC DESIGN SYSTEMS, 8201 E. Pacific Pl., Denver CO 80231. (303)750-5000. Art Director: Jim Pinigis. Computer video animation producer. Clients: international broadcasters; advertising agencies; industrial, corporate and medical institutions; filmmakers and numerous independent clients who utilize broadcasting in their advertising.
Needs: Works with 1 illustrator and 1-2 graphic artists/year. Uses artists for storyboards, background illustration, print ads and production art. Artwork done daily.
First Contact & Terms: Send resume and samples (animated graphics on video cassette, samples of illustration, storyboards, graphic design and printed pieces). Samples not returned. Provide resume and business card to be kept on file one year for possible future assignments. Payment varies.

STARWEST PRODUCTIONS, 1391 N. Speer Blvd., Denver CO 80204. (303)623-0636. Creative Director: Steve Pettit. Ad agency/audiovisual firm. Clients list provided upon request with SASE.
Needs: Works with 2-4 freelance artists/year. Local artists only, experienced in audiovisual, print, storyboard. Works on assignment only. Uses artists for full concept to paste-up. Especially seeks paste-up skills.
First Contact & Terms: Send resume and slides, tear sheets, Photostats to be kept on file. Samples not

filed are returned. Reports within 30 days. Write for appointment to show portfolio. Pays by the project, $1,000. Considers client's budget, and skill and experience of artist when establishing payment. Negotiates rights purchased.
Tips: "Always looking for someone with 'new' ideas."

***STRADE INDUSTRIES**, 12600 W. Colfax, Lakewood CO 80222. Production Manager: Sharon Adams. Audiovisual firm. "We are a communications firm specializing in print and slide presentation and computer graphics." Clients: banks, telecommunication companies, oil companies, aerospace companies, design firms, newspapers and real estate.
Needs: Works with 3 freelance artists/year. Assigns 20 jobs/year. Prefers local, experienced artists. Works on assignment only. Uses freelance artists for animation, charts/graphs, computer graphics and slide production.
First Contact & Terms: Send query letter with brochure or resume and slides. Samples are filed. Samples not filed are returned only if requested by artist. Reports back within months only if interested. Write to schedule an appointment to show a portfolio, which should include original/final art, final reproduction/product, slides and video disks. Pays for design and illustration by the hour, $8-15. Considers complexity of project, client's budget, turnaround time and skill and experience of artist when establishing payment. Buys all rights.
Tips: "Do not just drop in. Contact by letter or phone. Please keep in mind that schedules can be very hectic for managers and be patient (never rude). A delay in answer does not always mean 'no.' "

Connecticut

***AUDIOVISUAL DESIGN STUDIOS, INC.**, 1823 Silas Deane Hwy., Rocky Hill CT 06067-0588. (203)529-2581. President: Joseph J. Wall. Audiovisual firm. "We are a multimedia firm creating, producing and staging presentations worldwide." Clients: corporations, institutions, businesses, trade associations, government.
Needs: Works with approximately 10 artists/year. Assigns 300 jobs/year. Works on assignment only. Uses artists for design, illustration, brochures, catalogs, books, newspapers, P-O-P displays, mechanicals, retouching, animation, lettering, logos, charts/graphs, advertisements and slide production.
First Contact & Terms: Send query letter with resume. Samples are not filed. Samples not filed are not returned. Reports back only if interested. Write to schedule an appointment to show a portfolio, which should include final reproduction/product. Pays for design by the hour, $10-25. Pays for illustration by the hour, $15-35. Considers turnaround time and skill and experience of artist when establishing payment. Buys all rights.
Tips: "Do your best work always."

THE BERNI COMPANY, Marketing Design Consultants, 666 Steamboat Rd., Greenwich CT 06830. (203)661-4747. Contact: Jeff Burnham. Clients: manufacturers and retailers of consumer package goods. Buys 50 illustrations/year. Write or call for interview; local professionals only.
Needs: Uses artists for illustration, layout, lettering, paste-up, retouching and type spec for annual reports, catalogs, letterheads, P-O-P displays, packaging, design, production and trademarks. Pays $15-50. Pays promised fee for unused assigned work.

***BRADFORD ADVERTISING, INC.**, Two Pratt St., Essex CT 06426. (203)767-0173. Art Director: Jim Ladner. Ad agency. Clients: automotive, industrial, bank, modular home manufacturer and sporting goods.
Needs: Works with approximately 10 freelance artists/year. Prefers local artists. Works on assignment only. Uses freelance artists for design, illustration, brochures, catalogs, P-O-P displays, mechanicals, billboards, posters, direct mail packages, press releases, logos and advertisements.
First Contact & Terms: Send brochure. Samples are filed. Samples not filed are returned only if requested. Does not report back. Call to schedule an appointment to show a portfolio, which should include thumbnails, roughs, original/final art, tear sheets and slides. Pays for design by the hour, $25-100; by the project, $250-1,500; by the day, $250-500. Pays for illustration by the hour, $50-300; by the project, $100-1,000; by the day, $250-1,500. Considers complexity of project, client's budget, turnaround time, skill and experience of artist, how work will be used and rights purchased. Negotiates rights purchased; rights purchased vary according to project.
Tips: "When contacting our firm, please send samples of work."

EAGLEVISION, INC., Box 3347, Stamford CT 06905. (203)359-8777. Principal/Creative Director: Michael Macari, Jr. Audiovisual firm. Clients: corporate/industrial, music and arts and consumer home

video programmer, also cable TV.
Needs: Works with 25-50 freelance artists/year. Works on assignment only. Uses artists for computer and digital graphics and animation footage, as well as scriptwriters.
First Contact & Terms: "Good quality and creativity" are especially important. Send query letter and samples to be kept on file. Prefers ¾" or ½" VHS or BETA Hi-Fi videotapes as samples. Samples not filed are returned by SASE. Reports within 1 week only if interested. Write for appointment to show portfolio. Pays by the project or by amount of material/footage. Considers complexity of project, skill and experience of artist, and rights purchased when establishing payment. Buys one-time rights, all rights or variable rights according to project.

EDUCATIONAL DIMENSIONS GROUP, Box 126, Stamford CT 06904. (203)327-4612. Visual Editors: Marguerite Mead and Greg Byrnes. AV producer. Audience: businesses, schools and libraries. Produces filmstrips, motion pictures, slide sets and videotapes.
Needs: Works with illustrators and designers. Works on assignment only. Uses designers and mechanical artists for catalogs, filmstrips, direct mail flyers and brochures, etc.
First Contact & Terms: Send query letter with resume, photocopied samples and Photostats. Samples returned only if requested. Reports in 2 weeks. Provide resume to be kept on file for future assignments. Originals only returned at job's completion when return has been negotiated earlier. Pays by job for filmstrip, slide and film illustrations, charts, graphics and diagrams. "Payment depends totally on type of project."
Tips: Looks for neatness, organization, fresh ideas and versatility.

ERIC HOLCH/ADVERTISING, 49 Gerrish Lane, New Canaan CT 06840. President: Eric Holch. Clients: companies who advertise in trade magazines.
Needs: Works with 10 freelance artists/year. Works on assignment only. Prefers food, candy, packages, and seascapes as themes for advertising illustrations for brochures, ads, etc. Pays $100-2,000 average.
First Contact & Terms: Send query letter with brochure showing art style or samples to be kept on file. Write to schedule an appointment to show a portfolio, which should include roughs, photocopies and original/final art. Pays for design by the hour, $25-50. Pays for illustration by the project, $100-2,000. Buys one-time rights, all rights or negotiates rights purchased depending on project. Considers skill and experience of artist and client's preferences when establishing payment.

***JACOBY/STORM PRODUCTIONS INC.**, 22 Crescent Rd., Westport CT 06880. (203)227-2220. President: Doris Storm. AV/TV/film producer. Clients: schools, corporations and publishers. Produces filmstrips, motion pictures, slide sets, sound-slide sets and videotapes.
Needs: Assigns 6-8 jobs/year. Uses artists for lettering, illustrations for filmstrips and to design slide show graphics.
First Contact & Terms: Prefers local artists with filmstrip and graphics experience. Query with resume and arrange interview. SASE. Reports in 2 weeks. Usually buys all rights. Pays $20-30/frame, lettering; $50-100/frame, illustrations. Pays on acceptance.

***LISTENING LIBRARY, INC.**, 1 Park Ave., Old Greenwich CT 06870. (203)637-3616. Catalog Editor: Ronnie Lipton. Produces educational AV productions.
Needs: Requires illustrators for front covers for 8-10 catalogs/year. Uses artists for catalog and advertising design; advertising illustration; catalog and advertising layout, and direct mail packages.
First Contact & Terms: Local (New York City, Westchester County, Fairfield County, etc.) artists only. Works on assignment only. Send resume and nonreturnable samples to be kept on file for possible future assignments. Samples not returned. Original work not returned to artist after job's completion. "Payment is determined by the size of the job, and skill and experience of artist." Buys all rights.

THE McMANUS COMPANY, Box 446, Greens Farms CT 06436. (203)255-3301. President: John F. McManus. National advertising/marketing/PR agency. Serves clients in data processing, corporate, consumer, industrial, social agencies, automotives and other industries.
Needs: Works with 4 illustrators/month. Works on assignment only. Uses artists for art direction (TV commercials), graphic design (print ads and collateral pieces), illustration, publications, filmstrips, multimedia kits, storyboards and packaging.
First Contact & Terms: Send resume (to be kept on file for future assignments). Samples returned by SASE; reports back on future assignment possibilities. Write for interview to show portfolio. "Payment is determined on use of creative work, whether it will appear in national or regional media."

MARKETING EAST INC., 520 West Ave., Norwalk CT 06850. (203)866-2234. Contact: W. Greene. Ad agency.

Needs: Works with 2-3 freelance artists/year. Experienced artists only. Uses artists for mechanicals, etc.
First Contact & Terms: Send Photostats, photographs, slides or tear sheets as samples to be kept on file. Samples not filed are returned only if requested. Reports only if interested. Call for appointment to show portfolio. Pays by the job. Buys all rights

PALM, DEBOMIS, RUSSO, INC., 800 Cottage Grove Rd., Bloomfield CT 06002. (203)242-6258. Art Director: Lynn Schultz. Ad agency. Clients: consumer and industrial products and services.
Needs: Works with 2-3 illustrators/month. Works on assignment only. Uses illustrators for consumer magazines, trade magazines and technical illustration. Also uses artists for layout, illustration, technical art, paste-up, retouching, lettering and storyboards for TV, newspapers, magazines, radio, billboards, direct mail and collateral.
First Contact & Terms: Submit samples or call for interview. Prefers slides, photographs, photostats, b&w line drawings and originals as samples. Samples returned by SASE "if requested." Reports within 4 weeks. Provide business card, resume, samples and tear sheets of work to be kept on file for future assignments. No originals returned at job's completion. Pays by the project, $100-1,000 average. Considers complexity of project, client's budget, skill and experience of artist and turnaround time when establishing payment.
Tips: "Try not to submit too many styles of work—only what one is best at."

***SMITH, DORIAN & BURMAN, INC.**, 1100 New Britain Ave., Hartford CT 06110. Production Manager: Richard A. Mikush. Industrial clients.
Needs: Uses artists for layout, illustration and retouching for trade magazines, collateral, direct mail and P-O-P display.
First Contact & Terms: Call for interview; local artists only. Prefers photographs and Photostats as samples. Samples returned *only* if requested. Reports in 2 weeks. Works on assignment only. Provide business card and tear sheets to be kept on file for possible future assignments. Payment by the project varies.

THE WESTPORT COMMUNICATIONS GROUP INC., 155 Post Rd. E., Westport CT 06880. (203)226-3525. Art Director: H. Lindsay. AV producer. Clients: educational and corporate. Produces filmstrips, multimedia kits, slide sets, sound-slide sets and booklets.
Needs: Works with 10-15 illustrators/year. Uses artists for filmstrip, slide, booklet and brochure illustrations.
First Contact & Terms: Send query letter and tear sheets to be kept on file. Reports within 1 month. Arrange interview to show portfolio. Pays $35/educational filmstrip frame; negotiates pay on other assignments.

Delaware

ALOYSIUS, BUTLER, & CLARK, Bancroft Mills, 30 Hill Rd., Wilmington DE 19806. (302)655-1552. Creative Director: Isaac Segal. Ad agency. Clients: banks, industry, restaurants, real estate, hotels, small, local businesses, transit system, government offices.
Needs: Assigns "many" freelance jobs/year. Works with 3-4 freelance illustrators and 3-4 freelance designers/month. Uses artists for trade magazines, billboards, direct mail packages, brochures, newspapers, stationery, signage and posters.
First Contact & Terms: Local artists only "within reason (Philadelphia, Baltimore)." Send query letter with resume, business card and slides, photos, stats, photocopies to be kept on file all except work that is "not worthy of consideration." Samples not kept on file returned only if requested. Reports only if interested. Works on assignment only. Call for appointment to show portfolio. Pays by the project. Considers complexity of project, client's budget, and skill and experience of artist when establishing payment. Buys all rights.

CUSTOM CRAFT STUDIO, 310 Edgewood St., Bridgeville DE 19933. AV producer.
Needs: Works with 1 illustrator and 1 designer/month. Works with freelance artists on an assignment basis only. Uses artists for filmstrips, slide sets, trade magazine and newspapers. Also uses artists for print finishing, color negative retouching and airbrush work.
First Contact & Terms: Send query letter with slides or photographs, brochure/flyer, resume, samples and tear sheets to be kept on file. Samples returned by SASE. Reports in 2 weeks. No originals returned to artist at job's completion. Pay varies.

LYONS, INC., 715 Orange St., Wilmington DE 19801. (302)654-6146. Vice President: P. Coleman DuPont. Advertising and graphic design/AV & video. Clients: consumer, corporate and industrial.

Needs: Has need for art directors, graphic designers, illustrators, photographers, storyboard artists and multi-image designers. Works on assignment only. Uses artists for advertising, collateral materials, publications, multimedia presentations, displays.
First Contact & Terms: Send resume. Prefers nonreturnable samples, slides or copies to be kept on file for future assignments. Samples returned by SASE. Pays by the hour or by assignment, $6-20/hour average. Complexity of assignment, overall budget, and skill/experience of artist considered when establishing rate.

SHIPLEY ASSOCIATES INC., 1300 Pennsylvania Ave., Wilmington DE 19806. (302)652-3051. Creative Director: Jack Parry. Ad/PR firm. Serves clients in harness racing, industrial and corporate accounts, insurance, real estate and entertainment.
Needs: Works with 2 illustrators and 1 designer/month. Assigns 9 jobs/year. Works with freelance artists on assignment only. Uses artists for annual report illustrations, mechanicals, brochure and sign design.
First Contact & Terms: Query with previously published work. Prefers layouts (magazine & newspaper), mechanicals, line drawings and finished pieces as samples. Samples not returned. Reports within 2 weeks. Provide resume, samples and tear sheets to be kept on file for possible future assignments. No originals returned at job's completion. Pays for design by the hour, $8 minimum. Negotiates payment.
Tips: Looks for "versatility and technique, individual style, good production skills."

District of Columbia

JAFFE ASSOCIATES, Suite 200, 2000 L St. NW, Washington DC 20036. (202)331-1227. Office Manager: Lora Wegman. PR and marketing firm. Clients: commercial real estate, banks, national associations, architectural and engineering, health care, law firms and accounting. Places advertising only to limited extent.
Needs: Works with several designers. Uses artists for stationery design, multimedia kits, direct mail, television, slide sets and brochures/flyers.
First Contact & Terms: Send resume and portfolio for review. "Freelancers are employed on basis of past experience, personal knowledge or special expertise." Provide brochures, flyers, business cards, resumes and tear sheets to be kept on file for future assignments. Originals returned only if prearranged. Negotiates payment based on client's budget, amount of creativity required from artist and artist's previous experience/reputation.
Tips: "Interested in samples of produced work and details regarding availability and ability to produce work on short time schedules. *Do not* deluge account executives with calls."

***KROLOFF, MARSHALL & ASSOCIATES**, Suite 500, 1730 Rhode Island Ave. NW, Washington DC 20036. Vice President: Susanne Roschwalb. PR firm. Clients: major corporate, public interest and governmental; client list provided upon request.
Needs: Works with 12 illustrators/year. Uses freelance artists for advertising layouts.
First Contact & Terms: Query with resume of credits to be kept on file. Prefers photocopies or photographs as samples. Samples returned by SASE "if necessary." Reports only if interested. Works on assignment. Provide business card, brochure/flyer, resume, samples and tear sheets to be kept on file for possible future assignments. Pays by the hour, $40 minimum. Considers complexity of project, client's budget and turnaround time when establishing payment.
Tips: "It helps to pick up and deliver work; it helps to speak directly to the person giving the assignment. We receive many inquiries. Be patient. Frequently decisions are based on availability, turnaround time and always the suitability of the artist to the task."

MANNING, SELVAGE & LEE, INC., Suite 300, 1250 Eye St. NW, Washington DC 20005. (202)682-1660. Contact: Creative Director. PR firm. Clients: pharmaceutical firms, nonprofit associations, real estate developers, corporations and high-tech firms.
Needs: Uses artists for illustration, paste-up and design.
First Contact & Terms: Send tear sheets, photostats, photocopies, slides and photographs. Call or write to schedule an appointment to show a portfolio, which should include best work. Pays for design by the hour, $15-65; by the project, $150-5,000.

***O'KEEFE COMMUNICATIONS, INC.**, 2135 Wisconsin Ave. N.W., Washington DC 20007. (202)333-7832. Art Director: Jane P. Anderson. "We produce multimedia audiovisual presentations, films and video as well as some printed media. We have a fully equipped photo lab, art department, video and editing department. We also produce set designs and convention displays with multi-image

back-up." Clients: large trade associations and corporations. Types range from banking to food industry as well as direct marketing.
Needs: Works with 15 freelance artists/year. Prefers local artists with previous AV knowledge. Will consider outside illustrators. "Good production skills are a must." Uses artists for design, illustration, brochures, mechanicals, animation, posters and lettering.
First Contact & Terms: Send query letter with resume, tear sheets, photocopies and slides. "Personal interviews are great if we have the time." Samples are filed. Samples not filed are returned only if requested by artist. Reports back only if interested. Call or write to schedule an appointment to show a portfolio, which should include roughs, original/final art, final reproduction/product and slides. Pays for mechanicals production and paste-up by the hour, $7.50-12. Pays for design and illustration by the hour, $12-100. Considers complexity of project, client's budget and skill and experience of artist when establishing payment. Buys all rights. Rights purchased vary according to project.
Tips: "Our busy seasons are spring and early fall. All resumes and samples received throughout the year will be filed and reviewed at those times. The more samples of your work you include, the better your chances are of being called in during the crunch. Gear your samples to those you feel would translate well into A.V. communication and stress any A.V. experience you have in a cover letter."

Florida

JOSEPH ANTHONY ADVERTISING AGENCY, INC., 8300 Congress Ave., Boca Raton FL 33499. (305)994-2660. Art Director: L.J. Moscariello. In-house direct mail firm. Clients: American consumer homes.
Needs: Works with 3-4 artists/year. Artist must have direct mail experience. Works on assignment only. Uses artists for advertising design and catalog layout; brochure design.
First Contact & Terms: Send query letter with resume, copies or print. Samples not filed are returned only if requested. Reports back within 3 months. Write to schedule an appointment to show a portfolio, which should include thumbnails, roughs, original/final art and final reproduction/product. Pays for design by the hour, $8-15. Pays for mechanical paste-up/keyline by the hour, $7-10. Considers complexity of project, client's budget, how work will be used, turnaround time and rights purchased when establishing payment.

***CHENOWETH & FAULKNER, INC.**, 5201 W. Kennedy Blvd., Tampa FL 33609. (813)877-1409. Creative Director: James Barr. Ad agency specializing in aerospace, finance, telecommunications.
Needs: Works with 20 freelance artists/year. Assigns 50 jobs/year. Uses artists for design, illustration, brochures, catalogs, trade magazines, P-O-P displays, mechanicals, retouching, animation, press releases, lettering, logos and advertisements.
First Contact & Terms: Send query letter with brochure or resume. Samples are filed. Samples not filed are returned by SASE. Reports back within 10 days. Write to schedule an appointment to show a portfolio. Pays for design and illustration by the project, $200-5,000. Other methods of payment are negotiatiable. Considers complexity of project, client's budget, turnaround time, skill and experience of artist, how work will be used and rights purchased when establishing payment. Buys first rights, one-time rights, all rights, reprint rights; rights purchased vary according to project.
Tips: "Write, then call."

COVALT ADVERTISING AGENCY, 12907 N.E. 7th Ave., North Miami FL 33161. (305)891-1543. Creative Director: Fernando Vasquez. Ad agency. Clients: automotive, cosmetics, industrial banks, restaurants, financial, consumer products.
Needs: Prefers local artists; very seldom uses out-of-town artists. Artists must have minimum of 5 years of experience; accepts less experience only if artist is extremely talented. Works on assignment only. Uses artists for illustration (all kinds and styles), photography, mechanicals, copywriting, retouching (important), rendering and lettering.
First Contact & Terms: Send query letter with brochure, resume, business card, tear sheets, Photostats, and photocopies to be kept on file. Samples not filed not returned. Reports only if interested. Call for appointment to show portfolio, which should include Photostats, photographs, slides, original final art or tear sheets. Pays for design by the hour, $35 minimum; by the project, $150 minimum. Pays for illustrations by the project, $200 minimum. Considers complexity of project, client's budget, skill and experience of artist, and turnaround time when establishing payment. Buys all rights or reprint rights.
Tips: "If at first you don't succeed, keep in touch. Eventually something will come up due to our diversity of accounts. If I have the person, I might design something with his particular skill in mind."

CREATIVE RESOURCES INC., 2000 S. Dixie Hwy., Miami FL 33133. (305)856-3474. Chairman and CEO: Mac Seligman. Ad agency/PR firm. Clients: travel, hotels, airlines and resorts.
Needs: Works with 6 illustrators/designers/year. Local artists only. Uses artists for layout, type spec and design for brochures, ads, posters and renderings.
First Contact & Terms: Send query letter with resume and samples. No file kept on artists. Original work returned after completion of job. Call or write to schedule an appointment to show a portfolio, which should include thumbnails. Pays for design $20-40/hour or negotiates pay by job or day. Pays for illustration by the hour, $40; amount varies by the project and day. Considers complexity of project, client's budget, and skill and experience of artist when establishing payment.

***IMAGEWORKS® INC.**, Box 8628, Naples FL 33941. (813)598-3040. President: J. Paul Jodoin. Audiovisual firm. "We provide speaker-support slides, slide/tape programs, etc. for conventions, seminars, inhouse training, marketing, general information transfer." Clients: real estate developers, bankers, physicians, engineers, photographers, entertainers, attorneys, TV news personnel, PR and advertising agency representatives.
Needs: Works with 6 freelance artists/year. Assigns 20 jobs/year. Prefers local artists. Works on assignment only. Uses artists for P-O-P displays, mechanicals, retouching, animation, lettering, logos, charts/graphs and advertisements.
First Contact & Terms: Send query letter with resume and slides. Samples are filed. Samples not filed are not returned. Reports back only if interested. To show a portfolio, mail slides. Pays for design and illustration by the hour, $10-25. Considers complexity of project, client's budget, turnaround time, skill and experience of artist and how work will be used when establishing payment. Rights purchased vary according to project.

***IMPACT GRAPHICS, INC.**, 5205 NW 33rd Ave., Ft. Lauderdale FL 33309. (305)733-9414. President: William Henkel. Audiovisual firm. "We are a multi-media firm providing slide presentations (consisting of computer-generated visuals and photography), computer-generated artwork for print, brochure design and production and over visual media. We service all types of corporations including advertising companies, banks, manufacturers, real estate brokers, developers, engineers, architects, publishers and producers." Client list provided upon requested.
Needs: Works with 2 freelance artists/year. Assigns 12 jobs/year. Prefers local artists. Works on assignment only. Uses artists for design, illustration, brochures, charts/graphs and advertisements.
First Contact & Terms: Send query letter with resume and slides. Samples are filed. Samples not filed are returned only if requested by artist. Reports back only if interested. Write to schedule an appointment to show a portfolio, which should include slides. Pays for design by the hour, $5-15. Pays for illustration by the hour, $10-20. Considers skill and experience of artist when establishing payment. Rights purchased vary according to project.

MEDIA DESIGN GROUP, (formerly Starr Productions, Inc.), 4862 SW 72nd Ave., Miami FL 33155. (305)663-3327. Production Coordinator: Tab Licca. AV producer. Clients: industry (80%) and advertising (20%). Produces "sales and marketing primarily, with some financial reporting and a little training."
Needs: Assigns approximately 100 jobs/year. Works with 2-3 illustrators and 1-2 designers/month. Works on assignment only. Uses artists for overall show design, cartoon work, paste up and board work.
First Contact & Terms: "We prefer AV experience and demand a high energy level." Send resume, then arrange interview by phone. Provide resume and business card to be kept on file for possible future assignments. No originals returned after publication. Buys all rights.

PRUITT HUMPHRESS POWERS & MUNROE ADVERTISING AGENCY, INC., 516 N. Adams St., Tallahassee FL 32301. (904)222-1212. Ad agency. Clients: business-to-business, consumer. Media used includes billboards, consumer and trade magazines, direct mail, newspapers, P-O-P displays, radio and TV.
Needs: Uses artists for direct mail, brochures/flyers, trade magazines and newspapers. "Freelancers used in every aspect of business and given as much freedom as their skill warrants."
First Contact & Terms: Send resume. Provide materials to be kept on file for future assignments. Negotiates payment based on client's budget and amount of creativity required from artist. Pays set fee/job.
Tips: In portfolio, "submit examples of past agency work in clean, orderly, businesslike fashion including written explanations of each work. Ten illustrations or less."

Georgia

***ANDERSON EILERS & BLUMBERG**, Suite 710, Five Piedmont Center, Atlanta GA 30305. (404)261-0831. Art Director: Joe Erni. Ad agency. Clients: primarily agricultural and industrial accounts.
Needs: Works with "many" illustrators/month; may have occasional use for designers. Uses freelance artists for billboards, consumer and trade magazines, direct mail, P-O-P displays, brochures, catalogs, posters, signage, newspapers, TV and AV presentations.
First Contact & Terms: Arrange interview to show portfolio. Samples returned. Reports in 1 week-2 months. Usually works on assignment basis. Pays $100-2,000 (average) by the project for illustration. Negotiates payment according to client's budget.
Tips: "Show me or send me *only* a few of your best samples."

***ATLANTA AUDIO-VISUALS**, 66 12th St., Atlanta GA 30303. Telex: 6501072756 MCI. Director: Robert Foah. AV producer. Serves clients in corporations. Produces multi-image materials.
Needs: Works with 3 illustrators/month.
First Contact & Terms: Send resume. Provide business card to be kept on file for possible future assignments only. Works on assignment only. Reports within 3 months. Pays by the project. Amount of payment is negotiated with the individual artist and varies with each client's budget. No originals returned after publication. Negotiates rights purchased.

***CAMP COMMUNICATIONS**, 1718 Peachtree St. NW, Atlanta GA 30309. (404)874-3989. Creative Director: Wayne Hood. Ad agency for the business-to-business, industrial segment. Clients: electronics, chemical, manufacturing, mining.
Needs: Works with 6 freelance artists/year. Assigns 20-30 jobs/year. Works on assignment only. Uses artists for design, illustration, brochures, trade magazines, retouching, lettering, logos and charts/graphs.
First Contact & Terms: Send query letter with brochure. Samples are filed. Does not report back. Call to schedule an appointment to show a portfolio. Pays for design by the hour, $25-50; by the project, $100-5,000. Pays for illustration by the project, $100-13,000. Considers complexity of project, client's budget, turnaround time and skill and experience of artist when establishing payment. Buys all rights; ("will *not* negotiate.")
Tips: "Set appointment; keep presentation short, show materials that relate to *our* clients. Follow up once a month."

***CHANNEL ONE INC.**, 1727 Clifton Rd., Atlanta GA 30329. President: W. Horlock. AV producer. Clients: educational, nonprofit, religious.
Needs: Works with 3-4 illustrators/month. Uses artists for album covers, motion pictures and graphic and set design.
First Contact & Terms: Prefers slides, photographs, photostats and b&w line drawings as samples. Samples returned by SASE. Reports in 2 months. Works on assignment only. Provide business card, brochure/flyer, resume and samples to be kept on file for possible future assignments. Originals returned to artist at job's completion if part of job contract. Payment depends on project.

WILLIAM COOK ADVERTISING/ATLANTA, (formerly Smith McNeal Advertising), 368 Ponce De Leon, Atlanta GA 30308. (404)892-3716. Senior Art Director: Darryl Elliott. Ad agency. Clients: hotels, industry and food.
Needs: Works with very few freelance artists. Works on assignment only. Uses artists for illustrations, mechanicals and layouts. Artist should have "good layout skills, visualization, speed, accuracy."
First Contact & Terms: Send query letter with resume and samples. Samples not filed are returned by SASE. Reports only if interested. Write to schedule an appointment to show a portfolio, which should include roughs, final reproduction/product and tear sheets. Pays for design by the hour, $14-50. Pays for illustration by the project, $100-2,000. Considers complexity of project, client's budget, how work will be used and turnaround time when establishing payment. Buys all rights.

***FILMAMERICA, INC.**, Suite 209, 3177 Peachtree Rd. NE, Atlanta GA 30305. (404)261-3718. President: Avrum M. Fine. Audiovisual firm. Clients: corporate producer, advertising agencies.
Needs: Works with 2 freelance artists/year. Works on assignment only. Uses artists for film campaigns. Especially important are illustration and layout skills.
First Contact & Terms: Send query letter with resume and photographs or tear sheets to be kept on file. Samples not filed are returned only if requested. Reports back only if interested. Write for appointment to show portfolio. Pays by the project, $1,000-2,000. Pays for illustration by the project,

$1,500-2,500. Considers complexity of the project and rights purchased when establishing payment. Rights purchased vary according to project.
Tips: "Be very patient!"

PAUL FRENCH AND PARTNERS, INC., 503 Gabbettville Rd., LaGrange GA 30240. (404)882-5581. Contact: Ms. Gene Byrd. Audiovisual firm. Client list provided upon request.
Needs: Works with 3 freelance artists/year. Works on assignment only. Uses artists for illustration.
First Contact & Terms: Send query letter with resume and slides to be kept on file. Samples not filed are returned by SASE. Reports back only if interested. To show a portfolio, mail appropriate materials. Pays for design and illustration by the hour, $25-100 average. Considers client's budget when establishing payment. Buys all rights.
Tips: "Be organized."

GARRETT COMMUNICATIONS, Box 53, Atlanta GA 30301. (404)755-2513. President: Ruby Grant Garrett. Production and placement firm for print media. Clients: banks, organizations, products-service consumer. Client list provided for SASE.
Needs: Assigns 24 freelance jobs/year. Works with 1 freelance illustrator and 1 freelance designer/month. Experienced, talented artists only. Works on assignment only. Uses artists for billboards, brochures, signage and posters.
First Contact & Terms: Send query letter with resume and samples to be kept on file. Samples returned by SASE if not kept on file. Reports within 10 days. Write to schedule an appointment to show a portfolio which should include roughs and tear sheets. Pays for design by the hour, $35-50; by the project, $100 minimum; by the day, $150 minimum. Pays for illustration by the hour, $35 minimum, by the project, $100 minimum; by the day, $100 minimum. Considers client's budget, skill and experience of artist and turnaround time when establishing payment. Negotiates rights purchased.
Tips: Send "6-12 items that show scope of skills."

***THE GORDON GROUP, INC.**, Suite 106, 3305 Breckinridge Blvd., Duluth GA 30136. (404)381-6662. President: M.J. Gordon. Ad agency/AV and PR firm; "full-service marketing communication programs." Clients: business-to-business, industry, service, non-retail, non-foods.
Needs: Assigns 20-30 freelance jobs/year. Uses artists for trade magazines, direct mail packages, brochures, catalogs, filmstrips, stationery, signage, P-O-P displays, AV presentations and posters. Artists should make contact "any way they can." Works on assignment only. Pays by the hour, $20 minimum. Pay "depends on the job and the budget. We pay hourly or on a project basis." Considers complexity of project, client's budget, skill and experience of artist, turnaround time and rights purchased when establishing payment. Buys all rights, material not copyrighted.
Tips: "Don't spend a lot of money on materials. Turn us on with a creative letter instead."

KAUFMANN ASSOCIATES, One Willow Sq., St. Simons Island GA 31522. (912)638-8678. Creative Director: S.C. Kaufmann. Ad agency. Clients: resort, food processor, bank.
Needs: Assigns "very few" freelance jobs/year. Works on assignment only. Works with 1 freelance illustrator/month. Uses artists for brochures.
First Contact & Terms: Send samples to be kept on file. Reports only if interested. Pays for design and illustration by the hour, $15-25; by the project, $100-800. Considers complexity of project, client's budget, and skill and experience of artist when establishing payment. Buys all rights.

LEWIS BROADCASTING CORP., Box 13646, Savannah GA 31406. Public Relations Director: C.A. Barbieri. TV producer.
Needs: Uses artists for direct mail brochures, billboards, posters, public service TV spots and motion picture work. Works on assignment only.
First Contact & Terms: Send query letter with resume and printed photocopied samples. Samples returned by SASE. Reports in 2 weeks. Provide business card and resume to be kept on file. Originals returned to artist at job's completion. Pay "depends on job."
Tips: "Be willing to flesh out others' ideas."

PRINGLE DIXON PRINGLE, Suite 1500, Marquis One Tower, 245 Peachtree Center Ave., Atlanta GA 30303. (404)688-6720. Creative Director: Perry Mitchell. Ad agency. Clients: fashion, financial, fast food and industrial firms; client list provided upon request.
Needs: Works with 2 illustrators/month. Local artists only. Works on assignment basis only. Uses freelance artists for billboards, consumer and trade magazines, direct mail, P-O-P displays, brochures, catalogs, posters, signage, newspapers and AV presentations.
First Contact & Terms: Arrange interview to show portfolio. Payment varies according to job and freelancer.

***THE PROJECT GROUP**, 2970 Peachtree Rd., Atlanta GA 30305. Contact: Creative Director. Ad agency. Project-oriented marketing/advertising/promotions firm. Clients: all types—business-to-business and consumer.
Needs: Works with 25 freelance artists/year. Assigns 30-40 jobs/year. Works on assignment only. Uses freelance artists for design, illustration, brochures, catalogs, newspapers, consumer and trade magazines, P-O-P displays, mechanicals, retouching, billboards, posters, direct mail packages, lettering and logos.
First Contact & Terms: Send query letter with brochure. Samples are filed. Reports back only if interested. Call or write to schedule an appointment to show a portfolio. Pays for design by the hour, $35-80; by the project, $250-2,000; by the day, $200 minimum. Pays for illustration by the hour, $40-80; by the project, $100-3,000. Considers complexity of project, client's budget, turnaround time and rights purchased when establishing payment. Buys all rights.
Tips: "Be patient and persistent."

J. WALTER THOMPSON COMPANY, One Atlanta Plaza, 950 East Paces Ferry Rd., Atlanta GA 30326. (404)365-7300. Executive Art Director: Bill Tomassi. Executive Creative Director: Mike Lollis. Ad agency. Clients: mainly financial, industrial and consumer. This office does creative work for Atlanta and the southeastern U.S.
Needs: Works with freelance illustrators. Works on assignment only. Uses artists for billboards, consumer magazines, trade magazines and newspapers.
First Contact & Terms: Send slides, original work, stats. Samples returned by SASE. Reports only if interested. No originals returned at job's completion. Call for appointment to show portfolio. Pays by the hour, $20-65 average; by the project, $100-6,000 average; by the day, $150-3,500 average. Considers complexity of project, client's budget, skill and experience of artist and rights purchased when establishing payment.
Tips: Wants to see samples of work done for different clients. Likes to see work done in different mediums. Likes variety and versatility. Artists interested in working here should "be *professional* and do top grade work." Deals with artists reps only.

Hawaii

PACIFIC PRODUCTIONS, Box 2881, Honolulu HI 96802. (808)531-1560. Production Manager: Bill Bennett. AV producer. Serves clients in industry, government and education. Produces almost all types of AV materials.
Needs: Assigns 2 jobs/year. Works with 3 illustrators, 2 animators and 2 designers/year. Uses artists for all types of projects.
First Contact & Terms: Artists located in Hawaii only. Send query letter and samples (Photostats or slides preferred). Samples returned. Provide resume to be kept on file for possible future assignments. Works on assignment only. Reports in 2 weeks. Pays by the project. Payment varies with each client's budget. No originals returned to artist following publication. Negotiates rights purchased.

Idaho

***I/D/E/A INC.**, 401 Main St., Caldwell ID 83605. (208)459-6357. Creative Director: Ben Shiley. Ad agency. Clients: direct mail.
Needs: Assigns 12-15 freelance jobs/year. Uses artists for direct mail packages, brochures, airbrush and photographs.
First Contact & Terms: Call before sending query letter with brochure, resume and samples to be kept on file. Write for artists' guidelines. Prefers the "most convenient samples for the artist." Samples not kept on file returned only if requested. Reports only if interested. Works on assignment only. Pays by the project, amount varies. Considers complexity of project, client's budget, and skill and experience of artist when establishing payment. Rights purchased vary with project.
Tips: "Most work goes into catalogs or brochures."

The asterisk before a listing indicates that the listing is new in this edition. New markets are often the most receptive to freelance submissions.

Illinois

***THE BEST COMPANY**, 3318 N. Main St., Rockford IL 61103. (815)877-4100. Vice President: Richard (Ric) Blencoe. Ad agency producing radio/TV commercials, brochures, newspaper and magazine ads, logo and corporate identity programs. Clients: mainly consumer accounts. Client list provided upon request.
Needs: Works with 10-20 freelance artists/year. Uses artists for design, illustration, brochures, consumer magazines, retouching, billboards, lettering and logos.
First Contact & Terms: Send query letter with brochure or resume, tear sheets, Photostats and slides. Samples are filed. Samples not filed are returned only if requested. Reports back within 2 weeks only if requested. Call or write to schedule an appointment to show a portfolio or mail roughs, original/final art and tear sheets. Pays for design by the hour, $20-45; by the project, $50 minimum. Pays for illustration by the hour, $50 minimum; by the project, $300 minimum. Considers complexity of project, client's budget and skill and experience of artist when establishing payment. Buys all rights; negotiates rights purchased.
Tips: "Do some research on agency and our needs to present portfolio in accordance. Will not see walk-ins."

• **BRAGAW PUBLIC RELATIONS SERVICES**, 800 E. Northwest Hwy., Palatine IL 60067. (312)934-5580. Principal: Richard S. Bragaw. PR firm. Clients: professional service firms, associations, industry.
Needs: Assigns 12 freelance jobs/year. Local artists only. Works on assignment only. Works with 1 freelance illustrator and 1 freelance designer/month. Uses artists for direct mail packages, brochures, signage, AV presentations and press releases.
First Contact & Terms: Send query letter with brochure to be kept on file. Reports only if interested. Write to schedule an appointment. Pays by the hour, $25-75 average. Considers complexity of project, skill and experience of artist and turnaround time when establishing payment. Buys all rights.
Tips: "Be honest."

CAIN AND COMPANY (ROCKFORD), 2222 E. State St., Rockford IL 61108. (815)399-2482. Senior Art Director: Randall E. Klein. Ad agency/PR firm. Clients: financial, industrial, retail and service.
Needs: Assigns 6 freelance jobs/year. Uses artists for consumer and trade magazines, billboards, direct mail packages, brochures, catalogs, newspapers, filmstrips, movies, stationery, signage, P-O-P displays, AV presentations, posters and press releases "to some degree."
First Contact & Terms: Send query letter with brochure, resume, business card, samples and tear sheets to be kept on file. Call or write for appointment to show portfolio. Send samples that show best one medium in which work is produced. Samples not kept on file are not returned. Reports only if interested. Works on assignment only. "Rates depend on talent and speed; could be anywhere from $5 to $30 an hour." Considers skill and experience of artist and turnaround time when establishing payment. Buys all rights.
Tips: "Have a good presentation, not just graphics."

JOHN CROWE ADVERTISING AGENCY, 1104 S. 2nd St., Springfield IL 62704. (217)528-1076. Contact: John Crowe. Ad/art agency. Clients: industries, manufacturers, retailers, banks, publishers, insurance firms, packaging firms, state agencies, aviation and law enforcement agencies.
Needs: Buys 3,000 illustrations/year. Works with 4 illustrators and 3 designers/month. Works on assignment only. Uses artists for color separations, animation, lettering, paste-up and type spec for work with consumer magazines, stationery design, direct mail, slide sets, brochures/flyers, trade magazines and newspapers. Especially needs layout, camera-ready art and photo retouching.
First Contact & Terms: "Send a letter to us regarding available work at agency. Tell us about yourself. We will reply if work is needed and request samples of work." Prefers tear sheets, original art, photocopies, brochure, business card and resume to be kept on file. Samples not filed returned by SASE. Reports in 2 weeks. Pays $25/hour illustration/camera-ready art; $4-15/per sketch. No originals returned to artist at job's completion. No payment for unused assigned illustrations.
Tips: Seeks neat, organized samples or portfolio. "Disorganized sloppy work in presenting talent" is the biggest mistake artists make. Foresees a trend toward computer art.

***CUMMINGS ADVERTISING**, 510 N. Church, Rockford IL 61103. (815)962-0615. Vice President/Creative Services: Stephen Thompson. Business-to-business advertising agency, full service. Clients: food (ingredients, food service), electronics, hardware and industrial.
Needs: Works with 20-25 freelance artists/year. Assigns 150-200 jobs/year. Prefers national and local illustrators; local retouchers and paste-up artists. Uses artists for illustration, mechanicals, retouching, direct mail packages and lettering.

First Contact & Terms: Send brochure or resume, tear sheets, Photostats, photocopies, slides or printed promos. Samples are filed. Samples not filed are returned by SASE only if interested. Call to schedule an appointment to show a portfolio, which should include tear sheets, final reproduction/product, color and b&w. Pays for design by the project, $250 minimum. Pays for illustration by the project, $150 minimum. Considers complexity of project, client's budget, turnaround time and skill and experience of artist when establishing payment. Negotiates rights purchased; rights purchased vary according to project.
Tips: "We need only professionals with specified or specialized skills—as we assign jobs per talent expertise, they must be reliable; we tend to assign to top-name talent with proven track record, but consider fresh talent if they can prove themselves."

DYNAMIC GRAPHICS, 6000 N. Forest Park Dr., Peoria IL 61614. Art Director: Frank Antal. Graphics firm for general graphic art user.
Needs: Works with 50 freelance artists/year. Works on assignment only. Uses artists for illustrations. Needs artists with "originality, creativity, professionalism."
First Contact & Terms: Send query letter with brochure showing art style or tear sheets and photocopies. Samples not filed are returned. Reports back within 1 month. To show a portfolio, mail appropriate materials, which should include final reproduction/product or Photostats. Pays by the project; "we pay highly competitive rates but prefer not to specify." Considers complexity of project, skill and experience of artist and rights purchased when establishing payment. Buys all rights.
Tips: "Submit styles that are the illustrators strongest and can be used successfully, consistently."

FILLMAN ADVERTISING INC., 304 W. Hill St., Champaign IL 61820. (217)352-0002. Art/Creative Director: Mary Auth. Ad agency. Serves clients in industry. Assigns 60 jobs and buys 10 illustrations/year.
Needs: Works with 1-2 illustrators and 2-3 designers/month. Uses mostly local artists. Works on assignment only. Uses artists for stationery design, direct mail, brochures/flyers, trade magazines.
First Contact & Terms: Send query letter with originals, photographs, b&w line drawings, photocopies of inputs or finished printed pieces. Samples returned by SASE. Reports in 2 weeks. Send business card and resume to be kept on file for possible future assignments. No originals returned to artist at job's completion. Pays $35-600/project; by the hour, $15-25 average. Pays promised fee for unused assigned illustrations. Considers skill and experience of artist when establishing payment.

● **FOLEY ADVERTISING INC.**, 17W715 Butterfield Rd., Oakbrook Terrace IL 60181. (312)782-1791. Ad agency. President: J.E. Foley. Industrial agency. Serves clients in equipment for science and manufacturing. Assigns 200 jobs/year.
Needs: Works with 3 designers/month. Local, industrial artists only. Works on assignment only. Uses artists for layout and mechanicals.
First Contact & Terms: Send query letter with samples to be kept on file and arrange interview to show portfolio. Considers complexity of project and client's budget when establishing payment.

IMPERIAL INTERNATIONAL LEARNING CORP., Box 548, Kankakee IL 60901. (815)933-7735. President: Spencer Barnard. AV producer. Serves clients in education. Produces filmstrips, illustrated workbooks, microcomputer software, video tapes.
Needs: Assigns multiple jobs/year. Works with variety of designers/year. Works on assignment only. Uses artists for original line art, color illustrations and graphic design, computer graphics.
First Contact & Terms: Send query letter and tear sheets to be kept on file. Samples returned only if requested. Reports back only if interested. Method and amount of payment are negotiated with the individual artist. No originals returned to artist following publication. Considers skill and experience of artist when establishing payment. Buys all rights.

ELVING JOHNSON ADVERTISING INC., 7804 W. College Dr., Palos Heights IL 60463. (312)361-2850. Art/Creative Director: Michael McNicholas. Ad agency. Serves clients in industrial machinery, construction materials, material handling, finance, etc.
Needs: Works with 2 illustrators/month. Local artists only. Uses artists for direct mail, brochures/flyers, trade magazines and newspapers. Also uses artists for layout, illustration, technical art, paste-up and retouching.
First Contact & Terms: Call for interview.

● **LERNER SCOTT CORP.**, 1000 Skokie Blvd., Wilmette IL 60091. (312)251-2447. Vice President/Managing Art Director: Mark Bryzinski. Direct marketing/ad agency. Clients: insurance and communications companies, wholesale distributors, entertainment and consumer products.
Needs: Works with 8 freelance artists/year. Chicago area artists only. Works on assignment only. Uses

artists for advertising design, illustration and layout; P-O-P displays, and signage.
First Contact & Terms: Send query letter with business card, photocopies or tear sheets to be kept on file. Samples not filed returned only if requested. Reports only if interested. Call for appointment to show portfolio. Pays for design by the hour, $20-80; by the project, $250. Pays for illustration by the project, $60 minimum. Considers complexity of project when establishing payment.
Tips: "I look for versatility—someone who can do a variety of styles and subjects. Also, I look for quality and seasoning. I don't have time for hand-holding or re-dos."

MARTINDALE & ASSOCIATES, #102, 350 West Kensington, Mount Prospect IL 60056. (312)437-6400. President: R. Martindale. Financial consultants. Clients: banks and savings and loans. Media used include billboards, consumer and trade magazines, direct mail, newspapers, radio and TV.
Needs: "Work load varies; usually our extra assignments (beyond what our regular staff can service efficiently) bunch up in active months such as January, May, September and October. Those extra assignments might be 5 or 6 newspaper ad layouts, 2 or 3 brochures, and perhaps a special design assignment." Works on assignment only. Uses artists for work in direct mail, brochures/flyers and newspapers.
First Contact & Terms: Write and request personal interview to show portfolio. Provide resume to be kept on file for future assignments. Reports within 10 days. Pays by the hour or by the project. Considers complexity of project, client's budget, skill and experience of artist, and turnaround time when establishing payment.
Tips: "We prefer to let the individual decide what he or she wants to show. If they can't show a strong portfolio, we can't expect them to be strong enough for our purposes." Artist should "stay within the *guidelines* of the assigned project."

ARTHUR MERIWETHER, INC., 1529 Brook Dr., Downers Grove IL 60515. (312)495-0600. Production Coordinator: Lori Ouska. Audiovisual firm, design studio and communications services. Clients: industrial corporations (electronics, chemical, etc.) plus consumer clients.
Needs: Works with 10-20 freelance artists/year. Artists should have minimum 2 years of experience. Prefers local artists, will occasionally work with out-of-state illustrators. Uses artists for keyline/paste-up, illustration and design. Especially important are knowledge of audiovisual and print production techniques.
First Contact & Terms: Send query letter with resume, business card, slides and tear sheets. Samples returned by SASE. Reports only if interested. Payment varies per project and artist's experience. Also considers client's budget, skill of artist and turnaround time when establishing payment. Rights purchased vary according to project; usually buys all rights.

MINDSCAPE, INC., 3444 Dundee Rd., Northbrook IL 60062. (312)480-7667. Art Director: Jack Nichols. Software publisher.
Needs: Works with 6-10 freelance artists/year. Minimum three years' experience. Works on assignment only. Uses artists for design, illustrations, brochures, catalog, books, mechanicals, retouching, animation and computer graphics. Artist must have design and production skills.
First Contact & Terms: Send query letter with brochure showing style or resume and samples. Samples not filed are returned by SASE. Reports only if interested. Call or write to schedule an appointment to show a portfolio, which should include roughs, original/final art, final reproduction/product, color and B&W. Pays for illustrations by the project, up to $3,000. Considers complexity of project, skill and experience of artist and turnaround time when establishing payment. Buys all rights.

MOTIVATION MEDIA INC., 1245 Milwaukee Ave., Glenview IL 60025. (312)297-4740. Contact: Creative Graphics Manager. Clients: consumer and industrial. Producers of multi-image programs, speaker support and sound-slide programs, filmstrips, motion picture and videotape productions.
Needs: Works with 10 production artists and 5 designers/month. Assigns approx. 675 jobs/year. Works on assignment only.
First Contact & Terms: Query with resume and nonreturnable samples (photocopies, duplicates, etc.). SASE. Replies in 2 weeks if interested. Provide resume to be kept on file for future assignments. Pays $10-18/hour, multi-image, charts/graphs art direction; $10-30/hour, illustrations; also pays by the job. Considers complexity of project, client's budget, skill and experience of artist and turnaround time when establishing payment. Pays 30 days after receipt of invoice.
Tips: "Send resume and copies of work. Our schedule does not allow us extensive time for interviewing. Though I need people who know slide production, I'm interested in people who know all areas of art production. Be able to see a project through from input to completion. In your resumes, be brief and to the point; list experience. In your portfolio, specify AV or slide experience."

***THE SCHRAM ADVERTISING CO.**, 450 Skokie Blvd., Northbrook, IL 60062. President: Ira P. Weinstein. Art Director: Ray Alpert. Ad agency.
Needs: Works with 2-3 illustrators/month and uses freelance designers. Uses artists and designers for collateral material and ads.
First Contact & Terms: Call for appointment to show portfolio. Samples returned by SASE. Reports in 1 week. Works on assignment only. Provide business card, brochure/flyer and samples to be kept on file for possible future assignments. Negotiates payment with freelancer.

TELEMATION PRODUCTIONS, INC., 3210 W. Westlake, Glenview IL 60025. (312)729-5215. Art Director: Mitch Levin. Video production house. Clients: automotive firms, corporate clients, advertising agencies and private producers.
Needs: Works with 3-5 freelance artists/year. Computer graphics experience and art background required. Works on assignment only. Uses artists for design, illustrations, animation, logos, charts/graphics and advertisements. Artists should have "good illustration skill, a strong sense of design and be visually-oriented."
First Contact & Terms: Send query letter with resume and samples. Samples not filed are not returned. Reports only if interested. Pays for design by the hour, $10-15. Considers skill and experience of artist when establishing payment. Buys all rights.
Tips: Artists should "be enthusiastic toward learning a new computer graphic system." Looks for "use of color, 3-D, texture."

***TRANSLIGHT MEDIA ASSOCIATES, INC.**, 931 W. Liberty Dr., Wheaton IL 60187. Executive Producer: John Lorimer. Audiovisual firm. Clients: office products industry, telecommunications, religious organizations, colleges.
Needs: Works with 10 freelance artists/year. Uses artists for logo development, design of AVs, layout, charts and graphs, special requirements, cartoons, "and more." Especially wants artists to have "an understanding of audiovisual and multi-image presentations and know how their art translates and fits into that medium."
First Contact & Terms: Works on assignment only. Send query letter with brochure, resume and samples (if available) to be kept on file. Samples not filed are returned only if requested. Reports back only if interested. Pays by the hour, $10-50 average. Considers client's budget, skill and experience of artist and turnaround time when establishing payment. Rights purchased vary according to project.

Chicago

***AUDITIONS BY SOUNDMASTERS**, Box 8135, Chicago IL 60680. (312)224-5612. Executive Vice President: R.C. Hillsman. Produces radio/TV programs, commercials, jingles and records.
Needs: Buys 125-300 designs/year. Uses artists for animation, catalog covers/illustrations, layout, paste-up, multimedia kits and record album design.
First Contact & Terms: Mail 8x10 art. SASE. Reports in 3 weeks. Material copyrighted. Pays $500 minimum, animation; $100-350, record jackets; $50-225, layout; $35-165, paste-up.

N.W. AYER, INC., One Illinois Center, 111 E. Wacker Dr., Chicago IL 60601. (312)645-8800. Contact: Iris Rogers. Ad agency. "We cover a very wide range of clients."
First Contact & Terms: Call for personal appointment to show portfolio. Negotiates payment based on client's budget and the amount of creativity required from artist.
Tips: Portfolio should consist of past work used by ad agencies and commercial art.

***E. H. BROWN ADVERTISING AGENCY, INC.**, 20 N. Wacker, Chicago IL 60606. (312)372-9494. Art Director: Arnold G. Pirsoul. Ad agency. Clients: insurance, schools, banks, corporations, electronics, high-tech, etc.
Needs: Works on assignment only. Uses artists for design, illustration, newspapers, retouching, lettering, charts/graphs and advertisements.
First Contact & Terms: Send Photostats, photocopies and photographs. Samples are filed. Samples not filed are not returned. Reports back only if interested. Call or write to schedule an appointment to show a portfolio, which should include roughs, tear sheets, color and b&w. Pays for design by the hour, $35-50. Pays for illustration by the project, $400-1,200. Considers complexity of project, client's budget, turnaround time, skill and experience of artist, how work will be used and rights purchased. Negotiates rights purchased; rights purchased vary according to project.
Tips: "Be precise and efficient about the job to be done. Avoid delays and be on time when the job is contracted. Stick with the estimate."

FRANK J. CORBETT, INC., 211 E. Chicago Ave., Chicago IL 60611. (312)664-5310. Associate Creative Director: Bill Reinwald. Ad agency. Serves clients in pharmaceuticals.
Needs: Works with 8-10 freelance illustrators/month. Uses freelancers "for almost everything."
First Contact & Terms: Call for appointment to show portfolio or make contact through artist's agent. Selection based on portfolio review. Negotiates payment based on client's budget.
Tips: Wants to see the best of artist's work including that used by ad agencies, and tear sheets of published art. Especially interested in good medical illustration, but also uses a wide variety of photography and illustration.

THE CREATIVE DEPARTMENT, LTD.,311 W. Superior, Chicago IL 60610. (312)440-9794. Vice President: Helen White. Estab. 1985. Ad agency/art studio. Clients: mostly industrial manufacturers of electronic components, railcars, T.V. components.
Needs: Works with 4 freelance artists 1 year. Prefers local artists only with minimum three years' experience. Works on assignment only. Uses artists for design, illustrations, brochures, catalog, P-O-P displays, retouching, posters, direct mail packages, lettering, logos and advertisements. Artists should have good lettering skills, marker renderings, creative ideas, knowledge of papers and inks, and varnishes.
First Contact & Terms: Send resume, tear sheets and photocopies. Samples not filed are returned by SASE only if requested. Reports back only if interested. Call to schedule an appointment to show portfolio, which should include thumbnails, roughs, original/final art, final reproduction/product, color, tear sheets photostats, photographs and b&w. Pays for design and illustration by the hour, $20 minimum. Considers complexity of project, client's budget and skill and experience of artist when establishing payment. Buys all rights.
Tips: "Don't show fashion illustrations when I'm interested in designing brochures for steel companies and faucet manufacturers!"

THE CREATIVE ESTABLISHMENT, 1421 N. Wells, Chicago IL 60610. (312)943-6700. President: Joan Beugen. Also: 115 W. 31st St., New York NY 10001. (212)563-3337, and 832 Sansome, San Francisco CA 94111. (415)982-0800. Chairman: Ira Kerns. AV/multimedia/motion picture producer. Clients: Fortune 500 and other major U.S. corporations. Audience: top level executives, managers, salesmen, distributors and/or suppliers of the specific client. "We produce slides, films and multimedia presentations primarily for industry. Our specialty is large sales and management meetings, using multiscreen slide projection. The slides we use range over every conceivable type and format, since we produce in the neighborhood of 30,000 slides a month."
Needs: Works with 1-5 illustrators and 1-10 designers/month. Local artists only. Works on assignment only. Uses artists for motion pictures and slides. "We use illustrators, cartoonists, designers, costume and set designers, sculptors, model-makers. . .you name it."
First Contact & Terms: "I am most interested in hearing from artists and art directors who have experience in slides as opposed to print work. However, we do use illustrators occasionally and show them how to prepare their work for reproduction into slides." Send resume, brochure/flyer, business card, tear sheets and sample slides to be kept on file. Samples not filed returned by SASE. Reports within 2 weeks. Call to schedule an appointment to show a portfolio, which should include photographs and storyboards—"actual slides." Originals returned at job's completion if special arrangements are made. Pays by the hour, $15-20; by the project, $450/week. Considers client's budget and turnaround time when establishing payment.

***DARBY MEDIA GROUP**, 4015 N. Rockwell St., Chicago IL 60618. Creative Director: Tony Christian. Production Manager: Dennis Cyrier. Audiovisual/offset printing firm. Clients: corporate, ad agencies, educational.
Needs: Works with 10-20 freelance artists and designers/year. Uses artists for production and illustration. Especially important for artists to have knowledge of audiovisual production.
First Contact & Terms: Local artists only (Chicago metropolitan area). Send query letter with resume and samples (if possible) to be kept on file. Write for appointment to show portfolio. Prefers slides as samples. Samples not filed are returned. Reports back only if interested. Pays by the hour, $10-25 average; by the project or by the day. Considers complexity of the project, client's budget, skill and experience of artist and turnaround time when establishing payment. Rights purchased vary according to project.
Tips: "Be design-oriented. Be knowledgeable on all aspects of AV and print production. Supply your own working tools."

FINANCIAL SHARES CORPORATION, 62 W. Huron, Chicago IL 60610. (312)943-8116. Contact: Art Director. Training and public relations firm. Helps financial institutions achieve profitable results through high-quality customized consulting services. Our services include: market research, strategic marketing planning, product design and pricing, public and investor relations, sales training. We also

develop and implement sales incentive and measurement programs. Clients: all financial institutions.
Needs: Works with 6 freelance artists/year. Assigns 50 jobs/year. Prefers local artists only. Uses artists for design, brochures, newspapers, logos, charts/graphs and advertisements.
First Contact & Terms: Send query letter with brochure. Reports back within two weeks. Write to schedule an appointment to show a portfolio, which should include original/final art, Photostats and final reproduction/product. Pays for design by the project. Considers client's budget, turnaround time and skill and experience of artist when establishing payment. Rights purchased vary according to project.

***GARFIELD-LINN & COMPANY**, 142 E. Ontario,, Chicago IL 60611. (312)943-1900. Contact: Art Directors or Creative Director. Ad agency. Clients: "wide variety" of accounts; client list provided upon request.
Needs: Number of freelance artists used varies. Uses freelance artists for billboards, consumer and trade magazines, direct mail, brochures, catalogs and posters.
First Contact & Terms: Query with samples; arrange interview to show portfolio. Works on assignment basis only. Payment is by the project; negotiates according to client's budget.

HILL AND KNOWLTON, INC., 1 Illinois Center, 111 E. Wacker Dr., Chicago IL 60601. (312)565-1200. Creative Director: Jacqueline Kohn. PR firm. Clients: corporate, financial, industrial products, medical, pharmaceutical, and public utilities.
Needs: Works with 1-2 illustrators/month. Works on assignment only. Uses artists for annual reports, brochures, employee publications and associated print and collateral.
First Contact & Terms: Call for appointment to show portfolio, which should include business card, brochure/flyer, samples and tear sheets to be kept on file. Prefers printed samples, slides or original photos and art as samples. Reports back whether to expect possible future assignments.
Tips: Has very broad needs of highest quality. Will discuss these and particular needs during initial call. Artists interested in working here should be "punctual on appointments; arrange portfolio to pertain to our needs only."

IMAGINE THAT!, Suite 4908, 405 N. Wabash Ave., Chicago IL 60611. (312)670-0234. President: John Beele. Ad agency. Clients: broadcast, insurance firm, University of Illinois sports program, pharmaceuticals, retail furniture stores, real estate and professional rodeo.
Needs: Assigns 25-50 jobs and buys 15 illustrations/year. Uses artists for layout, illustration, mechanicals and photography.
First Contact & Terms: Arrange interview to show portfolio with Sheila Dunbar. Pay is negotiable.

***INSIGHT, INC.**, 100 E. Ohio St., Chicago IL 60611. (312)467-4350. Executive Art Director: Maureen Pesek. Audiovisual firm. Clients: major corporations.
Needs: Works with 5-15 freelance artists/year. Uses artists for AV module and speaker support storyboards, theme graphics, production and art.
First Contact & Terms: Local artists only with a minimum of one year of experience. Call or write for appointment to show portfolio. Prefers to review slides. Reports back only if interested. Pays by the hour, $10-18 average, or by the project. Considers complexity of the project, client's budget, skill and experience of artist and the type of work the artist performs when establishing payment. Buys all rights.

KEROFF & ROSENBERG ADVERTISING, 444 N. Wabash, Chicago IL 60611. (312)321-9000. Creative Supervisor: Dan Oditt. Ad and design agency. Clients: realty, financing, hotels.
Needs: Works with 10-12 freelance artists/year. Local, experienced artists only. Uses artists for advertising illustration and layout, brochure illustration, model making and signage.
First Contact & Terms: Send query letter with resume and Photostats, photographs, slides or tear sheets to be kept on file. Samples not filed returned by SASE only if requested. Reports only if interested. Write for appointment to show portfolio. Considers complexity of project and turnaround time when establishing payment.
Tips: "Freelancers usually get the overflow, so it's frequently under a tight deadline. So be prepared."

MANDABACH & SIMMS, Suite 3620, 20 N. Wacker Dr., Chicago IL 60606. (312)236-5333. Creative Director: B. Bentkover. Ad agency. Clients: food services, financial, graphic arts and real estate.
Needs: Works with 5-10 freelance illustrators/month. Works on assignment only. Uses freelancers for print advertising and collateral material.
First Contact & Terms: Send business card and tear sheets to be kept on file. Samples not filed are not returned. Reports back whether to expect possible future assignments. Negotiates payment based on client's budget.
Tips: Wants to see work relating to their clients' needs. Artists interested in working here should be "creative, businesslike, and remember the objective."

MANNING, SELVAGE & LEE/MID-AMERICA, Suite 1713, 2 Illinois Center, 233 N. Michigan Ave., Chicago IL 60601. (312)819-3535. PR firm. Managing Director: James O. Ahtes. Clients: medical, industry, food, beverage and corporate.
Needs: Assigns 2-3 jobs/year. Local artists only. Uses artists for brochures/flyers, and company magazines.
First Contact & Terms: Query with samples (include prices on samples) and arrange interview to show portfolio. Wants only samples of finished work: "depending on your specialty—the best, most recent (within 2 years) work you have done for the largest clients you have." Samples returned by SASE within 2 weeks. Works on assignment only. Provide brochure/flyer to be kept on file for possible future assignments. Pays $300-5,000/project; $50-150/hour—"we ask for estimate in advance." Considers complexity of project, client's budget, skill and experience of artist, and turnaround time when establishing payment.
Tips: "Artists interested in working with us should have good selection of brochures, mailers, annual reports, as well as a list of clients. Usually we ask freelance artists to send us a background letter telling us about work done and specialty if any. If interested, we will set up an appointment to view work, ask for a card, brochure, or something to be left behind for our files. We already have a number of artists we work with, so new ones are most likely to be kept on file."

MARKETING SUPPORT INC., 303 E. Wacker Dr., Chicago IL 60601. (312)565-0044. Executive Art Director: Robert Becker. Clients: plumbing, heating/cooling equipment, chemicals, hardware, ski equipment, home appliances, crafts and window covering.
Needs: Assigns 300 jobs/year. Works with 2-3 illustrators/month. Local artists only. Works on assignment only. Uses artists for filmstrips, slide sets, brochures/flyers and trade magazines. Also uses artists for layout, illustration, lettering, type spec, paste-up and retouching for trade magazines and direct mail.
First Contact & Terms: Arrange interview to show portfolio. Samples returned by SASE. Reports back only if interested. Provide business card to be kept on file for future assignments. No originals returned to artist at job's completion. Pays $15/hour and up. Considers complexity of project, client's budget, and skill and experience of artist when establishing payment.

NYSTROM, division of Herff Jones, Inc., 3333 N. Elston Ave., Chicago IL 60618. Contact: Editorial Department. AV producer. Serves clients in education. Produces multimedia kits for elementary education, including filmstrips, booklets, transparencies, copymasters, picture cards and study prints.
Needs: Works with "a few" illustrators and animators and designers/year, "but most are for large assignments." Chicago area artists only. Works on assignment only. Uses artists for photos, original artwork, box design, and keylining and paste-up.
First Contact & Terms: Send resume, "samples optional," to be kept on file. Prefers "original work if convenient; otherwise Photostats will do." Samples returned by SASE if not kept on file. Reports in 2 weeks. Pays by the project or by the hour, "depending on project and type of work called for." Amount of payment is negotiated with the individual artist. Payment varies with each client's budget. No originals returned to artist following publication. Buys all rights.
Tips: "We do not wish to be contacted by phone."

O.M.A.R. INC., 5525 N. Broadway, Chicago IL 60640. (312)271-2720. Creative Director: Paul Sierra. Spanish language ad agency. Clients: consumer food, telephone communication, TV station and public utilities.
Needs: Number of freelance artists used varies. Local artists only. Works on assignment only. Uses artists for consumer magazines, posters, newspapers and TV graphics.
First Contact & Terms: Send query letter with resume of credits, slides or originals (color) and photostats (b&w); follow with phone call. Samples returned by SASE. Reports within 3 weeks. Payment is by the project; negotiates according to client's budget. Buys all rights.
Tips: Three trends in this field are: "messages aimed at young audiences, bilingual TV commercials and more sophisticated Spanish language commercials." Artists interested in working here "must have sensitivity to the Hispanic culture. An artist should never sacrifice pride in his/her work for the sake of a deadline, yet must nevertheless meet the specified time of completion. Show only your best work during an interview, and don't take too much time."

POLYCOM TELEPRODUCTIONS, 142 E. Ontario, Chicago IL 60611. (312)337-6000. Executive Producer/Director: Mr. Carmen V. Trombetta. Producer: Debbie Heagy. Videotape teleproducer. Clients: 60% are major Chicago advertising and PR firms and educational/industrial enterprises and 40% are corporate enterprises. Produces filmstrips, motion pictures, multimedia kits, overhead transparencies, slide sets, sound-slide sets, videotapes and films.
Needs: Works with 2-3 illustrators/month. Works on assignment only. Assigns 150-200 jobs/year. Uses artists for motion pictures, videotape teleproduction, television copy art, storyboard animation and computer animation.

First Contact & Terms: Query with resume, business card and slides which may be kept on file. Samples not kept on file are returned by SASE. Reports in 2-3 weeks. Original art returned to artist at job's completion. Negotiates pay by project.
Tips: "Artists must be familiar with film and videotape. We need more videotape and computer graphics artists."

SIEBER & McINTYRE, INC., 625 N. Michigan Ave., Chicago IL 60611. (312)266-9200. Contact: Creative Services Manager. Ad agency. Clients: pharmaceutical and health care fields.
Needs: Work load varies. Works on assignment only. Uses freelancers for medical trade magazines, journal ads, brochures/flyers and direct mail to physicians. Especially needs sources for tight marker renderings and comp layouts.
First Contact & Terms: Send query letter with resume and samples. Call for appointment to show portfolio, which should include roughs, original/final art, final reproduction/product, color, Photostats and photographs. Reports within 2 weeks. Pays by the hour, $10-50. Negotiates payment based on client's budget, where work will appear, complexity of project, skill and experience of artist and turnaround time.
Tips: "Rendering with markers very important." Prefers to see original work rather than reproductions, but will review past work used by other ad agencies. Needs good medical illustrators but is looking for the best person—one who can accomplish executions other than anatomical. Artists should send resume or letter for files.

SOCIETY FOR VISUAL EDUCATION, INC., 1345 W. Diversey Pkwy., Chicago IL 60614. Graphic Arts Manager: Cathy Mijou. Audiovisual and microcomputer firm. No outside clients; all work done for SVE products and services. Produces filmstrips, micro software, video disks and some print materials (but not books) for education market—schools, libraries, etc.
Needs: Works with 10 or more freelance artists/year. Works on assignment only. Uses artists for keyline/paste-up, illustration, design, photography, and computer graphics for filmstrips, micro software and print materials. Artist must have demonstrated ability in these areas.
First Contact & Terms: Send query letter and photostats, tear sheets, etc. to be kept on file. Nonreturnable samples only. Reports only if interested. "No phone calls." Payment varies according to scope and requirements of project. Considers complexity of the project, budget, skill and experience of artist, turnaround time and rights purchased when establishing payment. Buys all rights.

Indiana

***ADVIEW COMMUNICATIONS**, 3610 Westview Blvd., Muncie IN 47304. President: Ron Groves. Vice President/Media Director: Cindi Wheat. Art Director: Kevin Byrd. Ad agency. Clients: industrial, banks, food chains and religious publishers.
Needs: Works with 2 illustrators/month. Uses illustrators for consumer magazines, direct mail, television, brochures/flyers, trade magazines and newspapers.
First Contact & Terms: Provide brochure and/or resume to be kept on file for future assignments. No originals returned to artist at job's completion.
Tips: "Would welcome inquiries from writers, photographers, designers and retouchers for industrial, technical and financial printed communications. Call in person and show samples. Formal appointment and presentation are not necessary, just let us know a few hours ahead of time that you plan to stop by. Leave your business card and keep in touch."

***ASHER AGENCY**, 511 W. Wayne, Fort Wayne IN 46802. (219)424-3373. Creative Director: Renee Wright. Ad agency and public relations firm. Clients: automotive firms, hospitals, convention centers, apartment development, area economic development agencies.
Needs: Works with 10 freelance artists/year. Assigns 50 jobs/year. Prefers area artists. Works on assignment only. Uses freelance artists for design, illustration, brochures, catalogs, consumer and trade magazines, retouching, billboards, posters, direct mail packages, logos and advertisements.
First Contact & Terms: Send query letter with brochure showing art style or tear sheets and photocopies. Samples are filed. Samples not filed are returned by SASE. Reports back only if interested. Write to schedule an appointment to show a portfolio, which should include roughs, original/final art, tear sheets and final reproduction/product. Pays for design by the hour, $20 minimum. Pays for illustration by the hour. Considers complexity of project, client's budget, turnaround time and skill and experience of artist when establishing payments. Buys all rights.
Tips: In portfolios, "we'd like to see rough or comp layouts as well as finished, printed work."

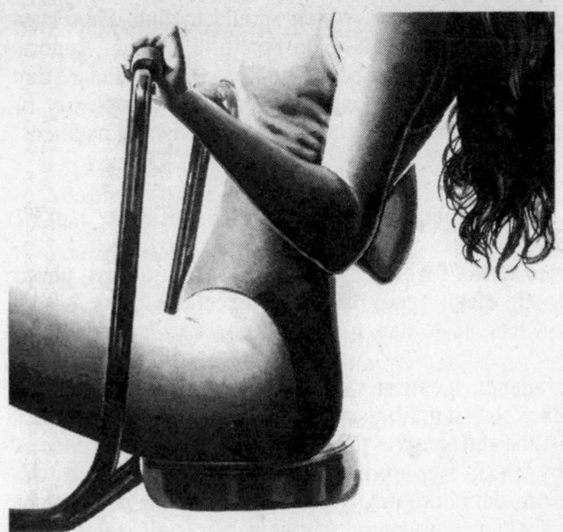

Artist: Merlen Seslar

Renee Wright, creative director of the Asher Agency in Fort Wayne, Indiana, had worked with illustrator Merlen Seslar of Churubusco, Indiana, for years and therefore asked Seslar to illustrate an ad for a new health club when the assignment arose. Wright bought all rights to the ad, which was designed for a newspaper campaign.

C.R.E. INC., 400 Victoria Centre, 22 E. Washington St., Indianapolis IN 46204. Senior Art Director: Roger Dobrovodsky. Ad agency. Clients: industrial, banks, agriculture and consumer.
Needs: Works with 15 freelance artists/year. Works on assignment only. Uses artists for line art, color illustrations and airbrushing.
First Contact & Terms: Send query letter with resume, and photocopies to be kept on file. Samples not filed are returned. Reports back only if interested. Call or write to schedule an appointment to show a portfolio, or mail original/final art, final reproduction/product and tear sheets. Pays by the project, $100 minimum. Considers complexity of the project, client's budget, skill and experience of artist and rights purchased when establishing payment. Buys all rights.
Tips: "Show samples of good creative talent."

CALDWELL-VAN RIPER, INC. ADVERTISING-PUBLIC RELATIONS, 1314 N. Meridian St., Indianapolis IN 46202. (317)632-6501. Creative Coordinator: Kathy Hendry. Ad agency/PR firm. Clients are a "good mix of consumer (banks, furniture, food, etc.) and industrial (chemicals, real estate, insurance, heavy industry)."
Needs: Assigns 100-200 freelance jobs/year. Works with 10-15 freelance illustrators/month. Works on assignment only. Uses artists for consumer and magazine ads, billboards, direct mail packages, brochures, catalogs, newspaper ads, P-O-P displays, storyboards, AV presentations and posters.
First Contact & Terms: Send query letter with brochure, samples and tear sheets to be kept on file. Call for appointment to show portfolio. Accepts any available samples. Samples not filed are returned by SASE only if requested. Reports only if interested. Pay is negotiated. Considers complexity of project, client's budget, skill and experience of artist and rights purchased when establishing payment. Buys all rights.
Tips: "Send 5 samples of best work (copies acceptable) followed by a phone call."

HANDLEY & MILLER, INC., 1712 N. Meridian, Indianapolis IN 46202. (317)927-5545. Art Director/Vice President: Irvin Showalter. Ad agency. Clients: package goods, sales promotion, retail, direct response, institutional and financial.
Needs: Works with 2 freelance illustrators/month. Works on assignment only. Uses freelancers for consumer and trade magazines, brochures/flyers, newspapers and P-O-P displays.

"Our clients are very pragmatic. They want work that is not 'art for art's sake' but related to their image and marketing goals."

—Alison Davis, Davis, Hays & Company, Hackensack, New Jersey

First Contact & Terms: Call for appointment to show portfolio, which should include Photostats, slides, computer graphic samples and original work. Selection based on portfolio review. Reports within 5 days if interested. Send business card and brochure/flyer to be kept on file. Pays standard day rate; by the hour, $40-100; by the project, $400-2,500; also by contract. Considers complexity of project, client's budget, skill and experience of artist, and turnaround time when establishing payment.
Tips: Likes to see a variety of techniques.

***HEMINGER ADVERTISING**, 318 Westwood Dr., Michigan City IN 46360. President: Jack R. Heminger. Ad agency. Clients: hardware/industrial.
Needs: Works with 2-6 freelance artists/year. Uses artists for illustrations, keyline/paste-ups, photo retouching, catalog work. Especially seeks "good, clean type, keylines, excellent reproductive qualities; willingness to do what client/art director wants; up-to-date materials/processes; and ability to meet deadlines on time."
First Contact & Terms: Local artists only for agency location working conditions. Artists must "purchase own supplies; have transportation to agency or fast mailing conditions; and be experienced, 5 years at least." Works on assignment only. Send resume and samples to be kept on file. No preference as to type of samples. Samples not filed are returned by SASE. Reports back only if interested. Pays by the hour, $15-20 average; catalog work, $25/page. Considers complexity of the project, client's budget, skill and experience of artist and rights purchased when establishing payment. Buys all rights.
Tips: "Neatness and presentation of work are important as is fulfilling all obligations at time agreed upon."

KARTES VIDEO COMMUNICATIONS, 10 E. 106th St., Indianapolis IN 46280. Senior Art Director: Susan Thomas. Video production company and publishing facility.
Needs: Works with 20-50 freelance artists/year. Artist must have experience and samples. Works on assignment only. Uses artists for design, illustrations, books, P-O-P displays, mechanicals, retouching, direct mail packages and lettering.
First Contact & Terms: Send query letter with brochure showing art style or tear sheets. Samples not filed are returned only if requested. Reports only if interested. Call or write to schedule an appointment to show a portfolio, which should include thumbnails, roughs, original/final art, final reproduction/product, color, tear sheets, Photostats, photographs, b&w and representative work in any area. Pays for illustrations by the project, $50-1,000. Considers how work will be used when establishing payment. Rights purchased vary according to project.

Iowa

***ADMARK ADVERTISING**, 109 1st St. SE, Box 779, Mason City IA 50401. (515)424-0191. Art Director: Jackie Loterbour. Ad agency providing catalogs, brochures, newspaper and magazine ads, radio, etc. Clients: business-to-business banks, battery manufacturer, I.D. tag manufacturer.
Needs: Works with 10 freelance artists/year. Assigns 10-25 jobs/year. Works on assignment only. Uses artists for illustration, brochures, catalogs, newspapers, magazines, mechanicals, retouching and animation.
First Contact & Terms: Send query letter with brochure or resume, tear sheets, Photostats, photocopies, slides and photographs. Samples not filed are returned only if requested. Reports back within days. Call or write to schedule an appointment to show a portfolio, which should include thumbnails, roughs, original/final art, Photostats, tear sheets, final reproduction/product, photographs, color, b&w and slides. Pays for design by the project, $200. Pays for illustration by the project, $30-400. Considers complexity of project, client's budget, skill and experience of artist when establishing payment. Buys all rights. Rights purchased vary according to project.
Tips: "Be prepared when contacting firm.

LA GRAVE KLIPFEL CLARKSON INC., Suite 300, 2700 Grand Ave., Des Moines IA 50312. (515)283-2297. Art Director: Rex Anthony. Ad agency. Clients: "wide range" of accounts—financial, industrial and retail; client list provided upon request.
Needs: Works with 3-4 illustrators or designers/month. Local artists only. Works on assignment only. Uses freelance artists for billboards, consumer and trade magazines, direct mail, P-O-P displays, brochures, catalogs, posters, signage, newspapers, TV art direction and AV presentations.
First Contact & Terms: Phone first and follow with mailed information. Negotiates payment by the project and on freelancer's previous experience.
Tips: "Present resume or self-promotion piece. Have a portfolio of no more than 20 pieces. Be neat and clean with presented pieces. Be brief and concise in talking about work; avoid speeches."

Kansas

LANE & LESLIE ADVERTISING AGENCY INC., Petroleum Bldg., Box 578, Wichita KS 67201. President: David W. Lane. Ad agency. Clients: banks, savings and loans, consumer products and fast food.
Needs: Works with 1 illustrator and 6 designers/month. Uses artists for storyboards, billboards, P-O-P displays, filmstrips, multimedia kits, direct mail, slide sets, brochures/flyers, trade magazines and newspapers. Also uses artists for photography and retouching.
First Contact & Terms: Send query letter with resume, tear sheets, photostats, photocopies, slides and photographs. Call or write to schedule an appointment to show a portfolio, which should include original final art, final reproduction/product, tear sheets, photostats and photographs. No originals returned to artist at job's completion. Pays by the hour and by the project; payment based on project. "We prefer to buy all rights."

MARKETAIDE, INC., Box 500, Salina KS 67402-0500. (913)825-7161. Production Manager: Eric Lamer. Full-service advertising/marketing/direct mail firm. Clients: financial, agricultural machinery, industrial, some educational, and fast food.
Needs: Prefers artists within one-state distance and possessing professional expertise. Works on assignment only. Uses freelance artists for illustrations, retouching, signage.
First Contact & Terms: Send query letter with resume, business card and samples to be kept on file. Accepts any kind of accurate representation as samples, depending upon medium. Samples not kept on file are returned only if requested. Reports only if interested. Write for appointment to show portfolio. Pays by the hour, $15-75 average; "since projects vary in size we are forced to estimate according to each job's parameters." Considers complexity of project, skill and experience of artist, how work will be used, turnaround time and rights purchased when establishing payment.
Tips: Artists interested in working here "should be highly-polished in technical ability, have a good eye for design and be able to meet all deadline commitments."

MARSHFILM ENTERPRISES, INC., Box 8082, Shawnee Mission KS 66208. (816)523-1059. President: Joan K. Marsh. Audiovisual firm. Clients: schools.
Needs: Works with 1-2 freelance artists/year. Works on assignment only. Uses artists for illustrating filmstrips. Artists must have experience and imagination.
First Contact & Terms: Send query letter, resume and slides or actual illustrations to be kept on file "if it is potentially the type of art we would use." Samples not filed are returned. Reports within 1 month. Write for appointment to show portfolio. Considers client's budget when establishing payment. Buys all rights.

TRAVIS-WALZ AND ASSOCIATES, INC., 8417 Santa Fe Dr., Overland Park KS 66212-2749. Contact: Gary Otteson. Ad agency. Serves clients in food, finance, broadcasting, utilities, pets, gardening and real estate.
Needs: Works with 2-4 illustrators/month. "We generally work with in-town talent because of tight deadlines." Commissioned work only. Uses illustrators for billboards, P-O-P displays, consumer magazines, direct mail, brochures/flyers, trade magazines and newspapers. Also uses artists for retouching. Does not buy design or layout. Agency has its own design staff.
First Contact & Terms: Send query letter with brochure showing art style or tear sheets, Photostats and photocopies. Samples returned by SASE. Reports only if interested. Call to schedule an appointment to show portfolio, which should include final reproduction/product and tear sheets. No originals returned to artist at job's completion. Pays for design by the project, $100 minimum. Pays ofr illustration by the project, $150 minimum. Consider complexity of project, client's budget and turnaround time when establishing payment.
Tips: "We must see your work to buy. The best way to sell yourself is by your samples shown in person or brochure mailed to us. We see 4 to 5 freelancers a week. More and more illustrators are entering the market. Our market is flooded so the competition is very stiff. We are using about the same amount of illustration and photography as a year before. Try to find a specialty that no one else is doing."

"Work is being quoted by the project. Companies are becoming more conservative. Clients are becoming more sophisticated and using art for more applications."

—Peter Schwartz, Imagematrix
Cincinnati, Ohio

Kentucky

DAN BURCH ASSOCIATES, 2338 Frankfort Ave., Louisville KY 40206. (502)895-4881. Art Director: Joe Burch. Specializes in business-to-business and packaged goods advertising, marketing and technical communications, brand and corporate identity, bruchures, catalogs, direct mail, P-O-P displays, trade show exhibits, AV, packaging and signage. Clients: industrial, technical and consumer goods manufacturers and services.
Needs: Uses freelance artists for illustration, cartooning and photo retouching on advertising and collateral materials.
First Contact & Terms: Send query letter with samples of work to be kept on file for future assignments. Pays for illustration and photoretouching by the project, $50-1,000.
Tips: Looks for "the ability to *finish* the work regardless of subject, style, etc., to the point of completion." A common mistake freelancers make in presenting samples is "not researching our needs before presenting and making us sit through too many pieces of inappropriate samples."

FESSEL, SIEGFRIEDT & MOELLER ADVERTISING, 1500 Heyburn Building, Box 1031, Louisville KY 40201. (502)585-5154. Vice President/Executive Art Director: James A. Berry. Ad agency. Clients: mostly consumer firms, some industrial.
Needs: Works with 3 illustrators/year. Works primarily with local freelancers. Uses freelance artists for billboards, consumer and trade magazines, direct mail, P-O-P displays, brochures, catalogs, posters, signage, newspapers and AV presentations.
First Contact & Terms: Arrange interview to show portfolio. Works on assignment only. Payment varies according to project estimates.

Louisiana

BENJAMIN ADVERTISING , (formerly Herbert S. Benjamin Associates), 2736 Florida St., Box 2151. Baton Rouge LA 70821. (504)387-0611. Art Director: Ana Espinosa. Clients: food, financial, industrial, retail fashion/furniture, etc.
Needs: Works with 2-3 illustrators/month. Works with freelance artists on assignment only. Uses artists for industrial, trade and business journals; newspapers, TV, brochures/flyers, newsletters.
First Contact & Terms: Call for appointment to show portfolio. Provide resume and samples to be kept on file for possible future assignments. Especially needs good retail illustrator in advertising areas such as furniture, fashion, etc. Illustrators must conform to area rates.
Tips: When reviewing an artist's work, particularly looks for "competence in drawing and lettering and knowledge of type, originality in ideas, simplicity and strength of design, and technique."

CARTER ADVERTISING INC., 800 American Tower, Shreveport LA 71101. (318)227-1920. President: Bill Bailey Carter. Ad agency. Clients: banks, real estate, airline, toy manufacturing, fast food and hospital. Assigns 150 jobs and buys 50 illustrations/year.
Needs: Works with 2-3 illustrators and 2-3 designers/month. Prefers local artists. "Must have heavy production experience." Uses artists for billboards, P-O-P displays, filmstrips, consumer magazines, stationery design, multimedia kits, direct mail, television, slide sets, brochures/flyers, trade magazines, album covers, newspapers, books and mechanicals.
First Contact & Terms: Query with resume or arrange interview to show portfolio. SASE. Reports within 2 weeks. Provide brochure, flyer, business card, resume, tear sheets, etc., to be kept on file for future assignments. No originals returned at job's completion unless otherwise agreed upon. Pay negotiated by project. Considers complexity of project, client's budget, skill and experience of artist, geographic scope of finished project, turnaround time and rights purchased when establishing payment.

CUNNINGHAM, SLY ADVERTISING, (formerly Cunningham, Sly & Associates, Inc.) Box 4503, Shreveport LA 71134-0503. Creative Director: Harold J. Sly. Ad agency. Clients: industrial/financial.
Needs: Works with 6-10 freelance artists/year. Works on assignment only. Uses artists for layout/design, illustrations, photo retouching, mechanical art and airbrushing. Especially looks for mechanical skills.
First Contact & Terms: Send query letter with brochure, resume, business card and samples to be kept on file. Samples not filed are returned only by request. Reports back only if interested. Pays by the hour, $20-50 average. Considers complexity of the project, client's budget and turnaround time when establishing payment. Rights purchased vary according to project.

DUKE UNLIMITED, INC., Suite 205, 1940 I-10 Service Road, Kenner LA 70065. (504)464-1891. President: Lana Duke. Ad agency. Clients: industrial, investment, medical, restaurants, entertainment, fashion and tourism.
Needs: Assigns 50 freelance jobs/year. Works with 2 freelance illustrators and 1 freelance designer/month. Works on assignment. Uses artists for consumer and trade magazines, billboards, direct mail packages, brochures, catalogs, newspapers, filmstrips, movies, stationery, signage, P-O-P displays, AV presentations, posters and press releases.
First Contact & Terms: Send query letter with brochure, business card, Photostats and tear sheets to be kept on file. Samples returned only if requested. Reports only if interested. Pays by the project, $150-1,000 average. The artist must provide a firm quotation in writing. Considers complexity of project, client's budget, skill and experience of artist, turnaround time and rights purchased when establishing payment. Buys all rights.

Maryland

***ALBAN BRUCE COMMUNICATIONS**, 1001 Cromwell Br. Rd., Towson MD 21204. (301)828-1220. Contact: Vice President. "We provide speaker support slides, AV multi-image, computer graphics."
Needs: Works with 30 freelance artists/year. Assigns 50 jobs/year. Uses artists for design and charts/graphs.
First Contact & Terms: Send query letter or resume and photocopies. Samples are filed. Samples not filed are returned only if requested by artist. Reports back only if interested. Write to schedule an appointment to show a portfolio, which should include original/final art and slides. Pays for design by the hour, $20 minimum; by the project, $100 minimum. Considers complexity of project, client's budget, turnaround time and how work will be used when establishing payment. Buys all rights; negotiates rights purchased.

SAMUEL R. BLATE ASSOCIATES, 10331 Watkins Mill Dr., Gaithersburg MD 20879-2935. (301)840-2248. President: Samuel R. Blate. Audiovisual and editorial services firm. Clients: business/professional, U.S. government, some private.
Needs: Works with 5 freelance artists/year. "We prefer to work with artists in the Washington-Baltimore-Richmond metro area." Works on assignment only. Uses artists for cartoons (especially for certain types of audiovisual presentations), illustrations (graphs, etc.) for 35mm slides, pamphlet and book design. Especially important are "technical and aesthetic excellence and ability to meet deadlines."
First Contact & Terms: Send query letter with resume and tear sheets, Photostats, photocopies, slides and photographs to be kept on file. "No original art, please. SASE for return." Call or write for appointment to show portfolio, which should include final reproduction/product, color, photographs and b&w. Samples are returned by SASE. Reports only if interested. Pays by the hour, $20-40. "Payment varies as a function of experience, skills needed, size of project, and anticipated competition, if any." Also considers complexity of the project, client's budget, turnaround time and rights purchased when establishing payment. Rights purchased vary according to project, "but we prefer to purchase first rights only. This is sometimes not possible due to client demand, in which case we attempt to negotiate a financial adjustment for the artist."
Tips: "The demand for technically-oriented artwork has increased. At the same time, some clients who used artists have been satisfied with computer-generated art."

COE COMMUNICATIONS, INC., Suite 2, 131 Rollins, Rockville MD 20852. (301)881-2820. Executive Vice President: Janice V. Long. Audiovisual firm. Clients: associations, corporations and nonprofits.
Needs: Works with 25-30 freelance artists/year. Works on assignment only. Uses artists for photography, artwork and editing.
First Contact & Terms: Send resume to be kept on file. Samples not filed are returned by SASE. Reports only if interested. Pays by the project, $500-15,000 average. Buys all rights.

***STEFAN DOBERT PRODUCTIONS**, 471 Fairhaven Rd., Fairhaven MD 20734. Producer/Director: Stefan Dobert. Film producer. Produces 16mm films and videotapes (training, technical and scientific, educational, etc.).
Needs: Works with 2 illustrators and 2 animators/year. Uses artists for animation and illustrations.
First Contact & Terms: Artists "should have some previous experience and be close enough for

contact." Send resume and query letter; arrange interview by mail. Returns samples by SASE. Provide resume to be kept on file for possible future assignments. Reports in 10 days. Works on assignment only. Method and amount of payment are negotiated with the individual artist. Considers complexity of project and client's budget when establishing payment. Original artwork returned to artist following publication. Buys all rights.
Tips: "My need for animators and illustrators is very rare and quite sporadic. It all depends on the requirement of the contract on which we are working. (My need in the past has been for technical animation explaining scientific concepts.) I would, however, like to maintain a file on who can do what, for how much, should the need arise. I would like to give an opportunity to an animator just beginning."

IMAGE DYNAMICS, INC., Suite 1400, 1101 N. Calvert St., Baltimore MD 21202. (301)539-7730. Art Director: Erin Ries. Ad agency/PR firm. Clients: wide mix, specializing in restaurants and hotels, associations, colleges, hospitals and land developers.
Needs: Local artists only. Uses artists for illustration, design and paste-up; frequently buys humorous and cartoon-style illustrations.
First Contact & Terms: Call to arrange interview to show portfolio; "please do not drop in or write. Bring lots of b&w and 2-color samples; have printed or produced work to show." Samples are returned. Reports only if interested. Provide business card and samples to be kept on file for possible future assignments. Pays flat fee or by the hour, depending on project and budget. Considers complexity of project, client's budget, skill and experience of artist and turnaround time when establishing payment.
Tips: "We are able to use freelance illustrators more towards a more creative product."

***RICHARDSON, MYERS AND DONOFRIO AD AGENCY**, 120 W. Fayette St., Baltimore MD 21201. Art Directors: Joe Herrick and David Curtis.
First Contact & Terms: Provide brochure/flyer to be kept on file for future assignments.

THE SANDLER GROUP, (formerly Gilbert Sandler & Associates, Inc.), 4 E. Madison St., Baltimore MD 21202. (301)837-7100. Senior Art Director: Erin J. Wease. Ad agency. Clients: institutional advertising (financial, industrial) and PR.
First Contact & Terms: Call for an appointment to show portfolio. Negotiates payment based on client's budget and particular job. "Prefers to get an estimate from the freelancer and negotiate payment based on the budget."
Tips: Wants to see a little bit of all freelancer can do in portfolio but especially specific style and best work. Uses many types of art and prefers to see artist's speciality.

SHECTER & LEVIN ADVERTISING/PUBLIC RELATIONS, 2205 N. Charles St., Baltimore MD 21218. (301)889-4464. Production Executives: Virginia Lindler. Ad agency/PR firm. Serves clients in real estate, finance, professional associations, social agencies, retailing, apartments and manufacturing.
Needs: Works with 3-4 illustrators/month. Uses designers for billboards, consumer magazines, stationery design, direct mail, television, brochures/flyers, trade magazines and newspapers. Also uses artists for layouts and mechanicals for brochures, newspaper and magazine ads.
First Contact & Terms: Write for an interview to show portfolio. No originals returned to artist at job's completion. Negotiates pay.

MARC SMITH CO., Box A, Severna Park MD 21146. (301)647-2606. Art/Creative Director: Marc Smith. Advertising agency. Clients: consumer and industrial products, sales services and public relations firms.
Needs: Works with 6 illustrators/month. Local artists only. Uses artists for layout, illustration, lettering, technical art, type spec, paste-up and retouching. Uses illustrators and designers for direct mail, slide sets, brochures/flyers, trade magazines and newspapers; designers for billboards, P-O-P displays, film strips, consumer magazines, stationery, multimedia kits and TV. Occasionally buys humorous and cartoon-style illustrations.
First Contact & Terms: Send query letter with brochure showing art style or tear sheets, Photostats, photocopies, slides or photographs. Keeps file on artists; does not return original artwork to artist after completion of assignment. Call or write to schedule an appointment to show a portfolio which should include thumbnails, roughs, original/final art, final reproduction/product, color and tear sheets. Pays by the hour, $25-150.
Tips: "More sophisticated techniques and equipment are being used in art and design. Our use of freelance material has intensified. Project honesty, clarity and patience."

VAN SANT, DUGDALE & COMPANY, INC., The World Trade Center, Baltimore MD 21202. (301)539-5400. Executive Creative Director: Stan Paulus. Creative Director: Glen Bentley. Ad agency.

Clients: consumer, corporate, associations, financial, and industrial.
Needs: Number of freelance artists used varies. Works on assignment basis only. Uses freelance artists for consumer and trade magazines, brochures, catalogs, newspapers and AV presentations.
First Contact & Terms: Negotiates payment according to client's budget, amount of creativity required, where work will appear and freelancer's previous experience.

Massachusetts

***ALLIED ADVERTISING AGENCY INC.**, 800 Statler Office Bldg., Boston MA 02116. (617)482-4100. Creative Director: Garrett A. Queen. Ad agency and public relations firm. "We are a full-service ad agency providing advertising and collateral material for clients in the print, video and audio media." Clients: electronic, consumer products, film industry, food.
Needs: Works with 25-50 freelance artists/year. Assigns 75-200 jobs/year. Prefers local artists but will go farther for specific talents." Uses artists for illustration, retouching, animation, motion pictures, logos and advertisements.
First Contact & Terms: Send query letter with brochure, or resume, tear sheets, photostats, photocopies, slides and photographs. Samples are sometimes filed. Samples not filed are returned by SASE. Reports back only if interested. Call or write to schedule an appointment to show a portfolio. Pays for design by the hour, $15-100. Pays for illustration by the project, $50 minimum. Considers complexity of project, skill and experience of artist and rights purchased when establishing payment. Buys all rights or reprint rights; negotiates rights purchased. Rights purchased vary according to project.

COSMOPULOS, CROWLEY & DALY, INC., 250 Boylston St., Boston MA 02116. (617)266-5500. Chairman of the Board/Creative Director: Stavros Cosmopulos. Advertising and marketing agency. Clients: banking, restaurants, industrial, package goods, food and electronics.
Needs: Works with 6 illustrators and 1 animator/month. Works on assignment only. Uses artists for billboards, P-O-P displays, filmstrips, consumer magazines, stationery design, multimedia kits, direct mail, television, slide sets, brochures/flyers, trade magazines and newspapers.
First Contact & Terms: Send business card, Photostats or slides. Samples not filed are returned by SASE. Reports only if interested. Make an appointment to show portfolio. No originals returned to artist at job's completion. Pays for design by the project, $250 minimum. Pays for illustration by the project, $100 minimum. Considers complexity of project, client's budget, geographic scope of finished project, turnaround time and rights purchased when establishing payment.
Tips: "Give a simple presentation of the range of work you can do including printed samples of actual jobs—but not a lot of samples. I look for specific techniques that an artist may have to individualize the art."

HBM/CREAMER, INC., 1 Beacon St., Boston MA 02108. (617)723-7770. Art Buyer: Anne Mary Blevins. Ad agency. Clients: consumer, financial, high-tech, fashion, cosmetic, and sportswear.
Needs: Will look at storyboard artists and illustrators; strong preference for advertising illustrators. Works on assignment only.
First Contact & Terms: Dropoff policy for portfolios. Pays for illustration by the project, $300-4,000.
Tips: Looks for a "strong personal style." Common mistakes freelancers make in presenting portfolios or samples are: 1. presenting "too much work. 12-15 pieces of excellent work is sufficient. 2. Unprofessionally packaged. I don't want sketches and original work. Have it reproduced and laminated. Also, no slides. 3. No leave-behinds. How am I supposed to remember this person? I see several illustrators' work each month. Yes. This is expensive and time-consuming but it depends on how committed you are to being an illustrator or artist. There's a tremendous amount of competition. You must convince me you are terrific."

HILL HOLLIDAY CONNORS COSMOPULOS INC., John Hancock Tower, 200 Clarendon St., Boston MA 02116. (617)437-1600, ext. 3487. Art Buyer: Lowry Maclean. Ad agency. Clients: computer firm, banks, consumer products, *Globe* newspaper, lottery, etc.
Needs: Works with 750 freelance artists (illustrators, designers; photographers)/year. Works on assignment only. Uses artists for illustration and photography. Fast turn-around time is important.
First Contact & Terms: Send nonreturnable samples to be kept on file. Samples not filed are not returned. Does not report back. Write for appointment to show portfolio. Pays by the project. Considers complexity of the project, client's budget, turnaround time and rights purchased when establishing payment. Rights purchased vary according to project.

Close-up

Stavros Cosmopulos

Creative Director
Cosmopulos, Crowley & Daly, Inc.
Boston, Massachusetts

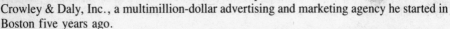

"I've always had confidence that I would succeed, and I'm a hard worker." That's how Stavros Cosmopulos explains his success in advertising.

Cosmopulos' confidence was tested early in his career when he had to show his portfolio to 180 advertising agencies to get his first job as an art director. He is now Chairman of the Board and Creative Director of Cosmopulos, Crowley & Daly, Inc., a multimillion-dollar advertising and marketing agency he started in Boston five years ago.

As Creative Director, he works with freelancers on a regular basis. Virtually all the agency's design is done inhouse, but there are no illustrators on staff. Freelance illustrators are hired to work on a wide range of projects including posters, magazine ads, billboards, brochures and annual reports.

When reviewing a portfolio, Cosmopulos looks for craftsmanship and style. Like most art directors, he needs illustrators who can produce quality work in a selected style. He suggests that freelancers include two or three pieces of the same style in their portfolios to indicate they can be consistent.

Some art directors want to see printed pieces in a portfolio to indicate you can prepare work suited for printing. But Cosmopulos isn't concerned about whether a portfolio contains printed pieces or not; artistic aptitude shown in drawings will suffice. "All I'm buying is the person's talent." If he likes the work of an inexperienced artist, he will work with the artist to assure a printable piece.

"All artwork in a portfolio should have commercial applications," Cosmopulos stresses. Like other art directors, he doesn't want to see framed paintings.

Cosmopulos cautions that the clothes an artist wears when presenting a portfolio may influence whether or not the artist gets an assignment. "Look neutral; act businesslike," he advises. "Let your work speak for itself. Creative clothes can upstage your work." Also, dressing neatly helps convince the art director that the artist will be dependable and will meet deadlines. "However," he adds, "a great portfolio will overcome anything."

Freelance artists face tough competition; Cosmopulos looks at the portfolios of hundreds of artists a year. It's important that freelancers do something to make themselves remembered. He recommends leaving something unusual and imaginative behind or sending it later. One artist gave Cosmopulos a director's chair with the artist's name and phone number on it. The reminder doesn't have to be that expensive—a printed card with your name, address, phone number and artwork on the same side will do—but Cosmopulos stresses that it should be unique.

To develop contacts, Cosmopulos suggests joining the art directors club in your locality. "Young illustrators should target in on young art directors; they have fewer loyalties." An illustrator might also consider doing a job without pay. For example, unpaid work for an advertising agency's business pitch can lead to a well-paying assignment later when the agency gets the new business.

He also recommends that freelancers consider paying to have their work printed in books such as the *Society of Illustrators Annual* and the *Creative Black Book*. This type of publicity may be too expensive for beginning freelancers, but it's worthwhile for those who can afford it. Many art directors refer to these books when choosing an illustrator for a project.

Cosmopulos also has advice for freelancers once they get assignments: "Get as much information and reference material as possible. Have the specifications (delivery date, proportions, color/b&w, style and price) written down on the purchase order by the person giving instructions. Make sure you have a clear understanding of what you are expected to do. Otherwise, you may have to redo an illustration at your own expense."

Cosmopulos' theory of design is as practical as his advice to freelancers. He laments that some designers think only of design and produce advertisements that are difficult to read. "People lead busy lives and don't have time to look at advertisements. Advertising design must attract attention and convey the message clearly and quickly."

—Mary Tonnies

Artist: John Thompson

To emphasize the stability of a long-established insurance company, Cosmopulos asked illustrator John Thompson to render a historical event (in this case, Wyatt Earp's shootout in Dodge City) that occurred in the early days of the company's founding. Cosmopulos chose the Jersey City, New Jersey, illustrator because of his realistic style which was needed for the assignment. Cosmopulos found Thompson through an artist's representative whom he had known for years.

MARCOA DR GROUP INC., (formerly The DR Group Inc.), 40 Broad St., Boston MA 02109-4359. Creative Director: William Allen. Direct marketing ad agency. Clients: industrial, financial, publishing firms.
Needs: Number of freelance artists used varies; has 5 art directors. Usually works with local freelancers. Works on assignment basis only. Uses freelance artists for direct mail and collateral.
First Contact & Terms: Arrange interview to show portfolio. Payment varies according to job.

PHOTOGRAPHERS' COLOR SERVICE, 10 Harvard St., Worcester MA 01609. (617)752-1921. President: Alice Richmond. Photographic studio. Clients: educational, industrial and business. Produces filmstrips, slide sets and color prints.
Needs: Assigns 30 jobs/year. Uses artists for slide and ad illustrations.
First Contact & Terms: Query with resume and samples. Samples returned with SASE. Reports in 2 weeks. Provide business card to be kept on file for possible future assignments. Negotiates pay by the project.

***SIMMONS PRODUCTIONS**, 660 Main St., Woburn MA 01801. President: Peter Simmons. AV/video producer. Clients: corporations. Main uses: sales and marketing.
Needs: Works with 2 designers/art directors/month. Uses designers for multi-image slide shows and video graphics. Some storyboarding and illustration.
First Contact & Terms: Write for interview to show portfolio, or send resume, business card or brochure/flyer to be kept on file for future assignments. SASE. Works on assignment only. Pays going rates. Negotiates pay based on amount of creativity required and artist's previous experience/reputation.

TR PRODUCTIONS, 1031 Commonwealth Ave., Boston MA 02215. (617)783-0200. Production Manager: Tom Cramer. Audiovisual firm. Clients: industrial and high-tech.
Needs: Works with 5-10 freelance artists/year. Assigns 20-50 jobs/year. Prefers local artists. Works on assignment generally. Uses artists for slide graphics, layout, mechanical, computer graphics, charts/graphs, advertisements, and 2-color and 4-color collateral design. Especially important is clean, accurate board work.
First Contact & Terms: For slide work, artist must have experience in design and mechanicals for slides/multi-image. Send query letter with brochure showing art style, resume and slides to be kept on file. Samples not filed are not returned. Reports only if interested. Call to schedule an appointment to show a portfolio. Pays by the hour, $10-25 average. Considers complexity of project, client's budget, skill and experience of artist and turnaround time when establishing payment. Buys all audiovisual rights.

Michigan

BLAVIN, HARTZ & MOLNER, INC., Suite 153, 23077 Greenfield Rd., Southfield, Michigan 48075. (313)557-8011. President: Monroe "Bob" Molner. Clients: Variety of industries.
Needs: Buys 100-150 illustrations/year. Local artists only. Works on assignment only. Uses artists for print ads, TV storyboards, layouts, and fashion and furniture illustrations.
First Contact & Terms: Query. SASE. Reports in 1 week. Pays $10-50, fashion or furniture illustration; $20-30/hour, layout. Pays original fee as agreed for unused assigned illustrations. No originals returned to artist at job's completion.

LEO J. BRENNAN ADVERTISING, 2359 Livernois, Troy MI 48083-1692. (313)362-3131. Financial and Administrative Manager: Virginia Janusis. Ad agency and public relations firm. Clients: mainly industrial, automotive, banks and C.P.A.s.
Needs: Works with 10 freelance artists/year. Artist must be well experienced. Uses artists for design, illustrations, brochures, catalog, retouching, lettering, keylining and typesetting.
First Contact & Terms: Send query letter with resume and samples. Samples not filed are returned only if requested. Reports only if interested. Call or write to schedule an appointment to show a portfolio, which should include thumbnails, roughs, original/final art, final reproduction/product, color, tear sheets, Photostats, photographs and b&w. Considers complexity of project, client's budget, skill and experience of artist, and turnaround time when establishing payment. Buys all rights.

***BROGAN KABOT ADVERTISING CONSULTANCY, INC.**, #475, 3000 Town Center, Southfield MI 48075. (313)353-9160. Creative Director: Ann Kabot. "We are a multimedia firm specializing in TV, print and radio." Clients: retail (convention center) and political.

Needs: "Doesn't use much freelance work but interested in increasing usage." Prefers local artists "but not exclusively." Works on assignment only. Uses artists for design, illustration, brochures, catalogs, P-O-P displays, mechanicals, direct mail packages, lettering, logos, layouts and storyboards.
First Contact & Terms: Send query letter with brochure or resume, tear sheets, Photostats, photocopies, slides and photographs; "anything that shows style and ability." Samples are filed. Samples not filed are returned only if requested. Reports back within 30 days. Call to schedule an appointment to show a portfolio or mail thumbnails, roughs, Photostats, tear sheets and slides. Pays for design by the project, $100-1,000. Pays for illustration by the project, $100-1,500. Considers complexity of project, client's budget and skill and experience of artist when establishing payment. Rights purchased vary according to project.
Tips: "Be prepared, be brief and be flexible."

COMMON SENSE COMMUNICATIONS, INC., 602 S. Michigan Ave., Saginaw MI 48602. (517)790-7404. Art Director: James Kinnaman. Serves clients in machinery, automobiles, insurance, building supplies and banking.
Needs: Buys 25 full-color illustrations/year. Works on assignment only. Uses artists for illustrations, color separations, layout, lettering, paste-up, retouching and type spec for ads, annual reports, billboards, catalogs, letterheads, packaging, P-O-P displays, posters, TV and trademarks.
First Contact & Terms: Send slides, printed samples, business card, brochure/flyer, resume, tear sheets or "all the information an artist has available for analyzing assignments" to be kept on file for possible future assignments. SASE. Reports within 4 weeks. Agency pays for unused completed work ("assignments usually approved or disapproved at tissue stage").
Tips: "Have a complete portfolio of work showing how you developed a project right through the finished project."

CREATIVE HOUSE ADVERTISING INC., Suite 301, 30777 Northwestern Hwy., Farmington Hills MI 48018. (313)737-7077. Executive Vice President/Creative Director: Robert G. Washburn. Advertising/graphics/display/art firm. Clients: residential and commercial construction, land development, consumer, retail, finance and manufacturing. Assigns 20-30 jobs and buys 10-20 illustrations/year.
Needs: Works with 3 illustrators and 2 designers/month. Local artists only. Uses artists for filmstrips, consumer magazines, multimedia kits, direct mail, television, slide sets, brochures/flyers, trade magazines and newspapers. Also uses artists for illustration, design and comp layouts of ads, brochures, catalogs, annual reports and displays.
First Contact & Terms: Query with resume, business card and brochure/flyer to be kept on file. Samples returned by SASE. Reports in 2 weeks. No originals returned to artist at job's completion. Arrange interview to show portfolio, which should include originals, reproduced and published pieces. Pays $50-5,000/project; $10-60/hour. Considers complexity of project, client's budget and rights purchased when establishing payment. Reproduction rights are purchased as a buy-out.
Tips: There is a trend toward "computerization to expedite research, reference and techniques. Maintain the basics of art, illustration and medium. Be flexible in pricing/budgeting."

***DELEEUW FERGUSON BASHAW**, 26555 Evergreen, Southfield MI 48076. Senior Art Director: Brad Phillips. Full service ad agency. Clients: food, hospital, retail, banking, radio stations.
Needs: Works with 10 freelance artists/year. Assigns 25 jobs/year. Prefers Detroit-based artists. Works on assignment only. Uses artists for illustration, animation and billboards.
First Contact & Terms: Contact through artist's agent or send query letter with brochure, photocopies and slides. Samples are filed. Samples not filed are returned by SASE. Reports back within 1 week. Write to schedule an appointment to show a portfolio. Pays for design by the hour, $50 minimum. Pays for illustration by the hour, $75 minimum. Considers client' budget, turnaround time and skill and experience of artist when establishing payment. Buys all rights or negotiates rights purchased.
Tips: "Don't call—write."

LAMPE COMMUNICATIONS, INC., Box 5339, West Bloomfield MI 48033. (313)332-3711. Production Manager: A.M. Lampe. PR firm. Clients: industry.
Needs: Assigns 100 freelance jobs/year. Works with 1 freelance illustrator and 2 freelance designers/month. Works on assignment only. Uses artists for trade magazine ads, brochures, stationery, signage and press releases.
First Contact & Terms: Send query letter with business card to be kept on file. Samples not kept on file are returned by SASE. Reports only if interested. Considers complexity of project, client's budget, and skill and experience of artist when establishing payment. Buys all rights.

***MARTIN, WINDSOR & ASSOCIATES, INC.**, 234 Federal Square Bldg., Grand Rapids MI 49503. Creative Director: Steve Yankee. Ad agency. "We are a full-service agency providing print, collateral, direct mail, public relations and audiovisual materials. Clients: business-to-business, industrial.
Needs: Works with 10 freelance artists/year. Assigns 20 jobs/year. Prefers local/regional artists, in most cases. Works on assignment only. Uses artists for illustration, mechanicals, retouching and animation.
First Contact & Terms: Send query letter with tear sheets and photocopies. Samples are filed. Samples not filed are returned by SASE. Reports back only if interested. Write to schedule an appointment to show a portfolio, which should include original/final art, tear sheets, photographs, color and b&w. Pays for illustration by the hour, $15 minimum; by the project, $50 minimum. Considers complexity of project, client's budget, turnaround time and skill and experience of artist when establishing payment. Buys all rights.
Tips: "Tell us what you're most capable of doing best, and be honest about it! Nothing bothers me more than a freelancer who can't get a contracted job done within a predetermined time frame!"

THE MESSAGE MAKERS, (formerly Synchronous Media International), 1217 Turner, Lansing MI 48906. Contact: Terry Terry. Audiovisual firm. Clients: industrial, commercial, government. Client list provided for SASE.
Needs: Works with 10-20 freelance artists/year. Works on assignment only. Uses artists for voice and camera talent, photography and graphics. Especially looks for communication skills and professional attitude.
First Contact & Terms: Send query letter with brochure showing art style or resume and tear sheets, photostats, photocopies, slides and photographs. Reports back only if interested. Write to schedule an appointment to show a portfolio, which should include thumbnails, roughs, original/final art, final reproduction/product, tear sheets, photostats and photographs. Pays for design and illustration by the hour, $8 minimum. Considers complexity of the project, client's budget, and skill and experience of artist when establishing payment. Rights purchased vary according to project.

PHOTO COMMUNICATION SERVICES, INC., 6410 Knapp NE, Ada MI 49301. (616)676-2429. President: Michael Jackson. Audiovisual firm. Clients: commercial and industrial; "local to international, large variety."
Needs: Works with 10 freelance artists/year. Works on assignment only. Uses artists for multi-image slide presentations, film and video. Especially important is knowledge of animation and pin registration.
First Contact & Terms: Send query letter with brochure, resume, business card, photographs or slides to be kept on file. Samples not filed are returned by SASE only if requested. Reports back only if interested. Call or write for appointment to show portfolio. Negotiates payment by project. Considers complexity of the project, client's budget, skill and experience of artist, geographic scope for the finished product, turnaround time and rights purchased when establishing payment. Negotiates rights purchased.

THOMPSON ADVERTISING PRODUCTIONS, INC., 31690 W. 12 Mile Rd., Farmington Hills MI 48018. (313)553-4566. Vice President: Clay Thompson. Ad agency. Clients: automotive, marine and industrial.
Needs: Works with 20 freelance artists/year. Works on assignment only. Uses artists for design, illustrations, layout, retouching, and creative concept. Artist should have a "strong sense of design communication."
First Contact & Terms: Send query letter with resume and samples. Samples not filed are returned only if requested. Call or write to schedule an appointment to show a portfolio, which should include thumbnails, roughs and original/final art. Pays for design and illustration by the hour or by the project. Considers complexity of project, client's budget, and skill and experience of artist. Rights purchased vary according to project.
Tips: Artist should "be prepared to show samples of layout work and demonstrated skills and be prepared to quote a price."

J. WALTER THOMPSON COMPANY, 600 Renaissance Center, Detroit MI 48243. (313)568-3800. Assistant Art Administrator: Maryann Inson. Ad agency. Clients: automotive, consumer, industrial, media and retail-related accounts.
Needs: Usually does not use freelancers; deals primarily with established artists' representatives and art/design studios.
First Contact & Terms: Contact only through artist's agent. Assignments awarded on lowest bid. Write to schedule an appointment to show a portfolio, which should include thumbnails, roughs,

original/final art, final reproduction/product, color, tear sheets, Photostats and photographs. Pays for design and illustration by the project.
Tips: Agency deals with proven illustrators from an "approved vendor's list." New vendors are considered for list periodically. "Portfolio should be comprehensive but not too large. Organization of the portfolio is as important as the sample. Mainly, consult professional rep."

Minnesota

ART & COPY OVERLOAD, Suite 2, 2010 Marshall Ave., St. Paul MN 55104. (612)644-3443. Contact: John Borden. Ad agency. Clients: food, ice, medical, financial, industrial, manufacturing.
Needs: Works with 8 freelance artists/year. Requires 2 years of commercial experience; prefers local artists. Works on assignment only. Uses artists for layout, paste-up, drawing and illustration. Especially important is an understanding of layout.
First Contact & Terms: Send brochure, resume, business card and Photostats or photocopies to be kept on file up to 1 year. Samples not filed are returned by SASE. Does not report back. Call for appointment to show portfolio. Pays by the hour, $18-50 average or by the day, $40-180 average. Considers complexity of the project, client's budget, skill and experience of artist and rights purchased when establishing payment. Rights purchased vary according to project.

***BADIYAN PRODUCTIONS INC.**, 720 W. 94 St., Minneapolis MN 55420. (612)888-5507. President: Fred Badiyan. Audiovisual firm. Client list provided upon request.
Needs: Works with 50 freelance artists/year. Works on assignment only. Uses freelance artists for design, brochures, mechanicals, press releases and motion pictures.
First Contact & Terms: Send query letter with brochure or resume, tear sheets, photocopies and slides. Samples are filed. Samples not filed are returned. Write to schedule an appointment to show a portfolio or mail appropriate materials. Pays for design and illustration by the hour or by the project.
Tips: "Send a letter and sample of work."

JOHN BORDEN & ASSOCIATES, Suite 2, 2010 Marshall Ave., St. Paul MN 55104. (612)644-3443. Contact: John Borden. Ad agency. Clients: business, industrial, financial, food and food-related and advertising. Assigns 15 jobs and buys 50 illustrations/year.
Needs: Works with 4 illustrators/month. Local professionals only. Uses artists for layouts, finished art, type spec, consumer and trade magazines, stationery design, direct mail, billboards, TV, brochures/flyers and newspapers.
First Contact & Terms: Query with samples or call to arrange interview to show portfolio. Prefers photographs, Photostats and b&w line drawings as samples. Especially looks for layout ability, and styles of art. Samples returned by SASE. Reports in 2 weeks. Provide brochure/flyer, Photostats or reprints of samples to be kept on file for possible future assignments. Works by assignment only. Originals become client's property at job's completion. Reports in 2 weeks. Pays $18-50/hour; $300-10,000/project.
Tips: Also owns Art and Copy Overload Service supplying freelancers to other companies that need them (for annual reports, etc.).

***BUTWIN & ASSOCIATES ADVERTISING, INC.**, Suite 202, 3601 Park Center Blvd., Minneapolis MN 55416. (612)929-8525. President: Ron Butwin. Ad agency. "We are a full-line ad agency working with both consumer and industrial accounts on advertising, marketing, public relations and meeting planning." Clients: banks, restaurants, clothing stores, food brokerage firms, corporations, full range of retail and service organizations, etc.
Needs: Works with 12-15 freelance artists/year. Prefers local artists when possible. Uses artists for design, illustration, brochures, catalogs, newspapers, consumer and trade magazines, P-O-P displays, retouching, animation, direct mail packages, motion pictures and lettering.
First Contact & Terms: Send brochure or resume, tear sheets, Photostats, photocopies, slides and photographs. Samples are filed. Samples not filed are returned only if requested. Reports back only if interested. Call to schedule an appointment to show a portfolio. Considers client's budget, skill and experience of artist and how work will be used when establishing payment. Buys all rights.

FABER SHERVEY ADVERTISING, 160 W. 79th St., Minneapolis MN 55420. (612)881-5111. Creative Director: Paul D. Shervey. Ad agency. Clients: business-to-business, industrial and farm.
Needs: Works with 25 freelance artists/year. Prefers local artists. Uses artists for retouching, line art, keyline, illustration.

First Contact & Terms: Send brochure and business card. Do *not* send samples. Does not report back. Call or write for appointment to show portfolio. Pays by the hour, $20-80 average. Considers complexity of project when establishing payment. Buys all rights.

LINHOFF PRODUCTIONS, Box 24005, 4400 France Ave. S, Minneapolis MN 55424. (612)927-7333. Art Director: Lynn Koskiniemi. Audiovisual firm. Clients: banks, computer companies and financial services companies.
Needs: Works with 8-15 freelance artists/year. Local artists only; must work inhouse. Works on assignment only, or as vacation replacement. Uses artists for keylining, artwork and typesetting. Especially important are ruling; an eye for layout; good word skills for proofreading; copy camera capabilities; graphic arts computer; typesetting knowledge a plus (Comp-Edit 5810). Experience with audio-visual preparation preferred.
First Contact & Terms: Send query letter with resume and photocopies to be kept on file. Samples not filed are returned by SASE. Reports within 2 weeks. Call to schedule an appointment to show a portfolio, which should include color and original/final art, AV projects (slides, viewgraphs). Pays by the hour, $8 minimum. Considers skill and experience of artist when establishing payment. Buys all rights.
Tips: "Much of our art preparation is predesigned and often 'mechanical' or repetitive. This is not a forum for an artist with flamboyant design skills. Instead, we want people that can envision the final AV product and can create clean yet exciting visuals."

***EDWIN NEUGER & ASSOCIATES**, 1221 Nicollet Mall, Minneapolis MN 55403. (612)333-6621. President: Ed Neuger. "We are a full-service public relations firm which specializes in financial relations for companies of all sizes." Clients: general. Client list provided upon request.
Needs: Works with 10 freelance artists/year. Assigns 25 jobs/year. Prefers local artists because "most assignments are not extremely large or time is a factor." Uses artists for design, illustration, brochures, catalogs and annual reports.
First Contact & Terms: Samples are filed. Samples not filed are not returned. Does not report back. Call or write to schedule an appointment to show a portfolio. Pays by the project, such as on annual reports. Considers complexity of project, client's budget and skill and experience of artist. Buys all rights.

PEDERSON HERZOG & NEE INC., 219 Logan Pkwy., Minneapolis MN 55432. (612)333-1234. Art Director: Ann Taylor. Ad agency. Serves clients in automotive, sporting equipment, farming equipment and industrial supplies. Assigns 12 illustrations/year.
Needs: Works with 2 illustrators and 1 designer/month. Local artists only. Uses artists for billboards, P-O-P displays, consumer magazines, television, trade magazines, newspapers and brochures.
First Contact & Terms: Query with samples to be kept on file for future assignments. No originals returned at job's completion. Pays $50-2,000/job.

VANGUARD ASSOCIATES INC., Suite 485, 15 S. 9th St., Minneapolis MN 55402. (612)338-5386. Ad agency. Clients: aluminum foil manufacturer, fashion and food firms, governmental agencies; client list provided upon request.
Needs: Work with 12 illustrators/month; occasionally uses freelance designers. Works on assignment basis only. Uses freelance artists for billboards, consumer and trade magazines, direct mail, P-O-P displays, brochures, posters, newspapers, multimedia campaigns and AV presentations.
First Contact & Terms: Must see samples. Out-of-town artists query with resume and samples; local artists arrange interview to show portfolio. Payment is by the project; negotiates according to client's budget.

Missouri

FRANK BLOCK ASSOCIATES, Chase Park Plaza, St. Louis MO 63108. (314)367-9600. Art Director: Dave Meinecke. Ad agency. Clients: primarily industrial firms; client list provided upon request.
Needs: Works with 6 illustrators/month. Works on assignment only. Uses freelance artists for billboards, consumer and trade magazines, direct mail, brochures, catalogs, posters, signage, newspapers, TV and AV presentations.
First Contact & Terms: Arrange interview to show portfolio. Negotiates payment by the project and on freelancer's ability.

BRYAN/DONALD, INC. ADVERTISING, Suite 2712, 2345 Grand, Kansas City MO 64108. (816)471-4866. President: Don Funk. Ad agency. Clients: food, fashion, pharmaceutical, real estate.
Needs: Works on assignment only. Uses artists for design, illustration, brochures, catalogs, books, newspapers, consumer and trade magazines, P-O-P displays, mechanicals, retouching, animation, billboards, posters, direct mail packages, lettering, logos, charts/graphs and advertisements.
First Contact & Terms: Samples are filed. Reports back only if interested. Call to schedule an appointment to show a portfolio.

BRYANT, LAHEY & BARNES, INC., Suite 210, 4200 Pennsylvania, Kansas City MO 64111. (816)561-9629. Art Director: Terry Pritchett. Ad agency. Clients: agricultural and veterinary.
Needs: Local artists only. Uses artists for illustration and production, including keyline and paste-up, consumer and trade magazines and brochures/flyers.
First Contact & Terms: Query by phone. Send business card and resume to be kept on file for future assignments. Negotiates pay. No originals returned to artist at job's completion.

FREMERMAN, ROSENFIELD & LANE, Suite 2102, 106 W. 14th St., Kansas City MO 64105. (816)474-8120. Creavtive Director: Marvin Fremerman. Art Director: Leanne Zembrunner. Ad agency. Clients: retail, consumer and trade accounts; client list provided upon request.
Needs: Works with 10-15 illustrators/month. Works primarily with local artists. Uses freelance artists for billboards, consumer and trade magazines, direct mail, P-O-P displays, brochures, catalogs, posters, signage, newspapers and AV presentations.
First Contact & Terms: Arrange interview to show portfolio. Query with resume of credits and samples. Payment is by the project or by the day; negotiates according to client's budget and where work will appear.

GARDNER ADVERTISING, 10 S. Broadway, St. Louis MO 63102. (314)444-2000. Director of Creative Services: Bob Fanter. Ad agency. Clients: consumer food, dog food, health care, financial, recreation, restaurant and services.
Needs: Works with about 15 illustrators/month and occasionally uses designers for packaging. Uses artists for consumer print and TV.
First Contact & Terms: Call for appointment to show portfolio or contact through artist's rep. Negotiates pay based on budget and where work will appear, whether color or b&w, etc.

GEORGE JOHNSON, ADVERTISING, 763 New Ballas Rd. S., St. Louis MO 63141. (314)569-3440. Art Director: Dean Weiler. Ad agency. Serves clients in real estate, financial and social agencies.
Needs: Works with 1-2 illustrators/month. Local artists only. Uses artists for illustrations, animation, layout, lettering, paste-up, retouching, type spec and design for annual reports, billboards, catalogs, print ads, letterheads, packaging, P-O-P displays, posters, TV and trademarks.
First Contact & Terms: Write or call for appointment to show portfolio, which should include tear sheets, roughs and work done for other ad agencies. SASE. Reports within 1 week. Originals returned at job's completion.

PREMIER FILM VIDEO & RECORDING, 3033 Locust St., St. Louis MO 63103. (314)531-3555. Secretary/Treasurer: Grace Dalzell. AV/film/animation/TV producer. Serves clients in business, religion, education and advertising. Produces videotape, motion 35mm, 16mm and Super 8mm, strip films, cassette dupes, 8-tracks, TV and radio spots.
Needs: Assigns 50-60 jobs/year. Works with 8-10 illustrators, "a few" designers/month. Works on assignment only. Uses artists for strip film and slide presentations, TV commercials and motion picture productions.
First Contact & Terms: Send resume to be kept on file. "We do not accept samples; we review them during interviews only." Reporting time varies with available work. Pays by the project; method and amount of payment are negotiated with the individual artist. Pay varies with each client's budget. No originals returned to artist following publication; "copies supplied when possible." Buys all rights, but sometimes negotiates.
Tips: "In developing a brochure, begin by simply stating work capability and area of work most capable of producing, i.e., animation, cartoons, production, direction or editing—whatever you want to do for a living. Be specific."

STOLZ ADVERTISING CO., Suite 500, 7701 Forsyth Blvd., St. Louis MO 63105. (314)863-0005. Art Director/Creative Supervisor: Paul MacFarlane. Ad agency. Clients: consumer firms.
Needs: Works with 2-4 illustrators/month; occasionally uses freelance designers. Works on assignment only. Uses freelance artists for billboards, consumer and trade magazines, direct mail, P-O-P displays, brochures, posters, newspapers and AV presentations.

First Contact & Terms: Arrange interview to show portfolio or query with samples. Pays for design by the hour, $25-50. Pays for illustration by the project, $100 minimum.
Tips: "I give more work to less-experienced people who have real vision—outstanding or potentially outstanding, yet 'unknown' work. I respond to professional, buttoned-down books." The most common mistakes freelancers make in presenting samples or portfolios are "too much work shown and showing unrelated or poorly presented work."

Montana

SAGE ADVERTISING/BILLINGS, Box 20977, Billings MT 59104. (406)652-3232. Art Director: Lori Richards-Burda. Ad agency/AV/PR firm/radio and TV; "a full-service agency." Clients: financial, utilities, industry, hotel/motel, health care.
Needs: Assigns 24 freelance jobs/year. Works with 2 freelance illustrators/month. Works on assignment only. Uses artists for filmstrips, AV presentations, photography and illustration.
First Contact & Terms: Send query letter with resume and photocopies to be kept on file. Samples not kept on file are returned only if requested. Reports within 2 weeks. Call or write to schedule an appointment to show a portfolio, which should include roughs, final reproduction/product, color, tear sheets, Photostats and photographs. Pays for illustration by the project, $150. Considers complexity of project, client's budget, skill and experience of artist, geographic scope of finished project, turnaround time and rights purchased when establishing payment. Negotiates rights purchased.

Nebraska

MILLER FRIENDT LUDEMANN INC., 300 Corporate Center, 1235 K St., Lincoln NE 68508. Senior Art Director: Michael Edholm. Art Director: Dave Christiansen. Ad agency/PR firm. Clients: bank, industry, restaurants, tourism and retail.
Needs: Works on assignment only. Uses artists for consumer and trade magazines, billboards, direct mail packages, brochures, newspapers, stationery, signage, P-O-P displays, AV presentations, posters, press releases, trade show displays and TV graphics. "Freelancing is based on heavy workloads. Most freelancing is paste-up but secondary is illustrator for designed element."
First Contact & Terms: Send query letter with resume and slides to be kept on file. Samples not kept on file are returned by SASE. Reports within 10 days. Write for appointment to show portfolio, "if regional/national; call if local." Portfolio should include thumbnails, roughs, original/final art, final reproduction/product, color, tear sheets and Photostats. Pays by the project, $100-1,500 average. Considers complexity of project, client's budget, skill and experience of artist, turnaround time and rights purchased when establishing payment. Buys all rights.
Tips: "Be prompt, have work done on time and be able to price your project work accurately. Make quality first."

J. GREG SMITH, Suite 102, Burlington Place, 1004 Farnam St., Omaha NE 68102. (402)444-1600. Art Director: Shelly Bartek. Ad agency. Clients: financial, banking institutions, associations, agricultural, travel and tourism.
Needs: Works with 3 illustrators/year. Works on assignment only. Uses freelance artists for consumer and trade magazines, brochures, catalogs and AV presentations.
First Contact & Terms: Send query letter with brochure showing art style or photocopies. Reports only if interested. To show a portfolio, mail original/final art, final reproduction/product, color and b&w. Payment is by the project; negotiates according to client's budget.
Tips: Current trends include a certain "flexibility." Agencies are now able "to use any style or method that best fits the job."

The asterisk before a listing indicates that the listing is new in this edition. New markets are often the most receptive to freelance submissions.

Nevada

***STUDIOS KAMINSKI PHOTOGRAPHY LTD.**, 1040 Matley Lane, Reno NV 89502. (702)786-2615. President: T.J. Kaminski. AV/TV/film producer. Clients: educational, industrial and corporate. Produces filmstrips, motion pictures, multimedia kits, overhead transparencies, slide sets, sound-slide sets and videotapes.
Needs: Works with about 3 illustrators/year. Has need of illustrators to paint portraits from photos once in a while. Uses artists for slide illustration and retouching, catalog design and ad illustration.
First Contact & Terms: Arrange interview to show portfolio. Samples returned by SASE. Reports within 1 week. Works on assignment only. Provide brochure/flyer, resume or tear sheet to be kept on file for possible future assignments. Pays $20-50/hour; $150-400/day.
Tips: Have good samples and be qualified.

New Jersey

SOL ABRAMS ASSOCIATES INC., 331 Webster Dr., New Milford NJ 07646. (201)262-4111. President: Sol Abrams. Public relations firm. Clients: real estate, food, fashion, beauty, entertainment, government, retailing, sports, nonprofit organizations, etc. Media used include billboards, consumer magazines, trade magazines, direct mail, newspapers, P-O-P displays, radio and TV.
Needs: Assigns 6 freelance jobs/year. "For practical purposes, we prefer using artists in New Jersey-New York area." Works on assignment only. Uses artists for consumer magazines, billboards, brochures, catalogs, newspapers, stationery, signage, AV presentations and press releases.
First Contact & Terms: Send query letter with photographs and Photostats which may be kept on file. Samples not kept on file returned by SASE. Reports only if interested. Pay varies according to client and job. Considers client's budget, and skill and experience of artist when establishing payment. Buys all rights.
Tips: "As one who started his career as an artist before deciding to become a public relations consultant, I empathize with young artists. If material interests me and I cannot use it, I might develop leads or refer it to people and firms which may use it. Artists should be honest and sincere. Dedication and integrity are as important as talent."

DAVID H. BLOCK ADVERTISING, INC., 33 S. Fullerton Ave., Montclair NJ 07042 (201)744-6900. Executive Art Director and Vice President: Karen Deluca. Clients: finance, industrial, consumer, real estate, bio-medical. Buys 100-200 illustrations/year.
Needs: Prefers to work with "artists with at least 3-5 years experience in paste-up and 'on premises' work for mechanicals and design." Uses artists for illustrations, layout, lettering, type spec, mechanicals and retouching for ads, annual reports, billboards, catalogs, letterheads, brochures and trademarks.
First Contact & Terms: Arrange interview. SASE. Reports in 2 weeks. Pays for design by the hour, $15-50.
Tips: "Please send some kind of sample of work. If mechanical artist; line art printed sample. If layout artist; composition of some type and photographs or illustrations."

***ERIK L. BURRO, THE MARKETING & COMMUNICATIONS GROUP**, Box 477, Willingboro NJ 08046. (609)877-3704. President: Erik L. Burro. Ad agency. Clients: companies related to cultural institutions and industrial and commercial organizations.
Needs: Works with 2-3 illustrators/month. Uses artists for layout, color separations, lettering, paste-up, retouching and type spec for ads, image programs, multimedia programs and AV work, stationery design, direct mail, brochures/flyers, trade magazines, annual reports, letterheads and trademarks.
First Contact & Terms: Prefers Philadelphia and New Jersey artists. Query with resume and samples. SASE. Contacts artists as needs arise. Provide business card and/or resume to be kept on file for future assignments. "We return art only if we have purchased 'use rights'. We pay prevailing market price for work." Pays promised fee for unused assigned work.

CABSCOTT BROADCAST PRODUCTIONS, INC., 517 7th Ave., Lindenwold NJ 08021. (609)346-3400. President: Larry Scott. Audiovisual firm, production company. Clients: retail, broadcasters (radio and TV), ad agencies and industrial users.
Needs: Works with 5 freelance artists/year. Prefers local artists experienced in television

storyboarding. Works on assignment only. Uses artist for art, layout and storyboard creation. Especially important are freehand skills.

First Contact & Terms: Send query letter with brochure showing art style, resume and slides to be kept on file. Prefers any type sample that gives an idea of artist's style. Samples are returned by SASE if requested. Reports only if interested. To show a portfolio, mail appropriate materials, which should include tear sheets, Photostats and photographs. Negotiates payment by the project. Considers complexity of project, client's budget, skill and experience of artist and turnaround time when establishing payment. Negotiates rights purchased.

CHAMPION ADVERTISING AGENCY, 86 Davison Place, Englewood NJ 07631. Art/Creative Director: Jerry Hahn. Clients: jewelers, manufacturing and retail.

Needs: Assigns 100-150 jobs/year. Need for freelance illustrators varies and uses 2 design studios for needed work. Works on assignment or on speculation basis if okay. Uses freelancers for fine line art, scratchboard of jewelry products for newspaper reproductions. Uses artists for catalog design, illustrators for packaging and display concepts.

First Contact & Terms: Query in person or via direct mail with proofs, Photostats or repros of line art, tear sheets or previously published work. Do not send original art or slides unless specifically requested. Samples returned only if requested. Reports in 1 week. Provide business card, brochure/flyer, resume, sample proofs and tear sheets to be kept on file for possible future assignments. Pays $25-65 depending on product, scratchboard or pen & ink; $100 average, full color rendering of product; $250 +, full color realistic illustration. Considers complexity of project and client's budget when establishing payment.

Tips: "My agency is a prospect for photographers, retouchers and scratchboard or line artists with jewelry or cosmetic experience, but hourly rates vary and are confidential. I look for graphic honesty . . . true product renderings in pen & ink for newspaper reproduction."

***COOPER COMMUNICATIONS & PRODUCTIONS, INC.**, 2115 Millburn Ave., Maplewood NJ 07040. Vice President: Al Keeney. Full-service ad agency with print, video and multi-image capabilities. Clients: all except retail—specialize in technology communications. Client list provided upon request.

Needs: Works with 4-5 freelance artists/year. Assigns 25 jobs/year. Prefers local artists. Works on assignment only. Uses artists for design, illustration, brochures, catalogs, newspapers, P-O-P displays, mechanicals, animation, posters, direct mail packages, press releases, logos, charts/graphs and advertisements.

First Contact & Terms: Send query letter with brochure or resume. Samples are filed. Samples not filed are returned only if requested by artists. Reports back only if interested. Call or write to schedule an appointment to show a portfolio. Pays for design and illustration by the hour, $30 minimum. Considers complexity of project and turnaround time when establishing payment. Rights purchased vary according to project.

***CREATIVE ASSOCIATES**, 626 Bloomfield Ave., Verona NJ 07044. (201)499-0044. Producer: Harrison Feather. Audiovisual firm. "We are a multimedia production facility providing photography, video post-production, slide shows; computer graphics, computer typesetting, scriptwriting for sales meetings, trade shows, speaker support and entertainment." Clients: high-tech, pharmaceutical, computer, R&D labs, engineering and marine. Client list provided with an SASE.

Needs: Works with 5 freelance artists/year. Assigns 10 jobs/year. Works on assignment only. Uses artists for design, illustration, motion pictures and charts/graphs.

First Contact & Terms: Send query letter with brochure or resume and slides. Samples are filed. Samples not filed are returned by SASE. Call to schedule an appointment to show a portfolio, which should include original/final art, slides and video cassette. Pays for design by the project, $300 minimum. Pays for illustration by the project, $150 minimum. Considers complexity of project, client's budget, skill and experience of artist and how work will be used when establishing payment. Rights purchased vary according to project.

CREATIVE PRODUCTIONS, INC., 200 Main St., Orange NJ 07050. (201)676-4422. Partner: Gus J. Nichols. Audiovisual firm. Clients: pharmaceutical firms, paper manufacturers, chemical and financial firms.

Needs: Works with 30 freelance artists/year. Artists must be within 1 hour travel time to studio with 1 year of experience. Uses artists for mechanicals, paste-ups, charts and graphs. Especially important is "accuracy, neat work and the ability to take direction."

First Contact & Terms: Send resume to be kept on file. Call for appointment to show portfolio. Reports back only if interested. Pays by the hour, $8-12 average. Considers skill and experience of artist when establishing payment.

Tips: Artists "need to do mechanicals in the conventional way and also operate a graphic computer."

DAVIS, HAYS & COMPANY, 426 Hudson St., Hackensack NJ 07601. (201)641-4910. Contact: Art Director. Public relations and promotional consulting firm. Clients: service industries, business-to-business, marketing research, health and beauty.
Needs: Works with 3-5 freelance artists/year. Artist must have experience working with agencies. Uses artists for design, layout, mechanicals, illustration and production. "Professionalism and deadline and budget restrictions awareness are important."
First Contact & Terms: Send query letter with Photostats to be kept on file. Samples not filed are returned only if requested. Reports within 1 month. Call or write to schedule an appointment to show a portfolio, which should include roughs and original/final art. Pays for design by the hour, $20-50. Pays for illustration by the project, $200 minimum. Considers complexity of the project, client's budget and turnaround time when establishing payment. Buys all rights.
Tips: "We are looking for positive thinkers: those who say 'we'll find a way to do it' even when there are no easy answers. Also looking for artists with knowledge of MacIntosh graphics."

DIEGNAN & ASSOCIATES, Box 298, Oldwick NJ 08858. (201)832-7951. President: Norman Diegnan. PR firm. Clients: commercial.
Needs: Assigns 25 freelance jobs/year. Works on assignment only. Uses artists for catalogs and AV presentations.
First Contact & Terms: Send brochure and resume to be kept on file. Write for appointment to show portfolio; may also send portfolio. Reports only if interested. Pays artist's rate. Considers client's budget when establishing payment. Buys all rights.

GRAPHIC WORKSHOP INC., 466 Old Hook Rd., Emerson NJ 07630. (201)967-8500. Creative Director: Al Nudelman. Sales promotion agency. Clients: AV, computer accounts, industrial tools, men's wear, ladies' wear.
Needs: Works with 10-15 freelance artists/year. Prefers local artists with a minimum of 3-5 years of experience; "retail layout and some design background helpful." Works on assignment only. Uses artists for illustration, paste-up and mechanical, design comps. Especially looks for knowledge of type and good design sense.
First Contact & Terms: Send query letter with business card and slides or "whatever shows work off the best". Samples not filed are returned only if requested. Reports back only if interested. Pays by the hour, $10-15 average; by the day, $75-100 average. Considers client's budget, complexity of the project, and skill and experience of artist when establishing payment. Buys all rights.

***INSIGHT ASSOCIATES**, Bldg. E, 373 Rt. 46 W., Fairfield NJ 07006. (201)575-5521. Audiovisual firm. "Full-service business communicators; multimedia, videotape, print materials, sales meetings . . . all of the above from concept to completion." Clients: organization in need of any audiovisual, audio and/or print." Client list provided upon request.
Needs: Works with 50-100 freelance artists/year. Assigns 50 jobs/year. Works on assignment only. Uses artists for design, illustration, brochures, catalogs, P-O-P displays, mechanicals, retouching, animation, direct mail packages, press releases, lettering, logos, charts/graphs and advertisements.
First Contact & Terms: Send query letter with brochure or resume. Samples are filed. Samples not filed are returned by SASE. Reports back within 3 weeks only if interested. Write to schedule an appointment to show a portfolio or mail brochure or resume. Payment varies. Considers complexity of project, client's budget, turnaround time and how work will be used when establishing payment. Rights vary according to project.
Tips: Artists need "experience with audiovisual productions, i.e., multi-image, video, etc."

JANUARY PRODUCTIONS, 249 Goffle Rd., Hawthorne NJ 07507. (201)423-4666. Art Director: Karen Neulinger. AV producer. Serves clients in education. Produces videos, sound filmstrips and read-along books and cassettes.
Needs: Assigns 5-10 jobs/year. Works with 5 illustrators/year. "While not a requirement, an artist living in the same geographic area is a plus." Works on assignment only, "although if someone had a project already put together, we would consider it." Uses artists for artwork for filmstrips, sketches for books and layout work.
First Contact & Terms: Send query letter with resume, tear sheets, photocopies and photographs. To show a portfolio, call to schedule an appointment. Portfolio should include original/final art, color and tear sheets. Pays for illustration by the project. No originals returned following publication. Buys all rights.

J. M. KESSLINGER & ASSOCIATES, 37 Saybrook Place, Newark NJ 07102. (201)623-0007. Art Director: J. Dietz. Advertising agency. Serves business-to-business clients.
Needs: Uses 1-2 illustrators/month for illustrations, mechanicals, direct mail, brochures, flyers, trade

magazines and newspapers. Prefers local artists. Works on assignment only.
First Contact & Terms: Phone for appointment. Prefers Photostats, tear sheets, slides as samples. Samples returned by SASE only if requested. Reports only if interested. Does not return original artwork to artist unless contracted otherwise. Negotiates pay. Pays by the hour, $15-50 average. Pay range depends on the type of freelance work, i.e. mechanicals vs. creative. Considers complexity of project, client's budget, skill and experience of artist, and rights purchased when establishing payment.

***SAI GROUP INC.**, SAI Building, 900 Dudley Ave., Cherry Hill NJ 08002. (609)665-8833. Advertising Manager: Ellen IuLiucci.
Needs: Works with 3 designers. Uses artists for consumer magazines, direct mail, brochures/flyers and newspapers.
First Contact & Terms: Local artists only. Call for interview. Artists must have experience in designing mailings and/or ads for major consumer direct mail business, preferably in insurance, financial services, etc. Provide brochure, flyer, business card, resume and tear sheets, etc. No originals returned at job's completion. "We generally work on a per job basis not an hourly one, and we find that we are paying the generally accepted fees in this area of the country."

SPOONER & CO., Box 126, Verona NJ 07044. (201)857-0053. President: William B. Spooner III. Industrial ad agency. Clients: mills, mixers, vacuum pumps, metals and ores, plastic blow molding machines and conveyor belts.
Needs: Works with 2 illustrators and 2 designers/month. Works on assignment basis only. Uses artists for stationery design, slide sets, brochures/flyers and trade magazines. Also uses artists for layout, illustration, technical art, type spec, paste-up, retouching and lettering for newspapers, trade magazines, direct mail, technical literature and trade shows.
First Contact & Terms: Call first or send letter with qualifications and experience. Provide brochure, flyer, business card and resume to be kept on file. Do not send original work. Samples returned by SASE. Reports back only if interested. Payment negotiated. Considers complexity of project, client's budget, and skill and experience of artist when establishing payment.

STARBUCK CREATIVE SERVICES, 26 Steven Tr., West Orange NJ 07052. Senior Vice President: B. Siegel. Ad agency. Clients: health care. Client list provided for SASE.
Needs: Works with 2-5 freelance artists/year. Uses artists for special projects and back-up.
First Contact & Terms: Send query letter with brochure, resume, business card and Photostats, photographs, slides or tear sheets to be kept on file. Samples not filed are returned by SASE only if requested. Reports within 3 weeks. Write for appointment to show portfolio. Payment open. Considers complexity of the project, client's budget, skill and experience of artist, geographic scope for the finished product, turnaround time and rights purchased when establishing payment. Rights purchased vary according to project.

***TROLL ASSOCIATES**, 100 Corporate Dr., Mahwah NJ 07430. Vice President, Production: Marian Schecter. AV producer/book publisher. Audience: children. Produces books, records, filmstrips and multimedia.
Needs: Buys approximately 200 designs/year. Uses artists for catalog covers/illustrations, direct mail brochures, multimedia kits, record album designs and book illustrations.
First Contact & Terms: Local artists only. Query with resume and samples (slides preferred). SASE. Reports in 4 weeks. Provide resume, samples, brochure/flyer or business card to be kept on file for future assignments. No originals returned to artist at job's completion. Pays by the project. Buys all rights.

***DOUGLAS TURNER, INC.**, 11 Commerce St., Newark NJ 07102. (201)623-4506. Senior Vice President/Creative Director: Gloria Spolan. Ad agency. Clients: banking institutions, window covering, toys and office equipment firms.
Needs: Number of illustrators used varies. Uses freelance artists for trade magazines, direct mail, brochures, catalogs, posters and newspapers.
First Contact & Terms: Send in literature first—if interested will contact artist. Works on assignment basis only. Payment is by the project; negotiates according to client's budget.

WREN MARKETING COMMUNICATIONS CO., (formerly Wren Associates, Inc.), 5 Independence Way, Princeton NJ 08540. (609)924-8085. Production Manager: Debbie Goodkin. Communications consulting firm. Clients: industrial, Fortune 500 (automotive, pharmaceutical, financial, etc.)
Needs: Works with 10-25 freelance artists/year. Artists should have minimum of 1-2 years of experience. Uses artists for mechanical preparation, photography, storyboard and design, video crew, typesetting, Forox photography, computer slide generation, project management. Especially important are de-

sign and mechanical preparation skills, slide preparation skills, multi-image training, Forox experience, computer slide experience, rendering and storyboarding.
First Contact & Terms: Send query letter with resume and slides and videocassettes of completed shows. Letter and resume are filed; samples are returned if postage is paid by the artist. Reports back only if interested. Call for appointment to show portfolio. Pays by the hour, $8-35; by the project, $100 minimum; by the day, $100-350. Design rates vary according to skill level and project; photography rates vary according to project. Considers client's budget, and skill and experience of artist when establishing payment. Rights purchased vary according to project.
Tips: "Wren Associates is very interested in attracting experienced multimedia designers and producers. We are most interested in seeing videotapes of completed projects which include photography direction, narration, soundtrack direction and strong conceptual skills. Freelance artists who are interested in our firm but do not fulfill this experience level should be able to show their level of expertise in the production of slides, print and/or video."

ZM SQUARED, 903 Edgewood Lane, Cinnaminson NJ 08077. (609)786-0612. Executive Director: Mr. Pete Zakroff. AV producer. Clients: industry, business, education and unions. Produces slides, filmstrips, overhead transparencies and handbooks.
Needs: Assigns 8 jobs/year. Works with 2 illustrators/month. Prefers artists with previous work experience who specialize. Works on assignment only. Uses artists for cartoons, illustrations and technical art.
First Contact & Terms: Send resume and samples (slides preferred). Samples returned by SASE. Provide samples and brochure/flyer to be kept on file for possible future assignments. Reports in 3 weeks. Pays by the project, $100-2,500. Payment varies with each client's budget. No originals returned to artist following publication. Buys all rights.
Tips: "We look for simplicity in style, facial expressions in cartoons."

New York

ACKERMAN ADVERTISING COMMUNICATIONS INC., 31 Glen Head Rd., Glen Head NY 11545. (516)759-3000. Creative Director: Skip Ackerman. Art Director: Maxine Brenner. Serves clients in food, finance and tourism.
Needs: Works with 4 illustrators and 2 designers/month. Local artists only. Uses artists for layout, paste-up, illustration and retouching for newspapers, TV, magazines, transit signage, billboards, collateral, direct mail and P-O-P displays.
First Contact & Terms: Arrange interview. No originals returned.

***ASSOCIATED INDUSTRIAL DESIGNERS, INC.**, 32 Court St., Brooklyn Heights NY 11201. (718)624-0034. President: Robert I. Goldberg. Ad agency. Clients: manufacturers.
Needs: Works with 6 freelance artists/year. Uses artists for design, illustration, mechanicals, retouching, lettering and logos.
First Contact & Terms: Send query letter with samples showing art style. Samples are filed. Pays for design by the hour, $18 minimum. Pays for illustration by the hour, $15 minimum. Considers complexity of project and client's budget when establishing payment. Buys all rights.

CAMPUS GROUP COMPANIES, 24 Depot Sq., Tuckaho NY 10707. (914)961-1900. Contact: Melanie Suskin. Audiovisual firm.
Needs: Works with 25 freelance artists/year. Works on assignment only. Uses artists for design, illustrations, brochures, catalogs, books, mechanicals, animation, posters, direct mail packages, press releases, motion pictures, logos, charts/graphs and advertisements. "Artists must have computer art skills, good design and board skills."
First Contact & Terms: Send query letter with resume and samples. Samples not filed are returned only if requested by artist. Reports within 12 weeks. Write to schedule an appointment to show a portfolio, which should include as much as is relative. Pays for design by the hour, $10-30. Pays for illustration by the hour, $10-30. Considers complexity of project, skill and experience of artist and turnaround time when establishing payment. Purchases all rights.
Tips: "Our company does not train artists; we have only skilled experienced artists."

***CHANNEL ONE PRODUCTIONS, INC.**, 82-03 Utopia Pkwy., Jamaica Estates NY 11432. (718)380-2525. President: Burton M. Putterman. Audiovisual firm. "We are a multimedia, film and video production company for broadcast, image enhancement, and P-O-P displays. Clients: multi-national corporations, recreational industry, PBS.

Needs: Works with 25 freelance artists/year. Assigns 100 jobs/year. Prefers local artists. Works on assignment only. Uses artists for brochures, catalogs, P-O-P displays, animation, direct mail packages, motion pictures, logos and advertisements.
First Contact & Terms: Send query letter with resume, slides and photographs. Samples are not filed. Samples not filed are returned by SASE. Reports back within 2 weeks only if interested. Call to schedule an appointment to show a portfolio, which should original/final art, final reproduction/product, slides, video disks and videotape. Pays for design by the project, $400 minimum. Considers complexity of project and client's budget when establishing payment. Rights purchased vary according to project.

***COMMAND COMMUNICATIONS** , 62 Bowman Ave., Rye Brook NY 10573. (914)937-7000. Studio Manager: J. Meyerowitz. Clients: industrial and corporate. Produces video animation, multimedia, slide presentations, videotapes and print materials.
Needs: Assigns 25 jobs/year. Uses artists for slide graphics, layout of brochures, design catalogs, corporate brochures, annual reports, filmstrips, slide shows, layouts, mechanicals, computer graphics and desk-top publishing.
First Contact & Terms: Local artists only (New York City, Manhattan and Westchester). "Send note on availability and previous work." SASE. Reports in 2 weeks. Provide materials to be kept on file for future assignments. No originals returned at job's completion. Pays $10-20/hour.

ALAN G. EISEN CO. INC., R.D. 2, Box 310, Narrowsburg NY 11804. President: Alan G. Eisen. PR firm. Clients: consumer and individual product manufacturers, service organizations and financial firms.
Needs: Works with 6-8 freelance artists/year. Assigns 2-3 jobs/year. Works on assignment only. Uses illustrators for jobs dealing with direct mail, brochures/flyers, trade magazines, annual reports and newspapers.
First Contact & Terms: Send query letter with resume and photographs. Samples not returned. Reports within weeks. To show a portfolio, mail Photostats upon request only. Pays for design by the project, $200 minimum. Pays for illustration by the project, $100 minimum. Considers complexity of project, how work will be used and rights purchased when establishing payment. Total rights purchased.

***FORAY ASSOCIATES**, Division of IMC Magnetics Corp., Suite 221, 100 Jericho Quadrangle, Jericho NY 11753. (516)938-0800. In-house advertising agency. Manager: Don Cronan. Serves clients in industry.
Needs: Uses artists for ads.
First Contact & Terms: Query with previously published work. Reports in 2 weeks. Originals not returned. Pays $50 minimum, spot drawings.

***FORDHAM EQUIPMENT & PUBLISHING CO.**, 3308 Edson Ave., Bronx NY 10469. (212)379-7300. President: Al Robbins. AV producer. Clients: schools. Produces filmstrips, multimedia kits, overhead transparencies and children's books.
Needs: Uses artists for filmstrip animation and children's book illustrations.
First Contact & Terms: Arrange interview to show portfolio. Prefers b&w line drawings as samples. Samples returned. Provide brochure/flyer to be kept on file for future assignments. Reports in 2 weeks. Works on assignment only. Pays by job.

HEALY, SCHUTTE & COMSTOCK, 1207 Delaware Ave., Buffalo NY 14209. (716)884-2120. Associate Creative Director: John Brooks. Ad agency. Clients: food service, industrial, retail department stores, consumer food, financial and health-related accounts; client list provided upon request.
Needs: Works with 5 illustrators/month. Uses freelance artists for consumer and trade magazines, direct mail, P-O-P displays, brochures, catalogs, posters, signage, newspapers and AV presentations.
First Contact & Terms: Contact is usually through representative—illustrator or design group. Payment is by the project.

***LLOYD S. HOWARD ASSOCIATES INC.**, Box N, Millwood NY 10546. Art/Creative Director: L. Howard. Ad agency. Serves clients in interior furnishings, lighting, swimming pools, recreation and publishing.
Needs: Works with 2 illustrators and up to 5 designers/month. Uses artists for consumer magazines, direct mail, brochures/flyers, trade magazines and newspapers. Also uses artists for mechanicals and finished art for newspapers, magazines, catalogs and direct mail. Especially needs layout/comp artists.
First Contact & Terms: Local or New York City artists only. Works on assignment only. Call for interview between 9 a.m.-noon. Prefers layouts, dupes, finished samples or Photostats as samples. Samples

not returned. Reports in 2 weeks. Provide business card and tear sheets to be kept on file for possible future assignments. No originals returned to artist at job's completion. Pays by the project; pay "depends on assignment."
Tips: "Show actual comps or roughs."

HUMAN RELATIONS MEDIA, 175 Tompkins Ave., Pleasantville NY 10570. (914)769-7496. Editor-in-Chief: Michael Hardy. Audiovisual firm. Clients: junior and senior high schools, colleges, hospitals, personnel departments of business organizations.
Needs: Works with 5 freelance artists/year. Prefers local artists. Uses artists for illustrations for videotape, filmstrip and slide programs. "It is helpful if artists have skills pertaining to science-related topics."
First Contact & Terms: Send query letter with resume and samples to be kept on file. Samples not filed are returned by SASE. Reports back only if interested. Call for appointment to show portfolio, which should include slides or tear sheets. Pays for illustration by the project, $65-1,500. Considers complexity of the project, number of illustrations in project, client's budget, skill and experience of artist and turnaround time when establishing payment. Rights purchased vary according to project.
Tips: "It is important that samples are seen before face-to-face interviews. We look for a strong, simple graphic style since the image may be on screen only 10 seconds. We require the ability to research and illustrate scientific subjects accurately."

KOPF & ISAACSON, 35 Pinelawn Rd., Melville NY 11747. Art Directors: Art Zimmermann or Evelyn Rysdyk. Ad agency. Clients: technical, i.e. telephones, computer firms etc.; some consumer, i.e. clothing manufacturing, travel agencies.
Needs: Works on assignment only. Uses some illustrations and some layout/comp.
First Contact & Terms: Send query letter with resume and slides or tear sheets to be kept on file. No phone queries. Samples not filed are returned by SASE only if requested. Reports back only if interested. Write for appointment to show portfolio. Pays for design by the project, $200-1,000. Pays for illustration by the project, $200-6,000. Considers complexity of the project, client's budget, skill and experience of artist, and geographic scope for the finished product when establishing payment. Rights purchased vary according to project.

McANDREW ADVERTISING, 2125 St. Raymond Ave., Bronx NY 10462. (212)892-8660. Art/Creative Director: Robert McAndrew. Ad agency. Clients: industrial and technical firms. Assigns 200 jobs and buys 120 illustrations/year.
Needs: Works with 2 illustrators and 4 designers/month. Uses mostly local artists. Uses artists for stationery design, direct mail, brochures/flyers and trade magazines.
First Contact & Terms: Query with photocopies, business card and brochure/flyer to be kept on file. Samples not returned. Reports in 1 month. No originals returned to artist at job's completion. Call or write to schedule an appointment to show a portfolio, which should include roughs and final reproduction/product. Pays $20-40/hour and $100 minimum by the project for annual reports, catalogs, trade magazines, letterheads, trademarks, layout and paste-up. Considers complexity of project, client's budget, and skill and experience of artist when establishing payment.

McCUE ADVERTISING & PUBLIC RELATIONS INC., 91 Riverside Dr., Binghamton NY 13905. Contact: Donna McCue. Ad/PR firm. Clients: retailers, nonprofit and industrial.
Needs: Artists with at least 2 professional assignments only. Uses artists for direct mail, television, brochures/flyers, trade magazines, newspapers, mechanicals and logo design.
First Contact & Terms: Send a query letter with resume, brochure or flyer, business card and tear sheets to be kept on file. Reports in 3-4 weeks. No originals returned at job's completion. Negotiates payment.

***THE NOTEWORTHY CO.**, 100 Church St., Amsterdam NY 12010. (518)842-2660. Contact: Tom Constantino. Advertising specialty manufacturer. Clients: advertising specialty jobbers with clients in real estate, banks, chain stores, state parks and community service groups. Buys 150 illustrations/year.
Needs: Uses artists for catalogs, packaging and litterbags, coloring books and pamphlets.
First Contact & Terms: Query with samples. SASE. Reports in 2 weeks. Provide resume and brochures to be kept on file for future assignments. No originals returned to artist at job's completion. Pays $200 minimum, litterbag design.

RICHARD-LEWIS CORP., Box 598, Scarsdale NY 10583. President: R. Byer. Clients: machinery, tool, publishers, office supplies, chemical, detergent, film and printing supplies.
Needs: Local artists only. Uses artists for illustrations, retouching and some ad layout and mechanicals.

First Contact & Terms: Query with resume or arrange interview to show portfolio. SASE. Reports in 2-3 weeks. Negotiates pay.

RONAN, HOWARD, ASSOCIATES, INC., 11 Buena Vista Ave., Spring Valley NY 10977-3040. (914)356-6668. President: Muriel Brown. Ad/PR firm. Clients: video production products; lighting products; electronic components.
Needs: Works with 2-3 freelance artists/year. Uses artists for mechanicals, retouching, charts/graphs and AV presentations.
First Contact & Terms: Send query letter. "Samples and/or other material will not be returned. Please do not send unordered material with a demand for return. It is an unwarranted burden on our shipping department." SASE. Reports immediately. Pays $25 minimum for illustrations, layout, lettering, paste-up, retouching and mechanicals for newspapers, magazines, catalogs and P-O-P displays. Pays promised fee for unused assigned illustrations.

SADOWSKY ART/ADVERTISING, 21 Pinetree Rd., Westbury NY 11590. (516)333-1427. President/Creative Director: Fanny Sadowsky. Clients: industrial, medical, electronics, housewares, giftwares, building contractors.
Needs: Local artists only. Works on assignment only. Uses designers for brochures/flyers and trade magazines. Uses artists for layout, illustration, technical art, paste-up and retouching for magazines, direct mail, brochures, annual reports and corporate promotions.
First Contact & Terms: Send query letter with resume and samples. Reports only if interested. Call to schedule an appointment to show a portfolio, which should include roughs, original/final art and photographs. Pays by the hour, $10 minimum. Considers client's budget, and skill and experience of artist when establishing payment. No originals returned to artist at job's completion.
Tips: "Call for appointment in advance. Do *not drop in*. Bring current portfolio to interview."

RIK SHAFER ASSOC. INC., 260 Main St., Northport NY 11768. (516)754-1750. President: Rik Shafer. Full-service agency.
Needs: Works with 12 freelance artists/year. Prefers artists in the Northeast region. Works on assignment only. Uses artists and graphic designers for advertising and brochure design and layout, brochure illustration, and posters.
First Contact & Terms: Send query letter, brochure, resume and Photostats to be kept on file. Samples not kept on file are returned. Reports back to artist. Pays by the project. Considers complexity of project, skill and experience of artist, and how work will be used when establishing payment.

WALLACK & WALLACK ADVERTISING, INC., 33 Great Neck Rd., Great Neck NY 11021. Art Director: John Napolitano. Ad agency. Clients: fashion eyewear, entertainment, computer and industrial.
Needs: Works with 10-15 artists/year. Uses artists for mechanicals, layout and design, illustration, photography and retouching. Mechanical and print production skills are important.
First Contact & Terms: Send query letter with brochure showing art style or resume, business card and photocopies to be kept on file. Samples returned only if requested. Reports only if interested. To show a portfolio, mail roughs and final reproduction/product. Pays for design by the hour, $10-20; by the day, $100-200. Pays for illustration by the project, $75-1,000. Considers complexity of the project, client's budget, skill and experience of artist, turnaround time, geographic scope for the finished product and rights purchased when establishing payment. Rights purchased vary according to project.
Tips: "Only present work at which you are most proficient. If you have made a commitment to the design profession—be professional. Develop your talents—don't demand only the high-priced, ambitious assignments. Put your best efforts into every job—especially your portfolio."

WINTERKORN LILLIS INC., Hiram Sibley Bldg., 311 Alexander at East Ave., Rochester NY 14604. (716)454-1010. Creative Director: Wendy Nelson. Ad agency. Clients: medical/health care and industrial firms; national level only—few regional accounts.
Needs: Works with 8-10 new illustrators/year; 6-10 new designers/year. Works on assignment only. Uses freelance artists for trade and consumer magazines, direct mail, P-O-P displays, brochures, posters, AV presentations and literature, and coverage for sales promotions and sales meetings.
First Contact & Terms: Query with samples to be kept on file. Prefers slide carousel or laminated tear sheets as samples. Samples returned only if requested. Reports only if interested. Pays by the project, $700-8,000 average. Considers complexity of project, client's budget, skill and experience of artist, turnaround time and rights purchased when establishing payment.
Tips: "Present only top professional work, 18 pieces maximum, in a very organized manner."

WOLF MANSFIELD ADVERTISING, INC., (formerly Lloyd Mansfield Co., Inc.), Suite 900, 237 Main St., Buffalo NY 14203. (716)854-2762. Executive Art Director: Joseph Lennert. Ad/PR firm, marketing communications. Serves clients in a variety of industries.

Needs: Assigns a minimum of 3 jobs and buys 25 illustrations/year. Uses artists for illustrations, mechanicals, layout and retouching.
First Contact & Terms: Local artists primarily. Works on assignment only. Query with resume and arrange interview to show portfolio. Especially looks for "neatness and creativity of presentation." SASE. Reports in 3 weeks. Provide business card, brochure/flyer or resume to be kept on file for possible future assignments. Pays $12-50/hour.

New York City

ADMASTER INC., 95 Madison Ave., New York NY 10016. (212)679-1134. Director of Visual Services: Andrew Corn. Clients: businesses. Produces slide sets, multimedia kits, multiple images, video cassettes and brochures. Assigns 300 jobs/year.
Needs: Works with 5 illustrators and 1 designer/month. Local artists only. Uses artists for slides, motion pictures and TV.
First Contact & Terms: Send query letter with resume. Reports in 1 week. Write to schedule an appointment to show a portfolio, which should include storyboards, slides and video. Samples returned by SASE if not kept on file. No originals returned to artist at job's completion. Buys all rights. Pays by the project. Considers skill and experience of artist when establishing payment.
Tips: Artists should have "good clean corporate samples."

***ALTAMONT ADVERTISING AGENCY**, 1457 Broadway, New York NY 10036. (212)921-7180. Contact: Creative Director. "We are a full-service advertising agency specializing in the print media." Clients: fashion, real estate, food. Client list provided upon request.
Needs: Prefers local artists. Uses artists for design, illustration, brochures, catalogs, newspapers, consumer and trade magazines, mechanicals, retouching, billboards, lettering, logos and advertisements.
First Contact & Terms: Send query letter with resume and photocopies. Samples are filed. Samples not filed are returned only if requested. Reports back only if interested. Call to schedule an appointment to show a portfolio, which should include Photostats, tear sheets and photographs. Pays for design by the hour, $25 minimum. Pays for illustration by the hour, $50 minimum. Considers complexity of project, client's budget, turnaround time and skill and experience of artist when establishing payment. Buys all rights.

***BIRD & FALBORN**, 220 E. 23rd St., New York NY 10010. Production Manager: Leonard Grow. Art Director: Charlie Deny. Ad agency. Clients: financial, insurance and publishers.
Needs: Works with several freelance artists/year. Uses artists for design, illustration and paste-up.
First Contact & Terms: Send query letter with resume to be kept on file. Reports only if interested. Pays by the hour, $10-30 average. Considers skill and experience of artist when establishing payment.

JOHN BRANSBY PRODUCTIONS, LTD./EFFECTIVE COMMUNICATION ARTS, INC. (ECA), 221 W. 57th St., New York NY 10019. Vice President: W. Comcowich. Clients: "Federal government and Fortune 500; we concentrate in the fields of science, medicine and technology." Produces filmstrips, videotapes and interactive video disk programs and print materials. Assigns 40 jobs/year.
Needs: Works with 2-3 illustrators and 1-2 designers/month. Works on assignment only. Uses artists for motion pictures, computer graphic design and professional monographs. Also uses artists for 16mm film animation design and graphics, 35mm slide illustration and graphics, and medical illustrations.
First Contact & Terms: Query with resume and slides, photographs and color prints (no originals). SASE. Reports in 4 weeks. Provide brochure/flyer and resume to be kept on file for future assignments. Pays for design by the hour, $25 minimum. Pays for illustration by the project, $150 minimum.
Tips: "There is greater need for medical artists and animators."

ANITA HELEN BROOKS ASSOCIATES, PUBLIC RELATIONS, 155 E. 55th St., New York NY 10022. (212)755-4498. President: Anita Helen Brooks. PR firm. Clients: fashion, "society," travel, restaurants, politics and diplomats, books. Special events; health and health campaigns.
Needs: Number of freelance jobs assigned/year varies. Works on assignment only. Uses artists for consumer magazines, newspapers and press releases. "We're currently using more abstract designs."
First Contact & Terms: Call for appointment to show portfolio. Reports only if interested. Payment determined by client's needs. Considers client's budget and skill and experience of artist when establishing payment.
Tips: Artists interested in working with us must provide "rate schedule, partial list of clients and media outlets. We look for graphic appeal when reviewing samples."

***LAWRENCE BUTNER ADVERTISING, INC.**, 228 E. 45th St., New York NY 10017. (212)682-3200. Vice President: Nevil Cross. Ad agency specializing in direct response, consumer and trade advertising. Clients: publishers, discount brokerage and insurance companies.
Needs: Prefers local artists only. Uses freelance artists for design, brochures, newspapers, consumer and trade magazines, P-O-P displays, mechanicals, retouching, posters and direct mail packages.
First Contact & Terms: Send query letter with brochure or resume and tear sheets. Samples are filed. Samples not filed are returned only if requested. "We pay by experience."

CANAAN COMMUNICATIONS INC., 310 E. 44th St., New York NY 10017. (212)682-4030. President: Lee Canaan. PR firm. Clients: restaurants, hotels, celebrities, authors, corporate accounts, advertising agencies, political, art museums and galleries. Client list provided for SASE.
Needs: Assigns 12 freelance jobs/year. Works on assignment only. Uses artists for consumer and trade magazines, brochures, catalogs, newspapers, filmstrips and stationery.
First Contact & Terms: Send query letter with brochure, resume, business card, samples and tear sheets to be kept on file.

CANON & SHEA ASSOCIATES, INC., 875 Ave. of Americas, New York NY 10001. (212)564-8822. Art Director: Richard Long. Ad/PR/marketing firm. Clients: business-to-business and financial services.
Needs: Assigns 20-40 jobs and buys 50-60 illustrations/year. Mostly local artists.
First Contact & Terms: Send query letter with brochure showing art style or resume and tear sheets. To show a portfolio, mail original/final art or write to schedule an appointment. Pays by the hour: $20-35, animation, annual reports, catalogs, trade and consumer magazines; $25-50, packaging; $50-250, corporate identification/graphics; $8-28, layout, lettering and paste-up.
Tips: "Artists should have industrial or financial materials as samples and should understand the marketplace."

THE CREATIVE ESTABLISHMENT, 115 W. 31st St., New York NY 10001. (212)563-3337. Producer: Diana Davis. AV/film/multi-image producer. Serves clients in industry. Produces materials for business meetings, product introductions, corporate image and P-O-P.
Needs: Assigns 20 jobs/year. New York metropolitan area artists only. "Artists must have at least 3 years of experience in work applied for." Works with 5 board artists, 1 animator and 2 designers/month. Uses artists for most projects.
First Contact & Terms: Send resume and samples (12 or more slides preferred). Samples not filed are returned with SASE. Reporting time depends on current needs. Call or write to schedule an appointment to show a portfolio, which should include storyboards/final slides. Pays for design by the day, $400 maximum; pays for illustration by the project, $50-200 maximum. No originals returned to artist after publication. Negotiates rights purchased.
Tips: "With more use of computer art, freelancers now need a more technical background."

DA SILVA ASSOCIATES, 137 E. 38h St., New York NY 10016. (212)696-1657. Executive Producer: Raul da Silva. TV/film/animation/AV producer and limited publishing firm. Clients: business, industrial, institutional, educational and entertainment.
Needs: Works with 3-4 illustrators and 1 designer/month. "Seeking several artists with experience in slide/multimedia production, layout and materials. Also seeking designers, plus illustrators capable of rendering sci-fi/fantasy art in the *Heavy Metal* style—see the magazine for the years '77-'79." Works on assignment only. Uses artists for filmstrips, motion pictures, record jackets, multimedia kits, storyboards and titles.
First Contact & Terms: Send resume including references with phone numbers and addresses, and electrostatic copies which will *not* be returned. Samples returned by SASE only if requested; samples "always kept on file if they merit space. Do not send any original work without obtaining our request for it." Returns only solicited work. Reports within 2 weeks only if interested. Payment for illustrations and layout "depends completely on end use." Storyboards, $15-50/frame; continuity design, $300 and up/program. Considers complexity of project, client's budget, skill and experience of artist, turnaround time and rights purchased when establishing payment.
Tips: "We are a small, highly professional studio using only committed, *skilled* professionals who enjoy having their good work appreciated and rewarded. Hobbyists, dabblers usually do not make the grade for us."

DANCER-FITZGERALD-SAMPLE INC., 405 Lexington Ave., New York NY 10174. Director of Art Services: James Hushon. Ad agency. Serves clients in food, household products, beauty products, publishing, hosiery and automobiles.

Needs: Works with 25 illustrators and 3 designers/month. Works on assignment only. Uses artists for billboards, P-O-P displays, filmstrips, consumer and trade magazines, TV, slide sets, brochures/flyers and newspapers; cartoons and humorous and cartoon-style illustrations (4-5 each year). Also uses artists for layout, retouching and lettering.
First Contact & Terms: Send printed pieces, slides or flyers as samples. Samples returned by SASE. No originals returned to artist at job's completion. Pays $200-5,000, depending upon use and degree of difficulty. Considers complexity of project, client's budget and rights purchased when establishing payment.

DARINO FILMS, 222 Park Ave. S, New York NY 10003. (212)228-4024. Creative Director: Ed Darino. Film/animation producer. Clients: educational, some industrial, TV station and corporate.
Needs: Works with 5-8 illustrators, 2-3 animators/month, plus airbrush artists and lettering artists. Also works with freelance designers. Uses artists for motion pictures. Works on assignment only.
First Contact & Terms: "No visits and no calls." Provide business card, brochure/flyer to be kept on file for future assignments. Reports back on future assignment possibilities. Payment to illustrators by illustration or by week; animators, within union salary; background artist, per background only (union scale). 3-6 month internship program.
Tips: Especially looks for "flexible communication of the graphic message in mailed submissions."

DITTMAN INCENTIVE MARKETING, 22 W. 23rd St., New York NY 10010. (212)741-8040. Art Director: W. Whetsel. AV producer/print sales promotion agency. Serves clients in corporations.
Needs: Uses mechanical artists, photographers, illustrators and hand letterers.
First Contact & Terms: Provide resume and slides, original publications to be kept on file for possible future assignments. Reports within weeks. Pays by the project or by the hour, "depending on task." Considers complexity of project, client's budget, turnaround time and sometimes skill and experience of artist and rights purchased when establishing payment. No originals returned to artist following publication. Negotiates rights purchased.
Tips: "We maintain extremely high standards, and only those artists who feel that their work is extraordinary in creation and execution should contact us. We work only with artists who have a high level of imagination and intense pride in the finished product—supported, of course, by samples that prove it."

JODY DONOHUE ASSOC., INC., 32 E. 57th St., New York NY 10022. (212)688-8653. Contact: Interview, Review Portfolios Department. PR firm. Clients: fashion and beauty. Media used includes direct mail and P-O-P displays.
Needs: Works with 1-5 illustrators and 1-5 designers/month. Uses artists for P-O-P displays, stationery design, multimedia kits, direct mail, slide sets and brochures/flyers.
First Contact & Terms: Send brochure to be kept on file. Call for personal appointment to show portfolio. No originals returned to artist at job's completion. Negotiates payment based on client's budget, amount of creativity required from artist, and where work will appear.
Tips: Wants to see recent work that has been used (printed piece, etc.) and strength in an area (i.e., still life, children, etc.).

***ERICKSEN/BASLOE ADVERTISING, LTD.**, 12 W. 37th St., New York NY 10018. Contact: Production Manager. Full-service advertising agency providing all promotional materials and commercial services for clients. Clients: entertainment, home video, television, television syndication, movies, etc..
Needs: Works with 50 freelance artists/year. Assigns 50 jobs/year. Works on assignment only. Uses artists for illustration, advertising, video packaging, brochures, catalogs, trade magazines, P-O-P displays, mechanicals, posters, lettering and logos.
First Contact & Terms: Contact through artist's agent or send query letter with brochure or tear sheets and slides. Samples are filed. Samples not filed are not returned unless requested; unsolicited samples are not returned. Reports back within 1 week only if interested. Does not report back to all unsolicited samples. Call or write to schedule an appointment to show a portfolio; "only on request should a portfolio be sent." Pays for illustration by the project, $500 minimum. Considers complexity of project, client's budget, turnaround time, skill and experience of artist, how work will be used and rights purchased when establishing payment. Buys all rights and retains ownership of original.

RICHARD FALK ASSOC., 1472 Broadway, New York NY 10036. (212)221-0043. PR firm. Clients: industry, entertainment and Broadway shows.
Needs: Uses 5 artists/year. Uses artists for consumer magazines, brochures/flyers and newspapers; occasionally buys cartoon-style illustrations.

First Contact & Terms: Send resume. Provide flyer and business card to be kept on file for future assignments. No originals returned to artist at job's completion. Pays for illustration and design by the project, $50-500.
Tips: "Don't get too complex—make it really simple."

TONI FICALORA PRODUCTIONS, 28 E. 29th St., New York NY 10016. (212)679-7700. Film/TV commercial producer. Serves clients in advertising.
Needs: Assigns 50 jobs/year. Prefers artists who specialize. Works on assignment only. Uses artists for "elaborate sets requiring freelance stylist and prop persons."
First Contact & Terms: Send query letter with resume, no samples. Call to schedule an appointment to show a portfolio, which should include color and photographs. Reports within weeks. Pays by the project. Amount of payment is negotiated with the individual artist and varies with each client's budget. No originals returned to artist after publication. Buys all rights.

FLAX ADVERTISING, 1500 Broadway, New York NY 10036. (212)944-9797. Assistant Art Director: Linda Ely. Clients: women's fashions, menswear and fabrics. Assigns 100 jobs and buys around 20 illustrations/year.
Needs: Uses artists for mechanicals, illustrations, technical art, retouching and lettering for newspapers, magazines, fashion illustration, P-O-P displays, some cartooning and direct mail.
First Contact & Terms: Local artists only. Arrange interview to show portfolio. Reports in 1 week. Pay varies.

ALBERT FRANK-GUENTHER LAW, 71 Broadway, New York NY 10006. (212)248-5200. Senior Art Director: D. Algieri. Ad agency. Clients: financial, general consumer.
Needs: Works with varying number of illustrators and designers/month. Uses artists for trade papers, consumer papers, and magazines.
First Contact & Terms: Contact only through artist's agent, who should send query letter with tear sheets. Call to schedule an appointment to show portfolio, which should include original/final art, final reproduction/product, color, tear sheets, photostats, photographs and b&w. Pays for design by the hour, $35 minimum; by the day, $250 minimum. Pays for illustration by the project, $150 minimum.
Tips: "Show excellent work only."

***PAUL FROEHLICH, PRODUCER**, #8E, 910 West End Ave., New York NY 10025. (212)865-8630. Producer: Paul Froehlich. Audiovisual firm. "I produce multimedia presentations, audiovisual presentations, video shows for industrial and broadcast application." Clients: corporate communication departments, high-tech firms and a variety of associations.
Needs: Works with 4 freelance artists/year. Assigns 10-15 jobs/year. Uses artists for brochures, press releases, charts/graphs, storyboards, slide show design, set design and costuming for video.
First Contact & Terms: Send query letter with brochure. Samples are filed. Samples not filed are returned only if requested. Call to schedule an appointment to show a portfolio. Pays for design by the hour, $15-30; or by the project. Pays for illustrations by the project. Considers complexity of project, how work will be used and rights purchased when establishing payment. Rights purchased vary according to project.

***GETO & DE MILLY, INC.**, 130 East 40th St., New York NY 10024. (212)686-4551. Senior Account Executive: Stuart Fischer. Public relations specializing in providing public relations, governmental affairs, political consulting. Clients: real estate developers and builders, nonprofit organizations and public officials.
Needs: Works with 15 freelance artists/year. Assigns 15 jobs/year. Prefers local artists. Uses freelance artists for design, illustration, brochures, mechanicals, direct mail packages, lettering, charts/graphs and advertisements.
First Contact & Terms: Send query letter. Samples are not filed. Samples not filed are returned by SASE if requested. Reports back only if interested. Write to schedule an appointment to show a portfolio. Pays for design and illustration by the project, $250 minimum. Considers complexity of project, client's budget, turnaround time, skill and experience of artist, how work will be used and rights purchased. Rights purchased vary according to project.

***MARC GLAZER AND COMPANY, INC.**, Suite 405, 249 W. 34th St., New York NY 10001. (212)244-3010. Administrative Assistant: Pam Hartmann. "We are a party planning and special events coordinator." Clients: banks, ad agencies, PR firms and other corporate accounts. Client list provided upon request.
Needs: Works with 15-20 freelance artists/year. Works on assignment only. Uses freelance artists for design, brochures, posters, direct mail packages, press releases, lettering, logos and advertisements.

First Contact & Terms: Send query letter with brochure or resume. Samples are filed. Reports back only if interested. Call to schedule an appointment to show a portfolio. Pays for design by the project, $100 minimum. Pays for illustration by the project, $200 minimum. Considers client's budget and skill and experience of artist when establishing payment. Rights purchased vary according to project.

***THE GRAPHIC EXPERIENCE INC.**, 341 Madison Ave., New York NY 10022. (212)867-0806. Contact: Production Manager. Ad agency/direct marketing firm. Clients: national corporations and financial institutions. Assigns 800 jobs/year.
Needs: Uses 3-4 illustrators and 6-10 designers/month. Uses artists for consumer magazines, direct mail and brochures/flyers. Also uses artists for annual reports, catalogs, direct mail brochures, packaging, P-O-P displays and print media advertising.
First Contact & Terms: Query with nonreturnable samples or arrange interview. No work returned. Provide brochures/flyers and business card to be kept on file for possible future assignments. Originals returned to artist at job's completion "only if a prior agreement has been made. If not, all art becomes property of agency." Pays $15-20/hour, mechanicals. Negotiates payment by job for color separations, design, illustrations, layout, paste-up, retouching, lettering and type spec.

GREY ADVERTISING INC., 777 3rd Ave., New York NY 10017. Print Business Manager: Gerda Henge. Needs ad illustrations.
Needs: Works on assignment only.
First Contact & Terms: Contact only through artist's agent. Call for an appointment to show a portfolio, which should include/original final art. Pays by the project, $500 minimum. Considers client's budget and rights purchased when establishing payment.
Tips: "Most of our advertising is done with photography. We use illustrations on a very limited basis."

***GREY FALCON HOUSE**, Suite 443, 496-A Hudson St., New York NY 10014. Art Director: Ann Grifalconi. General agency—audiovisual, public relations, market research and design firm. Clients: public service, corporate and research.
Needs: Occasionally uses outside artists for paste-up, lettering, occasional specialized art and illustration. Especially important are animation and layout, and specialized skill, such as medical, cartoon, storyboard, etc.
First Contact & Terms: Local artists only, minimum 3 years of experience. Works on assignment only. Call and outline special skills and background; send simple resume and 1 sample only to be kept on file for 1 year. Prefers Photostat or tear sheet as sample. Sample not filed is not returned. Reports only if interested. Pays by the hour, $15-30 average; by the project, $250-1,000 average; by the day, $50-200 average. Considers complexity of the project, client's budget, skill and experience of artist, geographic scope for the finished product, turnaround time and rights purchased when establishing payment. Negotiates rights purchased according to project.

CHARLES HANS FILM PRODUCTIONS INC., 25 W. 38th St., New York NY 10018. (212)382-1280. Art Director: Evelyn Simon. AV producer. Clients: industrial and corporate. Produces filmstrips, motion pictures, multimedia kits, overhead transparencies, slide sets, sound-slide sets, slide-a-motion and videotapes.
Needs: Works with 10-15 illustrators/year. Works on assignment only. Uses artists for "all phases of artwork," including chart work, paste-ups, mechanicals and some illustration and design as in animation or spot illustrations. The majority of the work is for slides.
First Contact & Terms: Send query letter with slides to be kept on file. SASE. Reports within 2 weeks. Call to schedule an appointment to show a portfolio, which should include original/final art. Pays for design by the hour, $15-20; payment for illustration varies.

HERMAN & ASSOCIATES INC., 488 Madison Ave., New York NY 10022. President: Paula Herman. Serves clients in insurance, electronics/computers, travel and tourism.
Needs: Prefers local artists who have worked on at least 2-3 professional assignments previously. Works on assignment only. Uses artists for mechanicals, illustrations and retouching for newspapers and magazines.
First Contact & Terms: Send brochure showing art style and whatever best represents artist's work as samples. Samples returned by SASE. Reporting time "depends on clients." Reports back whether to expect possible future assignments. Write to schedule an appointment to show a portfolio. Pays by the project.
Tips: "There is a trend toward more illustration. Artists interested in working with us should be persistent—keep following up. The illustrator should be an 'idea' contributor as well. Add to the concept or see another possiblity. Freelancers need to provide 'leave behinds,' reminders of their work."

JOCOM INTERNATIONAL, Suite 701, 250 W. 57th St., New York NY 10019. (212)586-5544. Vice President, Marketing: Patricia Crane. TV producer. Serves clients in industry, education and government. Produces films, videotape, teleconferences and multi-city closed-circuit satellite telecasts.
Needs: Assigns 6-12 jobs/year. Works with 2 illustrators and 2 designers/month. Uses artists for film and videotape.
First Contact & Terms: Send query letter. Works on assignment only. Provide samples, business card and tear sheets to be kept on file for possible future assignments. Reports in 2 weeks. Method and amount of payment are negotiated with the individual artist. No originals returned to artist following publication. Negotiates rights purchased.

***J. J. LANE, INC.**, 420 Lexington Ave., New York NY 10170. (212)661-0360. Art Director: Val Johnson. Ad agency and public relations firm. Clients: scientific, technical, business, automotive, aviation, marine, chemicals, plastics, electronics, computers, books, etc.
Needs: Works with 12 freelance artists/year. Assigns 4-5 jobs/month. Works on assignment only. Uses artists for design, illustration, brochures, catalogs, books, newspapers, consumer and trade magazines, mechanicals, retouching, direct mail packages, press releases, lettering, logos, charts/graphs and advertisements.
First Contact & Terms: Send query letter with brochure showing art style or resume, tear sheets and photocopies. Samples are filed. Samples not filed are returned by SASE if requested. Reports back within 1 week. Call to schedule an appointment to show a portfolio, which should include roughs, original/final art, and tear sheets. Pays for design by the hour, $5-50. Pays for illustration by the hour, $5-50. Considers skill and experience of artist when establishing payment. Buys all rights.

CHRISTOPHER LARDAS ADVERTISING, Box 1440, Radio City Station, New York NY 10101. (212)688-5199. President: Christopher Lardas. Ad agency. Clients: paper products, safety equipment, chocolate-confectionery, real estate, writing instruments/art materials.
Needs: Works with 6 freelance artists/year. Local artists only; must have heavy experience. Works on assignment only. Uses artists for illustration, layout, mechanicals.
First Contact & Terms: Send query letter with brochure showing art style or photocopies to be kept on file. Looks for "realistic product illustrations." Samples not filed are returned only if requested. Reports back only if interested. Write for appointment to show portfolio, which should include roughs, original/final art, color, b&w or tear sheets. Pays by the hour, $20-30. Considers client's budget when establishing payment. Buys all rights.
Tips: "Artists generally don't follow-up via mail! After artists make initial phone contact, we request a mail follow-up: e.g. photocopies of samples and business card for future reference. Few comply."

WILLIAM V. LEVINE ASSOCIATES, 31 E. 28th St., New York NY 10016. (212)683-7177. Vice President: Steve Gnamerl. AV producer. Serves clients in industry and consumer products. Produces sales meeting modules, slides for speaker support and printed literature.
Needs: Assigns 10 jobs/year. Works with 1-2 artists/month. Works on assignment only. Uses artists primarily for cartoons or design of booklet, brochures.
First Contact & Terms: Send resume. Reports in 2 weeks. Pays by the project. No originals returned to artist after publication. Negotiates rights purchased.

***LIGHTSCAPE PRODUCTIONS**, 420 W. 45th St., New York NY 10036. Associate Producer: Mari Geraci. "We are a video and film production company, producing commercials, news releases and industrials. Clients: advertising agencies and industrial institutions.
Needs: Works with 10 freelance artists/year. Assigns 10 jobs/year. Uses artists for mechanicals, animation and lettering.
First Contact & Terms: Send query letter with brochure. Samples are filed. Samples not filed are returned only if requested by artist. Reports back only if interested. Write to schedule an appointment to show a portfolio. Considers complexity of project, client's budget and skill and experience of artist when establishing payment. Buys all rights.

***McFRANK & WILLIAMS ADVERTISING AGENCY INC.**, 1501 Broadway, New York NY 10036. Executive Art Director: Harry Stahl.
Needs: Uses designers and artists for layout, illustration, type spec and lettering for newspaper recruitment ads.
First Contact & Terms: Send nonreturnable samples. Prefers "sharp, crisp graphics that can withstand the ravages of newsprint reproduction."

MALLORY FACTOR INC., 1500 Broadway, New York NY 10036. PR firm. Clients: Fortune 500 companies, hotels. Client list provided for SASE.

Needs: Assigns 25 freelance jobs/year. Works with 4 freelance illustrators and 2 freelance designers/month. Artists must be local. Works on assignment only. Uses artists for brochures, stationery, posters and advertising.
First Contact & Terms: Call or write for appointment to show portfolio. Samples not kept on file are not returned. Reports only if interested. Pays for design by the hour, $15; by the project, $200. Pays for illustration by the project, $150. Considers client's budget and turnaround time when establishing payment. Buys all rights.
Tips: "Have sample of a project that was done for business and is completed."

MANHATTAN VIDEO PRODUCTIONS, INC., 12 West 27th St., New York NY 10001. Video production firm serving banks, Fortune 500 companies.
Needs: Works with 3-5 freelance artists/year. Works on assignment only. Uses artists for brochures, mechanicals, logos and ads.
First Contact & Terms: Send query letter with brochure showing art style. Samples not filed are returned by SASE. Reports only if interested. To show a portfolio, mail appropriate materials. Pays for design by the hour, $10 minimum. Pays for illustration by the hour, $10 minimum. Considers client's budget, skill and experience of artist and turnaround time when establishing payment. Rights vary according to project.
Tips: "No phone calls."

MARTIN/ARNOLD COLOR SYSTEMS, 150 5th Ave., New York NY 10011. (212)675-7270. President: Martin Block. Vice President Marketing: A.D. Gewirtz. AV producer. Clients: industry, education, government and advertising. Produces slides, filmstrips and Vu Graphs, large blow-ups in color and b&w.
Needs: Assigns 20 jobs/year. Works with 2 illustrators and 2 designers/month. Works on assignment only.
First Contact & Terms: Send query letter with resume to be kept on file. Call or write to schedule an appointment to show a portfolio, which should include original/final art and photographs. Pays for design by the hour, $15 minimum; pays for illustration by the hour, $25 minimum. Original artwork returned to artist after publication. Negotiates rights purchased.

PETER MARTIN ASSOCIATES, INC., 770 Lexington Ave., New York NY 10021. Art Director: Sherry McCloskey. PR firm/AV/ad agency providing sales materials, consumer packaging, advertising and layouts. Clients: travel, wine and spirits, consumer and food.
Needs: Works with approximately 15 freelance artists/year. Assigns 50-75 jobs/year. Prefers local artists only. Works on assignment only. Uses artists for posters, catalogs, magazines, direct mail packages, brochures, signage, P-O-P displays, mechanicals, animation, posters, press releases, lettering, logos and advertisements.
First Contact & Terms: Send query letter with brochure, resume, business card, photocopies and tear sheets to be kept on file except for "those that do not interest us." Samples not kept on file are returned by SASE if requested. Reports only if interested. Write for appointment to show portfolio or mail Photostats. "Payment depends upon job, but conforms to artists' usual scales." Considers complexity of project, client's budget and turnaround time when establishing payment. Buys all rights.
Tips: "We seek bold, imaginative work. Show us only your best and not a lot of that either."

MEDICAL MULTIMEDIA CORP., 211 E. 43rd St., New York NY 10017. AV/motion picture/TV producer. Clients: pharmaceutical manufacturers and manufacturers of diagnostic equipment (e.g. x-ray, ultrasound, CAT scanning, nuclear imaging). Audiences: health care industry—sellers and/or users. Produces educational programs in health sciences. Buys 20-30 illustrations and designs/year.
Needs: Works with 1-2 illustrators and designers/month. New York artists only. Uses artists for album covers, books, catalogs, filmstrips and motion pictures. Also uses artists for layout, multimedia kits, paste-up, technical charts and medical illustrations.
First Contact & Terms: Send brochure/flyer, resume and tear sheets to be kept on file for future assignments. No originals returned to artist at job's completion. Buys all rights. Pays $12-15/hour, mechanicals; $25-40/hour, illustration and design.

MUIR CORNELIUS MOORE, INC., 750 Third Ave., New York NY 10017. Art Buyer: Virginia Martin. Specializes in business-to-business advertising, sales promotion, corporate identity, displays, direct mail and exhibits. Clients: financial, high-technology and industrial.
Needs: Works with 15-25 freelance artists/year. Works on assignment only. Uses artists for design, illustration, mechanicals and lettering; brochures, catalogs, books, P-O-P displays, posters, direct mail packages, charts/graphs, AV materials, logos, exhibits and advertisements.

First Contact & Terms: Send query letter with tear sheets and photographs to be kept on file. Prefers samples that do not have to be returned, but will return unfiled material by SASE. Reports only if interested. To show a portfolio, mail final reproduction/product, tear sheets, photographs and b&w or call to schedule an appointment. Pays by the project. Considers complexity of project, client's budget, skill and experience of artist, how the work will be used, turnaround time and rights purchased when establishing payment.

MULLER, JORDAN, WEISS, INC., 666 5th Ave., New York NY 10103. (212)399-2700. Contact: Art Director. Ad agency. Clients: fashion, agricultural, plastics, food firms, financial, corporate—"wide variety of accounts."
Needs: Works with 25 illustrators/year. Uses freelance artists for consumer and trade magazines, direct mail, P-O-P displays, brochures, posters, newspapers and AV presentations.
First Contact & Terms: Phone for appointment. Works on assignment basis only. Payment varies according to job.

NEWMARK'S ADVERTISING AGENCY INC., 253 W. 26th St., New York NY 10001. Art/Creative Director: Al Wasserman. Art/ad agency. Clients: manufacturing, industrial, banking, leisure activities, consumer, real estate, and construction firms.
Needs: Works with 1 designer/every 2 months. Uses artists for billboards, P-O-P displays, consumer magazines, slide sets, brochures/flyers and trade magazines. Also uses artists for figure illustration, cartoons, technical art, paste-up and retouching.
First Contact & Terms: Provide stat samples to be kept on file for future assignments. No originals returned to artist at job's completion. Pays $8-15/hour, paste-up and $75-3,000 or more/job.

NOSTRADAMUS ADVERTISING, Suite 1128-A, 250 W. 57th St., New York NY 10107. Creative Director: B.N. Sher. Specializes in annual reports, corporate identity, publications, signage, flyers, posters, advertising, logos. Clients: ad agencies, book publishers, nonprofit organizations and politicians.
Needs: Works with 5 freelance artists/year. Uses artists for advertising design, illustration and layout; brochure design, mechanicals, posters, direct mail packages, charts/graphs, logos, catalogs, books and magazines.
First Contact & Terms: Send query letter with brochure, resume, business card, samples and tear sheets to be kept on file. Do *not* send slides as samples; will accept "anything else that doesn't have to be returned." Samples not kept on file are not returned. Reports only if interested. Call for appointment to show portfolio. Pays for design, mechanicals, and illustration by the hour, $15-25 average. Considers skill and experience of artist when establishing payment.

OVATION FILMS INC., 15 W. 26th St., New York NY 10010. (212)686-4540. Contact: Art Petricone.
Needs: Works on assignment only. Uses artists for design and animation.
First Contact & Terms: Arrange interview. Prefers "original art where possible" as samples. Samples returned by SASE. Provide samples and tear sheets to be kept on file for possible future assignments.

PERPETUAL MOTION PICTURES, INC., 17 W. 45th St., New York NY 10036. (212)481-4120. Producer: Hal Hoffer. Animation/TV/film producer. Clients: industrial, corporate, ad agencies and TV networks.
Needs: Local artists only. Uses artists for comps and animatics, and animation design. "Use very little freelance work."
First Contact & Terms: Query with resume and samples. SASE. Reports in 2 weeks. Pays $30-100/panel or going rate by day. Pays $150 minimum.

PHOENIX FILMS INC., 468 Park Ave. S., New York NY 10016. (212)684-5910. President: Heinz Gelles. Vice President: Barbara Bryant. Director of Advertising/Promotion: Ren Patterson. Clients: libraries, museums, religious institutions, U.S. government, schools, universities, film societies and businesses. Produces and distributes motion pictures and educational films. Assigns 20-30 jobs/year.
Needs: Local artists only. Uses artists for motion picture catalog sheets, direct mail brochures, posters and study guides.
First Contact & Terms: Query with samples (tear sheets and photocopies). SASE. Reports in 3 weeks. Buys all rights. Keeps all original art "but will loan to artist for use as a sample." Pays for design by the hour, $12-20. Pays for illustration by the hour, $12-20; by the project $200-2,000. Free catalog.

***PUBLIC RELATIONS ANALYSTS, INC.**, 210 E. 47 St., New York NY 10017. (212)838-6330. President: Eileen Millingi. Multimedia public relations consultants. Clients: technical, educational, health care. Client list provided upon request with an SASE.

Needs: Works with a few freelance artists/year. Works on assignment only. Uses freelance artists for design, mechanicals, retouching, lettering and logos.
First Contact & Terms: Send query letter with brochure or resume and tear sheets. Samples are filed. "Will contact artists only if there is a need for a specific assignment or the possibility of a job." Payment is negotiated. Considers complexity of project, client's budget, turnaround time and how work will be used when establishing payment. Rights purchased vary according to project.
Tips: "Determine if there is an immediate need for services; follow up; honor time/date of appointment; keep references current."

RICHARD H. ROFFMAN ASSOCIATES, Suite 6A, 697 West End Ave., New York NY 10025. (212)749-3647. President: Richard R. Roffman. PR firm. Clients: restaurants, art galleries, boutiques, hotels and cabarets, nonprofit organizations, publishers and all professional and business fields.
Needs: Assigns 24 freelance jobs/year. Works with 2 freelance illustrators and 2 freelance designers/month. Uses artists for consumer and trade magazines, brochures, newspapers, stationery, posters and press releases.
First Contact & Terms: Send query letter and resume to be kept on file; call or write for appointment to show portfolio. Prefers photographs and Photostats as samples. Reports only if interested. Pays by the hour, $10-25 average; by the project, $75-250 average; by the day, $150-250 average. Considers complexity of project, client's budget, and skill and experience of artist when establishing payment. Buys first rights or one-time rights. Returns material only if SASE enclosed.
Tips: "Realize that affirmative answers cannot always be immediate—do have patience."

PETER ROTHHOLZ ASSOCIATES INC., 380 Lexington Ave., New York NY 10017. (212)687-6565. President: Peter Rothholz. PR firm. Clients: government (tourism and industrial development), publishing, pharmaceuticals (health and beauty products), business services.
Needs: Works with 2 illustrators, 2 designers/month. Works on assignment only.
First Contact & Terms: Call for appointment to show portfolio which should include resume or brochure/flyer to be kept on file. Samples returned by SASE. Reports in 2 weeks. Assignments made based on freelancer's experience, cost, style and whether he/she is local. No originals returned to artist at job's completion. Negotiates payment based on client's budget.

PHOEBE T. SNOW PRODUCTIONS, INC., 240 Madison Ave., New York NY 10016. (212)679-8756. Vice President: Lisbeth Bagnold. AV production company. Serves clients in industry. Produces slides, film and video materials.
Needs: Assigns 50 jobs/year. Works on assignment only. Uses artists, designers and illustrators for slides, film and video materials.
First Contact & Terms: Send resume to the attention of Barbara Bagnold, Production Coordinator; arrange interview by phone. Reports within 1 week. Pays by the project or by the hour. No originals returned following publication. Buys all rights.

THE SOFTNESS GROUP INC., 3 E. 54th St., New York NY 10022. President: Carol Blades. PR firm. Clients: corporations and manufacturers.
Needs: Works with 3 illustrators, 1 designer/month. Uses artists to work with filmstrips, consumer magazines, stationery design, multimedia kits, slide sets, brochures/flyers, trade magazines and newspapers.
First Contact & Terms: Query with resume and samples. SASE. Reports in 2 weeks. Provide brochure or flyer to be kept on file for future assignments. No originals returned to artist at job's completion. Negotiates pay.

SSC&B, INC., 1 Dag Hammarskjold Plaza, New York NY 10017. (212)605-8000. Senior Art Buyer: Patti Harris. Ad agency. Clients: home products, cosmetics, and food.
Needs: Works with 150 freelance artists/year. Works on assignment only. Uses photographers and illustrators for magazines, newspapers, and billboard advertisements. Artist should have "good design sense, color quality and reproduction knowledge."
First Contact & Terms: Send letter with tear sheets. Samples filed are not returned. Does not report back. Call to schedule an appointment to show a portfolio, which should include tear sheets, photographs and b&w. Negotiates payment. Considers complexity of project, client's budget, how work will be used, turnaround time and rights purchased when establishing payment. Rights purchased vary according to project.
Tips: Artist should contact art buyers "only if work is applicable to agency's accounts."

TALCO PRODUCTIONS, 279 E. 44th St., New York NY 10017. (212)697-4015. President: Alan Lawrence. TV/film producer. Clients: nonprofit organizations, industry, associations and public relations firms. Produces motion pictures, videotapes and some filmstrips and sound-slide sets.
Needs: Assigns 4-10 jobs/year. Works with an average of 1 illustrator/month for filmstrips, motion pictures, animation and charts/graphs. Prefers local artists with professional experience.
First Contact & Terms: Send query letter with resume. SASE. Reports only if interested. Portfolio should include roughs, final reproduction/product, color, Photostats and photographs. Pay varies according to assignment; on production. On some jobs originals returned to artist after completion. Buys all rights. Considers complexity of project, client's budget and rights purchased when establishing payment.
Tips: "Do not send anything but a resume!"

THE TARRAGANO COMPANY, 230 Park Ave., New York NY 10169. (212)972-1250. President: Morris Tarragano. Ad agency and PR firm. Clients: manufacturers of products and services of all types. Media used include consumer and trade magazines, direct mail, newspapers, radio and TV.
First Contact & Terms: Write for an appointment to show portfolio and/or send resume. Selection based on review of portfolio and references. Negotiates payment based on amount of creativity required from artist and previous experience/reputation.

TOGG FILMS, INC., 630 9th Ave., New York NY 10036. (212)974-9507. Producer/Director: Grania Gurievitch. AV/film producer. Serves clients in industry, education and government. Produces educational documentaries. Receives foundation grants.
Needs: Experienced New York City area artists only. Works on assignment only. Uses artists for opticals and credits design.
First Contact & Terms: Send query letter. Reports only if interested. Pays by the project. Amount of payment is negotiated with the individual artist. Considers complexity of project, client's budget, skill and experience of artist, turnaround time and rights purchased when establishing payment. Original artwork not returned after publication. Buys all rights, but will negotiate.
Tips: "The chances are *very* slim that we could hire an artist!"

***TOTAL VISUALS**, 145 W. 45 St., New York NY 10036. (212)944-8788. Vice President: Joanne Breiter. Audiovisual firm providing slide presentations. Clients: investment firms, ad agencies, banks and PR firms.
Needs: Prefers artists from New York City and boroughs; "mainly need chartists, mechanical artists." Works on assignment only. Uses freelance artists for illustration, mechanicals, lettering and charts/graphs.
First Contact & Terms: Send resume, photocopies and slides; "call." Samples are filed. Reports back within weeks. Call to schedule an appointment to show a portfolio, which should include original/final art, Photostats, final reproduction/product and slides. Pays for mechanical art by the hour, $15-20. Pays for illustration by the project. Considers complexity of project, client's budget, turnaround time and skill and experience of artist when establishing payment.
Tips: Artists "must produce neat work under pressure!"

VAN VECHTEN & ASSOCIATES PUBLIC RELATIONS, 427 E. 74th St., New York NY 10021. (212)570-6510. President: Jay Van Vechten. PR firm. Clients: medical, consumer products, industry. Client list provided for SASE.
Needs: Assigns 20+ freelance jobs/year. Works with 2 freelance illustrators and 2 freelance designers/month. Works on assignment only. Uses artists for consumer and trade magazines, brochures, newspapers, stationery, signage, AV presentations and press releases.
First Contact & Terms: Send query letter with brochure, resume, business card, photographs or Photostats. Samples not kept on file are returned by SASE. Reports only if interested. Write for appointment to show portfolio. Pays by the hour, $10-25 average. Considers client's budget when establishing payment. Buys all rights.

MORTON DENNIS WAX & ASSOCIATES INC., Suite 1260, 1560 Broody, New York NY 10036. (212)247-2159. President: Morton Wax. Public relations firm. Clients: entertainment, communication arts and corporate.
Needs: Artists must have references and minimum 3 years of experience. Works on assignment only. Uses artists for trade magazine ads, brochures and other relevant artwork.
First Contact & Terms: Send query letter with resume, Photostats or tear sheets to be kept on file. Samples not filed are returned by SASE. Reports only if interested. Write for appointment to show portfolio. "We select and use freelancers on a per project basis, based on specific requirements of clients. Each project is unique." Considers complexity of project, client's budget, turnaround time and rights purchased when establishing payment. Rights vary according to project.

North Carolina

CAROLINA BIOLOGICAL SUPPLY, 2700 York Rd., Burlington NC 27215. (919)584-0381. Art Director: Dr. Kenneth Perkins. AV producer. Serves clients in education. Produces filmstrips, charts and booklets, educational games.
Needs: Assigns 20 jobs/year. Works with 2 illustrators/month. Prefers artists located in the southeast who do good line work and use watercolor, acrylic or airbrush. Works on assignment only. Uses artists for illustration work, both biological and medical. "We buy some cartoons for our pamphlets, filmstrips and advertising and some cartoon-style illustrations."
First Contact & Terms: Send query letter with resume and samples (prefers Photostats or slides) to be kept on file. Samples returned by SASE not filed. Reports within 1 month. Call or write to schedule an appointment to show a portfolio, which should include roughs, original/final art, final reproduction/product and tear sheets. Amount of payment is negotiated with the individual artist; by the hour, $12 minimum. Considers complexity of project, skill and experience of artist and rights purchased when establishing payment. No originals returned to artist following publication. Buys all rights.

CLASSROOM WORLD MEDIA PRODUCTIONS, 14 Glenwood Ave., Raleigh NC 27603. Contact: E.E. Carter. AV producer. Clients: educational, industrial, governmental and religious. Produces filmstrips, multimedia kits, sound-slide sets and video programs.
Needs: Works with 1 designer/month. Uses artists for filmstrip animation, slide illustrations and catalog design.
First Contact & Terms: Query with resume and samples. Reports in 1-4 weeks. Provide brochures, flyers, resume and samples to be kept on file for future assignments. Negotiates pay; sometimes pays royalties.

GARNER & ASSOCIATES, INC., Suite 350, 3721 Latrobe Dr., Charlotte NC 28211. (704)365-3455. Art Directors: Arkon Stewart, Lynn Aquino. Ad agency. Clients: "wide range" of accounts; client list provided upon request.
Needs: Works with 2 illustrators/month. Works on assignment only. Uses freelance artists for billboards, consumer and trade magazines, direct mail, P-O-P displays, brochures, catalogs, posters, signage, newspapers and AV presentations.
First Contact & Terms: Send printed samples or phone for appointment. Payment is by the project; negotiates according to client's budget.

HEGE, MIDDLETON & NEAL, INC., Box 9437, Greensboro NC 27408. President: J.A. Middleton, Jr. Ad agency.
Needs: Assigns 200 freelance jobs/year. Works with 5 freelance illustrators and 5 freelance designers/month. Works on assignment only. Uses artists for consumer and trade magazines, billboards, direct mail packages, brochures, catalogs, newspapers, stationery, signage, P-O-P displays and posters.
First Contact & Terms: Send query letter with brochure, resume, business card, photographs and tear sheets to be kept on file. Samples returned by SASE if requested. Reports only if interested. Write for appointment to show portfolio. Pays by the project, $20-6,000 average. Considers complexity of project, client's budget, skill and experience of artist, geographic scope of finished project, turnaround time and rights purchased when establishing payment. Buys all rights.

LEWIS ADVERTISING, INC., 1050 Country Club Ln., Rocky Mount NC 27804. (919)443-5131. Senior Art Director: Scott Brandt. Ad agency. Clients: fast food, communications, convenience stores, financials. Client list provided upon request with SASE.
Needs: Works with 20-25 freelance artists/year. Works on assignment only. Uses artists for illustration and part-time paste-up. Especially looks for "consistently excellent results, on time and on budget."
First Contact & Terms: Send query letter with resume, business card and samples to be kept on file. Call for appointment to show portfolio. Artists should show examples of previous work, price range requirements and previous employers." Samples not filed returned by SASE only if requested. Reports only if interested. Pays by project. Considers complexity of the project, client's budget, turnaround time and ability of artist when establishing payment. Buys all rights.

MORPHIS & FRIENDS, INC., Drawer 5096, 230 Oakwood Dr., Winston-Salem NC 27103. (919)723-2901. Art Director: Joe Nemoseck. Ad agency. Clients: banks, restaurants, clothing, cable, industry and furniture.
Needs: Assigns 20-30 freelance jobs/year. Works on assignment only. Works with approximately 2 freelance illustrators/month. Uses artists for consumer and trade magazines, billboards, direct mail packages, brochures and newspapers.
First Contact & Terms: Send query letter with photocopies to be kept on file. Samples not filed are

returned only if requested. Reports only if interested. Call to schedule an appointment to show a portfolio, which should include roughs and final reproduction/product. Pays by the hour, $20 minimum. "Negotiate on job basis." Considers complexity of project, client's budget, skill and experience of artist, geographic scope of finished project, turnaround time and rights purchased when establishing payment. Buys all rights.
Tips: "Send a letter of introduction with a few samples to be followed up by phone call."

***MORRIS INTERNATIONAL**, 301 E. Boulevard, Charlotte NC 28203. (704)376-0736. Creative Director: Sid Morris. Ad agency. Clients: consumer, sports, construction, nonprofit organizations, retail, food, communications, manufacturing.
Needs: Assigns 5-15 freelance jobs/year. Uses artists for consumer and trade magazines, billboards, direct mail packages, brochures, catalogs, newspapers, stationery, signage, P-O-P displays, AV presentations and posters.
First Contact & Terms: Send query letter with samples. Call for appointment to show portfolio. Prefers originals, reproduced, as samples. Samples returned by SASE if not kept on file. Reports only if interested. Works on assignment only. Pays by the hour, $10-60 average; by the project, $25-1,500 average. Considers complexity of project, client's budget, and skill and experience of artist when establishing payment. Buys all rights.
Tips: There is a "trend toward more illustration using airbrush techniques. An artist's portfolio should include a wide variety of subjects/projects—emphasis on detail—with ability for marketing."

THOMPSON AGENCY, Suite 200, 1 Tyron Centre, 112 S. Tyron St., Charlotte NC 28284. (704)333-8821. Art Director: Jennifer Owens. Ad agency. Clients: banks, fast food, soft drink, TV station, resort, utility and automotive services.
Needs: Assigns approximately 200 freelance jobs/year. Works with 5 freelance illustrators/month. Works on assignment only. Uses artists for consumer and trade magazines, billboards, direct mail packages, brochures, newspapers, signage, P-O-P displays and posters.
First Contact & Terms: Send query letter with brochure showing art style or photocopies to be kept on file. Samples returned by SASE if requested. To show portfolio, mail appropriate materials or write to schedule an appointment; portfolio should include final reproduction/product. Reports only if interested. Pays for design by the project, $500-7,500; pays for illustration by the project, $350-3,000. Considers complexity of project, client's budget, skill and experience of artist, turnaround time and rights purchased when establishing payment. Buys all rights.
Tips: "In general, we see a bolder use of ideas and techniques. We try to screen all work before appointment. Work must be professional and very creative.

Ohio

***FAHLGREN & SWINK ADVERTISING INC.**, 120 E. 4th St., Cincinnati OH 45202. (513)241-9200. Ad agency. Serves clients in household products, utilities, industrial equipment manufacturers.
Needs: Works with 1-2 illustrators/month. Uses artists for billboards, consumer and trade magazines, direct mail, newspapers, P-O-P displays and brochures/flyers.
First Contact & Terms: Call for appointment to show portfolio (illustrations, designs and photography). Works on assignment only. Provide sample folders, brochures, etc. small enough to be kept on file for future assignments. Negotiates pay based on client's budget and amount of creativity required from artist/photographer.

FAHLGREN & SWINK, INC., Suite 901, 1 Seagate, Toledo OH 43604. (419)247-5200. Creative Director: Steve Drongowski. Ad agency. Serves clients in healthcare and finance.
Needs: Works with 5-6 freelance illustrators/month. Uses freelancers for consumer and trade magazines, A/V direct mail, brochures/flyers, newspapers and P-O-P displays.
First Contact & Terms: Call for appointment to show portfolio or make contact through artist's rep. Selection is usually based on reviewing portfolios through reps but will see individual freelancers. Negotiates payment based on client's budget, amount of creativity required from artist and where work will appear.
Tips: Pieces that are produced are best in portfolio. "Printed pieces have a lot more credibility."

FARRAGHER MARKETING SERVICES, 7 Court St., Canfield OH 44406. (216)533-3347. Creative Director: Linda Nicholas. Marketing service firm. Serves clients in industry and technical science. Assigns 20+ jobs/year.
Needs: Works on assignment only. Uses artists for P-O-P displays, stationery design, direct mail,

brochures/flyers and trade magazines. Also uses artists for annual reports, catalogs, brochures, corporate identity, newsletters and promotional materials.
First Contact & Terms: Query with resume, photographs and originals. Samples returned by SASE. Reports as soon as possible. Provide resume, brochure/flyer and business card to be kept on file. Originals returned to artist at job's completion if requested. Negotiates pay.
Tips: "Be practical and businesslike."

THE FILM HOUSE INC., 6058 Montgomery Rd., Cincinnati OH 45213. (513)631-0035. President: Ken Williamson. TV/film producer. Clients: industrial and corporate. Produces filmstrips, motion pictures, sound-slide sets and videotapes.
Needs: Assigns 30 jobs/year. Uses artists for filmstrip animation and ad illustrations. Works on assignment only.
First Contact & Terms: Send a query letter with resume and business card to be kept on file. Samples returned by SASE. Reports in 1 week. Negotiates pay; pays by the project.
Tips: "Maintain contact every 45 days."

GERBIG, SNELL, WEISHEIMER & ASSOC., Suite 600, 425 Metro Pl. N., Dublin OH 43017. (614)764-3838. Vice President, Creative Director: Christopher J. Snell. Senior Art Director: Diane Hay. Ad agency. Clients: business-to-business, financial and medical.
Needs: Works with 30 freelance artists/year. Works on assignment only. Uses artists for illustration, design, keyline and photography.
First Contact & Terms: Send query letter with brochure, resume, business card and photostats, photographs, slides or tear sheets to be kept on file. Samples not filed returned only if requested. Reports only if interested. Write for appointment to show portfolio. Pays for design by the hour, $25-60 and by the project, $25-1,000. Considers complexity of the project, client's budget, skill and experience of artist, geographic scope for the finished product and turnaround time when establishing payment. Rights purchased vary according to project.
Tips: Looks for "work which we can use at a reasonable fee and the ability to turn around quickly with a minimum of direction."

GRISWOLD INC., 55 Public Sq., Cleveland OH 44114. (216)696-3400. Executive Art Director: Tom Gilday. Ad agency. Clients: consumer and industrial firms; client list provided upon request.
Needs: Works with 30-40 illustrators/year. Works primarily with local artists, but occasionally uses others. Uses freelance artists for billboards, consumer and trade magazines, direct mail, P-O-P displays, brochures, catalogs, posters, newspapers and AV presentations.
First Contact & Terms: Works on assignment only. Arrange interview to show portfolio. Provide materials to be kept on file for possible future assignments. Payment is by the project; negotiates according to client's budget.

HAYES PUBLISHING CO. INC., 6304 Hamilton Ave., Cincinnati OH 45224. (513)681-7559. Office Manager: Marge Lammers. AV producer/book publisher. Produces educational books, brochures and audiovisuals on human sexuality and abortion. Free catalog.
Needs: Uses artists for direct mail brochures and books.
First Contact & Terms: Send slides and photographs. Samples returned by SASE. Reports in 2 weeks. Provide business card to be kept on file for possible future assignments. Pays by job.

IMAGEMATRIX, 2 Garfield Pl., Cincinnati OH 45202. (513)381-1380. President: Peter Schwartz. Total communications for business.
Needs: Works with 25 freelance artists/year. Local artists only; must have portfolio of work. Uses artists for paste-up, mechanicals, airbrushing, storyboards, photography, lab work, illustration for AV; buys cartoons 4-5 times/year. Especially important is AV knowledge, computer graphics for video and slides and animation understanding.
First Contact & Terms: Works on assignment only. Artwork buy-out. Send business card and slides to be kept on file. Samples not filed are returned by SASE. Reports within 2 months. Write for appointment to show portfolio. Pays for design by the hour, $8-35; by the project, $90 minimum. Pays for illustration by the hour, $8-15; by the project, $150 minimum. Considers complexity of the project, client's budget, skill and experience of artist and turnaround time when establishing payment. Buys all rights.
Tips: "Specialize your portfolio; show an understanding of working for a 35mm final product. We are using more design for video graphics and computer graphics."

GEORGE C. INNES & ASSOCIATES, Box 1343, 110 Middle Ave., Elyria OH 44036. (216)323-4526. President: George C. Innes. Ad/art agency. Clients: industrial and consumer. Assigns 25-50 jobs/year.
Needs: Works with 3-4 illustrators/month. Works on assignment only. Uses illustrators for filmstrips,

stationery design, technical illustrations, airbrush, multimedia kits, direct mail, slide sets, brochures/flyers, trade magazines, newspapers and books. Also uses artists for layout and design for reports, catalogs, print ads, direct mail/publicity, brochures, displays, employee handbooks, exhibits, products, technical charts/illustrations, trademarks, logos and company publications.
First Contact & Terms: Send query letter with brochure showing art style or tear sheets, Photostats, photocopies, slides and photographs. Samples not filed are not returned. Reports in 2 weeks. To show a portfolio, a freelance artist should mail appropriate materials. No originals returned to artist at job's completion. Pays for design by the hour, $5-15; pays for illustration by the hour, $5-15.

THE JONETHIS ORGANIZATION, Suite 401, 159 S. Main St., Akron OH 44308. (216)375-5122. Project Manager: Jane Byrd. Marketing services firm. Clients: industrial, consumer and retail. Client list provided upon request.
Needs: Works with 6-8 freelance artists/year. Uses artists for design and production. Especially important are design sense, language understanding and production sense.
First Contact & Terms: Send query letter with resume to be kept on file. Call for appointment to show portfolio. Reports only if interested. Pays by the project. Considers complexity of project, client's budget, skill and experience of artist, and turnaround time when establishing payment. Buys all rights.

***MERVIN N. LEVEY CO.**, 3338 Kingsgate Blvd., Toledo OH 43606. (419)536-8186. President: M.N. Levey. Advertising agency and marketing consultant to manufacturers of consumer products in the U.S., Canada, Europe and the Far East. Clients: manufacturers, distributors, land developers, real estate, insurance, machinery, home furnishings, major appliances, floor coverings, foods, automotive, pet foods, health and beauty aids, department stores, supermarket and drug store chains.
Needs: Original art, layout and paste-up for newspapers, magazines, TV, direct mail and P-O-P.
First Contact & Terms: Area artists only. Prefers Photostats as samples. Samples returned. Reports within 4 weeks. Pays by the hour, $12-20 average. Considers client's budget, and skill and experience of artist when establishing payment.
Tips: "We'd like to have a group located in nearby cities to do keyline and lettering (full page newspaper ads) once monthly."

LIGGETT-STASHOWER (formerly Lang, Fisher & Stashower), 1010 Euclid Ave., Cleveland OH 44115. (216)771-0300. Executive Art Director: Larry Pillot. Full service ad agency. Clients: consumer firms.
Needs: Works with 8 illustrators/year. Local artists primarily. Works on assignment only. Uses freelance artists for billboards, consumer and trade magazines, direct mail, P-O-P displays, brochures, catalogs, posters, signage, newspapers and AV presentations.
First Contact & Terms: Query with resume of credits and samples. Payment is by the project; negotiates according to client's budget, amount of creativity required, where work will appear and freelancer's previous experience. Pays for design and illustration by the hour, $10 minimum.

LOHRE & ASSOCIATES, 1420 E. McMillan St., Cincinnati OH 45206. (513)961-1174. Art Director: Charles R. Lohre. Ad agency. Clients: industrial firms.
Needs: Works with 2 illustrators/month. Local artists only. Works on assignment only. Uses freelance artists for trade magazines, direct mail, P-O-P displays, brochures and catalogs.
First Contact & Terms: Send query letter with resume and samples. Call or write to schedule an appointment to show portfolio, which should include final reproduction/product. Especially looks for "excellent line control and realistic people or products." Pays for design by the hour, $12 minimum; pays for illustration by the hour, $6 minimum.
Tips: Looks for artists who can draw well and have experience in working with metal inks.

***LOWE MARSCHALK, INC.**, 601 Rockwell Ave., Cleveland OH 44114. (216)687-8800. Creative Director: Stephen M. Fechtor. Ad agency. Clients: manufacturers, bank, grocery store chain, phone company, restaurant chain.
Needs: Uses artists and photographers for consumer and trade magazines and newspapers.
First Contact & Terms: Call for appointment to show portfolio.
Tips: Wants to see current work and "imaginative ideas, either published or unpublished."

CHARLES MAYER STUDIOS INC., 168 E. Market St., Akron OH 44308. (216)535-6121. President: C.W. Mayer, Jr. AV producer since 1934. Clients: mostly industrial. Produces film and manufactures visual aids for trade show exhibits.
Needs: Works with 1-2 illustrators/month. Uses illustrators for catalogs, filmstrips, brochures and slides. Also uses artists for brochures/layout, photo retouching and cartooning for charts/visuals.
First Contact & Terms: Send slides, photographs, Photostats or b&w line drawings or arrange

interview to show portfolio. Samples not kept on file are returned. Reports in 1 week. Provide resume and a sample or tear sheet to be kept on file for future assignments. Originals returned to artist at job's completion. Negotiates pay.

ART MERIMS COMMUNICATIONS, 750 Prospect Ave., Cleveland OH 44115. (216)664-1113. President: Arthur M. Merims. PR/advertising firm. Clients: industry.
Needs: Assigns 10 freelance jobs/year. Prefers local artists. Works on assignment only. Works with 1-2 freelance illustrators and 1-2 freelance designers/month. Uses artists for trade magazines, brochures, catalogs, signage and AV presentations.
First Contact & Terms: Send query letter with samples to be kept on file. Call or write for appointment to show portfolio, which should include "copies of any kind" as samples. Pays by the hour, $10-30 or by the project. Considers complexity of project, client's budget, and skill and experience of artist when establishing payment.
Tips: When reviewing samples, looks for "creativity and reasonableness of cost."

***V. STEFANELLI & ASSOCIATES**, Suite B, 5970 Walnut Circle, Toledo OH 43615. (419)865-5928. Producer: Vincent Stefanelli. Estab. 1986. Audiovisual firm. Film/video producer of commericals, industrials, training tapes, documentaries, fashion and music videos. Clients: advertising agencies, corporations, educators, retail, etc. Client list provided with a SASE.
Needs: Works with 25-30 freelance artists/year. Assigns 50 jobs/year. Works on assignment only. Uses artists for design, illustration, consumer and trade magazines, P-O-P displays, mechanicals, animation, direct mail packages, press releases, motion pictures, charts/graphs and advertisements.
First Contact & Terms: Send brochure. Samples are filed. Reports back within 3 weeks. Call to schedule an appointment to show a portfolio, which should include photographs. Pays for design and illustration by the hour, $30-75. Considers complexity of project, client's budget, turnaround time and skill and experience of artist when establishing payment. Rights purchased vary according to project.
Tips: "We are always looking for new styles and ideas."

TRIAD, (Terry Robie Industrial Advertising, Inc.), 124 N. Ontario St., Toledo OH 43624. (419)241-5110. Vice President/Creative Director: Janice Robie. Ad agency/graphics/promotions. Clients: industrial, consumer, medical.
Needs: Assigns 30 freelance jobs/year. Works with 1-2 freelance illustrators/month and 2-3 freelance designers/month. Works on assignment only. Uses artists for consumer and trade magazines, brochures, catalogs, newspapers, filmstrips, stationery, signage, P-O-P displays, AV presentations, posters and illustrations (technical and/or creative).
First Contact & Terms: Send query letter with resume and slides, photographs, Photostats or printed samples to be kept on file. Samples returned by SASE if not kept on file. Reports only if interested. To show a portfolio, mail appropriate materials or write to schedule an appointment; portfolio should include roughs, original/final art, final reproduction/product and tear sheets. Pays by the hour, $10-60; by the project, $25-2,500. Considers client's budget, and skill and experience of artist when establishing payment. Negotiates rights purchased.
Tips: "We are interested in knowing your specialty."

Oklahoma

THE ECONOMY COMPANY, 1200 N.W. 63rd St., Oklahoma City OK 73116. (405)840-1444. Art Director: Gayla Goodell.
Needs: Works with 100 freelance artists/year. Works on assignment only. Uses artists for illustrations in educational books. Artist "must have experience, and include several full-color samples of editorial and book illustrations in portfolio."
First Contact & Terms: Send query letter with resume and tear sheets, photocopies or slides. Samples not filed are returned only if requested. Reports only if interested. Buys all rights.

LOWE RUNKLE COMPANY, 6801 N. Broadway, Oklahoma City OK 73116. Senior Art Director: Doug Bowman. Ad agency. Clients: banks, petroleum, food manufacturer. Client list provided for SASE.
Needs: Works with 30 freelance artists/year. Local artists preferred, but out-of-towners used for longer project work. Works on assignment only. Uses artists for design, illustrations, brochures, P-O-P displays, mechanicals, retouching, animation, billboards, posters, direct mail packages, lettering, logos, charts/graphs and advertisements.
First Contact & Terms: Send query letter with brochure showing art style or resume and slides.

Samples not filed are returned by SASE. Reports back within 3 weeks. Call or write to schedule an appointment to show a portfolio, which should include thumbnails, roughs, original/final art, final reproduction/product and color. Pays for design by the hour, $35-100. Pays for illustration by the hour, $35-100. Considers complexity of project, client's budget, skill and experience of artist, and turnaround time when establishing payment. Buys all rights.
Tips: Artist should have "a varied portfolio (client-wise)."

Oregon

BOAZ-GREEN ADVERTISING, 1176 W. 7th St., Box 2565, Eugene OR 97402. (503)343-2548. Art Director: Robert E. Smith. Full-service ad agency with marketing and PR services.
Needs: Assigns 10-20 jobs/year. Uses artists for illustration, layout, mechanicals, occasional design work. Prefers experienced local artists. Works on assignment only. "We use freelancers primarily for overlow work and for special projects. Out-of-area artists are considered only if their specialized skills are better suited to a particular job than those of our inhouse staff."
First Contact & Terms: Send query letter with resume and samples to be kept on file. "Photocopies will do if they adequately show artist's work." Samples not filed are returned by SASE. Reports only if interested. Pays by the hour for inhouse production work, by the project for outside services. Considers nature of project, client's budget, and artist's skill when establishing payment. No originals returned unless agreed to in advance. Negotiates rights purchased.
Tips: "Our needs are as varied as our clients, so present a wide range of samples. Strong production skills a must."

CREATIVE COMPANY, INC., 345 Court St. NE, Salem OR 97301. (503)363-4433. President/Owner: Jennifer Larsen. Specializes in corporate identity and packaging. Clients: local consumer-oriented clients, professionals and trade accounts on a regional and national level, all in the Salem/Valley area.
Needs: Works with 3-4 freelance artists/year. Prefers local artists. Works on assignment only. Uses artists for design, illustration, retouching, airbrushing, posters and lettering. "Clean, fresh designs!"
First Contact & Terms: Send query letter with brochure, resume, business card, photocopies and tear sheets to be kept on file. Samples returned only if requested. Reports only if interested. Call for appointment to show portfolio. "We require a portfolio review. Years of experience not important if portfolio is good. We prefer one-on-one review to discuss individual projects/time/approach. Pays for design and illustration by the hour, $20-50 average. Considers complexity of project and skill and experience of artist when establishing payment.
Tips: Common mistakes freelancers make in presenting samples or portfolios are: "1) poor presentation, samples not mounted or organized, 2) not knowing how long it took them to do a job to provide a budget figure, 3) not demonstrating an understanding of the printing process and how their work will translate into a printed copy, 4) just dropping in without an appointment, 5) not following up periodically to update information or a resume that might be on file."

Pennsylvania

ANIMATION ARTS ASSOCIATES INC., Lee Park, Suite 301, 1100 E. Hector St., Conshohocken PA 19428. (215)825-8530. President: Harry E. Ziegler. AV/motion picture/TV producer. Clients: government, industry, education and TV. Audience: engineers, doctors, military, general public. Produces 35/16mm films, sound/slide programs and filmstrips.
Needs: Works with designers and illustrators. Uses artists for filmstrips, motion pictures and animation.
First Contact & Terms: Call for interview. Provide resume to be kept on file for possible future assignments. No work returned at job's completion. Pays $5-10/hour, cartoon and technical animation.

BAKER PRODUCTIONS INC., 4159 Main St., Philadelphia PA 19127. (215)482-2900. President: Alan Baker. Produces TV film and videotape commercials, documentaries, industrial films, and computer graphics.
Needs: Buys approximately 100 designs/year. Uses artists for computer graphics and medical illustration. Uses very few freelancers.
First Contact & Terms: Local artists only. Prefers artists with broadcast art or ad agency experience. Write for interview. Prefers photographs as samples. Samples not returned. Reports within 1 week "if prospect is pending"; otherwise, in 3 weeks. Works on assignment only. Provide resume to be kept on file for possible future assignments. Buys all rights. Pays $9/panel, storyboards; $12/title card, titles.
Tips: Most graphics used are computer generated.

TED BARKUS CO. INC., 1512 Spruce St., Philadelphia PA 19102. Executive Vice President/Creative Director: Allen E. Barkus. Ad agency/PR firm. Serves clients in finance, retailing, industrial products, consumer products, appliance manufacturers, fashion, food, publishing, travel destinations, and interior design.
Needs: Works with 2 illustrators and 1 designer/month. Local and New York artists with experience working with similar firms only. Works on assignment only. Uses designers for billboards, P-O-P displays, consumer and trade magazines, stationery design, multimedia kits, direct mail, TV, slide sets and newspapers. Uses illustrators for brochures/flyers.
First Contact & Terms: Send business card, slides, photographs and b&w line drawings to be kept on file. Samples returned by SASE. Reports in 2 weeks. No original work returned after job completed. Pays by the project or by the hour, $10-25 average. Considers complexity of project and skill and experience of artist when establishing payment.

***GENIGRAPHICS**, 3 Ben Franklin Pkwy., Philadelphia PA 19102. (215)568-5839. Production Manager: Richard P. Banse, Jr. Audiovisual firm. "We provide business graphics (computer-generated and optical), slides, overheads, prints, etc. We design and execute print projects." Clients: everything.
Needs: Works with 10 freelance artists/year. Assigns various jobs/year. Prefers local artists—within commuting distance. Works on assignment only. Uses artists for computer graphics (console operator).
First Contact & Terms: Send query letter with resume and slides. Samples are filed. Samples not filed are returned only if requested. Reports back only if interested. Call or write to schedule an appointment to show a portfolio, or mail original/final art, final reproduction/product, photographs and slides. Pays $10-25/hour for console time. Considers skill and experience of artist when establishing payment. Buys all rights.
Tips: "Only trained Genigraphic operators need apply."

HARDMAN EASTMAN STUDIOS, INC., 1400 E. Carson St., Pittsburg PA 15203. (412)481-4450. General Manager: Barbara Jost. Audiovisual firm. Clients: audiovisual and industrial.
Needs: Works with 1-2 freelance artists/year. Local artists only. Works on assignment only. Uses artists for design, illustration, mechanicals and charts/graphs. Artists should have the "experience to design art for 35mm slide and TV crop format, also the ability to communicate with clients and translate input into what is required for end use."
First Contact & Terms: Send query letter with resume. Samples not filed are not returned. Reports only if interested. Write to schedule an appointment to show a portfolio, which should include roughs, original/final art, color and photographs. Payment varies. Considers complexity of project, client's budget, skill and experience of artist, and turnaround time when establishing payment. Buys all rights.
Tips: "Do not call. Send letter and resume!"

***HARWYN MEDICAL PHOTOGRAPHERS**, 1001 City Ave., 918 W.B., Philadelphia PA 19151. (215)896-7137. President: Barnett Steinsnyder. Clients: colleges, hospitals and senior high schools. Produces 35mm photo-micrographs.
Needs: Assigns 50 jobs/year. Works with 2 illustrators/month. Uses artists for illustrations of micro-organisms. Pays $20 minimum/hour, illustrations; can negotiate.
First Contact & Terms: Query with resume and sample (1 slide). Samples are returned by SASE if not kept on file. Reports only if interested. Works on assignment only. Negotiates payment and rights purchased by the project. Considers complexity of project when establishing payment.

JERRYEND COMMUNICATIONS, INC., Rt. #2, Box 356H, Birdsboro PA 19508. (215)689-9118. Vice President: Gerard E. End, Jr. Advertising/PR firm. Clients: industry, banks, technical services, professional societies and automotive aftermarket.
Needs: Assigns 3-5 freelance jobs/year. Works "primarily with local artists for time, convenience and accessibility." Works on assignment only. Uses 1-2 freelance illustrators/month. Uses artists for trade magazines, brochures, signage, AV presentations, posters and press releases.
First Contact & Terms: Send query letter with brochure showing art style to be kept on file. Samples not filed returned by SASE. Reports within 2 weeks. Call to schedule an appointment to show a portfolio, which should include roughs, final reproduction/product and tear sheets. Pays for design by the hour, $25-50 average. Considers complexity of project, client's budget, turnaround time and rights purchased when establishing payment. Buys all rights.
Tips: Have a "realistic approach to art; clients are conservative and not inclined to impressionistic or surrealistic techniques."

***MUDERICK MEDIA**, 101 Earlington Rd., Havertown PA 19083. (215)449-6970. President: Michael Muderick. Audiovisual firm providing video production, meeting planning/AV. Clients: corporate, financial and education.

Needs: Works with 3 freelance artists/year. Assigns 5 jobs/year. Prefers local artists. Uses artists for mechanicals, motion pictures, logos and charts/graphs.
First Contact & Terms: Send query letter with brochure. Samples are not filed. Samples not filed are returned by SASE. Reports back only if interested. Call to schedule an appointment to show a portfolio. Pays for design and illustration by the project. Considers complexity of project, client's budget and turnaround time when establishing payment. Buys all rights.

NEW YORK COMMUNICATIONS, INC., 207 S. State Rd., Upper Darby PA 19082. Creative Director: Paul Greeley. Motion picture/TV/marketing consulting firm. Clients: radio & TV stations.
Needs: Uses artists for motion pictures and storyboards. Works with 2 illustrators and 1 designer/month.
First Contact & Terms: Query with resume. Reports within 1 week. Works on assignment only. Provide resume, sample storyboards, business card, brochure/flyer to be kept on file for future assignments. Samples not kept on file returned by SASE. No originals returned to artist at job's completion. Pays for design by the project, $300-1,200. Considers skill and experience of artist and turnaround time when establishing payment.
Tips: Looks for "the ability to capture people's faces, detail and perspective."

PERCEPTIVE MARKETERS AGENCY LTD., Suite 903, 1920 Chestnut St., Philadelphia PA 19103. (215)665-8736. Art Director: Marci Mansfield-Fickes. Ad agency. Clients: retail furniture, contract furniture, commuter airline, lighting distribution company; several nonprofit organizations for the arts, and a publishing firm.
Needs: Works with 15-20 freelance artists/year. Uses mostly local talent. In order of priority, uses artists for mechanicals, photography, illustration, comps/layout, photo retouching and design/art direction. Concepts, ability to follow instructions/layouts and precision/accuracy are important.
First Contact & Terms: Send resume and photostats, photographs and tear sheets to be kept on file. Accepts as samples—"whatever best represents artist's work—but preferably not slides." Samples not filed are returned by SASE only. Reports only if interested. Call for appointment to show portfolio. Pays by the hour, $10 minimum; by the project, $50 minimum. Considers complexity of the project, client's budget and turnaround time when establishing payment. Buys all rights.
Tips: "Freelance artists should approach us with unique, creative and professional work. And it's especially helpful to follow-up interviews with new samples of work, (i.e., to send a month later a 'reminder' card or sample of current work to keep on file.)"

THE REICH GROUP, INC., 230 S. Broad St., Philadelphia PA 19102. (215)546-1636. Art Director: Yvonne Mucci. Ad agency. Specializes in print media and direct mail/collateral material. Clients: banks, insurance companies, business to business services, associations, religious groups.
Needs: Works with 15-20 freelance artists/year. Uses artists for advertising and brochure design and illustration, design of direct mail kits and illustrations for association magazines. Rarely uses unusual techniques; prefers primarily realistic styles. No cartoons.
First Contact & Terms: Send query letter with photocopies or nonreturnable samples to be kept on file. Reports only if interested. Works on assignment only. Write for appointment to show portfolio. Pays by the hour, $12-25 average; by the project, $125-400 average. Considers skill and experience of artist, turnaround time and rights purchased when establishing payment.
Tips: "Show commercial work that has been used in print. No school samples or experimentals."

***THE SLIDEING BOARD, INC.**, 322 Blvd. of the Allies, Pittsburgh PA 15222. (412)261-6006. Production Manager: Cindy Len. "Audiovisual and multi-image firm for sales, marketing, training and capabilities presentations." Clients: consumer, industrial, financial, business-to-business.
Needs: Works with 20-30 artists/year. Assigns 75-100 jobs/year. Prefers local artists only. Uses artists for design, mechanicals, lettering and charts/graphs.
First Contact & Terms: Send query letter with resume and slides. Samples are filed. Samples not filed are returned. Reports back within 10 days only if interested. Call to schedule an appointment to show a portfolio. Pays for design and illustration by the hour, $5-20. Considers complexity of project, client's budget, turnaround time and skill and experience of artist when establishing payment. Buys all rights.
Tips: Artists must "have produced art for multi-image presentations before."

E.J. STEWART, INC., 525 Mildred Ave., Primos PA 19018. (215)626-6500. Production Coordinator: Karen Brooks. TV producer. Serves clients in industry, education, government, interactive video and advertising. Produces videotape programs and commercials.
Needs: Assigns 50+ jobs/year. Works with 2 illustrators and 2 designers/month. Philadelphia area artists only. Works on assignment only. Uses artists for set design and storyboards.
First Contact & Terms: Send resume, brochure/flyer and business card to be kept on file. Reports in 3

weeks. Method and amount of payment are negotiated with the individual artist. No originals returned to artists following publication. Buys all rights.
Tips: "There is more interest in computer generated animation in our field. 10% of work is cartoon-style illustrations."

***TOM WEIGAND, INC.**, 717 N. Fifth St., Reading PA 19601. (215)374-4431. AV Manager: Dan Kruse. Art Director/Producer: Joe Reighn. Audiovisual firm. "We provide multi-image/video production for corporate image, product introduction and sales meetings." Clients: manufacturers, financial, medical, chemical.
Needs: Works with 3-5 freelance artists/year. Assigns 10-15 jobs/year. Prefers local or regional artists. Works on assignment only. Uses artists for design, animation and AV programming.
First Contact & Terms: Send query letter with resume. Samples are filed. Samples not filed are returned if requested. Reports back only if interested. Write to schedule an appointment to show a portfolio, which should include tear sheets and slides. Pays for design by the hour, $6-20. Pays for illustration by the hour, $10-30, or by the project. Considers complexity of project, client's budget and turnaround time when establishing payment. Rights purchased vary according to project.
Tips: "I look to see what style(s) artists handle best and how creative their solutions have been while still matching the requirements of the project. They sometimes fail to present materials as solutions to certain communication objectives—as all our projects are."

Artist: Martha Freeman

"To present Epson as a creative company and create the mood of an outdoor barbeque" was the message illustrator Martha Freeman of Fleetwood, Pennsylvania, wanted to convey in this pen-and-ink invitation, assigned by art director/designer Joseph Reighn of Tom Weigand Inc. in Reading, Pennsylvania. Freeman requested an interview and portfolio review from Reighn, who then assigned this piece to her. Reighn says that Freeman "took direction well and was a pleasure to work with." Reighn bought all rights.

South Carolina

***BROOM & BUSSELL, INC.**, 2927 Devine St., Box 50710, Columbia SC 29250. (803)256-3337. Creative Director: Ralph Broom. Full-service advertising agency. Clients: real estate, banks, health care, department stores, radio station, government agencies, child care centers, car dealers.
Needs: Works with 20 freelance artists/year. Assigns 400 jobs/year. Works on assignment only. Uses artists for design, illustration, mechanicals, retouching, animation, posters, direct mail packages, lettering, logos and charts/graphs.
First Contact & Terms: Send query letter with brochure or tear sheets, Photostats, photocopies, slides and photogaphs. Samples are filed. Samples not filed are returned only if requested. To show a portfolio, mail thumbnails, roughs, Photostats, tear sheets, photographs and color. Pays for design and illustration by the project, $50 minimum. Considers complexity of project, client's budget and turnaround time when establishing payment.
Tips: "Send photocopied samples with cost charged on each."

***SYNERGY PRODUCTIONS, INC.**, 614 Meeting St., West Columbia SC 29169. (803)796-0173. Art Director: Carey Lee. Audiovisual firm. "We are an audio-visual communications company specializing in multi-image slide presentations. We are also involved in the production of computer-generated slides." Clients: corporations, banks, industrial plants. Client list provided upon request.
Needs: Works with 3 freelance artists/year. Assigns a few jobs/year. Prefers local artists. Works on assignment only. Uses artists for design, illustration and mechanicals.
First Contact & Terms: Send query letter with brochure or slides and photographs. Samples are filed. Reports back within 2 weeks only if interested. To show a portfolio, mail Photostats, tear sheets, photographs and slides. Pays for design and illustration by the project, $65 minimum. Considers complexity of project, client's budget and turnaround time when establishing payment. Rights purchased vary according to project.

Tennessee

JANUARY & ASSOCIATES, 5560 Franklin Pike Circle, Brentwood TN 37027. (615)377-9111. Owner/CEO: John January; Creative Director: Pam Karl. Ad agency. Clients: banks, fast food restaurants, industry, hospitals, music, entertainment and retail stores.
Needs: Assigns 26 freelance jobs/year. Works with 2 freelance illustrators and 2-5 freelance designers/month. Local artists only. Works on assignment only. Uses artists for trade magazines, billboards, brochures, catalogs, newspapers and filmstrips.
First Contact & Terms: Send resume to be kept on file. Write or call for appointment to show portfolio. Prefers slides, photographs or Photostats as samples. Pays by the hour or by the project. Considers complexity of project and client's budget when establishing payment. Negotiates rights purchased.

Texas

ALAMO AD CENTER INC., 217 Arden Grove, San Antonio TX 78215. (512)225-6294. Art Director: Mike Villanueva. Ad agency/PR firm. Serves clients in medical supplies, animal breeding, food, retailing (especially jewelry), real estate and manufacturing.
Needs: Works with 6 illustrators and 4 designers/month. Local artists only. Works on assignment only. Uses artists for work in consumer magazines, brochures/flyers, trade magazines, album covers, architectural renderings and "overflow work."
First Contact & Terms: Send brochure, flyer, business card, resume and tear sheets to be kept on file. SASE. Reports within 4 weeks if interested. Arrange interview to show portfolio, which should include tear sheets. No originals returned at job's completion. Pay is negotiable. Considers skill and experience of artist when establishing payment.

AVW PRODUCTIONS, 2241 Irving Blvd., Dallas TX 75207. (214)634-9060. Vice President: Bob Walker; Art Director: Lynn Leuck. AV/film/animation producer. Serves clients in industry and advertising. Produces multi-image materials, multiple-exposure slides, etc.
Needs: Works with 1-2 illustrators, 1-2 animators and 1-2 designers/year. Artists must work at the company's facility in Dallas. Works on assignment only. Uses artist for "any projects that the inhouse staff can't handle."

First Contact & Terms: Send resume, samples (slides preferred) and arrange interview by phone. Samples not kept on file are returned. Provide resume, samples, brochure/flyer and business card to be kept on file for possible future assignments. Reports within weeks. Pays by the project or by the hour. Method and amount of payment are negotiated with the individual artist. Payment varies with each client's budget. No originals returned to artist following publication. Negotiates rights purchased.

***BERNETA COMMUNICATIONS, INC.**, 701 Park Pl., Amarillo TX 79101. (806)376-7237. Vice President: Gladys Pinkerton. Ad agency and audiovisual firm. "We are a full-service communications and production firm." Clients: banks, automotive firms, museums, various businesses, hotels, motels, jewelry stores and politicians. Client list provided upon request.
Needs: Works with 12 freelance artists/year. Assigns 1,000 jobs/year. Works on assignment only. Uses freelance artists for design, illustration, brochures, catalogs, animation, posters, direct mail packages, lettering, logos, charts/graphs and advertisements.
First Contact & Terms: Send query letter with brochure. Samples are filed. Samples not filed are returned only if requested. Reports back only if interested. To show a portfolio, mail thumbnails, roughs, original/final art, Photostats, tear sheets, final reproduction/product, photographs, color, b&w, slides and video disks. Pays for design by the project, $100-1,500. Pays for illustration by the project, $100-1,900. Considers complexity of project, client's budget, turnaround time, skill and experience of artist, how work will be used and rights purchased when establishing payment. Rights purchased vary according to project.
Tips: "Be organized. Be able to present yourself in a professional manner."

BOZELL JACOBS KENYON & ECKHARDT, Box 619200, Dallas-Ft. Worth Airport TX 75261-9200. (214)556-1100. Creative Directors: Ron Spataro, Neil Scanlan, Artie McGibbens. Ad agency. Clients: all types.
Needs: Works with 4-5 freelance illustrators/month. Works on assignment only. Uses freelancers for billboards, newspapers, P-O-P displays, TV and trade magazines.
First Contact & Terms: Call for appointment to show portfolio. Reports within 3 weeks. Provide business card, brochure/flyer, resume and samples to be kept on file for possible future assignments. Samples not kept on file are returned. Payment is negotiated.
Tips: Wants to see a wide variety including past work used by ad agencies and tear sheets of published art.

CLAYPOOLE, BURK & HUMMEL, (formerly Womack/Claypoole), Suite 501, 8585 N. Stemmons Fwy., Dallas TX 75247-3805. Senior Art Director: Mary Davis. Ad agency. Clients: petroleum, aviation, financial, insurance, retail and plastics firms.
Needs: Works with 2-3 illustrators/month. Uses freelance artists for billboards, brochures, AV presentations, print and collateral pieces.
First Contact & Terms: Send query letter with brochure showing art style or tear sheets, Photostats and photocopies. Write to schedule an appointment to show a portfolio, which should include original/final art and final reproduction/product. Pays for design by the hour, $30-50 or by the project. Pays for illustration by the project, $200-1,500. Considers client's budget or where work will appear when establishing payment.
Tips: "In the field, there are more promotions to complement advertising campaigns. Also, computer graphics should be a strong medium for the last part of the twentieth century. As for approaching our firm, set reasonable prices on the total layout of artwork. Don't show consumer applications to a business-to-business shop."

DYKEMAN ASSOCIATES INC., 4115 Rawlins, Dallas TX 75219. (214)528-2991. Contact: Alice Dykeman or Laurie Christopher. PR/marketing firm. Clients: business, industry, sports, environmental, energy, health. Assigns 150 jobs/year.
Needs: Works with 5 illustrators/designers per month. "We prefer artists who can both design and illustrate." Local artists only. Uses artists for design of brochures, exhibits, corporate identification, signs, posters, ads, title slides, slide artwork and all design and finished artwork for graphics and printed materials.
First Contact & Terms: Arrange interview to show portfolio. Provide business card and brochures. No originals returned to artist at job's completion. Pays by the project, $250-3,000 average; "artist makes an estimate; we approve or negotiate." Considers complexity of project, creative compatibility, client's budget, skill and experience of artist and turnaround time when establishing payment.
Tips: "Be enthusiastic. Present an organized portfolio with a variety of work. Have a price structure but be willing to negotiate per project."

EVANS WYATT ADVERTISING, Gibralter Savings Bldg., 5151 Flynn Pkwy., Corpus Christi TX 78411. (512)854-1661. Contact: Mr. E. Wyatt. Advertising/exhibit/display/director.
Needs: Assigns 400 freelance illustrations/year; uses some cartoons and humorous and cartoon-style illustrations. Works on assignment only.
First Contact & Terms: Send a query letter with resume, brochure/flyer, tear sheets and photocopies to be kept on file. "No originals, please." Samples not filed are returned. Reports in two weeks. Arrange an interview to show portfolio, which should include scrapbook, slides or stats. Pays by the project, by the day, or by the hour, $75-150, with a $500 maximum. Considers client's budget and skill and experience of artist when establishing payment. "We pay flat for all rights."
Tips: More "by the project" assignments at negotiated charge. "Send 6-12 samples or copies of general scope of work plus best specialty and price expected."

***GOODMAN & ASSOCIATES**, 601 Penn St., Fort Worth TX 76102. (817)332-2261. Production Manager: Susan Whittenberger. Ad agency. Clients: financial, fashion, industrial, manufacturing and straight PR accounts.
Needs: Works with 3-6 illustrators/month. Uses freelance artists for billboards, consumer and trade magazines, direct mail, P-O-P displays, brochures, catalogs, posters, signage and AV presentations.
First Contact & Terms: Local artists only. Arrange interview to show portfolio. Works on assignment basis only. Payment is by the project, by the hour or by the day; negotiates according to client's budget.

GULF STATE ADVERTISING AGENCY, 3410 West Dallas, Houston TX 77019-3892. (713)521-1010. Art Director: Karen Gregory. Vice President: Irv Kauffman. Ad agency. Clients: financial, restaurant and industrial firms; client list provided upon request.
Needs: Number of freelance artists used varies. Local artists only. Works on assignment only. Primarily uses freelance artists for brochures and newspaper ads. Production work only.
First Contact & Terms: Send business card and Photostats to be kept on file. Pays for design and illustration by the hour, $15.

HEPWORTH ADVERTISING CO., 3403 McKinney Ave., Dallas TX 75204. (214)525-7785. Manager: S.W. Hepworth. Ad agency. Clients: finance, food, machinery and insurance.
Needs: Works with 2 illustrators and 2 designers/month. Local artists only. Uses artists for billboards, consumer magazines, direct mail, slide sets, brochures/flyers and trade magazines.
First Contact & Terms: Send a query letter with tear sheets to be kept on file. No originals returned to artist at job's completion.
Tips: Looks for variety in samples or portfolio.

***INFORMEDIA**, Box 13287, Austin TX 78711. (512)327-3227. President: Michael Sidoric. AV producer. Serves clients in industry, advertising, government and education. Produces new product introductions, marketing presentations, historical and educational slide multimedia presentations; single to 125 projector; single or multi-screen format; presentations both fixed and touring.
Needs: Assigns 60+ jobs/year. Works with 2 illustrators and 2 animators/month. Uses artists for specialized areas (historical, industrial) shows.
First Contact & Terms: Prefers "Southwestern artists who have backgrounds in strong graphics (line work) and who are familiar with 35mm slides as a medium. To be considered, one must have an unbounded imagination." Send query letter and a "representative sample of Photostats or slides." Arrange interview by mail. Samples not returned. Provide samples, brochure/flyer and business card to be kept on file for possible future assignments. Works on assignment only. Reports in 1 month. Method and amount of payment are negotiated with individual artist. Payment varies according to client's budget. No originals returned to artist after publication. Negotiates rights purchased.
Tips: "AV demands rigid time and mechanical restrictions (i.e., pin registration). Artist must know capabilities and limitations of AV and be willing to experiment in this exciting new medium!"

KNOX PUBLIC RELATIONS, Suite A, Guthrie Creek Park, 708 Glencrest, Longview TX 75601. (214)758-6439. President: Donna Mayo Knox. PR firm. Clients: civic, social organizations, private schools and businesses.
Needs: Works on assignment only. Uses artists for billboards, stationery design, multimedia kits, direct mail and brochures/flyers.
First Contact & Terms: Send query letter with brochure showing art style or resume and samples. Samples returned by SASE. Reports in 3 weeks. Call or write to schedule an appointment to show a portfolio. Originals returned to artist at job's completion. Pays for design by the hour, $30 minimum. Pays for illustration by the hour, $20 minimum.
Tips: "Please query first."

LEVEL FOUR COMMUNICATIONS, Three Dallas Communications Complex LB134, Irving TX 75039-3510. (214)869-7620. President: Doris Seitz. Ad agency. Clients: corporate and banking.
Needs: Works with 5-6 freelance artists/year. Uses local artists with a minimum of three years of experience. Works on assignment only. Uses artists for design, illustrations, brochures, catalogs, books, magazines, newspaper, P-O-P displays, mechanicals, retouching, billboards, posters, direct mail packages, press releases, motion pictures, lettering, logos, charts/graphs and advertisements. Looks for "first-quality, high-level, corporate design capability: a clean, sophisiticated style."
First Contact & Terms: Contact through artist's agent or send query letter with resume and samples. Samples not filed are not returned. Reports only if interested. To show a portfolio, mail original/final art, final reproduction/product, color, tear sheets and photographs. On a typical brochure, pays for design by the project, $200 minimum. Pays for illustration by the project, $200 minimum. Considers client's budget, skill and experience of artist, turnaround time and rights purchased when establishing payment. Purchases all rights but can negotiate; rights purchased vary according to project.

LOWE-MARSCHALK, (formerly Metzdorf-Marschalk), 3040 Postoak, Houston TX 77056. (713)840-0491. Art Director: Mike Lyons. Ad agency. Clients: consumer, food, financial and some industrial firms.
Needs: Works with 12 illustrators/year. Works on assignment only. Uses freelance artists for billboards, consumer and trade magazines, direct mail, catalogs, posters, newspapers and advertising.
First Contact & Terms: Send slides, tear sheets, Photostats or cards showing style used, or contact through artist representative. Reports only if interested. Usually deals with artist representative about payment for illustrators. Pays by the project, $125-4,000 average. Considers complexity of project and rights purchased when establishing payment.
Tips: "We are looking for artists with specific styles or specialties or unusual treatments to otherwise mundane subjects. Send examples of your work before attempting to make an appointment. Postcard mailings have been successful."

McCANN-ERICKSON WORLDWIDE, Briar Hollow Bldg., 520 S. Post Oak Rd., Houston TX 77027. (713)965-0303. Senior Vice President/Creative Director: Jesse Caesar. Ad agency. Clients: all types including industrial, gasoline, transportation/air, entertainment, computers and high tech.
Needs: Works with about 20 freelance illustrators/month. Uses freelancers in all media.
First Contact & Terms: Call for appointment to show portfolio. Selection based on portfolio review. Negotiates payment based on client's budget and where work will appear.
Tips: Wants to see full range of work including past work used by other ad agencies and tear sheets of published art in portfolio.

McNEE PHOTO COMMUNICATIONS INC., 9261 Kirby, Houston TX 77006. (713)796-2633. President: Jim McNee. AV/film producer. Serves clients in industry and advertising. Produces slide presentations, videotapes, brochures and films. Also a brokerage for stock photographs.
Needs: Assigns 20 jobs/year. Works with 4 illustrators/month. Prefers local artists with previous work experience. Uses artists for brochures, annual reports and artwork for slides, film and tape.
First Contact & Terms: "Will review samples by appointment only." Provide resume, brochure/flyer and business card to be kept on file for possible future assignments. Works on assignment only. Reports within 1 month. Method of payment is negotiated with the individual artist. Pays by the hour, $30-60 average. Considers client's budget when establishing payment. No originals returned after publication. Buys all rights, but will negotiate.

ROMINGER ADVERTISING AGENCY, 3600 Commerce, Dallas TX 75226. Art Director: G. Nelson Greenfield. Ad agency. Clients: hotels, real estate, corporate and industrial.
Needs: Works with 2-3 illustrators/year. Local artists only. Works on assignment basis only. Uses freelance artists for billboards, consumer and trade magazines, direct mail, P-O-P displays, brochures, catalogs, posters, signage, newspapers, and AV presentations and production.
First Contact & Terms: Query with resume of credits and samples. Payment is by the day or by project.

NEAL SPELCE COMMUNICATIONS, Suite 400, 333 Guadalupe, Two Republic Plaza, Austin TX 78701. (512)476-4644. Creative Director: D. Childress. Ad agency. Serves clients in finance, hospitals, professional associations and real estate.
Needs: Works with 3 illustrators and 4 designers/month. Works on assignment only. Uses artists for consumer and trade magazines, direct mail, newspapers, P-O-P displays, brochures/flyers and TV.
First Contact & Terms: Write requesting interview to show portfolio (illustrations and printed pieces incorporating the illustrations); send resume, slides or Photostats or make contact through the artist's

rep. Samples returned by SASE. Reports within 2 weeks. Provide resume, brochure or promotional materials showing work and/or samples to be kept on file for future assignments. Pay is negotiable.
Tips: "We tend to use illustrators, rather than designers, for freelance work."

TEXAS PACIFIC FILM VIDEO, INC., 501 N. I35, Austin TX 78702. (512)478-8585. Producer: Laura Kooris. Film/video production firm. Clients: ad agencies, music companies, etc. Client list provided for SASE.
Needs: Works with many freelance artists/year. Uses artists for set design, logos and signs, and costumes and makeup.
First Contact & Terms: Works on assignment only. Send query letter with samples to be kept on file. Prefers reels as samples. Samples not filed are returned by SASE. Reports only if interested. Write for appointment to show portfolio. Pays by the project or by the day. Considers client's budget and skill and experience of artist when establishing payment. Rights purchased vary according to project.

ZACHRY ASSOCIATES, INC., Box 1739, 709 N. 2nd, Abilene TX 79604. (915)677-1342. General Manager: Phil Ritz. Ad agency, audiovisual and printing firm. Clients: industrial, institutional and religious service. Client list provided for SASE.
Needs: Works with 6 freelance artists/year. Works on assignment only. Uses artists for illustration, calligraphy and mechanical preparation.
First Contact & Terms: Send query letter with samples, if available, to be kept on file. Samples not filed are returned by SASE. Call or write to schedule an appointment to show portfolio, which should include roughs, final reproduction/product or anything pertinent to talent offered. Pays for design by the hour, $10 minimum. Pays for illustration by the project, $35 minimum. Considers complexity of the project, client's budget and turnaround time when establishing payment. Rights purchased vary according to project.

Utah

***CINEPHONICS VIDEO**, 5898 Salem Ave., Kearns UT 84118. (801)968-3333. Owner/Manager: Eldon Hamblin. A video publishing and production house providing how-to and informational tapes and some multi-slide programs for various large and small businesses and individuals. Client list provided with a SASE.
Needs: Works with 2 freelance artists/year. Assigns 4-15 jobs/year. Works on assignment only. Uses artists for design, illustration, brochures, P-O-P displays, animation, motion pictures and logos.
First Contact & Terms: Send query letter with brochure showing art style or resume and slides. Samples are filed. Reports back within 10 days. Write to schedule an appointment to show a portfolio, which should include roughs, original/final art, final reproduction/product, photographs, color, slides and ¾ or VHS tape. Pays for design by the project, $350 minimum. Pays for illustration by the hour, $11-35 or by the project, $200 minimum. Considers complexity of project, client's budget, turnaround time, skill and experience of artist and rights purchased when establishing payment for freelance work. Rights purchased vary according to project.
Tips: "Be honest about your skills and projections."

FRANCOM ADVERTISING, INC., Suite D-100, 5282 S. 320 West, Salt Lake City UT 84107. (801)263-3125. President: A. Sterling Francom. Ad agency. Clients: banks, car dealers, restaurants, industrial, video rental. Client list provided upon request.
Needs: Assigns 120 freelance jobs/year. Local artists only. Works on assignment only. Works with 3 freelance illustrators and 2 freelance designers/month. Uses artists for billboards, direct mail packages, brochures, catalogs, newspapers and signage.
First Contact & Terms: Send query letter with resume and tear sheets and Photostats to be kept on file. Samples returned by SASE if not kept on file. Reports within 2 weeks. Call or write to schedule an appointment to show a portfolio, which should include original/final art, final reproduction/product, tear sheets and Photostats. Pays by the project, $25-1,500; amount of payment negotiated with artist in advance. Considers complexity of project, client's budget and turnaround time when establishing payment. Material not copyrighted.
Tips: Artists should possess "creativity and professionalism, and full-service capability from design concept to printer. Portfolio must include current commercial work similar to or complimentary to advertising agency's regular types of art work. Artwork submitted must be *commercial* art, not portraits, scenes, etc., either the original or published art of sample brochures, ads from newspapers, magazines, etc. It needs to look professional—on matboard, with tissue cover." Current trends include contemporary and computer-generated design using high-tech colors.

Vermont

***MEDIA FORUM INTERNATIONAL, LTD.**, Box 65, Peacham VT 05862; Box 8, FW, Mt. Vernon NY 10552. (802)592-8444; (914)667-6575. Contact: Managing Director. Media specialists, consultants for multi-lingual publications; photo typesetting, translations, international filler, video projects, consultants (overseas projects). Clients: multi-national corporations; academic institutional; etc.
Needs: Works with few freelance artists/year. Uses artists for design, illustration, animation, and motion pictures.
First Contact & Terms: Send query letter with resume. "Send samples ony when requested." Reports back only if interested." Payment depends on the project.
Tips: "Have your name, address, telephone and type of work information in our file—we call."

Virginia

GOLDMAN & ASSOCIATES, (formerly Dan Advertising & Public Relations), 408 W. Bute St., Norfolk VA 23510. (804)625-2518. Art Director: Oliver Raust. Ad/PR firm.
Needs: Uses artists for work in building and mechanical renderings, airbrushing, animation, TV animation, TV/film production, P-O-P displays, filmstrips, consumer magazines, multimedia kits, slide sets, brochures/flyers and finished work. Negotiates pay.
First Contact & Terms: Query with samples of previously published work. SASE. Provide brochures, flyers, resume, tearsheets, samples and 3/4" video tape when possible to be kept on file for future assignments. Originals returned at completion on some jobs.

PAYNE ROSS & ASSOCIATES ADVERTISING, INC., 206 E. Jefferson St., Charlottesville VA 22901. (804)977-7607. Creative Director: Lisa Ross. Ad agency. Clients: resorts, service industries, manufacturing, banks.
Needs: Works with 12-20 freelance artists/year. Uses artists for photography, illustration and copy-writing; occasionally for paste-up.
First Contact & Terms: Send query letter with brochure showing art style or resume and tear sheets, Photostats, slides, photographs and other printed pieces. Reports back only if interested. To show portfolio, mail appropriate materials, which should include original/final art, final reproduction/product, Photostats and photographs. Pays for design by the hour, $15-40; pays for illustration by the project, $200-1,500. Pay varies according to "experience, type of work, etc." Considers skill and experience of artist and turnaround time when establishing payment. Rights purchased vary according to project.
Tips: "There is increasing popularity in use of illustration for brochure and print advertising. Also there is more acceptance of this by client, particularly photography and illustration together. We find more integration between copy and design in conceptual stage. Therefore designer, illustrator, photographer must be flexible."

WILLIAM C. PFLAUM CO. INC., Reston International Center, Reston VA 22091. (703)620-3773. Art Director: John Cuddahy. PR firm.
Needs: Works with 1-2 designers/month. Uses artists for stationery design, direct mail, brochures/flyers, trade magazines and newspapers.
First Contact & Terms: Local artists only. Query with samples. No originals returned at job's completion.

SIDDALL, MATUS AND COUGHTER, Fidelity Bldg., 9th & Main Sts., Richmond VA 23219. Art Directors: Jessica Welton, Bob Shira, Suzanne Dashiell. Ad agency/PR firm. Clients: industrial, travel, land development, bank, chemical, computer, retail.
Needs: Assigns 50 freelance jobs/year. Works on assignment only. Works with 4 freelance illustrators/month. Uses artists for consumer and trade magazines, billboards, direct mail packages, brochures, newspapers and posters.
First Contact & Terms: Send query letter with samples and tear sheets to be kept on file. Call or write for appointment to show portfolio, which should include printed samples to be kept on file. Samples returned only if requested. Reports only if interested. Pays for design by the hour, $30-60. Pays for illustration by the project, up to $15,000. Considers complexity of project, client's budget, skill and experience of artist, geographic scope of finished project, turnaround time and rights purchased when establishing payment. Buys all rights.

Washington

INLAND AUDIO VISUAL COMPANY, N. 2325 Monroe St., Spokane WA 99205. (509)328-0706. President: Larry Ellingson. Audiovisual firm. Clients: advertising agencies and associations.
Needs: Works with 5 freelance artists/year. Works on assignment only. Uses artists for design, illustrations, retouching, animation, lettering, logos, charts/graphs and multi-image. Artist must have multi-image design skills.
First Contact & Terms: Send query letter with resume. Reports only if interested. Write to schedule an appointment to show a portfolio. Considers complexity of project, client's budget and turnaround time when establishing payment. Rights purchased vary according to project.

***MAGICMATION INC.**, Suite 1560, 1100 Olive Way, Seattle WA 98101. (206)682-8235. Vice President: Robert T. O'Dell. Audiovisual firm. "Magicmation is a computer graphics service center using state-of-the-art technology, talented artists and sales staff to create, produce, and image high-resolution business graphics, pictures, paintings, photographs, etc. Clients: advertising, corporations, printers, photographers, software companies, research and development.
Needs: Works with 2 freelance artists/year. "Artists must have basic knowledge of computer graphics machines." Uses artists for design, illustration, mechanicals, retouching and charts/graphs.
First Contact & Terms: Send query letter with brochure or resume and slides. Samples not filed are returned only if requested. Reports back only if interested. Write to schedule an appointment to show a portfolio, which should include roughs, photographs, color and slides. Pays for design and illustration by the hour, $12-25. Considers skill and experience of artist when establishing payment. Buys all rights.
Tips: "Color, design, speed and *knowledge* of our equipment are very important."

West Virginia

GUTMAN ADVERTISING AGENCY, 600 Board of Trade Bldg., Wheeling WV 26003. (304)233-4700. President: Milton Gutman. Ad agency. Clients: finance, glass, resort, media, industrial supplies (tools, pipes) and furniture.
Needs: Works with 3-4 illustrators/month. Local artists only except for infrequent and special needs. Uses artists for billboards, stationery design, television, brochures/flyers, trade magazines and newspapers. Also uses artists for retouching work.
First Contact & Terms: Send materials to be kept on file for possible future assignments. Call for an appointment to show a portfolio. No originals returned at job's completion. Negotiates payment.

Wisconsin

BARKIN, HERMAN, SOLOCHECK & PAULSEN, INC., 777 E. Wisconsin Ave., Milwaukee WI 53202. (414)271-7434. Contact: John Erickson. Wisconsin's oldest PR firm. Clients: educational organization, financial, manufacturing, hospital, insurance, brewery, leisure time and real estate development.
Needs: Works with freelance illustrators and designers according to individual needs. Uses artists for all communications media.
First Contact & Terms: Call account executive for appointment to show portfolio. Negotiates payment depending on job requirements.

HOFFMAN YORK & COMPTON, 330 E. Kilbourne Ave., Milwaukee WI 53202. (414)289-9700. Art Director: Reed Allen. Ad agency. Serves clients in machinery, food service.
Needs: Works with "many" illustrators/month. Needs vary. Uses freelancers and studios for all print media.
First Contact & Terms: Call for appointment to show portfolio. Negotiates payment.
Tips: Wants to see best work. Will probably use freelancer's area of specialty.

***BRIEN LEE & COMPANY**, 2025 N. Summit Ave, Milwaukee WI 53202. (414)277-7600. President/Creative Director: Brien Lee. Audiovisual firm. Video tape producer and agency specializing in wide range of sales and marketing presentations both on a per project and speculative basis. Clients: business, industry, the arts.
Needs: Works with 10 freelance artists/year. Assigns 20 jobs/year. Works on assignment only. Uses

artists for design, illustration, P-O-P displays, mechanicals, animation, motion pictures and storyboards.
First Contact & Terms: Send query letter with resume, tear sheets, Photostats, photocopies and slides. Samples are filed. Samples not filed are returned. Reports back within 10 days. Write to schedule an appointment to show a portfolio, or mail photostats, tear sheets, slides and videotape. Pays for design by the hour, $25-80. Pays for illustration by the hour, $40-100. Considers complexity of project, client's budget and turnaround time when establishing payment. Negotiates rights purchased.
Tips: Artists need "an understanding of videotape and motion/animation design."

L. QUILLIN & ASSOCIATES, INC., V.I.P. Bldg., 2101 Victory St., La Crosse WI 54601. (608)788-8292. Vice President: Barbara Lea. Ad agency. Clients: manufacturing, business to business.
Needs: Works with 6-8 freelance artists/year. Especially important are skills, creativity and understanding needs. Works on assignment only.
First Contact & Terms: Send query letter with resume and samples to be kept on file. Samples not filed are returned only if requested. Reports back only if interested. Call for appointment to show portfolio. Pay varies. Considers complexity of the project, client's budget and turnaround time when establishing payment. Buys all rights.

SORGEL-STUDIOS, INC., 205 W. Highland Ave., Milwaukee WI 53203. (414)224-9600. Contact: Art Director. AV producer. Clients: business, corporate, multi-image and videotapes. Assigns 100 jobs/year.
Needs: Works with 10 illustrators/year. Uses artists for stylized illustrations, human figures and animation.
First Contact & Terms: Query with resume and samples (slides). SASE. Reports in 3 weeks. Provide resume and brochures/flyers to be kept on file for possible future assignments. No originals returned to artist at job's completion. Negotiates pay.
Tips: "Most of our artwork is now computer generated and that limits our use of freelancers."

***VISUALS PLUS INC.**, 810 N. Plankinton Ave., Milwaukee WI 53203. Vice President/Creative Director: John D. Peterman. Audiovisual firm. "We are a multimedia firm specializing in computer-generated business graphics. We also have a complete art department and inhouse b&w/color photographic labs." Clients: private amateur/professional photographers. Produce graphics, art and multi-images for corporate and commercial businesses.
Needs: Works with 5 freelance artists/year. Assigns 40-50 jobs/year. Prefers local metro-Milwaukee artists. Works on assignment only. Uses artists for design, illustration, brochures, catalogs, books, newspapers, trade magazines, mechanicals, animation, direct mail packages, press releases, lettering, logos, charts/graphs and advertisements.
First Contact & Terms: Send query letter with brochure or resume and slides. Samples are filed. Reports back within 10 days "if applicable." Write to schedule an appointment to show a portfolio or mail roughs, tear sheets, final reproduction/product and slides. Pays for design by the hour, $4-10; by the project, $30-350. Pays for illustration by the hour, $8-20; by the project, $60-700. Considers turnaround time and skill and experience of artist when establishing payment. Buys all rights.
Tips: "Provide an honest response by mail with representative samples depicting experience and specific skills in area requested."

Canada

NORM DREW ENTERTAINMENT FEATURES, Suite 608-L, Laurier House, 1600 Beach Ave., Vancouver, B.C. V6G 1Y6 Canada. (604)689-1948. Contact: Norman Drew. Producer of audiovisual and print graphic art, TV commercials, slide shows, TV animated series, cartoon art-comic strips, panels, greeting cards, books for educational, advertising and entertainment use. Clients: TV networks, stations, ad agencies, corporations, government, publishers, newspapers and multimedia.
Needs: Freelance assistants for animation, comic strip, comic panels, lettering, children's books.
First Contact & Needs: Send query letter, photocopies of your best examples. "Do not send animation demo films/tapes unless requested. Unsolicited films/tapes will not be returned without adequate return postage/shipping fee included. Please include SAE with U.S./Canadian postage or IRC if replies to questions required. Keeps sample page/letter on file pending possible assignments." Animation paid by footage; graphic art by piecework. Buys all rights.

***DYNACOM COMMUNICATIONS**, Box 702, Snowdon Station, Montreal, Quebec H3X 3X8 Canada. Director: David P. Leonard. Audiovisual/TV/film producer. Clients: large industries,

government, education and health institutions.
Needs: Produces motion pictures, multimedia kits, overhead transparencies, slide sets, sound-slide sets, color videotapes and multiscreen mixed media "for training, motivation, sales, orientation and entertainment." Uses artists for album covers.
First Contact & Terms: Query with resume. Reports "only if we have a requirement." Buys all rights. Negotiates time of payment. Pays $20-40/frame, animated cartoons; $15-60, charts/graphs and technical art. Payment by hour: $5-15, advertising and illustrations; $5-10, lettering and mechanicals.

INSIGHT COMMUNICATIONS, 1850 Champlain Ave., Box 363, Whitby, Ontario L1N 5S4 Canada. (416)686-1144. Art Director: Garnet McPherson. AV firm. Clients: corporate, industry and travel industry.
Needs: Assigns 45 freelance jobs/year. Works with 2 freelance illustrators and 3 freelance designers/month. Prefers "local artists for assignment; any artist for stock art or photography." Uses artists for brochures, filmstrips, P-O-P displays, AV presentations, posters and graphics.
First Contact & Terms: Send query letter with business card and samples to be kept on file. Samples not kept on file are returned by SAE (nonresidents include IRC) only if requested. Reports within 3 weeks. Call for appointment to show portfolio, which should include slides and tear sheets. Pays by the project, $25-2,500 average. Considers complexity of project, client's budget, skill and experience of artist and rights purchased when establishing payment. Negotiates rights purchased.
Tips: "In contacting us, artists should send query with samples, then call 2 weeks later for an appointment."

LOWE MARSCHALK GOODGOLL LIMITED, (formerly Campbell-Ewald Limited), 20 Richmond St. E., Toronto, Ontario Canada. (416)362-8600. Creative Director: Trevor F. Goodgoll. Ad agency. Clients: airlines, liquor, financing, insulation products, candy, plastics and tires.
Needs: Assigns 25 freelance jobs/year. Works on assignment only. Uses artist for consumer and trade magazines, newspapers and some occasional brochures.
First Contact & Terms: Send resume, samples and tear sheets to be kept on file. Samples not kept on file are returned. Nonresidents include IRC. Reports within 15 days. Call or write for appointment to show portfolio. Payment is "entirely dependent on artist's skills. Illustrators are usually paid on a project basis." Considers complexity of project, client's budget, skill and experience of artist and turnaround time when establishing payment. Buys all rights.
Tips: Artists should "understand that the creative director is reponsible for a tremendous amount of day to day work and should be prepared for for polite 'put-offs.' Keep trying! Artists will always receive clear briefings from us and will be given the creative freedom necessary to do their very best. Don't show or bring too much. Quality, not quantity. Be patient and keep trying for an appointment."

McCANN-ERICKSON ADVERTISING OF CANADA, Britannica House, 151 Bloor W, Toronto, Ontario MS5 1S8 Canada. (416)925-3231. Contact: Art Directors. Ad agency. Clients: consumer food, beverage and service industry accounts.
Needs: Local artists only. Works on assignment only. Uses freelance artists and photographers on all accounts.
First Contact & Terms: Especially looks for a "unique style" in a portfolio—also "enthusiasm and dedication." Call to schedule an appointment to show portfolio with individual art directors. Payment is by the project; negotiates according to client's budget and freelancer's previous experience.
Tips: "Artists should be more selective in the work they show. One poor piece of work lets down the whole portfolio."

WARNE MARKETING & COMMUNICATIONS, Suite 810, 111 Avenue Rd., Toronto, Ontario M5R 3M1 Canada. (416)927-0881. President: Keith Warne.
Needs: Works with 8 freelance artists/year. Works on assignment only. Uses artists for design, illustrations, brochures, catalog, P-O-P displays, mechanicals, retouching, billboards, posters, direct mail packages, logos, charts/graphs and advertisements. Artists should have "creative concept thinking."
First Contact & Terms: Send query letter with resume and photocopies. Samples not filed are not returned. Reports only if interested. Write to schedule an appointment to show a portfolio, which should include roughs and final reproduction/product. Pays for design by the project, $85-125. Pays for illustration by the project, $125-200. Considers complexity of project, client's budget, and skill and experience of artist when establishing payment. Buys all rights.
Tips: Artist should "send samples (photocopies) and wait for assignment. There is an increasing need for technical illustration in the field."

Architectural, Interior & Landscape Design Firms

Architectural firms come in all sizes from a one-man operation that remodels homes to full-service firms that plan office complexes. Some firms do a little of everything, while others specialize in such areas as city planning or designing corporate office buildings. Residential clients are the exclusive domain of some firms, while others mix commercial, residential, corporate and industrial clients.

Firms vary in the type of artwork they need. All firms use architectural renderings to conceptualize a project. Model builders give renderings a three-dimensional form by constructing buildings, complexes and even cities from wood, plastic or plaster. Architectural drafters make detailed drawings that builders use in the preparation of blueprints. Landscape designers redesign natural settings, planning not only the placement of greenery but also traffic flow. Before the client is ready to move in, interior designers plan, supervise and coordinate the design and furnishing of the interior space. Interior designers often specialize in either contract (commercial) or residential clients; those involved in contract work further specialize in offices, hotels, restaurants or space planning (arranging interior spaces).

Each facet of architectural art requires good draftsmanship, a knowledge of blueprints and building materials plus a good sense of perspective. Renderings must be technically precise so a client knows what to expect. Formally drafted renderings are giving way to the use of shade and shadows in order to make drawings more realistic without being misleading.

Select firms which suit your style and work habits. Some projects require on-site construction visits, while others call for renderings which can be done at home or at the office. Mail a sample package which contains a query letter, slides or photographs of your projects. Architectural renderers should send samples of their rendering skills and photographs of model-making projects. Landscape designers should submit not only drafting or rendering samples but also photos of gardens or grounds they have designed; they should send sequential photos showing the grounds in different seasons. Interior designers should demonstrate their specialty, whether it is industrial space planning or residential decoration, with before and after shots.

Architectural and interior design firms often acquire paintings and sculpture for corporate clients. Corporations require a large amount of artwork to enhance executive offices and workspaces when building new headquarters or remodeling existing offices. Scan the business section of your local paper for news of corporations or businesses relocating to new offices. Then contact the art buyer (who may be the president of a smaller company or an art consultant for a large corporation) for the company, who will give you the name of the architect or interior designer.

Magazines which provide essential information on the industry are *Architectural Digest*, *The AIA Journal*, *Architectural Record* and *Interior Design*, as well as *House & Garden*, *House Beautiful* and *Better Homes and Gardens*. Names and addresses of architectural firms are available in *ProFile* and names of interior designers can be found in the membership lists of the local chapters of the American Society of Interior Designers (ASID's national chapter is at 1430 Broadway, New York NY 10018).

A&E DESIGN, INC., 5644 N. Dale Mabry, Tampa FL 33614. (813)885-4605. President: Gordon Amato, AIA. Architectural/engineering firm. Clients: residential, commercial and institutional.
Needs: Works with 2 freelance artists/year. Works on assignment only. Uses artists for advertising design, interior, landscape and architectural renderings, and model making.
First Contact & Terms: Send query letter with brochure showing art style or resume and samples. Samples not filed are returned only if requested. Reports only if interested. To show a portfolio, mail photographs and brochure. Pays for illustrations by the project, $600-2,000. Considers complexity of project, skill and experience of artist, and turnaround time when establishing payment.

***AKIYAMA/KEKOOLANI ASSOCIATES**, Suite 311, 1110 University Ave., Honolulu HI 96826. Partner: Geo. H. Kekoolani, Jr. Architectural firm. Clients: residential, commercial, housing; government (federal, state), institutional.
Needs: Works with 2-3 freelance artists/year. Uses artists for brochure illustration, interior and architectural renderings, and model making.
First Contact & Terms: Send query letter with resume, business card and samples to be kept on file; call for appointment to show portfolio. Prefers photographs as samples. Samples not kept on file are returned only if requested. Reports only if interested. Considers complexity of project, client's budget, skill and experience of artist and how work will be used when establishing payment.

***ANDERSON ASSOCIATES ARCHITECTS**, 422 E. Oak St., Ft. Collins CO 80524. (303)484-0306. Owner: Dick Anderson. Architectural/Interior design firm serving residential and commercial clients.
Needs: Works with 1 freelance artrist/every other year. Prefers versatile artists. Works on assignment only. Uses artists for advertising design, illustration and layout, brochure design, interior design and renderings, architectural renderings; design consulting and model making.
First Contact & Terms: Send brochure or resume. Samples are not filed. Does not report back. To show a portfolio, mail thumbnails, roughs, tearsheets and b&w. Pays for illustration by the project, $200-1,000. Considers client's budget, skill and experience of artist and turnaround time when establishing payment. Buys all rights.

***ANGEL, MULL & ASSOCIATES, INC.**, 3049 Sylvania Ave., Toledo OH 43613. (419)474-5496. Vice President: Melvin Henry Mull. Architectural firm providing architectural services for new buildings and renovations of existing buildings. Clients: institutional, government, educational, commercial, etc.
Needs: Works with 2-3 freelance artists/year. Works on assignment only. Uses artists for interior design, architectural renderings and model making.
First Contact & Terms: Send query letter with brochure. Samples are filed. Samples not filed are returned only if requested. Reports back within 30 days. Call or write to schedule an appointment to show a portfolio, which should include original/final art, final reproduction/product, color and photographs. Pays for illustration by the project, $100-3,000. Considers complexity of project, client's budget, skill and experience of artist, how work will be used and turnaround time when establishing payment.
Tips: "Call or write for an appointment, bring samples of your work and a cost schedule (if you have one)."

***ARCHITECTURAL PLANNING & DESIGN GROUP**, 495 Main St., Boise ID 83702. (208)345-4698. Partner: Ronald Thurber. Clients: commercial.
Needs: Works with 1 artist for architectural renderings; 1, signage design; and 1, stained glass.
First Contact & Terms: Western U.S. artists only. Query. SASE. Reports in 1 week. Provide brochure to be kept on file for future assignments. Pays for renderings by the job, $150-400. Pays for design by the hour, $12-16 average, and by the project, $150-400 average.

ARCHITRONICS, Suite D-44, 3 Sunset Way, Henderson NV 89015. (702)435-1150. President: David F. Welles. Architectural/interior design firm.
Needs: Works with 2 freelance artists/year. Works on assignment only. Uses artists for interior design, interior renderings and architectural renderings and model making.
First Contact & Terms: Send query letter with brochure showing art style or resume, tear sheets, Photostats, photocopies, slides and photographs. Samples not filed are returned only if requested. Reports only if interested. Call or write to schedule an appointment to show a portfolio, which should include thumbnails, roughs, original/final art, final reproduction/product, color, tear sheets, Photostats, photographs and b&w. Payment varies. Considers complexity of project, client's budget, skill and experience of artist, turnaround time and rights purchased when establishing payment.

MILLARD ARCHULETA/EDDY PAYNTER ASSOCIATES, 7440 N. Figueroa St., Los Angeles CA 90041. (213)254-9121. Director of Design: Frank J. Wong, AIA. Architectural firm. Clients: financial institutions, shopping centers, corporate office buildings.

Needs: Works with 12 freelance artists/year. Uses artists for interior and architectural renderings, landscape design, and model making.
First Contact & Terms: Contact only through artist's agent, who should send brochure, slides and photographs to be kept on file. Reports only if interested. Call for appointment to show portfolio, which should include final reproduction/product and color. Pays for illustration by the project, $500-2,000 average. Considers complexity of budget and skill and experience of artist when establishing payment.
Tips: "A very popular current trend is abstract design."

ARNOLD & STACKS ARCHITECTS, Box 69, 527 W. Washington, Jonesboro AR 72403. (501)932-5530; Box 1560, 901 Central Ave., Hot Springs AR 71902. (501)624-4678. Contact: Doug Arnold. Architectural/interior and landscape/design firm providing planning, design, architecture, landscape, graphic and interior design, and construction administration. Clients: private, public residential, governmental, educational, industrial.
Needs: Works with 1-2 freelance artists/year. Uses artists for advertising design, brochure design, illustration and layout; landscape and interior design, architectural and interior renderings, design consulting and furnishings.
First Contact & Terms: Send query letter with brochure, resume, business card, slides, photographs and tear sheets to be kept on file. Reports within 2 weeks. Call for appointment to show portfolio. Pay rate "depends on work, circumstances, etc." Considers complexity of project, client's budget, skill and experience of artist and turnaround time when establishing payment.

ASSOCIATED INDUSTRIAL DESIGNERS, INC., 32 Court St., Brooklyn Heights NY 11201. (718)624-0034. President: Dr. Robert I. Golberg. Specializes in brand and corporate identity, displays, interior design, packaging, and signage. Clients: "all major firms."
Needs: Works with "many" artists/year. Works on assignment only. Uses artists for brochure and direct mail, package illustration; P-O-P displays, mechanicals, retouching, model making, lettering and logo design.
First Contact & Terms: Send brochure/flyer, resume and Photostats. Samples returned. Pays by the hour for design; by the project for illustration; also negotiates.

LEON BARMACHE DESIGN ASSOCIATES LTD., 225 East 57th St., New York NY 10022. (212)759-3840. Executive Designer: Leon Barmache F.A.S.I.D. Interior space planners and designer. Clients: private.
Needs: Needs artists to render interiors, furniture, rugs, etc., from rough sketches; b&w or color, for presentations. Also uses artists for design, illustration, displays and model making.
First Contact & Terms: Send query letter with brochure, resume and Photostats, copies or tear sheets to be kept on file. Samples not filed returned by SASE only if requested. Reports within 2 weeks if interested. Call or write for appointment to show portfolio. Pays by the project, $250-500 average for design and illustration. Considers the skill and experience of artist when establishing payment.
Tips: Artist should have "a portfolio of renderings showing his drawing capabilities using the means available—pencil, ink, marker, gouache, airbrush, etc."

***BARNOUW & VASI, INC.**, Box 364, Katonah NY 10536. President: Alan A. Barnouw. Interior design firm. Clients: shopping centers, department stores, shops, showrooms, offices, banks, restaurants.
Needs: Works with 2-3 freelance artists/year. Uses artists for design and illustration.
First Contact & Terms: "Working with local artists is easier" and some experience is preferred because "we can't run a training program." Send query letter with resume and samples to be kept on file; "if representative samples of the artist's work are sent, we will contact the artist whose work and rates best suit our needs for a given project." Accepts "any medium" as samples, but "work will be filed. Photographs, if clear, are fine." Samples not filed are not returned. Reports within 2-3 weeks. Payment varies "based on the work to be performed, the type of project and the contractual arrangements." Considers the complexity of the project, skill and experience of the artist, turnaround time and "our 'budgeted' amount for artwork for any given project" when establishing payment.
Tips: "Give as much information as possible with your submitted sample—what the fee was, how long it took to complete, what information you were given. The more information we have to use in making a decision, the happier everyone will be in the end."

DWIGHT E. BENNETT & ASSOCIATES, 3929 Long Beach Blvd., Long Beach CA 90807. (213)595-1691. Contact: Dwight Bennett. Architecture firm. Clients: industrial, residential and commercial.
Needs: Assigns 6 jobs/year. Local artists only. Uses artists for architectural renderings.
First Contact & Terms: Query with brochure or samples. Reports within 1 week. Pays $400-2,500.

***LYNWOOD BROWN AIA AND ASSOCIATES, INC.**, 1220 Prince St., Alexandria VA 22314. (703)836-5523. President: L. Brown. Architectural firm providing architecture and engineering. Clients: commercial, industrial, institutional.
Needs: Works with 2-3 freelance artists/year. Uses artists for interior design, architectural renderings and model making.
First Contact & Terms: Works on assignment only. Send query letter with brochure; call for appointment to show portfolio. Prefers "photos or prints" as samples. Samples not filed are returned by SASE only if requested. Reports within 30 days. Pays for design by the hour, $9-20 average; for illustration by the hour, $8-18 average. Considers client's budget, skill and experience of artist and turnaround time when establishing payment.

L.M. BRUINIER & ASSOC. INC., 1304 SW Bertha Blvd., Portland OR 97219. (503)246-7412. President: Lou Bruinier. Architectural design/residential planner/publisher of plan books. Clients: contractors and individuals.
Needs: Works with 1-3 freelance artists/year. Uses artists for design and illustration, brochures, catalogs and books. Especially needs 3-dimensional perspectives (basically residential).
First Contact & Terms: Send resume and Photostats or photocopies to be kept on file. Material not filed is not returned. Reports only if interested. Pays for design by the hour, $6-15 average; for illustration by project, $50-700 average. Considers the complexity of project and skill and experience of the artist when establishing payment.

***BRUNNER & BRUNNER, ARCHITECTS & ENGINEERS, INC.,**, Blue Valley Building, 106 S. 7th St., St. Joseph MO 64501. (816)279-0809. President: William A. Brunner. Architectural firm providing architectural and engineering services. Clients: airport hangar analysis, commercial, industrial, institutional, governmental, residential and multifamily construction.
Needs: Uses artists for interior design and interior/architectural renderings.
First Contact & Terms: Artists with three years of experience only. Send brochure to be kept on file; write for appointment to show portfolio. Considers complexity of project, client's budget, skill and experience of artist, turnaround time and rights purchased when establishing payment.

CAMBRIDGE ARCHITECTS INTERNATIONAL INC., 1033 Massachusetts Ave., Cambridge MA 02138. (617)661-4100. Estab. 1985. Architectural/interior design/landscape design firm providing architectural, interior, and landscape design, programming, planning; construction supervision for commercial, industrial, residential and institutional clients.
Needs: Works with 1-5 freelance artists/year. Works on assignment only. Uses artists for interior, landscape and architectural renderings; model making.
First Contact & Terms: Send query letter with brochure showing art style or resume, tear sheets, photostats and photographs. Samples not filed are returned only if requested. Reports only if interested. Call or write to schedule an appointment to show a portfolio, which should include final reproduction/product, color, photographs and b&w. Payment varies. Considers complexity of project, client's budget, skill and experience of artist, and turnaround time when establishing payment.

***THOMAS PAUL CASTRONOVO, ARCHITECT**, 1175 Main St., Akron OH 44310. Clients: Residential and commercial. Mail slides or b&w photos. Reports in 10 days.
Needs: Uses artists for architectural and interior renderings, paintings, sculpture and model building. Pays by job.

CBT/CHILDS BERTMAN TSECKARES & CASENDINO INC., 306 Dartmouth St., Boston MA 02116. (617)262-4354. Architectural/interior and landscape design/urban design planning firm. Clients: developers and owners of offices and multifamily housing projects; institutions (schools and universities, churches, hospitals); government (municipal, state and federal).
Needs: Works with 3 freelance artists/year. Experienced artists in the greater Boston area only. Works on assignment only. Uses artists for brochure design, illustration and layout; landscape, interior and architectural renderings; and model making.
First Contact & Terms: Send query letter with brochure, resume, business card, photostats, slides, photographs and tear sheets to be kept on file; nothing that has to be returned (2-3 samples maximum). Samples not kept on file not returned. Does not report back. Pays for design by the project, $100-1,000 average; for illustration by the project, $50-600 average. Considers complexity of project, skill and experience of artist, and turnaround time when establishing payment.

CHRISMAN, MILLER, WOODFORD, INC., 326 S. Broadway, Lexington KY 40508. (606)254-6623. Contact: Karen A. Jones, ASID. Architectural, interior and landscape design and planning engineering firm. Clients: corporate (commerical, industrial); private (residential—large commissioning only); lo-

cal, state and federal government agencies; and institutional (educational, health care, religious).
Needs: Works with varied number of freelance artists/year. "Artist must be able to come into our offices or to visit job site per project demands. More than 90% of our work is conducted in Kentucky." Works on assignment only. Uses artists for architectural renderings.
First Contact & Terms: Send query letter with brochure/flyer or resume; write for appointment. Samples returned by SASE. Reporting time depends on circumstances of individual projects. Reports back whether to expect possible future assignments. Provide business card, brochure, flyer, samples and tear sheets to be kept on file for possible future assignments. Amount and method of payment vary according to client's budget and contractual agreement.
Tips: "We'll work with anyone, regardless of location. Persons we work with must make themselves readily available to our clients and staff. We will appreciate good art without regard to reputation of artist, etc."

MARK CHRISTY ASSOCIATES, INC., 5135 Liberty Ave., Pittsburgh PA 15224. (412)687-5135. Office Manager: Michael McCallian. Specializes in interior design. Clients: hotels, corporations, medical institutions and residences.
Needs: Works with 3 freelance artists/year. Prefers local artists. Especially needs watercolor. Uses artists for illustrations and renderings of interior settings.
First Contact & Terms: Send query letter with resume and photographs. Samples not filed are returned only if requested. Reports only if interested. Call to show a portfolio, which should include original/final art and color. Considers complexity of project, how work will be used and turnaround time when establishing payment.
Tips: "We like to see the ability of the artist to handle a mixture of styles: traditional, contemporary, architectural and furniture-oriented. Presentation must be finished and professional looking."

FJ CLARK INCORPORATED, 201 S. Murray Ave., Anderson SC 29624. (803)261-3902. President: Frank J. Clark, AIA. Architectural/interior/urban design firm. Clients: institutional, governmental, college and university, industrial and residential.
Needs: Works with approximately 4 freelance artists/year. Works on assignment only. Uses artists for brochure design and layout, interior and landscape design, interior and architectural renderings, and model making.
First Contact & Terms: Send query letter with resume, brochure, photographs, tear sheets or photocopies to be kept on file. Samples are not returned. Reports back only if interested. Pays by the project for design and illustration. Considers complexity of the project, skill and experience of artist and how work will be used when establishing payment.

CONNELLY ABBOTT TRULL P.A., 222 N. Pine, Magnolia AR 71753. (501)234-7008. President: T.G. Connelly. Architectural firm providing complete architectural-engineering services. Clients: residential, institutional, commercial and industrial.
Needs: Works with 4-6 freelance artists/year. Works on assignment only. Uses artists for interior, landscape and architectural renderings; interior design consulting; furnishings; and model making.
First Contact & Terms: Requires 5+ years of experience in artist's area of specialty. Send brochure and color photographs or photocopies to be kept on file. Samples not filed are returned by SASE only if requested. Reports back to artist. Write for appointment to show portfolio. Pays by the hour or by the project for design and illustration. Pay is negotiated. Considers complexity of the project, client's budget, skill and experience of artist, how work will be used, turnaround time and rights purchased when establishing payment.

***COOLIDGE ARCHITECTURAL SERVICES**, 603 Topeka Blvd., Topeka KS 66603. Owner: Phil W. Coolidge. Architectural firm providing architecture, interior architecture and planning for commercial, institutional and industrial clients.
Needs: Works with 1-2 freelance artists/year. Works on assignment only. Uses artists for interior design and renderings, architectural renderings and furnishings. Special needs include liturgical wood carving for a gothic restoration project.
First Contact & Terms: Send query letter with brochure. Samples are filed. Samples not filed are not returned. Reports back only if interested. To show a portfolio, mail photographs. Payment is by contract or service based on artist's proposal. Considers client's budget, skill and experience of artist and how work will be used when establishing payment. Buys all rights.
Tips: "Send descriptive information and photographs. We will contact you for further details."

COPE LINDER ASSOCIATES, 30 South 15th St., Philadelphia PA 19102. (215)981-0200. Contact: Lynda Cloud. Architectural/landscape design firm providing full range of architectural, landscape, urban design and planning services; consulting, planning, design, working drawings, supervision. Cli-

ents: residential, industrial, developer.
Needs: Works on assignment only. Uses artists for brochure design, illustrations and layout; interior, architectural and landscape renderings; and model making.
First Contact & Terms: Send query letter with brochure and photostats, photographs or original work to be kept on file. Call or write for appointment to show portfolio. Samples not filed are returned by SASE. Reports only if interested. Considers complexity of project, client's budget, skill and experience of artist and turnaround time when establishing payment.

***C.R. CORDA, P.A. ARCHITECTURE PLANNING INTERIORS**, Suite 1000, New Tower, 1101 Brickell Ave., Miami FL 33131. (305)579-9126. President: Charles Corda. Architectural/interior design firm providing corporate interiors and architecture. Clients: banks, insurance companies, law firms.
Needs: Works with 6 freelance artists/year. Prefers local artists only. Works on assignment only. Uses artists for interior and architectural renderings and model making.
First Contact & Terms: Send query letter with brochure or resume and samples. Samples are filed. Does not report back. To show a portfolio, mail roughs, color, Photostats and photographs. Considers complexity of project, client's budget, skill and experience of artist and turnaround time when establishing payment. Buys all rights.

***CORRELL/BRADLEY ARCHITECTS**, Box 178, Seymour IN 47274. President-Architect: David W. Correll. Vice President-Architect: Donald H. Bradley. Architectural firm offering all ranges of architectural services. Clients: all types.
Needs: Works with 2-3 freelance artists/year. Uses artists for advertising, brochure, interior and landscape design and architectural renderings.
First Contact & Terms: Send query letter with brochure to be kept on file; write for appointment to show portfolio. Material not filed is returned by SASE only if requested. Reports back only if interested. Pays by contract negotiation. Considers complexity of the project, client's budget, and skill and experience of artist when establishing payment.

MAURICE COURLAND & SON/ARCHITECTS-ENGINEERS-PLANNERS, Central Savings Bank Building, 2112 Broadway, New York NY 10023. (212)362-7018. Contact: R.H. Courland or N.M. Courland. Architecture/engineering/space planning/design firm. Clients: industrial, banks, residential, commercial, restaurants, corporate, financial institutions, government, public and semi-public, institutional and educational.
Needs: Buys 2-6 renderings of new buildings and building restoration work/year. Works on assignment only. Uses artists for architectural and interior renderings, murals/graphics and scale models. Occasionally purchases artwork (paintings; sculputre; etc.).
First Contact & Terms: Send query letter with brochure, resume, business card, and tear sheets to be kept on file. Portfolio should include color photos. SASE. Reports within "weeks." Negotiates pay/project. Certain projects require design and execution; murals; sculpture; paintings; graphics; logos; presentation (color) renderings; exteriors and interiors. Considers complexity of project, client's budget, skill and experience of artist and how work will be used when establishing payment.

THE CRAYCROFT ARCHITECTS, INC., Suite 1200, 4131 N. Central, Dallas TX 75204, (214)522-6060. Vice President: Don H. Price. Architectural firm providing programming, design, construction documents, project administration. Clients: multifamily housing, hotels, country club facilities, commercial office buildings, retail shopping centers.
Needs: Works with 2-3 freelance artists/year. Local artists mainly; credentials necessary. Works on assignment only. Uses artists for architectural renderings and model making; more presentation type material is needed for neighborhood opposition meetings, planning and zoning meetings, public hearings, governmental approvals, etc.
First Contact & Terms: Call for appointment to show portfolio. Pays for illustration by the project, $500-1,500. Considers complexity of project, client's budget, skill and experience of artist, how work will be used and turnaround time when establishing payment.

CREATIVE RETAILING, INC., Suite 265, 2222 Martin St., Irvine CA 92715. (714)476-8611. President: Clark Richey. Store planning and design firm. Plans, designs and installs retail speciality chain stores including space planning, fixturing, decor design, visual merchandise presentation and establishment of image.
Needs: Works on assignment only. Uses artists for advertising and brochure design and illustration, brochure layout, interior design, interior and architectural renderings, design consulting, furnishings, charts and model making.
First Contact & Terms: Send query letter with brochure showing art style or resume, tear sheets, Photostats, photocopies and photographs. Reports within 30 days. Call to schedule an appointment to

show a portfolio, which should include final reproduction/product, color, Photostats, and photographs. Pays for design by the project, $250-4,000. Pays for illustration by the project, $250-1,500 average. "All creative work becomes the property of Creative Retailing." Considers complexity of project, client's budget, and skill and experience of artist when establishing payment.
Tips: "Artist should have the ability to put on paper what the project designer visualizes, also a progressional presentation."

JERRY CUMMINGS ASSOCIATES INC., Suite 301, 420 Boyd St., Los Angeles CA 90013. (213)621-2756. Contact: Jerry Cummings. Landscape architecture firm. Clients: commercial and residential.
Needs: Assigns 20-30 freelance renderings/year. Works with artists for landscape architectural renderings. Works on assignment only.
First Contact & Terms: Send query letter with brochure showing art style or resume and photographs. Reports within 2 weeks. Samples returned by SASE. Reports back on future possibilities. Call or write to schedule an appointment to show portfolio, which should include original/final art. Pays for illustration by the hour, $25-35. Considers complexity of project, client's budget, and skill and experience of artist when establishing payment.

DAT CONSULTANTS LTD., SFA, 118 W. 16th St., New York NY 10011. (212)741-2121. Architect: S. Fernandez. Architecture and interior design firms. Clients: industrial, residential, commercial and institutional.
Needs: Assigns 10 jobs and buys 10 renderings/year. Prefers local artists. Uses artists for renderings, interior design, sculptures, graphics and scale models.
First Contact & Terms: Query with resume or arrange interview to show portfolio. Reports in 1 week. Pays $200-400/job or $15-25/hour.

JOHN LAWRENCE DAW & ASSOCIATES, 912 Baltimore Ave., Kansas City MO 64105. (816)474-9410. Architect: J.L. Daw; Interior Design: Ms. Becky Beilharz. Architectural/interior design firm. Clients: commercial, institutional.
Needs: Uses artists for brochure design and layout, interior design, architectural renderings and model making.
First Contact & Terms: Send query letter with brochure and resume to be kept on file. Accepts "whatever artist feels is expendable" as samples. Samples not returned. Reports back to artist. Call or write for appointment to show portfolio.

DESIGN COLLABORATIVE ARCHITECTS P.C., 765 Fairfield Ave., Bridgepert CT 06604. (203)576-1720. Managing Architect: Patrick Rose. Architectural/interior design firm. Services: architecture, planning, interior design, master planning. Clients: commercial, residential, corporate and industrial facilities.
Needs: Works with 10 freelance artists/year. Works on assignment only. Uses artists for advertising, brochure and interior design; advertising and interior illustrations; architectural renderings, design consulting, furnishings, charts and model making.
First Contact & Terms: Send query letter with brochure showing art style or resume, slides and photographs. Samples not filed are returned by SASE. Reports only if interested. Call or write to schedule an appointment to show a portfolio, which should include roughs, final reproduction/product, color and photographs. Negotiates payment. Considers complexity of project, skill and experience of artist, and turnaround time when establishing payment.
Tips: "Quality work and timely service response to requested need."

THE DESIGNPOINT, 307 Laurel St., San Diego CA 92101. (619)234-2565. President: R. Milberg. Art Director: Kerry Summers. Interior and graphic design firm also providing space planning, corporate identity, package design. Clients: commercial.
Needs: Works with 10 freelance artists/year. Local, qualified artists only. Works on assignment only. Uses artists for brochure illustration, interior and architectural renderings, and model making.
First Contact & Terms: Send query letter with brochure showing art style or resume to be kept on file. Reports only if interested. Call for appointment to show portfolio, which should include original/final art and final reproduction/product. Pays for design and illustration by the project, $200 minimum. Considers complexity of project, client's budget, and skill and experience of artist when establishing payment.

ROBERT E. DES LAURIERS, A.I.A., ARCHITECT & ASSOCIATES, 9349 El Cajon Blvd., La Mesa CA 92041. (619)469-0135. President: Robert E. Des Lauriers, A.I.A. Architectural firm providing architectural services for churches, schools, commercial and residential interior design.
Needs: Works with 6-10 freelance artists/year. Local artists only with strong background. Works on as-

signment only. Uses artists for brochure illustration; interior and landscape design and renderings; architectural renderings, design consulting, furnishings and model making.
First Contact & Terms: Send query letter with brochure, resume, business card and photographs to be kept on file. Samples returned only if requested. Reports within 10 days. Write for appointment to show portfolio. Pays for design and for illustration in lump sum. Considers complexity of project, client's budget, skill and experience of artist and how work will be used when establishing payment.

WILLIAM DORSKY ASSOCIATES, 23200 Chagrin Blvd., Cleveland OH 44122. (216)464-8600. Contact: Alex Espinosa. Architecture firm. Clients: commercial, residential, institutional.
Needs: Works with artists for architectural renderings, interior design, graphic design, signage design, model making, sculpture, and landscape design. Works on assignment only.
First Contact & Terms: Call for interview to show photos or transparencies. Samples returned by SASE; reports back on future assignment possibilities. Provide resume and brochure to be kept on file.
Tips: "Prepare reproducible examples of work that can be kept on file for ready reference."

DURRANT GROUP, One Cycare Plaza, Dubuque IA 52001. (319)583-9131. Interior Designer: Jane Jewell-Vitale. Architectural firm. Services: architectural, interior design, engineering and construction management. Clients: commercial and some residential.
Needs: Works with 4-5 freelance artists/year. Works on assignment only. Uses artists for interior design. "Currently looking for a weaver for custom work."
First Contact & Terms: Send query letter with brochure showing art style. Samples not filed are returned only if requested. Reports only if interested. Call to show a portfolio, which should include original/final art and photographs. Negotiates payment. Considers client's budget when establishing payment.
Tips: Artist should "be organized and efficient."

EHNI ASSOCIATES, LTD., ARCHITECTS & INTERIOR DESIGNERS, 16 Charlotte St., Charleston SC 29403. (803)577-0410. Contact: Scott Sampson. Architectural/interior design firm providing complete services.
Needs: Works with 6-8 freelance artists/year. Works on assignment only. Uses artists for brochure illustration, interior and architectural renderings, design consulting, model making and photography.
First Contact & Terms: Send query letter with brochure, resume, photographs and tear sheets to be kept on file. Reports back to artist. Call or write for appointment to show portfolio. Pay varies according to artistic talents and project needs. Considers complexity of project, client's budget, skill and experience of artist, how work will be used, turnaround time and rights purchased when establishing payment.

FALICK/KLEIN PARTNERSHIP, INC., Suite 1900, 5847 San Felipe, Houston TX 77057-3005. (713)782-9000. Contact: David G. Puckett. Architectural/interior design firm providing full services. Clients: institutional (hospitals), developers, governmental, financial, professional office buildings.
Needs: Works with 10-30 freelance artists/year. "Experienced, innovative" artists only. Uses artists for advertising illustration and layout, brochure design; interior, landscape and architectural renderings and model making.
First Contact & Terms: Send query letter with brochure to be kept on file. Reports only if interested. Write for appointment to show portfolio.

FEICK ASSOCIATES, 224 E. Water St., Sandusky OH 44870. (419)625-2554. Architect: John A. Feick. Architectural firm providing complete architectural services. Clients: residential, commercial and industrial.
Needs: Works with 1 freelance artist/year. Works on assignment only. Uses artists for architectural renderings.
First Contact & Terms: Send query letter with brochure showing art style. Reports only if interested. Call to schedule an appointment to show a portfolio, which should include thumbnails, roughs and original/final art. Pays for design and illustration by the project, $200 minimum. Considers complexity of project and client's budget when establishing payment.
Tips: "Be brief and concise in contact."

FEREBEE, WALTERS AND ASSOCIATES, Box 2029, Charlotte NC 28211. (704)542-5586. Architectural/planning/interior/graphics and landscape design firm providing complete environmental design and planning services. Clients: residential, commercial, industrial, institutional.
Needs: Works with 2-3 freelance artists/year. Uses artists for interior and architectural renderings.
First Contact & Terms: Send query letter with brochure, resume and tear sheets; also send samples and business cards. Prefers to see samples that are best illustration of talent. Samples not returned. Does not report back. Considers complexity of project, client's budget, skill and experience of artist, how work will be used, turnaround time and rights purchased when establishing payment.

ROBERT P. GERSIN ASSOCIATES, 11 E. 22nd St., New York NY 10010. President: Robert P. Gersin. Industrial design firm providing interiors, architecture, graphics, packaging, products and exhibits.
Needs: Works with freelance designers/technicians for implementation assistance to permanent staff on various projects.
First Contact & Terms: Send query letter with resume tear sheets, photostats, photocopies, slides or photographs. Prefers slides as samples. Samples returned by SASE. Reports in 2-3 weeks. To show portfolio, mail thumbnails, roughs, final reproduction/product, photographs or b&w. Negotiates payment. Considers client's budget, skill and experience of designer/technician and how work will be used when establishing payment.
Tips: "Be professional and pay attention to details. Develop skills and interest in professional work instead of focusing on money and short-term commitments."

***GERSON/OVERSTREET**, #804, 57 Post St., San Francisco CA 94104. (415)989-3830. President: Harry L. Overstreet. Architectural firm providing a complete spectrum of services in architecture, planning and urban design. Clients: residential, industrial and governmental.
Needs: Works with 2 freelance artists/year. Prefers local artists with 5 years of experience. Works on assignment only. Uses artists for brochure design and illustration, interior design, architectural renderings and model making.
First Contact & Terms: Send resume and samples. Samples are filed. Reports back. Call to schedule an appointment to show a portfolio, which should include final reproduction/product and color. Pays for design by the hour, by the project and by the day. Pays for illustration by the project. Considers client's budget and skill and experience of artist when establishing payment.

GHOTING ASSOCIATES, 8501 Potomac Ave., College Park MD 20740. (301)474-3719. Contact: Vinod M. Ghoting, AIA. Architectural/interior design/urban design firm providing complete architectural, urban design and interior design services, from schematic design through construction documents and management. Clients: residential, institutional, medical, commercial and industrial.
Needs: Works with 1 freelance artist/year. Local artists only at this time. Works on assignment only. Uses artists for interior design and renderings.
First Contact & Terms: Send query letter with photographs and photostats to be kept on file. Reports within 15 days. To show a portfolio, mail appropriate materials, which should include photostats. Pays for design by the hour, $12-20; pays for illustration by the project, $250-500. Considers clients budget, complexity of project, skill and experience of artist when establishing payment.

GIFFELS ASSOCIATES INC., 25200 Telegraph, Southfield MI 48086-5025. Administrator: D. Lewis. Architectural firm providing architecture and engineering. Clients: industrial, institutional and commercial.
Needs: Works with 3-4 freelance artists/year. Local artists only with 5 years of experience. Works on assignment only. Uses artists for advertising and brochure design and layout.
First Contact & Terms: Send query letter with brochure showing art style. Samples not filed are returned by SASE. Reports only if interested. To show a portfolio, write to schedule an appointment. Pays by the project. Considers complexity of project, skill and experience of artist, and turnaround time when establishing payment.

GREEN & ASSOCIATES, Suite C-26, 105 S. Alfred, Alexandria VA 22314. (703)370-3078. Contact: James F. Green. Interior design firm providing residential and contract interior design and space planning plus custom furniture design. Clients: residential, corporate offices and retail design.
Needs: Number of freelance artists used/year varies. Prefers local artists; "sometimes we require onsite inspections." Works on assignment only. Uses artists for interior design and interior and architectural renderings.
First Contact & Terms: Send query letter with brochure, resume and photostats or photographs, color preferred, to be kept on file. Reports only if interested. Pays for design and illustration by the project, $250 minimum. "Persons we work with must be able to make themselves available to our clients and staff. We will appreciate good art without regard to reputation of artist, etc." Considers complexity of project, client's budget and skill and experience of artist when establishing payment.

GRESHAM, SMITH AND PARTNERS, 504-A Brookwood Blvd, Birmingham AL 35209. (205)870-4455. Interior Architecture Administrative: Angela A. Lackey. Architectural/interior/landscape/engineering firm for corporate, commercial, healthcare and government clients.
Needs: Works with a various number of freelance artists/year. Works on assignment only. Uses artists for interior design.
First Contact & Terms: Send query letter with brochure showing art style or resume, tear sheets and photographs. Samples not filed are returned by SASE only if requested by artist. Reports back only if in-

terested. To show a portfolio, mail appropriate materials that are representative. Pays for design and illustration by the project. Considers client's budget, skill and experience of artist, how work will be used and price of artwork when establishing payment.

JOHN HAINES, ASSOCIATES, INC., (formerly John D. Haines, Architects and Planners, Inc.) Route 7, Manchester VT 05254-0403. (802)362-3776. Contact: Marian Louise. Architectural firm providing total design/planning services. Clients: commercial, governmental, residential, educational, cultural.
Needs: Works with 5-6 freelance artists/year. Works on assignment only. Uses artists for brochure illustration, landscape design and renderings, architectural renderings, furnishings and model making. Especially needs artists for renderings.
First Contact & Terms: Send resume and business card to be kept on file. Reports back only if interested. Considers complexity of the project, skill and experience of artist and turnaround time when establishing payment.

HANSEN LIND MEYER, 455 S. Orange Ave., Orlando FL 32801. (305)422-7061. Director of Design: Charles W. Cole, Jr. Architectural/interior design firm providing complete architecture and engineering services. Clients: commercial, health care, justice and government.
Needs: Works with 6 freelance artists/year. Works on assignment only. Uses artists for interior, landscape and architectural renderings, maps and model making.
First Contact & Terms: Send query letter with resume and samples. Samples not filed are returned only if requested. Reports only if interested. To show a portfolio, mail thumbnails, final reproduction/product, color and photographs. Pays for illustrations by the project, $400-3,500. Considers complexity of project, client's budget, skill and experience of artist, and turnaround time when establishing payment.

***A. CALVIN HOILAND ARCHITECT**, 2826-3rd Ave. S., Great Falls MT 59405. (406)761-0594. Owner: Cal Hoiland. Architectural firm providing architectural, interior design, acoustical, mechanical, landscaping, structural and electrical design services. Clients: commercial, public, institutional, residential, industrial, educational and fraternal.
Needs: Works with 1 freelance artist/year. Works on assignment only. Uses artists for brochure layout, architectural renderings, design consulting and furnishings.
First Contact & Terms: Send query letter with brochure. Samples are filed. Samples not filed are returned. Reports back only if interested. Call to schedule an appointment to show a portfolio. Payment "depends on services required." Considers complexity of project, client's budget, skill and experience of artist and how work will be used when establishing payment. Buys all rights.

***HOLLYRIDE GALLERY**, Interior Planning Consultants, 1208 22nd Ave., Meridian MS 39301. Planner/Designer: Judith McMullan. Interior design firm and designers' showroom stocking consignment artwork. Clients: institutional and residential.
Needs: Works with 4 freelance artists/year. Uses artists for brochure layout, and interior and architectural renderings; also "we place paintings and graphics, weavings, sculpture, etc., in interiors of public institutions."
First Contact & Terms: Experienced artists only. Works on assignment only. Send brochure to be kept on file. Write for artists' guidelines. Prefers slides or photographs as samples; may also consider original work. Samples not kept on file are returned only if requested. Reports only if interested. Pay varies according to assignment. Considers complexity of project, client's budget, and skill and experience of artist when establishing payment.

***HOLSHOUSER & ASSOCIATES**, 219 N. Clark Ave., Cape Girardeau MO 63701. (314)334-6422. Architect: Thomas C. Holshouser, AIA. Architectural firm providing architectural design services. Clients: commercial (90%), residential (10%).
Needs: Uses artists for architectural renderings.
First Contact & Terms: Send brochure to be kept on file. Reports only if interested. Works on assignment only. Pays for design and illustration by the project, $400-1,000 average. Considers complexity of project and skill and experience of artist when establishing payment.

HUNTER/MILLER & ASSOCIATES, 225 N. Fairfax St., Alexandria VA 22314. (703)548-0600. President: Jeffrey Miller. Architectural/interior design/landscape design firm offering comprehensive services. Clients: commercial, institutional, government.
Needs: Works with 1-2 freelance artists/year. "Experienced, quality artists" only. Works on assignment only. Uses artists for brochure design, illustration and layout; interior design and renderings; architectural renderings, design consulting, furnishings, charts, maps and model making.
First Contact & Terms: Send query letter with brochure, resume, business card and samples to be kept

on file. Reports back only if interested. Call or write to schedule an appointment to show a portfolio, which should include orignal/final art. Pays for design and illustration by the hour, $5-25. Considers skill and experience of artist and client's budget when establishing payment.

***JOHN A. IACOPI & ASSOC., LTD.**, 3182 Doolittle Dr., Northbrook IL 60062. (312)498-3994. President: John A. Iacopi. Architectural/engineering firm serving medical, institutional, educational clients.
Needs: Uses freelance artists for interior and architectural renderings.
First Contact & Terms: Send query letter with brochure. Samples are filed. Samples not filed are returned only if requested. Write to schedule an appointment to show a portfolio, which should include original/final art. Pays for design and illustration by the day, $200-500. Considers client's budget and skill and experience of artist when establishing payment. Buys all rights.
Tips: "We use traditional works of art, and watercolors."

IDENTITA INCORPORATED, Suite 515, 1000 N. Ashley Dr., Tampa FL 33602. (813)221-3326. Interior and graphic design firm providing consultative services to health care facilities. Clients: institutional, hospitals, courthouses and parking garages.
Needs: Works with 3 freelance artists/year. Works on assignment only. Uses artists for architectural renderings, interior and graphic design and signage.
First Contact & Terms: Send query letter. Samples returned. Reports within 2 weeks. Payment varies according to job.

THE IMAGE GROUP, 398 S. Grant Ave., Columbus OH 43215. (614)221-1016. Contact: Richard Henry Eiselt. Architecture/interior design firm. Clients: commercial.
Needs: Uses artists for restaurant design, architectural and full-color renderings, graphic and interior design, paintings, sculpture, signs and wall art.
First Contact & Terms: Mail photos or transparencies. Pay varies according to client's budget, and skill and experience of artist.

INTERACTIVE RESOURCES, INC., 117 Park Place, Pt. Richmond CA 94801. (415)236-7435. Marketing Director: Donna Sidel Straus. Architecture/interior design, investigation of construction defects and structural engineering. Clients: corporations, municipal governments, attorneys and lenders.
Needs: Works with 1-3 freelance artists/year. Uses artists for architectural renderings.
First Contact & Terms: Send query letter with resume and samples. Samples not filed are returned only if requested. Call to schedule an appointment to show a portfolio. Considers complexity of project, client's budget and skill and experience of artist when establishing payment.
Tips: "Be direct to our needs and show me only examples of your renderings that relate to our types of projects."

***INTRAPRO/ATLANTA**, Box 7962, Atlanta GA 30357. Executive Director: James J. Bachteler. Architectural/interior and landscape design/photography/graphics firm. Clients: residential, commercial. Specializes in greeting cards, displays, automobile racing promotion and photography, package design and point-of-purchase.
Needs: Works with 10 freelance artists/year. Uses artists for advertising and brochure design, landscape and interior design, architectural and interior renderings, design consulting and furnishings.
First Contact & Terms: Send query letter with brochure, resume and business card to be kept on file. Write for appointment to show portfolio; write for artists' guidelines. Reports within days. Pay varies according to assignment. Considers complexity of project, client's budget, skill and experience of artist, how work will be used, turnaround time and rights purchased when establishing payment.

JAMES ARCHITECTS & ENGINEERS, INC., Suite 122, 120 Monument Cir., Indianapolis IN 46204. (317)631-0880. Director Corporation Communications: Theresa Thompson. Architectural/interior design firm providing architectural, engineering, interior design, planning design and construction administration. Clients: government, corporate, institutional, criminal justice, commercial and industrial.
Needs: Works with 3-4 freelance artists/year. "Some projects/clients would prefer local artists." Works on assignment only. Uses artists for advertising design, brochure design and illustration, architectural renderings, photographs, environmental art and sculpture.
First Contact & Terms: Send query letter with brochure showing art style or resume, tear sheets, photostats, slides and photographs. Samples filed, returned only if requested. Reports only if interested. Call to schedule an appointment to show a portfolio, which should include roughs, final reproduction/product, color and photographs. Pays for design by the hour, $15-70. Pays for illustration by the hour, $15-70. Considers complexity of project, client's budget, skill and experience of artist, and turnaround time when establishing payment.

***JAMES, DURANT, MATTHEWS & SHELLEY A.I.A.**, 128 E. Liberty St., Sumter SC 29150. (803)773-3318. Architects: J.E. Matthews and W.D. Shelley. Architectural firm. Clients: educational, commercial, ecclesiastical.
Needs: Works with 1 freelance artist/year. Uses artists for architectural renderings.
First Contact & Terms: Seeks "good, imaginative work." Works on assignment only. Send query letter with brochure to be kept on file; call or write for appointment to show portfolio. Material not filed returned by SASE. Reports only if interested. Pays for illustration by the project, $250-800 average. Considers complexity of project, client's budget, and skill of artist when establishing payment.

BEN H. JOHNSON & ASSOCIATES, Suite 123, Executive Plaza, 12835 Bellevue-Redmond Rd., Bellevue WA 98005. (206)455-5502. Principal: Ben H. Johnson, AIA. Architectural/interior design firm providing architecture, planning and interior design. Clients: single family and multi-family residential, retail, offices, churches, libraries; yacht and corporate aircraft interiors.
Needs: Works with 6 freelance artists/year. Artists must exhibit "a willingness to meet time and/or cost deadline (or not accept the commission)." Works on assignment only. Uses artists for brochure illustration, interior and architectural renderings, landscape design and model making.
First Contact & Terms: Send query letter with resume, business card, photostats, slides, photographs, photocopies or tear sheets. Reports within 1 week. Call for appointment to show portfolio. Pays by the hour, $8-22 average for design, $6-18 average for illustration. Considers complexity of the project, client's budget, skill and experience of artist, and rights purchased when establishing payment.
Tips: "There is a tremendous hesitancy to use artistic graphics except in the largest projects. It is only after a design and contract drawings are nearly complete that graphic art is required for sales and/or publicity presentations."

LAWRENCE KASSER ASSOCIATES, ARCHITECTS AND PLANNERS, Box 495, Bellows Falls VT 05101. (802)463-9576. President: Lawrence Kasser. Architectural/interior design/landscape design firm providing design, construction documents and promotional material. Clients: commercial, residential, institutional, developers.
Needs: Works with 3 freelance artists/year. Uses artists for brochure design, illustration and layout; interior and landscape design and renderings; architectural renderings, design consulting, furnishings, architectural photography, promotional film production, and model making.
First Contact & Terms: New England area artists only, with 3 years of experience. Works on assignment basis. Send query letter with brochure and samples to be kept on file; write for appointment to show portfolio. Prefers slides as samples. Reports within 3 weeks. Pays for design and illustration by the hour. Considers client's budget when establishing payment.

GEROLD F. KESSLER & ASSOCIATES INC., 2101 S. Clermont, Denver CO 80222. (303)756-1536. Contact: Gerold Kessler. Landscape/architecture/project planning firm providing consulting services as project planners/land planners/landscape designers. Clients: residential and industrial.
Needs: Works with 1 artist for architectural renderings; 1, graphic design; 1, model making; and 1, landscape design. Local artists only. Works on assignment only. Also uses artists for site plans and subdivision development layout.
First Contact & Terms: Send query letter with resumes. Reports within 1 week. Call or write to schedule an appointment to show a portfolio, which should include Photostats and photographs. Samples returned by SASE. Pays $500-700, landscape and general site renderings; $600-1,000, subdivision land plan; $20-50/hour for design and illustration.

FRANCIS KOO & ASSOCIATES, INC., Suite 105, 601 University Ave., Sacramento CA 95825. (916)924-1375. Chief Architect: Francis Koo. Clients: commercial, industrial, military, institutional and residential.
Needs: Assigns 20 jobs/year. Works on assignment only. Works with 3 artists for architectural renderings; 3, interior design; 1, graphic design; 1, advertising art; 2, signage design; 2, model making; 2, murals; 1, wall hangings; 2, landscape design; and 1, charts/graphs.
First Contact & Terms: Send query letter with resume, business card and brochure to be kept on file. SASE. Reports in 1 week. Samples returned by SASE; reports back on future assignment possibilities. To show a portfolio, mail appropriate materials or write to schedule an appointment; portfolio should include anything that indicates quality. Maximum payment: $1,600, architectural renderings; $1,500, art

The asterisk before a listing indicates that the listing is new in this edition. New markets are often the most receptive to freelance submissions.

renderings; $3,000, graphic design; $15,000, scale models; $5,000, signs; $250,000, murals and sculpture. Pays minimum $500. Negotiates payment for paintings and wall art. Considers complexity of project, skill and experience of artist and turnaround time when establishing payment.
Tips: "We like to have a name list in different type of service artists provide, then we can contact them when we need that kind of service."

***KORDYS PUZIO & DITOMASSO, ARCHITECTS & PLANNERS**, 1310 Hamburg Tpk., Wayne NJ 07470. Partner: Henry Puzio. Architectural firm providing architectural design, construction administration and interior design. Clients: residential, commercial, public, industrial and medical.
Needs: Works with 1-2 freelance artists/year. Artists "must be experienced; quality of work is most important." Uses artists for interior and landscape design, architectural renderings and model making.
First Contact & Terms: Send query letter with brochure. Samples are not filed. Samples not filed are returned only if requested. Reports back only if interested. Write to schedule an appointment to show a portfolio, which should include photographs. Pays for design and illustration by the project, $500 minimum. Considers skill and experience of artist when establishing payment. Buys all rights.
Tips: "Send a brochure or copies of several projects. We are looking for work in pen & ink, pencil and tempera."

***KROCHINA ARCHITECTS, AIA**, Suite 303, 3501 Denali St., Anchorage AK 99803. (907)276-2241. Owner: Pat Krochina. Architectural firm.
Needs: Works with 6 freelance artists/year. Uses artists for brochure layout and architectural renderings. Especially needs color work (acrylics, oils, water) and renderings of architectural projects from blueprints.
First Contact & Terms: Send query letter with brochure, resume, business card and architectural renderings. Samples will be filed. Samples not filed are returned by SASE if requested. Reports back only if interested. Pays for illustration by the project, $300-900. Considers complexity of project, client's budget, skill and experience of artist and turnaround time when establishing payment.

LABUNSKI ASSOCIATES ARCHITECTS, Suite A3, 3301 S. Expressway 83, Harlingen TX 78550. (512)428-4334. President: R.A. Labunski. Architectural firm providing architecture, planning, construction, management, design, space planning, interiors, advertising. Clients: commercial, retail, residential, corporate, banks, hotel/motel/restaurant and schools.
Needs: Works with 5 freelance artists/year. Works on assignment only. Uses artists for advertising design, illustration and layout; brochure design, interior and architectural renderings, design consulting, furnishings and model making.
First Contact & Terms: Desires "affordable, practical" artists with referrals/references. Send query letter with brochure, resume and business card to be kept on file; also send samples. Samples returned by SASE. Reports within 2 weeks. Call or write for appointment to show portfolio. Pays by the project. Considers complexity of project, client's budget, and skill and experience of artist when establishing payment.

JOSEPH LADD & ASSOCIATES, P.C., 2405 Westwood Ave., Richmond VA 23230. (804)355-0849. President: Joseph N. Ladd, AIA, CCS. Architectural firm providing architecture, interior design and space planning. Clients: private sector; federal, state and local governments.
Needs: Works with 1 freelance artist/year. Artist must have work experience. Works on assignment only. Uses artists for architectural renderings, interior, landscape and graphic design, furnishings, design consulting, model making and signage.
First Contact & Terms: Send brochure/flyer, business card and resume to be kept on file. Reports in 1 week. Payment varies according to the job.
Tips: Artists "must maintain quality workmanship."

LANDOW AND LANDOW ARCHITECTS, PC, 3000 Marcus Ave., Lake Success NY 11042. (516)326-1111. President, AIA: Lloyd J. Landow. Architectural/interior design firm providing complete architectural, space planning and interior design services. Clients: corporate and institutional.
Needs: Uses artists for architectural renderings and model making. Also commissions for buildings.
First Contact & Terms: Send query letter with brochure, resume, business card, Photostats, photographs and tear sheets to be kept on file. Samples returned by SASE if not kept on file. Reports only if interested. Considers complexity of project, client's budget, skill and experience of artist and turnaround time when establishing payment.

LANE & ASSOCIATES, ARCHITECTS, 1318 N. "B", Box 3929, Fort Smith AR 72913. (501)782-4277. Contact: John E. Lane, AIA-ASID. Architectural and interior design firm providing architecture and interiors for remodeling and new construction; also art consultant. Clients: residential, multifamily,

commercial and industrial.
Needs: Works with 10-12 freelance artists/year. Uses artists occasionally for architectural renderings, charts, graphic design and advertising illustration; selects or commissions art pieces for clients; paintings, drawings, sculpture, photographs, macrame, tapestry (all mediums). Arranges art exhibits for large local bank—"would like sources of talent for various mediums, painting, sculptures, photography, drawings, etc."
First Contact & Terms: Prefers to be able to meet in person with artist. Send query letter with resume, business card, tear sheets slides or photos of work and brochure to be kept on file. Samples returned by SASE, but "would prefer to retain." Write to schedule an appointment to show a portfolio. Payment varies. Considers complexity of project, client's budget, skill and experience of artist, how work will be used, turnaround time and rights purchased when establishing payment.

LOUISVILLE ART GLASS STUDIO, 1110 Baxter Ave., Louisville KY 40204. (502)585-5421. Specializes in art glass and design fabrication. President: Gary D. Meeker. Clients: commercial, residential, churches and related liturgical.
Needs: Works with 2 artists for interior design; 3, graphic design; 2, sculpture; and 4, stained glass. Also uses artists for leaded glass design. Prefers artists with previous glass experience. Works on assignment only.
First Contact & Terms: Query with resume and samples to be kept on file. Reports within 4 weeks. Samples not filed returned by SASE. Prefers slides or photos as samples. Pays by the job, based on square footage and size of work; or by the hour. Pays for design by the hour, $15-50; by the project, 10-25%; or by the day $100-500.
Tips: There are "more good freelance artists availiable now than at any other time but not enough good, qualified craftsmen to execute the work." Artists approaching this firm should have "confidence that our execution will be of the very best quality and the newest techniques."

***McCAULEY ASSOC. INC.**, 1400 S. 20th St., Birmingham AL 35205. (205)933-7100. President: R. Mack Freeman, Jr. Architectural/interior design firm providing design, bid documents, bids, observation of construction. Clients: institutional, health care, commercial.
Needs: Works with 2-3 freelance artists/year. Uses artists for brochure design, interior and landscape design, architectural renderings, design consulting and furnishings.

MAHER & ASSOC. ARCHITECTS SC., 810 N. Plankinton Ave., Milwaukee WI 53203. (414)276-0811. President: J. Thomas Maher A.I.A. Architectural firm providing total architectural and interior design. Clients: industrial, commercial, hotel and medical.
Needs: Works with several freelance artists/year. Works on assignment only. Uses artists for interior and landscape design, interior and architectural renderings, design consulting, furnishings and model making.
First Contact & Terms: Send query letter with brochure showing art style or resume, photostats, photocopies, slides and photographs that can be retained. Samples not filed are returned only if requested. Reports back within 5 days. To show a portfolio, mail photographs and b&w. Pays by the project. Considers design, skill and experience of artist, complexity of project, how work will be used and turnaround time when establishing payment.
Tips: "We use greater freelance artists because we are doing a great deal more work. Contact us immediately."

MARTIN & DETHOFF REGISTERED ARCHITECTS, 422 Franklin St., Reading PA 19602. Contact: Robert S. Martin. Architectural/interior design firm providing architectural, engineering and interior design. Clients: commercial.
Needs: Works with 4 freelance artists/year. Works on assignment only. Uses artists for architectural renderings and furnishings.
First Contact & Terms: Send query letter with resume to be kept on file. Reports back only if interested. Pays for design by the hour, $25-50. Pays for illustration by the project, $500-1,000. Considers complexity and size of project when establishing payment.
Tips: Needs illustrators who are "fast and not expensive." Looks for "strong delineation and color."

THE MATHES GROUP, 201 St. Charles Ave., 23rd Floor, New Orleans LA 70170. (504)586-9303. President: Edward C. Mathes. Architectural/interior design/landscape design firm providing all services associated with architecture, landscape architecture and interior design. Clients: commercial (90%) and residential (10%).
Needs: Works with 10 freelance artists/year. Works on assignment only. Uses artists for interior design, architectural renderings, design consulting, furnishings, model making and as sources for artwork.
First Contact & Terms: Send query letter with brochure, resume, samples and tear sheets to be kept on

file unless unsuitable. Prefers slides, photographs, clear photocopies as samples. Samples not kept on file returned only if requested. Reports only if interested. Write for appointment to show portfolio. Pays by the project for design and illustration. Considers complexity of project, client's budget, and skill and experience of artist when establishing payment.

***MCA—MALCOLM CAMPBELL & ASSOCIATES**, 19640 Hwy. 305 NE, Poulsbo WA 98370. (206)779-2249. Architect: Malcolm Campbell. Architectural firm providing architecture, planning and feasibility studies for residential, commercial, institutional clients.
Needs: Works with 3-4 freelance artists/year. Works on assignment only. Uses artists for advertising design and illustration, brochure design, interior design, landscape design and renderings, architectural renderings, furnishings and model making.
First Contact & Terms: Send brochure showing art style or resume and photocopies. Samples are filed. Samples not filed are returned only if requested by artist. Reports back within 1 month. Write to schedule an appointment to show a portfolio which should include roughs, original/final art and final reproduction/product. Pays for design by the hour, $10-30. Pays for illustration by the hour, $10 minimum, "maximum open." Considers complexity of project, client's budget and how work will be used when establishing payment. Buys all rights.

METCALF HAEFNER ARCHITECTS, 1052 Main St., Stevens Point WI 54481. (715)344-7205. Partner: Michael Metcalf. Architectural firm providing building design, planning, energy design, interior design and rendering. Clients: residential, commercial, industrial, medical and religious.
Needs: Works with 3 freelance artists/year. Uses artists for advertising, interior and landscape design; landscape and architectural renderings, furnishings and model making.
First Contact & Terms: Send brochure, resume, business card and samples to be kept on file. Call or write for appointment to show portfolio. Pays by the project. Considers complexity of the project, client's budget, and skill and experience of artist when establishing payment.
Tips: "We occasionally enter national competitions in partnership with artists of our choosing."

MEYER SCHERER AND ROCKCASTLE, LTD., 325 Second Ave. N., Minneapolis MN 55401. Principal: Garth Rockcastle. Architecture/interior and landscape design firm providing design, document preparation and construction supervision. Clients: residential, commercial, institutional and industrial.
Needs: Works with 5-6 freelance artists/year. Works on assignment only. Uses artists for exterior, interior and landscape design; brochure design and layout, design consulting. "We occasionally enter national competitions in partnership with artists of our choosing without reimbursement to the artist unless we are winners. Contact for details. We also collaborate with artists on special projects such as stained glass or building furniture."
First Contact & Terms: Send query letter with resume and slides. Samples not filed are returned by SASE. Reports only if interested. Write to schedule an appointment to show a portfolio, which should include roughs, original/final art and color. Pays for design and illustration by the hour, $15-40; or by the project. Considers complexity of project, client's budget, skill and experience of artist, how work will be used, turnaround time and rights purchased when establishing payment.
Tips: Looks for "innovation and understanding of architecture. Don't ask questions about what we might be particularly interested in."

***NOE & NOE ARCHITECTS**, 539 Cooke St., Honolulu HI 96813-5235. (808)533-7836. Contact: Joyce or Leon Noe. Architectural/interior design firm providing planning, design, special services, and consultant services. Clients: commercial, institutional, governmental.
First Contact and Terms: Artists must be "technically competent in their chosen field and able to provide accurate drawings and budgets to demonstrate adequately how their work fits in with the project." Send query letter with resume and samples to be kept on file. Call or write for appointment to show portfolio. Prefers to see original work. Samples returned if not kept on file. Reports within 2 weeks. Works on assignment only. Payment figures "are negotiated with each artist individually and privately." Considers complexity of project, client's budget, skill and experience of artist, how work will be used, and turnaround time when establishing payment.

CHARLES E. NOLAN JR & ASSOCIATES, Box 1788, Alamogordo NM 88310. (505)437-1405. Additional office: Suite 212, 6121 Indian School Rd. NE, Albuquerque NM 87110. (505)881-0821. President: Charles E. Nolan, Jr. Architectural firm providing architectural design, interior design, feasibility studies and master planning. Clients: commercial, institutional, educational, government.
Needs: Works with 2-3 freelance artists/year. Uses artists for architectural renderings, furnishings, murals and sculpture in building design.
First Contact & Terms: Send query letter with brochure, slides and photos (color or b&w) to be kept on file. Samples returned if not kept on file. Reports within 14 days. Pays for design by the hour, $10-40

average; by the day, $100-300 average. Pays for illustration by the hour, $10-15 average. Considers complexity of project, skill and experience of artist and how work will be used when establishing payment.

THE OSBORNE ASSOCIATES, 161 W. Wisconsin Ave., Milwaukee WI 53203. (414)271-0123. Principal: Edward Osborne. Architectural firm offering full architectural and engineering services for any type of project. Clients: residential developers, commercial and cemetery owners (mausoleums).
Needs: Works with freelance artists 6 times/year. Works on assignment only. Uses artists for landscape design and architectural renderings.
First Contact & Terms: Send query letter with brochure and resume to be kept on file. Call for appointment to show portfolio. Accepts any type of samples. Samples not filed are returned. Reports within 10 days. Pays for illustration by the project, $300-700 average. Considers complexity of the project, and skill and experience of artist when establishing payment.
Tips: Especially looks for "accuracy, life-like quality and detail" in samples or portfolio.

OSSIPOFF, SNYDER & ROWLAND (ARCHITECTS) INC., 1210 Ward Ave., Honolulu HI 96814. President: Sidney E. Snyder, Jr., AIA. Architecture/interior design firm. Clients: commercial (offices), residential, institutional and religious.
Needs: Works with 5-10 freelance artists/year. Artist should be in Hawaii for this contact. Works on assignment only. Uses artists for interior design, architectural renderings, furnishings, model making and fine arts in building projects.
First Contact & Terms: Send query letter with brochure showing art style. Reports back. Write to schedule an appointment to show a portfolio. Payment determined by job.
Tips: Interested in high quality.

***PARKEY & PARTNERS ARCHITECTS**, Suite 1310, 3710 Rawlins, Dallas TX 75219. (214)522-4321. Architectural firm providing complete range of architectural services. Clients: commercial, governmental and some residential.
Needs: Works with 6 freelance artists/year. Uses artists for landscape and interior design renderings, architectural renderings, design consulting, furnishings and model making.
First Contact & Terms: Desires artists who are "able to respond quickly to our needs within a reasonable fee." Send query letter with brochure, resume, business card and tear sheets to be kept on file. Call for appointment to show portfolio. Reports only if interested. Works on assignment only. Pay rate depends on artist and project. Considers complexity of project, client's budget, skill and experience of artist and turnaround time when establishing payment.
Tips: Sees artists/designers operating "in a more business-like manner."

PDT & COMPANY ARCHITECTS/PLANNERS, 7434 Montgomery Rd., Cincinnati OH 45236. (513)891-4605. Contact: Ray Gephart.
Needs: Works with 2 artists for architectural renderings; 5, interior design; 1, model making; and 3, landscape design. Uses artists for architectural renderings. Works on assignment only.
First Contact & Terms: Mail samples (examples of finished work). Samples returned by SASE; reports back on future possibilities. Provide business card and brochure to be kept on file. Pays by job.

***PHILLIPS SWAGER ASSOCIATES**, 3622 N. Knoxville, Peo IL 61603. (309)688-9511. Vice President/Design Coordinator: Jim Matarelli. Full-service architectural/engineering/interiors firm serving governmental, health care, education, general practice clients.
Needs: Works with 2-3 freelance artists/year. Works on assignment only. Uses freelance artists for brochure design and architectural renderings.
First Contact & Terms: Send resume and slides. Samples are filed. Samples not filed are not returned. Reports back only if interested. Call or write to schedule an appointment to show a portfolio, which should include thumbnails, color, Photostats, photographs and b&w. Pays for illustration by the hour, $10-20 minimum; by the project, $200 minimum. Considers complexity of project, client's budget, skill and experience of artist, how work will be used and turnaround time.

QUINN ASSOCIATES INC. - ARCHITECTS AIA, 114 W. Main St., New Britain CT 06051. (203)224-2688. President: Richard W. Quinn AIA. Architectural firm providing architectural design, interior design and planning. Clients: commercial, institutional, residential.
Needs: Works with various numbers of freelance artists/year. Works on assignment only. Uses artists for brochure design, interior and architectural renderings, and furnishings.
First Contact & Terms: Send query letter with brochure, resume and samples to be kept on file. Prefers slides or photographs as samples. Samples returned by SASE only if requested. Reports within 30 days. Call or write for appointment to show portfolio. Payment varies with assignment. Considers complexity of project, client's budget, and skill and experience of artist when establishing payment.

***JOHN CREWS RAINEY ASSOCIATES**, 310 E. 55th St., New York NY 10022. Architecture firm. Clients: 95% commercial.
Needs: Works with 3 freelance artists/year. Uses artists for architectural renderings, interior design and building interiors.
First Contact & Terms: Send query letter with samples. Reports within 2 weeks. Provide resume, business card, samples to be kept on file for possible future assignments.

RESEARCH PLANNING ASSOCIATES, 1831 Chestnut St., Philadelphia PA 19103. (215)561-9700. Designer: Susan Klinker. Architectural and interior design firm providing architectural interior design, feasibility studies and architecture. Clients: commercial.
Needs: Works with 1 or 2 freelance artists/year. Uses artists for architectural renderings; interior, graphic and brochure design; interior and landscape art renderings; mural artwork and model making.
First Contact & Terms: Send query letter. Samples returned by SASE. Works on assignment only. Provide resume, business card, brochure, flyer, samples and tear sheets to be kept on file for possible future assignments. Negotiates payment. Pays for design and illustration by the hour. Considers complexity of project, client's budget, skill and experience of artist and turnaround time when establishing payment.

RKT&B (ROTHZEID KAISERMAN THOMSON & BEE, P.C., ARCH & PLANNERS), 134 Charles St., New York NY 10014. Partner: Carmi Bee. Architectural firm that designs buildings (new construction, restoration, rehab., medical facilities, retail, housing, offices).
Needs: Works with 3-10 freelance artists/year. Works on assignment only. Uses artists for brochure design and architectural renderings.
First Contact & Terms: Send query letter with brochure showing art style. Samples not filed are returned by SASE. Reports only if interested. To show a portfolio, mail appropriate materials. Payment varies. Considers complexity of project, client's budget, skill and experience of artist, how work will be used, turnaround time and rights purchased when establishing payment.
Tips: "We rarely use people—we are a longshot."

ROBERT AND COMPANY, 96 Poplar St. NW, Atlanta GA 30335. (404)577-4000. Contact: Marketing Department. Architecture/engineering/planning firm providing marketing and support graphics for company and clients. Clients: industrial, governmental/municipal, educational, military, medical, multi-residential.
Needs: Works with 5-6 freelance artists/year. Local artists preferred. Uses artists for advertising and brochure illustration; landscape, interior and architectural renderings; charts, maps and model makings; also uses photographers.
First Contact & Terms: Send query letter with resume, samples and tear sheets to be kept on file. Prefers photostats, slides, photographs as samples; original work only necessary for interview. Samples not kept on file returned by SASE only if requested. Reports only if interested. Write for appointment to show portfolio. Pays by the project; requests artist's estimate/bid. Considers complexity of project, skill and experience of artist, and turnaround time when establishing payment.

ROE/ELISEO, INC., 576 5th Ave., New York NY 10036. (212)398-1078. Vice President: Phyllis R. Ghougasian. Architecture/interior design firm providing architectural planning, design, interior design and construction services. Clients: health, commercial, industrial, government.
Needs: Works on assignment only. Uses artists for brochure design, illustration and layout; interior and landscape design; interior, landscape and architectural renderings; model making.
First Contact & Terms: Send query letter with resume, slides, photographs or original work to be kept on file. Samples not kept on file are returned by SASE. Reports only if interested. Pays by the project; rate depends on scope of project, fee, structure, etc. Considers client's budget when establishing payment.

***JANET SCHIRN INTERIORS**, 919 N. Michigan Ave., Chicago IL 60611. President: Janet Schirn. Interior design firm providing contract and residential interior design. Clients: business, restaurant and mercantile (wholesale).
Needs: Uses artists for graphics and fine art.
First Contact & Terms: Send letter with resume and samples. Pays by the project. Considers client's budget, and skill and experience of artist when establishing payment.
Tips: "Better quality work is necessary; there is greater client sophistication. Just show your work—no sales pitch."

JEAN SEDOR DESIGNS, 305 S. Main St., Janesville, WI 53545. Interior Designer: Jean Sedor. Interior design firm. "We function as interior designers doing everything from finish schedules to supervising and contracting for entire art programs for various installations." Clients: contract, i.e., banks, insurance companies, utilities, etc.

Needs: Works with freelance artists. Works on assignment only. Uses artists for art furnishings.

First Contact & Terms: Send query letter with brochure, resume, business card, slides, photographs, original work and tear sheets to be kept on file. Samples returned only if requested. Reports only if interested. Call or write for appointment to show portfolio. Pays for design and illustration by the project, $100-12,000 average. Considers client's budget, skill and experience of artist and how work will be used when establishing payment.

RICHARD SEIDEN INTERIORS, 238 N. Allen St., Albany NY 12206. (518)482-8600. President: Richard Seiden. Interior design firm. Provides residential and contract interior design. Clients: residential.

Needs: Works with 4 artists for graphic design; 3, signage design; 2, model making; 3, murals; 4, wall hangings; 3, landscape design; 2, charts/graphs; and 2, stained glass. Works on assignment only.

First Contact & Terms: Send query letter with resume, tear sheets and Photostats. SASE. Reports in 3 weeks. Provide materials to be kept on file for future assignments. Pays $150-1,800, original wall decor; also according to project. To show a portfolio, mail roughs. Pays for design by the hour, $25 minimum. Considers complexity of project, skill and experience of artist, and client's budget when establishing payment.

Tips: Prefers to see photos rather than slides, if possible.

***SEM PARTNERS, INC.**, 100 E. Prince St., Drawer Q, Beckley WV 25802. (304)255-6181. Contact: J. Blair Frier, AIA. Architectural firm offering architectural, planning, engineering, programming, construction administration, consulting. Clients: commercial, residential, education, state and federal, health care.

Needs: Uses artists for interior design, design consulting and model making.

First Contact & Terms: Works on assignment only. Send brochure and samples to be kept on file. Call for appointment to show portfolio. Samples not filed are returned only if requested. Reports within 1 month. Pays for design by the project. Considers complexity of the project and client's budget when establishing payment.

SINCLAIR ASSOCIATES, INC., 15 N. Ellsworth Ave., San Mateo CA 94401. (415)348-6865. Principal Architect: George L. Sinclair. Estab. 1985. Architectural firm providing full architectural design services. Clients: residential, commercial, retail, public and industrial.

Needs: Works with 2-5 freelance artists/year. Works on assignment only. Uses artists for advertising and brochure design and layout; brochure illustration; interior and landscape design, and architectural renderings.

First Contact & Terms: Send query letter with brochure showing art style or resume and photocopies. Samples not filed are not returned. Reports only if interested. Call or write to schedule an appointment to show a portfolio. Considers complexity of project, client's budget, skill and experience of artist, and how work will be used when establishing payment.

SKIDMORE OWINGS AND MERRILL, 1 Maritime Plaza, San Francisco CA 94111. Associate Partner: W. Weber. Architectural firm.

Needs: Works with 10 freelance artists/year. Works on assignment only. Uses artists for interior, landscape and architectural renderings, maps and model making. Especially needs "high quality work."

First Contact & Terms: Send query letter with brochure showing art style or resume, tear sheets, Photostats, photocopies and photographs. Samples not filed are not not returned. Does not report back. To show a portfolio, mail appropriate materials.

Tips: Artist should "show a few excellent examples."

"With the increased competition for the sale of buildings of all types, graphics play a larger role in marketing for an architectural firm. Graphics are also important in marketing the architect's services to potential clients."

—Ben H. Johnson, Ben H. Johnson & Assoc. Bellevue, Washington

SPACE DESIGN INTERNATIONAL, INC., Suite 445, 309 Vine St., Cincinnati OH 45202. (513)241-3000. Director of Communications: Cecily Hudson. Architectural interior and graphic design firm providing programming, space planning, store planning, interior and graphic design. Clients: corporate, professional, retail, institutional.
Needs: Prefers artists with experience; it helps if artists are nearby. Works on assignment only. Uses freelance artists for architectural and interior design renderings, graphic design and model making.
First Contact & Terms: Send query letter with samples and brochure/flyer or resume to be kept on file. Write for appointment to show a portfolio, which should include original work if reviewed in person; if mailed in, prefers reproductions. Samples returned by SASE. Negotiates payment by the project or by the hour; varies according to client's budget.

GEORGE STATEN & ASSOCIATES INC., ARCHITECTS & PLANNERS, Suite 101, 4849 N. Mesa, El Paso TX 79912. (915)544-7000. Contact: George Staten, AIA. Architecture/interior design firm. Clients: residential, institutional, hotel, medical and commercial.
Needs: Works with 3 artists for architectural renderings; 1, interior design; 2, graphic design; 2, signage design; 1, model making; 2, sculpture; 2, landscape design; and 2, stained glass.
First Contact & Terms: Query or write for interview. SASE. Reports in 1 week. Works on assignment only. Provide resume, business card and brochure to be kept on file for future assignments. Pays $200-2,500, architectural renderings; $50-1,000, building interiors; $300-3,000, full-color renderings; $100 minimum, landscape design.

D.J. STEPHANS, AIA, ARCHITECT, 4705 Crescent Rd., Madison WI 53711. (608)274-9235. Architect: Daniel Stephans. Architectural firm providing full architectural services and construction management. Clients: multi and single family housing, churches and offices.
Needs: Works with 1 freelance artist/year. Works on assignment only. Uses artists for advertising and brochure illustration, and interior, landscape and architectural renderings.
First Contact & Terms: Send query letter with brochure and photographs to be kept on file. Samples not filed are returned. Reports back only if interested. Pays for illustration by the project, $85-600 average. Considers complexity of the project, client's budget, skill and experience of artist, how work will be used and turnaround time when establishing payment.

ROBERT J. STURTCMAN—ARCHITECT, Drawer TT, Taos NM 87571. (505)758-4933. Owner: R. Sturtcman. Architectural/interior design firm. Clients: residential, schools and office-retail.
Needs: Uses artists for advertising and brochure design; interior and architectural renderings and model making.
First Contact & Terms: Send query letter with brochure showing art style. Samples not filed are returned by SASE. Reports back within 30 days. Write to schedule an appointment to show a portfolio. Pays for design by the hour, $15 minimum. Considers client's budget when establishing payment.

SUNDBERG, CARLSON AND ASSOCIATES, INC., 914 West Baraga Ave., Marquette MI 49855. (906)228-2333. Designer/Illustrator: Mike Lempinen. Architectural/interior design/engineering firm providing architectural design, interior design, graphic design, illustration architectural renderings, and model making. "We have used freelance rendering and model making services on an as needed basis in the past. We are currently testing the market for brochure, advertising and architectural rendering services, and are especially interested in beginning a file on available art services; freelance, art houses, publication firms, etc. Our firm is also interested in obtaining information on the market demand for art services."
First Contact & Terms: Send query letter with brochure showing art style or resume, tear sheets, Photostats and printed pieces. Samples not filed are not returned. Reports only if interested. To show a portfolio, mail appropriate materials. Pays for design by the hour, $8-50. Pays for illustration by the hour, $10-50. Considers complexity of project, client's budget, and skill and experience of artist when establishing payment.
Tips: "Please do not send returnable pieces, slides or photos. We can not return unsolicited materials."

SWAIN ASSOCIATES, INC., 222 Third St., Cambridge MA 02142. (617)661-3773. Associate: Robyn Jones. Architectural/land design firm providing architecture, urban design, land planning, landscape design, architectural interiors/space planning for residential, commercial and institutional clients.
Needs: Works with 3 freelance artists/year. Uses artists for brochure design, architectural renderings, furnishings/furniture/cabinetry and model making.

First Contact & Terms: Send query letter with brochure showing art style or resume and photo sheets, Photostats, photocopies, slides, photographs or "whatever best represents work." Samples not filed are returned only if requested. Reports only if interested or if requested. To show a portfolio, mail appropriate materials or call or write to schedule an appointment; portfolio should include thumbnails, roughs, original/final art, final reproduction/product, color, Photostats, photographs, b&w or best appropriate representation of work." Payment depends *entirely* on product/skills needed."

THE TARQUINI ORGANIZATION, A Professional Association of Architects and Planners, 1812 Federal St., Camden NJ 08105. (609)365-7270. Vice President: Robert Giacomelli AIA. Architectural firm. Clients: commercial, residential, municipal.
Needs: Works with 2 freelance artists/year. Uses artists for advertising, brochure and interior design; architectural renderings and model making.
First Contact & Terms: Send query letter with brochure and business card to be kept on file. Samples returned by SASE if requested by artist. Reports only if interested. To show a portfolio, mail thumbnails. Works on assignment only. Pays per job basis. Considers client's budget and how work will be used when establishing payment.

THOMAS-CAMPBELL-PRIDGEON, INC., 735 E. Main St., Box 3028, Spartanburg SC 29304. (803)583-1456. Vice President: Richard Campbell. Architectural firm offering design services with interior and landscape design. Clients: commercial, education, governmental, industrial, residential, religious.
Needs: Works with 1-2 freelance artists/year. Works on assignment only. Uses artists for brochure design and architectural renderings.
First Contact & Terms: Send query letter with brochure to be kept on file. Prefers to review photocopies. Reports only if interested. Pays for illustration by project. Considers complexity of the project, client's budget, and skill and experience of artist when establishing payment.

***ODIE K TUCKER**, 2738 Danbury Dr., New Orleans LA 70114. (504)393-7969. Owner: Odie K. Tucker. Architectural, interior design, landscape design firm providing complete architectural services to commercial clients.
Needs: Works with some CAD consultants.
First Contact & Terms: Send query letter with tear sheets. Samples are filed. Samples not filed are not returned. Reports back only if interested. To show a portfolio, mail tear sheets. Pays for design and illustration by the project. Considers complexity of project, client's budget and skill and experience of artist when establishing payment. Buys first rights.

TUGGLE & GRAVES, INC.-ARCHITECTS, 215 Broadway, San Antonio TX 78205. (512)222-0194. Contact: Tuggle or Graves. Architectural/interior design firm offering architectural and space planning. Clients: school districts, commercial, government, industrial, residential.
Needs: Works with 3 freelance artists/year. Artists with three years of experience only. Works on assignment only. Uses artists for brochure and interior design, architectural renderings, maps and model making.
First Contact & Terms: Reports within 1 day if interested. Call or write for appointment to show portfolio. Pays for design by the project, $200-1,000 average. Considers complexity of project, client's budget, skill and experience of artist and how work will be used when establishing payment.

PHILIP TUSA DESIGN INC., Box 14, Roosevelt Island Station, New York NY 10044. (212)753-2810. President: Philip M. Tusa. Specializes in interior design. Clients: commercial firms, corporations and residential.
Needs: Works on assignment only. Uses artists for illustration, model making, interior rendering and drafting.
First Contact & Terms: Send query letter with resume, tear sheets, Photostats, photocopies, slides and photographs. Reports back only if interested. Call to schedule an appointment to show a portfolio, which should include thumbnails, roughs, original/final art, final reproduction/product, color, tear sheets, Photostats, photographs and b&w. Pays for illustration by the hour, $10 minimum; by the project, $100 minimum. Considers complexity of project, client's budget, skill and experience of artist, how work will be used, turnaround time and rights purchased when establishing payment.
Tips: "The need for 'low overhead' prompts small companies to increase the use of freelance work. Keep in touch!!"

VALENTOUR ENGLISH AND ASSOCIATES, 470 Washington Rd., Pittsburgh PA 15228. (412)561-7117. Architect: James Howell. Architectural/interior design firm providing full architectural and interior design services for commercial, institutional, multifamily residential clients.

Needs: Works on assignment only. Uses artists for brochure design and layout, interior and architectural renderings, model making and conceptual sketches. Prefers artists with capability of illustrating a "visually real" scene from technical drawings.
First Contact & Terms: Send brochure or resume and samples. Samples are filed. Samples not filed are returned only if requested. To show a portfolio, mail appropriate material. "An appointment made if interested." Pays for design and illustration by the project. Considers client's budget, skill and experience of artist and turnaround time when establishing payment. Negotiates rights purchased.
Tips: "Be available when we contact you. Examples should address architectural and interior design needs. Establish parameters concisely at interview."

VERCESI & SCHARFSPITZ, ARCHITECTS, 353 Broad Ave., Leonia NJ 07605. Contact: Tony Vercesi. Architectural firm providing full architectural services. Clients: residential (custom homes and apartment houses); commercial (space improvements, office and industrial buildings).
Needs: Works with several freelance artists/year. Artists "must be talented and productive." Works on assignment only. Uses artists for interior design, architectural renderings, design consultation, furnishings and model making.
First Contact & Terms: Send query letter with brochure showing art style. Reports only if interested. Write to schedule an appointment to show a portfolio, which should include photographs. Pays for design by the hour, $15-25; by the day, $50-150. Pays for illustration by the hour, $15-50; by the day, $100-200. Considers complexity of project, client's budget, and skill and experience of artist when establishing payment.
Tips: "Possess the necessary credentials in the form of examples of work, etc."

VICKREY/OVRESAT/AWSUMB ASSOCIATES, INC., 500 S. Magnolia Ave., Orlando FL 32801. (305)425-2500. Principal: John K. Awsumb, AIA. Coordinator-Project Development: Sandra Moore. Architectural/Interior Design firm providing architecture, planning, interior design, space planning and construction administration services. Clients: industrial, office, residential, religious, military, hotel and restaurant, educational, medical, and recreational facilities.
Needs: Works with 1-5 freelance artists/year. Works on assignment only. Uses artists for interior and architectural renderings, and model making.
First Contact & Terms: Send letter of interest with brochure showing art style and slides to be kept on file. Samples not kept on file are returned only if requested. Call for appointment to show portfolio, which should include original/final art and color. Pays for design by the project, $1,000-25,000, relative to client's budget.
Tips: "Please send brochures and then follow up with a call."

LORRIN L. WARD, ARCHITECT INC., 341 W. 4th St., Chico CA 95928. (916)342-4265. President: Lorrin Ward. Architecture firm. Provides architectural design, planning, project administration. Clients: governmental, industrial and commercial. Buys 2-5 renderings/year.
Needs: Works with 2 artists for architectural renderings; 1, model making; and 1, landscape design. Prefers artists who have worked with other firms of this type.
First Contact & Terms: Query with brochure. SASE. Reports within 1-2 weeks. Provide resume, business card and brochure to be kept on file for future assignments. Pays for design by the hour, $15-35 average; by the project, $100-900 average; by the day, $120-280 average. Pays for illustration by the hour, $20-40 average; by the project, $200-900 average; by the day, $150-400 average. Considers complexity of project, skill and experience of artist, turnaround time and rights purchased when establishing payment.

***WARD ASSOCIATES ARCHITECTS**, 4064 Cresthaven Dr., Westlake Village CA 91362. (805)495-3030. Principal: Burton Ward. Architectural firm providing computer drawing, architectural drawings and airbrush renderings. Clients: commercial developers (real estate).
Needs: Works with 2 freelance artists/year. Works on assignment only. Uses artists for interior design and renderings, architectural renderings and model making.
First Contact & Terms: Send query letter with brochure. Samples are filed. Samples not filed are not returned. Does not report back. Write to schedule an appointment to show a portfolio, which should include photographs. Pays for design and illustration by the project. Considers skill and experience of artist when establishing payment. Negotiates rights purchased.

***THE WEBER GROUP, INC.**, (formerly Christian A. Weber), 530 Chestnut St., W. Reading PA 19611. (215)374-4178. Contact: Chris Weber. Architectural firm providing full architectural and engineering services. Clients: "all types."
Needs: Works with "several" freelance artists/year. Uses artists for landscape design, interior and architectural renderings, furnishings and model making.

First Contact & Terms: Send query letter, resume and Photostats, slides or photocopies. Samples not filed are returned only if requested. Reports back only if interested. Pays by the hour according to quote. Considers skill and experience of artist when establishing payment.

HENRY P. WILHELMI, LANDSCAPE ARCHITECT/COMMUNITY PLANNER, 420 E. Genesee, Syracuse NY 13202. (315)474-7567. Contact: Henry P. Wilhelmi. Clients: government and institutions.
Needs: Works with 3-4 artists for architectural renderings; 1-2, graphic design; occasional, signage design; occasional, model making; 1-2, murals; and 1-2, sculpture. Local artists only. Works on assignment only.
First Contact & Terms: Mail photos or transparencies. Samples returned by SASE; and reports back on future possibilities. Provide resume, business card, brochure, flyer and tear sheet or any combination which will provide basic data to be kept on file for future assignments. Pays by job.

CLIFFORD N. WRIGHT ASSOC. ARCHITECTS, 4066 W. Maple, Birmingham MI 48010. (313)647-2022. President: William L. Baldner A.I.A. Vice President: William D. Shiels A.I.A. Architectural firm providing total architectural services. Clients: residential, commercial, light industrial.
Needs: Works with 10 freelance artists/year. Works on assignment only. Uses artists for landscape and interior design, interior and architectural renderings, design consulting and furnishings.
First Contact & Terms: Send brochure and resume to be kept on file. Reports only if interested. Call for appointment to show portfolio. Pays by the project for design and illustration. Considers complexity of project, client's budget, and skill and experience of artist when establishing payment.

“Artists rarely ever show sketches in their portfolios. Sketches help indicate how the person 'thinks'. In illustration they should show both the art and how it was used.”

—Robert M. Boeberitz, Bob Boeberitz Design
Asheville, North Carolina

Art/Design Studios

The scope of work handled by a studio can range from mechanicals and retouching to designing annual reports, to packaging products and creating logos. There are art studios which specialize in illustration, such as your local airbrush studio which illustrates book covers. Then there are design studios which conceptualize and produce annual reports and corporate identity programs.

Designers are idea people. As master designer Seymour Chwast says in this section's Close-up, "I'm a problem solver." Designers are called upon to develop total programs that include not only a visual image but also a marketing strategy. As a result of this growing involvement in marketing and promotion, studios increasingly need the services of freelance artists. Freelancers are needed for retouching, layout, paste-up, illustration, design and the preparation of graphs and charts. In addition to the listings here, research the talents needed by studios in your region and approach only those who request your specialties. Consult the *Yellow Pages* and the *Business-to-Business Directory* to locate local studios and then the *Design Directory* to learn their areas of specialization.

Because of the need to meet tight deadlines, many studios prefer to work with local artists. So it's very possible you will be asked to present your portfolio in person. Your portfolio should reflect good organizational skills and a graphic plan. Art directors like to see more than a finished product; they want to see your ideas. So that your samples convey your thought process, show thumbnails, roughs, comprehensives and the final product. These materials must be displayed so that they can be easily reviewed in order. Include only your best work which applies to the firm's needs. Product designers should include photos of manufactured products or prototypes as well as drafting and rendering samples. On projects involving the construction of models, keep a running photographic account of the project so you will have appropriate examples in your portfolio. Samples of work that have appeared in print help to establish a designer's credibility. It is also a good idea to have more than one portfolio to cover the portfolio drop-off policy and the submission of a portfolio through the mail. If mailing pieces, send photographs of thumbnails through the finished product as a sequential slide show accompanied by an information sheet. Follow your mailing with a phone call.

In addition to looking at your artwork, directors look for professionalism in your manner; well-designed and illustrated promotional pieces left for their files; and the ability to communicate with printers, studio personnel and clients.

***A.T. ASSOCIATES**, 63 Old Rutherford Ave., Charlestown MA 02129. (617)242-6004. Partner: Daniel N. Kovacovic. Specializes in industrial design, model making, corporate identity, signage, displays and packaging. Clients: design firms, corporate clients, small business and ad agencies.
Needs: Works with 10-25 freelance artists/year. Prefers local artists, some experience necessary. Uses artists for model making, mechanicals, logos, brochures, P-O-P displays, charts/graphs and design.
First Contact & Terms: Send resume and nonreturnable samples. Samples are filed. Reports back within 30 days only if interested. Call or write to schedule an appointment to show a portfolio, which should include thumbnails, roughs, original/final art, final reproduction/product, tear sheets, Photostats, photographs, b&w and color. Pays for design and illustration by the hour, $10-25; by the day, $48-200. Considers complexity of project, client's budget, skill and experience of artist, turnaround time and rights purchased when establishing payment. Rights purchased vary according to project.

AARON, SAUTER, GAINES & ASSOCIATES/DIRECT MARKETING, Suite 230, 320 E. McDowell Rd., Phoenix AZ 85004. (602)265-1933. President: Cameron G. Sauter. Specializes in brand identity, direct marketing, direct response ads, catalogs and P-O-P displays for retail stores, banks, industrial, mail order and service companies.
Needs: Works with 5-10 freelance artists/year. Uses artists for advertising, brochure and catalog design and illustration, mechanicals, retouching and direct mail packages.
First Contact and Terms: Seeks artists with professionalism, speed and experience only. Works on assignment basis. Send query letter with brochure, resume and business card to be kept on file. Prefers original work, photos or slides as samples. Samples returned by SASE if not kept on file. Reports only if interested. Pays for design, by the hour, $15-50 average; by the project, $100-1,000 average; by the day, $50-100 average. Pays for illustration, by the hour, $25-75 average; by the project, $100-2,000 average; by the day, $100-150 average. Considers complexity of project, client's budget, skill and experience of artist and turnaround time when establishing payment. "All art is purchased with full rights and no limitations."

***AD SYSTEMS INC.**, 723 S. Wells St., Chicago IL 60607. (312)427-4025. Creative Director: Patricia Kestler. Art agency. Specializes in print advertising and promotions relating to it. Clients: manufacturers and retailers.
Needs: Uses artists for P-O-P displays, direct mail, signage, brochures/flyers and slide sets.
First Contact & Terms: Local artists only. Arrange interview to show portfolio. SASE. Prefers Photostats, b&w line drawings, layout, roughs, comps, marker rendering, and previously published work as samples. Provide material to be kept on file for future assignments. No originals returned.

ADLER, SCHWARTZ INC., 140 Sylvan Ave., Englewood Cliffs NJ 07632. (201)461-8450. Art Director: Fred Witzig. Specializes in brand identity, corporate identity, displays and direct mail. Clients: ad agencies.
Needs: Works with 100 freelance artists/year. Uses artists for design, illustrations, mechanicals and retouching.
First Contact & Terms: Send query letter with brochure showing art style or resume and samples. Samples not filed are returned only if requested. Reports only if interested. Call to schedule an appointment to show a portfolio, which should include roughs, original/final art, final reproduction/product, tear sheets and photographs. Considers complexity of project, client's budget, skill and experience of artist, how work will be used, turnaround time and rights purchased when establishing payment.

ANCO/BOSTON, 216 Tremont St., Boston MA 02116. (617)482-7600. Graphic Director: Fran Jarvis. Art agency. Clients: educational publishers, commercial and industrial.
Needs: Works with 10 illustrators. Local artists only. Uses artists for books, charts, graphs, technical art and paste-up. Most of the artwork required is one-color line art.
First Contact & Terms: Send query letter with resume and photocopies. All art becomes the property of Anco/Boston. To show portfolio, mail appropriate materials or call to schedule an appointment; portfolio should include original/final art, final reproduction/product, tear sheets and Photostats. Pays for design by the project, $25 minimum; pays for illustration by the project, $10 minimum.
Tips: "We are interested only in b&w line art. Our work is for educational materials and is frequently of a technical nature."

ANDREN & ASSOCIATES INC., 6400 N. Keating Ave., Lincolnwood IL 60646. (312)267-8500. Contact: Kenneth E. Andren. Clients: beauty products and tool manufacturers, clothing retailers, laboratories, banks, cameras and paper products.
Needs: Assigns 6-7 jobs/month. Local artists only. Uses artists for catalogs, direct mail brochures, flyers, packages, P-O-P displays and print media advertising.
First Contact & Terms: Query with samples or arrange interview. SASE. Reports in 1-2 weeks. Pays $15 minimum/hour for animation, design, illustrations, layout, lettering, mechanicals, paste-up, retouching and type spec.

ANTISDEL IMAGE GROUP, INC., 3242 De La Cruz Blvd., Santa Clara CA 95054. (408)988-1010. President: G.C. Antisdel. Specializes in annual reports, corporate identity, displays, interior design, packaging, publications, signage and photo illustration. Clients: high technology 80%, energy 10%, and banking 10%.
Needs: Works on assignment only. Uses artists for illustration, mechanicals, retouching, airbrushing, direct mail packages, model making, charts/graphs, AV materials and lettering.
First Contact & Terms: Send query letter with resume, business card and tear sheets to be kept on file. Reports back only if interested. Call or write to schedule an appointment to show a portfolio, which should include color, tear sheets, photographs and b&w. Pays for design by the hour, $10-40 or by the

project $40-18,000. Pays for illustration by the project, $40-10,000. Considers complexity of project, client's budget, skill and experience of artist, how work will be used, turnaround time and rights purchased when establishing payment. .
Tips: "Our top grade clients are not subject to 'trendy' fads."

THE ART WORKS, 4409 Maple Ave., Dallas TX 75219. (214)521-2121. Creative Director: Fred Henley. Specializes in annual reports, brand identity, corporate identity, packaging, publications, signage, illustration and photography.
Needs: Works with 15-20 freelance artists/year. Uses artists for advertising, brochure, catalog and book design and illustration; advertising, brochure and catalog layout; P-O-P displays, mechanicals, retouching, posters, direct mail packages, lettering and logos.
First Contact and Terms: Send brochure, business card slides, original work to be kept on file. Samples returned by SASE only if requested by artist. Reports within 7 days. Call or write for appointment to show portfolio. Pays for design and illustration by the project. Considers complexity of project, client's budget, skill and experience of artist and turnaround time when establishing payment.

ARTHUR RITTER, INC., 45 W. 10th St., New York NY 10011. (212)505-0241. Art Director: Valerie Ritter. Specializes in annual reports, corporate identity, brochures, catalogs and promotion for publishers, corporations, public service organizations and hospitals.
Needs: Works with 5 freelance artists/year according to firm's needs. Does not always work on assignment only; "sometimes we need a freelancer on a day-to-day basis at the studio." Uses artists for advertising design and illustration, brochure design, mechanicals, charts and graphs.
First Contact & Terms: Prefers experienced artists, although "talented 'self-starters' with design expertise/education are also considered." Send query letter with brochure, resume and samples to be kept on file. "Follow up within a week of the query letter about the possibility of arranging an appointment for a portfolio review." Prefers printed pieces as samples. Samples not filed are returned by SASE. Pays for design by the hour, $10-20 average; by the project, $100-500 average; or by the day, $65-120 average. Pays for illustration by the project, $50-500 average. Considers complexity of the project, client's budget, skill and experience of the artist and turnaround time when establishing payment.

BAKER STREET PRODUCTIONS LTD.,216 Belgrade Ave., Mankato MN 56001. (507)625-2448. Contact: Karyne Jacobsen. Specializes in publications. Clients: publishers.
Needs: Works with 2 freelance artists/year. Prefers colorful juvenile-style art. Uses artists for illustrations, catalogs and books.
First Contact & Terms: Send query letter with resume and tear sheets. Samples not filed are returned by SASE only if requested. Reports within 2 months. Write to schedule an appointment to show a portfolio, which should include roughs, tear sheets and photographs. Pays for design and illustration by the project, $250 minimum. Considers complexity of project, client's budget and skill and experience of artist when establishing payment.

CAROL BANCROFT & FRIENDS, 185 Goodhill Rd., Weston CT 06883. (203)226-7674. President: Carol Bancroft. Specializes in art for children. Clients: publishing companies, ad agencies, studios and major corporations.
Needs: Works with 30 freelance artists/year. Uses artists for advertising, brochure, catalog and book illustration.
First Contact & Terms: Send slides, tear sheets and photos to be kept on file. Samples not kept on file are returned by SASE. To show a portfolio, mail appropriate materials, which should include final reproduction/product, color and tear sheets. Pays by the project, 70-75% of total job. Considers complexity of project, client's budget, turnaround time and rights purchased when establishing payment.
Tips: "Send a lot of good color samples we can keep on file."

BANKA-MANGO, Room 274, Merchandise Mart, Chicago IL 60654. (312)467-0059. Director of Graphic Design: Joseph R. Mango. Specializes in brand and corporate identity, displays, exhibits and shows, interior design and signage. Clients: retail stores and manufacturers of retail products.
Needs: Works with 1-2 freelance artists/year. Works on assignment only. Uses artists for packaging design and illustration, brochure design, mechanicals, retouching, poster illustration, model making, charts/graphs, lettering and logo design.
First Contact & Terms: Send query letter with brochure/flyer or resume to be kept on file. Call or write for appointment to show portfolio. Pays by the project on completion for design and illustration.
Tips: "Have good, current samples."

BARNSTORM DESIGN/CREATIVE, Suite 301, 2502½ W. Colorado Ave., Colorado Springs CO 80904. (303)630-7200. Owner: Douglas D. Blough. Specializes in corporate identity, brochure design,

multi-image slide presentations and publications. Clients: ad agencies, high-technology corporations, restaurants.
Needs: Works with 2-4 freelance artists/year. Works with local, experienced (clean, fast and accurate) artists on assignment. Uses artists for design, illustration, brochures, mechanicals, retouching, AV materials and lettering.
First Contact & Terms: Send query letter with resume and samples to be kept on file. Prefers "good originals or reproductions, professionally presented in any form" as samples. Samples not filed are returned by SASE. Reports only if interested. Call or write for appointment to show portfolio. Pays for design by the project, $100 minimum. Pays for illustration by the project, $50 minimum, b&w; $100, color. Considers client's budget, skill and experience of artist, and turnaround time when establishing payment.
Tips: "Trend toward New Wave design/pastel colors. Portfolios should reflect an awareness of these trends. We try to handle as much inhouse as we can, but we recognize our own limitations (particularly in illustration)."

***BASIC/BEDELL ADVERTISING SELLING IMPROVEMENT CORP.**, 2040 Alameda Padre Serra, Santa Barbara CA 93103. President: C. Barrie Bedell. Specializes in publications, advertisements and direct mail. Clients: national and international newspapers, publishers, direct response marketers, retail stores, hard lines manufacturers and trade associations plus extensive self-promotion.
Needs: Uses artists for publication design, book covers and dust jackets, direct mail layout and pasteup. Especially wants to hear from publishing and "direct response" pros. Negotiates payment by the project. Considers client's budget, and skill and experience of artist when establishing payment.
Tips: "Substantial increase in use of freelance talent and increasing need for true professionals with exceptional skills and responsible performance (delivery as promised and 'on target'). It is very difficult to locate freelance talent with expertise in design of advertising and direct mail with heavy use of type. If work is truly professional and freelancer is business-like, contact with personal letter and photocopy of one or more samples of work that needn't be returned."

LAWRENCE BENDER & ASSOCIATES, 512 Hamilton Ave., Palo Alto CA 94301. (415)327-3821. President: Lawrence Bender. Specializes in annual reports. Clients: electronic manufacturers.
Needs: Works with 12 freelance artists/year. Uses artists for design, illustration, mechanicals, retouching and airbrushing.
First Contact & Terms: Send query letter with resume, business card and samples to be kept on file. Samples not kept on file returned only if requested. Reports only if interested. Call or write for appointment to show portfolio. Pays for design by the hour, project or day. Pays for illustration by the project. Considers complexity of project, client's budget, skill and experience of artist and rights purchased when establishing payment.

***MAY BENDER DESIGN ASSOCIATES, INC.**, 247 W. 30th St., New York NY 10001. (212)695-7107. President: May Bender. Specializes in brand identity, corporate identity, displays, packaging, product design and signage. Clients: manufacturers of products, i.e. R-J Reynolds, Bausch and Lomb.
Needs: Works with variable freelance artists/year. Uses artists for illustrations, mechanicals, retouching, airbrushing and lettering.
First Contact & Terms: Send brochure. Samples are filed. Samples not filed are returned only if requested. Call or write to schedule an appointment to show a portfolio, which should include original/final art. Pays for design by the hour, $15-25, or by the project, $10-20. Considers complexity of project, client's budget and turnaround time when establishing payment. Rights purchased vary according to project.
Tips: "I like to see a few 'how they got theres', finished art and repros if possible."

***SUZANNE BENNETT AND ASSOCIATES**, 251 Fifth Ave., New York NY 10011. (212)686-6454. Contact: Suzanne Bennett. Specializes in direct mail, publications and book design. Clients: PR firms, magazines, book publishers and nonprofit organizations.
Needs: Works with 15 freelance artists/year. Uses artists for mechanicals, retouching, airbrushing and charts/graphs.
First Contact & Terms: Samples not filed are not returned. Does not report back. Write to schedule an appointment to show a portfolio. Considers client's budget, skill and experience of artist, how work will be used and turnaround time when establishing payment. Rights purchased vary.
Needs: Works with 15 freelance artists/year. Uses artists for mechanicals, retouching, airbrushing and charts/graphs.
First Contact & Terms: Samples not filed are not returned. Does not report back. Write to schedule an appointment to show a portfolio. Considers client's budget, skill and experience of artist, how work will be used and turnaround time when establishing payment. Rights purchased vary according to project.

***BARRY DAVID BERGER & ASSOCIATES, INC.**, 9 East 19th St., New York NY 10003. (212)477-4100. Contact: Monya Steele. Specializes in brand and corporate identity, P-O-P displays, product and interior design, exhibits and shows, corporate capability brochures, advertising graphics, packaging, publications and signage. Clients: product manufacturers and marketing organizations.
Needs: Works with 10 freelance artists/year. Uses artists for advertising illustration, mechanicals, retouching, direct mail package design, model making, charts/graphs, photography, AV presentations and lettering.
First Contact & Terms: Send query letter, then call for appointment. Works on assignment only. Prefers "whatever is necessary to demonstrate competence" as samples. Samples returned if not kept on file. Reports immediately. Provide brochure/flyer, resume, business card, tear sheets and samples to be kept on file for possible future assignments. Pays by the project for design and illustration.

J.H. BERMAN AND ASSOCIATES, Suite 621, 2025 I St. NW, Washington DC 20006. (202)775-0892. Senior Vice President: Jackie Deitch. Specializes in annual reports, corporate identity, publications and signage. Clients: real estate developers, architects, high-technology corporations and financial-oriented firms (banks, investment firms, etc.).
Needs: Works with 10-15 (6 consistently) freelance artists/year. Uses artists for design, illustration, brochures, magazines, books, P-O-P displays, mechanicals, retouching, airbrushing, posters, model making, AV materials, lettering and advertisements. Especially needs designers, illustrators, technical illustrators, architectural renderers and mechanical/production artists.
First Contact & Terms: "Artists should be highly professional, with at least 5 years of experience. Highest quality work required. Restricted to local artists for mechanicals only." Send query letter with brochure, resume, business card and samples to be kept on file. Call or write for appointment to show portfolio or contact through agent. "Samples should be as compact as possible; slides not suggested." Samples not kept on file returned by SASE. Reports only if interested. Pays for design by the hour, $12-50 average. Pays for illustration by the project, $200 minimum. Considers complexity of project, skill and experience of artist, how work will be used, turnaround time and rights purchased when establishing payment.
Tips: Artists should have a "totally professional approach."

***THE BERNSTEIN DESIGN GROUP, INC.**, Suite 918, 500 N. Dearborn, Chicago IL 60610. (312)644-2474. President: Daniel Bernstein. Specializes in annual reports, corporate identity and direct mail. Clients: direct clients and PR firms.
Needs: Works with 3 freelance artists/year. Prefers local artists only. Works on assignment only. Uses artists for illustrations and retouching.
First Contact & Terms: Send query letter with brochure. Samples are filed. Samples not filed are not returned. Reports back within months only if interested. To show a portfolio, mail limited print promotional material. Pays for illustration by the project, $50-500. Considers complexity of project, client's budget and time involved when establishing payment. Buys all rights.
Tips: "I do not have time for personal contact until the need arises. I want printed material only, not originals. They will be kept on file until needed. My freelancer needs are minimal."

***THE BLANK COMPANY**, 1048 Lincoln Ave., San Jose CA 95125. (408)289-9095. Art Director: Jerry Blank. Specializes in annual reports, corporate identity, direct mail, packaging and all collateral materials. Clients: high-tech firms, variety and food service.
Needs: Works with 3 freelance artist/year. Prefers artists with "experience that is reflected in a strong portfolio presentation; local artists only." Works on assignment only. Prefers sophisticated, contemporary and creative artists. Uses artists for design, illustrations, brochures, catalogs, P-O-P displays, mechanicals, posters, lettering, logos and advertisements.
First Contact & Terms: Send query letter with resume, tear sheets, Photostats, photocopies and photographs. Samples are filed. Samples not filed are returned by SASE only if requested. Reports back only if interested. Call or write to schedule an appointment to show a portfolio.

BOB BOEBERITZ DESIGN, 247 Charlotte St., Asheville NC 28801. (704)258-0316. Owner: Bob Boeberitz. Graphic design studio. Clients: galleries, retail outlets, restaurants, textile manufacturers, land developers, computer software, record companies and publishers.
Needs: Works with freelance artists on occasion. Uses artists primarily for illustration; occasionally buys humorous or cartoon-style illustrations.
First Contact & Terms: Send query letter with brochure, resume, Photostats, photocopies, photographs, business card, slides and tear sheets to be kept on file. "Anything too large to fit in file" is discarded. Reports only if interested. To show a portfolio, mail appropriate materials or write to schedule an appointment; portfolio should include original/final art, final reproduction/product, color and b&w. Pays for illustration by the project, $50 minimum. Considers complexity of project, client's budget,

skill and experience of artist and turnaround time when establishing payment. Buys all rights.
Tips: "Show sketches. Sketches help indicate how the person thinks. In illustration, show both the art and how it was used."

THE BOOKMAKERS, INCORPORATED, 298 E. South St., Wilkes-Barre PA 18702. (717)823-9183. President: John Beck. Specializes in publications and technical illustrations. Clients: mostly book publishers.
Needs: Works with 10-20 freelance artists/year. Uses artists for illustrations, brochures, catalogs, retouching, airbrushing, posters and charts/graphs.
First Contact & Terms: Send query letter with resume, tear sheets, Photostats, photocopies, slides and photographs. Samples not filed are returned by SASE. Reports only if interested. Write to schedule an appointment to show a portfolio, which should include thumbnails, roughs, original/final art, final reproduction/product, tear sheets, Photostats and b&w. Pays for illustration by the project, $20-2,400. Considers complexity of project, client's budget, skill and experience of artist, how work will be used and turnaround time when establishing payment. Buys all rights.
Tips: "We are especially interested in versatility."

BOWYER ASSOCIATES, INC., 160 Broadway Ave., Toronto, Ontario M4P 1V9 Canada. (416)484-8848. President: Robert Bowyer. Studio. Clients: retail, industrial and commercial.
Needs: Assigns approximately 200 jobs/year to freelance artists. Works with 2 freelance illustrators/month. Sometimes works on assignment. Uses artists for illustrations and finished artwork.
First Contact & Terms: Send resume to be kept on file if interested. Reports only if interested. Pays for design by the project, $50-1,000. Pays for illustration by the project, $50-1,500. Considers complexity of project, client's budget, and skill and experience of artist when establishing payment. Buys all rights.
Tips: Looks for "good, clean, commercial artwork." Artists should "show only top quality work, anything artist thinks is good, in a range from brochures to advertisements. Do not show artwork that you did in school."

BRODSKY GRAPHICS INC., 270 Madison Ave., New York NY 10016. (212)684-2600. Art Director: Ed Brodsky. Specializes in corporate identity, direct mail, promotion and packaging. Clients: ad agencies and corporations.
Needs: Works with 10 freelance artists/year. Works on assignment only. Uses artists for illustration, mechanicals, retouching, airbrushing, charts/graphs, AV materials and lettering.
First Contact & Terms: Send business card and tear sheets to be kept on file. Reports back only if interested. Considers complexity of project, client's budget, skill and experience of artist and turnaround time when establishing payment.

BROOKS STEVENS DESIGN ASSOC., 1415 W. Donges Bay Rd., Mequon WI 53092. (414)241-3800. President: Kipp Stevens. Specializes in corporate identity, packaging and industrial design. Clients: manufacturing companies.
Needs: Works with 5 freelance artists/year. Uses artists for illustrations, P-O-P displays, retouching, model making and logos.
First Contact & Terms: Send query letter with resume. Samples not filed are returned only if requested. Reports only if interested. Call or write to schedule an appointment to show a portfolio, which should include roughs, original/final art, final reproduction/product and color. Pays for design by the hour, $11 minimum; by the project, $100 minimum. Pays for illustrations by the hour, $11 minimum; by the project, $100 minimum. Considers complexity of project, client's budget, skill and experience of artist, and turnaround time when establishing payment.

***BUTLER KOSH BROOKS**, 940 N. Highland Ave., Los Angeles CA 90038. (213)469-8128. Estab. 1987. Specializes in corporate identity, displays, direct mail, fashion, packaging and publications. Clients: film companies, fashion, medical and home video distributors.
Needs: Works with 12 freelance artists/year. Works on assignment only. Uses artists for design, brochures, catalogs, books, P-O-P displays, mechanicals, retouching, posters, model making, direct mail packages, lettering and logos.
First Contact & Terms: Send query letter with brochure or resume. Samples are filed. Samples not filed are returned by SASE. Reports back within 1 week only if interested. To show a portfolio, mail appropriate materials. Pays for design and illustration by the hour, $15. Considers complexity of project, client's budget, skill and experience of artist, how work will be used, turnaround time and rights purchased when establishing payment. Rights purchased vary according to project.

CANYON DESIGN, # 102, 20945 Devonshire St., Chatsworth CA 91311. (818)700-1173. Art Director/Owner: David O'Connell. Specializes in brand identity, corporate identity, displays and packaging. Clients: manufacturers, distributors and others.
Needs: Works with 28 freelance artists/year. Uses artists for design, illustrations, P-O-P displays, retouching, and lettering. "We are looking for an office manager/production manager and junior designer."
First Contact & Terms: Send query letter with brochure showing art style. Samples not filed are returned by SASE. Reports only if interested. Call to schedule an appointment to show a portfolio, which should include roughs, original/final art, final reproduction/product, color and tear sheets. Pays for design by the project, $500-4,500. Pays for illustration by the project, $500-1,500. Considers complexity of project, client's budget, skill and experience of artist, how work will be used, turnaround time and rights purchased when establishing payment.
Tips: "Check the going rates in the area before asking for Madison Ave. fees. Location of an agency or studio has a lot to do with determining the prices charged to a client. Don't include pieces in your portfolio that you have to make excuses for. More emphasis on creativity and less on production. The L.A. market has a strong color palette—atomic and neon colors." Looks for "innovations in materials and techniques. Airbrushed photrealism is dead. Photo illustration is very exciting. We like the concept of modifying reality by work over a real photograph with paint and other media."

THE CHESTNUT HOUSE GROUP INC., 540 N. Lakeshore Dr., Chicago IL 60611. (312)222-9090. Creative Directors: Norman Baugher and Miles Zimmerman. Clients: major educational publishers. Arrange interview.
Needs: Illustration, layout and assembly. Pays by job.

WOODY COLEMAN PRESENTS, INC., 490 Rockside Rd., Cleveland OH 44131. (216)661-4222. President: Woody Coleman. Artist's agent. Clients: ad agencies, PR firms and direct corporations.
Needs: Works with 25 freelance artists/year. Artists must have three years of experience. Especially needs photorealistic with figure and product. Uses artists for illustrations.
First Contact & Terms: Send query letter with brochure showing art style or tear sheets, slides and 4x5 transparencies. Samples not filed are returned by SASE. Reports only if interested. To show a portfolio, mail color and 4x5 transparencies. Pays for illustration by the project, $400-10,000. Considers complexity of project, client's budget, skill and experience of artist, how work will be used, turnaround time and rights purchased when establishing payment.
Tips: Artist should send "8 of their 10 best samples within their area of expertise."

***COLLS DESIGN, INC.**, 716 Yarmouth Rd., Palos Verdes Estates CA 90274. (213)541-8433. President: William J. Colls. Specializes in annual reports, corporate identity, displays and exhibits. Clients: industry and public relations firms.
Needs: Works with 3 freelance artists/year. Uses artists for advertising, brochure and catalog design, illustration and layout; P-O-P displays, exhibits, mechanicals, retouching and logo design.
First Contact & Terms: Prefers artists in or near the South Bay area of Los Angeles. Works on assignment only. Send query letter with resume. Reports in 2 weeks. Prefers Photostats and printed work as samples. Write for appointment to show portfolio. Provide resume, business card and sample copies to be kept on file for possible future assignments. Pays $50-500 average/project for design; $50-300 average/project for illustration. Pays for design by the hour, $5-20 average. Pays for illustration by the hour, $10-25 average; also negotiates. Considers client's budget, and skill and experience of artist when establishing payment.
Tips: "A successful freelance artist is usually talented, business-like, professional, dependable and knowledgeable about his specialty."

***COMITE: PLUS DESIGN ASSOCIATES**, 75 Bayview Dr., Swampscott MA 01907. Owner: Michael Comite. Graphic production consulting service. Clients: printers, ad agencies, design studios and companies.
Needs: Works with 10 freelance artists/year. Prefers artists with 5 years minimum of experience. Works on assignment only. Uses artists for design, illustrations, brochures, mechanicals, retouching, airbrushing, posters, direct mail packages, logos, advertisements, graphic art and production consulting servicing.
First Contact & Terms: Send query letter with resume and samples. Samples are filed. Samples not filed are returned by SASE. Reports back only if interested. Write to schedule an appointment to show a portfolio. Pays for design by the hour, $15-75. Pays for illustration by the project, $100-5,000. Considers complexity of project, client's budget, skill and experience of artist and turnaround time when establishing payment. Buys all rights; rights purchased vary according to project.

***COMMERICAL ARTS, LTD./MARKET DIRECT**, 5929 Rockhill Rd., Kansas City MO 64110-3155. (816)523-0482. President: Lanie Bethka. Specializes in corporate identity, direct mail and publications. Clients: real estate companies, banks, software houses, light manufacturers, engineering firms, colleges, insurance groups and medical groups.
Needs: Works with 1-5 freelance artists/year. Prefers local artists. Works on assignment only. Uses artists for illustrations, retouching, airbrushing, charts/graphs, AV materials and lettering.
First Contact & Terms: Send query letter with brochure or resume, tear sheets, Photostats, photocopies, slides and photographs. Samples are filed. Samples not filed are returned only if requested. Write to schedule an appointment to show a portfolio, which should include thumbnails, roughs, original/final art, final reproduction/product, tear sheets, Photostats, photographs, b&w and color. Pays for design by the project, $50-5,000 or more. Pays for illustration by the project, $35-2,000 or more. Considers complexity of project, client's budget, skill and experience of artist, how work will be used and turnaround time when establishing payment. Buys all rights.

CONTOURS CONSULTING DESIGN GROUP, INC., 864 Stearns Rd., Bartlett IL 60103. (312)837-4100. Director, Graphics Group: Pat King. Specializes in annual reports, brand identity, corporate identity, displays, direct mail, packaging and signage. Clients: various corporations.
Needs: Works on assignment only. Uses artists for illustration, mechanicals and retouching.
First Contact & Terms: Send query letter with tear sheets. Call to schedule an appointment to show portfolio, which should include roughs, final reproduction/product, color and b&w. Pays for design by the hour, $30-50; pays for illustration by the project, $200-800. Considers client's budget when establishing payment.
Tips: "In the field, there are more copy solutions to problems than visuals. There is a limited use of art because budgets have reduced art buy outs. We are looking for strong concept solutions rather than style alternatives."

***THE CORPORATE COMMUNICATIONS GROUP**, 43 W. 33rd St., New York NY 10001. Director: Barry L.S. Mirenburg. Specializes in annual reports, brand identity, corporate identity, packaging, publications, image development, advertising, graphic design and marketing. Clients: industrial and commercial manufacturers, and publishers.
Needs: Works with 6-10 freelance artists/year. Uses artists for illustration, brochures, catalogs, mechanicals, retouching, airbrushing, charts/graphs, lettering, advertisements and paste-up.
First Contact & Terms: Professional artists only. Works on assignment only. Send brochure, resume and samples to be kept on file. "Do not call. All information/samples will be reviewed and kept on file for future needs." Wants samples that give the best presentation and best clarity. Samples not filed are not returned. Pay varies. Considers complexity of project, client's budget, skill and experience of artist, how work will be used, turnaround time and rights purchased when establishing payment.

***COUSINS DESIGN**, 599 Broadway, New York NY 10012. (212)431-8222. Vice President: Morison Cousins. Specializes in packaging. Clients: manufacturing companies.
Needs: Works with 6 freelance artists/year. Prefers local artists. Works on assignment only. Uses artists for design, illustrations, mechanicals, retouching, airbrushing, model making, lettering and logos.
First Contact & Terms: Send query letter with brochure or resume, tear sheets and photocopies. Samples are filed or not filed. Samples not filed are returned only if requested. Reports back within 2 weeks only if interested. Write to schedule an appointment to show a portfolio, which should include roughs, final reproduction/product and Photostats. Pays for design by the hour, $20 minimum. Pays for illustration by the hour, $15 minimum. Considers skill and experience of artist when establishing payment. Buys all rights.

***CREATIVE COMPANY, INC.**, 345 Court St. NE, Salem OR 97301. (503)363-4433. President/Owner: Jennifer Morrow. Specializes in corporate identity and packaging. Clients: local consumer-oriented clients, professionals, and trade accounts on a regional and national level, all in the Salem/Valley area.
Needs: Works with 3-4 freelance artists/year. Uses artists for design, illustration, retouching, airbrushing, posters and lettering. "We are always looking for illustrators and cartoonists."
First Contact & Terms: Prefers local artists. "We also require a portfolio review. Years of experience not important if portfolio is good." Works on assignment only. Send query letter with brochure, resume, business card and samples to be kept on file. Accepts photocopies or tear sheets as samples. "We prefer one-on-one review of portfolio to discuss individual projects/time/approach." Samples returned only if requested. Reports only if interested. Call for appointment to show portfolio. Pays for design by the hour, $20-40 average. Pays for illustration by the hour $25-40 average. Considers complexity of project, and skill and experience of artist when establishing payment.
Tips: "Don't drop in, always call and make an appointment. Have a clean and well-organized portfolio, and a resume or something to keep on file."

CREATIVE DESIGN CENTER, INC., 23141-K La Cadena Dr., Laguna Hills CA 92653. President: Clair Samhammer. Specializes in corporate identity, displays, interior design, packaging, technical illustration and product design and development. Clients: manufacturing and marketing groups (medical, data processing/office equipment and consumer products).
Needs: Works with 15 freelance designers/year. Prefers designers with "minimum 3-5 years of experience, except in exceptional cases, and proven ability." Works on assignment only. Uses designers for design, illustration, brochures, P-O-P displays, mechanicals, model making and logos.
First Contact & Terms: Send query letter with brochure, resume, business card and samples to be kept on file. Samples not kept on file are returned only if requested. Write for appointment to show portfolio. Pays for design by the hour, $15 minumum. Pays for illustration by the project. Considers client's budget, skill and experience of designers and turnaround time when establishing payment.
Tips: "In a portfolio, subjects should be pertinent to our need at the time. Styles should be fresh with high-quality design content. Can be conservative through leading-edge/radical if the assignment justifies it."

***THE CREATIVE SOURCE, INC.**, 123 W. 44th St., New York NY 10036. (212)302-0059. Design Director: Dante Calise. Vice President: Adam J. D'Addari. Specializes in brand identity, corporate identity, displays and packaging design for blue-chip clients.
Needs: Works with 20-30 freelance artists/year. Prefers artists with at least 5 years of experience that meet committed deadlines. Uses artists for illustrations, brochures, airbrushing and hand lettering. "Floral, decorative illustrators always in need. We work for a lot of paper companies."
First Contact & Terms: Send query letter with brochure showing art style or resume and tear sheets. Samples are filed. Reports back only if interested. Write to schedule an appointment to show a portfolio, which should include original/final art, photographs and color. Pays for illustration by the hour, $27 or by the project, $300. Considers complexity of project, client's budget and skill and experience of artist when establishing payment. Buys all rights.
Tips: "Neat portfolios only."

CREATIVE WORKS, Suite A, 8295 N. Military Trail, Palm Beach Gardens FL 33458. (305)627-3388. Interior Designer (Drafting): Suzi Addessa. Art Director (Mechanicals): Ken Roscoe. Specializes in corporate identity, displays, interior design, packaging, signage, product and sales offices. Clients: ad agencies, public relations firms, real estate developers, manufacturers and promoters.
Needs: Works with 50 freelance artists/year. Uses local (work inhouse), experienced artists. Uses artists for design, illustration, mechanicals, airbrushing, model making and drafting. Especially needs drafting/mechanical people.
First Contact & Terms: Send query letter with resume to be kept on file. Samples not kept on file are returned by SASE only if requested. Reports within 1 week. Write to schedule an appointment to show a portfolio, which should include original/final art and photographs. Pays by the project for drafting and mechanicals. Considers complexity of project, client's budget, skill and experience of artist and turnaround time when establishing payment.
Tips: "Send resume for interest and follow by appointment."

CREEL MORRELL INC., Suite 1000, 301 Congress Ave., Austin TX 78701. Graphic Designer: Mary Conrade. Specializes in annual reports, corporate identity, displays, landscape design, interior design, technical illustrations, publications and signage.
Needs: Uses artists for illustrations, mechanicals, retouching, airbrushing, model making, copywriting and AV materials.
First Contact & Terms: Send query letter with brochure, resume, business card and whatever samples available to be kept on file. Samples not filed are returned only if requested. Reports only if interested. To show a portfolio, mail appropriate materials or call to schedule an appointment; portfolio should include final reproduction/product, color, tear sheets, Photostats, photographs or slides of work. Payment depends on each situation. Considers client's budget, skill and experience of artist, how work will be used and rights purchased when establishing payment.

CSOKA/BENATO/FLEURANT INC., 134 W. 26th St., New York NY 10001. (212)242-6777. President: Robert Fleurant. Clients: insurance, national retail chains and communications.
Needs: Uses artists for record jacket covers and sales promotion projects.
First Contact & Terms: Assigns 10-20 jobs/year. Arrange interview. Pays $15-25/hour, layout; $8-15/hour, paste-up and mechanicals; $500 maximum/job, record jacket covers. Negotiates payment by job for annual reports, catalogs, packaging, posters and P-O-P displays.
Tips: Professional presentation of work is a *must*.

DANMARK & MICHAELS, INC., Suite 308, 5728 Major Blvd., Orlando FL 32819. (305)351-6311. Art Directors: Mark de Stefano or Michael de Stefano. Specializes in technical illustrations. Clients: publishers of textbooks.
Needs: Works with several freeelance artists/year. Artist should have some experience in technical illustrations. Uses artists for illustrations, airbrushing, charts/graphs and maps. "We are always looking for good illustrators."
First Contact & Terms: Send query letter with resume and photocopies. Samples not filed are returned only if requested. Reports only if interested. Call or write to schedule an appointment to show a portfolio, which should include original/final art. Payment varies. Considers complexity of project, skill and experience of artist, and turnaround time when establishing payment.
Tips: "Artist must meet the deadlines required and have the ability to do the job."

***DEMARTIN*MARONA*CRANSTOWN*DOWNES**, 911 Washington St., Wilmington DE 19801. (302)654-5277. Vice President: Richard Downes. Specializes in annual reports, corporate identity, direct mail, packaging and publications. Clients: banks, radio stations and chemical companies.
Needs: Works with 3 freelance artists/year. Prefers 4-7 years of experience. Prefers mechanical artists. Uses artists for mechanicals and retouching.
First Contact & Terms: Send query letter. Samples are filed. Samples not filed are not returned. Reports back only if interested. Call to schedule an appointment to show a portfolio, which should include photographs. Pays for design by the hour and by the day. Pays for illustration by the project, amount varies. Considers skill and experience of artist when establishing payment. Buys all rights.

DESIGN & PRODUCTION INCORPORATED, 7110 Rainwater Pl., Lorton VA 22079. (703)550-8640. Design Director: Daniel Murphy. Specializes in displays, interior design, signage and exhibition design. Clients: ad agencies, PR firms, architectural firms, institutions and major corporations.
Needs: Works with 10-20 freelance artists/year. Uses artists for design, illustration, brochures, catalogs, mechanicals, model making and exhibit design.
First Contact & Terms: Prefers local artists who are established professionals. Works on assignment only. Send query letter with brochure, resume and samples to be kept on file; call for appointment to show portfolio. Prefers slides or tear sheets as samples. Samples not filed are returned by SASE. Reports within 2 weeks. Pays for design by the hour, $50-200 average; by the project, $1,000-15,000 average. Pays for illustration by the hour, $25-50 average; by the project, $1,000-3,000 average. Considers complexity of project, client's budget, and skill and experience of artist when establishing payment.
Tips: "Only experienced freelancers need apply. Develop a style, a definite, recognizable trait that can be associated to you exclusively."

***DESIGN HORIZONS INTERNATIONAL**, 520 W. Erie St., Chicago IL 60610. (312)664-0006. Creative Director: Carl Miller. Specializes in annual reports, corporate identity and publications. Clients: ad agencies, PR firms, builders/developers and travel firms.
Needs: Works with 6 freelance artists/year. Prefers artists with minimum 5 years of experience. Uses artists for illustrations, mechanicals, retouching, airbrushing and charts/graphs.
First Contact & Terms: Send query letter with brochure or resume, tear sheets, Photostats and photocopies. Samples are filed. Reports back only if interested. To show a portfolio, mail roughs, final reproduction/product, tear sheets and Photostats. Pays for design by the hour, $15-30. Considers complexity of project, client's budget and skill and experience of artist when establishing payment. Buys all rights; negotiates rights purchased.

DESIGN NORTH, INC., 8007 Douglas Ave., Racine WI 53402. (414)639-2080. Design Directors: Dennis Wolken (corporate), Jim Neill (promotional). Specializes in annual reports, brand identity, corporate identity, displays, all internal and external collateral. Clients: direct accounts—financial/medical, consumer/industrial products.
Needs: Works with 10 freelance artists/year. "Freelancer must not call directly or be in competition with us on accounts." Works on assignment only. Uses artists for illustration, photography, retouching, airbrushing and lettering.
First Contact & Terms: Send query letter with brochure and Photostats, slides, photocopies and tear sheets to be kept on file. Samples not kept on file are returned in 2 weeks with SASE. Pays by the project. Considers client's budget, skill and experience of artist, and turnaround time when establishing payment.
Tips: "Show an accurate representation, be professional, honest and service-oriented."

THE DESIGN OFFICE OF STEVE NEUMANN & FRIENDS, Suite 103, 3000 Richmond Ave., Houston TX 77098. (713)629-7501. Contact: Cynthia J. Whitney. Specializes in corporate identity and signage. Clients: architects, interior designers, developers, hospitals, universities, etc.

Needs: Works with 2-4 freelance artists/year. Artists must be local with "good background." Uses artists for design, illustration, retouching, model making, drafting and signage. Especially needs full-time and/or part-time production person.
First Contact & Terms: Send query letter with brochure, resume, references, business card and slides to be kept on file. Reports back within 15 days. Write for appointment to show portfolio. Pays for design by the hour based on job contract. Considers complexity of project, client's budget, skill and experience of artist, and how work will be used when establishing payment.

THE DESIGN QUARTER, 2900 4th Ave., San Diego CA 92103. (619)297-7900. Executive Vice President/Design: Brian Lovell. Specializes in annual reports, corporate identity, direct mail and publications. Clients: corporations and publishers.
Needs: Works with 6 freelance artists/year. Uses artists for catalogs, books, mechanicals, retouching, airbrushing, model making and charts/graphs.
First Contact & Terms: Send business card to be kept on file. Prefers Photostats, photocopies and tear sheets as samples. Samples not kept on file are returned only if requested by SASE. Reports back only if interested. Call for appointment to show portfolio. Pays for design by the hour, $10-30 average; by the project, $25-1,800 average. Pays for illustration by the hour, $25-50 average; by the project, $100-5,000 average. Considers complexity of project, client's budget, and skill and experience of artist when establishing payment.

DESIGNS FOR MEDICINE, INC., 301 Cherry St., Philadelphia PA 19106. (215)925-7100. President: Peter W. Bressler. Specializes in annual reports, corporate identity, packaging, technical illustrations, product design and graphic design. Clients: ad agencies, manufacturers and inventors.
Needs: Works with 8 freelance artists/year. "Local artists only to work in our office primarily; experience required varies." Works on assignment only. Uses artists for design, illustration, brochures, mechanicals, airbrushing, model making, lettering, logos and advertisements.
First Contact & Terms: Send query letter with brochure, resume, business card and samples to be kept on file, except for slides which will be returned to sender. Prefers slides and tear sheets as samples. Samples not filed returned. Reports within 3 weeks. Write for appointment to show portfolio. Pays for design by the hour, $5-20 average (quotation basis). Considers complexity of project, client's budget, and skill and experience of artist when establishing payment.
Tips: "Be aggressive, very talented and creative."

***DESIGN TRANSLATIONS**, 1 Tracy Ln., Milford OH 45150. (513)248-0629. Contact: Richard Riggs. Specializes in graphic design. Clients: technical firms, medical firms, and miscellaneous businesses.
Needs: Works with 1-2 freelance artists/year. Uses artists for mechanicals.
First Contact & Terms: "Artist must have superb craft and meticulous attention to detail; must be able to understand directions." Send query letter with resume and stats and/or slides to be kept on file. Samples not kept on file are returned by SASE only if requested. Reports back only if interested. Pays on a per job basis. Considers complexity of project, client's budget, skill and experience of artist, and turnaround time when establishing payment.

DESIGNWORKS, INC., Davis Square, 48 Grove St., Somerville, MA 02144. (617)628-8600. Art Directors: Sally Bindari, Jennie R. Bush. Provides design for publishing industry. Specializes in educational publications. Clients: book publishers.
Needs: Works with 10 freelance artists/year. Works on assignment only. Uses artists for book illustration, charts/graphs. Prefers styles "appropriate for educational materials."
First Contact & Terms: Send query letter with brochure showing art style or resume and samples. To show a portfolio, mail appropriate materials or write to schedule an appointment. Portfolio should include final reproduction/product, tear sheets, b&w or anything showing final product. Pays for design either by the hour or by the project, $12-20. "We hire designers to work in the studio for a specific project and pay hourly." Pays for illustration by the project, $200 minimum. Considers complexity of project, client's budget, and skill and experience of artist when establishing payment.
Tips: "We like samples for our files but we do not have a lot of office time for reviewing portfolios as we are producing during work hours ourselves. We do mostly textbook illustration."

DESKEY ASSOCIATES, INC., 45 W. 36th St., New York NY 10018. Director of Graphic Operations: Emmitt B. Sears. Specializes in brand and/or corporate identity, displays, packaging, illustration and mechanical art. Clients: corporations.
Needs: Works with freelance artists for design, illustration, P-O-P displays, mechanicals, retouching, airbrushing, model making, lettering and logos.
First Contact & Terms: "Artists should present their resume, hourly wages and make a written request

to present their work." Send query letter and resume to be kept on file. Prefers to see "best final samples of areas in which artist may be of help and very rough conceptual sketches." Samples are not returned. Write to schedule an appointment to show a portfolio, which should include thumbnails, roughs and "whatever is possible to show that will not be returned." Pays for design by the hour, $10 minimum or by contract. Pays for illustration by the project, $250 minimum. Considers complexity of project, client's budget, skill and experience of artist, and turnaround time when establishing payment.
Tips: "Too often artists present work that is a finished product—one wonders what efforts or contributions were made to develop the final product."

GABRIEL DI FIORE ASSOC., 625 Stanwix St., Pittsburgh PA 15222. (412)471-0608. Owner: Gabe Di Fiore. Specializes in annual reports, corporate identity, direct mail and publication. Clients: ad agencies, PR firms and corporations.
Needs: Works with 20 freelance artists/year. Uses artists for illustrations, mechanicals, retouching, charts/graphs and lettering. Especially needs mechanicals and illustrations.
First Contact & Terms: Send query letter with brochure showing art style or resume, tear sheets and slides. Samples not filed are returned by SASE. Reports only if interested. Call or write to schedule an appointment to show a portfolio, which should include thumbnails, roughs, original/final art and tear sheets. Pays for design by the hour, $10 minimum; pays for illustration by the hour, $10 minimum. Considers complexity of project, client's budget and how work will be used when establishing payment.

DI FRANZA-WILLIAMSON INC., 1414 Ave. of the Americas, New York NY 10019. (212)832-2343. Contact: Jack Williamson. Clients: businesses and advertising agencies.
Needs: Assigns 250 jobs/year; local artists with 5 years minimum of experience only. Uses artists for layout, comps, illustration, cartoons, lettering and retouching for catalogs, direct mail brochures, flyers, packaging, P-O-P displays and slides.
First Contact & Terms: Send query letter with resume and request interview. No work returned. Payment by the hour: $12-20, design and layout; $15-50, illustrations; $15-20, mechanicals and paste-up; $15-22, type spec. Considers complexity of project, client's budget, skill and experience of artist, and how work will be used when establishing payment.
Tips: "Show me good work." There is a "need for designers who can draw. Show me roughs and layouts, not just finished pieces. Illustration is coming back."

ANTHONY DI MARCO, ADVERTISING AND DESIGN AGENCY, 2948 Grand Route St. John, New Orleans LA 70119. (504)948-3128. Creative Director: Anthony Di Marco. Specializes in brand identity, packaging, publications, and technical illustration. Clients: individuals and major corporations.
Needs: Works with 5-10 freelance artists/year. Seeks "local artists with ambition. Artists should have substantial portfolios and an understanding of business requirements." Uses artists for design, illustration, mechanicals, retouching, airbrushing, posters, model making, charts/graphs. Computer-generated graphics are a current interest.
First Contact & Terms: Send query letter with resume, business card and slides and tear sheets to be kept on file. Samples not kept on file are returned by SASE. Reports back within 1 week if interested. Call or write for appointment to show portfolio. Pays for design and illustration by the project, $50-500 average. Considers complexity of project, skill and experience of artist, turnaround time and rights purchased when establishing payment.
Tips: "Keep professionalism in mind at all times. Artists should put forth their best effort. Apologizing for imperfect work" is a common mistake freelancers make when presenting a portfolio.

DIAMOND ART STUDIO LTD., 11 E. 36th St., New York NY 10016. (212)685-6622. Creative Directors: Gary and Douglas Diamond. Vice Presidents: John Taylor, Mary Nittolo, Phil Rowley. Art studio. Clients: advertising agencies, corporations, manufacturers and publishers. Assigns 500 jobs/year.
Needs: Employs 10 illustrators/month. Uses artists for comprehensive illustrations, cartoons, charts, graphs, illustrations, layout, lettering, logo design, paste-up, retouching, technical art and type spec.
First Contact & Terms: Send resume and tear sheets to be kept on file. SASE. Write for interview to show a portfolio. Pays for design by the hour. Pays for illustration by the project. Considers complexity of project, client's budget, skill and experience of artist, and turnaround time when establishing payment.
Tips: "Leave behind something memorable and well thought out."

DIMENSIONAL DESIGN, 11046 McCormick, North Hollywood CA 91601. (213)877-5694. Contact: Design Director. Specializes in brand and corporate identity, displays, exhibits and shows, packaging, publications, signage and technical illustration, direct mail marketing, movie titles and film production. Clients: multi-field corporations, manufacturers, shopping centers and advertising agencies.
Needs: Works with 20-30 freelance artists/year. Works on assignment only. Uses artists for advertis-

ing, brochure and catalog design, illustration and layout; P-O-P displays, mechanicals, retouching; poster, book and direct mail package design and illustration; model making, charts/graphs, lettering and logo design.
First Contact & Terms: Send query letter with brochure/flyer, resume and tear sheets, Photostats, photocopies, slides and photographs "as one unit to us." Samples returned by SASE, "but would like to keep samples, resume/brochure, etc. on file." Reports in 2 months. Call or write for appointment. Pays for design, $15-40 average/hour; pays for illustration, $20-60; also negotiates.
Tips: "Become as professional as possible, not only in art, but also in art reproduction."

DONATO & BERKLEY INC., 386 Park Ave. S, New York NY 10016. (212)532-3884. Contact: Sy Berkley or Steve Sherman. Advertising art studio. Specializes in direct mail response advertising, annual reports, brand identity, corporate identity and publications. Clients: ad agencies, public relations firms, direct response advertisers and publishers.
Needs: Works with 1-2 illustrators and 1-2 designers/month. Local experienced artists only. Uses artists for consumer magazines, direct mail, brochures/flyers, newspapers, layout, technical art, type spec, paste-up, lettering and retouching. Especially needs illustrations, retouching and mechanical paste-up.
First Contact & Terms: Call for interview. Send brochure showing art style, flyers, business card, resume and tear sheet to be kept on file. No originals returned to artist at job's completion. Call to schedule an appointment to show a portfolio, which should include thumbnails, roughs, original/final art and final reproduction/product. Pays for design by the hour,$25-50. Pays for illustration by the project, $75-1,500. Considers complexity of project and client's budget when establishing payment.
Tips: "We foresee a need for direct response art directors and the mushrooming of computer graphics. Clients are much more careful as to price and quality of work."

EDITING, DESIGN & PRODUCTION, INC., 4th Floor, 400 Market St., Philadelphia PA 19106. (215)592-1133. Production Manager: Jacqui Brownstein. Specializes in publications. Clients: publishers.
Needs: Works with approximately 18 freelance artists/year. Uses artists for design, illustrations, books and mechanicals. Especially needs designers of college textbook interior and/or covers.
First Contact & Terms: Send query letter with brochure showing art style or resume, tear sheets and photocopies. Samples not filed are returned only if requested. Reports within 2 weeks. Call to schedule an appointment to show a portfolio, which should include roughs, final reproduction/product, tear sheets and Photostats. Pays for design by the project, $200-500. Pays for illustration by the project, $10-30/piece. Considers complexity of project and client's budget when establishing payment.
Tips: "Our textbooks can be very complex and we require typed specifications and tissue layouts for every element in the book. We find we need a larger number of designers because we need the diversity to please various publishers. Some designers use the same elements in their design all the time and the publishers want each book to look different and unique." In presenting samples or portfolios, freelancers "usually have some beautiful artwork that they did and love but that is not appropriate to my needs. If they are informed up front before they come to see me, they should know what would apply to my needs."

EHN GRAPHICS, INC., 244 E. 46th St., New York NY 10017. (212)661-5947. President: Jack Ehn. Specializes in annual reports, book design, corporate identity, direct mail, publications and signage.
Needs: Works with 10-12 freelance artists/year. Uses artists for illustrations, books, mechanicals, retouching and direct mail packages.
First Contact & Terms: Send query letter with samples. Samples not filed are returned only if requested. Reports only if interested. Call or write to schedule an appointment to show a portfolio, which should include original/final art and final reproduction/product. Considers complexity of project, client's budget, and skill and experience of artist when establishing payment.

DAVE ELLIES INDUSTRIAL DESIGN, INC., 2015 W. Fifth Ave., Columbus OH 43212. (614)488-7995. Creative Manager: Ron Bushman. Specializes in corporate identity, displays, interior design, packaging and signage.
Needs: Works with 10 freelance artists/year. Prefers regional freelance artists with 3-5 years of experience. Works on assignment only. Uses artists for design, illustration, mechanicals, model making, AV materials and logos.
First Contact & Terms: Send query letter with resume, business card and slides to be kept on file. Samples not kept on file returned by SASE. Reports within 2 weeks. Call or write for appointment to show portfolio. Considers complexity of project, client's budget, skill and experience of artist and turnaround time when establishing payment.
Tips: Especially looks for "quality not quantity, professionalism, variety and effective problem solving" in samples.

ENSIGN DESIGN INC., 201 College Ave., Salem VA 24153. (703)389-0482. President: Jim Edgell. Specializes in corporate identity, displays, packaging, publications, signage, technical illustrations, product design prototypes and models. Clients: industry, communications and consumer products.
Needs: Works with "a few" freelance artists/year. Prefers local artists and that they work on premises. Uses artists for illustration, airbrushing and model making. Especially needs a good airbrush artist.
First Contact & Terms: Send query letter with resume to be kept on file. Samples not filed are returned by SASE. Reports only if interested. To show a portfolio, mail appropriate materials, which should include roughs, original/final art and final reproduction/product. Pays by the hour, $6-20 average. Considers complexity of project, client's budget, and skill and experience of artist when establishing payment.
Tips: "Assemble a portfolio showing broadest range of skills as those who can overlap into more than one area of design."

MEL ERIKSON/ART SERVICES, 31 Meadow Rd., Kings Park NY 11754-3812. (516)544-9191. Art Director: Toniann Dillon. Specializes in publications and technical illustration. Clients: book publishers.
Needs: Works with 8-10 freelance artists/year. Local artists only. Uses artists for advertising illustration, book design and illustration, mechanicals, retouching and charts/graphs.
First Contact & Terms: Send query letter with resume and photocopies to be kept on file. Samples not kept on file are not returned. Does not report back. Call to schedule an appointment to show a portfolio, which should include final reproduction/product. Pays for design by the hour, $4.50-20; by the project, $50-1,000; by the day, $40-100. Pays for illustration by the hour, $4.50-$9; by the project, $25-$100; by the day, $40-80. Considers complexity of project and client's budget when establishing payment.
Tips: "Call first—show only work relative to my needs."

ETC COMMUNICATIONS GROUP, INC., 61 W. 23rd St., 7th Floor, New York NY 10010. (212)645-6800. Principal: Edward T. Chin. Specializes in direct mail and marketing-oriented corporate brochures. Clients: Fortune 500 corporations, ad agencies, PR firms, magazine publishers, small- and medium-size companies.
Needs: Works with 17 freelance artists/year. Minimum 2-3 years of experience. Works on assignment only. Uses artists for design, illustration, mechanicals, retouching, airbrushing and comp rendering.
First Contact & Terms: Send query letter with resume, brochure, business card and tear sheets or photocopies to be kept on file. Write for appointment to show portfolio. Pays for design by the hour, $10-30; for illustration by the hour, $10-30, or by the project. Considers complexity of project, client's budget, skill and experience of artist, how work will be used, turnaround time and rights purchased when establishing payment.

FINN STUDIO LIMITED, 154 E. 64th St., New York NY 10021. (212)838-1212. Creative Director: Finn. Clients: theatres, boutiques, magazines, fashion and ad agencies.
Needs: Uses artists for T-shirt designs, illustrations, calligraphy; creative concepts in art for fashion and promotional T-shirts.
First Contact & Terms: Mail slides. SASE. Reports within 4 weeks. Pays $50-500; sometimes also offers royalty.

5 PENGUINS DESIGN, INC., 1648 W. Glenoaks Blvd., Glendale CA 91201. (818)502-1556. President: Dauri Pallas. Specializes in corporate identity and packaging. Clients: advertising for the motion picture industry, television and home video.
Needs: Works with varying number of freelance artists/year. Uses artists for design, mechanicals and production.
First Contact & Terms: Artists should be "very experienced and professional." Send query letter with resume, business card, tear sheets, photocopies, etc. to be kept on file. Samples not kept on file are not returned. Reports back only if interested. Pays for design by the hour at varying rates. Considers skill and experience of artist when establishing payment.

HANS FLINK DESIGN INC., 7-11 S. Broadway, White Plains NY 10601. (914)328-0888. President: Hans D. Flink. Specializes in brand identity, corporate identity, packaging and signage. Clients: corporate, packaged products.
Needs: Works with 10-20 freelance artists/year. Uses artists for design, illustration, P-0-P displays, mechanicals, retouching, airbrushing, model making, lettering, logos and package-related services.
First Contact & Terms: Send query letter with brochure and resume to be kept on file. Reports back only if interested. Call or write for appointment to show portfolio. Pays for design by the hour, $10-35 average; by the project, $500-3,000 average; by the day, $100-250 average. Pays for illustration by the project, $250-2,000 average. Considers complexity of project, client's budget, skill and experience of artist, how work will be used, turnaround time and rights purchased when establishing payment.

***FORREST ASSOCIATES INC.**, 5 Bridge St., Watertown MA 02172. (617)926-1131. President: Jess Forrest. Specializes in corporate identity, displays, interior design and product design.
Needs: Works with 2-3 freelance artists/year. Prefers local artists only. Works on assignment only. Uses artists for brochures, charts/graphs, AV materials, lettering and advertisements.
First Contact & Terms: Send query letter with resume. Call to schedule an appointment to show a portfolio. Pays for design by the hour, $15-25. Considers complexity of project, skill and experience of artist and turnaround time when establishing payment.
Tips: "We're a full-service industrial design firm."

FREE LANCE EXCHANGE, INC., 111 E. 85th St., New York NY 10028. (212)722-5816. Multi-service company.
Needs: Uses artists for cartoons, charts, graphs, illustrations, layout, lettering, logo design and mechanicals.
First Contact & Terms: Mail resume and photocopied samples that need not be returned. "Say you saw the listing in *Artist's Market*." Provide materials to be kept on file for future assignments. No originals returned to artist at job's completion.

FREEMAN DESIGN GROUP, 415 Farms Rd., Greenwich CT 06831. (202)968-0026. Specializes in annual reports, corporate identity, packaging, publications and signage. Clients: corporation.
Needs: Works with 5-10 freelance artists/year. New York City/Fairfield County artists only. Works on assignment only. Uses artists for illustration, mechanicals, retouching and airbrushing.
First Contact & Terms: Send query letter with brochure and business card to be kept on file. Call for appointment to show portfolio. Prefers to review slides, tear sheets or original work at time of interview *only*. Material not filed is returned by SASE only if requested. Reports back only if interested. Pays for design by the hour, $15-20 average, or by the project, $50-2,500 average; for illustration by the project, $50-1,000 average. Considers complexity of project, client's budget, how work will be used and rights purchased when establishing payment.
Tips: "Present a clean portfolio of your best work, not necessarily printed samples."

STEPHANIE FURNISS DESIGN, 1327 Via Sessi, San Rafael CA 94901. (415)459-4730. Contact: Stephanie Furniss. Specializes in corporate identity, architectural and environmental graphics, supergraphics, interior design, packaging, sculpture and signage.
Needs: Works with 5 freelance artists/year. Uses artists for lettering and production work.
First Contact & Terms: Send query letter with resume and business card. Call or write to schedule an appointment to show a portfolio, which should include thumbnails, roughs, original/final art, final reproduction/product, color, tear sheets, Photostats, photographs and b&w. Pays for design by the hour, $8-25. Considers complexity of project, skill and experience of artist, and turnaround time when establishing payment.
Tips: "Write first. Call second for appointment. Show up for appointment promptly and with *good* portfolio (nothing just thrown together)."

GAILEN ASSOCIATES, INC., Suite 105, 800 Oak St., Winnetka IL 60093. (312)446-5003. President: Bob Gailen. Specializes in annual reports, brand identity, corporate identity, packaging, publications and signage. Clients: direct mail, ad agencies, marketing firms.
Needs: Works with 5 freelance artists/year. Works on assignment basis. Uses artists for illustration, photography, airbrushing and model making.
First Contact & Terms: Send query letter with resume and samples to be kept on file. Does not report back. Pays for design by the hour, $25 minimum; for illustration, per illustrator's quote. Considers complexity of project, client's budget, and skill and experience of artist when establishing payment.

GARRETT COMMUNICATIONS, INC., Box 53, Atlanta GA 30301. (404)755-2513. President: Ruby Grant Garrett. Specializes in brand identity, corporate identity and packaging. Clients: manufacturers, public relations firms and ad agencies.
Needs: Works with 6 freelance artists/year. Works on assignment only. Uses artists for illustration, mechanicals, retouching, airbrushing, P-O-P displays, model making and lettering. Buys 3 cartoons, 6 cartoon-style and 6 humorous illustrations/year.
First Contact & Terms: Send resume, business card and samples to be kept on file. Samples not kept on file are returned only if requested. Reports within 10 days. Call to schedule an appointment to show a portfolio, which should include thumbnails, original/final art and photostats. Pays by the hour, $35 minimum. Considers client's budget, turnaround time and rights purchased when establishing payment.
Tips: "State what you cannot do. Live with your quote and place conditions in writing."

***GEMINI II ADVERTISING AND GRAPHICS, INC.**, 8580 Production Ave., San Diego CA 92121. (619)695-6955. Vice President: Barbara A. Brewer. Specializes in high-tech and business-to-business advertising. Clients: business and high-tech.

Needs: Works with 4 freelance artists/year. Prefers illustrators, designers and layout artists. Works on assignment only. Uses artists for design, illustrations, brochures, catalogs, magazines, P-O-P displays, mechanicals, retouching, airbrushing, direct mail packages and advertisements.

First Contact & Terms: Send query letter with resume and photocopies. Samples are filed. Reports back only if interested. "We will call to schedule an appointment to show a portfolio." Pays for design and illustration by the project, $200-5,000. Considers complexity of project, turnaround time and rights purchased when establishing payment. Buys all rights.

Tips: Artists "must have experience with agency work. No freelancer considered without having three years or more agency experience inhouse."

ERIC GLUCKMAN COMMUNICATIONS, INC., 60 E. 42nd St., New York NY 10165. (212)697-3670. President: Eric Gluckman. Specializes in corporate identity, direct mail, publications, industrial advertising and promotion, corporate capability brochures and sales promotion (trade). "We usually deal directly with client."

Needs: Works with 20 freelance artists/year. Artists should have 3 years of experience minimum. "All rights to art and photography revert to client." Works on assignment only. Uses artists for design, illustration, brochures, mechanicals, retouching, airbrushing, direct mail packages, posters, charts/graphs, lettering, logos and advertisements.

First Contact & Terms: Send query letter with resume and samples to be kept on file. No slides as samples. Samples not kept on file returned by SASE. Reports only if interested. Call or write for appointment to show portfolio. Pay is negotiable. Considers complexity of project, client's budget, skill and experience of artist, and turnaround time when establishing payment. Buys all rights.

Tips: "Be professional, make deadlines."

GOFF DESIGN GROUP, 69 Water St., San Francisco CA 94133. (415)441-5084. Art Director: Andrea Bryck. Specializes in annual reports, corporate identity, direct mail, packaging, publications, marketing and communications planning and design. Clients: ad agencies and major corporations.

Needs: Works with 10-15 freelance artists/year. Prefers three years of experience. Uses artists for design, illustrations, mechanicals, retouching, airbrushing, model making, AV materials and lettering.

First Contact & Terms: Send query letter with resume, tear sheets, Photostats, photocopies, slides and photographs. Samples not filed are returned by SASE. Reports only if interested. Call or write to schedule an appointment to show a portfolio, which should include roughs, original/final art, final reproduction/product, color, tear sheets, Photostats, photographs, b&w or whatever form will best represent artist's work. Pays for design by the hour, $18 minimum. Considers complexity of project, client's budget, skill and experience of artist, how work will be used, turnaround time and rights purchased when establishing payment.

GOLDSMITH YAMASAKI SPECHT INC, Suite 510, 900 N. Franklin, Chicago IL 60610. (312)266-8404. Industrial design consultancy. Chairman: William M. Goldsmith. Specializes in corporate identity, packaging, product design and graphics. Clients: industrial firms, institutions, service organizations, ad agencies, government agencies, etc.

Needs: Works with 6-10 freelance artists/year. "We generally use local artists, simply for convenience." Works on assignment only. Uses artists for design (especially graphics), illustration, retouching, model making, lettering and production art.

First Contact & Terms: Send query letter with resume and samples to be kept on file. Samples not kept on file are returned only if requested. Reports only if interested. Call or write to schedule an appointment to show a portfolio, which should include roughs and final reproduction/product. Pays for design by the hour, $20 minimum. Pays for illustration by the project; payment depends on project. Considers complexity of project, client's budget, skill and experience of artist, how work will be used, turnaround time and rights purchased when establishing payment.

Tips: "If we receive many inquiries, obviously our time commitment may necessarily be short. Please understand. We use very little outside help, but it is increasing (mostly graphic design and production art)."

ALAN GORELICK DESIGN, INC., Marketing Communications, One High St., Morristown NJ 07960-6807. President/Creative Director: Alan Gorelick. Specializes in corporate identity, displays, direct mail, signage, technical illustration and company and product literature. Clients: health care and pharmaceutical corporations, industrial, manufacturing.

Needs: Works with 6-10 freelance artists/year. Works with "seasoned professional or extremely talented entry-level" artists only. Uses artists for design, illustration, brochures, mechanicals, retouching, airbrushing, posters, direct mail packages, charts/graphs, logos and advertisements.

First Contact & Terms: Send query letter with brochure, resume, business card, Photostats, slides,

photocopies and tear sheets to be kept on file. Samples not filed are returned by SASE only if requested. Reports only if interested. Write for appointment to show portfolio, which should include thumbnails, roughs, original/final art, final reproduction/product, color, tear sheets, Photostats, photographs and b&w. Pays for design by the hour, $20-50. Pays for illustration by the hour, $15-50; by the project, $250-5,000. Considers complexity of project, client's budget, and skill and experience of artist when establishing payment.
Tips: Requires "straight talk, professional work ethic and commitment to assignment."

***GRAPHIC DESIGN INC.**, 23844 Sherwood, Center Line MI 48015. (313)758-0480. General Manager: Norah Heppard.
Needs: Works on assignment only. Uses artists for brochure design, catalog design, illustration and layout, direct mail packages, advertising design and illustration and posters.
First Contact & Terms: Send query letter with resume and photocopies. Samples are filed. Samples not filed are returned only if requested. Reports back within 1 week. Write to schedule an appointment to show a portfolio or mail thumbnails, roughs, original/final art, final reproduction/product, color, b&w, tear sheets, Photostats and photographs. Pays by the project, $50-2,000. Considers complexity of project, available budget, turnaround time and rights purchased when establishing payment. Buys all rights.
Tips: Artists must have the "ability to make deadlines and keep promises."

***GRAPHIC GROUP**, 203 Mamaroneck Ave., White Plains NY 10601. (914)948-3151. Studio Manager: Leslie Matteson. Specializes in annual reports and corporate identity. Clients: Fortune 500.
Needs: Works with 10 freelance artists/year. Uses artists for design, illustrations, brochures, catalogs, books, magazines, newspapers, P-O-P displays, mechanicals, posters, direct mail packages, charts/graphs, AV materials and logos.
First Contact & Terms: Send query letter with resume and slides. Samples are filed. Reports back only if interested. Write to schedule an appointment to show a portfolio, which should include roughs, Photostats and b&w. Pays for design and illustration by the hour, $15-20. Considers client's budget and turnaround time when establishing payment. Buys first rights.

GRAPHICUS, 11046 McCormick, North Hollywood CA 91601. (213)877-5694. President: Wayne Hallowell. Specializes in annual reports, brand and corporate identity, displays, exhibits and shows, packaging, publications, signage and technical illustration. Clients: advertising agencies, corporations, manufacturers (in all fields); "we supply all areas of corporate communications."
Needs: Works with 20 freelance artists/year. Prefers at least 5 years of experience. Works on assignment only. Uses artists for advertising, brochure and catalog design and illustration, advertising layout, P-O-P displays, mechanicals, poster, book and direct mail package design and illustration; model making, AV presentations, lettering, and logo and package design. Especially needs "good, clean, knowledgeable artists who are true professionals and know what happens to their work after it leaves the drawing boards."
First Contact & Terms: Send query letter with resume, tear sheets, Photostats, slides and photographs. Samples returned by SASE "only when requested; it is far better to have samples available in our offices." Reports in 4 weeks. Reports back on whether to expect possible future assignments. Call or write to schedule an appointment to show portfolio, which should include thumbnails, roughs, original/final art, final reproduction/product, tear sheets and photographs. Pays for design by the project, $1,000-$10,000. Pays for illustration by the project, $1,000-15,000.
Tips: "An artist should know the profession, become more business-like and train as an athlete does. Be creative, be yourself, be clean."

***GRIMALDI DESIGN INC.**, Box 864, Murray Hill Station, New York NY 10016. (212)532-3773. Assistants to Director: James Moksette, Andrew Thornley. President: Joseph Grimaldi. Specializes in displays, interior design, packaging and signage.
Needs: Works with 6-8 freelance artists/year. Uses artists for illustration, mechanicals and model making.
First Contact & Terms: Prefers 3 years of experience. Works on assignment only. Send resume and samples to be kept on file. Prefers slides as samples. Samples not kept on file returned. Reports within 2 weeks. Write for appointment to show portfolio. Pays for design by the hour, $10 maximum. Illustration rates on request. Considers complexity of project and client's budget when establishing payment.

GROUP FOUR DESIGN, 147 Simsbury Rd., Avon CT 06001-0717. (203)678-1570. Production Manager: Mike Doviak. Specializes in corporate communications, product design and packaging design. Clients: corporations dealing in consumer products and office products.
Needs: Works with 5-10 freelance artists/year. Artists must have at least two years of experience. Uses artists for illustrations, mechanicals, airbrushing and model making.

First Contact & Terms: Send query letter with resume and slides. Samples not filed are returned. Reports only if interested. To show a portfolio, mail roughs and original/final art. Pays for design by the hour, $12-20. Considers client's budget, and skill and experience of artist when establishing payment.
Tips: "We look for creativity in all artists seeking employment and expect to see that in their resume and portfolio."

***HALL DESIGN**, 707 California St., Mountain View CA 94041. (415)969-4255. President: Jack Hall. Specializes in brand identity, corporate identity, displays, interior design and packaging. Clients: corporations such as Motorola, Fujitsu and Scott Paper.
Needs: Works with 4 freelance artists/year. Prefers artists with 5 or more years of experience, local only. Works on assignment only. Prefers abstract graphic design, typography-based designs. Uses artists for design, P-O-P displays, mechanicals, model making, direct mail packages, AV materials and logos.
First Contact & Terms: Send resume and slides. Samples are filed. Samples not filed are returned. Reports back only if interested. To show a portfolio, mail original/final art and color. Pays for design by the project, $200-5,000. Considers complexity of project, client's budget, skill and experience of artist, how work will be used, turnaround time and rights purchased when establishing payment. Buys all rights.
Tips: "Be patient. The right job may not come along right away."

HAMILTON DESIGN, INC., 2130 Stella Ct., Columbus OH 43215. (614)481-8016. Contact: Bill Hamilton or Joan Etter. Specializes in brand identity, displays, packaging, publications and direct mail—merchandising and selling ads. Clients: publications and manufacturers.
Needs: Works on assignment only. Uses artists for advertising and brochure layout; catalog design and layout, P-O-P displays, mechanicals, retouching and direct response packages.
First Contact & Terms: Send query letter with resume and slides. Samples not kept on file are returned. Reports in 2 weeks. Call for appointment to show portfolio. Pays for design and illustration by the hour, $30-70 average. Considers how work will be used and rights purchased when establishing payment.

PAIGE HARDY & ASSOCIATES, 1731 Kettner Blvd., San Diego CA 92101. (619)233-7238. Contact: Paige Hardy or Lorie Kennedy. Specializes in corporate identity, publications, technical illustration and advertising art. Clients: retail firms and publications.
Needs: Works with 25 freelance artists/year. Usually works on assignment only. Uses artists for advertising, brochure and catalog design, illustration and layout; mechanicals, retouching and logo design. Especially needs production artist/paste-up with heavy experience.
First Contact & Terms: Send query letter with resume. Samples not returned. Reports in 1 week. Call or write for appointment to submit portfolio for review. Pays by the hour and project; negotiates payment.

HARPER & ASSOCIATES, INC., 2285 116th Ave. NE, Bellevue WA 98004. (206)462-0405. Creative Director: Randi Harper. Office Manager: Kelley Wood. Specializes in brand and corporate identity. Clients: high-tech, manufacturers, professional services (i.e., architects, doctors, attorneys, yacht brokers, stockbrokers, etc.), food, fashion, etc.
Needs: Works with 10-12 freelance artists/year. Works on assignment only. Uses artists for illustration and airbrush.
First Contact & Terms: Send resume and slides. Samples returned by SASE. Reports only if interested. Pays for design by the hour, $8-20; for illustration by the hour, $10-30, or by the project. Considers complexity of project, client's budget, skill and experience of artist, how work will be used, turnaround time and rights purchased when establishing payment.
Tips: "Be honest about your abilities and do not be afraid to turn down an assignment if it is not appropriate for you."

***LEE HELMER DESIGN**, 54 John St., Charleston SC 29403. (803)723-4570. President: Lee Helmer. Specializes in corporate identity, direct mail and publications. Clients: ad agencies, theatre and fine arts organizations, retail businesses and corporations.
Needs: Works with approximately 6 freelance artists/year. Uses artists for illustration, charts/graphs, lettering and map making.
First Contact & Terms: No restrictions "other than price." Works on assignment only. Send query letter with samples to be kept on file. Call for appointment to show portfolio. Reports back only if interested. Pays for illustration by job quotation; by the project, $150-750 average. Considers complexity of project, client's budget, skill and experience of artist, how work will be used, turnaround time and rights purchased when establishing payment.
Tips: "Charleston has a very limited market for illustrators demanding high fees."

HERBST, LAZAR, ROGERS & BELL, INC., 37 North Duke St., Lancaster PA 17602. (717)291-9042. Office Manager: Sarah Preston. Specializes in brand identity, corporate identity, displays, interior design, packaging, publications, signage, technical illustration, human factors, market placement research, product design and cost reduction. Clients: manufacturers, ad agencies and retailers.
Needs: Works with 20 freelance artists/year. Artists should be within driving distance; "prefer freelancers to work inhouse." Works on assignment only. Uses artists for illustration, brochures, catalogs, mechanicals, model making, charts/graphs, lettering, logos advertisements and market research.
First Contact & Terms: Send query letter with brochure, resume and business card to be kept on file; slides to be returned. Samples not kept on file are returned. Reports within 30 days. To show a portfolio, mail appropriate materials or write to schedule an appointment; portfolio should include thumbnails, roughs, final reproduction/product and photographs. Pays for design by the hour, $7-25; pays for illustration by the hour, $10-$25. Considers complexity of project, and skill and experience of artist when establishing payment.

HILLMAN ADVANCED DESIGN STUDIO, 1021 Pearl, Boulder CO 80302. (303)443-6099. President: Jack L. Hillman. Specializes in corporate identity, displays, industrial design and packaging. Clients: manufacturers.
Needs: Works with 12 freelance artists/year. Prefers local and experienced artists. Works on assignment only. Uses artists for design, brochures, mechanicals, posters, model making, charts/graphs, AV materials, lettering and logos. Especially needs "an experienced, well-rounded industrial designer."
First Contact & Terms: Send query letter with brochure, resume, business card and samples to be kept on file. Samples "originally should be any medium appropriate to the subject. In person I like to see originals or the finished piece." Samples not filed are returned by SASE only if requested. Reports within 1 week. Pay varies. Considers client's budget and skill and experience of artist when establishing payment.
Tips: "Only the best are considered: ability to meet schedules, professionalism, neatness; organization."

DAVID HIRSCH DESIGN GROUP, INC., 205 W. Wacker Dr., Chicago IL 60606. President: David Hirsch. Specializes in annual reports, corporate identity, publications and promotional literature. Clients: PR, real estate, financial and industrial firms.
Needs: Works with over 30 freelance artists/year. Uses artists for design, illustrations, brochures, retouching, airbrushing, AV materials, lettering, logos and photography.
First Contact & Terms: Send query letter with promotional materials showing art style or samples. Samples not filed are returned by SASE. Reports only if interested. Call to schedule an appointment to show a portfolio, which should include roughs, final reproduction/product, tear sheets and photographs. Considers complexity of project, client's budget and how work will be used when establishing payment.
Tips: "We're always looking for talent at fair prices."

GRANT HOEKSTRA GRAPHICS, INC., 333 N. Michigan Ave., Chicago IL 60601. (312)641-6940. President: Grant Hoekstra. Specializes in publications. Clients: publishers, ad agencies and corporations.
Needs: Works with 15 freelance artists/year. Local artists with experience only. Works on assignment only. Uses artists for design, illustration, brochures, retouching and lettering. Especially needs "illustrator who understands 'fundamental Christian' market."
First Contact & Terms: Send samples and prices to be kept on file. Call for appointment to show portfolio. Prefers photocopies as samples. Pays for design by the hour, $15-50 average. Pays for illustration by the project, $10-1,000 average. Considers complexity of project, client's budget and how work will be used when establishing payment.

THE HOLM GROUP, 3rd Floor, 405 Sansome, San Francisco CA 94111. (415)397-7272. Specializes in corporate identity and collateral. Clients: corporations.
Needs: Works with 5-10 freelance artists/year. Uses artists for illustration, mechanicals, retouching, airbrushing, lettering and logos.
First Contact & Terms: "Artist must send 'leave behind' first; then, we may call at a later date to see portfolio." Send query letter with leave behind and/or resume to be kept on file (except for bulky items or items requested returned). "Photocopies of samples are fine if they demonstrate the quality of work." Samples not kept on file are returned by SASE. Reports only if interested for a specific project (may be much later). Pays for illustration by the project, $350-1,000 average. Pays $15-20 in production. Considers complexity of project, client's budget and turnaround time when establishing payment.
Tips: "Put together an eye-catching resume to leave behind."

FRANK HOSICK DESIGN, Box H, Vashon Island WA 98070. (206)463-5454. Contact: Frank Hosick. Specializes in brand identity, corporate identity, packaging, product design and model building. Clients:

manufacturers.
Needs: Works on assignment only. Uses artists for illustration, mechanicals, retouching, airbrushing and model making.
First Contact & Terms: Send query letter with brochure, resume, business card and samples to be kept on file. Samples not kept on file are returned only if requested. Reports only if interested. Call for appointment to show portfolio. Pays for design by the hour, $15-50 average; by the project, $100 minimum; or by the day, $75-350 average. Pays for illustration by the hour, $15-50 average; by the project, $100-1,500 average; or by the day, $75-350 average. Considers complexity of project, client's budget, skill and experience of artist, and how work will be used when establishing payment.
Tips: Especially looks for "creativity, craftsmanship and quality of presentation" when reviewing a portfolio. Changes in the field include "big influence by computers, both in concept work and execution. Computer knowledge is helpful."

THE HOYT GROUP, INC., Box 686, Franklin Lakes NJ 07417-0688. President: Earl Hoyt. Specializes in corporate identity and packaging, and develops package structures. Clients: Fortune 500 firms.
Needs: Works with 10-15 freelance artists/year. Seeks experienced professionals. Works on assignment only. Uses artists for design, mechanicals, airbrushing, model making, lettering and logos.
First Contact & Terms: Send brochure to be kept on file. Send reproductions only as samples—no original art. Reports only if interested. Write for appointment to show portfolio. Pays for design by the project, $350-2,000. Pays for illustration by the project, $200-1,500. Considers client's budget, and skill and experience of artist when establishing payment.
Tips: Looks for "artistic flair." The most common mistake freelancers make in presenting samples or portfolios is "showing old, old work, plus everything they have ever done."

HUSTON AND BECK DESIGNERS, INC., 120 Lake St., Burlington VT 05402-1034. (802)864-5928. Principal: B. Huston. Specializes in displays, interior design, packaging, publications and signage. Clients: manufacturers, communication departments, museums and corporations.
Needs: Works with 24-50 freelance artists/year. Works on assignment only. Uses artists for design, illustrations, books, P-O-P displays, mechanicals, model making, charts/graphs and AV materials.
First Contact & Terms: Send query letter with resume. Samples not filed are returned only if requested. Reports only if interested. Call to show a portfolio, which should include thumbnails, roughs and photographs. Pays for design by the hour, $9-15. Pays for illustration by the hour, $25-75. Considers complexity of project, client's budget, skill and experience of artist, and turnaround time when establishing payment.

IDENTITY CENTER, 955G N. Plum Grove Rd., Schaumburg IL 60173. President: Wayne Kosterman. Specializes in brand identity, corporate identity, publications and signage. Clients: corporations, hospitals and banks.
Needs: Works with 6-10 freelance artists/year. Prefers 3-5 years of experience minimum. Uses artists for illustration, mechanicals, retouching and lettering.
First Contact & Terms: Send resume and photocopies. Samples are filed. Samples not filed are returned. Reports back within 1 week. To show a portfolio, mail original/final art, Photostats and photographs. Pays for design by the hour, $15-20. Pays for illustration by the hour, $10-25. Considers client's budget, skill and experience of artist and how work will be used when establishing payment. Buys one-time rights; rights purchased vary according to project.
Tips: "Not interested in amateurs or 'part-timers'."

***IMAGE DYNAMICS, INC.**, 5820 Oberlin Dr., San Diego CA 92121. (619)546-3900. Art Director: Kirsten Tiemeier. Specializes in annual reports, corporate identity, direct mail, publications and technical illustrations. Clients: auto manufacturers, computer companies and medical products.
Needs: Works with 10 freelance artists/year. Works on assignment only. Uses artists for design, illustrations, brochures, catalogs, books, magazines, newspapers, mechanicals, retouching, airbrushing, posters and direct mail packages.
First Contact & Terms: Send query letter with resume and photocopies. Samples are filed. Samples not filed are returned only if requested by artist. Reports back only if interested. Call to schedule an appointment to show a portfolio, which should include roughs, original/final art, b&w and color. Pays for design by the hour, $15-50. Pays for illustration by the project $100-2,000. Considers client's budget and skill and experience of artist when establishing payment. Buys all rights.

IMAGES, 1835 Hampden Ct., Louisville KY 40205. (502)459-0804. Creative Director: Julius Friedman. Specializes in annual reports, corporate identity, poster design and publications. Clients: corporate.
Needs: Works with approximately 100 freelance artists/year. Prefers experienced artists only. Uses art-

ists for advertising illustration and layout, brochure and catalog design and illustration, brochure layout, mechanicals, retouching, poster design, book design and illustration, charts/graphs, lettering and logo design.
First Contact & Terms: Send brochure/flyer or resume and business card as samples to be kept on file. Samples not filed returned by SASE. Works on assignment only; reports whether to expect possible future assignments. Pays by the project for design and illustration.

***INDIANA DESIGN CONSORTIUM, INC.**, Box 180, 300 River City Market Bldg., Lafayette IN 47902. (317)423-5469. Senior Art Director: Bryce Culverhouse. Specializes in corporate identity, displays, direct mail, publications, signage, technical illustrations, advertising and marketing communications. Clients: industrial, agricultural.
Needs: Works with 10-20 freelance artists/year. Prefers very experienced illustrators. Uses artists for illustrations, mechanicals, retouching, airbrushing, model making and lettering.
First Contact & Terms: Send brochure. Samples are filed. Samples not filed are returned by SASE. Reports back only if interested. Call or write to schedule an appointment to show a portfolio, which should include roughs, original/final art, final reproduction/product, photographs, b&w and color. Pays for design and illustration by the project. Considers complexity of project, client's budget, skill and experience of artist and turnaround time when establishing payment. Negotiates rights purchased.

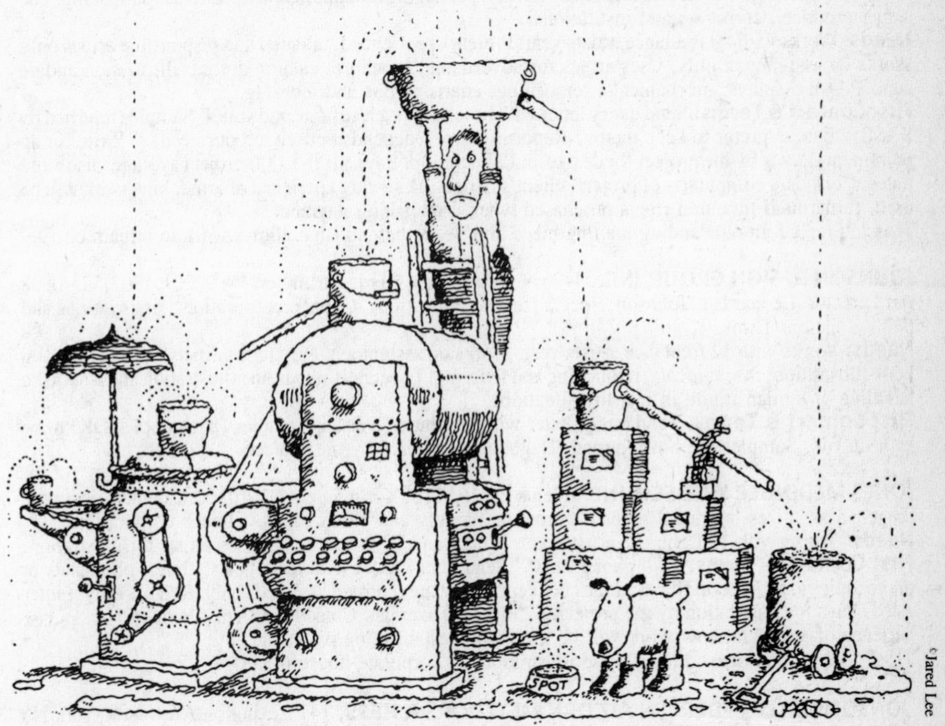

Jared Lee of Lebanon, Ohio, received this assignment for a humorous illustration from Bryce Culverhouse, art director for the Indiana Design Consortium in Lafayette, Indiana. Looking for an illustrator with a "humorous style," Culverhouse found Lee through the Creative Black Book. This ad conveys the futility of "people trying to jerrybuild a solution." Lee says humorous illustration differs from cartoons because it "solves a problem. You have something to work with, like ad copy or a storyboard, whereas cartoons come when an idea pops into your head." Culverhouse bought all rights to the illustration.

***INK DESIGNS**, 4839 N. Seeley, Chicago IL 60625. (312)989-8809. Production Manager: Bill Steffener. Specializes in corporate identity, direct mail and publications. Clients: corporations.
Needs: Works with 2-3 freelance artists/year. Works on assignment only. Uses artists for illustrations.
First Contact & Terms: Send query letter or resume and photocopies. Samples are filed. Reports back only if interested. To show a portfolio, mail thumbnails, roughs, original/final art and final reproduction/product. Pays for design and illustration by the hour, $10-35. Considers client's budget when establishing payment. Buys all rights.

INNOVATIVE DESIGN & GRAPHICS, Suite 214, 1234 Sherman Ave., Evanston IL 60202-1343. (312)475-7772. Contact: Tim Sonder and Maret Thorpe. Specializes in publications. Clients: magazine publishers, corporate communication departments, associations.
Needs: Works with 3-15 freelance artists/year. Local artists only. Uses artists for illustration and airbrushing.
First Contact & Terms: Send query letter with brochure showing art style or resume, tear sheets, Photostats, slides and photographs. Reports only if interested. Write to schedule an appointment to show a portfolio, which should include original/final art, final reproduction/product, tear sheets and Photostats. Pays for illustration by the project, $100-700 average. Considers complexity of project, client's budget and turnaround time when establishing payment.
Tips: "Interested in meeting new illustrators, but have a tight schedule. Looking for people who can grasp complex ideas and turn them into high-quality illustrations. Ability to draw people well is a must."

JMH CORPORATION, Suite 300, 247 S. Meridian, Indianapolis IN 46225. (317)639-2535. President: Michael Hayes. Specializes in corporate identity, packaging and publications. Clients: publishing, consumer products, corporate and institutional.
Needs: Works with 10 freelance artists/year. Prefers experienced, talented and responsible artists only. Works on assignment only. Uses artists for advertising, brochure, catalog design, illustration and design, P-O-P displays, mechanicals, retouching, charts/graphs and lettering.
First Contact & Terms: Send query letter with brochure/flyer, resume and slides. Samples returned by SASE, "but we prefer to keep them." Reporting time "depends entirely on our needs." Write for appointment. Pay is by the project for design and illustration. Pays $100-1,000/project average; also negotiates. Considers complexity of project, client's budget, skill and experience of artist, how work will be used, turnaround time and rights purchased when establishing payment.
Tips: "Prepare an outstanding mailing piece and 'leave-behind' that allows work to remain on file."

JOHNSON DESIGN GROUP, INC., 3426 N. Washington Blvd., Arlington VA 22201. (703)525-0808. Art Director: Leonard A. Johnson. Specializes in publications. Clients: corporations, associations and public relations firms.
Needs: Works with 12 freelance artists/year. Works on assignment only. Uses artists for brochure and book illustration, mechanicals, retouching and lettering. Especially needs line illustration and a realistic handling of human figure in real life situations.
First Contact & Terms: Send query letter with brochure/flyer and samples (photocopies OK) to be kept on file. Samples are not returned. Negotiates payment by the project.

JONES MEDINGER KINDSCHI INC., Fields Ln., RFD 2, North Salem NY 10560. Contact: Wynn Medinger. Specializes in annual reports, corporate identity and publications. Clients: corporations.
Needs: Works with 15 freelance artists/year. Works on assignment only. Uses artists for illustration.
First Contact & Terms: "*No* phone calls!" Send query letter with tear sheets, slides, photostats or photocopies to be kept on file. Samples not kept on file are returned by SASE only. Reports only if interested. Pays for illustration by the project, $250-5,000 average. Considers client's budget, skill and experience of artist and how work will be used when establishing payment.
Tips: "We mainly use editorial-style illustration for corporate house organs."

JONSON PIRTLE PEDERSEN ALCORN METZDORS & HESS, 141 Lexington Ave., New York NY 10016. Clients: corporations and publishers.
Needs: Prefers local artists and photographers for annual reports, publications, catalogs, etc. Pays $15-20, mechanicals and paste-up. Negotiates pay for color separations, illustrations, lettering, retouching and technical art.
First Contact & Terms: Query. SASE.

FREDERICK JUNGCLAUS, Designer/Illustrator, 145 E. 14th St., Indianapolis IN 46202. (317)636-4891. Owner: Fred Jungclaus. Specializes in annual reports, corporate identity, displays, architectural renderings and 3-D photo props. Clients: ad agencies and architects.
Needs: Works with 3-5 freelance artists/year. Works on assignment only. Uses artists for retouching

and airbrushing. Seeks artists capable of illustrating Indy-type race cars or antique cars.
First Contact & Terms: Send samples to be kept on file. Prefers slides or tear sheets as samples. Samples not filed are returned only if requested. Reports by SASE only if interested. Call for appointment to show portfolio. Pays by the project. Considers skill and experience of artist and turnaround time when establishing payment.

DAVID KAGEYAMA DESIGNER, 2119 Smith Tower, Seattle WA 98104. Contact: David Kageyama. Specializes in annual reports, corporate identity, displays, packaging, publications and signage. Clients: public service agencies, corporations, banking and insurance, attorneys and other professionals.
Needs: Works with 12 freelance artists/year. Works on assignment only. Uses artists for advertising, brochure, posters, direct mail packages, book and catalog illustration; retouching, AV presentations and calligraphy. Especially needs good, quick line/wash, humorous illustrator.
First Contact & Terms: Send brochure/flyer or resume, business card and samples to be kept on file for possible future assignments. Prefers photos (prints), actual illustrations and printed pieces as samples. Call for appointment. Pays $100-300 average/project for quick line illustrations. Considers client's budget, skill and experience of artist and turnaround time when establishing payment.
Tips: "We are much more apt to respond to the artist with a specific style or who specializes in a particular topic rather than the generalist. Keep in touch with your latest work. I like to see rough sketches as well as finished work. My firm buys all photography and virtually all illustration used for our clients."

KEITHLEY & ASSOCIATES, INC., 32 W. 22nd St., New York NY 10010. (212)807-8388. Art Director: Nancy P. Danahy. Specializes in publications. Primary clients: publishing (book and promotion departments); secondary clients: small advertising agencies.
Needs: Works with 3-6 freelance artists/year. "Except for artists doing retouching and some design work, all work must be done in our studio. We prefer experienced artists (2 years minimum)." Uses artists for design, brochures, catalogs, books (design and dummy), mechanicals, retouching and charts/graphs.
First Contact & Terms: Call for appointment to show portfolio. Do not send samples. Reports only if interested. Pays for design by the hour, $10-15 average. Pays for mechanicals by the hour, $6-15 average. Considers client's budget, and skill and experience of artist when establishing payment.
Tips: "We will be most likely to use you if you can handle the assignment completely—concept, presentation comps, type specs, mechanicals—or efficiently pick up a project in mid-course." A mistake artists make in presenting their portfolio is "not pointing out the obstacles they had to overcome during the course of a job."

***KELLY & CO., GRAPHIC DESIGN, INC.**, 5530 First Ave. N., St. Petersburg FL 33710. (813)341-1009. Art Director: Ken Kelly. Specializes in annual reports, brand identity, corporate identity, displays, direct mail, packaging, publications, signage and technical illustrations. Clients: industrial, banking, auto, boating, real estate, accountants, furniture, travel and ad agencies.
Needs: Works with 6 freelance artists/year. Prefers artists with a minimum of 5 years of experience. "Local artists preferred, in my office. Nonsmokers. Must be skilled in all areas. Must operate stat camera. Must have a good working attitude. Must be balanced in all styles." Uses artists for design, illustrations, brochures, catalogs, magazines, newspapers, P-O-P displays, mechanicals, retouching, airbrushing, posters, model making, direct mail packages, charts/graphs, lettering and logos.
First Contact & Terms: Send query letter with resume, tear sheets and photocopies, or "copies of work showing versatility." Samples are filed. Reports back only if interested. Write to schedule an appointment to show a portfolio, which should include roughs, tear sheets and b&w photocopies. Pays for design by the hour, $7.50-12.50; by the day, $50-60. Pays for illustration by the hour, $10-12.50; by the day, $60-75. Considers complexity of project, client's budget, skill and experience of artist and turnaround time when establishing payment. Buys all rights.
Tips: "Don't smoke! Be highly talented in all areas with reasonable rates. Must be honest with a high degree of integrity and appreciation."

LARRY KERBS STUDIOS INC., 419 Park Ave. S., New York NY 10016. (212)686-9420. Contact: Larry Kerbs or Jim Lincoln. Specializes in sales promotion design, some ad work and placement, annual reports, corporate identity, publications and technical illustration. Clients: industrial, chemical, insurance and public relations.
Needs: Works with 3 illustrators and 1 designer/month. New York, New Jersey and Connecticut artists only. Uses artists for direct mail, layout, illustration, slide sets, technical art, paste-up and retouching for annual reports, trade magazines, product brochures and direct mail. Especially needs freelance comps through mechanicals; type specification.
First Contact & Terms: Mail samples or call for interview. Prefers b&w line drawings, roughs, previously published work as samples. Provide brochures, business card and resume to be kept on file for fu-

ture assignments. No originals returned to artist at job's completion. Pays $14-18/hour, paste-up; $18-20/hour, comprehensive layout; $18-22/hour average, design; negotiates payment by the project for illustration.
Tips: "Improve hand lettering for comps; strengthen typographic knowledge and application."

***ANDRÉ RICHARDSON KING—ARCHITECTURAL GRAPHICS DESIGNERS**, Suite 2200, 220 S. State St., Chicago IL 60604. (312)922-7757. Owner: André R. King. Specializes in corporate identity, displays, publications, signing and technical illustrations. Clients: developers, architects, landscape architects, planners, manufacturers and municipalities, etc.
Needs: Works on contract only. Uses artist for design, brochures, catalogs, charts/graphs, logos and advertisements.
First Contact & Terms: Send resume and tear sheets. Samples are filed. Samples not filed are returned only if requested by artist.

***KMH, INC.**, 161 S. Twelve Mile Rd., Ceresco MI 49033. (616)979-1221. President: Douglas F. Wolff. Specializes in brand identity, corporate identity, packaging and signage. Clients: manufacturers.
Needs: Prefers product designers and prototype makers. Uses artists for design, brochures, mechanicals, retouching, airbrushing, model making, AV materials and logos.
First Contact & Terms: Send query letter with resume, Photostats, photocopies and slides. Samples are filed. Samples not filed are returned. Reports back within 5 days. To show a portfolio, mail roughs and original/final art. Pays for design by the hour, $15 minimum. Pays for illustration by the project, $250 minimum. Considers complexity of project, client's budget, skill and experience of artist and turnaround time when establishing payment. Buys all rights.

KNT PLUSMARK INC., Suite A, 1200 Main St., Irvine CA 92715. (714)261-1161. Senior Designer: John Hamlin. Specializes in brand identity, corporate identity and packaging. Clients: Fortune 500 companies.
Needs: Works with 15-25 freelance artists/year. Uses artists for design, illustrations, mechanicals, retouching, airbrushing, model making, lettering, logos and marker comps.
First Contact & Terms: Send query letter with resume. Samples not filed are returned by SASE. Reports only if interested. Call to schedule an appointment to show a portfolio, which should include roughs, original/final art, final reproduction/product, color, photographs and b&w. Pays for design by the hour, $12-18 and by the project. Pays for illustration by the project. Considers client's budget, skill and experience of artist and turnaround time when establishing payment.

ARVID KNUDSEN AND ASSOCIATES, 592 A Main St., Hackensack NJ 07601. (201)488-7857. Contact: Arvid Knudsen. Specializes in books and publications. Clients: publishing companies, advertising agencies and manufacturers.
Needs: Works with 12 freelance artists/year. Artists with "creativity, technical skills, experience and dependability" only. Uses artists for catalog design, illustration and layout; book and magazine design and illustration, mechanicals, children's books and greeting cards.
First Contact & Terms: Send tear sheets of full color work, photocopies of b&w work, to be kept on file. Samples not kept on file are returned by SASE only if requested. Reports only if interested. Works on assignment only. Pay for all work "is negotiated and related to client's budget," also complexity of project.
Tips: "First, find out precisely what kind of work we are interested in. Then, if possible, send in tear sheets or photocopies of work that comes close to that need. I need drawings that tell a story, are instructive, clear. For the children's books, I need imagination and sense of fantasy."

***KRUDO DESIGN ATELIER, LTD.**,, Suite 220, 540 N. Lakeshore Dr., Chicago IL 60611. (312)644-0737. Contact: Shlomo Krudo. Specializes in annual reports, corporate identity, displays, direct mail, fashion, publications, signage and environment design. Clients: banks, law firms, financial service firms, cultural and educational institutions.
Needs: Works with about 6 freelance artists/year. Works on assignment only. Uses artists for illustration, mechanicals, keyline and paste-up.
First Contact & Terms: Send query letter with resume and samples. Samples are filed. Samples not filed are returned only if requested by artist. Reports back only if interested. Call or write to schedule an appointment to show a portfolio, which should include "whatever is appropriate to the individual's experience." Payment varies. Considers complexity of project, client's budget, skill and experience of artist, how work will be used, and turnaround time when establishing payment. Negotiates rights purchased; rights purchased vary according to project.

F. PATRICK LA SALLE DESIGN/GRAPHICS, 225 Sheridan St., Rockford IL 61103. (815)963-2089. Contact: F. Patrick La Salle. Specializes in corporate identity, displays, direct mail, packaging, publica-

Artist: Myron Cavender

This logo was designed by Myron Cavender of Salem, Oregon, for Lee Erickson, owner/art director of Lee Graphics Design, also of Salem. The logo, created with a technical pen and press-on type, was used by a bookkeeping and tax firm for a card, letterhead and envelope plus various office application forms. Erickson, who had worked with the artist for many years, says the logo "denotes a systematic approach to business."

tions and signage. Clients: small corporations, ad agencies, book publishers and hospitals.
Needs: Works with 10-15 freelance artists/year. Experienced artists only. Uses artists for design, illustration, brochures, catalogs, books, magazines, newspapers, P-O-P displays, mechanicals, photography (studio and on-location), retouching, airbrushing, posters, direct mail packages, model making and AV materials.
First Contact & Terms: Send query letter with brochure and samples to be kept on file. Call for appointment to show portfolio. "Photocopies as samples okay if technique is clear." Samples not kept on file are not returned. Reports back only if interested. Pays for design by the hour, $10-25 average. Pays for illustration by the hour, $20-35 average. Considers complexity of project, client's budget and turnaround time when establishing payment. "Artist will be paid after client has paid invoice."
Tips: "Most freelancers work here at the studio with provided supplies. Payment schedules set up with client *before* work is begun. Frequently, there is a 45-60 day wait for payment after billing has been completed. Recently, our clients have depended a great deal on our co-ordination and consultation with small to elaborate audiovisual presentations. Some have included live actors with slide support for demonstrations. Many artists, in the form of freelance support and production companies, have been involved."

***JIM LANGE DESIGN**, 213 W. Institute Pl., Chicago IL 60610. (312)943-2589. Contact: Jim Lange. Specializes in lettering, logo design and corporate communications. Clients: agencies, PR firms.
Needs: Works with 12 freelance artists/year. Prefers expert craftsmanship. Uses artists for illustration and retouching.
First Contact & Terms: Send samples. Samples are filed. Pays for illustration by the project, $75-800. Considers complexity of project, client's budget, skill and experience of artist, how work will be used, turnaround time and rights purchased when establishing payment. Buys all rights.

LEE GRAPHICS DESIGN, 395 19th St. NE, Salem OR 97301. (503)364-0907. Owner/Art Director: Lee Ericksen. Specializes in annual reports, brand identity, corporate identity, displays, landscape design, interior design, direct mail, packaging, publications, signage and technical illustrations. "We are a full-service graphics studio." Clients: individuals, ad agencies and PR firms.
Needs: Works with approximately 3-5 freelance artists/year. Artist must have talent, creativity and basic design ability. Uses design, illustrations, brochures, catalogs, books, magazines, newspapers, P-O-P displays, mechanicals, airbrushing, posters, direct mail packages, charts/graphs, AV materials, lettering, logos, advertisements and anything that appears in print form.
First Contact & Terms: Send query letter with resume. Reports only if interested. Call to schedule an appointment to show a portfolio, which should include thumbnails, roughs, original/final art, final reproduction/product, color, tear sheets, Photostats, photographs and b&w. Pays for design by the hour, $10-25; by the project, $10-25. Pays for illustrations by the hour, $10-25; by the project, $10-25. "Usually get estimate by artist." Considers complexity of project, client's budget, skill and experience of artist, how work will be used, turnaround time and rights purchased when establishing payment.
Tips: "Always show respect for your artwork with presentation; follow directions. Be versatile in all areas of graphics."

LEGAL ARTS, 711 Twelfth Ave., San Diego CA 92101. (619)231-1551. Contact: James Gripp. Specializes in displays; technical illustration; and forensic exhibits including: medical illustration, scale diagrams and models; and charts and graphs. Clients: law firms.
Needs: Works with 3-5 freelance artists/year. Prefers "degreed artists (AA or BA); local to San Diego County." Works on assignment only. Uses artists for illustration, airbrushing, model making, charts/graphs and AV materials. Especially needs medical illustrator and model maker.

First Contact & Terms: Send query letter with resume and samples to be kept on file. Write for appointment to show portfolio. "Samples may be shown by appointment in lieu of portfolio. Artist must send at least 5 photocopy samples with query letter." Reports back within 5 days. Pays for design and illustration by the hour, $7.50 minimum. Considers skill and experience of artist, and turnaround time when establishing payment. "Always 'work for hire' due to legal application of original art."
Tips: Especially looks for "diversity of media, specific applications towards my needs and superior craftsmanship" in samples for portfolio. "If you are a 'generalist', good! We do work that will be used as evidence in court—it must be accurate *every* time. In the legal field, the background of the artist (i.e. degrees), is of great importance to the courts. One must qualify as being educationally capable rather than just physically capable of preparing exhibits for trial use. Hence, the freelancer must have some documented background that a non-artist (judge or juror), will deem as being necessary before the artist can truthfully, accurately and honestly portray whatever is in the exhibit."

***LEKASMILLER**, 3210 Old Tunnel Rd., Lafayette CA 94549. Chief Operating Officer: John Lekas. Specializes in annual reports, brand identity, corporate identity, publications and advertising. Clients: corporate clients, health care.
Needs: Works with 4 freelance artists/year. Prefers at least 1 year of experience. Works on assignment. Prefers designers, production artists. Uses artists for design, illustrations and mechanicals.
First Contact & Terms: Send resume and photocopies. Samples are filed. Samples not filed are returned by SASE. Reports back only if interested. Write to schedule an appointment to show a portfolio, or mail original/final art, Photostats and photographs. Pays for design and illustration by the hour, $9-12. Negotiates rights purchased.
Tips: "Mail resume and three samples."

***LEO ART STUDIO**, Suite 610, 320 Fifth Ave., New York NY 10001. (212)736-8785. Art Director/ Owner: Mr. Leopold Schein. Specializes in textile design for home furnishings. Clients: wallpaper manufacturers/stylists, glassware companies, furniture & upholstery manufacturing.
Needs: Works with 12-15 freelance artists/year. Prefers artists trained in textile field, not fine arts. Must have a portfolio of original art designs. Should be able to be in NYC on a fairly regular basis. Works both on assignment and speculation. Prefers contemporary and/or traditional styles. Uses artists for design, airbrushing, coloring and repeats. "We are always looking to add full-time artists to our in-house staff (currently at 9). We will also look at any freelance portfolio to add to our variety of hands."
First Contact & Terms: Send query letter with resume and slides. "We prefer to see portfolio in person. Contact via a phone is OK—we can set up appointments within a day or two notice." Samples are not filed. Samples not filed are returned. Reports back within 5 days. Call or write to schedule an appointment to show a portfolio, which should include original/final art. Pays for design by the project, $200-500. "Payment is generally two-thirds of what design sells for—slightly less if reference material, art material, or studio space is requested." Considers complexity of project, skill and experience of artist and how work will be used when establishing payment. Buys all rights.
Tips: "Do not call if you are not a textile artist. Artists must be able to put design in repeat, do color combinations and be able to draw well on large variety of subjects—florals, Americana, graphics, etc. We will look at student work and advise if in correct field. We do not do fashion or clothing design."

***LEONE DESIGN GROUP INC.**, 7 Woodland Ave., Larchmont NY 10538. President: Lucian J. Leone. Specializes in corporate identity, displays, publications, signage and museum exhibition design. Clients: museums, corporations, government agencies.
Needs: Works with 10-15 freelance artists/year. Uses artists for design, brochures, catalogs, mechanicals, model making, charts/graphs, AV materials and logos. Prefers freelancers with exhibition design skills.
First Contact & Terms: Send query letter with resume, samples, photocopies and photographs. Samples are filed unless otherwise stated. Samples not filed are returned only if requested. Reports back within 2 weeks. Write to schedule an appointment to show a portfolio, which should include thumbnails, original/final art, final reproduction/product, photographs, b&w and color. Pays for design by the hour, $10-20. Considers client's budget and skill and experience of artist when establishing payment.

WES LERDON ASSOCIATES, INDUSTRIAL DESIGN, 3070 Riverside Dr., Columbus OH 43221. (614)486-8188. Owner: W.E. Lerdon. Specializes in corporate identity and technical illustrations. Clients: manufacturers.
Needs: Works with 4 freelance artists/year. Prefers Ohio area designers with skill. Uses artists for design, illustrations, brochures, mechanicals, model making and logos.
First Contact & Terms: Send query letter with resume. Samples not filed are returned only if requested. Reports only if interested. Call or write to schedule an appointment to show a portfolio, which should include thumbnails, roughs, original/final art and photographs. Pays for design by the hour, $7-

25. Pays for illustration by the hour, $10-30. Considers complexity of project, client's budget, skill and experience of artist, and turnaround time when establishing payment.
Tips: "In presenting samples or portfolios, freelancers need to put them in time-ordered sequence of old work first and newest work last. . .to show improvement. Too often they are a jumble of old and recent work that confuses the impression of the artist's skill."

LESLEY-HILLE, INC., 32 E. 21st St., New York NY 10010. (212)677-7570. President: Valrie Lesley. Specializes in annual reports, corporate identity, publications, advertising and sales promotion. Clients: financial, fashion, nonprofit organizations, hotels, restaurants, investment firms, oil and real estate firms.
Needs: Works with "many" freelance artists/year. "Experienced and competent" artists only. Uses artists for illustration, mechanicals, airbrushing, model making, charts/graphs, AV materials and lettering.
First Contact & Terms: Send query letter with resume, business card and samples to be kept on file. Accepts "whatever best shows work capability" as samples. Samples not filed are returned by SASE. Reports only if interested. Call or write for appointment to show portfolio. Pay varies according to project. Considers complexity of project, client's budget, skill and experience of artist, and turnaround time when establishing payment.
Tips: Designers and artists must "be *able to do* what they say they can and agree to do . . . professionally and on time!"

***LIBBY-PERSZYK-KATHMAN-L.P.K.**, 225 E. 6th St., Cincinnati OH 45202. (513)241-6330. Design Director: James Gabel. Specializes in corporate identity and packaging. Clients: industrial firms.
Needs: Works with 12-20 freelance artists/year. Uses artists for illustration, mechanicals, retouching, airbrushing, model making and lettering. Especially needs illustration.
First Contact & Terms: Works on assignment only. Send query letter with brochure and samples/slides to be kept on file. Prefers slides, printed material or printed sheet as samples. Samples not kept on file are returned only if requested. Reports back only if interested. Write for appointment to show portfolio. Pays for illustration by the project, $50-3,000 average. Considers complexity of project, client's budget, skill and experience of artist, and turnaround time when establishing payment.

***LON DEN DESIGN**, 132 W. 12th Ave., Denver CO 80204. (303)534-1243. Creative Director: John F. Tunison. Specializes in annual reports, corporate identity, displays, direct mail, signage and technical illustrations. Clients: ad agencies, PR firms, real estate developers, manufacturers, entertainment industry, financial concerns, healthcare companies, retail.
Needs: Works with 6-12 freelance artists/year. Prefers local artists. Uses artists for illustrations, brochures, catalogs, magazines, newspapers, mechanicals, retouching and airbrushing.
First Contact & Terms: Send query letter with brochure or resume. Samples are filed. Samples not filed are not returned. Reports back only if interested. Call to schedule an appointment to show a portfolio, which should include final reproduction/product and tear sheets. Pays for design by the hour, $8-24. Pays for illustration by the project, $50-1,250. Considers complexity of project, client's budget, skill and experience of artist, how work will be used, turnaround time and rights purchased when establishing payment. Negotiates rights purchased; rights purchased vary according to project.
Tips: "Send examples of completed projects; show execution as well as conceptual skills."

JAN LORENC DESIGN, INC., #460, 3475 Lenox Rd., Atlanta GA 30326. (404)266-2711. President: Mr. Jan Lorenc. Specializes in corporate identity, displays, packaging, publications, architectural signage design and industrial design. Clients: developers, product manufacturers, architects and institutions.
Needs: Works with 10 freelance artists/year. Local artists only—senior designers. Uses artists for design, illustration, brochures, catalogs, books, P-O-P displays, mechanicals, retouching, airbrushing, posters, direct mail packages, model making, charts/graphs, AV materials, lettering and logos. Especially needs architectural signage designers.
First Contact & Terms: Send brochure, resume and samples to be kept on file. Prefers slides as samples. Samples not kept on file are returned. Call or write for appointment to show portfolio, which should include thumbnails, roughs, original/final art, final reproduction/product, color, Photostats and photographs. Pays for design by the hour, $10-25 average; by the project, $100-3,000 average. Considers complexity of project, client's budget, and skill and experience of artist when establishing payment.

***JODI LUBY & COMPANY**, 808 Broadway, New York NY 10003. (212)473-1922. Contact: Jodi Luby. Specializes in corporate identity, direct mail, publications and signage. Clients: corporate, publishing, manufacturing.
Needs: Works with various number of freelance artists/year. Works on assignment only. Uses artists for

illustrations, mechanicals, retouching, airbrushing and lettering.
First Contact & Terms: Send query letter with brochure or resume, tear sheets, Photostats and photocopies. Samples are filed. Samples not filed are not returned. Reports back only if interested. Call to schedule an appointment to show a portfolio. Pays for design by the hour, $10-30. Considers complexity of project, client's budget, how work will be used and rights purchased.

MCGRAPHICS DESIGN, Suite 206, 1010A W. Magnolia Blvd., Burbank CA 91506. (213)841-1266. Owner: Kathleen McGuinness. Specializes in brand identity, corporate identity, direct mail and packaging. Clients: corporations (manufacturers and distributors), some public relation firms and printers.
Needs: Works with 10 freelance artists/year. "Local artists only, personable and presentable in the corporate environment." Works on assignment only. Uses artists for illustration, catalogs, mechanicals, retouching, airbrushing and newsletters. Especially needs b&w line illustration.
First Contact & Terms: Send brochure, business card and samples to be kept on file. Call or write for appointment to show portfolio. Prefers brochures with some information about artist and samples of work. Samples not kept on file are not returned. Reports back "only if the artist calls and follows up." Pays for design by the hour, $10-20 average. Pays for illustration line products by the project, $100-250 average. Considers complexity of project, client's budget, and skill and experience of artist when establishing payment.
Tips: "Send samples first then make an appointment. Show up on time and *follow up* if we say we are interested."

MCGUIRE WILLIS & ASSOCIATES, 249 E. Cook Rd., Columbus OH 43214. (614)262-8124. Contact: Sue Willis. Specializes in annual reports, audiovisual and publications. Clients: schools, training departments of companies, sales and banking.
Needs: Works with 20 freelance artists/year. Works on assignment only. Uses artists for advertising, brochure, catalog, poster, direct mail package and book design and illustration, and mechanicals.
First Contact & Terms: Send query letter with Photostats, slides, brochure/flyer and samples to be kept on file. Samples returned by SASE if not kept on file. Reports in 2 weeks. Reports back on whether to expect possible future assignments. Negotiates payment.

ROB MacINTOSH COMMUNICATIONS, INC., 93 Massachusetts Ave., Boston MA 02115. President: Rob MacIntosh. Specializes in annual reports, advertising design and collateral. Clients: manufacturers, graphic arts industry, nonprofit/public service agencies.
Needs: Works with 12 freelance artists/year. Portfolio and work experience required. Uses artists for advertising and brochure design, illustration and layout, mechanicals, retouching and charts/graphs. Occasionally uses humorous and cartoon-style illustrations.
First Contact & Terms: Send samples to be kept on file. Irregular sizes or abundant material will not be filed. "Never send original work unless it's a printed sample. A simple, compact presentation is best. Often Photostats are adequate." Reports only if interested and "generally only when we require more information and/or services." Write for appointment to show portfolio. Pays for design by the day, $100 minimum. Pays for illustration by the project, $100 minimum. Considers complexity of project, client's budget, skill and experience of artist and turnaround time when establishing payment.

MCS, 600 Valley Rd., Wayne NJ 07470. (201)628-9630. Director: Martin Eldridge. Specializes in brand identity, corporate identity, displays and packaging. Clients: consumer product companies.
Needs: Works with 10 freelance artists/year. Prefers local artists. Works on assignment only. Uses artists for illustration, retouching, airbrushing and AV materials.
First Contact & Terms: Call or write for appointment to show portfolio. Prefers slides and printed material as samples. Samples not kept on file returned by SASE. Reports only if interested. Pays for design and illustration by the hour. Considers complexity of project, client's budget and turnaround time when establishing payment.
Tips: "The cool fine artist approach is a turn-off. Professionalism, clean work, originality and a cooperative attitude is a plus. If excessive verbal explanation of work is necessary then obviously the visual doesn't communicate on its own."

MG DESIGN ASSOCIATES INC., 824 W. Superior, Chicago IL 60622. (312)243-3661. Contact: Michael Grivas or design director. Specializes in trade show exhibits, museum exhibits, expositions and commercial interiors. Clients: industrial manufacturers, consumer-oriented product manufacturers, pharmaceutical firms, state and federal government, automotive parts manufacturers, etc.
Needs: Works with 4-6 freelance artists/year. Artists must be local exhibit designers with minimum of five years of experience. Works on assignment only. Uses artists for design, illustration, detail drawings and model making.

First Contact & Terms: Send resume, slides and photocopies to be evaluated. Samples not kept on file are returned only if requested. Write for appointment to show portfolio. Considers complexity of project, client's budget, and skill and experience of artist when establishing payment.

***MILLER + SCHWARTZ**, Suite 310, 3518 Cahuenga Blvd., Los Angeles CA 90068. (213)876-0239. Creative Director: David Schwartz. Specializes in corporate identity. Clients: commercial real estate.
Needs: Works with 20 freelance artists/year. Works on assignment only. Uses artists for design, illustrations, brochures, catalogs, mechanicals, retouching, airbrushing, posters, model making, charts/graphs, lettering and advertisements.
First Contact & Terms: Send resume, tear sheets, Photostats and photocopies. Samples are filed. Samples not filed are not returned. Reports back only if interested. Call to schedule an appointment to show a portfolio, which should include roughs and printed pieces. Pays for design by the hour, $15-25. Pays for illustration by the project. Considers complexity of project, client's budget, skill and experience of artist, how work will be used, turnaround time and rights purchased when establishing payment. Rights purchased vary according to project.

***MIRENBURG & COMPANY**, 43 W. 33rd St., New York NY 10001. Creative Director: Barry L. Mirenburg. Specializes in annual reports, brand identity, corporate identity, packaging, publications, signage and technical illustrations. Clients: Fortune 500, PR firms, etc.
Needs: Uses artists for design, illustrations, brochures, catalogs, books, magazines, newspapers, P-O-P displays, mechanicals, retouching, airbrushing, posters, model making, direct mail packages, charts/graphs, AV materials, lettering, logos and advertisements.
First Contact & Terms: Send resume and tear sheets, Photostats, photocopies, slides and photographs. Samples are filed. Samples not filed are not returned. Reports back only if interetsed.

MIZEREK ADVERTISING, 48 E. 43rd St., New York NY 10017. (212)986-5702. President: Leonard Mizerek. Specializes in catalogs, fashion and technical illustration. Clients: corporations—various service-oriented clientele.
Needs: Works with 25-30 freelance artists/year. Experienced artists only. Works on assignment only. Uses artists for design, illustration, brochures, retouching, airbrushing and logos.
First Contact & Terms: Send query letter with tear sheets and Photostats. Reports only if interested. Call to schedule an appointment to show a portfolio, which should include original/final art and tear sheets. Pays by the project, $200-1,000. Considers client's budget and turnaround time when establishing payment.
Tips: "Contact by mail; don't press for interview. Let the work speak for itself. Show commercial product work, not only magazine editorial."

MOBIUM CORPORATION FOR DESIGN & COMMUNICATION, (formerly Kovach Associates, Inc.), 676 St. Clair, Chicago IL 60611. (312)951-0999. Vice President: Ronald Kovach. Specializes in annual reports.
Needs: Uses artists for advertising, brochure, poster and direct mail package illustration. Prefers a classic look for annual reports and packaging; "probably includes illustration for logotype or company mark when appropriate."
First Contact & Terms: Send query letter with brochure/flyer or resume. Prefers finished art or finished products as samples. Samples returned by SASE. Reports within 2 weeks. Provide resume, business card and brochure/flyer to be kept on file for possible future assignments. Call or write for appointment. Pays $100-3,000 average/project for design or illustration; also negotiates.
Tips: "Most good work relationships center on the personal relationship between parties. Although direct mail solicitation is effective, if you see a company you like, visit with them personally as often as possible."

MOODY GRAPHICS, 639 Howard St., San Francisco CA 94105. (415)495-5186. President: Carol Moody. Specializes in annual reports, corporate identity, direct mail, publications and technical illustration. Clients: executives, printers and printing brokers.
Needs: Works with 3-5 freelance artists/year. "Artists work in my studio. They should have mechanical experience and good mechanical abilities; stat camera experience helpful." Works on assignment only. Uses artists for design, illustration, brochures, catalogs, mechanicals, retouching, airbrushing, direct mail packages, charts/graphs, lettering, logos and advertisements.
First Contact & Terms: Call or write for appointment to show portfolio. Samples not kept on file returned by SASE. Reports only if interested. Pays for design, mechanical assembly by the hour, $15-25 average. Pays for illustration, technical drawing by the hour, $15-25 average. Considers skill and experience of artist when establishing payment.
Tips: "Show paste-ups as well as printed samples."

***JOHN MORNING DESIGN, INC.**, 866 United Nations Plaza, New York NY 10017. (212)688-0088. Specializes in annual reports and publications. Clients: financial and service corporations, foundations and cultural institutions.
Needs: Works with 6 freelance artists/year. Uses artists for mechanicals, retouching, charts/graphs and lettering.
First Contact & Terms: Send brochure and samples to be kept on file "depending on appropriateness." Prefers printed samples or tear sheets as samples. Reports only if interested. Works on assignment only. Considers complexity of project, client's budget and skill and experience of artist when establishing payment.

***BARBARA MOSES DESIGN**, 225 W. Ohio, Chicago IL 60610. (312)644-2882. Contact: Barbara Moses. Clients: Direct response advertising.
Needs: Works with 20 freelance artists/year. Prefers local illustrators and keyline artists. Uses artists for advertising and brochure design and illustration and design consulting.

MARTIN MOSKOF & ASSOCIATES, INC., 154 W. 57th St., New York NY 10019. (212)333-2015. President: Martin Moskof. Specializes in annual reports, corporate identity, exhibits and shows, publications and signage. Clients: corporations and institutions, colleges (e.g., IBM, Carnegie Hall).
Needs: Works with 30-40 freelance artists/year. Local artists only, 2-3 years of experience. Works on assignment only. Uses artists for brochure and catalog design, illustration and layout; book design and illustration; mechanicals, retouching, direct mail packages, charts/graphs, AV presentations and logos.
First Contact & Terms: Send query letter with tear sheets, photocopies, slides and photographs to be kept on file. Reports only if interested. Call or write for appointment to show portfolio, which should include roughs, final reproduction/product, color and tear sheets. Pays for design by the hour, $12-20; by the day, $90-200. Pays for illustration by the project, $150-5,000. Considers complexity of project, client's budget and skill and experience of artist when establishing payment.

MOSSMAN DESIGN ASSOCIATES, 2800 S. Ocean Blvd.-PH-H, Boca Raton FL 33342. Account Supervisor: Stanley Mossman. Specializes in corporate identity, direct mail, publications, health care institution brochures, book jacket and book design. Clients: publishers, manufacturers, hospitals, agencies, nonprofit institutions, etc.
Needs: Works with 3-5 freelance artists/year. Interested in "local artists with strong portfolio, a few years of experience, neat work and understanding of mechanicals." Uses artists for design, mechanicals, charts/graphs and photography.
First Contact & Terms: Send query letter with resume, business card and samples to be kept on file. Prefers copies, tear sheets and mock-ups as samples. Reports back within 5 days. Call or write for appointment to show portfolio. Pays for design and illustration by the hour, $5-20 average. Considers complexity of project, and skill and experience of artist when establishing payment.
Tips: Especially looks for creative samples or portfolio, clean and organized. A mistake artists make is "not knowing their own limitations, not being honest about their skills."

***MULLER & COMPANY**, 112 W. Ninth St., Kansas City MO 64105. Associate Creative Director: Mark Sackett. Specializes in annual reports, corporate identity, displays, interior design, direct mail, fashion, packaging, publications and signage.
Needs: Works with 50-60 freelance artists/year. Works on assignment only. Uses artists for illustrations, brochures, catalogs, books, airbrushing, posters, charts/graphs, AV materials, lettering, advertisements and comp artists.
First Contact & Terms: Send resume, tear sheets, slides and photographs. Samples are filed. Reports back only if interested. To show a portfolio, mail thumbnails, roughs, original/final art, final reproduction/product and tear sheets. Considers complexity of project, client's budget, how work will be used and rights purchased when establishing payment.

MURAMATSU INCORPORATED, 10716 Reagan St., Los Alamitos CA 90865. Art Director: Amy Tarmira. Specializes in trade show exhibits, displays and interior design. Clients: various manufacturers in consumer electronics field.
Needs: Works with 10-15 freelance artists/year. Local artists preferred. Works on assignment. Uses artists for exhibit design, technical illustration, P-O-P displays, model making, mechanicals, posters and interior design support services.
First Contact & Terms: Send query letter with brochure, resume and business card to be kept on file. Samples not kept on file are returned by SASE only if requested. Reports only if interested. To show a portfolio, mail appropriate materials or call or write to schedule an appointment. Pays by the hour, $10-35. Considers complexity of project, client's budget, skill and experience of artist, how work will be used, turnaround time and rights purchased when establishing payment.
Tips: "Contemporary design philosophy."

MUSICAL IMAGE DESIGNS, 1212 Ardee Ave., Nashville TN 37216. (615)226-1509. Creative Director: Stacy Slocum. Specializes in art work for the music industry, i.e. record labels and covers, logo designs, advertisements and greeting cards.
Needs: Works with a limited number of freelance artists/year. Uses artists to design logos, album covers for various country artists, ads for magazines, and to develop a line of musical greeting cards.
First Contact & Terms: Send samples to be kept on file. Samples not kept on file will be returned by SASE. Prefers samples to be production perfect. "All samples that have been approved are put in a catalog. Those selected to be purchased from the catalog at different points during the year stand a better chance of being selected if they are sharp. Logo designs should be placed on a page as a logo would naturally appear. Album covers should be on card stock and be about the same size. Greeting cards should be a 7X10 card folded in half to make a 5x7 card. Art work will be purchased when it is selected and ready to go to print, but no artwork will be printed before being purchased. We buy all rights."

***CAROL NAUGHTON & ASSOCIATES, INC.**, 213 W. Institute Place, Chicago IL 60610. (312)951-5353. President: Carol Naughton. Specializes in corporate identity, displays, interior design and signage. Clients: real estate developers, manufacturers and hospitals.
Needs: Works on assignment only. Uses artists for illustrations, model making, lettering, renderings and maps.
First Contact & Terms: Send query letter with resume, tear sheets and photocopies. Samples are filed. Samples not filed are not returned. Reports back only if interested. Call to schedule an appointment to show a portfolio, or mail original/final art, tear sheets, photographs, b&w and color. Pays for design and illustration by the hour, $10-50. Considers complexity of project, client's budget and skill and experience of artist when establishing payment. Buys all rights.

SID NAVRATIL ART STUDIO, 1305 Clark Bldg., Pittsburgh PA 15222. Contact: Sid Navratil. Specializes in annual reports, corporate identity, direct mail, publication, signage, technical illustration and 3-dimensional designs. Clients: ad agencies and corporations.
Needs: Works with 5 freelance artists/year. Experienced artists only with a minimum of 5 years of experience; "I prefer artist to work on my premises at least during revision work, if that is possible." Works on assignment only. Uses artists for design, illustration, brochures, mechanicals, retouching, airbrushing, charts/graphs, lettering, logos and advertisements.
First Contact & Terms: Send resume, photocopies and business card to be kept on file. Material not filed is returned only if requested. Reports within 10 days. Write for appointment to show portfolio. Pays for design and illustration by the hour, $20-30 average. Considers complexity of project, client's budget, and skill and experience of artist when establishing payment.
Tips: "In illustration, we prefer the daring, innovative approach. The subject is usually industrial in nature, done for corporations such as PPG, USS, Alcoa, Rockwell. Do not send expensive photos and brochures. A brief resume with few photocopies of work is sufficient."

LOUIS NELSON ASSOCIATES INC., 80 University Pl., New York NY 10003. (212)620-9191. Contact: Judy Moskowitz. Specializes in brand identity, corporate identity, displays, interior design, packaging, publications, signage, product design, exhibitions and marketing. Clients: corporations, associations and governments.
Needs: Works with 8+ freelance artists/year. Works on assignment only. Uses artists for design, illustration, mechanicals, model making and charts/graphs.
First Contact & Terms: Considers "quality, point-of-view for project and flexibility." Send query letter with brochure showing art style or tear sheets, slides and photographs. Samples are returned only if requested. Reports within 2 weeks. Write to schedule an appointment to show a portfolio, which should include roughs, final reproduction/product, color and photographs. Pays for design by the hour, $8-35 average; by the project, $60-5,000 average. Pays for illustration by the project, $100-500 average. Considers complexity of project, client's budget, skill and experience of artist and rights purchased when establishing payment.
Tips: "I want to see how the person responded to the specific design problem and to see documentation of the process—the stages of development. The artist must be versatile and able to communicate a wide range of ideas. Mostly, I want to see the artist's integrity reflected in his/her work."

NIIMI DESIGN ASSOCIATES INC., 451 N. Racine, Chicago IL 60622. (312)666-8383. Contact: B. Hoolehan. Clients: hardware consumer products.
Needs: Assigns 20-100 jobs/year. Uses mostly local artists. Uses artists for design, illustrations, layout, lettering, paste-up, retouching and technical art for packaging, P-O-P displays, catalogs, charts/graphs, exhibits and print media advertising.
First Contact & Terms: Query with samples or arrange interview. SASE. Pay determined by job.

***NOSTRADAMUS ADVERTISING**, #1128A, 250 W. 57, New York NY 10107. Creative Director: Barry N. Sher. Specializes in publications. Clients: ad agencies, PR firms, nonprofit organizations, political candidates.
Needs: Works with 7 freelance artists/year. Uses artists for design, illustrations, mechanicals, logos and advertisements.
First Contact & Terms: Send resume and samples. Samples are filed. Samples not filed are not returned. Does not report back. Pays for design by the hour, $15 minimum. Pays for illustration by the project, $25 minimum. Considers complexity of project, client's budget and skill and experience of artist when establishing payment. Buys all rights.

NOTOVITZ & PERRAULT DESIGN, INC., 47 E. 19 St., New York NY 10003. (212)677-9700. President: Joseph Notovitz. Specializes in corporate design (annual reports, literature, publications), corporate identity and signage. Clients: finance and industry.
Needs: Works with 10 freelance artists/year. Uses artists for brochure, poster, direct mail and booklet illustration, mechanicals, charts/graphs and logo design.
First Contact & Terms: Send resume, slides, printed pieces and tear sheets to be kept on file. Samples not filed are returned by SASE. Reports in 1 week. Call for appointment to show portfolio, which should include roughs, original/final art and final reproduction/product. Pays for design by the hour, $15-50; by the project, $200-1,500. Pays for illustration by the project, $100-2,000; also negotiates.
Tips: "Send pieces which reflect our firm's style and needs. They should do a bit of research in the firm they are contacting. If we never produce book covers, book cover art does not interest us."

***ANNA OHALLA GRAPHIC DESIGN**, 317 Market St., Rockford IL 61104. (815)968-1533. Art Director: Anna Ohalla. Specializes in annual reports, brand and corporate identity, direct mail, packaging, publications and signage for corporations.
Needs: Works with 5 freelance artists/year. Prefers artists with 5 years plus of experience. Works on assignment only. Uses artists for illustrations, retouching and airbrushing.
First Contact & Terms: Contact through artist's agent or send query letter with samples. Samples are filed. Samples not filed are returned only if requested. Reports back only if interested. To show a portfolio, mail thumbnails, roughs, original/final art, final reproduction/product, tear sheets or photographs. Pays for design by the hour, $20-50 or by the day, $150-500. Pays for illustration by the hour, $20-50. Considers client's budget, skill and experience of artist, turnaround time and rights purchased when establishing payment. Buys all rights.

***OVERLOCK HOWE CONSULTING GROUP**, 4484 W. Pine Blvd., St. Louis MO 63108. (314)533-4484. Executive Creative Director: Robert Leu. Specializes in annual reports, brand identity, corporate identity, displays, packaging and signage. Clients: regional, national and international companies.
Needs: Works with 20-30 freelance artists/year. Prefers local artists with three years of experience, and national illustrators. Works on assignment only. Uses artists for illustrations, P-O-P displays, mechanicals, retouching, airbrushing, model making, direct mail packages, charts/graphs, AV materials, lettering and advertisements.
First Contact & Terms: Send query letter with resume and tear sheets, Photostats, photocopies, slides and photographs. Samples are filed. Reports back only if interested. Write to schedule an appointment to show a portfolio or mail original/final art, final reproduction/product, tear sheets, Photostats, photographs, b&w and color. Pays for illustration by the project, $200 minimum. Considers complexity of project, client's budget, skill and experience of artist, how work will be used, turnaround time and rights purchased when establishing payment. Rights purchased vary according to project.
Tips: Artist should be "well-organized, show full capabilities and be very professional."

PERSECHINI & COMPANY, #303, 1575 Westward Blvd., Los Angeles Ca 90024. (213)478-5522. Contact: Phyllis Persechini. Specializes in annual reports, corporate identity, displays, packaging, publications and signage. Clients: ad agencies, public relations firms and internal communications departments.
Needs: Works on assignment basis only. Uses artists for design, illustration, mechanicals, retouching, airbrushing and lettering. Occasionally uses humorous and cartoon-style illustrations.
First Contact & Terms: Send query letter with brochure, business card and Photostats and photocopies to be kept on file. Samples not kept on file are returned by SASE. Reports back only if interested. Pays for design by the hour, $10-20 average. Pays for illustration by the project, $100-2,500 average. Considers complexity of project, client's budget, skill and experience of artist, how work will be used, turnaround time and rights purchased when establishing payment.
Tips: "Our clients seem to want a very sophisticated look for their ads, brochures, etc. Occasionally we have a call for humor."

***PGD INC.**, Box 98, Syracuse NY 13201-0098. General Manager: Mr. James. Specializes in corporate identity, publications and technical illustrations. Clients: educational, institutional, industrial and commercial.
Needs: Works with 10-15 freelance artists/year. Prefers local, versatile, fast designers and technical illustrators. Works on assignment only. Uses artists for design, illustrations, brochures, catalogs, books, magazines, mechanicals, retouching, airbrushing, posters, charts/graphs, logos and advertisements.
First Contact & Terms: Send query letter with resume, Photostats and photographs. Samples are filed. Samples not filed are returned. Reports back within 4 weeks. Write to schedule an appointment to show a portfolio or mail thumbnails, roughs and final reproduction/product. Pays for design by the hour, $25 minimum. Pays for illustration by the hour, $20-40 minimum. Considers complexity of project, turnaround time and rights purchased when establishing payment. Buys all rights.

PHARES ASSOCIATES INC., Consultant Designers-Industrial Design, 37624 Hills Tech Dr., Farmington Hills MI 48018. (313)553-2232. Administrative Assistant: Penelope Phares. Specializes in interior design and product design. Clients: manufacturing and architectural firms and advertising agencies.
Needs: "At least 2 years of experience, speed and accuracy a must." Works on assignment only. Uses artists for design, illustration and model making. Special needs include architectural rendering, product design and drafting.
First Contact & Terms: Send query letter with brochure, resume, business card, slides, tear sheets or photographs to be kept on file. Samples not filed are returned by SASE. Reports within 2 weeks. Call or write for appointment to show portfolio. Pays for design by the hour, $8-20 average. Pays for illustration by the hour, $8-15 average. "Speed and quality are the determining factors regarding pay." Considers complexity of project, and skill and experience of artist when establishing payment.
Tips: "Our firm likes to use the work of artists who can take direction and meet short deadlines with quality work."

***HERBERT PINZKE DESIGN INC.**, 1935 N. Kenmore, Chicago IL 60614. (312)528-2277. President: Herbert Pinzke. Specializes in annual reports, corporate identity and publications. Clients: corporations.
Needs: Works with 4 freelance artists/year. Works on assignment only. Uses artists for illustrations, brochures, catalogs, books, magazines, mechanicals and model making.
First Contact & Terms: Send query letter with brochure or resume and samples. Samples are filed. Samples not filed are returned by SASE. Reports back only if interested. Call or write to schedule an appointment to show a portfolio, which should include thumbnails, roughs, original/final art and final reproduction/product. Pays for illustration by the hour, $15-50. Considers complexity of project, client's budget, skill and experience of artist, how work will be used, turnaround time and rights purchased when establishing payment. Rights purchased vary according to project.

***PORCELLI ASSOCIATES INC.**, 225 Lafayette St., New York NY 10012. (212)226-5500. President: V. Lorenzo Porcelli. Specializes in industrial design. Clients: corporations, ad agencies, retail.
Needs: Works with 3-5 freelance artists/year. Works on assignment only. Uses artists for design, mechanicals, model making and renderings.
First Contact & Terms: Send query letter with resume, tear sheets and photocopies. Samples are filed. Samples not filed are not returned. Reports back only if interested. Call to schedule an appointment to show a portfolio, which should include final reproduction/product. Pays for design by the hour, $8-15. Pays for illustration by the project, $300-1,000. Considers complexity of project and client's budget when establishing payment. Rights purchased vary according to project.

> ***"In the area of industry publications, we see a rapidly growing sophistication of visual information, in both design and illustration. Styles once reserved for upscale consumer publications have become accepted, with no dilution whatsoever. This is especially encouraging in the previously tight confines of technology trades."***
>
> ***—Michael Walters, Computer Reseller***
> ***Los Angeles, California***

Close-up

Seymour Chwast
Graphic Designer
Phyllis Rich Flood
Vice President
Pushpin Group
New York City

Seymour Chwast is one of the founding fathers of this internationally recognized studio. Known worldwide as a master designer, Chwast has maintained his individuality as a member of the group, though the work of the studio bears his recognizable style (the use of bright, flat colors and nostalgic, humorous figures). He is the backbone of the studio's design services and therefore leaves business matters to the care of Phyllis Rich Flood, who, as senior vice president, coordinates various aspects of the studio. Chwast and Flood enhance each other's talents by working together.

Chwast is the Left-Handed Designer (the title of one of his books), the man who sets his own stamp on design. "I am a designer who illustrates," he explains. A designer must organize various elements of a piece (such as type and illustration) into a unified statement. "As a designer, I put different elements together to form a piece. I observe the formal principles of design, but I might work with my own illustration or someone else's, or whatever, to solve the design problem. I'm a problem solver."

Design is more satisfying to him than gallery art because it allows him to make a personal statement while reaching millions of people. "As a designer, I can do anything a painter or sculptor could do. In fact, there are things I can do in design that I couldn't do in a painting. I also like the input of information that I translate into visual form. That's easier for me than creating my own problems to solve, as in painting."

The way Chwast usually solves design problems is through what he calls "visual puns." He explains: "I borrow styles from the past, and sometimes I exaggerate stereotypical people in situations to make a point." Familiarity with classical typefaces and illustration techniques keeps Chwast open to new discoveries. He encourages young designers to do likewise, because familiarity with classic forms lays a good foundation for creating new classics.

Chwast also feels that keeping up with trends stultifies personal taste. "Keeping up with trends means you don't have any vision of your own. The best designers don't look at what other people are currently doing in order to copy it. Your work has to have its own personality in order to be recognized."

Designers must always remember that they do not work for themselves; they work for clients. Young designers trying to make a name for themselves often forget they must consider clients' needs above personal aesthetics. "They don't listen to what the client needs or has to say," Chwast observes, "and that doesn't work. You have to listen carefully to a client first, then you can do anything you want as long as the message is conveyed and the solution is appropriate."

When presenting a portfolio, designers should show appropriate samples that demonstrate a knowledge of the client's focus and their own professionalism and creativity. Chwast adds, "They should narrow their range of work as much as possible, because a wide range confuses the person who's looking at it, who should, instead, have a sense of what the artist is good at and what he likes to do."

Portfolio reviewing is the domain of Phyllis Flood, the personable and discerning businesswoman behind the scenes of the Group. She coordinates the design services (corporate identity, packaging and editorial presentation) and representation of freelance artists. Since she decides which artists the studio will represent, she knows a good portfolio when she sees one.

"A portfolio presentation should be well-organized, and it should have pacing." Phyllis suggests having "high spots" at the beginning, middle and end of your presentation. Like a watchful houseguest, she doesn't tolerate sloppiness. "You don't invite somebody into your home and say, 'You should see it without the piles of laundry on the floor.' If you're not going to care about the way your portfolio looks, then I'm not."

Flood also advises artists to let their portfolios speak for themselves. "Quite often you won't be there to present it yourself. So you can't explain things away." Show only your best work that demonstrates your strengths.

Both Flood and Chwast look for that "extra something" in a design or illustration. In order to foster that creative spark, Chwast suggests that aspiring designers look through design annuals and review the work of past masters. "You'll find that you respond to certain things. Act on that response. Then you'll know what you want to do. You must go after that, especially if you think you can do better than what you see."

—Susan Conner

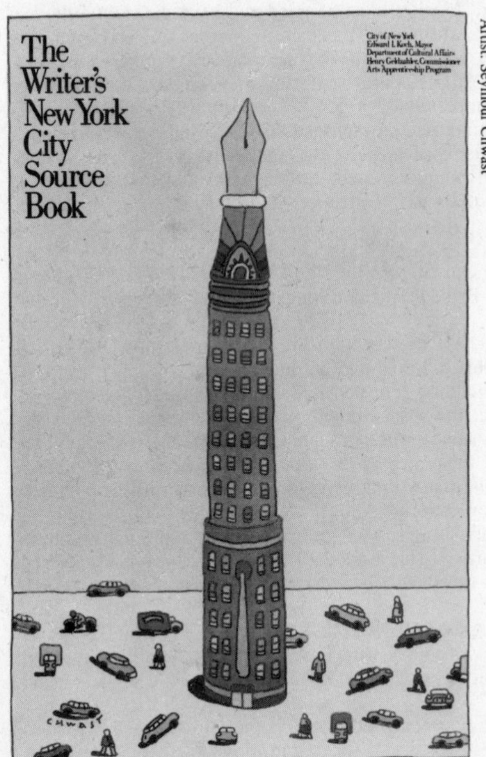

The Writer's New York City Source Book
City of New York
Edward I. Koch, Mayor
Department of Cultural Affairs
Henry Geldzahler, Commissioner
Arts Apprenticeship Program
CHWAST

Artist: Seymour Chwast

Chwast's own style has shaped that of the Pushpin Group. This piece is typical of the witty and expressive graphic style Chwast has made famous. Chwast is one of the founding fathers of the Group, which is viewed as one of the two dominant schools of the international movement of graphic design—the other is the Bauhaus School.

PULSE, INC. COMMUNICATIONS, 7516 W. Madison St., Forest Park IL 60130. (312)366-1770. Creative Director: Frank G. Konrath. Specializes in annual reports, corporate identity, displays, landscape design, interior design, packaging, publications, signage and technical illustration. Clients include corporations.
Needs: Works with 5-15 freelance artists/year. "Local artists preferred. I will always consider talent over experience." Works on assignment only. Uses artists for projects involving many different specialities.
First Contact & Terms: Send query letter with resume and business card to be kept on file. "Please don't call. Send your business card and give me an idea of what you're best at; I'll call you to arrange an interview when something comes up in your area. Save your samples until I ask to see them." Reports only if interested. Considers complexity of project, client's budget, turnaround time and rights purchased when establishing payment.
Tips: "Know what area you want to work in. We hire freelance artists for their talent in specific areas of discipline and for what they can produce consistently. "

THE PUSHPIN GROUP, 215 Park Ave. S., New York NY 10003. (212)674-8080. Senior Vice President: Phyllis Rich Flood. Specializes in annual reports, brand identity, corporate identity, packaging, publications and signage. Clients: individuals, ad agencies, corporations, PR firms, etc.
Needs: Works with 5-6 freelance artists/year. Generally prefers designers to illustrators. Uses artists for design, illustrations, brochures, books, magazines, mechanicals, retouching, airbrushing, charts/graphs and lettering.
First Contact & Terms: Send query letter with resume, tear sheets, Photostats and photocopies. Samples not filed are returned only if requested. Reports only if interested. Call or write to schedule an appointment to show a portfolio, which should include roughs, original/final art, final reproduction/product, color, tear sheets, Photostats, photographs and b&w. Pays for design by the hour, $15-20. Considers complexity of project, client's budget, skill and experience of artist, and turnaround time when establishing payment.

QUALLY & COMPANY INC., #2502, 30 E. Huron, Chicago IL 60611. (312)944-0237. Creative Director: Robert Qually. Specializes in advertising, graphic design and new product development. Clients: major corporations.
Needs: Works with 20-25 freelance artists/year. "Artists must be good and have the right attitude." Works on assignment only. Uses artists for design, illustration, mechanicals, retouching and lettering.
First Contact & Terms: Send query letter with brochure, resume, business card and samples to be kept on file. Samples not kept on file are returned by SASE. Reports back within several days. Call or write for appointment to show portfolio. Considers complexity of project, client's budget, skill and experience of artist, how work will be used, turnaround time and rights purchased when establishing payment.
Tips: Looks for talent, point of view, style, craftsmanship, depth and innovation in portfolio or samples. Sees "too many look-alikes. Very little innovation. Few people who understand how to create an image, who know how to conceptualize, who can think." Artists often "don't know how to sell or what's involved in selling."

THE QUARASAN GROUP, INC., Suite 7, 1845 Oak St., Northfield IL 60093. (312)446-4777. President and Director of Creative Services: Randi S. Brill. Production Manager: Joy Christensen. Specializes in books. Clients: book publishers.
Needs: Works with 100-300 freelance artists/year. Artists with publishing experience only. Uses artists for illustration, books, mechanicals, charts/graphs, lettering and production.
First Contact & Terms: Send query letter with brochure or resume and samples to production manager to be kept on file. Prefers "anything that we can retain for our files; Photostats, photocopies, tear sheets or dupe slides that do not have to be returned" as samples. Reports only if interested. Pays for production by the hour, $8-15 average; for illustration by the project, $75-3,500 average. Considers complexity of project, client's budget, how work will be used and turnaround time when establishing payment. "For illustration, size and complexity are the key factors."
Tips: "More publishers are finding that solid publishing service groups, with strength in art procurement, are an asset. They want us to work with the artists. This is good for artists, too. By working with us their work and talents can be displayed to all of our clients. It works well!"

***MIKE QUON DESIGN OFFICE, INC.**, 568 Broadway, New York NY 10012. (212)226-6024. President: Mike Quon. Specializes in corporate identity, displays, direct mail, packaging, publications and technical illustrations. Clients: corporations and ad agencies (e.g. American Express, Chemical Bank, PaineWebber).
Needs: Works with 5-10 freelance artists/year. Prefers good/great people "local doesn't matter." Works on assignment only. Prefers graphic style. Uses artists for design, brochures, P-O-P displays,

mechanicals, model making, charts/graphs and lettering. Especially needs precision inking people.
First Contact & Terms: Send query letter with resume, tear sheets and photocopies. Samples are filed. Samples not filed are returned if accompanied by a SASE. Reports back only if interested. Write to schedule an appointment to show a portfolio or mail thumbnails, roughs and tear sheets. Pays for design by the hour, $10-25. Pays for illustration by the project, $50-500 and up. Considers complexity of project, client's budget, skill and experience of artist, turnaround time and rights purchased when establishing payment. Buys one-time rights; rights purchased vary according to project.

R.H.GRAPHICS, INC.251 Park Ave. S., New York NY 10010. (212)246-0040. President: Roy Horton. Specialized in brand identity, corporate identity, displays, direct mail and packaging.
Needs: Works with 5-8 freelance artists/year. Artists must have ten years of experience. Especially needs mechanicals and ruling. Uses artists for P-O-P displays, mechanicals, retouching, airbrushing and lettering.
First Contract & Terms: Send query letter with brochure showing art style or resume and tear sheets. Reports only if interested. Write to show a portfolio, which should include roughs and original/final art. Pays for design by the hour, $18-25. Pays for illustration by the project, $50-250. Considers client's budget, and skill and experience of artist when establishing payment.

***JOHN RACILA ASSOCIATES**, 340 W. Butterfield Rd., Elmhurst IL 60126. (312)279-0614. Creative Director: John Neher. Specializes in brand identity, corporate identity, displays, interior design, packaging, publications and signage. Clients: manufacturers of consumer goods.
Needs: Prefers local artists to work on premises, minimum three years of experience or consumer product experience. Works on assignment only. Uses artists for design, illustrations, mechanicals, retouching, airbrushing, model making, AV materials, lettering and advertisements.
First Contact & Terms: Send query letter with brochure. Samples are filed. Samples not filed are returned only if requested. Reports back only if interested. Call to schedule an appointment to show a portfolio, which should include roughs, original/final art, final reproduction/product, tear sheets and color. Pays for design by the hour, $8 minimum. Pays for illustration by the project, $50 minimum. Considers complexity of project, client's budget, skill and experience of artist and turnaround time when establishing payment. Buys all rights.

COCO RAYNES GRAPHICS, INC., 35 Newbury St., Boston MA 02116. (617)536-1499. President: Coco Raynes. Specializes in brand identity, corporate identity, displays, direct mail, packaging, publications and signage. Clients: corporations, institutions (private and public) and architects.
First Contact & Terms: Send query letter with resume, tear sheets, and photocopies to be kept on file. Reports only if interested. Write to schedule an appointment to show a portfolio, which should include original/final art, photographs and b&w. Payment varies. Considers client's budget, and skill and experience of artist when establishing payment.
Tips: "Be on time, present yourself well. Show only your best pieces; smile, laugh."

RENAISSANCE COMMUNICATIONS, INC., 7835 Eastern Ave., Silver Spring MD 20910. (301)587-1505. Art Director: Joseph Giacalone. Specializes in corporate identity, publications, technical illustration, general illustrations and audiovisual presentations. Clients: government design and graphic departments, high-tech firms.
Needs: Works with 30-40 freelance artists/year. Uses artists for design, illustration, mechanicals, retouching, airbrushing, charts/graphs, AV materials and lettering.
First Contact & Terms: Send query letter with resume to be kept on file. Reports back only if interested. Pays for design and illustration by the hour, $10-20 average; for art production by the hour, $6-15 average. Considers complexity of project, skill and experience of artist and turnaround time when establishing payment.

RENQUIST/ASSOCIATES, INC., 2300 Washington Ave., Racine WI 53405. (414)634-2351. Vice President/Design: Dick Huennekens. Specializes in annual reports, brand identity, corporate identity, displays, landscape design, interior design, direct mail, fashion, packaging, publications, signage and technical illustrations. Clients: consumer and industrial.
Needs: Works with 10-12 freelance artists/year. Uses artists for illustrations, retouching, airbrushing, AV materials and lettering.
First Contact & Terms: Send query letter with brochure showing art style or resume, slides and photographs. Samples not filed are returned only if requested. Reports within 2 weeks. Call or write to schedule an appointment to show a portfolio, which should include thumbnails, roughs, original/final art, final reproduction/product, color and tear sheets. Pays for design by the hour, $15-50. Pays for illustration by the hour, $15-50. Considers complexity of project, client's budget and turnaround time when establishing payment.

RICHARDS DESIGN GROUP, INC., 4722 Old Kingston Pk., Knoxville TN 37919. (615)588-9707. Contact: Stephanie Dixon Wright. Specializes in corporate identity. Clients: ad agencies, industrial and consumer businesses.
Needs: Works on assignment only. Uses artists for illustration, mechanicals, retouching and lettering.
First Contact & Terms: Send query letter with tear sheets to be kept on file. Call for appointment to show portfolio. Samples not kept on file are returned only if requested. Reports only if interested. Pays for design by the project, $50-150 average. Considers complexity of project, how work will be used, turnaround time and rights purchased when establishing payment.

ROSENBAUM ENTERPRISES, 41 Glen Avon Dr., Riverside CT 06878. (203)637-1088. Chief Designer: Jeanette Rosenbaum. Specializes in interior design and posters. Clients: corporate headquarters and our own projects.
Needs: Works with 3-4 freelance artists/year. Uses artists for illustrations, books, magazines, newspapers, retouching, airbrushing, posters, model making and lettering.
First Contact & Terms: Send query letter with brochure showing art style or photographs. Samples not filed are returned by SASE. Reports only if interested. To show a portfolio, mail original/final art and final reproduction/product. Pays for illustration by the hour, $25-75; by the day, $200-500. Considers complexity of project, client's budget, skill and experience of artist, how work will be used, turnaround time and rights purchased when establishing payment.
Tips: "We like to see various styles of work and often can use right away on project, but other times it takes longer to use an artist. We welcome different types of illustrations."

PHILLIP ROSS ASSOCIATES LTD., 310 W. Chicago Ave., Chicago IL 60610. Creative Director: Phillip Ross. Specializes in brand identity, corporate identity, displays, posters, direct mail, fashion, packaging, publications and signage. Clients: ad agencies, public relations firms, corporations and poster publishers.
Needs: Works with 10 freelance artists/year. Prefers artists with three years of experience. Uses artists for design, illustration, brochures, catalogs, P-O-P displays, mechanicals, retouching, airbrushing, posters, direct mail packages, lettering, logos and advertisements. Especially needs experienced artists for graphic design and art production.
First Contact & Terms: Send query letter with resume, Photostats and slides to be kept on file. Reports within 30 days. Call for appointment to show portfolio. Pays for design by the hour, $10-20 and by the project. Considers complexity of project and client's budget when establishing payment.
Tips: Especially looks for "visual impact, simplicity, sensitivity to typography and color, and clean line when reviewing work."

THE ANDREW ROSS STUDIO INC., 9th Floor, 15 W. 20th St., New York NY 10011. (212)807-6699. Contact: Andrew Ross. Graphic design studio. Clients: magazines, AV, sales presentations, sales promotions and direct mail.
Needs: Works with 1 or 2 illustrators/month. Local artists only. Uses artists for direct mail, slides, brochures/flyers, trade magazines, illustration, paste-up, lettering and retouching.
First Contact & Terms: Send brochures and tear sheets to be kept on file. Originals returned to artist upon request. Call for interview. Pays for illustration by the project, $100-1,000 average. Pays for mechanicals and paste-up approximately $15/hour. Doesn't buy design.

JOHN RYAN & COMPANY, 12400 Whitewater Dr., Minnetonka MN 55343. (612)936-9900. Senior Designer: Jim Henke. Specializes in brand identity, corporate identity, displays, interior design, fashion, packaging and signage. Clients: major national retail chains, book publishers and retailers, food, clothing and high-tech manufacturers and retailers.
Needs: Works with 30-50 freelance artists/year. "Local and regional artists are preferred, but I will work with talented people anywhere. Professionalism is more important than experience; quality must be of the highest. Artists must be fast and priced within normal market rates." Uses artists for illustration, brochures, books, P-O-P displays, mechanicals, retouching, airbrushing, posters, direct mail packages, AV materials, lettering, logos and advertisements. Especially looking for "fresh new talent in black-and-white, graphic, airbrush and classic painterly styles, plus people working in new media such as 3-D and paper sculpture."

The asterisk before a listing indicates that the listing is new in this edition. New markets are often the most receptive to freelance submissions.

First Contact & Terms: Send query letter with brochure, resume, business card and samples to be kept on file. Accepts color stats, slides, photocopies, Photostats or printed samples, "preferably in 8½x11 format so they can be filed." Samples not filed are returned by SASE only if requested. Reports within 1 month. Call for appointment to show portfolio. Pays for design by the hour, $30-75 average; by the project, $50-300 average. Pays for illustration by the project, $200-3,000 average. Considers complexity of project, client's budget, skill and experience of artist, turnaround time and rights purchased when establishing payment.
Tips: "Artist's work should be fresh in approach, superlative in execution, turned around in reasonable deadline, priced along normal rate guidelines. Creative problem solving and dazzling execution are premiums here."

***SANOSKI DESIGN**, (Division of The Sandra Sanoski Company, Inc.), 166 E. Superior St., Chicago IL 60611. (312)644-7795. President: Sandra Sanoski. Specializes in annual reports, brand identity, corporate identity, displays, fashion, packaging and signage.
Needs: Works on assignment only. Uses artists for design, illustrations, P-O-P displays, mechanicals, retouching, airbrushing, model making, lettering, logos and advertisements.
First Contact & Terms: Send query letter with brochure or resume and samples. Samples are filed. Samples not filed are returned by SASE if requested. Reports back only if interested. Call to schedule an appointment to show a portfolio, or mail appropriate materials. Pays upon according to project and customized agreement. Considers skill and experience of artist when establishing payment.

***SCHAFER ASSOCIATES VISUAL COMMUNICATIONS GROUP**, 2001 Spring Rd., Oak Brook IL 60521; 32A Mills Pl., Pasadena CA 91105. (312)572-1890; (818)304-0346. Senior Vice President: Nicholas Sinadinos. Specializes in annual reports, brand identity, corporate identity, interior design, packaging, signage and name development. Clients: direct, agencies, PR firms, marketing firms and developers.
Needs: Works with 10-25 freelance artists/year. Prefers competent artists. Works on assignment only. Uses artists for design, illustrations, mechanicals, retouching, model making, AV materials, lettering and writing.
First Contact & Terms: Send query letter. Samples are filed. Samples not filed are returned by SASE. Does not report back. Call to schedule an appointment to show a portfolio, which should include final reproduction/product and tear sheets. Pays for design by the hour, $20 minimum; by the project, $100 minimum. Pays for illustration by the project, $100 minimum. Considers complexity of project and client's budget when establishing payment. Rights purchased vary according to project.
Tips: "Send materials and/or call. Follow up consistently."

JACK SCHECTERSON ASSOCIATES INC., 6 E. 39th St., New York NY 10016. (212)889-3950. Contact: Jack Schecterson. Art/ad agency. Specializes in packaging, product design, annual reports, brand identity, corporate identity, displays, exhibits and shows, publications and signage. Clients: manufacturers of consumer/industrial products.
Needs: Uses local artists. Works on assignment only. Uses artists for annual reports, catalogs, direct mail brochures, exhibits, flyers, packaging, industrial design, slide sets, album covers, corporate design, graphics, trademark, logotype design, sales promotion, audiovisuals, P-O-P displays and print media advertising. Especially needs package and product designers.
First Contact & Terms: Send query letter with brochure showing art style or resume and tear sheets, or write for appointment. Samples returned by SASE. Reports "as soon as possible." Pays by the project for design and illustration; negotiates payment. Reproduction rights purchased.

***HENRY SCHMIDT DESIGN**, 7752 Fay, La Jolla CA 92037. (619)454-9747. Creative Director: Henry Schmidt. Specializes in brand identity, collateral material, advertising, packaging and publications.
Needs: Works with 3-5 freelance artists/year. Uses artists for illustrations, mechanicals, retouching, model making, comprehensive illustration and lettering.
First Contact & Terms: Send query letter with resume, tear sheets, Photostats, photocopies, slides and photographs. Samples are filed. Reports back only if interested. Call or write to schedule an appointment to show a portfolio, which should include roughs, original/final art, final reproduction/product, tear sheets, photographs and color. Pays for design by the hour, $15-25. Pays for illustration by the project, $100 minimum. Considers complexity of project, client's budget and how work will be used when establishing payment. Negotiates rights purchased; rights purchased vary according to project.

***R. THOMAS SCHORER & ASSOCIATES, INC.**, 710 Silver Spur Rd., Palos Verdes CA 90274. (213)377-0207. President: R.T. Schorer. Specializes in brand identity, corporate identity, interior design, packaging, publications and signage. Clients: "all kinds."

Needs: Works with 3 freelance artists/year. Works on assignment only. Uses artists for mechanicals, model making, charts/graphs and lettering.
First Contact & Terms: Send query letter with brochure. Samples are filed. Samples not filed are returned only if requested. Reports back within 14 days. Call or write to schedule an appointment to show a portfolio, which should include original work. Pays for design by the day, $80-150. Pays for illustration by the project, $100-3,000. Considers client's budget, how work will be used, rights purchased and creativity when establishing payment. Rights purchased vary according to project.

SCHROEDER BURCHETT DESIGN GROUP, 40 Park Ave., New York NY 10016. Design Consultant: Carla Schroeder. Specializes in packaging. Clients: manufacturers.
Needs: Works on assignment only. Uses artists for design, mechanicals, lettering and logos.
First Contact & Terms: Send resume and Photostat to be kept on file. Samples not kept on file are returned. Reports within 5 days. Write for appointment to show portfolio, which should include thumbnails, final reproduction/product and photographs. Pays for design by the project, $25-500. Pays for illustration by the project, $25-350. Considers skill and experience of artist when establishing payment.
Tips: "Creativity depends on each individual. In graphics, the trend is toward bold colors. Projects should be very realistic."

SEAY GROUP INTERNATIONAL, 4651-A Roswell Rd., Atlanta GA 30342. (404)257-0263. President: Jack Seay. Specializes in corporate identity, displays, packaging, technical illustration, product design and graphics. Clients: manufacturers and publishers.
Needs: Works with 5-6 freelance artists/year. Prefers local artists for fast turnaround. Works on assignment only. Uses artists for design, illustration, brochures, books, P-O-P displays, mechanicals, direct mail packages, model making, charts/graphs and logos.
First Contact & Terms: Send query letter with resume. Samples not kept on file are returned by SASE only if requested. Reports back only if interested. Call to schedule an appointment to show a portfolio, which should include final reproduction/product. Pays for design by the hour, $5-100 average. Considers complexity of project, client's budget, skill and experience of artist, and turnaround time when establishing payment.
Tips: "Send a few quality examples of current works."

***SERIGRAPHICS ETC.**, Box 7200, Dallas TX 75209. Contact: Michael Truly. Specializes in packaging, publications and technical illustration. Clients: electronic companies, direct mail catalog industry—wholesale and retail, household appliance, auto part and auto air conditioning manufacturers, decorators and restaurants.
Needs: Works with 2-3 freelance artists/year. Works on assignment. Uses artists for advertising and catalog design, illustration and layout; P-O-P displays, mechanicals, retouching, posters, signs, charts/graphs, logos and architectural models.
First Contact & Terms: Artists must be careful and accurate, and able to interpret rough layouts. Send query letter with brochure, resume and business card to be kept on file. Write for appointment to show portfolio, which should include photographs or Photostats. Samples returned only if requested. Reports only if interested. Pays for design and mechanical production work by the hour, $6-7 average. Considers complexity of project, client's budget, skill and experience of artist, how work will be used and turnaround time when establishing payment.
Tips: "Show neat, accurate samples, if possible, that have been used in publication."

***DEBORAH SHAPIRO DESIGNS**, 150 Bentley Ave., Jersey City NJ 07304. (201)432-5198. Owner: Deborah Shapiro. Specializes in annual reports, brand identity, corporate identity, direct mail, packaging and publications. Clients: corporations and manufacturers.
Needs: Works with 10 freelance artists/year. Works on assignment only. Uses artists for illustrations, retouching and airbrushing.
First Contact & Terms: Send query letter with brochure or resume, tear sheets, Photostats and photocopies. Samples are filed. Samples not filed are not returned. Reports back only if interested. To show a portfolio, mail original/final art, final reproduction/product, tear sheets and photographs. Pays for illustration by the project, $200-2,000. Considers complexity of project, client's budget, skill and experience of artist, how work will be used, turnaround time and rights purchased when establishing payment. Buys one-time rights.

SHERIN & MATEJKA, INC.404 Park Ave. S, New York NY 10016. (212)686-8410. President: Jack Sherin. Specializes in corporate communications, publications and sales promotion. Clients: banks, consumer magazines and insurance companies.
Needs: Works with 25 freelance artists/year. Prefers artists located nearby with solid professional experience. Works on assignment only. Uses artists for advertising and brochure design and illustration, me-

chanicals, retouching, model making, charts/graphs and lettering.
First Contact & Terms: Send query letter with brochure showing art style to be kept on file. Samples returned by SASE. Reports in 1 week. Call to schedule an appointment to show a portfolio, which should include original/final art and tear sheets. Pays $15-40/hour for design; negotiates illustration payment method. Considers complexity of project, client's budget, skill and experience of artist, and how work will be used when establishing payment.
Tips: "We buy many humorous illustrations for use in corporate publications."

***NICHOLAS SINADINOS & ASSOCIATES**, 315 S. Maple Ave., Oak Park IL 60302. (312)383-8506. Design Director: Nicholas Sinadinos. Specializes in annual reports, brand identity, corporate identity, packaging, signage and name development. Clients: ad agencies, PR firms, marketing firms, developers and direct accounts.
Needs: Works with 10 freelance artists/year. Prefers competent artists. Works on assignment only. Uses artists for design, illustrations, mechanicals, retouching, model making, AV materials and lettering.
First Contact & Terms: Send query letter. Samples are filed. Samples not filed are returned by SASE. Does not report back. Call to schedule an appointment to show a portfolio, which should include final reproduction/product and tear sheets. Pays for design by the hour, $20-50. Pays for illustration by the project, $50-10,000. Considers complexity of project and client's budget when establishing payment. Rights purchased vary according to project.
Tips: "Follow up."

SMITH & DRESS, 432 W. Main St., Huntington NY 11743. (516)427-9333. Contact: A. Dress. Specializes in annual reports, corporate identity, displays, direct mail, packaging, publications and signage. Clients: corporations.
Needs: Works with 3-4 freelance artists/year. Local artists only. Works on assignment only. Uses artists for illustration, retouching, airbrushing and lettering.
First Contact & Terms: Send query letter with brochure showing art style or tear sheets to be kept on file (except for works larger than 8½x11). Pays for illustration by the project. Considers client's budget and turnaround time when establishing payment.

SPLANE DESIGN ASSOCIATES, 10850 White Oaks Ave., Granada Hills CA 91344. (818)366-2069. Principal: Robson Lindsay Splane. Specializes in product design, corporate identity, displays, packaging, exhibitry and furniture design.
Needs: Local artists only. Works on assignment only. Uses artists for illustration, mechanicals, and model making.
First Contact & Terms: Send query letter with brochure showing art style to be kept on file. Reports only if interested. To show a portfolio, mail appropriate materials, which should include thumbnails, roughs, original/final art and photographs. Pays for design and illustration by the hour, $6-100. Considers complexity of project, client's budget, skill and experience of artist, and turnaround time when establishing payment.

***HARRY SPRUYT DESIGN**, Box 6500, New York NY 10128. Principal: Harry Spruyt. Specializes in structural packaging, product design and invention. Clients: product manufacturers, design firms, consultants and ad agencies.
Needs: Works with various freelance artists/year. Works on assignment only. Uses artists for illustrations, model making and accurate perspective drawings of products.
First Contact & Terms: Portfolio should include thumbnails, roughs, original/final art, final reproduction/product, photographs of models and color. Pays for design and illustration by the hour, $10-25. Considers "usable work, competence in doing job and rate of accomplishment with assignments" when establishing payment.
Tips: "Be succinct in conversation. Give a high value to our time together."

***THOMAS STARR & ASSOCIATES**, 23 E. 37th St., New York NY 10016. President: Thomas Starr. Specializes in corporate identity, direct mail and publications. Clients: ad agencies, film and video publishers, eyewear manufacturers, retail stores, restaurants and real estate developers.
Needs: Works with 8 freelance artists/year. Uses artists for illustration, mechanicals, retouching, airbrushing, model making, charts/graphs and logos.
First Contact & Terms: Works on assignment only. Send query letter with brochure, resume and tear sheets to be kept on file. Reports back only if interested. Pays for design by the hour, $15-30 average. Pays for illustration by the project, $250-1,500 average. Considers complexity of project, client's budget, skill and experience of artist, how work will be used, turnaround time and rights purchased when establishing payment.

LINDA STILLMAN INC., 114 E. 91st St., New York NY 10128. (212)410-3225. Art Director: Linda Stillman. Specializes in promotion, brochures and publications. Clients: cultural and art organizations, publishers, insurance companies and financial companies.
Needs: Works with numerous freelance artists. Local artists only. Uses artists for design, illustration, lettering, mechanicals, photography and retouching. "We mostly need mechanical artists."
First Contact & Terms: Send query letter, resume, tear sheets or photocopies to be kept on file. Considers complexity of project, client's budget, skill and experience of artist, how work will be used, turnaround time and rights purchased when establishing payment. Payment varies.

GORDON STROMBERG DESIGN, 5423 N. Artesian, Chicago IL 60625. (312)275-9449. President: Gordon Stromberg. Specializes in corporate identity, publications, interior design, direct mail and signage. Clients: building trade, book publishing, small businesses, manufacturers, public relations firms, nonprofit organizations, Christian groups/charities and magazine publishers.
Needs: Works with variable number of artists/year. Uses artists for illustration, brochures, calligraphy, retouching and charts/graphs.
First Contact & Terms: Looks for "quality, price and appropriateness in artists' work." Works on assignment only. Send query letter with brochure, resume and samples—"anything that will give me insight into your ability"—to be kept on file. "A phone call will only delay the process until you send brochure or samples or photocopies of samples." Prefers slides; accepts photocopies. Samples are returned by SASE only if requested. Write for appointment to show portfolio. Considers complexity of project, client's budget, skill and experience of artist, how work will be used, and turnaround time when establishing payment.

***STUDIO GRAPHICS**, 7337 Douglas St., Omaha NE 68114. (402)397-0390. Owner: Leslie Hanson. Specializes in corporate identity, displays, direct mail, packaging, publications and signage. Clients: advertising agencies, corporations, direct with print advertisers and marketing organizations and restaurant chains.
Needs: Works with 2 freelance artists/year. Works on assignment only. Uses artists for illustrations, retouching, airbrushing and AV materials.
First Contact & Terms: Send query letter with resume and samples "as available." Samples are filed. Samples not filed are returned by SASE only if requested. Reports back only if interested. Write to schedule an appointment to show a portfolio, which should include "samples as available." Pays for design and illustration by the project, $100 minimum. Considers complexity of project and client's budget when establishing payment. Negotiates rights purchased; rights purchased vary according to project.

***STUDIO KIDOGO**, 1233 S. LaCienega Blvd., Los Angeles CA 90035. (213)854-6274. Owner: Kidogo. Specializes in annual reports, corporate identity and direct mail. Clients: small companies, public agencies and small corporations.
Needs: Works with 4-6 freelance artists/year. Works on assignment only. Uses artists for design, illustrations, mechanicals, lettering and logos.
First Contact & Terms: Send resume, tear sheets and photocopies. Samples are filed. Call to schedule an appointment to show a portfolio, which should include roughs, original/final art, final reproduction/product and Photostats. Pays for design by the hour, $15-25. Pays for illustration by the hour, $35-50; by the project, $50-150. Pays for production by the hour, $10-15. Considers complexity of project and client's budget when establishing payment. Rights purchased vary according to project.
Tips: In portfolios "include hourly rate and time minimums and availability."

SYNTHEGRAPHICS CORPORATION, 940 Pleasant Ave., Highland Park IL 60035. (312)432-7774. President: Richard Young. Specializes in publications. Clients: PR agencies, ad agencies and book publishers.
Needs: Works with 4-5 freelance artists/year. "Prefer local artists, particularly ones good at juvenile, multi-ethnic illustrations." Works on assignment only. Uses artists for advertising and brochure design, illustration and layout; book design and illustration; mechanicals and charts/graphs.
First Contact & Terms: Send resume and photocopies to be kept on file. Reports only if interested. Call for appointment to show portfolio, which should include thumbnails, roughs, original/final art, color, tear sheets and Photostats. Pays for design by the hour, $15-25 average. Pays for illustration by the hour, $10-15 average. Considers complexity of project, client's budget, and skill and experience of artist when establishing payment.

DOUGLAS R. TERCOVICH ASSOC. INC., 575 Madison Ave., New York NY 10022. (212)838-4800. President: Douglas Tercovich. Specializes in packaging, brand identity, displays, sales promotion and fashion. Clients: cosmetic companies, industry and corporations.
Needs: Works with 15 freelance artists/year. Works on assignment only. Uses artists for design, illus-

tration, brochures, P-O-P displays, mechanicals, retouching, airbrushing, posters, lettering and logos.
First Contact & Terms: Send resume and samples to be kept on file. Prefers Photostats or tear sheets as samples. Reports back only if interested. Write for appointment to show portfolio. Pays by the project: design $75 minimum; illustration $150-1,100 average. Considers complexity of project and client's budget when establishing payment.
Tips: "Mechanicals should be of packaging quality."

TESA DESIGN INC., 6122 Nancy Ridge Dr., San Diego CA 92121. (619)453-2490. President: Thomas E. Stephenson. Specializes in brand identity, corporate identity, packaging, signage and technical illustration. Clients: original equipment manufacturers.
Needs: Works with 4 freelance artists/year. Works on assignment only. Uses artists for design, illustration, brochures, catalogs, P-O-P displays, mechanicals, airbrushing, model making and logos.
First Contact & Terms: Send brochure and resume to be kept on file. Samples not kept on file are returned by SASE. Reports only if interested. Call for appointment to show portfolio. Pays for design and illustration by the project. Considers complexity of project, skill and experience of artist, and how work will be used when establishing payment.
Tips: "Portfolio should include industrial or mechanical subject matter."

***TESSING DESIGN, INC.**, 3822 N. Seeley Ave., Chicago IL 60618. (312)525-7704. Principal: Arvid V. Tessing. Specializes in corporate identity and publications. Clients: publishers, educational institutions and nonprofit groups.
Needs: Works with 8-12 freelance artists/year. Works on assignment only. Uses artists for design, illustrations, books, magazines, mechanicals, retouching, airbrushing, charts/graphs and lettering.
First Contact & Terms: Send query letter with brochure. Samples are filed. Samples not filed are not returned. Reports back only if interested. Call to schedule an appointment to show a portfolio, which should include original/final art, final reproduction/product and photographs. Pays for design and illustration by the project. Considers complexity of project, client's budget, skill and experience of artist, how work will be used, turnaround time and rights purchased when establishing payment. Rights purchased vary according to project.

***THARP DID IT**, Suite 21, Fifty University Ave., Los Gatos CA 95030. Design Administrator: Sidney French. Specializes in brand identity, corporate identity, displays, packaging and signage. Clients: direct.
Needs: Works with 10-15 freelance artists/year. Prefers local artists/designers with experience. Works on assignment only. Uses artists for illustrations, P-O-P displays and retouching.
First Contact & Terms: Send query letter with brochure, resume or printed promotional material. Samples are filed. Samples not filed are returned by SASE. Reports back within 2 years only if interested. To show a portfolio, mail appropriate materials. Pays for illustration by the project, $50-5,000. Considers client's budget and how work will be used when establishing payment. Rights purchased vary according to project.
Tips: "Hang in there. If you're good we'll keep you on file. We may call this month, but if a project suited to you does not arise, you may not hear from us for a year or two."

THOMAS & MEANS ASSOCIATES, INC., 1428 Duke St., Alexandria VA 22314. (703)684-2215. Associate Director: Linda Kahn. Specializes in annual reports, corporate identity, publication, audio visual presentation and programs and communication consultation. Clients: corporations, government agencies, architects and developers, and associations.
Needs: Works with 12 freelance artists/year. Prefers local artists. Works on assignment only. Uses artists for design, illustration, brochures, magazines, mechanicals, retouching, airbrushing, charts/graphs, AV materials and logos.
First Contact & Terms: Send query letter with resume, tear sheets and photocopies to be kept on file. Samples not kept on file returned by SASE only if requested. Reports only if interested. Call for appointment to show portfolio. Pays for design by the hour, $15-35 average. Pays for illustration by the project, $300-2,500 average. Considers complexity of project, client's budget, skill and experience of artist, how work will be used, turnaround time and rights purchased when establishing payment.
Tips: "Be persistent and show enthusiasm. Budgets are getting smaller again and clients are looking for the lowest bidder."

TOKYO DESIGN CENTER, Suite 252, 703 Market St., San Francisco CA 94103. Contact: Curtis Tsukano. Specializes in annual reports, brand identity, corporate identity, packaging and publications. Clients: consumer products, travel agencies and retailers.
Needs: Uses artists for design and illustration.
First Contact & Terms: Send business card, slides, tear sheets and printed material to be kept on file.

Samples not kept on file are returned by SASE only if requested. Reports only if interested. Pays for design by the project, $50-1,000 average. Pays for illustration by the project, $100-1,500 average. Considers client's budget, skill and experience of artist, turnaround time and rights purchased when establishing payment.

***TRAVER AND ASSOCIATES, INC.**, 195 E. Columbia Ave., Battle Creek MI 49015. (616)963-7010. Vice President Operations: Chris Kreps. Specializes in brand identity, corporate identity, direct mail, packaging, publications and technical illustrations. Clients: food, auto, industry, health care, editorial design.
Needs: Works with 5 freelance artists/year. Prefers 2 years of experience. Works on assignment only. Uses artists for design, illustration, magazines, mechanicals, retouching, airbrushing, model making and AV material.
First Contact & Terms: Send query letter with brochure showing art style, resume, tear sheets, Photostats or photocopies. Samples are filed. Samples not filed are returned only if requested. Reports back within 1 month. Write to schedule an appointment to show a portfolio which should include final reproduction/product, tear sheets, photographs and color. Pays by the project. Considers complexity of project and skill and experience of artist when establishing payment. Rights purchased vary according to project.
Tips: Freelancers should "demonstrate an enthusiasm for their chosen field and willingness to take creative chances. Think beyond what is asked of them when appropriate. Have an awareness and interest in current trends and leaders in the industry."

***TRES DESIGN GROUP, INC.**, 2100 N. Magnolia Ave., Chicago IL 60614. Director of Design: Stephen Melamed. Specializes in industrial (product) design. Clients: manufacturers.
Needs: Works with 1-3 freelance artists/year. Prefers local artists. Works on assignment only. Prefers high-tech, contemporary style. Uses artists for illustrations, mechanicals and model making.
First Contact & Terms: Send query letter with brochure or resume. Samples are filed. Samples not filed are returned only if requested. Reports back only if interested. To show a portfolio, mail thumbnails, roughs and original/final art. Pays for illustration by the hour, $8-16. Considers complexity of project, client's budget, skill and experience of artist and how work will be used when establishing payment. Rights purchased vary according to project.
Tips: "Be professional and well organized. Carefully select appropriate companies to approach."

TRIBOTTI DESIGNS, 15234 Morrison St., Sherman Oaks CA 91403. (818)784-6101. Contact: Robert Tribotti. Specializes in annual reports, corporate identity, packaging, publications and signage. Clients: PR firms, ad agencies, corporations.
Needs: Works with 2-3 freelance artists/year. Prefers local artists only. Works on assignment only. Uses artists for illustrations, brochures, catalogs, mechanicals, retouching, airbrushing, charts/graphs, lettering and advertisements.
First Contact & Terms: Send query letter with brochure. Reports back only if interested. Call to schedule an appointment to show a portfolio, which should include thumbnails, roughs, original/final art, final reproduction/product, tear sheets, Photostats, photographs, b&w and color. Pays for design and illustration by the hour, $25-40 and by the project, $75-1,000. Considers complexity of project, client's budget, skill and experience of artist, how work will be used and rights purchased when establishing payment. Buys one-time rights; negotiates rights purchased. Rights purchased vary according to project.
Tips: "We will consider experienced artists only. Must be able to meet deadline."

THE T-SHIRT GALLERY LTD., 154 E. 64 St., New York NY 10021. (212)838-1212. Vice President: Flora Azaria. Specializes in t-shirts.
Needs: Works with 10 freelance artists/year. Uses artists for design and illustrations.
First Contact & Terms: Send query letter with resume and samples. Samples not filed are returned only if requested. Reports within weeks. To show a portfolio, mail appropriate materials. Pays for design by the project, $50-500. Pays for illustrations by the project, $50-500. Considers how work will be used when establishing payment.

***UNICOM**, 4100 W. River Lane, Milwaukee WI 53209. (414)354-5440. Production Manager: Sue Sorenson. Specializes in annual reports, brand identity, corporate identity, packaging, publications and signage. Clients: retailers, industrial firms, fashion and professionals.
Needs: Works with approximately 10 freelance artists/year. Uses artists for design, illustration, brochures, catalogs, mechanicals, retouching and airbrushing.
First Contact & Terms: Works on assignment only. Send samples to be kept on file. Samples not kept

on file returned by SASE. Reports only if interested. Call or write for appointment to show portfolio. Considers complexity of project, client's budget, skill and experience of artist, how work will be used and turnaround time when establishing payment.

UNIT 1, INC., 1556 Williams St., Denver CO 80218. (303)320-1116. President: Chuck Danford. Specializes in annual reports, brand identity, corporate identity, direct mail, packaging, publications and signage.
Needs: Uses artists for design, brochures, catalogs, P-O-P displays, mechanicals, posters, direct mail packages, charts/graphs, logos and advertisements.
First Contact & Terms: Send resume and samples to be kept on file. Samples not kept on file are returned. Reports only if interested. Call or write for appointment to show portfolio. Pays for design by the hour. Considers skill and experience of artist when establishing payment.

***UNIVERSAL EXHIBITS**, 9517 E. Rush St., South El Monte CA 91733. (213)686-0562. Design and Sales Administrator: Frank Meyer. Specializes in displays and interior design. Clients: ad agencies and companies.
Needs: Works with 5 freelance artists/year. Prefers local artists, up to 40 miles, with excellent sketching abilities. Works on assignment only. Uses artists for design and model making.
First Contact & Terms: Send resume and samples to be kept on file. Prefers slides as samples; reviews original art. Samples not kept on file are returned only if requested. Reports back within 5 days. Call for appointment to show portfolio. Pays for design by the hour, $10-25 average. Considers client's budget and turnaround time when establishing payment.

WALTER VAN ENCK DESIGN LTD., 3830 N. Marshfield, Chicago IL 60613. (312)935-9438. President: Walter Van Enck. Specializes in annual reports, brand identity, corporate identity, displays, direct mail, packaging, publications and signage. Clients: book publishers, financial associations, health care institutions, investment advisory corporations and medium-sized corporations.
Needs: Works with 2-3 freelance artists/year. Prefers local artists. Works on assignment only. Uses artists for design, illustration, mechanicals, retouching, model making and lettering.
First Contact & Terms: Send query letter with business card and "slides or Photostats that do justice to line art" to be kept on file. Samples not kept on file are returned only if requested. Reports within 1 week. Call or write for appointment to show portfolio. Pays for illustration by the project, $500-2,500 average.

VIE DESIGN STUDIOS, INC., 830 Xenia Ave., Yellow Springs OH 45387. (513)767-7293. President: Read Viemeister. Specializes in corporate identity, packaging, publications and signage.
Needs: Works with 2 freelance illustrators/photographers per year. Artists must be local, or have a "very special style." Works on assignment only. Uses keyliners for mechanicals and charts/graphs.
First Contact & Terms: Send query letter with resume to be kept on file. Prefers to review Photostats and prints. Samples not kept on file are returned by SASE. Reports only if interested. Write for appointment to show portfolio. Pays for design by the hour, $20-30. Pays for illustration by the project, $100-300. Considers turnaround time when establishing payment.
Tips: "Smaller budgets require that design solutions be designed around existing resources, thus freelancer must be a known quantity."

***BRUCE WASSERMAN & ASSOCIATES**, Suite 1107, 568 Broadway, New York NY 10012. (212)226-4500. President: Bruce Wasserman. Specializes in annual reports, corporate identity, displays, packaging and signage. Clients: manufacturers and ad agencies.
Needs: Works with 10-20 freelance artists/year. Prefers local/mechanical people and illustrators. Works on assignment only. Uses artists for illustrations, mechanicals, retouching, airbrushing and lettering.
First Contact & Terms: Send query letter with tear sheets. Samples are filed. Samples not filed are returned only if requested. Reports back only if interested. Call or write to schedule an appointment to show a portfolio, which should include thumbnails, original/final art, final reproduction/product, tear sheets and photographs. Pays by the project. Considers complexity of project and client's budget when establishing payment. Buys all rights.

WHITE FLEET, INE WIJTVLIET DESIGN, 440 E. 56th St., New York NY 10022. (212)319-4444. Contact: Design Production. Specializes in annual reports, brand and corporate identity, displays, exhibits and shows, packaging, publications, signage and slide shows. Clients: large corporation in computers, software computer, retail stores, hospitals, banks, architects and industry.
Needs: Works with 8 freelance artists/year. Uses artists for brochure and catalog layout, mechanicals,

retouching, model making, charts/graphs, AV presentations, lettering and logo design. Especially needs good artists for mechanicals for brochures and other print. Prefers Swiss graphic style.
First Contact & Terms: Send brochure/flyer and resume; submit portfolio for review. Prefers actual printed samples or color slides. Samples returned by SASE. Reports within 1 week. Provide brochure/flyer, resume and tear sheets to be kept on file for possible future assignments. Pays $10-15 average/hour for mechanicals; pays by the project for illustration.
Tips: Artists should "not start so high if unknown; give a break on the first 2 days to work in."

WISNER ASSOCIATES, Advertising, Marketing & Design, 1991 Garden Ave., Eugene OR 97403. (503)683-3235. Creative Director: Linda Wisner. Specializes in brand identity, corporate identity, direct mail, packaging and publications. Clients: small businesses, manufacturers, restaurants, service businesses and book publishers.
Needs: Works with 7-10 freelance artists/year. Prefers experienced artists and "fast clean work." Works on assignment only. Uses artists for illustration, books, mechanicals, airbrushing and lettering.
First Contact & Terms: Send query letter with resume, Photostats, photocopies, slides and photographs to be kept on file. Prefers "examples of completed pieces, which show the abilities of the artist to his/her fullest." Samples not kept on file are returned by SASE only if requested. Reports only if interested. To show a portfolio, call to schedule an appointment or mail thumbnails, roughs, original/final art and final reproduction/product. Pays for illustration by the hour, $10-20 average. Pays for paste-up/production by the hour, $8.50-10. Considers complexity of project, client's budget, skill and experience of artist, how work will be used and turnaround time when establishing payment.
Tips: "Bring a complete portfolio with up-to-date pieces."

BENEDICT NORBERT WONG MARKETING DESIGN, 55 Osgood Pl., San Francisco CA 94133. (415)781-7590. President/Creative Director: Ben Wong. Specializes in direct mail and marketing design. Clients: financial services companies (banks, savings and loans, insurance companies, stock brokerage houses) and direct mail marketing firms (ad agencies, major corporations).
Needs: Works with 15 freelance artists/year. Uses artists for design, illustration, brochures, catalogs, mechanicals, retouching, posters, direct mail packages, charts/graphs, lettering, logos and advertisements. Especially needs "experienced mechanical artists in area of direct mail production."
First Contact & Terms: Send query letter with resume, business card and samples to be kept on file. Prefers tear sheets as samples. Reports back only if interested. Call for appointment to show portfolio. "Payment depends on experience and portfolio." Considers complexity of project, client's budget, skill and experience of artist, how work will be used, turnaround time and rights purchased when establishing payment.
Tips: "Please show imaginative problem-solving skills which can be applied to clients in direct marketing."

***WW3/PAPAGALOS**, 313 E. Thomas, Phoenix AZ 85012. (602)279-2933. Creative Director: Lonnie Whittington. Specializes in annual reports, corporate identity, displays, packaging, publications and signage. Clients: business to business.
Needs: Works with 10 freelance artists/year. Works on assignment only. Uses artists for illustrations, retouching, airbrushing, model making, charts/graphs, AV materials and lettering.
First Contact & Terms: Send query letter with brochure or resume and samples. Samples are filed. Samples not filed are returned only if requested. Reports back within 5 days. Call or write to schedule an appointment to show a portfolio, which should include thumbnails, roughs, final reproduction/product, Photostats and photographs. Pays for design and illustration by the project, $100 minimum. Considers complexity of project, client's budget, skill and experience of artist, how work will be used, turnaround time and rights purchased when establishing payment. Rights purchased vary according to project.
Tips: In presenting samples or portfolios, "two or three samples of the same type/style are enough."

***ZIM-LERNER INC., Industrial and Residential Design Group**, 123 University Pl., New York NY 10003. (212)777-1907. Principals: Larry Zim, Mel Lerner. Specializes in corporate identity, displays, interior design, packaging and signage. Clients: department stores, shopping malls, boutiques.
Needs: Uses artists for design, P-O-P displays, mechanicals, retouching and model making. Especially needs interior rendering.
First Contact & Terms: Experienced artists only. Works on assignment only. Send resume to be kept on file; write for appointment to show portfolio. Do not send samples until requested. Reports back only if interested. Considers complexity of project when establishing payment.

Associations & Institutions

Associations and institutions vary in their purposes—from soliciting funds for education to furthering the goals of the federal legal profession—but they all seek to promote and enrich humanitarian values. Handling a diversity of projects, these groups have many art needs yet seldom employ large inhouse art staffs and thus turn to freelancers.

Although these groups inform, promote and solicit via print and film media, it's print that dominates the demand for artwork. Service-oriented associations rely heavily on various print media, including magazines, newsletters, posters, invitations, brochures and catalogs. Many times one piece of artwork is used to thematically unite several printed pieces, such as invitations, catalogs and flyers. Therefore, portfolio samples should reproduce well in print, exhibit low-cost design solutions and be flexible enough for application to several uses.

Some projects, such as layout and campaign designs, call for local artists to facilitate quick turnaround times. Other projects, however, such as magazine illustration or spot art for membership literature, often can be discussed, assigned and submitted via the mail.

This market particularly seeks artists who *listen* when the group "image" is explained to them and then can adapt their work to fit that image rather than working from their own preconceived notions. An artist's flexibility is an asset since he may be used for several different jobs, each requiring a different approach.

Some associations ask artists to contribute their work; the exposure gained through widely disseminated literature and posters often leads to referrals and paying jobs. Also, the work provides pieces for your portfolio, which is especially important if you are just beginning to build one.

For additional information, consult the *Encyclopedia of Associations*, *Barron's Profiles of American Colleges*, *Comparative Guide to American Colleges*, *Peterson's Annual Guide to Undergraduate Studies* and the *Directory of World Museums*.

ADRENAL METABOLIC RESEARCH SOCIETY OF THE HYPOGLYCEMIA FOUNDATION, INC., 153 Pawling Ave., Troy NY 12180. (518)272-7154. President: Marilyn Hamilton Light. Nonprofit association providing information and research on functional hypoglycemia and related endocrine disorders for lay and professional persons.
Needs: Works with 1 freelance artist/year. Prefers design representative of content of material—medical designs, etc. Works on assignment basis only.
First Contact & Terms: Send query letter with brochure, samples and resume. "Photostats are acceptable as samples." Samples returned by SASE if not kept on file. Reports in 2 weeks. Write for appointment. Payment is negotiable; varies according to available budget.

AESTHETICIANS INTERNATIONAL ASSOCIATION, INC., Suite D, 3606 Prescott, Dallas TX 75219. (214)526-0752. Chairman of the Board: Ron Renee. Promotes education and public awareness of skin care, make-up and body therapy. Produces seminars and holds an annual congress; produces a magazine, *Dermascope*, published bimonthly.
Needs: Works with 6 freelance artists/year. Works on assignment only. Uses artists for advertising design, illustration and layout, brochure and magazine/newspaper design, exhibits, displays and posters.
First Contact & Terms: Send query letter with brochure showing art style, tear sheets, Photostats, photocopies, slides or photographs to be kept on file. Samples not kept on file are returned by SASE. Reports only if interested. Call or write to schedule an appointment to show portfolio, which should include tear sheets, Photostats and photographs. Pays by the hour, $3.75-6 average. Considers available budget when establishing payment.
Tips: "Have something that is creative that reflects our profession."

AFFILIATE ARTISTS INC., 37 W. 65 St., New York NY 10023. Director, Communications: Katharine Walling. A national not-for-profit organization, producing residencies and concert series for performing artists of all disciplines. "Affiliate Artists supports the professional development of exceptionally talented performers and builds audiences for live performance. Residencies are sponsored by corporations and corporate foundations, and presented locally by arts institutions and community organizations. Roster represents every discipline."

Needs: Works with 3 freelance artists/year. Works on assignment only. Uses artists for advertising and brochure design and layout.

First Contact & Terms: Send query letter with resume and Photostats. Samples returned only if requested. Reports only if interested. Pays by the project. Considers available budget when establishing payment.

***AFS INTERNATIONAL/INTERCULTURAL PROGRAMS**, 313 E. 43rd St., New York NY 10017. (212)949-4242. Creative Director: Margaret Connelly. AFS is a nonprofit student and adult international exchange program. "Our International and U.S. headquarters is in New York. We have offices in 70 countries. Most of our exchanges are educational in nature, involving students, teachers, the school stystems."

Needs: Works with 5 freelance artists/year. Prefers local artists only. Works on assignment only. Uses artists for advertising and brochure illustration, magazine illustration and posters. "We are usually limited to black-and-white line work, although we might use color on occasion. We like to show an ethnically diverse situation, with people interacting in an educational situation."

First Contact & Terms: Send query letter with photocopies. Samples are filed. Samples not filed are not returned. Reports back only if interested. To show a portfolio, mail tear sheets, color and b&w. Pays for illustration by the project, $50 minimum. Considers available budget when establishing payment. Buys all rights.

©Jim Ceribello

Illustrator Jim Ceribello of Staten Island, New York, received this assignment for a brochure from Margaret Connelly, creative director of AFS International in New York City. The association, which promotes intercultural study, had not previously used illustration in its print materials. Connelly used this brochure to show that illustration can be used in a "sophisticated and interesting way." She found Ceribello through his ad in RSVP. "He has a refined, simple style, and is very cooperative, creative and pleasant to work with," notes Connelly. Ceribello, who was paid $500 for seven drawings, uses the piece in his portfolio.

AMERICAN ACADEMY OF PEDIATRICS, 141 Northwest Point Blvd., Elk Grove Village IL 60009-0927. Publications Editor: Michael Burke. "A professional organization serving more than 31,000 pediatricians in North, Central and South America who are dedicated to the health, safety and well-being of infants, children, adolescents and young adults."
Needs: Works with 6 freelance artists/year. "Local artists only, please." Works on assignment only. Quick turnaround necessary. Uses artists for newspaper illustration, and annual report design. Especially needs themes related to child health care improvement.
First Contact & Terms: Send query letter with resume and tear sheets. Samples not filed are not returned. Reports only if interested. Write to schedule an appointment to show a portfolio, which should include thumbnails, roughs, original/final art, final reproduction/product, tear sheets, Photostats, photographs and b&w. "Payment varies considerably; will pay for talent." Considers complexity of project, client's budget, skill and experience of artist, how work will be used, turnaround time and rights purchased when establishing payment.
Tips: "No telephone calls please. If and when an appointment/interview is scheduled, show me something I haven't seen before. Most important: show me art that *communicates*. We have added to newspaper's editorial staff and more than doubled our editorial content. We're growing. In turn, we need more and more creative talent."

***AMERICAN ASSOCIATION FOR ADULT CONTINUING EDUCATION**, Suite 230, 1201 16th St. NW, Washington DC 20036. Contact: Jane Melton. Merger of 2 previous associations. Promotes the development of adult education for educational administrators, researchers and teachers.
Needs: Works with 2 freelance artists/year. Prefers local artists. Uses artists for brochure design and magazine covers.
First Contact & Terms: Send query letter with brochure, or resume and photocopies. Samples are filed. Samples not filed are not returned. Reports back only if interested. Call to schedule an appointment to show a portfolio. Pays for design and illustration by the project. Considers complexity of project when establishing payment.

***AMERICAN CORRECTIONAL ASSOCIATION**, Suite L-208, 4321 Hartwick Rd., College Park MD 20740. (301)699-7627. Publications Manager/Art Director: Martin J. Pociask. 14,000-member nonprofit association dealing primarily with correctional personnel and services to improve the correctional field.
Needs: Works with 3-5 freelance artists/year. Call for appointment to show portfolio. Works on assignment only. Uses artists for advertising, brochure, catalog and magazine/newspaper layout and pasteup. Prefers themes on corrections.
First Contact & Terms: Prefers primarily local artists; "however, there may be infrequent exceptions." Send query letter with resume to be kept on file. Reports only if interested. Call for appointment to show a portfolio. Pays by the hour, $6 minimum. Considers complexity of project, available budget, skill and experience of artist and turnaround time when establishing payment.
Tips: "Artists' work should be clean, concise, with quick turnaround." Abilities should not be too specialized. "Most clients are not interested in dividing their work among several artists. They prefer to work closely with only one or two artists."

AMERICAN GEM SOCIETY, 5901 West Third St., Los Angeles CA 90036. Contact: Editor. "AGS is a nonprofit professional organization of jewelers and educators which seeks to build consumer confidence in the retail jeweler through promotion of ethical business standards and continuing advancement of the gemological professional (nationwide) serving retail jewelers, jewelry suppliers and jewelry consumers.'
Needs: Works with 5 freelance artists/year. Artist must have "ability to portray beauty and romance of jewelry." Uses artists for brochure design, illustration and layout; AV presentations and exhibits. Prefers "an effective blend of simplicity, quality, and the tastefulness exemplified by fine jewelry stores."
First Contact & Terms: Send query letter with brochure showing art style or resume and tear sheets. Samples not filed are returned by SASE. Reports only if interested. Write to schedule an appointment to show a portfolio, which should include roughs and final reproduction/product. "Bids are taken on projects." Considers available budget, bids and satisfaction with previous work when establishing payment.
Tips: "Visit AGS stores (listed in the Yellow Pages) to see the kind of clientele we serve."

***AMERICAN INDIAN ARCHAEOLOGICAL INSTITUTE**, Box 260, Washington CT 06793. Editor: Joan Cannon. Association dedicated to education and research, especially in the prehistory and history of the Northeast, especially Litchfield County, CT. Members are interested in archaeology and anthropology.
Needs: Occasionally uses freelance artists. Prefers Indian blood or special knowledge of Indian cultures. Uses freelance artists for advertising illustration; brochure design, illustration and layout; magazine design, illustration, and layout; exhibits; displays; signage and posters.

First Contact & Terms: Send query letter with resume, tear sheets, Photostats, photocopies and photographs. Samples are filed. Reports back only if interested. Pays for design by the hour, $10-25. Considers budget when establishing payment. Negotiates rights purchased.
Tips: "We are a nonprofit institution, working on a strictly limited budget, but with high standards for design and production. New artists interested in publishing small illustrations might find us of interest to them. We do several brochures each year, designed inhouse, but are always interested in quality, dignified work."

***AMERICAN INSTITUTE OF BIOLOGICAL SCIENCES**, 730 11th St. NW, Washington DC 20001-4584. (202)628-1500. Managing Editor: Anne Meltzer. Umbrella organization representing over 40 affiliated societies and 70,000 life scientists dealing with the biological sciences. Members are individual biologists and libraries.
Needs: Works with 1-2 freelance artists/year. Uses artists for brochure design and magazine illustration.
First Contact & Terms: Send query letter with brochure or resume, photocopies and slides. Samples are filed. Samples not filed are returned. Reports back within months. To show a portfolio, mail original/final art, final reproduction/product, photographs and slides. Pays for design by the hour, $10-20. Pays for illustration by the project, $15-60. Considers complexity of project and client's budget when establishing payment.
Tips: "Flexibility, convenience, speed and reasonable prices are key qualities." Looks for "biological, technical subjects, ability to work in black & white. Include a lot of variety in portfolio."

AMERICAN SCIENCE FICTION ASSOCIATION, Suite 95, 421 E. Carson, Las Vegas NV 89101. Vice President: M. Silvers. Promotion and publishing of *all* facets of science fiction and fantasy literature for science fiction fans mostly.
Needs: Works with 20-40 freelance artists/year. Uses artists for brochure and magazine design, illustration and layout; AV presentation, exhibits, displays, signage and posters. Prefers futuristic themes.
First Contact & Terms: Send query letter with resume and samples. Samples not filed are not returned. Reports back within 3 weeks. To show a portfolio, mail original/final art. Pays for design by the hour, $18.50 minimum; by the project, $500 minimum; by the day, $88 minimum. Pays for illustration by the project, $250 minimum. Considers complexity of project and rights purchased when establishing payment.
Tips: "Past experience seems to indicate that the more material submitted the better the chance of our using the artist's services."

AMERICAN SOCIETY FOR THE PREVENTION OF CRUELTY TO ANIMALS, 441 E. 92nd St., New York NY 10128. (212)876-7700. Contact: Editor of Publications. A nonprofit humane society which cares for 200,000 animals annually. Its members are animal lovers and those concerned about humane issues.
Needs: Often uses illustrations for posters, booklets and newsletters. Needs realistic depictions of animals, and cartoons.
First Contact & Terms: Write with samples. Samples returned by SASE. Provide resume, brochure/flyer and tear sheet samples to be kept on file for future assignments. Reports within 3 weeks. Pays $25/small illustration for a pamphlet. Pay for product design and illustration depends on job required and funds available.

AMUSEMENT AND MUSIC OPERATORS ASSOCIATION, Suite 600, 111 E. Wacker Dr., Chicago IL 60601. (312)644-6610. Executive Vice President: William W. Carpenter. Represents the coin-operated games, music and vending industry (primarily jukeboxes, electronic darts and videogames) with 1,600 member companies, operators, distributors, suppliers and manufacturers.
Needs: Works with 4 freelance artists/year. Local artists only. Works on assignment basis only. Uses artists for magazine/newspaper design, illustration and layout; exhibits, signage and posters. Prefers themes revolving around the coin-op entertainment industry.
First Contact & Terms: Send query letter with brochure, resume, business card, samples and tear sheets to be kept on file; do not call. Accepts Photostats, original work, slides or photographs as samples. Reports only if interested. Negotiates pay by the project. Considers complexity of project, available budget, turnaround time and rights purchased when establishing payment.

***APPALACHIAN CONSORTIUM PRESS**, University Hall, Boone NC 28608. (704)262-2064. Executive Director: Dr.Barry Buxton. A nonprofit educational organization dedicated to preserving the cultural heritage of Southern Appalachia. "Our 14 members are colleges and universities in the Southern Highlands, governmental agencies and organizations, a craft guild, and a folk school. Our service region covers 156 counties in seven states. We serve not only our member institutions but the local com-

munity in our 156 county service region."
Needs: Works with 3 freelance artists/year. Uses artists for brochure and catalog design and layout, exhibits and signage.
First Contact & Terms: Send query letter with brochure or resume and photographs. Samples are filed. Reports back only if interested. Call or write to schedule an appointment to show a portfolio. Pays for design by the project, $100 minimum. Considers complexity of project and turnaround time when establishing payment.

BIKECENTENNIAL, INC., Box 8308, Missoula MT 59807. (406)721-1776. Art Director: Greg Siple. Service organization for touring bicyclists; 18,000 members.
Needs: Works on assignment only. Uses artists for illustration. Considers various styles.
First Contact & Terms: Send query letter with brochure showing art style or resume, tear sheets, Photostats, photocopies, slides and photographs to be kept on file. Samples not filed are returned. Reports within 4 weeks. To show a portfolio, mail thumbnails, roughs, final reproduction/product, tear sheets, photostats, photographs and b&w. Pays by the project, $25-75. Considers complexity of project, available budget, skill and experience of artist and how work will be used when establishing payment.
Tips: "We assign specific illustrations and usually provide reference material."

BUCKNELL UNIVERSITY, Lewisburg PA 17837. (717)523-3200. Director of Public Relations and Publications: Sharon Poff. 3,400-student university; public relations department serves students, alumni (31,000), donors and students' parents.
Needs: Works with 3-4 freelance artists/year. Prefers freelancers with strong experience in college/university graphics and located within a 3-hour drive from campus. Uses artists for brochure, catalog and magazine/newspaper design, illustration and layout; graphic design and posters. Especially needs brochure design.
First Contact & Terms: Send query letter with samples, brochure/flyer and resume. Accepts any type samples. Looks for innovation, appropriateness of design concept to target audience and "sensitivity to our particular 'look'—rather classic and dignified, but not boring" when reviewing artist's work. Samples returned by SASE. Reports in 1 month. Call or write for appointment to show portfolio. Payment is by the project, $50-3,000 average or by the hour, $10-20 average; method is negotiable. Considers complexity of project, available budget and turnaround time when establishing payment.
Tips: Artists should "be able to help me produce graphically strong and cost-effective pieces."

CALIFORNIA BAPTIST COLLEGE, 8432 Magnolia Ave., Riverside CA 92504. (714)689-5771. Vice President for Public Affairs: Dr. Jay P. Chance.
Needs: Assigns 3-5 jobs/year. Local artists only. Uses artists for annual reports, catalog covers/layouts, direct mail/publicity brochures, displays, newspaper ad layouts, lettering, recruitment literature and company publications.
First Contact & Terms: Send query letter with samples to Division of Public Information on campus. SASE. Reports in 3 weeks. Call to schedule an appointment to a show a portfolio, which should include final reproduction/product. Pays by the hour.
Tips: "Call for appointment with Ken Miller."

***CALIFORNIA STATE UNIVERSITY, LONG BEACH**, University Publications, 1250 Bellflower Blvd., Long Beach CA 90840. (213)498-5453. Director of University Publications: Randi Wald Bass. CSULB is one of the 19 campuses in the California State University system. It offers 128 baccalaureate programs and 72 master's programs. There are 33,000 students enrolled. Publications are mailed to over 100,000 alumni and friends of the University in the community.
Needs: Works with 5-10 freelance artists/year. Works on assignment only. Uses artists for advertising and brochure design, illustration and layout, catalog layout, magazine illustration and layout and posters.
First Contact & Terms: Send query letter with resume, tear sheets, Photostats or photocopies. Samples are filed. Reports back within 2 weeks. Call or write to schedule an appointment to show a portfolio. Pays for design and illustration by the project, $50-1,500. Considers complexity of project and turnaround time when establishing payment. Rights purchased vary according to project.

CANCER CARE INC., 1180 Ave. of the Americas, New York NY 10036. (212)221-3300. Creative Services Director: F. Critchlow. Health agency for cancer patients and their families, "helping emotionally and financially."
Needs: Works with 2 freelance artists/year. Prefers local artists only. Uses artists for the design, illustration and layout of advertising and brochures and for posters. Prefers modern, contemporary styles.
First Contact & Terms: Send query letter with brochure. Samples not filed are returned if requested.

Reports back only if interested. Pays for design and illustration by the project. Considers skill and experience of artists when establishing payment.

***CCCO/An Agency for Military and Draft Counseling**, 2208 South St., Philadelphia PA 19146. (215)545-4626. Publications Director: Robert A. Seeley. "The largest national draft and military counseling organization in the country; publishes an extensive line of literature, a quarterly newsletter reaching 45,000 people, and one other special-interest newsletter." Serves CCCO contributors and conscientious objectors registered with CCCO. "All are peace-oriented and interested in issues surrounding the draft and military."
Needs: Uses artists for brochure and magazine/newspaper illustration, and possibly for brochure design. Interested in war and peace themes particularly as they affect individuals; open to any style. Graphics and illustrations considered on a case by case basis; especially interested in cartoons.
First Contact & Terms: Send query letter with samples to be kept on file. Reviews any type of sample; finished artwork must be camera-ready. Samples not kept on file returned by SASE. Reports within 3 weeks. "We pay only in contributors' copies, but since our material reaches 45,000 people nationwide, including a number of magazines, we also offer exposure."
Tips: "Send several samples if possible."

CHILD AND FAMILY SERVICES OF NEW HAMPSHIRE, 99 Hanover St., Box 448, Manchester NH 03105. (603)668-1920. Contact: Development Director. "Our purposes are to reduce social problems, promote and conserve wholesome family life, serve children's needs and guard children's rights."
Needs: Works with 1 illustrator and designer/year; February-May only. Uses artists for annual reports, direct mail brochures, exhibits/displays, posters, publicity brochures and trademarks/logotypes. Especially needs illustrations and photos of children and/or families. Prefers realistic portrayals of family life.
First Contact & Terms: Query with business card and tear sheets to be kept on file or arrange interview. Looks for human interest appeal when reviewing artist's work. Reports in 2 weeks. Works on assignment only. Samples returned by SASE. Pays for design by the project, $250-1,500. Pays for illustration by the project, $100-1,500. Considers complexity of project and available budget when establishing payment.
Tips: "In black-and-white work, we look for a balance—nothing too stark or horrific—but a snapshot of real people, children, families."

***CHILDREN'S ART FOUNDATION**, Box 83, Santa Cruz CA 95063. (408)426-5557. Co-director: Gerry Mandel. "The Children's Art Foundation is a nonprofit educational organization. We operate a museum of international children's art and an art school for children. We also publish *Stone Soup*, a national magazine of writing and art by children. We currently have about 9,000 members. We serve schools, libraries, children, teachers, parents, and the general public."
Needs: Works with 5 freelance artists/year. Prefers children up to age 13 only. Uses artists for magazine illustration.
First Contact & Terms: Send query letter with Photostats, photocopies, slides, photographs, or original drawings. Samples are filed. Samples not filed are returned by SASE. Reports back within 2 months. Pays $7.50 "for each illustration we publish." Buys all rights.
Tips: "We like illustrations that depict complete scenes and fill the entire page with detail."

COACHING ASSOCIATION OF CANADA, Department of Promotions and Communication, 333 River Rd., Ottawa, Ontario, K1L 8H9 Canada. (613)746-0036. Development Editor: Steve Newman. National nonprofit organization dedicated to coaching development and the profession of coaching.
Needs: Works with 4-5 freelance artists/year. Works on assignment only. Uses artists for advertising, brochure, catalog and magazine illustration. Prefers coaching (sport) themes in realistic styles.
First Contact & Terms: Send brochure and samples to be kept on file. Prefers slides or photographs as samples. Samples not kept on file are returned. Reports within 4 weeks. Pays by the project, $50-400 average. Considers how work will be used and rights purchased when establishing payment. Buys reprint rights.
Tips: "Artists must have a good understanding of sport. Humorous illustrations are helpful."

COLLEGE OF THE SOUTHWEST, 6610 Lovington Highway, Hobbs NM 88240. (505)392-6561. Contact: Public Information Officer. Privately supported, independently governed 4-year college offering professional studies on a foundation of arts and sciences, emphasizing Christian principles and the private enterprise system.
Needs: Works with varying number of freelance artists/year. Prefers to work with artists in the Southwest. Works on assignment only. Uses artists for advertising, brochure and graphic design; advertising and brochure illustration; and posters. Especially needs artwork "relating to Southwestern heritage."

First Contact & Terms: Send query letter; submit portfolio for review. Prefers 5-10 Photostats or slides as samples. Samples returned by SASE. Reports within 2 weeks. Provide resume and samples to be kept on file for possible future assignments. Negotiates payment.

THE CONTEMPORARY ARTS CENTER, 115 E. 5th St., Cincinnati OH 45202. (513)721-0390. Publications Coordinator: Carolyn Krause. The Center is a small organization (8-10 full-time positions) with changing exhibitions of contemporary art surveying individuals, movements, regional artists, etc., in all media. "We have a growing membership which is geared toward contemporary art and design."
Needs: Works with 2-5 freelance artists/year. Works on assignment only. Uses artists for advertising, brochure and catalog design, illustration and layout; magazine/newspaper design and layout; signage and posters. Prefers contemporary styles.
First Contact & Terms: Send query letter with brochure and resume to be kept on file. Reports only if interested. Pays by the project; "other payment arrangements can be devised as needed." Considers complexity of project, available budget, skill and experience of artist, and turnaround time when establishing payment.

CORE PUBLICATIONS, 1457 Flatbush Ave., Brooklyn NY 11210. (718)434-3580. Communications Coordinator: George Holmes. Nonprofit association providing civil rights publications.
Needs: Works with 20-30 freelance artists/year. Works on assignment only. Uses artists for advertising and magazine/newspaper design, illustration and layout.
First Contact & Terms: Send query letter with samples and resume. Especially looks for artistic skill, imagination, reproduction ability and originality when reviewing work. Samples not filed returned by SASE. Reports within 6 weeks. Negotiates payment by the project.

***COVENANT COLLEGE**, Scenic Highway, Lookout Mountain GA 37350. (404)820-1560. PR Director: Linda Elmore. "Convenant College is a four-year Christian liberal arts college affiliated with the Presbyterian Church in America."
Needs: Works with 2 freelance artists/year. Prefers local artists. Works on assignment only. Uses artist for AV presentations and displays.
First Contact & Terms: Send query letter with brochure and resume. Samples are filed. Samples not filed are returned only if requested. Reports back only if interested. To show a portfolio, mail final reproduction/product. Payment for design and illustration is negotiable. Considers client's budget when establishing payment. Buys all rights; rights purchased vary according to project.

CYSTIC FIBROSIS FOUNDATION, 6931 Arlington Rd., Bethesda, MD 20814. (301)951-4422. Assistant Manager, Publications: Joann Fallon. National, nonprofit organization. National office oversees activities of 60 chapters throughout the country.
Needs: Works with 3 freelance artists/year. "Because we're a nonprofit organization, cost is a crucial factor—we must contract with artist that gives lowest bid, but we still strive for quality." Uses artists for brochure design and illustration; magazine/newspaper design, illustration and layout; AV presentations, exhibits, displays and posters. Especially needs artwork for promotional, fund-raising pieces and for corporate solicitations. Prefers simple, yet professional styles.
First Contact & Terms: Send query letter with brochure showing art style or resume and samples. Samples not filed are returned only if requested. Reports only if interested. Call to schedule an appointment to show a portfolio, which should include roughs, original/final art and color. Pays for design and illustration by the hour, $50 maximum. Considers complexity of project, client's budget and turnaround time when establishing payment.
Tips: "We see more nonprofit origanizations competing for less dollars, which means fund-raising pieces will become slicker, more professional and business-oriented."

DISCOVERY: THE ARTS WITH YOUTH IN THERAPY, 3977 2nd Ave., Detroit MI 48201. (313)832-4357. Director: Fr. Russ Kohler. "We fund self-employed artists to work for 15 weekly house calls to youth with cancer and long-term illnesses."
Needs: Works with "artists as we need them upon referral of patients by physicians and medical social workers. We prefer artists who are somewhat isolated in their medium and willing to enter the isolation of the child overly identified with his disease. Prefer a minimum of psychological and medical jargon; emphasis on the language of art and visual expression and experience."
First Contact & Terms: Write with resume to be kept on file for future assignments.

DREXEL UNIVERSITY, Dept. of Public Relations, 32nd and Chestnut Sts., Philadelphia PA 19104. (215)895-2613. Director: Philip Terranova. Buys 10 illustrations/year.
Needs: Uses designers for books, pamphlets and posters; illustrators for covers, spot art, advertising, annual reports, charts, direct mail brochures, exhibits/displays, handbooks, publicity, recruitment liter-

ature, magazines, newsletters and trademarks/logos. Also uses mechanical artists for same as need permits.
First Contact & Terms: Send query letter with resume, b&w or color tear sheets (slides OK) or arrange interview. Looks for originality and sound production skills. SASE. Reports in 1 week. Pays for mechanicals by the hour, $7.50-10; for illustration by the project, $100-300. Considers available budget and skill and experience of artist when establishing payment.

EDUCATIONAL FILM LIBRARY ASSOCIATION, INC., Suite 301, 45 John St., New York NY 10038. (212)227-5599. Executive Director: Ron MacIntyre. "The leading professional association concentrating on 16mm films, video and other nonprint media for education and community use." Members include: public libraries, universities/colleges, museums, community groups, film programmers, filmmakers, film teachers, etc.
Needs: Works with 1 artist/year for all illustrations; 1 for ad design. "Artists must work within strict guidelines."
First Contact & Terms: Query by mail or write with samples. Works on assignment only. Samples returned by SASE. Reports back on future assignment possibilities. Provide resume, business card, brochure/flyer, tear sheet samples or "anything that gives a good idea of work experience" to be kept on file for future assignments. Pay is negotiable.
Tips: "Send samples that apply to film/video technology, film librarians, independent video and filmmakers."

EPILEPSY FOUNDATION OF AMERICA, Suite 406, 4351 Garden City Dr., Landover MD 20785. (301)459-3700. Director of Administrative Services: Hugh S. Gage. Nonprofit association providing direct and indirect programs of advocacy, public health education and information, research, government liaison and fundraising to persons with epilepsy, their families and professionals concerned with the disorder.
Needs: Works with 3-4 freelance artists/year. Prefers local artists "because of tight deadlines. Sometimes this is not a problem. However, it depends on the job." Works on assignment only. Uses artists for advertising layout, brochure design, illustration and layout; graphic design, exhibits, displays, signage, AV presentations, annual reports, illustrations and layouts for fundraising materials. Themes must be suitable to a publicly-funded, charitable organization.
First Contact & Terms: Provide business card to be kept on file. Looks for "diversity, taste, 'non-cute' approaches." Samples returned by SASE. Reports back on whether to expect possible future assignments. Call for appointment. Payment is by the project. Considers complexity of project and available budget when establishing payment.
Tips: "We're looking for the most value for our money. Don't bring banged-up, poorly printed samples."

ESSEX COMMUNITY COLLEGE, 7201 Rossville Blvd., Baltimore County MD 21237. (301)682-6202. Contact: Managing Director. Performing arts center; presents musicals, cabaret plays, open-air Shakespearean and other classical plays, children's theatre, and seminars. "Cockpit is in residence at Essex Community College. We try to use the services of the school graphics department as much as possible but sometimes must use freelance artists because the staff at the school is too overloaded or they are unable to give us what we want."
Needs: Works with 2 illustrators and 2 designers/year. "Our brochure is our most important tool for publicity as it creates an image for our theatre. Work on the brochure begins in early fall for the following summer season." Uses artists for advertising, billboards, designer-in-residence, direct mail brochures, flyers, graphics, posters, sets and technical art.
First Contact & Terms: Local artists only. Query with samples or arrange interview. SASE. Reports within 2 weeks. Works on assignment only. Samples returned by SASE; and reports back on future assignment possibilities. Provide resume, business card, brochure, flyer and tear sheet to be kept on file for future assignments. Negotiates payment.
Tips: "Cockpit in Court Summer Theatre is a rarity. We are self-supporting through subscription sales, box office receipts, grants and donations. We have started an apprenticeship program to supplement nearly every production area and seldom require the services of a freelance artist as college faculty and staff members can usually produce what we want." To those artists interested in working in the performing arts field, "keep artwork simple! Graphics and typeface must be reproducible, will most likely be reduced for flyers, newspapers ads, etc. The simpler the typeface the better."

***EXOTIC WORLD**, 29053 Wild Rd., Holendale CA 92342. President: Jennie Lee. Associated with Exotic Dancers League of North America. Members are exotic dancers, strippers and their fans.
Needs: Works with 1-2 freelance artists/year. Uses artists for advertising and brochure design, illustration and layout, catalog design, magazine design, displays, signage, posters, portraits and murals.

First Contact & Terms: Send brochure or resume, tear sheets, Photostats, photocopies, photographs and SASE. Samples are filed. Samples not filed are returned by SASE only if requested. Reports back within 2 weeks only if interested. Write to schedule an appointment to show a portfolio or mail Photostats, tear sheets, photographs and color. Pays for design by the project, $20-100. Pays for illustration by the project, $20-200. Negotiates rights purchased; rights purchased vary according to project.
Tips: "We are mostly interested in posters and murals. Please submit your ideas for our new brochure, using design, printing and color photos, folded in thirds."

FEDERAL BAR ASSOCIATION, Suite 408, 1815 H St. NW, Washington DC 20006. (202)638-0252. Director of Publications: Monica Goldberg. "Our 15,000-member association was founded in1920 to further the goals of the federal legal profession." Serves lawyers, magistrates, judges, district attorneys and members of the Military Judge Advocates Generals Corps.
Needs: Works with 4 freelance artists/year. Uses artists for magazine design and illustration.
First Contact & Terms: Send query letter with resume and samples. Samples not filed are returned by SASE. Reports only if interested. Call or write to schedule an appointment to show a portfolio, which should include roughs, original/final art and final reproduction/product. Pays for illustration by the project, $500 maximum. Considers client's budget when establishing payment.

THE FINE ARTS CENTER, CHEEKWOOD, Forrest Park Dr., Nashville TN 37205. (615)352-8632. Director: Kevin Grogan. Art museum; full-time staff of 9; collects, preserves, exhibits and interprets art with special emphasis on American painting. The Tennessee Botanical Gardens and Fine Arts Center, Inc., has a membership in excess of 8,000, drawn primarily from Nashville (Davidson County) and neighboring counties in the middle Tennessee, southern Kentucky region.
Needs: Works with 1-3 freelance artists/year. Prefers local artists. Uses artists for advertising, brochure and catalog design and layout; signage and posters.
First Contact & Terms: Send query letter with resume, business card, slides and photographs to be kept on file; "slides, if any, will be returned." Reports within 4 weeks. Write to schedule an appointment to show portfolio and for artists' guidelines. Pays by the hour, $5-20 average. Considers complexity of project, available budget, skill and experience of artist, how work will be used and turnaround time when establishing payment.

***FISK UNIVERSITY**, 1000 17th Ave., Nashville TN 37203. (615)329-8536. Director Public Information: Sandra Mintner. Predominantly Black liberal arts college with enrollment of 500 students. Oriented towards pre-professional training with high academic standards.
Needs: Works with 3 freelance artists/year. Prefers local artists. Works on assignment only. Uses artists for brochure design, magazine design and illustration, AV presentations and posters.
First Contact & Terms: Send query letter with brochure or tear sheets, slides and photographs. Samples are filed. Samples not filed are returned only if requested. Reports back within 5 days. Call to schedule an appointment to show a portfolio, which should include original/final art, tear sheets, color and b&w. Pays for design by the hour, $20-35. Pays for illustration by the project, $35-50. Considers complexity of project, skill and experience of artist and how work will be used when establishing payment. Rights purchased vary according to project.

FLORIDA MEMORIAL COLLEGE, 15800 NW 42nd Ave., Miami FL 33054. (305)625-4141. Public Affairs Director: Nadine Drew. Baptist-related, 4-year, accredited liberal arts college located on a 50-acre site with enrollment of 1,800 multi-racial students.
Needs: Works with 2-3 freelance artists/year. Works on assignment only. Uses artists for advertising, brochure and catalog design, illustration and layout.
First Contact & Terms: Send brochure/flyer with printed material, tear sheets and actual work. Samples returned upon request only with SASE. Reports immediately.

FOUNDATION OF HUMAN UNDERSTANDING, Box 811, 111 NE Evelyn St., Grants Pass OR 97526. (503)479-0549. Managing Editor: David Masters. "Nonprofit, Judeo-Christian church, whose daily radio program reaches millions of listeners nationwide. Purpose is to teach people how to control their emotions through observation exercise taught by Founder/President Roy Masters. We reach out and help people of all faiths."
Needs: Works with 100 freelance artists/year. Uses artists for advertising and brochure design and illustration; magazine design, illustration and layout. Prefers thought-provoking, iconolastic, controversial b&w, pen & ink, photos, cartoons, modern, classic, etc; variety of artwork designed to shock or stimulate ideas surrounding article content.
First Contact & Terms: Send query letter with tear sheets, Photostats, photocopies, slides, photographs and original artwork. Samples not filed are not returned. Reports within 2 weeks. To show a port-

folio, mail thumbnails, roughs, original/final art, final reproduction/product, color, tear sheets, Photostats, photographs and b&w.
Tips: "The more controversial the subject matter, the better."

FRANKLIN PIERCE COLLEGE, Public Relations Office, Rindge NH 03461. Director/Public Relations: Richard W. Kipperman.
Needs: Regional artists only. Uses artists for cover illustrations for brochure and catalog covers, occasionally for brochure design and logo/institutional identity designs.
First Contact & Terms: Query with previously published work. Looks for "quality, artistic ability" when reviewing samples. Works on assignment only. Samples returned by SASE; and reports back on future possibilities. Provide resume and business card to be kept on file for future assignments. Pays per completed assignment (includes concept/roughs/comps/mechanicals).

***THE FREEDONIA GAZETTE**, Darien 28, New Hope PA 18938. (215)862-9734. Director: Paul Wesolowski. The purpose of this organization is to gather information on the lives and careers of the Marx Brothers and their impact on the world. It is a membership organization with approximately 400 members. Members consist of anyone interested in the Marx Brothers: students, professionals, libraries, fans.
Needs: Works with 1 freelance artist/year. Uses artists for magazine illustration and layout of the *The Freedonia Gazette*. Prefers illustrations which relate in some way to the Marx Brothers.
First Contact & Terms: Send query letter with tear sheets, photocopies and photographs. Samples are filed. Reports back within 3 weeks. To show a portfolio, mail thumbnails, roughs, original/final art, tear sheets, photographs and b&w.
Tips: "TFG is a not-for-profit organization. All writers, artists and editors volunteer their services. The only payment we offer is a complimentary copy of any issue your work appears in."

GEORGIA INSTITUTE OF TECHNOLOGY, Office of Publications, Alumni/Faculty House, Atlanta GA 30332. (404)894-2450. Director: Thomas Vitale. University with 11,000 students; publications serving alumni, graduate and undergraduate students and faculty.
Needs: Works with 5 freelance artists/year. Works on assignment only. Uses artists for brochure design and illustration, magazine/newspaper illustration and posters. Themes and styles vary with each project.
First Contact & Terms: Send query letter with brochure and samples to be kept on file. Samples not filed are returned only if requested. Reports only if interested. Call or write for appointment to show portfolio. Pays by the hour, $25-100 average. Considers complexity of project, available budget, skill and experience of artist, how work will be used, turnaround time and rights purchased when establishing payment.
Tips: "We are a state school—budgets are tight, but the work is very high-quality."

HAMPDEN-SYDNEY COLLEGE, Hampden-Sydney VA 23943. (804)223-4382. Director of Publications: Dr. Richard McClintock. Nonprofit all-male liberal arts college of 750 students in a historic zone campus.
Needs: Works with 5-6 freelance artists/year. Works on assignment only. Uses artists for advertising, brochure, catalog and graphic design; brochure and magazine/newspaper illustration; brochure, catalog and magazine/newspaper layout; AV presentations and posters. Especially needs illustrations and mechanical preparations.
First Contact & Terms: Send query letter with resume and actual work. Write for appointment to show portfolio. Samples returned by SASE. Reports in 1 week. Pays for design by the project, $250-1,500. Pays for illustration by the project, $25-300.
Tips: "Changes in art and design include more formality, careful design and quality of 'look.' "

HARDWOOD PLYWOOD MANUFACTURERS ASSN., Box 2789, Reston VA 22090. (703)435-2900. President: E.T."Bill" Altman. National trade association of hardwood plywood and veneer manufacturers and prefinishers of hardwood plywood and suppliers to the industry. Prefinishers, printer, vinyl overlayers, paper overlayers, embossers, etc. of imported and domestic hardwood plywood wall paneling.
Needs: Works with 1 freelance artist/year. Uses artists for brochure and catalog illustration.
First Contact & Terms: Send query letter with resume and samples. Samples not filed are returned only if requested. Reports only if interested. To show a portfolio, mail appropriate materials. Considers association's budget when establishing payment.

***HOOD COLLEGE**, Frederick MD 21701. (301)663-3131. A women's residential college for the liberal arts. "Has about 12,000 alumnae who receive a quarterly magazine with articles about the college and subjects of interest."

Needs: Works with 10 freelance artists/year. Prefers Baltimore/Washington, D.C. artists. Works on assignment only. Uses artists for advertising illustration and layout and magazine illustration.
First Contact & Terms: Send query letter with brochure or tear sheets and photographs.

INSTITUTE OF INTERNATIONAL EDUCATION, Communications Division, 809 United Nations Plaza, New York NY 10017. Senior Production Editor: Ellen L. Goodman. Produces information flyers, paperback catalogs and statistical analysis; also annual report. Publishes 11 titles/year.
Needs: Works with many freelance artists/year. Works on assignment only.
First Contact & Terms: Send query letter with brochure, resume and samples to be kept on file. Reports within 2 weeks. Originals sometimes returned to artist after job's completion. Pays by the project. Rights purchased vary.

INTERNATIONAL ASSOCIATION OF INDEPENDENT PRODUCERS, Box 2801, Washington DC 20013. (202)775-1113. Executive Director/Editor: Dr. Edward VonRothkirch. Associate Director: Ted Edwards.
Needs: Works with 15-25 illustrators and 3-4 designers/year. Works on assignment only. Uses graphic designers for art which pertains to motion pictures, TV, records, tapes, advertising and book/record cover illustrations. Specific needs include layouts, logos and column heads.
First Contact & Terms: Send resume, brochure and tear sheet to be kept on file; also send tear sheets, photocopies or transparencies as samples. Samples returned by SASE; reports back on future assignment possibilities. Pays by job. Usually buys all rights.

***INTERNATIONAL BLACK WRITERS CONFERENCE, INC.**, Box 1030, Chicago IL 60690. A writers' organization that provides annual workshops and an annual awards banquet for writers and aspiring writers. There are 500 members nationally.
Needs: Works with approximately 150 freelance artists/year. Uses artists for magazine design, exhibits and displays. Prefers subjects relevant to writers.
First Contact & Terms: Send query letter with resume and photocopies.

***INTERNATIONAL FABRICARE INSTITUTE**, 12251 Tech Rd., Silver Spring MD 20904. (301)622-1900. Director of Communications: Karen Graber. Trade association for drycleaners and launderers serving 10,000 members.
Needs: Works with 2-3 freelance artists/year. Uses artists for brochure and catalog design, illustration and layout; and posters.
First Contact & Terms: Local artists only; "must have references, be reachable by phone, reliable and honor schedules." Works on assignment only. Call or write for appointment to show portfolio. Especially looks for "neatness, appeal to my own aesthetics and suitability to our company image." Reports only if interested. Pay varies according to project; "typical #10 brochure, $500-800." Considers complexity of project, available budget, and skill and experience of artist when establishing payment.
Tips: "Call for an appointment; don't 'drop in.' Have your portfolio ready and references available. Follow up if necessary; I'm busy and may forget by the time a suitable project comes up."

INTERNATIONAL PLATFORM ASSN., 2564 Berkshire Rd., Cleveland. Heights OH 44106. (216)932-0505. Newsletter Editor: Dose Hill, 2126 Saddleback, Mosreau OK 73072. "Approximately 200 artists within the organization, among some 40 exhibits at annual art shows." Serves all types of patrons from all parts of the country and some foreign.
Needs: Works with 50 freelance artists/year. "Most freelance artists are painters that we work with but many prizes have been awarded to photographers in the past." Uses artists for art shows.
First Contact & Terms: "Each artist must be a member of I.P.A. (International Platform Assn). Artists get a mention in the *Talent* newsletter when they win our award."

INTERNATIONAL RACQUET SPORTS ASSOCIATION, 132 Brookline Ave., Boston MA 02215. (617)236-1500. Editor: Catherine Masterson. Trade association for commercially operated, investor-owned racquet and fitness clubs.
Needs: Works with 6 freelance artists/year. Prefers local artists. Uses artists for advertising, brochure and magazine/newspaper design, illustration and layout; posters. Prefers fitness club operations, business scenes and club sports as themes.
First Contact & Terms: Send query letter with brochure showing art style. Samples not filed are returned by SASE. Reports only if interested. Call or write to schedule an appointment to show a portfolio. Pays for design by the project, $200 minimum. Pays for illustration by the project, $100 minimum. Considers complexity of project, client's budget, skill and experience of artist, and turnaround time when establishing payment.
Tips: "We have only begun budgeting for design and illustration work fairly recently, so our rates are

low. We are looking to build a stable of contacts—if you start with us, you can probably take on work from a variety of sources within our organization: monthly magazine, marketing department, meeting planning, etc. Opportunity to grow with us (we've jumped from 8 staff and $500,000 budget 2 years ago to 20 employees and $2 million budget)."

INTER-TRIBAL INDIAN CEREMONIAL ASSOCIATION, Box 1, Church Rock NM 87311. (505)863-3896. WATS Line: 1-800-233-4528. Executive Director: L.D. Linford. Teaches Indian culture to Indians and non-Indians.
Needs: Assigns 1 art job/year. Uses artists for direct mail brochures and posters. Indian artists only. Especially needs posters and advertising art. Prefers Indian motifs by Indian artists.
First Contact & Terms: Send query letter with brochure showing art style. SASE. Reports within 1 month. Write to schedule an appointment to show a portfolio, which should include original/final art and photographs. Pays $500 maximum/job, design.

IPI ADVERTISING GROUP, (formerly Invitational Promotions, Inc.), 6930 Owensmouth Ave., Canoga Park CA 91303. (818)999-6515. Vice President, Creative: John A. Buchanan. National agency serving over 2,500 financial institutions, and 2,500 auto dealers in over 120 cities. Works in areas of auto, loan promotion, furniture, travel promotion; also deals in incentives and sales promotion, credit card systems and insurance.
Needs: Works on assignment only. Uses artists for advertising, brochure, magazine/newspaper and catalog design, illustration and layout; exhibits, displays, signage, posters and retouching. Especially needs "life-style types, four-color illustrations and layouts for financial promotions, i.e. IRA, ATM, loans, savings and checking printed pieces."
First Contact & Terms: Send query letter with brochure showing art style or resume and tear sheets, Photostats and photocopies to be kept on file. "No originals." Samples not kept on file are returned. Reports within 1 week. Call or write to schedule an appointment to show portfolio, which should include thumbnails, roughs, final reproduction/product, color, tear sheets, Photostats, photographs, b&w and slides of work if available. Pays by the hour, $3.85 minimum; by the project, rate varies, generally normal L.A. freelance rates. "Projects are generally quoted as a result of the scale; artists must work in a do-not-exceed price structure." Considers complexity of project, available budget, skill and experience of artist and turnaround time when establishing payment.
Tips: Artists should "make sure their books are concise and self-explanatory, and show as wide a range of work as possible. We look for versatility in style. Since we work with over 2,500 banks, savings & loans and credit unions, each piece must be unique. We will work with artists on a national basis because we use printing facilities in over 120 cities. We have rapidly expanded into fullscale advertising and marketing in the financial marketplace. There has been rapid deregulation, thus more advertising."

***JEWISH VEGETARIAN SOCIETY, INC.**, Box 5722, Baltimore MD 21208-0722. (301)486-4948. Chairman: Izak Luchinsky. Membership organization with 1,300 members in North America. "Advocates of non-carnivorous life based on Old Testament precepts. Members are vegetarian Jews.
Needs: Works with 1 freelance artist/year. Prefers experienced Hebrew calligraphers and those artists who can design *original* vegetarian/Jewish graphics. Uses artists for displays, signage, posters, T-shirts, stationery and jewelry with logo. Prefers diet, religion, anti-vivisection, soil conservation as themes; modern and ancient Hebrew lettering as styles.
First Contact & Terms: Send query with photocopies. Samples are not filed. Samples not filed are returned by SASE. Reports back only if interested. To show a portfolio, mail thumbnails. Pays for design and illustration by the project, amount being negotiable. Considers originality and rights purchased when establishing payment. Rights purchased vary according to project.

***KONGLOMERATI: THE LITERARY NETWORK**, 239 Second Ave. S, St. Petersburg FL 33701. (813)821-4115. Associate Director/Curator: Louise Thorlin. "Konglomerati is a small letterpress publisher. We print fine books for sale to the general public, libraries and other institutions. We particularly print poems that are often illustrated."
Needs: Works with 5 freelance artists/year. Uses artists for advertising, brochure and catalog design, illustration and layout, magazine/newspaper design, illustration and layout.
First Contact & Terms: Send query letter with brochure or resume, tear sheets, photocopies and photographs. Samples are sometimes filed. Samples not filed are returned by SASE only if requested. Reports back within 30 days. Write to schedule an appointment to show a portfolio or mail original/final art, final reproduction/product and color. Pays for design and illustation by the project, $10 minimum; "certainly is conditional." Considers complexity of project when establishing payment. Rights purchased vary according to project.

LOYOLA UNIVERSITY OF CHICAGO, 820 N. Michigan Ave., Chicago IL 60611. (312)670-2974. Assistant Vice President/University Public Relations: James Reilly. One of the largest private universi-

ties in Illinois providing higher education to 15,000 students on 3 Chicago-area campuses and one in Rome, Italy.
Needs: Works with 6-7 freelance artists/year. Works on assignment basis only. Uses artists for brochure and catalog design and layout; graphic design, exhibits, displays, signage, AV presentations and posters.
First Contact & Terms: Send query letter. Prefers original work as samples. Samples returned. Reports in 6 weeks. Write for appointment to show portfolio. Payment varies according to job.
Tips: "Keep up with the latest trends."

MACALESTER COLLEGE, Office of Public Relations & Publications, 1600 Grand Ave., St. Paul MN 55105. (612)696-6203. Director: Nancy A. Peterson. Designer: Marnie Lilja Baehr. Four-year liberal arts college "with reputation as one of nation's finest." Produces materials for student recruitment, academic use, alumni relations, fundraising, etc.
Needs: Works with a few freelance artists/year. Works on assignment only. Uses artists for brochure and catalog design, illustration and layout; graphic design, magazine illustration; and posters. Prefers variety of themes and styles. Especially needs b&w illustrations and photographs.
First Contact & Terms: Send query letter with resume, tear sheets, photocopies, photographs and printed samples. Reports back on whether to expect possible future assignments. Call or write for appointment to show portfolio. Samples not kept on file are returned. Pays for design by the hour, $8 minimum and by the project, $50 minimum. Payment varies according to job and client's budget.
Tips: "We're conservative in our approach to design, but we like something fresh and clean." Looks for "clean design; well-organized format; eye catching; interesting/innovative use of two-color format; strong photographs with a photojournalistic flair."

McALLEN CHAMBER OF COMMERCE, Box 790, McAllen TX 78501. (512)682-2871. Public Relations Manager: Rick Arriola. Promotes conventions, tourism, community programs, industry and legislation for McAllen.
Needs: Assign 8-15 jobs and buys 12 illustrations/year. Uses artists for advertising, magazines, newsletters, publicity brochures, exhibits/displays and trademarks/logos. Especially needs economic/business-oriented artwork; international trade and commerce themes; and Hispanic-related art and information.
First Contact & Terms: Send query letter with samples. SASE. Reports in 1 week. Pays $10-20/illustration. Considers turnaround time when establishing payment.
Tips: "We have expanded our monthly newsletter to a monthly economic report."

METASCIENCE FOUNDATION, Box 32, Kingston RI 02881. Associate Editor/Art Director: Robert Adsit. "We publish a scholarly academic periodical covering all areas of consciousness research. Topics include telepathy, precognition, psychokinesis, astrology, graphology, ufology, metaphysics, neurophysiology and the quantum physics of consciousness."
Needs: Works with 4 freelance artists/year. Uses artists for advertising design, illustration and layout; exhibits, displays and features artists within periodicals. Prefers Egyptian, occult, futuristic themes; creative, abstract, representational styles.
First Contact & Terms: Send query letter with Photostats, slides and photographs possibly to be kept on file. Samples not kept on file are returned by SASE if requested. Reports within 2 months. Pays $15; "our journal goes out to over 30 countries and over 50 libraries. Payment is more in exposure and opportunity than in direct pecuniary rewards."
Tips: Current trends include "surreal, metaphysical, extradimensional and futuristic themes."

***METRO-HELP, INC.**, 2210 N. Halsted St., Chicago IL 60614. Executive Director: Baulkus C. Heard.
Needs: Works with 2 freelance artists/year. Uses artists for advertising, brochure and magazine/newspaper design, illustration and layout, AV presentations and posters.
First Contact & Terms: Send query letter with brochure, samples and tear sheets to be kept on file. Write for appointment to show portfolio. Prefers Photostats as samples. Samples not kept on file are returned only if requested. Reports within 6 weeks. Pays by the project, $25-1,000 average. Considers complexity of project, and available budget when establishing payment.

MID-AMERICA BIBLE COLLEGE, 3500 S.W. 119th, Oklahoma City OK 73170-9797. (405)691-3881. Director of College Relations: Bill Cissna. A single purpose institution that prepares leadership for Christian service; serves approximately 350 students (55% male, 45% female and 32% married).
Needs: Works with 2-3 freelance artists/year. Artists must be sympathetic with the Christian philosophy of life and have a well-balanced portfolio. Works on assignment basis only. Uses artists for advertising, brochure, catalog and magazine/newspaper design; advertising, brochure, catalog and magazine/newspaper illustration; brochure and catalog layout; signage and posters. Prefers religious themes; "lots of people." Especially needs posters for distribution to local churches nationwide; brochures and re-

sponse card for each degree program.
First Contact & Terms: Send query letter with samples, brochure/flyer and resume; submit portfolio for review. Prefers "whatever is most convenient and economical for the artist" as samples. "Appeal to Christian high school student; work in sympathy with a conservative college." Samples returned. Reports in 5 weeks. Provide business card, brochure, flyer and samples to be kept on file for possible future assignments. Negotiates payment. Considers available budget and how work will be used when establishing payment.
Tips: "We like one artistic concept to do a multiple number of things." There has been "addition of new degree programs" here.

***MUSIC TEACHERS NATIONAL ASSOCIATION**, Suite 2113, 441 Vine St., Cincinnati OH 45202. (513)421-1420. Graphics Consultant: Poppy Evans. Association of music teachers most of whom teach independently. MTNA publishes a bimonthly journal.
Needs: Works with 3 freelance artists/year. Prefers local artists. Works on assignment only. Uses artists for magazine design and illustration.
First Contact & Terms: Send query letter with brochure or resume, tear sheets, Photostats, photocopies, slides and photographs. Samples are filed. Samples not filed are returned only if requested. Does not report back. Call to schedule an appointment to show a portfolio, which should include original/final art, Photostats, tear sheets, final reproduction/product, photographs, slides and b&w. Pays for design and illustration by the hour, $10 minimum; by the project, $20 minimum. Considers complexity of project, turnaround time and skill and experience of artist when establishing payment. Negotiates rights purchased; rights purchased vary according to project.

THE NATIONAL ASSOCIATION FOR CREATIVE CHILDREN & ADULTS, 8080 Springvalley Dr., Cincinnati OH 45236. Editor: Ann Isaacs.
Needs: Works with 1 artist/year for advertising design. Also uses artists for books and brochures.
First Contact & Terms: Send query letter with samples. Samples returned by SASE. Reports back on future assignment possibilities. Provide business card, brochure and/or tear sheet samples to be kept on file for future assignments. Reports in 3 months. Payment is in copies of publications.

THE NATIONAL ASSOCIATION OF LIFE UNDERWRITERS, 1922 F St. NW, Washington DC 20006. (202)331-6070. Editor: Edward Keenan. Publishes *Life Association News*, the monthly official association magazine with a circulation of 140,000. Subscriptions are limited to members and affiliated organizations, schools and libraries. Also publishes numerous brochures and catalogs. Serves life underwriters (life insurance agents), financial brokers and consultants, and businesspersons associated with insurance in general.
Needs: Works with 5-10 freelance artists/year. DC metropolitan area artists only. Works on assignment only. Uses artists for brochure, catalog and magazine illustration. Prefers pen & ink, washes, drybrush and airbrush. Especially needs editorial calendar. Looks for "clarity, expression, realism and freshness" in themes and styles.
First Contact & Terms: Send query letter or telecon with resume, original work, Photostats or tear sheets to be kept on file. Material not filed returned by SASE only if requested. Reports only if interested. Write for appointment to show portfolio. Pays by the project, $50-75 average for spot art. Considers complexity of project and turnaround time when establishing payment.

***NATIONAL ASSOCIATION OF TOWNS & TOWNSHIPS**, Suite 730, 1522 K St. NW, Washington DC 20005. Director of Communications: Bruce G. Rosenthal. Professional association providing educational materials and representation for local elected officials from small communities.
Needs: Works with several freelance artists/year. Uses artists for brochure and magazine/newspaper design and illustration, brochure layout and signage.
First Contact & Terms: Prefers local artists with "references from similar associations and creative style/ideas for a relatively limited budget." Send query letter with brochure to be kept on file. Reports only if interested. Works on assignment only. Considers complexity of project, available budget, and skill and experience of artist when establishing payment.

NATIONAL BUFFALO ASSOCIATION, Box 565, Ft. Pierre SD 57532. (605)223-2829. Executive Director-Editor: Judi Hebbring. Breed organization representing commercial producers of buffalo (bison); also caters to collectors, historians, etc. Publishes bimonthly magazine of interest to buffalo enthusiasts, collectors and producers; circ. 1,400. Membership: 1,000.
Needs: Works with 4-5 freelance artists/year. "We feature artists in the magazine (must paint, sketch, sculpt, etc., buffalo); also feature artwork on cover."
First Contact & Terms: Send query letter with brochure and photographs. Material is kept on file until used, then it is returned to artist. Samples not kept on file are returned. Reports within 2-3 weeks. No

pay; "we trade magazine exposure for use of photos and story about the artist in *Buffalo!* magazine.
Tips: Especially looks for "a good representation of the American buffalo, as well as a well-rounded subject portfolio. Awards and credentials are also looked at but not as primary criteria—talent and salability of the work is number one." Current trends include "a back-to-basics movement where artists are doing native animals rather than the exotics that were the vogue a few years ago."

NATIONAL CAVES ASSOCIATION, Rt. 9, Box 106, McMinnville TN 37110. (615)668-3925. Secretary/Treasurer: Barbara Munson. "The NCA is an organization of show caves owners and operators, established to set and maintain standards of operation and to promote the visitation of show caves."
Needs: "As an organization, the NCA offers little opportunity for freelance artists."

NATIONAL COMMITTEE FOR CITIZENS IN EDUCATION, Suite 301, 20840 Little Patuxent Pkwy., Columbia MD 21044. (301)997-9300. Editor: Chrissie Bamber. Purpose is to improve the education of children by mobilizing and assisting citizens, including parents, to strengthen public schools; an advocate for citizens helping them gain and use information and skills to influence the quality of public education.
Needs: Works with 3-4 freelance artists/year. Local artists preferred except for newspaper illustration. Works on assignment only. Uses artists for advertising, brochure and catalog design and layout; brochure illustration, magazine/newspaper design and illustration, and AV presentations.
First Contact & Terms: Send query letter with Photostats and tear sheets to be kept on file. Write for artists' guidelines. Samples not kept on file returned by SASE. Reports within 2 weeks. Pays by the project, $25-50 average for single illustration for newspaper; rates for "design of book cover, brochure, AV aids, etc, are higher." Considers complexity of project, available budget, skill and experience of artist, how work will be used, turnaround time and rights purchased when establishing payment.
Tips: Artists should exhibit an "understanding of current education issues" in their work.

***NATIONAL COUNCIL ON ART IN JEWISH LIFE INC.**, 15 E. 84th St., New York NY 10028. (212)877-4500. President: Julius Schatz. Provides education, exhibits, publications, books and information.
Needs: Uses artists for exhibits/displays, promotions and mailings.
First Contact & Terms: Mail art, or query with samples or previously used work. SASE. Reports in 2 weeks.

NATIONAL INSTITUTE FOR AUTOMOTIVE SERVICE EXCELLENCE, 1920 Association Dr., Reston VA 22091. (703)648-3838. Contact: Barry McNulty.
Needs: Uses artists for magazine graphics, audiovisual materials, recruitment literature and public information brochures.
First Contact & Terms: Call or write. Looks at "quality and price" when reviewing artist's work. Buys all rights.

NATIONAL SAFETY COUNCIL, 444 N. Michigan, Chicago IL 60611. Publisher: Gordon Bieberle. Director of Art: Frank Waszak. Publications Designer: Kim Zarley. Non-governmental, not-for-profit public service organization aimed at saving lives in industry and private sectors through education serving manufacturing, business and environmental health areas.
Needs: Works with 24 freelance artists/year. Local artists preferred. "Contemporary style important. Superior technique and conceptual abilities essential." Uses artists for the design, illustration and layout of advertising, brochures, magazines and posters.
First Contact & Terms: Send query letter with brochure showing art style or tear sheets and slides. Samples not filed are returned by SASE. Reports back only if interested. To show a portfolio, mail appropriate materials or "if in area," call or write to schedule an appointment; portfolio should include thumbnails, roughs, final reproduction/product and color. Payment "determined solely on project size negotiated at time of assignment." Considers complexity of project and how work will be used when establishing payment.
Tips: "Interested artists should query with samples of work (tear sheets) by mail."

***NATIONAL SPACE SOCIETY**, 600 Maryland Ave. SW, Washington DC 20024. (202)484-1111. Art Director: Aleta Jackson. "We are a nonprofit educational organization, with 6,000 members worldwide, that promotes the permanent human habitation of space. Our membership consists of people who are interested in the human and technical aspects of space development. They are intelligent, knowledgable and appreciate good art."
Needs: Works with 30 freelance artists/year. Uses artists for advertising and brochure design and illustration, catalog and magazine illustration, AV presentations, exhibits, posters, logos, T-shirts and models. Prefers as themes people living, working and playing in space and on other planets.

First Contact & Terms: Send query letter with brochure or resume, tear sheets, Photostats, photocopies, slides, photographs or "whatever the artist thinks best displays his work." Samples are filed. Samples are returned only if requested. Reports back within 4 weeks. Call or write to schedule an appointment to show a portfolio or mail roughs, Photostats, tear sheets, photographs, slides, color, b&w or "whatever best display the artist's work." Pays for design and illustration by the project, $50 minimum; payment is negotiable. Considers complexity of project, skill and experience of artist, how work will be used and rights purchased when establishing payment. Negotiates rights purchased.
Tips: "We want quality color paintings, and black-and-white drawings and sketches (cartoons, too!) of people living, working, and playing in space. Hardware accuracy is important, but it is secondary to the people in the picture: those people should be having a good time. We are especially looking for groupings of husband and wife; husband, wife and child; mother and child; dad and child; grandpa and small fry, etc., all enjoying the freedom of weightlessness. We do not want bug-eyed monsters or any frightening, alien tableaux. We are willing to overlook technical accuracy if the picture is strong on human interest. We would like to see less of Mars and more of lunar and space colonies, expeditions to comets and asteroids, what a science station on Titan might look like, or a vacation to Saturn's rings. If the artist has any questions, or has a project he would like to discuss, we will be happy to review rough sketches. Letters and phone calls always welcome. Vertical format preferred."

***NATIONAL THEATRE OF THE DEAF**, 5 W. Main St., Chester CT 06412. (203)526-4971. Director of Publications: Marilaine Dyer. International touring theatrical company of deaf and hearing actors who perform using a combination of sign language and the spoken word at the same time. "Audiences hear and see every word. This medium has been hailed by critics as 'sculpture in the air.' " Audiences are both hearing and deaf.
Needs: Works with 4 freelance artists/year. Prefers artists in New York, Connecticut and Rhode Island. Works on assignment only. Uses artists for advertising and brochure layout, catalog design and layout, AV presentations, exhibits, displays and posters.
First Contact & Terms: Send query letter with brochure. Samples are filed. Samples not filed are returned by SASE only if requested. Reports back within 3 months. Call to schedule an appointment to show a portfolio. Payment varies. "We decide by fee basis on each job." Considers complexity of project when establishing payment. Buys all rights or reprint rights; rights purchased vary according to project.
Tips: "Looking for creative approach to marketing a theatrical company on a nonprofit budget; looking for very visual graphics to match our very visual medium of theatre; very interested in motion photography/illustrations."

THE NEW ALCHEMY INSTITUTE, 237 Hatchville Rd., E. Falmouth MA 02540. (617)563-2655. Publications: David Wills. A nonprofit research and educational institution working on ecologically sound methods of producing food, energy and shelter for about 2,000 members and another 5,000 visitors who come by each year to the farm site on Cape Cod.
Needs: Works with 0-3 freelance artists/year. Uses artists for brochure design and magazine/newspaper design and illustration; postcard designs. Prefers themes emphasizing alternative technology such as gardening, solar design, compost and greenhouses; prefers b&w line drawings, also schematics.
First Contact & Terms: Send query letter with brochure showing art style or photocopies. Samples not filed are returned by SASE. Reports only if interested. To show a portfolio, mail appropriate materials. Pays for design by the hour, $10 minimum; by the project, $25 minimum. Pays for illustrations by the hour, $10 minimum; by the project, $25 minimum. "We use donated skill whenever possible."
Tips: "We have to use mostly students and people who believe in us rather than pros."

NEW JERSEY ASSOCIATION OF OSTEOPATHIC PHYSICIANS & SURGEONS, 1212 Stuyvesant Ave., Trenton NJ 08618. Executive Director: Eleanore A. Farley. Nonprofit association serving a membership of approximately 1,000 osteopathic physicians and 295 medical students.
Needs: Works with 1 freelance artist/year. Works on assignment only. Uses artists for brochure and magazine/newspaper design, illustration and layout; graphic design, and signage. Prefers themes which are in keeping with the medical profession.
First Contact & Terms: Send query letter with Photostats of original work and actual work. Looks for "quality and originality" when reviewing artist's work. Samples returned by SASE. Reports in 1 month. Write for appointment. Negotiates payment according to client's budget.

NORTH AMERICAN NATIVE FISHES ASSOCIATION, 123 W. Mt. Airy Ave., Philadelphia PA 19119. (215)247-0384. President: Bruce Gebhardt. "A 400-member group dedicated to study of fishes (mostly non-game) native to North America. It serves ichthyologists, biologists, government officials, aquarists and naturalists."
Needs: Uses artists for magazine/newspaper illustration. "We need realistic b&w sketches of fishes

(non-game, mostly, native to North America)." Prefers accuracy, realism.
First Contact & Terms: Send query letter with resume and photocopies; include SASE. Samples not filed are returned by SASE. Reports back within 1 week. To show a portfolio, mail appropriate materials or call to schedule an appointment; portfolio should include Photostats. "Better to call first. We can't commission artwork; however, if someone had drawn a particular fish for another assignment and could legally and ethically use it again, it would be a way to pick up a couple of bucks."
Tips: "We may be expanding our operations and art needs in the next few years. We're no major market, but artists who draw fish for other clients might try us as a second user."

OCCIDENTAL COLLEGE, 1600 Campus Rd., Los Angeles CA 90041. (213)259-2677. Contact: Director of Public Information and Publications. Educational institution with approximately 1,600 students providing a liberal arts education and serving current students, alumni, faculty, administration, trustees, staff and the community.
Needs: Publishes a quarterly magazine, currently ranked as one of the "Top Five College Magazines" in the country. Magazine often showcases a single illustrator, who provides artwork for cover and four feature articles related by a common theme. Excellent exposure for aspiring illustrators in need of impressive portfolio piece. Occasionally uses illustrators for other publications, such as catalogs and fund-raising brochures. "We mostly use students or alumni. Perhaps use freelancers 3 or 4 times a year." Works on assignment only.
First Contact & Terms: Send query letter with business card and original work or photocopies. Looks for "originality, nice clean layout and realistic renderings, as opposed to fantasy pieces" when reviewing artist's work. Samples not returned. Reports in 2 weeks. Submit portfolio for review. Magazine showcase illustrators are paid $400 for the series of cover and feature illustrations. For other publications, artists must be willing to furnish high-quality illustrations or photographs at very modest cost. Payment varies according to job and client's budget.
Tips: "Tight financial picture demands development of one comprehensive illustration/publication that has components which can be reproduced on their own throughout the publication."

***OPTICIANS ASSOCIATION OF AMERICA**, 10341 Democracy Lane, Box 10110, Fairfax VA 22030. Editor: James H. McCormick. Managing Editor: Robert Rathbone and Editorial Assistant: Rachel Russell. Nonprofit association to advance the objectives of the retail dispensing optician and to serve 10,000 opticians.
Needs: "Not a major user or buyer of art or artist's work." Works with 8-9 freelance artists/year. Uses artists for brochure and magazine/newspaper design, illustration (b&w and full-color art) and layout (roughs; nonmechanical). Especially needs work relating to retail dispensing opticians at work.
First Contact & Terms: Send query letter with samples or brochure/flyer to be kept on file. Looks for the ideas the artwork communicates. Prefers several representative, nonreturnable Photostats as samples. Samples not returned. Reports in 1 month. Payment is by the project; $25-250 average—"covers for magazine usually are more." Considers complexity of project, available budget, skill and experience of artist, how work will be used and rights purchased ("we usually buy only optical industry rights") when establishing payment.
Tips: "Always query before doing any work for us. There is a trend toward greater use of semi-abstract art."

PLAN AND PRINT, Box 879, 9931 Franklin Ave., Franklin Park IL 60131. (312)671-5356. Editor: Janet A. Thill. Serves architects, engineers, design/drafters/computer-aided design users, reprographic firm owners and managers.
Needs: Works with 7-10 artists/year. Works on assignment only. Uses magazine article illustrations. Especially needs cover art.
First Contact & Terms: Send query letter with brochure showing art style or samples. Samples not filed are returned. Reports back within 10 days. Call or write to schedule an appointment to show a portfolio, which should include final reproduction/product, color, tear sheets and b&w. Pays for illustration by the project, $300-500. Considers complexity of project, client's budget and rights purchased when establishing payment. Buys all rights.

***POPAI**, 2 Executive Dr., Fort Lee NJ 07024. (201)585-8400. Public Relations Manager: L.Z. Eccles. Promotes and fosters the use of point-of-purchase advertisers to marketers of all consumer goods and services (this includes retailers). Members are producers, buyers and users of P-O-P.
Needs: Works with 4 freelance artists/year. Prefers local artists. Works on assignment only. Uses artists for advertising, brochure and catalog design, illustration and layout.
First Contact & Terms: Send query letter with brochure or Photostats. Samples are filed. Samples not filed are not returned. Reports back only if interested. Write to schedule an appointment to show a port-

folio. Pays for design and illustration by the project, payment varies. Considers complexity of project and available budget when establishing payment.
Tips: "Be flexible and able to turn work around quickly."

***QUEENS COLLEGE OF THE CITY UNIVERSITY OF NEW YORK**, 65-30 Kissena Blvd., Flushing NY 11367. Director: Ron Cannava. Higher education institution serving 18,000 students as well as faculty, alumni and the general public.
Needs: Works with 11 freelance artists/year. Works on assignment basis only. Uses artists for advertising, brochure, graphic and magazine/newspaper design; advertising and magazine/newspaper layout; magazine/newspaper illustration, exhibits, displays, signage, AV presentations and posters. Prefers dramatic situation involving people learning from others, such as teacher/student relationships in many different backgrounds with various age and ethnic groups represented—usually on a one-to-one basis. Also office situations with white collar, college-educated staff in action in various backgrounds. Needs originality at minimal cost.
First Contact & Terms: Send query letter with samples, brochure/flyer and resume. Write for appointment to show portfolio. Samples returned by SASE. Reports in 5 weeks. Provide resume, business card, brochure and 1 sample to be kept on file for possible future assignments. Payment is by the project: $25-300 average; by the hour: $10-15 average. Negotiable and can vary according to available budget, restriction on limited tax-levy funding, complexity of project, skill and experience of artist, how work will be used, turnaround time and rights purchased.
Tips: "There will be more use of freelance work by colleges and universities, more promotional effort for higher education. This is a low-paying market with high expectations—a place to grow, but not to depend on."

RIPON COLLEGE, Box 248, Ripon WI 54971. (414)748-8115. Director of College Relations: Andrew G. Miller. Four-year, coeducational, liberal arts college serving 950 students, alumni and prospective students.
Needs: Works with 3-4 freelance artists/year. Works on assignment basis only. Uses artists for advertising, brochure and magazine/newspaper illustration; graphic design and AV presentations; photography. Especially needs graphic design and photography. Buys 1-2 cartoon-style illustrations/year.
First Contact & Terms: Send query letter with resume and samples. Samples returned by SASE. Reports back on whether to expect possible future assignments. Call for appointment to show portfolio. Negotiates payment.

ST. VINCENT COLLEGE, Latrobe PA 15650. (412)539-9761. Director/Publications and Publicity: Don Orlando.
Needs: Assigns 25 jobs/year. Uses artists for advertising, annual reports, direct mail brochures, exhibits, flyers, graphics, posters and programs.
First Contact & Terms: Send query letter with samples. SASE. Reports in 1 month. Pays $10 minimum/hour, design, illustration and layout.

SLOCUMB GALLERY, East Tennessee State University, Department of Art, Box 23740A, Johnson City TN 37614-0002. (615)929-4247. Gallery Director: M. Wayne Dyer. Nonprofit university gallery.
Needs: Works with 0-2 freelance artists/year. Works on assignment only. Uses artists for advertising design, illustration and layout; brochure and catalog design; exhibits, signage and posters.
First Contact & Terms: Send query letter with slides to be kept on file. Samples not filed are returned only if requested. Reports within 1 month. Negotiates payment. Considers complexity of project and available budget when establishing payment.

***SOCIETY OF SCRIBES, LTD.**, Box 933, New York NY 10150. Corresponding Secretary: Will Farrington. "1,000 memberships of calligraphers, professional, amateur and calligraphiles (those interested in calligraphy). S.O.S. promotes through educational programs and exhibitions the enjoyment of calligraphy in the graphic arts. Members are professional calligraphers, typographers, publishers and educators.
Needs: Works with 15 freelance artists/year. Works on assignment only. Uses artists for advertising, brochure, catalog design, illustration and layout, magazine design, illustration and layout, AV presentations, exhibits, displays, signage and posters.
First Contact & Terms: Send query letter with brochure or resume and slides. Samples are not filed. Samples not filed are returned by SASE. Reports back only if interested.

***THE SONNECK SOCIETY**, 410 Fox Chapel Lane, Radnor PA 19087. The Sonneck Society is a tax-exempt, nonprofit, educational institution, incorporated in 1975 to carry out educational projects and to help disseminate accurate information and research dealing with all aspects of American music and mu-

sic in America. Members include musicologists, ethnomusicologists, students, performers, collectors, composers, librarians, archivists, historians, publishers, educators, music critics, Americanists.
Needs: Works with 6 freelance artists/year. Works on assignment only. Uses artists for advertising design and illustration; brochure design and layout; newspaper design, illustration and layout. Prefers music as a theme and classic style.
First Contact & Terms: Send brochure or tear sheets and photocopies. Samples are filed. Reports back only if interested. Pays for design by the project, $25 minimum. Pays for illustration by the project, $10 minimum. Considers complexity of project, turnaround time and how work will be used when establishing payment. Rights purchased vary according to project.
Tips: "We always need calligraphy work for presentation certificates, music transcripts for our publications and occasional design help."

***SOROPTIMIST INTERNATIONAL OF THE AMERICAS**, 1616 Walnut St., Philadelphia PA 19103. (215)732-0512. Editor: Darlene Friedman. 40,000-member classified service organization for professional and executive business women.
Needs: Uses artists for brochure and magazine/newspaper illustration.
First Contact & Terms: Send query letter with brochure, resume, business card and samples to be kept on file. Prefers copies of brochures, publications in which artwork has appeared as samples. Reports only if interested. Works on assignment only. Pays by the project, $50-300 average. Consider complexity of project and available budget when establishing payment.

SUNDAY SCHOOL BOARD OF THE SOUTHERN BAPTIST CONVENTION, 127 9th Ave. N., Nashville TN 37234. (615)251-2365. Supervisor, Special Ministries Design Section: Mrs. Doris Mae Adams. Religious publisher of periodicals, books, Bibles, records, kits, visual aids, posters, etc. for churches.
Needs: Works with 45-50 freelance artists/year. Artists must be "people with experience that meet our quality requirements." Works on assignment only. Uses artists for illustration. Especially needs four-color Biblical illustrations in a realistic style.
First Contact & Terms: Send query letter with brochure showing art style. Call or write for appointment to show portfolio, which should include original/final art, final reproduction/product and color. Originals are preferred, tear sheets are acceptable; do not send slides. Samples are returned. Reports within 2 weeks. Pays by the illustration, $80-200 average. "For the price range quoted here, we buy all rights and retain the work."

SWEDISH HOSPITAL MEDICAL CENTER, 747 Summit Ave., Seattle WA 98104. (206)386-2738. Assistant Director for Communications: Julie Hanger.
Needs: Works with 2 illustrators and 2 designers/year. Works on assignment only. Uses artists for brochures, reports and posters.
First Contact & Terms: Query with photocopies. SASE. Contacts artists as needs arise. To show a portfolio, mail final reproduction/product, photographs and b&w. Negotiates pay.

TECHNICAL ASSISTANCE PROJECT (TAP), Suite 36, 639 Broadway, New York NY 10012. (212)673-6343. Director: Donna Brady. Nonprofit organization serving the performing arts community as well as film, TV, advertising and fashion through referrals of qualified production personnel (designers, stage managers and technicians). TAP also maintains information files with wide ranging details on hard-to-find equipment.
Needs: Works with 50 freelance artists/year. Uses freelance artists for AV presentation, displays, signage, posters and theatrical application.
First Contact & Terms: Send query letter with brochure showing art style or resume. Samples not filed are returned by SASE. Call to schedule an appointment to show a portfolio, which should include original/final art, final reproduction/product and color. Payment varies. Considers complexity of project, available budget, skill and experience of artist, how work will be used, turnaround time and rights purchased when establishing payment.

THE TEXTILE MUSEUM, 2320 S St. NW, Washington DC 20008. (202)667-0441. Public Relations Manager: Joan Wessel. Private, nonprofit museum dedicated to the collection, study, preservation, education and exhibition of historic and handmade textiles and carpets.
Needs: Works with 1-2 freelance artists/year. Local artists only. Works on assignment only. Uses artists for brochure illustration and layout, catalog design and layout, exhibits, displays and posters.
First Contact & Terms: Send query letter with samples to be kept on file. Prefers original work as samples. Reports only if interested. Negotiates pay according to project.
Tips: "Send samples of newsletters, invitations, catalogs or posters as these are items most often used by the institution; keep in mind the low budget of client."

UNITED HOSPITAL, 333 N. Smith Ave., St. Paul MN 55102. (612)292-5531. Assistant Public Relations Director: Mary Farr.
Needs: Works with 5 illustrators and designers/year. Local artists only. Works on assignment only. Uses artists for brochure and newsletter design, programs and general publications artwork. Especially needs logo design, publication and brochure design and keyline.
First Contact & Terms: Query with resume. SASE. Looks for "fast service, reasonable price, and creative and well thought-out approaches to project goals" when reviewing artist's work. Reports in 2 weeks. Samples returned by SASE. Provide resume and business card to be kept on file for possible future assignments. Pays by the hour. Considers complexity of project, available budget and turnaround time when establishing payment.
Tips: Especially likes "clean, uncluttered, simple, striking design."

U.S. SPACE EDUCATION ASSOC., NEWS OPERATIONS DIV., 746 Turnpike Rd., Elizabethtown PA 17022-1161. Editor, *Space Age Times*: Stephen M. Cobaugh. International grassroots association dedicated to the promotion of the peaceful uses of outer space. Serves both laymen and professionals concerned with all aspects of space education and news.
Needs: Works with 3 freelance artists/year. "Artist should be able to demonstrate knowledge of current space issues—both domestic and foreign." Uses artists for magazine/newspaper design and illustration; exhibits; displays and particularly editorial cartoons. Prefers space-related topics; particularly space shuttle, space station, commercialization, spinoffs, etc.
First Contact & Terms: Send query letter with brochure showing art style or resume, tear sheets, Photostats and photocopies. Samples not filed are returned by SASE. Reports only if interested. To show a portfolio, mail roughs and original/final art. Pays for design and illustration by the project, $25 minimum. Considers complexity of project, client's budget, turnaround time and rights purchased when establishing payment.

UNIVERSITY OF NEW HAVEN, West Haven CT 06516. (203)932-7000. Public Relations Director: Sally Devaney.
Needs: Uses illustrations of campus architecture, still life (books, lab equipment, etc.), occassionally people, for program brochures. Especially interested in those with map experience. Looks for "simplicity of reproduction. Prefers b&w line art for illustrations. Contemporary style that would appeal to students (18-34)." Works on assignment only.
First Contact & Terms: Query with samples (brochures and other publications, especially those for educational or service organizations; cover designs; illustrations). SASE. No samples returned. Provide resume if available, business card, fee structure, and samples of work to be kept on file for future assignments. Considers complexity of project, available budget, skill and experience of artist and turnaround time when establishing payment.
Tips: "Our budget is modest. Most pieces are one or two colors. We'd like to see work that would appeal to younger and older students. We're interested in variety of styles. Also interested in area talent."

WASHINGTON UNIVERSITY IN ST. LOUIS, Campus Box 1070, St. Louis MO 63110. Art Director: Lewis Glaser. Educational institution publication office serving alumni development (alumni magazines) and various schools' recruiting and promotional needs.
Needs: Works with 20 freelance artists/year. Works on assignment only. Uses artists for advertising, brochure, catalog and magazine/newspaper illustration. Especially needs layout and paste-up, some design *with* art direction and illustration. Looks for diversity, versatility.
First Contact & Terms: Send query letter with brochure, resume, Photostats, slides, photographs and tear sheets to be kept on file. Samples not filed are returned by SASE only if requested. Reports only if interested. Call for appointment to show portfolio, which should include original/final art, final reproduction/product, color, tear sheets and b&w. Pays by the project, $50 minimum. Considers complexity of project, available budget, skill and experience of artist, how work will be used, turnaround time and rights purchased when establishing payment.
Tips: "Present a neat and clean portfolio, showing as much diversity as possible. Better to have only five strong pieces than twenty-five weak ones."

WOLF TRAP FARM PARK FOR THE PERFORMING ARTS, The Wolf Trap Foundation, 1624 Trap Rd., Vienna VA 22180. Assistant to the Public Affairs Director: Karen Hanna. The Foundation serves as the administrative arm of the Park with the National Park Service maintaining the Park grounds. Wolf Trap is the only national park for the performing arts. "As a national park, Wolf Trap serves the nation as well as international visitors."
Needs: Uses artists for the design, illustration and layout of advertising, brochures, and magazines plus AV presentations, exhibits and displays.
First Contact & Terms: Send a query letter with resume and tear sheets, which will be kept on file.

Samples not filed are returned only if requested. Reports back within 3-4 weeks. Call or write for an appointment to show a portfolio. Pays by the project. Considers available budget, skill and experience of the artist, and turnaround time when establishing payment.
Tips: "We are a nonprofit organization and do not have a large budget for outside services."

WORCESTER POLYTECHNIC INSTITUTE, 100 Institute Rd., Worcester MA 01609. (617)793-5609. Director of Publications: Kenneth McDonnell. Third oldest college of engineering and science in U.S. with 3,500 students in undergraduate and graduate programs.
Needs: Works with 2-6 freelance artists/year. Prefers local artists. Works on assignment only. Uses artists for advertising illustration; brochure design, illustration and layout; catalog illustration and layout; AV presentations, exhibits, displays, signage and posters.
First Contact & Terms: Send query letter with resume, Photostats, slides, photographs and tear sheets. Write for appointment to show portfolio. Samples are returned by SASE. Reports within 2 weeks. Negotiates payment. Considers complexity of project, available budget, skill and experience of artist, turnaround time and rights purchased when establishing payment.

> ***"Nonprofits are becoming more competitive, needing to upgrade their publications in order to be of interest to our fast-paced society. We have seen a need to focus more on design, less on copy."***
>
> ***—Ruth B. Zax, Child and Family Services of New Hampshire Manchester, New Hampshire***

Book Publishers

The three main freelance opportunities in book publishing are in book design, jackets/covers and text illustrations. Book design utilizes artists skilled in illustration, typography and layout. Jackets and covers might involve a freelancer for the entire design or just an assigned piece of illustrative art for the jackets/covers. Requirements for text illustration vary from realistic pen-and-ink drawings to full-color fantasy landscapes.

The overall appearance of a book conveys its own message apart from the text inside. Covers or jackets advertise the book in bookstores and catalogs to attract prospective buyers. They express the content and mood of the book through a design that can be grasped at a glance and seen at a distance in bookstores. Recently publishers have established "brand identity," whereby a series of books has a uniform cover design and a consistent editorial personality. Books in a series tend to be grouped together and displayed face out in bookstores, rather than being shelved, spine out, throughout the store; this placement provides a chance to develop a loyal readership.

The book publishing industry classifies publishers according to subject matter or field of activity, and each classification requires different art treatments. Trade books (scholarly works, instructional manuals and biographies) feature simple designs and straightforward, realistic artwork. Mass-market books (those that appeal to a wide audience and are sold on newsstands) require bold, eye-catching covers to grab potential customers. A realistic approach is needed for romance and historical novels, whose covers usually focus on one or two of the story's main characters. A look at nonfiction titles reveals a tendency toward pure, simplistic design, often with an emphasis on typography. Specialized publishers who produce books geared to one topic like cooking or gardening often want traditional, very detailed art/design representing their main focus. Textbooks usually require simple graphics and two-color printing.

Approximately 50,000 books went to press last year as quality fiction established itself as a hot item. Because of its daring editorial content, quality fiction by contemporary authors has spurred more sophisticated and more complex cover designs using either vibrant or pastel colors. Autobiographies and instructional home/gardening books headed the bestselling trade list, while westerns and historical novels topped the mass-market one. Popular collaterals such as video- and audio cassettes, calendars and posters provide additional freelance opportunities for artists within the industry.

Don't discount a firm because it publishes only a few books a year. With an emphasis on quality, many small press books are award winners, often because of the special attention given to the illustrations. Some small publishers that survived the acquisition mania that gripped the industry last year have commercial aspirations and are determined to make a mark for themselves.

Visit bookstores and examine the type of artwork each publisher favors. Write and request a catalog of the firm's products—there's hardly a book publisher that won't send you one. Also read the advice of Robert McGinnis, who has illustrated over 1,300 covers, in the Close-up in this section.

For additional information on this market, refer to *Writer's Market 1988*, *Literary Market Place*, *Books in Print*, and *International Directory of Little Magazines and Small Presses*. The trade magazine *Publisher's Weekly* provides weekly updates on book publishing.

ACS PUBLICATIONS, INC., Box 16430, San Diego CA 92116-0430. (619)297-9203. Editoral Director: Maritha Pottenger. Specializes in trade paperbacks and originals, especially in astrology, metaphysics and holistic health. Publishes 10 titles/year.
First Contact & Terms: Works with 3 freelance artists/year. Prefers local artists ony. Works on assignment only. Send query letter with tear sheets, Photostats, photocopies and photographs. Samples not filed are returned by SASE. Reports only if interested. Original work returned after job's completion. Considers complexity of project, skill and experience of artist, project's budget (biggest factor) and turnaround time when establishing payment. Buys first rights or reprint rights.
Jackets/Covers: Assigns 10 book covers/year to freelancers. Pays by the project, $100-500.
Tips: "Most of our covers involve people. Artist must be excellent with faces. We use almost no interior illustrations (by artists). We computer-generate our own horoscopes which are our most common interior illustrations. For covers, we are very fond of photo-realistic style. Also like some fantasy. Artwork must 'grab' the viewer immediately. Good covers sell books. Freelancers often choose inappropriate subjects in presenting samples. They think metaphysical means occult and send sketches better suited to horror novels or Halloween parties."

A.D. BOOK CO., 6th Floor, 10 E. 39th St., New York NY 10157-0002. (212)889-6500. Art Director: Doris Gordon. Publishes hardcover and paperback originals on advertising design and photography. Publishes 12-15 titles/year; 4-5 of which require designers, 1-2 use illustrators.
First Contact & Terms: Send query letter which can be kept on file and arrange to show portfolio (4-10 tear sheets). Samples returned by SASE. Buys first rights. Originals returned to artist at job's completion. Free catalog. Advertising design must be contemporary. Pays $100 minimum/book design.
Jackets/Covers: Pays $100 minimum.

ACROPOLIS BOOKS LTD., 2400 17th St. NW, Washington DC 20009. Production Manager: Lloyd Greene. Publishes how-to, self-help, educational, political and Americana.
Needs: Uses artists for jacket design and illustration and advertising layouts.
First Contact & Terms: Local artists only. Send query letter with information on your background and specialties.

ADDISON-WESLEY, Jacob Way, Reading MA 01867. (617)944-3700. Art Director: Marshall Henrichs. Publishes 100 titles/year; 50% require freelance designers. Handles higher educational books.
First Contact & Terms: Send proofs. Buys all rights. Works on assignment only. Reports back on future assignment possibilities. Provide resume, business card and tear sheet to be kept on file for future assignments. Check for most recent titles in bookstores.
Jackets/Covers: Needs trade cover designers. Pays $500-800.

***AEOLUS PUBLISHING LTD.**, Box 2643, Vista CA 92083. (619)724-5703. President: Chuck Banks. Specializes in hardcover and paperback originals and reprints on militaria. Publishes 12 titles/year.
First Contact & Terms: Works with 3 freelance artists/year. Send query letter. "No calls from artist or artist's agent." Samples returned only if requested. Reports within 1 month. Return of original work after job's completion depends on contract. Considers complexity of the project, skill and experience of artist, project's budget, turnaround time and rights purchased when establishing payment. Rights purchased vary according to project.
Book Design: Assigns 3 freelance jobs/year. Negotiates payment.
Jackets/Covers: Assigns 3 freelance illustration jobs/year. Negotiates payment.
Text Illustration: Assigns 2 freelance jobs/year. Negotiates payment.

AIR-PLUS ENTERPRISES, Box 190, Garrisonville VA 22463. (609)881-0724. Specializes in hardcover and paperback originals on women's interest (particularly case histories of abortion complications—physical or other) and human sexuality. Publishes 2 titles/year.
First Contact & Terms: Works with 2 freelance artists/year. "We give anybody a chance." Send query letter with original sketches or photographs to be kept on file "unless unsuitable." Samples not kept on file are returned by SASE. Reports within 2 months. No originals returned to artist at job's completion. Considers project's budget when establishing payment. Buys all rights.
Jackets/Covers: Assigns 2 freelance illustration jobs/year. Pays by the project, $35-100 average.
Text Illustration: Assigns 2 freelance jobs/year. Pays by the project, $25-250 average.
Tips: Uses medical illustrations. "We see an increased need for technical work and have found that our best people in this field don't do cartoons well at all, so we now seek cartoonists."

ALLYN AND BACON INC., College Division, 7 Wells Ave., Newton MA 02159. (617)964-5530. Cover Administrator: Linda Knowles Dickinson. Publishes hardcover and paperback textbooks.

Publishes 75-85 titles/year; 75% require freelance cover designers.
First Contact & Terms: Needs artists/designers experienced in preparing art and mechanicals for print production. Designers must be strong in book cover design and contemporary type treatment.
Jackets/Covers: Assigns 50-65 freelance design jobs/year; assigns 2-3 freelance illustration jobs/year. Pays for design by the project, $300-550. Pays for illustration by the project, $150-500. "Always looking for good calligraphers."
Tips: "Keep stylistically and technically up to date. Learn *not* to over-design: read instructions, and ask questions. Introductory letter must state experience and include at least photocopies of samples of your work. We prefer designers/artists based in the Boston area."

ALYSON PUBLICATIONS, INC., 40 Plympton St., Boston MA 02118. Publisher: Sasha Alyson. Book publisher emphasizing gay and lesbian concerns. Publishes 15 titles/year. Circ. 800. Sample copy catalog free for SASE with 45¢ postage.
First Contact & Terms: Works on assignment only. Send query letter with brochure showing art style or tear sheets, Photostats, photocopies and photographs. Samples returned by SASE. Reports only if interested.
Jackets/Covers: Buys 10 cover illustrations/year. Pays $200-500, b&w, $300-500, color; on acceptance.

APPLEZABA PRESS, Box 4134, Long Beach CA 90804. (213)591-0015. Publisher: D.H. Lloyd. Specializes in paperbacks on poetry and fiction. Publishes 2-4 titles/year.
First Contact & Terms: Works on assignment only. Send query letter with brochure, tear sheets and photographs to be kept on file. Samples not filed are returned by SASE. Reports only if interested. Originals returned to artist at job's completion. Considers project's budget and rights purchased when establishing payment. Rights purchased vary according to project.
Jackets/Covers: Assigns 1 freelance design job/year. Pays by the project, $30-100.

***APRIL PUBLICATIONS, INC.**, Box 1000, Staten Island NY 10314. Art Director: Verna Hart. Specializes in paperback nonfiction. Publishes 25 titles/year.
First Contact & Terms: Works with 10 freelance artists/year. Works on assignment only. Send query letter with samples to be kept on file. Prefers Photostats as samples. Samples not filed are returned by SASE. Reports only if interested. Considers project's budget and rights purchased when establishing payment. Buys all rights.

ARCsoft PUBLISHERS, Box 132, Woodsboro MD 21798. (301)845-8856. President: A.R. Curtis. Specializes in original paperbacks, especially in space science, computers, miscellaneous high-tech subjects. Publishes 12 titles/year.
First Contact & Terms: Works with 5 freelance artists/year. Works on assignment only. Send query letter with brochure, resume and non-returnable samples. Samples not filed are not returned. Reports back within 3 months only if interested. Original work not returned after job's completion. Considers complexity of project, skill and experience of artist, project's budget and turnaround time when establishing payment. Buys all rights.
Book Design: Assigns 5 freelance illustration jobs/year. Pays by the project.
Jackets/Covers: Assigns 1 freelance design and 5 freelance illustration jobs/year. Pays by the project.
Text Illustration: Assigns 5 freelance jobs/year. Pays by the project.
Tips: "Artists should not send in material they want back. All materials received become the property of ARCsoft Publishers."

ART DIRECTION BOOK CO., 6th Floor, 10 E. 39th St., New York NY 10157-0002. (212)889-6500. Art Director: Doris Gordon. Specializes in hardcover and paperback books on advertising art and design. Publishes 15 titles/year; 50% require freelance designers.
First Contact & Terms: Works with 5 freelance artists/year. Professional artists only. Call for appointment. Drop off portfolio. Samples returned by SASE. Originals returned to artist at job's completion. Buys one-time rights.
Book Design: Assigns 10 jobs/year. Uses artists for layout and mechanicals. Pays by the job, $100 minimum.
Jackets/Covers: Assigns 10 design jobs/year. Pays by the job, $100 minimum.

***ARTIFACTS PRESS OF SPVVVA**, Box 315, Ft. Ontario Park, Oswego NY 13126. Director: Carlos Steward. Specializes in hardcover and paperback reprints on environmental themes, art books and children's books. Publishes 4-5 titles/year.
First Contact & Terms: Works with 5-6 freelance artists/year. Prefers artists from NY state; offers residencies to NY state artists, at $1,200 per month. Send query letter with resume, slides and photo-

graphs. Samples are filed. Samples not filed are returned by SASE. Reports back within 3 months. Originals returned to artist at job's completion. To show a portfolio, mail photographs and slides. Considers complexity of project, skill and experience of artist and project's budget when establishing payment. Negotiates rights purchased.
Book Design: Assigns 5-6 freelance illustration jobs/year. Pays by the hour, $8 minimum; by the project, $75- 7,200.
Tips: "Interested in people working in residencies programs for $1,200 per month, workspace programs (materials furnished), and strong black-and-white photographs and artwork. Residencies available in art (all media), crafts, photography, film/video and animation."

ARTIST'S MARKET, Writer's Digest Books, 1507 Dana Ave., Cincinnati OH 45207. Contact: Editor. Annual hardcover directory of freelance markets for graphic artists. Send b&w samples—photographs, photostats or good quality photocopies—of artwork. "Since *Artist's Market* is published only once a year, submissions are kept on file for the next upcoming edition until selections are made. Material is then returned by SASE." Buys one-time rights.
Needs: Buys 50-60 illustrations/year. "I need examples of art that has sold to one of the listings in *Artist's Market*. Thumb through the book to see the type of art I'm seeking. The art must have been freelanced; it cannot have been done as staff work. Include the name of the listing that purchased the work, what the art was used for, and the payment you received." Pays $25 to holder of reproduction rights and free copy of *Artist's Market* when published.

ASHLEY BOOKS INC., Box 768, Port Washington NY 11050. (516)883-2221. President: Billie Young. Publishes hardcover originals; controversial, medical and timely, fiction and nonfiction. Publishes 50 titles/year; 40% require freelance designers or freelance illustrators. Also uses artists for promotional aids.
First Contact & Terms: Metropolitan New York area residents only; experienced artists with book publisher or record album jacket experience. Arrange interview to show portfolio. Buys first rights. Negotiates payment. Free catalog.
Book Design: Assigns 35 jobs/year. Uses artists for layout and paste-up.
Jackets/Covers: Assigns 35 jobs/year. "Cover should catch the eye. A cover should be such that it will sell books and give an idea at a glance what the book is about. A cover should be eye catching so that it draws one to read further."
Tips: "As a result of an upsurge in consumer interest in cooking, more cookbooks will be produced generating more illustrations and more artwork."

***THE ATHLETIC PRESS**, Box 80250, Pasadena CA 91108. Contact: Donald Duke. Publishes sports training and conditioning books.
First Contact & Terms: Query.
Needs: "We are looking for line art of sport movements, anatomical drawings, etc."

AUGSBURG PUBLISHING HOUSE, Box 1209, 426 S. 5th St., Minneapolis MN 55440. (612)330-3300. Manager, Editorial/Design Services: James Lipscomb. Publishes paperback Protestant/Lutheran books (45 titles/year); religious education materials; audiovisual resources; periodicals. Also uses artists for catalog cover design, advertising circulars, advertising layout, design and illustration. Negotiates pay, b&w and color.
First Contact & Terms: "We don't have a rule to only work locally, but the majority of the artists are close enough to meet here on assignments." Works on assignment only. Call, write, or send slides or photocopies. Reports in 5-8 weeks. Samples not filed are returned by SASE. Reports back on future assignment possibilities. Provide brochure, flyer, tear sheet, good photocopies and 35mm transparencies; if artist willing to have samples retained, they are kept on file. Buys all rights on a work-for-hire basis except for cartoons. May require artist to supply overlays on color work.
Book Design: Assigns 45 jobs/year. Uses artists primarily for cover design; occasionally inside illustration, sample chapter openers. Pays $500-900 for cover design.
Text Illustration: Negotiates pay, 1-, 2-, and 4-color.
Tips: Buys 20 cartoons/year. Uses material on family, church situation and social commentary. Pays $15-20 minimum for one-time use.

AVON BOOKS, Art Department, 150 Madison Ave., New York NY 10016. (212)481-5663. Publisher: Rena Wolner. Art Director: Tom Egner. Publishes paperback originals and reprints—mass market, trade and juvenile. Publishes 300 titles/year; 80% require freelance illustrators.
First Contact & Terms: Works with 100 freelance artists/year. Works on assignment only. Send resume and samples to be filed. Drop-off portfolio. Accepts any type sample. Samples returned only by request. Reports within 1 month. Works on assignment only. Original work returned to the artist after

job's completion. Considers complexity of the project, skill and experience of the artist and project's budget when establishing payment.
Book Design: Assigns 20 jobs/year. Uses artists for all aspects. Payment varies.
Jackets/Covers: Assigns 150 freelance design and 150 freelance illustration jobs/year.
Text Illustration: Assigns 20 freelance jobs/year.
Tips: "Look at our books to see if work is appropriate for us before submitting."

AZTEX CORP., Box 50046, 1126 N. 6th Ave., Tucson AZ 85703. (602)882-4656. President: W. R. Haessner. Publishes hardcover and paperback originals on sports, mainstream and how-to. Publishes 9-12 titles/year.
First Contact & Terms: Works on assignment only. Send query letter with resume and/or brochure showing art style and samples. Especially looks for realism and detail when reviewing samples. Reports in 6 weeks. Samples returned by SASE. Buys reprint or all rights. No originals returned to artist at job's completion. Free catalog.
Jackets/Covers: Assigns 4 jobs/year. "We need technical drawings and cutaways." Pays $50-150, opaque watercolors and oils.

BAKER BOOK HOUSE, 6030 E. Fulton Rd., Ada MI 49301. (616)676-9185. Art Director: Dwight Baker. Specializes in hardcovers, paperbacks, originals and reprints of religious trade and textbooks. Publishes 100 titles/year.
First Contact & Terms: Works with 10 freelance artists/year. Works on assignment only. Send query letter with brochure showing art style or resume, tear sheets, photostats, photocopies, slides and photographs. Samples not filed are returned by SASE only if requested. Reports only if interested. Original art work is returned after the job's completion if requested. Considers complexity of project, skill and experience of artist, and project's budget when establishing payment. Buys all rights.
Jackets/Covers: Assigns 12 freelance design and 12 freelance illustration jobs/year. Pays by the project, $250 minumum.
Text Illustration: Assigns 2 freelance jobs/year. Prefers pen & ink cartoons and line drawings. Pays $10-25/spot drawing.
Tips: "We are always looking for jacket designers who work primarily with type for our academic book covers. The most valuable illustrators are those who are able to envisage the completed cover design and compose their illustration to incorporate the type copy that will be added later. In presenting samples or portfolios the most common error we see is the tendency for artists to include weaker pieces that distract from their strong ones."

WILLIAM L. BAUHAN, PUBLISHER, Dublin NH 03444. Art Director: W.L. Bauhan. Publishes hardbound and paperback books on New England. Publishes 6-8 titles/year.
Needs: Uses artists for jackets, covers, text illustrations. Uses line drawings and block prints, all b&w.
First Contact & Terms: Works on assignment only. Send query letter. SASE. Reports in 4 weeks. Send resume and samples or just samples of work to be kept on file for future assignments; do not send originals. Check for most recent titles in bookstores. Purchases outright.

BENGAL PRESS, INC., 1885 Spaulding SE, Grand Rapids MI 49506. (616)949-8895. President: John Ilich. Specializes in paperback originals and reprints of nonfiction (business, history, law, how-to) and fiction (science fiction, religious, inspirational). Publishes 1-4 titles/year; 100% require freelance designers; 25% require freelance illustrators.
First Contact & Terms: Send query letter with samples to be kept on file. Accepts any samples the artist deems relevant to show quality and type of work. Reports only if interested. Works on assignment only. No originals returned to artist at job's completion. Considers complexity of project, skill and experience of artist and project's budget when establishing payment. Negotiates rights purchased.
Book Design: Assigns 1-3 freelance jobs/year. Pays by the project, $100-1,000.
Jackets/Covers: Assigns 1-3 freelance design and 1-4 freelance illustration jobs/year. Pays by the project, $100-1,000.
Text Illustration: Assigns 1-3 freelance jobs/year. Pays by the project, $100-1,000.
Tips: "Good samples should be sent for our company files, so that when a project comes up, we can seek an artist based upon the samples filed."

BENNETT & MCKNIGHT PUBLISHING, 809 W. Detweiller, Peoria IL 61615. (309)691-4454. Director of Art/Design/Production: Donna M. Faull. Specializes in original hardcovers and paperbacks, especially in vocational education (industrial arts/high-tech/home economics/career education textbooks, filmstrips, software). Publishes over 100 titles/year.
First Contact & Terms: Works with over 30 freelance artists/year. Works on assignment only. Send query letter with brochure, resume and "any type of samples." Samples not filed are returned if request-

ed. Reports back in weeks. Original work not returned after job's completion; work-for-hire basis with rights to publisher. Considers complexity of the project, skill and experience of the artist, project's budget, turnaround time and rights purchased when establishing payment. Buys all rights.
Book Design: Assigns over 30 freelance design and over 30 freelance illustration jobs/year. Pays by the hour, $10-40; pays by the project, $300-3,000 and upward (very technical art, lots of volume).
Jackets/Covers: Assigns over 50 freelance design jobs/year. Pays by the project, $200 for 1-color; 4,000 for complete cover/interiors for textbooks.
Text Illustration: Assigns over 50 freelance jobs/year. Pays by the hour, $10-40; amount varies.
Tips: "Try not to call or never drop in without an appointment."

***BKMK PRESS**, College of Arts & Sciences, University of Missouri-Kansas City, 5100 Rockhill Rd., Kansas City MO 64110. (816)276-1305. Editor-in-Chief: Dan Jaffe. Specializes in paperback originals dealing with poetry, art, and quality short stories. Publishes 6 titles/year; 50% require freelance illustrators.
First Contact & Terms: Send query letter with photographs to be kept on file. "We want to see how things reproduce—no slides, please." Samples not kept on file are returned by SASE. Reports within 2 months only if interested. Works on assignment only. Originals returned to artist at job's completion. Write for appointment to show portfolio. Considers complexity of project, skill and experience of artist, project's budget, turnaround time and rights purchased when establishing payment. Negotiates rights purchased.
Jackets/Covers: Assigns 4-5 freelance design jobs/year.
Text Illustration: Pays by the project, $50 minimum.

BLACKTHORNE PUBLISHING INC., 786 Blackthorne Ave., El Cajon CA 92020. (619)463-9603. Art Director: Steven J. Schanes. Specializes in paperback originals and reprints, comic books, signed prints and trade books. Publishes 200 titles/year.
First Contact & Terms: Works with 50 freelance artists/year. "We look for professional standards in artists we work with." Send query letter with brochure, resume, and samples to be kept on file; originals will be returned. Prefers slides and Photostats as samples. Samples not filed are returned. Reports within 3 weeks. Originals returned to artist after job's completion. Considers complexity of the project, skill and experience of artist, project's budget and turnaround time when establishing payment. Rights purchased vary according to project.
Book Design: Assigns 50 jobs/year. Pays by the project, depending on the job, from $50 for a spot illustration to $15,000 for a complete comic book series.
Jackets/Covers: Assigns 15 freelance design and 30 freelance illustration jobs/year. Pays by the hour, $5-40 average; by the project, $50-10,000 average.
Text Illustration: Assigns 15 jobs/year. Prefers pen & ink. Pays by the hour, $5-40 average; by the project, $50-10,000 average.

BLACKWELL SCIENTIFIC PUBLICATIONS, INC., 52 Beacon St., Boston MA 02108. (617)720-0761. Production Manager: Elizabeth O'Neill McGuire. Specializes in hardcovers of medical and nursing books. Publishes 5 titles/year.
First Contact & Terms: Artists must have experience in medical illustration. "However, 95% of our authors supply finished art. We have hired freelance illustrators once in 5 years."
Jackets/Covers: Some cover design work for experienced designers.
Tips: Artists should "investigate the potential purchaser to see if their work is even appropriate."

***BONUS BOOKS**, 160 E. Illinois, Chicago IL 60611. Production Editor: Jane Marie Caplan. Specializes in hardcover and paperback nonfiction trade books, including sports, careers, guidebooks, general interest. Publishes 10-15 titles/year.
First Contact & Terms: Works with 10-15 freelance artists/year. Prefers local artists. Works on assignment only. Send query letter with slides and a SASE. "Do not send originals." Samples are filed. Samples not filed are returned by SASE. Reports back within 2 weeks only if interested. Originals returned to artist at job's completion "depending on job." Local artists can call or write to schedule an appointment to show a portfolio, which should include roughs and original/final art. Considers complexity of project, skill and experience of artist, project's budget, turnaround time and rights purchased when establishing payment.
Jackets/Covers: Assigns 30 freelance design and 2 freelance illustration jobs/year. Pays by the project, $100 minimum.
Text Illustration: Assigns 2 freelance jobs/year. Prefers line art (pen & ink). Pays by the project, $10 minimum.
Tips: "Unless your illustrations are book cover material, we probably aren't interested. We're most interested in talented book cover designers with a strong type sense. Many of our book covers use only type."

Close-up

Robert McGinnis

Illustrator

Old Greenwich, Connecticut

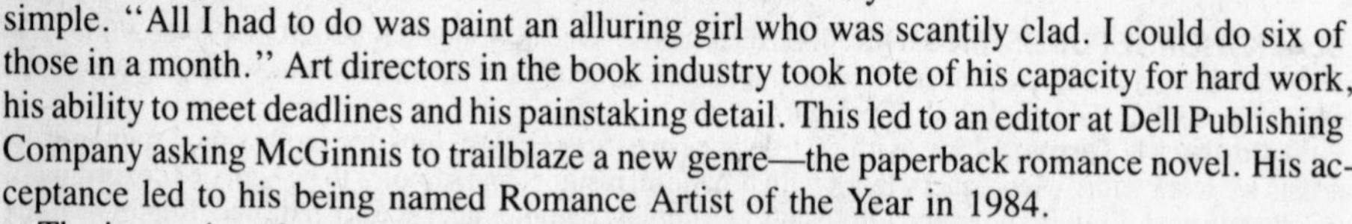

The book covers painted by Robert McGinnis—and he has done over 1,300—test the definition of illustration. McGinnis covers are illustrations—they are pictorial capsules of the editorial content—but they are also finely-crafted paintings.

His prolific output crosses over many literary genres. His first assignments were detective novels and were very simple. "All I had to do was paint an alluring girl who was scantily clad. I could do six of those in a month." Art directors in the book industry took note of his capacity for hard work, his ability to meet deadlines and his painstaking detail. This led to an editor at Dell Publishing Company asking McGinnis to trailblaze a new genre—the paperback romance novel. His acceptance led to his being named Romance Artist of the Year in 1984.

The impassioned prose of a romance novel is often accompanied by an equally sensuous cover. However, a sense of restraint sets apart McGinnis' work. "Too many covers are just a passionate clinch with costume and background. They're almost a format; they're more explicit and less cerebral than I like to be." He avoids clichés by hours of research into the book's plot, characters and setting.

His account of his working process attests to this penchant for going the extra mile: "Publishers either issue a reader's report (a short condensation of the book) or they send an entire manuscript. After reading the book or report, I explore the theme through pencil sketches of varying composition and staging until the design is solid. Through this process emotion builds and creates enthusiasm so essential to a successful painting."

Sketches are then sent to the art director, who consequently reviews them and writes notes or draws his own sketches in the margin. McGinnis proceeds with his painting, following both the art director's directions and his own sensibilities. Many artists submit roughs, finished sketches and then comprehensives before starting to paint, but McGinnis generally paints from sketches, upon the art director's approval.

"You have to remember books are aimed at different markets. Sometimes a book needs a strong, dramatic cover. For another book, something delicate, passive or serene is appealing." Occasionally the artist's conception of the project is at odds with the art director's. "You have to be flexible and considerate of an art director's position," says McGinnis. "You can't be temperamental." Otherwise deadlines are missed, and the artist builds a negative reputation in the industry.

However, McGinnis has developed a sixth sense for what's right for a certain situation from years of experience in commercial illustration. His interest in art began when he was growing up in Cincinnati, Ohio, where his mother enrolled him in art classes at the museum. These classes paid off when he received his first assignment from Cincinnati book publisher F&W Publications (the publisher of this book). The first assignment led to a variety of commercial jobs—motion picture posters, record jackets, sheet music cover illustration (his rendering of Audrey Hepburn in "Moon River" will always be remembered), annual reports and magazine illustration. He now completes choice assignments from book publishers while pursuing his interests in fine art, winning awards in galleries as well as in the commercial field.

Since he must complete a painting within a month or less, he uses egg tempera on a rabbit-skin gesso surface applied to masonite or illustration board. When he uses oils to gain a softer, more sensual touch, he hastens their drying time by adding a cobalt dryer, then varnish. He tries to avoid the crackling that sometimes occurs after a painting has been varnished. "I want my paintings to last. There's always that lurking desire for immorality."

He finds that wraparound covers (those in which the back is a continuation of the front cover) are annoying. "You have to look at two paintings at the same time. That makes it harder to organize the theme in your mind. You have to remember that the area that carries the copy must be kept light or dark, depending on the type." Because wraparounds take more planning, illustrators are paid more for them than for a front cover.

McGinnis continues to illustrate book covers because the field allows him to be creative. "There is no limit to creativity in book publishing. The field is wide open to ideas." His advice to artists interested in book illustration pertains to all creative people: "Do the best you can. Follow the feelings you have for a theme. Don't let anyone deter you from what you ultimately want to do. Follow your obsession."

—Susan Conner

McGinnis puts hours of research into a book's plot, characters and settings in order to produce a detailed painting like this cover for* Princess Daisy *(Bantam Books). McGinnis always looks beyond the "passionate clinch" for a more imaginative cover.

BOWLING GREEN UNIVERSITY POPULAR PRESS, Bowling Green University, Bowling Green OH 43403. (419)372-2981. Managing Editor: Pat Browne. Publishes hardcover and paperback originals on popular culture, folklore, women's studies, science fiction criticism, detective fiction criticism, music and drama. Publishes 15-20 titles and 8 journals/year.
First Contact & Terms: Send previously published work. SASE. Reports in 2 weeks. Buys all rights. Free catalog.
Jackets/Covers: Assigns 20 jobs/year. Pays $50 minimum, color washes, opaque watercolors, gray opaques, b&w line drawings and washes.

BRADY COMMUNICATIONS COMPANY, INC., a Prentice-Hall Company, 14999 Annapolis Rd., Bowie MD 20715. Executive Art Director: Jo DiDomenico, AMI. Publishes medical, allied health, emergency care, nursing and home computer textbooks.
First Contact & Terms: Works with 50 freelance artists/year. Artists must be experienced cover designers (high-tech computer covers for home computer books) or experienced textbook illustrators. Works on assignment only. Send resume and samples to be kept on file. Prefers tear sheets of illustrations or printed flat sheets of covers, both computer and medical, as samples. Samples not filed are returned by SASE. Reports back only if interested.
Jackets/Covers: Assigns cover designs, rough comprehensive full color to size. Considers the complexity of the project, skill and experience of artist, turnaround time and rights purchased when establishing payment. Pays by the project.
Text Illustration: Rough and final inking. Pays by the project.
Tips: "Work must be of a high quality, neat, clean. We prefer previously published examples only; no school work."

GEORGE BRAZILLER INC., 60 Madison Ave., New York NY 10010. (212)889-0909. Contact: Herman Figatner. Publishes hardcover and paperback originals on history of art and architecture; philosophy and religion. Publishes 20 titles/year. Also uses artists for advertising, paste-up, catalog layout and design, posters.
First Contact & Terms: Query with resume; local artists only. Works on assignment only. Provide resume and samples to be kept on file. Buys one-time rights.
Book Design: Assigns 25 jobs/year. Designer is responsible for type spec, composition arrangements, through finished mechanicals. Pays by the project, $2,000 maximum.
Jackets/Covers: Uses freelance designers and illustrators. Prefers line drawings, color wash, prints (wood blocks) as cover illustrations. Pays for design and illustration by the project, $150-300 average.
Tips: "Show work directly geared to a particular publisher."

BRIARCLIFF PRESS, 11 Wimbledon Court, Jericho NY 11753. (516)681-1505. Editorial/Art Director: Trudy Settel. Publishes hardcover and paperback cookbook, decorating, baby care, gardening, sewing, crafts and driving originals and reprints. Publishes 18 titles/year; 100% require freelance designers and illustrators. Uses artists for color separations, lettering and mechanicals; assigns 25 jobs/year, pays $5-10/hour. Also assigns 5 advertising jobs/year for catalogs and direct mail brochures; pays $5-10/hour.
First Contact & Terms: Send query letter; no samples until requested. Artists should have worked on a professional basis with other firms of this type. SASE. Reports in 3 weeks. Buys all rights. No advance. Pays promised fee for unused assigned work.
Book Design: Assigns 25/year. Pays $6 minimum/hour, layout and type spec.
Jackets/Covers: Buys 24/year. Pays $100-300, b&w; $250-500, color.
Text Illustration: Uses artists for text illustrations and cartoons. Buys 250/year. Pays $10-30, b&w; $25-50, color.

BRIDGE PUBLISHING, INC., 2500 Hamilton Blvd., South Plainfield NJ 07080. (201)754-0745. Art Director: Linda Bachert. Publisher of Christian books. Emphasizes books dealing with the practical aspects of the Christian life for a broad spectrum of Christian denominations and theological viewpoints; mainly adults. Publishes 12 titles/year.
First Contact & Terms: Buys 6-8 illustrations/year. Prefers Christian themes, nature (pastoral), figurative work. Send query letter with brochure, resume, Photostats, photocopies, slides, photographs and samples of book covers. Samples not filed are returned by SASE. Reports back only if interested. Pays for design by the hour, $7-10 or by the project, $400-700. Pays for illustration by the project, $300-700. Buys first rights and reprint rights; "we are paying the artist for rights to reproduce their work on book covers as well as any promotional materials and future reprints." Pays on acceptance.
Tips: "I look for good draftsmanship. That is, that a hand is drawn to look like a hand, not a claw. I also look for creative realism, interesting environments with an attention to detail."

BROADMAN PRESS, 127 9th Ave. N., Nashville TN 37234. (615)251-2630. Art Director: Jack Jewell. Religious publishing house.

First Contact & Terms: Artist must be experienced, professional illustrator. Works on assignment only. Send query letter with brochure and samples to be kept on file. Call or write for appointment to show portfolio. Send slides, tear sheets, Photostats or photocopies; "samples *cannot* be returned." Reports only if interested. Pays for illustration by the project, $250-900. Considers complexity of the project, client's budget and rights purchased when establishing payment. Buys all rights. Retains ownership of art.
Needs: Works with 50 freelance artists/year. Uses artists for illustration. "We publish for all ages in traditional and contemporary styles, thus our needs are quite varied."
Tips: "The quality of art in the Christian book publishing market has greatly improved in the last five years. We actively search for 'realist' illustrators who can work in a style that looks contemporary." Looks for " the ability to illustrate scenes with multiple figures, to accurately illustrate people of all ages, including young children and babies, and illustrate detailed scenes described in text."

ARISTIDE D. CARATZAS, PUBLISHER, Box 210, 481 Main St., New Rochelle NY 10802. (914)632-8487. Managing Editor: John Emerich. Publishes books about archaeology, art history, natural history and classics for specialists in the above fields in universities, museums, libraries and interested amateurs. Accepts previously published material. Send letter with brochure showing artwork. Samples not filed are returned by SASE. Reports only if interested. To show a portfolio, mail appropriate materials or call or write to schedule an appointment. Buys all rights or negotiates rights purchased.

CAREER PUBLISHING, INC., Box 5486, Orange CA 92613-5486. (714)771-5155. Secretary/Treasurer: Sherry Robson. Specializes in paperback original textbooks on trucking, medical office management, medical insurance billing, motorcycle dictionary, real estate dictionary, micro computer courses and guidance for jobs. Uses artists for advertising, direct mail and posters.
First Contact & Terms: Works with 3 freelance artists/year. Works on assignment only. Send query letter with brochure/flyer or resume, Photostats and line drawings or actual work to be kept on file. Submit portfolio for review. Guidelines given for each project. Samples returned by SASE. Reports in 2 months. No originals returned to artist at job's completion. Buys all rights.
Book Design: Assigns 12 jobs/year. Pays for design by the project, $50-300.
Jackets/Covers: Assigns 12 design and 150 illustration jobs/year. Prefers line drawings, paintings and cartoons for illustrations. Pays for illustration by the project, $50-100.
Text Illustration: Assigns approximately 10 jobs/year. Pays by the project, $50-100.
Tips: Uses some medical illustrations and technical drawings.

CARNIVAL ENTERPRISES, Box 19087, Minneapolis MN 55419. (612)870-0169. Editorial Director: Rosemary Wallner. "Carnival is a book producer, not a publisher. The titles we create are for clients who market them in many outlets and editions. Produces juvenile fiction and nonfiction. Produces 25-45 titles/year.
First Contact & Terms: Works with 25-45 freelance artists/year. "Experience in children's literature is *crucial*, including past published children's books and experience in picture book design." Works on assignment only. Send query letter with brochure, resume, photocopies, slides, printed excerpts—anything except original work—to be kept on file. "Carnival uses a file system and only contacts artists on an assignment basis. No specific submissions will be accepted; no queries are followed upon by Carnival due to the volume of our mail. We literally match up artists with appropriate styles. All samples are welcome, but bulk should be kept to a minimum for easy filing." Samples not filed are returned *only* by request with an SASE. Does not report back to the artist. Considers complexity of the project, skill and experience of artist, project's budget, (vital) turnaround time, rights purchased and going rates when establishing payment. Rights purchased vary from client to client.
Text Illustration: Assigns 25-45 titles/year. Considers watercolor, markers, colored pencil and gouache—any "flexible" medium for laser separation. Pays by the project, $2,000-6,000 for color. B&w line art pays less.

CATHOLIC BOOK PUBLISHING CO., 257 W. 17th St., New York NY 10011. (212)243-4515. Manager: Robert W. Cavalero. Specializes in hardcover and paperback originals. Publishes 10 titles/year; 50% require freelance illustrators.
First Contact & Terms: Works with 6 freelance artists/year. Works on assignment only. Send samples and tear sheets to be kept on file. Reports within 1 week. Call or write for appointment to show portfolio. No originals returned to artist at job's completion. Considers skill and experience of artist when establishing payment. Buys all rights.
Text Illustration: Assigns 10 freelance jobs/year.

THE CHILD'S WORLD, INC., Box 989, Elgin IL 60120. Editor: Diane Dow Suire. Specializes in hardcover originals on early childhood education. Publishes 40 titles/year; 50% require freelance designers and 100% require freelance illustrators.

First Contact & Terms: Works with 20 freelance artists/year. Prefers artists who have experience illustrating for children. Works on assignment only. Send samples and tear sheets to be kept on file except for original work. "Correspond please. Don't call." Reports only if interested. No originals returned to artist at job's completion. Considers complexity of project, skill and experience of artist, and project's budget when establishing payment. Buys all rights.
Book Design: Assigns 4-6 (by series) freelance jobs/year. Pays by the project for design and illustration.
Jackets/Covers: Assigns 4-6 (by series) freelance design jobs/year. Pays by the project for design and illustration.
Text Illustration: "We do about 40 books in series format. We publish in full-color and use very little black-and-white art." Pays by the project.
Tips: Looks for "art geared for the very young child—there's a big demand for more quality books for preschool children."

CHILTON BOOK CO., 201 King of Prussia Rd., Radnor PA 19089. (215)964-4711. Art Director: Edna H. Jones. Publishes hardbound and paperback arts and crafts, business, computer, technical, trade and automotive books. Publishes 80 titles/year; 50% require freelance designers, fewer than 5% require freelance illustrators.
First Contact & Terms: Query. "I prefer to deal in person rather than through the mail." Reports within 3 weeks. Buys world rights. No originals returned at job's completion. Works on assignment only. Samples returned by SASE. Provide resume, business card, flyer and tear sheet to be kept on file for future assignments. Check for most recent titles in bookstores. Artist sometimes supplies overlays for color work. Full payment for unused assigned work. Pays on acceptance.
Book Design: Assigns 40 jobs/year. Uses artists for layout, type spec and scaling art, castoffs. Pays by the project, $400-800 upon completion and acceptance. Price is discussed at beginning of the job with the designer.
Jackets/Covers: Assigns 80 freelance design and 30 freelance illustration jobs/year. Pays $400-1,000.
Text Illustration: Assigns 1-2 freelance jobs. Pays by the project.

CHRISTIAN BOARD OF PUBLICATION, Box 179, St. Louis MO 63166. Director of Product Development, Design and Promotion: Guin Tuckett. Publishes several paperbacks annually. Also publishes magazines, curriculum, catalogs and advertising pieces. Uses artists for design and illustration of curriculum, books, direct mail brochures and display pieces.
First Contact & Terms: Send query letter with resume, brochure or copies of work to be kept on file. SASE. Reports in 6-8 weeks. Buys all rights. No originals returned to artist at job's completion. Works on assignment only. Samples returned by SASE.
Jackets/Covers: Assigns a few jobs/year. Pays $200 minimum, 2-color and 4-color.
Text Illustration: Assigns many jobs/year. Pays $40 minimum, 2-color; $55 minimum, 4-color. "In a teen-age monthly magazine we use about 8-10 cartoons/issue."

CHRONICLE BOOKS, Suite 806, One Hallidie Plaza, San Francisco CA 94102. (415)777-7240. Production and Art Director: David Barich. Publishes hardcover and paperback originals on California and the West Coast, how-to, architecture, contemporary fine art books and cookbooks, California history, urban living, guidebooks, art and photography; some paperback reprints. Publishes 35-45 titles/year; 75% require freelance designers, 10% require freelance illustrators.
First Contact & Terms: Personal contact required. Query with resume or arrange interview to show portfolio. SASE. Reports within 2 weeks. Buys various rights. Free catalog.
Book Design: Assigns 25 jobs/year. Uses artists for layout, type spec and design. Pays by the project, $400-600 average. Payment upon completion of project.
Jackets/Covers: Assigns 40 jobs/year. Pays by the project, $400-600 average for design; by the project, $125-400 average for illustrations, b&w line drawings, washes and gray opaques; $400-650, color washes and opaque watercolors.
Text Illustration: Pays by the project, $200 minimum.

***CLIFFHANGER PRESS**, Box 29527, Oakland CA 94604-9527. Editor: Nancy Chirich. Estab. 1986. Specializes in paperback mystery and suspense. Publishes 4 titles/year.
First Contact & Terms: Works with 4 freelance artists/year for covers only. Works on assignment only. Send query letter with brochure, tear sheets or samples showing b&w techniques. "All our covers are 2-color (i.e. black and red). We are interested in line drawings, wash, watercolor—whatever will reproduce with black and a color for the covers, with or without a halftone." Samples are filed. Samples not filed are returned by SASE only if requested. Reports back within 2-3 weeks. To show a portfolio, mail disposable samples, such as thumbnails, tear sheets, roughs and final reproduction/product. Considers project's budget and turnaround time when establishing payment. Buys one-time rights for time

book is in print. "Artist keeps copyright to artwork."
Jackets/Covers: Assigns 4 freelance design jobs/year. "Artist gets synopsis or copy of manuscript." Pays by the project, $200-250, including "cover design by . . ." on cover.

CLIFFS NOTES INC., Box 80728, Lincoln NE 68501. Contact: Michele Spence. Publishes educational and trade (Centennial Press) books. Uses artists for educational posters.
First Contact & Terms: Works on assignment only. Samples returned by SASE. Reports back on future assignment possibilities. Send brochure, flyer and/or resume. No originals returned to artist at job's completion. Buys all rights. Artist supplies overlays for color art.
Jackets/Covers: Uses artists for covers and jackets.
Text Illustration: Uses technical illustrators for mathematics, science, miscellaneous.

COASTAR PUBLISHING, Subsidiary of Newtek Industries, Box 46116, Los Angeles CA 90046. (213)874-6669. Publisher: Jules Brenner. Publishes 1 original paperback—the *Brenner Restaurant Index*—each year. Also publishes a software program for home and office computers.
First Contact & Terms: "We are not yet working with artists, but would consider doing so." Send query letter with resume and samples to be kept on file. Accepts any type sample. Samples not filed are returned by SASE. Reports within 3 weeks. Original work returned to artist "if artist insists." Rights purchased vary according to project.
Jackets/Covers: Will probably assign 1 freelance illustration job/year. Pays 3 copies of book.
Text Illustration: Will consider using text illustration.

COMPCARE PUBLICATIONS, 2415 Annapolis Lane, Minneapolis MN 55441. (800)328-3330. Publisher: Margaret Marsh. Specializes in personal growth books including alcohol/chemical dependency, stress management, parenting and weight control. Publishes 6-8 titles/year. Uses artists for text illustrations and cover art.
First Contact & Terms: Works with 4 freelance artists/year. "We only consider artists who have illustrated for trade books." Works on assignment only. Send query letter with tear sheets. Negotiates payment arrangement with artist.
Book Design: Assigns 1-2 freelance design and 1-2 freelance illustration jobs/year.
Jackets/Covers: Assigns 6-8 freelance design and 2 freelance illustration jobs/year.
Text Illustration: Assigns 1-2 freelance jobs/year. Prefers line art—pencil illustration.

COMPUTER SCIENCE PRESS INC., 1803 Research Blvd., Rockville MD 20850. (301)251-9050. Publishes hardcover and paperback computer science, engineering, computers and math textbooks. Publishes 18 titles/year; 100% require freelance illustrators. Also uses artists for paste-up and for technical drawings using templates and form letters or Leroy lettering.
First Contact & Terms: Works on assignment only. Prefers local artists. Call or send query letter with template work, an illustration or line drawing as well as an upper and lower case alphabet and some words in Leroy or Berol lettering. Photocopy of work is OK. Samples not returned. Buys all rights. No originals returned to artist at job's completion. Check for most recent titles in bookstores. Artist supplies overlays for cover artwork. Send artwork to the attention of Ilene Hammer.
Book Design: Assigns 12 freelance design and 12 illustration jobs/year. Pays by the hour, $8 minimum.
Jackets/Covers: Assigns 12 freelance design jobs/year. Pays by the project, $100 minimum.
Text Illustration: Buys text illustrations (artist "reproduces our rough art"). Assigns 12 freelance text illustration jobs/year; prefers pen & ink drawings. Pays by the hour, $8 minimum.
Tips: "We would like to develop a file of freelance technical draftsmen familiar with Leroy or Berol lettering. Local artists preferred. We provide rough art to copy."

***COMPUTER TECHNOLOGY RESOURCE GUIDE**, Box 294, Rhododendron OR 97049. (503)622-4798. Editor: Michael P. Jones. Estab. 1986. Book about computers and computer accessories, computer services, books "and anything else related to computers" for beginners to advanced users of computers plus those involved with providing technical assistance to users. Circ. 2,500. Accepts previously published material. Original artwork returned to the artist after publication. Sample copy $8. Art guidelines for SASE with 1 first-class stamp.
Cartoons: Buys 1-3 cartoons/issue from freelancers. Prefers single-panel, double-panel and multi-panel with and without gagline; b&w line drawings, b&w washes and color washes. Send query letter with samples of style, roughs and finished cartoons. Samples are filed. Samples not filed are returned by SASE. Reports back within 2 weeks. Write for appointment to show a portfolio. Buys one-time rights. Pays in copies.
Illustrations: Buys 10 illustrations/issue from freelancers. Send query letter with brochure or resume, tear sheets, Photostats, photocopies, slides and photographs. Samples not filed are returned by SASE.

Reports back within 2 weeks. To show a portfolio, mail thumbnails, roughs, original/final art, final reproduction/product, color, tear sheets, Photostats, photographs and b&w. Buys one-time rights. Pays in copies on publication.
Tips: "I am looking for good quality black-and-white sketches. Give me a good sample of what you can draw, even if you haven't done much in the way of computers. Send me whatever you have, and I'll be able to get a good idea from the samples."

DAVID C. COOK PUBLISHING COMPANY, Chariot Books, 850 N. Grove Ave., Elgin IL 60120. (312)741-2400. Managing Editor: Catherine L. Davis. Publishes religious children's books for ages infant-junior high. Publishes 50 titles/year; 60% require freelance illustrators.
First Contact & Terms: Prefers artists with publishing experience. Send photocopies of work or 35mm slides with return package and postage. Samples returned by SASE. Provide "anything that can be kept or photocopied" to be kept on file for future assignments. Check for most recent titles in bookstores. Artist sometimes supplies overlays on inside illustrations.
Book Design: Assigns 20-35/year. Buys realistic illustrations. Uses artists for layout and full-color art. Illustrated books usually have an advance and royalty.
Jackets/Covers: Assigns 20-35/year. Buys realistic illustrations; prefers b&w and full-color. Uses artists for layout and full-color art. Pays by the job.

***CORONADO PUBLISHERS**, 1250 Sixth Ave., San Diego CA 92101. (619)699-6280. Art Director: Janet S. Taggart. Specializes in elementary and high school textbooks. Publishes series, 50 components involved in a series. Disciplines: English (language arts), science, biology, social studies, art and math.
First Contact & Terms: Works with 60-80 freelance artists/year. Works on assignment only. Send query letter with resume (if available), slides and tear sheets. Samples are filed "unless specifically requested to be returned to the illustrator." Write or call for appointment to show a portfolio. Samples not filed are returned. Reports back within 4 weeks. Originals not returned to artist after the job's completion. Work for hire. Considers complexity of project and project's budget when establishing payment. Buys all rights and ownership.
Jackets/Covers: Usually kept inhouse.
Text Illustration: Assigns hundreds of illustration jobs during the production of a series. Pays for illustration by the project, $15-1,000.
Tips: "We are always seeking the talent of freelance illustrators to illustrate in any number of different styles, color and black-and-white, as directed by the publisher. We work with freelance illustrators throughout the nation on a continuous basis and are always open to fresh new talent. All media and styles are openly considered. In particular we are interested in illustrators that exhibit a fine ability in any of the following categories: representational, realistic rendering of children in various classroom and normal everyday situations; representational and realistic illustration; scientific and biological illustration (including animal, wildlife, landscape, and medical); narrative and historical illustration; character development in illustration, based on given stories and/or poems (animals and people); stylized, humorous illustrations and technical illustration."

***CORTINA LEARNING INTERNATIONAL, INC.**, 17 Riverside Ave., Westport CT 06880. Publishes language teaching materials, art courses in commercial art, oil and watercolor painting, young people's arts, writing (fiction and nonfiction) and photography.
First Contact & Terms: Send "outline of proposed project or photocopies only of table of contents and sample chapters." No originals returned to artist at job's completion. Works on assignment only. Samples returned by SASE; reports back on future assignment possibilities. Provide resume and samples of style to be kept on file for future assignments. Artist supplies overlays for cover artwork.
Jackets/Covers: Uses artists for jacket design.
Text Illustration: Uses artists for text illustrations. Negotiates pay.
Tips: Also uses artists for direct mail promotion and advertising art.

***THE COUNTRYMAN PRESS; BACKCOUNTRY PUBLICATIONS**, Box 175, Woodstock VT 05091-0175. (802)457-1049. Production Manager: Louis Wilder. Specializes in hardcover and paperback originals and reprints on Vermont history and travel, contemporary fiction, poetry, how-to; reprints and originals of crime, suspense (Foul Play Press imprint). Publishes 25-30 titles/year.
First Contact & Terms: Works with 6-10 freelance artists/year. Works on assignment only. Send query letter with resume, tear sheets, Photostats, photographs and "relevant samples of work." Samples are filed. Samples not filed are returned by SASE if requested. Reports back within 3 months. Originals returned to artist at job's completion "if requested." Call or write to schedule an appointment. Considers complexity of project, budget, turnaround time and rights purchased. Negotiates rights purchased.
Book Design: Assigns 15-20 freelance design and 20-25 freelance illustration jobs/year. Pays by the hour, $7-35 "depending on dummies, paste-up and complexity."

Jackets/Covers: Assigns 14 freelance design jobs/year. Pays by the hour, $7-35.
Text Illustration: Assigns infrequent freelance jobs/year.
Tips: "Write for a catalogue. Take a preliminary look at some of our titles in a book shop or library. We are also interested in cartography."

CPI, 145 E. 49th St., New York NY 10017. (212)753-3800. Contact: Sherry Olan. Publishes hardcover originals, workbooks and textbooks for ages 4-14. Publishes 40 titles/year; 100% require freelance illustrators. Also uses artists for instructional materials, workbooks, textbook and scientific illustration.
First Contact & Terms: Local artists only. Works on assignment only. Send query letter with flyer, tear sheets and photocopies. Reports in 2 weeks. Samples returned by SASE. Reports back on future assignment possibilities. No originals returned to artist at job's completion. Buys all rights. Free artist's guidelines.
Text Illustration: Assigns 75 freelance jobs/year. "Submit color samples of action subjects. In general, realistic and representational art is required." Pays by the project, $35-150, opaque watercolors or any strong color medium except fluorescents. Also buys b&w line drawings.

THE CROSSING PRESS, Box 207, 22-D Roache Road, Freedom CA 95019. (408)722-0711. Publishers: John and Elaine Gill. Publishes hardcover and paperback cookbooks, how-to, feminist/gay literature, and greeting cards and calendars. Publishes 20 titles/year.
First Contact & Terms: Send photocopies.
Jackets/Covers: Assigns 15 jobs/year. Payment varies up to $200, b&w line drawings and washes.
Text Illustration: Assigns 3-4 jobs/year. Pays $10 and up/illustration or $300-1,000/book for b&w line drawings and washes.

CROWN PUBLISHERS, INC., 225 Park Ave. S., New York NY 10003. Design Director: Ken Sansone. Specializes in hardcovers, paperbacks and originals, especially general trade—fiction, nonfiction and illustrated nonfiction. Publishes 250 titles/year.
First Contact & Terms: Works with 50 artists/year. Prefers local artists. Works on assignment only. Contact only through artist's agent, who should send query letter with brochure showing art style. Samples not filed are returned by SASE. Reports only if interested. Original work returned at job's completion. Considers complexity of project, skill and experience of artist, project's budget, turnaround time and rights purchased when establishing payment. Negotiates rights purchased; rights purchased vary according to project.
Book Design: Assigns 20-30 freelance design and very few freelance illustration jobs/year. Pays by the project.
Jackets/Covers: Assigns 150 freelance design and 150 freelance illustration jobs/year. Pays by the project.
Text Illustration: Assigns very few jobs/year.

CUSTOM COMIC SERVICES, Box 50028, Austin TX 78763. Art Director: Scott Deschaine. Estab. 1985. Specializes in educational comic books for promotion and advertising for use by business, education, and government. "Our main product is full-color comic books, 16-32 pages long." Publishes 12 titles/year.
First Contact & Terms: Works with 24 freelance artists/year. "We are looking for artists who can produce finished artwork for educational comic books from layouts provided by the publisher. They should be able to produce consistently high-quality illustrations for mutually agreeable deadlines, with no exceptions." Works on assignment only. Send query letter with business card and nonreturnable samples to be kept on file. *Samples should be of finished comic book pages*; prefers Photostats. Reports within 6 weeks; must include SASE for reply. Considers complexity of project and skill and experience of artist when establishing payment. Buys all rights.
Text Illustration: Assigns 18 freelance jobs/year. "Finished artwork will be black-and-white, clean, and uncluttered. Artists can have styles ranging from the highly cartoony to the highly realistic." Pays $100-250/page of art.

DATA COMMAND, Box 548, 329 E. Court, Kankakee IL 60901. (815)933-7735. Editor: Patsy Gunnels. Specializes in educational software, teacher's guides, supplements to school curriculum in the language arts, math, science and social studies. Publishes 6 titles/year.
First Contact & Terms: Works with 4 freelance artists/year. Prefers artists with experience in marketing and cover design. Works on assignment only. Send resume and tear sheets, photocopies, slides and photographs. Samples not filed are returned by SASE. Reports back within 3 weeks. Original work not returned after job's completion. Considers complexity of project, skill and experience of artist and project's budget when establishing payment. Buys all rights.
Book Design: Pays by the project.

Jackets/Covers: Assigns 3-4 freelance design and 1-2 freelance illustration jobs/year. Pays by the project, $100 minimum.
Text Illustration: Assigns 1-2 freelance jobs/year. Pays by the project.
Tips: "All our products are aimed at educators and students from kindergarten to twelfth grade."

DAWN SIGN PRESS, #107, 2124 Kittredge St., Berkeley CA 94704. Art Director: Joe MacDougall. Specializes in paperbacks on education, juvenile fiction and parenting, sign language and deaf culture. Publishes 4 titles/year.
First Contact & Terms: Works with 2 freelance artists/year. All artists must go through interview process. Works on assignment only. Send query letter with resume, tear sheets, Photostats, photocopies, slides and photographs. Samples not filed returned only if requested. Reports within 90 days. Considers project's budget when establishing payment. Rights purchased vary according to project.
Book Design: Assigns 2 freelance design jobs/year and 2 freelance illustration jobs/year. Pays by the project, $150-750 average.
Jackets/Covers: Assigns 2 freelance design jobs/year and 2 freelance illustration jobs/year. Pays by the project, $250-550 average.
Text Illustration: Assigns 2 freelance jobs/year. Pays by the project, $20-45 average.
Tips: Artist should "specify their talents: i.e. graphic, cartoonist, illustrator, etc."

DECALOGUE BOOK INC., Box 2212, Mount Vernon NY 10550. (914)664-7944. Art Director: Rosemary Campion. Publishes paperback educational materials. Publishes 10 titles/year. Also uses artists for posters, direct mail brochure illustration, catalog and letterhead design. Negotiates pay.
First Contact & Terms: Send resume and samples; local and experienced artists only. SASE. Works on assignment only. Reports back within 1 month on whether to expect future assignments. Provide business card, flyer and tear sheet to be kept on file for possible future assignments. Originals not returned after completing assignment. "Samples supplied to artists we wish to consider." Buys all rights unless negotiated.
Book Design: Assigns 5-10 jobs/year. Uses artists for layout and type spec. Negotiates pay.
Jackets/Covers: Assigns 2 jobs/year. Buys color washes, opaque watercolors, gray opaques, b&w line drawings and washes. Negotiates pay.
Text Illustration: Assigns 5 jobs/year. Buys opaque watercolors, color washes, gray opaques, b&w line drawings and washes. Negotiates pay.
Tips: Buys small number of cartoons for use as cover art in educational material. Negotiates pay.

DELMAR PUBLISHERS INC., Box 15-015, 2 Computer Dr. W., Albany NY 12212. Contact: Karen Seebold. Specializes in original hardcovers and paperbacks, especially textbooks—science, computers, health, mathematics, professions and trades. Publishes 50 titles/year.
First Contact & Terms: Works with 35 freelance artists/year. Prefers artists with "professional technical art and photo preparation skills; dummy and page make-up skills; book publishing experience." Works on assignment only. Send query letter with brochure, resume, tear sheets, Photostats, photocopies, slides and photographs. Samples not filed are returned by SASE. Reports back only if interested. Original work not returned after job's completion. Considers complexity of project, project's budget and turnaround time when establishing payment. Buys all rights.
Book Design: Assigns 15 freelance design and 4-5 freelance illustration jobs/year. Pays by the project, $300-600.
Jackets/Covers: Assigns 15 freelance design and 15 freelance illustration jobs/year. Pays by the project, $200-400.
Text Illustration: Assigns 35 freelance jobs/year. Prefers ink and mylar or vellum; simplified style (axonometrics, schematics, diagrams and anatomical art). Pays by the project, $1,000-20,000.
Tips: "Quote prices for samples shown."

DILLON PRESS, 242 Portland Ave. S, Minneapolis MN 55415. (612)333-2691. Publisher: Uva Dillon. Specializes in hardcovers of juvenile fiction (Gemstone Books) and nonfiction for school library and trade markets. Publishes 40 titles/year.
First Contact & Terms: Works with 5 freelance artists/year. Works on assignment only. Send query letter with resume and samples to be kept on file. Call or write for appointment to show portfolio. Prefers slides and tear sheets as samples. Samples not filed are returned by SASE. Reports within 6 weeks. Originals not returned to artist. Considers complexity of the project, skill and experience of artist and project's budget when establishing payment. Rights purchased vary according to project.
Book Design: Assigns 10 jobs/year. Pays by the hour or by the project, negotiated so as competitive with other publishers in area.
Jackets/Covers: Assigns 10 freelance design and 10 freelance illustration jobs/year. Pays by the hour or by the project, negotiated so as competitive with other publishers in area.

Text Illustration: Assigns 10 jobs/year. Seeks a variety of media and styles. Pays by the hour or by the project, negotiated so as competitive with other publishers in area.

THE DONNING COMPANY/PUBLISHERS, 5659 Virginia Beach Blvd., Norfolk VA 23502. Publishes hardcover and paperback originals of pictorial histories, science fiction and fantasy, graphic novels, illustrated cookbooks, general and regional. Publishes 30-35 titles/year. Sample catalog $1.
First Contact & Terms: Works on assignment only. Send query letter to be kept on file for future assignments. Samples returned by SASE. Reports in 4 weeks. Buys first rights. Originals returned to artist at job's completion. Artist supplies overlays for cover artwork. Pays for illustration by the project, $60-2,000.
Tips: "We are concentrating on our graphic novels (high quality, extended-length comics) at present, so we need illustrators who can tell a story in pictures. Actually, our greatest need at present is probably for inkers and colorists." Looks for "believability—even in creating fantastic creatures or scenes; character- or people- oriented art; unique vision rather than slick copies of someone else's style." Common mistakes freelancers make are "sending entire portfolios when we only want samples; sending old work that doesn't reflect current abilities; failing to indicate whether we may keep the samples or if they are expected back; failing to include return postage; omitting a cover letter."

DORCHESTER PUBLISHING CO., INC. (publishers of Leisure Books), Suite 900, 6 E. 39th St., New York NY 10016. (212)725-8811. Production Manager: Lesley Poliner. Specializes in paperbacks, originals and reprints, especially mass market category fiction—historical romance, contemporary women's fiction, western, adventure, horror, mystery, romantic suspense war. Publishes 144 titles/year.
First Contact & Terms: Works with 24 freelance artists/year. "Should have experience doing paperback covers, be familiar with current design trends." Works on assignment only. Send brochure showing art style or resume, Photostats, slides and photographs. Samples not filed are returned by SASE. Reports within 2 weeks. Call for appointment to show portfolio. Original work returned after job's completion. Considers complexity of project and project's budget when establishing payment. Usually buys first rights, but rights purchased vary according to project.
Jackets/Covers: Pays by the project, $500 minimum.
Tips: "Talented new artists are welcome. Be familiar with the kind of artwork we use on our covers. If it's not your style, don't waste your time and ours."

DOUBLEDAY AND CO. INC., 245 Park Ave., New York NY 10167. (212)984-7561. Head Art Director: Alex Gotfryd. Publishes general adult, juvenile, western, science fiction, mystery, religious and special interest titles. Call Doug Bergstresser and Diana Klemin for interview.
Needs: Uses artists for jackets, inside illustrations.

***DOWN THERE PRESS/YES PRESS**, Box 2086, Burlingame CA 94010. Contact: Joani Blank. Specializes in paperback originals on sexuality, for adults and children. Publishes 1-2 titles/year.
First Contact & Terms: Works with 1 freelance artist/year. Local artists strongly preferred. Works on assignment only. Send brochure and samples. Brochure will be kept on file; samples may be. Prefers tear sheets or photocopies as samples. Samples not filed are returned by SASE. Original work is returned to the artist. Purchases one-time rights.
Jackets/Covers: Assigns 1 freelance design and 1 freelance illustration job/year. Pays by the project.
Text Illustration: Prefers b&w line drawings, no color work. Pays $200 minimum, plus royalties. Small advance sometimes given.

***EASTVIEW EDITIONS, INC.**, Box 783, Westfield NJ 07091. (201)964-9485. Manager: Mr. N. Glenn. Specializes in hardcover and paperback books on "all the arts"—fine arts, architecture, design, music, dance, antiques, hobbies, nature, history. Publishes 12 titles/year. Uses artists for book design, jacket/cover design and text illustrations. Also "looking for people who want cooperative publication."
First Contact & Terms: Send outline and description of work; "no samples that must be returned, only 'second generation' illustrations." Pays in royalties, fees.

WM. B. EERDMANS PUBLISHING COMPANY, 255 Jefferson Ave. SE, Grand Rapids MI 49503. (616)459-4591. Art Director: Randy Albosta. Specializes in hardcovers, paperbacks, originals and reprints. Publishes 70 titles/year.
First Contact & Terms: Works on assignment only. Send query letter with slides and photographs. Samples not filed are returned. Reports within 5 days. To show a portfolio, an artist should mail appropriate materials or call or write to schedule an appointment; portfolio should include original/final art. Buys one-time rights.
Jackets/Covers: Uses 40-50 freelance designs/year, 4 or 5 illustrations/year. Payment depends on the project.
Text Illustration: Payment depends on the project.

EMC PUBLISHING, 300 York Ave., St. Paul MN 55101. (612)771-1555. Editor: Eileen Slater. Specializes in educational books and workbooks for schools and libraries. Uses artists for book design and illustration.
First Contact & Terms: Works with 1-2 freelance artists/year. Prefers local artists with book experience. Works on assignment only. Send query letter with resume, business card and samples. Call for appointment to show a portfolio. Reports in 3 weeks. Buys all rights. Negotiates payment by the project.

ENSLOW PUBLISHERS, Box 777, Bloy St. & Ramsey Ave., Hillside NJ 07205. Vice President: Patricia Culleton. Specializes in hardcovers, juvenile young adult nonfiction; science, social issues, biography. Publishes 30 titles/year.
First Contact & Terms: Works with 3 freelance artists/year. Works on assignment only. Send query letter with brochure or photocopies. Samples not filed are not returned. Does not report back. Considers skill and experience of artist when establishing payment. Rights purchased vary according to project.
Book Design: Assigns 3 freelance design jobs/year. Pays by the project.
Text Illustration: Assigns 5 freelance jobs/year. Pays by the project.
Tips: "We're interested in b&w india ink work. We keep a file of samples by various artists to remind us of the capabilities of each."

ENTELEK, Ward-Whidden House/The Hill, Box 1303, Portsmouth NH 03801. Editorial Director: Albert E. Hickey. Publishes paperback education originals; specializing in computer books and software. Clients: business, schools, colleges and individuals.
First Contact & Terms: Query with samples. Prefers previously published work as samples. SASE. Reports in 1 week. Free catalog. Works on assignment only. Provide brochure, flyer and tear sheets to be kept on file for possible future assignments. Pays $300, catalogs and direct mail brochures.
Needs: Works with 1 artist for ad illustrations; 1, advertising design; and 1, illustration, for use on 6 products/year. Especially needs cover designs/brochure designs.

EXPOSITION PRESS OF FLORIDA, INC., Suite C., 1701 Blount Rd., Pompano Beach FL 33069. (305)979-3200. Coordinating Director: Steve Berner. Specializes in original and reprint hardcovers and paperbacks, particularly romance fiction, juvenile fiction, science textbooks; all subject except pornography and anti-ethnic material." Publishes 300 titles/year.
First Contact & Terms: Works with 5-10 freelance artists/year. Prefers, "but not restricted to," local artists. Works on assignment only. Send query letter with brochure, resume, and samples. Samples not filed are returned by SASE if requested. Reports back only if interested. Original work is returned but "depends on the specific needs of the assignment." Considers complexity of the project, skill and experience of the artist and the project's budget when establishing payment. Rights purchased vary according to project, but will buy all rights.
Book Design: Assigns 3 freelance design and 3 freelance illustration jobs/year. Pays by the hour, $25 minimum.
Jackets/Cover: Assigns 5 freelance design and 5 freelance illustration jobs/year. Pays for illustration by the hour, $25 minimum.

FARRAR, STRAUS & GIROUX INC., 19 Union Square W., New York NY 10003. Contact: Dorris Janowitz. Publishes general fiction, nonfiction, biography and juvenile. Publishes 90 titles/year; 75% require freelance designers, 20% require freelance illustrators. Send samples.
Book Design: Assigns 65 jobs/year. Requires castoff from mss, layouts, type spec sheets and followthrough on proofs.
Jackets/Covers: Uses artists for jacket designs. Pays $550, pre-separated 3-color jacket and $600-750 full-color illustration, with type.
Text Illustration: Uses artists for inside illustrations.
Tips: "Learn how to do the jacket typography as well as illustrate."

***FATHOM PUBLISHING COMPANY**, Box 1960, Cordova AK 99574. (907)424-3116. President/Manager: Connie Taylor. Specializes in paperback originals, newsletters, flyers, and cards on commercial fishing, poetry and Alaska. Publishes 2+ titles/year; 100% require freelance illustrators.
First Contact & Terms: Works with 3 freelance artists/year. Prefers local artists. Send query letter with photocopies to be kept on file. No originals. Reports within 2 weeks. Works on assignment only. No originals returned at job's completion. Considers complexity of project and rights purchased when establishing payment. Negotiates rights purchased.
Text Illustration: Assigns 5-10 freelance jobs/year. Prefers pen & ink. Pays by the hour, $15 minimum; by the project, $10-65 average.
Tips: "Bring me an idea that I can sell to the public."

FOREIGN SERVICES RESEARCH INSTITUTE/WHEAT FORDERS, Box 6317, Washington DC 20015-0317. (202)362-1588. Director: John E. Whiteford Boyle. Specializes in paperback originals of modern thought; nonfiction and philosophical poetry.
First Contact & Terms: Works with 2 freelance artists/year. Artist should understand the principles of book jacket design. Works on assignment only. Send query letter to be kept on file. Reports within 15 days. No originals returned. Considers project's budget when establishing payment. Buys first rights or reprint rights.
Book Design: Assigns 1-2 freelance jobs/year. Pays by the hour, $25-35 average.
Jackets/Covers: Assigns 1-2 freelance design jobs/year. Pays by the project, $250 minimum.
Tips: "Submit samples of book jackets designed for and accepted by other clients. SASE, please."

***GLORIA FOREMAN PUBLISHING CO.**, Box 405, Oklahoma City OK 73101. (918)723-5925. Advertising Director: Al Gould. Specializes in paperback children's activity books.
First Contact & Terms: Works on assignment only. Send query letter with photographs. Samples are filed. Samples not filed are returned only if requested by artist. Reports back within 10 days. Originals returned to artist at job's completion. Portfolio should include roughs. Considers rights purchased when establishing payment. Buys all rights.
Book Design: Pays by the project.
Jackets/Covers: Pays by the project.
Text Illustration: Prefers b&w ink. Pays by the project.

***LARRY FREDERICKS ASSOCIATES**,845 3rd Ave., 15th Floor, New York NY 10022. Contact: Larry Fredericks. Clients: book publishers, firms with quarterly house organs and retailers.
Needs: Uses artists for layout, illustration, type, spec, paste-up and retouching for consumer and trade magazines.
First Contact & Terms: Prefers local artists. Call for interview.

THE FREE PRESS, A DIVISION OF MACMILLAN, INC., 866 Third Ave., New York NY 10022. Manufacturing Director: W.P. Weiss. Specializes in hardcover and paperback originals, concentrating on professional and tradebooks in the social sciences. Publishes 70 titles/year.
First Contact & Terms: Works with around 10 artists/year. Prefers artists with book publishing experience. Works on assignment only. Send query letter with brochure showing art style or resume and nonreturnable samples. Samples not filed are returned by SASE. Reports only if interested. Original work returned after job's completion. Considers complexity of project, skill and experience of artist, project's budget, turnaround time and rights purchased when establishing payment. Buys all rights.
Book Design: Assigns around 70 freelance design and around 30 freelance illustration jobs/year. Pays by the project.
Jackets/Covers: Assigns around 70 freelance design and illustration jobs/year. Pays by the project, $250-750.
Text Illustration: Assigns around 35 freelance jobs/year. "It is largely drafting work, not illustration." Pays by the project.

C.J. FROMPOVICH PUBLICATIONS, RD 1, Chestnut Rd., Coopersburg PA 18036. (215)346-8461. Publisher: Catherine Frompovich. Specializes in self-help and technical books on nutrition, especially natural nutrition. Publishes 3 titles/year. Uses artists for jacket/cover design and illustration, text illustrations, games, cards, pamphlets.
First Contact & Terms: Works with 3 freelance artists/year. Send query letter with finished work and tear sheets; no sketches. Samples returned by SASE. Pays by the project.
Tips: "Do not solicit via telephone. Send a written resume and photocopies of some recently completed work."

FUNKY PUNKY AND CHIC, Box 601, Cooper Sta., New York NY 10276. (212)533-1772. Creative Director: R. Eugene Watlington. Specializes in paperback originals on poetry, celebrity photos and topics dealing with new wave, high fashion. Publishes 4 titles/year; 50% require freelance designers; 75% require freelance illustrators.
First Contact & Terms: Works with 20 freelance artists/year. Send query letter with business card, photographs and slides. Samples not kept on file are returned by SASE. Reports only if interested. Write for appointment to show portfolio. No originals returned to artist at job's completion. Considers complexity of project and project's budget when establishing payment. Buys all rights.
Book Design: Assigns 1 freelance job/year. Pays by the project, $100-300 average.
Jackets/Covers: Assigns 3 freelance illustration jobs/year. Pays by the project, $50-75 average.
Text Illustration: Assigns 2 freelance jobs/year. Pays by the project, $50-75 average.

GENERAL HALL INC., 5 Talon Way, Dix Hills NY 11746. Editor, for editorial and advertising work: Ravi Mehra. Publishes hardcover and paperback originals; college texts and supplementary materials. Publishes 4-6 titles/year; 100% require freelance designers, 10% require freelance illustrators.
First Contact & Terms: Local artists only. Query. SASE. Reports in 1-2 weeks. No originals returned to artist at job's completion. Works on assignment only. Provide brochure/flyer to be kept on file for future assignment. Artist provides overlays for color artwork. Buys all rights. Free catalog and artist's guidelines.
Book Design: Assigns 4-6 jobs/year. Uses artists for layout. Pays on job basis.
Jackets/Covers: Assigns 3-5 jobs/year. Pays by the project, $50-100 for design; $25-50 for illustration, b&w line drawings, washes, gray opaques and color washes.
Text Illustration: Assigns 1-2 jobs/year. Pays by the project, $10-25, b&w line drawings, washes and gray opaques.

GLENCOE PUBLISHING COMPANY, 15319 Chatsworth St., Mission Hills CA 91345. Design Director: Gary Hespenheide. Specializes in hardcovers and paperbacks, especially textbooks in all subjects. Publishes 120-150 titles/year.
First Contact & Terms: Works with 50-60 freelance artists/year. Looking for "quality work." Works on assignment only. Send resume and tear sheets. Samples not filed are returned by SASE. Reports back only if interested. Original work not returned after job's completion. Considers project's budget when establishing payment. Negotiates rights purchased but generally buys all rights.
Book Design: Assigns 20 freelance design and 50 freelance illustration jobs/year. Pays by the project, $300-1,500.
Jackets/Covers: Assigns 20 freelance design and 30 freelance illustration jobs/year. Pays by project, $200-600.
Text Illustration: Assigns 50 freelance jobs/year. Pays by the project, $50-200.

***GOLDEN WEST BOOKS**, Box 80250, San Marino CA 91108. Contact: Donald Duke. Publishes Americana railroad, steamship and transportation history books. Publishes 5 titles/year; 45% require freelance illustrators.
First Contact & Terms: Buys first rights. Catalog available.
Jackets/Covers: Uses artists for jacket design. Pays $250 minimum.

GORSUCH SCARISBRICK, PUBLISHERS, 8233 Via Paseo del Norte, E-400, Scottsdale AZ 85258. Production Manager: Gay L. Orr. Specializes in college textbooks for all disciplines.
First Contact & Terms: Works with 5 freelance artists/year. Works on assignment only. Send query letter with resume, photocopies or "any suitable sample." Samples not filed are not returned. Reports only if interested. Original work not returned after job's completion. Considers complexity of project, skill and experience of artist, project's budget and turnaround time when establishing payment. Buys all rights.
Book Design: Assigns 1-5 freelance design jobs/year. Pays by the project, $200-500.
Jackets/Covers: Assigns 15-18 freelance design and 15-18 freelance illustration jobs/year. Pays by the project, $150-600.
Text Illustration: Assigns 5 freelance jobs/year. Pays by the project, $100-600.
Tips: "We do not have a lot of work, but would like to establish some long-term working arrangments with a few good artists."

GRAPHIC IMAGE PUBLICATIONS, Box 6417, Alexandria VA 22306. Assistant Art Director: Ann Ross. Specializes in hardcover, paperback originals, mass market romance, calendars. Publishes 5-10 titles/year.
First Contact & Terms: Works with 5-10 freelance artists/year, on assignment only. Send query letter with brochure or resume, business card and samples to be kept on file; write for appointment to show portfolio. Prefers 2-5 slides, Photostats or photographs as samples. Samples not filed are returned by SASE. Reports within 3 months. Original work returned to artist unless all rights purchased. Considers complexity of the project, project's budget and rights purchased when establishing payment. Rights purchased vary according to project.

The asterisk before a listing indicates that the listing is new in this edition. New markets are often the most receptive to freelance submissions.

Book Design: Assigns 5-10 jobs/year. Pays by the hour, $10-50; by the project, up to $5,000.
Jackets/Covers: Assigns 2-5 freelance design and 2-5 freelance illustration jobs/year. Pays by the hour, $10-50; by the project, up to $1,000.
Text Illustration: Assigns 20-30 jobs/year. Pays by the hour, $10-50; by the project, negotiable.
Tips: Seeks "innovative designs. Artist should accept constructive criticism."

GREAT COMMISSION PUBLICATIONS, 7401 Old York Rd., Philadelphia PA 19126. (215)635-6515. Art Director: John Tolsma. Publishes paperback original educational and promotional materials for two Presbyterian denominations.
First Contact & Terms: Works with 6 freelance artists/year. Seeks experienced illustrators, usually local artists, but some may be from out-of-state. Works on assignment only. Send query letter with brochure, resume, business card and tear sheets to be kept on file. Material not filed is returned only if requested. Reports only if interested. No originals returned at job's completion. Considers complexity of project, skill and experience of artist, and the project's budget when establishing payment. Buys all rights.
Text Illustration: Assigns 100-150 jobs per year. Prefers stylized and humorous illustration, primarily figure work with some Biblical art; 1-, 2- and 4-color art. Pays by the project, $300 maximum. Assigns from 1-13 projects at one time.

GREEN HILL PUBLISHERS, INC./Jameson Books, 722 Columbus St., Ottawa IL 61350 . (815)434-7905. Contact: Jameson Campaigne. Specializes in hardcover and paperback originals and reprints. Specializes in politics/economics, Chicago themes and early American history, authentic pre-1840 fiction and nonfiction books. Publishes 10-20 titles/year.
First Contact & Terms: Works on assignment only. Send query letter with brochure showing art style or resume, slides and photographs. Samples not filed are returned by SASE if requested by artist and accompanied by SASE. Reports within 2 weeks. To show a portfolio, mail appropriate materials. Negotiates rights purchased. Pays $600-800 for color cover.
Book Design: Assigns 5-10 freelance design and 5-10 freelance illustration jobs/year. Pays by the project, $500 minimum.
Jackets/Covers: Assigns 5-10 freelance design and 5-10 freelance illustration jobs/year. Pays by the project, $500 minimum.

GUERNICA EDITIONS, Box 633, Station N.D.G., Montreal, Quebec H4A 3R1 Canada. President: Antonio D'Alfonso. Specializes in hardcover and paperback originals of poetry, translations and essays. Publishes 8 titles/year.
First Contact & Terms: Works with 5 local freelance artists/year. Works on assignment only. Send query letter with brochure and photographs to be kept on file. Samples not filed are returned by SASE. Reports only if interested. Write for appointment to show portfolio. Originals returned to artist at job's completion depending on royalty agreement. Buys all rights.
Book Design: Assigns 3 freelance jobs/year. Pays by the project, $200-500 average.
Jackets/Covers: Assigns 3 freelance design and 3 freelance illustration jobs/year. Pays by the project, $200-500 average.
Text Illustration: Assigns 1-2 freelance jobs/year. Pays by the project, royalties, $200 maximum.

***HARVEST HOUSE PUBLISHERS**, 1075 Arrowsmith, Eugene OR 97402. (503)343-0123. Manuscript Coordinator: Nancy Olson. Specializes in hardcovers and paperbacks of adult nonfiction, children's books, adult fiction and youth material. Publishes 55 titles/year.
First Contact & Terms: Works with 5 freelance artists/year. Works on assignment only. Send query letter with brochure or resume, tear sheets and photographs. Samples are filed. Reports back only if interested. Originals sometimes returned to artist at job's completion. Call or write to schedule an appointment to show a portfolio, or mail tear sheets and final reproduction/product. Considers complexity of project, skill and experience of artist, project's budget and turnaround time when establishing payment. Buys all rights.
Jackets/Covers: Assigns 50 freelance design and 10 freelance illustration jobs/year.
Text Illustration: Assigns 5 freelance jobs/year. Pays approximately $125/page.

***HEMISPHERE PUBLISHING CORPORATION**, 79 Madison Ave., New York NY 10016. Advertising & Promotion Manager: Suzan T. Mohamed. Specializes in hardcover originals, mainly technical and scientific books and journals. Publishes 70 titles/year.
First Contact & Terms: Works with 10-15 freelance artists/year. Prefers experienced direct mail and space ad artists, design through mechanicals. Works on assignment only. Send query letter with brochure, resume and tear sheets. Samples are filed. Samples not filed are not returned. Reports back only if interested. Originals are not returned to artist at job's completion. To show a portfolio, mail roughs,

original/final art, tear sheets, final reproduction/product and dummies. Considers complexity of project, project's budget and turnaround time when establishing payment. Buys all rights.
Book Design: Assigns 0-5 freelance design jobs/year. Pays by the project, $250.
Jackets/Covers: Assigns 0-5 freelance jobs/year. Pays $300.
Tips: "Meet those deadlines set forth and agreed to. Early birds are always remembered, and late ones stay hungry. Be polite and follow instructions. Never hesitate to offer good creative advice."

***HEMKUNT PRESS**, A-78 Naraina Indl. Area Ph.I, New Delhi 110028 India. Phone: 505079. Director: Mr. G.P. Singh. Specializes in educational text books, illustrated general books for children and also books for adults. Subjects include religion and history. Publishes 30-50 titles/year.
First Contact & Terms: Works with 7-8 freelance artists/year. Works on assignment only. Send query letter with resume and samples to be kept on file. Prefers photographs and tear sheets as samples. Samples not filed are not returned. Reports only if interested. Originals not returned to artist. Considers complexity of the project, skill and experience of artist and project's budget when establishing payment. Buys all rights.
Book Design: Assigns 40-50 titles/year. Payment varies from job to job.
Jackets/Covers: Assigns 30-40 freelance design jobs/year. Payment varies.
Text Illustration: Assigns 30-40 jobs/year. Pays by the project, $50-600.

***HERALD PRESS**, 616 Walnut Ave., Scottdale PA 15683. (412)887-8500, ext. 244. Art Director: James M. Butti. Specializes in hardcover and paperback originals and reprints of inspirational, historical, juvenile, theological, biographical, fiction and nonfiction books. Publishes 24 titles/year. Catalog available.
First Contact & Terms: Works with 3-4 freelance artists/year. Works on assignment only. Send query letter with brochure or resume, tear sheets, Photostats, slides and photographs. Samples are not filed. Samples not filed are returned by SASE. Reports back within 2 weeks. Originals not returned to artist at job's completion "except in special arrangements." To show a portfolio, mail original/final art, photostats, tear sheets, final reproduction/product, photographs and slides. Considers complexity of project, skill and experience of artist and project's budget when establishing payment. Buys all rights.
Jackets/Covers: Assigns 8 freelance design and 8 freelance illustration jobs/year. Pays by the project, $150 minimum.
Text Illustration: Assigns 6 freelance jobs/year. Pays by the project, $300-600 (complete project).
Tips: "We look for a light, free and easy style that will work well in children's books."

HOLLOWAY HOUSE PUBLISHING COMPANY, 8060 Melrose Ave., Los Angeles CA 90046. (213)653-8060. President: Ralph Weinstock. Specializes in paperbacks directed to the black reader, i.e., romance books, biographies, fiction, nonfiction, gambling-game books. Publishes 30-50 titles/year.
Needs: Assigns 25-50 book design and jacket/cover illustration jobs/year.
First Contact & Terms: Works with 6-10 freelance artists/year. Professional artists only. Works on assignment only. Send query letter with resume, slides, photostats, photographs or tear sheets to be kept on file. Samples not filed are returned by SASE only if requested. Reports only if interested. Call for appointment to show portfolio. Considers project's budget when establishing payment. Rights purchased vary according to project.

HOMESTEAD PUBLISHING, Box 193, Moose WY 83012. Art Director: Carl Schreier. Specializes in hardcover and paperback originals of nonfiction, natural history, Western art and general Western regional literature. Publishes 3+ titles/year.
First Contact & Terms: Works with 16 freelance artists/year. Works on assignment only. Send query letter with samples to be kept on file or write for appointment to show portfolio. Prefers to receive as samples "examples of past work, if available (such as published books or illustrations used in magazines, etc.). For color work, slides are suitable; for b&w technical pen, Photostats. And one piece of original artwork which can be returned." Samples not filed are returned by SASE only if requested. Reports within 10 days. No original work returned after job's completion. Considers complexity of project, skill and experience of artist, project's budget and turnaround time when establishing payment. Rights purchased vary according to project.
Book Design: Assigns 6 freelance jobs/year. Pays by the project, $50-3,500 average.
Jackets/Covers: Assigns 2 freelance design and 4 freelance illustration jobs/year. Pays by the project, $50-3,500 average.
Text Illustration: Assigns 26 freelance jobs/year. Prefers technical pen illustrations, maps (using airbrush, overlays, etc.), watercolor illustrations for children's books, calligraphy and lettering for titles and headings. Pays by the hour, $5-20 average; by the project, $50-3,500 average.
Tips: "We are using more graphic, contemporary designs."

***HUMAN KINETICS PUBLISHERS**, Box 5076, Champaign IL 61820. Production Director: Ernie Noa. Hardcover and paperback originals; trade, scholarly, textbooks in sports and sports science. Imprints: Human Kinetics; Leisure Press; Life Enhancement Publications. Publisher of YMCA of the USA materials. Publishes 75 titles/year; 90% require freelance illustrators for covers; 15% for interior art.
First Contact & Terms: Works with 10 freelance artists/year. Looking for quality and reasonable cost. Send query letter with brochure or samples to be kept on file; write for appointment to show portfolio. Prefers Photostats or photos as samples. Works on assignment only. Considers complexity of project, skill and experience of artist, project's budget and turnaround time when establishing payment. Buys all rights.
Jackets/Covers: Pays by the hour, $15-35 average.
Text Illustration: Prefers very graphic pen & ink. Pays by the hour, $15-35 average; by the project, $10 minimum/illustration. Artwork includes medical illustration.
Tips: "Don't call endlessly. First send a letter, then use a follow-up call. If we arrange to meet, come with a good variety of work that shows full range of talents."

HUMANICS LIMITED, Suite 201, 1389 W. Peachtree St., Atlanta GA 30309. (404)874-2176. Executive Editor: Sarah L. Gregory. Specializes in original paperback textbooks on early childhood education and development. Publishes 10 titles/year. Also uses artists for advertising, direct mail pieces, catalogs and posters.
First Contact & Terms: Works with 5 freelance artists/year. Prefers local artists. Send query letter with resume and business card to be kept on file. Call or write for appointment to show portfolio. Prefers line drawings, finished work, published ads and brochures as samples. Samples returned by SASE. Reports within 2 weeks. Works on assignment only. No originals returned after job's completion. Buys all rights.
Book Design: Assigns 10 freelance jobs/year. Pays by the job; $75 minimum.
Jackets/Covers: Assigns 10 illustration jobs/year. Prefers b&w line drawings and mechanical designs suitable for PMS colors. Pays for illustration by the project, $15-150 average.
Text Illustration: Assigns 10 jobs/year. Prefers line illustrations. Pays by the job; "we negotiate a per book rate; $150 minimum."
Tips: Looks for "excellent ability to draw children, and a childlike quality to artwork."

CARL HUNGNESS PUBLISHING, Box 24308, Speedway IN 46224. (317)244-4792. Editorial Director: Carl Hungness. Publishes hardcover automotive originals. Publishes 2-4 titles/year. Send query letter with samples. SASE. Reports in 2 weeks. Offers $100 advance. Buys book, one-time or all rights. No pay for unused assigned work. Free catalog.

***HUNTER HOUSE PUBLISHERS**, Box 1302, Claremont CA 91711. Production Manager: Paul J. Frindt. Specializes in hardcover and paperback originals on adult and young adult nonfiction, areas of health and psychology. Publishes 6-11 titles/year.
First Contact & Terms: Works with 2-3 freelance artists/year. Prefers local artists. Works on assignment only. Send query letter with resume, slides and photographs. Samples are filed. Samples not filed are returned by SASE. Reports back within weeks. Originals not returned to artist at job's completion. Write to schedule an appointment to show a portfolio, which should include thumbnails, roughs, original/final art, photographs, slides, transparencies and dummies. Considers complexity of project, skill and experience of artist, project's budget, turnaround time and rights purchased when establishing payment. Buys all rights.
Book Design: Assigns 2-3 freelance design and 2-4 freelance illustration jobs/year. Pays by the hour, $7.50-15; by the project, $250-750.
Jackets/Covers: Assigns 3-6 freelance design and 4-8 freelance illustration jobs/year. Pays by the hour, $10-25; by the project, $250-750.
Text Illustration: Assigns 1-3 freelance jobs/year. Pays by the hour, $10-18; by the project, $150-450.
Tips: "We work closely with freelancers and prefer designers/illustrators/artists who are open to suggestion, feedback, and creative direction. Much of the time may be spent consulting; we don't appreciate impatient or excessively defensive responses. In book design we are conservative, in cover and illustration rather conceptual and somewhat understated but interested in originality."

HURTIG PUBLISHERS LTD., 10560 105th St., Edmonton, Alberta T5H 2W7 Canada. (403)426-2359. Editor-in-Chief: Elizabeth Munroe. Specializes in hardcover and paperback originals of nonfiction, primarily on Canadian-oriented topics. Publishes 10-20 titles/year.
First Contact & Terms: Artists must have "considerable experience and be based in Canada." Send query letter to be kept on file; "almost all work is specially commissioned from current sources." Reports within 3 months. Considers complexity of project, skill and experience of artist, project's budget, turnaround time and rights purchased when establishing payment. Rights purchased vary according to project.

IGNATIUS PRESS, Catholic Publisher, 2515 McAllister St., San Francisco CA 94118. Production Editor: Carolyn Lemon. Art Editor: Roxanne Lum. Catholic theology and devotional books for lay people, priests and religious readers.
First Contact & Terms: Works on assignment only. Will send art guidelines "if we are interested in the artist's work." Accepts previously published material. Send brochure showing art style or resume and photocopies. Samples not filed are not returned. Reports only if interested. To show a portfolio, mail appropriate materials; "we will contact you if interested." Pays on acceptance.
Jackets/Covers: Buys cover art from freelance artists. Prefers Christian symbols/calligraphy and religious illustrations of Jesus, saints, etc. (used on cover or in text).

INSTITUTE FOR THE STUDY OF HUMAN ISSUES (ISHI PUBLICATIONS), 210 S. 13th St., Philadelphia PA 19107. (215)732-9730. Associate Director: Edward A. Jutkowitz. Publishes hardcover and paperback political science, anthropology, folklore, drug studies, and history—originals and paperback reprints. Uses artists for dust jackets, covers, maps, flowcharts, graphs, catalogs and advertising flyers. Publishes 16-20 titles/year.
First Contact & Terms: Prefers local artists. Especially likes artists with "directly-related experience in needed areas and whose estimated charges are appropriate to the job in question. Most jobs involve jacket design and mechanicals; text art limited. Mostly black-and-white; some 2-color, little 4-color work." Send query letter with resume and samples. Reports in 2 weeks. Buys all rights. No originals returned to artist at job's completion. Works on assignment only. Samples returned by SASE. Artist supplies overlays for cover artwork and advertising art. Pays promised fee for unused assigned work. Free catalog.
Book Design: Assigns 4 freelance design and illustration jobs/year. Pays by the project, $100-350 average.
Jackets/Covers: Assigns approximately 12 freelance design and 9 illustration jobs/year. Prefers line drawings or mezzotint and screened photos for cover illustrations. Pays by the project, $75-275 average; $250-350 for jacket mechanicals.
Text Illustration: Assigns approximately 4 freelance jobs/year. Prefers line art. Pays by the project, $100-300 average. Includes "maps, charts, graphs, other simple line art and labeling."
Tips: "In the nonfiction area the new emphasis is on simplicity of design; the use of decorative typefaces and strong color combinations is very much in evidence."

***INSTITUTE OF INTERNATIONAL EDUCATION**, Communications Division, 809 United Nations Plaza, New York NY 10017. Senior Production Editor: Ellen Goodman. Specializes in information flyers, paperback catalogs and statistical analysis; also annual report. Publishes 11 titles/year.
First Contact & Terms: Works with 4 freelance artists/year. Send query letter with brochure, resume and samples to be kept on file. Write for appointment to show portfolio. Rights purchased vary.
Book Design: Uses artists for various jobs depending on project. Pays by the project.
Text Illustration: Assigns "a few" jobs/year.

***INTERNATIONAL MARINE PUBLISHING CO.**, 21 Elm St., Camden ME 04843. (207)236-4342. Production Manager: Molly Mulhern. Specializes in hardcovers and paperbacks on marine (nautical) topics. Publishes 25 titles/year.
First Contact & Terms: Works with 12 freelance artists/year. Prefers local artists. Works on assignment only. Send resume and tear sheets. Samples are filed. Reports back only if interested. Originals are not returned to artist at job's completion. Write to schedule an appointment to show a portfolio, which should include roughs and tear sheets; "then follow with phone call." Considers project's budget when establishing payment. Buys one-time rights.
Book Design: Assigns 10 freelance design and 1 freelance illustration jobs/year. Pays by the project, $50-450.
Jackets/Covers: Assigns 15-25 freelance design and 3 freelance illustration jobs/year. Pays by the project, $200-700.

> ***"It's great to see people really drawing again. For too long, trendy illustrators were getting away with murder. It's not enough to be a good draftsman; you have to have a good concept."***
>
> ***—Pearl Law, Little, Brown & Company***
> ***Boston, Massachusetts***

Text Illustration: Assigns 3 freelance jobs/year. Prefers technical drawings. Pays by the hour, $15-40.
Tips: "Write with a resume and sample; then follow with a call; then come by to visit."

JALMAR PRESS, Bldg. 2, 45 Hitching Post Dr., Rolling Hill Estates CA 90274-4297. (213)547-1240. President: Bradley L. Winch.
First Contact & Terms: Works with 5-10 freelance artists/year. Works on assignment only. Send query letter with brochure showing art style. Samples not filed are returned by SASE. Reports only if interested. Considers complexity of project, client's budget and turnaround time when establishing payment. Buys all rights.

JANUS BOOK PUBLISHERS, 2501 Industrial Pkwy. W., Hayward CA 94545. (415)785-9625 or (415)887-7070. Production Manager: Carol Gee. Publishes hardcovers and remedial reading materials and soft-cover workbooks for high school and basic adult education. Publishes 25 titles/year.
First Contact & Terms: Works on assignment only. Send samples or arrange interview to show portfolio; prefers local artists. SASE. Reports within 3 weeks. Buys various rights. Provide resume and "photocopies of samples" to be kept on file for future assignments. Artist supplies overlays for 2-color cover artwork; sometimes for advertising art. Free catalog. Also uses artists for catalog design. Pays $25/hour.
Book Design: Assigns 10 jobs/year. Layout done inhouse. Offers advance "upon completion of acceptable roughs."
Jackets/Covers: Uses "2-color and 4-color, very direct and very simple designs." Pays for design and illustration by the project, $1,500-2,000 average.
Text Illustration: Assigns 12-15 jobs/year. Especially seeks realistic drawings. Pays $40-50 for ¼ or ½-page spot drawings; also pays by the project, $50 (single drawing)-2,400 (entire book). Buys b&w line drawings and washes. Offers advance "upon completion of acceptable roughs." Also uses a realistic type of cartoon. "Our 'cartoons' are used to illustrate meaning of words and phrases, either line or halftone wash work. Artist is given specifications, and asked to supply rough, revised, rough and finished art." Pays $35-50, b&w.
Tips: "Clear, concise, figure work with emphasis on minority groups (black, Chicano, Asian). Simple and direct, no fussy detail. Beginners should show their work to anyone who will take the time to look at it. Keep trying."

JUDSON PRESS, American Baptist Churches USA, Board of Educational Ministries, Publishing Division, Valley Forge PA 19481. Senior Artist: David E. Monyer. Specializes in paperbacks on religious themes (inspirational, Christian education, church administration, missions). Publishes 10-12 titles/year; 90% require freelance cover designers.
First Contact & Terms: Works with 4 or more freelance artists/year. Artists with book cover experience only. Send query letter, brochure/flyer, resume and samples to be kept on file. Prefers examples of book cover designs as samples. Samples not kept on file are returned by SASE. "We don't report on acceptance or rejection, but keep samples on file." Works on assignment only. No originals returned to artist at job's completion.
Jackets/Covers: Assigns 8-10 design and 1-2 illustration jobs/year. Prefers bold graphics, title dominant, for cover designs. Pays by the job, $500 average; "We pay for type and stats."
Text Illustration: Assigns 1-2 freelance jobs/year. Prefers realistic line drawings. Pays by the project.
Tips: "Stay with bold graphics, up-to-date typography."

***KALEIDOSCOPIX, INC., Children's Book Division**, Box 389, Franklin MA 02038-0389. President: J.A. Kruza. "Kaleidoscopix, Inc. has two new divisions: book publishing and audio cassette publishing. The products of both are marketed to an upscale audience like tourists through seacoast gift stores. Titles include historical and nautical material relevant to the area, tourism guides, and children's books for ages 3-7."
First Contact & Terms: "We are reviewing manuscripts and/or illustrations. And we are contracting with effective communicators with either in-depth knowledge, or storytelling or singing ability."
Text Illustration: Pays by the project, $300-1,000.
Tips: "We are looking for capability to produce quality illustrations that do not require excessive additional work on someone else's part to reproduce and print."

KAR-BEN COPIES, INC., 6800 Tildenwood Lane, Rockville MD 20852. Editor: Madeline Wikler. Specializes in hardcovers and paperbacks on juvenile Judaica. Publishes 8 titles/year.
First Contact & Terms: Works with 3-5 freelance artists/year. Send query letter with Photostats or tear sheets to be kept on file or returned. Samples not filed are returned by SASE. Reports within 2 weeks only by SASE. Originals returned after job's completion. Considers skill and experience of artist and turnaround time when establishing payment. Buys all rights.
Text Illustration: Assigns 3-5 freelance jobs/year. Pays by the project, $500-1,500 average, or royalty.

***B. KLEIN PUBLICATIONS INC.**, Box 8503, Coral Springs FL 33065. Editor: Bernard Klein. Publishes reference books, such as the *Guide to American Directories*. Publishes approximately 15-20 titles/year.
Needs: Uses artists for jacket design and direct mail brochures. Submit resume and samples. Pays $50-300.

***KNEES PAPERBACK PUBLISHING CO.**, 4115 Marshall St., Dallas TX 75210. (214)948-3613. Managing Editor: Dorothy J. Watkins. Specializes in paperback originals on poetry, children's and prose books. Publishes 2 titles/year; 15% require freelance designers; 15% require freelance illustrators.
First Contact & Terms: Works with 2 freelance artists/year. Local artists only. Send query letter with business card to be kept on file. Prefers slides as samples. Reports within 2 weeks. Works on assignment only. No originals returned to artist at job's completion. Considers complexity of project, and skill and experience of artist when establishing payment. Buys one-time rights or negotiates.
Book Design: Assigns 7 freelance jobs/year. Pays by the hour, the project or negotiates.
Tips: Artists should "always adhere to the given schedule." Current trends in the field are toward "more abstract design." Especially looks for "creativity, form and projection" when reviewing samples.

LACE PUBLICATIONS, Box 10037, Denver CO 80210-0037. Managing Editor: Artemis OakGrove. Specializes in paperbacks of lesbian fiction. Publishes 5 titles/year.
First Contact & Terms: Works with 10-15 freelance artists/year. Lesbians or sexually-sensitive women only. Works on assignment only. Send query letter with resume, b&w photographs or photocopies to be kept on file except for "the ones I don't like." Samples not filed are returned by SASE. Reports within 1 month. Original work returned after the job's completion; cover art returned only if requested. Considers complexity of project, skill and experience of artist, and project's budget when establishing payment. Rights purchased vary according to project; all rights purchased on cover art.
Jackets/Covers: Assigns 5 freelance design and varying number of freelance illustration jobs/year. Pays by the project, $75 minimum.

LIBRARIES UNLIMITED, Box 263, Littleton CO 80160-0263. (303)770-1220. Marketing Director: Shirley Lambert. Specializes in hardcover and paperback original reference books concerning library science and school media for librarians, educators and researchers. Publishes 45 titles/year.
First Contact & Terms: Works with 4-5 freelance artists/year. Works on assignment only. Send query letter with resume and photocopies. Samples not filed are returned only if requested. Reports within 2 weeks. No originals returned to artist at job's completion. Considers complexity of project, skill and experience of artist, and project's budget when establishing payment. Buys all rights.
Book Design: Assigns 2-4 freelance illustration jobs/year. Pays by the project, $100 minimum.
Jackets/Covers: Assigns 45 freelance design jobs/year. Pays by the project, $250 minimum.
Tips: "We look for the ability to draw or illustrate without overly-loud cartoon techniques. We need the ability to use two-color effectively, with screens and screen builds. We ignore anything sent to us that is in four-color. We also need a good feel for typefaces, and we prefer experience with books."

***THE PHILIP LIEF GROUP, INC.**, 319 E. 52nd St., New York NY 10022. Editor: Deborah Shina. Specializes in paperback originals. Produces 40 titles/year.
First Contact & Terms: Works with 20 freelance artists/year. Send brochure and resume to be kept on file. Reports within 2 months. Original work returned after job's completion. Negotiates rights purchased.
Book Design: Assigns 5 jobs/year. Uses artists for layout through mechanicals. Negotiates pay.
Jackets/Covers: Assigns 6 freelance design and 6 freelance illustration jobs/year. Negotiates pay.
Text Illustration: Assigns 18 freelance jobs/year. Prefers b&w, various styles. Negotiates pay.

LIFE CYCLE BOOKS, Box 792, Lewiston NY 14092-0792. (416)690-5860. Manager: Paul Broughton. Specializes in reprint paperbacks, pamphlets and brochures. Publishes 4-8 titles/year.
First Contact & Terms: Works with 2-3 freelance artists/year. Works on assignment only. Send query letter with resume, tear sheets, Photostats, photocopies, slides and photographs. Samples not filed are returned by SASE. Reports back only if interested. Original work not returned after job's completion. Considers complexity of project, skill and experience of artist and project's budget when establishing payment. Negotiates rights purchased.
Jackets/Covers: Assigns 2-3 freelance illustration jobs/year. Pays by the project, $200-500.

LITTLE, BROWN AND COMPANY ADULT TRADE DIVISION, 34 Beacon St., Boston MA 02106. (617)227-0730. Publishes mainstream hardcover originals. Publishes 150 + titles/year.
First Contact & Terms: Send samples or arrange interview to show portfolio. Buys first and reprint

rights. "We have no artist's guidelines but will gladly answer questions."
Jackets/Covers: Buys typographic design and all types of illustration and photography. Pays by the project, $800-2,000.

THE LITURGICAL PRESS, Collegeville MN 56321. (612)363-2218. Art Director: Don Bruno. Specializes in hardcovers and paperbacks. Publishes about 35-50 books/year concerning liturgy (worship) and scripture.
First Contact & Terms: Send query letter with resume and Photostats. Samples not filed are returned. Reports within 1 month. To show a portfolio, an artist should mail appropriate materials such as press sheets. Buys one-time rights.
Book Design: Assigns 5-10 freelance design and 2-5 freelance illustration jobs/year. Pays by the project, $500-1,000.
Jackets/Covers: Assigns 5-10 freelance design and 2-5 freelance illustration jobs/year. Pays by the project, $300-500.
Text Illustration: Assigns 2 freelance jobs/year. Prefers line art. Pays by the project, $300 minimum.

LLEWELLYN PUBLICATIONS, Box 64383, St. Paul MN 55164. Art Director: Terry Buske. Specializes in paperback originals. Publishes metaphysical, astrology and New Age books. Works with at least 6 freelance artists/year. Uses artists for book cover designs and inside art, color and b&w.
First Contact & Terms: Works on assigment only. Send query letter with samples to be kept on file. No preference regarding types of samples, but "must be professionally submitted. No roughs, fragments or photocopies of other than excellent quality. Do not send actual artwork." Samples not kept on file are returned by SASE only if requested. Reports within 2 weeks after receipt of submission if SASE is supplied. Negotiates payment. Considers project's budget, skill and experience of artist, and rights purchased when establishing payment. Negotiates rights purchased.
Jackets/Covers: Assigns 15 freelance illustration jobs/year. Pays by the project, $300-600.
Text Illustration: Assigns 5 freelance jobs/year. Prefers pen & ink. Pays per illustration, $20-40.
Tips: "People expect more of a high-tech, photo-realistic or refined look for the product. We are interested in artists who express our themes in more general terms reaching a broad audience. We are interested in realistic (photo-realism) art." Especially looks for "technique and professionalism" in artist's work. Uses many airbrush paintings.

LODESTAR BOOKS, division of E.P. Dutton, 2 Park Ave., New York NY 10016. (212)725-1818. Editor: Rosemary Brosnan. Publishes young adult fiction (12-16 years) and nonfiction hardcovers, fiction and nonfiction for ages 9-11 and 10-14 years and nonfiction picture books. Publishes 16-20 titles/year.
First Contact & Terms: Send query letter with samples or arrange interview. Especially looks for "knowledge of book requirements, previous jackets, good color, strong design and ability to draw people and action" when reviewing samples. Prefers to buy all rights.
Jackets/Covers: Assigns approximately 10-12 jackets/year. Pays $600 minimum, color.
Tips: In young adult fiction, there is a trend toward "covers that are more realistic with the focus on one or two characters. In nonfiction, strong, simple graphic design, often utilizing a photograph. Two-color jackets are popular for nonfiction; occasionally full color is used."

***LOLLIPOP POWER BOOKS**, Box 277, Carrboro NC 27510. Editor: Margaret Stephens. Publishes alternative picture books for ages 2-8, nonsexist, multi-racial.
First Contact & Terms: Works with 1 freelance artist/year. Works on assignment only. Send brochure showing art style and photocopies. Samples are filed. Samples not filed are returned if accompanied by a SASE. "We file until we have a manuscript ready, then send out letters to all our artists to see if they want to submit illustrations for that book." Considers project's budget when establishing payment.
Book Design: Pays by the project.
Jackets/Covers: Pays by the project.
Text Illustration: Pays by the project.

***MCDOUGAL, LITTELL & COMPANY**, One American Plaza, 1560 Sherman Ave., Evanston IL 60201. (312)869-2300. Senior Designer: Mary MacDonald. Specializes in elementary-high school textbooks.
First Contact & Terms: Send query letter with brochure or resume, tear sheets, Photostats, slides and photographs. Samples are filed. Samples not filed are returned. Call or write to schedule an appointment to show a portfolio. Considers complexity of project, skill and experience of artist and project's budget when establishing payment. Negotiates rights purchased.

***McGRAW HILL PUBLISHING**, College Division, 1221 6th Ave., New York NY 10020. Art Director, College and University Division: Merrill Haber. Submit samples.
Needs: Uses artists for book and jacket design; technical, medical and biological illustrations.

***MACMILLAN PUBLISHING CO.**, School Division, 866 Third Ave., New York NY 10022. (212)702-7925. Design Director: Zlata Paces. Publishes hardcover and auxiliary originals and reprints for elementary and high schools. Publishes 250 titles/year; 30% of which require freelance designers; 80% use freelance illustrators.
First Contact & Terms: Send letter of inquiry, resume and samples. Prefers tear sheets, stats, color photocopies, etc. as samples or drop off portfolio (overnight). Samples will be kept on file for future reference unless accompanied by SASE. Works on assignment only. Originals returned to artist at job's completion.
Book Design: Assigns 10 jobs/year. Uses freelance artists for layout and type specs. Pays by the hour, $10-15 average; also pays by the day.
Jackets/Covers: Assigns 30 jobs/year. Pays for illustration by the project; $200-400 average.
Text Illustration: Assigns 800-1,500 jobs/year. Pays by the project, "depends on assignment."

***MARVEL BOOKS**, 387 Park Ave. S., New York NY 10028. Art Director: Lillian Lovitt. Publishes liscened product children's books. Publishes 50-100 titles/year.
First Contact & Terms: Works with 50 freelance artists/year. Works on assignment only. Send query letter with tear sheets and photocopies. Samples not filed are not returned. Reports back only if interested. Originals are returned to the artist at job's completion. Considers complexity of project, skill and experience of artist, project's budget, turnaround time and rights purchased when establishing payment. Buys all rights.
Book Design: Assigns 10-20 freelance design and 50-100 freelance illustration jobs/year. Pays by the project, $2,000-8,000.
Jackets/Covers: Assigns 10-20 freelance design and 50-100 freelance illustration jobs/year. Pays by the project, $500-1,000.
Tips: "Send only your best work in photocopy form with card that has sample on it."

MASTERY EDUCATION, 85 Main St., Watertown MA 02172. Managing Editor: Elena Wright. Specializes in paperback originals of teacher-directed instruction books. Publishes 10 titles/year, K-8th grade materials.
First Contact & Terms: Works with 10 artists/year. Artists should have experience in educational textbooks. Works on assignment only. Send resume, tear sheets and photocopies. Samples not filed are returned by SASE. Reports only if interested. No originals returned to artist at job's completion. Considers complexity of project and project's budget when establishing payment. Buys all rights.
Book Design: Assigns 2 freelance design jobs/year. Pays by the project.
Text Illustration: Assigns hundreds of jobs/year. Pays by the project.
Tips: "Look at what is good in children's trade book art and show how you can transplant that excitement into elementary textbooks. School books require realistic line art of children at exact proportions for each year of age. No cartoon-style exaggerated features. We need real-looking kids, with dignity and intelligence."

***MECKLER PUBLISHING CORPORATION**, 11 Ferry Ln. W., Westport CT 06880-5808. (203)226-6967. Circulation Director: Al Henderson. Specializes in hardcover and paperback textbooks on computers, libraries, information and publishing. Publishes 50 titles/year.
First Contact & Terms: Works with 3 or more freelance artists/year. Send query letter with brochure. Samples are not filed. Samples not filed are returned by SASE. Does not report back. Originals not returned to artist at job's completion unless requested. To show a portfolio, mail appropriate materials. Buys all rights.
Tips: "We buy promotion design as well as occasional covers, illustrations, etc."

MEDIA PROJECTS INCORPORATED, Suite 340, 305 2nd Ave., New York NY 10003. (212)777-4510. Assistant Editorial Director: Ellen Coffey. Specializes in hardcover and paperback originals on juveniles, lifestyles and cookery. Publishes 15 titles/year.
First Contact & Terms: Works with 3-6 freelance artists/year. Works on assignment only. Send query letter with brochure showing art style or resume and tear sheets, Photostats, photocopies, slides and photographs. Samples not filed are returned by SASE. Reports within 2 weeks. Original work returned at job's completion. Considers project's budget when establishing payment. Negotiates rights purchased.
Book Design: Assigns 10 freelance design and 10 freelance illustration jobs/year. Pays by the project, negotiable amount.
Jackets/Covers: Assigns 10 freelance design and 10 freelance illustration jobs/year. Pays by the project, negotiable amount.
Text Illustration: Assigns 10 freelance jobs/year. Prefers line drawings. Pays by the project, negotiable amount.

***MERCURY PRINTING CO.**, 15126 Downey Ave., Paramount CA 90723. (213)531-4550. Vice President: Allen B. Hughes. Specializes in legal books. Publishes 4 titles/year.
First Contact & Terms: Works with 1 local freelance artist/year on assignment only. Send query letter with resume to be kept on file; call for appointment to show portfolio. Prefers tear sheets as samples. Samples not filed are returned by SASE. Reports only if interested. Originals returned to artist at job's completion. Considers project's budget when establishing payment. Buys all rights.

MILADY PUBLISHING CORP., 3839 White Plains Rd., Bronx, New York NY 10467. (800)223-8055. Editor: Mary Healy. Publishes textbooks and audiovisual aids for vocational schools.
First Contact & Terms: Works on assignment only. Send query letter with Photostats to be kept on file. Samples not filed are returned by SASE. Reports only if interested. Write for appointment to show portfolio. Pays by the hour, $5 minimum; by the project depending on nature of project and length of time needed for completion. Considers complexity of the project, client's budget and skill and experience of artist when establishing payment. Buys all rights. Catalog costs $1.
Needs: Works with 3 freelance artists/year during overloads. Especially important is ability to produce accurate and neat mechanicals and clean line illustrations. Uses technical and "fashion features and hairstyles" illustrations.
Tips: "Build up skills in illustrating hands and hair."

BARRY LEONARD STEFFAN MIRENBURG, DESIGN, 413 City Island Ave., New York NY 10464. Design Director: Barry L.S. Mirenburg. Specializes in hardcover and paperback nonfiction originals. Publishes 10 titles/year; 20% require freelance designers; 80% require freelance illustrators. Also uses artists for posters, annual reports, graphic design, trademarks, etc.
First Contact & Terms: Works with 12 freelance artists/year. Works on assignment only. Send brochure/flyer or resume and samples; samples not returned. Sometimes reports back whether to expect possible future assignments. Negotiates rights purchased.
Book Design: Assigns 12 jobs/year. Uses artists for layout, type spec and mechanicals. Pays "going rates."
Jackets/Covers: Assigns 20% to freelance designers and 80% of needs to freelance illustrators. Prefers b&w line drawings, paintings, color washes, gray opaques; no cartoon style. Payment varies.
Text Illustration: Number of jobs assigned/year varies. Prefers b&w line drawings, paintings, color washes, gray opaques; no cartoon style. Payment varies.

MODERN CURRICULUM PRESS, 13900 Prospect Rd., Cleveland OH 44136. (216)238-2222. Art Director: John K. Crum. Specializes in supplemental text books, readers and workbooks. Publishes 100 titles/year. Also needs local artists for advertising and mechanicals.
First Contact & Terms: All freelance. Works on assignment only. Send resume and tear sheets of children and animals to be kept on file. Samples not kept on file are returned by SASE. Reports back only if interested. Buys all rights.
Book Design: Assigns 6-10 freelance jobs/year. Uses artists for layout, mechanicals, type specs. Pays by the project, on acceptance. Payment varies.
Jackets/Covers: Pays by the project; payment varies.
Text Illustration: Prefers animated real life themes "nothing too cartoony; must be accurate." Pays by the project; payment varies.
Tips: Looks for "professional, serious illustrators who know production techniques. Don't drag in oil paintings, sculpture, etc."

MODERN PUBLISHING, 155 East 55th St., New York NY 10022. (212)826-0850. Art Director: Jill Steinberg. Specializes in hardcovers and paperbacks and coloring books. Publishes approximately 20 titles/year.
First Contact & Terms: Works with 15 freelance artists/year. Works on assignment only. Send query letter with resume and samples. Samples not filed are returned only if requested. Reports only if interested. Original work not returned at job's completion. Considers turnaround time and rights purchased when establishing payment. Buys all rights.
Jackets/Covers: Pays by the project, $100-200 average per cover, "usually 4 books per series."
Text Illustration: Pays by the project, $15-20 average per page (line art), "48-382 pages per book, always 4 books in series."

***MOTT MEDIA INC., PUBLISHERS**, 1000 E. Huron, Milford MI 48042. Contact: George Mott. Publishes hardcover and paperback Christian books and textbooks. Publishes 20-25 titles/year. Also uses artists for posters and mailables.
First Contact & Terms: Works on assignment only. Reports back in one month on future assignment

possibilities. Provide resume, flyer, tear sheet and letter of inquiry to be kept on file for possible future assignments. SASE. Buys all rights. No originals returned to artist at job's completion. Artist supplies all color overlays. Pays ½ on acceptance of sketch and ½ on submission of finished art. Free catalog.
Needs: Special need for book cover design, and internal illustration for children's books. Assigns 20-25 book design jobs/year. Minimum payment: $400 + for complete cover art and mechanicals; $150 for inside b&w sketch.

JOHN MUIR PUBLICATIONS, Box 613, Santa Fe NM 87504. (505)982-4078. President: Ken Luboff. Publishes trade paperback nonfiction. "We specialize in auto repair manuals and travel books and are always actively looking for new illustrations in these fields." Publishes 15 titles/year.
First Contact & Terms: Works with 5-6 freelance artists/year. Send query letter with resume and samples to be kept on file. Write for appointment to show portfolio. Accepts any type of sample "as long as it's professionally presented." Samples not filed are returned by SASE. Reports within months; "it depends on how harried our schedule is at the time." Originals returned at job's completion. Considers complexity of project, skill and experience of artist, project's budget, turnaround time and rights purchased when establishing payment. Buys all rights.
Jackets/Covers: Assigns 10-15 freelance design and freelance illustration jobs/year. Mostly 4 color. Negotiates payment.
Text Illustration: Assigns 10-15 freelance jobs/year. Usually prefers pen & ink. Negotiates payment.

***NAMASTE PUBLICATIONS**, Box 262, Marshfield MO 65706. Contact: Bob La Loge. Estab. 1986. Specializes in paperback poetry and nonfiction/fiction short stories and nonfiction new age books. Publishes 5 titles/year.
First Contact & Terms: Works with 3 freelance artists/year. Send Photostats. Samples not filed are returned by SASE. Reports back within 3 weeks. Originals not returned to artist at job's completion. To show a portfolio, mail Photostats. Considers project's budget when establishing payment. Buys first rights.
Book Design: Pays by the project, $5 minimum.
Text Illustration: Assigns 5 freelance jobs/year. Pays by the project, $5 minimum.
Tips: "We don't use that much art work during the year. So we would appreciate sending a query letter and a photocopy of one piece. This will give us some idea, and we can contact artists if and when we need something. On our last project, we contacted three different artists and will accept the best one submitted. This is the way we will be going in the future. If they want the work back, (which is not used) we suggest they send SASE. The work used is often spliced and dissected to use as we deem necessary, therefore, it's often difficult to return it. We give artist a free copy, however."

***NAVPRESS**, Box 6000, Colorado Springs CO 80934. (303)598-1212. Art Director: Wendy Reis or Naomi Trujillo. Publishes Christian books, Bible studies, and a bimonthly magazine, *Discipleship Journal*. Publishes 35 titles/year.
First Contact & Terms: Works with 15 freelance artists/year. Works on assignment only. Send query letter with brochure or tear sheets, slides and photographs. Samples are filed. Samples not filed are returned by SASE only if requested. Reports back within 1 month. Originals returned to artist at job's completion. Call or write to schedule an appointment to show a portfolio, which should include tear sheets, slides and transparencies. Considers complexity of project, skill and experience of artist, project's budget, turnaround time and rights purchased when establishing payment. Buys one-time rights.
Magazine Design: Assigns 15-20 freelance illustration jobs/year. Pays by the project, $350-1,000.
Jackets/Covers: Pays by the project, $350-1,000.
Tips: "Call or inquire by mail first. Include only what best represents your work and what is your best work. Sending updated samples as you get them is nice."

***NBM PUBLISHING CO.**, 35-53 70th St., Jackson Heights NY 11372. (718)458-3199. Publisher: Terry Nantier. Publishes graphic novels including *The Mercenary*, *Corfo Maltese* and *Roxanna* for an audience of 18-24 year olds. Genres: adventure, fantasy, mystery, science fiction, horror and social parodies. Themes: outer space, future science and social commentary. Circ. 5-10,000. Original artwork returned after publication. Sample copies available.
Illustrations: Uses freelance artists for lettering, paste-up and covers. Send query letter with resume and samples. Samples are filed. Samples not filed are returned by SASE. Reports back within 2 weeks. To show a portfolio, mail photocopies of original pencil art or inking. Negotiates payment for graphic novels.

***THOMAS NELSON PUBLISHERS**, Box 141000, Nashville TN 37214-1000. (615)889-9000. Vice President: Robert J. Schwalb. Specializes in hardcover and originals, Bibles and textbooks on religious subjects. Publishes 150 titles/year.
First Contact & Terms: Works with 30 freelance artists/year. Works on assignment only. Contact

Artist: Don Weller

As the cover of a Bible study this illustration conveys "a way to cross stormy seas, which is symbolic of a realization," according to illustrator Don Weller of Los Angeles. Weller designed this piece as part of a series of studies published by Navpress of Colorado Springs, Colorado. Weller used pen-and-ink and colored film to create the feeling of powerful forces which might capsize our human efforts. Weller, who has been an illustrator for over twenty years, is "very easy to work with, good at conceptualizing and always makes deadlines," according to Navpress art director Wendy Reis, who bought all rights to this illustration.

through artists' agent or send query letter with brochure or tear sheets, Photostats, slides and photographs. Samples are filed. Samples not filed are returned by SASE if requested. Reports back within 7 days. Return of originals depends on rights purchased. Call to schedule an appointment to show a portfolio, which should include roughs, tear sheets and slides. Considers project's budget and rights purchased when establishing payment. Negotiates rights purchased.

Jackets/Covers: Assigns 100 freelance design and 35 freelance illustration jobs/year. Pays by the project, $100-5,000.

Text Illustration: Assigns 20 freelance jobs/year. Pays by the project, $15-250.

Tips: "We also purchase art for advertising and newsletters." Prefers "people, Biblical scenes and artifacts, rendered in realistic style and interesting point of view. Prefer gouache, dyes, watercolor as well as pen & ink (Rapidograph style.)"

NELSON-HALL INC., 111 N. Canal St., Chicago IL 60606. Vice President: Stephen A. Ferrara. Publishes 85 titles/year; 100% require freelance designers, 50% require freelance illustrators. Also uses artists for technical illustration, advertising layout and catalog illustration.
First Contact & Terms: Submit resume and photocopies. Buys all rights. Pays on acceptance. Catalog available.
Book Design: Assigns 100 jobs/year.
Jackets/Covers: Pays $300, jacket design plus type.

***NEW PAGES: ALTERNATIVES IN PRINT & MEDIA**, 4426 S. Belsay Rd., Grand Blanc MI 48439. (313)743-8055. Publisher: Casey Hill. Publishes 3 issues/year.
First Contact & Terms: Send query letter with brochure. Samples are not filed. Samples not filed are returned by SASE. Reports back within 10 days. Originals returned to artist at job's completion. Considers complexity of project and skill and experience of artist when establishing payment. Buys first rights.
Tips: "We are looking for work relating to books, publishing, or other media. Wild, political, social-change oriented work wanted."

NEW SOCIETY PUBLISHERS, 4722 Baltimore Ave., Philadelphia PA 19143. (215)726-6543. Production Director: T.L. Hill. Specializes in hardcover and paperback originals and reprints on nonviolent social change. Publishes 15 titles/year.
First Contact & Terms: Works with 4 freelance artists/year. Works on assignment only. Send query letter with samples to be kept on file. Call for appointment to show portfolio. Prefers Photostats and photographs as samples. Samples not filed are returned only by SASE. Reports only if interested. Original work may or may not be returned to the artist. Considers complexity of the project, project's budget and rights purchased when establishing payment. Negotiates rights purchased.
Jackets/Covers: Assigns 8-10 freelance design jobs/year. Pays by the project, $50 for 3 sketches. "If one is accepted then $150 for completed mechanicals. Additional must be negotiated—normally on 2-color jobs only.
Text Illustration: Assigns 1-2 jobs/year. Prefers pen & ink line drawings. Pays by the hour, $5-10 or negotiated by the project.

NICHOLS PUBLISHING COMPANY, Box 96, New York NY 10024. (212)580-8079. President: Linda Kahn. Specializes in hardcover professional and reference books in architecture, business, education, technology and energy. Publishes 35 titles/year.
First Contact & Terms: Works with 4 freelance artists/year. Works on promotion assignment only. Artists must be in New York area. Send query letter with brochure and resume. Samples not kept on file are returned only if requested. Reports only if interested. Call or write for appointment to show portfolio, which should include promotion brochures. Considers complexity of project, skill and experience of artist and project's budget when establishing payment. Rights purchased vary.

OCTAMERON PRESS, 4805A Eisenhower Ave., Alexandria VA 22304. President: Anna Leider. Specializes in paperbacks—college money and college admission guides and travel guides. Publishes 10-15 titles/year.
First Contact & Terms: Works with 1 or 2 artists/year. Prefers local artists only. Works on assignment only. Send query letter with brochure showing art style or resume and photocopies. Samples not filed are returned. Reports within 1 week. Original work returned at job's completion. Considers complexity of project and project's budget when establishing payment. Rights purchased vary according to project.
Jackets/Covers: Works with variable number of freelance designers/year. Pays by the project, $75-250.
Text Illustration: Works with variable number of freelance artists/year. Prefers line drawings from photographs. Pays by the project, $35-75.

ODDO PUBLISHING, INC., Box 68, Fayetteville GA 30214. (404)461-7627. Vice President: Charles W. Oddo. Specializes in hardcovers on juvenile fiction. Publishes 6-10 titles/year; 100% require freelance illustration.
First Contact & Terms: Works with 3 freelance artists/year. Send query letter with brochure, resume, business card, samples or tear sheets to be kept on file. Accepts "whatever is best for artist to present" as samples. Samples not kept on file are returned by SASE only if requested. Reports only if interested. Works on assignment only. Write for appointment to show portfolio. No originals returned to artist at job's completion. Buys all rights.
Book Design: Assigns 3 freelance jobs/year. Pays for illustration and design combined by the project, $250 minimum.
Text Illustration: Assigns 3 freelance jobs/year. Artwork purchased includes science fiction/fantasy.

Tips: Portfolio should include "human form to show that artist can illustrate accurately. Chances are if an artist can illustrate people that look real, his or her talents are highly refined. We also look for quality cartoon-illustrating ability. We expect to see various styles to indicate the artist's versatility. Artists tend to want to show their entire portfolios without first determining what the publisher needs and what styles of art are in the portfolios that meet those needs.

ONCE UPON A PLANET, INC., 65-42 Fresh Meadow Lane, Fresh Meadows NY 11365. Art Director: Alis Jordan. Publishes trade paperback originals, greeting cards, pads and novelty books (humor). Uses artists for book design, cover and text illustration, mechanicals, displays, brochures and flyers.
First Contact & Terms: Prefers local artists. Send query letter with brochure showing art style or resume, tear sheets, photocopies and/or slides. Works on assignment only. If originals are sent, SASE must be enclosed for return. Reports in 3-5 weeks. Prefers to buy all rights, but will negotiate. Payment is negotiated.
Book Design: Assigns 8-12 jobs/year. Uses artists for layout, type specifications.
Jackets/Covers: Assigns 6 jobs/year. Uses 2-color art, occasionally 4-color art.
Text Illustration: Assigns 8-12 jobs/year. Uses b&w line drawings and washes.

101 PRODUCTIONS, 834 Mission St., San Francisco CA 94103. Art Director: Lynne O'Neil. Specializes in softcover trade books, cookbooks, travel guides and restaurant guides. Publishes 10-12 titles/year; 25% require freelance illustrators.
First Contact & Terms: Works with 4 freelance artists/year. Send query letter with resume and samples to be kept on file. Prefers good-quality photocopies of b&w line drawings, etc., related to food and food preparation; do not send original art. Samples returned with SASE only.
Jackets/Covers: Photography used for covers.
Tips: "Know your market—we look for food and cooking subjects and don't want to see portfolios that lack these. We also prefer to work with local illustrators. Will consider Southern California based artist."

***ONESS PRESS**, Box 336, Calpella CA 95418. (707)462-9957. Editor/Publisher: Mycall Sunanda. Specializes in paperback originals and reprints on children's liberation, natural sexual healing, wholistic health and group marriage.
First Contact & Terms: Prefers parents, nature lovers, sufi, new artists. Send query letter with resume, tear sheets, Photostats, slides and photographs. Samples are filed. Samples not filed are returned only if requested. Reports back within 3 weeks only if interested. Originals returned to artist at job's completion if requested. To show a portfolio, mail thumbnails, roughs, Photostats, tear sheets and photographs. Considers complexity of project, skill and experience of artist and project's budget when establishing payment.
Book Design: Assigns 2-7 freelance design and 5-10 freelance illustration jobs/year. Pays by the hour, $5-15; by the project, $15-100.
Jackets/Covers: Prefers kids, nature, coupling, healing as themes. Pays by the hour, $5-15; by the project, $10-100.
Text Illustration: Assigns 3 freelance jobs/year. Prefers line drawing or collage. Pays by the hour, $5-15; by the project, $10-100.
Tips: "Submit photocopy sample of alternative themes, mostly of people doing natural family trips, playful."

OTTENHEIMER PUBLISHERS, INC., 300 Reisterstown Rd., Baltimore MD 21208. (301)484-2100. Art Director: Diane Parameros Shea. Specializes in mass market-oriented hardcover and paperback originals and reprints—encyclopedias, dictionaries, self-help books, cookbooks, children's coloring and activity books, story books and novelty books. Publishes 200 titles/year.
First Contact & Terms: Works with 15-20 freelance artists/year. Local artists only, preferably professional graphic designers and illustrators. Works on assignment only. Send query letter with resume, slides, Photostats, photographs, photocopies or tear sheets to be kept on file, except for work style which is unsuitable for us. Samples not filed are returned by SASE. Reports only if interested. Call or write for appointment to show portfolio. Original work not returned at job's completion. Considers complexity of project, project's budget and turnaround time when establishing payment. Buys all rights.
Book Design: Assigns 20-40 freelance design jobs/year and 25 illustration jobs/year. Pays by the project, $75-500 average.
Jackets/Covers: Assigns 25 + freelance design and 25 + freelance illustration jobs/year. Pays by the project, $50-400 average, depending upon project, time spent and any changes.
Text Illustration: Assigns 30 + jobs/year. Prefers water-based color media and b&w line work. Prefers graphic approaches as well as very illustrative. "We cater more to juvenile market." Pays by the project, $50-2,000 average.

Tips: Looks for "clean work that will reproduce well. I also look for the artist's ability to render children/people well, which is a problem for some. A sure control of one's media should also be present. Very few freelancers are able to present a nice resume. I like it when people have taken the time and effort to record their art history. It helps me know something more about the person than they might let on during an interview and I respect them more for it."

OUTDOOR EMPIRE PUBLISHING INC., Box C-19000, 511 Eastlake Ave. E., Seattle WA 98109. (206)624-3845. Vice President/General Manager: Alec Purcell. Publishes paperback outdoor and how-to books on all aspects of outdoor recreation. Publishes 40 titles/year: 10% require freelance designers, 50% require freelance illustrators. Also uses artists for advertising layout and illustration. Minimum payment: $10-15, b&w; $25-50, color.
First Contact & Terms: Arrange interview or mail art. Especially looks for style, accuracy in rendering figures and technical illustrations when reviewing samples. Buys all rights. No originals returned at job's completion. Works on assignment only. Samples returned by SASE; and reports back within 3 weeks on future assignment possiblities. Send resume, flyer, business card, tear sheet, brochure and photocopies of samples that show style to be kept on file. Artist sometimes supplies overlays for color artwork. Gives minimum payment for unused assigned work. Pays on publication.
Book Design: Uses artists for layout and type spec. Pays by the hour, $10-35 average; by the project, $10-1,500; "depends upon project."
Jacket/Covers: Pays for design by the hour, $10-35 average; by the project, $50-1,000 average. Pays for illustration by the hour, $10-35 average; by the project, $10-500 average.
Text Illustration: Pays by the hour, $10-35 average; by the project, $10-100 average. Occasionally uses cartoons; buys 6 cartoons/year. Pays $10, b&w.
Tips: "Assignments sometimes depend upon timing—right style for the right project. Availability is important, especially with 'rush' projects. The competition is getting tougher. More people are trying to break into the field."

OXFORD UNIVERSITY PRESS, ELT Department, 200 Madison Ave., New York NY 10016. (212)679-7300. Art Director: Shireen Nathoo. Specializes in hardcover and paperback originals; educational materials for English as a second language. Publishes 20-25 titles/year: 15% require freelance designers; 100% require freelance illustrators.
First Contact & Terms: Works with 25 freelance artists/year. Prefers artists with experience in both publishing and magazine, color and b&w. Works on assignment basis only. Send query letter with resume, samples and tear sheets to be kept on file. Call to show portfolio, which should include Photostats, photocopies or printed samples. Samples not kept on file are returned by SASE. Reports only if interested. Works on assignment basis only. Considers complexity of project, skill and experience of artist and project's budget when establishing payment. Buys all rights.
Book Design: Assigns 5 freelance projects/year. Pays by the project.
Text Illustration: Assigns 15-20 freelance projects/year. Pays by the project.
Tips: Looks for "a developed sense of style, a good understanding of the problem and its visual solution, creativity within a set of tight specs and good renderings of ethnic features" when reviewing samples.

PADRE PRODUCTIONS, Box 1275, San Luis Obispo CA 93406. Editor/Publisher: Lachlan P. MacDonald. Publishes county and area, especially California, guidebooks. Publishes 6-10 titles/year; 5% require freelance designers; 40% require freelance illustrators.
First Contact & Terms: Query. Answers queries in 10 days; book decisions, 2 months. Samples returned by SASE. Provide resume, flyer, tear sheet, brochure and book jacket samples to be kept on file for future assignments. Artist provides overlays for color art. "We typeset all text, but want the artist to be responsible for complete preparation of art." Artists who produce quality, clarity and neat work only. "Actively seeking quality ink drawings in categories of: Western Americana, native and marine life, mystical, science fiction and contemporary humor." Need illustrations for short stories and novellas. Works on assignment only. Usually buys all book rights. Originals returned to artist at job's completion. Pays $10-1,000.
Tips: "Too few artists are familiar with book production, effects of reduction on their art, printing of process color, etc. Always query first. We are always in the market for complete manuscripts accompanied by simple line drawings."

PALADIN PRESS, Box 1307, Boulder CO 80306. (303)443-7250. Art Director: Fran Porter. Publishes hardcover and paperback originals and reprints; military-related (weaponry, self-defense, martial arts and survival) and titles of general interest. Publishes 40 titles/year. Catalog for SASE.
First Contact & Terms: Local artists only for book design. Works on assignment only. Send query letter with good quality photocopies of sample work to be kept on file. Samples returned by SASE. Artist

supplies overlays for all color artwork. Buys all rights.
Text Illustration: Assigns 8/year. Uses "99% pen & ink, b&w. Often technical." Buys b&w line drawings, washes and color washes. Pays for illustration by the project, $20-200.
Tips: "We prefer working with artists who have a strong background in mechanical and production skills (have they ever worked with a printer?). There is continued expansion into the martial arts market, financial survival, outdoor skills, etc. Also an increased demand for high caliber execution of how-to photo layouts."

PAULIST PRESS, 997 MacArthur Blvd., Mahwah NJ 07430. Specializes in hardcovers, paperbacks and originals—academic theology, philosophy, self-help, inspirational. Publishes 90-100 titles/year.
First Contact & Terms: Works with 20-30 freelance artists/year. "We look for local people. New York City and North New Jersey." Works on assignment only. Send resume, tear sheets, Photostats and photocopies. Samples not filed are returned only if requested. Reports only if interested. Original work returned at job's completion "if requested." Considers complexity of project and project's budget when establishing payment. Rights purchased vary according to project.
Book Design: Assigns 5-10 freelance design and 10-12 freelance illustration jobs/year. "With illustrators we often like to work out a royalty arrangement. For design, payment depends on the complexity."
Jackets/Covers: Assigns 9-10 freelance design and 5-10 freelance illustration jobs/year. Pays by the project, $100-250.
Text Illustration: Assigns "very few" jobs/year.
Tips: "We use little or no four-color art inside books. We look for artists with style that can be reproduced as b&w line art."

***PETER PAUPER PRESS, INC.**, 202 Mamaroneck Ave., White Plains NY 10601. (914)681-0144. Co-Publisher: Evelyn Beilenson. Specializes in hardcover adult gift books. Publishes 8 titles/year.
First Contact & Terms: Works with 4 freelance artists/year. Prefers local artists. Works on assignment only. Send query letter with brochure or Photostats. Samples are filed. Samples not filed are returned by SASE. Reports back within 2 weeks. Originals not returned to artist at job's completion. Call to schedule an appointment to show a portfolio or mail appropriate materials. Negotiates rights purchased.
Jackets/Covers: Assigns 8 freelance design jobs/year. Pays by the project, $300 minimum.
Text Illustration: Assigns 8 freelance jobs/year. Pays by the project, $700 for 7 full-page illustrations for 4¼x7¼ book with 3 PMS colors, separated on acetates on boards.
Tips: "Give us a call."

PEANUT BUTTER PUBLISHING, 329 2nd Ave. W., Seattle WA 98119. (206)281-5965. Specializes in paperback regional cookbooks and also speciality cookbooks for people who like to dine in restaurant and try the recipes at home. Publishes 30 titles/year.
First Contact & Terms: Works on assignment only. Send brochure showing art style or tear sheets, Photostats and photocopies. Samples not filed are returned only if requested. Reports only if interested. To show a portfolio, mail appropriate materials. Pays for design by the project, $400 minimum. Pays for illustration by the project, $100 minimum. Negotiates rights purchased.

***PEGASUS ORIGINALS, INC.**, Rt. 4, Box 362-A, Lexington SC 29072. (803)755-1141. Design Editor: Stephanie S. Hedgepath. Specializes in paperbacks on counted cross stitch and craft booklets. Publishes 10 titles/year.
First Contact & Terms: Works with variable freelance artists/year. Send query letter with chart and photo of model. Samples are filed. Reports back within 10 days. Originals not returned to artist at job's completion. Call to show a portfolio, which should include roughs and photos of any charted design work previously done, or charts, etc. Considers rights purchased and royalty.
Tips: "We prefer someone who is familiar with the counted cross stitch and craft market, but we are open to those artists who have never worked in charted design."

PELICAN PUBLISHING CO., Box 189, 1101 Monroe St., Gretna LA 70053. (504)368-1175. Assistant Production Manager: Sam Buddin. Publishes hardcover and paperback originals and reprints. Publishes 60-70 titles/year.
First Contact & Terms: Works on assignment only. Send query letter and 3-4 samples. SASE. No samples returned. Reports back on future assignment possibilities. No originals returned at job's completion. Buys complete rights.
Book Design: Assigns variable number of freelance artists. Payment varies.
Jackets/Covers: Assigns variable number of freelance artists. Payment varies.
Text Illustration: Assigns variable number of freelance artists. Payment varies.

***PEN NOTES INC.**, 134 Westside Ave., Freeport NY 11520. (516)868-5753 or 868-1966. President: Lorette Konezny. Produces books for children ages 3 and up; calligraphy age 8 and up.
First Contact & Terms: Buys designs and illustrations from freelance artists. Prefers New York area artists with toy-book experience. Send letter with brochure or Photostats and photocopies. Samples are filed. Reports back within 5 days. Call or write to schedule an appointment to show a portfolio or mail original/final art, Photostats, dummies, color and b&w. Original artwork is not returned to the artist after job's completion. Buys all rights.
Text Illustration: Also uses freelance artists for calligraphy, P-O-P displays, mechanicals and book illustrations. Prefers pen & ink. Pays by the project, $1,000 average.
Tips: Artists should "have strong experience in illustration for toy-book market and be able to complete work under deadline situation."

PENUMBRA PRESS, 920 S. 38th St., Omaha NE 68105. (319)455-2182. Contact: Bonnie O'Connell. Specializes in limited editions of hand-printed books—generally contemporary poetry with graphics or original prints as illustration. Subjects include contemporary poetry, very short fiction, graphics and original prints. Publishes 1-3 titles/year.
First Contact & Terms: Works with 1 artist every 2 years. Works on assignment only. Send query letter with good photocopies of line work, color slides which can be returned; material not suitable for letterpress book production will not be kept on file. Samples not kept on file are returned by SASE or adequate return postage. Reports within 4 weeks. Originals returned to artist at job's completion. Considers complexity of project and skill and experience of artist when establishing payment.
Book Design: Assigns 1-2 freelance illustration jobs/year. Pays by the project.
Text Illustration: Assigns 1-2 freelance jobs/year. Prefers pen & ink, high contrast work, original relief prints, collage and mixed media work. Pays price requested by artist and/or royalty copies.
Tips: "I provide hand-printed, hand-bound books in limited editions. I see more exciting styles of illustration in mixed media techniques entering fine press books."

PERGAMON PRESS INC., Fairview Park, Elmsford NY 10523. (914)592-7700. Art Department Manager: Angela Langston. Publishes scientific, technical, scholarly, educational, professional and business books and journals. Publishes 50 titles/year: 75% require freelance designers, 25% require freelance illustrators. Also uses artists for jacket designs, cover designs, text illustrations, advertising design, mechanicals and direct mail brochures. Mostly needs artists for 1-2-color promotion pieces. Produces about 75 pieces per year. 90% need freelance artists.
First Contact & Terms: Prefers local artists. Works on assignment only. Call for interview. No originals returned at job's completion. Check for most recent titles in bookstores. Pays net 90 days.

***PHILLIPS PUBLICATIONS, INC.**, Box 168, Williamstown NJ 08094. (609)567-0695. Director: Jacqueline White. Specializes in hardcovers. Publishes 3 titles/year.
First Contact & Terms: Works with 5 freelance artists/year. Send query letter with brochure or resume and photographs. Samples are filed. Reports back within 3 weeks. Originals returned to artist at job's completion. To show a portfolio, mail transparencies and dummies. Buys first rights, one-time rights or reprint rights; negotiates rights purchased.
Book Design: Assigns 5-10 freelance design and 25 freelance illustration jobs/year. Pays by the project.
Jackets/Covers: Pays by the hour, $5-20; by the project, $25 minimum.
Text Illustration: Assigns 25 freelance jobs/year.
Tips: "Send a small portfolio with return envelope with postage."

PICTURE BOOK STUDIO, 60 North Main St., Natick MA 01760. Editor: Robert Saunders. Produces children's picture books. Publishes 25 books/year with 10-12 illustrations in each.
First Contact & Terms: Send query letter with slides. Samples not filed returned by SASE. Reports within 1 month. "We always must see slides first. Do not call." Originals returned to artist at job's completion. Buys worldwide book rights.
Tips: Artist should "write us for a catalog to see if their work fits. Never call."

PLAYERS PRESS, Box 1132, Studio City CA 91604. Associate Editor: Marjorie Clapper. Specializes in children's books, covers to books, jackets, etc.
First Contact & Terms: Buys up to 30 illustrations/year from freelancers. Works on assignment only. Send query letter with brochure showing art style or resume and samples. Samples not filed are returned by SASE. Reports only if interested. To show a portfolio, mail thumbnails, original/final art, final reproduction/product, tear sheets, photographs and as much information as possible. Buys all rights. Payment varies.

PLAYMORE INC. PUBLISHERS, 1107 Broadway, New York NY 10010. (212)924-7447. President: John Horwich. Publishes hardcover and paperback juvenile, adult and mass market originals and reprints. Publishes 50 titles/year; 100% require freelance illustrators.
First Contact & Terms: Send query letter with samples. SASE. Reports in 2 weeks. Negotiates pay for design and illustration.

PLYMOUTH MUSIC CO., INC., 170 NE 33rd St., Ft. Lauderdale FL 33334. (305)563-1844. General Manager: Bernard Fisher. Specializes in paperbacks dealing with all types of music. Publishes 60-75 titles/year; 100% require freelance designers, 100% require freelance illustrators.
First Contact & Terms: Works with 10 freelance artists/year. Artists "must be within our area." Works on assignment only. Send brochure, resume and samples to be kept on file. Samples not kept on file are returned. Reports within 1 week. Call for appointment to show portfolio. No originals returned to artist at job's completion. Considers complexity of project when establishing payment. Buys all rights.
Jackets/Covers: Assigns 5 freelance design and 5 freelance illustration jobs/year. Pays by the project.

POCKET BOOKS, Art Department, Simon & Schuster Bldg., 1230 Ave. of the Americas, New York NY 10020. (212)698-7000. Art Director: Bruce Hall. Publishes paperback romance, science fiction, Westerns, young adult, fiction, nonfiction and classics. Publishes 250 titles/year; 80% require freelance illustrators.
First Contact & Terms: Works with 30 freelance artists/year. "We prefer artists who live close enough that they are able to deliver and discuss their work in person. We judge them on their portfolio work. We prefer color illustration." Send brochure/flyer and color slides, transparencies and prints. Submit portfolio for review, no appointment necessary. Samples not kept on file are returned by SASE. Reports in weeks. Works on assignment only. Provide brochure/flyer, samples, tear sheets to be kept on file for possible future assignments. Originals returned to artist at job's completion. Buys all rights.
Jackets/Covers: Assigns 220 freelance illustration jobs/year. Prefers paintings and color washes. Pays by the job, $800-4,000 average.

PORTER SARGENT PUBLISHERS, INC., 11 Beacon St., Boston MA 02108. (617)523-1670. Coordinating Editor: Peter Casey. Specializes in hardcover and paperback originals and reprints of college texts in the social sciences, particularly political science, sociology and history. Publishes 4-5 titles/year; 20% require freelance designers, 20% require freelance illustrators.
First Contact & Terms: Works with 2-4 freelance artists/year. Local artists only. Works on assignment only. Send query letter with resume, business card and tear sheets to be kept on file; write for appointment to show portfolio. "We are basically looking for samples of dust jacket cover designs." Samples not kept on file returned by SASE. Reports only if interested. No originals returned at job's completion. Considers complexity of project, and skill and experience of artist when establishing payment. Buys all rights.
Jackets/Covers: Assigns 1-2 freelance design jobs/year. Pays by the project, $200 minimum; negotiates.

CLARKSON N. POTTER INC., 1 Park Ave., New York NY 10016. (212)532-9200. Art Director: Gael Towey. Publishes hardbound and paperback books on Americana, fiction, interior decoration, satire, art, cooking, photographs, lifestyle. Publishes 35 titles/year; 80% require freelance designers, 10% require freelance illustrators.
First Contact & Terms: Prefers minimum of three years of experience, New York location. Send query letter with photocopies or call for an appointment. SASE. Reports within 2 weeks "if we like samples." Buys all rights.
Book Design: Assigns 30 jobs/year. Uses artists for all aspects of the book as a package. Pays $450-1,000 for jacket design, $500 for simple text design, more for lifestyle photography books, $50 full-page illustration and $15-20 for spot illustration.

***PRAEGER PUBLISHERS**, 521 Fifth Ave., New York NY 10175. (212)599-8400. Art Director: Carole A. Seylar. Specializes in hardcover and paperback trade and academic books on political, medical, business, science, economics, psychology and sociology themes. Publishes 200 titles/year.
First Contact & Terms: Works with 10-12 freelance artists/year. Works on assignment only. Send query letter with tear sheets. Samples are filed. Samples not filed are not returned. Reports back only if interested. Originals not returned to artist at job's completion. Call or write to schedule an appointment to show a portfolio, which should include roughs, original/final art and final reproduction/product. Considers skill and experience of artist and project's budget when establishing payment. Negotiates rights purchased.
Jackets/Covers: Assigns 30 freelance design jobs/year. Pays by the project, $350-500.
Tips: "Want to see type designs mainly; rarely use illustrations or photographs."

***THE PRAIRIE PUBLISHING COMPANY**, Box 264, Postal Station C, Winnipeg MB R3M 3S7 Canada. (204)885-6496. Publisher: Ralph E. Watkins. Specializes in paperback juvenile fiction and local history. Publishes 3 titles/year.
First Contact & Terms: Works with 3-4 freelance artists/year. Works on assignment only. Send query letter with resume and tear sheets. Samples are filed. Samples not filed are returned. Reports back within weeks. Originals not returned to artist at job's completion. To show a portfolio, mail appropriate roughs. Considers skill and experience of artist and project's budget when establishing payment. Negotiates rights purchased.
Book Design: Pays by the project, $100-150.
Jackets/Covers: Pays by the project, $100-150.
Text Illustration: Prefers line drawings. Pays by the project, $100-150.
Tips: "A freelancer should have other projects on which he is working. On the other hand, he must be able to carry out the work for which he has bid."

PRENTICE-HALL BOOKS FOR YOUNG READERS, A Division of Simon & Shuster, Inc.,1230 Ave. of the Americas, New York NY 10020. Art Coordinator: Rose Lopez. Specializes in hardcover and paperback juvenile trade books, for ages 3-10. Publishes 50 hardcover and 20 paperbacks/year.
First Contact & Terms: Assigns 50 jobs/year "but only to artists we have previously met and selected. We do not look at portfolios and have a stable on whom we rely. We pay an advance or flat fee."

PRICE/STERN/SLOAN PUBLISHERS, 410 N. La Cienega Blvd., Los Angeles CA 90048. Art Director: Gloria DeMuri. Publishes books (children's and humor), greeting cards and calendars.
First Contact & Terms: Send query letter with samples to be kept on file. Prefers photocopies or photostats as samples. Samples not filed are returned by SASE. Does not report back. Sometimes returns original art after reproduction. Negotiates rights purchased.
Illustrations: Buys 200+ illustrations/year from freelance artists. Seeks illustrations for children's books, inside and covers. Also uses artists for paste-up and mechanicals. Pay varies; "depends on illustration, book, size, colors, etc."

PRUETT PUBLISHING COMPANY, 2928 Pearl St., Boulder CO 80301. Project Editor: Jim Pruett. Specializes in hardcovers, paperbacks and originals on western history, outdoor themes, Americana and railroads. Publishes 20 titles/year. Also uses freelancers for brochure, catalog and advertising design. Assigns 20-25 projects/year. Pays by the project.
First Contact & Terms: Works with 4-5 freelance artists/year. Prefers local artists. Works on assignment only. Send query letter with brochure showing art style. Samples not filed are returned only if requested. Reports within 10 days. Original work returned at job's completion. Considers complexity of project, skill and experience of artist, project's budget and turnaround time when establishing payment. Rights purchased vary according to project.
Book Design: Assigns 20 freelance design and 0-1 freelance illustration jobs/year. Pays by the hour, $15-25.
Jackets/Covers: Assigns 20 freelance design and 5-10 freelance illustration jobs/year. Pays by the project, $250-450.
Text Illustration: Assigns 0-1 freelance jobs/year. Pays by the project, $75-400.

PUBLISHERS ASSOCIATES, Box 160361, Las Colinas TX 75016. (817)478-8564. Chief Operating Officer: Nicholas Lashmet. Established 1985. A consortium of 14 independent academic presses. Specializes in paperback originals on feminist/liberal subjects. Publishes 20 titles/year.
First Contact & Terms: Works with 7 freelance artists/year. Send query letter with brochure showing art style or photocopies. Samples not filed are returned by SASE only if requested. Reports within 45 days. "Never send original work until requested." Considers skill and experience of artist, project's budget and rights purchased when establishing payment. Buys all rights.
Book Design: Works with 10 freelance designers and 10 freelance illustrators/year. Pays by the project, $50 on up.
Jackets/Covers: Works with 10 freelance designers and 10 freelance illustrators/year. Pays by the project, $50 on up. "We need quality/realistic work for medieval books—primarily on women, some men illustrations."
Text Illustration: Works with 10 freelance artists/year. Prefers line drawings, ink only. Pays by the project, $100 on up. "We are in desperate need of artists who can draw men with/without clothing (no porno) in historic settings. Our preference is for realism; we do not wish da Vinci type males (small, effeminate, etc.) Will pay well. Our staff artists currently are capable only in area of women. Need freelance here, too."
Tips: "Never send original work. Write first, submit 2 or 3 examples in areas of our needs, include

SASE. We do not use cartoons, unless commissioned first. Cartoons are political (liberal) in nature. All other work must be realistic in style. Our primary emphasis is women—we will not accept 'Gibson Girl' or 'clip art' style work. Historic/period brings top dollars."

G.P. PUTNAM'S SONS, (Philomel Books), 51 Madison Ave., New York NY 10010. (212)689-9200. Art Director, Children's Books: Nanette Stevenson. Publishes hardcover and paperback juvenile books. Publishes 100 titles/year.
First Contact & Terms: "We take drop-offs on Tuesday mornings. Please call in advance with the date you want to drop off your portfolio." Originals returned to artist at job's completion. Works on assignment only. Samples returned by SASE. Provide flyer, tear sheet, brochure and photocopy or stat to be kept on file for possible future assignments. Free catalog.
Jackets/Covers: "Full-color paintings, tight style."
Text Illustration: "A wide cross section of styles for story and picture books."

RAINTREE PUBLISHERS GROUP, INC., 310 W. Wisconsin Ave., Milwaukee WI 53203. (414)273-0873. Art Director: Suzanne Beck. Specializes in educational material for children. Publishes 40 titles/year; 90% require freelance illustrators.
First Contact & Terms: Works with 12 freelance artists/year. Send slides, tear sheets or photocopies or submit portfolio for review. Do not call in person. Provide samples to be kept on file for possible future assignments. Samples not kept on file are returned by SASE. Reports in 2-3 weeks. Works on assignment only. Originals sometimes returned to artist at job's completion. Buys all rights.
Jackets/Covers: Assigns 12 illustration jobs/year. Payment varies depending on job and artist's experience.
Text Illustration: Assigns 12 jobs/year. Payment varies depending on job and artist's experience.

***RANDALL BOOK COMPANY**, 1182 N. Industrial Park Dr., Orem UT 84057. Production Manager: Lyle V. Mortimer. Specializes in hardcover religious books. Publishes 20 titles/year.
First Contact & Terms: Works with 5 freelance artists/year. Prefers local artists. Send query letter with brochure or photographs. Samples are filed. Samples not filed are returned by SASE. Reports back only if interested. Originals not returned to artist at job's completion. To show a portfolio, mail photographs. Considers complexity of project, skill and experience of artist, project's budget, turnaround time and rights purchased when establishing payment. Negotiates rights purchased.
Book Design: Assigns 30 freelance design and 5 freelance illustration jobs/year. Pays by the project, $50-1,100.
Jackets: Assigns 30 freelance design and 10 freelance illustration jobs/year. Pays by the project, $50-1,100.
Text Illustration: Assigns 3 freelance jobs/year. Pays by the project, $50-3,000.
Tips: "Send as much literature as possible. Do not call for appointment."

***READ'N RUN BOOKS**, Box 294, Rhododendron OR 97049. (503)622-4798. Publisher: Michael P. Jones. Estab. 1985. Specializes in fiction, history, environment, wildlife for children through adults. "Varies depending upon subject matter. Books for people who do not have time to read lengthy books." Publishes 2-6 titles/year. Accepts previously published material. Original artwork returned to the artist after publication. Sample copy: $6. Art guidelines for SASE with 1 first-class stamp.
Text Illustration: Buys 10 illustrations/year from freelancers. Send query letter with brochure or resume, tear sheets, Photostats, photocopies, slides and photographs. Samples not filed are returned by SASE. Reports back within 2 weeks. To show a portfolio, mail thumbnails, roughs, original/final art, final reproduction/product, color, tear sheets, Photostats, photographs and b&w. Buys one-time rights. Pays in copies, on publication.
Tips: "Oftentimes we can select an artist for a particular project, even though the individual may not specialize in that field, nor even attempt to do illustrations in what we need. Just show your talents, and we do the rest."

RESOURCE PUBLICATIONS INC., Suite 290, 160 E. Virginia, San Jose CA 95112. Editorial Director: Kenneth Guentert. Publishes paperback originals related to celebration and the arts. Publishes 12 titles/year. Also uses artists for advertising and production. Assigns 4 advertising jobs/year. Pays $4-25/hour; catalogs, direct mail brochures, letterhead and magazines. Assigns 12-16 production jobs/year. Pays $5-10/hour, paste-up.
First Contact & Terms: Send query letter with samples. SASE. Reports in 6-8 weeks. No advance. Buys all rights. Free catalog.
Book Design: Assigns 1-4/year. Pays $5-25/hour, layout and type spec.
Jackets/Covers: Buys 1-4/year. Pays $45-125, b&w; $50-250, color.

ROWAN TREE PRESS, 124 Chestnut St., Boston MA 02108. (617)523-7627. Specializes in paperback originals and reprints—poetry, mystery, juvenile and memoir. Publishes 6 titles/year; 100% require freelance designers, 50% require freelance illustrators.
First Contact & Terms: Area artists only. Works on assignment only. Send query letter with brochure, resume and samples to be kept on file. Call or write for appointment to show portfolio, which should include photographs. Samples not kept on file are returned by SASE. Reports within 2 months. Originals returned to artist at job's completion. Considers complexity of project, skill and experience of artist and project's budget when establishing payment. Negotiates rights purchased. Material not copyrighted.
Jackets/Covers: Assigns 6 freelance design and 2 freelance illustration jobs/year. Pays by the project, $200-300 average.
Text Illustration: Pays by the project, $100 maximum.

ROYAL HOUSE PUBLISHING CO., INC., Book Division of Recipes-of-the-Month Club, 9465 Wilshire Blvd., Box 5027, Beverly Hills CA 90210. (213)277-7220 or 550-7170. Director: Mrs. Harold Klein. Publishes paperbacks on entertaining, humor, sports and cooking. Publishes 10 titles/year. Also uses artists for brochures, ads, letterheads and business forms.
First Contact & Terms: Query with samples; local artists only. SASE. Reports in 4-6 weeks. Purchases outright. No originals returned to artist at job's completion. Works on assignment only. Provide brochure to be kept on file for future assignments. Check for most recent titles in bookstores. Negotiates pay.
Book Design: Assigns 8-12 jobs/year. Uses artists for layout and type spec.
Jackets/Covers: Assigns 8-12 jobs/year. Uses "4-color art; old-fashioned heirloom quality." Buys color washes, opaque watercolors and b&w line drawings.
Text Illustration: Assigns 8-12 jobs/year. Buys b&w line drawings.

WILLIAM H. SADLIER INC., 11 Park Place, New York NY 10007. (212)227-2120. Art Director: Grace Kao. Publishes hardcover and paperback Catholic adult education, religious, mathematics, social studies and language arts books. Publishes 60 titles/year. Also uses artists for direct mail pieces and catalogs. Pays $12-15/hour or $175-350/job.
First Contact & Terms: Query with samples. SASE. Reports within 2 weeks. Buys all rights.
Book Design: Assigns 40 jobs/year. Uses artists for layout, type spec and mechanicals. Pays $10-15/hour.
Text Illustration: Assigns 30 jobs/year. Pays $75-200, color washes and opaque watercolors; $60-200, gray opaques, b&w line drawings and washes.

SANTILLANA PUBLISHING CO. INC., 257 Union St., Northvale NJ 07647. (201)767-6961. President: Sam Laredo. Managing Editor: Bernard Cohen. Specializes in hardcover and paperback juvenile and teen textbooks and workbooks. Publishes 20 titles/year.
First Contact & Terms: Works with 8-10 freelance artists/year. Works on assignment only. Send query letter with brochure, tear sheets or "anything we don't have to return" to be kept on file. Call or write for appointment to show portfolio. Samples not filed are returned by SASE. Reports only if interested. No originals returned to artist at job's completion. Considers skill and experience of artist, project's budget and rights purchased when establishing payment. Buys all rights or negotiates rights purchased.
Text Illustration: All jobs assigned to freelancers. Pays by the project, $200-5,000 average.
Tips: Looks for "lots of details, strong lines, good color."

SCOTT, FORESMAN AND CO., 1900 E. Lake Ave., Glenview IL 60025. Design Manager: John Mayahara. Specializes in hardcover and paperback originals and reprints on elementary and high school textbooks for major subject areas. Publishes over 100 titles/year.
First Contact & Terms: Works with over 200 artists/year. Works on assignment only. Send query letter with slides or "any material that can be filed; *no* original art." Samples not filed are returned by SASE. Reports within 1 month. No originals returned to artist at job's completion. Considers complexity of project, skill and experience of artist and project's budget when establishing payment. Buys all rights.

CHARLES SCRIBNER'S SONS, A Division of MacMillan Publishing Co., 866 3rd Ave., New York NY 10022. (212)702-2000. Art Director for adult books: Ruth Kolbert. Send flyers or non-returnable copies of work before calling for appointment. "No slides or transparencies please."
Needs: Pays for design by the project, $650-1,000. Pays for illustration by the project, $650-12,000 depending on project. Adult book division uses illustrators and graphic designers for trade and paperback jackets and covers. Uses some freelance book designers for interior design.
Tips: "We want strong conceptual illustration, whether realistic or stylized; it should be well-drawn and carefully realized. We do not want science fiction, fantasy or juvenile illustration, or cartoons."

***SCROLL PRESS INC.**, 2858 Valerie Court, Merrick NY 11566. (516)379-4283. President: M. Albert. Specializes in hardcovers for juveniles.
First Contact & Terms: Works with 5 freelance artists/year. Prefers local artists. Send query letter with brochure. Samples are filed. Samples not filed are not returned. Reports back within 1 month. Outright purchase of original work. To show a portfolio, mail roughs and dummies. Considers rights purchased when establishing payment. Buys all rights.
Book Design: Assigns freelance design jobs. Pays by the project.
Jackets/Covers: Assigns freelance design jobs. Prefers character color illustrations. Pays by the project.
Text Illustration: Assigns freelance jobs. Prefers b&w children's illustrations. Pays by the project.
Tips: "Send color rough illustrations for the pre-school children learning category. Also looking for box design video field on classics to be animated in educational school and library sales."

***SERENDIPITY PRESS**, Building C, Suite 102, 3801 Kennett Pike, Wilmington DE 19807.
First Contact & Terms: Query with business card, tear sheet and brochure to be kept on file; local artists only. Buys various rights. Works on assignment only. Samples returned by SASE; and reports back on future assignment possiblities. Artist supplies overlays for cover artwork, inside illustrations and advertising art.
Needs: Uses artists for design of direct mail flyers, book interiors, posters, book end sheets, jackets and cartoons.

SIERRA CLUB BOOKS, 730 Polk St., San Francisco CA 94109. Publisher: Jon Beckmann. Editorial Director: Daniel Moses. Design Director: Eileen Max. Publishes books on natural history, science, ecology, conservation issues and related themes, calendars and guides.
First Contact & Terms: Send query letter with resume, tear sheets and/or business card to be kept on file.
Needs: Uses artists for book design and illustration (maps, juvenile art) and jacket design. Pays by the project, $450-700 for book design. Pays by the project, $450-1,000 for jacket/cover design; $175-500 for jacket/cover illustration; $1,000-2,000 average for text illustration. Buys U.S. or world rights.

SINGER COMMUNICATIONS, INC., 3164 Tyler Ave., Anaheim CA 92801. (714)527-5650. Contact: Natalie Carlton. Licenses paperback originals and reprints; mass market, Western, romance, doctor/nurse, mystery, science fiction, nonfiction and biographies. Licenses 200 titles/year through affiliates, 95% require freelance designers for book covers. Also buys 3,000 cartoons/year to be internationally syndicated to newspaper and magazine publishers—also used for topical books. Pays 50% of fee received.
First Contact & Terms: Send query letter with photocopies and tear sheets to be kept on file. Do not send original work. Material not filed is returned by SASE. Reports in 2 weeks. Buys first and reprint rights. Originals returned to artist at job's completion. Artist's guidelines $1.
Book Design: Assigns "many" jobs/year. Uses artists for reprints for world market. Prefers clean, clear uncluttered style.
Jackets/Covers: Popular styles include Western, romance, mystery, science fiction/fantasy, war and gothic. "We are only interested in color transparencies for paperbacks." Duplicates only. Offers advance.
Tips: "Study the market. Study first the best seller list, the current magazines, the current paperbacks and then come up with something better if possible or something new. We now utilize old sales for reprint." Looking for "new ideas, imagination, uniqueness. Every artist is in daily competition with the best artists in the field. A search for excellence helps. We get hundreds of medical cartoons, hundreds of sex cartoons. We are overloaded with cartoons showing inept office girls but seldom get cartoons on credit cards, senior management, aerobics, fitness, romance. We have plenty on divorce, but few on nice romance and love. We would like more positive and less negative humor. Can always use good travel cartoons around the world."

SOUTH END PRESS, 116 Botolph St., Boston MA 02115. (617)266-0629. Contact: Editorial Department. Specializes in hardcover and paperback books on contemporary problems, alternatives to oppression, movements for change. Publishes 15 titles/year. Uses artists for jacket/cover illustration.
First Contact & Terms: Works with varying number of freelance artists/year. "Artist must read the book and understand theme of leftist issues." Send samples of jacket covers of similar books. Prefers Photostats as samples. Pays for design by the project, $200-250.
Tips: Looks for "ability to work creatively with few colors; good political instinct."

***SOUTHERN HISTORICAL PRESS, INC.**, 300 South 1st St., Box 738, Easley SC 29641-0738. (803)859-2346. President: The Rev. Silas Emmett Lucas, Jr. Specializes in hardcover and paperback originals and reprints on genealogy and history. Publishes 40 titles/year.

First Contact & Terms: Works with 1 freelance artist/year. Works on assignment only. Send query letter and samples to be kept on file. Call or write for appointment to show portfolio. Prefers tear sheets or photographs as samples. Samples not filed are returned by SASE if requested. Reports back only if interested. Original work not returned after job's completion. Considers complexity of the project, skill and experience of artist, project's budget and turnaround time when establishing payment. Buys all rights.

Needs: Assigns 5 freelance book design, cover design and illustration, and text illustration jobs/year.

STANDARD PUBLISHING, 8121 Hamilton Ave., Cincinnati OH 45231. Advertising Manager: John Weidner. Art Director: Frank Sutton. Publishes religious, self-help and children's books.

First Contact & Terms: Artists with at least 4 years of experience. Send query letter with business card to be kept on file. SASE. Reports in 2 weeks. Buys all rights. Free catalog.

Needs: Art director uses artists for illustrations only. Advertising manager uses artists for advertising, books, catalogs, convention exhibits, decorative spots, direct mail brochures, letterheads, magazines, packages and posters.

STAR PUBLISHING, Box 68, Belmont CA 94002. Managing Editor: Stuart Hoffman. Specializes in original paperbacks and textbooks. Publishes 16 titles/year.

First Contact & Terms: Works with 10 artists/year. Send query letter with resume, tear sheets and photocopies. Samples not filed are returned only if requested. Reports back only if interested. Original work returned after job's completion "if arrangements are made." Rights purchased vary according to project but does buy one-time rights.

Book Design: Assigns 3 freelance design and 4 freelance illustration jobs/year. Pays by the project.

Jackets/Covers: Assigns 3 freelance design and 3 freelance illustration jobs/year. Pays by the project.

Text Illustration: Assigns 3-5 freelance jobs/year.

STEIN AND DAY, Scarborough House, Briarcliff Manor NY 10510. Art Director: Paul Scalenghe. Publishes hardcover, paperback, original and reprint mass market fiction and nonfiction. Publishes 100 titles/year; 10% require freelance designers, 20% require freelance cover illustrators.

First Contact & Terms: Prefers local artists with experience with other publishers, but young unpublished artists are welcome to submit. Send query letter with brochure showing art style or resume and nonreturnable samples. Especially looks for clean, smooth art, good color design and layout; also a variety of technical skills. SASE. Works on assignment only. Reports back on future assignment possibilities. Portfolios accepted at Westchester office for review. Artist provides overlays for color covers. Buys all rights. 15% kill fee. Pays on publication. Free catalog.

Jackets/Covers: Assigns 15 freelance design and 25 illustration jobs/year. Pays by the project, $500-1,200 average; mass market cover illustration, $700-1,500 average.

Text Illustration: Assigns 3-5 jobs/year. Pays by the project, $150-500 average. "We use very little text illustration but on occasion we require maps or b&w line drawings."

Tips: "Our covers are very diversified. All styles and designs are considered. A book can make it or break it by its cover. Simple design executed properly is the best design. Artist is selected for the best style that matches my layout and concept."

STEMMER HOUSE PUBLISHERS, INC., 2627 Caves Rd., Owings Mills MD 21117. (301)363-3690. President: Barbara Holdridge. Specializes in hardcover and paperback fiction, nonfiction, art books, juvenile and design resource originals. Publishes 20 titles/year; 50% require freelance designers, 75% require freelance illustrators.

First Contact & Terms: Works with 10 freelance artists/year. Works on assignment only. Send brochure/flyer, tear sheets, photocopies or color slides to be kept on file; submission must include SASE. Do not send original work. Material not filed is returned by SASE. Call or write for appointment to show portfolio. Reports in 6 weeks. Works on assignment only. Originals returned to artist at job's completion on request. Negotiates rights purchased.

Book Design: Assigns 1 freelance design and 5 illustration jobs/year. Uses artists for design. Pays by the project, negotiable amount.

Jackets/Covers: Assigns 2 freelance design jobs/year. Prefers paintings. Pays by the project, $300 minimum.

Text Illustration: Assigns 8 jobs/year. Prefers full-color artwork for text illustrations. Pays by the project on a royalty basis.

Tips: Looks for "draftmanship, flexibility, realism, understanding of the printing process." A common mistake freelancers make in presenting samples or portfolios is "presenting original work only without printed samples."

STONE WALL PRESS INC., 1241 30th St. NW, Washington DC 20007. Publisher: Henry Wheelwright. Publishes paperback and hardcover environmental, backpacking, fishing, beginning and advanced outdoor originals, also medical. Publishes 2-4 titles/year; 10% require freelance illustrators.
First Contact & Terms: Prefers artists who are accessible. Works on assignment only. Send query letter with resume and brochure to be kept on file. Samples returned by SASE. Reports in 2 weeks. Buys one-time rights. Originals returned to artist at job's completion.
Book Design: Assigns 1 job/year. Uses artists for composition, layout, jacket design. Prefers generally realistic style—photo, color or b&w. Artist supplies overlays for cover artwork. Pays cash upon accepted art.
Text Illustration: Buys b&w line drawings.

***STONEYDALE PRESS PUBLISHING COMPANY**, Drawer B, Stevensville MT 59870. (406)777-2729. Publisher: Dale Burk. Specializes in hardcover and paperback originals on outdoor recreation, nature and wildlife with emphasis on hunting and fishing. Publishes 4-6 titles/year.
First Contact & Terms: Works with 3-4 freelance artists/year. Works on assignment only. Send query letter with samples to be kept on file. Samples not filed are returned by SASE. Reports within 2-3 weeks. Original work not returned to artist. Considers complexity of the project, project's budget and rights purchased when establishing payment. Negotiates rights purchased.
Book Design: Assigns 2-3 jobs/year. Pays on the basis of artist's bid.
Jackets/Covers: Assigns 4-6 freelance design and 2-3 freelance illustration jobs/year for book and video covers. Pays on the basis of artist's bid.

***SWAMP PRESS**, 323 Pelham Rd., Amherst MA 01002. President: Ed Rayher. Specializes in hardcover and paperback originals of literary first editions. Publishes 2 titles/year.
First Contact & Terms: Works with 3 freelance artists/year. Send query letter with brochure or Photostats. Samples are filed. Samples not filed are returned by SASE. Reports back within 2 months. Originals are returned to artist at job's completion. To show a portfolio, mail Photostats, tear sheets and slides. Considers complexity of project and project's budget when establishing payment. Buys one-time rights.
Book Design: Assigns 3 freelance illustration jobs/year. Pays in copies of the book-$50 maximum.
Jackets/Covers: Assigns 3 freelance illustration jobs/year. Pays in copies-$25 maximum.
Text Illustration: Assigns 3 freelance jobs/year. Pays in copies-$50 maximum.
Tips: "Send four or five photocopies or slides. Woodcuts, engravings, linocuts are wonderful, especially if we can use your blocks."

TEN SPEED PRESS, Box 7123, Berkeley CA 94707. (415)845-8414. President: Phil Wood. Publishes hardcover and paperback cookbook, history, sports, gardening, career and life planning originals and reprints. Publishes 50 titles/year. Assigns 50 advertising jobs/year. Pays $1,500 maximum/job, catalogs; $1,000 maximum/job, direct mail brochures.
First Contact & Terms: Submit query. Reports within 4 weeks. Works on assignment only. Samples returned by SASE. Provide resume, flyer and/or sample art which may be kept on file for future assignments. Buys all rights, but may reassign rights to artist after publication. Pays flat fee. Offers advance. Pays promised fee for unused assigned work. Free catalog.
Book Design: Assigns 50 jobs/year. Pays by the project, $200 minimum.
Jackets/Covers: Assigns 50 freelance design jobs and 50 illustration jobs/year. Pays by the project, $200 minimum.
Text Illustration: Assigns 20 jobs/year. Pay varies.

TEXAS MONTHLY PRESS, Box 1569, Austin TX 78767. (512)476-7085. Design & Production Director: Cathy S. Casey. Specializes in hardcover and paperback originals and reprints on general trade books. Publishes 25-28 titles/year.
First Contact & Terms: Works with 15 freelance artists/year. Works on assignment only. Send resume, tear sheets and Photostats. Samples not filed are returned only if requested. Reports within 3 weeks. Originals returned at job's completion. Considers complexity of project and project's budget when establishing payment. Buys first rights.
Book Design: Assign 25-28 freelance design and 3 freelance illustration jobs/year. Pays by the project, $350-1,000.
Jackets/Covers: Assigns 25-28 freelance design and 3 freelance illustration jobs/year. Pays by the project, $350-1,200.
Text Illustration: Assigns 2 freelance jobs/year. Pays by the project, $200-500.

THORNDIKE PRESS AND NORTH COUNTRY PRESS, Box 159, Thorndike ME 04986. (207)948-2962. Art Director: Andrea Stark. Specializes in hardcover and paperback originals and reprints—large print books for the visually impaired. Publishes 136 titles/year.

First Contact & Terms: Works with 15-18 freelance artists/year. Prefers New England artists. "Demand experience in preparation of mechanicals for four-color process." Works on assignment only. Send query letter with tear sheets and slides. Samples not filed returned by SASE. Reports only if interested. Pays for design by the the project, $100-160. Pays for illustration by the project, $200. Considers project's budget when establishing payment. Rights purchased vary according to project.
Book Design: Assigns 12 freelance design jobs and 6 freelance illustration jobs/year. Payment is negotiable.
Jackets/Covers: Works with 16 freelance designers/year. Pays by the project, negotiable amount.
Text Illustration: Works with 6 freelance artists/year. Prefers pen & ink. Payment is negotiable.
Tips: "We are looking for artists/designers who have experience in four-color process on the trade book publishing level; textbook or magazine experience is *not* sufficient in most cases."

TOR BOOKS, 49 W. 24th St., New York NY 10018. Editor-in-Chief: Beth Meacham. Specializes in hardcover and paperback originals and reprints: espionage, thrillers, horror, mysteries and science fiction. Publishes 180 titles/year; heavy on science fiction.
First Contact & Terms: All covers are freelance. Works on assignment only. Send query letter with color photographs, slides or tear sheets to be kept on file "unless unsuitable"; call for appointment to show portfolio. Samples not filed are returned by SASE. Reports only if interested. Original work returned after job's completion. Considers skill and experience of artist, and project's budget when establishing payment. "We buy the right to use art on all editions of book it is commissioned for and in promotion of book."
Jackets/Covers: Assigns 180 freelance illustration jobs/year. Pays by the project, $500 minimum.

TROLL ASSOCIATES, Book Division, 100 Corporate Dr., Mahwah NJ 07430. Vice President: Marian Schecter. Specializes in hardcover and paperbacks for juveniles 5 to 15 years. Publishes 100+ titles/year; 30% require freelance designers and illustrators.
First Contact & Terms: Works with 30 freelance artists/year. Send query letter with brochure/flyer or resume and samples. Prefers photostats or photocopies as samples. Samples "usually" returned by SASE. Reports in 3 weeks. Works on assignment only. Originals "usually not" returned to artist at job's completion. Negotiates all rights.

TROUBADOR PRESS INC., Division of Price/Stern/Sloan, 410 N. La Cienega Blvd., Los Angeles CA 90048. (213)657-6100. Editor: Lisa Marsoli. Publishes mostly children's paperback project and activity books (coloring, cut-out, maze, puzzle and paperdoll books). Publishes 4-6 titles/year.
First Contact & Terms: Send query letter with resume, tear sheets and copies of b&w art outline of work. SASE must accompany submissions. Reports in 4 weeks. Originals returned to artist at job's completion, upon request. Check most recent titles in toy, art supply and bookstores for current style. All rights may be purchased or royalty contract arranged. Pays 4-6% royalty. Offers advance. Pays promised fee for unused assigned work. Catalog and artist's guidelines for SASE with 39¢ postage.
Needs: Uses artists for design and illustrations for coloring, game, cut-out books and some art books. Pays $25-100/illustration.
Tips: "Study our existing books in print for style, quality and interest range before sending material. See that art and ideas fit the publisher."

***THE TRUMPET CLUB/DELL PUBLISHING COMPANY**, 245 47th St., New York NY 10017. (212)605-3123. Art Director: Ann Hoffman. Estab. 1985. Mail-order school book club specializing in paperbacks and related promotional material. Publishes juvenile fiction and nonfiction.
First Contact & Terms: Works with 25 freelance artists/year. Prefers local mechanical people only. Prefers local illustrators, but out-of-towners okay. Send query letter with brochure, resume and tear sheets. Samples are filed. Samples not filed are not returned. Reports back only if interested. "We only report if we are interested or you can call for an appointment to show your portfolio. We prefer illustrators with children's experience, but we will consider others, too." Originals returned after job's completion. Call or write to schedule an appointment to show a portfolio, which should include Photostats, final reproduction/product, slides and transparencies. Considers complexity of project and project's budget when establishing payment.
Tips: "We are looking for freelance mechanical people, designers and illustrators. Designers and mechanical people may work or or off premises, depending on the complexity of the project. Designers must be able to carry a job through to production."

THE UNICORN PUBLISHING HOUSE, INC., 1148 Parsippany Blvd., Parsippany NJ 07054. (201)334-0353. Associate Editor: Heidi K.L. Corso. Specializes in original and reprint hardcovers, especially juvenile, issue-oriented and music books. Publishes 14 titles/year.
First Contact & Terms: Works with 8 freelance artists/year. Send query letter with brochure, resume,

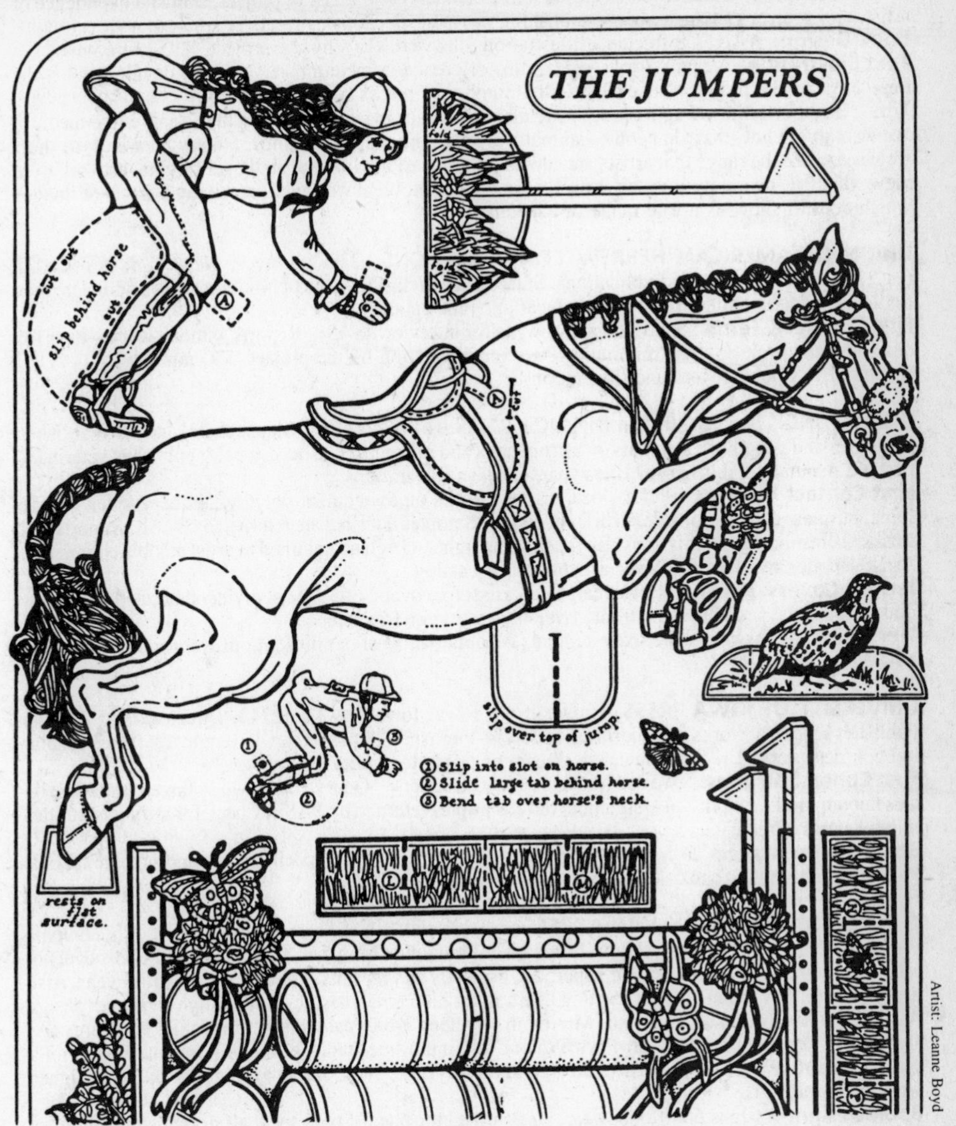

This illustration by Leanne Boyd of Denver, Colorado, was one of 16 in a color- and cut-out activity book for Troubador Press in San Francisco. Troubador's editorial director Malcolm K. Whyte says that Boyd had submitted samples that indicated she had worked with cut-out paper toy concepts before and assigned her this project. "She developed some very exciting roughs, and, with perserverance and good humor, produced excellent art and paper engineering." He felt the pen-and-ink drawings "perfectly conveyed the excitement, color and pageantry associated with horse shows." Boyd, who found Troubador through the Artist's Market, received a royalty with an advance of $500 for a buyout.

tear sheets and photocopies. Samples not filed are returned by SASE. Reports back within 3 months. Original work returned after job's completion. Considers complexity of project, skill and experience of artist, and project's budget when establishing payment. Negotiates rights purchased.
Book Design: Assigns 8 freelance illustration jobs/year. Pays by the project, $300 minimum.
Text Illustration: Assigns 8 jobs/year. "No preference in medium—art must be detailed and realistic." Pays by the project, "depends on the number of pieces being illustrated."
Tips: "In a portfolio, we're looking for realism in a color medium, and in a black-and-white medium. We want to see how they do people, animals, architecture, natural settings, fantasy creatures; in short, we want to see the range that artists are capable of. Occasionally we actually get original artwork to review which we do not want to see. Usually the biggest problem we have is receiving a group of images which doesn't show us a true range of capacity."

UNION OF AMERICAN HEBREW CONGREGATIONS, 838 5th Ave., New York NY 10021. (212)249-0100. Director of Publications: Stuart L. Benick. Produces books, filmstrips and magazines for Jewish school children and adult education. Free catalog.
First Contact & Terms: Send samples or write for interview. SASE. Reports within 3 weeks. Pays for design by the project, $150 minimum. Pays for illustration by the project, $50 minimum.
Needs: Buys book covers and illustrations.

UNIVELT INC., Box 28130, San Diego CA 92128. (619)746-4005. Manager: H. Jacobs. Publishes hardcover and paperback originals on astronautics and related fields; occasionally publishes veterinary first-aid manuals. Publishes 10 titles/year; all have illustrations.
First Contact & Terms: Prefers local artists. Works on assignment only. Send query letter with resume, business card and/or flyer to be kept on file. Samples not filed are returned by SASE. Reports in 4 weeks on unsolicited submissions. Buys one-time rights. Originals returned to artist at job's completion. Artist supplies overlays for cover artwork. Free catalog.
Jackets/Covers: Assigns 10 jobs/year. Uses artists for covers, title sheets, dividers, occasionally a few illustrations. Pays $50-100 for front cover illustration or frontispiece.
Tips: "Illustrations have to be space-related. We obtain most of our illustrations from authors and from NASA."

UNIVERSITY OF IOWA PRESS, University of Iowa, Iowa City IA 52242. Director: Paul Zimmer. Publishes scholarly works and short fiction series. Publishes 28 titles/year; 15 require freelance scholarly book designers, 2 require freelance illustrator or photographer.
First Contact & Terms: "We use freelance book designers." Query with "two or three samples; originals not required." Works on assignment only. Samples returned by SASE. Check for most recent titles in bookstores. Free catalog.
Book Design: Assigns 20 freelance jobs/year. Pays $250 to draw specifications and prepare layouts. Pays $300 minimum, book design; $250, jacket.

***UNIVERSITY OF PENNSYLVANIA PRESS**, Blockley Hall, 13th Floor, 418 Service Dr., Philadelphia PA 19104. Director: Thomas M. Rotell. Design & Production Manager: Carl E. Gross. Publishes scholarly books and texts; hardcover and paperback originals and reprints. Publishes 55-60 titles/year. Also uses artists for advertising layout, catalog illustration, direct mail design, book design and cover design. Assigns 20-30 advertising jobs/year. Minimum payment: $400, catalogs or direct mail brochures. Assigns 55-60 production jobs/year. Pays $9/hour minimum, mechanicals and paste-ups. Arrange interview; local artists only. SASE. Buys all rights. No advance. Negotiates payment for unused assigned work. Free catalog.
Book Design: Assigns 55-60 jobs/year. Uses artists for layout, type spec; all design shipped out-of-house. Pays $350-375/job, text layout; $75/job, type spec.
Jackets/Covers: Assigns 35-40 jobs/year. Pays for design by the job, $350-375 average; $300-350 b&w line drawings and washes, gray opaques and color-separated work.
Text Illustration: Pays $10-15/hour for maps, charts.
Tips: Production of books has doubled. Artists should have some experience in book and jacket design.

THE UNIVERSITY OF WISCONSIN PRESS, 114 N. Murray St., Madison WI 53715. (608)262-4978. Production Manager: Gardner R. Wills. Publishes scholarly hardcover and paperback books. Publishes 40-50 titles/year.
First Contact & Terms: Works on assignment only. Query first. Reports in 2 weeks. Buys all rights. No originals returned to artist at job's completion. Samples returned by SASE. Reports back on future assignment possibilities. Provide letter of inquiry and samples as agreed upon to be kept on file. Check for most recent titles in bookstores. Designer supplies overlays for cover artwork. No advance.
Book Design: Assigns 20-25/year. Pays upon completion of design. Pays by the project, $200-300 average.

Jackets/Covers: Assigns 30-40 freelance design jobs/year. Pays for design by the project, $175-250, average. "We do not purchase individual items of art."
Tips: "In presenting samples via mail, many freelancers do not personalize the presentation with either a cover letter or a note. So mechanical. Often, in-person presentations do not include work relevant to my needs."

***VONGRUTNORV OG PRESS, INC.**, Box 411, Troy ID 83871. (208)835-4902. Publisher: Steve E. Erickson. Specializes in paperback originals on philosophy, metaphysics, poetry, creative fiction.
First Contact & Terms: Works with 1-2 freelance artists/year. Works on assignment only. Send query letter with photostats or copies to be kept on file. Samples not filed not returned. Reports within 6 weeks. Whether original work is returned after the job's completion "depends on the type of assignment and agreement or contract with the artist." Considers complexity of project, project's budget and rights purchased when establishing payment. Rights purchased vary according to project.

J. WESTON WALCH, PUBLISHER, Box 658, Portland ME 04104-0658. (207)772-2846. Managing Editor: Richard Kimball. Specializes in supplemental secondary school materials including books, poster sets, filmstrips and computer software. Publishes 120 titles/year.
First Contact & Terms: Works with 20 freelance artists/year. Works on assignment only. Send query letter with resume and samples to be kept on file unless the artist requests return. Write for artists' guidelines. Prefers Photostats as samples. Samples not filed are returned only by request. Reports within 6 weeks. Original work not returned to the artist after job's completion. Considers project's budget when establishing payment. Rights purchased vary according to project.
Jackets/Covers: Assigns 20 freelance design and 20 freelance illustration jobs/year. Pays by the hour, $12-20 and by the project, $100 minimum.
Text Illustration: Assigns 10 freelance jobs/year. Prefers b&w pen & ink. Pays by the hour, $12-20 and by the project, $100 minimum.

WALKER & COMPANY, 720 Fifth Ave., New York NY 10019. (212)265-3632. Cable address: REKLAWSAM. Art Director: Laurie McBarnette. Publishes hardcover originals and reprints on mysteries, regency romance, children's science, adult trade, etc. Publishes 200 titles/year; 60% require freelance designers, 60% require freelance illustrators. Also uses artists for catalog design and layout, educational and adult/juvenile.
First Contact & Terms: Works with 20-30 freelance artists/year. Illustrators must be within 2 hours of New York; designers must have textbook experience. Works on assignment only. Send business card and samples to be filed. Prefers any sample except slides. Samples are returned by SASE. Reports only if interested. Buys all rights. Originals returned to artist at job's completion (except in special instances).
Book Design: Assigns 7 jobs/year. Uses freelance artists for complete follow-through on job, layout, type spec. Prefers classic style—modern conservative. Pays by the hour, $7.50-15 average, or by the project, $200-600 average; 60 days upon completion.
Jackets/Covers: Assigns 40 freelance illustration jobs/year. Pays by the project, $100 minimum.
Text Illustration: Assigns 3 freelance jobs/year. Prefers b&w line drawings or pencil. Pays by the project, $500 minimum.

WARNER BOOKS INC., 666 Fifth Ave., New York NY 10103. (212)484-3151. Creative Director: Jackie Meyer. Publishes 400 titles/year; 20% require freelance designers, 80% require freelance illustrators. Works with countless freelance artists/year. Buys hundreds of designs from freelance artists/year. Buys hundreds of illustrations from freelance artists/year.
First Contact & Terms: Works on assignment only. Send brochure or tear sheets and photocopies. Samples are filed. Samples not filed are returned by SASE. Reports back only if interested. To show a portfolio, mail appropriate materials. Originals returned to artist at job's completion (artist must pick up). Pays $650/design; $1,000/illustration. Negotiates rights purchased. Check for most recent titles in bookstores.
Jackets/Covers: Uses realistic jacket illustrations. Payment subject to negotiation.
Tips: Industry trends include "more graphics and stylized art. Looks for "photorealistic style with imaginative and original design and use of eyecatching color variations." Artists shouldn't "talk too much. Good design and art should speak for themselves."

***SAMUEL WEISER INC.**, Box 612, York Beach ME 03910. (207)363-4393. Production Manager: Kathryn Sky-Peck. Specializes in hardcover and paperback originals, reprints and trade publications on metaphysics/oriental philosophy/occult. Publishes 20 titles/year.
First Contact & Terms: Works with 4 freelance artists/year. Send query letter with resume, slides, book covers and jackets. Samples are filed. Samples not filed are returned by SASE only if requested by artist. Reports back within 1 month only if interested. Originals returned to artist at job's completion. To show a portfolio, mail tear sheets and slides. Considers complexity of project, skill and experience of

artist, project's budget, turnaround time and rights purchased when establishing payment. Buys one-time rights.

Jackets/Covers: Assigns 20 freelance design jobs/year. Pays by the project, $200-600.

Tips: "We're interested in artists with professional experience with cover mechanicals—from inception of design to researching/creating image to type design, color-separated mechanicals to logo in place. Don't send us drawings of witches, goblins and demons, for that is not what the occult field is. You should know something about us before you send materials."

WESTBURG ASSOC., PUBLISHERS, 1745 Madison St., Fennimore WI 53809. (608)822-6237. Editor/Publisher: John Westburg. Specializes in paperback originals of essays, criticism, short fiction, poetry, in the fields of literature and humanities. Publishes 1-3 titles/year.

First Contact & Terms: Works with 3-5 freelance artists/year. Send query letter with brochure and business card to be kept on file. Do not send samples until requested; do not send original work. Samples not filed are returned by SASE. No originals returned at job's completion. Considers project's budget when establishing payment. Buys all rights or negotiates rights purchased.

Jackets/Covers: Assigns 4-8 freelance design and illustration jobs/year. Pays for illustration by the project, $25-50 average.

Text Illustration: Assigns 4 freelance illustration jobs/year. Prefers b&w line drawings. Pays for illustration by the project, $25-50 average.

WHITE EAGLE PUBLISHER, Dept. A-0111, Box 1332, Lowell MA 01853. President: Jack Loisel. Specializes in paperbacks on religion and poetry. Publishes 5 titles/year; 100% require freelance designers, 100% require freelance illustrators.

First Contact & Terms: Works with 7 freelance artists/year. Artists should have experience. Send query letter with brochure or photographs and Photostats to be kept on file. Reports only if interested. Works on assignment only. No originals returned to artist at job's completion. Considers complexity of project and project's budget when establishing payment. Buys one-time or all rights. Material not copyrighted.

Book Design: Assigns 5 freelance jobs/year. Pays by the project, $500 minimum.

Jackets/Covers: Assigns 5 freelance design and 10 freelance illustration jobs/year. Pays by the project, $400 minimum.

Text Illustration: Assigns 2 freelance jobs/year. Pays by the project, $300 minimum.

ALBERT WHITMAN & COMPANY, 5747 W. Howard St., Niles IL 60648. Editor: Kathleen Tucker. Specializes in hardcover original juvenile fiction and nonfiction—many picture books for young children. Publishes 21 titles/year; 100% require freelance illustrators.

First Contact & Terms: Works with 18 freelance artists/year. Prefers working with artists who have experience illustrating juvenile trade books. Works on assignment only. Send brochure/flyer or resume and "a few slides and photocopies of original art and tear sheets that we can keep in our files. Do *not* send original art through the mail." Samples not returned. Reports to an artist if "we have a project that seems right for him. We like to see evidence that an artist can show the same children in a variety of moods and poses." Original work returned to artist at job's completion "if artist holds the copyright." Rights purchased vary.

Cover/Text Illustration: Cover assignment is usually part of illustration assignment. Assigns 18 jobs/year. Prefers realistic art. Pays by flat fee or royalties.

Tips: Especially looks for "an artist's ability to draw people, especially children."

WILSHIRE BOOK CO., 12015 Sherman Rd., North Hollywood CA 91605. (213)875-1711 or (818)983-1105. President: Melvin Powers. Publishes paperback reprints on psychology, self-help, inspirational and other types of nonfiction. Publishes 25 titles/year.

First Contact & Terms: Local artists only. Call. Buys first, reprint or one-time rights. Negotiates pay. Free catalog.

Jackets/Covers: Assigns 25 jobs/year. Buys b&w line drawings.

WOMEN'S AGLOW FELLOWSHIP, Publications Division, Box I, Lynnwood WA 98036. (206)775-7282. Art Director: Kathy Boice. Specializes in Bible studies and Christian literature, and a bimonthly magazine offering Christian women's material. Publishes 20 titles/year; 25% require freelance illustrators and calligraphers.

First Contact & Terms: Works with 20 freelance artists/year. Send slides, Photostats, line drawings and reproduced art as samples. Samples returned by SASE. Reports in 6 weeks. Call or write for appointment to show portfolio. Provide resume, business card, brochure/flyer, samples and tear sheets to be kept on file for possible future assignments. Originals returned to artist at job's completion. Buys one-time rights.

Pencil, cray-pas and ink washes were used by Lydia Halverson of Evanston, Illinois, to create this portrait of Amelia Earhart for a children's book published by Albert Whitman & Company of Niles, Illinois. Halverson wanted these illustrations to be reminiscent of the actual photos of the aviatrix. Joseph Boyd, president of Albert Whitman, bought all rights to the artwork.

Jackets/Covers: Pays for design and illustration by the job, $200 average.
Magazine Illustrations: Pays $80-175, b&w line drawings; $200-325, color, inside; $500, color, cover.
Text Illustration: Prefers b&w line drawings. Pays by the job, $35-200 average.
Tips: "Be aware of organization's emphasis. Be motivated to work for a women's organization."

WOODALL PUBLISHING COMPANY, 500 Hyacinth Pl., Highland Park IL 60035. (312)433-4550. Publications Manager: Debby Spriggs. Specializes in paperback annuals on camping. Publishes 3 titles/year.
First Contact & Terms: Works with 4 freelance artists/year. Works on assignment only. Call for appointment to show portfolio. Reports within 4 weeks. No original work returned at job's completion. Considers complexity of project, skill and experience of artist, and project's budget when establishing payment. Rights purchased vary according to project.
Book Design: Assigns 3-4 jobs/year. Pays by the project.
Jackets/Covers: Assigns 2 freelance design and illustration jobs/year. Pays by the project.
Text Illustration: Pays by the project.

WRITER'S DIGEST BOOKS/NORTH LIGHT, F&W Publishing, 1507 Dana Ave., Cincinnati OH 45207. Art Director: Carol Buchanan. Publishes 25-30 books annually for writers, artists, photographers, plus selected trade titles. Send photocopies of printed work to be kept on file. Works on assignment only.
Text Illustration: Uses artists for text illustration and cartoons.
Tips: Uses artists for ad illustration and design, book jacket illustration and design, and direct mail design.

***YANKEE PUBLISHING INC., BOOK DIVISION**, Main St., Dublin NH 03444. Assistant to Editorial Director: Rebecca Robinson. Specializes in hardcover and paperback originals on New England topics; cookbooks. Publishes 14 titles/year; 50% require freelance illustrators.
First Contact & Terms: Works with 10 freelance artists/year. Send query letter with resume and slides or photocopies to be kept on file. Samples not kept on file are returned by SASE. Works on assignment only. Originals returned to the artist at job's completion if stated in contract. Considers complexity of project, project's budget and rights purchased when establishing payment. Negotiates rights purchased.
Jackets/Covers: Pays by the project, $200-600 average, usually full color.
Text Illustration: Pays by the project, $50-500 average, usually b&w line art.

YE GALLEON PRESS, Box 25, Fairfield WA 99012. (509)283-2422. Editorial Director: Glen Adams. Publishes rare western history, Indian material, antiquarian shipwreck and old whaling accounts, and town and area histories; hardcover and paperback originals and reprints. Publishes 30 titles/year; 20% require freelance illustrators.
First Contact & Terms: Query with samples. SASE. No advance. Pays promised fee for unused assigned work. Buys book rights. Free catalog.
Text Illustration: Buys b&w line drawings, some pen & ink drawings of a historical nature; prefers drawings of groups with facial expressions and some drawings of sailing and whaling vessels. Pays for illustration by the project, $10-35.
Tips: " 'Wild' artwork is hardly suited to book illustration for my purposes. Many correspondents wish to sell oil paintings which at this time we do not buy. It costs too much to print them for short edition work."

"The most valuable illustrators are those who are able to envisage the completed cover design and compare their illustration to incorporate the type and copy that will be added later."

—Dwight Baker, Baker Book House
Ada, Michigan

Businesses

Product styling and the design of collateral materials that "sell" the company and/or its products are the main needs of the business listings in this section. Annual reports, print ads, brochures, point-of-purchase displays, plus innovative product lines, are a few of the diverse ways the services of freelance artists are used with these firms.

Opportunities exist for both illustrators and designers. Businesses most often need illustrations for newspaper ads and catalogs. When you read the Close-up of illustrator Kim Gromoll, you'll find how many opportunities there are in this section. Manufacturers need industrial and package designers. Industrial designers shape products, determining the characteristic look and quality one "feels" about a product. Some industrial designers move into toy designing, in which they work with miniature projects. A package designer must combine the three-dimensional skills of an industrial designer with the two-dimensional design sense of a graphic designer. He creates graphic symbols and works with the color and design of labels.

If you're interested in a particular product area, check the *Yellow Pages* and ask at your local library for suggestions of trade periodicals dealing with that specific interest. Additional manufacturers can be obtained from the *Thomas Register of Manufacturers*, which lists companies alphabetically and according to product.

The business world also has needs for fine art. We've included collectibles manufacturers in the listings, because they are always looking for new talent. Collectibles producers generally seek artists with a realistic style who can render idealized people and nostalgic settings. Collectible manufacturers can also be found in *The Bradford Book of Collector's Plates* and in *Plate World*.

Fashion firms have been singled out at the end of this section so you can locate them more easily. Their art needs revolve around a similar theme—clothing and the accessories that enhance it. The fashion world is adjusting to the loss of one of its major illustrators—Antonio—but will continue to use fine art touches in advertisements and editorial projects. Most opportunities for freelancers exist in laying out ads for department stores. Retail illustration requires a realistic style, because its purpose is to sell garments for department stores, boutiques and mail-order companies. Print advertisements which stress a certain look or style require editorial art, which entails a freer, more expressionistic touch. When contacting art directors of department stores or design houses, make appointments in advance, because time is at a premium in this industry. To keep aware of trends, refer to *Women's Wear Daily*, a leading trade newspaper or its sister magazine *W*.

Artist: Carolyn Hild

Created by Carolyn Hild of Hild-Nelson in Deerfield, Illinois, this and two other logos were used to promote a convention seminar for the employees of Banker's Life and Casualty Company. Hild was paid $300 for all rights to the work, which was used in a bulletin, brochure and a poster, plus promotional items.

ABBEY PRESS, Hill Dr., St. Meinrad IN 47577. Creative Director: Jo Anne Calucchia. Manufacturer/distributor/mail order catalog providing Christian products, greeting cards, wall decor and sculpture. Clients: Christian bookstores and retail catalog.
Needs: Works with 50 freelance artists/year. Buys 200-300 freelance designs/illustrations/year. Artist must have knowledge of art preparation for reproduction; prefers 3 years experience in greeting cards. Works on assignment only. Uses artists for 3-dimensional product design, illustration on product and model making. "Quick turnaround time is required."
First Contact & Terms: Send query letter with resume, tear sheets, slides and photographs. Samples not filed are returned by SASE. Reports back within 1 month. Pays for design by the project, $75 minimum. Pays for illustration by the project, $200 minimum.
Tips: "Our products are of a religious and/or inspirational nature. We need full-color illustrations from experienced artists who know how to prepare art for reproduction. Familiarize yourself with current looks and trends in the Christian market."

ABRACADABRA MAGIC SHOP, Box 450, Dept. AM87, Scotch Plains NJ 07076. (201)668-1313. President: Robert Bokor. Manufacturer/mail order specializing in fun products for boys, marketed via mail order. Clients: boys, as well as hobby and magic shops.
Needs: Works with 2-3 freelance artists/year. Local artists only. Works on assignment only. Uses artists for advertising and catalog design, illustration and layout; packaging design and layout.
First Contact & Terms: Send query letter with resume and photocopies. Samples not filed are returned by SASE. Reports back within 1 month. To show a portfolio, mail appropriate materials. Pays for design by the project, $50-1,000. Considers client's budget when establishing payment.
Tips: "Freelancers with past experience designing products/ads for boys and/or hobby products is a plus."

***ACADEMY HANDPRINTS LTD.**, 14-16 Irving Pl., Woodmere NY 11598. (516)569-4600. President: Leo Nichols. Manufacturer of wallcoverings.
Needs: Works with freelance artists/year. Works on assignment only. Usea artists for advertising design, illustration and layout.
First Contact & Terms: Send resume. Samples not filed are returned only if requested. Reports back only if interested. Call or write to schedule an appointment to show a portfolio. Pays for design by the project. Buys all rights.

ADELE'S II, INC., 17300 Ventura Blvd., Encino CA 91316. (818)990-5544. Contact: Shirley Margulis. Franchisor and retailer of personalized gifts including acrylic and oak desk accessories, novelty clocks, personalized gift items from any medium. Sells to "high-quality-conscious" customers.
Needs: Works with 100-150 freelance artists/year. Uses artists for product design, model making and lettering. "We always will consider any type of item that can be personalized in some way, shape or form."
First Contact & Terms: Send query letter with brochure or photocopies and photos to be kept on file. Samples not filed are returned by SASE. Reports only if interested. Write for appointment to show portfolio, which should include thumbnails and photographs. Pays for design by the hour, $10-20; by the project, $10-300. Considers rights purchased when establishing payment.
Tips: "Consider first that we only purchase items we can sell personalized. A beautiful picture can't be personalized. Common mistakes freelancers make in presenting samples or portfolios is to "talk too much and show sloppy samples. Also, they don't know how to cost out their item."

AERO PRODUCTS RESEARCH INC., 11201 Hindry Ave., Los Angeles CA 90045. Director of Public Relations: J. Parr. Aviation training materials producer. Produces line of plastic credit and business cards.
Needs: Works with about 2 illustrators/month. Prefers local artists. Uses artists for brochures, catalogs, advertisements, graphs and illustrations.
First Contact & Terms: Send query letter with resume, brochure/flyer, resume and tear sheets to be kept on file. No originals returned to artist at job's completion. Negotiates pay according to experience and project.

AHPA ENTERPRISES, Box 506, Sheffield AL 35660. Marketing Manager: Allen Turner. Media products producer/marketer. Provides illustrations, fiction, layouts, video productions, computer-printed material, etc. Specializes in adult male, special-interest material. Clients: limited-press publishers, authors, private investors, etc.
Needs: Seeking illustrators for illustration of realistic original fiction or concepts. Wants only those artists "who are in a position to work with us on an intermittent but long-term basis." Works on assignment only.

First Contact & Terms: Send query letter with resume and photocopies or tear sheets, photostats, photographs and new sketches to be kept on file. Samples not filed are returned by SASE only if requested. Reports back only if interested (within 3-7 days). Pays for illustration by the project, $30-1,000 average. Considers complexity of the project and number and type of illustrations ordered when establishing payment. Buys all rights.
Tips: "Samples should indicate capability in realistic (if 'glamorized') face-and-figure illustration. Continuity-art experience is preferred. This is an excellent place for capable amateurs to 'turn pro' on a part-time, open-end basis."

AK INTERNATIONAL, 1116 Marshall Ave., Lancaster PA 17601. (717)394-0202. President: O. Ali Akincilar. Full line of photo frames including brass, chrome and brass, exotic woods and aluminum. Clients: the gift industry, premium, department stores, photo stores.
Needs: Buys approximately 20 designs/year from freelance artists. Prefers line drawings for illustrations. Artists must have a knowledge of photo etching. Works on assignment only.
First Contact & Terms: Send query letter with brochure, resume and photographs to be kept on file. Samples not filed are returned only if requested. Reports only if interested. Call for appointment to show portfolio. Original art not returned after reproduction. Pays by the project, $50-500 average. Buys all rights.
Tips: Looks for "eye for proportion and exactness, feel for proper color, knowledge of current market trends."

ALBEE SIGN CO., 561 E. 3rd St., Mt. Vernon NY 10553. (914)668-0201. President: William Lieberman. Produces interior and exterior signs and graphics. Clients are commercial accounts, banks and real estate companies.
Needs: Works with 6 artists for sign design, 6 for display fixture design, 6 for P-O-P design and 6 for custom sign illustration. Local artists only. Works on assignment only.
First Contact & Terms: Query with samples (pictures of completed work). Previous experience with other firms preferred. SASE. Reports within 2-3 weeks. No samples returned. Reports back as assignment occurs. Provide resume, business card and pictures of work to be kept on file for future assignments. Pays by job.

ALL-STATE LEGAL SUPPLY CO., One Commerce Dr., Cranford NJ 07016. (201)272-0800. Advertising Manager: Paul Ellman. Manufacturer and distributor of supplies, stationery, engraving, printing. Clients: lawyers.
Needs: Works with 6 freelance artists/year. Experienced, local artists and designers only. Works on assignment only. Uses artists for advertising, brochure and catalog design, illustration and layout; display fixture design, and illustration on product. Especially needs cover illustrations and catalog work.
First Contact & Terms: Send query letter with photostats to be kept on file. Reports only if interested. Call for appointment to show portfolio. Pays by the project, $350-1,500 average. Considers complexity of project, skill and experience of artist and turnaround time when establishing payment.

***ALMOST HEAVEN HOT TUBS, LTD**, Attention: Art Dept., Route 5, Renick WV 24966. (304)497-3163. Art Director: Barry Glick. Manufacturer of hot water leisure products, i.e., hot tubs, spas, whirlpools, saunas. Clients: distributors, dealers, retailers, consumers.
Needs: Works with 5 freelance artists/year. Uses artists for advertising, brochure and catalog design, illustration and layout; product and display fixture design, illustration on product, P-O-P displays, posters, model making and signage.
First Contact & Terms: Send query letter with brochure, resume, business card, samples and tear sheets to be kept on file. Reports within 1 week. Pay varies. Considers complexity of project, skill and experience of artist, how work will be used, turnaround time and rights purchased when establishing payment.

***ALVA MUSEUM REPLICAS**, Division of Barrett Colea Inc., 24-39 44th St., Long Island City NY 11103. (718)726-4063. Contact: Gregory Glasson. Manufacturer and distributor of sculpture replicas. Clients: museum shops, department stores, libraries and universities. For contract casting, mail color slides or photos stating size, medium and showing all views. SASE.
Tips: There is a trend toward "categories such as Art Deco, animals and sculpture suitable for casting in "lalique" finish lucite."

ALVIMAR MANUFACTURING CO., INC., 51-02 21st St., Long Island City NY 11101. President: Alan P. Friedlander. Display firm and manufacturer of plastic inflatable swim toys, such as beach balls, rings, pools, mats. Also premium items, such as product replicas, like Little Green Sprout and Wrigley Spearmint Chewing Gum. Clients: Service advertising agencies, food and cosmetic manufacturers,

"any category as we make product replicas."
Needs: Uses artists for product and P-O-P design and model making.
First Contact & Terms: Call for appointment. Prefers to see originals or Photostats of work. Samples returned by SASE. Reports in 4 months. Provide resume and tear sheets to be kept on file for possible future assignments. Payment method is negotiable and varies according to client's budget.

AMERICAN ADVERTISING DISTRIBUTORS, 170 Changebridge Rd., Montville NJ 07045. (201)227-4607. President: Joesph O'Dowd. Distributor of direct mail advertising for retail and professional business.
Needs: Works with 3 freelance artists/year. Local artists only. Uses artists for advertising design and layout.
First Contact & Terms: Send query letter with brochure showing art style. Reports only if interested. Write to schedule an appointment to show a portfolio, which should include roughs and original/final art. Pays for design by the hour, $5-20. Considers complexity of project and turnaround time when establishing payment.

AMERICAN ARTISTS, Division of Graphics Buying Service, 225 W. Hubbard St., Chicago IL 60610. (312)828-0555. Advertising Coordinator: Lorraine Light. Manufacturer of limited edition plates and figurines. Specializes in horse, children, and cat themes, but considers others. Clients: wholesalers and retailers.
Needs: Works with 3 freelance artists/year. Does not work on assignment only. Uses artists for plate and figurine design and illustration; brochure design, illustration and layout. Open to most art styles.
First Contact & Terms: Send query letter with resume and samples to be kept on file unless return is requested or artwork is unsuitable. Prefers transparencies or slides but will accept photos—color only. Samples not filed are returned only if requested or if unsuitable. Reports within 1 month. Call or write for appointment to show portfolio. Payment varies and is negotiated. Rights purchased vary. Considers complexity of project, skill and experience of artist, how work will be used and rights purchased when establishing payment.

AMERICAN BOOKDEALERS EXCHANGE, Box 2525, La Mesa CA 92041. Editor: Al Galasso. Publisher of *Book Dealers World* targeted to self-publishers, writers and mail order book dealers. Clients: self-publishers, writers, business opportunity seekers.
Needs: Works with 3 freelance artists/year. Prefers artists with at least a year's experience. Works on assignment only. Uses artists for advertising, brochure and catalog design and illustration.
First Contact & Terms: Send query letter with photostats to be kept on file. Samples not kept on file are returned only if requested. Reports only if interested. Pays by the project, $25-200 average. Considers complexity of project, skill and experience of artist, turnaround time and rights purchased when establishing payment.

AMERICAN EAGLE COMPANY, 1130 E. Big Beaver, Troy MI 48083. (313)689-9458. Creative Director: Diane Chownyk. Provides teaching aid products and marketing products/programs for hospitals and nurses and foreign language teachers.
Needs: Works with 6 freelance artists/year. Local artists only. Works on assignment only. Uses artists for advertising, brochure and catalog design, illustration and layout; product design, illustration on product, posters and model making.
First Contact & Terms: Send query letter with resume and photocopies. Samples not filed are not returned. Reports only if interested. To show a portfolio, mail appropriate materials or call or write to schedule an appointment. Pays for design and illustration by the hour, $10-15. Considers complexity of project, skill and experience of artist, and how work will be used when establishing payment.
Tips: Artist should "show their best samples—our interview time is limited. Have a resume if possible."

***AMERICAN MANAGEMENT ASSOCIATION**, 135 W. 50th St., New York NY 10020. (212)903-8157. Art Director: Dolores Wesnak. Provides educational courses, conferences and topical briefings to business managers and support staff. Clients: business executives, managers and supervisors.
Needs: Works with 6-10 freelance artists/year. Uses artists for brochure design and layout, catalog design and layout, and posters.
First Contact & Terms: Prefers local artists experienced in 2-color brochures, full-time professionals. The ability to conceptually develop ideas is important. Works on assignment only. Call or write for appointment to show portfolio. Pays by the project, $450 minimum. Considers complexity of project and skill and experience of artist when establishing payment.
Tips: Artists "must have a knowledge of design for direct mail and of postal regulations."

AMERICAN PERMANENT WARE, INC. (APW), 729 Third Ave., Dallas TX 75226. (214)421-7366. Director of Advertising and Marketing: Mary M. Cardone. Manufacturer of stainless steel food service equipment for dealers, distributors and national accounts.
Needs: Works with 4 freelance artists/year. Prefers local artists. Works on assignment only. Uses artists for the design, illustration and layout of advertising brochures and catalogs plus P-O-P displays and trade publication ad layouts.
First Contact & Terms: Send query letter with brochure showing art style or photocopies. Samples not filed are returned only if requested. Reports back only if interested. Write to schedule an appointment to show a portfolio, which should include final reproduction/product and color. Considers complexity of project and client's budget when establishing payment. Buys all rights.
Tips: "See more sophistication in the field."

***ANNIS-WAY SIGNS LTD.**, 595 West St. S., Orillia, Ontario Canada. Contact: Lloyd H. Annis.
Needs: Uses artists for exhibit, trademark and display design, sign redesign and lettering.
First Contact & Terms: Send resume.

ARMSTRONG'S, 150 E. 3rd St., Pomona CA 91766. (714)623-6464. President: David W. Armstrong. Wholesale and retail manufacturer/gallery of collector plates, figurines and lithographs. Clients: wholesale and retail customers of all age groups.
Needs: Works on assignment only. Uses professional artists for plate design; limited edition art prints; advertising posters; advertising, brochure and catalog design, illustration and layout.
First Contact & Terms: Send query letter with brochure, resume, business card and photographs, transparencies and tear sheets to be kept on file. Samples not filed are returned. Reports within 2 weeks. Payment is determined on a case-by-case basis. Considers skill and experience of the artist and rights purchased when establishing payment.
Tips: "Make your initial contact by letter and do not make excessive telephone calls to our offices."

ARTISTS OF THE WORLD, 2915 N. 67th Place, Scottsdale AZ 85251. National Sales Manager: Thomas R. Jackson. Producer of plates, figurines and miniature plates and figurines. Clients: wholesalers and retailers.
Needs: Works with a variable number of freelance artists/year. Works on assignment only. Uses artists for the design and illustration of plates and figurines.
First Contact & Terms: Send query letter with brochure showing art style. Samples not filed are returned only if requested. Reports back within 2 weeks. To show a portfolio, mail appropriate materials, which should include original/final art, final reproduction/product and color. Pays for design by the project. Considers how work will be used when establishing payment.

THE ASHTON-DRAKE GALLERIES, 9333 Milwaukee Ave., Niles IL 60648. (312)966-2770, ext. 300. Product Development: Ed Bailey-Mershon. Marketer of limited edition collectibles, such as dolls, figurines, ornaments, and other uniquely executed artwork sold in thematic series. Clients: Collectible consumers represent all age groups.
Needs: Works with 200 freelance doll artists, coustume designers, illustrators, artists, sculptors a year. Works on assignment only. Uses artists for concept illustrations, collectible designs, prototype specifications and construction. Prior experience in giftware design, greeting card and book illustration a plus. Subject matter is children and mothers, animals, nostalgia scenes.
First Contact & Terms: Send query letter with resume, copies of samples to be kept on file, except for copyrighted slides which are duplicated and returned. Prefers slides, photographs, tear sheets, or photostats (in that order) as samples. Samples not filed are returned. Reports within 45 days. Concept illustrations are done "on spec" to $200 maximum. Contract for length of series on royalty basis with guaranteed advances. Considers complexity of the project, project's budget, skill and experience of the artist, and rights purchased.

AVALON LTD., 12217 Woodbine, Redford MI 48239. (517)332-4902. Vice President: Eric Fromm. Importer/distributor/retailer of rattan and bamboo home furnishings and furniture. Directed toward ages 20-45.
Needs: Works with 2-4 freelance artists/year. Uses artists for brochure and catalog design, illustration and layout; P-O-P displays, posters and direct mail.
First Contact & Terms: Send query letter with resume and samples. Samples not filed are returned only if requested. To show a portfolio, mail roughs, original/final art, color and tear sheets. Pays for design and illustration by the project, $10-100. Considers complexity of project and budget when establishing payment.

BAKER STREET PRODUCTIONS LTD., Box 3610, Mankato MN 56001. (507)625-2482. Contact: Karyne Jacobsen. Service-related firm providing juvenile books to publishers.
Needs: Works with 2 freelance artists/year. Artists must be able to meet exact deadlines. Works on assignment only. Uses artists for advertising illustration, illustration on product and book illustration.
First Contact & Terms: Send query letter with resume and tear sheet. Reports back within 3 months. Write to schedule an appointment to show a portfolio, which should include roughs, final reproduction/product, color and photographs. Fee is determined by the size of the project involved. Pays for design and illustration by the project. Considers complexity of the project and how work will be used when establishing payment. Buys all rights.

BANKERS LIFE & CASUALTY COMPANY, 1000 Sunset Ridge Rd., Northbrook IL 60062. (312)498-1500. Manager-Communications/Graphics: Charles S. Pusateri. Insurance firm.
Needs: Works with 5-10 freelance artists/year. Works on assignment only. Uses artists for advertising and brochure displays, illustration and layout; posters and signage.
First Contact & Terms: Send query letter with resume and printed pieces to be kept on file. Samples returned only if requested. Reports within 2 weeks only if interested. Write to schedule an appointment to show a portfolio, which should include thumbnails, roughs and final reproduction/product. Pays for design by the project. Considers complexity of project, skill and experience of artist and turnaround time when establishing payment. Rights purchased vary according to project.
Tips: "Follow rules but don't give up. Timing is essential."

***BARTON-MAKS COMPANY**, 1819 Floradale Ave., S. El Monte CA 91733. President: David Mak. Toy distributor/wholesaler to department stores, toy chains, supermarket, and drug stores, etc. Clients: department stores, discount stores and supermarket drug stores.
Needs: Works with 1 freelance artist/year. Prefers local (Los Angeles) artists. Works on assignment only. Uses artists for catalog design, illustration and layout, illustration and product and display fixture design.
First Contact & Terms: Send query letter with brochure or resume. Samples not filed are returned. Reports back only if interested. To show a portfolio, mail roughs and original/final art. Pays for design by the project. Considers skill and experience of artist when establishing payment. Negotiates right purchased.
Tips: "Need freelancers with experience in toy industry to apply in writing with a resume."

***BAY AREA RAPID TRANSIT (BART)**, 800 Madison St., Oakland CA 94619. (415)465-4100. Manager Passenger Service: Kay Springer. Transportation service firm providing passenger brochures, flyers, signs, information, advertising.
Needs: Works with 4-6 freelance artists/year. Uses artists for advertising and brochure design, illustration and layout; posters and signage.
First Contact & Terms: Local artists only (San Francisco Bay area). Send query letter with brochure, resume, business card and original work to be kept on file. Reports only if interested. Works on assignment only. Pays by the hour or by the project. Considers complexity of project and turnaround time when establishing payment.

BENJAMIN DIVISION, THOMAS INDUSTRIES, Box 180, Rte. 70 S. Rd., Sparta TN 38583. (615)738-2241. Advertising Manager: Cindy Jarvis. Manufacturer of commercial/industrial fluorescent/incandescent lighting, produce HID lighting for lighting distributors, architects, engineering firms, government agencies, schools, industrial firms and national chains.
Needs: Works with 1-2 freelance artists/year. Prefers artists with three years experience. Works on assignment basis only. Uses artists for the illustration layout of advertising, brochures and catalogs.
First Contact & Terms: Send query letter with brochure showing art style. Reports back only if interested. Call or write to schedule an appointment to show a portfolio, which should include original/final art, final reproduction/product, color and photographs. Pays for design and illustration by the project. Considers how work will be used and turnaround time when establishing payment.

BERMAN LEATHERCRAFT INC., 25 Melcher St., Boston MA 02120. (617)426-0870. President: Robert S. Berman. Manufacturer/importer/mail order firm providing leathercraft kits and leather supplies, diaries and notepads. Clients: shops, hobbyists, schools and hospitals. "We mail to 5,000-25,000 people every six weeks."
Needs: Works with 2-4 freelance artists/year. Local artists only "for the convenience of both parties." Uses artists for brochure design, illustration and layout; "we produce two- to four-page fliers." Especially needs line drawings with dimension.
First Contact & Terms: Send query letter with printed brochures; "follow up with a phone call three to five days later." Samples not filed are returned by SASE only if requested. Pays by the project. Considers complexity of project, and skill and experience of artist when establishing payment. Buys all rights.

BEROL, Berol Corp., Eagle Rd., Danbury CT 06813. (203)744-0000. Art Product Group Manager: Lance Hopkins. Manufactures writing instruments, drawing materials and art supplies (Prismacolor Art Pencils, Art Markers and Art Stix ® artist crayons).
Needs: Uses artists for illustrations and layout for catalogs, ads, brochures, displays, packages. Artists must use Prismacolor and/or Verithin products only.
First Contact & Terms: Query with photographs and slides to be kept on file. Samples returned only by request. Reports within 2 weeks. Call or write to schedule an appointment to show a portfolio; portfolios not necessary. Pays by the project, $300 maximum. Rights purchased vary according to project.
Tips: "Hand-colored photographs (with Prismacolor® Art Pencils) becoming very popular."

BEST WESTERN INTERNATIONAL INC., Best Western Way, Box 10203, Phoenix AZ 85064. (602)957-5763. Art Director: Barbara Lanterman. Motel inn/hotel resort chain. Clients: motels, hotels, resorts.
Needs: Assigns 200 jobs/year. Especially needs photography, illustration, production art, design.
First Contact & Terms: Query with samples. Prefers samples of printed or published pieces, illustrations.

***BLUE CROSS AND BLUE SHIELD OF MICHIGAN**, 600 Lafayette E., Detroit MI 48226. (313)225-8115. Art/Production Manager: Vivian K. Adams.
Needs: Uses 4 artists for product illustration/year. Also uses artists for designs for annual reports, brochures, posters, booklets, keylining and figure illustration.
First Contact & Terms: Local artists only. Query with printed samples. Artists must have at least 5 years in the field and a portfolio to back up professional experience. Payment negotiated.

***BON-TON WALLCOVERINGS, INC.**, Rte. 70 & Mansion Blvd., Pennsauken NJ 08109. (609)662-3605. President: Ted Lutz. Manufacturer and distributor of wallcoverings. Clients: wallcovering dealers, contractors, architects, etc.
Needs: Uses artists for product design.
First Contact & Terms: Send query letter with brochure. Samples are not filed. Samples not filed are returned only if requested. Reports back only if interested. Call to schedule an appointment to show a portfolio. Buys all rights.

THE BRADFORD EXCHANGE, 9333 Milwaukee, Niles-Chicago IL 60648. (312)966-2770, ext. 302. Artist Liaison: Janet Jensen. Marketers of collectible plates. Clients: plate collectors in all age groups and income groups.
Needs: Works with 200 freelance artists/year. Works on assignment only. Uses artists for plate design; interested in all media, 2-D, 3-D. Subject matter is predominately mothers, children; new areas: animals and movie themes. Especially needs professional artists of portraiture, landscape, sculptors, still life, wildlife, fantasy, nautical and religious. "Quality painting reproduced on plate."
First Contact & Terms: Send query letter with brochure, 18-20 slides, resume and samples to be kept on file. Prefers slides, photographs, photocopies, tear sheets or Photostats (in that order) as samples. Samples not filed are returned. Reports within 45 days. Call or write for appointment to show portfolio; portfolio should include roughs, original/final art, final reproduction/product, tear sheets, photographs and slides or transparencies. Pays "on spec"; $200 maximum. Contract negotiated for series. Considers complexity of the project, project's budget, skill and experience of the artist and rights purchased when establishing payment.
Tips: Artists "need good reference material illustrating ability to render the human figure and faces realistically. Include a resume or biography."

CANTERBURY DESIGNS, INC.. Box 4060, Martinez GA 30907. (800)241-2732 or (404)860-1674. President: Angie A. Newton. Publisher and distributor of charted design books; counted cross stitch mainly. Clients: needlework specialty shops, wholesale distributors (craft and needlework), department stores and chain stores.
Needs: Works with 12-20 freelance artists/year. Uses artists for product design.
First Contact & Terms: Send query letter with samples to be returned. Prefers stitched needlework, paintings, photographs or charts as samples. Samples not filed are returned. Reports within 1 month. Call for appointment to show portfolio. Payment varies. "Some designs purchased outright, some are paid on a royalty basis." Considers complexity of project, salability, customer appeal and rights purchased when establishing payment.
Tips: "When sending your work for our review, be sure to photocopy it first. This protects you. Also, you have a copy from which to reconstruct your design should it be lost in mail. Also, send your work by certified mail. You have proof it was actually received by someone."

KEN CAPLAN PRODUCT DESIGN, 4651 Fitch Ave., Lincolnwood IL 60646. (312)674-2643. Art Director: Ken Caplan. Product development of hobbycrafts, activity toys, Christmas ornaments, leather crafts, clock kits, toys and games. "We create, invent, design the product, its color and 'look' for child and adult shelf appeal." Clients: manufacturers.
Needs: Works on assignment only. Uses artists for advertising and catalog illustration and layout, brochure illustration, product design, illustration on product and model making. "We use whimisical illustrations that are conducive to game boards, cards and all children's products."
First Contact & Terms: Send query letter with resume, photocopies, photographs, tear sheets or proofs to be kept on file. Samples not returned. Reports within 10 days. To show a portfolio, mail appropriate material, which should include thumbnails, roughs and original/final art. Pays by the project. Considers complexity of the project, how work will be used and rights purchased when establishing payment. Buys all rights.
Tips: "There is a large do-it-yourself adult market and also juvenile market. There is a trend more towards the *fine-detail* illustration. Show-n-tell days are over. Let your work do *all* the talking for you."

***CARIBBEAN EXHIBITS, INC.**, Box 6806, Loiza Station, Santurce, Puerto Rico 00914. (809)726-4630. Contact: Design Director. Exhibit/display/sign firm.
Needs: Assigns 15-25 jobs/year. Uses artists for calligraphy, fine art, murals, neon signage and scale models. "We have regular need for skillful artists who can reproduce large blow-ups of figures, items or products, backgrounds such as landscapes; following small scaled original designs or drawings, etc. Some of these murals can be as large as 50' long by 15' high."
First Contact & Terms: Arrange interview; especially needs artists September-June. SASE. Reports in 2 weeks. Pays $50-300, decoration rendering; $75-400, scenery; $50-500, exhibits. Also pays by the hour $12-30 average; by the day $96-240 average. Considers complexity of project; and skill and experience of artist when establishing payment.
Tips: "Due to the distance that our firm is from the mainland US, the artist must be aware that he is to travel by air and must be willing to set aside various days until he has completed his services here in Puerto Rico."

CENIT LETTERS, INC., 7438 Varna Ave., North Hollywood CA 91605. (818)983-1234 or (213)875-0880. President: Don Kurtz. Sign firm producing custom cutout letters. Clients: building managers and their tenants (high rise), designers and architects. Assigns 25 jobs/year.
Needs: Local artists only. Works with artists for sign design, exhibit design, P-O-P design, and custom sign artwork. Also uses artists for layout and gold leaf work.
First Contact & Terms: Send query letter with resume. SASE. Reports in 1 week. Samples returned by SASE. Call to schedule an appointment to show a portfolio, which should include original/final art and photographs. Pays $100 minimum gold leaf. Pays for design and illustration by the hour, $10-15.
Tips: Especially looks for "proficiency in hand lettering and accurate full-scale layouts. Find an end-user for your artwork (e.g. a buyer for 3-dimensional graphics) and we could produce the end product."

CMA MICRO COMPUTER, Box 2080, 55888 Yucca Trail, Yucca Valley CA 92286-2080. (619)365-9718. Director/Advertising: Phyllis Wattenbarger. Manufacturer/distributor of computer software. Clients: computer software manufacturers and distributors.
Needs: Works with 10 freelance artists/year. Uses artists for advertising and brochure design and illustration.
First Contact & Terms: Send query letter with photostats, photographs, photocopies or tear sheets to be kept on file. Samples not filed returned only if requested. Reports only if interested. To show a portfolio, mail appropriate materials, which should include tear sheets and photostats. Pays for design by the hour, $8 minimum. Considers complexity of project, skill and experience of the artist, how work will be used and turnaround time ("very important") when establishing payment. Buys all rights.
Tips: "Just mail material appropriate to the computer industry. If we wish to respond, we will call or write."

***COLLECTIBLE RESOURCE GROUP, INC.**, 6700 Griffin Rd., Ft. Lauderdale FL 33314. Contact: Michael Couture. Wholesale manufacturer of collectibles such as prints, plates and figurines. Clients: retailers.
Needs: Uses artists for plate and figurine design, limited and unlimited edition fine art prints, and art posters.
First Contact & Terms: Send query letter with brochure. Samples not filed are returned only if requested. Reports back only if interested. Write to show a portfolio. Pays for a flat fee plate design, or $500-5,000. Negotiates rights purchased.

COLLINS-LACROSSE SIGN CORP., 222 Pine St., LaCrosse WI 54601. (608)784-8200. President/Manager: Charles C. Collins. Outdoor advertising sign firm. Clients: food manufacturers, beer and soft drink bottlers, oil companies; "any commercial enterprise."
Needs: Works with artists for sign design and custom sign illustration. Works on assignment only. Also uses artists for billboards, displays, neon signs and sign redesign.
First Contact & Terms: Send brochure showing art style, resume, tear sheets or photographs. Write to schedule an appointment to show a portfolio, which should include thumbnails, roughs, original/final art and photographs. Reports in 3 days. Samples returned by SASE. Pays $25-75, full color sketches; $6, rough pencil-$30, accurate pencil; by the hour, $8-12 average. Considers complexity of project, skill and experience of artist, and turnaround time when establishing payment. Rights purchased vary according to project.
Tips: "There is a trend toward animation. Freelance artists need to be able to provide fast service. Determine a need, supply roughs to start and get an okay for precise work."

COLORSCAN SERVICES, INC., 241 Stuyvesant Ave., Lyndhurst NJ 07071. (201)438-6729. President: J. Principato. Graphic services firm providing separations and printing services. Clients: ad agencies, printers, manufacturers and publishers.
Needs: Works with 3 freelance artists/year. Works on assignment only. Uses artists for advertising, brochure and catalog design, illustration and layout; product design; illustration on product; P-O-P displays; display fixture design; posters; model making; and signage.
First Contact & Terms: Send resume and tear sheets to be kept on file. Samples not filed are returned by SASE. Reports only if interested. Write for appointment to show portfolio. Pays by the project. Considers complexity of the project and rights purchased when establishing payment.

***COLORTEX CO.**, One Cape May St., Harrison NJ 07029. (201)482-5500. Product Manager: Margo Christensen. Manufacturer of needlecraft kits; counted and stamped cross-stitch, plastic canvas; crewel and line-work designs for wholesalers, shops and mass merchandiser.
Needs: Works with 15 freelance artists/year. Prefers artists with experience with stamped and counted cross stitch.
First Contact & Terms: Send query letter with brochure or tear sheets, photostats and photographs. Samples not filed are returned. Reports back within 1 week. Call or write to show a portfolio, which should include thumbnails, roughs and original/final art. Pays for design by the project, $75-450. Pays for illustration (color charts) by the project, $25-150. Considers complexity of project when establishing payment. Buys all rights.
Tips: I do not have enough artists for amount of development we would like to do. Look for overall design attractiveness and design balance. Need overall feeling of being filled out without undue complexity. Please, experienced designers only! We'll review all work. Please call before sending and/or bringing."

COMMUNICATION SKILL BUILDERS, INC., Box 42050, Tucson AZ 85733. (602)323-7500. Production Manager: Sharon Walters. Publisher of education materials for special education (K-12), gifted education and microcomputer education. Clients: teachers, special education professionals, hospitals, clinics, etc.
Needs: Works with 10 freelance artists/year. Prefers local artists, but "can work with out-of-town artists as well. Must have experience." Works on assignment only. Uses artists for advertising, brochure and catalog design, illustration and layout; product and display fixture design; illustration on product; and posters.
First Contact & Terms: Send query letter with brochure and slides, photos and printed work to be kept on file. Write for appointment to show portfolio. Reports within 2 weeks. Considers complexity of project, turnaround time and rights purchased when establishing payment.
Tips: "Artists should have experience doing materials for educational publishers."

COMMUNICATIONS ELECTRONICS, Dept. AM, Box 1045, Ann Arbor MI 48106-1045. (313)973-8888. Editor: Ken Ascher. Manufacturer, distributor and ad agency (10 company divisions). Clients: electronics, computers.
Needs: Works with 300 freelance artists/year. Uses artists for advertising, brochure and catalog design, illustration and layout; product design, illustration on product, P-O-P displays, posters and renderings.
First Contact & Terms: Send query letter with brochure, resume, business card, samples and tear sheets to be kept on file. Samples not kept on file returned by SASE. Reports within 1 month. Call or write for appointment to show portfolio. Pays for design and illustration by the hour, $15-100; by the project, $10-15,000; by the day, $40-800. Considers complexity of project, skill and experience of artist, how work will be used, turnaround time and rights purchased when establishing payment.

CONIMAR CORPORATION, Box 1509, Ocala FL 32678. (904)732-7235. Creative Director: Ray Mayer. Manufactures placemats, coasters, table hot pads, calendars, recipe cards, note cards, postcards.
Needs: Buys 10-15 designs/year. Designs include floral, abstract, Christmas and children's. Especially needs illustrations. Artist quotes price to be considered by Conimar. "Our designs are based a lot on designs of dinnerware, glassware and stationery items." Works on assignment only.
First Contact & Terms: Send query letter, resume and tear sheets, photocopies, slides and photographs. Reports in 1 week. Samples returned by SASE. To show portfolio, mail color, tear sheets, Photostats and photographs. Pays for design by the hour, $15-25; pays for illustration by the project, $50-350. Buys all rights.

CONSOLIDATED STAMP MFG. CO., 7220 W. Wilson Ave., Harwood Heights IL 60656. (312)867-5800. Director of Sales: Jim Kedzie. Manufacturer and distributor of customized stationery embossers and notarial seals, marking devices of all types, security badges, advertising medallions, transportation tokens, premiums for banks, store chains, etc. Clients: office and stationery supply stores, department stores, direct mail chains, security outfits, transportation systems, consumer direct mail.
Needs: Works with 2-3 freelance artists/year. Local, experienced artists only; "must not work for our competition." Works on assignment only. Uses artists for advertising design, illustration and layout; brochure, catalog and display fixture design and P-O-P displays. There is a trend in the field toward "a simplification of overall design with the use of more open spaces."
First Contact & Terms: Send query letter with resume, business card and samples to be kept on file. Prefers "whatever artist has available, original art, printed brochures, etc." as samples. Samples not filed are returned by SASE. Reports only if interested. Call or write for appointment to show portfolio. Pays by the project. "We prefer the artist to quote on the entire job." Considers complexity of project, and skill and experience of artist when establishing payment.
Tips: "At least be familiar with our product line. An artist who comes in and inquires as to what we do is given little consideration. Many artists make a fatal mistake of bringing dirty, worn-out samples, or poor examples of their work. Most come ill-prepared to explain their capabilities. An artist is a salesperson. In a large firm like ours we can't gamble with the unknown factors." When reviewing samples, especially looks for "originality, certainly, but of more importance is an artist's ability to understand our specific art problems or our promotional communication problems. Flexibility is also important."

CREATE YOUR OWN, INC., R.R. #2, Box 201A, Hickory Corner Rd., Milford NJ 08848. (201)479-4015. President: Catherine C. Knowles. Vice President: George S. Wetteland. Manufactures needlework and craft kits, including needlepoint, crewel, fabric dolls, crochet, stamped cross stitch and counted cross stitch, plastic canvas, candlewicking, lace net darning and a finished gift line. Clients: catalog houses, department store chains, needlework chains, retail stores, etc.
Needs: Works with 2-3 freelance artists/year. Prefers local artists with some experience in needleworking design, if possible. Works on assignment only. Uses artists for product design in needlework area only and model making.
First Contact & Terms: Send query letter with brochure, resume, business card and samples to be kept on file, except for original art work. Prefers photographs or tear sheets as samples. Samples returned only if requested. Pays by the project, $25-300. Considers skill and experience of the artist, how work will be used, turnaround time and rights purchased when establishing payment.
Tips: Looks for "designs suitable for silk screening (maximum 4 colors), possibly accented with minimum embroidery, designs for counted cross stitch, crewel embroidery, or finished gift ideas involving minimum assembly."

CREATIVE AWARDS BY LANE, 1575 Elmhurst Rd., Elk Grove IL 60007. (312)593-7700. President: Don Thompson. Distributor of recognition incentive awards consisting of trophies, plaques, jewelry, crystal, ad specialties and personalized premiums. Clients: companies, clubs, associations, athletic organizations.
Needs: Works with 3-4 freelance artists/year. Local artists only. Uses artists for advertising, brochure and catalog design, illustration and layout; and signage.
First Contact & Terms: Send query letter to be kept on file. Write for appointment to show portfolio, which should include Photostats, photographs or photocopies. Reports within 10 days. Pays by the project. Considers complexity of project when establishing payment.

CUSTOM HOUSE OF NEEDLE ARTS, INC., 197-200 Stow Rd., Marlborough MA 01752. (617)485-6699. Owner/President: Carolyn Purcell. Manufacturer of traditional crewel embroidery kits. Clients: needlework shops and catalogs.
Needs: Uses artists for product design. "We hope that artist is a crewel stitcher and can produce sample model."

First Contact & Terms: Send query letter with samples and any pertinent information to be kept on file. Prefers colored drawings or photos (if good closeup) as samples. Samples not filed are returned by SASE only if requested. Reports within 1 month. Pays royalty on kits sold.
Tips: "We emphasize *traditional* designs; use *some* current 'cutesy' type designs, but only if exceptional, for pictures, pillows, bellpulls, chair seats and clock faces."

CUSTOM STUDIOS INC., 1337 W. Devon Ave., Chicago IL 60660. (312)761-1150. President: Gary Wing. Custom T-shirt manufacturer. "We specialize in designing and screen printing of custom T-shirts for schools, business promotions, fundraising and for our own line of stock."
Needs: Works with 4 illustrators and 4 designers/month. Assigns 50 jobs/year. Especially needs b&w illustrations (some original and some from customer's sketch). Uses artists for direct mail and brochures/flyers, but mostly for custom and stock T-shirt designs.
First Contact & Terms: Send query letter with resume, photostats, photocopies or tear sheets; "do not send originals as we will not return them." Reports in 3-4 weeks. Call or write to schedule an appointment to show a portfolio, or mail tear sheets, photostats and b&w to be kept on file. Pays by the hour, $5-25 average. Considers turnaround time and rights purchased when establishing payment. On designs submitted to be used as stock T-shirt designs, pays 5-10% royalty. Rights purchased vary according to project.
Tips: "Send good copies of your best work. Do not get discouraged if your first designs sent are not accepted."

DEKA PLASTICS, INC., 914 Westfield Ave., Elizabeth NJ 07208. (201)351-0900. Design Director: David M. Hummer. Manufacturer and distributor of toys and children's products for trade-toy retailers and distributors.
Needs: Works with 6 freelance artists/year. Works on assignment only. Uses artists for the design, illustration and layout of advertising brochures and catalogs plus product design, illustration on product, P-O-P displays, display fixture design, model making and signage.
First Contact & Terms: Send query letter with brochure showing art style or resume, tear sheets, photocopies, slides and photographs. Samples not filed are returned by SASE. Reports back only if interested. Write to schedule an appointment to show a portfolio, which should include roughs, original/final art, final reproduction/product, photostats and photographs. Considers complexity of project, skill and experience of artist, turnaround time and rights purchased when establishing payment.

***GEORGE DELL, INC.**, 133 W. 25th St., New York NY 10001. (212)206-8460. President: George Dell. Manufacturer of display decorative materials, exclusively for use by stores in interior or window display. Clients: department stores, specialty stores, real estate.
Needs: Works with 2-3 freelance artists/year. Uses artists for advertising and brochure design, illustration and layout; product design and illustration on product.
First Contact & Terms: Prefers local artists with some experience. Send resume, tear sheets and photostats to be kept on file. Reports within 2 weeks. Pays by the project, $300-600. Considers complexity of project, skill and experience of artist, and rights purchased when establishing payment.
Tips: Artists should be "neat in their presentation."

***DISCOVERIES INC.**, 235 W. 1st St., Bayonne NJ 07002. Contact: Frank Latino. Submit tear sheets. Reports in 2-3 weeks.
Needs: Buys ideas for department store window and interior display props. Pays 10% of sales ($40-10,000) for display sold to individual store; 5% of sales ($1,000-100,000) for display purchased by chain. Pays when idea is sold.

DISPLAYCO, 2055 McCarter Hwy., Newark NJ 07104. (201)485-0023. Creative Art Director: Chris Byrd. Designers and producers of P-O-P displays in all materials. Clients: "any consumer products manufacturers."
Needs: Works with 12 freelance artists/year. Prefers artists experienced in P-O-P or display/exhibit. Works on assignment only. Uses artists for advertising layout, brochure illustration and layout, display fixture and P-O-P design, and model making. Especially needs P-O-P designers with excellent sketching and rendering skills.
First Contact & Terms: Send samples, brochure/flyer and resume. Submit portfolio for review or call for appointment. Prefers renderings, models, produced work, photos of models, work, etc., as samples. Samples not returned. Reports back on whether to expect possible future assignments. Provide resume, business card, brochure, flyer or tear sheets to be kept on file for possible future assignments. Payment is determined by the project; method is negotiable and varies according to job.
Tips: There is a "need for greater creativity and new solutions. Freelancers should have knowledge of P-O-P materials (plastics, wire, metal, wood) and how their designs can be produced."

DUKE'S CUSTOM SIGN CO., 601 2nd St. NE, Canton OH 44702. (216)456-2729. Clients: banks, merchants, architects, hospitals, schools and construction firms.
Needs: Assigns 5-10 jobs/year. Works with 1-2 artists/year for sign design. Prefers local artists. Works on assignment only. Especially needs sign shapes for outdoor and free-standing displays.
First Contact & Terms: Send query letter with resume to be kept on file. SASE. Reports within 2 weeks. Call to schedule an appointment to show a portfolio, which should include thumbnails. Pays for design by the hour, $4.50-10. Considers complexity of project, skill and experience of artist, and how work will be used when establishing payment.
Tips: "Please bring samples of what you think are quality sign displays. Know current graphic designing."

EBERSOLE ARTS & CRAFT SUPPLY, 11417 W. Highway 54, Wichita KS 67209. (316)722-4771. Buyer/Manager: Carolyn Hendryx. Art supply store providing full line of art supplies: brushes, canvas, paints (many kinds), easels, frames, wood products—some neeedlework, calligraphy supplies, books and some classes. Clients: other art stores and general public—mostly women from 20 to 60 age group.
Needs: Works with 4-6 freelance artists/year. Uses artists to teach classes.
First Contact & Terms: Send query letter with brochure showing art style. Samples not filed are returned by SASE. Reports only if interested. Call or write to schedule an appointment to show a portfolio. Payment varies. Considers skill and experience of artist when establishing payment. Rights purchased vary according to project.

EMBOSOGRAPH DISPLAY MFG. CO., 1430 W. Wrightwood, Chicago IL 60614. (312)472-6660. Vice President/Personnel: Jayne Legatowicz. Specializes in "complete creative art services and manufacturing in litho, silk screen, plastic molding of all kinds, spray, hot stamping, embossing, die cutting, metal work and assembly." Clients: brewery, beverage, food, automotive, hardware, cosmetics, service stations, appliances, clocks, plus consumer wall decor plus retail merchandisers.
Needs: Assigns 50-100 jobs/year. Works with 15 artists for sign design, display fixture design, costume design, model-making, P-O-P design, print advertising and custom sign illustration. Especially needs P-O-P design. Works on assignment only.
First Contact & Terms: Query with resume or call. Prefers roughs and previously published work as samples. Reports in 2 weeks. Samples returned by SASE. Provide resume and brochure to be kept on file for possible future assignments. Pays $25-45/hour.
Tips: "We have added consumer items, mostly wall decor." There is a trend toward "counter and wall cases and stands" in this business field.

ENVIRONMENTAL TECTONICS CORP., County Line Industrial Park, Southhampton PA 18966. (215)355-9100. Art Director: Larry Keffer. Manufacturer of environmental systems, hospital and industrial sterilizers, hyperbaric systems, aeromedical physiological training systems for clients in medicine, industry and government.
Needs: Works with a various amount of freelance artists/year. Works on assignment only. Uses artists for the design and illustration of advertising, brochures, and catalogs, plus technical illustration.
First Contact & Terms: Send query letter with brochure, resume, tear sheets, photostats and photocopies. Samples not filed are returned if requested. Reports back within 2 weeks. Call or write to schedule an appointment to show a portfolio or mail roughs, original/final art, final reproduction/product, color, tear sheets and photostats. Pays for design by the hour, $20 minimum; pays for illustration by the project, $75 minimum. Considers complexity of project, client's budget, skill and experience of artist, how work will be used, turnaround time and rights purchased when establishing payment.
Tips: Looking for "strong, clean, well-executed design and illustration shouting superior quality and originality capable of competing in high-tech international market. The particular subject or style is not important in judging the artist's capabilities. It is the concept and execution of the piece that is important. If the artist is successful in those areas, matching that style to fit the requirements of a project is a matter of judgement on the part of the art director."

***EPSILON DATA MANAGEMENT, INC.**, 50 Cambridge St., Burlington MA 01803. Creative Director, Design: Thomas Flynn. Full-service direct response advertising and direct mail for commercial and not-for-profit organizations. Clients: 250 diversified clients nationwide, nonprofit and commercial.
Needs: Works with 40 freelance artists/year. Uses artists for direct mail packaging; advertising, brochure and catalog design, illustration and layout; and signage.
First Contact & Terms: Local artists generally with three years direct response experience, plus "must work fast and accurately on very tight deadlines." Send query letter with brochure, resume, business card, samples and tear sheets to be kept on file. Considers photostats, slides, photographs or original work as samples. Samples not kept on file are not returned. Reports only if interested. Works on assignment only. Pays by the hour, $50-80 average; by the project, $150-3,000 average; by the day, $150-300

average. Considers complexity of project, skill and experience of artist and turnaround time when establishing payment.
Tips: "Be well experienced in direct response advertising."

EUREKA, Box 977, Scranton PA 18501. Marketing Manager: John A. Yourishen. Manufactures decorations and school and stationery supplies. Uses artists for party decorations, package design, greeting cards and lettering. Send samples. Reports in 30 days. Pays on acceptance.

***EVERTHING METAL IMAGINABLE, INC. (E.M.I.)**, 401 E. Cypress, Visalia CA 93277. (209)732-8126. Vice President: Dru McBride. Wholesale manufacturer. "We manufacture lost wax bronze sculpture. We do centrifugal white metal casting; we do resin casting (cold cast bronze, alabaster walnut shell, clear resin etc.). Clients: wholesalers, premium incentive consumers, retailers.
Needs: Works with "innumerable" freelance artists/year. Prefers artists that understand centrifugal casting, bronze casting and the principles of mold making. Works on assignment only. Uses artists for figurine and illustration and model making.
First Contact & Terms: Send query letter with brochure or resume, tear sheets, photostats, photocopies and slides. Samples not filed are returned only if requested. Reports back only if interested. Call to show a portfolio, which should include original/final art and photographs "or any samples." Pays for design by the project, $100 minimum. Considers complexity of project, client's budget, how work will be used, turnaround time and rights purchased. Buys all rights.
Tips: "Artists must be conscious of detail in their work, be able to work expediently and under time pressure. Must be able to accept criticism of work from client and price of program must include completing work to satisfaction of customers."

EXHIBIT BUILDERS INC., 150 Wildwood Rd., Deland FL 32720. (904)734-3196. Contact: J.C. Burkhalter. Produces custom exhibits, displays, scale models, dioramas, sales centers and character costumes. Clients: primarily manufacturers, ad agencies and tourist attractions.
Needs: Works on assignment only. Uses artists for exhibit/display design and scale models.
First Contact & Terms: Provide resume, business card and brochure to be kept on file. Samples returned by SASE. Reports back on future possibilities. Considers complexity of project, skill and experience of artist, how work will be used, turnaround time and rights purchased when establishing payment.
Tips: "Wants to see examples of previous design work for other clients; not interested in seeing school-developed portfolios."

FRANKLIN ELECTRIC, 400 Spring St., Bluffton IN 46714. Manager of Corporate Communications: Mel Haag. Manufacturer of submersible and fractional H.P. motors for original equipment manufacturers and distributors.
Needs: Works with 8 freelance artists/year. "Freelance artists must be proven." Works on assignment only. Uses artists for the design, illustration and layouts of advertising and brochures, the design and layout of catalogs and for posters.
First Contact & Terms: Send query letter with brochure showing art style or resume, tear sheets, slides and photographs. Samples not filed are returned only if requested. Reports only if interested. Call to schedule an appointment to show a portfolio, which should include roughs, original/final art, final reproduction/product, color and tear sheets. Pays for design and illustration by the hour, $30 minimum; payment is negotiated.
Tips: "I look for all styles and subjects. I am very interested in new techniques and styles."

FRELINE, INC., Box 889, Hagerstown MD 21740. Art Director: Mark Kretzer. Manufacturer and developer of library promotional aids—posters, mobiles, bookmarks, t-shirt transfers, reading motivators and other products to promote reading, library services and resources. Clients: school and public libraries, classroom teachers.
Needs: Works with 10-15 freelance artists/year. Works on assignment only. Uses artists for illustration and graphic design and promotional materials. Most assignments for 4-color process.
First Contact & Terms: Experienced designers or illustrators only. Send query letter with resume and tear sheets to be kept on file. Slides sent for review will be returned. Reports within 15 days. Pays by the project, $250-800. Considers complexity of the project, skill and experience of the artist, turnaround time and rights purchased when establishing payment.
Tips: "We love good idea and concept artists."

G.A.I. AND ASSOCIATES, INC., Box 30309, Indianapolis IN 46230. (317)257-7100. President: William S. Gardiner. Licensing agents. "We represent artists to the collectibles and gifts industries. Collectibles include high-quality prints, collector's plates, figurines, bells, etc. There is no up-front fee for our services. We receive a commission for any payment the artist receives as a result of our efforts." Clients:

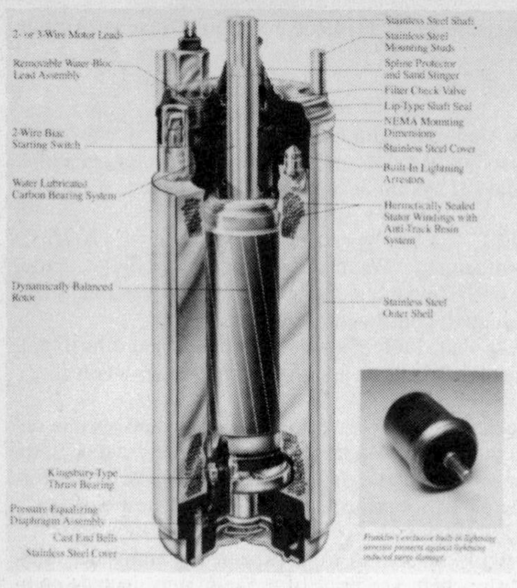

Artist: Shepp Parr

Originally done in watercolor, this rendering "illustrates the many features of Franklin Submersible Motors," according to Mel Haag, manager of corporate communications at Franklin Electric in Bluffton, Indiana. Artist Shepp Parr of Milwaukee, Wisconsin, was paid $850 for all rights.

manufacturers of high-quality prints and lithographs, porcelain products.
Needs: Works with 30-40 freelance artists/year. Works on assignment only. "We are not interested in landscapes, still lifes, or modern art. We are looking for 'people-oriented' art that will appeal to the average person."
First Contact & Terms: Send query letter with resume and color photographs; do *not* send original work. Samples not kept on file are returned by SASE. Reports in 1 month. Payment: "If we are successful in putting together a program for the artist with a manufacturer, the artist is usually paid a royalty on the sale of the product using his art. This varies from 4%-10%." Considers complexity of project, skill and experience of artist, how work will be used and rights purchased when establishing payment; "payment is negotiated individually for each project."
Tips: "We are looking for art with broad emotional appeal."

GADSDEN COUNTY CHAMBER OF COMMERCE, Box 389, Quincy FL 32351. (904)627-9231. Executive Director: Ben Ellinor.
Needs: Assigns 2 jobs/year. Uses artists for direct mail/publicity brochures, newspaper ad layouts, trade magazine ads and publications.
First Contact & Terms: Arrange interview or mail art. SASE. Reports in 1 month. Negotiates payment.

***GALAXIE HANDPRINTS, INC.**, 38 William St., Amityville NY 11701. (516)789-4224. Vice President: Andrea Reda. Self-contained manufacturer of wallpaper for national clients.
Needs: Uses artists for wallpaper.

GALLERY CLASSICS, 13726 Seminole Dr., Chino CA 91710. (714)627-8533. President: Robert A. Perkins. Manufacturer of wholesale and retail ceramic collector items (plates, bowls, etc.). Clients: wholesalers, retailers and consumers (direct mail) age 30-65 female.
Needs: Works with 3 freelance artists/year. Works on assignment only. Uses artists for plate and figurine design and illustration. Prefers "realistic wildlife (water fowl, baby animals endangered species, etc.) generally in their natural habitat and children (cute, soft, gentle) real, not animated."
First Contact & Terms: Send query letter with brochure showing art styles or slides. Samples not filed returned only if requested. Reports within 10 days. To show a portfolio, mail appropriate materials or call or write to schedule an appointment. Portfolio should include original/final art and photographs. Pays for design by the project, $1,500/subject, plus royalties. Considers complexity of project, skill and experience of artist, how work will be used and rights purchased when establishing payment.
Tips: "We deal with series of 2-4 subjects. Artists must think of continuity of subjects."

GARDEN STATE MARKETING SERVICES, INC., Box 343, Oakland NJ 07436. (201)337-3888. President: Jack Doherty. Service-related firm providing public relations and advertising services, mailing services and fulfillment. Clients: associations, publishers, manufacturers.

Needs: Works with 6 freelance artists/year. Works on assignment only. Uses artists for advertising and brochure design, illustration and layout; display fixture design, P-O-P displays and posters.
First Contact & Terms: Send query letter with resume, business card and copies to be kept on file. Samples not kept on file are returned. Reports only if interested. To show a portfolio, mail appropriate materials, which should include thumbnails, original/final art, final reproduction/product, color, tear sheets, photographs and b&w. Pays for design by the hour, $8-15. Considers complexity of project, skill and experience of artist and how work will be used when establishing payment.
Tips: "We have noticed a movement toward one color with use of bendays."

GARON PRODUCTS INC., 1924 Highway 35, Wall NJ 07719. (201)449-1776. Marketing Manager: Christy Karl. Industrial direct marketers of maintenance products, i.e., concrete repair, roof repair. Clients: maintenance departments of corporations, government facilities, small businesses.
Needs: Works with 3 freelance artists/year. Uses artists for brochure and catalog design, illustration and layout. Seeks "local artists and ones who will work within the organization so that corrections and additions can be done on the spot."
First Contact & Terms: Send query letter with brochure, resume, business card, photographs or photostats to be kept on file. Reports only if interested. Pays by the page or by the project. Considers complexity of project, and skill and experience of artist when establishing payment.
Tips: "Professionalism is a must! Work should be camera-ready for commercial printing upon completion. I need experienced catalog artists with creative ideas."

GARTH PRODUCTS, INC., 32-4 Littell Rd., East Hanover NJ 07936. (201)887-8487. President: Garth Patterson. Manufacturer of silkscreened ceramic glass souvenirs. Clients: banks, museums, amusement parks, restored villlages, tourist attractions, resorts, hotels and retail stores.
Needs: Works with 5 artists/year. Uses artists for illustrations on products. Especially needs line drawing of buildings, statures, flowers and songbirds.
First Contact & Terms: Send query letter, Photostats, brochure/flyer or actual work. Samples returned by SASE. Reports within 3-4 weeks. Provide business card, brochure and samples to be kept on file for possible future assignments. Payment is by the project, $25-100 average. Considers complexity of job and skill and experience of artist when establishing payment.
Tips: "Understand the type of line work needed for silkscreening. We now also use pencil work. Better artwork is more appreciated."

***GENERAL MOTORS CORP.**, 3044 W. Grand Blvd., Detroit MI 48202. (313)556-2017. Contact: Art Director, Public Relations Staff. Manufactures cars and trucks. Call for interview or send fees and samples for files; local artists only. SASE. Buys all rights.
Needs: Uses artists for annual reports, employee/student handbooks, technical charts/illustrations and company publications. Pay varies.

GOLDBERGS' MARINE, 201 Meadow Rd., Edison NJ 08818. (201)819-3500. Vice President Marketing: Richard Goldberg. Produces 9 mail order catalogs of pleasure boating equipment and water-sport gear for the active family.
Needs: Works with 6 freelance artists/year. Artists must be "flexible with knowledge of 4-color printing, have a willingness to work with paste-up and printing staff, and exhibit the ability to follow up and take charge." Uses artists for brochure and catalog design, illustration and layout; retail events and signage. "Seasonal freelance work also available."
First Contact & Terms: Send query letter with brochure, business card, printed material and tear sheets to be kept on file. "Original work (mechanicals) may be required at portfolio showing." Reports only if interested. Call for appointment to show portfolio. Pays by the project. Considers complexity of project, how work will be used and turnaround time when establishing payment.
Tips: "Boating experience is helpful and a willingness to do research is sometimes necessary. Long-term relationships usually exist with our company. We have plenty of work for the right people."

THE GREAT MIDWESTERN ICE CREAM COMPANY, Box 1717, 209 N. 16 St., Fairfield IA 52556. (515)472-7595. President: Fred Gratzon. Manufacturer and franchiser. "We manufacture an excellent ice cream which we feel is the new standard in the industry. We sell it through supermarkets, restaurants and our beautiful franchise stores." Clients are grocery shoppers and ice cream lovers.
Needs: Works with 15+ freelance artists/year. Uses freelance artists for the design, illustration and layout of advertising, brochures and catalogs plus product design, illustration of the product, P-O-P displays, display fixture design, posters, model making, signage, and fashion clothing design for franchise employees and customers (t-shirts, etc.).
First Contact & Terms: Send query letter with resume and samples. Samples not filed are returned with SASE. Reports back only if interested. Call to schedule an appointment to show a portfolio. Pays

for design by the project, $3,000; pays for illustration by the project, $1,000. Considers complexity of project, client's budget, skill and experience of artists, how work will be used and rights purchased when establishing payment.
Tips: "We are a highly creative company that prefers art on the cutting edge. We are looking for all types of art—from painting to cartoons—that uses ice cream as the theme."

GUILFORD PUBLICATIONS INC., 200 Park Ave. S., New York NY 10003. (212)674-1900. Art Director: Denise Adler. Produces professional, educational and industrial audiovisuals and books.
Needs: Assigns 20 jobs/year. Local artists only. Uses artists for catalog design, book jackets and ads.
First Contact & Terms: Query. SASE. Reports within 4 weeks. Pays by job.

THE HAMILTON COLLECTION, Suite 1000, 9550 Regency Square Blvd., Jacksonville FL 32211. Vice President, Product Development: Melanie Hart; Senior Design and Production Director (for commercial art/advertising): Deorah Levine. Direct marketing firm for collectibles: limited edition art, plates, sculpture, and general gifts. Clients: general public, specialized lists of collectible buyers and retail market.
Needs: Works with 5 freelance artists in creative department and 15 in product development/year. Only local artist with three years experience for mechanical work. For illustration and product design, "no restricion on locality, but must have quality work and flexibility regarding changes which are sometimes necessary. Also, a 'name' and notoriety help." Uses artists for advertising mechanicals, brochure illustration and mechanicals, product design and illustration on product.
First Contact & Terms: Send query letter with samples to be kept on file, except for fine art which is to be returned (must include a SASE or appropriate container with sufficient postage). Samples not kept on file are returned only if requested by artist. Reports within 2-4 weeks. Call or write for appointment to show portfolio. Pays for design by the hour, $10-50. Pays for illustration by the project, $50-5,000. Pays by the hour for mechanicals, $20 average. Considers complexity of project, skill and experience of artist, how work will be used and right purchased when establishing payment.
Tips: Prefers conservative, old fashioned, realistic style. "Attitude and turnaround time important." In presenting portfolio, don't "point out mistakes, tell too much, tell not enough, belittle work or offer unsolicited opinions. Be prepared to offer sketches on speculation."

***HAMPSHIRE PEWTER COMPANY**, Box 1570, 9 Mill St., Wolfeboro NH 03894-1570. (603)569-4944. Vice President: J.H. Milligan. Manufacturer of handcast pewter tableware, accessories, and Christmas ornaments. Clients: jewelry stores, department stores, executive gift buyers, tabletop and pewter speciality stores, churches, and private consumers.
Needs: Works with 3-4 freelance artists/year. "We prefer New-England based artists for convenience." Works on assignment only. Uses artists for brochure an catalog design, product design, illustration on product and model making.
First Contact & Terms: Send brochure or slides and photographs. Samples are not filed. Samples not filed are returned only if requested. Reports back to the artist within weeks. Call to schedule an appointment or mail roughs, photographs and b&w. Pays for design and illustration by the project. Considers complexity of project, client's budget and rights purchased. Buys all rights.
Tips: "Inform us of your capabilities. We commission work by the project. For artists who are seeking a manufacturing source, we will be happy to bid on manufacturing of designs, under private license to the artists, all of whose design rights are protected. If we commission a project, we intend to have exclusive rights to the "designs by contract" as defined in the Copyright Law and we intend to protect those rights."

***HARRIS CORP.**, Computer Systems Division, 2101 W. Cypress Creek Rd., Fort Lauderdale FL 33309. Advertising Manager: Debbie Coller. Uses local artists for sales literature, employee handbooks, design projects, special awards, cover design, paste-up and mechanicals.
First Contact & Terms: Pay is on project basis for design, comps, camera ready and/or separations.

HERFF JONES, Box 6500, Providence RI 02940-6500. (401)331-1240. Art Director: Fred Spinney. Manufacturer of class ring jewelry; motivation/recognition/emblematic awards—service pins, medals, medallions and trophies. Clients: high-school and college-level students; a variety of companies/firms establishing recognition programs.
Needs: Works with 6 freelance artists/year. "Previous experience in this field helpful but not necessary. Must be strong in illustration work." Works on assignment only. Uses artists for illustration of product.
First Contact & Terms: Send query letter with brochure, resume, business card, slides and photos to be kept on file; originals will be returned if sent. Samples not kept on file returned by SASE. Reports only if interested. Write for appointment to show portfolio. Pays by the project, $25-100 average. Con-

siders complexity of project, skill and experience of artist, and turnaround time when establishing payment.
Tips: Artists approaching this firm "should be of a professional level. The artist should have a good versatile background in illustrating as well as having some mechanical drawing abilities, such as hand lettering."

***HOUSE OF GLOBAL ART**, 350 Fellowship Rd., Morrestown NJ 08057. (609)234-4242. Vice President Marketing: Kenneth G. LeFevre. Wholesale giftware distributor of figurines, porcelain collector dolls, rag and vinyl dolls and crystal. Clients: retailers.
Needs: Works with varied number of freelance artists/year. Works on assignment only. Uses artists for figurine design.
First Contact & Terms: Send query letter with resume and "any available material as examples of work." Samples are filed. Samples not filed are returned. Reports back within 30 days. Write to show a portfolio or mail original/final art, final reproduction/product, b&w, tear sheets and photographs. Considers complexity of project, skill and experience of artist and client's budget when establishing payment.

HUTCHESON DISPLAYS, INC., 517 S. 14th St., Omaha NE 68102. (402)341-0707. Vice President: Harvey W. Schutte. Manufacturer of screen printed display materials. Clients: advertisers.
Needs: Works with 6 freelance artists/year. Uses artists for advertising layout. Especially needs graphic design.
First Contact & Terms: Send query letter with brochure showing art style. Samples returned. Portfolio should include photographs. Pays by the project. Pays for design and illustration by the project. Considers complexity of project when establishing payment. Buys one-time rights.

IGPC, 460 W. 34th St., 10th Floor, New York NY 10001. (212)869-5588. Contact: Art Department. Agent to foreign governments; "we produce postage stamps and related items on behalf of 40 different foreign governments."
Needs: Works with more than 100 freelance artists/year. Artists must be within metropolitan (NY) or tri-state area. "No actual experience required except to have good tight art skills (four-color) and excellent design skills." Works on assignment only. Uses artists for postage stamp design.
First Contact & Terms: Send samples. Reports back within 5 weeks. Pays by the project, $500-1,500 average. Considers government allowance per project when establishing payment.
Tips: "Artists considering working with IGPC must have excellent 4-color abilities (in general or specific topics, i.e., flora, fauna, transport, famous people, etc.); sufficient design skills to arrange for and position type; the ability to create artwork that will reduce to postage stamp size and still hold up to clarity and perfection. All of the work we require is realistic art. In some cases, we supply the basic layout and reference material; however, we appreciate an artist who knows where to find references and can present new and interesting concepts. Initial contact should be made by mail."

INTERNATIONAL RESEARCH & EVALUATION, 21098 Ire Control Ctr., Eagan MN 55121. (612)888-9635. Art Director: Ronald Owon. Private, nonpartisan, interdisciplinary research firm that collects, stores and disseminates information on line, on demand to industry, labor and government on contract/subscription basis.
Needs: Works with 30-40 freelance artists/year. Works on assignment only. Uses artists for advertising, brochure and catalog design, illustration and layout; product design and P-O-P displays.
First Contact & Terms: Artists should request "Capabilities Analysis" form from firm. Reports only if interested. Pays by the hour, $50-250 average. Considers how work will be used when establishing payment.

JOULÉ INC., 1245 Rt. 1 S., Edison NJ 08837. (201)494-6500. Marketing Manager: Carl Tuosto. Engineering firm.
Needs: Works on assignment only. Uses artists for advertising gimmicks, graphic sales promotion, audiovisual presentations and exhibit equipment. Needs artists for general design, layout and comps.
First Contact & Terms: Send query letter, brochure and resume to be kept on file for possible future assignments. Reports back. Call or write to schedule an appointment to show a portfolio, which should include thumbnails, roughs, final reproduction/product, photographs and b&w. Pays $500-1,000 average for camera-ready art.

The asterisk before a listing indicates that the listing is new in this edition. New markets are often the most receptive to freelance submissions.

Close-up

Kim Gromoll
Illustrator
Bensalem, Pennsylvania

Kim Gromoll's artwork doesn't hang on people's walls, but it is seen in thousands of homes every day. It appears on postage stamps, game box covers, newspaper ads, posters, can labels and even doormats. By working with a variety of businesses, Gromoll has made a name for himself as a successful freelance artist.

"I've done some publication work," says the young, energetic illustrator, "but I find that it's much more consistent to work with businesses. For example, if I do a magazine cover, they might not use me for another year, but if I do 30 pieces of line work for a newspaper ad for a department store, they'll be running another ad with *different* merchandise in a couple of weeks." Businesses not only provide steady work but also a diversity of subjects—stamps for Africa, toy catålogs and automotive posters, to name a few.

Businesses most often need illustrations for newspaper ads and catalogs, and Gromoll's realistic style and attention to detail fit their needs. After graduating from art school, Gromoll worked inhouse for a toy retailer. "This job really prepared me for eventual freelancing. We did black-and-white art for newspaper ads. The deadlines were tight, and the pressure was always on."

After hours he would also freelance, illustrating topical stamps for the Inter-Governmental Philatelic Corporation (I.G.P.C.), an agent who produces and markets stamps for foreign governments. "The deadline was two weeks for four or five stamps, and I still had a fulltime job. I did the stamps nights and weekends, and I delivered them on time."

As I.G.P.C. continued to ask him to illustrate stamps, Gromoll realized there were only so many hours in a day. He had to make a decision whether to hold on to the security of a fulltime job or to freelance. "It sure is scary to give up that paycheck and benefits," he says. But he opted for freelancing, which had been his goal for eight years. "I've never regretted it. Freelancing has its peaks and valleys, but if you can work through those valleys, it's one heck of a way to live. Sometimes I put in 10 to 14 hours a day for weeks on end. But no one is looking over my shoulder or punching the clock."

When Gromoll struck out on his own, he had two steady clients. He advises other potential freelancers to follow suit. "Make sure you can put a list of clients together before you leave your fulltime job. Don't stop trying; everybody out there needs artwork. You just have to convince a few of them that you're the one that should do theirs."

Gromoll maintains a market list of his own and uses promotional pieces to get his foot into the door. He has both black-and-white and color pieces that he mails to markets he finds in directories such as the *Artist's Market*. He prints 5x7s of portfolio pieces to "target" a client. "If they seem interested, I'll leave tear sheets and more 8x10s of additional samples." He also makes contacts through attending trade shows, where he also distributes his 5x7s.

Now that he's in a position to turn down work ("I refer clients to other artists"), Gromoll has a quick answer to what he enjoys most about freelancing: "Finishing the piece I'm working on." He also enjoys the cooperative effort in working with an art director. "I enjoy taking someone's idea and giving it life. I'd do it even if no one paid me." He keeps his enjoyment alive by retaining a creative edge. "I can't just sit down and crank 'em out. I usually have a crisis or two in each piece. When I put the last dab of paint on a piece, I'm relieved, but I'm already thinking about what's next."

He has solid advice to any freelancer for maintaining good clients. "Make your deadlines! The quickest way to cut your own throat is to blow deadlines. Also—and this one is tough for most artists—keep records, write down everything. After all, you're a businessman. When Uncle Sam wants to see the books, you're the bookkeeper."

—Susan Conner

Artist: Kim Gromoll

Gromoll has completed four stamp assignments for the Inter-Governmental Philatelic Corporation (IGPC). This set of stamps commemorated the fortieth anniversary of the International Civil Aviation Organization for the country of Sierre Leone. He was paid $1,200 for all rights to the five-stamp set.

KELCO, Division of Merck & Co., Inc., 8355 Aero Dr., San Diego CA 92123. (619)292-4900. Advertising and Communications: Yolanda Nunez. Specialty chemical firm. Clients: food companies, industrial users and oil field companies.
Needs: Works with 1-2 freelance artists per year. Works on assignment only. Uses artists for advertising and brochure design and illustration; employee annual report, and AV presentations.
First Contact & Terms: Send query letter. Reports in 3 weeks. Negotiates payment.

KIMBALL I.D. PRODUCTS, 151 Cortlandt St., Belleville NJ 07109. Art Director: John Larimer. Manufacturer providing artwork pertaining to the airline sortation industry. Clients: airlines, steam ships, hotels and trains.
Needs: Works with 20 freelance artist/year. Local artists only with 5 years experience minimum. Works on assignment only. Uses artists for brochure design and illustration; catalog layout; and P-O-P displays.
First Contact & Terms: Send query letter with resume and slides. Samples not filed are not returned. Reports only if interested. Write to schedule an appointment to show a portfolio, which should include roughs, original/final art, final reproduction/product and photostats. Pays for design by the project, $50-250. Pays for illustration by the project, $25-500. Considers complexity of project, skill and experience of artist, turnaround time and rights purchased when establishing payment.

KLITZNER IND., INC., 44 Warren St., Providence RI 02901. (401)751-7500, ext. 242. Design Director: Louis Marini. Manufacturer; "four separate divisions that serve uniquely different markets: ad specialty, fraternal, direct mail and retail."
Needs: Works with "several" freelance artists/year. Artists must be "qualified to provide the desired quality of work within our time frame." Works on assignment only. Uses artists for product design, illustration on product and model making.
First Contact & Terms: Send query letter with resume to be kept on file. Reviews Photostats, photographs, photocopies, slides or tear sheets; "they must clearly illustrate the quality, detail, etc. of artist's work." Materials not filed are returned by SASE. Reports back only if interested. Write for appointment to show portfolio. Pays by the project; "a mutually agreed upon figure *before* the project is undertaken."
Tips: "Turn-around time on most projects has been virtually cut in half. More competitive market warrants quick, dependable service. This change has created a bigger need for outside assistance during heavy backlog periods."

***KOZAK AUTO DRYWASH, INC.**, 6 S. Lyon St., Box 910, Batavia NY 14020. (716)343-8111. President: Ed Harding. Manufacturer and direct marketer of automotive cleaning and polishing cloths and related auto care products distributed by direct mail and retail. Clients: stores with car care lines, consumers and specialty groups.
Needs: Works with up to 2 freelance artists/year. Uses artists for advertising design and illustration, P-O-P displays, packaging design and direct response advertising.
First Contact & Terms: Prefers artist located within a convenient meeting distance with experience in desired areas (P-O-P, packaging, direct response). Works on assignment only. Send query letter with brochure, resume and business card to be kept on file. Material not filed returned only if requested. Reports within 2 weeks. Pays by the project. Considers complexity of project, skill and experience of artist, and how work will be used when establishing payment.

KRISCH HOTELS, INC., Box 14100, Roanoke VA 24022. (703)342-4531. Director of Communications: Julie Becker. Estab. 1985. Service-related firm providing all advertising, in-room and P-O-P pieces for camping (inhouse department). Clients: hotel/motels and restaurants/lounges.
Needs: Works with 10-20 freelance artists/year. Prefers local artists. Works on assignment only. Uses artists for advertising and brochure illustration; illustration on product, P-O-P displays, posters and signage.
First Contact & Terms: Send query letter with resume and photocopies. Samples not filed are not returned. Reports only if interested. Call or write to schedule an appointment to show a portfolio, which should include roughs, original/final art, tear sheets and photostats. Pays for design and illustration by the hour, $25 minimum; by the project, $75 minimum; by the day, $200 minimum. Considers complexity of project, client's budget, how work will be used, turnaround time and rights purchased when establishing payment.
Tips: "Increased competition in all markets leads to more sophisticated work attitudes on the part of our industry. Artists should know their own abilities and limitations and be able to interact with us to achieve best results."

KVCR—TV/FM RADIO, 701 S. Mount Vernon Ave., San Bernardino CA 92410. (714)888-6511 or 825-3103. Program Director: Lew Warren. Specializes in public and educational radio/TV.

Needs: Assigns 1-10 jobs/year. Uses artists for graphic/set design, set design painters and camera-ready cards.
First Contact & Terms: Query and mail photos or slides. Reports in 2 weeks. Samples returned by SASE. Pays $20-30, camera-ready cards.

LARAMI CORPORATION, 340 North 12 St., Philadelphia PA 19107. (215)923-4900. Director of Research & Development: Anne Pitrone. Produces toys.
Needs: Uses local artists only. Works on assignment only. Uses artists for mechanicals.
First Contact & Terms: Send query letter with brochure showing art style and/or resume and samples. Samples not filed are not returned. Reports only if interested. To show a portfolio, mail thumbnails, roughs, original/final art, final reproduction/product, color, tear sheets, photostats, photographs and b&w.

LASER ART DIVISION-LASER LABORATORY, Laser Art Gallery-The Light Fantastic, Laser Research Laboratory, Cincinnati OH 45208. (513)321-4804. Director: Leon Goldman, MD. Develops all phases of laser art. Members are those interested in training, in laser art and art for laser companies. Special exhibits of many forms of laser art.
Needs: Works with 4 freelance artists/year. Artists must have training or interest in laser technology. Uses artists for advertising, exhibits, brochure and catalog design, illustration and layout, exhibits, displays, signage and posters. Prefers any phase of laser art design, sculpture, photography, interferommentry: holography, lapidary, etching, ceramics.
First Contact & Terms: Schedule at times available for training in laser art. Send query letter with photocopies and slides to be kept on file. Samples are returned. Reports within 2 weeks. Write to schedule an appointment to show a portfolio, which should include original/final art, color, photostats and photographs. Considers complexity of project and available budget when establishing payment.
Tips: "Accepts exhibits for laser art in laser art gallery, the Light Fantastic."

LEISURE AND RECREATION CONCEPTS INC., 2151 Fort Worth Ave., Dallas TX 75211. (214)942-4474. President: Michael Jenkins. Designs and builds amusement and theme parks.
Needs: Assigns 200 jobs/year. Uses artists for exhibits/displays and sketches of park building sections and bird's eye views of facilities.
First Contact & Terms: Query with samples or previously used work, or arrange interview. SASE. Reports in 1 week. Pay determined by job.

LEISURE LEARNING PRODUCTS INC., 16 Division St. W., Box 4869, Greenwich CT 06830. (203)531-8700. Advertising/Sales Promotion Manager: Richard Bendett. Manufactures children's games, activities, books and educational products.
Needs: Uses artists for illustration and design for sales literature, inhouse publications, recruitment literature, catalogs, exhibits and displays. Also needs cartoon-type color illustrations similar to the style of Walt Disney illustrations, Peanuts and Nancy strips. Must appeal to 3-8 year olds.
First Contact & Terms: Query with photocopies or art. Pays $10-25 minimum for product illustration.

LILLIAN VERNON CORP., 510 S. Fulton Ave., Mount Vernon NY 10550. (914)699-4131. Vice President: David Hochberg. Direct mail giftware firm that produces greeting cards, giftwrap, calendars, stationery and paper tableware products. Also produces toiletries, housewares, textiles, dinnerware and toys. Two divisions: one serves general consumers, the other serves retail stores.
Needs: Buys 250 designs and 100 illustrations/year from freelance artists. Only artists within 250 miles "for ease in communication." Works on assignment only. Considers all types of media for illustrations. "We are heavily oriented toward Christmas merchandise"; submit seasonal artwork in January or February.
First Contact & Terms: Send query letter with brochure, resume, Photostats, photographs or tear sheets to be kept on file. "Please don't call!" Samples not filed are returned only if requested. Reports within 2 weeks. Original art not returned after reproduction. Pays flat fee. Buys first rights.
Tips: "We are *always* on the lookout for good talent!"

LIVING ARTS, INC., 250 West 57th St., New York NY 10019. Director: Peter Klein. Theatrical agency. Clients: musicians, Broadway productions, and major ballet and dance companies.
Needs: Buys 10-15 illustrations/year. Uses artists for catalog layouts, stationery design, posters and publicity brochures.
First Contact & Terms: Query. SASE. Reports in 2 weeks. Provide brochures/flyers and tear sheets to be kept on file for future assignments. Originals returned to artist at job's completion. Minimum payment: $1,000, brochure design; $500, poster design.

LOON MOUNTAIN RECREATION CORP., Kancamagus Hwy., Lincoln NH 03251. (603)745-8111. Marketing Director: Rick Owen. Ski resort with inn, restaurants and lounges.
Needs: Works with 2 advertising designers/year. Assigns 6 jobs and buys 2 illustrations/year. Uses artists for design and illustration of brochures, signs, displays, mailings and other promotional materials. Especially needs renderings of future projects.
First Contact & Terms: Arrange interview. SASE. Reports within 2 weeks. Negotiates pay; pays by the hour, $10 average. Considers skill and experience of artist, and turnaround time when establishing payment.

***LORENZ STUDIO**, (formerly Window Display Service), Rt. 109, Lakeside CA 06758. (203)567-4280. Owner: Larry Livolsi. Manufactures custom furniture, signage and prop design; does window display design and consultation; sells new and used store fixtures (racks, mannequins). Clients: banks, stores, private firms, building managements, private clients, corporations, theaters and country clubs.
Needs: Works with 15 freelance artists/year. Uses artists for advertising design, illustration and layout; product design; P-O-P displays; display fixture design; model making; signage; and prop design.
First Contact & Terms: Send resume, business card and samples to be kept on file; write for art guidelines. Prefers slides as samples. Samples not filed are returned by SASE. Reports only if interested. Pays generally by the project. Considers skill and experience of the artist when establishing payment.

***McALLEN CHAMBER OF COMMERCE**, Box 790, McAllen TX 78502. (512)682-2871. Public Relations Director: Rick Arriola. Promotes conventions, tourism, community programs, industry and legislation for McAllen.
Needs: Assigns 8-15 jobs and buys 12 illustrations/year. Uses artists for advertising, magazines, newsletters, publicity brochures, exhibits/displays and trademarks/logos. Especially needs economic/business oriented artwork; international trade and commerce themes; and Hispanic-related art and information.
First Contact & Terms: Query with samples. SASE. Reports in 1 week. Pays $10-20/illustration. Considers turnaround time when establishing payment.
Tips: "We have expanded our monthly newsletter to a monthly economic report."

***MARBURG WALL COVERINGS**, 7601 Cicero, Chicago IL 60652. General Manager: Mike Vukosavich. Manufacturer and distributor which designs, styles and manufactures decorative wall coverings. Clients: wholesale distributors, contractors and architects.
Needs: Works with 2 freelance artists/year. Prefers bilingual English/German artists. Works on assignment only. Uses artists for product design.
First Contact & Terms: Send query letter with brochure or tear sheets. Samples are filed. Samples not filed are returned only if requested. Reports back only if interested. To show a portfolio, mail thumbnails, tear sheets and color. Payment is negotiable. Considers client's budget and skill and experience of artist when establishing payment. Buys first rights or reprint rights.

METROPOLITAN WATER DISTRICT OF SOUTHERN CALIFORNIA (MWD), Box 54153, 1111 Sunset Blvd., Los Angeles CA 90054. (213)250-6496. Graphic Arts Designer: Mario Chavez. Supplies water for southern California. "MWD imports water from the Colorado River and northern California through the state water project, it imports about half of all the water used by some 13 million consumers in urban southern California from Ventura to Riverside to San Diego counties. MWD wholesales water to 27 member public agencies which, along with about 130 subagencies, deliver it to homes and businesses in MWD's 5,200-square-mile service area."
Needs: Works with 4-6 freelance artists/year. "Color artwork for publication is separated on scanner, it should be flexible; final agreement (contract) is purchase order, based upon verbal agreement of artist accepting assignment. All artwork is vested in Metropolitan Water Distict unless agreed upon." Works on assignment only. Uses artists for brochure/publications design, illustration and layout.
First Contact & Terms: Send query letter with brochure showing art style. Samples not filed are returned by SASE. Reports only if interested. Call to schedule an appointment to show a portfolio, which should include roughs, original/final art, color, tear sheets and b&w. Pays for design by the project, $100 minimum. Pays for illustration by the project, $50 minimum. Considers complexity of project, client's budget, skill and experience of artist, how work will be used, turnaround time and rights purchased when establishing payment.
Tips: "Phone calls should be kept short and to a minimum. Public affairs of MWD is interested in skillful execution of conceptual artwork to illustrate articles for its publication program. Number of projects is limited."

***J. MICHAELS INC.**, 182 Smith St., Brooklyn NY 11201. (718)852-6100. Advertising Manager: Lance Davis. Retailer of furniture and home furnishings for young married couples ages 20-45.

Needs: Works with 5-6 freelance artists/year. Uses artists for advertising illustration, P-O-P displays, calligraphy, paste-up, mechanicals and posters. "We use a lot of line, ink furniture illustrations."
First Contact & Terms: Send query letter with brochure or nonreturnable samples, such as photocopies. Samples are filed. Samples not filed are not returned. Reports back only if interested. "Mail photocopies. If I want to see more, I will call." Pays for illustration by the project, $50 for items like charts on TV. Considers complexity of project and skill and experience of artist when establishing payment. Buys all rights.
Tips: "We are a furniture retailer. Show me furniture illustrations that can print in newspapers."

MILWAUKEE SIGNS CO., 1964 Wisconsin Ave., Grafton WI 53024. (414)377-8920. Director of Marketing: Bob Aiken.
Needs: Local artists only. Works on assignment only. Works with 3 artists for sign design and P-O-P design. Also uses artists for custom sign faces, brochure and ad design.
First Contact & Terms: Arrange interview to show portfolio. Samples returned by SASE. Reports back on future possibilities. Send resume, business card and brochure to be kept on file. Considers complexity of project, skill and experience of artist, and how work will be used when establishing payment.

***MORTON JONAP LTD.**, 195 Engineers, Hauppauge NY 11787. (516)931-6777. Director of Design: Isreal Fiedler. Manufacturer and distributor of wallcoverings and related fabrics to the consumer and contract market.
Needs: Works with 10 freelance artists/year. Uses artists for product design.
First Contact & Terms: Send query letter with resume, tear sheets and slides. Samples not filed are returned. Write to schedule an appointment to show a portfolio, which should include original/final art. Considers complexity of project and skill and experience of artist when establihsing payment. Buys all rights.
Tips: "Originality!"

MURPHY INTERNATIONAL SALES ORGANIZATION, 11444 Zelzah Ave., Granada Hills CA 91344. (818)363-1410. President: F.S. Murphy. Distributor and service-related firm providing retrofit, covering materials, new products and patents. Clients: building and home owners.
Needs: Works with 2 freelance artists/year. Uses artists for advertising, brochure and catalog design, and illustration on product.
First Contact & Terms: Send samples to be kept on file. Write for art guidelines. Prefers photocopies as samples. Samples not filed are not returned. Reports back only if interested. Pays by the project. Considers how work will be used when establishing payment.
Tips: "Design should be realistic. Art is becoming more simple and less dramatic."

MURRAY HILL PRESS, 43 N. Village Ave., Rockville Centre NY 11570. (516)764-6262. President: Ralph Ceisler. Printer. Clients: paint manufacturers, window treatment magazines and general commercial.
Needs: Assigns 12 jobs/year; uses mostly local artists. Uses artists for catalogs, direct mail brochures, flyers and P-O-P displays. Especially needs P-O-P displays in retail stores, paint and hardware stores in particular. "Need good catalog-brochure art. Must be creative. We compete with originals by supplying full package. Artist preferably should be from Long Island for better access."
First Contact & Terms: Send query letter with tearsheets. SASE. Reports in 2 weeks. Call or write to schedule an appointment to show a portfolio, which should include thumbnails, roughs, original/final art and final reproduction/product. Pays for design and illustration by the project, $100 minimum. Pay depends strictly on job and is negotiable. Considers complexity of project, skill and experience of artist, and how work will be used when establishing payment. Rights purchased vary according to project.
Tips: "Have samples showing rough through completion."

***MUSEUM COLLECTIONS**, 2840 Maria Ave., Northbrook IL 60062. Creative Director: Donna Benson.
Needs: Uses artists for product illustration, advertising, design and collateral materials. Needs realistic portraitists—artists specializing in children and animals, and sculptors of human or animal figures.
First Contact & Terms: Call or write for appointment; Chicago and local artists only. Prefers photos or slides or actual sample pieces as samples. Solicited samples returned. Works on assignment only; reports back whether to expect possible future assignments. Provide business card to be kept on file for possible future assignments. Negotiates pay.

NEIBAUER PRESS, INC., 20 Industrial Dr., Warminister PA 18974. (215)322-6200. Contact: Nathan Neibauer. Publishers and printers of religious publications.
Needs: Works with 12 freelance artists/year. Works on assignment only. Uses artists for advertising,

brochure and catalog design, illustration and layout; illustration on product, and posters.
First Contact & Terms: Send query letter with photocopies. Reports only if interested. Write for appointment to show portfolio. Pays by the hour, $10 minimum; or by the project. Considers skill and experience of artist when establishing payment.

NORTON OUTDOOR ADVERTISING, 5280 Kennedy Ave., Cincinnati OH 45213. (513)631-4864. Contact: Tom Norton. Outdoor advertising firm.
Needs: Assigns 30-60 jobs/year. Local artists only. Uses artists for billboards.
First Contact & Terms: Call for interview. Pays $25 minimum, roughs; $75-100, finished sketch.

O'DONNELL-USEN FISHERIES, 255 Northern Ave., Boston MA 02210. (617)542-2700. Executive Vice President: Arnold S. Wolf. Processes frozen seafoods.
Needs: Assigns 20-30 jobs and buys 15 illustrations/year. Uses artists for packaging, point of sale material and letterheads, etc. Especially needs new packaging design.
First Contact & Terms: Query with samples (rough sketches, mock up design). SASE. Reports in 3 weeks. Provide resume to be kept on file for possible future assignments. Pays compensation based on agreement by the project. Considers complexity of project and rights purchased when establishing payment.
Tips: "Present boxes are being redesigned and made more modern." Artists should "have past experience in design of packaging."

***OHIO PRODUCTS, INC.**, 2554 Needmore, Dayton OH 45414. (513)276-392. President: J.E. Ryan. Manufacturer of custom plastic displays and parts for many clients; many including department stores, art stores, museums, malls.
Needs: Works with 2 freelance artists/year. Works on assignment only. Uses artists for advertising, brochure and catalog design, illustration and layout, illustration on product, P-O-P displays and display fixture design.
First Contact & Terms: Send query letter with brochure. Samples are not filed. Samples not filed are returned only if requested. Reports back only if interested. To show a portfolio, mail appropriate materials; portfolio should include final reproduction/product and photographs. Payment is negotiable. Considers complexity of project, skill and experience of artist and turnaround time when establishing payment. Negotiates rights purchased.
Tips: "We can only use two artists at a time. Have patience."

O'KEEFFE'S INC., 75 Williams Ave., San Francisco CA 94124. (415)822-4222. Marketing Manager: Abby Lipman. Manufacturer of skylights, aluminum building products and fire-rated glass door, window and wall systems for architects, contractors and builders.
Needs: Works with 1-5 freelance artists/year. Works on assignment only. Uses artists for advertising, brochure and catalog design, illustration and layout.
First Contact & Terms: Reports back only if interested. Call or write for appointment to show portfolio. Pays by the hour, $25-50 average. Considers complexity of the project, skill and experience of artist, and turnaround time when establishing payment.
Tips: "Work more on planning, not necessarily on the finished piece—that's the printer's art."

***P.O.P. DISPLAYS, INC.**, 11-12 30 Drive Astoria, New York NY 11102. (212)721-6700. Creative Director: Tom Haas. Display/P-O-P firm. Clients: distillers, cosmetic firms and various others.
Needs: Assigns 400-500 jobs/year. Works with six artists for P-O-P design.
First Contact & Terms: Query with samples. SASE. Reports in 1 week. Works on assignment only. Samples returned by SASE. Provide resume and brochure to be kept on file for future assignments. Pays $20/hour.

***PALMLOOM CO.**, Box 1541, New York NY 10017. (212)688-8797. Advertising Manager: N. Tyler. Direct response (mail order) marketer (magazines) and catalogs.
Needs: Works with 2-3 freelance artists/year. Uses artists for advertising design (mail order), brochure and catalog design and layout, and paste-up.
First Contact & Terms: Send query letter with samples to be kept on file. Prefers tear sheets (nonreturnable printed matter) as samples. Reports back only if interested. Pays $10/hour for paste-up; $20/hour for design and layout.

***PARAGON NEEDLECRAFT COPR.**, 57-07 31st. Ave., Woodside NY 11377. Vice President: Susan Goldsmith. Manufacturer of needlework kits including embroidery, cross-stitch, Christmas, latch hook rugs, etc. Clients: needlework shops, craft chains, mass merchants, mail order catalogs.
Needs: Works with about 20 freelance artists/year. Uses artists for product design.

First Contact & Terms: Send query letter to request catalog or tear sheets, slides, photographs and finished pieces. Samples not filed are returned. Reports back within 1 month. Call or write to schedule an appointment to show a portfolio. Pays for design by the project, $75-500. Considers complexity of project and how work will be used when establishing payment. Buys one-time rights for kit reproduction.
Tips: "Artists should be somewhat familiar with the needlecraft industry. We need approximately 250-300 new pieces of art yearly. Most popular themes are florals, scenes and children's designs. Very interested in new needlework techniques."

PERFECT PEN & STATIONERY CO. LTD., #42, 1241 Denison St., Markham, Ontario L3R 4B4 Canada. (416)474-1866. President: S. Szlrtes. Distributor of advertising specialties, office specialties and gifts. Clients: "all businesses across Canada."
Needs: Works with 6 freelance artists/year. Artists must have a minimum of 5 years of experience and references. Works on assignment only. Uses artists for advertising, brochure and catalog design and layout; photography and film work.
First Contact & Terms: Send query letter with brochure to be kept on file. Prefers tear sheets as samples. Samples not filed are not returned. Reports back only if interested. Write for appointment to show portfolio. Pays by the project. Considers complexity of the project when establishing payment.
Tips: "Apply only if you're experienced in direct mail advertising or a closely related area."

PHILADELPHIA T-SHIRT MUSEUM, 235 N 12th St., Philadelphia PA 19107. (215)625-9230. President: Marc Polish. Manufacturer and distributor of imprinted t-shirts and sweatshirts for retail shops and national mail order firms.
Needs: Uses artists for imprinted sportwear.
First Contact & Terms: Send query letter with brochure showing art style or photocopies. Samples not filed are returned. Reports within 1 week. To show a portfolio, mail roughs and Photostats. Pays in percent of sales or outright purchase.

PICKARD, INC., 782 Corona Ave., Antioch IL 60002. President: Henry A. Pickard. Manufacturer of wholesale fine china dinnerware and collector plates. Clients: retailers.
Needs: Works with 3-4 freelance artists/year. Works on assignment only. Uses artists for patterns for dinnerware and fine art for collector plates. Prefers realistic and classical styles. Seeks "fine art as opposed to illustration for our limited edition plates."
First Contact & Terms: Send query letter with brochure, resume and slides. Samples not filed are returned only if requested. Reports within 1 month. Write to schedule an appointment to show a portfolio, which should include color, b&w, photographs, slides and transparencies. Negotiates payment; generally a flat fee and/or royalties. Considers complexity of project, project's budget, skill and experience of the artist, how work will be used, turnaround time and rights purchased when establishing payment. Negotiates rights purchased.

***PICKHARDT & SIEBERT USA**, 700 Prince Georges Blvd., Upper Marlboro MD 20772. (301)249-7900. Studio Manger: Kathy McConaughy. Manufacturer/importer of wallcoverings. "We sell to distributors, who service retail wallcoverings stores."
Needs: Uses artists for product design and styling, and "purchases wallpaper designs from freelancers on an ongoing basis."
First Contact & Terms: Send query letter with resume. Samples are filed. Samples not filed are returned only if requested. Reports back only if interested. Write to schedule an appointment to show a portfolio, which should include roughs, original/final art, slides and color. Pays by the project, $200-900.
Tips: "Designs need to be right scale and layout to appear in repeat on a wall."

PICTURESQUE PRODUCTS, Box 41630, Tucson AZ 85717. President: B.B. Nelson. Mail order firm of general gift items. Clients: consumers.
Needs: Works with 2 freelance artists/year. Uses artists for advertising, brochure and catalog design, illustration and layout; and P-O-P displays.
First Contact & Terms: Send query letter to be kept on file. Reports only if interested. Pays by the project, $100-500 average. Considers skill and experience of artist, how work will be used and rights purchased when establishing payment.
Tips: "Originality in the presentation sells me."

PITTSBURGH DISPLAY, 200 Federal St., Pittsburgh PA 15212. (412)322-5800. President: Art Pearlman. Distributes decorative material, fabrics, papers, plastics, and photographic arts. Clients: malls, shopping centers, banks, utilities and retail merchants.
Needs: Works with 8-12 freelance artists/year. Uses artists for brochure and catalog design, illustration

and layout; P-O-P displays; display fixture design; posters; and signage.
First Contact & Terms: Send query letter with brochure, photographs, photocopies and tear sheets to be kept on file. Samples not filed are returned by SASE. Does not report back. Call for appointment to show portfolio. Pays by the project, $60-200 average. Considers complexity of the project when establishing payment. Amount allowed within bid to customer.

PLANET-TRANS, INC., 5 Blake Ave., Brooklyn NY 11212. (718)773-3332. President: Marino Bonilla. Manufacturer of iron-on heat transfers in all types of designs—adults, children, souvenir, babies—with worldwide distribution.
Needs: Works with 10 freelance artists/year. Works on assignment only. Uses artists for advertising illustration.
First Contact & Terms: Send query letter with original work, slides or photos to be kept on file. Samples not filed are returned by SASE. Reports only if interested. Call or write for appointment to show portfolio. Pays by the project, $125-200 average. Considers skill and experience of artist when establishing payment.
Tips: Prefers airbrush artwork on boards.

POURETTE MFG. INC., 6910 Roosevelt Way NE, Seattle WA 98115. (206)525-4488. President: Don Olsen. Manufacturer and distributor specializing in candle making supplies and soap making supplies. Clients: anyone interested in selling candle making supplies or making candles.

PRECISION GRAPHICS, 119 W. Washington St., Champaign IL 61820. (217)359-6655. President: Jeff Mellander. Specializes in technical illustration for book publishers.
Needs: Works with 1-5 freelance artists/year. Uses artists for one-color, two-color and four-color work including airbrush illustration.
First Contact & Terms: Seeks artists experienced in drawing with technical pens and with highly developed skills in the area of technical illustration. Send query letter with brochure showing art style or resume, tear sheets, Photostats, photocopies and slides to be kept on file. Samples not filed are returned by SASE only if requested. Reports only if interested. Write for appointment to show portfolio, which should include original/final art. Pays according to accepted job bid of artist. Considers complexity of project, skill and experience of artist, and turnaround time when establishing payment.
Tips: Looks for "quality—not quantity—and consistency" when reviewing work. "Beginning artists just out of school tend to show too much; try to hit on too many areas. Show what you *like* to do and what you do best."

PRESTIGELINE INC., 5 Inez Dr., Brentwood NY 11717. (516)273-3636. Director of Marketing: Ken Golden. Manufacturer of lighting products.
Needs: Buys various illustrations from freelance artists/year. Uses artists for advertising and catalog design, illustrations and layout; and illustration on product. Prefers b&w line drawings. Produces seasonal material for Christmas, Mother's Day, Father's Day, Thanksgiving, Easter, back-to-school and graduations; submit work 3-4 months before season.
First Contact & Terms: Send resume, business card and Photostats. Call for appointment to show a portfolio. Samples returned by SASE. Reports within 2 weeks. Buys all rights. Payment method is negotiable.
Tips: "There is an increased demand for b&w line art for newspaper advertisements."

***PRISS PRINTS, INC. (a subsidiary of ISSC)**, Rte. 3, Box 490-B, Falls Mills VA 24613. (800)543-4971. President: Toni Fischer Morath. Manufacturer. "We manufacture pressure sensitive wall decorations used ordinarily in children's rooms." Clients: retail stores selling wallcoverings and/or children's products to the parents of infants and children.
Needs: works with 4-5 freelance artists/year. Uses artists for advertising and brochure design, illustration and layout, product design, illustration on product and signage.
First Contact & Terms: Send query letter with photostats. Samples are filed. Samples not filed are returned. Reports back only if requested; if not interested, all submissions returned. To show a portfolio, mail photostats. Pays for design and illustration by the project, $100 minimum. Considers complexity of project and interpertation of instructions when establishing payment. Buys all rights.
Tips: "Don't overwhelm me with long letters and too many samples. Don't sent any originals unless requested."

PUCCI MANIKINS, 578 Broadway, New York NY 10012. (212)219-0142. Manufacturer of manikins—art work on faces, clay for sculptures. Clients: department stores.
Needs: Uses artists for model making.

PULPDENT CORPORATION OF AMERICA, 75 Boylston St., Brookline MA 02147. (617)232-2380. Director of Product Information: Jane Hart Berk. Manufacturer/distributor of dental supplies including instruments, pharmaceuticals, X-ray supplies, sterilizers, needles, articulating paper, etc. Clients: dental supply dealers and dentists.

Needs: Works with 3-5 freelance artists/year. Prefers local artists. Works on assignment only. Uses artists for advertising, brochure and catalog design, illustration and layout; photography and technical illustration.

First Contact & Terms: Send query letter with business card, photostats and tear sheets. Samples returned by SASE if not kept on file. Reports within 6 weeks. Call or write for appointment to show portfolio. Pays by the project, $40 minimum. Considers complexity of project, and skill and experience of artist when establishing payment; "how much our product is worth determines to some extent the amount we are willing to invest in designing, etc."

Tips: "We prefer simple, not-too-trendy designs aimed at the dental professional."

REALTORS NATIONAL MARKETING INST., Suite 500, 430 N. Michigan, Chicago IL 60611-4092. (312)670-3780. Editorial Assistant: Paula Ludman. Trade organization for real estate brokers.

Needs: Works with 4-8 freelance artists/year. Prefers local artists. Works on assignment only. Uses artists for advertising and brochure illustration.

First Contact & Terms: Send query letter with resume, tear sheets and photocopies. Samples not filed are not returned. Reports only if interested. Call or write to schedule an appointment to show a portfolio, which should include original/final art, final reproduction/product and b&w. Pays for illustration by the hour, $10-50; by the project, $25-250. Considers complexity of project, how work will be used and turnaround time when establishing payment.

RECO INTERNATIONAL CORPORATION, Collector's Division, Box 951, 138-150 Haven Ave., Port Washington NY 11050. (516)767-2400. Manufacturer/distributor of limited editions collectors plates, lithographs and figurines. Clients: stores.

Needs: Works with 4 freelance artists/year. Uses artists for plate and figurine design, and limited edition fine art prints. Prefers romantic and realistic styles.

First Contact & Terms: Send query letter and brochure to be filed. Write for appointment to show a portfolio. Reports within 3 weeks. Negotiates payment.

RECO INTERNATIONAL CORPORATION, Kitchen Gourmet Accessories Division, 138-150 Haven Ave., Port Washington NY 11050. (516)767-2400. President: Heio W. Reich. Publisher and manufacturer.

Needs: Designers to design houseware and kitchen utensils on an exclusive basis for production according to designs. Works on assignment only.

First Contact & Terms: Send query letter and brochure showing art style or resume; submit portfolio for review. Prefers to see "anything that will show artist's ability." Reports "when needed." Negotiates payments.

***REYNOLDS PRINTASIGN CO.**, 9830 San Fernando Rd., Pacoima CA 91331. (213)899-5281. Art Director: Macy Clark. Manufacturer of sign printing equipment for retailers.

Needs: Works with 3 freelance artists/year. Uses artists for advertising and brochure design and illustration; illustration on product and photography.

First Contact & Terms: Local artists only. Send query letter with brochure, resume, business card, samples and/or tear sheets to be kept on file. Prefers "photostats, photographs, printed brochure, slides or anything that will not have to be returned" as samples. Samples returned only if requested. Reports only if and when interested. Works on assignment only. Pays by the project, $25 minimum. Considers complexity of project, skill and experience of artist and turnaround time when establishing payment.

BOB ROBINSON MARKETING INC., 963 Brush Hollow Road, Westbury NY 11590. (516)334-8600. President: Bob Robinson.

Needs: Assigns 100 jobs/year. Uses artists for display/P-O-P design and scale models.

First Contact & Terms: Arrange interview to show portfolio. SASE. Reports in 2 weeks. Pays $50-300/sketch or $100-1,000/job for design of permanent displays.

***ROCKING HORSE**, Box 306, Highland NY 12528. Convention center, ranch-resort. Clients: social vacationers—business meeting executives, senior citizens, couples, families.

Needs: Works with 2 ad illustrators, 2 ad designers, 2 or 3 product designers and 2 illustrators for products/year. Uses artists for descriptive brochures, exhibits, signs and meeting room decorations. Especially needs caricatures, brochures, rate schedule line work or design as samples.

First Contact & Terms: Send published samples (resort ads around a western scene). Prefers "bartering" as payment method.
Tips: "Foresees more use of artists" in the field. Artists should "make their abilities and offerings known to potential clients."

***ROCKY POINT PARK**, Warwick RI 02889. (401)737-8000. General Manager: David Cascioli. Clients: general public.
Needs: Uses artists for direct mail brochures, programs, trade magazine ads, bumper stickers, and pennants.
First Contact & Terms: Submit photos, roughs or tear sheets of published work. Pays going rates.

***S. ROSENTHAL & CO. INC.**, 9933 Alliance Rd., Cincinnati OH 45242. (513)984-0710. Creative Director: Claire Schwarberg. Clients: publishers, manufacturers, associations and schools.
Needs: Works with 1-3 artists/month for paste-up. Uses artists for layout and retouching for direct mail, magazines, catalogs and brochures.
First Contact & Terms: Local artists only. Query by mail. No originals returned to artist at job's completion. Pay varies.

***THE ROSENTHAL JUDAICA COLLECTION**, by Rite Lite, 946 McDonald Ave., Brooklyn NY 11218. (718)436-7070. President: Alex Rosenthal. Manufacturer and distributor of a full range of Judaica ranging from mass-market commercial goods to exclusive numbered pieces. Clients: gift shops, museum shops and jewelry stores.
Needs: Works with 3-4 freelance artists/year. Works on assignment only. Uses artists for brochure and catalog design, illustration and layout and product design.
First Contact & Terms: Send query letter with brochure or resume, tear sheets and photographs. Samples are filed. Reports back only if interested. Call to schedule an appointment to show a portfolio, which should include original/final art, tear sheets, photographs, slides and color. Pays for design by the project, $500 minimum. Considers complexity of project, client's budget, skill and experience of artist and turnaround time when establishing payment. Buys all rights.

ROYAL COPENHAGEN INC., Formerly Bing & Grondahl, 27 Holland Ave., White Plains NY 10603. Creative Director: Cami Messina. Wholesale manufacturer of collectibles, figurines, plates and dinnerware. Clients: wholesalers, retailers, corporations.
Needs: Uses artists for limited and unlimited edition plate and figurine design, model making, mechanicals, advertising posters and design, illustration and layout of advertising and brochures. "We prefer a Scandinavian look."
First Contact & Terms: Send a query letter with a brochure, resume and a sample, either a tear sheet, a slide or photograph. Samples not filed are returned by SASE. Reports back only if interested. Write to schedule an appointment to show a portfolio or mail roughs, original/final art, color, tear sheets, photographs and b&w. Payment depends "on the project and what is involved." Considers complexity of project, client's budget, skill and experience of artist, how work will be used; turnaround time and rights purchased.

***ROYALEIGH DESIGNS, LTD.**, 1784 Pitkin Ave., Broolkyn NY 11212. (718)495-3700. President: Robin B. Leigh. Manufacturer of handprinted wallcoverings. Clients: wallcovering distributors and interior designers.
Needs: Works with 3-4 freelance artists/year. Prefers local artists only.
First Contact & Terms: Send query letter with tear sheets or "call." Samples are not filed. Samples not filed are returned only if requested. Reports back within 10 days. Call to schedule an appointment to show a portfolio, which should include roughs and original/final art. Pays for design by the project. Considers client's budget, skill and experience of artist and rights purchased when establishing payment. Buys all rights.
Tips: Artists should "have wallcovering or fabric design experience."

RSVP MARKETING, Suite 5, 450 Plain St., Marshfield MA 02050. (617)837-2804. President: Edward C. Hicks. Direct marketing consultant services—catalogs, direct mail and telemarketing. Clients: primarily industry and distributors.
Needs: Works with 7-8 freelance artists/year. Desires "primarily local artists; must have direct marketing skills." Uses artists for advertising, copy brochure and catalog design, illustration and layout.
First Contact & Terms: Send query letter with resume and finished, printed work to be kept on file. Reports only if interested. Pays for design by the job, $400-1,000. Pays for illustration by the hour, $25-85. Considers skill and experience of artist when establishing payment.

S.E. RYKOFF & CO., 761 Terminal St., Los Angeles CA 90021. (213)622-4131. Advertising Manager: Paul Mayeda. Distributor of wholesale food and equipment to restaurants and institutions nationwide, serving restaurants, hospitals, schools and food establishments.
Needs: Works with 2 or 3 freelance artists/year. Prefers local artists. Works on assignment only. Uses artists for catalog design and layout, and also signage.
First Contact & Terms: Send query letter with resume. Reports only if interested. Write to schedule an appointment to show a portfolio, which should include final reproduction/product. Pays by the hour, $8 minimum. Considers complexity of project when establishing payment.
Tips: Looks for "accurate literal renderings and the ability to execute product illustrations with properly weighted emphases."

***CLAUDIA SABIN FINE ARTS**, 710 SW 27th St., Gainesville FL 32607. (904)378-4240. President: Claudia Sabin. Art consultants specializing in fine original art in all media. Clients: architects, designers, retail art galleries and private collectors, corporations and art in public places.
Needs: Works with up to 45 artists/year. Artists need to live in Florida. Works on consignment—slides only.
First Contact & Terms: Send query letter with brochure, resume and slides. Slides not filed are returned by SASE. Reports back within 30 days.

***SANDICAST, INC.**, 8480 Miralani Dr., San Diego CA 92126. (619)695-9611. Administrative Assistant: Myrna I. Lybarger. Manufacturer of gift and home decorating items for all age groups. Clients: retail outlets, department stores, furniture stores, Hallmark stores, gift shops, etc.
Needs: Works with 10 freelance artists/year. Uses artists for catalog design, illustration and layout and product design.
First Contact & Terms: Send query letter with brochure or photographs. Photos are not filed. Photos not filed are returned by SASE. Reports back within 1 month. Write to schedule an appointment to show a portfolio, which should include photographs and slides. Pays for design by the project, $100 minimum. Buys all rights.
Tips: Need "freelance artists/sculptors, experienced in clay (bas-relief and sculptors)."

SANTA FE PARK SPEEDWAY, 9100 S. Wolf Rd., Hinsdale IL 60521. (312)839-1050. Public Relations: Mary Lou Tiedt. Stock car racetrack. Clients: "We are a public family entertainment establishment and service a wide variety of manufacturers, patrons and small businesses locally. A large portion of advertisers, which need the work of our artists, are auto shops, motorcycle shops and restaurants."
Needs: Works with 2 artists/year for advertising design. Uses artists for advertising, direct mail brochures, posters, publicity brochures, yearly programs, bumper stickers and road signs. "We are looking for new original layouts and designs for racing." Especially needs speedway logo to be used on t-shirts, mailings and the program cover.
First Contact & Terms: Mail art. Will review basic pencil sketches or photos; previously published work is preferred. SASE. Reports in 2-4 weeks. Provide business card to be kept on file for possible future assignments. Call or write to schedule an appointment to show a portfolio, which should include original art, final reproduction, color or photographs. Negotiates pay. Considers how work will be used, turnaround time and rights purchased when establishing payment. Rights purchased vary according to project.
Tips: "Artist must keep up to date on the car models on the market for designs as we run a 'late model stock car' division; also on trends in t-shirt design and what will work well for printing (silkscreen). Keep in touch and be persistent, as we get very busy. Send samples with envelope to return work in-...this allows a quick return and response to work. The best time to contact us for work is in November or late January. The spring season is much too late. By March, we are already set for the summer season."

***SCAN AM IMPORT INC.**, 205 9th Ave. S., Great Falls MT 59405. (406)452-1230. President: Peter L. Madsen. Wholesaler/importer of tabletop. Clients: department stores and gift shops.
Needs: Works with designers. Uses artists for catalog and product design.
First Contact & Terms: Send query letter with brochure. Samples are filed. Samples not filed are returned only if requested. To show a portfolio, mail roughs. Pays for design by the project.

***THE J.H. SCHULER CO.**, 1649 Broadway, Hanover PA 17331. (717)632-5000. Director of Product Development: Bruce N. Wolff. Distributor of giftware for fundraising. Clients: nonprofit groups.
Needs: Uses illustrators and dimensional designers.
First Contact & Terms: Send query letter with samples. Prefers printed pieces as samples. Samples returned by SASE only if requested.

***SITKA STORE FIXTURES**, Box 410247, Kansas City MO 64141. (816)531-8290. Manufacturer of wood store fixtures and merchandisers. Clients: pharmacies, hardware, paint and wallpaper stores, bakers, jewelers and department stores.
Needs: Works with artists for fixture design.
First Contact & Terms: Query. Reports within 3 weeks. Works on assignment only. Samples returned by SASE; and reports back on future possibilities. Provide resume to be kept on file for future assignments. Pay determined by job.

SLADE CREATIVE MARKETING, Box 484, Santa Barbara CA 93102. (805)687-5331. President: S. Richard Slade. Service-related firm providing graphics, brochures, technical drawings, collateral material and general advertising. Clients: technical and consumer.
Needs: Works with 10-12 freelance artists/year. Artists must be able to communicate directly with company. Works on assignment only. Uses artists for advertising, brochure and catalog design, illustration and layout; illustration on product, P-O-P displays, signage, photography and technical writing.
First Contact & Terms: Send query letter with resume, photostats, photographs, photocopies, slides or tear sheets to be kept on file. Samples not filed are returned by SASE only if requested. Reports only if interested. Write for appointment to show portfolio. Pays by project, $100-750 average. Considers complexity of project, how work will be used and rights purchased when establishing payment.
Tips: "Be flexible and open to any job within your range."

SNAP-ON TOOLS CORP., 1801 80th St., Kenosha WI 53140-2801. (414)656-5348. Advertising Manager: William Tower. Manufacturer of tools and provides retouching of hand tool photos for dealers and marketing needs.
Needs: Works with 5 freelance artists/year on a daily basis, 5 outside freelancers. Prefers artists with three years of experience. Uses artists for the design, illustration and layout of advertising brochures and catalogs plus product design, illustration on product, P-O-P displays, display fixture design, posters, model making and signage.
First Contact & Terms: Contact only through artist's agent. Samples not filed are not returned. Reports back only if interested. Call or write to schedule an appointment to show a porfolio, which should include thumbnails, roughs, original/final art, final reproduction/product, color, tear sheets, Photostats, photographs and b&w. Pays for design by the hour, $15-55. Pays for illustration by the hour, $15-55. Considers complexity of project, client's budget, skill and experience of artist, how work will be used, turnaround time and rights purchased when establishing payment.

***TOM SNYDER PRODUCTIONS, INC.**, 123 Mt. Auburn St., Cambridge MA 02138. Art Director: Peter Reynolds. Developer of educational computer software for ages 5-adult; develops software, documentation, ancillary materials (music, art, books). Clients: schools, department stores, program stores.
Needs: Works with 3+ freelance artists/year. Uses artists for brochure design, illustration and layout; illustration on product and package design.
First Contact & Terms: Works on assignment only. Send query letter with resume and samples to be kept on file. Prefers photocopies as samples. Samples not filed are returned by SASE only if requested. Reports back only if interested. Pays by the hour, $15-25 average. Considers complexity of the project, skill and experience of the artist, how work will be used and turnaround time when establishing payments.
Tips: Let your work speak for itself. Just send photocopies and be patient. When an appropriate job comes up and your work is on file, we'll call you."

SOFTSYNC, INC., 162 Madison Ave., New York NY 10016. (212)685-2080. President: Sue Currier. Manufacturer of software for a variety of home computers. Subject matter includes education, personal productivity. Clients: computer and mass market retail stores.
Needs: Works with 5 freelance artists/year. Works on assignment only. Uses artists for advertising and brochure design, illustration and layout; illustration on product, P-O-P displays and posters.
First Contact & Terms: Send query letter with brochure and photographs, slides or tear sheets to be kept on file. Samples not filed are returned only if requested. Reports within days. Call or write for appointment to show portfolio. Pays by the hour, $10-15 average, or by the project, $350-1,000 average. Considers complexity of project, skill and experience of artist and how work will be used when establishing payment.
Tips: "For mechanical artists, we need people who are quick and accurate. For illustrators, bring us samples that are colorful, zippy and innovative."

SPENCER GIFTS, INC., 1050 Black Horse Pike, Pleasantville NJ 08232. (609)645-5526. Art Director: James Stevenson. Retail gift chain located in approximately 440 malls in 43 states; gifts range from wall decorations to 14k gold jewelry.

Needs: Assigns 150-200 jobs/year. Prefers artists with professional experience in their field of advertising art. Uses artists for package design illustration, hard line art, fashion illustration, newspaper ads and toy, poster, package and product design, T-shirt design and other soft goods.
First Contact & Terms: Query with samples, previously published work or arrange interview to show portfolio. With samples, enclose phone number where you can be reached during business hours. Reports within 2 weeks. Negotiates pay.

STAMP COLLECTORS SOCIETY OF AMERICA, Box 3, W. Redding CT 06896. Executive Vice President and Creative Director: Malcolm Decker. Philatelic marketing firm. Develops mail order/direct response buyers of stamps using publications and mailing lists.
Needs: Works with 6 freelance artists/year. Prefers local (Westchester, New Haven, Fairfield County and New York City) artists; "experience requirement is determined by the job complexity." Works on assignment only. Uses artists for advertising and brochure design, illustration and layout; product design, album and editorial design, and "full-dress" direct mail packages.
First Contact & Terms: Send query letter and resume; "if interested, we'll call you. Show your portfolio and leave behind or send in samples or photocopies as requested." Pays by the hour, by the project, or offers a retainer. Considers complexity of project, and skill and experience of the artist when establishing payment.
Tips: "Send a comprehensive, detailed resume listing all the clients served, noting those for whom the most work was done."

SURCO PRODUCTS, INC., Box 777, Braddock PA 15104. General Manager: Arnold Howard. Manufacturer of air fresheners, cleaners and related products.
Needs: Works with 3 freelance artists/year. Uses artists for advertising, brochure and catalog design, illustration and layout; product design, illustration on product, P-O-P displays, display fixture design, posters, model making and signage.
First Contact & Terms: Send query letter with brochure showing art style or resume, tear sheets, photostats and photocopies. Samples not filed are not returned. Reports only if interested. Write to schedule an appointment to show a portfolio, which should include original/final art, final reproduction/product, tear sheets, photographs and b&w. Negotiates payment. Considers complexity of project, client's budget, skill and experience of artist, how work will be used and turnaround time when establishing payment.

SWEET STOP INC., 11 Tompkins Ave., Staten Island NY 10304. (718)447-8400. President: Igor Reverson. Produces candy novelties for card and gift shops.
Needs: Buys 4 designs and 4 illustrations from freelance artists/year. Prefers local artists only. Also uses artists for P-O-P displays and mechanicals. Prefers watercolors.
First Contact & Terms: Send resume, tear sheets and photographs. Samples not filed are returned. Reports within 10 days. Call to schedule an appointment to show a portfolio, which should include thumbnails and photographs. Original artwork returned. Pays flat fee. Negotiates rights purchased.

TEACH YOURSELF BY COMPUTER SOFTWARE, INC., 2128 W. Jefferson Rd., Pittsford NY 14534. (716)427-7065. President: Lois B. Bennett. Publisher of educational software for microcomputers. Clients: schools, individuals, stores.
Needs: Local artists only. Works on assignment only. Uses artists for advertising, brochure and catalog design, illustration and layout; and illustration on product.
First Contact & Terms: Send query letter with brochure, resume, Photostats, photographs, photocopies, slides or tear sheets to be kept on file. Samples not filed are returned by SASE. Reports within 6 weeks. Write for appointment to show portfolio, which should include roughs, photostats and photographs. Pays for design and illustration by the hour. Considers complexity of project, skill and experience of artist, how work will be used, turnaround time and rights purchased when establishing payment. Buys all rights.

***TERRAGRAFICS, INC., Subsidiary of R. Dakin & Co.**, 7000 Marina Blvd., Brisbane CA 94005. Product Development Manager: Elaine-Wolf Baker. Produces frames and giftware for women 18 and over and children.
Needs: Works with 20 freelance artists/year. Buys 100 designs from freelance artists/year. Buys 30 illustrations from freelance artists/year. Works on assignment only. Prefers watercolor, goauche. Produces material for Christmas, Mother's Day, Valentines; submit 9 months before holiday.
First Contact & Terms: Send query letter with brochure showing art style. Samples are filed. Samples not filed are not returned. Reports back only if interested. Write to schedule an appointment to show a portfolio, which should include original/final art and final reproduction/product, dummies or color. Original artwork is returned to the artist after job's completion. Pays average flat fee of $100/design;

\$100/illustration; by the hour, \$20; or royalties of 2½%. "Payment is customed to each individual artist based on mutual agreement." Negotiates rights purchased.
Tips: "Look at Terragraphics products first. We primarily need 3-D art for children's ceramic accessories or frame designs."

***THOG CORPORATION**, Box 424, Tallmadge OH 44278. Sales Manager: Don Martin. Provides equipment for the graphic arts industry.
Needs: Works with 2-3 freelance artists/year. Uses freelance artists for advertising, brochure and catalog design, illustration and layout and product design.
First Contact & Terms: Send query letter. Samples are filed. Reports back only if interested. Write to schedule an appointment to show a portfolio, which should include roughs and photostats. Pays for design and illustration by the project, \$25 minimum. Considers complexity of project, client's budget and rights purchased when establishing payment. Buys all rights.
Tips: "We use a lot of custom line art.

THOMAS NELSON PUBLISHERS, Box 141000, Nelson Place, Elm Hill Pike, Nashville TN 37214. (615)889-9000. Vice President Advertising and Marketing: Robert J. Schwalb. Manufacturer and distributor of religious materials, Bibles, Christian books; also secular markets from subsidiary companies. Clients: retailers, book stores.
Needs: Works with 60 freelance artists/year. Works on assignment only. Uses artists for advertising, brochure and catalog design, illustration and layout; product and display fixture design; illustration on product; P-O-P displays; posters; model making and signage.
First Contact & Terms: Send query letter with brochure showing art style or tear sheets, Photostats, photocopies, slides and photographs. Samples not kept on file are returned. Reports only if interested. Call or write to schedule an appointment to show a portfolio, which should include original/final art, final reproduction/product and photographs. No set pay range; "project budget sets price." Payment terms of 10 days or 30-day turnaround. Firm reserves publishing rights. Buys all rights.
Tips: Industry trends are toward "a clean-cut motif with simple design." When reviewing work, evaluates "presentation of work, cleaness and creative concept." Artists should "research the type of work or creative needs of the business they interview with."

THUMB FUN AMUSEMENT PARK, Box 128, Hwy. 42, Fish Creek WI 54212. (414)868-3418. Contact: Doug Butchart. Send samples.
Needs: Uses artists for direct mail brochures, posters, newspaper ads, costume design, signs, bumper stickers, designs for t-shirt printing and tie-in products.
First Contact & Terms: Send query letter with brochure showing art style or resume and photocopies. To show a portfolio, mail appropriate materials or write to schedule an appointment; portfolio should include roughs, Photostats and photographs. Rights purchased varies according to project. Pays by the project. Considers complexity of project, skill and experience of artist, how work will be used, turnaround time and rights purchased when establishing payment.

***TREASURE CRAFT/POTTERY CRAFT**, 2320 N. Alameda, Compton CA 90222. President: Bruce Levin. Manufacturer of earthenware and stoneware housewares and gift items. Clients: department stores and gift shops.
Needs: Works with 3 freelance artists/year. Uses artists for advertising and product design, illustrations, layout and model making.
First Contact & Terms: Prefers local area artists. Send query letter. Reports in 3 weeks. Works on assignment basis only. Provide business card and flyer to be kept on file for possible future assignments. Payment determined by the project.

TRW OPTOELECTRONICS DIVISION, 1207 Tappan Circle, Carrollton TX 75006. (214)323-2200. Marketing Manager: J. Scott Bechtel. Manufacturer providing optoelectronic components for electronic equipment. Clients: manufacturers of electronic equipment, e.g. computers.
Needs: Works with 10 freelance artists/year. Artists must have experience in technology-related areas such as electronics or mechanical illustration. Uses artists for illustration on product.
First Contact & Terms: Send query letter with resume. Samples not filed are not returned. Reports only if interested. Write to schedule an appointment to show a portfolio, which should include original/final art, photostats and photographs. Pays for design and illustration by the hour, \$25-45. Considers skill and experience of artist, and how work will be used when establishing payment.
Tips: "All successful candidates must be significantly more competitive than existing vendors. Names are kept on file and called in to bid on project."

TURNROTH SIGN CO., 1207 E. Rock Falls Rd., Rock Falls IL 61071. (815)625-1155. Contact: R. Neil Turnroth. Clients: banks, business, retail and industry.
Needs: Works with artists for billboards ($25-50), neon signage ($20-75), sign redesign ($20-100). Works primarily with out-of-town artists. Assigns 15-20 jobs/year.
First Contact & Terms: Send query letter with samples. SASE. Reports within 1 week. Payment by the job.
Tips: "Artists should have some nice photos of sketch work."

UARCO, INC., 121 N. Ninth St., Dekalb IL 60115. Advertising Manager: Melinda Newtson. Direct mail catalog providing computer supplies and business forms to businesses with computers.
Needs: Works with 1-2 freelance artists/year. Works on assignment only. Uses artists for brochure design and layout and cover designs.
First Contact & Terms: Send query letter with resume, tear sheets and photocopies. Samples not filed are returned only if requested. Reports only if interested. To show a portfolio, mail roughs, final reproduction/product and tear sheets. Pays for design by the project, $100 minimum. Considers complexity of project, skill and experience of artist, and turnaround time when establishing payment.

UMSI INCORPORATED, Box 450, Scotch Plains NJ 07076. (201)668-1313. President: Robert Bokor. Mail order firm. Offers magic tricks and novelties marketed to boys and men.
Needs: Works with 2 freelance artists/year. Local artists only "who have samples of similar product links (hobbies or children's products)." Works on assignment only. Uses artists for advertising and catalog design, illustration and layout.
First Contact & Terms: Send query letter with brochure, resume and samples to be kept on file "unless the samples exhibit that the artist does not have closely related experience." Prefers samples that need not be returned. Samples not kept on file are returned by SASE. Reports only if interested. Call for appointment to show portfolio. Pays by the project, $500 minimum for catalog design and typesetting, less for smaller projects (ads, etc.). Considers complexity of project and skill and experience of artist when establishing payment.

***THE UNGAME COMPANY**, 761 Monroe Way, Placentia CA 92670. (714)993-9800. Vice President Marketing: Martin H. Magdaleno. Manufacturer and distributor of educational and entertainment games and toys with the theme "games and toys with a heart." Clients: chain toy stores, department stores, specialty and Christian bookstores.
Needs: Works with 4-6 freelance artists/year. Prefers local artists. Works on assignment only. Uses artists for advertising, brochure and catalog design, illustration and layout, product design, illustration on product, P-O-P displays, posters and magazine design.
First Contact & Terms: Send query letter with brochure. Samples are not filed. Samples not filed are returned only if requested. Reports back only if interested. Call or write to schedule an appointment to show a portfolio. Pays for design and illustration by the project, $100-5,000. Considers complexity of project, client's budget, skill and experience of artis, turnaround time and rights purchased when establishing payment. Negotiates rights purchased.

***VERMONT T'S**, Main St., Chester VT 05143. (802)875-2091. Manager: Richard Glennon. Commercial screen printer, specializing in t-shirts and sweatshirts. Vermont T's produces custom as well as tourist-oriented silkscreened sportwear. Does promotional work for business, ski-resorts, tourist attractions and events.
Needs: Works with 6 freelance artists/year. Uses artists for graphic designs for t-shirt silkscreening.
First Contact & Terms: Send query letter with brochure. Samples are filed. Samples not filed are returned only if requested. Reports back within 10 days. Mail Photostats. Pays for design by the project, $75-150. Considers complexity of project, client's budget, skill and experience of artist and how work will be used when establishing payment. Negotiates rights purchased.
Tips: "Have samples showing rough through completion. Understand the type of linework needed for silkscreening."

VISUAL AID/VISAID MARKETING, Box 4502, Inglewood CA 90309. (213)473-0286. Manager: Lee Clapp. Distributes sales promotion (aids), marketing consultant (service)—involved in all phases. Clients: manufacturers, distributors, publishers and graphics firms (printing and promotion) in 23 SIC code areas.
Needs: Works with 3-5 freelance artists/year. Uses artists for advertising, brochure and catalog design, illustration and layout; product design, illustration on product, P-O-P displays, display fixture design and posters. Buys some cartoons and humorous and cartoon-style illustrations. Additional media: fiber optics, display/signage, design/fabrication.
First Contact & Terms: Works on assignment only. Send query letter with brochure, resume, business

card, photostats, duplicate photographs, photocopies and tear sheets to be kept on file. Originals returned by SASE. Reports within 2 weeks. Write for appointment to show portfolio. Pays for design by the hour, $5-75. Pays for illustration by the project, $100-500. Considers complexity of project, skill and experience of artist and turnaround time when establishing payment.
Tips: "Do not say 'I can do anything.' We want to know best media you work in (pen/ink, line, illustration, layout, etc.)."

WELLS CONCRETE PRODUCTS, PRESTRESSED BUILDINGS DIV., Box 308, Hwy. 109 E., Wells MN 56097. Advertising Manager: Bruce Borkenhagen. Manufacturer of commercial/industrial/office buildings, building components and bridges. Clients: business owners, developers, architects and government.
Needs: Works with 6 freelance artists/year. Works on assignment only. Uses artists for advertising, brochure and catalog design, illustration and layout; illustration on product and signage.
First Contact & Terms: Send query letter. Samples not filed are returned by SASE. Reports only if interested. Call or write to schedule an appointment to show a portfolio, which should include roughs. Pays for design and illustration by the hour, $10 minimum; by the project, $30 minimum. Considers complexity of project when establishing payment.
Tips: "Outside work would be primarily doing line perspective drawings by photographs supplied by us (work on buildings by quote)."

WEST SUPPLY, INC., 103 Smokey St., Fort Collins CO 80525. (303)223-2322. Vice President: Mark H. West. Manufactures gift items and several lines of belt buckles. Clients: retail stores, distributors, syndicators and wholesalers.
Needs: Works with 7 freelance artists/year. Uses artists for illustration on product; black on white pen & ink art to be reproduced on belt buckles and wall hangings.
First Contact & Terms: "We prefer to purchase reproduction rights." Send query letter with photocopies to be kept on file, originals which will be returned if not used. Samples are kept on file or are returned if requested. Reports within 2 weeks. Pays per piece by mutual agreement. Pays for design by the project, $20-200. Considers complexity of project, how work will be used and rights purchased when establishing payment.
Tips: "We are price conscious, but easy to work with."

WINDSOR ART PRODUCTS, INC., 9101 Perkins St., Pico Rivera CA 90660. (213)723-6301. Design Director: Pauline Raschella. Manufacturer of decorative framed artwork and mirrors for retail stores.
Needs: Works with 5 freelance artists/year. Prefers local artists. Works on assignment only. Uses artists for product design.
First Contact & Terms: Send query letter with brochure showing art style and photographs. Samples not filed are returned only if requested. Reports only if interested. Call or write to schedule an appointment to show a portfolio, which should include roughs, original/final art, final production/product and photographs. Pays for design by the project, $300 minimum. Pays for illustration by the project, $100 minimum. Considers complexity of project when establishing payment.

WOODMERE CHINA INC., Box 5305, New Castle PA 16105. (412)658-1630. President: L.E. Tway. Manufacturer and importer of all types of collectible plate and porcelain figurines, dinnerware and giftware. Clients: wholesalers, retailers and corporations.
Needs: Works with 6-12 freelance artists/year. Works on assignment only. Uses artists for plate and figurine design; mechanicals; advertising, brochure and catalog design, illustration and layout.
First Contact & Terms: Send query letter with resume and samples to be filed unless return requested. Accepts any type sample. Reports within 2 weeks. Pays by the project, $1,000-10,000 or on an advance and royalty basis. Considers complexity of the project, skill and experience of the artist and reputation of artist in market when establishing payment.
Tips: Be professional. Seeks "only art styles that fit our markets and that are good, tight quality work."

***YUMA CIVIC CONVENTION CENTER**, Box 6468, Yuma AZ 85364. (602)344-3800. Director: Suzanne Murray.
Needs: Works with 2-3 advertising illustrators and designers/year. Assigns 20 jobs/year. Uses artists for illustration, design, layout, lettering and production for ads, direct mail brochures, posters, publicity brochures and trademarks/logo.
First Contact & Terms: Works mostly with local artists. Works on assignment only. Mail art or query for advertising art with samples (1/4 page in magazine). SASE. Reports in 2 weeks. No samples returned. Provide business card and brochure to be kept on file for future assignments.
Tips: Current trends include "clean ads—simple with a specific message being broadcast."

Fashion

ACT YOUNG IMPORTS INC., 49 W. 37th St., New York NY 10018. (212)354-8894. Executive Vice President: Joe Hafif. Manufacturers and importers of printed totes, diaper bags, knapsacks, school bags, ladies handbags, clutches made of canvas, vinyl, oxford, nylon, etc.
Needs: Buys 300-600 designs/year. Especially needs experienced designers. Local artists only.
First Contact & Terms: Query with samples. Designs on paper only, no sample manufacturing necessary.

ADVERTIR, LTD., 990 Avenue of the Americas, New York NY 10001. (212)629-8755. President: Eve Denbaum.
Needs: Works with many freelance artists/year. Local artists only. Works on assignment only. Uses artists for illustrations, brochures, catalogs, magazines, newspapers, mechanicals, retouching, airbrushing and advertisements.
First Contact & Terms: Send query letter with brochure showing art style or samples. Samples not filed are returned only if requested. Reports only if interested. Call to schedule an appointment to show a portfolio, which should include final reproduction/product, color, tear sheets and b&w. Pays by the project. Considers complexity of project, client's budget, skill and experience of artist, and how work will be used when establishing payment.
Tips: "Respond only if professional."

***AFRICAN FABRIC PRINTS/AFRICAN GARMENTS INC.**, Box 91, New York NY 10108. (212)725-1199. Contact: Vince Jordan.
Needs: Uses artists for fashion and textile design and ready-to-wear patterns.
First Contact & Terms: Mail tear sheets, original art or design ideas. Reports in 5-6 weeks. Pays $50 minimum.

BAIMS, 408 Main, Pine Bluff AR 71601. (501)534-0121. Contact: David A. Shapiro. Retailer. Carries Haggar, Van Heusen and other labels.
Needs: Works with 2-3 illustrators/designers/year. Assigns 25-100 jobs/year. Uses artists for ad illustrations.
First Contact & Terms: Send a query letter with resume, business card and samples to be kept on file. Reports in 2 weeks. Call or write to arrange an appointment to show a portfolio. Pays $5-20/job.

BEACON SHOE COMPANY, INC., Lions Estates Dr., Jonesburg MO 63351. (314)488-5444. Advertising Manager: Jennifer Turnbaugh. Manufacturer of women's casual footwear for department stores, independent merchants and mail order firms.
Needs: Works with 2 freelance artists/year. Works on assignment only. Uses artists for illustration on product, the design and layout of advertising and catalogs and also advertising illustrations. Especially needs line art and wash drawings.
First Contact & Terms: Send query letter with tear sheets, photostats and photocopies. Samples not filed are returned only if requested. Reports within 10 days. Call to schedule an appointment to show a portfolio, which should include roughs, original/final art, tear sheets, b&w photostats and photographs. Pays for illustration by the shoe, $10-65. Considers complexity of project, client's budget, skill and experience of artist, how work will be used and turnaround time. Buys all rights or reprint rights.
Tips: "The shoe industry—at least domestically—is becoming harder and harder each year. Because of that the advertising has had to become much more aggressive. Trade advertising has become much more sophisticated. Obviously our company must follow those changes with our work. Be flexible!"

BENO'S, 1515 Santee St., Los Angeles CA 90015. (213)748-2222. Director of Advertising and Sales Promotion: Gregg Seaman. Department and family apparel chain in California and Oregon.
Needs: Works with 4-5 freelance artists/year. Local artists only. Uses artists for illustrations of men's, women's and children's fashions, some hard lines and domestics (pillows, blankets, sheets) for newspapers ads and direct mail coupon books.
First Contact & Terms: Arrange interview to show portfolio. Prefers b&w line drawings, airbrush, charcoal, and previously published work as samples. SASE. Reports in 1-2 weeks. Pays by the project, $10-75 average; negotiates payment based on experience and skill of artist, and turnaround time.

BODY FASHIONS/INTIMATE APPAREL, 545 5th Ave., New York NY 10017. (212)503-2910. Editor/Associate Publisher: Jill Gerson. Information for merchandise managers, buyers, manufacturers and

suppliers about men's and women's hosiery and underwear and women's intimate apparel and leisurewear. Monthly. Circ. 13,500.
Illustrations: Interested in fashion illustrations of intimate apparel. Do not mail artwork. Arrange interview to show portfolio. Works on assignment only. Keeps file consisting of editor's comments on portfolio review and samples of work. Reports in 4 weeks. Pays on publication.

BRITCHES OF GEORGETOWNE, The Extension 229 Adver. Agency, 2213 Mt. Vernon Ave., Alexandria VA 22301. (703)548-0200. Art Director: Janet K. Daniel. Upscale retailer and manufacturer of men's and women's clothing, providing exclusive designs at the best possible prices. High level of customer service. Casual, business and formal wear. Clothing "reflects a level of taste that makes building a Britches wardrobe a continual investment in quality, fashion and enjoyment that will last for years to come." Produces casual and rugged outerwear and also elegant and sophisticated business and evening wear.
Needs: Works with 6-8 freelance artists/year. Works on assignment only. Uses artists for advertising, brochure and product illustration, model making and signage.
First Contact & Terms: Send query letter with brochure showing art style or resume, tear sheets, photostats, photocopies, slides and photographs. Samples not filed are returned only if requested. Reports only if interested. Call or write to schedule an appointment to show a portfolio, which should include original/final art, final reproduction/product, color, tear sheets, photostats, photographs, b&w, slides and prints. Pays for design by the project, $50 minimum. Pays for illustration by the project, $50-1,000. Considers complexity of project, client's budget, skill and experience of artist, how work will be used, turnaround time and rights purchased when establishing payment.

CATALINA/Division of Kayser Roth, 6040 Bandini Blvd., Los Angeles CA 90040. (213)726-1262, ext. 281. Art Director: Rhonda Thomason. Manufacturer of women's, men's, juniors, and girls' swimwear and sportswear; Catalina.
Needs: Works with 10 freelance artists/year. Uses artists for fashion illustration, paste-up and mechanicals. Seeks "contemporary but not 'high' fashion look" in art styles. Prefers b&w work, in markers or wash with charcoal pencil line. Watercolors and markers are generally used in color work.
First Contact & Terms: Local artists only. Send photostats and photographs to be kept on file. Reports to the artist only if interested. Call for appointment to show portfolio. Pays by the hour, $18-25 for production; by the project, $125-250 for illustration/per figure. "For catalogs that are totally illustrated, we would like to make arrangements according to budget." Considers complexity of project, available budget and how work will be used when establishing payment.

EARNSHAW'S REVIEW, 225 W. 34th St., New York NY 10001. (212)563-2742. Publisher: Thomas Hudson. Managing Editor: Catherine Connors. Art Director: Bette Gallucci. For designers, manufacturers, buyers and retailers in the children's fashion industry. Monthly. Circ. 10,000.
Needs: Buys 180 illustrations/year on fashion (infants to pre-teenagers). Works with 12-15 illustrators/year. Especially needs color fashion sketches.
First Contact & Terms: Send tear sheets with an SASE or call. Reports in 1 week. Call to schedule an appointment to show a portfolio, which should include original/final art, color, tear sheets, photographs and b&w. Pays for design by the project, $20-250; for illustration by the project, $15-250.
Tips: "There is more fashion orientation and color in the field. We are interested in new people. Know children's body shapes, size, and age differences."

GELMART INDUSTRIES, INC., 180 Madison Ave., New York NY 10016. (212)889-7225. Vice President and Head of Design: Ed Adler. Manufacturer of high fashion socks, gloves, headwear, scarves, and other knitted accessories. "We are prime manufacturers for many major brands and designer names."
Needs: Uses artists for fashion accessory design.
First Contact & Terms: Call for appointment to show portfolio.
Tips: "Keep the products in mind and show us how your ideas can adapt."

***GIVENCHY ACTIVEWEAR AND SWIMWEAR**, 1411 Broadway, 27th Floor, New York NY 10018. (212)840-7888. Contact: Jim Quinn. Estab. 1985. Importer of men's active sportswear for the 25-50 age group.
Needs: Works with 1 freelance artist/year. Works on assignment only. Uses artists for brochure design, fashion design, paste-up and mechanicals.
First Contact & Terms: Send resume and tear sheets. Samples not filed are returned only if requested. Reports back within 1 week. Pays for design and illustration by the project, $250 minimum. Considers complexity of project and skill and experience of artist when establishing payment.

***JOHN PAUL GOEBEL**, 10 Park Ave., New York NY 10016. Vice President: Suzette Lynch. Specializes in fashion. Clients: fibers, textiles and ready to wear.
Needs: Works with 2-6 freelance artists/year. Uses artists for illustrations, brochures, catalogs, newspapers and model making.
First Contact & Terms: Works on assignment only. Send query letter with brochure, business card and samples to be kept on file. Write for appointment to show portfolio, which should include photostats, photocopies or tear sheets. Reports back only if interested. Pays for illustration by the project, $100-5,000 average. Considers complexity of project, client's budget and how work will be used when establishing payment.
Tips: "Submit examples of their fashion illustrations. We deal primarily with men's apparel."

HOSIERY AND UNDERWEAR, 545 Third Ave., New York NY 10017. (212)503-2910. Managing Editor: Lynn Rhodes. Emphasizes hosiery; directed to hosiery buyers (from department and specialty stores, mass merchandisers, etc.) and hosiery manufacturers nationwide. Monthly. Circ. 10,000. Returns original artwork after publication if requested. Sample copy for SASE; art guidelines available.
Illustrations: Considers illustrations of hosiery; "we look for a clean style that pays attention to detail, but has a fresh, '80s look." Works on assignment only. Send query letter with brochure, resume and samples to be kept on file. Accepts photostats, tear sheets or photocopies as samples; no slides and photographs. Samples not filed are returned only if requested. Reports back. Write for appointment to show portfolio. Buys all rights. Pays $8/b&w figure; $75-100 for color spread. Pays on acceptance.

***IKA ENT. INC.**, 50 W. 34th St., 21-A10, New York NY 10001. Contact: Jerry Mossberg or Mike Bass. Manufacturer of men's apparel and sales. Labels: Roevelle, Visitor.
Needs: Works with 8 freelance artists/year. Uses artists for advertising, product, fashion and pattern design.
First Contact & Terms: Send query letter with brochure. Samples not filed are returned. Reports back within weeks. Call to schedule an appointment to show a portfolio, which should include roughs, original/final art, color and photographs. Pays for design by the project. Considers complexity of project when establishing payment.
Tips: Artists should have "openmindedness with an ability to give us direction, since if we had the direction we wouldn't need the artist."

IZOD LACOSTE WOMENSWEAR, 11 Penn Plaza, 6th Floor, New York NY 10001. Advertising PR: Anica Archip. Manufacturer of knit sportwear (shirts, bottoms, outerwear) with classic, updated traditional styling, alligator emblem, for ages 25-50 and up. Labels: Izod, Izod Lacoste (alligator).
Needs: Works with 5-6 freelance artists/year. Prefers artists experienced with sportswear. Uses artists for the design and illustration of advertising and brochures, the layout of brochures, fashion illustration, window design, P-O-P displays, calligraphy and mechanicals. Prefers "sophisticated, traditional, realistic, feminine styles."
First Contact & Terms: Send query letter with brochure showing art style or resume and tear sheets, slides and photographs. Samples not filed are returned by SASE. Reports only if interested. To show a portfolio, mail appropriate materials; portfolio should include final reproduction/product, color, tear sheets and photographs. Pays for illustration by the project, $200 minimum. Considers complexity of project, skill and experience of artist, how work will be used and turnaround time when establishing payment.
Tips: "We need very good turnaround; consultation during development of project."

***KICK BACK SPORTWEAR INC.**, 5058 Venice Blvd., Los Angeles CA 90019. (213)937-5007. President: Craig Hiller. Manufacturer of beach wear for young men and boys. Label: Kick Back.
Needs: Works with many freelance artists/year. Prefers local artist from Orange County or Los Angeles. Works on assignment only. Uses artists for fashion design and illustration, textile and pattern design and paste-up.
First Contact & Terms: Samples not filed are returned. Reports back within 7 days. Call to schedule an appointment to show a portfolio, which should include thumbnails, roughs, original/final art and color. Pays for design by the project, $200-1,000. Pays for illustration by the project, $150-750. Considers complexity of project, turnaround time and rights purchased when establishing payment. Buys all rights.
Tips: Artists should have "confidence, skill and ability to accept advice."

KNITTING TIMES, (formerly Apparel World), 386 Park Ave. S., New York NY 10016. (212)683-7520. Editor: David Gross. Official publications of the National Knitwear and Sportwear Association

emphasizing apparel manufacturing, management and marketing. It covers the latest trends in fabrics, color and technology. Monthly. Circ. 11,000.
Needs: Local artists with a knowledge of fashion to do interpretive work in the editorial area. "Artists must be able to do interpretive work, to use their imagination. If I tell them I want a long dress or a tunic sweater over a short skirt, they have to know what I need. If you can only work with figure models, you can't work with me." Prefers an "interesting" contemporary look but no avant garde.
First Contact & Terms: Send a query letter with photocopies. Samples are filed for future reference. "Artists must show the ability to meet tight deadlines." Call to schedule an appointment to show a portfolio.

LEE CO., Division of Lee Byron Corp., Suite 2819, Empire State Building, New York NY 10118. (212)244-4440. Contact: Dan L. Lieberfarb. Produces belts and personal leather goods. Mail samples or call for interview; prefers New York City artists.
Needs: Uses artists for fashion design of men's, ladies' and boys' belts, sales promotion/ad layouts, package design and direct mail brochures.

***MARATHON MARKETING CORP.**, 5 Lamont Ct., Brooklyn NY 11225. (718)363-0300. President: Rolando Royce. Manufacturer, importer and design studio providing menswear for boys and men ages 4-90. Labels: Nero Bianco, Charles Jourdan.
Needs: Works with 2 freelance artists/year. Uses artists for advertising design and illustration, fashion and accessory design, fashion illustration, textile, package and package design and posters.
First Contact & Terms: Send brochure, tear sheets and photocopies. Samples are not filed. Samples not filed are returned only if requested by artist. Reports back only if interested. Write to schedule an appointment to show a portfolio, which should include tear sheets, photostats and photographs. Pays for design and illustration by the project. Considers complexity of project, skill and experience of artist, client's budget, how work will be used, turnaround time and rights purchased when establishing payment. Buys first rights, one-time rights, reprint rights or all rights.

MAYFAIR INDUSTRIES INC., 1407 Broadway, New York NY 10018. President: Robert Postal. Manufacturer of T shirts, sweat shirts and sportswear. Prefers screen printed tops and bottoms (fun tops). Directed towards ages 2 to 21. B. J. Frog, Jane Colby and Rrribbit Rrribbit labels.
Needs: Works with 10 freelance artists/year. Uses artists for pattern design. Prefers cartoon style, young in look.
First Contact & Terms: Send query letter with brochure showing art style. Samples not filed are returned only if requested. Reports only if interested. To show a portfolio, mail appropriate materials. Pays for illustrations by the project, $100-500. Considers complexity of project when establishing payment.

***MS. LIZ**, 61 W. 68th St., New York NY 10023. Design studio providing designs for apparel, gifts; television production, advertising (animation); Ms. Liz label.
Needs: Works with 10 freelance artists/year. Uses artists for advertising and brochure design, illustration, and layout; fashion design, fashion accessory design, package design, graphics, illustration on product and animation. Prefers "cartoon art—high fashion—adult appeal."
First Contact & Terms: Artists with heavy experience, New York City area only. Send query letter with brochure, resume, samples and tear sheets to be kept on file. Write for appointment to show portfolio. Accepts "anything but original work" as samples. Samples returned by SASE if not kept on file. Reports within 2-3 weeks. Pays for design by the hour, $12-25 average; by the project, $100-5,000 average; by the day, $75-200 average. Pays for illustration by the hour, $10-20 average; by the project, $75-1,000 average; by the day $75-150 average. Considers complexity of project, available budget, and skill and experience of artist when establishing payment.

NAZARETH/CENTURY MILLS, 350 5th Ave., New York NY 10118. (212)613-0500. Designers: Marie Millelo (girls'/ladies' sportswear); Eileen Kornbluh (boys'/mens' sportswear); Martha Deutsch (sleepwear). Manufactures children's sleepwear, mens', boys', girls' and ladies' sportswear and underwear; cotton and polyester/cotton; Nazareth Mills, Savage and Lady Nazareth labels.
Needs: Buys 50-100 illustrations/year. Works with 6 local freelance artists/year.
First Contact & Terms: Query with samples. Reports within 4 weeks. Works on assignment only. Samples returned by SASE; and reports back on future assignment possibilities. Provide flyer to be kept on file for future assignments. Pays $100-200/job, artwork for screen printing.

NETWORK IND./CLASS KID LTD., 350 Fifth Ave., New York NY 10118. Design Director: Debbie Kuhfahl. Importer of men's and boys sportswear.
Needs: Works with 4-6 seasonal freelance artists/year. Uses artists for fashion, textile, and graphic

screen print design.
First Contact & Terms: Send query letter with resume and photocopies. Samples not filed are not returned. Reports back only if interested. To show a portfolio, mail appropriate materials; portfolio should include roughs (concepts), original/final art and color. Pays for design by the hour, $10-20; by the project, $15-100. Pays for illustration by the hour, $10-15; by the project, $10-100. Considers complexity of project and skill and experience of artist when establishing payment.

LOUIS NICHOLE, INC., Office and showroom location 105 E 29th St., New York NY 10016. (212)685-0395. Design studio location 54 New Haven Rd., Prospect CT 06712. (203)758-3160. President: Louis Nichole. Design company for home furnishings and decorative arts products providing very detailed romantic European 18th and 19th century designing of wallcovering, fabrics, dinnerware, glassware, stationery, greeting cards, dolls, furniture lace, bridal and children apparel.
Needs: Works with 20 freelance artists/year. Uses artists for product design, illustration on product, posters, signage and illustration.
First Contact & Terms: Artists must have only quality, European style and detail craftsmanship. Send query letter with brochure, resume, samples and tear sheets to be kept on file or call for appointment to show a portfolio. Samples returned by SASE only if requested by artist. Reports within 1 week. Pays by the hour, $10-50 average. Considers complexity of project, skill and experience of artist, and turnaround time when establishing payment.

***NOW (BY R.B. INC.)**, 777 NW 72nd Ave., (Showroom #3E1), Miami FL 33126. (305)262-3200. President: Ricardo Bisio. Wholesaler of men's accessories (exotics belts). Labels: Now by R.B.
Needs: Works on assignment only. Uses artists for advertising and brochure illustration and catalog design.
First Contact & Terms: Send brochure. Samples are not filed. Samples not filed are returned. Reports back within 1 week. Write to schedule an appointment to show a portfolio, which should include original/final art, color and photographs. Pays for design by the project, $100-400. Pays for illustration by the project, $200-400. Considers complexity of project when establishing payment.
Tips: "Show punctuality."

***OMEGA SLACKS LTD.**, 3140 Maiden Ln., Manchester MD 21102. (301)239-2367. President: Bill Garden. Manufacturer of mens dress slacks, Safari sets, leisure wear and shirt sets for fashion-oriented men ages 35 and up.
Needs: Uses artists for product and fashion design.
First Contact & Terms: Send query letter with brochure or samples. Samples are filed. Reports back within 10 days. Call to schedule an appointment to show a portfolio, which should include roughs. Pays for design by the hour, $10 minimum. Buys first rights.

PENDLETON WOOLEN MILLS, 218 SW Jefferson, Portland OR 97201. Menswear Communications Manager: Carolyn A. Zelle; Womenswear Communications Manager: Pat McKevitt. Manufacturer of men's and women's sportswear, blankets and piece goods; all 100% pure virgin wool. Pendleton Woolen Mills.
Needs: Works with 1 or 2 freelance artist/year directly and "through our agency more." Seeks local artist for line art. Uses artists for advertising illustration.
First Contact & Terms: Send query letter with samples to be kept on file. Call for appointment to show portfolio. Reports to the artist within 3 weeks. Considers complexity of project, available budget and how work will be used when establishing payment. Pays for illustration by the project, $40 minimum.

PERSONAL LEATHER DESIGN, INC., Box 9155, Wethersfield CT 06109. (203)721-0270. President: Larry Bell. Imports leather clothing and accessories under the "Louis Baron" label.
Needs: Works on assignment only. Works with illustrators in New York and New England for advertising and promotional material. Buys 40+ sketches/year. Uses illustrations for tradepaper ads and direct mail. Looks for unique fashion style. Prefers illustrators that have a feeling for current retail trends.
First Contact & Terms: Query. SASE. Reports in 2 weeks. Provide photocopy of recent work to be kept on file for future assignments. Pays by the project.

PINEHURST TEXTILES INC., Box 1628, Asheboro NC 27204. (919)625-2153. Contact: Lloyd E. Milks Jr. Manufactures ladies' lingerie, sleepwear and leisurewear; nylon tricot, woven polyester/cotton, brushed tricot and fleece; Pinehurst Lingerie label.
Needs: Works with 2 illustrators/year. Seasonal needs: spring and summer due September 1; fall and winter due March 1.

PLYMOUTH MILLS, INC., 330 Tompkins Ave., Staten Island NY 10304. (718)447-6707. President: Alan Elewson. Manufacturer of imprinted sportswear—t-shirts, sweatshirts, fashionwear, caps, aprons and bags. Clients: mass merchandisers/retailers.
Needs: Works with 6 freelance artists/year. Uses freelance artists for advertising and catalog design, illustration and layout; product design.
First Contact & Terms: Send brochure and resume. Reports back only if interested. Pays for design and illustration by the hour, $10; by the project, $100.. Considers complexity of the project and how work will be used when establishing payment.

PROPHECY CORP., 1302 Champion Circle, Carrollton TX 75006. (214)245-7807. Director of Advertising: Jayme Stoutt. Manufacturer of missy and petite fashions: jackets, blouses, skirts, sweaters, pants and dresses in the upper moderate price range. Prefers a variety of themes from casual, career, to dressy. Directed toward 25-60 years. Prophecy and Anna Ellero label.
Needs: Works with 6 freelance artists/year. Artists must constantly produce professional work quickly. Uses artists for fashion illustration, textile and pattern design, calligraphy, paste-up, mechanicals and photography.
First Contact & Terms: Send query letter with any type of sample that does not need to be returned. Samples not filed are not returned. Reports only if interested. Call to schedule an appointment to show a portfolio. Pays for design by the project, $50-100. Pays for illustration by the project, $50-250. Considers complexity of project, skill and experience of artist, and turnaround time when establishing payment.
Tips: "I look for a portfolio that specializes in fashion illustration or textiles. For illustration I want to see high contrast artwork with strong, flowing lines, and for design, I want to see a knowledge of pattern repeat and printing technique. . .and creative ability in both cases. Many artists feel that it is important to show how versatile they are, however, when I look at a portfolio, I look for consistency of style. I want to know what I will be getting. Too many times I have requested a style that the artist could not duplicate."

***PROTECH LEATHER APPAREL, INC.**, 155 Webster St., Hanover MA 02339. Advertising/PR: James Goodson. Manufacturer and importer of leather outerwear "with a youthful sporty appeal," mostly a motorcycle-type theme for ages 18-35. Labels: Protech Leather Apparel.
Needs: Works with 3-4 freelance artists/year. Prefers artists experienced in fashion or experience with models. Uses artists for advertising and brochure design and layout, catalog design, illustration and layout, product design and direct mail.
First Contact & Terms: Send query letter with resume, tear sheets, photostats and photocopies. Samples are filed. Reports back only if interested. To show a portfolio, mail roughs, original/final art, color, photostats and photographs. Pays for design and illustration by the project, $50-200. Considers complexity of project, skill and experience of artist and client's budget when establishing payment. Negotiates rights purchased.

QUEEN CASUALS, INC., 1411 Broadway, New York NY 10018. (212)398-9977. Advertising Director: Tillie Smith. Manufacturer of misses' and womens' sizes 38-46 sportswear, misses sizes 8-20, womens sizes 38-46 in polyester knits; Queen Casuals, Lady Queen and Smith, Smith & Jones misses sizes, Smith & Jones for Her, Smith & Jones Petites labels.
Needs: Works with a varied number of freelance artists/year. Works on assignment only. Prefers artists in New York, New Jersey, Pennsylvania and Connecticut areas primarily. Uses artists for fashion illustration and mechanicals.
First Contact & Terms: Send query letter with resume, tear sheets and photocopies. To show a portfolio, mail appropriate materials or call or write to schedule an appointment; portfolio should include original/final art, b&w or color, and tear sheets. Samples returned by SASE. Does not report on acceptance or rejection; "artist should call." Pays for design by the project, $2-300. Pays for illustration by the project.
Tips: "Check the kind of work done by the client."

R-TEX DECORATIVES CO., INC., 59 Sea Cliff Ave., Glen Cove NY 11542. (516)671-7600. President: Lillian Sturm. Manufacturer of high-fashion decorative yard goods, posters, panels and banners. Clients: department stores.
Needs: Works with 3-4 freelance artists/year. Works on assignment only. Uses artists for product design and posters.
First Contact & Terms: Send query letter with brochure and samples to be kept on file. Call or write for appointment to show portfolio. Accepts any type sample. Samples not filed are returned only if requested. Reports back only if interested. Pays by the project. Considers complexity of the project and artist's bid when establishing payment.

Artist: Jacques Alscheck

Fashion illustrator Jacques Alscheck has worked with Jayme Stoutt, advertising manager of Prophecy Corporation, for seven years. Alscheck, from New Hope, Pennsylvania, used pastels to illustrate a line of fall career wear. The piece was used in advertising materials distributed to Prophecy accounts and for newspaper ads. Stoutt notes that Alscheck's style is consistent and, "because he knows the fashion industry well, he does not need much direction." Stoutt, who bought all rights to the work, originally heard about the artist through an art director at Nieman-Marcus.

***THE SAMPLE**, 1927 Elmwood Ave., Buffalo NY 14207. (716)874-1730. Director of Advertising: Bruce Barber. Retailer (fashion specialty stores).
Needs: Prefers local experienced artists. Works on assignment only. Uses artists for retail illustration.
First Contact & Terms: Send query letter with brochure or tear sheets. Samples are filed. Reports back only if interested. Call or write to schedule an appointment to show a portfolio. Pays for illustration by the hour, $8-25. Considers skill and experience of artist when establishing payment. Buys all rights.

SEW NEWS, News Plaza, Box 1790, Peoria IL 61656. Art Director: Denise M. Koch Parr. Tabloid emphasizing home sewing and fashion for primarily women, average age 49. Monthly. Does not accept previously published material. Original artwork is not returned to the artist after publication. Sample copy and art guidelines are not available.
Needs: Buys up to 10 illustrations per issue. Works on an assignment basis only.
First Contact & Terms: Send query letter with resume. Write for appointment to show portfolio. Reports back to the artist only if interested. Purchases all rights. Pays on acceptance.

PRESTON STUART ART SERVICES, 69 W. 9th St., New York NY 10011. Director: Preston Stuart. Specializes in corporate presentations. Clients: fashion and corporate companies and ad agencies.
Needs: Works with 10 freelance artists/year. Desires "a professional relationship and good work." Works on assignment only. Uses artists for design and illustration, mechanicals and retouching.

First Contact & Terms: Send query letter with samples and tear sheets to be kept on file. "Photocopied samples are best." Reports only if interested. Pays for illustration by the project, $150-800 average. Considers client's budget, skill and experience of artist, how work will be used, turnaround time and rights purchased when establishing payment.

***SUN BRITCHES MFG.**, 6620 White Dr., W. Palm Beach FL 33407. Director Marketing and Sales: T.S. Steele. Manufacturer of surf trunks and beach wear for surfers' lifestyle clothing for ages 10 to 19 years. Labels: Sun Britches.
Needs: Works with 2-3 freelance artists/year. Prefers artists with knowledge of the surfwear market. Works on assignment only. Uses artists for advertising design and illustration, pattern design and mechanicals.
First Contact & Terms: Send query letter with brochure. Samples are filed. Samples not filed are returned only if requested by artist. Reports back only if interested. Write to schedule an appointment to show a portfolio, which should include thumbnails or "as required for project." Pays for design by the project, $200-450. Pays for illustration by the project, $150-350. Considers how work will be used and rights purchased when establishing payment. Buys first rights.
Tips: Artists should have "knowledge of the surfwear market, with working experience."

***SURVIVORS, INC.**, #16C10, 50 W. 34th St., New York NY 10001. (212)594-6776. Contact: K. Cho. Estab. 1985. Importer of young men's apparel for ages 16-35 years. Labels: Chavalier and Victorio Uomo.
Needs: Uses artists for brochure, catalog and fashion design.
First Contact & Terms: Send query letter with brochure or resume. Write to schedule an appointment to show a portfolio. Payment depends on agreement between the parties.

TRIBORO QUILT MFG. CORP., 172 S. Broadway, White Plains NY 10605. (914)428-7551. Sales Manager: Alvin Kaplan. Produces infants' wear and bedding under the Triboro label; for chain and department stores.
Needs: Works with freelance artists for infants' and childrens' embroidery and fabric designs.
First Contact & Terms: Call for interview or provide resume, business card and brochure to be kept on file. Reports in 1 week. Samples returned by SASE; and reports back on future assignment possibilities.

***UFO**, 466 Bloome St., New York NY 10013. Vice President: Lorna Brody. Manufacturer of contemporary sportswear for ages 16 to 40. Labels: UFO jeans and sportswear; Surplus by UFO.
Needs: Works with 4-5 freelance artists/year. Prefers local artists only. Works on assignment only. Uses artists for advertising design and illustration, brochure design and layout, catalog design, illustration and layout, fashion illustration, package design and direct mail.
First Contact & Terms: Send query letter with resume, tear sheets, photostats and photocopies. Samples are filed. Reports back only if interested. Write to schedule an appointment to show a portfolio. Pays for design and illustration by the project. Considers complexity of project, skill and experience of artist, client's budget, how work will be used and turnaround time when establishing payment. Negotiates rights purchased.

UNIFORMS MANUFACTURING INC., Box 5336, W. Bloomfield MI 48033. (313)332-2700. President: L.P. Tucker. Manufacturer of all types of wearing apparel—smocks, lab coats, shirts, trousers, coveralls, dresses, aprons, gloves in cotton, polyester and knits; Uniform label.
Needs: Works with 3 freelance artists/year. Works on assignment only. Uses artists for advertising, brochure and catalog design; advertising illustration and direct mail promotions.
First Contact & Terms: Send brochure/flyer and slides as samples. Samples returned by SASE. Reports as soon as possible. Reports back whether to expect possible future assignments. Negotiates payment.

U.S. SHOE CORPORATION, One Eastwood Dr., Cincinnati OH 45227. (513)527-7000. Promotion Services Director: Philip Gleeson. Manufacturer of shoes featuring current fashion trends; Red Cross, Socialites, Cobbies, Joyce, Selby, Pappagallo and Capezio.
Needs: Works with 3 freelance artists/year. "Experience is normally necessary." Uses artists for advertising, brochure and catalog design, illustration and layout; fashion design and illustration; paste-up and mechanicals.
First Contact & Terms: Send query letter with samples to be kept on file. Call or write for appointment to show portfolio. Accepts any type sample. Samples not kept on file are returned only if requested by artist. Reports to the artist only if interested. Pays by the hour, $25-30 for design; $30-35 for illustration. Considers complexity of project, available budget and turnaround time when establishing payment.

Greeting Cards and Paper Products

Let us count the ways we can say, "I love you." As far as the greeting card industry is concerned, there is no limit. Last year, more than 7 billion cards were bought, making "social expression" a $3.6 billion business.

This lucrative industry has an insatiable appetite for ideas and artwork. Alternative card companies have expanded the market with cards dealing irreverently with touchy subjects such as divorce and dieting. Since ninety percent of card purchases are made by women, card makers are addressing contemporary lifestyles by offering "business" cards for the boss, babysitter and househusband. Cartoon cards prove that "funny is money," as Zai Zatoon of Strings Attached has declared.

There is a truism within the industry that the art attracts the buyer and the messages sells the card. Artists who can develop both the message and the artwork have a better chance of selling their work, because companies look for a complete greeting card concept. Publishers look for work that elicits an immediate emotional response, since cards must compete with each other in grocery stores and stationery shops.

The doors are open for every artistic style, medium and technique in cards. Traditionally the most popular painting mediums are watercolor and designer's gouache, but some companies, such as Albion Cards, specialize in pen-and-ink designs. Though cards appear in every size and shape, most follow a vertical format, the standard size being 4⅝ by 7½.

Most publishers prefer contact by mail. Study first-hand the card lines in stationery and card shops, book stores and novelty shops. Find the companies whose style and message fit your work, then write to request a catalog, which will give you an overview of all the lines they offer. When you're ready to submit work, your mailing package should include a cover letter, resume or brochure, 10-12 samples and a SASE that is large enough to return your work. Send slides, Photostats and tear sheets to show how your work appears in printed form. Some companies want only lines of cards, so 8-10 cards with the same theme or central character should be developed.

Also listed in this section are calendar firms, who also use artists for stationery, desk accessories, and other knickknack designs. Giftwrap manufacturers need year-round and seasonal designs for their hundreds of giftwrapping papers. Licensing agents have developed a multibillion dollar business matching artists with manufacturers who, in turn, are always looking for a unique, marketable product. Through licensing their designs, many greeting card artists are able to resell their designs to other companies who produce peripheral products such as coffee mugs, plates and school items.

Payment for cards is usually a flat fee for each illustration or a royalty. Many companies prefer to buy all rights because they will use your design throughout a line of paper products; make sure that you are adequately compensated.

To keep current with the greeting card industry, consult *Greetings Magazine*. *Thomas Register of Manufacturers* lists paper products manufacturers and can be found in your local library. Ron Lister's *Designing Greeting Cards and Paper Products* and Susan Evart's *The Art & Craft Of Greeting Cards* give overviews of the industry. *A Guide to Greeting Card Writing* by Larry Sandman points out the opportunities in the field. *The Complete Guide to Greeting Card Design & Illustration* by Eva Szela is a comprehensive guide to all aspects of greeting card design and illustration.

ACCORD PUBLICATIONS (US) INC., 1a Mt. Vermont St., Rigefield Park NJ 07660. (201)440-8210. President: Richard Storr. Produces greeting cards and giftwrap. Produces general cards, soft lines cards, everyday humorous, whimsical, fine art and Victorian cards.
Needs: Works with many freelance artist/year. Buys 250 designs from freelance artist/year. Buys 40 illustrations from freelance artist/year. Prefers watercolors. Prefers 5x7. Produces material for Christmas, Valentines, Mother's Day, Easter, Halloweeen and Thanksgiving; submit 1 year before holiday.
First Contact & Terms: Send query letter with brochure or photostats, photocopies and slides or "whatever is at hand." Samples are filed. Samples not filed are returned. Reports back within 10 days. Call or write to schedule an appointment to show portfolio, which should include roughs. Original artwork is sometimes returned to artist after job's completion. Pays average flat fee of $150/design; royalties of 5%. Buys one-time rights.
Tips: "We are an alternative card company, study the market. We like stylized work that stands out from what is generally available, cut-out cards, pop-up cards, button cards, anything ingenious is in.

***AFRICA CARD CO. INC.**, Box 91, New York NY 10108. (212)725-1199. President: Vince Jordan. Publishes greeting cards and posters.
Needs: Buys 25 designs/year.
First Contact & Terms: Mail art, or arrange interview. SASE. Reports in 6 weeks. Pays $50 minimum, greeting cards and posters. Buys all rights.

***AGENT ANDY, INC.**, 221 Orient Way, Lyndhurst NJ 07071. (201)933-0917. President: Andrew Abrams. Licenses new product concepts to manufacturers of games, toys, calendars, posters, stationery, paper tableware, mugs, novelties, housewares, desk accessories, home decor items, plush toys, pens, ceramics, and musical giftware.
Needs: New product concepts submitted on 8½"x11" format. "We work with non-artists who have an original, marketable concept as well as top designers."
First Contact & Terms: Send query letter with brochure or resume and photocopies. Samples are filed. Samples not filed are returned only if requested by artist. Reports back only if interested. "Non-disclosure forms are signed to protect new concepts." Call or write to schedule and appointment to show a portfolio. Negotiates royalties of 5-10%, $1,000 to $10,000 advance plus guarantees $5,000-25,000/year.
Tips: "We're more concerned with subject matter that shows creativity as opposed to technical skills. Concepts leading to extensive lines of product are most important.

***ALASKA MOMMA, INC.**, 303 Fifth Ave., New York NY 10016. (212)679-4404. President: Shirley Henshel. "We are a licensing company representing artists, illustrators and designers with regard to design concepts and cartoon characters." Licenses artwork to toy, clothing, giftware, stationery and houseware manufacturers of consumer products.
Needs: Considers work that demonstrates a unique style. "An artist must have a distinctive style that a manufacturer can't get from his own art department and that can be applied to the product." Prefers figurative and "cartoony" styles.
First Contact & Terms: "Artists may submit work in any visual format that they choose, as long as it is a fair representation of their style." Henschel prefers to see several color samples "in a mailable size." No originals. Charges royalties of 7-10% with an advance available. Earned royalties "depending on whether the products sell."
Tips: "We are interested in the work of freelance artists in so far as that we would be interested in representing them, if they are any good for licensing purposes. What we look for in an artist before we undertake a licensing program is somebody who is distinctive in what he does."

ALBION CARDS, Box 102, Albion MI 49224. Owners: Maggie and Mike LaNoue. Produces greeting cards, prints, note cards, postcards, catalogues and brochures. Uses b&w, line art, realistic, detailed, old-fashioned, clear; must hold line quality when reduced—to "jump out"—high contrast. Directs products to women, older people, tourists, nostalgia buffs and sports enthusiasts.
Needs: Buys approximately 100 designs from freelance artists/year. Uses artists for calligraphy and mechanicals. Considers pen & ink and watercolors. Size of originals 9x12 or proportionate; important elements of design and artist's signature should be one inch from all edges of the drawing. Produces material for Christmas and summer (skiing, golfing, bicycling, boating); other subjects: animals (cats & ducks especially), landscapes, wild flowers and herbs. Catalog $2; art guidelines free for SASE. Theme must be "upbeat" and positive, but not cutesy.
First Contact & Terms: Send query letter with brochure, showing art style and photocopies. Samples not filed are not returned. Reports back within 3 months. Do not send originals. Send color photographs, b&w and photocopies. Pays for illustration by the project, 5% minimum. Payment depends entirely on sales; artists can boost sales and earn sales commission as well. Buys copyright outright to be used for

cards only and prints; artist retains some rights for other items. Buys only scenes that have not been published as cards to date. "Looking for artists who seek long-term arrangement not fast cash."
Tips: "We are interested in producing series of cards relating to scenic tourist areas, seascapes, street scenes and landmarks. Need scenes of Washington D.C. for 1988. We can help promote other artists' works in their own locale. The card market is expanding; nostalgia is gaining in popularity. Our needs for freelance work have increased dramatically. There is a greater appreciation of quality work—we can no longer produce all the new card scenes that our customers would like to purchase—so we are using more freelance work. We are interested in serious artists. Please do not send quick sketchy work or designs that display bad taste. Work must reproduce well and give the viewer a good feeling."

AMBERLEY GREETING CARD CO., 11510 Goldcoast Dr., Cincinnati OH 45249-1695. Art Director: Ned Stern. Publishes studio, humorous and everyday cards.
Needs: Assigns 200 jobs/year. Local artists only. Uses freelance artists for product illustration. Especially needs humorous cards.
First Contact & Terms: Call first. Buys all rights. No original work returned at job's completion. Call or write to schedule an appointment to show portfolio, which should include original/final art and final reproduction/product. Pays for design and illustration by the project, $60; on acceptance.
Tips: Visit greeting card shops to get a better idea of the types of cards published by Amberley. When reviewing an artist's work, "the first thing I look for is the professionalism of the presentation, i.e. samples neatly displayed (no loose drawings, scraps of paper, etc.); creativity—what has the artist done differently and effectively; use of color, and lettering." An artist's biggest mistake is having a sloppy portfolio; "I'd rather see 5 good examples of work than 25 poorly done."

AMCAL, 1050 Shary Ct., Concord CA 94518. (415)689-9930. Publishes calendars and greeting cards. Markets to all major gift, book and department stores throughout U.S. Some sales to Europe and Japan. Rapidly expanding company looking for distinctive card and gift ideas for growing market demand. "All subjects considered that fit our quality image."
Needs: Prefers work in 5x7 vertical card format. Send photos, slides or published work.
First Contact & Terms: Responds within 2 weeks. Send samples or call for appointment to show a portfolio. Pays for design by the hour, $20-50. Pays for illustration by the project $200-700.
Tips: "Know the market. Go to gift shows and visit lots of stationery stores. Read all the trade magazines. Talk to store owners to find out what's selling and what isn't."

AMERICAN GREETINGS CORP., 10500 American Rd., Cleveland OH 44102. (216)252-7300. Director Creative Recruitment: Mary Ellen Knot. Publishes humorous, studio and conventional greeting cards, calendars, giftwrap, posters, stationery and paper tableware products. Manufactures candles and ceramic figurines.
First Contact & Terms: Query with resume. Forms for submitting portfolio will be mailed. Portfolios received without necessary paperwork will be returned unreviewed.
Tips: "We are staffed to generate our own ideas internally, but we will review portfolios for full-time or freelance employment."

***ARTFAIRE**, 600 E. Hancock St., Appelton WI 54911. (414)738-4284. Art Director: Marilyn Wolf. Produces giftwrap and paper tableware products.
Needs: Works with 25 freelance artists/year. Buys 100 designs from freelance artists/year. Buys 100 illustrations from freelance artists/year. Prefers artists experienced in giftwrap and party goods designing. Prefers watercolors, acrylics, etc. Produces material for everyday, Christmas, Valentine's Day, Halloween.
First Contact & Terms: Send query letter with brochure or tear sheets. Samples not filed are returned by SASE. Reports back within 2 months. To show a portfolio, mail original/final art, tear sheets, photographs and b&w. Original artwork is not returned after job's completion. Pays for design by the project, $100-700. Pays for illustration by the project, $250-700. Buys all rights.
Tips: Looks for "newness, strong style and excellence in execution. Also, knowledge of our product and the application of design to meet our products' needs."

BARNSTABLE ORIGINALS, 50 Harden Ave., Camden ME 04843. (207)236-8162. Art Director: Marsha Smith. Produces greeting cards, posters, gift books, paper sculpture cards and memo pads. Directed towards tourists travelling in New England, and sailors or outdoors people—"nature and wildlife lovers."
Needs: Buys 50 designs and illustrations from freelance artists/year. Prefers 5x7 cards, vertical or horizontal.
First Contact & Terms: Send query letter with brochure showing art style and resume, tear sheets, photostats, photocopies, slides or photographs. Samples not filed are returned by SASE. Reports back

within 1 month. To show a portfolio, mail tear sheets, photostats, color photographs or slides of originals. No originals returned to artist at job's completion. Pays $50 minimum per design/illustration. Pays on acceptance. Buys all rights.

Tips: "We're looking for quality art work—any creative and fresh ideas. The artist must display a sound background in art basics, exhibiting strong draftsmanship in a graphic style. Colors must be harmonious and clearly expected."

BARTON-COTTON INC., 1405 Parker Rd., Baltimore MD 21227. (301)247-4800. Contact: Creative/Art Department. Produces religious greeting cards, commercial Christmas cards, wildlife designs and spring note cards. Free guidelines and sample cards; specify area of interest: religious, Christmas, spring, etc.

Needs: Buys 150-200 illustrations each year. Submit seasonal work "any time of the year."

First Contact & Terms: Send query letter with resume, tear sheets, photocopies, photostats, slides and photographs. Previously published work and simultaneous submissions accepted. Reports in 4 weeks. To show a portfolio, mail original/final art, final reproduction/product, color and tear sheets. Submit full-color work only (watercolors, gouache, pastels, oils and acrylics); pays $150-500/illustration; on acceptance.

Tips: "Good draftsmanship is a must, particularly with figures and faces. Spend some time studying market trends in the greeting card industry to determine current market trends." There is an increased need for creative ways to paint traditional Christmas scenes with up-to-date styles and techniques."

BEACH PRODUCTS, 1 Paper Pl., Kalamazoo MI 49001. (616)349-2626. Creative Director: Steven G. Mueller. Publishes paper tableware products; general and seasonal, birthday, special occasion, invitations, announcements, stationery, wrappings and thank you notes for children and adults.

Needs: Buys designs from freelance artists. Uses artists for product designs and illustration. Sometimes buys humorous and cartoon-style illustrations. Prefers flat 4-color designs; 5 1/4 wide x 5 1/2 high for luncheon napkins. Produces seasonal material for Christmas, Mother's Day, Thanksgiving, Easter, Valentine's Day, St. Patrick's Day, Halloween and New Year's Day. Submit seasonal material before June 1; everyday (not holidays) material before March.

First Contact & Terms: Send query letter 9x12 SASE so catalog can be sent with response. Disclosure form must be completed and returned before work will be viewed. Call or write to schedule an appointment to show a portfolio, which should include original/final art and final reproduction/product. Previously published work OK. Originals not returned at artist at job's completion; "all artwork purchased becomes the proverty of Beach Products. Items not purchased are returned." Buys all rights. Pays average flat fee of $100/design; on acceptance. Considers product use when establishing payment.

Tips: "When asking for specifications and catalog the SASE should be large enough to accommodate the catalog, for example a 9x12 SAE. Artwork should have a clean, professional appearance and be the specified size for submissions, as well as a maximum of four flat colors."

CAROLYN BEAN PUBLISHING, LTD., 2230 W. Winton Ave., Hayward CA 94545. Art Director: Tom Drew. Publishes alternative and traditional greeting cards and stationery; diverse themes.

Needs: Buys 100-150 designs/illustrations per year from freelance artists. Uses artists for product design. Produces greatly expanded occasions and holiday images; submit material 12-18 months in advance.

First Contact & Terms: Send query letter with slides or photocopies. Samples returned only if accompanied by SASE. Reports in 4-8 weeks. Originals returned to artist at job's completion. Do not call or write to schedule an interview. Provide samples, business card and tear sheets to be kept on file for possible future assignments. Negotiates rights purchased; royalty arrangement if possible. Payment is made according to time schedule established in contract.

Tips: "Think about *cards*. I see good work all the time, but rarely things that have been created with greeting cards in mind. Do something different! We are not interested in seeing more of what is already available on the market."

***ANITA BECK CARDS**, 3409 W. 44th St., Minneapolis MN 55410. General Manager: Jean Johnson. Produces greeting cards, calendars and stationery. Products directed to female market.

Needs: Buys 15-20 designs/year from freelance artists. Considers watercolors and paper cut-outs for product illustrations. Prefers final art of 4 1/4x5 1/2. Produces seasonal material for Christmas and holidays; submit art by February 1 for Christmas.

First Contact & Terms: Send query letter with samples. Accepts slides, photostats or photographs as samples; submit only with SASE. Samples not filed are returned by SASE. Reports within 3 weeks. Returns original art after reproduction. Pays flat fee, $50-75 average/design. Buys reprint rights.

Tips: "Submit work that is similar in style to designs in our catalog. Artists are encouraged to write for our catalog. Cost is $1 for our catalog; you also receive a sample note, gift enclosure, recipe card and $1 coupon redeemable with your first order."

BLOOMIN' IMAGES, 70 W. Cedar St., Box H, Poughkeepsie NY 12602. (914)471-3110. Administrative Services Manager: Vera Lawrence. Estab. 1983. Produces a unique variety of greeting cards and stationery sold primarily on the east coast.
Needs: Buys 20 designs and illustrations from freelance artists/year. Works on assignment only. Uses artists for calligraphy and paste-up. Prefers pen & ink.
First Contact & Terms: Send query letter with tear sheets to be kept on file. Samples not filed are returned. Reports within 2 months. Returns original artwork after reproduction. Negotiates payment and rights purchased.

BRETT-FORER GREETINGS, INC., 105 73rd St., New York NY 10021. Art Director: Barbara T. Schaffer. Publishes cute and whimsical greeting cards; Christmas and everyday.
Needs: Uses artists for design of 6x9 and 4½x6 Christmas cards, and 4¾x6½ everyday cards. Considers all media. Produces seasonal cards for Valentine's Day and Mother's Day.
First Contact & Terms: Send samples. Reports in 4 weeks. No originals returned to artist at job's completion. Buys all rights. Pays average flat fee of $125/design. Considers complexity of project when establishing payment.

BRILLIANT ENTERPRISES, 117 W. Valerio St., Santa Barbara CA 93101. Art Director: Ashleigh Brilliant. Publishes postcards.
Needs: Uses up to 300 designs/year. Artists may submit designs for word-and-picture postcards, illustrated with line drawings.
First Contact & Terms: Submit 5½x3½ horizontal b&w line drawings. SASE. Reports in 2 weeks. Buys all rights. "Since our approach is very offbeat, it is essential that freelancers first study our line. Ashleigh Brilliant's books include *I May Not Be Totally Perfect, But Parts of Me Are Excellent* and *Appreciate Me Now and Avoid the Rush*. We supply a catalog and sample set of cards for $2." Pays $40 minimum, depending on "the going rate" for camera-ready word-and-picture design.
Tips: "Since our product is highly unusual, freelancers should familiarize themselves with it by sending for our catalog ($2 plus SASE). Otherwise, they will just be wasting our time and theirs."

BURGOYNE, INC., (formerly Sidney J. Burgoyne & Sons Inc.), 2030 E. Byberry Rd., Philadelphia PA 19116. (215)677-8000. Art Director: Jon Harding. Publishes greeting cards and calendars; Christmas, winter and religious themes.
Needs: Buys 75-100 designs/year. Prefers artists experienced in greeting card design. Uses freelance artists for products design and illustration, and calligraphy. Will review any media; prefers art proportional to 5¼x7⅛. Produces seasonal material for Christmas; will review new work at any time.
First Contact & Terms: Send query letter with original art or published work or actual work. Samples returned by SASE. Simultaneous submissions OK. Reports in 2 weeks. No originals returned to artist at job's completion. To show a portfolio, mail appropriate materials or call to schedule an appointment; portfolio should include original/final art and final reproduction/product. Pays for design by the project, $100-300. Buys all rights; on acceptance.
Tips: "Familiarize yourself with greeting card field. Spend time in card stores."

CAPE SHORE PAPER PRODUCTS, INC., 42A N. Elm St., Box 537, Yarmouth ME 04096. Art Director: Anne W. Macleod. Produces notes, giftwrap and stationery products predominantly nautical in theme. Directs products to gift and stationery stores/shops.
Needs: Buys 25-50 designs and illustrations/year from freelance artists. Prefers watercolor, acrylics, cut paper and gouache. Specific sizes for final art listed in guideline letter. Produces material for Christmas cards; June deadline for finished artwork.
First Contact & Terms: Send query letter with brochure to be kept on file. Reports within several weeks. Pays by the project, $25-200. Prefers to buy all rights. Originals returned to artist if not purchased.
Tips: "We do not use black-and-white artwork, photographs, greeting card prose. Please pay close attention to specification requirements—otherwise, problems can occur."

***CARING CARD CO.**, Box 90278, Long Beach CA 90809. President: Shirley Hassell. Produces greeting cards, especially contemporary cards and "significant loss" cards for Hospice Programs for all ages and groups.
Needs: Buys 90% of designs used from freelance artists. Buys illustrations from freelance artists. Also uses artists for P-O-P displays. Prefers pen & ink and watercolors; looks for "simplicity and elegance."
First Contact & Terms: Send brochure or photostats, photocopies and slides. Samples are filed. Samples not filed are returned only if requested by artist. Reports back only if interested. To show a portfolio, mail slides, tear sheets, photostats, photographs, color and b&w. Original artwork is not returned after job's completion. Pays average flat fee of $25/design; $40/illustration. Buys all rights.

Shirley Hassell, president of the Caring Card Company, says, "a third party who knows I'm always looking for artists" suggested she contact freelance artist Carol Abrahams of Long Beach, California, to illustrate this significant loss card. Rendered in pen and ink, the card shows "reflections of a person's life when looking back and remembering the love and heartaches shared." All rights were purchased.

***CARLTON CARDS**, Box 660270, Dallas TX 75266-0270. (214)638-4800. Creative Coordinator: Laurel Milton. Produces greeting cards, calendars and paper tableware products. Produces announcements, general cards, informal cards, inspirational cards, invitations, contemporary cards, juvenile cards, soft line cards and studio cards.
Needs: Prefers 3 years experience in the industry. Works on assignment only. Produces material for all seasos.
First Contact & Terms: Send query letter with SASE. Samples are filed. Samples not filed are returned by SASE. Reports back within 15 days. To show a portfolio, mail final reproduction/product, slides, photographs and color. Original artwork is not returned after job's completion. Pays average flat fee of $250/illustration. Buys all rights.
Tips: "Keep current with trends and endeavor to tailor your work to fit the trends."

CASE STATIONERY CO., INC., 179 Saw Mill River Rd., Yonkers NY 10701. (914)965-5100. President: Jerome Sudwow. Vice President: Joyce Blackwood. Produces stationery and tins for mass merchandisers in stationery and housewares departments.
Needs: Buys 50 designs from freelance artists/year. Works on assignment only. Uses artists for mechanicals and ideas. Produces materials for Christmas; submit 6 months in advance.
First Contact & Terms: Send query letter with resume and tear sheets, Photostats, photocopies, slides and photographs. Samples not filed are returned. Reports back. Call or write to schedule an appointment to show a portfolio. Original artwork is not returned. Pays a flat fee, by the hour, by the project or by royalties. Buys first rights or one-time rights.
Tips: "Get to know us. We're people who are creative and who know how to sell a product."

H. GEORGE CASPARI, INC., 225 Fifth Ave., New York NY 10010. (212)685-9726. President: Douglas H. Stevens. Publishes greeting cards, Christmas cards, invitations, giftwrap and paper napkins. The line maintains a very traditional theme.
Needs: Buys 80-100 illustrations/year from freelance artists. Prefers watercolors, color pencil and oth-

er color media. Produces seasonal material for Christmas, Mother's Day, Father's Day, Easter and Valentine's Day.
First Contact & Terms: Arrange an appointment with Lisa Fingeret to review portfolio. Prefers unpublished original illustrations as samples. Reports within 4 weeks. Negotiates payment on acceptance; pays for design by the project, $200 minimum.
Tips: "Caspari and many other small companies rely on freelance artists to give the line a fresh, overall style rather than relying on one artist. We feel this is a strong point of our company."

CELEBRATION GREETINGS, Box 9500, Boulder CO 80301. (303)530-1442. Product Manager: Jane Knutson. Produces greeting cards, calendars, posters and stationery. Product is directed mainly towards females between 20-45 years of age, both working and non-working.
Needs: Buys 100 designs/year from freelance artists. Prefers artists with previous publication experience and/or knowledge of reproduction and of the greeting card industry. Works on assignment only. Also uses freelance artists for calligraphy and greeting card illustration. Considers watercolors, acrylics, airbrush and torn paper. Prefers sizes proportionate to 5x7 with space for 1" bleeds. Seasonal material includes Christmas cards; submit material for the holiday any time of the year.
First Contact & Terms: Send query letter with brochure, resume, tear sheets, slides, photographs and originals. Samples not filed are returned. Call or write to schedule an appointment to show a portfolio, which should include original/final art; final reproduction/product, color, tear sheets and photographs. Original work sometimes returned after publication. Pays a flat fee, $150-200/illustration. Payment is also negotiable. Artists will receive 25 free samples of each illustration. Buys all rights.
Tips: "Most of our accounts are Christian bookstores. Our product tends to have a warm and friendly feel, as opposed to a highly graphic feel. Art may suggest a religious theme, but not usually unless it is specifically for Christmas. We are looking for contemporary art, not dated or traditional themes."

***CHARACTER CARDS**, 14 North St., Maynard MA 07154. President: Conne Hollander. Produces juvenile cards and activity cards for children. Target market is generally adults, parents, friends, grandparents, other relatives who are buying cards for children. They live primarily in urban and suburban areas.
Needs: Works with freelance artists. Prefers "artists who live in the greater Boston, MA area who are experienced cartoonists or are last year art students who are cartoonists and are willing to work with the company's ideas. Artists may give input for ideas." Works on assignment only. Also uses artists for mechanicals. Prefers size that can be adequately reduced for standard 5x7 greeting cards.
First Contact & Terms: Send query letter with resume and photocopies. Samples are filed. Samples not filed are returned by SASE. Reports back within a month's time only if interested. Call or write to schedule an appointment to show a portfolio, which should include tear sheets, photostats, color or b&w. Original artwork is not returned after job's completion. Pays for illustration by the project, $500. Buys all rights.
Tips: "Be professional in your approach."

***CLASSICO SAN FRANCISCO INC.**, 16 Golden Gate Dr., San Rafael CA 94901. (415)459-3830. Vice President: Dolores Dietz. Produces contemporary postcards, cartoon postcards and art photography postcards.
First Contact & Terms: Send query letter with brochure or photostats and photocopies. Samples are filed. Samples not filed are returned only if requested. Reports back within 2 weeks. Call or write to schedule an appointment to show a portfolio, which should include slides, tear sheets and photographs. Pays royalties of 5%. Negotiates rights purchased.
Tips: "Art must be applicable to postcard size."

THE COLORTYPE COMPANY, 1640 Market St., Coronua CA 91720. (714)734-7410. Vice President/ Marketing: Mike Gribble. Produces greeting cards, stationery, mugs and bulletin boards.
Needs: Buys 150 designs from freelance artists/year. Experienced artists only. Uses artists for P-O-P displays, paste-up and mechanicals. Prefers pen & ink, watercolors and acrylics.
First Contact & Terms: Send query letter with brochure showing art style or samples. Samples not filed are returned by SASE. Reports back within 2 weeks. To show a portfolio, mail appropriate materials. No originals returned to artist at job's completion. Pays average flat fee of $120/design and illustration.
Tips: Artist should "be knowledgeable about the card business."

CPS INDUSTRIES, INC., Columbia Highways, Franklin IN 37064. (615)794-8000. Art Director: Michelle Rosenberg. Produces giftwrap.
Needs: Buys 70-75 designs from freelance artists/year. "We solicit speculatives at the concept stage." Prefers pattern repeat, an even division of 18. Produces 50% of material for Christmas, the rest for occasions such as weddings, showers, baby, etc.; submit 1½ years in advance.

First Contact & Terms: Send query letter with resume and photocopies. Samples not filed are returned by SASE. Reports only if interested; will always send guidelines. Call for an appointment to show a portfolio, which should include original/final art, roughs, tear sheets and photostats. Original artwork is returned sometimes. Pays by the project, $100-300 average. Buys rights for giftwrap.
Tips: Designs should be appropriate for one or more of the following categories; wedding, baby shower, birthday, masculine, feminine and abstract.

***CREATIF LICENSING**, Suite 106, 587 Main St., New Rochelle NY 10801. (914)632-2232. President: Stan Cohen. Licensing manager. "We handle artists and their properties with the purpose of licensing their art and concepts to companies that produce products compatible to those art styles." Serves gift, stationery, clothing and toy companies.
Needs: Works with 12 freelance artists/year. "We are looking for creative artists who have a unique, distinguishable style which lends itself to merchandise licensing." Prefers simple line drawings depicting children, animals or cartoons characters.
First Contact & Terms: Send query letter with brochure, photocopies and SASE. Samples are filed except for "styles we feel are not applicable for licensing." Samples not filed are returned by SASE. Reports back within 2 weeks. Call or write for appointment to show portfolio. "We work on 50% commission on all royalties our company receives."

CREATIVE DIRECTIONS, INC., 2955 W. 5th Ave., Gary IN 46404. (219)949-5000. Director: Barbara A. Woods. Estab. 1986. Produces greeting cards, which include announcements, invitations, all-occasion, general, informal, inspirational, contemporary, juvenile, soft line and studio cards.
Needs: Works with a maximum number of freelance artists/year. Buys 100 designs and 100 illustrations from freelancers/year. "We welcome new artists." Material will be cropped to 8½x5½. Produces material for all occasions; submit 12 months before holiday.
First Contact & Terms: Send query letter with resume, photocopies, slides, transparencies, photocopies and SASE. Samples are not filed; samples not filed are returned by SASE. Reports back within 6 weeks. Original artwork is returned by SASE. Pays royalties of 1%. Buys first rights or reprint rights; negotiates rights purchased.

CREATIVE PAPER PRODUCTS, INC., 1523 Prudential, Dallas TX 75235. (214)634-1283. President: David Hardenbergh. Novelty pens, pencils, costume jewelry etc. for children 6-14 years old. "Hello Kitty"-type merchandise. Everyday themes for women.
Needs: Buys "simplistic flat art that is very colorful" from freelance artists. Uses artists for product design and illustration. Produces seasonal material; submit art 6 months before holiday.
First Contact & Terms: Send samples. Prefers photostats and slides as samples. Samples returned on request. Reports within 3 weeks. Provide samples to be kept on file for possible future assignments. Material not copyrighted. Negotiates payment on acceptance.

CREATIVE PAPERS BY C.R. GIBSON, The C.R. Gibson Co., Knight St., Norwalk CT 06856. (203)847-4543. Vice President Creative Papers: Steven P. Mack. Publishes stationery, note paper, invitations and silk-screened giftwrap. Interested in material for lines of products. "Two to three designs are sufficient to get across a concept. We don't use too many regional designs. Stationery themes are up-to-date, fashion oriented. Designs should be somewhat sophisticated without being limiting. Classic designs and current material from the giftware business do well."
Needs: Buys 100-200 designs/year. Especially needs new 4-color art for note line and invitations; "we need designs that relate to current fashion trends as well as a wide variety of illustrations suitable for boxed note cards. We constantly update our invitation line and can use a diverse selection of ideas." Uses humorous illustrations especially for invitation line. Speculation art has no size limitations. Finished size of notes is 4x5½ and 3¾x5; folded invitations, 3¾x5; card style invitations 4¾x6; and giftwrap repeat, 8x8 minimum.
First Contact & Terms: Send query letter with brochure showing art style or resume, photocopies and slides. Prefers 4-6 samples (slides or chromes of work or originals), published or unpublished. Previously published, photocopied and simultaneous submissions OK, if they have not been published as cards and the artist has previous publishers' permissions. SASE. Reports in 6 weeks. Call or write to schedule an appointment to show a portfolio, which should include thumbnails, roughs, original/final art and tear sheets. Pays $35 for rough sketch. Pays for design by the hour, $20 minimum; by the project, $35 minimum. Pays for illustration by the project, $175 minimum. Negotiates payment. Considers complexity of project, skill and experience of artist, reproduction expense and rights purchased. Usually buys all rights; sometimes buys limited rights.
Tips: "Almost all of the artists we work with or have worked with are professional in that they have a background of other professional assignments and exhibits as well as a good art education. We have been fortunate to make a few 'discoveries,' but even these people have been at it for a number of years and

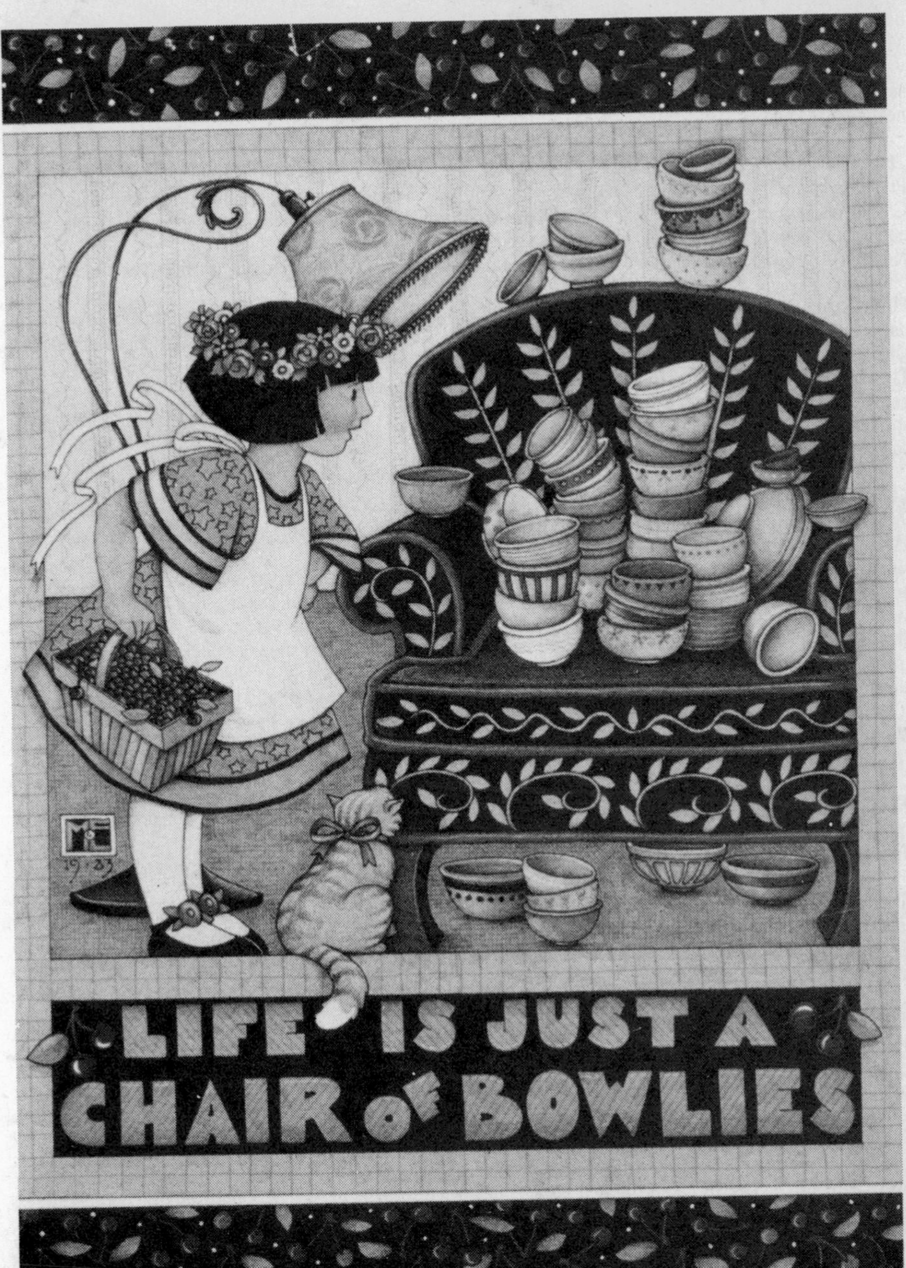

© Mary Engelbreit.

This design by Mary Engelbreit of St. Louis, Missouri, was originally used as a greeting card. Licensed by Creatif Licensing in New Rochelle, New York, to Sunrise Publications for a 5% net of profits, the design was subsequently used in book marks, figurines, limited edition prints, and ceramic picture frames. Engelbreit says the design (executed in markers, colored pencil and pen and ink) "is very popular and continues to sell well after seven years. This design has helped considerably with my name being recognized within the greeting card industry."

have a very distinctive style with complete understanding of printing specifications and mechanicals. More artists are asking for royalties and are trying to develop licensed characters. Most of the work is not worthy of a royalty and people don't understand what it takes to make a 'character' sell. Keep your presentation neat and don't send very large pieces of art. Keep the submission as varied as possible and neat. Good quality slides also will show the artwork in a better light."

THE CROCKETT COLLECTION, Rt. 7, Box 1428, Manchester Center VT 05255. (802)362-2913. President: James Alden. Publishes mostly traditional, some contemporary, humorous and whimsical Christmas and everyday greeting cards, postcards, note cards. Christmas themes geared to sophisticated, upper-income individuals. Free artist's guidelines.
Needs: Buys up to 100 designs/year from freelance artists. Produces products by silkscreen method exclusively.
First Contact & Terms: Send query letter. Request guidelines which are mailed out once a year in January, one year in advance of printing. Submit unpublished, original designs only. Art should be in finished form. Art not purchased returned by SASE. Buys all rights. Pays $75-125 per design.
Tips: "Designs must be suitable for silkscreen process. Airbrush and watercolor techniques are not amenable to this process. Bold, well-defined designs only. Our look is mostly traditional and realistic, so that is a must. Artists should find out what a company specializes in and submit only appropriate work."

CURRENT INC., 1005 E. Woodmen Rd., Colorado Springs CO 80901. Art Director: Pierre De Bernay. Produces greeting cards, giftwrap, calendars and stationery for working women and housewives—all ages.
Needs: Buys 200 designs and illustrations from freelancers/year. Experienced, professional artists only. Uses artists for calligraphy, paste-up and mechanicals. Prefers full color illustrations—no pen & ink. Produces material for all seasons and holidays; submit 2 months before.
First Contact & Terms: Send query letter with brochure showing art style or slides. Samples not filed are returned by SASE. Reports back within 2 weeks. Mail appropriate materials or call or write to schedule an appointment to show a portfolio, which should include original/final art, final reproduction/product and color. Originals sometimes returned to artist at job's completion. Pays average flat fee of $250/design and illustration.
Tips: "Send only small sampling of best art showing variety of styles and quality illustration."

DECORAL INC., 232 Route 109, Farmingdale NY 11735. In NY (516)752-0076; outside NY (800)645-9868. President: Walt Harris. Produces decorative, instant stained glass plus sports and wildlife decals.
Needs: Buys 50 designs from freelance artists/year; buys 50 illustrations from freelance artists/year. Uses artists for P-O-P displays. Prefers watercolors.
First Contact & Terms: Send query letter with brochure showing art style or resume and samples. Samples not filed are returned. Reports back within 30 days. To show a portfolio, mail appropriate materials or call or write to schedule an appointment; portfolio should include original/final art, final reproduction/product and photostats. Original artwork is not returned. Pays average flat fee. Buys all rights.

***DESIGNER GREETINGS, INC.**, Box X, Staten Island NY 10314. (718)981-7700. Art Director: Fern Gimbelman. Produces greeting cards, general cards, informal cards, inspirational cards, invitations, contemporary cards, juvenile cards, soft line cards and studio cards.
Needs: Works with 16 freelance artists/year. Buys 100-150 designs and illustrations from freelance artists/year. Works on assignment only. Also uses artists for calligraphy, P-O-P displays and airbrushing. Prefers pen & ink, airbrush. No specific size. Produces material for all seasons; submit 6 months before holiday.
First Contact & Terms: Send query letter with brochure or tear sheets, photostats or photocopies. Samples are filed. Samples not filed are returned only if requested. Reports back within 3-4 weeks. Call or write to schedule an appointment to show a portfolio, which should include original/final art, final reproduction/product, tear sheets and photostats. Original artwork is not returned after job's completion. Pays average flat fee. Buys all rights.
Tips: "We are willing to look at any work through the mail, (photocopies, etc.). Appointments are given after I personally speak with the artist (by phone).

***DHARMART DESIGNS**, 2425 Hillside Ave. Berkeley CA 94704. (415)548-5407. Director of Sales: Rima Tamar. Specializes in calendars and cards. Publishes 6 calendars.
Needs: Works on assignment only. Works with 2-4 freelance artists/year. Prefers local artists, but not necessary. Works on assigment only.
First Contact & Terms: Send query letter with brochure or small sampling. Samples are filed. Samples not filed are returned by SASE. Reports back within 3 weeks only if interested. Originals returned

to artist at job's completion. Call or write to schedule an appointment to show a portfolio, which should include photographs. Considers skill and experience of artist, project's budget and rights purchased when establishing payment.

DICKENS COMPANY, 59-47 Fresh Meadow Lane, Flushing NY 11365. (718)357-5700, (800)445-4632. Vice President: James Chou. Art Director: David Podwal. Produces greeting cards including musical greetings.
Buys: Buys 300 designs from freelance artists/year; also buys illustrations. Prefers watercolors mainly. Final art size 5¾x8. Produces material for everyday, Valentine's Day, Mother's Day, Father's Day and Christmas; submit 9 months in advance.
First Contact & Terms: Prefers local artists with experience in greeting card design. Send resume and photographs or slides to be kept on file. Prefers photographs or slides as samples. Samples not filed are returned only if requested. Reports within 1 month. Call or write for appointment to show portfolio. Originals are not returned to artist at job's completion unless agreed differently in advance. Pays average flat fee of $100-500/design; $20-300/illustration; or royalties. Negotiates rights purchased.
Tips: "We need experienced artist for greeting card artwork badly."

***DIEBOLD DESIGNS**, High Bridge Rd., Lyme NH 03768. Principals: Martha or Peter Diebold. Produces greeting cards. Specializes in general cards for business and invididuals with specific interests.
Needs: Buys some designs and illustrations from freelance artists/year. Prefers professional looking work. Works on assignment only. Also uses artists for calligraphy, paste-up and mechanicals. Uses any media. Prefers 5x7. Produces material for Christmas, primarily.
First Contact & Terms: Send query letter with brochure or samples that illustrate style with a SASE. Samples are not filed. Samples not filed are returned by SASE. Reports back within 1 month. Write to schedule an appointment to show portfolio. Original artwork is negotiable. Pays average flat fee of $100/design. Buys all rights.
Tips: "Let us see your work and be the judge of whether or not we can use your talents. Let us tell you what *we* need/want."

EARTH CARE PAPER CO., 325 Beech Lane, Harbor Springs MI 49740. (616)526-7003. Art Director: Carol Magee. Produces greeting cards, giftwrap, notecards and stationery. "All of our products are printed on recycled paper and are targeted toward nature enthusiasts and environmentalists."
Needs: Buys 25-40 illustrations from freelance artists/year. Considers all media. Produces Christmas cards; seasonal material should be submitted 10 months before the holiday.
First Contact & Terms: "For initial contact, artists should submit samples which we can keep on file." Reports back within 1 month. Original artwork is usually returned after publication. Pays 5% royalties plus a cash advance on royalties or a flat fee, $75 minimum. Buys reprint rights for cards.
Tips: "We primarily use a nature theme but will consider anything. The artwork should evoke an emotional response. We consider graphic or traditional designs. We would like to develop a humor line based on environmental and social issues, and a cute or whimsical animal line."

***EISNER ADVERTISING**, 2421 Traymore Rd., Unviersity Dr., University Heights OH 44118. (216)932-2669. President: Adele Eisner. Produces greeting cards, calendars and advertising. Publishes announcements, general cards, informal cards, invitations and judaica.
Needs: Works with 10 freelance artists/year. Buys 100 illustrations and other finished art logo from freelance artists/year. Prefers local artists. Also uses artists for calligraphy, P-O-P displays, paste-up and mechanicals. Prefers pen & ink. Produces material for mostly Jewish holidays and nonseasonal, informal, get well, thank you's, etc.; submit 4 months before holiday.
First Contact & Terms: Send query letter with brochure. Samples are filed. Samples not filed are not returned. Reports back only if interested. Call or write to schedule an appointment to show a portfolio, which should include thumbnails, roughs, original/final art and final reproduction/product. Original artwork is not returned to the artist after job's completion. Pays by the project, $15-350. Buys all rights.

THE EVERGREEN PRESS, INC., 3380 Vincent Rd., Pleasant Hill CA 94523. (415)933-9700. Art Director: Malcolm K. Nielsen. Publishes greeting cards, giftwrap, and stationery; high quality art reproductions, Christmas cards and Christmas postcards.
Needs: Buys 200 designs/year from freelance artists. Uses artists for product design (any design that can be used to produce greeting cards, giftwrap, stationery and other products sold through book, stationery, card and gift stores). Uses only full-color artwork in any media in unusual designs, sophisticated art and humor or series with a common theme. No super-sentimental Christmas themes, single greeting card designs with no relation to each other, or single color pen or pencil sketches. Roughs may be in any size to get an idea of work; final art must meet size specifications. Produces seasonal material for

Christmas, Easter and Valentine's Day; "we examine artwork at any time of the year to be published for the next following holiday."
First Contact & Terms: Send query letter with brochure showing art style or slides and actual work; write for art guidelines. Samples returned by SASE. Reports within 2 weeks. To show a portfolio, mail roughs and original/final art. Originals returned at job's completion. Negotiates rights purchased. "We usually make a cash down payment against royalties; royalty to be negotiated. Royalties depend upon the type of product that is submitted and the state of readiness for publication." Considers product use and reproduction expense when establishing payment. Pays on publication.

EXCLUSIVE HANDPRINTS INC., 96 NW 72nd St., Miami FL 33150. (305)751-0281. Vice President: Stanley Bercovitch. Wallpaper firm.
Needs: Buys 12 designs from freelance artists/year. Artists who are "well experienced in wallpaper and fabric designs" only. Uses artists for wallpaper and fabric patterns. If design is repeated, accepts 18" repeat pattern; will also consider nonrepeated designs.
First Contact & Terms: Call or write for appointment to show portfolio. No originals returned at job's completion. Pays flat fee/design. Buys all rights.

FRAVESSI-LAMONT INC., 11 Edison Place, Springfield NJ 07081. Art Director: Helen M. Monahan. Publishes greeting cards; general, cute and some humorous.
Needs: Buys "thousands" of designs and "few" illustrations/year from freelance artists. Uses artists for greeting card design and illustration. Especially needs seasonal and everyday designs; prefers color washes or oil paintings for illustrations. Pays $50 minimum.
First Contact & Terms: Send query letter and samples of work. Prefers roughs as samples. Produces seasonal material for Christmas, Mother's Day, Father's Day, Thanksgiving, Easter, Valentine's Day and St. Patrick's Day; submit art 10 months before holiday. SASE. Reports in 2-3 weeks. No originals returned to artist at job's completion. Provide samples to be kept on file for possible future assignments. To show a portfolio, mail roughs and color. Buys all rights. Negotiates payment; pays $75 minimum; on acceptance. Considers product use and reproduction expense when establishing payment. Free artist's guidelines.
Tips: "Just send a few samples of type of work to see if it fits in with our line."

FREEDOM GREETINGS, Box 715, Bristol PA 19007. (215)945-3300. Vice President: Jay Levitt. Produces greeting cards featuring flowers and scenery.
Needs: Buys 100 designs from freelance artists/year. Works on assignment only. Considers watercolors, acrylics, etc. Call for size specifications. Produces material for all seasons and holidays; submit 14 months in advance.
First Contact & Terms: Send query letter with resume and samples. Samples are returned by SASE. Reports within 10 days. To show a portfolio, mail roughs and original/final art. Originals returned to artist at job's completion. Pays for design by the project, $150-200. Buys all greeting and stationery rights.

THE C.R. GIBSON CO., 32 Knight St., Norwalk CT 06856. (203)847-4543. Director of Creative Services: Gary E. Carpenter. Publishes stationery, baby and wedding books, paper tableware and other gift products. SASE. Reports in 6 weeks. No finished art, paid for, is returned. Buys all rights.
Needs: Buys 200 designs/year. Uses artists for illustration and calligraphy. Assigns specific art needs for individual projects. Does not usually buy unsolicited finished art.
First Contact & Terms: Send query letter with samples to the attention of Creative Services Coordinator: Marilyn Schoenleber.

THE C.R. GIBSON CO., Creative Papers/Greeting Cards, 32 Knight St., Norwalk CT 06856. (203)847-4543. Product Manager: John C.W. Carroll. Produces greeting cards.
Needs: Buys 100-200 designs and illustrations from freelance artists/year. Considers most media except collage. Scale work to a minimum of 5x7. Prefers vertical image. Submit seasonal material 12 months before the holiday.
First Contact & Terms: Send query letter with brochure showing art style and or resume and tear sheets, Photostats, photocopies, slides, photographs and other sample materials. Prefers samples; do not send originals. Samples not filed are returned by SASE. Reports in 2 months. Call or write for appointment to show portfolio, which should include final reproduction/product, color, tear sheets, Photostats, photographs and transparencies along with representative originals. Write for art guidelines. Original artwork returned at job's completion. Pays by the project, $150 minimum. Negotiates rights purchased.
Tips: "If your images are appropriate for card use ("sendability"), then accompanying text should follow relatively easily; artists *can* write . . . it's a complete concept. Our orientation is toward fashion. Humor is important category, and our need for it is growing."

GRAND RAPIDS CALENDAR CO., 906 S. Division Ave., Grand Rapids MI 49507. (616)243-1732. Art Director: Rob Van Sledright. Publishes calendars; pharmacy, medical and family themes.
Needs: Buys approximately 15 designs/year. Uses artists for advertising art and line drawings.
First Contact & Terms: Send query letter and SASE for information sheet. Reports in 2 weeks. Previously published, photocopied and simultaneous submissions OK. Pays $10 minimum.

GRAND SLAM GREETINGS, INC., 35 York St., Brooklyn NY 11201. President: Kent Wood. Produces t-shirts, sweatshirts and children's wear.
Needs: Buys 30 designs/year from freelance artists. Local artists only. Also uses artists for paste-up and mechanicals. Considers pen & ink for illustrations.
First Contact & Terms: Send query letter with resume and photographs to be kept on file; "I'll make contact when interview time is available." Samples not filed are returned by SASE. Reports back only if interested. Pays by the hour, $10-15 average; by the project, $100-350 average. Negotiates rights purchased.
Tips: "Stop expecting me to pay a good hourly rate when you don't know your craft. Learn painting, learn about separations. Don't expect me to pay for your education."

GREAT LAKES CONCEPTS DESIGNED, Box 2107, Traverse City MI 49685. (616)941-1372. General Manager: Ardana J. Titus. Estab. 1983. Produces note cards. Seeks "creative, romantic and humorous designs with one or two subjects. We need colorful and imaginative designs for all-occasion notecard line." No landscapes. Sample cards $3.
Needs: Buys 12 designs from freelance artists/year. Considers primarily watercolor—bright, distinct colors and designs—no washes. Final art size 8x11; allow ¼" on all sides for trim. Prefers vertical designs but will consider horizontal.
First Contact & Terms: Prefers Michigan artists; will consider work from Great Lakes area. Send query letter with samples to be kept on file. Write for art guidelines with SASE. Prefers photographs or originals as samples. Samples not filed are returned by SASE. Reports back within 3 months. Original art returned after reproduction. Pays flat fee of $50 for design. Purchases first rights and/or reprint rights.
Tips: "When submitting material, send bright designs using imaginative approaches. An example is a white lily on a bright yellow background. We will consider a series. We're looking for designs of one or two children as subjects. Designs must be of easily recognizable subjects. Customers want designs of distinct subject work, landscapes don't seem to do well on stationery cards."

***GREAT NORTHERN PUBLISHING**, 116 W. Denny Way, Seattle WA 98119. (206)285-6838. President: Jeffrey Ross. Produces calendars.
Needs: Works with variable number of freelance artists/year. Buys designs and illustrations from freelance artists/year. Works on assignment only. Also uses artists for P-O-P displays and mechanicals. Prefers calendar format, 11¾x16½.
First Contact & Terms: Send query letter with brochure or photocopies and slides. Samples are not filed. Samples not filed are returned. Reports back within 1 month. Call or write to schedule an appointment to show a portfolio, which should include original/final art, slides, photographs, color and b&w. Original artwork is returned to artist after job's completion. Pays by the project, $800 minimum. Buys first rights, one-time rights, reprint rights, or all rights; negotiates rights purchased.
Tips: "We are always looking for fresh and artistic calendar ideas. We tend to produce calendars that are more trendy in appearance. Not the basic cats, dogs and landscapes, etc."

THE GREAT NORTHWESTERN GREETING SEED COMPANY, Box 776, Oregon City OR 97045. (503)631-3425. Art Director: Betty Barrett. Produces greeting cards. Uses pastel watercolor, black overlay; whimsical, botanical and natural themes.
Needs: Works on assignment with local artists only. Uses artists for calligraphy, P-O-P displays, paste-up and mechanicals. Prefers pen & ink and watercolor. Produces material for Christmas, Mother's Day, Father's Day and Valentine's Day.
First Contact & Terms: Send query letter with samples to be kept on file. Accepts slides, Photostats, photographs, photocopies and tear sheets as samples. Samples not filed are returned. Reports within several weeks. No originals returned to artist at job's completion. Buys all rights.

GREEN TIGER PRESS, 1061 India St., San Diego CA 92101. (619)238-1001. Art Director: Sandra Darling. Publishes greeting cards, giftwrap, calendars, posters, stationery and books; fantasy, nostalgia, The World of the Child themes.
Needs: Uses artists for cards, book and calendar illustration.
First Contact & Terms: Send color slides. Provide samples to be kept on file for possible future assignments. Samples not kept on file are returned by SASE. Reports in 2 months. Originals returned to artist

Close-up

Victoria Marshall

Greeting card illustrator
Kansas City, Missouri

Once a year, roughly one out of every 15 Americans sends a printed, mass-produced sentiment called a greeting card. "A greeting card must communicate a message," says greeting card artist Victoria Marshall, "and I feel that message should contain some love." Victoria, who designs cards for C.R. Gibson Greeting Cards, believes that the situation depicted on a card should convey a positive response for both the sender and the receiver. The card should visually symbolize a message that two people share, be it an inside joke or a deep emotion.

In order to express this message, Marshall relies on her artistic skills to capture the right emotion. Many of her cards depict animals which personify human qualities. "For a forgotten birthday, I'll have a rabbit looking at the world with an embarrassed look. Subtle things, like the position of the eyebrow or the look in a character's eye, captures the right expression."

Those expressions might work for her, but what about for the rest of us? She shows her cards to friends to test their reactions. "Some comments are very useful. I have changed some designs because of them."

Victoria's art career evolved from an interest in fashion and costume design. After graduate school at the University of Missouri, she worked on a Bible storybook for C.R. Gibson, a project that used not only her skills in drawing costumes but also in drawing simple, clean lines to capture dramatic Biblical characters. C.R. Gibson's artistic director J.W. Carroll was so impressed with her work that he asked her to illustrate a series of greeting cards. "It seems that everything works together to help you in whatever creative endeavor you're in," says Marshall.

Greeting card companies differ in their demands on freelance artists. Some expect the artist to provide both the artwork and the message, while others allow the artist to originate the idea and the artwork, then the company adds the copy. Marshall and Carroll work together on developing the concept and the artwork. Then she works out the details, referring to an extensive reference file for realistic touches to imaginary characters. Almost any style is permissible in greeting cards, but Victoria has found that a stylized figure with simple, clean lines conveys the direct message needed in a card.

Victoria is constantly rearranging her portfolio to accommodate the needs of a market she is pursuing. "What you submit depends upon the work you're going after. I generally rely on printed samples of work I have published." Along with individual cards, she includes a series of work and also examples from her storybook, since many companies produce not only cards but publications.

As a freelancer, Victoria has learned to be a businessperson. "You usually are paid a set fee, and no taxes are taken out. Remember, some of this money is not for keeps when you receive it. Regularly set aside money for quarterly tax payments."

The freedom of freelancing requires personal discipline. Artists are often caught in the "feast or famine" situation, where they are overwhelmed with work for a few months, then are faced with "dry" periods. Victoria sends out her portfolio during busy periods to help offset 'dry' periods.

Victoria's final advice applies to all aspects of freelancing: "You must balance your working life and your personal life. Keep excited. Keep up your energy. It's important to learn how to get away from your work. Refresh your mind and don't dwell on your work constantly. Come back to it fresh, then you'll have a whole new way of looking at it."

—*Susan Conner*

Artist: Victoria Marshall

Marshall uses subtleties in expressions and gestures to convey the emotions she wants to impart in greeting cards. She uses reference material as a base for drawing animals and then adds her own touches to express the appropriate message.

at job's completion. Negotiates rights purchased. Negotiates payment.
Tips: Artists should have a "good variety of samples; include human figures, especially children, if available. "(Does not use cartoon-style work.)"

GREETING SEEDS, Box 776, Oregon City OR 97045. (503)631-3425. Contact: Betty Barrett. Produces greeting cards.
Needs: Buys 24 illustrations from freelance artists/year. Local artists only. Works on assignment only. Uses artists for calligraphy, P-O-P displays, paste-up and mechanicals. Prefers watercolors. Prefers final size of art to be equal to 150% of product. Produces material for Christmas, Mothers Day and Fathers Day; submit 6 months in advance.
First Contact & Terms: Send query letter with resume and samples. Samples not filed are returned by SASE. Reports back ony if interested. Call or write to schedule an appointment to show a portfolio, which should include thumbnails, roughs, original/final art, final reproduction/product and color. Original artwork is not returned. Pays by the project. Buys all rights.
Tips: "Artist should be familiar with our products, botanical subjects, watercolor, whimsical designs and black line."

GREETWELL, D-23, M.I.D.C., Satpur, Nasik 422 007 India. Chief Executive: H.L. Sanghavi. Produces greeting cards, calendars and posters. Specializes in wildlife, flowers, landscapes; general purpose only.
Needs: Buys 50 designs from freelance artists/year.
First Contact & Terms: Send color photos and samples to be kept on file. Samples not filed are returned only if requested. Reports within 4 weeks. Original art returned after reproduction. Pays flat fee of $60/design. Buys reprint rights.
Tips: "Submit printed proof of past work so that we can send guidelines and a sample of our requirements."

***H & L ENTERPRISES, INC.**, 76 Dover Ave., Trenton NJ 08638. (609)882-3080. President: Jerry Wagner. Produces greeting cards and incense matches.
Needs: Buys 8 designs and illustrations/year from freelance artists. Also uses artists for mechanicals. Considers pen & ink and acrylics for illustrations.
First Contact & Terms: Works on assignment only. Call for appointment to show portfolio. Sometimes returns original work after reproduction. Pays by the project.

***HAND DRAWN GREETINGS, INC.**, Box 39055, Philadelphia PA 19136. (215)969-3391. Art Director: Ira Weinstein. Produces greeting cards (general and contemporary cards) for collegiates and working people 18-50.
Needs: Works with 2-4 freelance artists/year. Buys 24-36 designs from freelance artists/year. Prefers local artists (NY to Washington DC). Prefers pen & ink, b&w or watercolor. Prefers 5x7 vertical format. Produces material for Christmas, Hannukah and Valentines Day; submit 1 year before holiday.
First Contact & Terms: Send query letter with tear sheets, photocopies and SASE. Samples are filed. Samples not filed are returned by SASE. Reports back within 6 weeks. To show a portfolio, mail roughs, slides and tear sheets. Original artwork is returned to the artist after job's completion. Pays average flat fee of $50/illustration. "We will negotiate a royalty if there is special interest." Negotiates rights purchased.
Tips: "Remember that a greeting card is essentially a vehicle which one person uses to send a communication to another. Our cards are a humorous way to do that. For each card possiblity, ask yourself the questions: who could send this card? Who could receive it? Also, think in terms of a coherent line of cards that work together as well as separately. We publish 50% birthdays and 50% other occasions."

***HARTLAND CARDS**, Box 210, Woodstock VT 05091. (802)457-3905. General Manager: Jack Anderson. Produces greeting cards, announcements, invitations and humorous cards for ages 18 to 65.
Needs: Works on assignment only. Prefers pen & ink, watercolors and acrylics. Prefers 4⅞x7⅜, vertical format mostly; horizontal OK. Produces material for Christmas, Valentines, Easter, Mother's Day and Father's Day, Graduation, St. Patrick's Day; submit 1 year before holiday. Also produces all-occasion, everyday cards.
First Contact & Terms: Send query letter with photocopies or card roughs and SASE. Samples are not filed. Samples not filed are returned by SASE. Reports back only if interested. "We need an adjunct line or lines to market in concert with that of the company's major artist, Nadine Westcott. Primarily looking for humor, but will look at other themes. Would like to see at least 12-24 cards in a line to start with a commitment to building the line. Humor should be "cute," not "sappy" or "raunchy." Slightly risque is OK. Occasions and themes should address real life, contemporary situations. Colorful cartooned styles preferred." Original artwork is returned after job's completion. Pays royalties of 3-5%, with usual

Ruth Ann Epstein of Woodland Hills, California, learned of Intercontinental Greetings, Ltd. in the Artist's Market. She submitted several designs on speculation, some of which Robin Lipner, Intercontinental's art/creative marketing director, purchased for use in greeting cards. Lipner was impressed by Epstein's "good presentation and willingness to take direction." Epstein realized that licensing companies look for original and marketable ideas, and therefore presented a series of drawings showing highly-marketable animals in various poses.

advancement on royalties of $50-100 per design. All payments negotiated.
Tips: "Send cover letter and 12 cards at least roughed out, final art work is not necessary. Reports only if interested. Originals or slides will be treated carefully and returned with SASE."

***MARIAN HEATH GREETING CARDS, INC.**, 9 Kendrick Rd., Wareham MA 02175. (617)291-0766. Art Director: Susan Bint. Produces greeting cards, giftwrap, stationery and children's books. Produces announcements, general cards, informal cards, inspirational cards, invitations and juvenile cards.
Needs: Works with 12 freelance artists/year. Buys 100 designs from freelance artists/year. Prefers full color. Produces material for Christmas, Valentine, Easter, Thanksgiving; submit 1 year before holiday.
First Contact & Terms: Send query letter with brochure or Photostats, photocopies, slides and SASE. Samples are filed. Samples not filed are returned by SASE only if requested. Reports back within 3 weeks. Call or write to schedule an appointment to show a portfolio or mail thumbnails, roughs, original/final reproduction/product and slides. Original artwork is sometimes returned to artist after job's completion. Pays average flat fee of $150/design. Negotiates rights purchased.
Tips: "We look for tight rendering especially. Will consider roughs if accompanied by a finished piece of work, either original or reproduction; color important."

***HOS INTERNATIONAL INC.**, 5-2 Heiwajima Ohta-Ku, Tokyo Japan. 03-767-0651. President: Mr. A. Hanaoka. Produces greeting cards, giftwrap, calendars, posters and stationery.
Needs: Uses artists for illustration and calligraphy. Considers any kind of medium for illustration. Produces seasonal material for Christmas; submit art before April.
First Contact & Terms: Works on assignment only. Send query letter with samples to be kept on file. Write for appointment to show portfolio; write for art guidelines. Any type of samples are acceptable "if picture can be seen well." Samples not filed are returned only if requested. Reports back within weeks. Sometimes returns original art after reproduction. Negotiates payment. Buys all rights.

IDEA SOURCE, 77 Park Ave., New York NY 10016. (212)532-5831. President: Ted Tamarkin. Produces greeting cards, stationery, plastic glassware, ceramics, giftware and lighting.
Needs: Buys 100 designs from freelance artists/year; buys 120 illustrations from freelance artists/year. Prefers local artists only. Works on assignment only. Uses artists for P-O-P displays. Submit material 10 months to a year in advance.
First Contact & Terms: Send query letter with brochure showing art style, Photostats and photographs. Samples not filed are returned by SASE. Reports within 1 month. Call or write to schedule an appointment to show a portfolio, which should include thumbnails, roughs, original/final art and final reproduction/product. Original artwork is returned sometimes. Pays average flat fee; pays by the hour, $30-60 average; by the project, $50-200 average. Buys all rights.

INTERCONTINENTAL GREETINGS LTD., 176 Madison Ave., New York NY 10016. (212)683-5830. Creative Marketing Director: Robin Lipner. Sells reproduction rights on a per country per product basis. Licenses and syndicates to 4,500-5,000 publishers and manufacturers in 50 different countries. Industries include greeting cards, calendars, prints, posters, stationery, books, textiles, heat transfers, giftware, china, plastics, toys and allied industries, scholastic items and giftwrap.
Needs: Assigns 400-500 jobs and 1,500 designs and illustrations/year. "The trend is to more graphic—clean, modern work." Uses some humorous and cartoon-style illustrations. Prefers full-color original artwork, C-prints or transparencies.
First Contact & Terms: Send query letter and/or resume, tear sheets, slides and photographs. SASE. To show a portfolio, mail appropriate materials or call or write to schedule an appointment; portfolio should include original/final art, color, tear sheets, photographs and originals. Pays for design and illustration by the project $30-500+. Pays by the project, design and illustration. Pays royalties upon sale of reproduction rights on all selected designs. Contractual agreements made with artists and licensing representatives, will negotiate reasonable terms. Considers skill and experience of artist, product use, turnaround time and rights purchased when establishing payment. Provides worldwide promotion, portfolio samples (upon sale of art) and worldwide trade show display.
Tips: "More and more of our clients need work submitted in series form, so we have to ask artists for work in a series or possibly reject the odd single designs submitted. Make as neat and concise a presentation as possible with commerical application in mind."

***INTRAPRO/ATLANTA**, Box 7962, Atlanta GA 30357. Director: Mr. J. Bach. Produces greeting cards, calendars, posters and stationery with 1930's-'40s look.
Needs: Buys 6 designs and 12 illustrations/year from freelance artists. Also uses artists for calligraphy, P-O-P displays, paste-up and mechanicals. Considers all media. Produces products for all seasons.
First Contact: Works on assignment only. Send query letter with brochure, business card and samples to be kept on file. Accepts any type sample. Samples not filed are returned by SASE. Reports only if interested. Original artwork returned to the artist after reproduction.

JOLI GREETING CARD CO., 2520 W. Irving Park Rd., Chicago IL 60618. (312)588-3770. President: Joel Weil. Produces greeting cards and stationery.
Needs: Number of designs and illustrations bought/year varies. Artists must not have worked for Joli's immediate competition. Uses artists for P-O-P displays. Considers airbrush for product illustration. Prefers finished art of 4x9 for studio cards and 5x7 for 5x7 line. Publishes seasonal material for Christmas, St. Valentine's Day, Mother's Day, Father's Day.
First Contact & Terms: Send query letter with samples to be kept on file. Accepts "whatever is available" as samples. Samples not filed are returned by SASE. Reports within 1 month. Sometimes returns original art after reproduction. Pays flat fee; "open, depending on project." Buys all rights.
Tips: "We are looking for a 'today-look', primarily in the medium of airbrushing and cartooning."

KOGLE CARDS, INC., Box 3744, Englewood CO 80155. President: Patty Koller. Produces greeting cards.
Needs: Buys 50 designs from freelance artists/year; buys 50 illustrations from freelance artists/year. Works on assignment only. Considers all media for illustrations. Prefers 5x7 for final art. Produces material for Christmas and all major holidays, plus birthdays; material accepted all year round.
First Contact & Terms: Send resume and slides. Samples not filed are returned by SASE. Reports back within 2 weeks. To show a portfolio, mail original/final art, color, Photostats, photographs and b&w. Original artwork is not returned. Pays on royalty basis. Buys all rights.

LAFF MASTERS STUDIOS INC., 557 Oak St., Copiague NY 11726. (516)789-8361. Also: Robin Lane Art Studios (counter card division), same address and phone number. Creative Art Director: Sylvia Hacker. Publishes greeting cards: humorous, sophisticated, conventional and youth-oriented. "Robin Lane is concerned with all categories of everyday counter cards, from birth congratulations to formal sympathy cards. Its art standards are extremely high and its freelance work and inhouse requirements are handled by top professionals." In most cases, prefer artists who are nearby and can work with inhouse staff.
Needs: Buys 150-250 illustrations/year. Especially needs humorous and conventional art on assignment only. Artists must be well-versed in knowledge of latest greeting card printing and finishing techniques. Also requires artists who are skilled in juvenile style artwork for future juvenile lines.
First Contact & Terms: Submit published samples only. "Never send unsolicited unpublished material. All samples submitted must have SASE. We cannot return unsolicited samples which do not have SASE and correct postage." Reports within 1 week. No originals returned at job's completion. Pays $100 and up; on completion. Buys all rights.
Tips: "We assign work. We never buy unsolicited art. We require artists who are familiar with all phases of greeting card finishing and printing requirements. We see a trend toward more sophisticated and stylized art."

***LATIN AMERICAN ART By Furlong Companies**, 1799 Chatham Ave., Arden Hills MI 55112. Product Manager: Zulay Varges. Distributes paintings and posters, and produces greeting cards and paper products with Latin themes in English and/or Spanish language. Products convey the warmth and friendliness of Latin America in non-stereotypic way.
Needs: Buys "hundreds" of designs/year from freelance artists. Uses cartoons and humorous or cute drawings in Spanish.
First Contact & Terms: Send original or copies. Samples returned by SASE only. Pays flat fee/design. Royalties paid for exceptional work. Buys all rights.
Tips: "Hispanic culture has its own brand of humor that has universal appeal. Show that you understand it. Also, this year I am searching for one or more Latin American cartoon characters that create pathos and laughter. For example, a character could be called "Pepe." How does he view life in the United States?"

LEANIN' TREE PUBLISHING CO., Box 9500, Boulder CO 80301. (303)530-1441. Product Manager: Jane Knutson. Publishes greeting cards, calendars, posters and stationery. Product is directed mainly towards females between 20-45 years of age, both working and non-working.
Needs: Buys 100 designs/year from freelance artists. Prefers artists with previous publication experience and/or knowledge of reproduction and of the greeting card industry. Works on assignment only. Also uses freelance artists for calligraphy and greeting card illustration. Considers watercolors, acrylics, airbrush and torn paper. Prefers sizes proportionate to 5x7" with space for 1" bleeds. Seasonal material includes Christmas cards; submit material for the holiday any time of the year.
First Contact & Terms: Send query letter with brochure, resume, tear sheets, slides, photographs and originals. Samples not filed are returned. Call or write to schedule an appointment to show a portfolio, which should include original/final art; final reproduction/product, color, tear sheets and photographs. Original work sometimes returned after publication. Pays a flat fee, $150-200/illustration; payment is

Art director Ann Richardson of Leanin' Tree, a greeting card company in Boulder, Colorado, bought all rights to several pieces from artist Catherine Cleary for $150 each. "Catherine Cleary had worked with several greeting card companies. Her color choices, attention to details, and the human expression in her animals created a winning package."

also negotiable. Artists will receive 25 free samples of each illustration. Buys all rights.
Tips: "The majority of our product has a warm, friendly feel, as opposed to a slick, graphic feel. Be sure to take a look at our product."

LEAVERLY GREETINGS, (formerly Grandma Jenny Greeting Cards), 10502 Magnolia Blvd., N. Hollywood CA 91601. President: Benson Goldenberg. Produces greeting cards with cartoon theme.
Needs: Buys illustrations from freelance artists/year. Uses artists for calligraphy. Prefers pen & ink, watercolors, color pencils and acrylics. Prefers larger than 5x7 for final art. Produces material for Christmas, Hanukkah, Valentine's Day, Mother's and Father's Days—"all in addition to everyday cards"; submit 9 months in advance.
First Contact & Terms: Send query letter with resume, photostats and tear sheets to be kept on file. Samples not filed are not returned. Reports within 2 weeks. no originals returned to artist at job's completion. Pays average flat fee of $100-250/illustration. Buys all rights.

PAUL LEVY-DESIGNER, 2993 Lakewood Lane, Hollywood FL 33021. (305)981-9550. President: Paul Levy. Produces wallpaper and fabrics.
Needs: Buys 12-24 designs from freelance artists/year. Uses artists for original designs for wallcovering and fabric. Prefers gouache - watercolor designers colors for illustrations; side repeats divisible into 27" and down repeats 18" to 27".
First Contact & Terms: Send resume and original sketches. Call or write to schedule an appointment to show a portfolio, which should include original/final art, final reproduction/product and color. Pays for design by the hour, $8-10; "price depends on experience of artist."
Tips: "Designs in fabrics and wall covering will continue in a contemporary fashion with a modest blending of 'transitional' which is a combination of traditional and contemporary. It is most critical to be as original as possible. Designs of "me too" nature will not be acceptable in marketplace. Have eyes everywhere as design is universal. Search out the unusual and try to apply it to the medium and field you are designing for. Keep up with color trends as color is as important if not more so than design."

***LIFE GREETINGS**, Box 468, Meeting House Lane, Little Compton RI 02837. (401)635-8535. Art Director: Kathy Brennan. Produces greeting cards, specialized religious announcements and inspirational cards.
Needs: Works with 6 freelance artists/year. Buys 100 designs from freelance artists/year. Buys 100 illustrations from freelance artists/year. Prefers pen & ink, pencil, charcoal and some watercolor. Produces material for Christmas, Mother's Day, Father's Day, graduation, First Communion, Confirmation and all occasion; submit 6 months before holiday.
First Contact & Terms: Send query letter with brochure; "would like some representation of type of work." Samples are filed. Samples not filed are returned by SASE only if requested by artist. Reports back within 1 month. Pays average flat fee of $25/design. Buys all rights.

***LITTLE CONTESSA ENTERPRISES, INC.**, Box 81485, San Diego CA 92138. (619)297-2153. President: Tessa Carson. Greeting card manufactuer.
Needs: Works with 5 freelance artists/year. Prefers pastels, watercolors, mixed media and airbrush.

First Contact & Terms: Send query letter with brochure or Photostats, photographs and photocopies. Samples are filed. Samples not filed are returned by SASE only if requested. Reports back only if interested. To show a portfolio, mail thumbnails, roughs, original/final art, Photostats, tear sheets, transparencies (4x5) and color. Pays flat fee; $50-500; 5% royalties. Buys first or all rights.

MAINE LINE COMPANY, Box 418, Rockport ME 04856. (207)236-8536 or 1-800-624-6363. Contact: Liz Stanley or Marjorie MacClennen. Publishes greeting cards for contempory women from college age up, with primary concentration on women in their 30s, and also both men and women. Most of the cards are humorous and deal with women's contemporary concerns. Also publishes humorous postcards and notepads.
Needs: Buys 300-400 illustrations a year from freelance artists; most work is commissioned. "We're looking for illustrators with a sense of humor, whose style is contemporary, funky and colorful. You need not write your own copy to illustrate cards for us, but we're also looking for illustrators who write as well." Most often commissions a group or series of cards, rather than a single card. Also reviews artists or designers concepts for greeting card and postcard series.
First Contact & Terms: Send query letter with photocopies, Photostats, tearsheets, slides or photographs. SASE needed for return of samples. Sample card $1 each; creative guidelines for SASE with 60¢ postage. Turnaround time 4-6 weeks. To show a portfolio, mail appropriate materials, which should include final reproduction/product, color, tear sheets, photographs, b&w and slides. Pays advance against royalties for commissioned work.
Tips: "We are using more and more full-color art and have more need for illustrators and designers. Please send organized work, labeled, with SASE."

ALFRED MAINZER INC., 27-08 40th Ave., Long Island City NY 11101. (718)392-4200. Art Director: Arwed H. Baenisch. Publishes calendars, greeting cards and postcards; religious, traditional and ethnic European. Submit seasonal work 12 months in advance. Previously published work OK. SASE. Reports in 2 weeks. Originals returned to artist at job's completion. Purchases outright.
Needs: Buys 500-1,000 illustrations/year. Pays $25-250, color; on acceptance.
Tips: Does not accept unsolicited artwork sent by *registered* mail.

MARCEL SCHURMAN CO. INC., 954 60th St., Oakland CA 94608. (415)428-0200. Art Director: Sandra McMillan. Produces greeting cards, giftwrap and stationery. Specializes in "very fine art work with many different looks: traditional, humorous, graphic designs, photography, juvenile designs, etc."
Needs: Buys 800-1000 designs/year from freelance artists. Prefers final art sizes proportionate to 5x7", 4x6"; Produces seasonal material for Valentine's Day, Easter, Mother's Day, Father's Day, graduation, Halloween, Christmas, Hanukkah and Thanksgiving. Submit art by March for Valentine's Day and Easter, end of June for Mother's and Father's Day, graduation; November for Christmas, Halloween, Thanksgiving and Hanukkah. Interested in all-occasion cards also.
First Contact & Terms: Send query letter with slides, printed material or photographs. Reports within 1 month. Returns original art after reproduction. Buys all rights.
Tips: "Please send work; we are very open to see new designs."

MARK I INC., 1733 W. Irvine Park Rd., Chicago IL 60613. (312)281-1111. Creative Director: Alex H Cohen. Publishes greeting cards and stationery products for adult and juvenile markets.
Needs: Buys 200 designs from freelance artists/year. Will work on assignment. Uses artists for calligraphy. Prefers contemporary and traditional designs. Prefers total line concept of 18-36 pieces. Considers all media. Categories in humorous and sensitivity; everyday, Christmas, Valentine's Day Mother's Day.
First Contact & Terms: Send query letter to be kept on file. Write for art guidelines. Samples not filed are returned by SASE. Reports within 2 weeks. Originals returned to artist at job's completion. Write for appointment to show portfolio. Pays for design by the project, $100 + royalties. Pays for illustration by the project, $100/design-$250/design. Buys exclusive world-wide rights for greeting cards. Will pay usage fee against a royalty.
Tips: "We look for images that are neutral enough to be sold to an unlimited portion of this buying market."

MASTERPIECE STUDIOS, 5400 W. 35th St., Chicago IL 60650. (312)656-4000. Creative Director: Frank Stockmal. Publishes Christmas cards, stationery and notes. Free artist's guidelines. Buys all rights.
Needs: Interested in original material for lines of cards and stationery. "We are interested in reviewing any Christmas art on spec, regardless of experience." Submit seasonal work "any time."
First Contact & Terms: Send query letter with brochure showing art style or resume and samples. Prefers samples of unpublished Christmas cards and stationery. SASE. Reports in 3-4 weeks. Write to

schedule an appointment to show a portfolio, which should include original/final art and final reproduction/product. No originals returned to artist at job's completion. Pays for design by the project, $50-75; pays for illustration by the project, $150-350. Considers complexity of project and skill and experience of artist when establishing payment.
Tips: "Originate highly stylized, updated designs with plenty of emphasis on originality, color and design."

MICHEL'S DESIGNS, INC.,—DIVISION OF THE VIOLA GROUP, INC., 8 Engineers Lane, Farmingdale, Long Island NY 11735. (212)585-1577. Creative Coordinator: Arthur D. Viola. Produces period and high fashion (contemporary) hand-silk screen wallcoverings for interior designers/interior decorators; home-furnishings; showrooms; and major wallcovering distribution companies.
Needs: Buys 18-36 designs from freelance artists/year. Priority to local artists having contacts and a presence in the home furnishings and or Interior Decorator/Interior Designer markets. Ability to create artwork; produce color separations on acetate, thus creating camera-ready artwork. Uses artists for paste-up and mechanicals. Prefers watercolor or color pencils initially, and subsequently reproduction on acetates to produce the wallcovering design samples at our factory. Prefers 28" to 32" pattern repeat, initially on notepaper, and subsequently reproduced on acetate in color separations by creating freelance artists. Coloring of designs must be current and applicable to the season the line is launched—which is usually fall or spring.
First Contact & Terms: Contact only through artist's agent, who should send query letter with resume, tear sheets, Photostats, photocopies and photographs. Samples not filed are returned by SASE. Reports back within 4 weeks. To show a portfolio, mail appropriate materials or call or write to schedule an appointment. Portfolio should include thumbnails, original/final art, final reproduction/product, color, Photostats and photographs. No originals returned to artist at job's completion. Payment is reimbursement of reasonable expenses, a royalty arrangement which includes publicly trading common stock in our parent company; and if the line (you help create) goes, a permanent creative consulting position in the division created to house your line and others. Buys all rights.
Tips: "We are looking for a freelancer with sufficient business acumen and commitment to act as manager of a division of a small public company. This division of our parent company will be created around the line her artwork helps to create. A block of stock in the company may be available at the "insider" price to the right candidate should her creative ability produce a profitable line. She will gain through capital gains on the stock and through profit-sharing percentage on the line created."

***MIDWEST ART PUBLISHERS**, 1123 Washington Ave., St. Louis MO 63101. (314)241-1404. Contact: Sales Manager. Publishes calendars, combination of paper and vinyl products such as pad and pen sets, photo albums, pocket calendars and recipe books with mixed themes—cute children, animals, outdoor scenes, scenic for women.
Needs: Uses artists for product illustrations and catalog design, illustration and layout. Main product size approximately 3½x6½ (checkbook size) and 3¾x5¼.
First Contact & Terms: Send query letter with Photostats and original work showing artist's style. Unsolicited samples returned only if requested by SASE. Provide resume and samples to be kept on file for possible future assignments. Pays an average flat fee; also negotiates.

***MIMI ET CIE**, Box 32-B, Balboa Island CA 92662. Owner: Mimi Singleton. Produces giftwrap and stationery for high-end gift stores and boutiques.
Needs: Prefers artists who understand the way giftwrap is printed and can design for flexographic printing. Prefers flat color for flexographic prints. Prefers repeat 7½x10. Produces material for all seasons; submit 1 year before holiday.
First Contact & Terms: Send query letter with brochure or tear sheets. Samples are filed. Samples not filed are returned only if requested by artist. Reports back only if interested. Write only to schedule an appointment to show a portfolio, which should include tear sheets and color. Original artwork is not returned after job's completion; retained for copyright protection. Pays average flat fee of $150 minimum/design. Buys all rights.
Tips: "No cutsie or exceptionally seasonal designs wanted. Our company is known for its quality and good clean design and color both in traditional American and European-looking designs and exceptionally modern designs and materials."

MUSICAL IMAGE DESIGNS, 1212 Ardee Ave., Nashville TN 37216. Creative Director: Stacy Slocum. Estab. 1985. Produces greeting cards, stationery designs, logo designs and album covers for the music industry, and occasionally the non-music industry.
Needs: Uses artists to design logo designs for stationery letterheads, album covers for country music stars, and greeting cards with a musical motif.
First Contact & Terms: Send samples to be kept on file. Samples not kept on file will be returned

SASE. Prefers samples to be "production perfect." All samples that have been approved are put in a catalog. Those selected from the catalog are purchased. The designs stand a better chance of being selected if they are clean, sharp, creative, and in the appropriate place on the page. Logo letterheads should be placed on a 8½x11" page where it would appear on the finished stationery. Album covers should be sharp and clean and on cardstock the size of an album cover. Greeting cards are on a 10x7" card folded to a 5x7" card (7" high). Artwork will be purchased when it is selected and ready to go into print, but no artwork will be printed before it is purchased. We buy all rights." Pays by the project, $100 minimum.

***NATIONAL ANNOUNCEMENTS INC.**, 34-24 Collins Ave., Flushing NY 11753. (718)353-4002. Vice President: David Rosner. Produces wedding invitations (blank stock, ready for printing) for women ages 18 up.
Needs: Works with freelance artists/year. Prefers local artists with greeting card background.
First Contact & Terms: Send query letter with brochure. Samples are not filed. Samples not filed are returned only if requested by artist. Reports back only if interested. Call or write to schedule an appointment to show a portfolio, which should include final reproduction/product. Original artwork is not returned to the artist after job's completion. Pays by the project, $50-250. Buys all rights.
Tips: "Greeting card experience is necessary plus it's helpful to understand the graphic arts process."

OATMEAL STUDIOS, Box 138, Rochester VT 05767. (802)767-3171. Art Director: Helene Lehrer. Publishes greeting cards; creative ideas for everyday cards and holidays.
Needs: Buys 100-150 designs/illustrations per year from freelance artists. Uses artists for greeting card design and illustration. Considers all media; prefers 5x7, 6x8½, vertical composition. Produces seasonal material for Christmas, Mother's Day, Father's Day, Easter, Valentine's Day and Hanukkah. Submit art in August for Christmas and Hanukkah, in January for other holidays.
First Contact & Terms: Send query letter with slides, roughs, printed pieces, brochure/flyer to be kept on file; write for artists' guidelines. "If brochure/flyer is not available, we ask to keep one slide or printed piece." Samples returned by SASE. Reports in 2-4 weeks. Negotiates payment arrangement with artist.
Tips: "We're looking for exciting and creative illustrations and graphic design for greeting cards. Also, light humor with appeal to college age and up."

***OUTREACH PUBLICATIONS**, Box 1010, Siloam Springs AR 72761. (501)524-9381. Art Director: Darrell Hill. Produces greeting cards and stationery. Produces announcements, general cards, informal cards, inspirational cards, invitations, contemporary cards, soft line cards and studio cards.
Needs: Works with 12 freelance artists/year. Buys 100 designs from freelance artists/years. Prefers experienced greeting card artists. Works on assignment only. Also uses artists for calligraphy. Prefers designers gouache colors and watercolors. "Greeting card sizes range from 4½x6½ to 5½x8½, prefer same size, but not more than 200% size." Produces material for Valentine's, Easter, Mother's Day, Father's Day, Confirmation, Graduation, Thanksgiving, Christmas; submit 1 year before holiday.
First Contact & Terms: Send query letter with brochure or photocopies, slides and SASE. Samples are not filed. Samples not filed are returned by SASE. Reports back within 4-6 weeks. To show a portfolo, mail original/final art, final reproduction/product, slides, photographs and color. Original artwork is not returned after job's completion. Pays by the project, $50-200. Buys all greeting card rights.
Tips: "Outreach Publications produce Dayspring Greeting cards, a Christian card line. Suggest interested artists request our guidelines for freelance artists. Experienced greeting cards artists preferred."

PACIFIC PAPER GREETINGS, INC., (formerly Snap Dragon Floral Design), Box 2249, Sidney British Columbia V8L 3S8 Canada. (604)656-0504. President: Louise Rytter. Produces greeting cards and stationery.
Needs: "Prefers experience and artists that will develop a theme to their artwork thus creating a series for greeting cards." Uses artists for paste-up. Prefers illustrations for card reproductions only. Prefers greeting cards of stand-up size, 5x7. Produces material for Christmas, Mother' Day, Easter, Father's Day and Valentines Day; submit 1 year before holiday.
First Contact & Terms: Send query letter with brochure showing art style or resume, tear sheets, Photostats, photocopies, slides and photographs. Samples not filed returned by SASE. Reports within 1 month. To show a portfolio, mail appropriate materials. Negotiates payment and rights purchased.
Tips: "Remember we are looking for a theme artist to create a card line."

PAPEL, INC., Box 9879, North Hollywood CA 91609. (818)765-1100. Art Coordinator: Helen Scheffler. Produces souvenir and seasonal ceramic giftware items: mugs, photo frames, greeting plaques.
Needs: Buys 300 illustrations from freelance artists/year. Artists with minimum 3 years of experience in greeting cards only; "our product is ceramic but ceramic experience not necessary." Uses artists for product and P-O-P design, illustrations on product, calligraphy, paste-up and mechanicals. Produces

material for Christmas, Valentine's Day, Easter, St. Patrick's Day, Mother's and Father's Day; submit 1 year before holiday.
First Contact & Terms: Send query letter with brochure, resume, Photostats, photocopies, slides, photographs and tear sheets to be kept on file. Samples not kept on file are returned by SASE if requested. Reports within 2 weeks. No originals returned to artist at job's completion. To show a portfolio, mail appropriate materials, which should include final reproduction/product, color, tear sheets, Photostats, photographs and b&w. Pays by the project, $50-350. Buys all rights.
Tips: "I look for an artist who has realistic drawing skills but who can temper everything with a decorative feeling. I look for a 'warm' quality that I think will be appealing to the consumer. We still depend a tremendous amount on freelance talent. Send samples of as many different styles as you are capable of doing well. Versatility is a key to having lots of work."

PAPER ART COMPANY INC., 3500 N. Arlington Ave., Indianapolis IN 46218. (800)428-5017. Creative Director: Jo Anne Madry. Produces paper tableware products, invitations and party decor.
Needs: Buys 25% of line from freelance artists/year. Prefers flat watercolor, designer's gouache for designs. Prefers 5x5 design area for luncheon napkin designs; 4x4 for cocktail napkins; 9¼ for plate design. Produces general everyday patterns for birthday, weddings, casual entertaining, baby and bridal showers; St. Patrick's Day, Easter, Valentine's Day, Fall, Halloween, Thanksgiving, Christmas and New Year; submit 8-10 weeks in advance.
First Contact & Terms: Send query letter with brochure showing art style, photocopies and printed samples. Samples are not returned. Reports back within 2 weeks. Call to schedule an appointment to show a portfolio, which should include original/final art, final reproduction/product, color and designs. Original artwork is not returned if purchased. Pays by the project, $150-250.
Tips: "Color coordinating and the mixing and matching of patterns are prevalent. Need sophisticated designs. In paper products, the biggest change is in non-drinking type cocktail napkins. For us, we require professional, finished art that would apply to our product."

***PAPER PEDDLER, INC.**, 1201 Pennsylvania Ave., Richmond CA 94801. Art Director: Britta Kreps. Produces greeting cards, calendars, postcards and boxed notes. "Our greeting card line tends to be more conservative with a fine arts appeal. They are directed towards a more sophisticated market. Our postcards have a variety of subject matter. Humor, fine arts, black-and-white, and contemporary. The postcards are generally directed towards the younger, more style-conscious crowd."
Needs: Buys 15-20 designs and illustrations from freelance artists/year. Prefers 5x7 or proportional for greeting cards and 4⅛x5⅞ or proportional for postcards. Produces material for Christmas, Valentines, summer; submit 12 months before holiday.
First Contact & Terms: Send query letter with slides or originals. Samples are filed. "Please include SASE. Reports back within 4-6 weeks. To show a portfolio, mail original/final art, photographs or slides. Original artwork is returned after job's completion. Pays average of $50-150/design; $50-150/illustration; advance against royalties of 5%. Buys reprint rights.
Tips: "Paper Peddler, Inc. is largely an importer of greeting cards, postcards, calendars, and boxed notes. However, we also do our own publishing. Our greeting cards are directed towards a more conservative, sophisticated market. We generally don't go for the cartoony look but lean toward a fine arts style. Elegant watercolor, country, Americana, nostalgia and contemporary florals are some of our categories. On the other hand, our postcard line covers a variety of subject matter including humor, black-and-white or color photo, fine arts, Americana, and nature images, and the market tends to be the younger, more style-conscious crowd."

PECK INC., 3963 Vernal Pike, Box 1148, Bloomington IN 47402. Art Director: Jane Ackerman. Manufactures Christmas tags; Christmas, Halloween, Valentine and Easter cutouts; and educational bulletin board aids.
Needs: Uses artists for product design and illustrations. Specific needs include juvenile characters, animals, traditional Christmas, Halloween and/or all occasion design.
First Contact & Terms: Send a query letter with color samples or slides. SASE. Reports in approximately 2 months. Pays by the project; negotiates payment according to complexity of project and product use.
Tips: Especially looks for "full-color work and emphasis on clarity of color and design. It would be helpful if the artist has worked with a large format."

***PEGASUS, The Greeting Card Company Inc.**, 1611 Edith St., Berkeley CA 94703. (415)849-3535. President: Sheila Maccallum. Produces greeting cards, giftwrap, calendars and tri-fold cards with calligraphic greetings for sophisticated, literate, educated market ages 25 and up.
Needs: Works on assignment only. "Our finished tri-fold cards are 7x15, folded 7x5. Produces material for Christmas and Valentines; submit 9 months before holiday.

First Contact & Terms: Send query letter with brochure or tear sheets, photocopies and SASE. Samples are not filed. Samples not filed are returned by SASE only if requested. Reports back within 6 weeks. "We do not review portfolios." Original artwork is sometimes returned after job's completion. Pays royalties of 5%. Buys all rights.
Tips: "We would like artists to be familiar with our line before approaching us."

***PENNYROYAL PAPERS & PUBLICATIONS, INC.**, Suite E, 4000 E. 96th St., Indianapolis IN 46240. President: B. Brookie White. Produces greeting cards, giftwrap, stationery and cookbooks. Also publishes announcements, general cards, informal cards and invitations for "men and women who are looking for quality writing papers." Customers include American art and historical museums, restored villages, traditional and country shops.
Needs: Uses artists for concepts. Considers pen & ink, watercolors, acrylics, needlework, etc. "May be in the style and materials used by traditional and folk artists of 18th and 19th century." Size should not exceed 150% of final size. All occasion cards are standard announcement sizes: A-2, A-6, A-7. Produces material for Christmas; submit 1 year before holiday.
First Contact & Terms: Send query letter with resume, tear sheets and SASE. Samples are filed. Samples not filed are returned by SASE. Reports back within 30 days. To show a portfolio, mail original/final art, final reproduction/product and photographs. Pays minimum flat fee of $50/concept or royalties; fees are based on originality, quality of finished artwork. Buys all rights.
Tips: "Work should be suitable for two- to three-color registry or four-color process."

***PLUM GRAPHICS INC.**, Box 136, Prince Station, New York NY 10012. President: Yvette Cohen. Produces greeting cards for ages 18-45.
Needs: Needs illustrations from freelance artists. Prefers local artists, but not a requirement. Prefers tight watercolors, oil, airbrush. Illustrations must be colored in reproducible colors. Prefers 5x7 or larger to be reproduced in 5x7 format.
First Contact & Terms: Send query letter with brochure or tear sheets and photocopies. Samples are filed. Samples not filed are returned by SASE or not returned. Reports back within 2 months only if interested. After photocopies were considered and found acceptable, call or write to schedule an appointment to show a portfolio, which should include original/final art, final reproduction/product, tear sheets and color. Original artwork is sometimes returned after job's completion. Pays average flat fee of $150-300/illustration; by the project; or may provide negotiable flat fee for future reprints. Buys greeting card rights.

PLYMOUTH INC., 361 Benigno Blvd., Bellmawr NJ 08031. Art Director: Nancy Yarnall. Produces posters, stationery and paper products, such as 3x5 wire-bound memo books, wire-bound theme books, porfolios, scribble pads, book covers, pencil tablets, etc., all with decorative covers for school, middle grades and high school. "We use contemporary illustrations. Some of our work is licensed. We are expanding into the gift trade with various paper products aimed toward an older age group 19 and up."
Needs: Buys 300 designs and 300 illustrations from freelance artists/year. Works on assignment only. Uses artists for illustration, logo design, design, paste-up and mechanicals. Prefers full color.
First Contact & Terms: Send query letter with brochure showing art style or resume, tear sheets, Photostats, photocopies, slides and photographs. Samples returned by SASE. Reports only if interested. Mail appropriate materials or write to schedule an appointment to show a portfolio, which should include final reproduction/product, color and tear sheets. Pays according to project and based upon experience. Buys all rights or negotiates rights purchased.
Tips: "Plymouth is looking for professional illustrators and designers. The work must be top notch. It is the art that sells our products. We use many different styles of illustration and design and are open to new ideas."

***POPSHOTS, INC.**, 167 East Ave., Norwalk CT 06851. (203)838-5777. Art Director: Paul Zalon. Produces pop-up greeting cards for women ages 18 to 32, college-educated.
Needs: Works with 50 freelance artists/year. Buys 50 designs from freelance artists/year. Buys 50 illustrations from freelance artists/year. Works on assignment only. Prefers all media. Job specs given. Produces material for Valentine's Day, Christmas, birthday, get well; submit 1 year before holiday.
First Contact & Terms: Contact only through artist's agent or send query letter with brochure or Photostats and photocopies. Samples are filed. Samples not filed are returned by SASE. Reports back only if interested. To show a portfolio, mail tear sheets and Photostats. Original artwork is sometimes returned after job's completion. Pays average flat fee of $1,500-2,000 illustration. Negotiates rights purchased.

POTPOURRI PRESS, 6210 Swiggett Rd., Greensboro NC 27410; mailing address: Box 19566, Greensboro NC 27419. (919)852-8961. Director of New Product Development: Janet Pesther. Produces paper

tableware products, tins, plastics, stoneware and fabric items for giftshops, the gourmet shop trade, and department stores.
Needs: Buys 10-20 designs from freelance artists/year; buys 10-20 illustrations from freelance artists/year. Works on assignment only. Uses artists for calligraphy, mechanicals and art of all kinds for product reproduction. Prefers watercolor, acrylics and mechanical work. Produces everyday and seasonal products; submit material 1-2 years in advance.
First Contact & Terms: Send query letter with resume and tear sheets, Photostats, photocopies, slides and photographs. Samples not filed are returned by SASE. Reports back as soon as possible. Call or write to schedule an appointment to show a portfolio, which should include anything to show ability. "Artist must have good portfolio showing styles the artist is comfortable in." Original artwork not returned. Pays for illustration by the project $150-1,200. Buys all rights.
Tips: "Business is booming. Our art needs are increasing. We need artists who are flexible and willing to meet deadlines. Provide references that can tell us if you meet deadlines, are easy, medium or tough to work with, etc."

PREFERRED STOCK, INC., 2301 N.W. 334d Court #9, Pompano Beach FL 33069. President: Ann C. Cohen. Produces greeting cards, stationery, bags, pads, pencils and invitations using graphics and illustrations.
Needs: Buys 200 designs and 150 illustrations from freelance artists/year. Also uses artists for calligraphy and mechanicals. Works on assignment only. Considers watercolors, acrylics, etc. Prefers 5x7 size for final art. Produces material for everyday, Christmas, Valentine's Day, Mother's Day, Father's Day, Graduation, Chanukkah and Jewish New Year; submit 1 year in advance.
First Contact & Terms: Send query letter with brochure, resume, business card, slides, colored Photostats and printed pieces to be kept on file as samples. Samples not filed are returned by SASE. Reports only if interested. Originals sometimes returned to artist at job's completion. To show a portfolio, mail non-returnable roughs. Pays by the project, $100-200. Buys all rights for use on paper items.

PRELUDE DESIGNS, 1 Hayes St., Elmsford NY 10523. Art Director: Madalyn Grano. Produces paper tableware products and wallpaper/fabric.
Needs: Buys 10 designs and 1-5 illustrations from freelance artists/year. Local artists only. Works on assignment only. Uses artists for paste-up and color paint-ups. Prefers tempera, oil, watercolor and acrylic. Prefers 36x27 (or fractions thereof).
First Contact & Terms: Send query letter with resume. Samples not filed are returned. Reports within 7 days. To show a portfolio, which should include original/final art, final reproduction/product, color and photographs. Originals sometimes returned to artist at job's completion. Pays average flat fee of $200-500. Negotiates rights purchased.

THE PRINTERY HOUSE OF CONCEPTION ABBEY, Conception MO 64433. Art Director: Rev. Norbert Schappler. A publisher of religious greeting cards; religious Christmas and all occasion themes for people interested in religious yet contemporary expressions of faith. "Our card designs are meant to touch the heart and feature strong graphics, calligraphy and other appropriate styles."
Needs: Works with 25 freelance artists/year. Uses artists for product illustrations. Prefers silk-screen, oil, watercolor, line drawings; classical and contemporary calligraphy. Produces seasonal material for Christmas and Easter.
First Contact & Terms: Send query letter with brochure showing art style or resume, tear sheets, Photostats, photocopies, slides and photographs. Samples returned by SASE. Reports within 3 weeks. To show a portfolio, mail appropriate materials only after query has been answered. Portfolio should include final reproduction/product, color, tear sheets and photographs. "In general, we continue to work with artists year after year once we have begun to accept work from them." Pays by the project; $100-250. Usually purchases exclusive reproduction rights; for a specified format occasionally buys complete reproduction rights.
Tips: "Abstract or semi-abstract background designs seem to fit best with religious texts. Color washes and stylized flowers sometimes appropriated. Simple designs and fresh, clean calligraphy are looked for. Computerized graphics are beginning to have an impact in our field; multi-colored calligraphy is a new development. Remember our specific purpose of publishing greeting cards with a definite Christian/religious dimension but not piously religious. Wedded with religious dimension, it must be good quality artwork. We sell mostly via catalogs so artwork has to reduce well for catalog."

PRODUCT CENTRE-S.W. INC./THE TEXAS POSTCARD CO., Box 708, Plano TX 75074. (214)423-0411. Art Director: Susan Hudson. Produces greeting cards, calendars, posters, melamine trays, coasters and postcards. Themes range from nostalgia to art deco to pop/rock for contemporary buyers.
Needs: Buys 150 designs from freelance artists/year. Uses artists for P-O-P display, paste-up and mechanicals. Considers any media, "we do use a lot of acrylic/airbrush designs." Final art must not be

larger than 8x10. "Certain products require specific measurements; we will provide these when assigned. Produces Christmas material; submit 1 year in advance.
First Contact & Terms: Send resume, business card slides, Photostats, photographs, photocopies and tear sheets to be kept on file. Samples not filed are returned only by request with SASE including return insurance. Reports within 1 month. No originals returned to artist at job's completion. Call or write for appointment to show portfolio. Pays average flat fee of $100/design maximum. Buys all rights.
Tips: "Artist should be able to submit camera-ready work and understand printer's requirements. The majority of our designs are assigned."

RAINBOW ARTS, 488 Main St., Fitchburg MA 01420. (617)345-4476. Art Director: Ian Michaels. Produces greeting cards, specializing in everyday, all occasion and Valentine's Day cards.
Needs: Buys 75-100 designs/illustrations from freelance artists/year. Uses artists for product design and illustration on product. Considers wide variety of media for illustrations; "we've used just about every medium—watercolor, acrylics, colored line work, markers, airbrush, gouache, silkscreen, batik, etc. We *do not* use still lifes, nature studies or abstract art. Prefers artwork "larger than our 5⅛x6½ format, but in direct proportion; otherwise you have a card with disproportionate borders or have to crop part of the artwork." Produces seasonal material for Valentine's Day, Mother's Day, Father's Day, Easter and Christmas, but "each work should be able to relate to other occasions, such as, blanks (cards with no verse), birthday, anniversary, etc." Submit seasonal material 6-12 months before holiday. "We also design and manufacture stickers."
First Contact & Terms: Send query letter with brochure showing art style or tear sheets, photocopies, slides and photographs; possibly to be kept on file. "We can't be responsible for original art unless otherwise stated." Samples not kept on file are returned by SASE *provided* by the artist. Usually reports within 1 month, but does vary during the year. Originals returned to artist at job's completion. To show a portfolio, mail appropriate materials, which should include final reproduction/product, color, tear sheets and slides; "we prefer to view slides." Pays royalties of 8% and advances ranging from $100-150. Buys reprint rights for greeting cards and we do licensing. Pays for design by the project 5-8%..
Tips: "With new freelance artists we look more for new looks. The market surge is in cartoon-style illustration, in both the cute category and the risque market. Send us your samples with a *self-addressed stamped envelope*. Request it and we'll send you *The Artist's Guide to the Freelance Market* by Ian Michaels with our response. Include a self-addressed stamped post card with your work. Write on it: "Date received," so you can keep track of your work without the worry. An artist should first have this work okayed as being relevant to what a card company is currently producing before taking the time to tailor this work to that company's size and schedule. I look for the art and the message to be more commercially viable and or better in substance than work currently produced for us by our regular freelancers."

RAINBOWORLD CARDS, 319 A St., Boston MA 02210. (617)350-0260. Assistant Sales Manager: Sandra Hubbard. Publishes die cut, stamped and embossed greeting cards, stationery and invitations. General themes.
Needs: Buys 20 designs and 50 illustrations/year from freelance artists. Works on assignment only. Uses artists for advertising illustration. Considers any color media sized 10x14 or larger. Produces seasonal material for Christmas, Spring (Easter, Mother's Day, Father's Day, Graduation) and Valentine's Day; submit art 6-12 months before holiday.
First Contact & Terms: Send resume and samples. No originals or slides. "If work is suitable, we will arrange to review portfolio and other work." Reports as soon as possible. Originals returned to artist at job's completion. Buys first rights and reprint rights. Negotiates payment, $250 and up/project; on publication. Considers complexity of project, skill and experience of artist, product use and rights purchased when establishing payment.
Tips: "For initial contact, artists should submit copies of their work which we can *keep* on file—even photocopies. This allows us to keep a 'review' file to use as projects develop and allows us to quickly discover which artists are suitable for our market with a minimum of inconvenience to both parties. Do not send resumes without samples and do not bother to write asking for further information on firm. Send samples. This is a visual medium, not verbal."

The asterisk before a listing indicates that the listing is new in this edition. New markets are often the most receptive to freelance submissions.

How to Work with Greeting Card Companies

If you've never worked with greeting card companies before but would like to try, here is some inside information on the steps a greeting card passes through from conception to publication from Bob Van Steinberg. A landscape artist from Ilion, New York, who was looking for commercial markets for his fine art, he submitted samples of his landscapes to many companies and was accepted by Prudent Publishing. These are some of his experiences:

"First, the company carefully reviews the best-selling card designs from the previous year in a concept review. They try to objectively determine what qualities made certain cards bestsellers. For example, they ask, 'Is there a trend toward city scenes as opposed to country scenes? Did the embossed cards outsell the four-color printed cards?'

The next approach is to review any artwork currently in their files to find anything they might use for next year's sales based on what type of card sold well the previous year. The marketing department then determines how many new cards will most likely be added to the line for the next selling season.

The company lists the subjects and the types of cards that will be developed. The company may decide to work on two city scenes, one to be printed four-color, the other to be embossed with foil accents. After the company determines its line, the art director contacts the artists who are best suited to render the needed style. After accepting the assignment, the artist will render actual-size pencil and/or watercolor roughs. The art director reviews these and returns them with comments for additions or suggests a completely new idea.

From this point on, anything can happen. For example, with the 'Covered Bridge' design, no changes or revisions were done. Final production was authorized at once.

With the 'Starry Night' design, the art director requested a complete repainting of the design using different color tones for most areas and redoing the painting to the correct proportion of the card for the Gallery Collection line.

On two other cards, the art director initiated the subject, colors, perspective, proportion and style. I did three or four versions, in addition to many sketches with extensive changes and revisions before final approval. In some cases, the company doesn't know exactly what they want until they see it.

The design then goes under the scrutiny of the color separator. Even at this stage, little changes are done and some areas are reworked. Color revisions are often left up to the color separator to solve in order to enhance a color that is perhaps weak or maybe needs a little strengthening.

After the color separations are completed (this usually involves three, four, or more film negatives, one for each color), the design is printed. It is not unusual for three or more press changes to take place, since color mixing and register must be accurate.

For an artist, this is an all-year endeavor. The companies I render for require work nine to twelve months ahead of production time. I also spend a great deal of time looking for information and reference material for possible card designs."

It's unusual when there are no revisions in a greeting card design, but the art director of Prudent Publishing decided Van Steinburg's "Covered Bridge" fit his needs perfectly without changes. The artist says final production was authorized upon acceptance. Van Steinburg says that he is basically a realist landscape artist. "I find both the fine art approach and that of the commercial aspect very compatible today."

The artist's "Starry Night" design is a different story. Van Steinburg had to repaint the scene after the art director decided to use different color tones and different proportions for the company's Gallery Collection line. The final painting features a red barn and a pale blue-violet sky, which imparts an appropriately restful feeling to the scene.

RECYCLED PAPER PRODUCTS INC., 3636 N. Broadway, Chicago IL 60613. Art Director: Melinda Gordon. Publishes greeting cards, calendars, and buttons; unique subjects. Artist's guidelines available.
Needs: Buys 1,000-2,500 designs and illustrations/year from freelance artists. Uses artists for product design and illustrations. Considers b&w line and color—"no real restrictions." Prefers 5x7 vertical format for cards, 10-14 maximum. "Our primary concern is card design." Produces seasonal material for Christmas, Hanukkah, Mother's Day, Father's Day, Thanksgiving, Easter, Valentine's Day, St. Patrick's Day and Halloween. Submit seasonal material 18 months in advance; everyday cards are reviewed in April and September.
First Contact & Terms: Send query letter with roughs and printed pieces or actual work. Samples returned by SASE. Reports in 2 months. Original work usually not returned at job's completion, but "negotiable." Buys all rights. Pays average flat fee of $75-150/design or illustration; also negotiates payment "if we have major interest"; on acceptance.
Tips: "Study our product before submitting work. Remember that a greeting card is primarily a message sent from one person to another. The art must catch the customer's attention, and the words must deliver what the front promises. We are looking for unique points of view and manners of expression. Our artists must be able to do concepts, art and messages. The must be able to work with a minimum of direction, and meet deadlines."

RED FARM STUDIO, 334 Pleasant St., Box 347, Pawtucket RI 02862. (401)728-9300. Creative Director: Mary M. Hood. Produces greeting cards, giftwrap, coloring books, paper dolls, story coloring books, paper party ware, playing cards, Christmas cards, gift enclosures, notes, invitations, postcards and paintables. Specializing in nautical and country themes and fine watercolors. Art guidelines available upon request if SASE is provided.
Needs: Buys approximately 200 designs and illustrations/year from freelance artists. Considers watercolor artwork. Prefers final art of 6¾x8⁷⁄₁₆ (³⁄₁₆ bleed) for Christmas cards; 4¾x6¾ (⅛ bleed) for everyday cards; and 6³⁄₁₆x8¹³⁄₁₆ (³⁄₁₆ bleed) for notes. Submit Christmas artwork 1 year in advance.
First Contact & Terms: Send query letter with slides, photographs, photocopies or original art. Call for appointment to show portfolio. Samples not filed are returned by SASE. Reports within 2 weeks. Original artwork not returned after reproduction. "Pays for illustration by the project, $150 minimum. Buys all rights.
Tips: "We are interested in realistic, fine art watercolors of traditional subjects like country and nautical scenes, flowers, birds, shells and baby animals. We do not reproduce photography."

C.A. REED, INC., 99 Chestnut St., Box 3128, Williamsport PA 17701-0128. Art Director: Carol Cillo. Publishes paper tableware products; birthday, everyday, seasonal and holiday.
Needs: Buys 100-150 designs/year. Uses artists for product design and illustration. Interested in material for paper tableware, i.e. plates, napkins, cups, etc. Some invitations.
First Contact & Terms: Query with samples or photocopies. SASE. Reports in 6-8 weeks. Photocopied and simultaneous submissions OK. "Buys all rights within our field of publication." Pays for design by the project,$100-200 minimum. Pays for illustration by the project, $150 minimum. "Requests for artist's guidelines only granted with SASE and review of samples."
Tips: Artist should visit stationery shops, party stores and discount store party goods sections. There is a greater expansion of the party goods field. We need more variation within traditional subject parameters. There is trend towards more sophistication in design.".

***REED PRODUCTIONS**, 1102 Chruch St., San Francisco CA 94114. (415)282-8752. Partner/Art Director: Susie Reed. Produces postcards, stationery, notebooks, address books, etc.
Needs: Works with few freelance artists/year. Buys various number of design and illustrations from freelance artists/year. Prefers local artists with experience. Works on assignment only. Also uses artists for paste-up and mechanicals. Prefers color or b&w illustrations.
First Contact & Terms: Send query letter with brochure or resume, tear sheets, Photostats, photocopies or slides and SASE. Samples are filed. Samples not filed are returned by SASE. Reports back only if interested. Call or write to schedule an appointment to show a portfolio, which should include original/final art, final reproduction/product, slides, tear sheets, Photostats or photographs, color and b&w. Original artwork is returned after job's completion. Pays royalties of 5-10%. Negotiates rights purchased.
Tips: "We primarily sell products with images of celebrities, current and old, on them."

REGENCY & CENTURY GREETINGS, 1500 W. Monroe St., Chicago IL 60607. (312)666-8686. Art Director: David Cuthbertson. Publishes Christmas cards; traditional and some religious Christmas.
Needs: Buys 200 illustrations and designs/year.
First Contact & Terms: Send query letter with samples. Submit seasonal art 8 months in advance. Reports in 6 weeks. Previously published work OK. Buys *exclusively Christmas* card reproduction rights.

Originals returned to artist at job's completion. Pays $90 minimum, b&w; $125, color; $90-150, design. Pays on acceptance.
Tips: Artist should visit stationery shops for ideas, and request artist's guidelines to become familiar with the products. "Traditional still sells best in more expensive lines."

RENAISSANCE GREETING CARDS, Box 127, Springvale ME 04083. Art Director: Janet Ledoux. Publishes greeting cards; "current approaches" to all occasion cards, seasonal cards, Christmas cards and nostalgic Christmas themes.
Needs: Buys 200 illustrations/year from freelance artists. Full-color illustrations only. Prefers art proportional to 8½x11 and 5x7. Produces everyday occasions—birthday, Get Well, friendship and seasonal material for Christmas, Valentine's Day, Mother's Day, Father's Day, Easter, graduation, St. Patrick's Day, Halloween, Thanksgiving, Passover, Jewish New Year and Hanukkah; submit art 18 months in advance for Christmas material; approximately 1 year for other holidays.
First Contact & Terms: Send query letter with printed pieces, tear sheets and/or slides; write for artists' guidelines. Samples returned by SASE. Reports in 3 months. To show a portfolio, mail appropriate materials, which should include original/final art, color tear sheets and slides or transparencies. Originals returned to artist at job's completion. Pays for design by the project,$200-500. Pays for illustration by the project, $125-500, plus royalties.
Tips: "Start by sending a small (10-12) sampling of 'best' work, preferably printed samples or slides of your best work (with SASE for return). This allows a preview for possible fit, saving time and expense."

REPRODUCTA CO. INC., 11 E. 26th St., New York NY 10010. Art Director: Thomas B. Schulhof. Publishes stationery, postcards and greeting cards; religious and general.
Needs: Buys 750 designs/year. Works with all occasions—religious plus floral, wildlife and "cutes."
First Contact & Terms: Mail art. SASE. Seasonal: Christmas, Mother's Day, Easter and Father's Day themes. No originals returned to artist at job's completion. Request artist's guidelines. Buys all rights. Pays $50-200; payment negotiated.

RIVERSIDE PAPER COMPANY, Box 179, Appleton WI 54912-0179. (414)733-6651. Marketing Manager: Patrick Georgia. Produces fine printing papers.
Needs: Buys 10 designs for freelance artists/year; buys 4-5 illustrations from freelance artists/year. Works on assignment only. Prefers brochures, top sheets, etc.

ROCKSHOTS, INC., 8th Floor, 632 Broadway, New York NY 10012-2416. (212)420-1400. Art Director: Ron Petro. Publishes greeting cards, calendars, posters and stationery; humorous, erotic and satirical themes for "anyone who loves well-designed, outrageous, humorous, sexy cards."
Needs: Buys 150 designs and 150 illustrations/year from freelance artists. Uses artists for card, calendar and catalog illustration layout and catalog design. No airbrush, prefer cartoon—bright, full-color artwork. Produces seasonal material for birthday, Christmas, Mother's Day, Father's Day, Easter, Valentine's Day and Halloween; submit art 10 months before holiday.
First Contact & Terms: Send resume and actual work. Prefers slides and examples of artist's style of original work as samples. Samples returned by SASE. Reports within 2 weeks. Originals returned to artist at job's completion. Provide tear sheets to be kept on file for possible future assignments. Call for appointment, submit portfolio for review. Buys all rights. Negotiates payment; on acceptance.

ROUSANA CARDS, 28 Sager Pl., Hillside NJ 07205. Art Director: Dorothy Chmielewski. Produces seasonal (all) and everyday greeting cards.
Needs: Established greeting card designers only.
First Contact & Terms: "Submit printed samples of your style, no original art. Write to schedule an appointment to show a portfolio, which should include final reproduction/product and color. Pays for illustration by the project, $150 minimum; varies with complexity of project.
Tips: We see a leaning towards smart, sophisticated designing."

THE ROYAL STATIONERY, INC., 1650 Tower Blvd., North Mankato MN 56001. National Sales: Linda Stevens. Produces stationery, greeting cards, novelty items, postcards, note cards, mugs, key chains and soaps; floral, scenic, animal, children and novelty. Interested in material for lines of products.
Needs: Buys 50 designs/year. Uses artists for product design, and b&w and color illustrations.
First Contact & Terms: Submit 4-5 illustrations. Prefers unpublished samples. SASE. Reports within 1 month. No originals returned at job's completion. Buys all rights. Terms negotiable.

***RUBY STREET, INC.**, 16 E. 23rd St., New York NY 10010. (212)529-0400. Art Director: Peter Nevraumont. Produces calendars and trade paperbacks.
Needs: Works on assignment only. Also uses artists for calligraphy, paste-up and mechanicals.

Produces material for Christmas; submit 2 months before holiday.
First Contact & Terms: Send query letter with brochure or tear sheets. Photostats and slides. Samples are not filed. Samples not filed are returned by SASE. Reports back within 1 month only if interested. To show a portfolio, mail slides, tear sheets, Photostats and photographs. Original artwork is returned after job's completion. Pays royalties. Negotiates rights purchased.
Tips: "Develop general audience calendar concepts."

SACKBUT PRESS, 2513 E. Webster Place, Milwaukee WI 53211. Contact: Angela Peckenpaugh. Publishes poem postcards and notecards.
Needs: "A few line drawings for very specific themes."
First Contact and Terms: Send query letter with Photostats. Samples returned. Reports in 1 month. Send Photostats. Buys one-time rights. Pays for illustration by the project, $10; on publication.
Tips: "I went from publishing a literary magazine to publishing poem postcards and notecards. I have little time or money to market my product. I sell at fairs. Produce sporadic direct mail ads and classifieds. Usually my prices only appeal to beginners or hobbyists."

ST. CLAIR-PAKWELL PAPER PRODUCTS, Box 800, Wilsonville OR 97070. (503)638-9833. Art Director: Anna Mack. Publishes gift boxes, giftwrap and various packaging.
Needs: Buys 100 designs/year. Uses artists for product design and illustration. "For use in department stores as courtesy wrap or used for pre-wrapped box coverings."
First Contact & Terms: Send query letter with resume and tear sheets, Photostats, photocopies, slides, photographs and "anything available." Prefers 15" repeat and even divisions thereof for giftwrap. SASE. Reports in 2 weeks. Call or write to schedule an appointment to show a portfolio, which should include original/final art and final reproduction/product. No originals returned to artist at job's completion. Pays for design by the hour, $4.50 minimum; pays for illustration by the project, $50-500. Buys all rights.
Tips: "We're seeing more and more use of freelance artists. Work should be geared toward the resale market—not the fine arts."

STONEWAY LTD., Box 548, Southeastern PA 19399. (215)272-4400. Art Director: RoseAnne Flynn. Publishes coloring books and brochures, children cartoon themes for 2-8 year-olds.
Needs: Buys 10 designs and 125 illustrations/year from freelance artists. Needs artists experienced in children's illustration line. Uses artists for product design and illustrations plus advertising and catalog design, illustration and layout. Prefers b&w line drawings and color washes; 17x22 and 8½x11,for coloring books. Children's craft books 9x12; frame tray puzzles 17x22; and 11x17, 8½x11, 17x22 for brochures. Also produces seasonal material.
First Contact & Terms: Send query letter with roughs and resume to be kept on file. Samples not kept on file are returned by SASE. Reports in 3 weeks. No originals returned to artist at job's completion. Write for appointment. Buys all rights. Payment varies per type of job or project. Pays on acceptance *only*.

***STORY CARDS**, Box 11575, Washington DC 20008-0075. (202)462-3263. Editor: Bill Adler. Estab. 1986. Produces greeting cards. "The card format is a vehicle—like a book, journal or magazine—for circulating short stories. Only in form do Story Cards bear any resemblance to greeting cards. We believe that fiction shouldn't be limited to these traditional media. Inside each Story Card is an original short story about a particular occasion—such as birthdays, anniversaries, Valentine's Day, or April Fool's day. On the front of each Story Card is an original illustration based on that story, plus the holiday greeting. Story Cards is aimed toward an educated audience—people who may have once enjoyed reading short fiction, but haven't for a while."
Needs: Works with 20-40 freelance artists/year. Buys 20-40 illustrations from freelance artists/year. Works on assignment only. Prefers pen & ink, line art. "The cards 5x7 and artwork can range from that to 12x15.
First Contact & Terms: Send query letter with resume, tear sheets, Photostats, photocopies and SASE. Samples are filed. Reports back within 3 months. Write to schedule an appointment to show a

> ***"The greeting card field is expanding to a more alternative, contemporary market. We follow the home furnishing and fashion trends."***
>
> ***—Laurel Milton, Carlton Cards***
> ***Dallas, Texas***

"A sense of fun and curiosity" is what publisher Bill Adler of Story Cards, Inc., in Washington D.C., wanted artist John Heinly to convey in this card. "When first looking at the illustration, people wonder why anyone would draw a bear at a dining room table," says Adler. Heinly, of Burke, Virginia, selected the most expressive image from the story "without giving too much away." He was paid $200 for limited rights, meaning the illustration could not be reproduced on another greeting card.

portfolio, which should include tear sheets, Photostats and photocopies. Original artwork is sometimes returned after job's completion. Pays average flat fee of $100-600/illustration; average $200, plus 25 copies. Buys limited rights; artist retains rights to publish in other markets except greeting cards.
Tips: "We're a literary magazine in disguise. We match artwork to the story. Often the illustrations freelancers send are too amatuerish or not detailed enough. Illustrators who aren't familiar with the kind of art Story Cards uses frequently don't send what we need."

***STRINGS ATTACHED**, Box 132, Mill Valley CA 94942-0132. (415)459-5300. Administrative Executive: Zai Zatoon. Produces greeting cards, especially general cards.
Needs: Works with 5-10 freelance artists/year. Buys approximately 50 illustrations from freelance artists/year. Prefers cartoonists. Works on assignment only. Also uses freelance artists for paste-up. Prefers pen & ink. Prefers 2x2½ cartoons. Produces material for everyday, Christmas, Valentines, Mother's Day, Father's Day, Graduation; submit 1 year before holiday.
First Contact & Terms: Send query letter with brochure or photocopies and SASE. Samples are filed. Samples not filed are returned by SASE only if requested. Reports back only if interested. To show a portfolio, mail thumbnails. Original artwork is not returned after job's completion. Pays average flat fee of $5-10/illustration (2x2½ frame); by the hour, $4.75-10 average. Buys all rights.

STUART HALL CO., INC., Box 419381, Kansas City MO 64141. Director of Advertising and Art: Judy Riedel. Produces stationery, school supplies and office supplies.
Needs: Buys 40 designs and illustrations from freelance artists/year. Artist must be experienced—no beginners. Works on assignment only. Uses artists for design, illustration, calligraphy, paste-up and mechanicals. Considers pencil sketches, rough color, layouts, tight comps or finished art; watercolor, gouache, or acrylic paints are preferred for finished art. Avoid fluorescent colors. "All art should be prepared on heavy white paper and lightly attached to illustration board. Allow at least one inch all around the design for notations and crop marks. Avoid bleeding the design. In designing sheet stock, keep the design small enough to allow for letter writing space. If designing for an envelope, first consult us to avoid technical problems."
First Contact & Terms: Send query letter with resume, tear sheets, Photostats, slides and photographs. Samples not filed returned by SASE. Reports only if interested. To show a portfolio, mail roughs, original/final art, final reproduction/product, color, tear sheets, Photostats and photographs. No originals returned to artist at job completion. 'Stuart Hall may choose to negotiate on price but generally accepts the artist's price." Buys all rights.

SUNRISE PUBLICATIONS INC., Box 2699, Bloomington IN 47402. (812)336-9900. Manager of Creative Services: Lorraine Merriman Farrell. Publishes greeting cards and other paper products. Art guidelines available.
Needs: Generally works on assignment but picks up existing pieces from unsolicited submissions. Purchases 300-350 designs and illustrations/year. Considers any medium. Full-color illustrations scaled to 5x7 vertical, but these can vary. "We are interested in full range of styles for everyday and seasonal use, from highly illustrated to simple and/or humorous." Produces seasonal material for Christmas, Valentine's Day, St. Patrick's Day, Easter, Mother's Day, Father's Day, graduation, Halloween and Thanksgiving.
First Contact & Terms: Send query letter with slides as samples. "Indicate whether or not samples may be kept on file." Reports in 3 weeks. Samples returned only by SASE. Originals returned to artist at job's completion. Offers an advance against royalty program.
Tips: "First, study our cards in your local card shops or send for our catalogs to get an idea of our look. To best fulfill the consumers' needs, we have begun to purchase rights to a much broader scope of contemporary subject matter and application."

***TECH STYLES**, Box 1877, Winter Haven FL 33880. President: Dean Bagley. Estab. 1986. Produces greeting cards, calendars, posters, stationery, postcards and notepads. Types of greeting cards include announcements, general, informal, contemporary, juvenile and studio cards and invitations for "computer people and those not into computers, but buy gifts for a computer person."
Needs: Prefers cartoonists, graphic designers and illustrators. "Will look at anything." Prefers line art. Produces material for Christmas; submit 6 months before holiday.
First Contact & Terms: Send query letter with tear sheets, ideas on paper and SASE. Samples are filed. Samples not filed are returned. Reports back within 6-8 weeks. To show a portfolio, mail roughs, tear sheets and dummies. Original artwork is sometimes returned after publication. Pays average flat fee of $200/design, $300/illustration; by the project, $100-300; royalties of 5% (negotiable). Buys all rights.
Tips: "Currently we print just black-and-white. We need cartoons, poster designs and calendar ideas. We will make assignments to the right artist. We would like to find someone to draw "Dick and Jane"-style of the old textbooks. All must be about computers."

***TEXAN HOUSE, INC.**, 40214 Industrial Park Circle, Georgetown TX 78626. (512)863-9460. President: Joan K. Davis. Produces greeting cards, giftwrap, stationery and paper tableware products. Publishes general cards and invitations.
Needs: Works with 7 freelance artists/year. Works on assignment only. Also uses artists for calligraphy. Produces material for Christmas; submit 8 months before holiday.

First Contact & Terms: Send query letter with brochure or Photostats and photocopies. Samples are returned. Reports back within 2-4 weeks. Call or write to schedule an appointment to show a portfolio, which should include thumbnails, original/final art and photographs. Original artwork is not returned after job's completion. Pays flat fee. Buys all rights.

***ARTHUR THOMPSON & COMPANY**, 1260 S. 16th St., Omaha NE 68108. (402)342-2162. General Manager: Jim Ogden. Publishes greeting cards and letterheads; holiday and special occasion designs.
Needs: Uses 6 freelance artists/year for product illustrations. Prefers oils, acrylic paintings or mixed media; fall and winter scenes, Christmas and Thanksgiving background designs, birthday and special occasion designs.
First Contact & Terms: Write and send samples if possible. Prefers transparencies, slides of original art or original art as samples. Samples returned. Reports in 6 weeks. Provide sample and tear sheets to be kept on file for possible future assignments. Pays flat fee or negotiates payment. Considers product use and rights purchased when establishing payment.

***TO COIN A PHRASE**, 104 Forrest Ave., Narberth PA 19072. (215)664-3130. Owner: Gerri Rothman. Produces stationery, general cards, informal cards, invitations, contemporary cards and juvenile cards for ages 30 upwards in age and affluent.
Needs: Uses freelance artists for calligraphy.
First Contact & Terms: Send query letter with photocopies or call. Samples not filed are returned only if requested. Reports back only if interested. Call or write to schedule an appointment to show a portfolio. Pays for calligraphy, $10 per hour or by the piece.

***TWINROCKER HANDMADE PAPER INC.**, Box 246, Brookston IN 47923. (317)563-3119. Contact: Kathryn Clark. Produces stationery and fine artist papers for fine artists, graphic artists, calligraphers, book binders, nonsilver photographers and letterpress printers.
Needs: Buys 5 designs from freelance artists/year. Prefers local artists. Works on assignment only. Also uses artists for calligraphy and mechanicals. Prefers pen & ink.
First Contact & Terms: Buys reprint or all rights.
Tips: "Our need for advertising art work is growing. We need graphic designers who are also excellent calligraphers." Looks for "a classic, traditional style."

VAGABOND CREATIONS INC., 2560 Lance Dr., Dayton OH 45409. (513)298-1124. Art Director: George F. Stanley, Jr. Publishes stationery and greeting cards with contemporary humor. 99% of artwork used in the line is provided by staff artists working with the company.
Needs: Uses 120 designs/year. Uses own artists for product design and illustration; line drawings, washes and color-separations; material should fit in standard size envelope.
First Contact & Terms: Query. SASE. Reports in 2 weeks. Submit (everyday, graduation, Christmas, Mother's Day, Father's Day and Valentine's Day) material at any time. Originals only returned upon request. Pays $10-25.
Tips: Visit stationery shops and request artist's and writer's guidelines for writing and illustrating for cute-humorous copy. Does *not* encourage artwork to be submitted by freelance contributors because of own group of five staff artists.

WILD CARD©, Box 3960, Berkeley CA 94703-0960. Art Director: Leal Charonnat. Publishes greeting cards and stationery; current, avant-garde themes for 20-40 year-olds—"young, upwardly mobile urbanites." Send $2.50 for sample cards and submittal pak. Many designs die-cut. Specializes in animals (graphic), cats, zoo, dinosaurs, etc.
Needs: Imaginative die-cut designs that fit the basic greeting card market themes (birthday, Christmas, Valentine's, friendship, etc.); must be very graphic as opposed to illustrated. Specializes in die-cut, 3-D cards."
First Contact & Terms: Please "submit after receiving our guidelines. Cannot review submittals that have not received our guidelines." Send submittal pak, and brochure/flyer or resume to be kept on file. All materials 8½x11 only. Prefers brochure of work with nonreturnable pen & ink Photostats or photocopies as samples; do not send original work. "If your project is accepted, we will contact you. But we cannot always promise to contact everyone who submits." Pays for design by the project or royalties, $75-250; flat fee of $75-250/illustration. Also pays royalties for card line ideas. Considers complexity of project, product use and reproduction expense when establishing payment. "We will have all publishing rights for any work published. Artist may retain ownership of copyright." Pays on publication.
Tips: "Present only commercially potential examples of your work. Prefer to see only die-cut ideas. *Do not* present work that is not of a professional nature or what one would expect to see published. Know what is already in the market and have a feeling for the subjects the market is interested in. Go out and look at *many* card stores before submitting. Ask the owner or buyer to 'review' your work prior to submitting."

CAROL WILSON FINE ARTS, INC., Box 17394, Portland OR 97217. (503)283-2338 or 281-0780. Contact: Gary Spector. Produces greeting cards, postcards, posters and stationery that range from contemporary to nostalgic. "At the present time we are actively looking for unusual humor to expand our contemporary humor line. We want cards that will make people laugh out loud! Another category we also wish to expand is fine arts."

Needs: Uses artists for product design and illustration. Considers all media. Produces seasonal material for Christmas, Valentine's Day and Mother's Day; submit art preferably 1 year in advance.

First Contact & Terms: Send query letter with resume, business card, tear sheets, Photostats, photocopies, slides and photographs to be kept on file. No original artwork on initial inquiry. Write for an appointment to show portfolio or for artists' guidelines. "All approaches are considered but, if possible, we prefer to see ideas that are applicable to specific occasions, such as birthday, anniversary, wedding, new baby, etc. We look for artists with creativity and ability." Samples not filed are returned by SASE. Reports within 2 months. Negotiates return of original art after reproduction. Payment ranges from flat fee to royalties. Buys all rights.

Tips: "We have noticed an increased emphasis on humorous cards for specific occasions, specifically, feminist and 'off-the-wall' humor. We are also seeing an increased interest in fine arts cards."

***WORLD GREETINGS, INC.**, Suite 49, 77 Ives St., Providence RI 02906. (401)351-3520. President: Barry Beckham. Produces greeting cards and posters. Publishes general cards and contemporary cards for a black audience.

Needs: Works with 3-4 freelance artists/year. Buys 36 designs from freelance artists/year. Buys 36 illustrations from freelance artists/year. Also uses artists for paste-up and mechancials. Prefers photographs; 3-color art of all media. Submit seasonal material 6 months before holiday.

First Contact & Terms: Send query letter with brochure or photocopies, slides and SASE. Samples are filed. Samples not filed are returned by SASE. Call or write to schedule an appointment to show a portfolio, which should include roughs and photographs. Original artwork is returned after job's completion. Pays average flat fee of $100/design; royalties of 5-10%. Negotiates rights purchased.

Tips: "We need upbeat, high-quality art only."

***ZINGERS**, Suite 1639, 500 E. 77th St., New York NY 10162. (212)861-9209. Contact: Helen Alberts. Produces greeting cards, especially contemporary cards with angry or humorous themes for all ages to 55, all sexes, every education.

Needs: Prefers artists with a great sense of humor and imagination. Prefers pen & ink or magic marker. Prefers 5x7 (but can be smaller). Produces material for Valentines, Mother/Father Days, Easter, Christmas, Hanakkah, Passover, New Years' Day, political organizations; submit 6-9 months before holiday or election dates.

First Contact & Terms: Send query letter with brochure or tear sheets, Photostats and photocopies. Samples are filed. Reports back within 10 days. Call or write to schedule an appointment to show a portfolio, which should include roughs, dummies, color and b&w. Original artwork sometimes returned after job's completion. Pays the going rate.

Tips: "Zingers embrace the theory that greeting cards can be used to express emotional disappointment and political anger. They are cynical, but have a sense of humor. The graphics would have to be tailored to the words. My needs have changed from using words only on my cards to cards that are more graphic but tailored to the words."

"I get photocopies of rough sketches in portfolios, and it is difficult to tell by looking at these sketches whether or not they are capable of doing a finished drawing. Since the only thing I have to go by when I receive a design or illustration is what artists send me, samples need to be the very best work they are capable of doing."

—Charion Slocum, Musical Image Designs
Nashville, Tennessee

Magazines

This section offers one of the best and most consistent markets for freelance art. The magazines listed in this section are planning to buy 16,853 illustrations and 12,443 cartoons this year. Not only do magazines have art needs that must be filled consistently, but most magazine art directors work entirely by mail. If you can follow directions and meet deadlines, plus produce quality work, you can submit your samples to the more than 700 magazines listed in this section.

Understanding a magazine's category is important in gearing your work to the appropriate market. There are four basic categories. The consumer magazine is geared towards the general public. Artwork, like the editorial content, is used to both inform and entertain the reader. The second and largest category of magazines consists of trade or business publications. These are directed towards a certain profession, trade or industrial group. To the busy professional who reads these magazines, "less is more," and graphic images are designed therein to communicate messages quickly. The third category is inhouse publications (or company publications) produced by companies for their employees or stockholders. Outside the company, this type of magazine becomes an extension of the annual report. Finally, there are literary magazines that combine fiction, poetry, essays and artwork to make an alternative statement apart from the mainstream of thought. Literary magazines are known for their quality artwork, much of which has a lithographic feel to it.

After deciding the type of magazine most suited to your interests, focus the subject matter of your artwork in that area. Read at least four to six issues of each publication you plan to submit to, reviewing its topics, themes and styles of artwork. Keep in mind that the more general the magazine's audience, the keener the art competition. As a newcomer, start with the less-circulated and more focused publications to increase your chance for sales.

Illustrators often specialize in a certain area, such as science fiction or medicine. Art directors look for artists with a certain style or treatment when they assign work, and specialists have a better chance of developing unique approaches to often esoteric subjects. Illustrations are used for covers, editorial content and also for spot art. Spot illustrations are usually a column wide and are needed on demand, meaning they are more likely to be bought from your samples. Send nonreturnable Photostats or photocopies for black-and-white work and photos or slides to represent color.

"Cartoons have returned," says Greg Paul of Brady & Paul Communications, a design consultant firm specializing in magazines. "They provide a buffer to the grimness of angst-ridden expressionism in so many illustrations." Cartoons are used not just as filler but as unique parts of the editorial content. Art directors prefer to receive original work and will often buy cartoons unsolicited. Send twelve to sixteen finished or rough cartoons, each cartoon labeled on the back with your name, address and phone number, plus a cartoon reference number. When an art director selects one or more cartoons, he notifies you and refers to the cartoon by the number or caption.

Comic books have changed dramatically over the last decade. Read the Close-up of Mary Wilshire to find how the comic book industry is open to new creative expression.

Check the mastheads of magazines to note any changes in the staff, particularly the art director. Consult the following directories for further names and addresses, but no marketing information: the *Standard Periodical Directory*, the *Internal Publications Directory*, the *Gebbie Press All-in-One Directory of Publications*, *Magazine Market Place*, and *Ulrich's International Periodical Directory*. If you are a cartoonist seeking to learn or refine your craft, write the Joe Kubert School of Cartoon Art (37 Myrtle Ave., Dover NJ 07801) for a catalog of its courses.

***ABORIGINAL SF**, Box 2449, Woburn MA 01888-0849. Editor: Charles C. Ryan. Estab. 1986. Science fiction tabloid for adult science fiction readers. Bimonthly. Circ. 13-15,000. Sample copy $3; art guidelines for SASE with 1 first-class stamp.
Cartoons: Buys 2-8 cartoons from freelancers. Prefers science fiction, science and space themes. Prefers single panel or double panel with or without gagline; b&w line drawings, b&w washes and color washes. Send finished cartoons. Samples are filed. Samples not filed are returned by SASE. Reports back within 2 months. Buys first rights and nonexclusive reprint rights. Pays $15, b&w; $15, color.
Illustrations: Buys 8-16 illustrations/issue from freelancers. Works on assignment only. Prefers science fiction, science and space themes. "Generally, we prefer art with a realistic edge, but surrealistic art will be considered." Send query letter with photocopies and slides. Samples not kept on file are returned by SASE. Reports back within 2 months. To show a portfolio, mail photocopied samples and/or color slides. Buys first rights and nonexclusive reprint rights. Pays $250, color, cover; $200, color, inside; on publication.

ACCENT ON LIVING, Box 700, Bloomington IL 61702. Editor: Betty Garee. Emphasis on success and ideas for better living for the physically handicapped. Quarterly. Original artwork returned after publication, if requested. Sample copy $2.
Cartoons: Buys approximately 12 cartoons/issue from freelancers. Receives 5 submissions/week from freelancers. Interested in people with disabilities in different situations. Send finished cartoons. SASE. Reports in 2 weeks. Buys first-time rights (unless specified). Pays $20 b&w; on acceptance.
Illustrations: Uses 3-5 illustrations/issue. Interested in illustrations that "depict articles/topics we run." Works on assignment only. Provide samples of style to be kept on file for future assignments. Samples not kept on file are returned by SASE. Reports in 2 weeks. To show a portfolio, mail color and b&w. Buys all rights on a work-for-hire basis. Pays $250-300, color, cover; on acceptance.
Tips: "Send a sample and be sure to include various styles of artwork that you can do."

ACROSS THE BOARD, 845 Third Ave., New York NY 10022. (212)759-0900. Art Director: Josef Kozlakowski. Emphasizes business-related topics for Chief Executive Officers in the business field and industry. Monthly. Returns original artwork after publication. Sample copy for SASE.
Illustrations: Buys 4-6 illustrations/issue from freelancers. Works on assignment only. Send brochure and samples to be kept on file. Prefers tear sheets or photocopies as samples. Samples not filed are returned by SASE. Reports back only if interested. Call for appointment to show portfolio. Buys first rights. Pays $400 for color cover; $200 for b&w inside; on publication.

ACTION, 901 College Ave., Winona Lake IN 46590. (219)267-7656. Contact: Vera Bethel. For ages 9-11. Circ. 25,000. Weekly. SASE. Reports in 1 month.
Cartoons: Buys 1/issue on school, pets and family. Pays $10, b&w; on publication. Send finished artwork.
Illustrations: Uses color illustrations on assignment. Send samples or slides. Pays $75 for full-color drawings (no overlays); on acceptance.

ADIRONDAC, 174 Glen St., Glens Falls NY 12801. Editor: Neal Burdick. Emphasizes the Adirondack Mountains and conservation for members of the Adirondack Mountain Club, conservationists and outdoor-oriented people in general. Published 10 times/year. Circ. 9,000. Accepts previously published material and simultaneous submissions. Original artwork returned after publications. Sample copy $1.75; art guidelines for SASE.
Cartoons: Interested in environmental concerns, conservation, outdoor activities as themes. Prefers single panel with gagline; b&w line drawings. Send query letter to be kept on file. Reports within 4 weeks. Negotiates rights purchased. No payment.
Illustrations: Prefers maps, specific illustrations for articles. Send query letter to be kept on file. Reports within 4 weeks. No payment.

AFTA-THE ALTERNATIVE MAGAZINE, Second Floor, 147 Crater Ave., Wharton NJ 07885. (201)828-5467. Editor: Bill-Dale Marcinko. Emphasizes rock music, films, TV and books for young (18-35) male readers who are regular consumers of books, records, films and magazines; and socially and politically aware. 60% are gay; 50% are college educated or attending college. Quarterly. Circ. 25,000. Receives 10 cartoons and 30 illustrations/week from freelance artists. Previously published material and simultaneous submissions OK. Original work returned after publication. Sample copy $3.50. Especially needs political satire; rock and film illustrations, surreal, erotic work.
Cartoons: Uses 50 cartoons/issue; buys all from freelancers. Interested in satires on social attitudes, current political events, films, TV, books, rock music world, sexuality; single and multiple-panel with gagline, b&w line drawings. No color work accepted. Send query letter with samples of style. Samples returned. Buys one-time rights. Pays in contributor copies; on publication.

Illustrations: Uses 75 illustrations/issue; buys all from freelancers. Interested in illustrations from films, rock music stars, books and TV programs. No color work accepted. Send query letter with samples of style to be kept on file. Samples not kept on file are returned. Reports in 1 week. Buys one-time rights. Pays in contributor copies; on publication.
Tips: "Read a sample copy of *AFTA* before submitting work."

Adam Niklewicz, who emigrated four years ago from Poland to Moberly, Missouri, submitted this piece on speculation to* Amelia Magazine. *Editor Frederick A. Raborg, Jr., not only bought one-time rights for $15 but was so impressed with the work that Niklewicz has become a regular contributor. "Niklewicz's illustrations are like what out-of-the-body experiences must be," says Raborg. "He is easy to work with and understands the print problems inherent in various media."

AIM, Box 20554, Chicago IL 60620. (312)874-6184. Editor-in-Chief: Ruth Apilado. Managing Editor: Dr. Myron Apilado. Art Director: Bill Jackson. Readers are those "wanting to eliminate bigotry and desiring a world without inequalities in education, housing, etc." Quarterly. Circ. 16,000. Sample copy $3; artist's guidelines for SASE. Reports in 3 weeks. Previously published, photocopied and simultaneous submissions OK. Receives 12 cartoons and 4 illustrations/week from freelance artists.
Cartoons: Uses 1-2 cartoons/issue; all from freelancers. Interested in education, environment, family life, humor through youth, politics and retirement; single panel with gagline. Especially needs "cartoons about the stupidity of bigotry." Mail finished art. SASE. Reports in 3 weeks. Buys all rights on a work-for-hire basis. Pays $5-15, b&w line drawings; on publication.
Illustrations: Uses 4-5 illustrations/issue; half from freelancers. Interested in current events, education, environment, humor through youth, politics and retirement. Provide brochure to be kept on file for future assignments. No samples returned. Reports in 4 weeks. Prefers b&w for cover and inside art. Buys all rights on a work-for-hire basis. Pays $25 for b&w illustrations, cover; on publication.
Tips: "Because of the possibility of nuclear war, people are seeking out ways for survival. They are feeling more alienated from society and are more conscious of the importance of getting together. Their submissions reflect their concern. For the most part, artists submit material omitting black characters. We would be able to use more illustrations and cartoons with people from all ethnic and racial backgrounds in them. We also use material of general interest."

ALFRED HITCHCOCK MYSTERY MAGAZINE, Davis Publications, 380 Lexington Ave., New York NY 10017. (212)557-9100. Art Director: Jerry Hawkins. Art Editor: Ron Kuliner. Emphasizes mystery fiction.
Needs: Line drawings, minimum payment: $100.
First Contact & Terms: Call for interview. Reports in 1 week. Pays on acceptance. Buys first rights.

***THE ALTADENA REVIEW**, Box 212, Altadena CA 91001. Editor: Ralph Rubino. Literary magazine emphasizing poetry. "We publish poetry, reviews of books of poetry, occasional interviews with poets." Published 1-2 times/year. Circ. 250-300. Original artwork returned after publication if requested. Sample copy $2.50.
Illustrations: Buys 4-12 illustrations/year from freelancers. Send query letter with camera-ready b&w artwork; prefer 4x5 or smaller. Samples are not filed. Samples not filed are returned by SASE. Reports back within 5 weeks by SASE. To show a portfolio, mail original/final art, final reproduction/product or b&w. "These should be things we could actually publish, not samples." Buys first rights. Pays 2 copies on publication.
Tips: "Look through a copy of the magazine to see what we do and how the artwork fits in, but remember, we like variety from issue to issue."

***AMAZING HEROES**,4359 Cornell Rd., Agoura CA 91301. (818)706-7606. Art Director: Dale Crain. Magazine emphasizing news and features on popular comic books. Circ. 15,000. Original artwork is returned to the artist after publication. Sample copy $3.50.
Illustrations: Prefers b&w spot illustrations and gags dealing with comics. Send query letter with samples. Buys one-time North American rights. Pays $2.50 +, b&w; inside; on publication.

AMELIA, 329 "E" St., Bakersfield CA 93304. (805)323-4064. Editor: Frederick A. Raborg, Jr. Magazine; also publishes 2 supplements—*Cicada* (haiku) and *SPSM&H* (sonnets) and illustrated postcards. Emphasizes fiction and poetry for the general review. "Our readers are drawn from a cross-section of reading tastes and educational levels, though the majority tend to be college-educated." Quarterly. Circ. 1,250. Accepts some previously published material from illustrators. Original artwork returned after publication if requested with SASE. Sample copy $5.95; art guidelines for SASE.
Cartoons: Buys 3-5 cartoons/issue from freelancers for *Amelia*. Prefers sophisticated or witty themes (see Cynthia Darrow's or Jessica Finney's work). Prefers single panel with or without gagline (will consider multi panel on related themes); b&w line drawings, b&w washes. Send query letter with finished cartoons to be kept on file. Material not filed is returned by SASE. Reports within 1 week. Buys first rights or one-time rights; prefers first rights. Pays $5-25, b&w; on acceptance.
Ilustrations: Buys 80-100 illustrations and spots annually from freelancers for *Amelia;* 24-30 spots for *Cicada*; 15-20 spots for *SPSM&H*; and 50-60 spots for postcards. Considers all themes; "no taboos except no explicit sex; nude studies in taste are welcomed, however." Send query letter with resume, Photostats and/or photocopies to be kept on file; unaccepted material returned immediately by SASE. "See work by H. E. Knickerbocker, Richard Dahlstrom, Walt Phillips, Gregory Powell, Steve Del Monte, Cliff Johnson, Ford Button, L. John Creslinski, Carol Gale Anderson." Reports in 1 week. Buys first rights or one-time rights; prefers first rights; Pays $25, b&w, $100, color, cover; $5-25, b&w, inside; on acceptance, "except spot drawings which are paid for on assignment to an issue."
Tips: "We use virtually every subject and style that would fit into a literary quarterly's range. Above all we look for skill and sophistication with wit. Wit and humor above all in cartoons. In illustrations, it is

very difficult to get excellent nude studies (such as one we used by Carolyn G. Anderson to illustrate a short story by Judson Jerome in our Fall 1986 issue.) everyone seems capable of drawing an ugly woman; few capture sensuality, and fewer still draw the nude male tastefully."

AMERICAN AGRICULTURIST, Box 370, Ithaca NY 14851. (607)273-3507. Art Director: Maureen Viele. Emphasizes agriculture in the Northeast, specifically New York, New Jersey and New England. Monthly. Circ. 72,000. Original artwork not returned after publication. Art guidelines for SASE.
Cartoons: Buys 3 cartoons/issue from freelancers. Prefers agriculture theme. Single panel, 2⅛" wide by 2¾-3¼" high or similar proportions, with gagline; b&w line drawings. Send query letter with finished cartoons. Material returned. Reports within 3 weeks. Buys first rights or one-time rights. Pays $10, b&w; on acceptance.

THE AMERICAN ATHEIST, Box 2117, Austin TX 78768. (512)458-1244. Editor: R. Murray-O'Hair. For atheists, agnostics, materialists and realists. Monthly. Circ. 30,000. Simultaneous submissions OK. Free sample copy, send 9x12 envelope or label.
Cartoons: Buys 10 cartoons/issue. Cartoons, $15 each. Especially needs 4-seasons art for covers and greeting cards. Send query letter with resume and samples.
Illustrations: Buys 1 illustration/issue on acceptance. "Illustrators should send samples to be kept on file. We do commission artwork based on the samples received. All illustrations must have bite from the atheist point of view and hit hard." To show a portfolio, mail original/final art, final reproduction/product, photographs and b&w. Pays $75-100, cover and $25 inside.
Tips: "*The American Atheist* looks for clean lines, directness and originality. We are not interested in side-stepping cartoons and esoteric illustrations. Our writing is hard-punching and we want artwork to match. The mother press of the *American Atheist*, the American Atheist Press, buys book cover designs and card designs."

AMERICAN BABY INC., Cahners Publication, 575 Lexington Ave., New York NY 10022. (212)752-0775. Art Director: Blair Davis. Four publications emphasizing babies, children and parents. Monthly, quarterly and annually. Circ. 1,000,000. Returns original artwork after publication. Sample copy for SASE, art guidelines available.
Illustrations: Buys 3-5 illustrations/issue from freelancers. Works on assignment only. Send business card and samples to be kept on file. Samples not filed are not returned. Reports back only if interested. Buys one-time rights. Pays on publication.

AMERICAN BANKERS ASSOCIATION-BANKING JOURNAL, 345 Hudson St., New York NY 10014. (212)620-7256. Art Director: Rob Klein. Emphasizes banking for middle and upper-level banking executives and managers. Monthly. Circ. 42,000. Accepts previously published material. Returns original artwork after publication.
Illustrations: Buys 4 illustrations/issue from freelancers. Themes relate to stories, primarily, financial; styles vary, realistic, cartoon, surreal. Works on assignment only. Send query letter with brochure and samples to be kept on file. Prefers tear sheets, slides or photographs as samples. Samples not filed are returned by SASE. Negotiates rights purchased. Pays $350-500 for color cover and $75-100 for b&w or color inside; on acceptance.

THE AMERICAN BAPTIST MAGAZINE, Box 851, Valley Forge PA 19482-0851. (215)768-2441. Managing Editor: Ronald Arena. Executive Editor: Philip Jenks. Manager of Print Media Services: Richard Schramm. National publication of American Baptist Churches in the USA. Contains feature articles, news, and commentary of interest to the American Baptist (1.5 million) constituency. Circ. 100,000. Bimonthly. Guidelines available.
Illustrations: All artwork on assignment for specific themes/subjects. (May make occasional use of freelance line art and cartoons.) Compensation negotiable. Portfolio samples and resume welcomed; enclose SASE for material to be returned.
Tips: "Artists should be willing to work promptly and creatively within stated guidelines for both specific and thematic art work."

AMERICAN BIRDS, National Audubon Society, 950 3rd Ave., New York NY 10022. Editorial Assistant: F. Baumgarten. Emphasizes ornithology—migration, distribution, breeding and behavior of North and Middle American birds, including Hawaii and the West Indies for amateur and professional birders, scientists, researchers, schools and libraries. Published 5 times/year (seasonal and Christmas Bird Count issue). Circ. 11,000. Original artwork returned after publication. Sample copy $3. Art guidelines free for SASE with 1 first-class stamp.
Illustrations: Buys 5-10 illustrations/issue from freelancers. Prefers detailed drawings of birds of the Americas; drawings to aid in identification (anatomically correct a must); artistic renderings for inside

material; outstanding artwork for cover." Send query letter with Photostats and slides. Samples not filed are returned only if requested. Reports back within 4 months. Buys first rights. Pays up to $100, b&w or color, cover; $10-25, b&w or color, inside; on publication.

AMERICAN BOOKSELLER, Booksellers Publishing Inc., Suite 1410, 122 E. 42nd St., New York NY 10168. Editor-in-Chief: Ginger Curwen. Art Director: Amy Bogert. For booksellers interested in trends, merchandising, recommendations, laws and industry news. Monthly. Circ. 8,700. Original artwork returned after publication. Sample copy $3.

Cartoons: Uses 2 cartoons/year; buys all from freelancers. Receives 5-10 submissions/week from freelancers. Interested in bookselling, authors and publishing; single panel with gagline. Send finished cartoons. SASE. Reports in 4 weeks. Buys first North American serial rights.

Illustrations: Uses 4 illustrations/issue; buys 4/issue from freelancers. Prefers local artists due to tight deadlines. Receives 10 submissions/week from freelancers. Looks for strong concepts and an original style. Interested in books, inventory or material for specific assignments. Works on assignment only. Send query letter with samples. Provide business card, flyer and tear sheet to be kept on file for future assignments. SASE. Reports back only if interested. Call to schedule an appointment to show a portfolio, which should include Photostats, tear sheets and final reproduction/product. Considers project's budget and rights purchased when establishing payment. Buys first North American serial rights. Pays $50 minimum for b&w line drawings, washes and gray opaques; on acceptance.

Tips: "I have a greater and greater need for strong conceptual work. Yet the mailing pieces I get don't give me enough sense of the artist's ability to solve a visual problem with a visual idea. Please send more than one sample of work, as it gives me a sense of the artist's range and aids in the decision-making process."

AMERICAN DEMOGRAPHICS, Box 68, Ithaca NY 14851. (607)273-6343. Managing Editor: Caroline Arthur. Emphasizes demographics and population trends. Readers are business decision makers, advertising agencies, market researchers, newspapers, banks and professional demographers and business analysts. Monthly. Circ. 35,000. Original artwork returned after publication. Sample copy $6.

Cartoons: Uses 1-3 cartoons/issue, all from freelancers. Receives 5-10 submissions/week from freelancers. Interested in population trends including moving, aging, families, birth rate, the census, surveys, changing neighborhoods, women working, data (use, computers, etc.), market research, business forecasting and demographers. Format: single panel b&w line drawings and b&w washes with gagline. Prefers to see finished cartoons. SASE. Reports in 2 weeks. Buys one-time rights. Pays $50-100 on publication.

Illustrations: Uses 2 illustrations/issue. Interested in demographic themes. Needs "styles that reproduce best in b&w. Spare statements with a light approach to the subject." Prefers to see portfolio; contact Caroline Arthur. SASE. Provide photocopies of work to be kept on file for future needs. Reports in 1 month. Buys one-time rights. Inside: pays $50, under ½ page; $75, ½ page; $100, full page.

***AMERICAN FAMILY PHYSICIAN**, 1740 W. 92nd St., Kansas City MO 64114. Managing Publisher: Clayton Raker Hasser.

Cartoons: Uses 2 cartoons/issue, all from freelancers. Receives 30 submissions/week from freelancers. Original artwork not returned after publication. Interested in medical and hospital themes. Prefers finished cartoons. SASE. Reports in 1 week. Buys all rights on a work-for-hire basis. Pays $35; on acceptance.

AMERICAN FITNESS, (formerly Aerobics & Fitness), Suite 310, 15250 Ventura Blvd., Sherman Oaks CA 91403. (818)905-0040. Editor: Peg Angsten. Magazine emphasizing fitness, health and exercise for sophisticated, college-educated, very active lifestyles. Bimonthly. Circ. 30,000. Accepts previously published material. Original artwork returned after publication. Sample copy $1.

Cartoons: Buys 1 cartoon/issue from freelancers. Material not kept on file is returned if requested. Buys one-time rights. Pays $35.

Illustrations: Buys 1-2 illustrations/issue from freelancers. Works on assignment only. Prefers very sophisticated line drawings. Send query letter with brochure showing art styles and tear sheets. Reports back within 2 months. To show a portfolio, mail thumbnails and roughs. Buys one-time rights. Pays $50; on publication.

THE AMERICAN LEGION MAGAZINE, Box 1055, Indianapolis IN 46206. Contact: Cartoon Editor. Emphasizes the historical development of the world at present, and milestones of history; general interest magazine for veterans and their families. Monthly. Original artwork not returned after publication.

Cartoons: Uses 2-3 cartoons/issue, all from freelancers. Receives 100 submissions/week from freelancers. Especially needs general humor, in good taste. "Generally interested in cartoons with a broad, mass appeal. Prefer action in the drawing, rather than the illustrated joke-type gag. Those which have a beguiling character or ludicrous situation that attract the reader and lead him to read the caption rate the highest attention. No-caption gags purchased only occasionally. Because of the tight space problem, we're not in the market for the spread-type or multipanel cartoon but use both vertical and horizontal format single panel cartoons. Themes should be home life, business, sports and everyday Americana. Cartoons which pertain only to one branch of the service may be too restricted for this magazine. The service-type gag should be recognized and appreciated by any ex-serviceman or woman. Cartoons in bad taste, off-color or which may offend the reader not accepted. Liquor, sex, religion and racial differences are taboo. Ink roughs not necessary, but are desirable. Finish should be line, Ben-Day." Send query letter with brochure showing art style with promotional material that will not be returned. Usually reports within 30 days. Call to schedule an appointment to show a portfolio, which should include final reproduction/product. Buys first rights; "pays on receipt of Ben-Day acceptance." Pays $95-125; on publication.

Tips: "Artists should submit their work as we are always seeking a new slant or more timely humor. Black-and-white representational art is primarily what we seek. Note: Cartoons are a separate department from the art department."

***AMERICAN LIBRARIES**, American Library Association, 50 E. Huron St., Chicago IL 60611. (312)944-6780. Editor-in-Chief: Arthur Plotnik. Executive Editor: Susan E. Brandehoff. Associate Editor: Edith McCormick. For professional librarians, library employees and individuals in business-related fields. Published 11 times/year. Circ. 46,000. Sample copy $4. Free artist's guidelines.

Cartoons: Buys 4-10/year on libraries and library-patron interaction; single panel with gagline. Avoid stereotypes. Query with samples or with resume and portfolio. SASE. Reports only if interested. Buys first North American serial rights. Pays $30-75, b&w line drawings and washes, depending on assignments.

Illustrations: Buys 4-8/year on libraries, library-patron interaction and assigned themes. Query with samples or with resume and portfolio. SASE. Reports only if interested. Buys first North American serial rights. Cover: Pays $50-200, b&w; $300 maximum, color. Inside: Pays $15-200, color and b&w; on acceptance.

Tips: "Review a few issues of our magazine at your public library so you are familiar with the type of articles we illustrate and sophistication of audience being addressed. Avoid stereotypical images of librarians."

AMERICAN MOTORCYCLIST, American Motorcyclist Association, Box 6114, Westerville OH 43081-6114. (614)891-2425. Executive Editor: Greg Harrison. Managing Editor: Bill Wood. Associate Editor: John Van Barriger. Monthly. Circ. 130,000. For "enthusiastic motorcyclists, investing considerable time and money in the sport." Sample copy $1.50.

Cartoons: Uses 2-3 cartoons/issue; all from freelancers. Receives 5-7 submissions/week from freelancers. Interested in motorcycling; "single panel gags." Prefers to receive finished cartoons. SASE. Reports in 2 weeks. Buys all rights on a work-for-hire basis. Pays $15 minimum, b&w washes; on publication.

Illustrations: Uses 1-2 illustrations/issue, almost all from freelancers. Receives 1-3 submissions/week from freelancers. Interested in motorcycling themes. Works on assignment only. Provide resume and tear sheets to be kept on file. Prefers to see samples of style and resume. Samples returned by SASE. Reports in 3 weeks. Buys first North American serial rights. Pays $75 minimum, color, cover: $30-100, b&w and color, inside; on publication.

***AMERICAN MUSIC TEACHER**, Suite 2113, 441 Vine St., Cincinnati OH 45202-2982. Graphics Consultant: Poppy Evans. Trade journal emphasizing music teaching. Features historical and how-to articles. "*AMT* promotes excellence in music teaching and keeps music teachers informed. It is the official journal of the Music Teachers National Association, an organization which includes concert artists, independent music teachers and faculty members of educational institutions." Bimonthly. Circ. 25,000. Accepts previously published material. Original artwork returned after publication. Sample copies available.

Illustrations: Buys 1 illustration/issue from freelancers. Buys 6 illustrations/year from freelancers. Prefers musical theme. "No interest in cartoon illustration." Send query letter with brochure or resume, tear sheets, slides and photographs. Samples are filed. Samples not filed are returned only if requested. Reports back within 3 months. To show a portfolio, mail original/final art, tear sheets, photographs, slides, color and b&w. Buys one-time rights. Pays $50, b&w; $100, color, cover; on publication.

AMERICAN SALON, 7500 Old Oak Blvd., Cleveland OH 44130. Editor: Jody Byrne. Concerns the art of cosmetology and related fashion; for beauty salons. Monthly. Circ. 158,000. Simultaneous submissions OK "if trade exclusive." Receives 1-2 cartoons and 2-3 illustrations/month.

Illustrations: Buys themes on hairstyling. Especially needs drawings of men and women with current

or avant garde hairstyles. Uses b&w line drawings and photos. Query with resume and samples or arrange interview to show a portfolio. SASE. Reports only if interested. Negotiates pay. Buys all rights.
Tips: Work "must have a professional look."

THE AMERICAN SHOTGUNNER MAGAZINE, Box 3351, Reno NV 89505. Story Editor: Simon Grimes. Emphasizes high-grade and competition shotguns; hunting and the outdoors; trap and skeet competitions; industry news; reloading for upscale hunters, collectors and outdoorsmen; competition shooters. Monthly. Circ. 120,000. Original artwork returned after publication.
Illustrations: Uses approximately 4 b&w line drawings and 7 wildlife paintings or bronze sculptures. Prefers skeet or trap shooters; hunters (with dogs) as themes. Send query letter with resume, business card and samples to be kept on file. To show a portfolio, mail final reproduction/product, color, Photostats, photographs, b&w and Kodachrome slides of high-grade wildlife art and wildlife bronze sculptures. Samples not kept on file are returned by SASE. Reports within 2 months. Buys first rights. Pays $10-20, b&w; $30-50, color, inside; $75 color, cover; on publication.
Tips: "Our art editor is constantly looking for new names in the field so we can profile them as the up-and-coming wildlife artists."

THE AMERICAN SPECTATOR, Box 10448, Arlington VA 22210. Managing Editor: Wladyslaw Pleszczynski. Concerns politics and literature. Monthly. Circ. 43,000. Original artwork returned after publication. Sample copy.
Illustrations: Uses 2-3 illustrations/issue, all from freelancers. Interested in "caricatures of political figures (for portraits with a point of view)." Works on assignment only. Samples returned by SASE. Reports back on future assignment possibilities. Provide resume, brochure and tear sheets to be kept on file for future assignments. Prefers to see portfolio and samples of style. Reports in 2 weeks. Buys first North American serial rights. Pays $150 minimum, b&w line drawings, cover. Pays $35 minimum, b&w line drawings, inside; on publication.

***AMERICAN SPORTS**, Box 6100, Rosemead CA 91770. Art Director: Michael Harding. Magazine emphasizing prep, collegiate, professional and recreational sports. Features general interest, historical, how-to, inspirational, interview/profile, personal experience, travel articles and experimental fiction (all sports-related). Monthly. Circ. 400,500. Accepts previously published material. Original artwork returned after publication.
Illustrations: Buys 5 illustrations/issue from freelancers. Buys 60 illustrations/year from freelancers. Send query letter with resume, tear sheets, slides and photographs. Samples are filed. Samples not filed are returned. Reports back within 1 week. To show a portfolio mail tear sheets, final reproduction/product, photographs, slides, color and b&w. Buys first rights, one-time rights, reprint rights and all rights. Pays on acceptance.
Tips: "Be consistent in style and quality."

***AMERICAN SQUAREDANCE**, Box 488, Huron OH 44839. Editors: Stan and Cathie Burdick. For squaredancers, callers and teachers. Emphasizes personalities, conventions and choreography. Monthly. Original artwork returned after publication if requested. Free sample copy.
Cartoons: Uses 1 cartoon/issue; buys 6/year from freelancers. Interested in dance theme; single panel. Send finished cartoons. SASE. Reports in 1 week. Buys all rights on a work-for-hire basis. Pays $10-20, halftones and washes; on publication.
Illustrations: Uses 5 illustrations/issue; buys 1/issue from freelancers. Interested in dance themes. Send finished art. SASE. Reports in 1 week. Buys all rights on a work-for-hire basis. Pays $25-50, b&w line drawings, washes and color-separated art, cover; $5-15, b&w line drawings and washes inside; on publication.

AMERICAN TRUCKER MAGAZINE, Box 9159, Brea CA 92622. Editor: Cal Calvert. Emphasizes trucks and trucking topics of interest to the single truck owner operator and the small truck fleet businessman. Monthly. Circ. 80,000. Accepts previously published material only in exceptional circumstances. Original artwork returned if requested. Sample copy for SASE.
Illustrations: Buys 1 illustration/issue from freelancers. Prefers realistic styles. Works on assignment only. Send query letter. Write for appointment to show portfolio. Buys first rights. Pays $100/page for b&w; on publication.

AMIGA WORLD AND RUN MAGAZINES, C W Communications/Peterborough, 80 Pine St., Peterborough NH 03458. Art Director: Rosslyn A. Frick. Emphasizes computing for business and families who own and operate Commodore computers. Monthly. Circ. 225,000. Original artwork returned after publication.
Illustrations: Prefers exciting, creative styles and Amiga-generated artwork. Works on assignment

only. Send tear sheets, photographs, or promotional material. Reports only if interested. Negotiates rights purchased. Pays $300-600, b&w; $500-1,000, color, cover; $300-600 b&w; $500-1,000, color, inside; on acceptance.

***ANIMALS**, 350 S. Huntington Ave., Boston MA 02130. Photo Researcher: Laura Ten Eyck. "*Animals* is a national full-color, bimonthly magazine published by the Massachusetts Society for the Prevention of Cruelty to Animals. We publish articles on and photographs of wildlife, domestic animals, conservation, controversies involving animals, animal-welfare issues, pet health and pet care. Circ. 50,000. Original artwork usually returned after publication. Sample copy $2.50.
Illustrations: Buys 5 illustrations/year from freelancers. Prefers pets or wildlife illustrations relating to a particular article topic. Send query letter with brochure or tear sheets. Samples are filed. Samples not filed are returned by SASE. Reports back within 1 month. Write to schedule an appointment to show a portfolio, which should include roughs, original/final art, tear sheets, final reproduction/product and color. Negotiates rights purchased. Pays minimum $50, b&w; minimum $100, color, inside; on acceptance.

ANTIC, The Atari Resource, 544 Second St., San Francisco CA 94107. Art Director: Marni Tapscott. Magazine emphasizing computers for Atari enthusiasts. Monthly. Circ. 100,000. Original artwork returned after publication.
Illustrations: Buys 3-5 illustrations/issue from freelancers. Works on assignment only. Prefers sophisticated, highly realistic styles using airbrush, colored pencil, pastels, or acrylics. Send brochure showing art style or resume and tear sheets, Photostats, photocopies, slides and photographs; "color work should be in color though." Samples not filed are returned. Reports back only if interested. To show a portfolio, mail appropriate materials, which should include original/final art, final reproduction/product, color and tear sheets. Buys one-time rights. Pays $800-1,000, color, cover; $50-150, b&w; $75-700, color, inside; 30 days from acceptance date.

THE ANTIQUARIAN, Box 798, Huntington NY 11743. (516)271-8990. Editors: Marguerite Cantine and Elizabeth Kilpatrick. Concerns antiques, arts, shows and news of the market; for dealers and collectors. Monthly. Circ. 15,000.
Illustrations: Receives 2 illustrations/week from freelance artists. "We are one magazine that hates the use of photography but it's more available to us than good illustrations. We ran a complete history of the teddy bear and would have used all drawings if we could have found an illustrator. Instead we had to use photos. We've also recently started using many illustrations of colonial and Victorian buildings." Buys b&w line drawings. Especially needs illustration for ad designs. Query with resume, samples and SASE. "No phone calls, please!" Include 8½x11" SASE with $1.25 if sample copy is requested. Reports in 4-8 weeks. Buys all rights. Pay "depends on the size of the article. We commission the entire article or issue if possible to one artist. I like for the artist to quote his/her rates." Pays $10 maximum, b&w; on acceptance.
Tips: "Our covers are us. They are children's illustrations from fine, usually German, books circa 1850-1875. If an artist can get the feel of what we're trying to convey with our covers, the rest is easy. We specialize in totally designed magazines. I think we're a leader in the antiques trade field and people will follow the trend. We are heavily illustrated—we use few photos. Send 5-10 illustrations *after* reviewing the publications. Suggest a price range. If the illustration is good, needed, usable, the price is never a problem. So suggest one. Only the artist knows the time involved. We buy *all rights only*. Please quote prices accordingly."

AOPA PILOT, 421 Aviation Way, Frederick MD 21701. (301)695-2353. Emphasizes general aviation (no military or airline) for aircraft owners and pilots. Monthly. Circ. 270,000. Original artwork returned after publication. Sample copy $2.
Illustrations: Buys 1-3 illustrations/issue. Uses illustrations specifically for manuscripts. Works on assignment only. Send query letter with tear sheets, Photostats, photocopies, slides and photographs. Samples returned by SASE. Reports only if interested. Call to schedule an appointment to show a portfolio, which should include original/final art and tear sheets. Buys first rights. Pays for illustration by the project,$250-2,500. Pays on acceptance.
Tips: Looks for "strong conceptual abilities, technical competence, solid design and confidence." Don't include pencil drawings in samples or portfolio. "Avoid duplicating photographs, as such an illustration is an unnecessary extra step. If I can use photography, I will."

APPALACHIAN TRAILWAY NEWS, Box 807, Harpers Ferry WV 25425. (304)535-6331. Editor: Judith Jenner. Emphasizes the Appalachian Trail for members of the Appalachian Trail Conference. 5 issues/year. Circ. 22,000. Sometimes accepts previously published material. Returns original artwork after publication. Sample copy $1 for serious inquiries; art guidelines for SASE with first-class postage.

Cartoons: Buys 0-1 cartoons/issue from freelancers. Prefers themes on hikers and trailworkers on Aplachian Trail. Open to all formats. Send query letter with roughs and finished cartoons. Only materials pertinent to Appalachian Trail are considered. Material not filed is returned by SASE. Reports within 1 month. Negotiates rights purchased. Pays $25-50 for b&w; on acceptance.
Illustrations: Buys 2-5 illustrations/issue from freelancers. Themes/styles are assigned to particular story ideas. Send query letter with samples to be kept on file. Prefers Photostats, photocopies or tear sheets as samples. Samples not filed are returned by SASE. Reports within 1 month. Negotiates rights purchased. Pays $75-150, b&w and $150 up, color (watercolor only) for covers; $25-100, b&w for inside; pays on acceptance.

***APPLE PRESS, INC.**, Box 787, Bethel CT 06801. (203)798-2988. Publisher: Michael Catron. Estab. 1986. Publishes comic books including *Elfquest*, *Fantasci*, *Space Ark*, *Thunderbunny*, and *Unicorn Isle*. Genres: adventure, fantasy, romance and science fiction. Themes: outer space, future science and social commentary. "We are attempting to publish a range of comics titles in the sf/fantasy arena—particularly those that will have a dual male/female appeal." Bimonthly. Circ. 30,000. Original artwork returned after publication. Sample copy for SASE with 79¢ postage.
Illustrations: Uses artists for inking, lettering, pencilling, color work, paste-up, posters and covers. Send query letter with samples. Samples are not filed. Samples not filed are returned by SASE. Reports back within 2 months. To show a portfolio, mail 2-4 pages of action continuity and photocopies of original pencil art or inking one-and-one half times up. Rights purchased are "subject to negotiation but generally we are interested in all publishing and licensing rights. Creators retain copyright." Pays advance against royalty on acceptance.

APPLIED RADIOLOGY, Brentwood Publishing, 1640 5th St., Santa Monica CA 90401. Publisher: Martin Waldman. Art Director: Tom Medsger. Emphasizes technological, medical and professional news.
Illustrations: Submit brochure/flyer to be kept on file for possible future assignment. Reports only when assignment available. Buys all rights. Pays $60 and up, spot art; $400, full-color cover; on acceptance.

ARARAT, 585 Saddle River Rd., Saddle Brook NJ 07662. Contact: Leo Hamalian. For those interested in Armenian life and culture, for Americans of Armenian descent, and Armenian immigrants. Quarterly. Circ. 2,000.
Illustrations: SASE. Pays on publication.

ARIZONA LIVING MAGAZINE, Suite C, 5046 N. 7th St., Phoenix AZ. (602)264-4295. Art Director: Margie Diguiseppe. Magazine emphasizing Arizona lifestyle and strong issues for 28-45 age group; salary of $30,000 or more a year; yuppie type. Monthly. Circ. 18,000. Accepts previously published material. Original artwork returned after publication. Sample copy free for SASE with 50¢ postage.
Cartoons: Buys 0-1 cartoon/issue from freelancers. Prefers funny yet strong themes. Prefers single or multi panel with gagline; b&w washes. Send samples of style to be kept on file. Call for appointment to show a portfolio. Samples not filed returned only if requested. Reports only if interested. Buys one-time rights.
Illustrations: Buys 3 illustrations/issue from freelancers. Works on assignment only. Prefers themes dealing with people and subjects pertaining to story. Send query letter with resume, tear sheets and Photostats. Samples not filed returned only if requested. Reports only if interested. Call or write to schedule an appointment to show a portfolio, which should include original/final art, tear sheets and Photostats. Buys one-time rights. Pays by project, $25-250.

***ART BUSINESS NEWS**, 60 Ridgeway Plaza, Stamford CT 06905. Editor: Jo Yanow-Schwartz. Trade journal emphasizing business of selling art and frames, trends, new art editions, limited editions, posters and framing supplies. Features general interest, interview/profile and technical articles. Weekly. Circ. 25,000. Original artwork returned after publication. Sample copies available. Art guidleines available for SASE.
Cartoons: Buys some cartoons/issue from freelancers. Prefers "sophisticated, light business orientation." Prefers single panel, b&w line drawings and b&w washes. Send query letter with samples of style. Samples are filed. Samples not filed are returned. Reports back within weeks. Pays $35-50, b&w; $50-100, color.
Illustrations: Works on assignment only. Send query letter with brochure showing art style, tear sheets and slides. Samples are filed (excluding slides). Samples not filed are returned. Reports back within weeks. Write to schedule an appointment to show a portfolio or mail tear sheets, photographs, color and b&w. Buys one-time rights. Pays by the project, $35-100.

ART DIRECTION, 10 E. 39th St., 6th Floor, New York NY 10157-0002. (212)889-6500. Editor: Hedi Levine. Emphasizes advertising for art directors. Monthly. Circ. 12,000. Original work returned after publication. Sample copy $2.50. Receives 7 illustrations/week from freelance artists.
Illustrations: Uses 2-3 illustrations/issue; all from freelancers. Interested in themes that relate to advertising. Send query letter. Provide information to be kept on file for possible future assignments. Samples not returned. Reports in 1 month. No payment for cover or editorial art.

***ART EXPRESSIONS**, Box 2074, California City CA 93505. President/Publisher: Dennis W. Sumrow. Six column, 13.5" tabloid for active artists, professional and amateur. Features central coast California, cultural arts and fine arts. Bimonthly. Circ. 30,000. Accepts previously published material. Original artwork not returned after publication. Sample copies and art guidelines free for SASE with $1.27 postage.
Cartoons: Buys 6 cartoons/year from freelancers. Prefers single panel with gagline; b&w line drawings and b&w washes. Send query letter with samples of style. Samples are filed. Reports back only if interested. Buys one-time rights. Pays $10, b&w.
Illustrations: Buys 6 illustrations/issue from freelancers. Prefers fine art themes. Send query letter with resume and photographs. Samples are filed. Samples not filed are returned by SASE. Reports back only if interested. To show a portfolio mail tear sheets, photographs and b&w. Buys one-time rights. Pays $100, b&w, cover; $20, b&w, inside; on publication.

ART MATERIAL TRADE NEWS, 6255 Barfield Rd., Atlanta GA 30328. (404)256-9800. Editor: Charles Craig. Emphasizes art material business, merchandising and selling trends, products, store and manufacturer profiles for dealers, manufacturer, wholesalers of artist supplies. Monthly. Circ. 11,500. Accepts previously published material. Original artwork returned after publication. Sample copy $2.
Cartoons: Themes and styles open. Send query letter with samples of style to be kept on file "if desired by artist." Write for appointment to show portfolio. Material not kept on file returned by SASE. Reports "ASAP." Negotiates rights purchased. Payment negotiable. Pays on publication.
Illustrations: Works on assignment only. Send brochure, resume, samples and tear sheets to be kept on file. Write for an appointment to show portfolio. Prefers "anything but originals" as samples. Samples returned by SASE if not kept on file. Reports "ASAP." Negotiates rights purchased. Pays on publication.

***ARTFUL DODGE**, Box 1473, Bloomington IN 47402. (812)966-2096. Art Editor: Karen Kovacik. Emphasizes literature (all genres). "Our readers are interested in challenging poetry, fiction, and drama, both from the U.S. and abroad (particularly Eastern Europe)." Bianually/irregularly. Circ. 750. Original artwork returned after publication. Latest issue (double) costs $5.75; art guidelines available for SASE and 1 first class stamp.
Illustrations: Prefers pen & ink drawings, woodcuts—high contrast b&w work that reproduces well. "Please no science fiction or cat cartoons. We look for visually interesting work that can stand on its own apart from our literary offerings." Prefers good photocopies or samples. Samples cannot be returned. Reports within 2-3 months. Buys first rights or one-time rights. Pays in copies (2).

THE ARTIST'S MAGAZINE, 1507 Dana Ave., Cincinnati OH 45207. Editor: Mike Ward. Emphasizes the techniques of working artists for the serious beginning and amateur artist. Published 12 times/year. Circ. 185,000. Occasionally accepts previously published material. Returns original artwork after publication. Sample copy $2 with SASE and 50¢ postage.
Cartoons: Contact Mike Ward, editor. Buys 3-4 "top-quality" cartoons/issue from freelancers. Most cartoons bought are single-panel finished cartoons with or without gagline; b&w line drawings, b&w washes. "We're also on the lookout for color, multi panel (4-6 panels) work with a theme to use on our "P.S." page. Any medium." All cartoons should be artist-oriented, appealing to the working artist (versus the gallery-goer), and should not denigrate art or artists. Avoid cliche situations. For single panel cartoon submissions, send query letter with 4 or more finished cartoons. For "P.S." submissions, query first. Material not filed is returned only by SASE. Reports within 1 month. Pays $50 and up for b&w single panels; pays $200 and up for "P.S." work. Buys first North American serial rights. Pays on acceptance.
Illustrations: Contact Carol Buchanan, art director. Buys 2-3 illustrations/issue from freelancers. Works on assignment only. Send query letter with brochure, resume and samples to be kept on file. Prefers Photostats or tear sheets as samples. Samples not filed are returned by SASE. Buys first rights. Pays on acceptance.

ARTSLINE, 2518 Western Ave., Seattle WA 98121. (206)441-0786. Editor: Alice Copp Smith. Magazine emphasizing performing and visual arts. Monthly. Circ. 79,000. Original artwork returned after publication. Sample copy free for 9x12 SASE and 3 first-class stamps; art guideline free for SASE with 1 first-class stamp.

Cartoons: Buys 6 cartoons/year from freelancers. Prefers single panel with or without gagline; b&w line drawings. Send query letter with finished cartoons "which will be returned if accompanied by SASE," or photocopies. Reports within 6 weeks. Buys first rights. Pays $25-50, b&w.
Illustrations: Buys 1 illustration/issue from freelancers. Works on assignment only. Prefers spot art, "Seattle scenes; arts-related themes; *New Yorker*-style spot art." Send query letter with brochure showing art style or tear sheets and Photostats. Samples not filed are returned by SASE. Reports back within 6 weeks. To show a portfolio, mail appropriate materials or call to schedule an appointment. Buys first rights. Pays $25-50, b&w, inside; on acceptance.

ASSOCIATION AND SOCIETY MANAGER, Brentwood Publishing, 1640 5th St., Santa Monica CA 90401. Publisher: Martin H. Waldman. Art Director: Tom Medsger. Devoted to the interests of managers of professional membership societies.
First Contact & Terms: Send brochure/flyer to be kept on file for possible future assignment. Reports only when assignment available. Buys all rights. Pays $60 and up, spot art; $400, full-color cover; on acceptance.

ATLANTIC CITY MAGAZINE, 1637 Atlantic Ave., Atlantic City NJ 08401. (609)348-6886. Art Director: Jeff Roth. Emphasizes the growth, people and entertainment of Atlantic City for residents and visitors. Monthly. Circ. 50,000.
Illustrations: Buys 2-4 illustrations/issue. Mainly b&w, some 4-color. Works on assignment only. Send query letter with brochure showing art style and tear sheets, slides and photographs to be kept on file. Call or write to schedule an appointment to show a portfolio, which should include original/final art, final reproduction/product, color, tear sheets, photographs and b&w. Buys first rights. Pays $50-250, b&w, $150-400, color; on publication.
Tips: "We are looking for intelligent, reliable artists who can work within the confines of our budget and time frame. Deliver good art and receive good tear sheets."

ATLANTIC SALMON JOURNAL, 1435 St. Alexandre, Montreal, Quebec H3A 2G4 Canada. (514)842-8059. Managing Editor: Joanne Eidinger. Emphasizes conservation and angling of Atlantic salmon; travel, biology and cuisine for educated, well-travelled, affluent and informed anglers and conservationists, biologists and professionals. Quarterly. Circ. 20,000. Does not accept previously published material. Returns original artwork after publication. Sample copy free for SASE. Art guidelines available.
Cartoons: Uses 2-4/issue. Prefers environmental or political themes, specific to salmon resource management, travel and tourism—light and whimsical. Prefers single panel with or without gagline; b&w line drawings. Send query letter with samples of style to be kept on file. Material not filed is returned. Reports within 8 weeks. Buys first rights and one-time rights. Pays $25-50, b&w; on publication.
Illustrations: Uses 4-6/issue. Prefers themes on angling, environmental scenes and biological drawings. Send query letter with samples to be kept on file. Prefers Photostats, tear sheets, slides or photographs as samples. Samples not filed are returned. Reports within 8 weeks. Buys first rights and one-time rights. Pays $50-150, b&w, and $100-250, color, inside; on publication.

AUTO TRIM NEWS, 1623 Grand Ave., Baldwin NY 11510. Contact: Nat Danas. "For the small businessman." Does not return original artwork after publication.
Cartoons: Buys 2/issue from freelancers. Prefers to see roughs; reports in 2 weeks. Pays on publication.
Illustrations: Buys 1/issue from freelancers. Works on assignment only. Send query letter with roughs and samples of style; samples returned. Reports in 2 weeks. Buys all rights on a work-for-hire basis. Pays $10, spot drawings; $25-50, cover design; on publication.
Tips: Artists should "visit a shop" dealing in this field.

AUTOMATIC MACHINING MAGAZINE, 100 Seneca Ave., Rochester NY 14621. (716)338-1522. Editor: Donald Wood. For metalworking technical management. Readers are management and engineering personnel. Monthly. Circ. 16,000. Purchased artwork not returned.
Cartoons: Uses 3-4 cartoons/issue, all from freelancers. Receives 1 submission/week from freelancers. Interested in engineering and metalworking. Prefers single panel b&w line drawings with gag lines. Prefers finished cartoons. SASE. Reports in 1 week. Buys one-time rights. Pays $5-10; on acceptance.
Tips: There is a trend toward "use of computers and numerical control" in our field. Artists should "get a copy of our magazine" before making submissions.

AUTOMOBILE QUARTERLY, 1449 Monrovia Ave., Newport Beach CA 92663. (714)720-5300. Art Director: Michael Pardo. Concerns autos and auto history. Circ. 30,000. Quarterly. Original artwork returned after publication, by arrangement.

Illustrations: Uses 8-10 illustrations/issue, all from freelancers. Interested in antique, classic cars and cutaway technical illustrations. Works on assignment only. Send query letter with Photostats, photocopies, slides and photographs. Provide "sample of rendering" to be kept on file for future assignments. SASE. Reports in 2 weeks. Buys various rights. Negotiates pay (part of payment may be posters of work); pays on publication.

AXIOS, The Orthodox Journal, 800 S. Euclid Ave., Fullerton CA 92632. (714)526-2131. Editor: David Gorham. Emphasizes "challenges in ethics and theology, some questions that return to haunt one generation after another, old problems need to be restated with new urgency. *Axios* tries to present the 'unthinkable'." Circ. 6,478. Accepts previously published material and simultaneous submissions. Original artwork returned after publication. Sample copy $2.
Illustrations: Buys 5-10 illustrations/issue from freelancers. Prefers bold line drawings, seeks icons, b&w; "no color *ever*; use block prints—do not have to be religious, but must be *bold*!" Send query letter with brochure, resume, business card or samples to be kept on file. Samples not filed are returned by SASE. Reports within 5 weeks. To show a portfolio, mail final reproduction/product and b&w. Buys one-time rights. Pays $100, b&w cover and $50-75, b&w inside; on acceptance.

***B.C. OUTDOORS**, 202-1132 Hamilton St., Vancouver, British Columbia Canada V6B 2S2. (604)687-1581. Editor: George Will. Emphasizes fishing, hunting, RV camping, wildlife/conservation. Published 10 times/year. Circ. 36,000. Original artwork returned after publication unless bought outright. Free sample copy.
Cartoons: Uses 3-4 cartoons/issue; buys all from freelancers. Cartoons should pertain to outdoor recreation: fishing, hunting, camping, wildlife in British Columbia. Format: single panel b&w line drawings with or without gagline. Prefers finished cartoons. SAE (nonresidents include IRC). Pays on acceptance. Reports in 2 weeks. Buys one-time rights.
Illustrations: Uses 12 illustrations/year. Interested in outdoors, creatures and activities as stories require. Freelancers selected "generally because I've seen their work." Format: b&w line drawings for inside, rarely for cover; b&w washes for inside; and color washes for inside and cover. Works on assignment only. Samples returned by SAE (nonresidents include IRC). Reports back on future assignment possibilities. Arrange personal appointment to show portfolio or send samples of style. When reviewing samples, especially looks at how their subject matter fits the publication and the art's quality. Reports in 2-6 weeks. Buys first North American serial rights or all rights on a work-for-hire basis. Payment negotiable, depending on nature of assignment. Pays on acceptance.

***BACK HOME IN KENTUCKY**, 7460 Rt. 64 W., Mt. Morris IL 61054. (815)734-4073. Managing Editor: Mayron J. Cockrel. "*Back Home In Kentucky* is a magazine for all those having a genuine interest in the Bluegrass State—its heritage, its people, its places and its events. This magazine reflects a contemporary and dynamic Kentucky, yet one that maintains its traditions." Features general interest, historical, interview-profile, personal experience, travel, historical and humorous stories. Bimonthly. Circ. 20,000. Accepts previously published material. Original artwork returned after publication. Sample copies free for SASE with $1.09 postage.
Illustrations: Buys 2 illustrations/year from freelancers. Prefers actual places or events in Kentucky as themes. Send query letter with slides and photographs. Samples are filed. Samples not filed are returned by SASE. Reports back within 2 weeks. To show a portfolio, mail appropriate materials. Buys one-time rights. Pays $15, b&w; $15, color, cover; $15, b&w; $15, color, inside; on publication.

BAJA TIMES, Box 755, San Ysidro CA 92073. (706)612-1244. Editorial Consultant: John W. Utley. Emphasizes Baja California, Mexico for tourists, other prospective visitors and retirees living there. Monthly. Circ. 50,000. Accepts previously published material. Original artwork returned after publication. Sample copy for 9x12 or larger SASE with 85¢ postage.
Cartoons: All must be Baja California-oriented. Prefers single panel with gagline; b&w line drawings. Send query letter with sample of style to be kept on file. Material not filed returned by SASE. Reports within 1 month. Buys one-time rights. Payment not established. Pays on publication.
Illustrations: Theme: Baja California. Send query letter with samples, tear sheets or photocopies to be kept on file. Samples not filed are returned by SASE. Reports within 1 month. Buys one-time rights. Payment not established. Pays on publication.
Tips: "We have not used art, mostly because it has not been offered to us. If properly oriented to our theme (Baja California), we would consider on an occasional basis."

BAKERSFIELD LIFESTYLE MAGAZINE, 123 Truxtun Ave., Bakersfield CA 93301. (805)325-7124. Editor: Steve Walsh. City magazine aimed at local lifestyles of college-educated males/females, ages 25-65. Monthly. Circ. 10,000. Accepts previously published material. Original artwork returned after publication. Sample copy $3; art guidelines free for SASE.

Cartoons: Buys 4 cartoons/issue from freelancers. No political humor. Prefers single panel with gagline; b&w line drawings or b&w washes. Send finished cartoons to be kept on file. Material not filed is returned by SASE. Reports only if interested. Buys one-time rights or reprints rights. Pays $5, b&w; on publication.
Illustrations: Buys 6 illustrations/issue from freelancers. Send Photostats, tear sheets or photocopies to be kept on file. Write for appointment to show portfolio. Samples not filed are returned by SASE. Reports only if interested. Buys one-time rights or reprint rights. Pays $100, b&w and $150, color, cover; $50, b&w and $75, color, inside; on publication.

***BALLOON LIFE MAGAZINE**3381 Pony Express Dr., Sacramento CA 95834. (916)922-9648. Editor: Tom Hamilton. Estab. 1985. Monthly magazine emphasizing the sport of ballooning. This is a "four-color magazine covering the life of sport ballooning, contains current news, feature articles, calendar and more. Audience is sport balloon enthusiasts." Circ. 2,500. Accepts previously published material. Original artwork returned after publication. Sample copy for SASE with $1.25 postage.
Cartoons: Buys 10-15 cartoons/year from freelancers. Prefers gag cartoons, editorial or political cartoons, caricatures and humorous illustrations. Prefers single panel with or without gaglines; b&w line drawings. Send query letter with samples, roughs and finished cartoons. Samples are filed. Samples not filed are returned. Reports back within 2 weeks. Buys first rights. Pays $25, b&w; on publication.
Illustrations: Buys 1-3 illustrations/year from freelancers. Send query letter with business card and samples. Samples are filed. Samples not filed are returned. Reports back within 2 weeks. Buys first rights. Pays $50, color, cover; $40, color, inside; on publication.

BALTIMORE JEWISH TIMES, 2104 North Charles St., Baltimore MD 21218. (301)752-3504. Art Director: Kim Muller-Thym. Assistant Art Director: Carol Steuer. Tabloid emphasizing special interest to the Jewish community for largely local readership. Weekly. Circ. 20,000. Returns original artwork after publication, if requested. Sample copy available.
Illustrations: Buys 2-3 illustrations/issue from freelancers. Works on assignment only. Prefers high-contrast b&w illustrations. Send query letter with brochure showing art style or tear sheets and photocopies. Samples not filed are returned by SASE. Reports back only if interested. To show a portfolio, mail appropriate materials or write to schedule an appointment; portfolio should include original/final art, final reproduction/product, color, tear sheets and Photostats. Buys first rights. Pays $100-150, b&w, cover and $200-300, color, cover; $30-100, b&w, inside; on publication.

***BAM PRODUCTIONS**, 1070 Baldwin Ave., Sharon PA 16146. (412)962-3522. Manager: Merry L. Frable. Estab. 1985. Publishes fantasy comic books with future science themes. Bimonthly. Circ. 25,000. Original artwork not returned after publication. Sample copy for SASE. Art guidelines for SASE with 1 first-class stamp.
Illustrations: Prefers circular panels. Uses freelance artists for inking, lettering, pencilling, color work, paste-up, posters and covers. Send query letter with resume. Samples are filed. Samples not filed are returned if requested. Reports back within 2 months. Call or write to schedule an appointment to show a portfolio, which should include photocopies of original pencil art or inking twice up. Buys all rights. Payment varies. Pays on publication.

BANJO NEWSLETTER, INC., Box 364, Greensboro MD 21639. (301)482-6278. Editor/Publisher: Hub Nitchie. Emphasizes banjo 5-string music for musicians and instrument collectors. Monthly. Circ. 7,000. Accepts previously published material. Original artwork returned after publication. Sample copy $1; deductible on subscription..
Cartoons: Buys 1 cartoon/issue from freelancers. 5-string banjo related. Prefers single panel; b&w line drawings. Send query letter with sample of style to be kept on file. Material not filed is returned by SASE. Reports within 2 weeks. To show a portfolio, mail thumbnails. Buys one-time rights. Pays $20-25, b&w; on publication.
Illustrations: Buys 1-2 illustrations/issue from freelancers. Send query letter to be kept on file. Samples returned by SASE. Reports within 2 weeks. Buys one-time rights. Pays approximately $30, b&w, cover; $20-30, b&w, inside; on publication.

BANKERS MONTHLY, Suite 31E, 870 Seventh Ave., New York NY 10019. (212)399-1084. Art Director: Elaine Kursch. Trade journal emphasizing banking for top management of banks. Features general interest, how-to and interview/profile articles. Monthly. Circ. 10,000. Accepts previously published material. Returns original artwork after publication "unless we bought." Sample copy available.
Cartoons: Prefers gagline; b&w line drawings. Send query letter with samples of style to be kept on file. Samples not filed are returned only if requested. Reports only if interested. Buys first rights. Pays $25-100, b&w.

Illustrations: Buys 1-3 illustrations/issue from freelancers. Works on assignment only. Prefers banking and finance-related themes. Send query letter with brochure showing art style. Samples not filed are returned only if requested. Reports only if interested. Call or write to schedule an appointment to show a portfolio, which should include tear sheets, color and b&w. Buys first rights. Pays $600, color, cover; $125, b&w; $250 color, inside; on publication.

***BANKING TODAY**, Florida Bankers Association, Box 53-6847, Orlando FL 32853-6847. Editor: Tina Kautter. Communicates educational, legislative and other material relevant to Southeastern U.S. bankers and businesspersons. Published 6 times/year. Circ. 6,500. Sample copy $3.50.
Cartoons: Buys very few cartoons/issue. Interested in banking; single, double and multi panel with gaglines. Prefers to see roughs. SASE. Reports in 8-12 weeks only if SASE included.

***BASKETBALL DIGEST**, 1020 Church St., Evanston IL 60201. (312)491-6440. Art Director: Thomas M. Miller. Emphasizes pro basketball, some college for "the serious sports fan who wants all the scores, stats, and stories behind the action." Monthly. Circ. 130,000. Accepts previously published material. Original artwork returned after publication.
Cartoons: Basketball themes. Prefers single panel; b&w line drawings. Send query letter. Write for appointment to show portfolio. Material not filed is returned by SASE. Reports only if interested. Pays on publication.
Illustrations: Basketball themes. Works on assignment only. Send query letter. Write for appointment to show portfolio. Samples not filed are returned by SASE. Reports only if interested. Pays on publication.

BAY AND DELTA YACHTSMAN, Recreation Publications, 2019 Clement Ave., Alameda CA 94501. (415)865-7500. Editor: Dave Preston. Art Director: David Hebenstreit. Concerns boating and boat owners in northern California. Monthly. Circ. 20,000. Previously published and simultaneous submissions OK (if not published in northern California). Original artwork returned after publication if requested. Sample copy $1.50.
Cartoons: Buys 4-5/year on boating. Prefers to see roughs. SASE. Reports in 2 weeks. Buys all rights on a work-for-hire basis. Pays $5 minimum, b&w line drawings; on publication.
Illustrations: Uses 2-3 charts and technical drawings/issue on boating. Prefers to see roughs. SASE. Send query letter with resume to be kept on file. Reports in 2 weeks. Buys all rights on a work-for-hire basis. Pays $5 minimum, b&w line drawings; on publication.

BEND OF THE RIVER® MAGAZINE, 143 W. Third St., Box 239, Perrysburg OH 43551. Editors-in-Chief: Chris Raizk Alexander and R. Lee Raizk. For local history enthusiasts. Monthly. Circ. 3,000. Previously published and photocopied submissions OK. Original artwork returned after publication. Sample copy $1.
Cartoons: Buys 12 cartoons/issue from freelancers. Interested in early Americana; single panel with gagline. SASE. Buys first North American serial rights or all rights on a work-for-hire basis. Pays $1-3, b&w line drawings.
Illustrations: Buys 20 illustrations/year. Interested in "historic buildings for ads." Works on assignment only. Prefers to see roughs. SASE. No samples returned. Reports in 6 weeks. Buys first North American serial rights or all rights on a work-for-hire basis. Pays $10-15, b&w line drawings, inside. Especially needs antiques, nostalgic items, landscapes and riverscapes.

THE BERKELEY MONTHLY, 1301 59th St., Emeryville CA 94608. Art Director: Laura Cirolia. Tabloid emphasizing art/ad mix and exciting graphics for Bay area residents. Monthly. Circ. 90,000. Accepts previously published material. Original artwork returned after publication. Sample copy for SASE.
Cartoons: Buys 1-2 cartoons/issue from freelancers. Prefers single, double or multiple panel; b&w line drawings. Send samples of style to be kept on file. Material not filed is returned by SASE. Reports only if interested. Buys one-time rights. Pays $50-75.
Illustrations: Buys 5 illustrations/issue from freelancers. Works on assignment only. Send query letter. Samples not filed are returned by SASE. Reports only if interested. To show a portfolio, mail final reproduction/product, tear sheets and photographs. Buys one-time rights. Pays $200, color, cover; $50-100, b&w, and $100, color, inside; on publication.

***BETTER HEALTH AND LIVING MAGAZINE**, 800 2nd Ave., New York NY 10017. (212)986-9600. Art Director: Cornelia Walworth. Associate Art Director: Robin Zachary. Magazine emphasizing healthy lifestyles, exercise, food, people and new products. Features general interest, how-to, interview/profile and personal experience articles. Bimonthly. Circ. 100,000. Original artwork returned after publication. Sample copy $3.

Illustrations: Buys 175 illustrations/year from freelancers. Works on assignment only. Prefers "upbeat, funky, colorful, nice healthy faces." Send query letter with brochure showing art style or tear sheets. Samples are filed. Samples not filed are returned by SASE. Reports back only if interested. Call or write to schedule an appointment to show a portfolio, or mail tear sheets or slides and color. Buys one-time rights. Payment varies.
Tips: "Call in advance or just drop off book to attention of one of us. Appointments granted if time is available."

BETTER HOMES & GARDENS, Meredith Corp., 1716 Locust, Des Moines IA 50336. Contact: Cartoon Editor. For "middle-and-up income, homeowning and community-concerned families." Monthly. Circ. 8,000,000. Original artwork not returned after publication. Free artist's guidelines.
Cartoons: Uses 2 cartoons/issue; buys all from freelancers. Receives 50-75 submissions/week from freelancers. Interested in current events, education, environment, family life, humor through youth, politics, religion, retirement, hobbies, sports and businessmen; single panel with gag line. Prefers finished cartoons. SASE. Reports in 2 weeks. Buys all rights. Pays $300 minimum, b&w line drawings; on acceptance.

BEVERAGE WORLD MAGAZINE, 150 Great Neck Rd., Great Neck NY 11021. (516)829-9210. Art Director: Alice Cosby. Managing Editor: Jeanne Lukasick. Emphasizes beverages (beers, wines, spirits, bottled waters, soft drinks, juices) for soft drink bottlers, breweries, bottled water/juice plants, wineries and distilleries. Monthly. Circ. 30,000. Accepts simultaneous submissions. Original artwork returned after publication if requested. Sample copy $2.50.
Illustrations: Uses 5 illustrations/issue; buys 3-4 illustrations/issue from freelancers. Works on assignment only. Send query letter with Photostats, slides or tear sheets to be kept on file. Write for appointment to show portfolio. Reports only if interested. Negotiates rights purchased. Pays $350 color, cover; $30, b&w, inside; on acceptance. Uses color illustration for cover. Usually black-and-white for sport illustrations inside.

BICYCLE USA, Suite 209, 6707 Whitestone Rd., Baltimore MD 21207. (301)944-3399. Art Director: David Borucki. Readers are members of BICYCLE USA; publication is also sold in bicycle stores. Monthly. Circ. 15,000. Previously published material OK "if not in overlapping market." Original artwork returned after publication. Sample copy and art guidelines available.
Cartoons: Buys 3 cartoons/year from freelancers. Interested in recreational or utilitarian use of bicycles, road design, legislation and technical topics; single panel with gagline. Send query letter with finished cartoons. Samples are filed. Samples not filed are returned. Reports back within 1 month. Buys first rights. Pays $100, b&w; on acceptance.
Illustrations: Buys 3 illustrations/year from freelancer. Works on assignment only. Send query letter with brochure or resume and slides. Samples are filed. Reports back within 1 month. Call to schedule an appointment to show a portfolio which should include thumbnails, roughs, original/final art and final reproduction/product. Buys first rights. Pays $150, color, cover; $100, b&w; $100, color,inside; on acceptance.
Tips: "Bicycle geometry is critical. Illustrations of real bicycles are preferable to ones with funny frames and parts missing."

THE BIG REEL, Rt. 3, Box 83, Madison NC 27025. (919)427-5850. Publisher: Donald R. Key. Tabloid. Emphasizes motion picture films, videotapes, movie photos and material for movie buffs and serious movie material collectors. Features general interest, historical, interview/profile and personal experience articles. "We cater to film hobbyists—anything having to do with movies and celebrities." Monthly. Circ. 5,000. Accepts previously published material. Original artwork returned after publication if requested. Sample copy $3.
Cartoons: Uses up to 3 cartoons/issue. Format open. Send query letter with finished cartoons to be kept on file. Material not kept on file returned by SASE only if requested. No payment.
Illustrations: Accepts 4 or more/issue.
Tips: "Submit movie, TV and entertainment materials . . . only!"

BIKEREPORT, Box 8308, Missoula MT 59807. (406)721-1776. Editor: Daniel D'Ambrosio. Magazine. Emphasizes long-distance bicycle touring for bicycle enthusiasts. Circ. 18,000. Accepts previously published material. Original artwork returned after publication. Sample copy and art guidelines free for SASE.
Illustrations: Uses 3-6 illustrations/issue. Themes/styles are open. Works on assignment only. Send query letter with samples to be kept on file. Samples not kept on file are returned. Reports within 1 month. To show a portfolio, mail tear sheets and Photostats. Buys first rights. Pays $75, b&w, cover; $20-50, b&w, inside; on publication.

BIRD TALK, Box 6050, Mission Viejo CA 92690. (714)240-6001. Editor: Karyn New. Magazine emphasizing information about caring for pet birds, plus entertainment for owners of pet birds. Monthly. Circ. 125,000. Accepts previously published material. Original artwork returned after publication. Sample copy $3. Art guidelines free for SASE with first-class postage.
Cartoons: Buys 2-8 cartoons/issue from freelancers. Prefers themes dealing with pet birds (some wild). No "Polly want a cracker" takeoffs! Prefers single-panel, with gagline; b&w line drawings. Send finished cartoons; to be kept on file. Samples not filed are returned by SASE. Reports within 30 days. Buys one-time rights. Pays $35, b&w.
Illustrations: Buys 1 illustration/issue from freelancers. Prefers pet birds (fairly lifelike) as themes. Send originals. Samples not filed are returned by SASE. Reports within 30 days. No portfolios. Only a few drawings need to be sent in the mail. Buys one-time rights. Pays $20-150, b&w, inside; after publication.

BIRD WATCHER'S DIGEST, Box 110, Marietta OH 45750. (614)373-5285. Editor: Mary B. Bowers. Emphasizes birds and bird watchers for "bird watchers and birders (backyard and field; veteran and novice)." Bimonthly. Circ. 40,000. Previously published material OK. Original work returned after publication. Sample copy $3.
Cartoons: Uses 1-3 cartoons/issue; buys all from freelancers. Interested in themes pertaining to birds and/or bird watchers. Single panel with or without gagline, b&w line drawings. Send roughs. Samples returned by SASE. Reports in 1 month. Buys one-time rights and reprint rights. Pays $10, b&w; on publication.

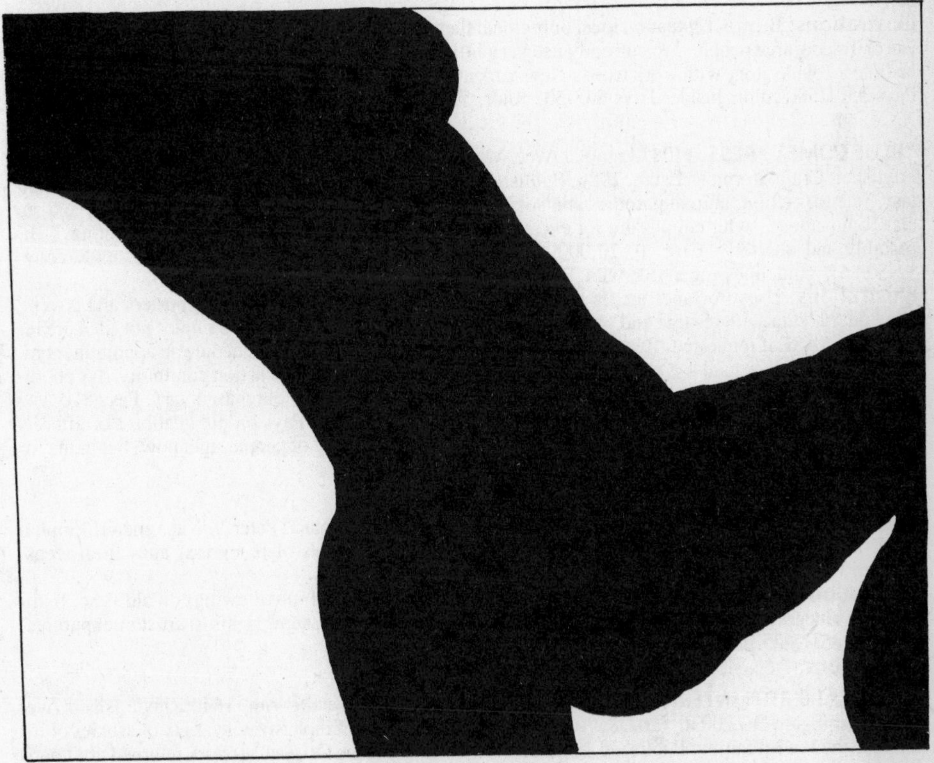

©Robert J. Bixby

Publisher Ave Jean of Black Bear Publications of Croydon, Pennsylvania bought one-time rights to this pen-and-ink silhouette for the cover of a poetry collection. Artist Robert J. Bixby of Kalamazoo, Michigan, says the image conveys a spirit of "abandon, sophistication and grit." Bixby is also a poet and found Black Bear through CODA, the magazine of Poets and Writers, Inc.

BLACK BEAR PUBLICATIONS, 1916 Lincoln St., Croydon PA 19020-8026. (215)788-3543. Editor: Ave Jeanne. Associate Editor: Ron Zettlemoyer. Magazine emphasizing social, political, ecological, environmental subjects for a mostly well-educated audience, any age group. Semiannual. Circ. 400. Accepts previously published material. Original artwork returned after publication with SASE. Sample copy $2 (for back issues); art guidelines for SASE with first-class postage. Current copy $3 postpaid in U.S. and Canada.
Illustrations: Buys 12 illustrations/issue from freelancers. Prefers collage, woodcuts, pen & ink. Send query letter with SASE, resume and photocopies. Samples not filed returned by SASE. Reports within 10 days. To show a portfolio, mail photocopies. Buys one-time rights or reprint rights. Pays in copies; on publication, for the magazine. Pays cash on acceptance for chapbook illustrators.

THE BLACK COLLEGIAN MAGAZINE, 1240 S. Broad St., New Orleans LA 70125. (504)821-5694. Art Director: Bonnie Bart. Managing Editor: Kuumba Kazi-Fettouillet. For black college students and recent graduates with a concentration on career-oriented subjects and job opportunities. Bimonthly. Circ. 171,000. Sample copy $2.50; art guidelines for SASE.
Illustrations: Uses 6 illustrations/issue; buys 4/issue from freelancers. Send query letter with samples to be kept on file; original work is returned. Prefers Photostats or tear sheets as samples. Samples not kept on file are returned by SASE only if requested. Reports within 30 days. Call or write for appointment to show portfolio. Buys one-time rights or reprint rights. Pays $150, b&w and $275, color, for covers; $20 and up for b&w and color, inside. Pays on publication.

***THE BLADE "TOLEDO" MAGAZINE**, 541 Superior St., Toledo OH 43660. Editor: Sue Stankey. Weekly. Circ. 210,000. Query. Previously published and simultaneous submissions OK. Free sample copy.
Illustrations: Buys 6-12/year on local or regional themes. "Most of our original art is done by staff artists or Toledo-area people. We currently use very little outside freelance illustration since it is hard to illustrate a Toledo story with work from a New York artist." Query. SASE. Buys one-time rights. Cover: Pays $50-150, color. Inside: Pays $35-50, color; $20-30, b&w; on publication.

***BLUE COMET PRESS**, 1708 Magnolia Ave., Manhattan Beach CA 90266. (213)545-6887. President/Publisher: Craig Stormon. Estab. 1986. Publishes limited edition comic books. Genres: adventure, fantasy, science fiction, animal parodies and social parodies. Themes: outer space, future science and social commentary. "Our comics are for everybody—for kids and grown ups. We have PG rating." Bimonthly and quarterly. Circ. 10-20,000. Original artwork returned after publication. Sample copy $2.50. Art guidelines for SASE with 1 first-class stamp.
Illustrations: Uses freelance artists for inking, lettering, pencilling, color work, posters and covers. Send query letter with resume and photocopies of work, story form 4-8 pages. Samples not filed are returned by SASE if requested. Reports back within 1 month. Call or write to schedule an appointment to show a portfolio, or mail 4-8 pages of pencil or ink drawings, 4-8 pages of action continuity, 4-8 photocopies of original pencil art or inking and 4-8 pages of lettering. Rights purchased vary. Pays $10-35/page for pencilling, $15-25/page for inking and $5-10 for lettering. Pays on publication "or after."
Tips: "We are interested in new ideas and artists. I may not need a lot of people right now, but in the future I will."

***BLUEGRASS UNLIMITED**, Box 111, Broad Run VA 22014. Contact: Peter V. Kuykendall. Emphasizes old-time traditional country music for musicians and devotees of bluegrass, ages from teens through the elderly.
Illustrations and Cartoons: Uses 5-6 pen & ink cartoons/year and spot drawings on old-time, traditional or bluegrass country music. Buys all rights, but sometimes reassigns rights to artist after publication. Pays $15-25 plus; on publication.

THE B'NAI B'RITH INTERNATIONAL JEWISH MONTHLY, B'nai B'rith, 1640 Rhode Island Ave. NW, Washington DC 20036. (202)857-6645. Editor: Marc Silver. Emphasizes a variety of articles of interest to the Jewish family. Published 10 times/year. Circ. 200,000. Original artwork returned after publication. Sample copy $1. Also uses artists for "design, lettering, calligraphy on assignment. We call or write the artist, pay on publication."
Illustrations: Buys 2 illustrations/issue from freelancers. Theme and style vary, depending on tone of story illustrated. Works on assignment only. Write or call for appointment to show portfolio, which should include tear sheets, slides or photographs. Reports within 3 weeks. Samples returned by SASE. Buys first rights. Pays $150, b&w and $250, color, cover; $100, b&w and color, inside; rates vary regarding size of illustration; on publication.

Artist: Glenn Wong

Craig Stormon, owner and president of Blue Comet Press in Manhattan Beach, California, was signing comics at a store when artist Glenn Wong showed him samples of his work. The impromptu review resulted in a continuing comic book series titled "Crime Smasher." The artwork, rendered in pen and ink, will be used for a poster, t-shirt and a portfolio piece. Stormon owns all rights.

BOATING, 1 Park Ave., New York NY 10016. (212)503-3976. Art Director: Victor Mazurkiewicz. Emphasizes boating for boat owners. Monthly. Circ. 180,000. Original artwork returned after publication.
Illustrations: Occasionally uses illustrations; buys all from freelancers. Works on assignment only. Send samples and tear sheets to be kept on file. Write or call for appointment to show portfolio. Prefers Photostats or photographs as samples. Samples returned only by SASE if not kept on file. Buys first rights. Pays $1,000, color, cover. Pays $100-500, b&w, inside; $1,000, color, 2-page spread, inside. Pays after publication.

BOSTON MAGAZINE, 300 Massachusetts Ave., Boston MA 02115. Associate Art Director: Suzanne Heine Peterman. Emphasizes regional/city subjects/issues of the Boston area for young professionals. Monthly. Circ. 110,000. Original artwork returned after publication.
Illustrations: Uses 8 illustrations/issue. Works on assignment only. Send query letter with brochure showing art style or resume and tearsheets to be kept on file. Call for appointment to show portfolio, which should include final reproduction/product, color and tear sheets. Reports only if interested. Buys first rights. Pays on publication.
Tips: "We accept no responsibility for unsolicited art work or photographs."

BOTH SIDES NOW, Rt. 6, Box 28, Tyler TX 75704. (214)592-4263. Contact: Editor. Magazine emphasizing the new age for people seeking holistic alternatives in spiritual, lifestyle and politics. Irregular publication. Circ. 2,000 printed. Accepts previously published material. Original artwork returned by SASE. Sample copy 75¢.
Cartoons: Buys various number of cartoons/issue from freelancers. Prefers fantasy, political satire, religion and exposes of hypocrisy as themes. Prefers single or multi panel; b&w line drawings. Send query letter with samples of style such as good photocopies. Samples not filed are returned by SASE. Reports within 3 months. Pays in copies only.
Illustrations: Buys variable amount of illustrations/issue from freelancers. Prefers fantasy, surrealism, spirituality and realism as themes. Send query letter with resume and photocopies. Samples not filed are returned by SASE. Reports back within 3 months. Pays in copies; on publication.

BOW & ARROW MAGAZINE, Box HH, Capistrano Beach CA 92624. (714)493-2101. Managing Editor: Roger Combs. Emphasizes bowhunting and bowhunters. Bimonthly. Original artwork not returned after publication. Art guidelines available.
Cartoons: Uses 2-3 cartoons/issue; buys all from freelancers. Prefers single panel, with gag line; b&w line drawings. Send finished cartoons. Material not kept on file returned by SASE. Reports within 2 months. Buys all rights. Pays $7.50-$10, b&w. Pays on acceptance.
Illustrations: Uses 1-2 illustrations/issue; buys all from freelancers. Prefers live animals/game as themes. Send samples. Prefers photographs or original work as samples. Especially looks for perspective, unique or accurate use of color and shading, and an ability to clearly express a thought, emotion or event. Samples returned by SASE. Reports in 2 months. Buys all rights or negotiates rights purchased. Pays $100-150, color, cover; payment for inside b&w varies. Pays on acceptance.

BOWHUNTER, Editorial Offices, 3720 S. Calhoun, Fort Wayne IN 46807. (219)456-3580. Editor-in-Chief: M.R. James. For "readers of all ages, background and experience. All share two common passions—hunting with the bow and arrow and a love of the great outdoors." Bimonthly. Circ. 180,000.
Cartoons: Uses few cartoons; but considers all submissions. Interested in "bowhunting and wildlife. No unsafe hunting conditions; single panel." Prefers to see roughs. SASE. Reports in 6 weeks. Buys all rights on a work-for-hire basis; will reassign rights. Pays $20-25, line drawings; on acceptance.
Illustrations: Buys b&w and color illustrations/issue, all from freelancers. Interested in "wildlife-bowhunting scenes." Send query letter with slides and photographs. SASE. Reports in 6 weeks. To show a portfolio, mail roughs. Buys first rights. Pays $200 color, cover; $20 + b&w and $50 + color, inside; on acceptance.
Tips: "We are presently overstocked with cartoons but need good wildlife art." Artist must convey "a feeling and understanding for the game represented. Call it atmosphere or mood, or whatever, it's something that is either there or not. The art we select for publication has this extra something the viewer immediately senses. We are using more color on inside pages. This opens up additional possibilities for freelance artists with good wildlife art. Study the magazine before contacting us. Know what we use before making suggestions or submitting ideas. Know the subject down to the finest details."

***BOWLERS JOURNAL**, John Hancock Center, 875 N. Michigan Ave., Chicago IL 60611. (312)266-7171. Managing Editor: Jim Dressel. Monthly. Circ. 22,000. Emphasizes bowling. Also uses artist for design; specific assignments to suit editorial themes. Query with previously published work.
Illustrations: Needs art to illustrate specific articles. Send query letter with brochure showing art style. SASE. Reports in 2 months. Buys one-time rights. Call to schedule an appointment to show a portfolio, which should include a representative variety of their work." Pays $200 b&w; $325 color, cover; $100 b&w; $150 color, inside; on acceptance.
Tips: "We've stepped up our use of illustration for our more conceptual articles. We've been bearing down to customize the artwork to the article rather than depend so heavily on our file of stock art. Humorous and cartoon-style illustrations are assigned on a need basis."

***BOWLING DIGEST**, 1020 Church St., Evanston IL 60201. Art Director: Thomas M. Miller. Emphasizes pro and amateur bowling. Bimonthly. Circ. 115,000. Original artwork returned after publication.
Cartoons: Considers sports themes. Prefers single panel; b&w line drawings or color washes. Send query letter. Write for appointment to show portfolio. Material not filed is returned by SASE. Reports only if interested. Pays on publication.
Illustrations: Considers sports—bowling themes. Works on assignment only. Send query letter. Write for appointment to show portfolio. Samples returned by SASE. Reports only if interested. Pays on publication.

BREAD, 6401 The Paseo, Kansas City MO 64131. (816)333-7000. Editor-in-Chief: Karen DeSollar. Christian leisure reading magazine for ages 12-17 with denominational interests. Monthly. Circ. 25,000. Previously published and simultaneous submissions OK. Free sample copy and artist's guidelines *with* SASE.
Cartoons: Buys 10 cartoons/year; buys all from freelancers. Receives 10 submissions/week from freelancers. Interested in humor through youth—teen, school, religious, dating. Prefers single panel with gagline. Prefers to see finished cartoons. Reports in 4-6 weeks. Buys first rights. Pays $6-15, b&w line drawings; on acceptance.
Illustrations: Uses 15 illustrations/year. Works on assignment only. Prefers to see samples. Pays $150-200, color, cover; $25-30, b&w, inside; on acceptance.

BREAKFAST WITHOUT MEAT, Room 188, 1827 Haight St., San Francisco CA 94117. Art Director: G. Obo. Magazine emphasizing music and satire. "We want outrageous stuff only; please no mainstream cartoons!" We have world-wide distribution, mainly to fans of humor and punk music. Quarter-

ly. Circ. 700. Sample copy $1.25. Art guidelines free for SASE with first-class postage.
Cartoons: Buys 2 cartoons/issue from freelancers. Prefers single or multi panel with gagline; b&w line drawings. Send query letter with finished cartoons. Samples not filed are returned by SASE. Reports back within 4 weeks. Negotiates rights purchased. Pays $10, b&w.

BRIGADE LEADER, Box 150, Wheaton IL 60189. (312)665-0630. For Christian laymen and adult male leaders of boys enrolled in the Brigade man-boy program. Circ. 14,000. Published 4 times/year. Original artwork returned after publication. Sample copy for $1.50 and large SASE; artist's guidelines for SASE.
Cartoons: Contact: Cartoon Editor. Uses 1 cartoon/issue, all from freelancers. Receives 3 submissions/week from freelancers. Interested in sports, nature and youth; single panel with gagline. "Keep it clean." SASE. Buys first rights only. Pays $20, b&w line drawings; on publication.
Illustrations: Art Director: Lawrence Libby. Uses 2 illustrations/issue. Interested in man and boy subjects, sports, camping—out of doors, family. Works on assignment only. Samples returned by SASE. Reports back on future assignment possibilities. Provide resume and flyer to be kept on file for future assignments. Prefers to see portfolio and samples of style. Reports in 2 weeks. Pays $85-100, for inside use of b&w line drawings and washes; on publication.
Tips: Looks for "good crisp handling of black & white line work, clean washes and skill in drawing. Copying is very obvious in amateur portfolios. Portfolios should have more printed samples of work."

BROTHERHOOD OF MAINTENANCE OF WAY EMPLOYES JOURNAL, 12050 Woodward Ave., Detroit MI 48203. Associate Editor/Director of Public Relations: R.J. Williamson. For members of international railroad workers' union who build, repair and maintain tracks, buildings and bridges. Monthly. Circ. 120,000. Previously published, photocopied and simultaneous submissions OK. Original artwork returned after publication. Free sample copy available.
Cartoons: Buys 2 cartoons/year from freelancers. Receives less than 1 submission/week from freelancers. Interested in railroad/trackwork themes; single panel with gagline, b&w line drawings. Send query letter with photocopies. Samples returned by SASE. Reports in 1 week. Buys one-time rights. Pays $10, b&w; on acceptance.

***BUILDER/DEALER** (formerly Alternative Housing Builder), 16 1st Ave., Corry PA 16407. Production Director: William Stright. Emphasizes log, dome, modular, timber, post and beam, component, precut and panelized construction and any other type of industrialized housing for kit package manufacturers and builder-dealers of these homes. Monthly. Circ. 21,500. Original artwork returned after publication if requested. Sample copy and art guidelines for SASE.
Cartoons: Buys 1-2 cartoons/issue from freelancers. Considers anything pertaining to the industrialized housing industry or the problems faced by the men and women who are building or selling these homes. Prefers single panel with or without gagline; b&w line drawings or b&w washes. Send query letter with finished cartoons, slides and photographs to be kept on file. Material not filed is returned only if requested. Reports within 2 weeks. Buys all rights. Pays $15-25, b&w; on publication.
Illustrations: Buys 1-2 illustrations/issue. Send query letter with slides, photographs and illustrations. To show a portfolio, mail appropriate materials.
Tips: "We're sprucing up the appearance of our magazine and, as such, may be more receptive to freelancer's work."

BUILDER MAGAZINE, Suite 475, 655 15th St. NW, Washington DC 20005. (202)737-0717. Art Director: Karen Polard. Emphasizes the housing industry for the National Association of Home Builders members and subscriptions. Monthly. Circ. 185,000. Original artwork not returned after publication unless requested. Sample copy and art guidelines available.
Illustrations: Uses 4-7 illustrations/issue. Prefers b&w line drawings. Works on assignment only. Send query letter with samples to be kept on file. Prefers tear sheets, Photostats or photocopies as samples. Looks for "originality, a distinct style and creativity" when reviewing samples. Reports only if interested. Buys one-time rights. Call for appointment to show portfolio. Pays $75-150, b&w; payment negotiable for color, inside. Pays on acceptance.

The asterisk before a listing indicates that the listing is new in this edition. New markets are often the most receptive to freelance submissions.

BULLETIN OF THE ATOMIC SCIENTISTS, 5801 S. Kenwood, Chicago IL 60637. (312)363-5225. Art Director: Lisa Grayson. Emphasizes arms control; science and public affairs for audience of 40% scientists, 40% politicians and policy makers, and 20% interested, educated citizens. Monthly. Circ. 25,000. Original artwork returned after publication. Sample copy $2.50; free artist's guidelines for SASE.

Cartoons: Buys about 5-10 cartoons/issue including humorous illustrations from freelancers. Considers arms control and international relation themes. "We are looking for new ideas. Please, no mushroom clouds or death's heads." Prefers single panel without gagline; b&w line drawings. Send finished cartoons. Cartoon portfolios are not reviewed. Material returned by SASE. Reports within 1 month. Buys first rights. Pays $25, b&w; on acceptance.

Illustrations: Buys 2-8 illustrations/issue from freelancers. Considers serious b&w themes. "Do not even consider sending work until you have viewed a few issues. The name of the magazine misleads artists who don't bother to check; they wind up wasting time and postage." Works on assignment only. Send query letter with brochure and samples to be kept on file, except for completely unsuitable work which is returned promptly by SASE. Artist may write or call for appointment to show portfolio but prefers mailed samples. Prefers tear sheets or Photostats as samples. Samples not filed are returned by SASE. Reports within 1 month. Buys first world-wide rights. Pays $300, b&w, cover; $100/ 1/4 page, $150/1/2 page, $250/full page, b&w, inside; on acceptance.

***BUSINESS & COMMERCIAL AVIATION**, Hangar C-1, Westchester City Airport, White Plains NY 10604. Art Director: Mildred Stone. Technical publication for corporate pilots and owners of business aircraft. Monthly. Circ. 55,000.

Illustrations: Especially needs full page spot art of a business-aviation nature. "We generally only use artists with a fairly realistic style. This is a serious business publication—graphically conservative. We have a monthly section for the commuter industry and another for the helicopter industry. These magazines will have a more consumer-magazine look and will feature more four-color illustration than we've used in the past. Need artists who can work on short deadline time." Query with samples. SASE. Reports in 4 weeks. Photocopies OK. Buys all rights, but may reassign rights to artist after publication. Pays on acceptance. Cover: Pays $350-1,100, color. Inside: Pays $100-300, color; $50-300, b&w. Pays $5/hour minimum, paste-up/mechanicals; local artists only. Pays $100 minimum, portraits of editors for monthly columns, printed size 2x3".

Tips: "Send or bring samples. I like to buy based more on style than whether an artist has done aircraft drawings before."

BUSINESS TODAY, Aaron Burr Hall, Princeton NJ 08540. (609)921-1111. Contact: Production Manager. For college undergraduates interested in business, politics and careers in those fields. Published 3 times/academic year. Circ. 205,000. Receives 10 cartoons and 2 illustrations/week from freelance artists. Especially needs illustrations and political cartoons. Query with samples to be kept on file; do not send originals, photocopies only. Will contact artists as needed. Previous work as magazine illustrator preferred. Reports in 2 months. Previously published, photocopied, and simultaneous submissions OK. Buys one-time, reprint or simultaneous rights. Pays on publication. Original artwork returned after publication. Sample copy $2.

Cartoons: Buys 4-5/issue on current events, education, environment, politics, business, college life and careers. "Keep the student readership in mind; *no typical scenes with executives and secretaries*."

Illustrations: Buys 4-5/issue on current events, education, environment, politics, college life and careers. "We like the style of *The New Yorker* and op-ed cartoons in *The New York Times*." Prefers to have samples of style and topic areas covered. Provide business card and letter of inquiry to be kept on file for future assignments. Cover: Pays $50 minimum, color; $10-20, b&w. Inside: Pays $20 minimum, color; $10 minimum, b&w; on publication.

Tips: There is a trend toward "more quality, less quantity of artwork; we like to have artwork that says something. We need both concrete and abstract photos, as long as they are of quality and in sharp focus."

BUTTER FAT MAGAZINE, Box 9100, Vancouver B.C., V6B 4G4 Canada. (604)420-6611. Managing Editor: Carol A. Paulson. Editor: Nancy L. Ryder. Emphasizes dairy farming, dairy product processing, marketing and distribution for dairy cooperative members and employees in British Columbia. Monthly. Circ. 3,500. Free sample copy and art guidelines for SAE (non-resident include IRC).

Cartoons: Uses 2 cartoons/issue; buys all from freelancers. Receives 10 submissions/week from freelancers. Interested in agriculture, dairy farming, farming families and Canadian marketing systems. No cartoons unrelated to farming, farm family life or critical of food prices. Prefers single panel b&w line drawings or washes with gagline. Send query letter with finished cartoons. Reports in 2 weeks. Negotiates rights purchased. Pays $10, b&w; on acceptance.

Illustrations: Uses 1 illustration/issue; buys mostly from freelancers. Interested in making assignments for specific issues—variable technical, food. Works on assignment only. Send brochure. Samples

not kept on file are returned by SASE. Provide resume and samples to be kept on file for possible future assignments. Reports in 2 weeks. To show a portfolio, mail original/final art. Negotiates rights purchased. Pays $75-150 minimum for b&w inside; on acceptance.
Tips: "We prefer to meet artists as well as see their work. Most assignments are short notice: 10-14 days." Prefers "gentle, nostalgic" style.

***C.S.P. WORLD NEWS**, Box 2608, Station D, Ottawa, Ontario K1P 5W7 Canada. Contact: Guy F. Claude Hamel. Concerns book reviews and poetry. Monthly.
Cartoons and Illustrations: Buys 24/year. Needs b&w. Query on cartoons; send samples for illustrations. Reports in 1 week. Negotiates pay; pays on acceptance.

***THE CALIFORNIA FIREMAN**, Suite 1, 2701 K St., Sacramento CA 95816. (916)441-4153. Editor: Grant Beebe. Fire service related magazine. "Our publication is geared towards our association's members. They are all firefighters from throughout California." Monthly. Circ. 30,000. Accepts previously published material. Original artwork sometimes returned after publication if requested. Sample copies available.
Cartoons: Prefers fire service/safety related. Send query letter with samples of style. Samples are not filed. Samples not filed are returned if requested. Reports back only if interested.
Illustrations: Prefers fire service/safety related. Send query letter. Samples not filed are returned only if requested. Reports back only if interested.

***CALIFORNIA GARDEN**, San Diego Floral Association, Casa del Prado, Balboa Park, San Diego CA 92101-1619. (619)232-5762. Editor: Elizabeth B. Glover. Magazine emphasizing horticulture. Bimonthly. Circ. 3,000. Accepts previously published material. Original artwork returned after publication. Sample copy $1.
Illustrations: "Anything pertaining to horticulture." Send query letter with photographs or illustrations. Samples not filed are returned if requested. Reports back within 15 days. Pays in 3 contributor's copies.

CALLI'S TALES, Box 1224, Palmetto FL 33561. Editor: Annice E. Hunt. Magazine emphasizing wildlife and pets for animal lovers of all ages. Quarterly. Circ. 100#. Accepts previously published material. Original artwork returned after publication. Sample copy $2. Art guidelines free for SASE with first-class postage.
Cartoons: Buys 1 cartoon/issue from freelancers. Prefers animals, wildlife and environment in good taste as themes. Prefers single panel with gagline; b&w line drawings. Send query letter with samples of style and finished cartoons to be kept on file. Samples not filed are returned by SASE. Reports back within 6 weeks. Buys one-time rights. Payment is one free copy of issue.
Illustrations: Buys 2-3 illustrations/issue from freelancers. Prefers wildlife, pets and nature scenes as themes. Send query letter with resume and tear sheets. Samples not filed are returned by SASE. Reports within 6 weeks. Payment is one free copy of issue.

CAMPUS LIFE, 465 Gundersen Dr., Carol Stream IL 60188. Art Director: Jeff Carnehl. For high school and college students. "Though our readership is largely Christian, *Campus Life* reflects the interests of all kids—music, activities, photography and sports." Monthly. Circ. 175,000. Original artwork returned after publication. "No phone calls, please. Show us what you can do."
Cartoons: Uses 3-5 single-panel cartoons/issue plus cartoon features (assigned). Receives 5 submissions/week from freelancers. Buys 50/year on high school and college education, environment, family life, humor through youth, and politics; apply to 13-23 age groups; prefers single panel, especially vertical format. Prefers to receive finished cartoons. Reports in 4 weeks. Pays $50 minimum, b&w; on acceptance.
Illustrations: Uses 2 illustrations/issue; buys all from freelancers. Receives 5 submissions/week from freelancers. Works on assignment only. "Show us what you can do, send photocopies, transparencies or tearsheets. Samples returned by SASE." Reporting time varies; is at least 2 weeks. Buys first North American serial rights; also considers second rights. Pays $250-400, color; $225-300, b&w; on acceptance.
Tips: "The best way to see what we can use is to ask for several sample copies ($2 each)."

CANADIAN FICTION MAGAZINE, Box 946, Station F, Toronto, Ontario M4Y 2N9 Canada. Editor: Geoffrey Hancock. Anthology devoted exclusively to contemporary Canadian fiction. Quarterly. Canadian artists or residents only. Sample copy $5.50.
Illustrations: Uses 16 pages of art/issue; also cover art. SAE (nonresidents include IRC). Reports in 4-6 weeks. Pays $10/page; $25, cover. Uses b&w line drawings, photographs.
Tips: "Portraits of contemporary Canadian writers in all genres are valuable for archival purposes."

CAPE COD LIFE, Box 222, Osterville MA 02655. (617)428-5706. Art Director: Betsy Morin. Magazine emphasizing Cape Cod people, places, arts and concerns for a wide range of ages, from 40-70. Bimonthly. Circ. 32,000. Original artwork returned to artists after publication. Sample copy $3; art guidelines available.
Illustrations: Buys 8-10 illustrations/issue from freelancers. Prefers Cape Cod scenes, a realistic style. "When subject is an identifiable area or building, we are more likely to use the illustration." Send query letter with tear sheets and photocopies. Samples not filed are returned by SASE. Reports back only if interested. Call or write to schedule an appointment to show a portfolio, which would include original/final art, final/reproduction/product and tear sheets. Buys one-time rights. Pays $15-30, b&w; $20-40, color, inside; on publication.

CAR CRAFT, Petersen Publishing Co., 8490 Sunset Blvd., Los Angeles CA 90069. (213)657-5100. Editor-in-Chief: Cameron Benty. Managing Editor: Tracey Hurst. Art Director: Todd Westover. "We feature articles on automotive modifications and drag racing. Monthly. Circ. 425,000. Original artwork not returned unless prior arrangement is made. Free sample copy and artist's guidelines.
Illustrations: Uses 1 or more illustrations/issue; buys 1/issue from freelancers. Interested in "automotive editorial illustration and design with a more illustrative and less technical look." Works on assignment only. Query with business card, brochure, flyer and tear sheet to be kept on file for future assignments. SASE. Reports in 2 weeks. Pays for design and illustration by the project, $100-1,000. Buys all rights on a work-for-hire basis.

***CARDIOLOGY MANAGEMENT**, 1640 5th St., Santa Monica CA 90401. Publisher: Martin Waldman. Art Director: Tom Medsger. Emphasizes medical technologial and professional news.
Illustrations: Submit brochure/flyer to be kept on file for possible future assignment. Reports only when assignment available. Buys all rights. Pays $60-up, spot art; $400, full-color cover; on acceptance.

***CAROLINA COUNTRY**, Box 27306, Raleigh NC 27611. Editor: Owen Bishop. General interest family magazine. Monthly.
Cartoons: Buys about 6/year. "We do not know from one month to the next what art we need, and when we do need it, the subject matter is specific and must be received promptly. We have a tight deadline." Submit published samples. Buys first rights. Pays $10; on acceptance.

***CAROLINA QUARTERLY**, Greenlaw Hall 066A, University of North Carolina, Chapel Hill NC 27514. Editor: Emily Stockard. Magazine emphasizing literature for libraries and readers all over the U.S. who are interested in contemporary poetry and fiction. Publishes 3 issues/year. Circ. 1,000. Returns original artwork after publication. Sample copy $5 (includes postage and handling). Art guidelines free for SASE with first-class postage.
Illustrations: Buys up to 5/issue. Prefers small b&w sketches. Send query letter with samples. Prefers photographs as samples. Reports within 2 months. Buys first rights. Pays $10, b&w, covers; and $5, b&w inside; on publication.

***CARTOONS**, 8490 Sunset Blvd., Los Angeles CA 90069. Contact: Dennis Ellefson. For young males who like cars and bikes. Original artwork returned after publication if requested.
Cartoons: Buys 150 pages of cartoon stories and 60 single panel cartoons annually. Should be well-drawn, identifiable, detailed cars. Prefers to see roughs. SASE. Reports in 2-4 weeks. Pays $75 minimum/page; $15/single panel; $15, spot drawings.
Tips: "Check out the automotive scene in *Hot Rod* and *Car Craft* magazines. And then look at *Cartoons*."

CAT FANCY, Fancy Publications Inc., Box 6050, Mission Viejo CA 92690. (714)240-6001. Editor: Linda W. Lewis. For cat owners, breeders and fanciers. Readers are men and women of all ages interested in all phases of cat ownership. Monthly. Circ. 130,000. Simultaneous submissions and previously published work OK. Sample copy $3; free artist's guidelines.
Cartoons: Buys 12/year; single, double and multi panel with gagline. "Central character should be a cat." Send query letter with Photostats or photocopies as samples. SASE. Reports in 6 weeks. Pays $20-50, b&w line drawings; on publication. Buys first rights.
Illustrations: Buys 12/year of domestic and wild cats. Send query letter with resume and samples. SASE. Reports in 6 weeks. Inside: Pays $50-125, b&w line drawings; on publication. Buys first rights.
Tips: "We need good cartoons."

CATHOLIC FORESTER, 425 W. Shuman Blvd., Naperville IL 60566. (312)983-4920. Editor: Barbara Cunningham. Magazine. "We are a fraternal insurance company but use general interest art and photos.

Audience is middle-class, many small town as well as big city readers, patriotic, somewhat conservative. We are distributed nationally." Bimonthly. Circ. 150,000. Accepts previously published material. Original artwork returned after publication if requested. Sample copy for SASE with 56¢ postage.
Cartoons: Considers "anything *funny* but it must be clean." Prefers single panel with gagline; b&w line drawings. Send query letter with roughs. Material returned by SASE if requested. Reports within 3 months; "we try to do it sooner." Buys one-time rights or reprint rights. Pays $25, b&w; on acceptance.
Illustrations: Send query letter with Photostats, tear sheets, photocopies, slides, photographs, etc. to be kept on file. Samples not filed are returned by SASE. Reports within 3 months. Write for appointment to show portfolio. Buys one-time rights or reprint rights. Payment depends on work and negotiation with artist. "We have large and small needs, so it's impossible to say." Pays on acceptance.

CATHOLIC SINGLES MAGAZINE, Box 1920, Evanston IL 60204. (312)731-8769. Founder: Fred C. Wilson. Magazine for single, widowed, separated and divorced Catholic persons. Circ. 10,000. Accepts previously published material. Original artwork returned after publication by SASE. Sample copy $3. Art guidelines free for SASE with fist-class postage.
Cartoons: Buys variable amount of cartoons/issue from freelancers. Prefers anything that deals with being single (no porn) as themes. Send query letter with finished cartoons to be kept on file. Write or call to schedule an appointment to show a portfolio. Material not filed returned by SASE only if requested. Reports only if interested. Buys one-time rights. Pays on publication.
Illustrations: Works on assignment only. Prefers anything dealing with singledom as themes. Send query letter with samples. Samples not filed returned by SASE. Reports only if interested. To show a portfolio, mail original/final art Buys one-time rights. Payment varies.

***CATS MAGAZINE**, Box 37, Port Orange FL 32029. Editor: Linda J. Walton. Emphasizes household pet cats and show cats. Monthly. Circ. 126,000. Returns original artwork after publication on request. Sample copy and art guidelines for SASE.
Cartoons: Buys 1 cartoon/issue from freelancers. Considers line work suitable for b&w publication with or without gaglines. Send finished cartoons to be kept on file. Material not filed is returned by SASE. Does not report back. Buys first rights. Payment varies; made on publication.
Illustrations: Buys 3-5 illustrations/issue from freelancers. Prefers cats or cat-oriented themes. Send samples; copies are not returned, originals are returned by SASE. Does not report back. Buys first rights. Payment varies; made on publication.

THE CATTLEMAN, 1301 W. Seventh St., Fort Worth TX 76102. (817)332-7155. For Southwestern cattle producers and cattlemen. Monthly. Circ. 19,169. Sample copy $2.
Cartoons: Contact Carolyn Brimer. Uses 3 cartoons/issue. Receives 10 submissions/week from freelancers. Interested in beef cattle raising and the Old West. Prefers single panel with gagline. Prefers to see finished cartoons. SASE. Reports in 1 month. Buys first North American serial rights. Pays $10 minimum, b&w line drawings; on acceptance.
Illustrations: Contact Dale Segraves, editor. Buys limited number of illustrations. Interested in beef cattle, raising cattle and horses, western art. Send query letter with resume and samples to be kept on file. Samples not kept on file are returned by SASE. Reports in 2 weeks. Buys first North American serial rights or buys all rights on a work-for-hire basis. Pays $100 minimum, color washes, cover. Pays $15-25, color washes and opaque watercolors; $15-20, b&w line drawings, washes and gray opaques, inside; on acceptance.

CAVALIER, Dugent Publishing Corp., 2355 Salzedo St., Coral Gables FL 33134. Contact: Nye Willden. "For young men and college students interested in good fiction, articles and sex." Monthly. Circ. 250,000. Sample copy $3; guidelines free. Receives 50-75 cartoons and 3-4 illustrations/week from freelance artists. Original work only; no simultaneous submissions.
Cartoons: Buys 5/issue on erotica; single panel with gagline. Send query letter with samples. SASE. Reports in 2 weeks. Buys first rights. Pays $50-100, b&w line drawings and washes; 30 days before publication.
Illustrations: Buys 3/issue on erotica and assigned themes, including some humorous and cartoon-style illustrations. Works on assignment only. Send query letter with samples. SASE. Reports in 2 weeks. Buys first rights. Pays $150 minimum, b&w line drawings and washes; $200/page, $300/spread, color washes and full-color work, inside; 30 days before publication.
Tips: "Send 35mm slide samples of your work that art director can *keep* in his file, or tear sheets of published work. We have to have samples to refer to when making assignments. Large portfolios are difficult to handle and return. Also send samples *related* to our publication, i.e., erotica or nude studies. We are an excellent market for unpublished but very talented artists and cartoonists. Many of the top people in both fields — Mort Drucker, Peter Max, Ed Arno, Sid Harris—started with us, and many of them still work for us. Study *our* magazine for samples of acceptable material. *Do not submit* original artwork for our evaluation; slides, photos or stats only."

CENTRAL PARK/A JOURNAL OF THE ARTS & SOCIAL THEORY, Box 1446, New York NY 10023. (212)382-9151. Co-editor; Stephen-Paul Martin. Magazine emphasizing experimental or politically progressive statements of art and social theory for intellectuals and artists of all kinds. Twice/year. Circ. 1,000. Accepts previously published material. Original artwork returned after publication. Sample copy $5. Art guidelines free for SASE with first-class postage.
Illustrations: Also accepts photographs and collages. Buys 20 illustrations/issue from freelancers. Prefers social realism, surrealism and expressionalism as themes. Send resume and photographs. Samples not filed returned by SASE. Reports within 6 weeks. Buys first rights. "Until further notice, payment is two copies of the issue in which the work appears."
Tips: "Artists should keep in mind that our medium is the 8x10 page and that their artwork will be considered in relation to experimental and political literary texts."

***CENTRIFUGAL BUMBLE PUPPY**, 4359 Cornell Rd., Agoura CA 91301. Editor: Joe Sacco. Monthly magazine of cartoon humor and fiction. Cir. 10,000. Original artwork is returned after publication. Sample copy $3.50.
Cartoons: "Gags or strips with a bit of biting satire (cultural, political, etc.) are desired but not a requirement. Being funny is. No preferred format. That's up to the artist." Send query letter with samples. Samples are filed. Reports back within 1 month. Buys one-time North American rights. Pays $30/page for everything; on publication.

CHAIN STORE AGE, 425 Park Ave., New York NY 10022. (212)371-9400. Emphasizes retail stores. Readers are buyers, retail executives, merchandise managers, vice presidents of hard lines and store personnel. Monthly. Circ. 30,000.
Cartoons: Occasional use of line art *by assignment only*. Send samples of style to art director. SASE. Keeps file on artists. Pays $50-125 on publication for b&w cartoons. Buys all rights on a work-for-hire-basis.
Illustrations: Uses 1-2 illustrations/issue, all from freelancers. We "keep samples on file; must be in NY area. Must see portfolio." Uses inside b&w line drawings and washes, four-color cover. Send roughs, tear sheets and samples of style, and/or arrange personal appointment to show portfolio to art director. SASE. Reports in 1 week. Pays $50-125 on publication for inside b&w, $300 maximum for color cover, $150-250 for inside color. Buys all rights.

CHANGING TIMES, 1729 H St. NW, Washington DC 20006. Cartoon Editor: Joseph Yacinski. For general, adult audience interested in personal finance, family money management and career advancement. Monthly.
Cartoons: Buys 1 cartoon/issue from freelancers. Receives 800 submissions/month from freelancers. Interested in financial topics, home budgeting, insurance, stocks, taxes, etc. or of seasonal nature. Uses 1 cartoon/month on letters to editor page. Send query letter with tear sheets. Prefers to see finished drawings. SASE. Reports in 1 month. Pays $250, b&w; on acceptance.

CHARIOT, Ben Hur Life Association, Box 312, Crawfordsville IN 47933. Editor: Loren Harrington. Emphasizes fraternal activities and general interest for members of the Association, a fraternal life insurance benefit society. Quarterly. Circ. 10,000. Accepts previously published material. Original artwork returned after publication if requested. Sample copy for 9x12 SASE with 88¢ postage; art guidelines for #10 SASE with first-class postage.
Cartoons: Rarely buys cartoons from freelancers. Considers humor and some satire. Prefers single panel with gagline; b&w line drawings or washes. Send finished cartoons to be kept on file. Material not filed is returned by SASE. Reports within 1 month. Negotiates rights purchased. Pays $1-20; on acceptance.
Illustrations: Rarely buys illustrations from freelancers but may work on assignment basis. Prefers line and wash, b&w only. Send query letter with resume and samples to be kept on file. Write for appointment to show portfolio. Accepts any type of sample that portrays quality of work. Reports in 1 month. Negotiates rights purchased and payment. Pays by the project, $5-200. Pays on acceptance, sometimes on publication.

CHARLOTTE MAGAZINE, Box 36639, Charlotte NC 28236. (704)375-8034. Editor: Diane Clemens. Consumer magazine emphasizing lifestyle of the inhabitants of Charlotte, North Carolina. Features general interest, historical, interview/profile and travel articles. Monthly. Circ. 20,000. Does not accept previously published material. Original artwork sometimes returned after publication. Sample copy $3.
Cartoons: Buys various number of cartoons/issue from freelancers. Prefers single panel, b&w line drawings, b&w and color washes. Send query letter with samples of style. Samples are filed. Reports back within 2 weeks. Pays $20, b&w; $50, color.
Illustrations: Buys various number of illustrations/issue from freelancers. Works on assignment only. Send query letter with resume and tear sheets. Samples are filed. Samples not filed are returned by

SASE. Reports back wtihin 2 w[illegible]tment to show a portfolio, which should include thumbnail[illegible]color and b&w. Buys first rights. Pays $20-50, b&w; $50, [illegible]
Tips: "Contact editor before submitting art."

CHESS LIFE, 186 Route 9W, New Windsor NY 12550. (914)562-8350. Art Director: Bruce R. Helm. Official publication of the United States Chess Federation. Contains news of major chess events with special emphasis on American players, plus columns of instruction, general features, historical articles, personality profiles, cartoons, quizzes, humor and short stories. Monthly. Circ. 56,000. Accepts previously published material and simultaneous submissions. Sample copy for SASE with $1.07 postage; art guidelines for SASE with first-class postage.
Cartoons: Buys 1-2 cartoons/issue from freelancers. All cartoons must have a chess motif. Prefers single panel, with gagline; b&w line drawings. Send query letter with brochure showing art style. "We may keep a few cartoons on hand, but most are either bought or returned." Material not kept on file returned by SASE. Reports within 2-4 weeks. Negotiates rights purchased. Pays $10-25, b&w; on publication.
Illustrations: Buys 1-2 illustrations/issue from freelancers. All must have a chess motif; uses some humorous and occasionally cartoon-style illustrations. "We use mainly b&w." Works on assignment, but will also consider unsolicited work. Send query letter with Photostats or original work for b&w; slides for color, or tear sheets to be kept on file. Reports within 4 weeks. Call to schedule an appointment to show a portfolio, which should include roughs, original/final art, final reproduction/product and tear sheets. Negotiates rights purchased. Pays by the project, $25-150. Pays on publication.
Tips: "I look for work that is clean, well-executed, well thought out and which will reproduce well in print."

CHICAGO, 414 N. Orleans, Chicago IL 60610. (312)565-5100. Editor: Hillel Levin. Art Director: Cynthia Hoffman. For active, well-educated, high-income residents of Chicago's metropolitan area concerned with quality of life and seeking insight or guidance into diverse aspects of urban/suburban life. Monthly. Circ. 220,000. Original artwork returned after publication.
Illustrations: Uses 7-8 illustrations/issue, all from freelancers. Interested in "subjective approach often, but depends on subject matter." Works on assignment only. Query with brochure, flyer and tear sheets, Photostats, photocopies, slides and photographs to be kept on file. Accepts finished art, transparencies or tear sheets as samples. Samples not filed are returned by SASE. Reports in 4 weeks. Call to schedule an appointment to show a portfolio, which should include original/final art, tear sheets and Photostats. Buys first North American serial rights. Negotiates pay for covers, color-separated and reflective art. Inside: Pays $600, color; $400 minimum, b&w ($100-200 for spot illustrations); on publication.

CHIEF FIRE EXECUTIVE, 33 Irving Place, New York NY 10003. (212)475-5400. Managing Editor: A. Saly. Art Director: Michael B. Delia. Estab. 1986. Magazine emphasizing management issues relative to community fire protection for fire chiefs, corporate safety officers, fire marshals, architects and engineers. Bimonthly. Circ. 42,000. Accepts previously published material. Sample copy and art guidelines for SASE.
Cartoons: Uses various cartoons/issue. Send query letter with finished cartoons. Call to schedule an appointment to show a portfolio. Material not filed is returned by SASE. Reports only if interested. Buys one-time rights.
Illustrations: Buys various illustrations/issue from freelancers. Works on assignment only. Send query letter with resume and tear sheets. Samples not filed are not returned. Reports only if interested. Call to schedule an appointment to show a portfolio, which should include tear sheets. Buys one-time rights. Pays $100-800; on publication.
Tips: "I prefer realistic over a cartoon or looser style. I like very tight drawings."

CHILD LIFE, 1100 Waterway Blvd., Box 567, Indianapolis IN 46206. (317)636-8881. Art Director: Janet K. Moir. For children 7-9. Monthly except bimonthly February/March, April/May, June/July and August/September. Receives 3-4 submissions/week from freelance artists. Sample copy 75¢.
Illustrations: Buys 30 (average)/year on assigned themes. Especially needs health-related (exercise, safety, nutrition, etc.) themes, and stylized and realistic styles of children 7-9 years old. Send query letter with brochure showing art style or resume and tear sheets, Photostats, photocopies, slides, photographs and SASE. Especially looks for an artist's ability to draw well consistently. SASE. Reports in 4 weeks. To show a portfolio, mail appropriate materials or call or write to schedule an appointment; portfolio should include original/final art, b&w and 2-color and/or 4-color pre-separated art. Buys all rights. Pays $225/illustration, color, cover. Pays for illustrations inside by the job, $60-125 (4-color), $50-100 (2-color), $25-65/page (b&w); thirty days after completion of work. "All work is considered work for hire."

Tips: "I look for the ability to accurately portray children's ages and to portray children in group situations. Consistency of style and the ability to tell a story in pictures is very important. I see lots of very well done single illustrations when I really need to see how the artist can tell the story with pictures. Artists should obtain copies of the magazine to ensure proper submission of art styles. I rarely have a need for cartoons or 'cutesy' animals and kids, for example."

***CHILDREN'S ALBUM**, Box 6086, Concord CA 94524. Literary Editor: Debra Wittenberg. Crafts Editor: Kathy Madsen. Magazine featuring children's stories and plays written by children 8-14. Quarterly. Original artwork is returned after publication if SASE enclosed. Sample copy $3.
Cartoons: Buys 1-5 cartoons/issue from freelancers. Interested in "anything having to do with children's lives, creative writing or crafts. Seasonal, holidays, children at school, at play, with families. Pensive, humorous, inspiring, sense of accomplishment." Prefers single panel, double panel, multi panel, with or without gagline; b&w line drawings. Send finished cartoons. Samples are filed. Samples not filed are returned by SASE. Reports back within 2 months. Buys all rights. Pays $5-20, b&w.
Illustrations: Covers only. Pays $50 on publication.

***CHILDREN'S DIGEST**, Box 567, Indianapolis IN 46206. (317)636-8881. Art Director: Lisa A. Nelson. Special emphasis on health, nutrition, safety and exercise for boys and girls 8-10 years of age. Monthly except bimonthly February/March, April/May, June/July and August/September. Accepts previously published material and simultaneous submissions. Sample copy 75¢; art guidelines free for SASE.
Illustrations: Uses 25-35 illustrations/issue. Works on assignment only. Send query letter with brochure, resume, samples and tear sheets to be kept on file. Write for appointment to show portfolio. Prefers Photostats, slides and good photocopies as samples. Samples returned by SASE if not kept on file. Reports within 4 weeks. Buys all rights. Pays $225, color, cover; $25-65, b&w; $50-100, 2-color; $60-125, 4-color, inside. Pays on acceptance. "All artwork is considered work for hire."
Tips: Likes to see situation and story-telling illustrations with more than 1 figure. When reviewing samples, especially looks for artists' ability to bring a story to life with their illustrations. "Contemporary artists, by and large, are more experimental in the use of their mediums, and are achieving a greater range of creativity. We are aware of this and welcome the artist who can illustrate a story that will motivate a casual viewer to read."

CHILDREN'S PLAYMATE, Box 567, Indianapolis IN 46206. (317)636-8881. Art Director: Linda Simmons. For ages 5-7; special emphasis on health, nutrition, exercise and safety. Published 8 times/year. Sample copy sent if artist's work might be used.
Illustrations: Uses 25-35 illustrations/issue; buys 10-20 from freelancers. Interested in "stylized, humorous, realistic themes; also nature and health." Especially needs b&w and 2-color artwork for line or halftone reproduction; text and full-color cover art. Works on assignment only. Prefers to see portfolio and samples of style. SASE. Provide brochure or flyer, tear sheet, stats or good photocopies of sample art to be kept on file. Buys all rights on a work-for-hire basis. Pays $225, 4-color, cover; $25-65, b&w; $50-100, 2-color; $60-125, full-color inside. Will also consider b&w art, camera-ready for puzzles, such as dot-to-dot, hidden pictures, crosswords, etc. Payment will vary. "All artwork is considered work for hire."
Tips: "Look at our publication prior to coming in; it is for *children*. Also, gain some experience in preparation of two-color and four-color overlay separations."

CHINA PAINTER, 2641 N.W. 10th St., Oklahoma City OK 73107. (405)521-1234 or (405)943-3841. Founder/Trustee: Pauline Salyer. Emphasizes porcelain china painting for those interested in the fine art. Bimonthly. Circ. 9,000. Original artwork returned after publication. Sample copy $2.75 plus 95¢ postage.
Illustrations: Send query letter. Prefers art designs in color or photographs of hand-painted porcelain china art as samples. Samples returned by SASE only if requested.

THE CHRISTIAN CENTURY, 407 S. Dearborn St., Chicago IL 60605. (312)427-5380. Production Manager: Eugene Roehlkepartain. Emphasizes religion and comments on social, political and religious subjects; includes news of current religious scene, book reviews, humor. Weekly. Circ. 38,000. Original artwork not returned after publication. Sample copy free for SASE.
Cartoons: Occasionally uses cartoons. Prefers social, political, religious (non-sexist) issues. Prefers single panel with gagline; b&w line drawings. Send query letter with finished cartoons to be kept on file unless "we can't possibly use them." Material not filed is returned only if requested. Reports only if interested. Buys one-time rights. Pays $20, b&w; on publication.
Illustrations: Uses 4 illustrations/issue; buys 1-2 from freelancers. Prefers religious and general scenes, people at various activities, books. Send query letter with resumes and photocopies to be kept on file. Samples not filed are returned by SASE. Reports only if interested. Buys one-time rights. Pays

$50, cover and $20, inside b&w; on publication.
Tips: "Because of our newsprint, bold, uncluttered styles work the best. Too much detail gets lost. We need more inclusive illustrations—non-sexist."

CHRISTIAN HERALD, 40 Overlook Dr., Chappaqua NY 10514. (914)769-9000. Editor: Dean Merrill. Grassroots magazine for Christian adults (30 and up); specializes in people stories, real-life examples. Monthly. Circ. 180,000. Original artwork returned after publication. Receives 3 illustrations/week from freelance artists. Sample copy $2.
Cartoons: Should have religious flavor.
Illustrations: Uses 2-3 illustrations/issue; buys all from freelancers. Prefers pen & ink, airbrush, washes, oils, acrylics; "pencil drawings are unacceptable." Works on assignment only. Send query letter with resume and tear sheets, Photostats and slides. Samples not kept on file are returned by SASE. Reports in 4 weeks or less. Negotiates rights purchased. Pays $75-200 inside, b&w line drawings or b&w washes; $100-350 inside, color washes; upon publication.
Tips: "Present your best work only, and make contacting you as easy as possible."

CHRISTIAN HOME & SCHOOL, 3350 E. Paris Ave. SE, Grand Rapids MI 49508. (616)957-1070. Associate Editor: Judy Zylstra. Emhasizes current, crucial issues affecting the Christian home for parents who support Christian education. Published 8 times/year. Circ. 13,000. Original artwork returned after publication. Sample copy free for SASE with 75¢ postage; art guidelines free for SASE with 22¢ postage.
Illustrations: Buys approximately 2 illustrations/issue from freelancers. Prefers family or school life themes. Works on assignment only. Send query letter with resume, tear sheets, photocopies or photographs. Samples returned by SASE. Reports only if interested. Buys first rights. Pays on publication.

THE CHRISTIAN MINISTRY, 407 S. Dearborn St., Chicago IL 60605. (312)427-5380. For the professional clergy (primarily liberal Protestant). Bimonthly. Circ. 12,000.
Cartoons: Buys 3 cartoons/issue on local church subjects. Send query letter with brochure showing art style or resume, tear sheets, Photostats, photocopies and photographs. SASE. Reports in 2 weeks. Pays $20 minimum, b&w; on publication.
Illustrations: Uses 4 spot drawings/issue on local church issues; preaching, counseling, teaching, etc. Illustrations and cartoons should reflect the diversity of professional clergy—male, female, black, white, young, old, etc. To show a portfolio, mail thumbnails, original/final art, final reproduction/product, Photostats, photographs and b&w. Pays $50, b&w, cover; $20, b&w, inside; on publication.
Tips: "We tend to use more abstract than concrete artwork. We insist on a balance between portrayals of male and female clergy."

THE CHRONICLE OF THE HORSE, Box 46, Middleburg VA 22117. Editor: John Strassburger. Emphasizes horses and English horse sports for dedicated competitors who ride, show and enjoy horses. Weekly. Circ. 22,000. Occasionally accepts previously published material. Sample copy available.
Cartoons: Buys 1-2 cartoons/issue from freelancers. Considers anything about English riding and horses. Prefers single panel with or without gagline; b&w line drawings or b&w washes. Send query letter with finished cartoons to be kept on file if accepted for publication. Material not filed is returned. Reports within 2 weeks. Buys first rights. Pays $20, b&w; on publication.
Illustrations: "We use a work of art on our cover every week. The work must feature horses, but the medium is unimportant. We do not pay for this art, but we always publish a short blurb on the artist and his or her equestrian involvement, if any." Send query letter with samples to be kept on file until published. If accepted, insists on high-quality, b&w 8x10 photographs of the original artwork. Samples are returned. Reports within 2 weeks.

THE CHURCHMAN, 1074 23rd Ave. N., St. Petersburg FL 33704. (813)894-0097. Editor: Edna Ruth Johnson. Published 9 times/year. Circ. 10,000. Original artwork returned after publication. Sample copy available.
Cartoons: Uses 2-3 cartoons/issue. Interested in religious, political and social themes. Prefers to see finished cartoons. SASE. Reports in 1 week. Pays on acceptance.
Illustrations: Uses 2-3 illustrations/issue. Interested in themes with "social implications." Prefers to see finished art. Provide tear sheet to be kept on file for future assignments. SASE. Reports in 1 week. Pays $5, b&w spot drawings; on acceptance.
Tips: "Read current events news so you can apply it humorously."

CINCINNATI MAGAZINE, Suite 300, 35 E. 7th St., Cincinnati OH 45202. (513)421-4300. Editor: Laura Pulfer. Art Director: Thomas Hawley. Emphasizes Cincinnati living. For college-educated, ages 25+ with an excess of $35,000 incomes. Monthly. Circ. 30,000. Previously published and simultane-

ous submissions OK. Original artwork returned after publication. Buys all rights. Pays on acceptance.
Cartoons: Uses 2 cartoons/issue, all from freelancers. Receives 3 submissions/week from freelancers. Interested in current events, education and politics; single panel. Send finished cartoons. SASE. Reports in 3 weeks. Buys all rights on a work-for-hire basis. Pays $15-25, b&w washes; on acceptance.
Illustrations: Uses 3 illustrations/issue, all from freelancers. Receives 3 illustrations/week from freelance artists. Buys cover art and article illustrations on assigned themes. Works on assignment only. Prefers to see portfolio or samples of style. Samples returned by SASE. Reports in 3 weeks. Buys all rights on a work-for-hire basis.

CINEFANTASTIQUE, Box 270, Oak Park IL 60303. Editor-in-Chief: Frederick S. Clarke. Emphasizes science fiction, horror and fantasy films for "devotees of 'films of the imagination.' " Bimonthly. Circ. 20,000. Original artwork not returned after publication. Sample copy $6.
Cartoons: Buys 0-1 cartoon/issue; buys all from freelancers. Interested in a variety of themes suited to magazine's subject matter; formats vary. Send query letter with resume and samples of style. Samples not returned. Reports in 3-4 weeks. Buys all rights. Pays $75/page or proportionally for fraction thereof; b&w; on publication.
Illustrations: Uses 1-2 illustrations/issue; buys all from freelancers. Interested in "dynamic, powerful styles, though not limited to a particular look." Works on assignment only. Send query letter with resume, brochure and samples of style to be kept on file. Samples not returned. Reports in 3-4 weeks. Buys all rights. Pays $75 maximum, inside b&w line drawings; $75 maximum, inside b&w washes; $150 maximum, cover color washes; $75 maximum, inside color washes; on publication.

CIRCLE TRACK MAGAZINE, 8490 Sunset Blvd., Los Angeles CA 90069. (213)854-2350. Art Director: Mike Austin. Magazine emphasizing oval-track racing for enthusiasts, ages 18-40. Monthly. Circ. 100,000. Original artwork returned after publication. Sample copy and art guidelines available.
Cartoons: Buys 3-4 cartoons/issue from freelancers. Prefers technical, automotive themes. Prefers single panel, b&w line drawings. Send samples of style to be kept on file. Call for appointment to show portfolio. Material not filed is returned. Reports only if interested. Negotiates rights purchased. Pays $100, b&w; $200, color.
Illustrations: Buys 0-1 illustrations/issue from freelancers. Works on assignment only. Prefers automotive themes. Send resume. Samples not filed are returned. Reports only if interested. Call to schedule an appointment to show a portfolio, which should include original/final art. Negotiates rights purchased. Pays $200, b&w; $400, color, inside; on publication.

CIVIL WAR TIMES ILLUSTRATED, Box 8200, 2245 Kohn Rd., Harrisburg PA 17105. (717)657-9555. Art Director: Jeanne Collins. For the general public interested in well-researched historical articles. Monthly except July and August. Circ. 120,000.
Illustrations: Works on assignment only. Prefers American history (1861-1865) themes. Send query letter with Photostats of historical illustration work to be kept on file. Provide rates and deadline requirements with work samples. SASE. Reports in 4 weeks. Pays $10-500, b&w or color; on acceptance or publication.
Tips: "Please send photostatic samples of historical illustration work, to be kept on file. We accept no unsolicited submissions. All freelance work is on assignment. All freelancers should provide their rates and deadline requirements with work samples. We use no cartoons."

CLAVIER, 200 Northfield Rd., Northfield IL 60093. Editor: Barbra Barlow Kreader. For teachers and students of keyboard instruments. Published 10 times/year. Buys all rights. Sample copy available with magazine-sized SASE.
Cartoons: Buys 10-20/year on music, mostly keyboard music. Receives 1 set of cartoons/week from freelance artists. Pays $15 on acceptance.

CLEVELAND MAGAZINE, 1621 Euclid Ave., Cleveland OH 44115. (216)771-2833. City magazine emphasizing local news and information. Monthly. Circ. 50,000.
Illustrations: Buys 5-6 editorial illustrations/issue on assigned themes. Sometimes uses humorous illustrations. Send query letter with brochure showing art style or samples. Call or write to schedule an appointment to show a portfolio, which should include original/final art, final reproduction/product, color, tear sheets and photographs. Payment varies.
Tips: "Artists used on the basis of talent. We use many talented college graduates just starting out in the field. We do not publish gag cartoons but do print editorial illustrations with a humorous twist. Full page editorial illustrations usually deal with local politics, personalities and stages of general interest. Generally, we are seeing more intelligent solutions to illustration problems and better techniques."

CLUBHOUSE, Box 15, Berrien Springs MI 49103. (616)471-9009. Editor: Elaine Meseraull. Magazine emphasizing stories, puzzles and illustrations for children ages 9-15. Published 10 times/year. Circ. 17,000. Accepts previously published material. Returns original artwork after publication if requested. Sample copy for SASE with postage for 3 oz.
Cartoons: Buys 2/issue. Prefers animals, kids and family situation themes; single panel with gagline, vertical format; b&w line drawings. Accepts previously published material. Pays $10-12 on acceptance.
Illustrations: Buys 19-20/issue on assignment only. Assignments made on basis of samples on file. Send query letter with resume and samples to be kept on file. Samples returned by SASE within 1 month. Portfolio should include final reproduction/product, tear sheets, Photostats and b&w. Usually buys one-time rights. Pays according to published size: $30 b&w, cover; $25 full page, $18 half page, $15 third page, $12 quarter page, $7.50 spots, b&w inside; on acceptance.
Tips: Prefers "natural, well-proportioned, convincing expressions for people, particularly kids."

***COAL AGE**, 1221 Avenue of the Americas, New York NY 10920. (212)512-6518. Art Director: Barney Edelman. Trade journal emphasizing coal mining. Features technical articles on coal mining engineers and owners. Monthly. Circ. 30,000. Original artwork is returned after publication.
Illustrations: Buys various amount of illustrations/issue from freelancers. Works on assignment only. Send brochure or resume, tear sheets and photocopies. Samples are filed. Samples not filed are not returned. Does not report back. Call to schedule an appointment to show a portfolio or mail original/final art, tear sheets, slides, color and b&w. Buys first rights, one-time rights or reprint rights. Pays on acceptance.

COBBLESTONE MAGAZINE, 20 Grove St., Peterborough NH 03458. (603)924-7209. Editor: Carolyn Yoder. Emphasizes American history; features stories, supplemental nonfiction, fiction, biographies, plays, activities, poetry for children between 8 and 14. Monthly. Circ. 45,000. Accepts previously published material and simultaneous submissions. Sample copy $3.95. Material must relate to theme of issue; subjects/topics published in guidelines which are available for SASE.
Illustrations: Uses variable number of illustrations/issue; buys 1-2/issue from freelancers. Prefers historical theme as it pertains to a specific feature. Works on assignment only. Send query letter with brochure, resume, business card, photocopies or tear sheets to be kept on file. Samples not kept on file are returned by SASE. Write for appointment to show portfolio. Buys all rights. Payment varies. Artists should request illustration guidelines. Pays on publication.
Tips: "Study issues of the magazine for style used. Send samples and update samples once or twice a year to help keep your name and work fresh in our minds."

COINS MAGAZINE, 700 E. State St., Iola WI 54990. (715)445-2214. Editor: Arlyn G. Sieber. Emphasizes coin collecting as a hobby or business for collectors of all forms of coins, paper money, medals, etc. Monthly. Circ. 70,000. Previously published material and simultaneous submissions OK. Original artwork not returned after publication. Sample copy for SASE.
Illustrations: Buys 1-2/issue from freelancers. Works on assignment only. Provide brochure and samples to be kept on file. Reports in 2 weeks. Buys first rights and reprint rights. Pays $10-50, inside b&w line drawings; $10-50, inside b&w washes; $75-200, cover color washes; $25-100, inside color washes; on acceptance.

***COLLEGIATE MICROCOMPUTER**, Rose-Hulman Institute of Technology, Terre Haute IN 47803. (812)877-1511. Managing Editor: Brian J. Winkel. Emphasizes uses of microcomputers in *all* areas of college life, teaching, administration, residence, recreation, etc. for college libraries, college faculty and college students. Quarterly. Circ. 5,000. Original artwork returned after publication. Accepts previously published material and simultaneous submissions.
Cartoons: Plans to use 8-10 cartoons/issue. Prefers activities surrounding microcomputers and the educational environment—spoofs of uses—as themes. Prefers single, double, or multi panel, with or without gagline; b&w line drawings or b&w washes. Query with samples of style, roughs or finished cartoons to be kept on file. Material not kept on file is returned by SASE. Reports within 2 weeks. Negotiates rights purchased and payment. Pays on acceptance.

COLLISION MAGAZINE, Box M, Franklin MA 02038. (617)528-6211. Has an audience of new car dealers, auto body repair shops, and towing companies. Articles are directed at the managers of these small businesses. Published 9 times/year. Circ. 28,000. Prefers original material but may accept previously published material. Sample copy $3.
Cartoons: Buys 1 cartoon/issue. Prefers themes that are positive or corrective in attitude. Send rough versions or finished cartoons. Reports back in 2 weeks or samples returned by SASE. Buys first rights and reprint rights. Pays $12.50/single panel b&w line cartoon.
Illustrations: Buys about 2 illustrations/issue from freelancers based upon a 2-year advance editorial

schedule. "A query letter with samples, tear sheets or photocpies of art is helpful." Samples are returned within 2 weeks. Buys first rights or reprint rights. Pays $25 and up for b&w illustrations; on acceptance.

THE COLORADO ALUMNUS, Koenig Alumni Center, University of Colorado, Boulder CO 80309. (303)492-8484. Editor: Ronald A. James. For university administrators, alumni, librarians and legislators. Published 6 times/year. Circ. 94,000. Previously published work and simultaneous submissions OK. Original artwork not returned after publication. Free sample copy.
Cartoons: Uses 1 cartoon/issue from freelancers. Receives 2-3 submissions/week from freelancers. Interested in sports, humor through youth, environment, campus and problems in higher education. Prefers to see finished cartoons. SASE. Reports in 2 weeks. "Work becomes the property of the University of Colorado." Pays $25 minimum, line drawings and halftones; on acceptance.
Illustrations: Uses 2-3 illustrations/issue from freelancers. Receives 1-2 submissions/week from freelancers. Interested in sports, campus and higher education. Send query letter with samples, SASE. Reports in 2 weeks. "Work becomes the property of the University of Colorado." Call or write to schedule an appointment to show a portfolio, which should include roughs, original/final art and final reproduction/product. Pays $25 minimum, b&w line drawings cover and inside; on acceptance.

COLUMBIA, Drawer 1670, New Haven CT 06507. (203)772-2130, ext. 263-64. Editor: Elmer Von Feldt. Art Director: John Cummings. Fraternal magazine of the Knights of Columbus; indepth interviews on family life, social problems, education, current events and apostolic activities as seen from the Catholic viewpoint. Monthly. Circ. 1,405,411. Original artwork not returned after publication. Buys all rights. Sample copy available.
Cartoons: Buys 3 cartoons/issue from freelancers. Interested in pungent, captionless humor. Send roughs or finished cartoons to be kept on file. SASE. Reports in 2 weeks. Buys all rights. Pays $50; on acceptance.
Illustrations: Buys 1 cover illustration/issue; buys all from freelancers. Send query letter with tear sheets or slides to be kept on file for future assignments. SASE. Reports in 4 weeks. To show a portfolio, mail color, tear sheets and photographs. Buys all rights. Pays $1,000, full-color cover design; on acceptance.

COLUMBIA JOURNALISM REVIEW, 700 Journalism Bldg., Columbia University, New York NY 10027. Contact: Managing Editor or Art Director. Emphasizes analysis of the performance of various communications media. For professional journalists, government leaders, opinion makers and students. Bimonthly. Circ. 33,000. Query with resume and samples. Previously published work OK. Original artwork returned after publication.
Illustrations: Uses 1-10 illustrations/issue, all from freelancers. Interested in political and satirical themes and caricatures. Works on assignment only. Samples returned "only if necessary"; prefers "photocopies or other disposable material." Reports back on future assignment possibilities. Provide calling card, brochure, flyer, tear sheet or photocopies to be kept on file for future assignments. Prefers to see portfolio or samples of style. Reporting time varies. Buys one-time reproduction rights. Pays $500-800; 4-color. Inside: Pays $100-200, spot drawings; on publication.

COLUMBUS MONTHLY, Columbus Monthly Publishing Corp., 171 E. Livingston Ave., Columbus OH 43215. (614)464-4567. Editor: Max S. Brown. Art Director: Jane Fuller. Regional/city publication. Emphasizes subjects of general interest primarily to Columbus and central Ohio. Circ. 40,000. Sample copy $1.75.
Illustrations: Uses 4-6 illustrations/month; buys most from freelancers. Interested in contemporary editorial illustration. Works on assignment only. Samples returned with SASE. Provide resume, business card, letter of inquiry and brochure or tear sheets to be kept on file for future assignments. Prefers to see portfolio (finished art). Buys publication rights. Pays $200-350, color washes and full-color art, cover; $75 minimum, b&w line drawings and washes, inside.

***COMICO THE COMIC COMPANY**, 1547 DeKalb St., Norristown PA 19401. Editor-in-Chief: Diana Schutz. Publishes limited edition comic books and graphic novels. Titles include *Elementals*, *Grendel*, *Jonny Quest*, *Justice Machine*, *Robotech The Macross Saga*, *Robotech The New Generation*, *Robotech Masters*, *Star Blazers*, *Gumby*, *Fathom*, *Rocketeer Adventure Magazine*, *The World of Ginger Fox*, *Space Ghost*, *Night and the Enemy* and *Rio*. "We are not restrictive in our choice of material and are willing to look at any and all genres. All of our publications strive to maintain a high degree of quality, both in art and writing. Comico is presently publishing an eclectic assortment of comic book titles, with a wide audience appeal—from the very young to the elderly." Circ. 70,000. Original artwork returned 60 days after publication. Sample copy and art guidelines available.
Illustrations: Uses three-tier page of 6 panels, vertical panels, horizontal panels, inset panels, border-

less panels, circular panels, double-page spreads and sequential narrative (any form). Uses freelance artists for inking, lettering, pencilling, color work, posters, covers and cover paintings and pin-ups. Send query letter with resume and samples. Samples are filed. Samples not filed are returned by SASE. Reports back within 6 weeks. To show a portfolio, an artist should mail photocopies of original pencil art or inking. Rights purchased vary. Negotiates payment. Pays on acceptance.
Tips: "We are looking for the artist's ability to tell a story through pictures. Due to the comic book market's preference for realism coupled with highly detailed renderings, we also look for the artist's abilities in anatomy, perspective, proportion, composition, good use of negative space. Artists should never send original art, unless they want to risk losing it. We are not responsible for unsolicited submissions. Don't send single illustrations instead of storytelling samples. Don't send more than five pages. Generally, the thicker a submissions package is, the longer it takes the editor to get around to looking at it."

***THE COMICS JOURNAL**, 4359 Cornell Rd., Agoura CA 91301. (818)706-7606. Art Director: Dale Crain. Magazine emphasizing the news and people of the world of comic books and strips. Circ. 8,000. Original artwork is returned to the artist after publication. Sample copy $4.50.
Illustrations: Prefers b&w spot illustrations and gags dealing with comics. Send query letter with samples. Buys one-time North American rights. Pays $2.50+, b&w, inside; on publication.

COMMON LIVES/LESBIAN LIVES, Box 1553, Iowa City IA 52264. Contact: Editorial Collective. Magazine emphasizing lesbian lives for lesbians of all ages, races, nationalities, and sizes. Quarterly. Circ. 2,000. Original artwork returned after publication if SASE provided. Sample copy $4.
Cartoons: Prefers lesbian themes. Prefers vertical format 8½x5½ page. Send finished cartoons to be kept on file. Material not kept on file is returned only if SASE provided. Reports within 4 months.
Illustrations: Prefers lesbian themes. Prefers vertical format 8½x5½ page. Samples not filed are returned only if SASE provided. Reports back within 3 months.

COMMONWEAL, 15 Dutch St., New York NY 10038. (212)683-2042. Editor: Peter Steinfels. National journal published by Catholic laypeople emphasizing political, social, cultural and religious issues. Biweekly. Circ. 18,000. Accepts previously published material. Original artwork not returned after publication.
Cartoons: Buys 1-3 cartoons/issue from freelancers. Prefers single panel without gagline; b&w line drawings. Send finished cartoons to be kept on file. Material not filed is not returned. Reports only if interested. Buys one-time rights. Pays $10-15, b&w; on publication.
Illustrations: Buys 0-1 illustration/issue from freelancers. Prefers political/social/religious themes; simple drawings. Send query letter with brochure showing art style or samples and tear sheets. Samples not filed are not returned. Reports only if interested. Write to schedule an appointment to show a portfolio, which should include original/final art. Buys one-time rights. Pays $25, cover, b&w; $10-15, inside, b&w; on publication.

COMMUNICATION WORLD, % IABC, Suite 940, 870 Market St., San Francisco CA 94102. (415)433-3400. Editor: Gloria Gordon. Emphasizes communication, public relations (international) for members of International Association of Business Communicators: corporate and nonprofit businesses, hospitals, government communicators, universities, etc. who produce internal and external publications, press releases, annual reports and customer magazines. Monthly except June/July combined issue. Circ. 17,000. Accepts previously published material. Original artwork returned after publication. Sample copy available.
Cartoons: Buys 1-5 cartoons/issue from freelancers. Considers international communication and publication themes. Prefers single panel with or without gagline; b&w line drawings or washes. Send query letter with samples of style or finished cartoons to be kept on file. Material not filed is returned only if requested. Reports only if interested. Write or call for appointment to show portfolio. Buys first rights, one-time rights or reprint rights; negotiates rights purchased. Pays $25-50, b&w; on publication.
Illustrations: Buys 3-10 illustrations/issue from freelancers. Theme and style are compatible to individual article. Send query letter with samples to be kept on file; write or call for appointment to show portfolio. Accepts Photostats, tear sheets, photocopies, slides or photographs as samples. Samples not filed are returned only if requested. Reports only if interested. Buys first rights, one-time rights or reprint rights; negotiates rights purchased. Pays $100, b&w and $250, color, cover; $150-250, b&w and $200, color, inside; on publication.
Tips: Artwork "must be professionally displayed. Show understanding of subject, discipline in use of media, general knowledge of working with editorial design problems."

COMPUTER AND COMMUNICATIONS DECISIONS, 10 Mulholland Dr., Hasbrouck Heights NJ 07604. Art Director: Bonnie Meyer. For computer-involved management in industry, finance, academia, etc.; well-educated, sophisticated and highly-paid. Monthly. Circ. 110,000.

Illustrations: Buys 2-3/issue. Assigned to illustrate columns and some feature stories. Works on assignment only. Prefers to see portfolio or samples of style. Send query letter with brochure or samples to be kept on file. Reports in 1 week. Call or write to schedule an appointment to show a portfolio, which should include original/final art, final reproduction/product, color and tear sheets. Buys all rights. Pays $150, b&w and $350, color, inside; on acceptance.
Tips: "Chartists with good ideas needed. No cartoons—realistic, slick drawings/renderings only. Ability to draw people well."

COMPUTER RESELLER, International Thomson Retail Press, Suite 660, 3550 Wilshire Blvd., Los Angeles CA 90010. (213)383-5800. Art Director: Michael Walters. Emphasizes the business of selling computers; "we publish industry magazines directed to reach retailers of high-technology products." Monthly. Circ. 40,000. Does not accept previously published material. Returns original artwork after publication.
Illustrations: Buys 8-10 illustrations/issue from freelancers. Prefers concept-oriented work of any medium. Works on assignment only. Send brochure and tear sheets, Photostats or photocopies to be kept on file. Samples not filed are not returned. Reports back only if interested. Call for appointment to show portfolio. Buys first-time North American rights. Pays $150 for b&w and $300 for color, inside; on publication.
Tips: "I'm very unconcerned with particular subjects or styles. Talent is talent, and I am confident it will manifest itself in whatever form. I do look for a particular personal vision of what illustration should be. This is not to say I shy away from a person using many different mediums, rather if that sense of 'vision' is present I am all-the-more encouraged. Most important is a sure sense of concept, conceiving, and capturing the essence of an idea."

CONFIDENT LIVING, (formerly Good New Broadcaster), Box 82808, Lincoln NE 68501. Managing Editor: Norman Olson. Interdenominational magazine for adults ages 16 and up. Monthly. Circ. 125,000. Previously published work OK. Original artwork returned after publication. Sample copy $1.50.
Illustrations: Interested in themes that are "serious, related to the subjects of the articles about the Christian life." Works on assignment only. Send query letter with brochure showing art style. Samples returned by SASE. "Helps to know if person is a Christian, too, but not necessary." Reporting time varies. Buys first North American serial rights. Pays $80 color, cover; $20 b&w and $50 color, inside; on publication.
Tips: Trends in the field today include "more realism, more primary colors and more oil painting than pencil/pen." When reviewing work, "we ask how well does it fit the story and does it have a truly professional look? Artists should think of the publication's needs and pay attention to small, but important, details in artwork that will complement the details in the writing."

CONNECTICUT MAGAZINE, 789 Resevoir Ave., Bridgeport CT 06606. (203)374-3388. Art Director: Joan Barrow. Emphasizes issues and entertainment in Connecticut for "upscale, 40-50's, Connecticut residents." Monthly. Circ. 66,000. Accepts previously published material. Original artwork returned after publication.
Illustrations: Uses 1-3 illustrations/issue; buys all from freelancers. Works on assignment only. Send query letter with brochure, business card, samples or tear sheets to be kept on file. Drop-off portfolios on Wednesdays, pick-up on Thursdays. Samples not filed are not returned. Pays $200-600, color, cover; $75-400, b&w, $200-600, color, inside; on publication.

CONSERVATORY OF AMERICAN LETTERS, Box 123, South Thomaston ME 04858. (207)354-6550. Editor: Bob Olmsted. Estab. 1986. Newsletter emphasizing literature for literate, cultured adults. Quarterly. Accepts previously published material with proper written evidence of right to re-use. Original artwork returned after publication. Sample copy for SASE with first-class postage.
Illustrations: Send brochure showing art style or samples. Samples not filed are returned by SASE. Reports back within 15 days. To show a portfolio, mail appropriate materials, which should include photographs. Buys first rights, one-time rights or reprint rights. Pays $100, color, cover; on acceptance.

CONSTRUCTION EQUIPMENT OPERATION AND MAINTENANCE, Construction Publications, Inc., Box 1689, Cedar Rapids IA 52406. (319)366-1597. Editor-in-Chief: C.K. Parks. Concerns heavy construction and industrial equipment for contractors, machine operators, mechanics and local government officials involved with construction. Bimonthly. Circ. 67,000. Simultaneous submissions OK. Original artwork not returned after publication. Free sample copy.
Cartoons: Uses 8-10 cartoons/issue, all from freelancers. Interested in themes "related to heavy construction industry" or "cartoons that make contractors and their employees 'look good' and feel good about themselves"; multiple panel. Send finished cartoons. SASE. Reports within 2 weeks. Buys all

rights but may reassign rights to artist after publication. Pays $10-15, b&w.
Illustrations: Uses 20+ illustrations/issue; "very few" are from freelancers. Pays $80-125; on acceptance.

THE CONSTRUCTION SPECIFIER, 601 Madison St., Alexandria VA 22314. (703)684-0300. Editor: Kimberly C. Smith. Emphasizes commercial (*not* residential) design and building for architects, engineers and other A/E professionals. Monthly. Circ. 18,000. Returns original artwork after publication if requested. Sample copy for SASE with $2.07 postage.
Illustrations: Buys 1-2 illustrations/issue from freelancers. Works on assignment only. Send query letter with Photostats, tear sheets, photocopies, slides or photographs. Samples not filed are returned by SASE. Reports back only if interested. Buys one-time rights. Pays on publication.

CONSUMERS DIGEST, 5705 N. Lincoln Ave., Chicago IL 60659. (312)275-3590. Senior Art Director: Craig Smith. Magazine emphasizing consumer products for post 30 consumers. Monthly. Circ. 1,200,000. Accepts previously published material. Original artwork returned after publication.
Illustrations: Buys 5-10 illustrations/issue from freelancers. Works on assignment only. "No restraints except we buy more realistic art than cartoon art." Send query letter with brochure showing art style or tear sheets, Photostats and slides. Samples not filed are returned by SASE. Does not report back. To show a portfolio, mail original/final art, final reproduction/product, color, tear sheets, Photostats and photographs. Buys reprint rights. Pays $2,000, color, cover; $100-700, b&w; and $200-900, color, inside; on acceptance.

CONSUMER GUIDE PUBLICATION INTERNATIONAL, (formerly Video Movies™ Magazine), 3841 W. Oakton, Skokie IL 60076. (312)676-3470. Art Directors: Terry Kolodziej and Mike Johnson. Emphasizes publications from cookbooks to medical journals. Does not return original artwork after publication.
Illustrations: Works on assignment only. Send samples to be kept on file. "Photocopies are fine as samples, whatever the artist usually sends." Samples not filed are returned only if requested. Reports back only if interested. Write for appointment to show portfolio. Buys all rights. Payment varies according to project; pays on acceptance.

CONTEMPORARY CHRISTIAN MAGAZINE, Box 6300, Laguna Hills CA 92653. Art Director: Lynn Schrader. Reviews and comments on personalities, music, arts, entertainment and issues relevant to Christian adults. Emphasis on music. Monthly. Circ. 40,000. Accepts previously published material and simultaneous submissions if specified with which publications. Originals returned to artist after publication only if requested and accompanied by required postage. Sample copy $1.95.
Cartoons: Interested in using cartoons as editorial fillers. Should be music oriented. Prefers single panel with hand-lettered gagline; *New Yorker* style. Mail prints or reproducible photocopies of finished cartoons to be kept on file; do not call. Material not kept on file is not returned. Reports only if cartoon is used. Buys one-time rights or negotiates. Pays $15-25, b&w; 30 days after publication. Return address, phone and credit information must be on the back of each cartoon.
Illustrations: Buys 1 illustration/issue from freelancers. Works on assignment only. Send query letter with brochure showing art style or photocopies to be kept on file. Samples not kept on file are returned by SASE. Reports only if interested. Call to schedule an appointment to show a portfolio, which should include original/final art, final reproduction/product and b&w. Buys one-time rights or negotiates. Pays $25-150, b&w, inside; 30 days after publication.
Tips: "Include a self-addressed stamped postcard as a response card. That way it will be sent back (usually right away). Type inquiries, it looks more professional."

CONTRACT, Gralla Publications, 1515 Broadway, New York NY 10036. Editor: Len Corlin. Executive Editor: Roberta Walton. Provides "ideas for interior installations, product information, and news on developments in the commercial interior design industry." Monthly. Circ. 35,000.
Illustrations: Buys 2-4/year on interior design; all on assignment only. Mail art or samples, or arrange interview to show portfolio. SASE. Reports in 3 weeks. Buys one-time rights. Pays $300, full-color renderings, cover; pays $150-250, b&w line drawings and washes, inside; on publication.
Tips: "Illustrators should not be shy. Call editor(s) to show portfolio."

DAVID C. COOK PUBLISHING CO., 850 N. Grove Ave., Elgin IL 60120. (312)741-2400. Director of Design Services: Randy R. Maid. Publisher of magazines, teaching booklets, visual aids and film strips. For Christians, "all age groups."
Illustrations: Buys about 30 full-color illustrations/week from freelancers. Send tear sheets, slides or photocopies of previously published work; include self-promo pieces. No samples returned unless requested and accompanied by SASE. Reports in 2-4 weeks to personal queries only. Works on assignment only. Pays on acceptance $50 minimum for inside b&w; $275-300, for color cover and $100 mini-

mum for inside color. Considers complexity of project, skill and experience of artist and turnaround time when establishing payment. Buys all rights. Originals can be returned in most cases.
Tips: "We do not buy illustrations or cartoons on speculation. We welcome those just beginning their careers, but it helps if the samples are presented in a neat and professional manner. Our deadlines are generous but must be met. We send out checks as soon as final art is approved, usually within 2 weeks of our receiving the art. We want art radically different from normal Sunday School art. Fresh, dynamic, the highest of quality is our goal; art that appeals to preschoolers to senior citizens; realistic to humorous, all media."

CORPORATE FITNESS, 1640 5th St., Santa Monica CA 90401. Publisher: Martin Waldman. Art Director: Tom Medsger. Emphasizes health/fitness corporate programs and professional news.
First Contact & Terms: Submit brochure/flyer to be kept on file for possible future assignment. Reports only when assignment available. Buys all rights. Pays $60 and up, spot art; $400, full-color cover; on acceptance.

CORVETTE FEVER MAGAZINE, Box 44620, Fort Washington MD 20744. (301)839-2221. Editor: Patricia Stivers. For "Corvette owners and enthusiasts, ages 25-55." Bimonthly. Circ. 35,000. Original artwork not returned after publication. Sample copy $2; general art guidelines for SASE.
Cartoons: Uses 2 cartoons/issue; buys 2-4 from freelancers. Themes "must deal with Corvettes"; single panel with gagline, b&w line drawings. Send roughs. Samples returned by SASE. Reports in 6 weeks. Buys first rights and reprint rights. Pays $15-35, b&w; on publication.
Illustrations: Uses 4-6 illustrations/issue; buys 3-6 from freelancers. Themes "must deal with Corvettes." Provide resume, brochure and tear sheets to be kept on file for possible future assignments. Send roughs with samples of style. Samples returned by SASE. Reports in 6 weeks. Buys first rights and reprint rights. Pays $10-75, inside, b&w line drawings; on publication.

COSMOPOLITAN, 224 W. 57th St., New York NY 10019. Cartoon Editor: Parker Reilly. For career women, ages 18-34.
Cartoons: Works largely with extensive present list of cartoonists. Receives 200 cartoons/week from freelance artists. Especially looks for "light, sophisticated, female-oriented cartoons."
Tips: "Less and less freelance work is purchased—the competition is tougher. Choose your topics and submissions carefully. We buy only sophisticated cartoons that stress a *positive* view of women—females as the subject of the cartoon but not the butt of the joke. Please read the magazine—there are only about 20 cartoonists who really understand our needs. I can't stress this enough." When reviewing an artist's work, "appropriateness to the magazine comes first. Sense of humor comes next, then quality of art. We like pretty people to be featured in our magazine—even in the cartoons. Be aware of *all* the outlets available to you—papers, ad agencies—then study the market *you're* trying to break into. Every magazine has its own slant. Read half a dozen issues and then ask yourself—can I describe, in two or three sentences, a typical reader's concerns, interests, age and economic background?"

THE COVENANT COMPANION, 5101 N. Francisco Ave., Chicago IL 60625. (312)784-3000. Editor: James R. Hawkinson. Emphasizes Christian life and faith. Monthly. Circ. 27,500. Original artwork returned after publication if requested. Sample copy $1.50.
Illustrations: Uses b&w drawings or photos about Easter, Advent, Lent, and Christmas. Works on assignment only. Write or submit art 10 weeks in advance of season. SASE. Reports "within a reasonable time." Buys first North American serial rights. Pays in month after publication.

CREATIVE IDEAS FOR LIVING, 820 Shades Creek Pkwy., Birmingham AL 35202. (205)877-6000. Art Director: Lane Gregory. Magazine emphasizing lifestyle for women 28-40. Monthly. Circ. 850,000. Original artwork returned after publication. Sample copy for SASE.
Cartoons: Buys 1 cartoon/issue. Prefers b&w line drawings; b&w or color washes. Send samples of style to be kept on file. Write or call for an appointment to show a portfolio. Material not filed is returned only if requested. Reports only if interested. Negotiates rights purchased. Negotiates payment.
Illustrations: Buys 0-10 illustrations/issue from freelancers. Send query letter with brochure showing art style or resume and samples. Samples returned only if requested. Reports only if interested. To show a portfolio, mail final reproduction/product, color and tear sheets. Negotiates rights purchased. Negotiates payment. Pays on acceptance.

***CRICKET, The Magazine for Children**, Box 300, Peru IL 61354. Art Director: Maryann Leffingwell. Emphasizes children's literature for children, ages 6-12. Monthly. Circ. 140,000. Accepts previously published material. Original artwork returned after publication. Sample copy $1; art guidelines free for SASE.
Illustrations: Uses 70 illustrations/issue; buys 45 illustrations/issue from freelancers. Prefers realistic

© Jay Ossip

Cartoonist Jay Ossip of Miami, Florida, studied magazines on the newsstands and found that Cosmopolitan "accomodated my style of cartooning." The cutline reads, "There is nothing wrong with your set. We are experiencing technical difficulties in the studio." The magazine purchased one-time rights to the single-panel cartoon for $25. It was also used by Ossip as part of a mailer to advertising agencies. Ossip says the cartoon conveys the "humor of technology in everyday life."

styles (animal or human figure); occasionally accepts caricature. Works on assignment only. Send query letter with brochure, samples and tear sheets to be kept on file, "if I like it." Prefers Photostats, tear sheets or original work as samples. Samples are returned by SASE if requested or not kept on file. Reports within 2-3 weeks. Buys reprint rights. Pays $500, color, cover; $150/full page, b&w. Pays on acceptance.
Tips: "Very little chance of cartoon sales at *Cricket*."

CROSSCURRENTS, 2200 Glastonbury Rd., Westlake Village CA 91361. Graphic Arts Editor: Michael Hughes. "This is a literary quarterly that uses graphic art as accompaniment to our fiction and poetry. We are aimed at an educated audience interested in reviewing a selection of fiction, poetry and graphic arts." Circ. 3,000. Original artwork returned after publication. Sample copy $5; art guidelines available for SASE.
Illustrations: Uses 5-7 illustrations/issue; buys 75% from freelancers. Considers "any work of high quality and in good taste that will reproduce b&w, 5x7", with clarity, including but not limited to line drawings, charcoal sketches, etchings, lithographs, engravings; vertical format. No pornography." Send brochure, resume, tearsheets, Photostats, slides and photographs. No simultaneous submissions or previously published material. SASE. Reports in 3 weeks. To show a portfolio, mail appropriate material. Buys first rights. Pays $10 minimum cover or inside b&w line drawings and b&w washes; $15 minimum cover, color washes; on acceptance.
Tips: "Study a sample copy of our publication and read our guidelines to understand what it is that we use, and what styles we publish." When reviewing an artist's work, "we look for technical excellence, strength of style, something of worth. A professional, neat submission is a must, of course."

CRUISING WORLD, 524 Thames St., Newport RI 02840. (401)847-1588. Assistant Art Director: Rachel Cocroft. Magazine emphasizing cruising sailboats for audience with a $98,000 average income, most own their own boat, approx. 40-50 years old. Circ. 118,000. Sample copy and art guidelines available "if we're interested in their work."
Illustrations: Buys 10 or more illustrations/issue from freelancers. Works on assignment only. Prefers b&w or four-color marine, boat-oriented editorial illustrations as well as b&w technical line illustra-

tions. Send query letter with brochure showing art style or tear sheets, Photostats, photocopies, slides and photographs. To show a portfolio, mail color tear sheets, Photostats, photographs, b&w. Buys first rights. Pays $100-300, b&w; $200-650, color, inside; on publication.
Tips: "Freelance artists must be familiar with boats, what they look and feel like when sailing. An artist must have ability to render human anatomy accurately in scale with marine equipment and also to interpret editorial matter creatively. We are using more airbrushed material, more four-color and we are looking for diversity of styles. We are, however, increasingly interested in spot illustrations that are not necessarily marine-oriented."

CRUSADER, Baptist Brotherhood Commission, 1548 Poplar, Memphis TN 38104. (901)272-2461. Art Director: Herschel Wells. Christian-oriented mission magazine for boys grades 1-6. Monthly. Circ. 100,000. Photocopied and simultaneous submissions OK. Original artwork returned after publication, if requested.
Illustrations: Uses 10 illustrations/issue; buys 2/issue from freelancers. Interested in boys' activities. Works on assignment only. Sample copy provided "if we consider using the artist after we've seen samples." Send roughs or samples of style, which may be returned or duplicated to be kept on file. Samples not filed are returned by SASE. Reports in 3 weeks. To show a portfolio, mail original/final art, tear sheets and Photostats. Buys first North American serial rights. Pays $100, b&w, and up to $250, color, cover; $35-$120, b&w, inside; on acceptance.
Tips: "Please send several samples if you have more than one style. We must see human figure work as most of our art requires this."

CRYPTOLOGIA, Rose-Hulman Institute of Technology, Terre Haute IN 47803. (812)877-1511. Managing Editor: Brian J. Winkel. Emphasizes all aspects of cryptology: data (computer) encryption, history, military, science, ancient languages, secret communications for scholars and hobbyists. Quarterly. Circ. 1,000. Accepts previously published material and simultaneous submissions. Original artwork returned after publication.
Cartoons: Uses 1-2 cartoons/issue. Prefers plays on language, communication (secret), ancient language decipherment, computer encryption. Prefers single, double or multi panel, with or without gagline; b&w line drawings or b&w washes. Send query letter with samples of style, roughs, or finished cartoons to be kept on file. Material not kept on file is returned by SASE. Reports within 2 weeks. Negotiates rights purchased. Pays on acceptance.

CURRENTS, Box 6847, 314 N. 20th St., Colorado Springs CO 80904. Editor: Eric Leeper. Magazine emphasizing whitewater river running for kayakers, rafters and canoeists; from beginner to expert; middle-class, college-educated. Bimonthly. Circ. 10,000. Accepts previously published material. Original artwork returned after publication. Sample copy 75¢. Art guidelines for SASE with first-class postage.
Cartoons: Buys 0-1 cartoon/issue from freelancers. Themes *must* deal with whitewater rivers or river running. Prefers single panel with gagline; b&w line drawings. Send query letter with roughs of proposed cartoon(s) to be kept on file. Samples not kept on file are returned by SASE. Reports within 6 weeks. Buys one-time rights. Pays $10-35, b&w.
Illustrations: Buys 0-2 illustrations/issue from freelancers. Works on assignment only. Themes must deal with rivers or river running. Send query letter with proposed illustrations. Samples not filed returned by SASE. Reports within 6 weeks. To show a portfolio, mail appropriate materials, which should include "whatever they feel is necessary." Buys one-time rights. Pays $10-35, b&w; inside. Pays on publication.
Tips: "Make sure you have seen a sample copy of *Currents* and our guidelines. Be sure you know about rivers and whitewater river sports."

CURRICULUM REVIEW, 517 S. Jefferson St., Chicago IL 60607. (312)939-3010. Editor-in-Chief: Irene M. Goldman. Emphasizes material of interest to teachers, superintendents, curriculum coordinators, librarians (schools of education and school libraries). Bimonthly. Circ. 10,000. Original artwork returned after publication. Sample copy for SASE with $1.75 postage.
Cartoons: Uses variable number of cartoons/issue. Prefers single, double or multi panel with gagline; b&w line drawings. Send query letter with samples of style to be kept on file. Material not kept on file is returned by SASE. Reports only if interested. Write for appointment to show portfolio. Negotiates payment. Pays on publication.
Illustrations: Send query letter with Photostats and tear sheets to be kept on file. Samples not kept on file are returned by SASE. Reports within 1 month only if interested. Buys reprint rights. Negotiates payment. Pays on publication.

CWC/PETERBOROUGH, 80 Elm St., Peterborough NH 03458. (617)924-9471. Creative Director: Christine Destrempes. "We publish 4 microcomputing monthlies and 2 bi-monthlies: *AmigaWorld*,

Computers in Science, *CD-ROM Review*, *80 Micro*, *RUN*, and *inCider*." Circ. 140,000-550,000. Accepts previously published material. Returns original artwork after publication. Sample copy for SASE.

Cartoons: Minimal number of cartoons purchased from freelancers. Prefers single panel without gaglines; b&w line drawings, b&w washes or color washes. Send query letter with samples of style or finished cartoons to be kept on file. Material not filed is returned only if requested. Reports within 5 weeks. Rights purchased and payment varies; pays within 30 days.

Illustrations: Buys 8-20 illustrations/issue from freelancers. Works on assignment only. Send query letter with resume and tear sheets to be kept on file. Samples not filed are returned only if requested. Reports within 5 weeks. To show a portfolio, mail final reproduction/product, color and b&w or call or write to schedule an appointment. Rights purchased and payments vary; pays on acceptance.

Tips: "The quality of presentation is very important."

CYCLE WORLD, 1499 Monrovia Ave., Newport Beach CA 92663. (714)720-5300. For active motorcyclists who are "young, affluent, educated, very perceptive." Monthly. Circ. 375,000. "Unless otherwise noted in query letter, we will keep spot drawings in our files for use as future fillers." Free sample copy and artist's guidelines.

Illustrations: Art Director: Elaine Anderson. Uses 7-8 illustrations/issue, all from freelancers. Receives 25-30 submissions/week from freelancers. Interested in motorcycling and assigned themes. Works on assignment only. Prefers to see resume and samples. Samples returned, if originals; kept if photocopies. Reports back on future assignment possibilities to artists who phone. Does not report back to artists who contact through mail. Call or write to schedule an appointment to show a portfolio, which should include original/final art, final reproduction/product, color, tear sheets and b&w. Provide brochure, tear sheet, letter of inquiry and business card to be kept on file for future assignments. Buys all rights. Pays $300-500, cover. Pays $25-150, b&w; $100-400, color; $75, spot drawings, on publication.

Tips: "We use a lot of spot drawings as fillers. black-and-white motorcyle illustrations used mostly. Call or write. Do not send original art or unsolicited art."

THE DALE CORP., 2684 Industrial Row, Troy MI 48084. (313)288-9540. Contact: Art Director. Publishes law enforcement, corrections and fire fighting publications. Circ. 240,000. Free sample copies and art guidelines.

Illustrations: Buys 12/year. Send query letter with previously published work. SASE. Reports in 4 weeks. Buys all rights, but may reassign rights to artist after publication. Cover: Pays $100-200, b&w line drawings; $75-200, color-separated work. Pays on acceptance.

***DC COMICS INC.**, 666 Fifth Ave., New York NY 10103. Executive Editor: Dick Giordano. Super-hero and adventure comic books for mostly boys 7-14, plus an older audience of high school and college age. Monthly. Circ. 6,000,000. Original artwork is returned after publication.

Illustrations: Buys 22 pages/comic. Works on assignment only. Send query letter with resume and photocopies. Do not send original artwork. Samples not filed are returned. Reports back within 2 months. Write to schedule an appointment to show a portfolio, which should include thumbnails and original/final art. Buys all rights. Payment varies on acceptance.

DEATH RATTLE, Kitchen Sink Enterprises, No. 2 Swamp Rd., Princeton WI 54968. (414)295-6922. Story Editor: Dave Schreiner. Serious comic book emphasizing science fiction and horror for serious readers and collectors of quality fantasy, science fiction and horror comics. Bimonthly. Circ. 20-25,000. Does not accept previously published material unless obscure publications. Original artwork returned after publication. Sample copy $2.50 postpaid; art guidelines for SASE with first-class postage.

Cartoons: "We *never* buy "gag" or single panel cartoons. This is a comic book featuring fully developed graphic stories." Prefers b&w line drawings. Send query letter with samples of style, roughs or photocopies of finished cartoons to be kept on file. Samples not filed are returned only by SASE. Does not send original art on query. Reports within 2 weeks. Negotiates rights purchased. Payment variable; generally $50-200/page, paid on royalty basis. "Higher earnings possible."

Illustrations: For cover only; "balance is fully-developed graphic stories.." Generally works on assignment only. Preferred style is simplified realism. Send query letter with brochure showing art styles or tear sheets, Photostats and photocopies. Samples returned by SASE. Reports within 2 weeks. "Portfolio presentations unrealistic for geographic reasons." Negotiates rights purchased. Pays $200-400, b&w, cover. Pays one-half on acceptance, one-half on publication.

DECOR, 408 Olive, St. Louis MO 63102. (314)421-5445. Associate Editor: Sharon Shinn. "Trade publication for retailers of art, picture framing and related wall decor. Subscribers include gallery owners/directors, custom and do-it-yourself picture framers, managers of related departments in department stores, art material store owners and owners of gift/accessory shops." Monthly. Circ. 20,000. Simulta-

neous submissions and previously published work OK. Original artwork not returned after publication. Sample copy $4.
Cartoons: Uses 6-10 cartoons/year; buys all from freelancers. Receives 5-10 submissions/week from freelancers. Interested in themes of galleries, frame shops, artists and small business problems; single panel with gagline. "We need cartoons as a way to 'lighten' our technical and retailing material. Cartoons showing gallery owners' problems with shows, artists and the buying public, inept framing employees, selling custom frames to the buying public and running a small business are most important to us." Send finished cartoons. SASE. Reports in 1 month. Buys various rights. Pays $20, b&w line drawings and washes; on acceptance.
Tips: "Most of our cartoons fill one-quarter-page spaces. Hence, cartoons that are vertical in design suit our purposes better than those which are horizontal. Send good, clean drawings with return envelopes; no more than 6 cartoons at a time."

DELAWARE TODAY MAGAZINE, 120A Senatorial Dr., Wilmington DE 19807 (302)656-1809. Art/Design Director: Ingrid Hansen-Lynch. Magazine emphasizing regional interest in and around Delaware. Features general interest, historical, humorous, interview/profile, personal experience and travel articles. "The stories we have are about people and happenings, in and around Delaware. They are regional interest stories. Our audience is middle-aged (40-45) people with incomes around $60,000, mostly educated." Monthly. Circ. 18,000. Accepts previously published material. Original artwork returned after publication. Sample copies available.
Cartoons: Buys 1 cartoon every other month from freelancers. Buys approximately 6 cartoons/year from freelancers. Open to all styles. Prefers no gagline; b&w line drawings, b&w and color washes. Send query letter with samples of style. Samples are filed. Reports back only if interested. Buys first rights or one-time rights. Pays $50 small; $100 large.
Illustrations: Buys 2 illustrations/issue from freelancers. Buys 24 illustrations/year from freelancers. Works on assignment only. Open to all styles. Send query letter with resume, tear sheets, slides and whatever pertains. Samples are filed. Reports back only if interested. Call to schedule an appointment to show a portfolio, which should include original/final art, tear sheets, final reproduction/product, color and b&w. Buys first rights and one-time rights. Pays $50, small b&w and color; $100 large b&w and color, inside; $250, cover; on publication.
Tips: "The most appropriate way to contact us is to send a resume, cover letter and a promo card or brochure showing black-and-white and color samples and different styles of the artist's work."

DENTAL HYGIENE, Suite 3400, 444 N. Michigan, Chicago IL 60611. Contact: Staff Editor. Emphasizes "professional concerns and issues involving dental hygienists and scientific topics concerning dental hygiene" for "a primarily female audience of dental hygientists." Monthly. Circ. 35,000. Original artwork returned after publication. Sample copy available.
Illustrations: Uses 1 cover illustration/issue; buys 1/issue from freelancers. Prefers a variety of styles. "The theme depends on the individual issue." Works on assignment only. Send query letter with brochure, resume, samples and tear sheets to be kept on file. Prefers slides or photographs of color work. Reports within 1 month. Write for appointment to show portfolio. Buys one-time rights. Payment depends on the artwork. Pays on publication.

DETROIT MAGAZINE, 321 W. Lafayette, Detroit MI 48231. (313)222-6446. Contact: Art Director. Sunday magazine of major metropolitan daily newspaper emphasizing general subjects. Weekly. Circ. 800,000. Original artwork returned after publication. Sample copy available.
Illustrations: Buys 1-2 illustrations/issue from freelancers. Uses a variety of themes and styles, "but we emphasize fine art over cartoons." Works on assignment only. Send query letter with samples to be kept on file unless not considered for assignment. Send "whatever samples best show artwork and can fit into 8½x11 file folder." Samples not filed are not returned. Reports only if interested. Buys first rights. Pays $250-300, color, cover; up to $200, color and up to $175, b&w, inside; on publication.

DETROIT MONTHLY MAGAZINE, 1400 Woodbridge, Detroit MI 48207. (313)446-6000. Emphasizes "features on local political, economic, style, cultural, lifestyles, culinary subjects, etc., relating to Detroit and region" for "middle and upper-middle class, urban and suburban, mostly college-educated professionals." Monthly. Circ. approximately 80,000. "Very rarely" accepts previously published material. Sample copy for SASE.
Illustrations: Uses 10 illustrations/issue; buys 10/issue from freelancers. Works on assignment only. Send query letter with samples and tear sheets to be kept on file. Call for appointment to show portfolio. Prefers anything *but* original work as samples. Samples not kept on file are returned by SASE. Reports only if interested. Pays $600, color, cover; $300-400 color, full page; $200-300, b&w, full page; $100, sport illustrations; on publication.

***DIRT RIDER MAGAZINE**, Petersen Publishing, 8490 Sunset, Los Angeles CA 90069. (213)854-2390. Art Director: John Thomas Sutton. Consumer magazine emphasizing dirt bike riding, riders and maintenance. Features how-to, humor, interview/profile, personal experience, technical, travel and humorous fiction. "Caters to athletic, younger readers." Monthly. Circ. 160,000. Original artwork not returned after publication. Sample copy $2.
Cartoons: Buys 12 cartoons/issue from freelancers. Buys 150 cartoons/year from freelancers. Prefers single panel, double panel or multi panel with or without gaglines; b&w line drawings, b&w or color washes. Send query letter with samples of style and roughs. Samples are filed. Samples not filed are not returned. Does not report back. Buys all rights. Pays $50, b&w.
Illustrations: Buys 12 illustrations/issue from freelancers. Buys 150 illustrations/year from freelancers. Send query letter with brochure showing art style or tear sheets, photocopies, slides and photographs. Samples are filed. Samples not filed are not returned. Does not report back. To show a portfolio, mail tear sheets, final reproduction/product, Photostats, photographs, color and b&w. Buys all rights. Pays $50, b&w; on acceptance or publication.

THE DISCIPLE, Christian Board of Publication, Box 179, St. Louis MO 63166. Editor: James L. Merrell. For ministers and laypersons. Monthly. Circ. 58,000. Photocopied and simultaneous submissions OK. Original artwork returned after publication, if requested. Sample copy $1.50; free artist's guidelines.
Cartoons: Buys 1 cartoon/issue from freelancers. Receives 10 submissions/week from freelancers. Interested in family life and religion; single panel. Church material only. "Originality in content and subject matter stressed. No clergy collars—ties or robes preferred." Especially needs "good religious cartoons along the lines of those which appear in *TV Guide*." Prefers to see finished cartoons. SASE. Reports in 4 weeks. Buys first North American serial rights. Pays $15 minimum, b&w line drawings and washes; on acceptance.
Illustrations: Uses 2 illustrations/issue; buys 1/issue from freelancers. Receives 10 submissions/week from freelancers. Interested in "seasonal and current religious events/issues." Also uses 4 cartoon-style illustrations/year. Send query letter with tear sheets, photocopies and photographs. SASE. Reports in 2 weeks. To show a portfolio, mail tear sheets, Photostats and photographs. Buys first North American serial rights. Payment depends on quality. Pays on acceptance.
Tips: "We would be very happy to look at samples of artists' work (covers), in case we want to commission. Read the magazine before submitting material. Send seasonal art, especially Easter and Christmas, at least six months in advance. Do not send 'dial-a-prayer' cartoons."

DISCIPLESHIP JOURNAL, Box 6000, Colorado Springs CO 80934. (303)598-1212, ext. 298. Art Director: Naomi Trujillo. Magazine/journal emphasizing Christian living and discipleship. Bi-monthly. Works with 15 freelance artists/year.
Illustrations: Buys 4-5 illustrations/issue from freelance artists. Send resume, tear sheets, Photostats, photocopies, slides, photographs. Samples not filed are returned if requested by SASE. Reports back only if interested. Buys one-time rights. Pays by the project, $150-1,000.

DISTRIBUTOR, Box 745, Wheeling IL 60090. (312)537-6460. Editorial Director: Steve Read. Emphasizes HVAC/R wholesaling for executives at management level in the wholesale field. Bimonthly. Circ. 11,000. Returns original artwork after publication. Sample copy $4.
Illustrations: Works on assignment only. Send query letter with brochure, Photostats, tear sheets, photocopies, slides or photographs, to be kept on file; *no* original work. Reports within 2 weeks. To show a portfolio, mail tear sheets, Photostats, photographs and b&w. Buys first rights. Negotiates payment; pays on publication.

DIVER MAGAZINE, Suite 295, 10991 Shellbridge Way, Richmond, British Columbia V6X 3C6 Canada. (604)273-4333. Editor: Neil McDaniel. Emphasizes scuba diving, ocean science and technology (commercial and military diving) for a well-educated, outdoor-oriented readership. Published 9 times yearly. Circ. 25,000. Sample copy $3; art guidelines for SAE (nonresidents include IRC).
Cartoons: Buys 1 cartoon/issue from freelancers. Interested in diving-related cartoons only. Prefers single panel b&w line drawings with gagline. Send samples of style. SAE (nonresidents include IRC). Reports in 2 weeks. Buys first North American serial rights. Pays $15 for b&w; on publication.
Illustrations: Interested in diving-related illustrations of good quality only. Prefers b&w line drawings for inside. Send samples of style. SAE (nonresidents include IRC). Reports in 2 weeks. Buys first North American serial rights. Pays $7 minimum for inside b&w; $100 minimum for color cover and $15 minimum for inside, color. Pays 1 month after publication.

DOG FANCY, Box 6050, Mission Viejo CA 92690. (714)240-6001. Editor: Linda Lewis. For dog owners and breeders of all ages, interested in all phases of dog ownership. Monthly. Circ. 100,000. Simultaneous submissions and previously published work OK. Sample copy $3.; free artist's guidelines with SASE.

Cartoons: Buys 12 cartoons/year; single, double or multiple panel. "Central character should be a dog." Mail finished art. SASE. Prefers Photostats or photocopies as samples. Reports in 6 weeks. Buys first rights. Pays $20-50, b&w line drawings; on publication.

Illustrations: Buys 12 illustrations/year on dogs. Query with resume and samples. SASE. Reports in 6 weeks. Buys first rights. Pays $50-100, b&w line drawings, inside; on publication.

Tips: "Spot illustrations are used in nearly every issue. I need dogs in action (doing just about anything) and puppies. Please send a selection that we can keep on file. We pay $20 for each spot drawing used. Drawings shoudl be scaled to reduce to column width (2¼)"

DOLLS—THE COLLECTOR'S MAGAZINE, 170 5th Ave., New York NY 10010. Art Director: Lisa Dayton. Magazine emphasizing antique and collectible dolls for doll collectors. Bimonthly. Circ. 52,500. Original artwork returned after publication. Sample copy $2. Art guidelines for SASE with first-class postage.

Illustrations: Buys 1-2 illustrations/issue from freelancers. Works on assignment only. Prefers realistic presentations, b&w line art or full-color for covers and how-to type drawings. Send query letter with resume, tear sheets and photocopies. Samples not filed returned by SASE. Reports only if interested. Write to schedule an appointment to show a portfolio, which should include roughs, original/final art, final reproduction/production, color, tear sheets, photographs and b&w. Negotiates rights purchased. Pays by the project, $100-1,000. Pays 30 days after submission.

Tips: Also accepts illustrations for *Dollmaking*, quarterly magazine emphasizing doll projects and plans (Circ. 50,000) and *Teddy Bear Review*, quarterly magazine emphasizing antique and collectible bears (Circ. 30,000).

THE DOLPHIN LOG, The Cousteau Society, 8440 Santa Monica Blvd., Los Angeles CA 90069. (213)656-4422. Editor: Pamela Stacey. Educational magazine covering "all areas of science, history and the arts related to our global water system, including marine biology, ecology, the environment, and natural history" for children ages 7-15. Quarterly. Circ. 60,000. Original artwork returned after publication. Sample copy for $2 and SASE with 56¢ postage; art guidelines for SASE with first-class postage.

Cartoons: Considers themes or styles related to magazine's subject matter. B&w line drawings or b&w or color washes. Send query letter with samples of style to be kept on file. Material not filed is returned by SASE. Reports within 1 month. Buys one-time rights and translation rights. Pays $25-50, b&w and color; on publication.

Illustrations: Buys 4-6 illustrations/issue from freelancers. Uses simple, biologically and technically accurate line drawings and scientific illustrations. Subjects should be carefully researched. Send query letter with tear sheets and photocopies to be kept on file unless otherwise notified. "No original artwork, please." Samples not filed are returned by SASE. Reports within 1 month. To show a portfolio, mail final reproduction/product, tear sheets and b&w. Buys one-time rights; the right to grant reprints for use in other publications; worldwide translation rights for inclusion in other Costeau Society publications. Pays $100, color, cover; $25-50, b&w and color, inside; on publication.

Tips: "Biological/technical accuracy a must. Stay within concept of magazine."

DOWN EAST, Box 679, Camden ME 04843. (207)594-9544. Art Director: F. Stephen Ward. Concerns Maine's people, places, events and heritage. Monthly. Circ. 75,000. Previously published work OK. Buys first North American serial rights. Sample copy $2.

Illustrations: Buys 50/year on current events, environment, family life and politics. Query with resume and samples or arrange interview to show portfolio. SASE. Reports in 4-6 weeks. Cover: Pays $75, color paintings in any medium; "must have a graphic, poster-like feel and be unmistakably Maine." Inside: Pays $25-200, b&w or color; on publication.

Tips: "Neatness in presentation is as important as the portfolio itself."

DRAGON MAGAZINE, TSR, Inc., Box 110, Lake Geneva WI 53147. Editor: Roger E. Moore. Art Director: Roger Raupp. For readers interested in role-playing games, paticularly Dungeons & Dragons. Circ. 90,000. Query with samples. SASE. Usually buys first rights only. Pays within 60 days after acceptance.

Cartoons: Buys 40-60/year on fantasy role-playing. Pays $35-80, b&w only.

Illustrations: Buys at least 100/year on fantasy and science fiction subjects. Pays $250/page, b&w; $700 and up for color cover art.

Tips: "Commissions are not likely unless the artist provides a sampling of work which demonstrates his ability to render realistic fantasy art. The more particular the work is to the Dungeons & Dragons game the better."

***DRAMATIKA**, 429 Hope St., Tarpon Springs FL 33589. Editor: J. Pyros. For persons interested in the performing arts, avant garde and traditional. Published semiannually. Sample copy $2.
Illustrations: Query first. SASE. Reports in 1 month. Cover: Pays $15, b&w. Inside: Pays $5, b&w line drawings; on acceptance.

EARTHWISE REVIEW, (formerly Earthwise: A Journal of Poetry), Box 680-536, Miami FL 33168. (305)940-7157. Publisher: Barbara Holley. Art Editors: Kathryn L. Vilips and Ted Wezyk. Emphasizes poetry, art and literature for an eclectic group of literate writers, artists and poets, mainly academic, collegiate and aimed at excellence in the field. Quarterly. Circ. 3,000+. Sometimes accepts previously published material; simultaneous submissions OK. Original artwork returned after publication. Sample copy $4; art guidelines for SASE.
Illustrations: Uses 4-8 illustrations/issue; buys some from freelancers. Send query letter with velox copies or originals (please insure). "We especially prefer samples, photocopies or stats which we can purchase and/or keep on file for future publication; our themes occasionally change depending on submissions." Samples returned by SASE "but would like something to keep on file." Reports in 3 months. Write to schedule an appointment to show a portfolio, which should include thumbnails, roughs, original/final art, final reproduction/product, color, tear sheets, Photostats, photographs and especially b&w. Buys first rights. Pays $10-50/b&w line drawings, cover; $10-25/b&w line drawings, inside. "Very negotiable depending on size, availability, etc." Pays on publication.
Tips: "We lean toward the environmental, nature, creatures, humankind. Send 4-6 black-and-white samples, either veloxes or insured originals with proper return envelope and appropriate postage for their prompt return. We use black-and-white in both the annual calendar and the newsletter also."

***EASYRIDERS MAGAZINE**, Box 3000, Agoura CA 91301. (818)889-8740. Art Director: Pat Taketa. Magazine emphasizing adult motorcyclists (specifically Harley-Davidsons). Features how-to and interview/profile articles. For adult men who own, or desire to own, large-displacement, custom street motorcycles, the individualist—a rugged guy who enjoys the freedom of motorcycling and all the good times derived from it." Monthly. Circ. 300,000. Original artwork not returned after publication. Sample copy $2.95.
Cartoons: Buys 12 cartoons/issue from freelancers. Prefers motorcycle-oriented themes. Send roughs and finished cartoons. Samples are filed. Samples not filed are returned. Reports back within 10 days. Buys first rights. Pays $35, color.
Illustrations: Buys 10 illustrations/issue from freelancers. Send brochure or slides and photographs. Samples are filed. Samples not filed are returned. Call to schedule an appointment to show a portfolio, which should include roughs, original/final art and photographs. Buys first rights. Pays $150, b&w, cover; $250, color, inside; on publication.

***ECLIPSE COMICS**, Box 1099, Forestville CA 95436. Editor-in-Chief: Catherine Yronwode. Publishes comic books and graphic albums. "All our comics feature fictional characters in action-adventures. Genres include super-heroes, science fiction, weird horror, western, detective adventure, funny-animal, etc. The emphasis is on drawing the human figure in action. Audience is adolescent to adult. The age varies with each series. (For instance, adolescents prefer *Airboy*, a teen hero, while adults prefer *Scout*, a post-holocaust science fiction series with strong romantic and political overtones.)" Publishes 24 comics/month on average. Most are monthlies, some bi-monthly; others are one-shots or mini-series. Circ. 30,000-80,000, depending on title. Does not accept previously published material except for reprint collections by famous comic book artists. Original artwork returned after publication. Sample copy $1.75; art guidelines for SASE.
Cartoons: "We buy entire illustrated stories, not individual cartoons. We buy approximately 6,250 pages of comic book art by freelancers/year—about 525/month." Interested in realistic illustrative comic book artwork—drawing the human figure in action; good, slick finishes (inking); ability to do righteous 1-, 2- and 3-point perspective required. "The bulk of our material continues to be color comics in the realistic action vein." Formats: b&w line drawings or fully painted pages with balloon lettering on overlays. Send query letter with samples of style to be kept on file. "Send minimum of 4-5 pages of full-size (10x15) photocopies of pencilled *storytelling* (and/or inked too)—no display poses, just typical action layout continuities." Material not filed is returned by SASE. Reports within 2 months by SASE only. Buys first rights and reprint rights. Pays $100-200/page, b&w; "price is for pencils plus inks; many artists only pencil for us, or only ink."; on acceptance (net 30 days). Pays $25-35/page for painted or airbrushed coloring of greylines made from line-art; on acceptance (net 30 days).
Illustrations: "We buy 12-15 cover paintings for science fiction and horror books per year." Science fiction paintings: fully rendered science fiction themes (e.g. outer space, aliens); horror paintings: fully rendered horror themes (e.g. vampires, werewolves, etc.). Send query letter with business card and samples to be kept on file. Prefers slides, color photos or tear sheets as samples. Samples not filed are returned by SASE. Reports within 2 months by SASE only. Buys first rights or reprint rights. Pays $200-500, color; on acceptance (net 30 days).

***EIDOS MAGAZINE: Erotic Entertainment for Women**, Box 96, Boston MA 02137-0096. (617)262-0096. Editor: Brenda L. Tatelbaum. Magazine emphasizing erotica and erotic entertainment for women and men. Quarterly. Original artwork returned after publication.
Illustrations: Works with 12-15 artists/year. Send query letter with resume, tear sheets, Photostats and photographs. Samples are filed. Samples not filed are returned by SASE. Reports back within 2 months. Write to schedule an appointment to show a portfolio, which should include original/final art, Photostats and photographs. Buys first rights. "We have standard payment terms."
Tips: "We look for sensuous, sensitive, sophisticated erotica depicting mutually respective sexuality and images of the human form. Alternative to commercial mainstream men's and women's magazines. More images of men and couples are published in *Eidos* than female images."

80 MICRO, 80 Pine St., Peterborough NH 03458. (603)924-9471. Art Director: Anne Fleming. Magazine for users of Tandy TRS-80 computers. Monthly. Circ. 80,000. Original artwork returned after publication. Art guidelines available.
Illustrations: Buys 4-7 illustrations/issue from freelancers. Works on assignment only. Prefers creative, original and new themes and styles. Send query letter with brochure showing art style or tear sheets, Photostats and photocopies. Samples not filed are returned only if requested. Reports back only if interested. Call or write to schedule an appointment to show a portfolio, which should include original/final art, final reproduction/product and tear sheets. Buys first rights. Pays $175, b&w; $100-850, color, inside; on acceptance.
Tips: "Don't write asking for a copy of magazine and guidelines without sending a sample. I also won't fill out questionnaires from illustrators if I don't know if I'm interested in them."

ELECTRICAL APPARATUS, Barks Publications, Inc., 400 N. Michigan, Chicago IL 60611. Contact: Elsie Dickson. Emphasizes industrial electrical maintenance and repair.
Cartoons: Receives 2-3 cartoons/week from freelance artists. "Always looking for applicable cartoons, as we use a strip (assigned), plus 4-6 individual column-size cartoons in every issue." Query with resume.
Tips: Artists should "know the magazine!"

ELECTRICAL WORLD, McGraw-Hill Inc., 1221 Avenue of the Americas, New York NY 10020. (212)512-2440. Art Director: Kiyo Komoda. Emphasizes operation, maintenance and use of electric utility facilities. For electric utility management and engineers. Monthly. Original artwork returned after publication, on request. Pays $50-150 b&w, $80-200 color; on acceptance.
Cartoons: Buys 1 cartoon/issue from freelancers, works on assignment only. Interested in industry-related situation cartoon, usually related to editorial articles. Buys one-time and reprint rights. Pays on acceptance.
Illustrations: Uses 20 illustrations/issue, buys 1/3 from freelancers. Interested in energy systems; 90% are mechanical line drawings, maps, flow designs, graphs and charts. Works on assignment only. Samples returned by SASE. Provide resume or business card to be kept on file for future assignments. Prefers to see portfolio or finished art. Reports in 1 week. Buys one-time and reprint rights. Cover: Pays $10-200, b&w line drawings, inside; $20-300 color, inside; on acceptance.
Tips: "We prefer artists with clean and crisp line work. They should know about color separation and overlays. Young artists welcomed."

ELECTRONIC COMMUNICATION, INC., Suite 220, 1311 Executive Center Dr., Tallahasee FL 32301. (904)878-4178. Art Director: Faye Howell. Three publications emphasizing educational technology for kindergarten to high school principals, teachers, and administrators and also college and upper educational teachers and administrators. Monthly, bimonthly and quarterly. Circ. 275,000; 70,000; 34,000. Original material not returned after publication. Sample copy for SASE with 56¢ postage.
Illustrations: Buys 0-3 illustrations/issue from freelancers. Works on assignment only. Send query letter with brochure showing art style. Samples not filed are returned only if requested. Reports only if interested. To show a portfolio, mail appropriate materials, which should include final reproduction/product, color and tear sheets. Negotiates rights purchased. Payment "varies widely;" on publication.

***ELECTRONICS**, McGraw-Hill Publishing Co., 1221 Avenue of the Americas, New York NY 10020. (212)997-2430. Art Director: Fred Sklenar. For college graduates, electronics engineers, marketing people and executives. Biweekly. Circ. 125,000. Original artwork returned after publication. Photocopied and simultaneous submissions OK.
Illustrations: Uses 30 illustrations/issue; buys all from freelancers. Receives 20-30 illustrations/week from freelance artists. Buys 26 covers/year on assigned themes. Works on assignment only. "Personal interview would be best way to contact." Especially needs engineering drafting, and creative and conceptual illustrations for cover. Samples returned by SASE. Provide tear sheet and sample art to be kept on file for future assignments. Prefers finished art, portfolio, samples of style, or tear sheets as samples.

Buys all first-time world rights. Cover: Pays $1,000 minimum, color. Inside: Pays $50-500; on acceptance.

Tips: "Prepare portfolio professionally and have samples ready to leave so they may be kept on file."

THE ELKS MAGAZINE, 425 W. Diversey Pkwy., Chicago IL 60614. Editor: Judith Keogh. Emphasizes general interest with family appeal. For members of the Elks. Monthly. Circ. 1,600,000. Original artwork not returned after publication. Pays on acceptance. Sample copy for 9x12 SASE.

Cartoons: Uses 1 cartoon/issue, buys from freelancers. Receives 50 submissions/week from freelancers. Buys 8-10/year; single panel. "Must have family appeal." Interested in general interest cartoons. Prefers to see finished cartoons. Reports in 1 month. Buys first and North American serial rights. Pays $50, line drawings; on acceptance.

Tips: "Many cartoonists are specializing in 'put-down' or 'insult' humor. Our publication has no use for this type of material; thus many technically excellent artists find themselves the recipients of our rejection slips." Needs "clean, well-rendered art; appropriate or adaptable subject matter; fresh, succinct captions."

EMERGENCY MEDICINE MAGAZINE, 475 Park Ave. S, New York NY 10016. (212)686-0555. Art Director: Lois Erlacher. Emphasizes emergency medicine for primary care physicians, emergency room personnel, medical students. Bimonthly. Circ. 139,000. Returns original artwork after publication.

Illustrations: Buys 3-4 illustrations/issue from freelancers. Works on assignment only. Send tear sheets, transparencies, original art or Photostats to be kept on file. Samples not filed are not returned. To show a portfolio, mail appropriate materials. Reports only if interested. Buys first rights. Pays $750 for color, cover; $250-500, b&w and $500-600, color, inside; on acceptance.

Tips: "Portfolios may be dropped off any day of the week. Art Director prefers to keep overnight—call first."

EMPLOYEE SERVICES MANAGEMENT MAGAZINE, NESRA, 2400 S. Downing Ave., Westchester IL 60153. (312)562-8130. Editor: Pamela A. Tober. Emphasizes the field of employee services and recreation for human resource professionals, employee services and recreation managers and leaders within corporations, industries or units of government. Published 10 times/year. Circ. 5,000. Accepts previously published material. Returns original artwork after publication. Sample copy for SASE with 56¢ postage; art guidelines for SASE with first-class postage.

Illustrations: Buys 0-1 illustration/issue from freelancers. Works on assignment only. Send query letter with resume and tear sheets or photographs to be kept on file. Samples not filed are returned only if requested. Reports within 1 month. Buys one-time rights. Pays $100-200 for b&w and $300-400 for color covers; on acceptance.

Tips: "We have noticed a change to a simpler, more dramatic style in art and design, one that is not so 'busy.' We have used freelancers who embrace this style."

THE ENSIGN, Official Publication of the United States Power Squadrons, Box 31664, Raleigh NC 27622. (919)821-0892. Editor: Carol Romano. Emphasizes boating safety and education for members of the United States Power Squadrons, a nonprofit organization of boating men and women across the country. Monthly. Circ. approximately 50,000. Returns original artwork after publication. Sample copy and art guidelines for SASE.

Cartoons: Prefers single panel, with gagline; b&w line drawings. Send query letter with finished cartoons; "material is reviewed and used or returned by SASE." Reports within 2 weeks. Acquires one-time rights.

Illustrations: Prefers boating themes. Send query letter with photocopies; "material is reviewed and used or returned by SASE." Reports within 2 weeks. Acquires all rights.

Tips: "We are happy to accept cartoons and drawings for use in the magazine and provide artists with copies of the magazine at no charge, a letter of appreciation and a certificate of appreciation for their contributions. We provide an opportunity for beginning freelancers to get nationwide exposure, but we have no freelance budget to pay artists at this time."

ENVIRONMENT, 4000 Albemarle St., Washington DC 20016. (202)362-6445. Production Graphics Editor: Ann Rickerich. Emphasizes national and international environmental and scientific issues. Readers range from "high school students and college undergrads to scientists, business and government leaders and college and university professors." Circ. 12,500. Published 10 times/year. Original artwork returned after publication if requested. Sample copy $4; cartoonist's guidelines available.

Cartoons: Uses 0-1 cartoon/issue; buys all from freelancers. Receives 2 submissions/week from freelancers. Interested in single panel b&w line drawings or b&w washes with or without gagline. Send finished cartoons. SASE. Reports in 1 month. Buys first North American serial rights. Pays $35, b&w cartoon; on acceptance.

Illustrations: Buys 0-5/year from freelance artists. Send query letter, brochure, tear sheets and photocopies. To show a portfolio, mail original/final art or reproductions. Pays $200 b&w, cover; $50-200 b&w, inside; on publication.
Tips: "Regarding cartoons, we prefer the witty to the slapstick." For illustrations, "we are looking for an ability to communicate complex environmental issues and ideas in an unbiased way."

ESQUIRE, 2 Park Ave., New York NY 10016. (212)561-8100. Art Director: Ms. Wendall Harrington. Emphasizes politics, business, the arts, sports and the family for American men.
Illustrations: Buys 1-10 illustrations/issue, depending on special sections. Send brochure showing art style or resume and tear sheets. To show a portfolio, mail original/final art, final reproduction/product, color, tear sheets, photographs and b&w. Pays on acceptance.

ETERNITY MAGAZINE, 1716 Spruce St., Philadelphia PA 19103. (215)546-3696. Design Coordinator: Olivia Fox. Emphasizes news and news trends from a Christian viewpoint. Monthly. Circ. 40,000. Accepts previously published material. Original artwork returned after publication. Sample copy $1; art guidelines available.
Illustrations: Buys 5-7 illustrations/issue from freelancers. Themes range from sports to politics to environment to family. Works on assignment only. Send query letter with resume, tear sheets, Photostats, photocopies, slides and photographs. "Please do not send original work." Samples returned by SASE. Reports only if interested. Call or write to schedule an appointment to show a portfolio, which should include original art, final reproduction/product, color, tear sheets and b&w. Buys one-time rights. Pays $200-400 , b&w, and $150-200, color, cover; $50-100 b&w or color, inside; on acceptance.

EUROPE, MAGAZINE OF THE EUROPEAN COMMUNITY, Seventh Floor, 2100 M St. NW, Washington DC 20037. (202)862-9500. Editor: Webster Martin. Emphasizes European affairs, US-European relations—particularly economics, trade and politics. Readers are businessmen, professionals, academics, government officials and consumers. Published 10 times/year. Circ. 65,000. Free sample copy.
Cartoons: Occasionally uses cartoons, mostly from a cartoon service. "The magazine publishes articles on US-European relations in economics, trade, business, industry, politics, energy, inflation, etc." Considers single panel b&w line drawings or b&w washes with or without gagline. Send resume plus finished cartoons and/or samples. SASE. Reports in 3-4 weeks. Buys one-time rights. Pays $25; on publication.
Illustrations: Uses 3-5 illustrations/issue. "At present we work exclusively through our designer and set up charts and graphs to fit our needs. We would be open to commissioning artwork should the need and opportunity arise. We look for economic graphs, tables, charts and story-related statistical artwork"; b&w line drawings and washes for inside. Send resume and photocopies of style. SASE. Reports in 3-4 weeks. To show a portfolio, mail original/final art. Buys all rights on a work-for-hire basis. Payment varies; on publication.

EVANGEL, 901 College Ave., Winona Lake IN 46590. (219)267-7656. Contact: Vera Bethel. Readers are 65% female, 35% male; ages 25-31; married; city-dwelling; mostly non-professional high school graduates. Circ. 35,000. Weekly.
Cartoons: Buys 1/issue on family subjects. Pays $10, b&w; on publication. Mail finished art.
Illustrations: Buys 1/issue on assigned themes. Pays $40, 2-color; on acceptance. Query with samples or slides. SASE. Reports in 1 month.

EVENT, Douglas College, Box 2503, New Westminster, British Columbia V3L 5B2 Canada. (604)520-5400. Editor: Dale Zieroth. For "those interested in literature and writing." Published 3 times/year. Circ. 1,000. Original artwork returned after publication. Sample copy $4.
Illustrations: Receives 3 illustrations/week from freelance artists. Buys 16-20 illustrations/issue from freelancers. Interested in experimental drawings and prints, and thematic or stylistic series of 12-20 works. SAE (nonresidents include IRC). Reporting time varies; at least 2 weeks. To show a portfolio, mail original/final art, b&w and color. Buys first North American serial rights. Pays $40 maximum, b&w line drawings, photographs and lithographs for cover and inside; work must reproduce well in one color. Pays on publication. Payment includes free copy.
Tips: "No photocopies—otherwise we welcome almost anything—no cartoons—no nudies."

EXPECTING MAGAZINE, 685 Third Ave., New York NY 10017. Art Director: Azade Erhun. Emphasizes pregnancy, birth and care of the newborn for pregnant women and new mothers. Quarterly. Circ. 1.2 million distributed through obstetrician and gynecologist offices nationwide. Original artwork returned after publication.
Illustrations: Buys approximately 6/issue. Color only. Works on assignment. "We have a drop-off policy for looking at portfolios; include a card to be kept on file." Buys one-time rights. Pays within 30 days after publication.

THE EYE MAGAZINE, 11th & Washington Sts., Wilmington DE 19801. (302)571-6978. Art Director: Paul A. Miles. Tabloid for high school students; all writing, cartoons, photographs, etc. are produced by high-school age cartoonists and artists. Monthly October through May. Circ. 25,000. Accepts previously published material. Original artwork returned after publication. Sample copy for SASE with 37¢ postage.
Cartoons: Uses 1 cartoon/issue. Prefers single panel with gagline; b&w line drawings. Prefers themes showing resourcefulness of young people. "We prefer ones that do not show teens in a derogatory manner." Send query letter with samples of style to be kept on file. Material not kept on file is returned by SASE. Reports within 30 days. Buys one-time rights.
Illustrations: Buys 1 illustration/issue from freelancers. Works on assignment only. Primary theme is teenagers; artist must be a teenager. Send query letter with resume and photocopies. Samples not filed are returned by SASE. Reports within 30 days. "We do not see portfolios." Buys one-time rights. Pays $25, b&w, cover; $10, b&w, inside. "Our publication is a non-profit publication to give students a voice to their peers and adults. We are a training ground and as such do not pay very much for editorial or artwork. We will gladly give copies of publication and letters of recommendations to high school students interested in getting something published."
Tips: "Don't expect very much from us. We are small and like to help artists; not monetarily, but through public work."

FACT MAGAZINE, 305 E. 46th, New York NY 10017. Art Director: Christopher Goldsmith. Emphasizes consumer money management and investment. Monthly. Returns original artwork after publication.
Illustrations: Buys 10-12 illustrations/issue from freelancers. Always works on assignment. Send Photostats, tear sheets, photocopies, slides or photographs to be kept on file. Samples not filed are returned only if requested. Reports only if interested. Portfolio should include final reproduction/product, color, tear sheets, Photostats, photographs and b&w. Buys first rights or reprint rights. Pays $500-800 for cover; $300-600 inside.

***FAMILY MOTOR COACHING**, 8291 Clough Pike, Cincinnati OH 45244. (513)474-3622. Contact: Editor. Emphasizes self-contained motor homes for families who own or enjoy the recreational use of such vehicles motorhomes. Monthly. Circ. 50,000. Original artwork returned after publication, "if requested." Sample copy $2.50; art guidelines available with SASE.
Cartoons: Uses 1-5 cartoons/issue; buys all from freelancers. Themes "must pertain to motorhoming, RV lifestyle, travel. No trailers." Prefers single, double, or multi panel with or without gagline, b&w line drawings, b&w washes. Send finished cartoons. Samples returned by SASE. Reports in 4-6 weeks. Buys first rights. Pays $20, b&w; on publication.

FAMILY PLANNING PERSPECTIVES, 111 5th Ave., New York NY 10003. (212)254-5656. Art Director: Mark Kellogg. Trade journal emphasizing family planning and contraceptive technology for health-care providers. Features technical articles. Bimonthly. Circ. 15,000. Original artwork returned after publication. Sample copy available.
Cartoons: Buys 1 cartoon/year from freelancers. Prefers single panel, without gagline; b&w line drawings. Send query letter with finished cartoons. Samples are filed. Samples not filed are returned by SASE. Reports back only if interested. Buys one-time rights. Pays $50, b&w.
Illustrations: Buys 1-2 illustrations/year from freelancers. Send query letter with brochure or resume. Samples are filed. Samples not filed are returned by SASE. Reports back only if interested. Call to schedule an appointment to show a portfolio, which should include original/final art, tear sheets and photographs. Buys one-time rights. Pays $250-400, b&w; $350-550, color, cover; $80-125, b&w, inside; on publication.

FANFARE, Box 720, Tenafly NJ 07670. (201)567-3908. Editor: Joel Flegler. Magazine emphasizing classical record reviews for classical record collectors. Bimonthly. Circ. 20,000. Accepts previously published material. Original artwork returned after publication. Sample copy $5.
Illustrations: Buys 1 illustration/issue from freelancers. Prefers anything to do with music as themes. Send query letter with resume and samples. Samples not filed are returned by SASE. Reports only if interested. Call to dicuss artwork; no appointments. Buys one-time rights. Pays $100, color, cover; on acceptance.

***FANTAGRAPHIC BOOKS**, 4359 Cornell Rd., Agoura CA 91301. (818)706-7606. Contact: Gary Groth. Publishes comic books and 1 graphic novel/year. Titles include *Love and Rockets*, *Amazing Heroes*, *Los Tejanos*, *Anything Goes*, *Lloyd Llewelyn* and *Neat Stuff*. All genres except superheroes. Bimonthly. Circ. 8-30,000. Sample copy $2.50.
Illustrations: Fantagraphic is looking for artists who can create an entire product or who can work as

part of an established team. Most of the titles are black and white. Send query letter with samples which display storytelling capabilities, or submit a complete package. All artwork is creator-owned. Buys one-time rights usually. Payment terms vary. Creator receives an advance upon acceptance and then royalties after publication.

***FANTASY GENERAL COMICS**, 17 W. 4th, Williamsport PA 17701. (717)322-5068. Art Director: Ren Koozer. Publishes 54 limited edition comic books/year, 4-6 series/month and 1 graphic novel/year. Titles include *Codename Tomahawk*, *Terra Nauts*, *Marauders of Black Sun*, *Future Course*, *Super Six*, *Haulers Inc.*, *One Shot Western* and *Time Warriors*. Genres: adventure, fantasy, science fiction and western. "We will look at other genres." Themes: outer space, future science, alternative lifestyles and film-like books. "Keep the story in guidelines for the 13- to 18-year-old market. We are attempting to create film-like stories and art." Circ. 25-50,000. Original artwork is returned after publication. Sample copy $1. Art guidelines for SASE with 1 first-class stamp.
Illustrations: Uses three-tier page of 6 panels, vertical panels, horizontal panels, inset panels, borderless panels, circular panels and double-page spreads. Uses freelance artists for inking, lettering, pencilling and posters. Send query letter with resume and photocopies of original art. Samples are filed. Samples not filed are returned by SASE if requested. Reports back within 1 month only if interested. Call or write to schedule an appointment to show a portfolio, or mail 5 pages of pencil or ink drawings, 2 pages of action continuity, 5 photocopies of original pencil art or inking, 2 pages of lettering twice up with sound effects, titles and display lettering. Pays $40/page for pencilling, $40/page for inking and $10-20/page for lettering. Negotiates payment for graphic novels. Pays on publication; "some cases on 50/50 basis."

FANTASY REVIEW, Meckler Publishing, 11 Ferry Lane W., Westport CT 06880. Editorial offices at: College of Humanities, Florida Atlantic University, Boca Raton FL 33431. (305)393-3839. Editor: Robert A. Collins. Emphasizes fantasy and science fiction for "collectors, book dealers, libraries, academics and fans in general." Monthly. Circ. 3,000. Original artwork returned after publication. Sample copy $2.50. Receives very few cartoons ("could use more") and 10 illustrations/week from freelance artists.
Cartoons: Horror, fantasy and science fiction subjects. "Publishing is caught in the Reaganomics squeeze; rates will stay the same."
Illustrations: Uses mainly cover illustrations; buys all from freelancers. Interested in themes pertaining to fantasy, science fiction, and horror. "Artists should *not* send originals on speculation—send PMT's, stats, or quality photocopies. Don't send copies larger than 9x12. If we need originals (as for cover illustration), we ask for them. All art is eventually returned, but we assume no responsibility for it." Samples returned "with SASE only." Reports in 4 weeks. Buys one-time publication rights only; all other rights retained by artist. Pays $100 cover (b&w with one-color overlay), $10-25 inside (various sizes), all media; pays on publication.

FARMSTEAD MAGAZINE, Box 111, Freedom ME 04941. (207)382-6200. Publisher: George Frangoulis. Focuses on home gardening and country living. Published 6 times/year. Circ. 125,000. Sample copy and artist's guidelines with 8½x11 SASE.
Illustrations: Buys 2 illustrations/issue. Receives 5 submissions/week from freelancers. Interested in farming, gardening, plants, livestock, wildlife, etc. (pen & ink, wood block, etching). Works on assignment only. Call to schedule an appointment to show a portfolio, which should include roughs, original/final art or final reproduction/product. SASE. Reports in 8 weeks. Buys all rights on a work-for-hire basis. Pays $125 color, cover; $25-100 b&w; $50-100 color, inside; on publication.
Tips: "Send attractive resume that is short and simple, and several samples (photocopies preferred) of work, slides for color work. Creative brochures are eye-catching. Artist should include a telephone number—we often call on short notice. No samples returned without SASE."

FARM SUPPLIER, Watt Publishing Co., Mount Morris IL 61054. Editorial Director: Clayton Gill. Editor: Marcella Sadler. For retail farm suppliers and dealers throughout the U.S. Monthly.
Illustrations: "We use color slides that match editorial material. They should relate to the farm supply retail business, including feed, custom application of chemicals and fertilizers." Send query letter with slides. To show a portfolio, mail photographs and slides. Pays $150 color, cover; on acceptance.

THE FIDDLEHEAD, Old Arts Bldg., University of New Brunswick, Frederiction, New Brunswick E3B 5A3 Canada. (506)454-3591. Editor: Michael Taylor. Emphasizes poetry, short stories, essays and book reviews for a general audience. Quarterly. Circ. 1,050. Original artwork returned after publication. Sample copy U.S. $4.25 plus postage (nonresidents include IRC).
Illustrations: Buys 3-5 illustrations/issue from freelancers. Send query letter with tear sheets, Photostats and photocopies to be filed "if considered suitable." Samples returned by SAE (include Canadian

stamps or IRC). Reports within 6-8 weeks. Buys first rights. Pays $50, b&w and $75, color, cover; $20, b&w, inside; on publication.
Tips: "There is a trend away from cartoons to line drawings and much more brush work; abstract work is becoming more desirable. When sending samples, doodles aren't acceptable; there needs to be some purpose."

FIELD & STREAM MAGAZINE, 1515 Broadway, New York NY 10036. (212)719-6552. Art Director: Victor J. Closi. Magazine emphasizing wildlife hunting and fishing. Monthly. Circ. 2 million. Original artwork returned after publication. Sample copy and art guidelines for SASE.
Illustrations: Buys 9-12 illustrations/issue from freelancers. Works on assignment only. Prefers "good drawing and painting ability, realistic style, some conceptual and humorous styles are also used depending on magazine article." Send query letter with brochure showing art style or tear sheets and slides. Samples not filed are returned only if requested. Reports only if interested. Call or write to schedule an appointment to show a portfolio, which should include roughs, original/final art, final reproduction/product and tear sheets. Buys first rights. Payment varies: $75-300 on simple spots; $500-1,000 single page; $1,000 and up on spreads, and $1,500 and up on covers; on acceptance.

***THE FINAL EDITION**, Box 294, Rhododendron OR 97049. (503)622-4798. Editor: Michael P. Jones. Estab. 1985. Investigative journal that deals "with a variety of subjects—environment, wildlife, crime, etc. for professional and blue collar people who want in-depth reporting." Monthly. Circ. 1,500. Accepts previously published material. Original artwork is returned after publication. Art guidelines for SASE with 1 first-class stamp.
Cartoons: Buys 1-18 cartoons/issue from freelancers. Prefers single panel, double panel, multi panel, with or without gagline; b&w line drawings, b&w or color washes. Send query letter with samples of style, roughs or finished cartoons. Samples are filed. Samples not filed are returned by SASE. Reports back within 2 weeks. Buys one-time rights. Pays in copies.
Illustrations: Buys 10 illustrations/issue from freelancers. Send query letter with brochure showing art style or resume and tear sheets, Photostats, photocopies, slides or photographs. Samples not filed are returned by SASE. Reports back within 2 weeks. To show a portfolio, mail thumbnails, roughs, original/final art, final reproduction/product, color, tear sheets, Photostats, photographs or b&w. Buys one-time rights. Pays in copies.
Tips: "We have a real need for nonfiction illustrations. *The Final Edition* deals with real things and real events, not science fiction. The type of illustrations we are looking for must deal with the subject matter of *The Final Edition* for that month. It may be on bison, wolves, wild horses, wiretapping or profiling the life history of an individual.

***FINS AND FEATHERS PUBLISHING COMPANY**, 401 N. 3rd St., Minneapolis MN 55401. Art Director: David Minix. "We're a state-oriented hunting and fishing magazine providing information to active outdoors people about hunting, fishing and boating opportunities close to home." Features how-to, humor, interview/profile, personal experience articles and humorous fiction. Monthly. Circ. 500,000. Original artwork is returned after publication. Sample copy for SASE.
Cartoons: Buys 24 cartoons/year from freelancers. Prefers sporting life themes—hunting, fishing. Prefers single panel; b&w line drawings. Send query letter with samples of style and roughs. Samples are filed. Samples not filed are returned by SASE. Reports back within 3 weeks. Pays $25-75, b&w.
Illustrations: Buys 7 illustrations/year from freelancers. Prefers hunting, fishing, mood pieces. Send query letter with tear sheets, slides and photographs. Samples are filed. Samples not filed are returned by SASE only if requested. Reports back within 30 days. Buys one-time rights. Pays $25-75, b&w; $250, color, cover; $50-200, color, inside; on publication.
Tips: "Our readership is very knowledgeable about the subjects we write about. Accuracy in representation of anatomy and terrain is essential. It's recommended interested persons look over a copy of *Fins & Feathers* to get a general idea of our state format and subject matter."

FIRST HAND LTD., 310 Cedar Ln., Teaneck NJ 07666. (201)836-9177. Art Director: Laura Patricks. Emphasizes homoerotica for a male audience. Monthly. Circ. 60,000. Original artwork can be returned after publication. Sample copy $3; art guidelines available for SASE.
Cartoons: Buys 5 cartoons/issue from freelancers. Prefers single panel with gagline; b&w line drawings. Send finished cartoons to be kept on file. Material not filed is returned by SASE. Reports within 2 weeks. Buys first rights. Pays $15 for b&w; on acceptance.
Illustrations: Buys 20 illustrations/issue from freelancers. Prefers "nude men in a realistic style; very basic, very simple." Send query letter with Photostats or tear sheets to be kept on file. Samples not filed are returned. Reports within 2 weeks. Call or write for appointment to show portfolio. Buys all magazine rights. Pays for design by the hour, $10. Pays $25-50 for inside b&w; on acceptance.
Tips: "I like to see current work, not work that is too old. And I prefer to see printed samples if that is possible."

***FIRST PUBLICATIONS**, 435 N. LaSalle, Chicago IL 60610. (312)670-6770. Art Director: Alex Wald. Publishes comic books and graphic novels including *Shatter* and *American Flagg*.
Illustrations: Prefers comic storytelling with well-realized figures. Uses freelance artists for inking, lettering, pencilling, color work and covers. Send query letter with photocopies of original art, which should be proportional to 10x15; include your name, address and phone number on every sample page. Samples are sometimes filed. Call to schedule an appointment to show a portfolio. Negotiates rights purchased and payment. All material is invoiced 30-60 days after acceptance.

***FISH BOAT**, (Incorporating *Fishing Gazette*), Box 2400, Covington LA 70434. Executive Editor: Bill Sarratt. Trade journal emphasizing commercial fishing. Features general interest and technical articles. Monthly. Circ. 19,500. Accepts previously published material. Original artwork returned after publication. Sample copy $3.
Cartoons: Buys all rights. Pays $75, b&w; $125, color.
Illustrations: Buys 2 illustrations/issue from freelancers. Buys 10 illustrations/year from freelancers. Send query letter with slides and photographs. Samples are filed. Samples not filed are returned. Reports back within 2 weeks. To show a portfolio, mail slides, color and b&w. Buys all rights. Pays $125, color, cover. Pays on acceptance.

FISHING WORLD, 51 Atlantic Ave., New York NY 11001. (516)352-9700. Editor: Keith Gardner. Emphasizes angling. Readers are adult male U.S. sport fishermen. Editorial content is a mix of how-to and where-to with emphasis on the former, this is, on advanced use of tackle and techniques. Bimonthly. Circ. 325,000. Original artwork returned after publication. Sample copy $1.
Illustrations: Buys 3-6 illustrations/year from freelancers. Interested in realistic illustrations. Uses inside color washes. Works on assignment only. Send query letter with slides. Samples are filed. Samples not filed are returned only if requested by artist. SASE. Reports in 3 weeks. Buys first North American serial rights. Pays $300 for color, cover; $200 color, inside; on acceptance.
Tips: "Know the sport and milieu."

FLING, Relim Publishing Co., 550 Miller Ave., Mill Valley CA 94941. (415)383-5464. Editor: Arv Miller. Bimonthly. Emphasizes sex, seduction, sports, underworld pieces, success stories, travel, adventure and how-to for men, 18-34. Sample copy for $4.
Cartoons: Prefers sexual themes. "The female characters must be pretty, sexy and curvy, with extremely big breasts. Styles should be sophisticated and well-drawn." Pays $30, b&w, $50-100, color; on acceptance.

***FLORIDA WATER RESOURCES JOURNAL**, Box 560027, Orlando FL 32856-0027. Managing Editor/Advertising Director: Emory Dawkins. "Dedicated to serving water and wastewater industry—heavy emphasis on Florida people, projects, related news. Features general interest, some humor, interview/profile and technical articles. Bimonthly. Circ. 6,500. Accepts previously published material. Original artwork sometimes returned after publication. Sample copy $2.
Cartoons: Related to some aspect of water, wastewater operations—plants or systems. Prefers single panel with gagline; b&w line drawings. Send query letter with samples of style. Samples are filed. Samples not filed are returned if requested. Reports back only if interested. Buys one-time rights. Pays $50, b&w.
Illustrations: Buys 3-5 illustrations/year from freelancers. Send query letter. Samples are filed. Samples not filed are not returned. Reports back only if interested. To show a portfolio, mail tear sheets. Buys one-time rights. Pays $25, b&w; $100, color, cover; $25, b&w; $50, color, inside. Pays on publication.

FLORIST, Florists Transworld Delivery Association, Box 2227, Southfield MI 48037. (313)355-9300. Editor-in-Chief: William Golden. Production Manager: Margaret Baumgarten. Managing Editor: Susan Nicholas. Emphasizes information pertaining to the operation of the floral industry. For florists and floriculturists. Monthly. Circ. 24,000. Reports in 1 month. Accepts previously published material. Does not return original artwork after publication.
Cartoons: Buys 3 cartoons/issue. Interested in retail florists and floriculture themes; single panel with gagline. Mail samples or roughs. SASE. Buys one-time rights. Pays $20, b&w line drawings; on acceptance.
Illustrations: Works on assignment only. Send query letter with Photostats, tear sheets, photocopies, slides or photographs. Samples not filed are returned by SASE. Reports within 3 months. To show a portfolio, mail final reproduction/product, tear sheets, Photostats and photographs. Buys first rights.

FLOWER AND GARDEN, 4251 Pennsylvania, Kansas City MO 64111. (816)531-5730. Editor: Rachel Snyder. Emphasizes "gardening for avid home gardeners." Bimonthly. Circ. 630,000. Sample copy $2.

Cartoons: Uses 1 cartoon/issue. Receives about 10 submissions/week. Needs cartoons related to "indoor or outdoor home gardening." Format: single panel b&w line drawings or washes with gagline. Prefers to see finished cartoons. SASE. Reports in 4 weeks. Buys one-time rights. Pays $20, b&w cartoon; on acceptance.

FLY FISHERMAN, Editorial Offices, Box 8200, 2245 Kohn Rd., Harrisburg PA 17105. (802)867-5951. Art Director: Jeanne Collins. Emphasizes fly fishing. Readers are 99% male; 79% are college graduates; 79% are married. Published 6 times a year. Circ. 143,988. Original artwork returned after publication. Sample copy $3; art guidelines for SASE.
Illustrations: Uses spots, maps and diagrams. Receives about 20 submissions/week from freelancers. Interested in "saltwater and freshwater fly-fishing or stream-scene in all areas of the country. Scenics including insects, fish—preferably not dead or braces of—and related subjects." Prefers b&w line drawings, b&w washes and color washes for inside magazine. Freelancers are selected from "samples and spot-filler-work kept on file." Send query letter or a sample of work preferably in the fly-fishing or stream area to be kept on file for future assignments. Prefers to see samples of style or arrange personal appointment to show portfolio. SASE. Reports in 4-6 weeks. Buys one-time North American magazine rights. Pays $25-200 for b&w "depending on size and use inside the magazine"; color payment negotiated; on publication.

THE FLYFISHER, 1387 Cambridge Dr., Idaho Falls ID 83401. (208)523-7300. Editor: Dennis G. Bitton. For members of the Federation of Fly Fishers. Concerns fly fishing and conservation. Quarterly. Circ. 10,000. Buys first North American serial rights. Sample copy $3 from Federation of Fly Fishers main office, Box 1088, West Yellowstone, MT 59758.
Cartoons: Buys 3-4 cartoons/issue. Pays $25 b&w; $25-150 color.
Illustrations: Interested in fly-fishing themes. Send query letter with tear sheets, Photostats and photocopies. Samples returned by SASE. Reports in 2 weeks. To show a portfolio, mail appropriate materials. Buys first North American serial rights. Pays $150-200 b&w and; $150-200 color, cover; $25-150 b&w and; $35-150 color, inside; on publication.
Tips: "We always encourage freelancers to submit material. The possibility for a sale is good with good material. We especially look for an artist's ability to illustrate an article by reading the copy. See a current issue of the magazine. In general there is better line art."

***FOCUS: NEW YORK**, 375 Park, New York NY 10022. Editor-in-Chief: Bodil W. Nielsen. Emphasizes shops, restaurants and galleries for the New York visitor. Annual circ. 250,000. Previously published material OK. Original artwork returned after publication. Sample copy $1.50.
Illustrations: Uses 10 illustrations/issue; buys 5 from freelancers. Interested in fashion, logos, children and gift items. Works on assignment only. Send query letter with resume and samples of style. Provide resume, business card and samples to be kept on file for possible future assignments. Reports in 3 weeks. Pays $50 minimum, inside b&w line drawings; on publication.

FOOD & SERVICE NEWS,Box 1429, Austin TX 78767. (512)444-6543. Editor: Bland Crowder. Art Director: Jane Yansky. Official trade publication of Texas Restaurant Association. Seek materials dealing with business problems of restaurant owners and foodservice operators, primarily in Texas, and including managers of clubs, bars and hotels. Published 11 times/year. Circ. 5,000. Simultaneous submissions OK. Sample copy for SASE.
Cartoons: Not used.
Illustrations: Seeks high-quality b&w or color artwork in variety of styles (airbrush, watercolor, pastel, pen & ink, etc.). Seeks versatile artists who can illustrate articles about foodservice industry, particularly business aspects. Works on assignment only. Query with resume, samples and tear sheets. Call for appointment to show portfolio. Pays for illustration by the project, $50-400. Negotiates rights and payment upon assignment. Returns original artwork after publication.
Tips: "We try to provide business solutions in *Food & Service*, and illustrations are often surreal depictions of the problems or solutions. I look for innovative, professional and unique styles."

FOOD & WINE, 1120 Avenue of the Americas, New York NY 10036. (212)382-5702. Art Director: Elizabeth Woodson. Emphasizes food and wine for "an upscale audience who cook, entertain and dine out stylishly." Monthly. Circ. 600,000.
Illustrations: Buys all from freelancers. Interested in sophisticated style. Works on assignment and pick up. Send brochure and samples of style to be kept on file; drop portfolio off on third Tuesday of the month only. Reports when assignment is available. Buys one-time rights. Pays $100 minimum, inside, b&w line drawings; on acceptance.

FOOD PROCESSING, Putman Publishing Co., 301 E. Erie, Chicago IL 60611. Editor/Publisher: Roy Hlavacek. Emphasizes equipment, new developments, laboratory instruments and government regulations of the food processing industry. For executives and managers in food processing industries. Monthly. Circ. 64,000. Photocopied submissions OK. Original artwork not returned after publication. Free sample copy and artist's guidelines.
Cartoons: Buys 1-2 cartoons/issue, from freelancers. Receives 10-15 submissions/week from freelancers. Interested in "situations in and around the food plant (e.g., mixing, handling, transporting, weighing, analyzing, government inspection, etc.)"; single panel with gagline. Prefers to see finished cartoons. SASE. Reports in 1 week. Buys all rights. Pays $20 minimum, b&w line drawings.
Tips: "Avoid most 'in-the-home' and all retailing cartoon situations. Stick to in-the-food-plant situations—meat packing, vegetable and fruit canning, candymaking, beverage processing, bakery, dairy—including any phase of processing, inspecting, handling, quality control, packaging, storage, shipping, etc."

***FOREIGN SERVICE JOURNAL**, 2101 E St. NW, Washington DC 20037. (202)338-4045. Contact: Assistant Editor. Emphasizes foreign policy for foreign service employees. Monthly. Circ. 9,000. Accepts previously published material. Returns original artwork after publication. Sample copy for SASE with 87¢ postage.
Cartoons: Write or call for appointment to show portfolio. Buys first rights. Pays on publication.
Illustrations: Buys 1-2 illustrations/issue from freelancers. Works on assignment only. Write or call for appointment to show portfolio. Buys first rights. Pays on publication.

***FOREST NOTES**, 54 Portsmouth St., Concord NH 03301. (603)224-9945. Editor: Richard Ober. Magazine emphasizing conservation and environmental news. "*Forest Notes* offers news of conservation, forestry and environmental issues in New Hampshire and New England. Quarterly. Circ. 8,000. Accepts previously published material. Original artwork sometimes returned after publication. Sample copy available.
Cartoons: Buys 1 cartoon/issue from freelancers. Buys 4 cartoons/year from freelancers. Prefers people-oriented, nonsensational art for upscale readers. Prefers single panel without gagline; b&w line drawings. Send query letter with samples of style. Samples are filed. Samples not filed are returned. Reports back within 3 weeks. Buys first or reprint rights. Pays $50 maximum, b&w.
Illustrations: Buys 1 illustration/issue from freelancers. Buys 4 illustrations/year from freelancers. Works on assignment only. Send query letter with brochure or tear sheets. Samples are filed. Reports back within 3 weeks. To show a portfolio, mail Photostats. Buys first or reprint rights. Pays $50, b&w. Pays on acceptance.
Tips: "Live and work in New Hampshire or New England."

4-H LEADER, The National Magazine for 4-H, 7100 Connecticut Ave., Chevy Chase MD 20815. (301)961-2800. Editor: Suzanne M. Carney. Emphasizes techniques for working with children, and interests of children, for adult and teenaged 4-H volunteers. Receives few cartoons and 2-3 illustrations/week from freelance artists.
Illustrations: Especially needs themes on families, teen interest and adults interacting with youngsters. Send query letter with brochure showing art style or Photostats, tear sheets or photocopies to be kept on file. No originals. May be any type b&w technique, watercolor, charcoal sketch, scratchboard, pen & ink or woodcuts. SASE. Reports in 1 month. Buys one-time rights. Pays $10-75; on acceptance.

4 WHEEL & OFF-ROAD MAGAZINE, 8490 Sunset Blvd., Los Angeles CA 90069. Art Director: Karen Hawley. Magazine emphasizing 4-wheel drive vehicles for males aged 16-35. Monthly. Circ. 350-400,000.
Cartoons: Buys 1-3 cartoons/issue from freelancers. Prefers single or multiple panel; b&w line drawings. Send samples of style to be kept on file. Call to schedule an appointment to show a portfolio. Material not kept on file is returned only if requested. Reports only if interested. Buys all rights.
Illustrations: Buys 0-3 illustrations/issue from freelancers. Works on assignment only. Send query letter with resume, tear sheets, Photostats and photocopies. Samples not filed are returned only if requested. Reports only if interested. Call or write to schedule an appointment to show a portfolio, which should include original/final art and final reproduction/product. Buys all rights. Pays on publication.

FREEWAY, Box 632, Glen Ellyn IL 60138. (312)668-6000. Designer: Mardelle Ayers. Sunday School paper emphasizing Christian living for teenagers for high school and college age teens from a conservative, evangelical Christian upbringing. Published 4 quarters/year, 13 issues/quarter. Circ. 60,000. Accepts previously published material. Returns originals after publication. Sample copy for SASE with first-class postage.
Cartoons: Buys 4-5 cartoons/quarter. Prefers any style or theme that appeals to teens. Prefers single,

double or multi panel with gagline; b&w line drawings or b&w washes. Send query letter with finished cartoons. Material not kept on file is returned by SASE. Reports within 4 weeks. Buys first rights. Pays $15, b&w.
Illustrations: Buys 1-3 illustrations/issue from freelancers. Works on assignment only. Prefers any theme or style appealing to teens. Send query letter with resume, Photostats and photocopies. Samples not filed are returned by SASE if requested. Reports only if interested. To show a portfolio, mail Photostats and b&w photos. Payment is variable; on acceptance.

THE FRIEND, 50 E. North Temple, Salt Lake City UT 84150. (801)531-2210. Contact: Art Director. Children's publication of the Church of Jesus Christ of Latter-day Saints. Emphasizes the cultures and children of different countries. Original artwork returned after publication, usually after about 1 year.
Illustrations: Uses 30-35 illustrations/issue; buys about 12/issue from freelancers. Interested in themes mostly specific to individual art assignments from our concepts (child-related, dealing with ages 1-12); excellent, competitive quality. Covers often emphasize seasons and holidays; wide spectrum of styles and ideas. Works with freelancers on assignment basis only, except for activity related things. Samples returned if artist requests. Provide printed samples to be kept on file for future assignments. Prefers roughs of ideas before finish art. SASE. Report depends on specific art assignment. Need to retain art for about a year. Pays $200-600, b&w and full-color; on acceptance.

FRONT PAGE DETECTIVE, RGH Publications, 20th Floor, 460 W. 34th St., New York NY 10001. Editor: Rose Mandelsberg. For mature adults—law enforcement officials, professional investigators, criminology buffs and interested laymen. Monthly.
Cartoons: Must have crime theme. Submit finished art. SASE. Reports in 10 days. Buys all rights. Pays $25; on acceptance.
Tips: "Make sure the cartoons submitted do not degrade or ridicule law enforcement officials. Omit references to supermarkets/convenience stores."

FUR-FISH-GAME, A.R. Harding Publishing Co., 2878 E. Main St., Columbus OH 43209. (614)231-9585. Editor/Art Director: Tom Glass. Monthly magazine with circulation of 180,000 for practical outdoorsmen, emphasizing trapping, fishing, hunting, woodsmanship and conservation. Previously published work OK in some cases. Sample copy $1; free artists' guidelines.
Covers: Uses 12/year, mostly from well-known artists. Receives about 1 submission/week from freelancers. Interested in game animals, gamebirds, gamefish and furbearers. Prefers to see color photograph or transparency of art. SASE. Reports in 6 weeks. Painting must be able to crop into square format for cover. Pays $75 for one-time rights for full-color covers; on acceptance.
Illustrations: Uses 50-150 b&w/year, mostly from submissions and freelancers responding to assigned work. Interested freelancers should send query letter with specific submissions or samples of work. Photostats or other reproductions preferred as submissions. SASE if needed. Pays $10-30 for most, on acceptance.
Tips: "We are seeking top-quality color paintings for our covers. We work at least 10 weeks in advance with covers and attempt to keep them seasonal. Subjects such as small game, common game fish, furbearers and outdoorsmen in a beautiful natural setting have the best chance of acceptance. Prefer artist's signature on right side of painting. Credit will be given in table of contents. We are looking for very realistic work that contains a certain freshness and vitality, especially for our covers. The work must not only be visually appealing, but also painstakingly accurate in its detail of wild animals or birds. We are also looking for good quality b&w art of animals in their natural setting. If the art tells a story—so much the better. Familiarize yourself with the magazine before making queries or sending samples."

THE FUTURIST, 4916 St. Elmo Ave., Bethesda MD 20814. (301)656-8274. Art Director: Cynthia Fowler. Managing Editor: Timothy H. Willard. Emphasizes all aspects of the future for a well-educated, general audience. Bimonthly. Circ. 30,000. Accepts simultaneous submissions. Return of original artwork following publication depends on individual agreement. Sample copy available.
Illustrations: Buys 3-4 illustrations/issue from freelancers. Uses a variety of themes and styles "usually line-drawings, often whimsical. We like an artist who can read an article and deal with the concepts and ideas." Works on assignment only. Send query letter with brochure, samples or tear sheets to be kept on file. Call or write for appointment to show portfolio. "Photostats are fine as samples; whatever is easy for the artist." Reports only if interested. Rights purchased negotiable. Pays $300-500, color, cover; $100-125, b&w, inside; on acceptance.

GALLERY MAGAZINE, 800 2nd Ave., New York NY 10017. (212)986-9600. Creative Director: Michael Monte. Emphasizes sophisticated men's entertainment for the middle-class, collegiate male. Monthly. Circ. 700,000. No art guidelines, editorial content dictates illustration style.
Cartoons: Buys 5 cartoons/issue from freelancers. Interested in sexy humor; single, double, or multi-

"Here she comes just a-walkin' down the street . . . singing 'Doo wah ditty . . . dum . . . ditty doo . . .' "

***"Hysterical laughter" was the message cartoonist Rick Stromoski wanted to convey in this single-panel cartoon published in* Gallery Magazine. *The Los Angeles-based cartoonist sold first North American serial rights for $60. He learned of the magazine through the* Artist's Market.**

ple panel with or without gagline, color and b&w washes, b&w line drawings. Send finished cartoons. Reports in 1 month. Buys first rights. Pays on publication. Enclose SASE. Contact: J. Linden.
Illustrations: Buys 4-5 full-page illustrations monthly from freelancers. Works on assignment only. Interested in the "highest creative and technical styles." Especially needs slick, high quality, 4-color work. Send flyer, samples and tear sheets to be kept on file for possible future assignment. Send samples of style or submit portfolio. Samples returned by SASE. Reports in several weeks. Negotiates rights purchased. Pays $1,000 maximum for inside color washes; on publication.

***GAMBLING TIMES**, 1018 N. Cole Ave., Hollywood CA 90038. (213)463-4833. Editor-in-Chief: Len Miller. Art Director: Jackie Yberra. Emphasizes gambling techniques and personalities in gambling. Monthly. Circ. 100,000. Original artwork returned after publication. Sample copy $1; free artist's guidelines.
Cartoons: Buys approximately 20/year on topic directly related to gambling. Prefers finished cartoon, full-page, single panel; b&w line drawings. SASE. Reports in 2 weeks. Buys all rights. Pays $25-100; on publication.
Illustrations: Uses 6-7 illustrations/issue; buys 5/issue from freelancers. Interested in simple and clean b&w line drawings; satirical or humorous visuals used occasionally. Works on assignment only. Samples returned by SASE. Provide business card or tear sheet to be kept on file for future assignments. Prefers to see portfolio. Reports in 1 week. Buys all rights on a work-for-hire basis. Pays $25-100; on publication.

GAMES, 1350 Avenue of the Americas, New York NY 10022. (212)421-5984. Contact: Art Director. Emphasizes games, puzzles, mazes, brain teasers, etc. for adults interested in paper and pencil games. Bimonthly. Circ. 600,000.
Cartoons: Buys 1 cartoon/issue from freelancers. Pays $100 b&w and $200 color.
Illustrations: Buys 5-15 illustrations/issue from freelancers. Illustrations should be lighthearted but not childish. Prefers b&w line drawings and color renderings for inside and cover. Send query letter with brochure showing art style or tear sheets. To show a portfolio, drop off on Wednesdays or mail tear sheets. Buys one-time rights. Pays $1,500 b&w; $2,500 color, cover.
Tips: "We encourage artists to create games or puzzles that they can execute in their own style after editorial approval. Illustrations are often required to be based on specific puzzles but can also be conceptual in nature."

GARDEN, New York Botanical Garden, Bronx NY 10458. Associate Editor: Jessica Snyder. Emphasizes all aspects of the plant world—botany, horticulture, the environment, etc. for "members of botanical gardens and arboreta—a diverse readership, largely college graduates and professionals, with a common interest in plants." Bimonthly. Circ. 30,000. Accepts previously published material. Original artwork returned after publication. Sample copy $3.
Illustrations: Works on assignment only. Send query letter with Photostats, photographs, tear sheets, slides or photocopies. Especially looks for "quality, botanical accuracy and style." Samples not kept on file are returned by SASE. Reports only if interested. To show a portfolio, mail appropriate materials. Buys one-time rights. Pays $25 minimum, b&w, inside; $150, color, cover; on publication.

GENERAL LEARNING CORPORATION, 60 Revere Dr., Northbrook IL 60062-1563. (312)564-4070. Photo & Graphics editor: Denise Cavanah. Produces 10 magazines—*Current Health I, Current Health II, Career World, Writing!* and *Current Consumer & Lifestudies* published monthly during the school year. Readership is 7-12th grade students. Remaining four titles are *Your Health & Fitness* and *Your Health & Safety*, both bimonthly. *Energy Sense* and *Money Plan* both quarterly. The readership is general audience. Accepts previously published material. Original artwork returned after publication. Sample copy free for 8x10 SASE.
Illustrations: Student publications use a varying number of b&w illustrations/issue. General magazines use 5-10 b&w and color illustrations/issue and work on an assignment basis only. Send query letter with photocopies or slides. Samples are returned only by request with SASE. Reports within 2-4 weeks. Buys one-time rights for student magazines, negotiates payment, pays on publication. Negotiates rights purchased and payment for general magazines; on acceptance.

GENT, Dugent Publishing Co., 2355 Salzedo St., Coral Gables FL 33134. Publisher: Douglas Allen. Editor: John Fox. Managing Editor: Nye Willden. For men "who like big women." Sample copy, $3.
Cartoons: Buys humor and sexual themes; "major emphasis of magazine is on large D-cup-breasted women." Mail cartoons. Buys first rights. Pays $50, b&w spot drawing; $75/page.
Illustrations: Buys 3-4 illustrations/issue on assigned themes. Submit illustration samples for files. Buys b&w only. Buys first rights. Pays $100-150.
Tips: "Send samples designed especially for our publication. Study our magazine. Be able to draw erotic anatomy. Write for artist's guides and cartoon guides *first*, before submitting samples, since they contain some helpful suggestions."

GENTLEMENS QUARTERLY, 350 Madison Ave., New York NY 10017. (212)880-6691. Art Director: Mary Shanahan. Emphasizes "men's fashions and lifestyles for middle- to upper-income professional males ranging in age from 20 to 40." Monthly. Circ. 650,000. No cartoons.
Illustrations: Uses less than 10 illustrations/issue, all supplied by freelancers. Selection based on review of portfolios ("we have a strict first-time drop-off policy") and by reviewing files maintained on freelancers. Send copied samples of b&w and color drawings to art assistant; do not send original work. SASE. Reports in 1 week. Pays 30 days after work is completed. Buys all rights on a work-for-hire basis.

GLAMOUR, 350 Madison Ave., New York NY 10017. (212)880-8800. Art Director: George Hartman. Emphasizes fashion, beauty, travel, lifestyle for women ages 18-35. Query with resume and arrange to show portfolio.
Needs: "All work done here is freelance." Pays $225/page.

GLASS DIGEST, 310 Madison Ave., New York NY 10017. Editor: Charles B. Cumpston. For management in the distribution, merchandising, and installation phases of the flat glass, architectural metal, and allied products industry (including stained, art glass and mirrors). Original artwork not returned after publication. Free sample copy.

Cartoons: Uses 0-3 cartoons/issue; buys about 2/issue from freelancers. Receives 5 submissions/week from freelancers. Interested in storefront and curtain wall construction and automotive glass industry. Prefers to see finished cartoons. SASE. Reports in 1 week. Pays $7.50; on acceptance.
Illustrations: Works on assignment only. Prefers to see roughs. Samples returned by SASE. Reports in 1 week. Buys first North American serial rights. Pays on acceptance.
Tips: "Stick to the subject matter."

GLASS NEWS, Box 7138, Pittsbrugh PA 15213. (412)362-5136. Manager: Liz Scott. Emphasizes glass manufacturing and industry news for glass manufacturers, dealers, and others involved in making, buying, and selling glass items and products. Semimonthly. Circ. 1,600. Sample copy for SASE with 56¢ postage.
Cartoons: Uses 1 cartoon/issue. Receives an average of 1 submisson/week from freelancers. Cartoons should pertain to glass manufacturing (flat glass, fiberglass, bottles and containers; no mirrors). Prefers single and multiple panel b&w line drawings with gagline. Prefers roughs or finished cartoons. SASE. Reports in 1 month. Buys all rights. Pays $25; on acceptance.
Tips: "Learn about making glass of all kinds."

***GLENFED TODAY**,700 N. Brand Blvd., 11th floor, Box 1709, Glendale CA 91209. (818)500-2732. Editor-in-Chief: Lisa Jason. Emphasizes the savings and loan industry and company events for employees of Glendale Federal. Monthly. Circ. 5,600.
Cartoons: Uses 1-2 cartoons/issue; buys 1-2 from freelancers. Interested in conservative themes. No anti-establishment themes. Prefers single, double, or multi-panel with or without gagline, color and b&w washes, b&w line drawings. Send query letter with samples of style. Samples not returned. Reporting time "depends on work load." Buys all rights. Negotiates payment; pays on publication.
Illustrations: Uses 1-2 illustrations/issue; buys 1-2 from freelancers. Interested in conservative themes. No anti-establishment themes. Works on assignment only; reports back whether to expect possible future assignments. Send query letter "that we can keep. Do not phone. Do not send unsolicited photos. We cannot return them." Reporting time "depends on work load." Buys all rights. Negotiates pay; pays on publication.
Tips: "We are becoming comprehensive family financial centers with a housing orientation. Changes within our operation include the introduction of interest-bearing checking accounts, credit cards, etc. Freelance artists should be sure to query first and send SASE."

GOLDEN YEARS MAGAZINE, 233 E. New Haven Ave., Melbourne FL 32901. Art Director: Debbie Billington. Statewide magazine for the mature market (50 and over). Monthly. Circ. 700,000. Accepts previously published material. Sample copy $1. Art guidelines available.
Illustrations: Pays $25-150.
Tips: Looks for "ability to illustrate an article in a way that isn't obvious, i.e., with a sense of humor or maybe looking at the subject from a different perspective. Photocopies aren't very impressive. Printed pieces attract attention."

GOLF JOURNAL, Golf House, Far Hills NJ 07931. (201)234-2300. Managing Editor: George Eberl. Readers are "literate, professional, knowledgeable on the subject of golf." Published 8 times/year. Circ. 135,000. Original artwork not returned after publication. Free sample copy.
Cartoons: Buys 2-3 cartoons/issue from freelancers. Receives 50 submissions/week from freelancers. "The subject is golf. Golf must be central to the cartoon. Drawings should be professional, and captions sharp, bright and literate, on a par with our generally sophisticated readership." Formats: single or multiple panel, b&w line drawings with gagline. Prefers to see finished cartoons. SASE. Reports in 1 month. Buys one-time rights. Pays $25, b&w cartoons; on acceptance.
Illustrations: Buys several illustrations/issue from freelancers. "We maintain a file of samples from illustrators. Our needs for illustrations—and we do need talent with an artistic light touch—are based almost solely on assignments, illustrations to accompany specific stories. We would assign a job to an illustrator who is able to capture the feel and mood of a story. Most frequently, it is light-touch golf stories that beg illustrations. A sense of humor is a useful quality in the illustrator; but this sense shouldn't lapse into absurdity." Uses color washes. Send samples of style to be kept on file for future assignments. SASE. Reports in 1 month. Buys all rights on a work-for-hire basis. Payment varies, "usually $300/page.
Tips: "We often need illustrations supporting a story. Knowledge of the game and a light touch, however, are imperative and, too often, sadly lacking. I can't call it a trend, but at times it seems that self expression supersedes the ability and willingness to underscore a point artistically."

GOLF MAGAZINE, Times Mirror Magazines, 380 Madison Ave., New York NY 10017. Art Director: Ron Ramsey. Emphasizes golf. Monthly. Circ. 850,000. Original artwork returned after publication.

Art guidelines for SASE.
Illustrations: Uses 3-6 illustrations/issue; buys 2-3/issue from freelancers. Works on assignment only. Send 35mm photographs or tear sheets to be kept on file. Samples not kept on file are returned by SASE. Reports only if interested. Buys first or all rights. Write for appointment to show portfolio; drop off policy. Pays $700, b&w and $1,000, color, cover; $300, b&w and $700, color, inside; on acceptance.

GOLF SHOP OPERATIONS, 5520 Park Ave., Trumbull CT 06611. (203)373-7000. Editor and Publisher: Nick Romano. Art Director: Nancy Graham. For golf professionals at public and private courses, resorts and driving ranges. Published 8 times/year. Circ. 13,200. Original artwork returned after publication. Free sample copy.
Illustrations: Buys 4-6 illustrations/issue. Works on assignment only. Soft goods oriented. Illustrations often used for conceptual pieces. Send query letter with brochure showing art style or tear sheets, slides and photographs. Samples returned by SASE. Reports back on future assignment possibilities. Reports in 2 weeks. Call to schedule an appointment to show a portfolio, which should include thumbnails, roughs, original/final art, final reproduction/product, color, tear sheets and b&w. Buys one-time reproduction rights on a work-for-hire basis. Pays $50-750; on acceptance.

GOOD HOUSEKEEPING, Hearst Corp., 959 8th Ave., New York NY 10019. (212)262-5700. Editor-in-Chief: John Mack Carter. Contact: Art Director. For homemakers. Emphasizes food, fashion, beauty, home decorating, current events, personal relationships and celebrities. Monthly. Circ. 5,000,000.
Cartoons: Buys 150/year on family life, animals and humor through youth; single panel. Arrange an interview to show portfolio. Buys all reproduction rights. Pays $250 maximum, b&w line drawings and washes; on acceptance.
Illustrations: Buys 15 illustrations/issue on romantic themes. "Drop off" policy for portfolios. Reports in 3 weeks. Buys all reproduction rights. Inside: pay for b&w line drawing and washes depends on complexity of job, $1,000-2,000, color washes and full-color renderings; on acceptance.

GOOD READING MAGAZINE, Box 40, Litchfield IL 62056. (217)324-3425. "Nonfiction magazine which emphasizes travel, business, human interest and novel occupations." Monthly. Circ. 12,000. Original artwork returned after publication, only if requested.
Cartoons: Buys 1 cartoon/issue from freelancers. Receives 15 submissions/week from freelancers. Interested in "business, points of interest, people with unusual hobbies and occupations, and wholesome humor." Prefers to see finished cartoons. SASE. Reports in 6-8 weeks. To show a portfolio, mail original/final art. Buys first North American serial rights. Pays $20 b&w; on acceptance.

***GORHAM**, 800 S. Euclid Blvd., Fullerton CA 92634. Publisher/Editor: Daniel J. Gorham. Emphasizes genealogy and history for people interested in their family's history. Monthly. Circ. 2,083. Accepts previously published material and simultaneous submissions. Original artwork returned after publication. Sample copy $2.
Illustrations: Uses 15-45 illustrations/issue; buys 20-30/issue from freelancers. Themes and styles are open, but desires "good, serious work." Send query letter with samples to be kept on file. Samples not kept on file are returned by SASE. Reports within 2 months. Write for appointment to show portfolio. Buys first rights. Pays $500-1,000, b&w, cover; $75-500, b&w, inside; on publication.
Tips: Seeks *neat* work, with a "timeless aspect."

GRADUATING ENGINEER, 1221 Ave. of the Americas, New York NY 10020. (212)512-3796. Art Director: Vincent Lomonte. Directed to the young engineer in his last year of school, who is about to enter job market. Quarterly with 3 special issues; computer, women, minority. Circ. 83,000. Returns original artwork after publication. Art guidelines available.
Illustrations: Buys 10-15 illustrations/issue from freelancers. Works on assignment only. Send brochure and business card to be kept on file. Will review Photostats, tear sheets, photocopies, slides or photographs. Reports back only if interested. Call art director for appointment to show portfolio. Negotiates rights purchased. Pays $200-300 for b&w and $500 for color, cover; $125-225 for b&w inside; on acceptance.

GRAND RAPIDS MAGAZINE, Gemini Publications, Suite 1040, Trust Building, 40 Pearl St. NW, Grand Rapids MI 49503. (616)459-4545. Editor: Ronald E. Koehler. Managing Editor: Carole Vallade Smith. For greater Grand Rapids residents. Monthly. Circ. 13,500. Original artwork returned after publication. Local artists only.
Cartoons: Buys 2-3 cartoons/issue from freelancers. Prefers Michigan, Western Michigan, Lake Michigan, city, issue or consumer/household themes. Send query letter with samples. Samples not filed are returned by SASE. Reports within 1 month. Buys all rights. Pays $25-35 b&w.
Illustrations: Buys 2-3 illustrations/issue from freelancers. Prefers Michigan, Western Michigan,

Lake Michigan, city, issue or consumer/household themes. Send query letter with samples. Samples not filed are returned by SASE. Reports within 1 month. To show a portfolio, mail original/final art and final reproduction/product or call to schedule an appointment. Buys all rights. Pays $100 color, cover; $20-30 b&w and $30-50 color, inside; on publication.
Tips: "Approach only if you have good ideas."

GRAPHIC ARTS MONTHLY, 875 3rd Ave., New York NY 10022. (212)605-9548. Editor: Roger Ynostroza. Managing Editor: Peter Johnston. For management and production personnel in commercial and specialty printing plants and allied crafts. Monthly. Circ. 90,000. Sample copy $5.
Cartoons: Buys 15 cartoons/year on printing, layout, paste-up, typesetting and proofreading; single panel. Mail art. SASE. Reports in 3 weeks. Buys first rights. Pays on acceptance.

GRAY'S SPORTING JOURNAL, 205 Willow St., So. Hamilton MA 01982. (617)468-4486. Editor-in-Chief: Ed Gray. Art Director: DeCourcy Taylor. Concerns the outdoors, hunting and fishing. Published 4 times/year. Circ. 35,000. Sample copy $6.50; artist's guidelines for SASE.
Illustrations: Buys 10 illustrations/year, 2-6/issue, on hunting and fishing. Send query letter with tear sheets or slides. SASE. Reports in 4 weeks. To show a portfolio, mail tear sheets and photographs. Buys one-time rights. Pays $350, color art; $75-200, b&w line drawings, inside.
Tips: "Will definately not accept original art."

GREAT LAKES TRAVEL & LIVING, 108 W. Perry St., Port Clinton OH 43452. (419)734-5774. Associate Editor: Carol B. Brown. Estab. 1986. Magazine emphasizing travel and tourism in the Great Lakes region for people who enjoy living and vacationing in the Great Lakes region. Monthly. Circ. 40,000. Accepts previously published material. Original artwork returned after publication. Sample copy for SASE with $1.25 postage. Art guidelines for SASE with 37¢ postage.
Cartoons: Prefers b&w line drawings. Send query letter with samples of style to be kept on file except for items artist requests back. Write or call for appointment to show a portfolio. Material not kept on file is returned by SASE. Reports within 4 weeks. Buys one-time rights. Negotiates payment.
Illustrations: Buys 1-3 illustrations/issue from freelancers. Works on assignment only. Prefers b&w line drawings, usually rendered from photos of locations featured in the editorial material. Send query letter with brochure showing art style. Samples not filed are returned by SASE. Reports within 4 weeks. Call or write to schedule an appointment to show a portfolio. Buys one-time rights or negotiates rights purchased. Pays $50-350. Pays on publication.
Tips: "Freelancers don't read the magazine to see our style of art. We're pretty conservative, but get lots of 'trendy' samples the opposite of our style!"

***GREATER PHOENIX JEWISH NEWS**, Suite G, 7220 N. 16th St., Phoenix AZ 85020. (602)870-9470. Production Manager: Debra Ross. Tabloid emphasizing topics of interest to Jewish residents of Phoenix and surrounding areas—both local, national and international news. Readers are 35-65; 60% are college graduates. Weekly. Circ. 7,000. Accepts previously published material. Sample copy for SASE with $1 postage. Art guidelines available.
Cartoons: Currently buys weekly cartoons, will consider others. Prefers Jewish issues and family life themes. Prefers single panel with gagline; b&w line drawings. Send query letter with samples of style to be kept on file. Write for appointment to show portfolio. Material not filed is returned by SASE. Reports within 2 weeks. Negotiates rights purchased and payment; pays on publication.
Illustrations: Buys 1-3/month. Works on assignment only. Send query letter with brochure, resume or business card and samples to be kept on file. Write for appointment to show portfolio. Accepts any type sample except slides. Samples not filed are returned by SASE. Reports within 2 weeks. Negotiates rights purchased and payment; pays on publication.

THE GRENADIER MAGAZINE, 3833 Lake Shore, Oakland CA 94610. (415)763-0928. Senior Editor: S.A. Jefferis-Tibbets. Emphasizes military simulation and its historical context for military professionals, war gamers and game theorists. Bimonthly. Circ. 5,600. Original artwork not returned after publication. Sample copy for 9x12 SASE with $1.25 postage; art guidelines for SASE with first-class postage.
Cartoons: Buys 0-1 cartoon/issue from freelancers. Military simulation theme. Prefers single panel with gagline; b&w line drawings or b&w washes. Send query letter with samples of style or finished cartoons to be kept on file. Material not filed is returned by SASE. Reports within 1 month. To show a portfolio, mail appropriate materials. Buys all rights. Pays $10-5, b&w; open rate, color; on acceptance.
Illustrations: Buys 0-12 illustration/issue from freelancers. Works on assignment only. Send query letter with brochure and samples to be kept on file. Photocopies OK as samples if they show the artist's style and capability. Samples not filed are returned by SASE. Reports within 1 week. To show a portfolio, mail appropriate materials. Buys all rights. Pays $250 +, color, cover; $10-25, b&w, inside; on acceptance.

GROUP, Thom Schultz Publications, Inc., Box 481, Loveland CO 80539. (303)669-3836. Editorial Director: Joani Schultz. Director of Design: Jean Bruns. For adult leaders of high-school-age Christian youth groups. Incorporates *Group Members Only Magazine* (also sold separately) for members of high-school-age Christian youth groups. Both published 8 times/year. Circ. 60,000. Previously published, photocopied and simultaneous submissions OK. Original artwork returned after publication, if requested. Sample copy $1.
Cartoons: Buys cartoons occasionally from freelancers. Interested in humor through youth and religion. Send finished artwork. Reports in 2 weeks. Buys first, reprint or all rights, but may reassign rights to artist after publication. Pays on acceptance.
Illustrations: Buys 6 illustrations/issue; buys all from freelancers. Send query letter with finished art, roughs, slides or tear sheets to be kept on file for future assignments. Reports in 2 weeks. Call to schedule an appointment to show a portfolio, which should include original/final art, tear sheets and photographs. Cover: Pays $200 minimum, color. Inside: Pays $25-300, b&w line drawings and washes, color. Buys first publication rights and occasionally additional rights.
Tips: "I find we're needing more black-and-white illustrations of a serious, more conceptual nature. However, we still seek humorous illustrations in a style appropriate for our adult audience (mature, not childish). I look for evidence of maturity and a well-developed style in the illustrator. I also look for good, artistically-sound renderings, particularly of people and ability to conceptualize well and approach subjects in an unusual way."

***GUIDEPOSTS**, 747 3rd Ave., New York NY 10017. (212)754-2200. Contact: Design Director. "*Guideposts* is an inspirational monthly magazine for all faiths in which men and women from all walks of life tell how they overcame obstacles, rose above failures, not sorrow, learned to master themselves, and became more effective people through the direct application of the religious principles by which they live." Monthly. Original artwork returned after publication. Free sample copy.
Illustrations: Uses 2-3 illustrations/issue; buys 2-3/month from freelancers. Receives 15 samples/month from freelancers. Works on assignment only. Call Larry Laukhuf for interview; prefers to see portfolio in conjunction with artist. Provide business card, brochure, flyer and tear sheet to be kept on file for future assignments. Buys one-time rights on a work-for-hire basis. Buys full-color illustrations, and washes.

GULFSHORE LIFE MAGAZINE, 2975 S. Horseshoe Dr., Naples FL 33942. (813)643-3933. Creative Director: Alyce Mathias. Magazine emphasizing lifestyle of southwest Florida for an affluent, sophisticated audience. Monthly. Circ. 18,000. Accepts previously published material. Original artwork returned after publication. Sample copy $3.
Illustrations: Send query letter with brochure, resume, tear sheets, Photostats and photocopies. Samples not filed are returned by SASE. Reports back only if interested. Write to schedule appointment to show a portfolio, which should include thumbnails, original/final art, final/reproduction/product and tear sheets. Negotiates rights purchased. Payment negotiated; pays on publication.

GYMNASTICS TODAY, 2006 Pine St., Philadelphia PA 19103. (215)235-4917. Publisher: Ron Alexander. Tabloid emphasizing gymnastics and fitness for teen gymnastic athletes, coaches, officials and fans. Bimonthly. Circ. 130,000. Accepts previously published material. Returns original artwork after publication. Sample copy for SASE with 60¢ postage; art guidelines for SASE with first-class postage.
Cartoons: Buys 1 cartoon/issue from freelancers. Prefers single panel; b&w line drawings or b&w washes. Send samples of style or roughs to be kept on file. Call for appointment to show portfolio. Material not kept on file is returned by SASE if requested. Buys one-time rights. Payment is negotiable.
Illustrations: Buys 3-5 illustrations/issue from freelancers. Prefers b&w line drawings and washes. Send query letter with resume, tear sheets, Photostats, photocopies, slides and photographs. Samples not filed are returned by SASE. Reports only if interested. Call or write to schedule an appointment to show a portfolio, which should include thumbnails, roughs, tear sheets, Photostats and b&w. Buys one-time rights. Pays $200-500, b&w; $300-600, color, cover; $150-300, b&w; $200-400, color, inside; on publication.

HADASSAH MAGAZINE, 50 W. 58th St., New York NY 10019. (212)355-7900. Editor-in-Chief: Alan M. Tigay. Advertising Director: Robert Kinney. Art Director: Meyer Fecher. For American Jewish families; deals with social, economic, political and cultural developments in Israel and Jewish communities in the U.S. and elsewhere. Monthly. Circ. 370,000. Sample copy $1.50. SASE. Reports in 6 weeks. Buys first rights. Pays on acceptance.

HAM RADIO, Greenville NH 03048. (603)878-1441. Editor-in-Chief: Rich Rosen. Managing Editor: Dorothy Rosa. Art Director: Susan Shorrock. Address inquiries to Dorothy Rosa. For licensed amateur radio operators and electronics experimenters. Monthly. Circ. 40,000.

Illustrations: Buys drafting (on assignment), cover art, illustration. Prefers to see photocopied samples; do not send original art unless requested to do so. Reports in 30 days. Minimum payment: cover art, $100; illustration, $20; on publication.
Tips: "On our covers we favor strong graphic interpretations of concepts in electronics. The use of bright, bold colors sets us apart from other publications in our field."

HANDS-ON ELECTRONICS, 500 B Bi-County Blvd., Farmingdale NY 11735. (516)293-3000. Editor: Julian Martin. Magazine emphasizing hobby electronics for consumer and hobby-oriented electronics buffs. Monthly. Circ. 120,000. Original artwork not returned after publication. Sample copy free.
Cartoons: Buys 3-5 cartoons/issue from freelancers. Prefers single panel with or without gagline; b&w line drawings and b&w washes. Send finished cartoons; "we purchase and keep! Unused ones returned." Samples are returned. Reports within 1 week. Buys all rights. Pays $25 b&w.
Illustrations: Does not buy illustrations currently, "but would like to start." Works on assignment only. Send query letter with brochure showing art style. Samples not filed are returned. Reports within 1 week. Write to schedule an appointment to show a portfolio, which should include thumbnails, roughs, original/final art, final reproduction/product, color, tear sheets, photographs and b&w. Buys all rights. Pays $300, color, cover; payment depends on usage for inside; on acceptance.

HARROWSMITH, Camden House Publishing Ltd., Ontario K0K 1J0 Canada. (613)378-6661. Editor-in-Chief: James Lawrence. Art Director: Pamela McDonald. Concerns alternative lifestyles, energy sources and architecture, the environment, country living and gardening. Publishes 6 issues/year. Circ. 164,000. Sample copy $5. Receives 4 cartoons and 6 illustrations/week from freelance artists.
Cartoons: Uses 2-3 cartoons/issue, all from freelancers. Single panel with gagline. Prefers roughs, samples for files and business card; SAE (nonresidents include IRC). Reports in 6 weeks. Pays $25-100 on acceptance.
Illustrations: Uses 12 illustrations/issue, all from freelancers. Interested in "high-quality color, drawings and some fine art on country living theme. Many have won awards." Works on assignment only. Likes to have samples on file. Reports back on future assignment possibilities; SAE (nonresidents include IRC). Reports in 6 weeks. Buys first North American serial rights. Cover: pays $500-1,200, color. Inside: pays $250-1,000 color; $150-500, b&w; on acceptance.

HARROWSMITH MAGAZINE, The Creamery, Charlotte VT 05445. (802)425-3961. Managing Editor: Tom Rawls. Estab. 1986. Magazine emphasizing country living in the northern U.S. for sophisticated, well-educated, between 25-45 years of age interested in country living. Bimonthly. Circ. 180,000. Original artwork returned after publication. Sample copy $4. Art guidelines for SASE with 39¢ postage.
Cartoons: Buys 1 cartoon/issue from freelancers. Prefers b&w line drawings. Send query letter with samples of style to be kept on file. Write to schedule an appointment to show a portfolio. Samples not filed returned by SASE. Reports within 4 weeks. Buys first or reprint rights. Negotiates payment.

***HEALTH MAGAZINE**, 41st Floor, 3 Park Ave., New York NY 10016. (212)340-9200. Art Director: Maxine Davidowitz. Circ. 1,000,000. Original artwork returned after publication.
Illustrations: Uses 10 illustrations/issue. Works on assignment only. Send samples to be kept on file. Buys first rights. Payment varies; on acceptance.

THE HERB QUARTERLY, Box 275, Newfane VT 05345. (802)365-4392. Editor and Publisher: Sally Ballantine. Magazine emphasizing horticulture for middle to upper class, affluent men and women with an ardent enthusiasm for herbs and all their uses—gardening, culinary, crafts, etc. Most are probably home-owners. Quarterly. Circ. 20,000. Accepts previously published material. Original artwork returned after publication if requested. Sample copy $5. Art guidelines available.
Illustrations: Prefers pen & ink illustrations, heavily contrasted. Illustrations of herbs, garden designs, etc. Artist should be able to create illustrations drawn from themes of manuscripts sent to them. Send query letter with brochure showing art style or resume, tear sheets, photocopies, slides and photographs. Samples not filed are returned by SASE only if requested. Reports within weeks. To show a portfolio, mail original/final art, final reproduction/product, photographs or b&w. Buys reprint rights. Pays on publication.

HIBISCUS MAGAZINE, Box 22248, Sacramento CA 95822. Editor: Margaret Wensrich. Estab. 1985. Magazine for "people who like to read poetry and short stories." Published three times/year. Circ. 2,000. Original artwork returned after publication if requested. Sample copy $3; art guidelines for SASE with 39¢ postage.
Illustrations: Buys 3-4 illustrations/issue from freelancers. Works on assignment only. Send query letter with resume and samples. Samples not filed are returned by SASE. Reports back only if interested. To show a portfolio, mail original/final art or photocopy of finished work. "We use pen & ink drawings

only. No color, slides, etc." Buys first rights. Pays for design and illustration by the project $10-25; on acceptance.
Tips: "We need clean pen & ink that can be reproduced exactly by printer. Subjects are assigned. The portfolio gives us an idea of artist's work."

HIGHLIGHTS FOR CHILDREN, 803 Church St., Honesdale PA 18431. Art Director: John R. Crane. Cartoon Editor: John Lansingh Bennett. For ages 2-12. Monthly, bimonthly in July/August. Circ. 1,600,000.
Cartoons: Buys 2-4 cartoons/issue from freelancers. Receives 20 submissions/week from freelancers. Interested in upbeat, positive cartoons involving children, family life or animals; single panel. Send roughs or finished cartoons. SASE. Reports in 4-6 weeks. Buys all rights. Pays $20-25, line drawings; on acceptance. "One flaw in many submissions is that the concept or vocabulary is too adult, or that the experience necessary for its appreciation is beyond our readers. Frequently, a wordless self-explanatory cartoon is best."
Illustrations: Uses 30 illustrations/issue; buys 25 from freelancers. Works with freelancers on assignment only. "We are always looking for good hidden pictures. We require a picture that is interesting in itself and has the objects well hidden. Usually an artist submits pencil sketches. In no case do we pay for any preliminaries to the final art." Also needs "original ideas and illustrations for covers and 'What's Wrong' illustrations for back cover. Send samples of style and flyer to be kept on file. SASE. Reports in 4-6 weeks. Buys all rights on a work-for-hire basis. Pays on acceptance.
Tips: No cartoons or artwork that uses sex-role sterotypes, "sick" humor or mocks authority. "We use very limited amounts of 'cartooning' type art."

***HISTORIC PRESERVATION**, 1785 Massachusetts Ave. NW, Washington DC 20036. Editor: Thomas J. Colin. For members of the National Trust for Historic Preservation; concerns national preservation of architectural and cultural heritage. Bimonthly. Circ. 180,000. Simultaneous submissions and previously published work OK. Artist's guidelines available.
Illustrations: Buys 12 illustrations/year on education, architecture, folk art and historical subjects. Query with previously published work. SASE. Reports in 2 weeks. Buys one-time rights. Inside: Pays $150 maximum, color washes; $75 minimum, b&w line drawings and washes; on publication.

HOME LIFE, 127 9th Ave. N, Nashville TN 37234. (615)251-2581. Artist/Designer: David Wilson MSN 191. Leisure/religious magazine for married, divorced, widowed adults ages 25-45. Monthly. Circ. 750,000. Art guidelines for SASE. Sample copy $1.
Illustrations: Buys 10-15 illustrations/issue from freelancers. Works on assignment only. Themes or styles vary. Send query letter with samples. Samples are filed. Samples not filed are returned by SASE. Reviews tear sheets, Photostats. No slides or photographs. Reports back only if interested. Buys all rights. Pays $100-175, b&w, inside; on acceptance.

THE HORROR SHOW, 14848 Misty Springs Ln., Oak Run CA 96069-9801. (916)472-3540. Editor: David B. Silva. Magazine emphasizing short horror fiction for "anyone who enjoys a good chill up their spine." Quarterly. Circ. 4,000. Original artwork not returned after publication. Sample copy $4.95; art guidelines for SASE with first-class postage.
Cartoons: Buys 1-2 cartoons/issue. Pays $5 b&w; on acceptance.
Illustrations: Buys 13-20 b&w illustrations/issue from freelancers. Works on assignment only. Send query letter with tear sheets and photocopies to be kept on file, except for slides, which will be returned. Samples not filed are returned by SASE. Reports within 2 weeks. Buys first rights or reprint rights. To show a portfolio, mail tear sheets, photographs and b&w. Pays $15, color, cover; $10, b&w, inside; on acceptance.

HORSE ILLUSTRATED, Box 6050, Mission Viejo CA 92690. (714)240-6001. Editor: Jill-Marie Jones. For people of all ages who own, show and breed horses, who are interested in all phases of horse ownership. Monthly. Circ. 60,000. Sample copy $3; art guidelines for SASE.
Cartoons: Buys several cartoons/issue. Prefers single, double or multi panel. "Central character should be a horse." Send finished art. SASE. Reports within 6 weeks. Buys one-time rights. Pays $25-50, b&w line drawings; on publication.
Illustrations: Buys several illustrations/year of horses. Send query letter with resume and samples. SASE. Reports within 6 weeks. Buys one-time rights. Pays $20-50, b&w line drawings, inside; on publication.
Tips: When reviewing an illustrator's work, "we look for realism and accurate portrayal of the horse. We don't use 'fantasy' or 'surrealistic' art. For cartoons, we look for drawing ability and humor. We will, however, accept good humor with adequate illustration over good illustration with poor humor.

Generally, we use free-standing illustrations as art rather than going to the illustrator and commissioning a work, but this is impossible if the artist sends us poor reproductions. Naturally, this also lessens his chance of our seeking out his services."

HORTICULTURE, THE MAGAZINE OF AMERICAN GARDENING, 755 Boylston St., Boston MA 02116. (617)247-4100. Illustration Editor: Sarah Boorstyn Schwartz. Magazine geared to homeowners. Monthly. Circ. 140,000. Very occasionally accepts previously published material. Original artwork returned after publication. Art guidelines available.
Illustrations: Buys 15 illustrations/issue from freelancers. Works on assignment only. Prefers gardening as a theme, 'how-to' illustrations and color floral pieces. Send query letter with tear sheets, Photostats, photocopies, slides or photographs. Samples not filed are returned. Reports within 2 months. To show a portfolio, mail appropriate materials or call or write to schedule an appointment. Buys one-time rights. Fee schedule depends on complexity of piece and the amount of material; pays on publication.
Tips: "Show as many different styles as possible. Bring in (or send in) lots of work—doesn't have to be only gardening or horticulture material. Besides illustrating plants and gardens, I look for ability to render hand manipulations and figures. We are doing far more how-to, step-by-step sorts of illustration to gear ourselves to the new gardeners."

HOSPITAL PRACTICE, 10 Astor Place, New York NY 10003. (212)477-2727. Design Director: Robert S. Herald. Emphasizes clinical medicine and science for practicing physicians throughout the U.S. 18 issues/year. Circ. 200,000. Original artwork returned after publication if requested.
Illustrations: Uses 40-50 illustrations/issue; buys 15-20 illustrations/issue from freelancers. Uses only non-symbolic medical and scientific (conceptual) illustrations in a style similar to *Scientific American*. Also charts and graphs. Works on assignment only. Send query letter with brochure showing art style, resume, Photostats, photographs and tear sheets to be kept on file. Does not report unless called. Call for appointment to show portfolio, which should include original/final art, color, tear sheets, Photostats and b&w. Returns material if SASE included. Negotiates rights purchased. Pays $900, color, cover; $100 and up, b&w, inside; on publication.
Tips: "If possible, review the publication before submitting work, to understand specific editorial style. There are a lot more skilled general illustrators, but surprisngly few good ones specializing in biomedical science."

HOUSE & GARDEN, 350 Madison Ave., New York NY 10017. (212)880-8800. Art Director: Karen Lee Grant. Readers are upper income home owners or renters. Monthly. Circ. 500,000.
Illustrations: Uses minimum number of illustrations/issue; all of which are commissioned by the magazine. Selection based on "previous work, samples on file, and from seeing work in other publications. Illustrations are almost always assigned to fit specific articles." Themes "vary with our current format and with article we want illustrated." Format: b&w line drawings or washes. Portfolios viewed on first Tuesday of every month. Send samples of style to Art Director. SASE. Reports "from immediately to 4 weeks." Payment on acceptance "varies depending on artist, size and type of illustration." Buys one-time rights.

HUMPTY DUMPTY'S MAGAZINE, Box 567, Indianapolis IN 46206. (317)636-8881. Art Director: Lawrence Simmons. Special emphasis on health, nutrition, safety and exercise for girls and boys, ages 4-6. Monthly except bimonthly February/March, April/May, June/July and August/September. Sample copy 75¢; art guidelines for SASE.
Illustrations: Uses 25-35 illustrations/issue. Works on assignment only. Send query letter with resume, Photostats, slides, good photocopies or tear sheets to be kept on file. Samples returned by SASE if not kept on file. Reports within 6-8 weeks. Buys all rights. To show a portfolio, mail original/final art, final reproduction/product, color, b&w and 2-color. Include SASE for return. Pays $225, cover; and $25-65, b&w; $50-100, 2-color; $60-125, 4-color, inside; on publication.
Tips: Illustrations should be figurative and should be composed of story-telling situations. "Be familiar with the magazines before submitting artwork or samples that are completely inappropriate."

IDEALS MAGAZINE, Box 141000; Nelson Place at Elm Hill Pike, Nashville TN 37214. (615)889-9000. Editor: Peggy Schaefer. Magazine emphasizing poetry and light prose. Published 8 times/year. Accepts previously published material. Sample copy $3.50.
Illustrations: Buys 1 illustration/issue from freelancers. Prefers seasonal themes rendered in a realistic style. Send query letter with brochure showing art style or tear sheets and slides. Samples not filed are returned by SASE. Reports within 2 months. To show a portfolio, mail appropriate materials; portfolio should include final reproduction/product and tear sheets. Do not send originals. Negotiate rights purchased. Pays on publication.

***IN BUSINESS**, Box 323, Emmaus PA 18049. (215)967-4135. Managing Editor: Nora Goldstein. Emphasizes small business start-up and management. Bimonthly. Circ. 50,000. Original artwork returned after publication. Sample copy $2.50; art guidelines for SASE.
Cartoons: Uses 2-3 cartoons/issue; buys all from freelancers. Prefers single panel, with gagline; b&w line drawings. Send query letter with roughs. Material not kept on file is returned by SASE. Reports within 4 weeks. Buys first rights. Pays $35, b&w; on publication.
Illustrations: Uses 5-6 illustrations/issue; buys all from freelancers. Uses themes related to article subject. Works on assignment only. Send query letter with brochure and tear sheets to be kept on file; call for appointment to show portfolio. Reports within 4 weeks. Buys first rights. Pays $35, b&w, inside; on publication.

INCENTIVE TRAVEL MANAGER, Brentwood Publishing, 1640 5th St., Santa Monica CA 90401. Publisher: Martin H. Waldman. Art Director: Tom Medsger.
Illustrations: Submit brochure/flyer to be kept on file for possible future assignment. Reports only when assignment available. Buys all rights. Pays $60 and up, spot art; $400 and up, full-color cover. Pays on acceptance.

INCIDER-THE APPLE II MAGAZINE, CW Communications-80 Pine St., Peterborough NH 03458. (603)924-9471. Art Director: Donna Wohlfarth. Magazine emphasizing Apple II computing. Monthly. Circ. 150,000. Original artwork returned after publication. Sample copy for SASE. Art guidelines available.
Illustrations: Buys 5-7 illustrations/issue from freelancers. Works on assignment only. Send query letter with resume and samples. Samples not filed are returned only if requested. Reports only if interested. Call or write to schedule an appointment to show a portfolio, which should incude original/final art or tear sheets. Buys first rights. Negotiates payment; on acceptance.

***INDEPENDENT AGENT MAGAZINE**, 100 Church St., New York NY 10007. (212)285-4255. Art Director: Bette Cowles. Trade journal emphasizing insurance. Features general interest, interview/profile, technical and travel articles. "*Independent Agent* is a trade publication promoting the interests of the independent insurance agent." Monthly. Circ. 62,000. Accepts previously published material. Original artwork is sometimes returned to artist after publication. Sample copy $5.
Cartoons: Buys 2-6 cartoons/year from freelancers. Uses various themes. Prefers color washes. Send query letter with samples of style. Samples are filed. Samples not filed are not returned. Reports back only if interested. Negotiates rights purchased. Pays $500 cover, color.
Illustrations: Buys 15 illustrations/year from freelancers. Works on assignment only. Uses various themes. Send query letter with brochure or photocopies. Samples are filed. Samples not filed are not returned. Reports back only if interested. Call to schedule an appointment to show a portfolio which should include original/final art and tear sheets. Negotiates rights purchased. Pays $500, color, cover; $100, b&w; $250, color, inside; on publication.
Tips: "Bring a card or photocopy with a sample to leave for our files."

INDIANAPOLIS 500 YEARBOOK, Box 24308, Speedway IN 46224. (317)244-4792. Publisher: Carl Hungness. Emphasizes auto racing for auto racing fans. Annually. Circ. 50,000. Previously published material OK. Original artwork returned after publication. Sample copy $12.95.
Illustrations: Works on assignment only. Send query letter plus information to be kept on file for possible future assignments. Samples returned by SASE. Reports in 2 weeks. Buys one-time rights. Pays on publication.

INDIANAPOLIS MAGAZINE, Suite 200, 32 E. Washington St., Indianapolis IN 46204. (317)639-6600. Art Director: Kurt Conner. "General interest city magazine targeting upscale audience in central Indiana." Features general interest, historical, humor, interview/profile and travel articles. Monthly. Circ. 27,000. Original artwork returned after publication. Sample copy $1.95.
Cartoons: Buys 1-2 cartoons/issue from freelancers. Open to varied themes and styles. Prefers single panel without gagline; b&w line drawings, b&w and color washes. Send query letter with samples of style and roughs. Samples are filed. Samples not filed are returned by SASE. Reports back only if interested. Buys one-time rights. Pays $30-75, b&w; $50-100, color.
Illustrations: Buys 1-2 illustrations/issue from freelancers. Works on assignment only; "dictated by editorial." Send query letter with resume, tear sheets and slides. Samples are filed. Samples not filed are returned by SASE. Reports back only if interested. Call to show a portfolio, which should include tear sheets, slides, color and b&w. Buys one-time rights. Pays $2-500, color, cover; $1-200, b&w; $1-300, color, inside. Pays on publication.
Tips: "Artists should, when possible, send a story package (illustration/manuscript) showing their ability to interpret editorial material in an intelligent, sophisticated fashion."

Artist: David Catrow

***Artist David Catrow of Springfield, Ohio, explored freelance possibilities in Indianapolis and set up an appointment to show his portfolio to* Indianapolis Magazine*'s art director Kurt Conner. He was then commissioned to draw this editorial illustration. "David is extremely quick and consistently comes up with clever solutions to illustration problems," says Conner, who bought all rights for $100. Catrow is now editorial cartoonist for* The Springfield News.**

INDUSTRIAL MACHINERY NEWS, division of Hearst Business Media Corp., Box 5002, 29516 Southfield Rd., Southfield MI 48086. (313)557-0100. Contact: L.D. Slace. For those in the metalworking industry responsible for manufacturing, purchasing, engineering, metalworking, machinery, equipment and supplies.
Illustrations: Contact publisher for guidelines.

INDUSTRY WEEK, 1000 Superior Ave., Cleveland OH 44114. (216)696-7000. Editor: Stanley J. Modic. Examines top- and middle-management problems in industry. Biweekly. Circ. 350,000. Original artwork returned after publication if requested. Buys first and reprint rights. Sample copy $2.
Cartoons: News Editor: John Carson. Uses freelance cartoons rarely. Receives 10 submissions/week from freelancers. Interested in management themes; single panel. SASE. Reports in 2 weeks. Buys various rights. Pays $35 minimum, b&w line drawings or washes; pays on acceptance.
Illustrations: Art Director: Nick Dankovich. Buys 2-4 illustrations/issue. Works on assignment only. Buys various rights. Cover and inside: buys b&w and color work, all media; pays on acceptance.
Tips: "Read and examine our magazine."

INSIDE, 226 S. 16th St., Philadelphia PA 19102. (215)893-5760. Contact: Art Director. Quarterly. Circ. 70,000. Original artwork returned after publication.
Illustrations: Buys 3 or more illustrations/issue from freelancers. Prefers color and b&w drawings. Works on assignment only. Send samples and tear sheets to be kept on file; call for appointment to show portfolio. Samples not kept on file are not returned. Reports only if interested. Buys first rights. Pays from $100, b&w, and from $300 full-color, inside; on acceptance. Prefers seeing sketches.

INSIDE DETECTIVE, RGH Publications, 20th Floor, 460 W. 34th St., New York NY 10001. (212)947-6500. Editor: Rose Mandelsberg. For mature adults—law enforcement officials, professional investigators, criminology buffs and interested laymen. Monthly.
Cartoons: Receives approximately 20 cartoons/week from freelance artists. Must have crime theme. Submit finished art. SASE. Reports in 10 days. Buys all rights. Pays $25; on acceptance.
Tips: "Make sure that the humor in the cartoons is *not* at the expense of police officers or law enforcement officials. Omit references to supermarket/convenience stores."

***INSIDE SPORTS**, 1020 Church St., Evanston IL 60201. Art Director: Thomas M. Miller. Emphasizes sports. Monthly. Circ. 325,000. Original artwork returned after publication.
Cartoons: Considers sports themes. Prefers single panel; b&w line drawings or color washes. Send query letter. Write for appointment to show portfolio. Material not filed is returned by SASE. Pays on acceptance.
Illustrations: Considers sports themes. Works on assignment only. Send query letter. Write for appointment to show portfolio. Samples not filed are returned by SASE. Pays on acceptance.

INSTANT AND SMALL COMMERCIAL PRINTER, Box 368, Northbrook IL 60062. Editor: Daniel Witte. Emphasizes the instant/quick and small commercial printing business and successful, profitable, technical and promotional methods for owners and/or managers of print shops, as well as interested employees. Bimonthly. Circ. 25,000. Accepts previously published work and simultaneous submissions "if material is so indicated." Sample copy $3.
Cartoons: Buys 1 cartoon/issue from freelancers. Prefers single panel with gagline; b&w line drawings. Send query letter with samples of style, roughs or finished cartoons to be kept on file. Material not kept on file is returned by SASE only if requested. Reports within 1 month. Buys all rights. Pays $25, b&w; on publication.
Illustrations: Buys 2 illustrations/issue from freelancers. Works on assignment only. Send query letter with brochure, resume, business card, samples and tear sheets to be kept on file. Samples not kept on file are returned by SASE only if requested. Reports within 1 month. Buys all rights. Pays $50-150, b&w, and $150-250, color, covers; $50-100, b&w, and $50-200, color, inside; on publication.

THE INSTRUMENTALIST, 200 Northfield Rd., Northfield IL 60093. (312)328-6000. Contact: Elaine Guregian. Emphasizes music education for "school band and orchestra directors and teachers of the instruments in those ensembles." Monthly. Circ. 22,500. Original artwork may be returned after publication. Sample copy $2.
Cartoons: Buys 3 cartoons/issue; buys all from freelancers. Interested in themes stating "music is wonderful." No themes stating "music is a problem"; single panel with gagline, if needed; b&w line drawings. Send finished cartoons. Samples not returned. Reports in 1-2 months. Buys all rights. Pays $20, b&w; on acceptance.
Illustrations: Buys Kodachrome transparencies or slides for covers. Query about suitable subjects. Pays $50-100 on acceptance.
Tips: Looks for "realistic or abstract closeups of performers and musical instruments. Style should be modern, with clean lines and sharp focus that will reproduce well. Black-and-white glossy photos are best; color slides for covers should be Kodachrome film. Inexperienced freelancers sometimes attach long lists of fees or policies, not understanding that each magazine sets its own acceptance and payment policies."

INSURANCE SALES, Rough Notes Publishing Co. Inc., Box 564, Indianapolis IN 46206. (317)634-1541. Editor: Roy Ragan. For life and health insurance salespeople; "emphasis on sales and marketing methods, and on the uses of life and health insurance to solve personal and business financial situations." Monthly. Circ. 25,000. Sample copy $1. Receives 15-20 cartoons/week from freelance artists.
Cartoons: Buys 50-60 cartoons/year from freelancers. Interested in life insurance salesmanship, tax payer and IRS situations, inflation, recession, vagaries of bankers and stock market; single panel. "No cartoons which show salesman holding prospect on ground, twisting arm, knocking doors down, etc." Send finished cartoons with SASE. Reports in 1 week. Buys all rights. Pays $15, b&w line drawings; on acceptance.

INTERNATIONAL MEDICAL CENTERS, INC. JOURNAL, 1515 NW 167th St., Miami FL 33169. (305)623-1091. Art Director: David Rison. Magazine emphasizing health, fitness, preventative medicine and fulfilled living. Quarterly. Circ. 200,000. Accepts previously published material. Original artwork returned after publication. Sample copy for SASE with 40¢ postage.
Illustrations: Prefers modern, contemporary and trend aware themes or styles. Send query letter with brochure showing art style or tear sheets, Photostats, photocopies, "or any sample that is non-returnable." Samples not filed are returned only if requested. Reports only if interested. Call to show portfolio, which should include final reproduction/product, original/final art, photographs and tear sheets. Buys one-time rights. Payment varies. Pays on publication.

INTERRACIAL BOOKS FOR CHILDREN BULLETIN, 1841 Broadway, New York NY 10023. Contact: Editor. Emphasizes "bias-free children's literature and learning materials" for teachers, librarians, parents, authors, and others concerned with children's materials. Published 8 times/year. Circ. 5,000. Accepts previously published material. Original artwork returned after publication. Sample copy $3.50; art guidelines for SASE.

Cartoons: Rarely uses cartoons. Prefers b&w line drawings. Send query letter with samples of style; samples will be kept on file if relevant. Material not kept on file is returned by SASE. Reports within 2 months.
Illustrations: Uses up to 15 illustrations/issue. Send query letter with Photostats and photographs; material will be kept on file if relevant. Samples returned by SASE if not kept on file. Reports within 4 weeks. Buys one-time rights. Pays $50, b&w, cover; $25, b&w, inside; on publication.

***INTERZONE**, 21 The Village St., Leeds LS4 2PR England. Co-Editor: Simon Ounsley. Magazine featuring science fiction and fantasy for "readers of intelligent imaginative fiction. Main age range 18-34." Quarterly. Circ. 2,500. Original artwork returned after publication. Sample copy $3.
Illustrations: Buys 6-10 illustrations/issue from freelancers. Interested in science fiction and fantasy. Works on assignment only. Send query letter with samples. "If we like the samples, we will send a story for illustration." Samples are filed. "We prefer to keep material, so photocopies, tear sheets, etc. are best." Reports back only if interested. Buys first rights. Pays £60, color, cover; £40, page, £20, half page, b&w inside; on publication.

INVESTMENT DECISIONS, 11 Elm Pl., Rye NY 10580. (914)921-0230. Publications Director: George G. Lindsey. Magazine emphasizing professional investing for upscale, investment and financial/managers. Monthly. Circ. 40,000. Accepts previously published material. Original artwork returned after publication. Sample copy available.
Cartoons: Buys 1 cartoon/issue from freelancers. Prefers single panel without gagline; b&w line drawings. Send query letter with samples of style to be kept on file. Call for appointment to show portfolio. Samples are returned only if requested. Reports only if interested. Negotiates rights purchased.
Illustrations: Buys 3 illustrations/issue from freelancers. Works on assignment only. Send query letter with resume and samples. Samples not filed are returned only if requested. Reports only if interested. Call or write to schedule an appointment to show a portfolio, which should include thumbnails, roughs, original/final art and tear sheets. Negotiates rights purchased. Pays on publication.

IOWA MUNICIPALITIES, League of Iowa Municipalities, Suite 100, 900 Des Moines St., Des Moines IA 50309. Editor-in-Chief: Robert W. Harpster. Managing Editor/Art Director: Sandy Pollard. Magazine for city officials. Monthly. Circ. 10,400. Previously published, photocopied and simultaneous submissions OK. Sample copy $1.
Cartoons: Buys none except from local artists; "would consider some really good political cartoons relating to the federal government and cities."
Illustrations: Buys 12 illustrations/issue from freelancers. Send query letter with tear sheets and Photostats. To show a portfolio, mail Photostats and b&w. Pays $75 b&w, cover; on publication.

JACK AND JILL,Box 567, 1100 Waterway Blvd., Indianapolis IN 46206. (317)636-8881. Art Director: Edward F. Cortese. Emphasizes entertaining articles written with the purpose of developing the reading skills of the reader. For ages 6-8. Monthly except bimonthly February/March, April/May, June/July and August/September. Buys all rights. Original artwork not returned after publication (except in case where artist wishes to exhibit the art. Art must be available to us on request.) Sample copy 75¢.
Illustration: Buys 25 illustrations/issue; buys 10-15/issue from freelancers. Receives 3-4 submissions/week from freelancers. Interested in "stylized, realistic, humorous, mystery, adventure, science fiction, historical and also nature and health." Work on assignment only. Send query letter with brochure showing art style or resume, tear sheets, Photostats, photocopies, slides and p hotographs to be kept on file; include SASE. Reports in 1 month. To show a portfolio, mail appropriate materials or call or writer to schedule an appointment; portfolio should include original/final art, color, tear sheets, b&w and 2-color pre-separated art. Buys all rights on a work-for-hire basis. Pays $225, color, cover; $60-125, 4-color; $50-100 2-color; $25-65 b&w, inside; thirty days after completion of work.
Tips: "There are more updates on realistic illustrations of people and stylized illustrations." Artist should "obtain copies of our current issues to insure proper submission of art styles needed. Like to see situation and story telling illustrations with more than 1 figure.

***JACKSONVILLE**, Box 329, Jacksonville FL 32201. Editor: Carolyn Carroll. Features community trends, civic and corporate leaders, new companies, history, sports, arts and other aspects of living and working on Florida's First Coast. Monthly except January/February, May/June, July/August. Circ. 16,250. Local artists only. Buys one-time and all rights. Pays on publication.

JAPANOPHILE, Box 223, Okemos MI 48864. (517)349-1795. Editor: Earl R. Snodgrass. Emphasizes cars, bonsai, haiku, sports, etc. for educated audience interested in Japanese culture. Quarterly. Circ. 800. Accepts previously published material. Original artwork not returned after publication. Sample copy $3; art guidelines free for SASE.

Cartoons: Buys 1 cartoon/issue from freelancer. Prefers single panel with gagline; b&w line drawings. Send finished cartoons. Material returned only if requested. Reports only if interested. Buys all rights. Pays $5; on publication.
Illustrations: Buys 1-5 illustrations/issue from freelancers. Prefers sumie or line drawings. Send Photostats or tear sheets to be kept on file if interested. Samples returned only if requested. Reports only if interested. Buys all rights. Pays $15, cover and $5, inside, b&w; on publication.

***JAZZTIMES MAGAZINE**, 8055 13th St., Silver Springs MD 20910. (301)588-4114. Publisher: Ira Sabin. Tabloid emphasizing jazz music. Features general interest, historical, how-to, inspirational, interview/profile, personal experience, technical and travel articles. Monthly. Circ. 50,000. Original artwork sometimes returned after publication. Sample copy $2.
Illustrations: Send query letter with brochure showing art style or slides and photographs. Samples are filed. Samples not filed are returned only if requested. Reports back only if interested. To show a portfolio, mail appropriate materials. Pays $10, b&w; $25, color.

JEMS JOURNAL OF EMERGENCY MEDICAL SERVICES, Box 1026, Solana Beach CA 92075. (619)481-1128. Managing Editor: Rick Minerd. Emphasizes emergency medical services for emergency room physicians, nurses, paramedics, emergency medical technicians and administrators. Monthly. Circ. 33,000. Accepts previously published material. Original artwork returned after publication. Sample copy for SASE with $1.07 postage; art guidelines for SASE with 22¢ postage.
Illustrations: Buys 3-5 illustrations/issue from freelancers. Works on assignment only. Send query letter with Photostats, tear sheets, photocopies, slides or photos to be kept on file. Samples not filed are returned by SASE. Reports within 2 weeks. Buys one-time rights. Pays $150-200, color, cover; $35-50, b&w, and $50-75, color, inside; on publication.

JOURNAL OF ACCOUNTANCY, 1211 Avenue of the Americas, New York NY 10036. (212)575-5268. Art Coordinator: Jeryl Costello. Magazine emphasizing accounting for certified public accountants. Monthly. Circ. 300,000. Original artwork returned after publication.
Illustrations: Buys 2 illustrations/issue from freelancers. Works on assignment only. Send query letter with brochure showing art style. Samples not filed are not returned. Reports only if interested. Call to schedule an appointment to show a portfolio, which should include original/final art, color, tear sheets and b&w. Buys first rights. Pays $1,200, color, cover; $150-600, color (depending on size), inside; on publication.
Tips: "Because the majority of our editorial content is very technical, graphic elements used in the past were simple and conservative. This is changing. We want colorful, conceptual artwork. It draws readers and helps them through the often lengthy, technical editorial. I look for indications that an artist can turn the ordinary into something extraordinary, whether it be through concept or style. In addition to illustrators, I also hire freelancers to do charts and graphs."

JOURNAL OF READING, Int'l Reading Assn., Box 8139, Newark DE 19714-8139. (302)731-1600. Graphic Design Co-ordinator: Larry Husfelt. Magazine emphasizing teaching for teachers, reading specialists and professors. Published monthly Oct.-May (8 issues/year). Circ. 19,000. Sample copy for SASE with 60¢ postage. Art guidelines available.
Cartoons: Buys 1 cartoon/issue from freelancers. Prefers double panel with or without gagline; b&w line drawings. Send finished cartoons. "We buy what we want immediately and return the rest." Reports within 14 days. Buys one-time rights. Pays $20, b&w.
Illustrations: Buys 1 illustration/issue from freelancers. Works on assignment only. Prefers themes about schools and reading. Send query letter with brochure showing art style or resume and photocopies. Samples not filed are returned only if requested. Reports within 20 days. Call to schedule an appointment to show a portfolio, which should include original/final art. Buys first rights. Pays $250-350, color, cover; on acceptance.

JOURNAL OF THE WEST, 1531 Yuma, Manhattan KS 66502. (913)532-6733. Editor: Robin Higham. Emphasizes the West for readers in public libraries and classrooms. Quarterly. Circ. 4,500 (readership). Original artwork returned after publication. Sample copy and art guidelines available.
Illustrations: Uses cover illustrations only; artist supplies 4-color separation. Send query letter with brochure or samples and/or tear sheets to be kept on file. Prefers either photographs, prints or preferably duplicate slides as samples. Samples not filed are returned only if requested. Reports within 4 days. Negotiates rights purchased. Payment: "We make a trade."
Tips: There is a trend toward "pastels with sometimes interesting and eye-catching results in Western scenes." Looks for work that is "original and not copied from a photograph; and is evidence of artistic talent and ability. We also are concentrating on the twentieth century. Artists send material that is unsuitable to our publication, often because they have never bothered to look at it or to send for a sample copy."

JUDICATURE, Suite 1600, 25 E. Washington, Chicago IL 60602. Contact: David Richert. Journal of the American Judicature Society. Published 6 times/year. Circ. 30,000. Accepts previously published material. Original artwork returned after publication. Sample copy for SASE with $1.07 postage.
Cartoons: Buys 1-2 cartoons/issue. Interested in "sophisticated humor revealing a familiarity with legal issues, the courts and the administration of justice." Send query letter with samples of style. SASE. Reports in 2 weeks. Buys one-time rights. Pays $35 for unsolicited cartoons.
Illustrations: Buys 2-3 illustrations/issue. Works on assignment only. Interested in styles from "realism to light cartoons." Prefers subjects related to court organization, operations and personnel. Send query letter with brochure showing art style. SASE. Reports within 2 weeks. Write to schedule an appointment to show a portfolio, which should include roughs and original/final art. Buys one-time rights. Negotiates payment. Pays $250, b&w, cover; $175, b&w, inside.

KEYNOTER, Kiwanis International, 3636 Woodview Trace, Indianapolis IN 46268. Executive Editor: Jack Brockley. Art Director: Jim Patterson. Official publication of Key Club International, nonprofit high school service organization. Published 7 times/year. Copyrighted. Circ. 130,000. Previously published, photocopied and simultaneous submissions OK. Original artwork returned after publication. Free sample copy.
Illustrations: Buys 3 illustrations/issue from freelancers. Works on assignment only. "We only want to work with illustrators in the Indianapolis area; it is otherwise too inconvenient because of our production schedule." SASE. Reports in 2 weeks. "Freelancers should call our Production and Art Department for interview." Buys first rights. Pays by the project, $100-500. Pays on publication.

***KITE LINES**, 7106 Campfield Rd., Baltimore MD 21207-4699. Publisher/Editor: Valerie Govig. Magazine emphasizing kites for the adult enthusiast only. Quarterly. Circ. 9,500. Original artwork returned after publication. Sample copy $3. Art guidelines available.
Cartoons: Buys 1 cartoon/year from freelancers. Prefers single panel; b&w line drawings—kites only. Send finished cartoons. Samples are filed. Samples not filed are returned by SASE. Reports back within 1 month only if interested. Buys first rights. Pays $15, b&w.
Illustrations: Buys 2-3 illustrations/year from freelancers; "would buy more if good work were available." Works on assignment primarily. Send query letter with brochure showing art style or photocopies. Samples are filed. Samples not filed are returned by SASE. Reports back within 1 month only if interested. To show a portfolio, mail final reproduction/product. Buys first rights. Pays $15 and up, b&w; inside. "We often pay in the form of subscriptions, kite books, etc."
Tips: "We use very little outside art anyway, and our rates are embarrassingly low—although we'd use more and pay more if we could get the kind of work we really need. We're talking working drawings here. No 'fine' art, no pretty for pretty's sake. You must be intensely interested in kites, enter into the life of our magazine and subordinate your skills to helping people who want to make and fly interesting kites. Choice of subject kites and style of drawing are both extremely circumscribed."

KIWANIS, 3636 Woodview Trace, Indianapolis IN 46268. (317)875-8755. Executive Editor: Chuck Jonak. Art Director: James Patterson. Magazine emphasizing civic and social betterment, business, education, religion and domestic affairs for business and professional men. Uses cartoons, illustrations, and photos from freelancers. Original artwork returned after publication. Published 10 times/year.
Cartoons: Buys 1-2 cartoons/issue, all from freelancers. Interested in "daily life at home or work. Nothing off-color, no silly wife stuff, no blue-collar situations." Prefers finished cartoons. Send query letter with brochure showing art style or tear sheets, slides and photographs. SASE. Reports in 3-4 weeks. Pays $50, b&w; on acceptance.
Illustrations: Buys 6-8 illustrations/issue from freelancers. Interested in themes that correspond to themes of articles. Works on assignment only. Keeps material on file after in-person contact with artist. Prefers portfolio, "anything and everything." SASE. Reports in 2 weeks. To show a portfolio, mail appropriate materials (out of town/state) or call or write to schedule an appointment; portfolio should include roughs, original/final art, final reproduction/product, color, tear sheets, Photostats, photographs and b&w. Buys first North American serial rights or negotiates. Pays $1,000, full-color, cover; $400-700, full-color, inside; $50-75, spot drawings; on acceptance.
Tips: "We deal direct—no reps. Have plenty of samples, particulary those that can be left with us. I see too much student or unassigned illustration in many portfolios."

The asterisk before a listing indicates that the listing is new in this edition. New markets are often the most receptive to freelance submissions.

L.A. WEST, (formerly Preview Magazine), Suite 245, 919 Santa Monica Blvd., Santa Monica CA 90401. (213)458-3376. Editor: Jan Loomis. Emphasizes community events for upper middle-class, well-educated, sophisticated audience. Monthly. Circ. 37,000. Original artwork returned after publication. Sample copy and art guidelines for SASE.
Cartoons: Buys 1-2 cartoons/issue from freelancers. Prefers single panel with gagline; b&w line drawings or washes. Send query letter with samples of style or roughs to be kept on file. Material not filed is returned by SASE. Reports within 1 month. Negotiates rights purchased. Write for appointment to show portfolio. Pays $17.50, b&w; on publication.
Illustrations: Uses only local artists, by assignment. Pays $25, minimum.

LACMA PHYSICIAN, Box 3465, Los Angeles CA 90054. (213)483-1581. Managing Editor: Howard Bender. "Membership publication for physicians who are members of the Los Angeles County Medical Association; covers association news and medical issues." Published 20 times/year, twice monthly except January, July, August and December. Circ. 11,000. Does not accept previously published material. Original artwork returned after publication "if requested." Sample copy for SASE with $1.50 postage.
Illustrations: "Occasionally use illustrations for covers." These are "generally medical, but can relate to a specific feature story topic." Works on assignment only. Send query letter with business card and samples to be filed. Samples not kept on file are returned by SASE. Reports only if interested. Call or write for appointment. Negotiates pay; pays on acceptance. Buys all rights.

LE BUREAU, Suite 1000, 1001 de Maisonneuve West, Montreal, Quebec H3A 3E1 Canada . (514)845-5141. Editor-in-Chief: Paul Saint-Pierre. For corporate and financial executives, office managers, electronic data processing experts and systems analysts. Bimonthly. Circ. 10,500. Free sample copy if artist sends samples.
Illustrations: Buys 12 illustrations/year on calculators, small computers, in-plant printing and word processing. All covers are freelance illustrations. Especially needs "outstanding drawings illustrating an office situation. We appreciate humor in good taste." Query with samples. SAE (nonresidents include IRC). Reports in 2 weeks. Buys all rights, but may reassign rights to artist after publication. Pays $125-200, color; on acceptance.

LEATHER CRAFTSMAN, (formerly Make It With Leather), Box 1386, Fort Worth TX 76101. (817)923-6787. Editor: Stanley Cole. For persons interested in leather crafts. 80% of articles are how-to-do-it, 15% are profiles of people producing leatherwork, 75% general interest. Bimonthly. Circ. 11,000. Previously published, photocopied and occasionally, simultaneous submissions OK. Free sample copy.
Illustrations: Buys leathercraft themes. "We are how-to-do-it oriented. Make the art relevant to the audience, and do some research on tools and terminology of the craft. The more accurate, the more usable." Send query letter with samples. SASE. Reports in 6-8 weeks. To show a portfolio, mail appropriate materials. Buys all rights. Pays $10-100, b&w line drawings, washes and reflective art; on publication.
Tips: "Most often we require a whole package, including an article and photographs or illustrations. Basically we are looking for journalists who can write a how-to-do-it or profile article who can also illustrate their piece, or for an artist who has teamed up with a writer to illustrate his/her submission. We do have an illustrator on staff who can draw good, clear photographs."

THE LEATHERNECK MAGAZINE, Magazine of the Marines, Box 1775, Quantico VA 22134. (703)640-6161. Art Director: John De Grasse. Emphasizes activities of Marines—air, land, sea ships, tanks, aircraft, physical fitness, etc. for Marines, dependents, retired, friends of the Corps, plus former Marines. Monthly. Circ. 95,000. Occasionally accepts previously published material. Only original cover artwork returned after publication. Sample copy available.
Cartoons: Uses 8 cartoons/issue; buys all from freelancers. Prefers Marine-related subjects and "correctly pictured uniforms particularly." Prefers single panel with gagline; b&w line drawings. Send query letter with samples of style. Material not kept on file is returned by SASE. Reports within 30 days. Buys first rights. Pays $25, b&w; on acceptance.
Illustrations: Uses 4 illustrations/issue. Send query letter with samples. Prefers illustrations for covers only. Pays $100-150, b&w, cover; on acceptance.

LEGAL ECONOMICS, A Magazine of the Section of Economics of Law Practice of the American Bar Assocation), Box 11418, Columbia SC 29211. (803)754-3563 or 359-9940. Managing Editor/Art Director: Delmar L. Roberts. For the practicing lawyer. Published 8 times/year. Circ. 28,000. Previously published work rarely used. Pays on publication.
Cartoons: Primarily interested in cartoons "depicting situations inherent in the operation and management of a law office, e.g., operating word processing equipment and computers, interviewing, office

meetings, lawyer/office staff situations, and client/lawyer situations. We are beginning to use 1-2 cartoons/issue. We almost never use material relating to trial law." Send query letter with resume. Reports in 90 days. Usually buys all rights. Pays $50 for all rights; on acceptance.
Illustrations: Uses inside illustrations and, infrequently, cover designs. Send query letter with resume. Reports in 90 days. Usually buys all rights. Pays $75-125; more for covers and for 4-color; on publication.
Tips: "There's an increasing need for artwork to illustrate high-tech articles."

LEGION, 359 Kent St., Ottawa Ontario K2P 0R6 Canada. (613)325-8741. Editor-in-Chief: Mac Johnston. Art Director: Dick Logan. For Royal Canadian Legion members. Published 10 times/year. Circ. 528,098. Original artwork returned after publication. Free sample copy.
Illustrations: Buys 6-8 illustrations/issue from freelancers. Interested in "various techniques." Works on assignment only. "Because of the invariable loss of time clearing illustrations through Canada Customs, Canadian artists are used to illustrate most stories." Provide 35mm slides to be kept on file for possible future assignments. Prefers to see portfolio. Reports immediately. Buys various rights. Cover: Pays $450-1,500, color. Inside: Pays $100-1,200, b&w; $100-1,500, color; on acceptance.

LEISURE WHEELS, Box 7302, Station E, Calgary, Alberta T3C 3M2 Canada. (403)263-2707. Publisher: Murray Gimbel. Emphasizes recreational vehicles, travel and outdoors for upper income, ages 30-65. Monthly. Circ. 100,000. Sample copy 50¢; free art guidelines.
Cartoons: Uses 4 cartoons/issue; buys all from freelancers. Receives 1 submission/month from freelancers. Especially needs cartoons. Subject matter should concern traveling and camping as it relates to trailering, motorhoming, fishing or hiking. Prefers b&w line drawings with gag line. Send samples of style. SASE (nonCanadians include International Reply Coupons). Reports in 2 weeks. Cartoons can appear in other publications. Pays $25 for b&w.
Illustrations: Uses 4 illustrations/issue; buys all from freelancers. Receives 1 submission/week from freelancers. Usually works on assignment. Illustration needs identical to cartoons. Prefers b&w line drawings for inside. Send samples of style. SASE (nonCanadians include International Reply Coupons). Reports in 3 weeks. "Prefer illustrations not appear in a similar magazine." Pays $50-100 for inside b&w on publication.
Tips: "We now feature a broader range of editorial content. Basically, any subject that applies to recreational activity outdoors."

LET'S LIVE, Box 74908, 444 N. Larchmont Blvd., Los Angeles CA 90004. (213)469-3901. Editor: Keith Stepro. Emphasizes nutrition, health and recreation. Monthly. Circ. 140,000. Sample copy $1.50; free art guidelines.
Illustrations: Uses 8-12 illustrations/issue; buys 2/issue from freelancers. Receives 2 illustrations from freelancers/week. Works on assignment only. "We like to check newspapers and magazines to find samples of the style we like to use or, we check the *Creative Black Book* for artists." Needs illustrations of inanimate objects: (e.g., salt shaker, vitamin bottles), sports action, charts, graphs, montages, spot illustrations, medical scenes (facilities, equipment), people, faces. "No mod or avant-garde styles, please." Especially needs good illustrations of various organs. Query first. Prefers samples, tear sheets and/or roughs. Originals should be sent certified mail. SASE. "Our medically-oriented graphics must be simple, non-technical, but accurate depictions of parts and their functional relationships in the body." Format: color and b&w washes. Reports in 2 weeks. Buys first North American serial rights. Pays $150-200 for color cover; $75-150 for inside color; $50-125 for inside b&w; on publication.
Tips: "There is more interest in preventive medicine and the use of natural foods and supplements, more interest among readers in seeing graphics explaining how their systems work, and more interest in exercise or therapeutic regimens. Also greater emphasis on top-flight rendering ability in illustrators doing expository and/or instructional graphics; we don't want "artistes" of the avant-garde school—we want artists who can illustrate with diagrammatic skills that can replace a lot of extraneous verbiage."

***A LETTER AMONG FRIENDS**, Box 1198, Groton CT 06340. Contact: Victoria Baker. Literary magazine emphasizing poetry and graphic art. Triannual. Circ. 400. Original artwork sometimes returned after publication. Sample copy $3. Art guidelines available for SASE with first class postage.
Illustrations: Buys up to 10 illustrations/issue from freelancers. Buys up to 120 illustrations/year from freelancers. Send query letter with Photostats, photocopies and photographs. Samples are not filed. Samples not filed are returned by SASE. Reports back within 6 months. Buys first rights. Pays 1 copy; on publication.

PETER LI, INC./PFLAUM PRESS, 2451 E. River Rd., Dayton OH 45439. (513)294-5785. Art Director: Jim Conley. Publishes three monthly magazines—*The Catechist*, *Classroom Computer Learning* and *Today's Catholic Teacher*.

Illustrations: Works with 20 freelance artists/year. "Local artists are, of course, more preferable but it's not an absolute." Uses artists for 4-color cover illustrations and b&w and 2-color spot illustrations. "We are only interested in *professional* illustrators, especially those with fresh, innovative styles. Experience a plus but not necessary." Works on assignment only. Send query letter with Photostats, photographs, slides or tear sheets. Samples returned by SASE. Reports only if interested. Pays by the project, $100-600 average. Considers complexity of the project when establishing payment. Buys all rights.

LIGHT & LIFE, 901 College Ave., Winona Lake IN 46590. (219)267-7656. Contact: Art Director. "Emphasizes evangelical Christianity with Wesleyan slant for a cross-section readership." Readers are mostly of Free Methodist denomination. Monthly. Circ. 43,500. Original artwork returned after publication, if requested and postage included. Sample copy $1.50.
Cartoons: Rarely used. Interested in religious themes. Format: single panel b&w line drawings with or without gagline. Prefers finished cartoons. SASE. Reports in 4 weeks. Buys all rights. Pays $5-20; on acceptance.
Illustrations: Buys 2-4 illustrations/issue from freelancers. Interested in art that illustrates themes of articles. Works on assignment only. Send query letter with brochure showing art style or resume and tear sheets. Reports in 4 weeks. To show a portfolio, mail original/final art, final reproduction/product, color and tear sheets. Buys all rights on a work-for-hire basis. Pays $25 and up, inside b&w and 2-color; on publication.
Tips: "Does the artwork have freshness rather than an overworked appearance? I look for an obvious use of adequate resources (models) to avoid human body distortion, and for consistency within a piece of artwork. Consider the media used; will it reproduce well? Use quality drawing paper or appropriate type of illustration board. Freelancers don't go to enough trouble and expense to 'show off' their work; they use cheap photo albums, photocopies. I would encourage availability of a list of their employment in the art field as well as their educational background, and the use of tear sheets of published work."

***LIVELY ARTS & FINE ART MAGAZINE**, 111 Willet Circle, Pajaro Dunes CA 95076. (408)728-1950. Publisher: Robert A. Stillman. Magazine emphasizing performing and fine arts for "upscale, sophisticated segment: married, post graduates, professionals with incomes between $35,000-60,000." Bimonthly. Circ. 20,000. Accepts previously published material. Original artwork returned after publication. Sample copy and art guidelines for SASE.
Cartoons: Send query letter with samples of style. Samples are filed. Samples not filed are returned by SASE. Write to schedule an appointment to show a portfolio. Reports back only if interested.
Illustrations: Works on assignment only. Send query letter with tear sheets and photographs. Samples not filed are returned by SASE. Reports back only if interested. To show a portfolio, mail tear sheets and photographs.

***LODESTONE PUBLISHING**, Suite 222, 1671 E. 16th St., Brooklyn NY 11229. (718)339-4488. Art Director: Marc Thorner. Publishes limited edition comic books, series and graphic novels. Genres: adventure, fantasy, science fiction and espionage. Themes: outer space, future science and family situations. Monthly and bimonthly. Original artwork returned after publication. Sample copy $1. Art guidelines free for SASE.
Illustrations: Uses three-tier page of 6 panels, vertical panels, horizontal panels, inset panels, borderless panels, circular panels and double-page spreads. Send query letter with resume and published samples or tear sheets. Samples are filed. Reports back within 2 weeks. To show a portfolio, mail 5 pages of pencil or ink drawings—twice up or one-and-one-half times up, 5 pages of action continuity or 5 photocopies of original pencil art or inking and 5 pages of lettering—one-and-one-half up or twice up with sound effects, titles and display lettering. Rights purchased vary; "we keep to Graphic Artists Guild standards." Negotiates payment. Pays on acceptance.

LOG HOME GUIDE FOR BUILDERS & BUYERS, Rt. 32 & 321, Cosby TN 37722. (615)487-2256. Editor: Doris Muir. Emphasizes buying and building log homes; energy-efficiency. Audience: ages 25-60, college educated, middle- upper-middle income; prefer country life. Quarterly. Circ. 150,000. Sometimes accepts previously published material. Original artwork returned after publication. Sample copy $3.50; art guidelines for SASE.
Cartoons: Buys 1-4 cartoons/issue from freelancers. Themes include renderings of log homes; warmth of log home living; amusing aspects of building with logs; and country living. Prefers single panel without gagline; b&w line drawings, b&w and color washes. Send query letter with samples of style or roughs to be kept on file. Material not filed is returned if accompanied by SASE. Reports within 6 weeks. Negotiates rights purchased. Pays $10-25, b&w; $25-50, color; on publication.
Illustrations: Buys 1-4 illustrations/issue from freelancers. Themes include log home renderings; log homes in rural scenes; and beavers and badgers in natural settings. Send query letter with brochure, re-

sume, business card and samples to be kept on file. Prefers tear sheets, slides and photographs as samples. Samples not filed are returned by SASE. Reports within 6 weeks. Negotiates rights purchased. Pays $15-35, b&w and $25-50, color, inside; on publication.

LONE STAR HUMOR, Lone Star Publications of Humor, Suite 103, Box 29000, San Antonio TX 78229. (512)271-2632. Editor/Publisher: Lauren Barnett. "Book-by-subscription" (magazine-type format). Audience: "comedy connoisseurs," and "others who like to laugh." Published about 3 times/year. Circ. 1,200. Sometimes accepts previously published material. Original artwork returned after publication. Inquire for update on sample copy; art guidleines for SASE with first-class postage.
Cartoons: Buys 20-25 cartoons/issue from freelancers. Prefers single, double or multiple panel with or without gagline; b&w line drawings. Send roughs or finished cartoons. Material returned by SASE. Reports within 3 months. Negotiates rights purchased. Pays on publication ("but we try to pay before"). Inquire for update on pay scale.

THE LOOKOUT, 8121 Hamilton Ave., Cincinnati OH 45231. (513)931-4050. Editor-in-Chief: Mark A. Taylor. For conservative Christian adults and young adults. Weekly. Circ. 140,000. Original artwork not returned after publication, unless requested. Sample copy and artists' guidelines available for 50¢.
Cartoons: Uses 1 cartoon/issue; buys 20/year from freelancers. Interested in church, Sunday school and Christian family themes. Send roughs or finished cartoons. Samples returned by SASE. Reports in 2 weeks. Buys one-time rights.
Illustrations: Buys 3-4 illustrations/issue. Interested in "adults, families, interpersonal relationships; also, graphic treatment of titles." Works on assignment only. Send query letter with brochure, flyer or tear sheets to be kept on file for future assignments to Frank Sutton, art director, at above address. Reporting time varies. Buys all rights but will reassign. Inside: Pays $125 for b&w, $150 for full-color illustrations, firm; on acceptance. Cover: "Sometimes more for cover work."

LOS ANGELES, 1888 Century Park E, Los Angeles CA 90067. (213)552-1021. Design Director: William Delorme. Emphasizes lifestyles, cultural attractions, pleasures, problems and personalities of Los Angeles and the surrounding area. Monthly. Circ. 170,000. SASE. Reports in 2-3 weeks. Especially needs very localized contributors—custom projects needing person-to-person concepting and implementation. Previously published work OK. Pays on publication. Sample copy $3.
Cartoons: Contact Geoff Miller, editor-in-chief. Buys 5-7/issue on current events, environment, family life, politics, social life and business; single, double or multi panel with gagline. Mail roughs. Pays $25-50, b&w line or tone drawings.
Illustrations: Buys 10/issue on assigned themes. Send or drop off samples showing art style (tear sheets, Photostats, photocopies and dupe slides). Pays $300-500, color, cover; $150-500, b&w and $200-800, color, inside; on publication.
Tips: "Show work similar to that used in the magazine—a sophisticated style. Study a particular publication's content, style and format. Then proceed accordingly in submitting sample work." There is a trend toward "imaginative imagery and technical brilliance with computer-enhanced art being a factor. Know the stylistic essence of a magazine at a gut level as well as at a perceptive level. Identify with Los Angeles or Southern California."

LOTTERY PLAYER'S MAGAZINE, 321 New Albany Rd., Morristown NJ 08057. Editor/Publisher: S.W. Valenza, Jr. Emphasizes lottery, gaming. Monthly. Circ. 200,000. Accepts previously published material and simultaneous submissions. Sample copy $1.
Cartoons: Occasionally uses cartoons. Prefers single panel, with gagline; b&w line drawings. Send samples of style to be kept on file. "If in the area, an appointment *may* be possible." Material not kept on file is returned by SASE. Reports in 4 weeks. Buys one-time rights. Pays $15-40, b&w; on publication.
Illustrations: Uses illustrations occasionally; occasionally buys from freelance artists. Themes or styles depend on content of issue; "we are 2-color." Send query letter with business card and Photostats or photocopies to be kept on file; no slides. Samples returned by SASE if not kept on file. Reports within 4 weeks. Buys one-time rights. To show a portfolio, mail appropriate materials. Pays $20-100, b&w, inside; on publication.

LOUISIANA LIFE MAGAZINE, 4200 S. I-10 Service Rd., Metairie LA 70002. (504)456-2220. Art Director: Theodora T. Tilton. Emphasizes the lifestyle of Louisiana (food, entertainment, work, etc.) for the upper-income Louisianian, "proud of the state and its diversity." Bimonthly. Circ. 50,000. Original artwork returned after publication. Sample copies available.
Illustrations: Buys 3 illustrations/issue from freelancers. Works on assignment only. Send query letter with brochure and tear sheets to be kept on file. Samples not kept on file are returned by SASE. Reports only if interested. Call or write to schedule an appointment to show a portfolio, which should include

original/final art (if possible), final reproduction/product, slides and tear sheets. Buys one-time rights. Pays $85, b&w; $250, color, cover; $185, color, inside; on publication.
Tips: "Do your homework. Explore the magazine before you submit any work. Tailor your selection based on your research."

***LUNA VENTURES**, Box 1064, Suisun CA 94585. Editor: Paul Doerr. Publishes *'Skinner*, emphasizing mountainmen, muzzleloading, subsistence farming; *Scifant*, emphasizing science fiction, fantasy, horror and fandom; *Luna City Press*, all space-related subjects. Accepts previously published material. Original artwork returned after publication. Sample copy $3. Art guidelines available for SASE with first class postage.
Tips: "New or nonprofessional artists welcomed."

THE LUTHERAN, 2900 Queen Lane, Philadelphia PA 19129. (215)438-6580. Editor-in-Chief: Edgar R. Trexler. General interest magazine of the Lutheran Church in America. Biweekly; monthly in July, August and December. Circ. 546,000. Previously published work OK. Original artwork returned after publication. Free sample copy.
Cartoons: Buys 1 cartoon/issue from freelancers. Receives 30 submissions/week from freelancers. Interested in humorous or thought-provoking cartoons on religion or about issues of concern to Christians; single panel. Prefers roughs or finished cartoons. SASE. Reports usually within a week. Buys first rights. Pays $10-50, b&w line drawings and washes; on publication.
Illustrations: Buys 2 illustrations/issue from freelancers. Interested in church-related family scenes, Christmas, Advent, Baptism, Communion, Confirmation, church entering, leaving, interior, exterior, choirs, funerals, Easter and Lent. Works on assignment only. Prefers to see portfolio or samples of style. Reports in 2 weeks. Buys all rights on a work-for-hire basis. Samples returned by SASE. Send resume or tear sheets to be kept on file for future assignments. Buys 30-40/year on assigned themes. Pays $150, b&w and 2-color; on publication.

***THE LUTHERAN JOURNAL**, 7317 Cahill Rd., Edina MN 55435. Contact: J.W. Leykom. Family magazine for Lutheran Church members, middle aged and older. Previously published work OK. Free sample copy.
Illustrations: Seasonal 1-, 2- or full-color covers. Mail art with price. Buys one-time rights. Pays on publication.

THE LUTHERAN STANDARD, Box 1209, 426 S. 5th St., Minneapolis MN 55440. (612)330-3300. Editor: Lowell G. Almen. Managing Editor: Donn S. McLellan. Emphasizes news in the world of religion, dealing primarily with the Lutheran church. For members of the American Lutheran Church. Published 20 times/year. Circ. 540,000. Free sample copy.
Cartoons: Buys 1-2 cartoons/issue; buys all from freelancers. Receives 10 submissions/week from freelancers. Interested in current events, education, family life, humor through youth and religious themes. Send finished cartoons. SASE. Reports in 3-4 weeks. Buys first or simultaneous rights. Pays $15-35, b&w line drawings and washes; on acceptance.
Illustrations: Buys 4 illustrations/issue from freelancers. Works on assignment only. Send query letter with photocopies and SASE. Reports in 3-4 weeks. Buys all rights on a work-for-hire basis. Inside: Pays $75-250, b&w and 2-color line drawings and washes.

LYNN, THE NORTH SHORE MAGAZINE, 45 Forest Ave., Swampscott MA 01907. CEO: Paula R. Hastings. Magazine emphasizing the general consumer, some emphasis on local geographical area (North Shore of Boston) for upscale homeowners, age 30 and up. Bimonthly. Circ. 75,000. Accepts previously published material. Original artwork returned after publication if requested. Sample copy for SASE with $1 postage.
Cartoons: Prefers lifestyle themes, human issues, sports or the ocean and wildlife. Prefers single panel with gagline; b&w line drawings and b&w washes. Send query letter with samples of style and finished cartoons. Samples not filed are returned by SASE. Reports only if interested. Buys one-time rights. Pays $50, b&w.
Illustrations: Buys 5 illustrations/issue from freelancers. Works on assignment only. Prefers "a generally realistic style, lifestyle material and mixed media. Send query letter with brochure showing art style or resume, tear sheets and photocopies. Samples not filed are returned by SASE. Reports only if interested. Buys one-time rights. Pays $300, b&w and $300, color, cover; $200, b&w and $200, color (full page), inside. Smaller pieces negotiable. Pays on publication.

***MAD DOG GRAPHICS**, Box 931686, Hollywood CA 90093. (213)464-2932. Publisher: Jan Strnad. Estab. 1986. Publishes comic books. Genres: adventure, science fiction, humor. "No romances or war sagas." "I am looking for individualistic visions rather than a 'house' look, presentations that are slight-

© Ronald Wilber

As editor of the new comic book* Splat! *(published by Mad Dog Graphics) Tom Mason of Hollywood, California, was looking for new artists and was referred to artist Ronald Wilber. The Liberty, New York, artist sent Mason copies of Grisleyworld, a story he had illustrated previously. Mason bought the story and artwork, purchasing one-time rights on a royalty basis. "It's hard to get into comics," says Wilber. "They're almost like a private club. But independents are more accessible."

ly rebellious and iconoclastic, not too sanitized. All the comics will be in black-and-white." Mostly continuing series, with some mini-series (3-6 issues).

Illustrations: Send photocopies and SASE. "A complete package is the best way to submit work, and also samples of continuity that show either an action sequence or dialogue sequence. Lettering is not necessary. Show that you have good storytelling abilities." All artwork is creator-owned. Buys all English language comic book rights. Payment is on a royalty basis.

***MAD MAGAZINE**, 485 Madison Ave., New York NY 10022. (212)752-7685. Art Director: Len Brenner. Humor magazine for teen and up. Published 8 times/year. Circ. 1,000,000. Art guidelines for SASE with first-class postage.

Cartoons: Prefers current topics; no single gag panels. Send query letter with samples of style and roughs. Samples are filed. "Styles we know we'll never use" are returned only if accompanied by SASE. Call for appointment to show portfolio. Reports back within 3 weeks. Buys all rights. Pays $300/page, b&w.

Illustrations: Prefers current topics. Send query letter with brochure showing art style or tear sheets, Photostats and photocopies. Samples not kept are returned by SASE. Reports back within 3 weeks. Call to schedule an appointment to show a portfolio. Buys all rights. Pays $900-1,200, color, cover; $300, b&w, inside; on acceptance.

MADE TO MEASURE, 600 Central Ave., Highland Park IL 60035. (312)831-6678. Publisher: William Halper. Emphasizes uniforms, career clothes, men's tailoring and clothing. Magazine distributed to retailers, manufacturers and uniform group purchasers. Semiannually. Circ. 24,000. Art guidelines available.

Cartoons: Buys 15 cartoons/issue from freelancers. Prefers themes relating to subject matter of magazine; also general interest. Prefers single panel with or without gagline; b&w line drawings. Send query letter with samples of style or finished cartoons. Any cartoons not purchased are returned to artist. Reports back. Buys first rights. Pays $20-25 b&w, on acceptance.

MAGIC CHANGES, 2S424 Emerald Green Dr., Warrenville IL 60555. (312)393-7856. Editor: John Sennett. Emphasizes fantasy and poetry for college students, housewives, teachers, artists and musicians: "People with both an interesting and artistic slant." Annually. Circ. 500. Accepts previously published material. Original artwork returned after publication. Sample copy $4; art guidelines for SASE.
Cartoons: Buys 2 cartoons/issue from freelancers. Considers space, art, animals and street activity themes. Single, double, or multi panel with or without gagline; b&w line drawings. Send query letter with finished cartoons. Material returned by SASE. Reports within 2 weeks. Acquires first rights. Pays $0-10.
Illustrations: Buys 10 illustrations/issue from freelancers. Considers city, wilderness, bird, space and fantasy themes. Send query letter with samples. Samples returned by SASE. Reports within 2 weeks. To show a portfolio, mail original/final art, final reproduction/product or b&w. Acquires first rights. Pays $0-10.
Tips: "Send imaginative b&w drawings."

MAGICAL BLEND, Box 11303, San Francisco CA 94101. Art Editor: Jeff Fletcher. Emphasizes spiritual exploration, transformation and visionary arts. Quarterly. Circ. 25,000. Original artwork sometimes returned after publication. Sample copy $4; art guidelines for SASE.
Cartoons: Buys 3 cartoons/issue from freelancers. Buys 24 cartoons/year from freelancers. Send query letter with Photostats.
Illustrations: Buys 5 illustrations/issue from freelancers. Receives 1 submission/week from freelancers. "We keep samples on file and work by assignment according to the artists and our time table and workability. We accept b&w line drawings, also pencil and pre-separated color work. We look for pieces with occult, psychic and spiritual subjects with positive, inspiring, uplifting feeling." Especially needs Oriental themes and strong cultural themes, i.e., African, Latin American, Zen brush work, Indian, etc. Send query letter with brochure or tear sheets, final reproduction/product, Photostats, photographs and slides. SASE. Reports in 6 months. Buys first North American serial rights. Rights revert to artist. Pays in copies.
Tips: "We are basically a print works from San Francisco's Visionary School, although we also print occasional abstract surreal, expressionist/impressionistic works. We want work that is energetic and thoughtful, and that has a hopeful outlook on the future. Our page size is 8½x11, although few full-page works are printed. Please send a SASE with your slides or artwork if you want them returned. High-quality, camera-ready reproductions are preferable over originals. The best way to see what we need is to send $4 for a sample copy of *Magical Blend*. If you are doing work of quality, that is positive and inspiring, we would like to see it."

MARRIAGE AND FAMILY LIVING, Abbey Press, St. Meinrad IN 47577. (812)357-8011. Contact: Art Director. For Christian families. Monthly. Circ. 40,000. Buys one-time rights. Pays on publication.
Cartoons: "We try to use one cartoon per month."
Illustrations: Buys 20 illustrations/year.

***MARVEL COMICS**, 387 Park Ave. S., New York NY 10016. (212)696-0808. Contact: Editors. Publishes comic books and graphic novels. Created superheroes like Spider Man and the Incredible Hulk. Produces up to 50 titles/month.
Illustrations: Uses freelance artists for inking, lettering, pencilling and color work. Most artists work in-house. Pencillers should send 4-5 samples of sketches one-and-one-half times up on kid-finish Bristol paper, which demonstrate skills at figure drawing and narration; there should be some continuity. "Draw any character you want, but show a variety of settings and situations. Prove that you can draw ordinary people, superheroes, action and quiet scenes." Inkers should submit 4-5 pages of pencil work which has been inked. Submit both the inked pencil drawing and the photocopy of the original pencil art. Letterers should submit samples of lettering one-and-one-half times up with sound effects, titles, and display lettering. Letter your samples in India ink on kid-finish Bristol paper. Colorists should photocopy pages of b&w comic book pages on bond paper, then color appropriate areas with Dr. Martin's watercolor dyes. Most in-house work is work-for-hire, with the artist receiving a royalty after a certain number of sales. Graphic novels are creator-owned, the artist retaining the copyright. Pays $70-100/page for pencilling and $45-70/page for inking.
Tips: "Before sending us anything, take time to give your work a long hard objective look. Is it really in the same league with the very best work you see printed in our publications? Be honest with yourself. If it isn't as good or better than our best, don't send it. Practice, study and work to get better instead."

MATURE YEARS, United Methodist Publishing House, 201 8th Ave. S., Nashville TN 37202. (615)749-6000. Art Director: Dave Dawson. For retired persons and those facing retirement; persons seeking help on how to handle problems and privileges of retirement. Quarterly. Circ. 103,000. Free

Close-up

Mary Wilshire

Illustrator
New York City

The comics industry can't be laughed away. Between 250 and 300 different titles are sold each month. Last year over 150 million comic books were sold in this country. Over the past few years some 70 independent comic book publishers have joined the mainstream publishers such as Marvel, DC and Archie Comics to spur the industry to new creative heights.

The booming comic book industry has created opportunities for talented young artists, including a growing number of women. One of the leading women comic book artists is Mary Wilshire. Wilshire specializes in drawing female characters. She has been a penciler for such popular Marvel Comics as *Red Sonja* and is presently working on an eight-page story for Renegade Press (an independent publisher headed by another woman, Denis Loubert).

"The comics industry is grossly unexplored," notes Wilshire. "It's going through a creative renaissance. New narrative techniques are being tried, and the subject matter is often revolutionary."

Comic books have changed drastically over the last decade. Appealing to an older, more sophisticated crowd, comics have become larger in scope and darker in content. In the past, adventures were spun around the superhero, with women emerging either as foils or foes. There have always been women wonders and witches, but now there are even "human beings" being penciled into stories.

Wilshire believes the time has come for strong women characters to reflect societal changes. "In the industry, artists are known for certain talents. Some have a reputation for drawing superpowers or military characters. I'm known for my drawing of women and children. I have a more human element in my drawing."

She explains that when an artist is needed for a comic, editors call upon certain specialists. Wilshire is known for her conceptual skills as a penciler, an artist who sketches characters and settings straight from a script. After the penciler draws the basic shapes and background, an inker emphasizes certain outlines and shadows to further dramatize the narrative. Then the bullpen artists (staff artists who are jack-of-all-trades) put on the final touches and assign PMS colors to the black-and-white work before sending the work to the printer.

Most comic book artists begin as assistants or apprentices, filling out areas for established name artists. To be a successful comic book artist, Wilshire emphasizes two fundamental abilities. Since a comic book tells a story in pictures, your art must possess a narrative flow. "You must show the story in pictures. It's very similar to storyboarding in this aspect." She also stresses that artists must have a knowledge of anatomy in order to draw quickly and accurately.

After all, speed equals money in the comic book world, where work is paid by the page. On the average, pencilers are paid $40-80 per page, while pencilers/inkers are paid $120 per page. Working with Marvel, Wilshire completed ten pages a week. "It doesn't make sense to do less than that to make a living in New York. You have to do a cost analysis, taking into account your living and operating costs, to determine how much work you should do."

Comic book art used to be a work-for-hire agreement, whereby all rights belonged to the publisher. Wilshire is among the many artists who have deplored this practice and have urged artists to demand their artistic rights. Now artists are paid a percentage of the net sales after a certain amount of copies are sold. Comic book creators also negotiate their own contracts to retain their rights, since many opportunities exist in the licensing world.

She encourages artists to set their sights high but to grab any available opportunities to draw. "Some artists aren't willing to put aside long-range plans and compromise a little by taking lesser jobs (such as penciling or inking instead of creating a new script), and these jobs will probably help them in the long run."

Wilshire also has some useful tips for artists in all disciplines: "Draw every day. Keep a sketch book. Always work at getting better. Being a good artist is like being a good athlete. If you keep in shape, then you're ready to compete. If you get sloppy, you lose your tone. When you're competing, you'll get left in the dust."

—Floyd Conner

Artist: Mary Wilshire

***Red Sonja** is among the comics Wilshire has penciled for Marvel Comics. Known for her storyboarding skills and her expressive female characters, Wilshire has found that the same skills used in penciling for comic books are used in storyboarding for advertisements, which she also does.*

catalog and artist's guidelines.
Cartoons: Buys 4 cartoons/year. Interested in current events relate to aging, religion and retirement. Send query letter with samples. SASE. Reports in 4 weeks. Buys all rights. Pays $25 minimum, b&w; on publication.
Illustrations: Buys full-color inside illustrations according to manuscript needs. Using more illustrations depicting intergenerational activities. Works on assignment only. Pays $80-150 depending on complexity.

***MATURITY MONTHLY**, Box 2074, California City CA 93505. President/Publisher: Dennis W. Sumrow. Six column x 13.5" tabloid for senior citizens (50 + market). Features travel, health, senior fitness, nutrition, local and state news. Monthly. Circ. 57,000. Accepts previously published material. Original artwork is not returned after publication. Sample copy and art guidelines for SASE with $1.27 postage.
Cartoons: Buys 6 cartoons/year from freelancers. Prefers single panel with gagline; b&w line drawings. Send query letter with samples of style. Samples are filed. Reports back only if interested. Buys one-time rights. Pays $10, b&w.
Illustrations: Buys 6 illustrations/issue from freelancers. Prefers senior themes. Send query letter with resume and photographs. Samples are filed. Samples not filed are returned by SASE. Reports back only if interested. To show a portfolio, mail tear sheets, photographs and b&w. Buys one-time rights. Pays $100, b&w, cover; $20, b&w, inside; on publication.

***MBA MAGAZINE**, 18 N. Main St., Chagrin Falls OH 44022. (216)622-4444. Art Director: Ben Kotowski. Trade journal emphasizing business articles about or of interest to alumni of graduate business schools. Features humorous, interview/profile and personal experience articles. Monthly. Circ. 100,000. Will sometimes accept previously published material. Original artwork is sometimes returned to the artist after publication. Sample copy $5.
Cartoons: Buys 5-10 cartoons/issue from freelancers. Buys 60-120 cartoons/year from freelancers. Prefers anything of a business nature. Prefers single panel with gagline; b&w line drawings, b&w and color washes. Send query letter with samples of style, roughs and photocopies of finished cartoons. Samples are filed. Samples not filed are returned if requested by artist. Reports back within 1 month only if interested. Negotiates rights purchased. Pays $75, b&w; $125, color.
Illustrations: Buys 3-4 illustrations/issue from freelancers. Buys 40 illustrations/year from freelancers. Works on assignment only. Send brochure or tear sheets, Photostats, photocopies, slides and photographs. Samples are filed. Samples not filed are returned only if requested by artist. Reports back within weeks only if interested. Call to schedule an appointment to show a portfolio, which should include original/final art, tear sheets, final reproduction/product, Photostats, photographs, slides, color and b&w. Buys first rights; negotiates rights purchased. Pays $125 and up, b&w; $300 and up, color, inside; on publication.

MEDIA & METHODS, 1511 Walnut St., Philadelphia PA 19102. (215)563-3501. Emphasizes the methods and technologies of teaching for all school teachers and administrators. Bimonthly. Circ. 40,000 +. Accepts previously published material. Returns original artwork after publication. Sample copy for SASE.
Illustrations: Buys 1-2 illustrations/issue from freelancers. Send query letter with brochure, business card, tear sheets, photocopies or photographs. Material not filed is returned by SASE. Reports back only if interested. To show a portfolio, mail original/final art, final reproduction/product, color, tear sheets, Photostats, photographs and b&w. Buys first rights or reprint rights. Pays $175 for b&w and $250 for color, cover; $150 for b&w and $175 for color, inside; on publication.
Tips: "We like to see consistency in artwork so that if we commission some art we have an idea of what we'll get."

MEDICAL ECONOMICS FOR SURGEONS, 680 Kinderkamack Rd., Oradell NJ 07649. (201)267-3030. Art Administrator: Ms. Grady Olley. Magazines for physicians, surgeons and financial specialists. Monthly. Circ. 45,000. Accepts previously published material. Original artwork returned after publication.
Cartoons: Buys 5-7 cartoons/issue from freelancers. Prefers medically-related themes. Prefers single panel with gagline; b&w line drawings and b&w washes. Send query letter with finished cartoons. Samples not filed are returned by SASE. Reports within 2 months. Buys all rights. Pays $50, b&w.
Illustrations: Buys 5-10 illustrations/issue from freelancers. Works on assignment only. Send query letter with resume, tear sheets, and slides. Samples not filed are returned by SASE. Reports back only if interested. Call to schedule an appointment to show a portfolio, which should include original/final art (if possible) and tear sheets. Buys one-time rights. Pays $300-1,000, color, cover; $50-300, b&w, $200-500, color, inside; on acceptance.

MEDICAL ECONOMICS MAGAZINE, 680 Kinderkamack Rd., Oradell NJ 07649. (201)599-8442. Art Administrator: Ms. Grady Olley. Magazine for those interested in the financial and legal aspects of running a medical practice. Bimonthly. Circ. 182,000. Accepts previously published material. Original artwork returned after publication.

Cartoons: Buys 10 cartoons/issue from freelancers. Prefers medically-related themes. Prefers single panel, with gagline; b&w line drawings and b&w washes. Send query letter with finished cartoons. Material not filed is returned by SASE. Reports within 8 weeks. Buys all rights. Pays $50, b&w.

Illustrations: Buys 10-12 illustrations/issue from freelancers. Works on assignment only. Send query letter with resume and samples. Samples not filed are returned by SASE. Reports only if interested. Call to schedule an appointment to show a portfolio, which should include original/final art (if possible) and tear sheets. Buys one-time rights. Pays $350-1,200, color, cover; $80-400, b&w and $300-850, color, inside; on acceptance.

Tips: "We are using more 3-D art. Always looking for new sources of medial illustration. A common mistake freelancers make is not having promotional pieces that are representational of their work to leave behind as reminders."

MEDICAL TIMES, 80 Shore Rd., Port Washington NY 11050. Executive Editor: Anne Mattarella. Emphasizes clinical medical articles. Monthly. Circ. 120,000. Sample copy $5.

Cartoons: Buys 5-6 cartoons/year from freelancers. Prefers medical themes, "but nothing insulting to our audience. Jokes about doctors' fees are *not* funny to doctors." Accepts single panel with gagline; b&w line drawings. Send query letter with finished cartoons; "we'll either accept and pay or return them within one month." Negotiates rights purchased. Pays $25, b&w; on acceptance.

Illustrations: Buys 2 or 3 illustrations/issue, 24-36/year from freelancers. Works on assignment only. Send query letter with resume and medical samples such as tear sheets, Photostats, photocopies, slides and photographs. Samples not filed are returned. Reports within 1 month. Write to schedule an appointment to show a portfolio, which should include original art (1 or 2 pieces only) and printed material "so we can see how the artist's work reproduces. Most of the portfolio should consist of printed pieces." Negotiates rights purchased. Payment varies; pays on acceptance.

Tips: "With the ever-increasing number of medical journals competing for the same ad budgets, competition and cost controls are becoming fierce. This may mean a cutback in the amount of artwork purchased by some of the marginally successful journals."

MEDICENTER MANAGEMENT, Brentwood Publishing, 1640 5th St., Santa Monica CA 90401. Publisher: Martin Waldman. Art Director: Tom Medsger. Emphasizes technological, medical and professional news. Send brochure/flyer to be kept on file for possible future assignment. Reports only when assignment available. Buys all rights. Pays $60 and up, spot art; $400, full-color cover; on acceptance.

MEMCO NEWS, Box 1079, Appleton WI 54912. Editor: Richard F. Metko. Emphasizes "welding applications as performed with Miller Electric equipment. Readership ranges from workers in small shops to metallurgical engineers." Quarterly. Circ. 44,000. Previously published material and simultaneous submissions OK. Original artwork not returned after publication.

THE MERCEDES-BENZ STAR, 1235 Pierce St., Lakewood CO 80214. (303)235-0116. Editor: Frank Barrett. Magazine emphasizing new and old Mercedes-Benz automobiles for members of the Mercedes-Benz Club of America and other automotive enthusiasts. Bimonthly. Circ. 25,000. Does not usually accept previously published material. Returns original artwork after publication. Sample copy for SASE with $1.75 postage.

Illustrations: Buys 0-1/issue. Prefers Mercedes-Benz related themes. Looks for authenticity in subject matter. Send query letter with resume, slides or photographs to be kept on file except for material requested to be returned. Write for appointment to show portfolio. Samples not filed are returned by SASE. Reports within 3 weeks. Buys first rights. Pays $100-1,500; pays on publication.

***MESSAGE MAGAZINE**, 55 West Oak Ridge Dr., Hagerstown MD 21740. Design Director: Lee Cherry. Interdenominational journal with an ethnic emphasis published by Seventh-day Adventist Church. "The goal is to bring Christianity to the reader in a relevant, engaging and contemporary manner." Send published samples. SASE. Buys all or one-time rights. Pays on acceptance.

Illustrations: Does not publish 'say nothing' artwork such as portraits, still lifes of Bibles, candles and the like, pretty, vacation-like scenics, clip-art style or anything similar. "We cover subject matter involved with current issues (drugs, crime, ecology), the Bible, health, family and home topics, science and nature, church history and current events in the world." Pays $300-500, full-color, cover. Pays $100-300/full color page; $50-150, b&w line drawings and 2-color, inside.

MICHIGAN OUT OF DOORS, Box 30235, Lansing MI 48909. Contact: Kenneth S. Lowe. Emphasizes outdoor recreation, especially hunting and fishing; conservation; and environmental affairs. Sample copy $1.
Illustrations: "Following the various hunting and fishing seasons we have a need for illustration material; we consider submissions 6-8 months in advance." Reports as soon as possible. Pays $15 for pen & ink illustrations in a vertical treatment; on acceptance.
Tips: "Our magazine has shifted from newsprint to enamel stock. We have our own art department and thus do not require a great deal of special material."

MILITARY LIFESTYLE MAGAZINE, 1732 Wisconsin Ave. NW, Washington DC 20007. Art Director: Judi Connelly. Emphasizes active-duty military lifestyles for military wives and families. Published 10 times/year. Circ. 500,000. Original artwork returned after publication.
Illustrations: Buys 2-6 illustrations/issue from freelancers. Theme/style depends on editorial content. Works on assignment only. Send brochure and business card to be kept on file. Accepts Photostats, tear sheets, photocopies, slides, photographs, etc. as samples. Samples returned only if requested. Reports only if interested. Buys first rights. Payment depends on size published, cover and inside; pays on publication.

MILITARY MARKET MAGAZINE, Springfield VA 22159-0210. (703)750-8676. Editor: Nancy M. Tucker. Emphasizes "the military's PX and commissary businesses for persons who manage and buy for the military's commissary and post exchange systems; also manufacturers and sales companies who supply them." Monthly. Circ. 10,000. Simultaneous submissions OK. Original artwork not returned after publication.
Cartoons: Buys 3-4 cartoons/issue from freelancers. Interested in themes relating to "retailing/buying of groceries and general merchandise from the point of view of the store managers and workers"; single panel with or without gagline, b&w line drawings. Send finished cartoons. Samples returned by SASE. Reports in 6 months. Buys all rights. Pays $25, b&w; on acceptance.
Tips: "We use freelance cartoonists only—*no* other freelance artwork."

***MILLER/FREEMAN PUBLICATIONS**, 500 Howard St., San Francisco CA 94105. (415)397-1881. Associate Art Director: Janet Duncan. Business magazines on paper and pulp, computers and medical subjects. Monthly. Circ. 100,000+. Returns original artwork after publication.
Illustrations: Buys 2 illustrations/month from freelancers. Works on assignment only. Send query letter with samples to be kept on file. Samples not filed are returned by SASE. Reports back only if interested. Negotiates rights purchased. Payment varies; on acceptance.

MPLS. ST. PAUL MAGAZINE, Suite 1030, 12 S. 6th St., Minneapolis MN 55402. (612)339-7571. Contact: Tara Christopherson. City/regional magazine. For "professional people of middle-upper income levels, college educated, interested in the arts, dining and the good life of Minnesota." Monthly. Circ. 48,000. Original artwork returned after publication.
Illustrations: Uses 12 illustrations/issue. Works on assignment only. Arrange interview to show portfolio. Provide business card, flyer or tear sheet to be kept on file for future assignments. Reports in 2 weeks. Buys first North American serial rights, and all rights on a work-for-hire basis. Pays $75-200, b&w; $600 maximum/full-page, color; on acceptance.

MISSOURI LIFE, 14327 Strawbridge Ct., Chesterfield MO 63017. (314)434-5556. Editor: Debra Gluck. Magazine about Missouri. Readers are people interested in where to go, what to do in the state, and the beauty and fascination of Missouri places and faces. Bimonthly. Circ. 30,000. Original artwork returned after publication. Sample copy $3; art guidelines for SASE.
Cartoons: Used to illustrate some departments and features.
Illustrations: Uses original artwork depicting Missouri places or people. Receives 2 illustrations/week from freelance artists. Especially needs variety of b&w and color line art and other types of art for illustration of specific stories, on assignment; interested in a variety of styles. Format: b&w, color cover washes, inside and cover color washes and original art that will reproduce for offset printing/web. Samples returned by SASE. Provide letter of inquiry, tear sheet, proposal and sample of work to be kept on file for future assignments. Reports in 4 weeks. Buys first North American serial rights. Pays $25-50 for b&w, on publication.
Tips: "Send samples of work that show the styles and media you are experienced and good at."

MISSOURI RURALIST, 2401A Vandiver, Columbia MO 65202. (314)474-9557. Editor: Larry Harper. r Missouri farm families. Biweekly (except monthly May through December). Circ. 80,000. Previ-ly published material OK. Original artwork not returned after publication.
oons: Buys 2 cartoons/issue from freelancers. Interested in farm and rural themes; single panel

with gagline. Send finished cartoons. Samples returned by SASE. Reports in 4 weeks. Negotiates rights purchased. Negotiates pay; pays on publication.
Tips: There is a "definite need for good agricultural cartoonists who understand the agriculture business. They must be able to write as well as draw. Puns on farming and agriculture are taboo. Good agricultural cartoonists are scarce. Most are artists, but not good gag writers."

MODEL RETAILER, Clifton House, Clifton VA 22024. (703)830-1000. Editor: Geoffey A. Wheeler. For hobby store owners. Monthly. Circ. 6,100. Previously published and simultaneous submissions ("must be notified") OK. Original artwork returned after publication. Also interested in art for covers, article illustrations, and headline/blurb blocks.
Cartoons: Buys 3 cartoons/issue, all from freelancers. Receives 10 submissions/month from freelancers. Interested in themes pertaining to hobbies, hobby stores or small businesses; double panel. "Query first, with brief summary of types of work done (ads, covers, headline art, cartoons, etc.); after positive response from us send samples of work (photocopies, etc.) and some references." SASE. Reports in 2 weeks. Buys "first time rights in our field." Pays $25 minimum, line drawings; on publication.
Tips: We are "trying to improve the look of the magazine to gain attention for articles and help emphasize key points through imaginative use of graphics. We want good artwork that could be used to dress up feature articles, especially artwork for the headline/blurb block. Basically, artwork that would look good as line or with color overlays."

MODERN DRUMMER, 870 Pompton Ave., Cedar Grove NJ 07009. (201)239-4140. Editor-in-Chief: Ronald Spagnardi. Art Director: David Creamer. For drummers, all ages and levels of playing ability with varied interests within the field of drumming. Monthly. Circ. 75,000. Previously published work OK. Original artwork returned after publication. Sample copy $2.95.
Cartoons: Buys 5-10 cartoons/year. Uses 1 cartoon/issue. Interested in drumming; single and double panel. "We want strictly drummer-oriented gags." Prefers finished cartoons or roughs. SASE. Reports in 3 weeks. Buys first North American serial rights. Pays $5-25; on publication.

MODERN MACHINE SHOP, 6600 Clough Pike, Cincinnati OH 45230. (513)231-8020. Editor: Ken M. Gettelman. Emphasizes the metalworking industry for production and engineering management in the metalworking industry. Monthly. Circ. 106,000. Free sample copy.
Cartoons: Uses 1 cartoon/issue; buys 1 from freelancers. Receives 5 cartoons/week from freelance artists. Interested in themes relating to the manufacturing environment; single panel with gag line. A topical cartoon can still be appropriate. Send finished cartoons. Samples returned. Reports in 2 weeks. Buys all rights. Pays $25-35, b&w; on acceptance.
Illustrations: Uses 25 illustrations/issue; industrial material only. Prefers illustrations with articles; especially needs those relating to the new trends of computer-assisted design and manufacturing. Provide samples and tear sheets to be kept on file for possible future assignments. Call for appointment. Samples returned. Buys all rights. Pays $300-500 for illustrations with articles; on acceptance.
Tips: "We see growth of manufacturing capabilities around the world and growth of computer-assisted manufacturing."

MODERN MATURITY, 3200 East Carson, Lakewood CA 90712. (213)496-2277. Picture Editor: Ms. M.J. Wadolny. Emphasizes health, lifestyles, travel, sports, finance and contemporary activities for members 50 years and over. Bimonthly. Previously published work OK. Original artwork returned after publication. Sample copy available.
Cartoons: Uses 4 cartoons/issue; buys 2/issue from freelancers. Receives 50 submissions/week from freelancers. Interested in general interest themes. Send finished cartoons, color and b&w. SASE. Reports in 2 months. Buys all rights on a work-for-hire basis. Pays $200, 8x10" finished cartoons.

***MODERN PLASTICS**, 1221 Avenue of the Americas, New York NY 10020. (212)512-3491. Art Director: Bob Barravecchia. Trade journal emphasizing technical articles for manufacturers of plastic parts and machinery. Monthly. Circ. 60,000. Original artwork is sometimes returned after publication.
Illustrations: Works on assignment only. Send brochure. Samples are filed. Does not report back. Call to schedule an appointment to show a portfolio, which should include tear sheets, photographs, slides, color and b&w. Buys all rights. Pays $500, color, cover; $75, color, inside; on acceptance.

MODERN TIRE DEALER, 110 N. Miller Rd., Akron OH 44313. (216)867-4401. Editor: Lloyd R. Stoyer. Circ. 33,000. For owners/operators of independent retail/wholesale tire shops. Buys all rights. Pays on publication.
Cartoons: Buys themes relating to automotive and tire services. Send actual cartoons with gagline. SASE. Pays $50, pen &ink, approximately 8x10 to be shot down to about 3x5; on publication.

Illustrations: Buys automotive services and tire-related themes, using line drawings of men performing services on tires, brakes, shocks and mufflers. Send query letter with samples of artistic style. SASE. Assignments given based on samples. Reports in 1 week. Pays $100-200, color, cover; pays $20-50, drawings inside; on publication.

MONEY MAKER, 5705 N. Lincoln Ave., Chicago IL 60659. Art Director: Debora Clark. Magazine emphasizing financial investments. Bimonthly. Circ. 300,000. Accepts previously published material. Original artwork returned after publication.
Illustration: Buys 15 illustrations/issue. Works on assignment only. Prefers financial themes in any art style. Send query letter with brochure showing art style, tear sheets, Photostats, photocopies and slides. Samples not filed, returned by SASE. Reports only if interested. To show a portfolio, mail appropriate material or write to schedule an appointment; portfolio should include original/final art and tear sheets. Buys reprint rights or negotiates rights purchased. Payment is negotiable.

THE MORGAN HORSE, Box 1, Westmoreland NY 13490. (315)735-7522. Production Manager: Carol Misiaszek. Emphasizes all aspects of the Morgan horse breed including educating Morgan owners, trainers and enthusiasts on breeding and training programs; the true type of the Morgan breed, techniques on promoting the breed, how-to articles, as well as preserving the history of the breed. Monthly. Circ. 10,000. Accepts previously published material and simultaneous submissions. Original artwork is returned after publication. Sample copy $3; art guidelines free for SASE.
Illustrations: Uses 2-5 illustrations/issue. "Line drawings are most useful for magazine work. We also purchase art for promotional projects dealing with the Morgan horse—horses should look like *Morgans*." Send query letter with samples and tear sheets. Accepts "anything that clearly shows the artist's style and craftsmanship" as samples. Samples are returned by SASE. Reports within 6-8 weeks. Call or write for appointment to show portfolio. Buys all rights or negotiates rights purchased. Pays $50 minimum, color cover; $10 minimum, b&w inside; on acceptance.

THE MOTHER EARTH NEWS, Box 70, Hendersonville NC 28791. Art Directors: Will Hopkins, Ira Friedlander. Magazine emphasizing self-reliant living, do-it-yourself products, natural foods, organic gardening, etc. for suburban, rural, small town, upper-middle income, family folks. Bimonthly. Circ. 700,000. Accepts previously published material. Original artwork returned after publication. Sample copy for SASE with $2.40 postage.
Cartoons: Buys 1 cartoon/issue from freelancers. Prefers single panel with or without gagline; b&w line drawings and b&w washes. Send query letter with samples of style and finished cartoons to be kept on file except for finished cartoons. Write or call for appointment to show portfolio. Material not kept on file is returned by SASE. Reports only if interested. Negotiates rights purchased. Pays $200, b&w.
Illustrations: Buys 1-2 illustrations/issue from freelancers. Works on assignment only. Send query letter with brochure showing art style or tear sheets, Photostats and photocopies. Samples not filed are returned by SASE. Reports only if interested. To show a portfolio, mail appropriate materials or write to schedule an appointment; portfolio should include roughs, original/final art, color, tear sheets and photographs. Negotiates rights purchased. Pays $200-400, b&w, and $300-500, color, inside; on acceptance.

MOTOR MAGAZINE, 555 W. 57th St., New York NY 10019. Art Director: Harold A. Perry. Emphasizes automotive technology, repair and maintenance for auto mechanics and technicians. Monthly. Circ. 135,000. Accepts previously published material. Original artwork returned after publication if requested. Never send unsolicited original art.
Illustrations: Buys 5-15 illustrations/issue from freelancers. Works on assignment only. Prefers realistic/technical line renderings of automotive parts and systems. Send query letter with resume and photocopies to be kept on file. Will call for appointment to see further samples. Samples not filed are not returned. Reports only if interested. Buys one-time rights. Write to schedule an appointment to show a portfolio, which should include final reproduction/product, color and tear sheets. Payment negotiable for cover, basically $300-1,500; pays $50-500, b&w, inside; on acceptance.
Tips: "*Motor* is an educational, technical magazine and is basically immune to illustration trends because our drawings *must* be realistic and technical. As design trends change we try to incorporate these into our magazine (within reason). Though *Motor* is a trade publication, we approach it, design-wise, as if it were a consumer magazine. We make use of white space when possible and use creative abstract and impact photographs and illustration for our opening pages and covers. But we must always retain a 'technical look' to reflect our editorial subject matter. There are more and more *Folio* and *Forbes* clones. A few of the elite say what is good and the rest fall into line. Publication graphics is becoming like TV programming, more calculating and imitative and less creative."

***MOUNTAIN FAMILY CALENDAR**, Box 294, Rhododendron OR 97049. (503)622-4798. Editor: Michael P. Jones. Newspaper emphasizing family activities, recreation, history, wildlife, environment. Monthly. Circ. 2,500. Accepts previously published material. Original artwork returned after publication. Sample copy for SASE with 50¢ postage. Art guidelines for SASE with first-class postage.

Cartoons: Buys 1-8 cartoons/issue from freelancers. Prefers single panel, double panel, multi panel with or without gagline; b&w line drawings, b&w or color washes. Send query letter with samples of style, roughs or finished cartoons. Samples are filed. Samples not filed are returned by SASE. Reports back within 2 weeks. Buys one-time rights. Pays in copies.

Illustrations: Buys 10 illustrations/issue from freelancers. Send query letter with brochure showing art style or resume, tear sheets, Photostats, photocopies, slides or photographs. Samples not filed are returned by SASE. Reports back within 2 weeks. To show a portfolio, mail thumbnails, roughs, original/final art, final reproduction/product, color, tear sheets, Photostats, photographs or b&w. Buys one-time rights. Pays in copies.

Tips: "We need more wildlife and recreational sketches that can easily be reduced without losing clarity."

MUSCLE MAG INTERNATIONAL, Unit 2, 52 Bramsteele Rd., Brampton, Ontario L6W 3M5 Canada. (416)457-3030. Editor-in-Chief: Robert Kennedy. For 16- to 50-year-old men and women interested in physical fitness and overall body improvement. Published 12 times/year. Circ. 210,000. Previously published work OK. Original artwork not returned after publication. Sample copy $3.

Cartoons: Buys 6 cartoons/issue from freelancers. Receives 30 submissions/week from freelancers. Interested in weight training and body building; single panel; "well-drawn work—professional." Send finished cartoons. SAE (nonresidents include IRC). Send $3 for return postage. Reports in 3 weeks. Buys all rights on a work-for-hire basis. Pays $15-25, color; $10-20, b&w; on acceptance. More for superior work.

Illustrations: Uses 2 illustrations/issue; buys 1/issue from freelancers. Receives 20 submissions/week from freelancers. Interested in "professionally drawn exercise art of body builders training with apparatus." Send query letter with tear sheets, photocopies, slides, photographs, and preferably finished art. SAE (nonresidents include IRC). Send $4 for return postage. Reports in 2 weeks. Call to schedule an appointment to show a portfolio, which should include original/final art. Buys all rights on a work-for-hire basis. Pays $300, color, cover; $100, color and $80, b&w, inside; on acceptance. "Pay can be triple for really professional or outstanding artwork."

Tips: "We only want to see top line work—we want only the best. Study our publication, then submit material to us."

MUSCULAR DEVELOPMENT, Box 1707, York PA 17404. (717)767-6481. Advertising Manager: Philip Redman. Emphasizes body building, powerlifting and strength sports. Bimonthly. Circ. 40,000. Accepts previously published material. Original artwork returned after publication. Sample copy for SASE with $1 postage; art guidelines available.

Illustrations: Buys variable number of illustrations/issue from freelancers. Prefers styles other than line art. Works on assignment only. Send query letter with resume and photocopies or any other good representation to be kept on file; present originals and printed material in person. Samples returned by SASE. Reports only if interested. Call for appointment to show portfolio. Buys one-time rights. Pays on publication as determined by artist and negotiations.

MUSIC EDUCATORS JOURNAL, 1902 Association Dr., Reston VA 22091. (703)860-4000. Editor: Karen Deans. Production Manager: Pamela Halonen. Art Director: Charlene Gridley. For music educators in elementary and secondary schools and universities. Monthly (September-May). Circ. 56,000.

Illustrations: Occasionally uses illustrations from freelancers. Interested in collages, drawings, paintings, designs on music education subjects. "Artwork should be geared toward people, faces, etc., in music—not very many abstracts are used. Depictions of instruments must be true to form, correct playing positions." Works on assignment. Send brochure, flyer or tear sheets to be kept on file for future assignments. Reports in "up to 6 months." Buys one-time rights on a work-for-hire basis. Cover: Pays $100-250, full-color art. Inside: Pays $25-100 per item: b&w line drawings, washes, gray opaques and color-separated work; on acceptance.

Tips: "Accepted artwork must be clean and appropriate for offset reproduction. Instruments must be accurately drawn and postures and fingerings must be correct. Artwork should show teaching, not just performing."

***MUSIC OF THE SPHERES**, Box 1751, Taos NM 87571. (505)758-0405. Editor: John Patrick Lamkin. Emphasizing new age art and music. Quarterly. Circ. 10,000. Accepts previously published material. Original artwork is returned to the artist after publication. Sample copy $4.50. Art guidelines available for SASE with first class postage.

Illustrations: Buys varied number of illustrations/issue from freelancers. Prefers "New Age"/visionary/spiritual/fantasy/future (positive) themes. Send query letter with resume, tear sheets, slides and photographs. Samples are filed. Samples not filed are returned by SASE. Reports back within 30 days. To show a portfolio, mail original/final art, final reproduction/product, photographs, slides, color and b&w. Buys one-time rights. Pays $100, color, cover; $25, b&w; $50, color, inside; on publication.
Tips: "We accept only positive/visionary/spiritual/etc. work. We also publish articles and short sketches on artists. For this we need photos, bio and articles about the artist, etc."

***MUSICIAN MAGAZINE**, 31 Commercial St., Gloucester MA 01930. Art Director: Gary Koepke. Consumer magazine emphasizing music. Features interview/profile. Monthly. Circ. 110,000. Original artwork returned after publication. Sample copy for SASE.
Cartoons: Send query letter with samples of style. Samples are filed. Reports back only if interested. Buys one-time rights. Pays $50, b&w; $100, color.
Illustrations: Buys 2 illustrations/issue from freelancers. Buys 24 illustrations/year from freelancers. Works on assignment only. Send query letter with brochure showing art style or slides. Samples are filed. Samples not filed are returned by SASE. Reports back only if interested. To show a portfolio, mail tear sheets, slides, color and b&w. Buys one-time rights. Pays $250, b&w; $500, color, cover; $50, b&w; $350, color, inside. Pays on publication.

THE NATIONAL FUTURE FARMER, Box 15130, Alexandria VA 22309. (703)360-3600. Editor-in-Chief: Wilson W. Carnes. For members of the Future Farmers of America who are students of vocational agriculture in high school, ages 14-21. Emphasizes careers in agriculture/agribusiness and topics of general interest to youth. Bimonthly. Circ. 422,528. Reports in 3 weeks. Buys all rights. Pays on acceptance. Sample copy available.
Cartoons: Buys 15-20 cartoons/year on Future Farmers of America or assigned themes. Receives 30 cartoons/week from freelance artists. Pays $15, cartoons; more for assignments.
Illustrations: "We buy a few illustrations for specific stories; almost always on assignment." Send query letter with tear sheets or photocopies. Write to schedule an appointment to show a portfolio, which should include final reproduction/product, tear sheets and Photostats. Negotiates payment.
Tips: "We suggest you send samples of work so we can keep your name on file as the need arises. We prefer b&w line art. Please include rates. We are a bimonthly publication and buy very little art. Study back issues and offer suggestions for improvement through the use of art. We need more youthful cartoons."

NATIONAL GEOGRAPHIC, 17th and M Sts. NW, Washington DC 20036. (202)857-7000. Contact: Art Director. Monthly. Circ. 10,500,000. Original artwork returned after publication, in some cases.
Illustrations: Number of illustrations bought/issue varies. Interested in "full-color, representational renderings of historical and scientific subjects. Nothing that can be photographed is illustrated by artwork. No decorative, design material. We want scientific geological cut-aways, maps, historical paintings." Works on assignment only. Prefers to see portfolio and samples of style. Samples are returned by SASE. "The artist should be familiar with the type of painting we use." Provide brochure, flyer or tear sheet to be kept on file for future assignments. Reports in 2 weeks. Minimum payment: Inside: $1,000, color; $200, b&w; on acceptance.

NATIONAL MOTORIST, Suite 300, One Market Plaza, San Francisco CA 94105. (415)777-4000. Graphic Artist: Lana Peters. Editor: Jane Offers. Emphasizes travel on the West Coast for all members of the National Automobile Club in California. Bimonthly. Circ. 205,000. Original artwork returned after publication. Sample copy 50¢ postage.
Cartoons: Uses 1 cartoon/issue; buys 1/issue from freelancer. Prefers auto- or travel-related themes. Prefers b&w line drawings with gaglines. Send query letter with roughs to be kept on file. Material not kept on file is returned. Reports within days. Buys first rights. Pays "on request", b&w and color; on acceptance.
Illustrations: Uses very few illustrations/issue. Prefers auto- or travel-related themes. Send query letter with samples to be kept on file. Prefers original work as samples. Samples not kept on file are returned. Buys first rights. Pays "all on request"; on acceptance.

THE NATIONAL NOTARY, 23012 Ventura Blvd., Box 4625, Woodland Hills CA 91365-4625. (818)347-2035. Contact: Production Editor. Emphasizes "notaries public and notarization—goal is to impart knowledge, understanding, and unity among notaries nationwide and internationally." Readers are notaries of varying primary occupations (legal, government, real estate and financial), as well as state and federal officials and foreign notaries." Bimonthly. Circ. 61,000. Original artwork not returned after publication. Sample copy $5.
Cartoons: May use. Cartoons "must have a notarial angle"; single or multi panel with gagline, b&w

line drawings. Send samples of style. Samples not returned. Reports in 4-6 weeks. Call to schedule an appointment to show a portfolio. Buys all rights. Negotiates pay; on publication.
Illustrations: Uses about 5 illustrations/issue; buys all from local freelancers. Works on assignment only. Themes vary, depending on subjects of articles. Send business card, samples and tear sheets to be kept on file. Samples not returned. Reports in 4-6 weeks. Call for appointment. Buys all rights. Negotiates pay; on publication.
Tips: "We are very interested in experimenting with various styles of art in illustrating the magazine. We generally work with Southern California artists, as we prefer face-to-face dealings."

NATIONAL REVIEW, 150 E. 35th St., New York NY 10016. Art Director: Anna Lieber. Emphasizes world events from a conservative viewpoint. Bimonthly. Original artwork returned after publication.
Cartoons: Buys 15 cartoons/issue from freelancers. Interested in "political, social commentary." Prefers to receive finished cartoons. SASE. Reports in 2 weeks. Buys first North American serial rights. Pays $25 b&w; on publication.
Illustrations: Uses 15 illustrations/issue. Especially needs b&w ink illustration, portraits of political figures and conceptual editorial art (b&w line plus halftone work). "I look for a strong graphic style; well-developed ideas and well-executed drawings." Works on assignment only. Send query letter with brochure showing art style or tear sheets and photocopies. No samples returned. Reports back on future assignment possibilities. Call to schedule an appointment to show a portfolio, which should include original/final art, final reproduction/product, tear sheets and b&w. SASE. Also buys small decorative and humorous spot illustrations in advance by mail submission. Buys first North American serial rights. Pays $15, small spots, $35, larger spot, $40; assigned illustration; $40 b&w, inside; $300 color, cover; on publication.
Tips: "Tear sheets and mailers are helpful in remembering an artist's work. Artists ought to make sure their work is professional in quality, idea and execution. Printed samples alongside originals help. Changes in art and design in our field include fine art influence and use of more halftone illustration."

NATIONAL RURAL LETTER CARRIER, Suite 100, 1448 Duke St., Alexandria VA 22314. (703)684-5545. Managing Editor: RuthAnn Saenger. Emphasizes news and analysis of federal law and current events. For rural letter carriers and family-oriented, middle-Americans; many are part-time teachers, businessmen and farmers. Weekly. Circ. 70,000. Mail art. SASE. Reports in 4 weeks. Original artwork returned after publication. Previously published, photocopied and simultaneous submissions OK. Buys first rights. Sample copy 24¢. Receives 1 cartoon and 2 illustrations/month from freelance artists.
Illustrations: Buys 12 covers/year on rural scenes, views of rural mailboxes and rural people. Buys 1 illustration/issue from freelancers. Interested in pen & ink or pencil on rural, seasonal and postal matter. Especially needs rural mailboxes and sketches of scenes on rural delivery. Works on assignment only. Send query letter with brochure showing art style or resume, tear sheets, photocopies, slides and photographs. Samples returned by SASE. Reports in 1 week, if accepted; 1 month if not accepted. Write to schedule an appointment to show a portfolio, which should include original/final art, final reproduction/product, color, tear sheets, Photostats, photographs and b&w. Buys all rights on a work-for-hire basis. Pays by the project, $60-150; on publication.
Tips: "Please send in samples when you inquire about submitting material." Have a definite need for "realistic painting and sketches. We need a clean, crisp style. Subjects needed are scenic, mailboxes, animals and faces. We need fine black-and-white, pen-and-ink, and watercolor."

NATIONAL SOCIETY OF PUBLIC ACCOUNTANTS, 1010 North Fairfax St., Alexandria VA 22314. Contact: Managing Editor. Send samples.
Illustrations: Buys assigned themes on accounting, business, finances, taxes and economics. Pays $20 minimum, line drawings. "Only send items relating to tax issues or small business."

NATURAL HISTORY, American Museum of Natural History, Central Park W. and 79th St., New York NY 10024. (212)769-5500. Editor: Alan Ternes. Designer: Tom Page. Emphasizes social and natural sciences. For well-educated professionals interested in the natural sciences. Monthly. Circ. 500,000. Previously published work OK.
Illustrations: Buys 23-25 illustrations/year; 25-35 maps or diagrams/year. Works on assignment only. Query with samples. Samples returned by SASE. Provide "any pertinent information" to be kept on file for future assignments. Reports in 1 week. Buys one-time rights. Inside: Pays $200 and up for color illustrations; on publication.
Tips: "Be familiar with the publication. Always looking for accurate and creative scientific illustrations, good diagrams and maps."

NEGATIVE CAPABILITY, 6116 Timberly Rd. N, Mobile AL 36609. Editor: Sue Walker. Journal. Emphasizes fiction, poetry, art, music and essays. Audience is interested in art/literature. Quarterly. Circ.

1,000. Original artwork returned after publication. Sample copy $3.50.
Cartoons: Buys 3 cartoons/issue from freelancers. Theme or style open. Prefers single or double panel with gagline; b&w line drawings, b&w washes. Send finished cartoons to be kept on file. Material not filed is returned by SASE. Reports within 6 weeks. To show a portfolio, mail original/final art, final reproduction/product, photographs and b&w. Acquires one-time rights. Pays in 2 contributor's copies.
Illustrations: Buys 8-10 illustrations/issue from freelancers. Themes or styles open. Send query letter with brochure showing art style and samples to be kept on file. Samples not filed are returned by SASE. Reports within 6 weeks. To show a portfolio, mail original/final art, final reproduction/product, photographs and b&w. Acquires one-time rights. Pays in 2 contributor's copies.

NEW AGE JOURNAL, 342 Western Ave., Brighton MA 02135. (617)787-2005. Art Director: Howie Green. Emphasizes alternative lifestyles, holistic health, ecology, personal growth, human potential, planetary survival. Bimonthly. Circ. 150,000. Accepts previously published material and simultaneous submissions. Original artwork returned after publication by request. Sample copy $3.00.
Illustrations: Uses 8-10 illustrations/issue. Illustrations accompany specific manuscripts. Send query letter with samples or tear sheets to be kept on file. Call for appointment to show portfolio. Prefers Photostats, photocopies or slides as samples. Samples returned by SASE if not kept on file. Buys one-time rights.

***THE NEWFOUNDLAND HERALD**, Box 2015, St. John's, Newfoundland A1C 5R7 Canada. (709)726-7060. 130-page informative entertainment magazine with TV listings for the province. Paid circ. 40,000. Weekly. Simultaneous submissions and previously published work OK. "Our publication is copyrighted."
Cartoons: Buys TV, movie, entertainment and Hollywood themes. Send roughs. Pays on publication.

NEW MEXICO MAGAZINE, 1100 St. Francis Dr., Santa Fe NM 87503. (505)827-0220. Art Director: Mary Sweitzer. Emphasizes the state of New Mexico for residents, and visiting vacationers and businespersons. Monthly. Circ. 100,000. Accepts previously published material and simultaneous submissions. Original artwork returned after publication. No printed artists' guidelines, but may call for information. Also interested in calligraphers.
Cartoons: Uses 12-20 cartoons/year, 1-2/issue. Prefers single panel; b&w line drawings, b&w washes. Send resume, tear sheets, Photostats, photocopies and slides. Call to schedule an appointment to show a portfolio, which should include original/final art, final reproduction/product, color, tear sheets, photographs and b&w. Material not kept on file is returned only if requested. Reports only if interested. Buys one-time rights. Pays $25-50, b&w; $50-100, color; two weeks after acceptance, on publication for stock material.
Illustrations: Uses 2 illustrations/issue. Works on assignment only. Send query letter with samples to be kept on file. Samples not kept on file are returned only if requested. Reports only if interested. Buys one-time rights. Pays for design $7-15; $40 for small illustrations to $300 for 4-color work, usually all inside; on acceptance.
Tips: Contact verbally or with written material first. Send appropriate materials and samples.

NEW ORLEANS, SEM Publishing Co., 6666 Morrison Rd., New Orleans LA 70126. (504)246-2700. Art Director: John Maher. Editor: Sherry Spear. Emphasizes entertainment, travel, sports, news, business and politics in New Orleans. For readers with high income and education. Monthly. Circ. 44,000. Previously published and photocopied submissions OK. Sample copy $2.50.
Illustrations: Query with samples. SASE. Buys assigned illustrations and cartoons on current events, education and politics. Especially needs assigned feature illustrations "specifically relating to and illustrating a concept in one of our main feature stories." Pays $40-100, spot drawings; $75-200, feature illustrations; on publication.
Tips: "Do not send unassigned, unsolicited work on speculation. It creates a burden for me to sift through work and return it. However, do send nonreturnable photocopies or stats of work so I can keep them on file when work becomes available."

NEW ORLEANS REVIEW, Box 195, Loyola University, New Orleans LA 70118. (504)865-2294. Editor: John Mosier. Journal of literature and culture. Published 4 times/year. Sample copy $7.
Illustrations: Uses 5-10 illustrations/issue. Cover: uses color, all mediums. SASE. Reports in 4 months. Inside: uses b&w line drawings, photos/slides of all mediums.

***THE NEW PHYSICIAN**, 1890 Preston White Dr., Reston VA 22091. Contact: Art Director: Mary Ellen Vehlow. For physicians-in-training; concerns primary medical care, political and social issues relating to medicine. Published 9 times/year. Circ. 42,000. SASE. Original artwork returned after publication. Buys one-time rights. Pays on publication.

Cartoons: Cartoon submissions welcome. Interested in medical education. Send finished artwork. Reports in 2 weeks.
Illustrations: Uses 5 illustrations/issue. Usually commissioned. Samples returned by SASE. Submit resume and samples of style. Reports in 2 weeks. Provide resume, letter of inquiry, brochure and flyer to be kept on file for future assignments. Buys one-time rights. Negotiates pay.

NEW REALITIES, %Heldref Publications, 4000 Albemarle St. N.W., Washington D.C. 20016. Editor/Publisher: Neal Vahle. Managing Editor: Shirley Christine. Concerns "holistic health and personal growth." Bimonthly. Pays on publication.
Cartoons: Buys 2 cartoons/issue on assigned themes.
Illustrations: Buys 2-3 illustrations/issue on assigned themes. Inside: $75-150, b&w.

THE NEW REPUBLIC, 1220 19th St. NW, Washington DC 20036. (202)331-7494. Copy Editor: Leona Hiraoka Roth. Emphasizes politics and culture for a "well-educated, well-off audience with a median age of 40." Weekly. Circ. 100,000. Accepts previously published material and simultaneous submissions. Original artwork returned after publication.
Cartoons: Buys 1 cartoon/month from freelancers. Send query letter with samples of style, finished cartoons and color work, if possible, to be kept on file. Material not kept on file returned only if requested and only if accompanied by SASE. Write or call for appointment to show portfolio. Reports only if samples are accompanied by cover letter or written inquiry. Negotiates rights purchased. Pays $50 b&w; on publication.
Illustrations: Uses 1 illustration/issue. Prefers political, literary themes. Works on assignment only. Send query letter with brochure, resume, business card, samples and tear sheets to be kept on file. Call or write for appointment to show portfolio. Negotiates rights purchased and payment. Pays on publication.

NEW WOMAN MAGAZINE, 215 Lexington Ave., New York NY 10016. (212)685-4790. Magazine emphasizing emotional self-help for women ages 25-34, 50% married. Most have attended college. Published monthly. Circ. 1.2 million. Accepts previously published material. Returns original artwork to the artist upon request.
Cartoons: Uses approximately 10 freelance cartoons/issue. Prefers single panel, with or without gagline; b&w line drawings. "We have changed quite a bit. We are still pro-women, but not as hard-hitting or as sexist in putting men down. We need cartoons every month for our word power quiz, Pin-ups and letters to the editor column. Look at recent issues of the magazine." Contact Rosemarie Lennon, cartoon editor, for more information, or to be added to the monthly mailing list, which tells which articles in upcoming issues will require cartoons. Cartoons are matched with editorial. Send finished cartoon and SASE. Purchases all serial rights. Pays $225 on acceptance.
Illustrations: Uses 3-4 freelance illustrations/issue. Works on assignment only. Send query letter with tear sheets and photocopies to be kept on file to Caroline Bowyer, art director. Samples not kept on file are not returned. Reports only if interested. Payment varies. Pays on acceptance.

***THE NEW YORK LAW SCHOOL REPORTER**, 57 Worth St., New York NY 10013. (212)431-2117. Contact: Editorial Board. Tabloid emphasizing law and music. Features technical articles, confession, humor, and science fiction for law school students and alumni—anti-racist, progressive. Bimonthly. Circ. 7,000. Accepts previously published material. Sample copy for SASE with 56¢ postage.
Cartoons: Prefers political left, progressive themes. Prefers double panel, with gagline, b&w line drawings. Send query letter with finished cartoons. Samples are filed. Samples not filed are returned by SASE. Reports back within 2 months. Negotiable fee. Buys one-time rights. Pays $7.
Illustrations: Send query letter with photocopies. Samples are filed. Samples not filed are returned by SASE. Reports back within 2 months. Buys one-time rights. Pays $15, b&w; inside.

NEW YORK MAGAZINE, 755 Second Ave., New York NY 10017. (212)880-0700. Design Director: Robert Best. Art Director: Josh Gosfield. Emphasizes New York City life; also covers all boroughs for New Yorkers with upper-middle income and business people interested in what's happening in the city. Weekly. Original artwork returned after publication.
Illustrations: Works on assignment only. Send query letter with tear sheets to be kept on file. Prefers Photostats as samples. Samples returned if requested. Call or write for appointment to show portfolio (drop-offs). Buys first rights. Pays $1,000, b&w and color, cover; $600 for 4-color, $400 b&w full page, inside; $225 for 4-color, $150 b&w spot, inside. Pays on publication.

NEW YORK/PHILADELPHIA ACTION, Suite 144, 1601 Easton Rd., Willow Grove PA 19090. Managing Editor: Don Conti. Tabloid emphasizing sex and adult entertainment for adult males. Monthly. Circ. 10,000. Sample copy for SASE with $1.50 postage. Cartoon guidelines for SASE with first-class postage.

Cartoons: Buys 12 cartoons/issue from freelancers. Prefers sex as themes. Prefers single panel with gagline; b&w line drawings. Send query letter with brochure showing art style or resume, tear sheets, Photostats, photocopies and finished cartoons. Material not kept on file is returned by SASE. Reports within 12-14 weeks. To show a portfolio, mail original/final art and b&w. Buys first rights or reprint rights. Pays $9.50, b&w; on publication or 30 days after acceptance, whichever comes first.
Tips: "No interest in non-sexual cartoons."

THE NEW YORKER, 25 W. 43rd St., New York NY 10036. Contact: Art Editor. Emphasizes news analysis and lifestyle features.
Needs: Buys cartoons, spots and cover designs. Receives 3,000 cartoons/week. Mail art or deliver sketches on Wednesdays. SASE. "Spots are now purchased every 4 months." Strict standards regarding style, technique, plausibility of drawing. Especially looks for originality. Pays $500 minimum, cartoons; top rates for spots and cover designs.
Tips: "Familiarize yourself with your markets."

THE NEWS CIRCLE, Box 3684, Glendale CA 91201. (818)240-1918. Contact: Laila Haiek. For Arab-Americans. Monthly magazine. Circ. 5,000.
Cartoons: Buys 5-8 cartoons/issue. Needs b&w. Send roughs. Reports in 3 weeks. Negotiates pay; pays on publication.
Illustrations: Buys b&w Arabic and arabesque designs. Send query letter with samples. Reports in 3 weeks. Negotiates pay; pays on publication.

NEXUS, 1110 N. Fillmore, Amarillo TX 79107. (806)376-6229. Editor: Vance Buck. Emphasizes games for game players. Quarterly. Circ. 10,000. Usually does not accept previously published material. Returns original artwork after publication with SASE. Sample copy for $5; art guidelines for SASE.
Illustrations: Buys 10-30/issue. Prefers themes related to games produced by Task Force Games Company—Star Fleet Battles, StarFire, History of WWII and Battlewagon, etc. Send query letter with Photostats, photocopies, slides and photographs. Reports within 3 weeks. To show a portfolio, mail color, tear sheets, Photostats, photographs and b&w. Buys one-time rights. Pays $200-300, color, cover; 75¢/square inch, b&w, inside; on publication.
Tips: "Artists should be familiar enough with our games to be able to do artwork which is consistent with game concepts."

NIT&WIT, Box 627, Geneva IL 60134. (312)232-9496. Publisher: Harrison McCormick. Magazine emphasizing the cultural arts for an affluent, art-oriented audience, 50% male, 50% married, median age 35. Bimonthly. Circ. 20,000. Original artwork sometimes returned after publication. Sample copy $3; art guidelines available.
Illustrations: Buys 6-10/issue from freelance artists. Buys 36 illustrations/year from freelancers. Prefers cultural arts themes. Send query letter with brochure, slides and photocopies. Samples not filed are returned by SASE. Reports back within 1 week. To show a portfolio, mail roughs, tear sheets and final reproduction/product. Buys first rights. Pays $0-50, b&w; $0-200, color, cover and inside; on publication.

NJEA REVIEW, 180 W. State St., Box 1211, Trenton NJ 08607. Editor-in-Chief: Martha O. DeBlieu. Nonprofit, for New Jersey public school employees. Monthly. Circ. 123,000. Previously published work OK. Original artwork not returned after publication. Free sample copy.
Cartoons: Buys 3-4/year from freelancers. Receives 20 submissions/week from freelancers. Interested in b&w cartoons with an "education theme—do not make fun of school employees or children"; single panel. Prefers to see finished cartoons. Buys all rights on a work-for-hire basis. Pays on acceptance. Limited budget.
Illustrations: Buys 1-2 illustrations/issue from freelancers. Receives 1-2 submissions/week from freelancers. Especially needs education-related spot art. Send query letter with brochure showing art style or resume, tear sheets, Photostats, photocopies and photographs. Reports as soon as possible. To show a portfolio, mail appropriate materials, which should include original/final art, tear sheets, photographs and b&w. Buys all rights on a work-for-hire basis. Pays $25 b&w, cover; $7.50-10 b&w, inside; on acceptance.
Tips: "Like bigger and bolder art rather than intricate work. Too much artwork we see is too finely detailed or on the other extreme, too simplistic, amateur looking. Look at our magazine and don't send us material not related to our type of magazine."

NORTH AMERICAN HUNTER, Box 35557, Minneapolis MN 55435. (612)941-7654. Managing Editor: Bill Miller. Publishes hunting material only for avid hunters of both small and big game in North America. Bimonthly. Circ. 100,000. Accepts previously published material. Original artwork returned after publication unless all rights are purchased. Sample copy $2; art guidelines available.

Cartoons: Buys 36 cartoons/year from freelancers. Considers humorous hunting situations. "Must convey ethical, responsible hunting practices; good clean fun." Prefers single panel with gagline; b&w line drawings or washes. 8½x11 vertical or horizontal format. Send query letter with roughs or finished cartoons. Returns unpurchased material immediately. Reports within 2 weeks. Buys all rights. Pays $15, b&w; on acceptance.
Illustrations: Buys 2 illustrations/issue from freelancers; usually includes 1 humorous illustration. Prefers line art, mostly b&w, occasionally color. "Work should be close to being photographically real in most case." Works on assignment only. Send query letter with samples. Samples not filed are returned. Reports within 2 weeks. Buys one-time rights. Pays $250, color, cover; $75-100, b&w or color, inside; on acceptance.
Tips: "Send only art that deals with hunting, hunters, wildlife or hunting situations. North American big and small game only. We accept only detailed and realistic-looking pieces—no modern art."

NORTH AMERICAN MENTOR, Drawer 69, Fennimore WI 53809. (608)822-6237. Editor-in-Chief: John Westburg. Managing Editor: Mildred Westburg. Send art submissions to Martial R. Westburg, art editor, North American Mentor, Box 558, Old Chelsea Station, New York NY 10011. For professional people, half of whom are age 60 or over. Quarterly. Circ. 400. Previously published, photocopied and simultaneous submissions OK. Original artwork not returned after publication. Sample copy $2.
Illustrations: Buys 1 (cover) illustration/issue. Receives less than 10 submissions/year from freelancers. Interested in b&w line drawings only. Send resume, brochure, flyer and tear sheets to be kept on file. Samples are not returned. Reports in "6 months or more." Buys all rights. Pays $25 minimum, b&w line drawings; on publication.

NORTH SHORE MAGAZINE, 874 Green Bay Rd., Winnetka IL 60093. (312)441-7892. Contact: Art Director. City/regional magazine; upscale readership. Monthly. Circ. 38,500 subscribers. Occasionally accepts previously published material. Returns original artwork after publication. Sample copy free for SASE with $1 postage.
Cartoons: Buys 1-5 cartoons/issue from freelancers. Prefers single panel with gagline; b&w line drawings. Send query letter with samples of style or finished cartoons to be kept on file. Material not filed is returned by SASE. Reports within 1 week. Buys one-time rights. Payment varies; pays on publication.
Illustrations: Buys 1-3 illustrations/issue from freelancers. Works on assignment only. Send query letter with resume, tear sheets and slides. Samples not filed are returned by SASE. Reports within 1 week. Call to schedule an appointment to show a portfolio, which should include original/final art, final reproduction/product, color and b&w. Buys first rights. Pays on acceptance.

NORTHEAST OUTDOORS, Box 2180, Waterbury CT 06722-2180. (203)755-0158. Editor: Debbie Nealley. For camping families in the Northeastern states. Monthly. Circ. 14,000. Original artwork returned after publication, if requested. Previously published material and simultaneous submissions OK if noted in cover letter. Editorial guidelines for SASE with 1 first-class stamp; sample copy for 9x12 SASE with 6 first-class stamps.
Cartoons: Buys 1 cartoon/issue on camping and recreational vehicle situations. Send query letter with samples. Reports in 2 weeks. Pays $10, b&w; on acceptance.
Illustrations: Buys 2-3 illustrations/year with manuscripts. To show a portfolio, mail appropriate materials. Pays $40 b&w, cover; $10-30 b&w, inside; on publication.
Tips: "Make it neat. Felt-tip pen sketches won't make it in this market any more. Query or send samples for illustration ideas. We occasionally buy or assign to accompany stories. Artists who have accompanying manuscripts have an extra edge, as we rarely buy illustrations alone."

THE NORTHERN LOGGER & TIMBER PROCESSOR, Northeastern Loggers Association Inc., Box 69, Old Forge NY 13420. (315)369-3078. Editor: Eric A. Johnson. Emphasizes methods, machinery and manufacturing as related to forestry. "For loggers, timberland managers and processors of primary forest products." Monthly. Circ. 13,000. Previously published material OK. Free sample copy; guidelines sent upon request.
Cartoons: Uses 1 cartoon/issue, all from freelancers. Receives 1 submission/week from freelancers. Interested in "any cartoons involving forest industry situations." Send finished cartoons with SASE. Reports in 1 week. Pays $10 minimum, b&w line drawings; on acceptance.
Tips: "Keep it simple and pertinent to the subjects we cover. Also, keep in mind that on-the-job safety is an issue that we like to promote."

NORTHWEST REVIEW, 369 PLC, University of Oregon, Eugene OR 97403. (503)686-3957. Editor: John Witte. Art Editor: Deb Casey. Emphasizes literature. "We publish material of general interest to those who follow American/world poetry and fiction." Original artwork returned after publication. Published 3 times/year. Sample copy $3.

Illustrations: Uses b&w line drawings, graphics and cover designs. Receives 20-30 portfolios/year from freelance artists. Arrange interview or mail slides. SASE. Reports as soon as possible. Acquires one-time rights. Pays in contributor's copies. Especially needs high-quality graphic artwork. "We run a regular art feature of the work of one artist, printed in b&w, 133-line screen on quality coated paper. A statement by the artist often accompanies the feature."

NOSTALGIA WORLD FOR COLLECTORS AND FANS, Box 231, North Haven CT 06473. Editor: Bonnie Roth. Collector's magazine for records, comics, toys, movie memorabilia, baseball cards, sheet music, etc. Bimonthly. Circ. 4,000. Accepts previously published material and simultaneous submissions. Original artwork returned after publication. Sample copy $2; art guidelines for SASE.
Cartoons: Uses 24-page comic strips presently bought through syndication. Prefers b&w line drawings. Send query letter with roughs to be kept on file. Material not kept on file is returned by SASE. Reports within 2-4 weeks. Buys all rights. Pays $7-15, b&w; on acceptance.
Illustrations: Uses 2-5 illustrations/issue; number bought from freelancers varies. Prefers topics relating to collectors. Send query letter with photocopies to be kept on file. Reports within 2-4 weeks. Buys all rights. Pays $35, b&w, cover; $15, b&w, inside; on publication.
Tips: "We are looking for outrageous concepts in the form of comic strip art as we are planning to publish more comic books in the future. We presently purchase comic strip art through syndication. Be bold, be daring, but have an original style."

NOTRE DAME, University of Notre Dame, 415 Main Bldg., Box M, Notre Dame IN 46556. Art Director: Don Nelson. For university alumni. Quarterly. Circ. 98,000. Uses 6 illustrations/issue, all from freelancers. Professional artists only. "Please don't request sample copies." Accepts previously published material. Original artwork returned after publication.
Illustrations: Seeks " 'graphic' solutions to communication problems." Buys 6 illustrations/issue from freelancers. Send query letter with brochure showing art style or tear sheets, Photostats and photocopies. Works on assignment only. Samples returned by SASE. Buys one-time rights. Pays $100 minimum; on acceptance.

© Tom Duckworth

Donald Nelson, art director of Notre Dame Magazine*, asked artist Tom Duckworth of Granger, Indiana, to illustrate a campus news story on housing for married students, many on whom are foreign. The artwork, rendered with airbrush and watercolor, conveys the "idea of a village of struggling student families, drying clothes the old-fashioned way." Nelson regularly works with Duckworth because he is "open to suggestions, prompt and reliable." Duckworth received $375 for the purchase of one-time rights.*

***NOW COMICS/THE NOW LIBRARY**, Box 8042, Chicago IL 60680-8042. (312)786-9013. Publisher: Tony Caputo. Estab. 1985. Publishes limited edition comic books and graphic novels. Titles include *Ralph Snart Adventures*, *Valor Thunderstar*, *Syphons*, *Vector* and *EB'NN*. Genres: adventure, mystery, science fiction, animal parodies and superheroes. Themes: outer space, future science and teenage exploits. "We are a 'creator-oriented' company which reaches males and females from age 13-34. We're looking for educated writers." Monthly and bimonthly. Average circ. 25,000. Original artwork returned after publication. Sample copy and art guidelines for SASE with 50¢ postage.
Illustrations: Uses freelance artists for inking, lettering, pencilling, color work and covers. Send query letter with photocopies of work. Samples are filed. Samples not filed are returned by SASE if requested. Reports back within 1 month. Call or write to schedule an appointment to show a portfolio, which should include 10 pages of pencil or ink drawings one-and-one half times up, 5 pages of action continuity and 3 pages of lettering—one-and-one-half up with sound effects. Creators retain own rights. Pays $25-30/page for pencilling, $15-30/page for inking, $8-15/page for lettering and $10-30/page for coloring. Negotiates payment for graphic novels. Pays on publication.
Tips: Looks for "storytelling talent and capability in drawing anatomy. A common mistake freelancers make is sending or showing too many samples."

NUCLEAR TIMES MAGAZINE, Suite 300, 1601 Connecticut Ave., NW, Washington DC 20009. (202)332-9222. Art Director: Elliott Negin. Provides straight news coverage of the anti-nuclear weapons movement. Bimonthly. Circ. 70,000. Accepts previously published material. Returns original artwork after publication. Sample copy $3; art guidelines available.
Illustrations: Buys 5 illustrations/issue from freelancers. Only anti-nuclear issues as themes. Primarily works on assignment. Write or call for appointment to show portfolio. Prefers to review photocopies and tear sheets in mail submissions. Samples not filed are returned by SASE only if requested. Reports within 2 weeks. Buys one-time rights. Pays $400-500 for b&w cover; $50-300 for b&w inside; on publication.

NUGGET, Dugent Publishing Co., 2355 Salzedo St., Coral Gables FL 33134. Editor: John Fox. Illustration Assignments: Nye Willden. For men and women with fetish interests.
Cartoons: Buys 10 cartoons/issue, all from freelancers. Receives 100 submissions/week from freelancers. Interested in "funny fetish themes." B&w only for spots, b&w and color for page. Prefers to see finished cartoons. SASE. Reports in 2 weeks. Buys first North American serial rights. Pays $50, spot drawings; $75, page.
Illustrations: Buys 4 illustrations/issue from freelancers. Interested in "erotica, cartoon style, etc." Works on assignment only. Prefers to see samples of style. No samples returned. Reports back on future assignment possibilities. Send brochure, flyer or other samples to be kept on file for future assignments. Buys first North American serial rights. Pays $125-150, b&w.
Tips: Especially interested in "the artist's anatomy skills, professionalism in rendering (whether he's published or not) and drawings which relate to our needs." Current trends include "a return to the 'classical' realistic form of illustration which is fine with us because we prefer realistic and well-rendered illustrations."

***NUTRITION TODAY**, 428 E. Preston St., Baltimore MD 21202. (301)528-8520. Art Director: James R. Mulligan. Trade journal emphasizing nutrition in the public and private sector directed to the practicing dietitian. Features general interest and technical articles. Bimonthly. Circ. 16,000. Accepts previously published material. Original artwork returned after publication. Sample copy available. Art guidelines for SASE with 30¢ postage.
Illustrations: Buys 8 illustrations/year from freelancers. Works on assignment only. Prefers technical illustrations of diverse topics. Send query letter with brochure or resume and photocopies. Samples are filed. Samples not filed are not returned. Repórts back only if interested. Write to schedule an appointment to show a portfolio, which should include original/final art, final reproduction/product, slides, color and b&w. Buys all rights. Pays $200, b&w; $400, color, cover; $100, b&w; $300, color, inside; on acceptance.
Tips: "Have a strong background in technical art, such as graphs and flow charts incorporating graphics."

OCEANS, 2001 W. Main St., Stanford CT 06902. Editor: Michael W. Robbins. "For those interested in the beauty, science, adventure and conservation of the oceans and the life therein.'' Bimonthly. Circ. 55,000. Original artwork returned after publication. Sample copy $3.50; free contributor guidelines.
Cartoons: Interested in sea-oriented themes. Uses very few authors. Prefers roughs. SASE. Buys first North American serial rights.
Illustrations: By assignment only, based on editorial need.

OFF DUTY, Suite C-2, 3303 Harbor Blvd., Costa Mesa CA 92626. Art Director: John Wong. Three editions: Europe, Pacific and America. Emphasizes general interest topics, e.g. leisure, sports, travel, food, photography, music, finance for military Americans stationed around the world. Combined circ: 708,000. Accepts previously published material and simultaneous submissions if not submitted to other military magazines. Assignment artwork returned after publication. Sample copy $1.
Cartoons: Uses occasional cartoons in two categories. First must relate to military personnel, families and military life. Off-duty situations preferred. Send to Bruce Thorstad, U.S. Editor. Second category relates to hobbies of audio, video, computers or photography. "A military angle in this category is ideal, but not necessary." Send to Gary Burch. Technical Editor. "Keep in mind that all readers are active duty military, not retirees or vets." Pays $40 minimum b&w; more by negotiation.
Illustrations: *Off Duty*'s America edition uses several illustrations per issue, by assignment only. Accepts photocopies or tearsheets of previous work that can be kept on file, but does not want originals or anything that must be returned. Pays $50-150 on acceptance for assignments.

***OFFICIAL DETECTIVE STORIES**, 20th Floor, 460 W. 34th St., New York NY 10001. Editor: Art Crockett. For readers of factual crime stories and articles. Monthly.
Cartoons: Buys crime genre themes. "Avoid cliche situations such as 2 convicts conversing in cell; cute, mild sex." Submit roughs. SASE. Reports in 2 weeks. Buys all rights. Pays $25; on acceptance.

OHIO MAGAZINE, 40 S. Third St., Columbus OH 43215. (614)461-5083. Managing Editor: Ellen Stein Burbach. Emphasizes feature material of Ohio for an educated, urban and urbane readership. Monthly. Circ. 110,000. Previously published work OK. Original artwork returned after publication. Sample copy $2.50.
Illustrations: Buys 1-3/issue from freelancers. Interested in Ohio scenes and themes. Works on stock and assignment. Send query letter with brochure showing art style or tear sheets, dupe slides and photographs. SASE. Reports in 2 weeks. On assignment: pays $75-150, b&w; $100-250, color, inside; on publication. Buys one-time publication rights.
Tips: Magazine is now realizing an "increased use of stock photography and artwork (illustration, paintings, prints). Artwork should exhibit a fine arts 'bent,' but not 'slick.' Uncontrived elegance, rich, noncommercial images that elevate 'real life' in Ohio."

OLD WEST, Box 2107, Stillwater OK 74076. (405)743-0130. Editor: John Joerschke. Emphasizes American western history from 1830 to 1910 for a primarily rural and suburban audience, middle-age and older, interested in Old West history, horses, cowboys, art, clothing and all things western. Quarterly. Circ. 90,000. Accepts previously published material and considers some simultaneous submissions. Original artwork returned after publication. Sample copy and art guidelines free for SASE.
Illustrations: Uses 5-10 illustrations/issue, including 2 or 3 humorous illustrations; buys all from freelancers. "Inside illustrations are usually, but need not always be pen & ink line drawings; covers are western paintings." Send query letter with samples to be kept on file; "we return anything on request." Call or write for appointment to show portfolio. "For inside illustrations, we want samples of artist's line drawings. For covers, we need to see full-color transparencies." Reports within 1 month. Buys one-time rights. Pays $100-150 for color transparency for cover; $15-40, b&w, inside; on acceptance.
Tips: We think the mainstream of interest in Western Americana has moved in the direction of fine art, and we're looking for more material along those lines. A recent cover that we were very pleased with is Fall 1986."

ONE WORLD, Box 1553, Williamsport PA 17703. (717)322-3252. Vice President: Dana Stuchell. Emphasizes animal rights for "the general public involved in the protection of animals and promotion of animal rights and the philosphical public interested in animal rights as a philosophical/ethical issue." Periodic. Circ. 10,000. Accepts previously published material. Original artwork returned after publication. Sample copy $1.
Cartoons: Prefers animal rights or environmental issue themes. Send query letter with tear sheets, Photostats, photocopies and finished cartoons to be kept on file. Material not filed is returned by SASE. Reports only if interested. Buys reprint rights. Pays negotiable rate, b&w and color; on publication.
Illustrations: Prefers animal rights and environmental issue as themes. Send query letter with tear sheets, Photostats, photocopies and photographs to be kept on file. Samples returned by SASE. Reports only if interested. Buys reprint rights. Pays negotiable rate, b&w and color, cover and inside; on publication.
Tips: "Artwork should have an immediate relevance to animal rights."

ONTARIO OUT OF DOORS, 7th Floor, 777 Bay St., Toronto, Ontario M5W 1A7 Canada. (416)596-5022. Editor-in-Chief: Burton Myers. Emphasizes hunting, fishing, camping and conservation.

Published 10 times/year. Circ. 55,000. Previously published work OK. Original artwork not returned after publication. Free sample copy and artist's guidelines.
Cartoons: Buys 2 cartoons/issue, all from freelancers. Receives 10-20 cartoons/month from freelance artists. Interested in fishing, hunting and camping themes; single panel. Send roughs. SASE (nonresidents include IRC). Reports within 6 weeks. Buys one time rights. Pays $50, b&w line drawings; 4 weeks after acceptance.
Illustrations: Uses 1-2 color illustrations plus 2-4 b&w line drawings/issue, all from freelancers. Interested in wildlife and fish themes. Especially needs cover artwork. Prefers to see roughs. SAE (nonresidents include IRC). Provide business card to be kept on file for future use. Reports in 6 weeks. Pays $250-500, color, cover; 4 weeks after acceptance.
Tips: "Strive for realism. Take the time to research the publication. Ask for a sample copy first before sending submissions." Especially looks for "the ability to depict nature or an activity in a clear-cut, informative fashion that supports the article."

OPPORTUNITY MAGAZINE, 6 N. Michigan Ave., Chicago IL 60602. Editor: Jack Weissman. Features articles dealing with direct (door-to-door) selling and on ways to start small businesses. For independent salesmen, agents, jobbers, distributors, sales managers, flea market operators, franchise seekers, multi-level distributors, route salesmen, wagon jobbers and people seeking an opportunity to make money full- or part-time. Monthly. Original artwork not returned after publication. Sample copy free for SASE with 50¢ postage.
Cartoons: Buys 2-3 cartoons/issue from freelancers. Interested in themes dealing with humorous sales situations affecting door-to-door salespeople. Considers single panel with gagline; b&w line drawings. Prefers roughs or finished cartoons. SASE. Buys all rights. Pays $5 on publication.
Tips: "Get sample copy beforehand and have an idea of what is appropriate."

THE OPTIMIST MAGAZINE, 4494 Lindell Blvd., St. Louis MO 63108. Editor: James E. Braibish. Emphasizes activities relating to Optimist clubs in U.S. and Canada (civic-service clubs). "Magazine is mailed to all members of Optimist clubs. Average age is 42, most are management level with some college education." Circ. 160,000. Accepts previously published material. Sample copy for SASE.
Cartoons: Buys 3 cartoons/issue from freelancers. Prefers themes of general interest; family-oriented, sports, kids, civic clubs. Prefers single panel, with gagline. No washes. Send query letter with samples. Submissions returned by SASE. Reports within 1 week. Buys one-time rights. Pays $30/b&w; on acceptance.

ORANGE COAST MAGAZINE, Suite 8, 245-D Fischer Ave, Costa Mesa CA 92626. (714)545-1900. Art Director:Leslie Freidson Lawicki. General interest regional magazine. Monthly. Circ. 35,000. Returns original artwork after publication. Sample copy and art guidelines available.
Illustrations: Buys 3 illustration/issue from freelancers. Considers airbrush. Works on assignment only. Send brochure showing art style or tear sheets, slides or transparencies to be kept on file. Samples not filed are returned only if requested. Reports only if interested. To show a portfolio, mail original/final art, final reproduction/product, color, tear sheets and photographs. Buys one-time rights. Pays for design by the hour, $5-10. Pays for illustration by the project, $50-500; on publication.
Tips: There is a need for "fluid free-style illustration and for more photojournalistic expression within an artists mode—i.e. the art meets needs to express a story exactly, yet in a creative manner and executed well. Please send samples soon."

***OREGON RIVER WATCH**, Box 294, Rhododendron OR 97049. (503)622-4798. Editor: Michael P. Jones. Estab. 1985. Books published in volumes emphasizing "fisheries, fishing, rafting, environment, wildlife, hiking, recreation, tourism, and everything that can be related to Oregon's waterways." Monthly. Circ. 2,000. Accepts previously published material. Original artwork returned after publication. Art guidelines for SASE with first-class postage.
Cartoons: Buys 1-3 cartoons/issue from freelancers. Prefers single panel, double panel, multiple panel with or without gagline; b&w line drawings, b&w or color washes. Send query letter with samples of style, roughs or finished cartoons. Samples are filed. Samples not filed are returned by SASE. Reports back within 2 weeks. Buys one-time rights. Pays in copies.
Illustrations: Buys 10-20 illustrations/issue from freelancers. Send query letter with brochure showing art style or resume and tear sheets, Photostats, photocopies, slides or photographs. Samples not filed are returned by SASE. Reports back within 2 weeks. To show a portfolio, mail thumbnails, roughs, original/final art, final reproduction/product, color, tear sheets, Photostats, photographs or b&w. Buys one-time rights. Pays in copies.
Tips: "We need b&w or pen & ink sketches. We have a lot of projects going on at once but cannot always find an immediate need for freelancer's talent. Being pushy doesn't help."

THE ORIGINAL NEW ENGLAND GUIDE, Historical Times, Inc., Box 8200, 2245 Kohn Rd., Harrisburg PA 17105. Editor: Kathie Kull. Consulting Editor: Mimi E.B. Steadman. Art Director: Jeanne Collins. Emphasizes New England travel of all kinds. Readers are "those planning on going on vacation trips, weekend jaunts, mini-holidays, day trips. For North American and overseas visitors to New England." Annually. Circ. 160,000. Sample copy $5.
Illustrations: "*The Guide* is almost always able to make its few assignments for artwork locally. However, we are certainly happy to know about freelancers and their special abilities, and welcome letters and/or samples (clips are fine)." Pays $50-150 on publication for inside b&w, depending on use. Send correspondence to Art Director.

THE OTHER SIDE, 300 W. Apsley St., Philadelphia PA 19144. (215)849-2178. Editor: Mark Olson. Art Director: Cathleen Boint. "We are read by Christians with a radical commitment to social justice and a deep allegiance to Biblical faith. We try to help readers put their faith into action." Published 10 times/year. Circ. 15,000. Receives 3 cartoons and 1 illustration/week from freelance artists. Sample copy $3.
Cartoons: Buys 6 cartoons/year on current events, environment, economics, politics and religion; single and multiple panel. Pays $25, b&w line drawings; on publication. "Looking for cartoons with a radical political perspective."
Illustrations: Especially needs b&w line drawings illustrating specific articles. Send query letter with tear sheets, photocopies, slide, photographs and SASE. Reports in 6 weeks. Photocopied and simultaneous submissions OK. To show a portfolio, mail appropriate materials or call to schedule an appointment; portfolio should include roughs, original/final art, final reproduction/product and photographs. Pays "within 4 weeks of publication." Pays $125-200, 4-color. Pays $40-150, b&w line drawings inside, on publication.
Tips: "We're looking for illustrators who share our perspective on social, economic and political issues, and who are willing to work for us on assignment."

OTTAWA MAGAZINE, 192 Bank St., Ottawa, Ontario K2P 1W8 Canada. (613)234-7751. Art Director: Peter de Gannes. Emphasizes lifestyles for sophisticated, middle and upper income, above average education professionals; most readers are women. Monthly. Circ. 42,500. Accepts previously published material. Sample copy available; include $1.06 Canadian funds to cover postage (nonresidents include 2 IRCs).
Illustrations: Buys 6-8 illustrations/issue from freelancers. Receives 3-4 submissions/week from freelancers. "Illustrations are geared to editorial copy and run from cartoon sketches to *Esquire*, *New Yorker* and *Psychology Today* styles. Subjects range from fast-food franchising to how civil servants cope with stress. Art usually produced by local artists because of time and communication problems." Open to most styles including b&w line drawings, b&w and color washes, collages, photocopy art, oil and acrylic paintings, airbrush work and paper sculpture for inside. Also uses photographic treatments. Send query letter with resume and photocopies. "Do not send original artwork." No samples returned. Reports in 1 month. To show a portfolio, mail appropriate materials, which should include tear sheets and Photostats. Buys first-time rights, or by arrangement with artist. Pays $35-150 for inside b&w; and $75-250 for inside color; on publication.
Tips: Prefers "work that shows wit, confidence in style and a unique approach to the medium used. Especially in need of artists who can look at a subject from a fresh, unusual perspective. There is a trend toward more exciting illustration, use of unusual techniques like photocopy collages or collages combining photography, pen & ink and watercolor. Freedom given to the artist to develop his treatment. Open to unusual techniques. Have as diversified a portfolio as possible. Remember that our average reader is an upper-middle-class woman, aged 40-50, married, with children."

OUTDOOR AMERICA MAGAZINE, Suite 1100, 1701 N. Ft. Meyer Dr., Arlington VA 22209. Editor: Carol Dana. Emphasizes conservation and outdoor recreation (fishing, hunting, etc.) for sportsmen and conservationists. Quarterly. Circ. 45,000. Accepts previously published material. Original artwork returned after publication. Sample copy $1.50.
Illustrations: Buys 2-3 illustrations/issue from freelancers. Send query letter with samples to be kept on file. Prefers tear sheets or photocopies as samples. Samples not filed are returned. Reports within 2 months. Buys one-time rights or reprint rights. Pays on publication.

***OUTDOOR CANADA MAGAZINE**, 801 York Mills Rd., Don Mills, Ontario M3B 1X7 Canada. Editor: Teddi Brown. Emphasizes wildlife and active people enjoying the Canadian outdoors. Stories for anglers, hikers, canoeists, campers, hunters, conservationists and the adventurous. Readers are 81% male. Publishes 7 regular issues a year and a fishing special in April. Circ. 150,000.
Illustrations: Buys approximately 10 drawings/issue. Buys all rights. Pays up to $400.

OUTDOOR LIFE, 380 Madison Ave., New York NY 10017. (212)687-3000. Art Director: Jim Eckes. Emphasizes hunting, fishing, boating and camping for "male and female, young and old who enjoy the outdoors and what it has to offer." Monthly. Circ. 1.5 million. Original artwork returned after publication "unless we buy all rights." Sample copy available "if work is going to be published."
Cartoons: Very seldom uses cartoons. Send finished cartoons to be kept on file, except for "those we won't ever use." Material not kept on file is returned by SASE. Reports only if interested. Buys first rights. Pays on publication.
Illustrations: Uses 1-2 illustrations/issue. Prefers "realistic themes, realistic humor." Works on assignment only. Send query letter with samples and tear sheets to be kept on file except "those which do not meet our standards." Prefers slides, tear sheets and originals as samples. Samples not kept on file are returned. Reports only if interested. Call for appointment to show portfolio. Negotiates rights purchased. Pays $800, color spread, $1,000, cover; on publication. Payment "depends on size and whether it is a national or regional piece."
Tips: "First of all, we're looking for 'wildlife, realists'—those who know how to illustrate a species realistically and with action."

OUTDOOR SPORTS & RECREATION, Box 65798, St. Paul MN 55165. (612)221-0596. Editor-in-Chief: John Hall. Magazine emphasizing hunting, fishing and outdoor recreation for fishermen and hunters in the upper Midwest (emphasis in Minnesota and Wisconsin). Bimonthly. Circ. 30,000. Original artwork returned after publication. Sample copy free for SASE with 56¢ postage.
Cartoons: Buys 1 cartoon/issue from freelancers. Prefers fishing/hunting humor themes. Prefers single panel with gagline; b&w line drawings. Send query letter with samples of style or roughs to be kept on file. Material not kept on file is returned by SASE. Reports back within 2 weeks. Buys one-time rights. Pays $10, b&w.

OUTSIDE, 1165 N. Clark St., Chicago IL 60610. (312)951-0990. Managing Editor: John Rasmus. Design Director: John Askwith. Concerns enjoyment and participation in the great outdoors. Published 12 times/year. Circ. 250,000+.
Illustrations: Uses 60 illustrations/year; buys 60/year from freelancers. Works on assignment only. Receives 3-4 submissions/week from freelancers. Ask for artists' guidelines. Especially needs spot (less than 1/2 page) 4-color art; "contemporary, communicative, powerful illustration. We are also interested in seeing any contemporary stills for assignment purposes." Send "good slides" or previously published work as samples. SASE. Reports in 2 weeks. Send samples or tear sheet to be kept on file for future assignments. Buys one-time rights. Pays $100-750, b&w line drawings, washes and full-color renderings, inside; on publication.
Tips: "Observe the 'front runners' for style and trends. We presently don't use cartoons."

OVERSEAS!, Kolpingstr 1, 6906 Leimen, West Germany. Editorial Director: Charles L. Kaufman. Managing Editor: Greg Ballinger. "*Overseas!* is the leading lifestyle magazine for the U.S. military male stationed throughout Europe. Primary focus is on European travel, with regular features on music, sports, video, audio and photo products, and men's fashion. The average reader is male, age 24." Sample copy for SAE and 4 IRCs; art guidelines for SAE and 1 IRC.
Cartoons: Buys 3-5 cartoons/issue. Prefers single and multiple panel cartoons. "Always looking for humorous cartoons on travel and being a tourist in Europe. Best bet is to send in a selection of 5-10 for placement of all on one-two pages. Looking for more *National Lampoon* or *Playboy*-style cartoons/humor than a *Saturday Evening Post*-type cartoon. Anything new, different or crazy is given high priority. On cartoons or cartoon features don't query, send nonreturnable photocopies. Pay is negotiable, $25-75/ cartoon to start."
Illustrations: Uses 3-5 illustrations/month. Send query letter with nonreturnable photocopies. "We will assign when needed." To show a portfolio, mail appropriate materials or call or write to schedule an appointment. Pays $75-200, negotiable.
Tips: "Not enough cartoonists send samples of work for consideration."

PACIFIC COAST JOURNAL, Box 254822, Sacramento CA 95865. Editor-in-Chief: Jill Scopinich. For horse breeders, trainers and owners interested in performance, racing and showing of quarter horses. Monthly. Circ. 7,800. Previously published and simultaneous submissions OK "if we are notified."
Cartoons: Buys 24 cartoons/year on horses; single panel. Send query letter with samples. SASE. Reports in 4 weeks. Buys first, reprint, all or simultaneous rights. Pays $7.50-20, washes; on acceptance.

PAINT HORSE JOURNAL, Box 18519, Fort Worth TX 76118. (817)439-3400. Editor: Bill Shepard. Art Director: Vicki Day. Official publication of breed registry for Paint horses. For people who raise, breed and show Paint horses. Monthly. Circ. 11,200. Receives 4-5 cartoons and 2-3 illustrations/week from freelance artists. Original artwork returned after publication if requested. Sample copy $2; artist's

guidelines free for SASE.
Cartoons: Buys 1 or 2 cartoons/issue, all from freelancers. Interested in *Paint* horses; single panel with gagline. Material returned by SASE only if requested. Reports in 1 month. Buys first rights. Pays $10, b&w line drawings; on acceptance.
Illustrations: Uses 1-3 illustrations/issue; buys few/issue from freelancers. Receives few submissions/week from freelancers. Send business card and samples to be kept on file. Prefers snapshots of original art or Photostats as samples. Samples returned by SASE if not kept on file. Reports within 1 month. Send query letter with brochure showing art style or photocopies and finished art. Buys first rights. Pays $5-25, b&w, inside; $50 color, cover; on publication.
Tips: "We use a lot of different styles of art, but no matter what style you use-you *must* include Paint horses with acceptable (to the APHA) conformation. As horses are becoming more streamlined-as in race-bred Paints, the older style of horse seem so out dated. We get a lot of art from older artists who still draw the Paint as stocky and squatty—which they are not."

***PALM BEACH LIFE**, 265 Royal Poinciana Way, Palm Beach FL 33480. (305)837-4762. Design Director: Anne Wholf. Emphasizes culture, cuisine, travel, fashion, decorating and Palm Beach County lifestyle. Readers are affluent, educated. Monthly. Circ. 32,000. Sample copy $3.50; art guidelines for SASE.
Illustrations: Uses 3-4 illustrations/issue; all from freelancers. Only assigned work. Uses line drawings to illustrate regular columns as well as features. Format: color washes for inside and cover; b&w washes and line drawings for inside. "Any technique that can be reproduced is acceptable." Send samples or photocopies and/or arrange appointment to show portfolio. No original artwork returned. SASE. Reports in 4-6 weeks. Buys all rights on a work-for-hire basis. Pays $300-500 on acceptance for color cover; $100-350 for inside color; $30-200 for inside b&w. Top price on covers only paid to established artists; "the exception is that we are looking for super-dramatic covers." Subjects related to Florida and lifestyle of the affluent. Price negotiable. Send slides or prints; do not send original work. *Palm Beach Life* cannot be responsible for unsolicited material.
Tips: "Look at magazines to see what we are like—make an appointment."

PANDORA, %Empire Books, Box 625, Murray KY 42071-0625. Editor: Jean Lorrah. Emphasizes science fiction and fantasy. Semiannually. Circ. 700. Accepts previously published material. Original artwork returned after publication but prefers Photostat. Sample copy $3.50.
Cartoons: Buys 1-2 cartoons/year from freelancers. Considers science fiction themes. Prefers single panel; b&w line drawings. Send query letter with roughs to be kept on file. Material not filed is returned by SASE. Reports within 6 weeks. Buys first North American serial rights. Pays $5, b&w; on acceptance.
Illustrations: Buys 5-7 illustrations/issue from freelancers. Style should suit story. Works on assignment only. Send query letter with tear sheets or photocopies to be kept on file. Samples not filed are returned by SASE. Reports in 6 weeks. Buys first North American serial rights. Pays $10, b&w, cover and inside; on acceptance. "We pay $15 for a Photostat, to avoid the hassles of handling originals."
Tips: "We have very little need for portraits; please send samples that indicate ability to portray action. If an artist sends us a slick, expensively-produced portfolio, a small-press shoestring-operated magazine like ours tends to think we can't afford to pay that artist's rates. If an artist sends us color work, we know he has neither read our listing nor seen a copy of the magazine."

PARADE MAGAZINE, 750 Third Ave., New York NY 10017. (212)573-7187. Director of Design: Ira Yoffe. Photo Editor: Brent Petersen. Emphasizes general interest subjects. Weekly. Circ. 31 million (readership is 60 million). Original artwork returned after publication. Sample copy and art guidelines available.
Illustrations: Uses varied number of illustrations/issue. Prefers various themes. Works on assignment only. Send query letter with brochure, resume, business card and tear sheets to be kept on file. Call or write for appointment to show portfolio. Reports only if interested. Buys first rights, and occasionally all rights.
Tips: "Provide a good balance of work."

PARAPLEGIA NEWS, Suite 111, 5201 N. 19th Ave., Phoenix AZ 85015. Art Director: Carol Beiriger. Magazine emphasizing wheelchair living for wheelchair users, rehabilitation specialists. Monthly. Circ. 24,000. Accepts previously published material. Original artwork not returned after publication. Sample copy free for SASE with 96¢ postage; art guidelies free for SASE with first-class postage.
Cartoons: Buys 1 cartoon/issue from freelancers. Prefers line art with wheelchair theme. Prefers single panel with gagline; b&w line drawings. Send query letter with samples of style or finished cartoons to be kept on file. Write for appointment to show portfolio. Material not kept on file is returned by SASE. Reports only if interested. Buys all rights. Pays $10, b&w.

Illustrations: Buys 1 illustration/issue from freelancers. Prefers wheelchair living or medical and financial topics as themes. Send query letter with brochure showing art style or tear sheets, Photostats, photocopies and photographs. Samples not filed are returned by SASE. Reports only if interested. To show a portfolio, include final reproduction/product, color, tear sheets, Photostats, photographs and b&w. Negotiates rights purchased. Pays on acceptance.

***PARENTGUIDE MAGAZINE**, Suite 2012, 2 Park Ave., New York NY 10016. (212)213-8840. Art Director: Bobbi Rosenthal. "We reach parents of children from birth through their elementary school years. We are an upbeat magazine for sophisticated parents." Features general interest, how-to and personal experience. Monthly. Circ. 1,250,000. Accepts previously published material. Original artwork returned after publication. Sample copy $1.50.
Cartoons: Buys 2-3 cartoons/issue from freelancers. Themes and styles vary. Prefers b&w line drawings without gagline. Send query letter. Samples are filed. Samples not filed are returned by SASE. Reports back only if interested. Buys first and one-time rights.
Illustrations: Buys 2-3 illustrations/issue from freelancers. Works on assignment only. Themes and styles vary. Send query letter with resume, tear sheets and photocopies. Samples are filed. Samples not filed are returned by SASE. Reports back only if interested. Write to schedule an appointment to show a portfolio, which should include roughs, color, tear sheets, Photostats or b&w. Buys first and one-time rights.

PARENT'S CHOICE, Box 185, Waban MA 02168. (617)332-1298. Editor: Diana Huss Green. Reviews children's media. Designed to alert parents to the best books, TV, records, movies, music, toys, computer software, rock-n-roll, home video cassettes. Quarterly. Original artwork returned after publication. Sample copy $2.50.
Illustrations: Uses 4 illustrations/issue, 2 from freelancers. Uses "work of exceptional quality." Format: b&w line drawings for inside and cover; no pencil. Works on assignment only. Send samples or arrange appointment to show portfolio. Samples returned. Prefers to see portfolio. SASE. Reports in 4-6 weeks. Pays on publication.

PARTNERSHIP, 465 Gundersen Dr., Carol Stream IL 60188. (312)260-6200. Art Director: Joan Nickerson. Estab. 1984. Emphasizes ministry wives. Bimonthly. Circ. 45,000. Accepts previously published material. Original artwork returned after publication only if requested. Sample copy free for SASE.
Cartoons: Buys 5 cartoons/issue from freelancers. Prefers inside humor having to do with the parish ministry. Prefers single panel with gagline; b&w line drawings. Send finished cartoons; call for appointment to show portfolio. All cartoons are returned. SASE. Reports within 2 weeks. Buys first rights. Pays on acceptance.
Illustrations: Buys 5-6 illustrations/issue from freelancers. Works on assignment only. Send query letter; write for appointment to show portfolio. Accepts Photostats, tear sheets, photocopies, slides, photographs, etc. as samples. Samples not filed are returned. Reports within 1 week. Negotiates rights purchased. Pays on acceptance.

PARTS PUPS, 2999 Circle 75 Parkway, Atlanta GA 30339. Editor: Don Kite. For automotive repairmen. Circ. 279,000. Monthly plus annual publication. Original artwork not returned after publication. Previously published material and simultaneous submissions OK. Free sample copy and artist's guidelines.
Cartoons: Buys 144/year on "girlie" themes, auto repairmen, general interest; single panel with gagline, b&w line drawings and washes. Receives 400 cartoons/week from freelance artists. Send finished artwork with SASE. Reports in 6 weeks. Pays $30, b&w line drawings and washes; on acceptance.
Tips: "Look over our publication before submitting material."

PASTORAL LIFE, The Magazine for Today's Ministry, Rt. 224, Canfield OH 44406. (216)533-5503. Editor: Rev. Jeffrey Mickler. Emphasizes religion and anything involving pastoral ministers and ministry for Roman Catholic priests (70%); the remainder are sisters, brothers, laity and ministers of other denominations. Monthly. Circ. 7,000. Original artwork returned after publication. Sample copy

"Artwork seems to have more of a bright, fun side. A bit of humor is good."

—Mario Chavez, Metropolitan Water District of Southern California

available.
Illustrations: Prefers religious, pastoral themes. Works on assignment only. Send query letter with photographs. Call or write for appointment to show portfolio, which should include b&w or photographs. Samples not kept on file are returned by SASE only if requested. Reports within 3 weeks. Buys first rights. Payment varies; on publication.

PEDIATRIC ANNALS, 6900 Grove Rd., Thorofare NJ 08086. (609)848-1000. Managing Editor: Sandra L. Patterson. Emphasizes pediatrics for practicing pediatricians. Monthly. Circ. 33,000. Original artwork returned after publication. Sample copy and art guidelines available.
Illustrations: Buys 4-5 illustrations/issue from freelancers. Send query letter with tear sheets, slides and photographs to be kept on file except for those specifically requested back. Reports within 2 months. Buys one-time rights or reprint rights. Pays $150, b&w and $250-450, color, cover; $25-30, b&w and $50-100, color, inside; on publication.
Tips: "*Pediatric Annals* continues to require that illustrators be able to treat medical subjects with a high degree of accuracy. We need people who are experienced in medical illustration, who can develop ideas from manuscripts on a variety of topics, and who can work independently (with some direction) and meet deadlines. We anticipate that our needs for illustration will continue to increase. We deal with medical topics specifically related to children."

PENNSYLVANIA ANGLER, Box 1673, Harrisburg PA 17105-1673. (717)657-4520. Editor: Art Michaels. Emphasizes fishing in Pennsylvania, published by the Pennsylvania Fish Commission. Monthly. Circ. 60,000. Sample copy and art guidelines for 9x12 SASE with 73¢ postage.
Illustrations: Uses 12 illustrations/issue; buys 2/issue from freelancers. Send query letter with samples and tear sheets to be kept on file. Accepts photocopies as samples. Samples not kept on file are returned by SASE. Reports back. Rights purchased vary. Pays $50-300, color, cover; $5-25, b&w, and $25-100, color, inside; on acceptance.

PENNSYLVANIA MAGAZINE, Box 576, Camp Hill PA 17011. (717)761-6620. Editor-in-Chief: Albert Holliday. For college-educated readers, ages 35-60+, interested in self-improvement, history, travel and personalities. Bimonthly. Cir. 24,000. Query with samples. SASE. Reports in 3 weeks. Previously published, photocopied and simultaneous submissions OK. Buys first serial rights. Pays on publication or on acceptance for assigned articles/art. Sample copy $2.50.
Illustrations: Buys 50-75 illustrations/year on history and travel-related themes. Minimum payment for cover, $100, inside color, $25-50; inside b&w, $5-50.

PENNWELL PUBLISHING CO., 1421 S. Sheridan, Tulsa OK 74112. (918)835-3161. Art Director: Mike Reeder. Emphasizes dental economics for practicing dentists; 24-65 years of age. Monthly. Circ. 100,000. Sample copy for SASE; art guidelines available.
Cartoons: Uses about 1 cartoon/2 issues. Prefers dental-related themes. Prefers single panel, with or without gagline; b&w line drawings. Send up to 12 cartoons in a batch. Material is returned by SASE only. Reports if interested. Pays on acceptance.

***PERINATOLOGY-NEONATOLOGY**, Brentwood Publishing Corp., 1640 5th St., Santa Monica CA 90401. Publisher: Martin Waldman. Art Director: Tom Medsger. Emphasizes technological, medical and professional news.
Illustrations: Submit brochure/flyer to be kept on file for possible future assignments. Reports only when assignment available. Buys all rights. Pays $60 and up, spot art; $400, full-color cover; on acceptance.

PERSONNEL JOURNAL, Suite B2, 245 Fischer, Costa Mesa CA 92626. (714)751-1883. Art Director: Susan Overstreet. Emphasizes the hiring, firing, training, recruiting of employees. Directed to directors or managers of corporate personnel departments in organizations with 500 or more employees. Monthly. Circ. 20,000. Original artwork returned after publication. Sample copy and art guidelines free for SASE.
Cartoons: Buys 1 cartoon/issue; buys 1/issue from freelancer. Prefers theme of the world of work, jobs, careers. "Please, no sexist or racist cartoons." Prefers single panel with gagline; b&w line drawings or b&w washes. Send query letter with samples of style to be kept on file. Reports within 3 weeks. Buys one-time rights. Pays $50, b&w; on acceptance.
Illustrations: Buys 3 illustrations/issue; buys all from freelancers. Prefers professional themes such as the workplace, office equipment, professionals (line drawings). Works on assignment; will also accept previously published material. Send query letter with resume, business card and Photostats to be kept on file. Call or write for appointment to show portfolio. Samples not kept on file are returned only if requested. Reports only if interested. Negotiates rights purchased. Pays $150-200, b&w, inside; on acceptance.

PET BUSINESS, 5400 N.W. 84th Ave., Miami FL 33166. Editor: Linda Mills. A monthly news magazine for the pet industry (retailers, distributors, manufacturers, breeders, groomers). Circ. 15,500. Sample copy $3.
Cartoons: Pet-related themes; single panel. SASE. Pays $10; on publication.
Illustrations: Anatomically correct line drawings of pet animals. Pays $10; on publication.

PETERSENS HUNTING MAGAZINE, Petersen Publishing Co., 8490 Sunset Blvd., Los Angeles CA 90069. (213)854-2222. Editor: Craig Boddington. Art Director: C. A. Yeseta. Emphasizes sport hunting for hunting enthusiasts. Monthly. Circ. 300,000. Sometimes returns originals after publication. Sample copy $2. Occasionally uses production paste-up artists on an hourly wage.
Cartoons: Uses 1-2 cartoons/year from freelancers on hunting scenes and wildlife. Prefers to see finished cartoons. Reports in 1 week. Pays on publication.
Illustrations: Buys 8-10 illustrations/year on "very realistic wildlife themes and action hunting scenes"; some "how-to" drawings. Works on assignment only. Prefers to see finished art, roughs, portfolio, samples of style or previously published work. Arrange interview to show portfolio. Samples returned by SASE. Provide resume, business card, letter of inquiry; also brochure or flyer containing examples of work to be kept on file for future assignments. Reports in 4 weeks. Buys various rights. Inside: Pays $75-150, b&w line drawings; on publication.

PGA MAGAZINE, 100 Avenue of the Champions, Palm Beach Gardens FL 33418. (305)626-3600. Editor/Advertising Sales Director: William A. Burbaum. Circulates to 28,000 golf club professionals and amateur golfers nationwide.
Needs: Works with 2 artists/year for magazine illustrations for *PGA Magazine*. Artists "should know something about golf and golf tournaments." Interested in title page art and golf tip illustrations for magazine that circulates to 14,500 professionals and 22,500 amateur golfers nationwide. Works on assignment most of the time.
First Contact & Terms: Write with tear sheets to be kept on file. Samples returned by SASE. Reports in 2 weeks. Reports back on future assignment possibilities. Negotiates pay by prior agreement.
Tips: "Read our magazine and read and check the artwork in golf's two major national publications: *Golf Magazine* and *Golf Digest*."

PHI DELTA KAPPAN, Box 789, Bloomington IN 47402. Editor-in-Chief: Robert W. Cole, Jr. Design Director: Kristin Herzog. Emphasizes issues, policy, research findings and opinions in the field of education. For members of the educational organization Phi Delta Kappa and subscribers. Published 10 times/year. Circ. 145,000. SASE. Reports in 2 weeks. "We return cartoons after publication." Sample copy $2.50—"the journal is available in most public and college libraries."
Illustrations: Uses 2-5 b&w illustrations/issue, all from freelancers, who have been given assignments from upcoming articles. "Quality of drawing and good concepts most important aspect-i.e., the kind of line, the graphic use of the space. Next is ability to depict appropriate image from editorial content and come up with an interesting concept. Most illustrations depict teachers or principals, theories of learning, testing principles, studies of excellence, international comparisons of education." Samples returned by SASE. To show a portfolio, mail a few slides or photocopies with SASE. Buys one-time rights. Payment varies.
Tips: "You need to take a lot of responsibility for marketing your work. I'd suggest going to the library and reading a couple of books on selling and salesmanship. It doesn't matter if the books are talking about selling cars or homes or soap—the skills are the same. Then please look at our magazine before you mail things. If your work doesn't look like what we are buying you probably should send it to another place."

PHILADELPHIA MAGAZINE, 1500 Walnut St., Philadelphia PA 19102. Contact: Art Director. For a professional, upper-middle-income audience. Monthly. Circ. 142,000. Simultaneous submissions OK. Original artwork returned after publication.
Cartoons: Buys 0-1 cartoons/issue.
Illustrations: Uses 10-16 illustrations/issue; buys all from freelancers. Interested in a variety of themes and styles. Works on assignment only. Send query letter with resume and tear sheets, photostats, photocopies, slides and photographs to be kept on file. Samples not returned. Buys one-time rights. To show a portfolio, mail appropriate materials, which should include original/final art, final reproduction/product, color, tear sheets and b&w. Pays $75-375 b&w; $100-500 color, inside; on acceptance.
Tips: "Variety is the key word. Accurate and intelligent interpretation of the editorial message is essential. Look at several issues of the magazine in the library. Understand the level of work expected."

PHOENIX HOME/GARDEN, 3136 N. 3rd Ave., Phoenix AZ 85013. (602)234-0840. Editor: Manya Winsted. Managing Editor: Nora Burba. Emphasizes homes, entertainment and gardens for Phoenix area residents interested in better living. Monthly. Circ. 33,000. Original artwork not returned after pub-

© Claudia Tantillo

Kirsten Herzog of* Phi Delta Kappan Magazine *of Bloomington, Indiana, regularly works with illustrator Claudia Tantillo of New York City because "she has been easy to work with and has always made deadlines. She is willing to make changes when needed. I especially like the fact that she thinks about articles I give her and doesn't just do the first and easiest solution that comes to mind." Tantillo used scratchboard to illustrate a special section on the Gallup Poll. Tantillo said she wanted to create "an atmosphere of determination, evaluation and inquiry with an overall positive, steadfast spirit." Herzog bought one-time rights for $250.

lication. Sample copy $2.50.

Illustrations: Uses 6-12 illustrations/year; buys 1-5 from freelancers. Interested in botanical illustrations and spot art relevant to topics. Also uses illustrations for promotional material in conjunction with the magazine. Works on assignment only. Send samples of style. Reports in 6 weeks. Provide tear sheets to be kept on file for possible future assignments. Buys all rights on assignments. Pays $30-50 average inside, b&w line drawings. Pays on publication.

PHYSICIAN'S MANAGEMENT, 7500 Old Oak Blvd., Cleveland OH 44130. (216)243-8100, ext. 808. Editor: Robert A. Feigenbaum. Art Director: David Komitau. Published 12 times/year. Circ. 110,000. Emphasizes business, practice management and legal aspects of medical practice for primary care physicians.

Cartoons: Receives 50-70/week from freelancers. Buys 10 cartoons/issue. Themes typically apply to medical and financial situations "although we do publish general humor cartoons." Prefers single and double panel; b&w line drawings with gagline. Uses "only clean-cut line drawings." Send query letter with brochure showing art style or resume and tear sheets, photostats, photocopies, slides and photographs. SASE. Reports in 2 weeks. Call or write to schedule an appointment to show a portfolio, which should include final reproduction/product and photographs. Buys one-time rights. Pays $80 for b&w; on acceptance. No previously published material and/or simultaneous submissions.
Illustrations: Buys 5 illustrations/issue. Accepts b&w and color illustrations. All work done on assignment. Send a query letter to editor or art director first or send examples of work. Fees negotiable. Buys first rights. No previously published and/or simultaneous submissions.
Tips: "First, become familiar with our publication, second, query the art director. Cartoons should be geared toward the physician—not the patient. No cartoons about drug companies or medicine men. No sexist cartoons. Illustrations should be appropriate for a serious business publication. We do not use cartoonish or comic book styles to illustrate our articles. We work with artists nationwide."

PIG IRON, Box 237, Youngstown OH 44501. (216)783-1269. Editors-in-Chief: Jim Villani and Rose Sayre. Emphasizes literature/art for writers, artists and intelligent lay audience with emphasis in popular culture. Annually. Circ. 1,000. Previously published and photocopied work OK. Original artwork returned after publication. Sample copy $2.50.
Cartoons: Uses 1-15 cartoons/issue, all from freelancers. Receives 1-3 submissions/week from freelancers. Interested in "the arts, political, science fiction, fantasy, alternative lifestyles, psychology, humor"; single and multi panel. Especially needs fine art cartoons. Prefers finished cartoons. SASE. Reports in 1 month. Buys first North American serial rights. Pays $2 minimum, b&w halftones and washes; on acceptance.
Illustrations: Uses 15-30 illustrations/issue, all from freelancers. Receives 1-3 submissions/week from freelancers. Interested in "any media: pen & ink washes, lithographs, silk screen, charcoal, collage, line drawings; any subject matter." B&w only. Prefers finished art or velox. Reports in 2 months. Buys first North American serial rights. Minimum payment: Cover: $4, b&w. Inside: $2; on publication.
Tips: "*Pig Iron* is a publishing opportunity for the fine artist; we publish art in its own right, not as filler or story accompaniment. The artist who is executing black-and-white work for exhibit and gallery presentations can find a publishing outlet with *Pig Iron* that will considerably increase that artist's visibility and reputation." Current theme: Third World.

PITTSBURGH MAGAZINE, 4802 5th Ave., Pittsburgh PA 15213. (412)622-1360. Art Director: Michael Maskarinec. Emphasizes culture, feature stories and material with heavy Pittsburgh city emphasis; public broadcasting television and radio schedule. Monthly. Circ. 58,000. Sample copy $2.
Illustrations: Uses 5-10 illustrations/issue; all from freelancers; inside b&w and 4-color illustrations. Works on assignment only. Prefers to see roughs. SASE. Buys one-time rights on a work-for-hire basis. Pays on publication.

***PLAN AND PRINT**, International Reprographic Association, 9931 Franklin Ave., Box 879, Franklin Park IL 60131. Editor: Janet Thill. For commercial reproduction company owners, managers and dealers in architects', engineers' and draftsmen's supplies and equipment, in-plant reproduction department supervisors, in-plant design and drafting specialists, computer-aided design users and architects. Monthly. Circ. 29,000. Originals not returned after publication. Free sample copy and artist's guidelines.
Illustrations: Buys 1 spot illustration/issue. Especially needs spots related to the industry. Interested in reprographics and design/drafting. Works on assignment only. Send samples of style. SASE. Keeps files of information on artists for future assignment possibilities. Reports in 1 week. Buys all rights on a work-for-hire basis. Pays $7.50-10, b&w spots. Payment for article illustrations and 4-color cover art varies from $50-450.
Tips: "Heavy use of computer-aided design."

PLANNING, American Planning Association, 1313 E. 60th St., Chicago IL 60637. (312)955-9100. Editor-in-Chief: Sylvia Lewis. Art Director: Richard Sessions. For urban and regional planners interested in land use, housing, transportation and the environment. Monthly. Circ. 25,000. Previously published work OK. Original artwork returned after publication, upon request. Free sample copy and artist's guidelines.
Cartoons: Buys 2 cartoons/year on the environment, city/regional planning, energy, garbage, transportation, housing, power plants, agriculture and land use. Prefers single, double and multi panel with gaglines ("provide outside of cartoon body if possible"). SASE. Reports in 2 weeks. Buys all rights. Pays $25 minimum, b&w line drawings; on publication.

Illustrations: Buys 20 illustrations/year on the environment, city/regional planning, energy, garbage, transportation, housing, power plants, agriculture and land use. Prefers to see roughs and samples of style. SASE. Reports in 2 weeks. Buys all rights. Pays $200 maximum, b&w drawings, cover. Pays $25 minimum, b&w line drawings inside; on publication.

PLAYBILL, Suite 320, 71 Vanderbilt Ave., New York NY 10169. (212)557-5757. Editor-in-Chief: Joan Alleman. Concerns theater in New York City. Monthly. Circ. 1,040,000.
Cartoons: Buys b&w line drawings on New York City theater. SASE. Reports in 4 weeks. Buys all rights. Pays on acceptance.
Illustrations: Assigns work on New York City theater. SASE. Reports in 4 weeks. Buys all rights. Pays on acceptance.

PLAYBOY, 919 Michigan Ave., Chicago IL 60611. Executive Art Director: Tom Staebler. Emphasizes celebrities, beautiful women, dining, humor and fiction. For the sophisticated, urban male. All work generally done on assignment. Reports in 3-4 weeks.
Cartoons: Submit roughs with one finished drawing to Michelle Urry, cartoon editor. Buys 30/month on satirical, sophisticated and other situtations. Prefers cartoons that deal with sex and are slanted toward young, urban male market. "Style and technique very important." Pays $350, b&w; $600, full-page color.
Illustrations: Submit samples to Kerig Pope, managing art director. Pays $1,200/page or $2,000/spread; $200-250, spot drawings.

PLAYGIRL, 801 Second Ave., New York NY 10017. Art Director: Ken Palumbo. Emphasizes entertainment, fiction, reviews, beauty, fashion, cooking and travel for women ages 18-40. Monthly. Circ. 850,000.
Cartoons: Uses 6-18 cartoons/issue; all by freelancers. Receives 200+ cartoons from freelancers/month. Cartoons should be "slanted towards women's problems, intellectual humor, and topical issues." Format: Single panel b&w washes with gagline. Especially needs 6-inch square, b&w cartoons dealing with women's issues, experiences. Prefers finished cartoons or excellent photocopies. SASE. Reports in 2 months. Pays on publication; $75 for b&w. Buys first North American serial rights. Call for appointment to show a portfolio.
Illustrations: Works on assignment only. Uses 4-12 illustrations/issue; all by freelancers. Artists are selected from "walk-ins" doing editorial artwork to illustrate fiction. Format: b&w line drawings and color washes for inside. Especially needs vertical color and b&w. Arrange personal appointment to show portfolio and/or send samples of style and tear sheets. SASE. Reports only if interested. Pays on publication. Buys all rights.
Tips: "There is a trend toward humor with a subliminal sexuality slant. Women are being depicted in a more liberal light, particularly regarding male nudity and in other sexual contexts. We want as strong and contemporary a visual style as possible."

POCKETS, Box 189, 1908 Grand Ave., Nashville TN 37202. (615)327-2700, ext. 455. Associate Editor: Janet Bugg. Devotional magazine for children 6 to 12. Monthly magazine except January/February. Circ. 68,000. Accepts previously published material. Original artwork returned after publication. Sample copy for SASE with 73¢ postage.
Illustrations: Uses variety of styles; 4-color, 2-color, flapped art appropriate for children. Realistic fable and cartoon styles. We will accept tear sheets, photostats and slides. Samples not filed are returned by SASE. Reports only if interested. Buys one-time or reprint rights. Pays $50-500 depending on size. Pays on acceptance. Decisions made in consultation with out-of-house designer.

PODIATRY MANAGEMENT MAGAZINE, 401 N. Broad St., Philadelphia PA 19108. (215)925-9744. President: Scott Borowsky. Emphasizes practice management for podiatrists, faculty and students. Published 8 times/year. Circ. 11,000. Original artwork returned after publication. Also uses paste-up artists; pays $7-8/hour.
Illustrations: Buys 2-3 b&w illustrations/issue from freelancers. Themes tie in with stories. Works on assignment only. Send query letter with resume to be kept on file; write for appointment to show portfolio. Prefers photostats and tear sheets as samples. Samples returned by SASE. Reports only if interested and if SASE is included. Buys all rights. Pays $100-175, b&w and $250, color, cover; $100, b&w, inside; on publication.

***POPULAR PHOTOGRAPHY**, 1 Park Ave., New York NY 10016. (212)503-3700. Art Director: Steven Powell. Magazine emphasizing photography with how-to and technical articles. Monthly. Circ. 800,000. Original artwork is returned after publication. Sample copy for SASE.
Illustrations: Buys 5 illustrations/issue from freelancers. Buys 60 illustrations/year from freelancers.

Works on assignment only. Prefers line drawings to illustrate photo techniques and equipment. Send brochure or tear sheets and photocopies. Samples are filed. Samples not filed are not returned. Reports back only if interested. Call to schedule an appointment to show a portfolio which should include original/final art, tear sheets, color and b&w. Buys one-time rights. Pays $75, b&w; $150, color, inside; on acceptance.
Tips: "Nearly all assigned work will pertain to photographic techniques or related equipment utilized."

POPULAR SCIENCE, Times Mirror Magazines, Inc., 380 Madison Ave., New York NY 10017. Art Director: David Houser. For the well-educated adult male, interested in science, technology, new products. Receives 3 illustrations/week from freelance artists. Original artwork returned after publication.
Illustrations: Uses 30-40 illustrations/issue; buys 30/issue from freelancers. Works on assignment only. Interested in technical 4-color art and 2-color line art dealing with automotive or architectural subjects. Especially needs science and technological pieces as assigned per layout. Samples returned by SASE. Reports back on future assignment possibilities. Provide tear sheet to be kept on file for future assignments. "After seeing portfolios, I photocopy or photostat those samples I feel are indicative of the art we might use." Reports whenever appropriate job is available. Buys first publishing rights.
Tips: "More and more scientific magazines have entered the field. This has provided a larger base of technical artists for us. Be sure your samples relate to our subject matter, i.e., no rose etchings, and be sure to include a tear sheet for our files."

POWER, McGraw-Hill, Inc., 11 W. 19th St., New York NY 10020. (212)337-4086. Art Director: Kiyo Komoda. Emphasizes the systems and equipment for the use and conservation of energy. For power generation and plant energy systems. Monthly plus 2 annuals. Original artwork returned after publication, on request only.
Illustrations: Uses 30 illustrations/issue on energy systems. Buys 30%/issue from freelancers; most are graphs, charts and mechanical line drawings. Especially needs "graphs, charts, diagrams with more imagination or creative dramatization of what they represent." Works on assignment only. Send query letter with brochure showing art style or tear sheets and Photostats. Samples returned by SASE. Reports in 1 week. Call to schedule an appointment to show a portfolio, which should include original/final art, final reproduction/product and tear sheets. Buys one-time and reprint rights. Cover: Pays $150-500, color. Inside: Pays $30-300, color; $10-200, b&w line drawings; on acceptance.
Tips: "We prefer artists with clean and crisp line works. They should know about color separation and the use of Zipatone. Young artists welcomed. Follow the specs—especially those arts with deadlines. I'll never recall any artist if he or she fails to meet specs or deadlines."

PRAYING, Box 410335, Kansas City MO 64141. (816)531-0538. Editor: Arthur N. Winter. Emphasizes spirituality for everyday living for lay Catholics and members of mainline Protestant churches; primarily Catholic, non-fundamentalist. "Starting point: The daily world of living, family, job, politics, is the stuff of religious experience and Christian living." Bimonthly. Circ. 15,000. Accepts previously published material. Original artwork not returned after publication. Sample copy and art guidelines available.
Cartoons: Buys 1-2 cartoons/issue from freelancers. Especially interested in cartoons that spoof fads and jargon in contemporary spirituality, prayer and religion. Prefers single panel with gagline; b&w line drawings. Send query letter with samples of style to be kept on file. Material not filed is returned by SASE. Reports within 2 weeks. Buys one-time rights. Pays $25, b&w; on acceptance.
Illustrations: Buys 2-3 illustrations/issue from freelancers. Prefers contemporary interpretations of traditional Christian symbols to be used as incidental art; also drawings to illustrate articles. Send query letter with samples to be kept on file. Prefers Photostats, tear sheets and photocopies as samples. Samples returned if not interested or return requested by SASE. Reports within 2 weeks. Buys one-time rights. Pays $25, b&w; on acceptance.

THE PRESBYTERIAN RECORD, 50 Wynford Dr., Don Mills, Ontario M3C 1J7 Canada. (416)441-1111. Production and Design: Mary Visser. Published 11 times/year. Deals with family-oriented religious themes. Circ. 73,759. Original artwork returned after publication. Simultaneous submissions and previously published work OK. Free sample copy and artists' guidelines.
Cartoons: Buys 1-2 cartoons/issue; buys from freelancers. Interested in some theme or connection to religion. Send roughs. SAE (nonresidents include IRC). Reports in 1 month. Pays on publication.
Illustrations: Buys 1 illustration/year on religion. "We use freelance material, and we are interested in excellent color artwork for cover." Any line style acceptable— should reproduce well on newsprint. Works on assignment only. Send query letter with brochure showing art style or tear sheets, photocopies and photographs. Samples returned by SAE (nonresidents include IRC). Reports in 1 month. To show a portfolio, mail appropriate materials; portfolio should include original/final art, color, tear sheets and b&w. Buys all rights on a work-for-hire basis. Pays $50, color washes and opaque watercolors, cover;

pays $20-30, b&w line drawings, inside; on publication.
Tips: "We don't want any 'cute' samples (in cartoons). Prefer some theological insight in cartoons; some comment on religious trends and practices."

PRESBYTERIAN SURVEY, 341 Ponce de Leon Ave. NE, Atlanta GA 30365. (404)873-1549. Art Director: Richard Brown. Emphasizes Presbyterian-related features and news, issues facing the church, Christian life. Monthly. Circ. 180,000. Sample copy for SASE.
Cartoons: Runs 1/issue on topics which speak to the issues of the day. Prefers finished cartoons. Reports in 6 weeks. Pays $20, b&w.
Illustrations: Buys 2/issue. Works on assignment only. Send query letter with brochure showing art style or tear sheets and photocopies. Samples not returned. Reports only if interested. To show a portfolio, mail final reproduction/product, tear sheets and Photostats. Negotiates rights purchased. Pays $250 b&w, cover; $250 b&w, inside; on acceptance.

PREVENTION, 33 E. Minor St., Emmaus PA 18049. (215)967-5171. Executive Art Director: Wendy Ronga. Emphasizes health, nutrition, fitness, cooking. Monthly. Circ. 3,500,000. Returns original artwork after publication. Sample copy available.
Cartoons: Buys 2-3 cartoons/issue from freelancers. Prefers themes of health, pets, fitness. Considers single panel with gagline; b&w line drawings, b&w washes. Samples of style are filed; unused roughs or finished cartoons are returned by SASE within 2 weeks. Reports back only if interested. Buys one-time rights.
Illustrations: Buys about 20 illustrations/issue from freelancers. Themes are assigned on editorial basis. Works on assignment only. Send samples to be kept on file. Prefers tear sheets or slides as samples. Samples not filed are returned by SASE. Reports back only if interested. Buys one-time rights. Pays $100-3,000.

PRIMAVERA, University of Chicago, 1212 E. 59th St., Chicago IL 60637. (312)324-5920. Contact: Editorial Board. Emphasizes art and literature by women for readers interested in contemporary literature and art. Annual. Circ. 800. Original artwork returned after publication. Sample copy $4; art guidelines available for SASE.
Illustrations: Buys 15-20 illustrations/issue from freelancers. Receives 5 illustrations/week from freelance artists. "We are open to a wide variety of styles and themes. Work must be in b&w with strong contrasts and should not exceed 7" high x 5" wide." Send finished art. Reports in 1-2 months. "If the artist lives in Chicago, she may call us for an appointment." Acquires first rights. "We pay in 2 free copies of the issue in which the artwork appears"; on publication.
Tips: "It's a good idea to take a look at a recent issue. Artists often do not investigate the publication and send work which may be totally inappropriate. We publish a wide variety of women artists. We have increased the number of graphics per issue. Send us a *variety* of prints. It is important that the graphics work well with the literature and the other graphics we've accepted. Our decisions are strongly influenced by personal taste and the work we know has already been accepted. Will consider appropriate cartoons and humorous illustrations."

***PRIME CUTS**, 4359 Cornell Rd., Agoura CA 91301. (818)706-7606. Editor: Gary Groth. Art Director: Dale Crain. An adult comic magazine devoted to "the work of the new breed of sophisticated comic artists. Any and all subjects considered (drama, humor, satire, etc.)." Stories consist of 1-10 b&w pages. Circ. 10,000. Sample copy $4.
Illustrations: Send query letter with samples. Buys one-time North American rights. "Creator retains copyright." Pays $30/page; on publication.

***PRINCETON PARENTS**, Princeton University, Stanhope Hall, Princeton NJ 08544. Senior Publications Editor: Laurel M. Cantor. Newsletter emphasizing Princeton University and subjects relevant to parents. Features general interest, historical, interview/profile, personal experience, technical and trav-

> ***"More and better editorial artists are on the scene now. Because of more publishing activity and because of long-distance communications, anyone can work with anyone else regardless of geographical location."***
>
> ***—Don Nelson, Notre Dame Magazine***
> ***Notre Dame, Indiana***

el articles. Quarterly. Circ. 14,000. Accepts previously published material. Original artwork returned after publication. Sample copy available.
Cartoons: Buys 2 cartoons/year from freelancers. Prefers very specifically about Princeton or students. Prefers multi panel with gagline; b&w line drawings. Send query letter with samples of style. Samples are filed. Samples not filed are returned. Reports back within 1 week. Buys one-time rights or negotiates rights purchased. Pays $50, b&w.
Illustrations: Buys 2 illustrations/year from freelancers. Prefers collegiate or something relevant to parents. Send query letter with brochure showing art style, resume, tear sheets and photocopies. Samples are filed. Samples not filed are returned. Reports back within 1 week. Call to schedule an appointment to show a portfolio or mail tear sheets, final reproduction/product, Photostats, photographs, slides, color and b&w. Buys one-time rights. Pays $200, color, cover; $25, b&w, inside; on publication.
Tips: "Must have samples, must schedule appointment if you desire one, could just send samples though."

PRIVATE PILOT/AERO/KITPLANES, Box 6050, Mission Viejo CA 92690. (714)240-6001. Contact: Editor. For owners/pilots of private aircraft, student pilots and others aspiring to attain additional ratings and experience. Circ. 80,000. Monthly. Receives 5 cartoons and 3 illustrations/week from freelance artists.
Cartoons: Buys 2-4 cartoons/issue on flying. Send finished artwork. SASE. Reports in 3 months. Pays $35, b&w; on publication.
Illustrations: Send query letter with samples. SASE. Reports in 3 months. Pays $50-100, b&w; $75-150, color. "We also use spot illustrations as column fillers; buys 1-2 spot illustrations/issue. Pays $25/spot."
Tips: "Know the field you wish to represent; we get tired of 'crash' gags submitted to flying publications."

PRIVATE PRACTICE, Suite 470, 3535 NW 58th St., Oklahoma City OK 73112. (405)943-2318. Art Director & Design Director: Rocky C. Hails. Editorial features "maintenance of freedom in all fields of medical practice and the effects of socioeconomic factors on the physician." Monthly. Circ. 180,000. Free sample copy and artists' guidelines.
Cartoons: Send query letter with resume and samples or arrange interview to show portfolio. SASE. Reports in 2-3 weeks. Negotiates pay; pays on acceptance.
Illustrations: Buys 1-4 illustrations/issue on politics, medicine and finance. Also uses artists for 4-color cover illustration. Uses some humorous illustrations and occasionally cartoon-style illustrations. Especially looks for "craftsmanship, combined with an ability to communicate complex concepts." Send a brochure showing art style or tear sheets, Photostats, slides and photographs. Call to schedule an appointment to show a portfolio, which should include original/final art, final reproduction/product, color, tear sheets, Photostats, photographs and b&w. Buys first and reprint rights. Pays $200-400, unlimited to media, all forms, cover; pays $60-110, color washes and opaque watercolors; $40-100, b&w line drawings and washes inside; on acceptance.
Tips: "Provide reproductions of several illustrations (that demonstrate the uniqueness of your style) to leave with the art director. Include a postcard requesting my response to the applicability of your work to *Private Practice*. This is efficient for both the art director and artist. It is encouraging to see the wide variety of 'accepted' styles and the design revisions going on in major journals. There is a rapid movement toward interactive production techniques freeing the designer for greater experimentation and creativity."

PROBE, Baptist Brotherhood Commission, 1548 Poplar, Memphis TN 38104. (901)272-2461. Art Director: Herschel Wells. Christian-oriented mission magazine for boys grades 7-12. Monthly. Original artwork returned after publication, if requested. Circ. 50,000. Previously published, photocopied and simultaneous submissions OK.
Illustrations: Uses 3 illustrations/issue; buys 1/issue from freelancers. Interested in family life with emphasis on boys and their interests. "Our freelance needs are usually directed toward a specific story; we frequently use humorous illustrations and sometimes use cartoon-style illustrations; we very seldom use art submitted on spec." Send brochure showing art style or resume and roughs to be kept on file. Reports in 3 weeks. Samples returned by SASE. Buys first North American serial rights. Cover: Pays $200-250, full-color; $100-180, b&w line drawings, washes and gray opaques. Inside: Pays $45-120, b&w line drawings, washes and gray opaques. Pays on acceptance.

PROCEEDINGS, U.S. Naval Institute, Annapolis MD 21402. (301)268-6110. Editor-in-Chief: Fred H. Rainbow. Emphasizes Navy, Marine Corps, Coast Guard, and related maritime and military topics for sea service professionals. Monthly. Circ. 100,000. Original artwork returned after publication. Sample copy and art guidelines available.

Cartoons: Buys a few cartoons/issue on various themes from freelancers. No rigid format guidelines. Prefers b&w line drawings. Send query letter with samples of style to be kept on file, except for rejections. Material not filed is returned only if requested. Reports within a few weeks. Negotiates rights purchased. Pays $25-50, b&w and color; on acceptance.
Illustrations: Buys approximately 5 illustrations/issue on varied themes from freelancers. Works on assignment only. Send query letter with tear sheets or photocopies. Samples returned only if requested. Reports within a few weeks. Negotiates rights purchased. Pays $200, color, cover; $25-50, b&w and color, inside; on acceptance.

PROFESSIONAL AGENT, 400 N. Washington St., Alexandria VA 22314. (703)836-9340. Editor: Eric R. Wassyng. For independent insurance agents and other affiliated members of the American Agency System. Monthly. Circ. 40,000. Original artwork returned after publication. Free sample copy.
Illustrations: Buys 3/issue from freelancers. Local artists preferred. Provide samples to be kept on file for future assignments. Pays by the project, $75-250. Buys first-time North America rights.
Tips: Conceptual approach often required. Trends are toward "more realism and fewer cartoons." Looks for "whether an artist's work is reproducible. Editorial experience is helpful."

PROFESSIONAL ELECTRONICS, 2708 W. Berry St., Ft. Worth TX 76109. (817)921-9062. Editor-in-Chief: Wallace S. Harrison. For professionals in electronics, especially owners, technicians and managers of consumer electronics sales and service firms. Bimonthly. Circ. 10,000. Samples of previously published cartoons furnished on request.
Cartoons: Buys themes on electronics sales/service, association management, conventions and directors' meetings. Prefers single panel with gagline. Submit art with SASE. Reports in 2 weeks. Buys first rights. Pays $10, b&w line drawings; on acceptance.
Illustrations: Buys assigned themes. Submit art and SASE. Reports in 2 weeks. Buys first rights. Pays $30-60, b&w line drawings, cover. Pays $10-15, b&w line drawings, inside; on acceptance.
Tips: "We need more diversity in subject matter. Most freelancers submit TV-only gags or computer-only. What might be funny to a consumer isn't necessarily funny to a professional (our market)."

PROFILES MAGAZINE, 533 Stevens Ave., Solana Beach CA 92075. (619)481-4352. Art Director: Rochelle Bradford. Magazine emphasizing computers. Monthly. Circ. 95,000. Original artwork returned after publication. Sample copy and art guidelines available.
Cartoons: Buys 4 cartoons/issue. Prefers multi panel, with or without gagline; b&w line drawings. Send finished cartoons to be kept on file. Write for appointment to show portfolio. Samples not filed are not returned. Does not report back. Buys first rights or one-time rights.
Illustrations: Buys 4 illustrations/issue from freelancers. Works on assignment only. Send tear sheets, Photostats, photocopies, slides and photographs. Samples not filed are not returned. Reports only if interested. To show a portfolio, mail original/final art, final reproduction/product, color, tear sheets, Photostats, photographs and b&w. Buys one-time rights. Payment varies.

PROFIT, Box 1132, Studio City CA 91604. (818)789-4980. Associate Editor: Marjorie Clapper. Magazine emphasizing business news for the business community. Circ. 10,000. Monthly. Original artwork not returned after publication. Sample copy $1.
Cartoons: Prefers single panel; b&w line drawings or b&w washes. Send query letter with samples of style to be kept on file if acceptable. Write for appointment to show portfolio. Samples not filed are returned by SASE. Reports only if interested. Buys all rights. Payment varies.
Illustrations: Buys 0-12 illustrations/issue from freelancers. Works on assignment only. Send query letter with brochure showing art style or resume and samples. Samples returned by SASE. Reports only if interested. To show a portfolio, mail thumbnails, original/final art, final reproduction/product, tear sheets, b&w photographs and as much information as possible. Buys all rights. Payment varies. Pays on publication.

THE PROGRESSIVE, 409 E. Main St., Madison WI 53703. (608)257-4626. Art Director: Patrick JB Flynn. Monthly. Circ. 50,000. Free sample copy and artists' guidelines.
Illustrations: Buys 10 b&w illustrations/issue from freelancers. Works on assignment only. Send query letter with tear sheets and photocopies. Samples returned by SASE. Reports in 2 months. Portfolio should include final reproduction/product and tear sheets. Cover pays $300, b&w. Inside pays $100-200, b&w line or tone drawings/paintings, inside; on publication, cover. Buys first rights.
Tips: Do not send original art. Send appropriate return postage. "The most obvious trend in editorial work is toward more artistic freedom in ideas and style. I think the successful art direction of a magazine allows for personal interpretation of an assignment."

***PSA**, East-West Network, Inc., 5900 Wilshire Blvd., Los Angeles CA 90036. (213)937-5810. Editor: Al Austin. Art Director: George Kenton. Emphasizes events, issues and business in California. For airline passengers. Monthly. Original artwork returned after publication. Sample copy $2.
Illustrations: Works on assignment only. Query with resume. Buys first rights. Pays $125 minimum, spot art; $450 maximum for full-page illustration; other formats negotiable.

PSYCHIC GUIDE MAGAZINE, Box 701, Providence RI 02901. (401)351-4320. Publisher: Paul Zuromski. Magazine emphasizing new age, natural living and metaphysical topics for people looking for tools to improve body, mind and spirit. Bimonthly. Circ. 150,000. Original artwork returned after publication. Sample copy for 9x12 SASE with $1.07 postage.
Cartoons: Prefers new age, natural living and metaphysical themes. Prefers single panel with gagline; b&w line drawings. Send query letter with samples of style and roughs to be kept on file. Write to show a portfolio. Material not kept on file is returned by SASE. Reports within 3 months. Buys one-time reprint rights. Negotiates payment.
Illustrations: Buys 5-10 illustrations/issue from freelancers. Works on assignment only. Prefers line art with new age, natural living and metaphysical themes. Send query letter with resume, tear sheets, Photostats, photocopies, slides and photographs. Samples not filed are returned by SASE. Reports within 3 months. To show a portfolio, mail original/final art and tear sheets. Buys one-time reprint rights. Negotiates payment. Pays on publication.

PUBLIC CITIZEN, #605, 2000 P St., Washington DC 20036. (202)293-9142. Editor: Catherine Baker. Emphasizes consumer issues for the membership of Public Citizen, a group founded by Ralph Nader in 1971. Bimonthly. Circ. 42,000. Accepts previously published material. Returns original artwork after publication. Sample copy available.
Illustrations: Buys up to 10/issue. Send query letter with samples to be kept on file. Write or call for appointment to show portfolio, which should include tear sheets or photocopies. Samples not filed are returned by SASE. Reports only if interested. Buys first rights or one-time rights. Pays $300, 3-color, cover; and $50-200, b&w or 2-color, inside; on publication.

QUARRY MAGAZINE, Box 1061, Kingston, Ontario K7L 4Y5 Canada. (613)376-3584. Editor: Bob Hilderley. Emphasizes poetry, fiction, short plays, book reviews—Canadian literature. Audience: Canadian writers; libraries (public, high school, college, university); persons interested in current new writing. Quarterly. Circ. 1,000. Original artwork returned after publication. Sample copy $3.
Illustrations: Buys 3-5 illustrations/issues from freelancers. No set preference on themes or styles; "we need high quality line drawings." Send query letter with originals or good Photostats to be kept on file. Contact only by mail. Reports within 12 weeks. Buys first rights. Pays $25, b&w, cover; $25, b&w, inside. Pays on publication.

ELLERY QUEEN'S MYSTERY MAGAZINE, Davis Publications, 380 Lexington Ave., New York NY 10017. (212)557-9100. Editor: Eleanor Sullivan. Emphasizes mystery stories and reviews of mystery books. Reports within 1 month. Pays $25 minimum, line drawings. All other artwork is done inhouse. Pays on acceptance.

QUICK PRINTING, 1680 S.W. Bayshore Blvd., Port St. Lucie FL 33452. (305)879-6666. Art Director: Jeff Macharyas. Emphasizes quick printing for owners/managers of quick print, copying and small commercial printshops. Monthly. Circ. 34,500. Occasionally returns original artwork after publication upon artist's request. Sample copy for SASE with 80¢ postage; call for art guidelines.
Cartoons: Buys 1 cartoon/issue from freelancers. Prefers themes related to quick printing/copying, the plight of managers and computers. Prefers double panel with gagline; b&w line drawings. Send query letter with roughs to be kept on file. Material not filed is returned by SASE only if requested. Reports within 1 month. Negotiates rights purchased. Pays $10 for b&w; on acceptance.
Illustrations: Buys 3 illustrations/issue from freelancers. Works on assignment only. Send query letter to be kept on file. "No samples necessary." Reports within 1 week. Negotiates rights purchased. Payment depends on use, size, complexity, and "general businesslike attitude of artist." Pays $50-400; on acceptance.
Tips: "We plan on using more illustration in the future. We've done a lot of airbrush, but we'll be trying some new media soon."

QUILT WORLD, Box 689, Seabrook NH 03874. Editor: Sandra L. Hatch. Concerns patchwork and quilting. Bimonthly. SASE. Previously published work OK. Original artwork not returned after publication. Sample copy with 9x12 SASE with 66¢ postage.
Cartoons: Buys 2 cartoons/issue from freelancers. Receives 25 submissions/week from freelancers.

Uses themes "poking gentle fun at quilters." Send finished cartoons. Reports in 3 weeks if not accepted. "I hold cartoons I can use until there is space." Buys all rights. Pays $20; on acceptance and/or publication.

R-A-D-A-R, 8121 Hamilton Ave., Cincinnati OH 45231. Editor: Margaret Williams. For children 3rd-6th grade in Christian Sunday schools. Original artwork not returned after publication.
Cartoons: Buys 1 cartoon/month on animals, school and sports. Prefers to see finished cartoons. Reports in 1-2 months. Pays $10-15; on acceptance.
Illustrations: Uses 5 or more illustrations/issue. "Art that accompanies nature or handicraft articles may be purchased, but almost everything is assigned." Send tear sheets to be kept on file. Samples returned by SASE. Reports in 1-2 months. Buys all rights on a work-for-hire basis. Pays $60, line drawing, cover; pays $35-40, inside.

RADIO-ELECTRONICS, 500-B Bi-County Blvd., Farmingdale NY 11735. (516)293-3000. Editorial Director: Arthur Kleiman. Monthly. For electronics professionals and hobbyists. Circ. 242,000. Previously published work OK. Free sample copy.
Cartoons: Buys 3 cartoons/issue on electronics, service, hi-fi, computers and TV games; single panel. Mail art. SASE. Reports in 1 week. Buys first or all rights. Pays $35 minimum, b&w washes; on acceptance.

RAG MAG, Box 12, Goodhue MN 55027. Contact: Beverly Voldseth. Emphasizes poetry, graphics, fiction and reviews for small press, writers, poets and editors. Semiannually: fall and spring. Circ. 300. Accepts previously published material. Original artwork returned after publication. Sample copy $3; art guidelines free for SASE.
Cartoons: Buys 2 cartoons/issue from freelancers. Any theme or style. Prefers single panel or multiple panel with gagline; b&w line drawings. Send samples of styles or finished cartoons. Material returned in 2 months by SASE if unwanted. Reports within 2 months. Write for appointment to show a portfolio. Acquires first rights. Pays in copies only.
Illustrations: Buys 6 illustrations/issue from freelancers. Any style or theme. Send tear sheets, photocopies, Photostats as samples. Samples returned by SASE. Reports within 1 month. Write for appointment to show portfolio, which should include thumbnails, final reproduction/product, Photostats, photographs, b&w PMTs. Acquires first rights. Pays in copies for b&w cover and inside.
Tips: "Realize I publish only 2 issues per year. I can use only 10-12 art pieces per year. I don't hold a lot in my files because I think artists should be sending their art work around. And even if I like someone's art work very much, I like to use new people."

RAILROAD MODEL CRAFTSMAN, Box 700, Newton NJ 07860. (201)383-3355. Editor: William Schaumburg. Emphasizes scale model railroads for all levels of enthusiasts. Covers full range of model railroading, including narrow-gauge, traction, period and modern-day equipment. Monthly. Buys all rights.
Illustrations: Uses scale line drawings of real railroad equipment and structures. Write for payment rates.
Tips: "Freelancers should be active in the field of model railroading. Contact prior to submitting unsolicited drawings."

***RANGER RICK**, 8925 Leesburg Pike, Vienna VA 22180. Design Director: Donna Miller. Emphasizes wildlife and conservational education for children 6-12 years old. Monthly. Circ. 800,000. Buys one-time North American rights.
Illustrations: Buys 3-6 illustrations/issue from freelancers. Works on assignment only. "All assignments involve wildlife, some require ability to draw children." Send query letter with brochure and samples to be kept on file, except for slides that artist needs back. Prefers tear sheets as samples. Samples not filed are returned by SASE. Reports within 2 months. Negotiates rights purchased. Pays $150 minimum, b&w and $250 minimum, color, inside; on acceptance.

REAL ESTATE CENTER JOURNAL, (formerly Tierra Grande), Real Estate Center, Texas A&M University, College Station TX 77843. (409)845-0369. Art Director: Bob Beals. Emphasizes real estate; "primarily for real estate practitioners, with a smattering of investors, attorneys, CPAs, architects and others interested in real estate." Quarterly. Circ. 75,000. Previously published material and simultaneous submissions OK. Free sample copy.
Illustrations: Uses 1-5 illustrations/issue; buys 1-5 from freelancers. Interested in "anything relating directly or indirectly to real estate." Works on assignment only. Send query letter. Provide samples and tear sheets to be kept on file for possible future assignments. Reports in 4 months. Negotiates rights pur-

chased. Pays $20-200, inside b&w line drawings; $50-200, inside b&w washes; on acceptance.
Tips: "There are a great many talented artists, making it unnecessary to consider the marginally talented or those with less than professional presentation of their material. I especially like the artist to know printing production, and I want to know how well the artist works in 1 or 2 colors."

REASON MAGAZINE, Suite 1062, 2716 Ocean Park Blvd., Santa Monica CA 90405. (805)963-5993. Contact: Art Director. Emphasizes current affairs, public policy from libertarian point of view for the "intelligent, literate person concerned with public issues." Monthly. Circ. 30,000. Original artwork returned after publication.
Cartoons: Uses 1 cartoon/issue ("could use more if funny"); buys all from freelancers. "Jokes should be *funny*, well-drawn, with an irreverent view toward government." Prefers single panel, with gagline; b&w line drawings, b&w washes. Send query letter with samples of style to be kept on file. Material not kept on file returned by SASE. Reports only if interested. Buys first rights. Call for appointment to show a portfolio. Payment depends on size, $25 and up.
Illustrations: Uses 8 illustrations/issue; buys all from freelancers. Works on assignment only. Send query letter with brochure showing art style, tear sheets, photocopies, slides or photographs to be kept on file. Write for appointment to show a portfolio, which should include original/final art, final reproduction/product, color, tear sheets, photographs and b&w. Samples returned by SASE if not kept on file. Reports in 3 weeks. Buys first rights. Pays color, cover, depending on size; $100 b&w; $175 color, inside; on publication.
Tips: "Basically, I look for originality, freshness, professionalism and ability to handle complex ideas visually."

***RELIX MAGAZINE**, Box 94, Brooklyn NY 11229. Manager: Toni A. Brown. Emphasizes music—rock, 60's groups, particularly the Grateful Dead for audience 16-39 years of age, 68% male, 32% female. Bimonthly. Circ. 15,000. Accepts previously published material. Original artwork not returned after publication. Sample copy $3; art guidelines for SASE.
Cartoons: Prefers music-related themes, especially "hippie humor." Prefers multi panel, with gagline; b&w line drawings. Send query letter with samples of style to be kept on file. Material not kept on file is returned by SASE. Reports only if interested. Buys all rights. Pay rate is open; pays on publication.
Illustrations: Uses 3-6 illustrations/issue. Prefers rock and roll themes. Send query letter with samples to be kept on file. Prefers Photostats or photographs as samples. Samples not kept on file are returned by SASE. Does not report back. Buys all rights. Pays $150, color, cover; negotiates payment for b&w, inside; pays on publication.
Tips: "We seriously consider anything. We have a lot of opportunities open including t-shirts. We are very accessible. We are especially looking for skeletal art—not morbid."

***RENEGADE**, 3908 E. 4th St., Long Beach CA 90814. Publisher: Deni Loubert. Publishes comic book series. Titles include *Ms. Tree*, *Wordsmith*, *Flaming Carrot*, *Ditko's World*, *Cases of Sherlock Holmes*, *Eternity Smith*, *Murder*, *The Silent Invasion*, *Neil the Horse*, *Maxwell Mouse Follies* and *Vickie Valentine*. Prints work "that hasn't been seen before." Circ. 12-15,000.
Illustrations: Send query letter with a one paragraph summary of the premise, and photocopies of a cover and an interior page. "The artist receives royalties based on sales. All titles are creator-owned, with the artist retaining the copyright."
Tips: "Artists who work for me need very little guidance. I work with people who write and draw the entire package and with people who have established themselves as a team."

***RENTAL EQUIPMENT REGISTER**, 2048 Cotner, Los Angeles CA 90025. (213)477-1033. Readers are independent owners of small and large rental centers including firms engaged in rental of tools and appliances, trucks, trailers, contractor equipment, home health care supplies and party goods. Monthly. Circ. 14,500.
Cartoons: Uses 2 cartoons/issue; buys all from freelancers. Interested in cartoons with slant to the rental center owner. Prefers single panel b&w line drawings or b&w washes. Send finished cartoons to Bob Keeley, editor. SASE. Reports in 2 weeks. Buys all rights. Pays $20-30 for b&w; on publication.

RESIDENT AND STAFF PHYSICIAN, 80 Shore Rd., Port Washington NY 11050. (516)883-6350. Executive Editor: Anne Mattarella. Emphasizes hospital medical practice from clinical, educational, economic and human standpoints. For hospital physicians, interns and residents. Monthly. Circ. 100,000.
Cartoons: Buys 3-4 cartoons/year. "We occasionally publish sophisticated cartoons in good taste dealing with medical themes." Interested in "inside" medical themes. Send query letter with brochure showing art style or resume, tear sheets, Photostats, photocopies, slides and photographs. Call or write to schedule an appointment to show a portfolio, which should include final reproduction/product, color,

tear sheets and b&w. Reports in 2 weeks. Buys all rights. Pays $25; varies for color; also buys spots; pays $10-50; on acceptance.
Illustrations: "We commission qualified freelance medical illustrators to do covers and inside material. Artists should send sample work." Pays $600, color, cover; payment varies for inside work; on acceptance.
Tips: "We like to look at previous work to give us an idea of the artist's style. Since our publication is clinical, we require highly-qualified technical artists who are very familiar with medical illustration. Sometimes we have use for nontechnical work. We like to look at everything. We need material from the *doctor's* point of view, *not* the patient's."

RESPIRATORY MANAGEMENT, 1640 5th St., Santa Monica CA 90401. Publisher: Martin Waldman. Art Director: Tom Medsger. Emphasizes technological, medical and professional news.
First Contact & Terms: Send brochure/flyer to be kept on file for possible future assignment. Reports only when assignment is available. Buys all rights. Pays $60 and up, spot art; $400, full-color cover; on acceptance.

RESTAURANT BUSINESS MAGAZINE, 633 Third Ave., New York NY 10017. Art Director: Charlie Ornett. Emphasizes restaurants/hotels/food for restaurateurs. Monthly. Circ. 110,000. Original artwork returned after publication. Art guidelines available.
Illustrations: Uses 8-10 illustrations/issue. Works on assignment only. Drop off portfolio. Prefers to see b&w portfolio with a few samples of color work. Negotiates rights purchased and payment. Pays $500-1,000 b&w and $500-1,000 color, cover; $100-250 b&w inside; within 60 days.

RESTAURANT HOSPITALITY, 1100 Superior Ave., Cleveland OH 44114. (216)696-7000. Associate Editor: David Farkas. Emphasizes commercial foodservice industry for owners, managers, chefs, etc. Circ. 121,000. Accepts previously published material "if exclusive to foodservice trade press." Original artwork returned after publication. Sample copy $4.
Illustrations: "We want to build a file of freelance illustrators to whom we can assign projects." Works on assignment only. Send query letter with brochure, resume, business card, samples and tear sheets to be kept on file. Prefers photographs as samples, 5x7 or larger, but will accept Photostats. Does not report back to the artist. Pays $350-400, cover; $100-300, inside; on acceptance.

THE RETIRED OFFICER, 201 N. Washington St., Alexandria VA 22314. (703)549-2311. Art Director: M.L. Woychik. For retired officers of the seven uniformed services; concerns current military/political affairs; recent military history, especially Vietnam and Korea; holiday anecdotes; travel; human interest; humor; hobbies; second-career job opportunities and military family lifestyle.
Illustrations: Buys illustrations on assigned themes. (Generally uses Washington DC area artists.) Send query letter with resume and samples.

***RIP OFF PRESS, INC.**, Box 14158, San Francisco CA 94114. (415)469-5800. Chief Copy Editor: Kathe Todd. Publishes comic books including *Fabulous Furry Freak Brothers*, *Rip Off Comics* and *Gyro Comics*. Genres: animal parodies and social parodies. Themes: social commentary and alternative lifestyles. "We publish 'underground' comix. Prefer submissions to be intelligent, funny and well-drawn, rather than heavily violent, graphically sexual or New Wave." Circ. 10-50,000. Original artwork returned after publication. Sample copy available. Send for free catalog listing retail prices. Art guidelines for SASE with first-class postage.
Illustrations: Prefers three-tier page of 6 panels or format 2 wide by 3 tall. Send query letter with photocopies of representative pages or stories. Samples are filed "depending on merit." Samples not filed are returned by SASE if requested. Call or write to schedule an appointment to show a portfolio, which should include 4-5 photocopies of original inking. Buys U.S. comic rights and first refusal on subsequent collections. "Our advance ranges $75-100 per b&w finished page against 10% of cover price on net copies sold (divided by number of pages)." Pays on acceptance and publication when earned royalties exceed advance.
Tips: Looks for "knowledge of successful techniques for b&w reproduction; ability to use comic narrative techniques well; knowledge of and facility with anatomy and perspective."

RISK MANAGEMENT, 205 E. 42nd St., New York NY 10017. (212)286-9292. Production Manager: Edith Reimers. Emphasizes the insurance trade for insurance buyers of Fortune 500 companies. Monthly. Circ. 10,500.
Illustrations: Uses 3-4 illustrations/issue; buys 2-4 every issue from freelancers. Prefers color illustration or stylized line; no humorous themes. Works on assignment only. Send card showing art style or tear sheets. Call for appointment to show portfolio, which should include original art and tear sheets. Prefers printed pieces as samples; original work will not be kept on file after 1 year. Samples not kept on file are

returned only if requested. Buys one-time rights. Pays $100 color, cover (2nd use); $175-225 b&w and $250-300 color, inside; on acceptance.
Tips: When reviewing an artist's work, looks for "neatness, strong concepts, realism with subtle twists and sharply-defined illustrations."

RN MAGAZINE, 680 Kinderkamack Rd., Oradell NJ 07649. (201)262-3030. Readers are registered nurses. Monthly. Circ. 275,000. Sample copy $3.
Illustrations: Buys 10 illustrations/issue from freelancers. Works on assignment only. Provide promo material to be kept on file for future assignments. Samples returned by SASE. Prefers b&w line drawings and washes for inside and color washes, oils, acrylics, etc. for cover. Editorial and medical art is bought. Buys first world serial rights, reprints and promotional rights. Pays $50-300 for inside b&w, $300-1,000 for color cover and $200-500 for inside color; on publication.
Tips: "The art director sees very little need for outside freelance design help but is willing to accept new ideas and their execution by freelancers if the need arises. Freelance artists should contact the art administrator to schedule an appointment."

ROAD KING MAGAZINE, Box 250, Park Forest IL 60466. (312)481-9240. Editor: George Friend. Emphasizes services for truckers, news of the field, CB radio and fiction; leisure-oriented. Readers are over-the-road truckers. Quarterly. Circ. 224,000.
Cartoons: Uses 4 cartoons/issue; buys all from freelancers. Receives 1-2 submissions/week from freelancers. Interested in over-the-road trucking experiences. Prefers single panel b&w line drawings with gagline. Send finished cartoons. SASE. Reports in 2-4 months. Buys first North American serial rights. Pays $25 and up for b&w; on acceptance.
Tips: "Stick to our subject matter. No matter how funny the cartoons are, we probably won't buy them unless they are about trucks and trucking."

RODALES PRACTICAL HOMEOWNER, (formerly *Rodales New Shelter*), 33 E. Minor St., Emmaus PA 18049. (215)967-5171. Art Director: John Pepper. Emphasizes "do-it-yourself home design, repair and management for 30-50-year-old, college-educated males; homeowners, handymen." Published 9 times/year. Circ. 700,000. Original artwork returned after publication "if requested." Smple copy for SASE "and samples of artist's work"; art guidelines available for SASE.
Illustrations: Buys 15-20 illustrations/issue from freelancers. Works on assignment only. Prefers technical illustrations in 4-color. Send business card, samples, and tear sheets—"anything to help us decide to use an artist"—to be kept on file for possible future assignments; call or write for appointment to show portfolio. Samples not kept on file are returned by SASE. Reports in 2-4 weeks. Pays $40-300, inside b&w line drawings; $50-1,500, inside color washes. Pays upon completion of assignment.
Tips: "Become familiar with the needs and style of publication. Have a unique, innovative, clear and accurate style that works with the nature of the magazine."

ROOM OF ONE'S OWN, Box 46160, Station G, Vancouver, British Columbia V6R 4G5 Canada. Contact: Editor. Emphasizes feminist literature for general and academic women, and libraries. Quarterly. Circ. 1,200. Original artwork returned after publication. Sample copy $2.75; art guidelines for SAE (nonresidents include IRC).
Illustrations: Buys 3-5 illustrations/issue from freelancers. Prefers good b&w line drawings. Send samples to be kept on file. Accepts Photostats, photographs, slides or original work as samples. Samples not kept on file are returned by SAE (nonresidents include IRC). Reports within 1 month. Buys first rights. Pays $50, b&w, cover; $25, b&w, inside; on publication.

ROSICRUCIAN DIGEST, Rosicrucian Order, AMORC, San Jose CA 95191. (408)287-9171, ext. 320. Editor/Art Director: Mr. Robin M. Thompson. Fraternal magazine featuring articles on science, philosophy, psychology, metaphysics, mysticism, and the arts for men and women of all ages—"inquiring minds seeking answers to the important questions of life." Bimonthly. Circ. 70,000. Does not accept previously published material. Returns original artwork to the artist. Sample copy available.
Illustrations: Buys a maximum of 10/year. Send query letter with samples. Prefers Photostats, tear sheets and photocopies as samples. Samples returned with SASE. Reports back within 30-60 days. Pays $10 minimum. Pays on acceptance.
Tips: "We are looking for new, fresh unknown artists who want to break in. We offer the opportunity to show off their fine work in a scholarly publication. We are looking for thought-provoking artwork. Nothing sensational or trendy. Freelancers should be familiar with our magazine—the format, style, etc.—before sending their samples or especially their portfolios."

THE ROTARIAN, 1600 Ridge Ave., Evanston IL 60201. Editor: Willmon L. White. Associate Editor: Jo Nugent. Art Director: P. Limbos. Emphasizes general interest and business and management articles.

Service organization for business and professional men, their families, and other subscribers. Monthly. Sample copy and editorial fact sheet available.
Cartoons: Buys 4-5 cartoons/issue. Interested in general themes with emphasis on business. Avoid topics of sex, national origin, politics. Send query letter with brochure showing art style. Reports in 1-2 weeks. Buys all rights. Pays $75 on acceptance.
Illustrations: Buys assigned themes. Most editorial illustrations are commissioned. Buys average 3 or more illustrations/issue; 6 humorous illustrations/year. Send query letter with brochure showing art style. Reports within 10 working days. Buys all rights. Call to schedule an appointment to show a portfolio, which should include original/final art, final reproduction/product, color and photographs. Pays $250-1,000 on acceptance.
Tips: "Artists should set up appointments with art director to show their portfolios. Preference given to area talent." Conservative style and subject matter.

RUBICON, 853, rue Sherbrooke ouest, Montréal Québec H3A 2T6 Canada. (514)286-0652. Art Director: Su Schnee. Magazine emphasizing contemporary writing and visual art for artists and writers. Biannual. Circ. 750. Sample copy $4.
Illustrations: Buys 50 illustrations/issue from freelancers. Prefers contemporary themes and styles. Send resume, tear sheets, Photostats, photocopies, slides and photographs, ("*not* originals"). Samples not filed are returned by SAE (nonresidents include IRC). Reports within 3 months. To show a portfolio, mail appropriate materials, which should include thumbnails, roughs, tear sheets, Photostats, photographs and b&w. Buys first rights. Payment is "minimal;" on publication.

RUNNER'S WORLD, (incorporating *The Runner*), 135 N. 6th St., Emmaus PA 18049. (215)967-5171. Art Director: Kay Douglas. Emphasizes serious, recreational running. Monthly. Circ. 470,000. Returns original artwork after publication. Sample copy available.
Cartoons: Buys 2/issue from freelancers. Prefers themes on running and general health and fitness. Considers single panel with gagline; b&w line drawings, b&w washes. Samples of style are filed; unused roughs or finished cartoons are returned by SASE within 1 month. Buys one-time rights. Pays $100, b&w on acceptance.
Illustrations: Buys average of 6/issue from freelancers. "Styles include tightly rendered human athletes, caricatures, and cerebral interpretations of running themes. Also, *RW* uses medical illustration for features on biomechanics." Works on assignment only. Send samples to be kept on file. Prefers tear sheets or slides as samples. Samples not filed are returned by SASE. Reports back only if interested. Buys one-time rights.

RUNNING TIMES, Suite 21, 2022 A Opitz Blvd., Woodbridge VA 22191. (703)643-1740. Emphasizes distance running. Readers include road runners, cross country and adventure runners; people interested in fitness. Monthly. Sample copy $1.95.
Illustrations: Uses 3-5 illustrations/issue, all from freelancers. Prefers b&w line drawings for inside, and color illustrations for inside and cover. Especially needs color illustrations for feature articles and small b&w drawings. Prefers to see finished art, portfolio or tear sheet to be kept on file. SASE. Reports in 4 weeks. Buys all rights on a work-for-hire basis. Pays $35-200 for inside and $250 minimum for cover; on publication. Buys first North American serial rights.
Tips: "We need more art and would like to see more samples or portfolios!"

RURAL HERITAGE, (formerly *The Evener*), Box 7, Cedar Falls IA 50613. (319)277-3599. Managing Editor: Suzanne Seedorff. Magazine. Emphasizes draft horses, mules and oxen. "*Rural Heritage*'s subscribers are primarily farmers, craftsmen, showmen and women. They are interested in horses, nostalgia—and, oftentimes—self-sufficiency. Some subscribers work horses, mules or oxen on their farm or ranch and look for features and quality artwork and photographs about people in the industry." Quarterly. Circ. 10,400. Accepts previously published material. Original artwork returned after publication. Sample copy for SASE with $1.07 postage; art guidelines for SASE with 39¢ postage.
Cartoons: Buys 1 cartoon/issue from freelancers.
Illustrations: Buys 2 illustrations/issue from freelancers. Usually works on assignment. Send query letter with brochure or Photostats, photographs and slides as samples. Samples not filed are returned by SASE. Reports within 4 months by SASE only. Negotiates rights purchased; prefers first-time rights. Pays $40-100, b&w, cover; $10-60, b&w, inside; on publication.

RURAL KENTUCKIAN, Box 32170, Louisville KY 40232. Editor: Gary Luhr. Magazine emphasizing Kentucky-related and general feature material for Kentuckians living outside metropolitan areas. Monthly. Circ. 300,000. Accepts previously published material. Original artwork returned after publication if requested. Sample copy available. All artwork is solicited by the magazine to illustrate upcoming articles.

Illustrations: Buys 2-3 illustrations/issue from freelancers. Works on assignment only. Prefers b&w line art. Send query letter with resume and samples. Samples not filed are returned only if requested. Reports within 2 weeks. Buys one-time rights. Pays $50, b&w, cover; $30-50, b&w, inside; on acceptance.

***RX HOME CARE**, Brentwood Publishing, 1640 5th St., Santa Monica CA 90401. Publisher: Martin Waldman. Art Director: Tom Medsger. Emphasizes technological, medical and professional news.
First Contact & Terms: Submit brochure/flyer to be kept on file for possible future assignment. Reports only when assignment is available. Buys all rights. Pays $60 and up, spot art; $400, full-color cover; on acceptance.

SACRAMENTO MAGAZINE, Box 2424, Sacramento CA 95811. (916)446-7548. Art Director: Chuck Donald. Emphasizes Sacramento city living for audience 25-54 years old, executives/professionals, married, middle-upper income. Monthly. Circ. 30,000. Accepts previously published material and simultaneous submissions. Sample copy for SASE.
Cartoons: Buys 6 cartoons/issue. Pays $25 b&w.
Illustrations: Uses 5 illustrations/issue. Send query letter with brochure showing art style or tear sheets, Photostats, slides and photographs to be kept on file. Accepts any type of samples which fairly represent artist's work. Reports only if interested. Negotiates rights purchased. Call or write to schedule an appointment to show a portfolio, which should include original/final art and final reproduction/product. Pays $300 color, cover; $125 b&w and $200 color, inside; on acceptance.

SAFETY & HEALTH, (formerly *National Safety and Health News*), National Safety Council, 444 N. Michigan Ave., Chicago IL 60611-3991. (312)527-4800. Editor: Roy Fisher. For those responsible for developing and administering occupational and environmental safety and health programs. Monthly. Circ. 56,000. Original artwork returned after publication. Free sample copy and artist's guidelines. Also uses artists for 4-color cover design, publication redesign and layout mock-ups. Contact: Gordon Bieberle, Director of Publications Department.
Cartoons: Contact: Susan-Marie Kelly. Uses 4-6 cartoons/issue, all from freelancers. Interested in occupational safety and health; single, double or multi panel with gagline. Prefers to see roughs. SASE. Reports in 4 weeks. Buys first North American serial rights or all rights on a work-for-hire basis. Pays $10 minimum, b&w line drawings.

SAILING, (formerly *Yacht Racing & Crusing*), 125 E. Main St., Port Washington WI 53074. (414)284-3494. Editor: William F. Schanen III. Emphasizes all aspects of sailing (sailboats only). Monthly. Circ. 30,000. Original artwork returned after publication upon special request. Previously published work OK. Sample copy $2.50.
Illustrations: Uses very few illustrations/year. Interested in action sailing only. Works on assignment. Send resume, finished art, or samples of style. Samples returned by SASE, if requested. Provide letter of inquiry to be kept on file for future assignments. Reports in 2-3 weeks. Buys one-time rights.

SAILING WORLD, 111 E Ave., Norwalk CT 06851. (203)853-9921. Editor: John Burnham. Managing Editor: Douglas O. Logan. Emphasizes racing events and instructional articles for "performance-oriented sailors." Published 12 times/year. Circ. 53,000. Original artwork returned after publication. Sample copy $1.75.
Illustrations: Works on assignment only. Send query letter with roughs. Samples returned by SASE. Buys first rights. Pays on publication.

THE ST. LOUIS JOURNALISM REVIEW, 8380 Olive Blvd., St. Louis MO 63132. (314)991-1699. Contact: Charles L. Klotzer. Features critiques of St. Louis media—print, broadcasting, TV, cable, advertising, public relations and the communication industry. Monthly. Circ. 12,000.
Cartoons: Subject should pertain to the news media; preferably local. Query with samples. SASE. Reports in 4-7 weeks. Pays $15-25 on publication.
Illustrations: Query with samples. SASE. Reports in 4-6 weeks. Pays $15-25 each (negotiable) for b&w and color illustrations pertaining to the news media (preferably local); on publication.

The asterisk before a listing indicates that the listing is new in this edition. New markets are often the most receptive to freelance submissions.

SALES AND MARKETING MANAGEMENT, 633 3rd Ave., New York NY 10017. (212)986-4800. Art Director: Tom Loria. For sales managers. Biweekly. Circ. 65,000. Simultaneous submissions OK. Pays on acceptance.
Cartoons: Buys 26 cartoons/year. Interested in sales management and selling; single panel. Prefers art. SASE. Reports in 1 week. Buys all rights but may reassign rights to artist after publication. Pays $30-45, b&w; on acceptance.

SALT LICK PRESS, 1804 E. 38½ St., Austin TX 78722. Editor/Publisher: James Haining. Published irregularly. Circ. 1,500. Previously published material and simultaneous submissions OK. Original artwork returned after publication. Sample copy $3.
Illustrations: Uses 12 illustrations/issue; buys 2 from freelancers. Receives 2 illustrations/week from freelance artists. Interested in a variety of themes. Send brochure showing art style or tear sheets, Photostats, photocopies, slides and photographs. Samples returned by SASE. Reports in 6 weeks. To show a portfolio, mail roughs, Photostats, photographs and b&w. Negotiates payment; pays on publication. Buys first rights.

SALT WATER SPORTSMAN, 186 Lincoln St., Boston MA 02111. (617)426-4074. Editor-in-Chief/Art Director: Barry Gibson. Emphasizes resorts, areas, techniques, equipment and conservation. For saltwater fishermen, fishing equipment retailers and resort owners. Monthly. Circ. 125,000. Original artwork returned after publication. Free sample copy and artists' guidelines.
Illustrations: Buys 3 illustrations/issue from freelancers. Receives 3 submissions/week from freelancers. Works on assignment only. Interested in themes covering all phases of salt water sport fishing—mood, how-to, etc. Send query letter with brochure to be kept on file. SASE. Reports in 4 weeks. Reports back on future assignment possibilities. Write to schedule an appointment to show a portfolio, which should include final reproduction/product. Buys first North American serial rights. Pays $400 b&w, cover, payment varies for inside; on acceptance.
Tips: "Let us see samples of work relevant to our topics/areas. New artists should strive for accuracy in portraying fish, equipment, etc."

SAN FRANCISCO FOCUS MAGAZINE, 680 8th St., San Francisco CA 94103. (415)553-2800. Art Director: Matthew Drace. The city magazine for the San Francisco Bay area. Audience is approx. 47-year-old average, male/female, professional-managerial, post-graduate, homeowner; average income $85,000. Monthly. Circ. 210,000. Sometimes accepts previously published material. Original artwork returned after publication.
Illustrations: Uses 3-6 illustrations/issue; buys 2-6 illustrations/issue from freelancers. Uses a variety of styles according to editorial content; top-level professional artists *only*. Assignments made on basis of individual style and proficiency. Send resume, business card and samples to be kept on file. No original work—only reproductions (prints, slides, tear sheets, photocopies, stats) as samples. Samples returned by SASE only if requested; prefers to keep on file. No "guidelines" sent. Reports only if interested. Please: no calls—only letters. Send samples to "Attn: Artists File". Buys one-time rights. Pays $100-500 color, cover; $50-150, b&w and $150-400, color, inside; on publication (30 days after receipt of invoice).
Tips: "Send samples for us to keep on file; please don't call just send letter or resume—we need to see the *work*."

SAN JOSE STUDIES, San Jose State University, San Jose CA 95192. (408)277-2841. Editor: Fauneil J. Rinn. Emphasizes the arts, humanities, business, science, social science; scholarly. Published 3 times/year. Circ. 500. Original artwork returned after publication. Sample copy $5.
Cartoons: Number of cartoons/issue varies. Interested in "anything that would appeal to the active intellect." Prefers single panel b&w line drawings. Send slides. SASE. Reports in 2 weeks. Buys first North American serial rights. Pays in 2 copies of publication, plus entry in $100 annual contest.
Illustrations: Number of illustrations/issue varies. Prefers b&w line drawings. Send slides. SASE. Reports in 2 weeks. To show a portfolio, mail Photostats, photographs and b&w. Buys first North American serial rights. Pays in 2 copies of publication, plus entry in $100 annual contest.
Tips: "We would be interested in cartoons, and humorous and cartoon-style illustrations especially if accompanied by some description of the artist's techniques, purpose, conception and development of the artwork."

SANTA BARBARA MAGAZINE, 123 W. Padre St., Santa Barbara CA 93105. Art Director: Kimberly Kavish. Magazine emphasizing Santa Barbara culture and community. Bimonthly. Circ. 11,000. Original artwork returned after publication if requested. Sample copy $2.95.
Illustrations: Buys about 3 illustrations/issue from freelance artists. Works on assignment only. Send query letter with brochure, resume, tear sheets and photocopies. Reports back within 6 weeks. To show

a portfolio, mail original/final art, final reproduction/product/color, tear sheets and b&w, will contact if interested. Buys first rights. Payment varies; on acceptance.

SATELLITE ORBIT, SATELLITE DIRECT, (formerly Satellite Orbit, Satellite Dealer), Box 53, Boise ID 83707. (208)322-2800. Magazine emphasizing satellite television industry for home satellite dish owners and dealers. Monthly. Circ. Satellite Orbit—650,000; Satellite Direct—20,000. Accepts previously published material. Original artwork returned after publication.
Cartoons: Buys 1-3 cartoons/issue from freelancers. Prefers single panel, with gagline; b&w washes. Send query letter with samples of style to be kept on file. Material not kept on file is returned by SASE. Reports within 1 month. Negotiates rights purchased. Pays $150, b&w; $200-250, color.
Illustrations: Buys 5-15 illustrations/issue from freelancers. Works on assignment only. Send query letter with tear sheets, photocopies, slides and photographs. Samples not filed are returned only if requested. Reports within 1 month. To show a portfolio, mail color, tear sheet, photographs and b&w. Negotiates rights purchased. Pays $100-1,000, b&w and $200-1,500, color, cover; $100-1,000, b&w and $100-1,000, color, inside; on publication.

THE SATURDAY EVENING POST, The Saturday Evening Post Society, 1100 Waterway Blvd., Indianapolis IN 46202. (317)636-8881. General interest, family-oriented magazine. Published 9 times/year. Circ. 600,000. Sample copy $1.
Cartoons: Cartoon Editor: Robert Grindy. Buys 20 cartoons/issue. Prefers single panel with gaglines. Receives 100 batches of cartoons/week from freelance cartoonists. "We look for cartoons with neat line or tone art. The content should be in good taste, suitable for a general-interest, family magazine. It must not be offensive while remaining entertaining. We prefer that artists first send SASE for guidelines and then review recent issues. Political, violent or sexist cartoons are not used. Need all topics, but particularly medical, health, travel and financial." SASE. Reports in 1 month. Buys all rights. Pays $125, b&w line drawings and washes, no pre-screened art; on publication.
Illustrations: Art Director: Chris Wilhoite. Uses average of 3 illustrations/issue; buys 90% from freelancers. Send query letter with brochure showing art style or resume and samples. To show a portfolio, mail original/final art. Buys all rights, "generally. All ideas, sketchwork and illustrative art are handled through commissions only and thereby controlled by art direction. Do not send original material (drawings, paintings, etc.) or 'facsimiles of' that you wish returned." Cannot assume any responsibility for loss or damage. "If you wish to show your artistic capabilities, please send unreturnable, expendable/sampler material (slides, tear sheets, photocopies, etc.)."

SAVINGS INSTITUTIONS, 111 E. Wacker Dr., Chicago IL 60601. (312)644-3100. Art Director: George Glatter. Emphasizes the savings and loan business for people in savings and loan or related businesses. Monthly. Circ. 35,000. Accepts previously published material. Original artwork returned after publication. Sample copy available.
Cartoons: Buys 0-1 cartoons/issue from freelancers.
Illustrations: Buys 0-2 illustrations/issue from freelancers; some are humorous or cartoon-style illustrations. Works on assignment only. Send query letter with samples to be kept on file. Call for appointment to show portfolio. Samples not kept on file are returned only if requested. Reports only if interested. Buys first rights, one-time rights, reprint rights or negotiates rights purchased. Negotiates payment. Pays on acceptance.

SCHOOL SHOP, Box 8623, Ann Arbor MI 48107. Publisher and Executive Editor: Alan H. Jones. For industrial and technical education personnel. Published 10 times/year. Circ. 45,000. Original artwork not returned after publication. Free artist's guidelines.
Cartoons: Buys 1+ cartoons/issue; buys all from freelancers. Interested in vocational/industrial education; single, double or multi panel. Send query letter, resume and finished cartoons. SASE. Reports in 6 weeks. To show a portfolio, mail roughs, tear sheets and b&w. Buys all rights. Pays $20, b&w line drawings; on publication.
Tips: "Must be related to industrial and technical education."

SCIENCE AND CHILDREN, National Science Teachers Association, 1742 Connecticut Ave. NW, Washington DC 20009. (202)328-5800. Editor-in-Chief: Phyllis Marcuccio. For elementary and middle school science teachers, educators, administrators and personnel. Published 8 times/year. Circ. 17,000. Original artwork not returned after publication. Free sample copy.
Cartoons: Buys 1 cartoon/issue; buys all from freelancers. Interested in science-technology and environment; multi-panel with gaglines. Reports in 2 weeks. Prefers finished cartoons. SASE. Buys all rights. Pays $15-25, b&w line drawings and washes; on publication.
Illustrations: Buys 10-15 illustrations/issue from freelancers. Works on assignment only. Interested in education and environment; light, stylized, realistic science illustrations (no stock illustrations). Sam-

ples returned by SASE. Send resume, brochure, flyer or photocopy of work to be kept on file for future assignments. Reports in 2 weeks. Prefers to see portfolio with samples of style. Buys all rights on a work-for-hire basis. Cover: Pays $50-150, b&w line drawings, washes and color. Pays $10-100, b&w line drawings and washes, inside; on publication.
Tips: "Looking for new talent. Realistic drawings of children important—scientific renderings secondary."

SCIENCE NEWS, 1719 N St. NW, Washington DC 20036. (202)785-2255. Art Director: Wendy McCarren. Emphasizes all sciences for teachers, students and scientists. Weekly. Circ. 200,000. Accepts previously published material. Original artwork returned after publication. Sample copy for SASE with 39¢ postage.
Illustrations: Buys 10 illustrations/year from freelancers. Prefers realistic style, scientific themes; uses some cartoon-style illustrations. Works on assignment only. Send query letter with Photostats or photocopies to be kept on file. Samples returned by SASE. Reports only if interested. Buys one-time rights. Write to schedule an appointment to show a portfolio, which should include original/final art. Pays $50-200; on acceptance.
Tips: Uses some cartoons and cartoon-style illustrations.

***THE SCIENCE TEACHER**, 1742 Connecticut Ave. NW, Washington DC 20009. (202)328-5800. Assistant Editor: Susan Burns. Emphasizes high school science. Features how-to and technical articles on new theories in science and science experiments for teenagers. Published 9 times/year. Circ. 24,000. Original artwork returned after publication upon request. Free sample copy.
Cartoons: Rarely buys cartoons.
Illustrations: Buys 2 illustrations/issue from freelancers. Works on assignment only. "Must be b&w—any medium accepted." Send query letter with photocopies. Samples are filed. Samples not filed are returned only if requested. Reports back only if intereted. Call to schedule an appointment to show a portfolio or mail original/final art or tear sheets. Buys first rights. Pays $80-120, b&w; $150, color, cover (photography). Pays on acceptance.
Tips: Artists "should live in the DC area. We are in search of new artists and photographers constantly, especially photographers who can shoot in a high school."

SCOTT STAMP MONTHLY MAGAZINE, Box 828, Sidney OH 45365. Art Director: Edward Heys. Magazine emphasizing stamp collecting for beginning through advanced collectors. Monthly. Circ. 22,000. Accepts previously published material. Original artwork returned after publication. Sample copy available for SASE with $1.24 postage.
Cartoons: Buys 1-2 cartoons/issue. Prefers single, double or multi panel with gagline; b&w line drawings; b&w washes. Send query letter with brochure showing art style, resume, tear sheets, Photostats, photocopies and slides. Material not kept on file is returned by SASE. Reports only if interested. Buys reprint rights. Pays $10-25, b&w.
Illustrations: Works on assignment only. Reports only if interested. To show a portfolio, mail roughs, Photostats and tear sheets. Samples not filed are returned by SASE. Buys one-time and reprint rights. Pays $300, color, cover; $25-100, b&w, and $50-200, color, inside; on acceptance. Also uses freelancers for paste-up.
Tips: Looks for "clean, accurate, meticuluous work."

SCREEN PRINTING MAGAZINE, 407 Gilbert Ave., Cincinnati OH 45202. (513)421-2050. Art Director: Ann Campbell. Emphasizes screen printing for screen printers, distributors and manufacturers of screen printing equipment and screen printed products. Monthly. Circ. 12,000. Accepts previously published material and simultaneous submissions in noncompeting magazines. Sometimes returns original artwork after publication. Sample copy available.
Illustrations: Uses 3 illustrations/issue. Send query letter with samples and tear sheets. Prefers Photostats as samples. Samples returned by SASE if requested. Reports only if interested. Call for appointment to show portfolio. Negotiates rights purchased. Pays for design and illustration by the project, $50-350. Pays on acceptance.
Tips: "Ask for sample copy of the magazine. Need competent technical illustrators with good sense of design. Large, "student-type portfolio with loose dog-eared samples makes for a lousy impression."

SEA, Box 1337, Newport Beach CA 92663. (714)646-0173. Contact: Art Director. Emphasizes recreational boating for owners or users of recreational boats, both power and sail, primarily for cruising and general recreation; some interest in boating competition; regionally oriented to 13 Western states. Monthly. Circ. 50,000. Whether original artwork returned after publication depends upon terms of purchase. Sample copy for SASE.
Illustrations: Uses 6-8 illustrations/issue; buys 90% from freelancers. "I often look for a humorous il-

lustration to lighten a technical article." Works on assignment only. Send query letter. Samples returned. Reports in 6 weeks. Provide business card and tear sheets to be kept on file for possible future assignments. Negotiates rights purchased and payment. Pays on publication (negotiable).
Tips: "We will accept students for portfolio review with an eye to obtaining quality art at a reasonable price. We will help start career for illustrators and hope that they will remain loyal to the publication which helped launch their career."

SECURITY MANAGEMENT, c/o ASIS, Suite 1200, 1655 N. Fort Myer Dr., Arlington VA 22209. (703)522-5800. Art Director: Cecily Roberts. For security managers who protect assets, personnel and information of organizations. Monthly. Circ. 25,000. Previously published and simultaneous submissions acceptable if not submitted to competitors. "Want exclusive in security market. Please state where else work has been submitted." Original artwork returned after publication.
Cartoons: Rarely uses cartoons. Prefers to see roughs. SASE.
Illustrations: Uses 5-6 illustrations/issue; buys all from freelancers. Works on assignment only. Send query letter with brochure, business card and Photostats to be kept on file. Pays $500-700, color, cover; $100-200, b&w and $200-500, color, inside; on publication.
Tips: There is an "increasing use of color in our operation. Artists should get a couple of copies and try to get to know the orientation of the content. Send samples of illustrations from other professional/business publications."

SEEK, 8121 Hamilton Ave., Cincinnati OH 45231. (513)931-4050, ext. 365. Emphasizes religion/faith. Readers are young adult to middle-aged adults who attend church and Bible classes. Quarterly in weekly issues. Circ. 45,000. Free sample copy and guidelines; SASE appreciated.
Cartoons: Editor: Eileen H. Wilmoth. Uses 1-2 cartoons/quarter. Buys "church or Bible themes—contemporary situations of applied Christianity." Prefers single panel b&w line drawings with gagline. Send finished cartoons, photocopies and photographs. SASE. Reports in 3-6 weeks. Buys first North American serial rights. Pays $10-15 on acceptance.
Illustrations: Art Director: Frank Sutton. Buys 13-15 illustrations/issue. Uses cover & inside b&w line drawings and washes. Works on assignment only; needs vary with articles used. Arrange appointment to show portfolio. Reports in 1 week. Pays $60, cover or full page art; $40, inside pieces; on acceptance. Buys first North American serial rights.
Tips: "We use only 2-color work. The art needs to be attractive as well as realistic. I look for detail, shading and realism."

THE SENSIBLE SOUND, 403 Darwin Dr., Snyder NY 14226. Editor: John A. Horan. Emphasizes audio equipment for hobbyists. Quarterly. Circ. 5,800. Accepts previously published material and simultaneous submissions. Original artwork returned after publication. Sample copy $2.
Cartoons: Uses 4 cartoons/year. Prefers single panel, with or without gagline; b&w line drawings. Send samples of style and roughs to be kept on file. Material not kept on file is returned by SASE. Reports within 30 days. Negotiates rights purchased. Pay rate varies; pays on publication.

SERVICE BUSINESS, 1916 Pike Pl., #345, Seattle WA 98101. (206)622-4241. Publisher: Bill Griffin. Submissions Editor: Martha M. Ireland. Technical, management and human relations emphasis for self-employed cleaning and maintenance service contractors. Quarterly. Circ. 4,500. Prefers first publication material, simultaneous submissions OK "if to non-competing publications." Original artwork returned after publication if requested by SASE. Sample copy $3.
Cartoons: Uses 1-2 cartoons/issue; buys all from freelancers. Must be relevant to magazine's readership. Prefers b&w line drawings.
Illustrations: Uses approximately 12 illustrations/issue including some humorous and cartoon-style illustrations; buys all from freelancers. Send query letters with samples. Samples returned by SASE. Buys first publication rights. Reports only if interested. Pays for design by the hour, $5-10. Pays for illustration by the project, $3-15. Pays on publication.
Tips: "Our budget is extremely limited. Those who require high fees are really wasting their time."

***S/F MAGAZINE**, 755 Mt. Auburn St., Watertown MA 02172. (617)924-2422. Editor-in-Chief: Alan R. Earls. Magazine for real estate and other professionals in New England. Monthly. Circ. 18,000. Sample copy for $2 postage or money order.
Cartoons: Buys 1-2 cartoons/issue from freelancers. Prefers real-estate-related topics. Prefers single panel. Send samples of style. Reports back within 1 month. Buys all rights. Pays $30 and up; on publication.
Illustrations: Works on assignment only. Send query letter with brochure showing art style to be kept on file. Prefers Photostats as samples. Samples not filed are returned by SASE only if requested by artist. Reports back only if interested. Material copyrighted. Payment varies. Pays on publication.

THE SHINGLE, One Reading Center, Philadelphia PA 19107. (215)238-6300. Managing Editor: Nancy L. Hebble. Law-related articles, opinion pieces, news features, book reviews, poetry and fiction for the Philadelphia Bar Association membership (9,400 members). Quarterly. Circ. 10,000. Sample copy free for SASE.
Illustrations: Buys 2 illustrations/issue. Works on assignment only. Prefers fine line drawings; themes vary with editorial content. Send query letter with brochure, resume, business card and Photostats to be kept on file. Samples not kept on file are not returned. Reports only if interested. Pay rate varies; pays on acceptance.

SHUTTLE SPINDLE & DYEPOT, 65 LaSalle Rd., West Hartford CT 06117. (203)233-5124. Art Director: Tracy McHugh. Emphasizes weaving and fiber arts for hobbyists and professionals. Quarterly. Circ. 18,500. Accepts simultaneous submissions. Original artwork returned after publication. Sample copy $6.50; art guidelines for SASE.
Illustrations: Uses 20-30 illustrations/issue; buys "very few" from freelancers. Works on assignment only. Prefers b&w line drawings. Send query letter with resume tear sheets, photocopies and slides to be kept on file. Reports within 6 weeks. To show a portfolio, mail color and b&w or write to schedule an appointment. Buys first American serial rights. Honorarium only on publication; no payment. Credit line given.

***SIGHTLINES**, Suite 301, 45 John St., New York NY 10038. (212)227-5599. Publisher: Marilyn Levin. Editor-in-Chief: Judith Trojan. Emphasizes film and video for the nontheatrical film/video world, including librarians in university and public libraries, independent filmmakers, film teachers on the high school and college levels, film programmers in the community, universities, religious organizations and film curators in museums." Quarterly magazine of Educational Film Library Association, Inc. Circ. 3,000. Previously published material OK; simultaneous submissions "OK if not with competitor." Original artwork returned after publication. Sample copy $3.50 plus $2 shipping.
Cartoons: "We sometimes buy cartoons which deal with library and film/video issues that relate to educational and community use of media"; b&w line drawings. Send query letter with samples of style and resume. Samples returned by SASE. Buys one-time rights. Pays approximately $25 (but negotiable), b&w; on publication.
Tips: "We use very little freelance artwork."

SIGN OF THE TIMES—A CHRONICLE OF DECADENCE IN THE ATOMIC AGE, Box 70672, Seattle WA 98107-0672. Contact: M. Souder. Magazine emphasizing fiction, phtography and graphics for sleazy up-scale college educated. Publishes twice yearly. Circ. 500. Accepts previousy published material. Original artwork returned after publication if requested. Sample copy $3.50.
Cartoons: Buys 1-2 cartoons/issue from freelancers. Prefers single or multiple panel with or without gagline; b&w line drawings. Send query letter to be kept on file. Material not kept onfile is returned by SASE. Reports within 6 weeks. Buys reprint rights. Negotiates payment.
Illustrations: Buys 1-2 illustrations/issue from freelancers. Prefers decadent themes. Send query letter with photocopies. Samples not filed are returned by SASE. Reports within 6 weeks. To show a portfolio, mail original/final art. Buys reprint rights. Negotiates payment on publication.

THE SINGLE PARENT, 8807 Colesville Rd., Silver Spring MD 20910. (301)588-9354. Editor: Donna Duvall. Assistant Editor: Jackie Conciatore. Emphasizes family life in all aspects—raising children, psychology, divorce, remarriage, etc.—for all single parents and their children. Bimonthly. Circ. 200,000. Accepts simultaneous submissions and occasionally accepts previously published material. Original artwork returned after publication. Sample copy available for 10"x12" SASE with 48¢ postage.
Cartoons: Uses 1-2 cartoons/issue; buys all from freelancers. Prefers divorce, children, family life topics with single parenthood as the theme. Prefers cartoons with gag line; b&w line drawings, b&w washes. Send finished cartoons to be kept on file. Write or call for appointment to show portfolio. Material not kept on file returned by SASE. Reports within 6 weeks. Negotiates rights purchased. Pays $15, b&w; on publication.
Illustrations: Uses 5-6 illustrations/issue; buys all from freelancers. Works on assignment only for specific stories. Assignments based on artist's style. Send query letter with brochure, resume, samples to be kept on file. Write or call for appointment to show portfolio. Prefers Photostats, photographs, tear sheets as samples. Samples returned by SASE if not kept on file. Reports within 6 weeks. Negotiates rights purchased. Pays $75, b&w, cover; $50-75, b&w, inside. Pays on publication.

SKI, 380 Madison Ave., New York NY 10017. Editor: Richard Needham. Emphasizes instruction, resorts, equipment and personality profiles. For new and expert skiers. Published 8 times/year. Previously published work OK "if we're notified."

Cartoons: Especially needs cartoons of skiers with gagline. "Artist/cartoonist must remember he is reaching experienced skiers who enjoy 'subtle' humor." Mail art. SASE. Reports immediately. Buys first serial rights. Pays $75, b&w skiing themes; on publication.
Illustrations: Mail art. SASE. Reports immediately. Buys one-time rights. Pays $100-500, full-color art; on acceptance.

SKIING, 1 Park Ave., New York NY 10016. (212)503-3900. Art Director: Barbara Rietschel. Emphasizes skiing, ski areas, ski equipment, instruction for young adults and professionals; good incomes. Published 7 times a year, September-March. Circ. 445,000. Original artwork returned after publication. Sample copy free for SASE.
Illustrations: Uses 2 illustrations/issue on average. Works on assignment basis. Send query letter with samples to be kept on file. Call for appointment to show portfolio. Prefers Photostats or photocopies as samples. Samples returned by SASE if not kept on file. Reports only if interested. Buys first or one-time rights. Pays $75-250, b&w, inside; on acceptance.
Tips: "Know the magazine. I find it very annoying when artists come in, never having looked at a copy of *Skiing*."

SKY AND TELESCOPE, 49 Bay State Rd., Cambridge MA 02238. Editor: L.J. Robinson. Art Director: Mr. Kelly Beatty. Concerns astronomy, building telescopes and space exploration for enthusiasts and professionals. Monthly. Circ. 75,000. Buys one-time rights. Pays on publication.
Cartoons: Buys 4/year on astronomy, telescopes and space exploration; single panel preferred. Pays $25-50, b&w line drawings, washes and gray opaques. Send query letter with samples.
Illustrations: Buys assigned themes. Send query letter with previously published work. Pays $50-150.

***SMALL BOAT JOURNAL**, Box 1066, Bennington VT 05201. (802)442-3101. Art Director: Adelaide Jaquith. Editor: Thomas Baker. Magazine emphasizing boats and boating for recreation boaters of all types—sailors, powerboaters and rowers. Bimonthly.
Illustrations: Works with 4 artists/year. Uses artists for illustrating technical details, boat building and repair techniques, perspective and profile views of boats. Cartoon ideas also welcomed. Send query letter with brochure or samples. Reports back only if interested. Call to schedule an appointment to show a portfolio, which should include roughs and original/final art. Pays by the hour, $10-20.
Tips: "Ability to render people is a plus. Familiarity with boats and nautical subjects is necessary."

THE SMALL POND MAGAZINE OF LITERATURE, Box 664, Stratford CT 06497. Emphasizes poetry and short prose. Readers are people who enjoy literature—primarily college-educated. Published 3 times/year. Circ. 300. Sample copy $2.50; art guidelines for SASE.
Illustrations: Editor: Napoleon St. Cyr. Uses 1-5 illustrations/issue. Receives 50-75 illustrations/year. Uses "line drawings (inside and on cover) which generally relate to natural settings, but have used abstract work completely unrelated." Especially needs line drawings; "fewer wildlife drawings and more unrelated-to-wildlife material." Send query letter with finished art or production quality photocopies, 2x3 minimum, 8x11 maximum. SASE. Reports in 1 month. Pays 2 copies of issue in which work appears on publication. Buys copyright in convention countries.
Tips: "Need cover art work, but inquire first or send for sample copy." Especially looks for "smooth clean lines, original movements, an overall impact. Don't send a heavy portfolio, but rather 4-6 black-and-white representative samples with SASE. Better still, send for copy of magazine ($2.50)."

SOAP OPERA DIGEST, 254 W. 31st St., New York NY 10001. Art Director: Andrea Wagner. Emphasizes soap opera and prime-time drama synopses and news. Biweekly. Circ. 825,000. Accepts previously published material. Returns original artwork after publication upon request. Sample copy available, with SASE.
Cartoons: Publishes 3/issue. Seeks humor on soaps, drama or TV. Accepts single or double panel with or without gagline; b&w line drawings, b&w washes. Send query letter to managing editor with samples of style to be kept on file. Material not filed is returned by SASE. Pays $50, b&w; on publication.
Illustrations: Buys 2 illustrations/issue from freelancers. Works on assignment only. Prefers humor and caricatures. Send query letter with brochure showing art style or resume, tear sheets and photocopies to be kept on file. Call to schedule an appointment to show a portfolio, which should include original/final art and tear sheets. Negotiates rights purchased. Pays $200-300 for b&w and $300-500 for color, inside; on publication. All original artwork is returned after publication.
Tips: "Familiarize yourself with the magazine before submitting your samples. They should be relevant to our topics and styles."

SOCIAL POLICY, 33 W. 42nd St., New York NY 10036. (212)840-7619. Managing Editor: Audrey Gartner. Emphasizes the human services—education, health, mental health, self-help, consumer educa-

tion, neighborhood movement, employment. For social action leaders, academics, social welfare practitioners. Quarterly. Circ. 5,000. Accepts simultaneous submissions. Original artwork returned after publication. Sample copy $2.50.
Cartoons: Accepts b&w only, "with social consciousness." Sometimes uses humorous illustrations; often uses cartoon-style illustrations. Call for appointment to show portfolio. Reports only if interested. Buys one-time rights. Pays on publication.
Illustrations: Buys 4-6 illustrations/issue from freelancers. Accepts b&w only, "with social consciousness." Send query letter and tear sheets to be kept on file. Call for appointment to show portfolio, which should include original/final art, final reproduction/product, tear sheets and b&w. Reports only if interested. Buys one-time rights. Pays $100, cover; $25, b&w, inside. Pays on publication.
Tips: When reviewing an artist's work, looks for "sensitivity to the subject matter being illustrated."

SOLDIERS MAGAZINE, Cameron Station, Alexandria VA 22304-5050. (202)274-6671. Editor-in-Chief: Lt. Col. Donald Maple. Lighter Side Compiler: Thomas Kiddoo. Provides "timely and factual information on topics of interest to members of the Active Army, Army National Guard, Army Reserve and Department of Army civilian employees." Monthly. Circ. 250,000. Previously published material and simultaneous submissions OK. Samples available upon request.
Cartoons: Purchases approximately 60 cartoons/year. Should be single panel with gagline. Prefers military and general audience humor. Submit work; reports within 3 weeks. Buys all rights. Pays $25/cartoon on acceptance.
Tips: "We are actively seeking new ideas, fresh humor and looking for new talent—people who haven't been published before. We recommend a review of back issues before making submission. Issues available upon request. Remember that we are an inhouse publication—anti-Army humor, sexist or racist material is totally unacceptable."

SOLIDARITY MAGAZINE, Published by United Auto Workers, 8000 E. Jefferson, Detroit MI 48214. (313)926-5291. Editor: David Elsila. "1.5 million member trade union representing U.S. and Canadian workers in auto, aerospace, agricultural-implement and other industries."
Illustrations: Works with 10-12 artists/year for illustrations. Uses artists for posters and magazine illustrations. Interested in graphic designs of publications, topical art for magazine covers with liberal-labor political slant. Especially needs illustrations for articles on unemployment, economy. Prefers Detroit-area artists, but not essential. Looks for "ability to grasp publication's editorial slant" when reviewing artist's work. Send query letter with resume, flyer and/or tear sheet. Samples to be kept on file. Pays $75/small b&w spot illustration; up to $400 for color covers; $400+/designing small pamphlet.

***SONOMA BUSINESS MAGAZINE**, Box 2525, Santa Rosa CA 95405. Art Director: Candi Cohen. Bimonthly. Tabloid emphasizing business with very local editorial content. Relates to business owners in Sonoma County. Circ. 12,000. Accepts previously published material. Returns original artwork after publication. Sample copy $3.50 with 12x9 SASE. Art guidelines not available.
Illustrations: Buys 3-6 illustrations/issue from freelancers. Works on assignment only. Send query letter with brochure. Samples are filed. Reports back only if interested. Write to schedule an appointment to show a portfolio, which should include original/final art, tear sheets, final reproduction/product, b&w and color. Buys one-time rights. Pays $25, b&w; $75, color, cover; $100, b&w; $200, color, inside; on acceptance.
Tips: "Keep trying. Must be well-drawn, clever, and we usually buy b&w."

SOUTH CAROLINA WILDLIFE, Box 167, Columbia SC 29202. (803)758-0001. Editor: John Davis. Art Director: Linda Laffitte. Deals with wildlife, outdoor recreation, natural history and environmental concerns. Bimonthly. Circ. 70,000. Previously published work OK. Sample copy and guidelines available.
Illustrations: Uses 10-20 illustrations/issue. Interested in wildlife art; all media; b&w line drawings, washes, full-color illustrations. "Particular need for natural history illustrations of good quality. They must be technically accurate." Subject matter must be appropriate for South Carolina. Prefers to see finished art, portfolio, samples of style, slides, or transparencies. Send resume, brochure, or flyer to be kept on file. SASE. Reports in 2-8 weeks. Acquires one-time rights. Does not buy art; accepts donations.
Tips: "We are interested in unique illustrations—something that would be impossible to photograph. Make sure proper research has been done and that the art is technically accurate."

SOUTH FLORIDA HOME BUYERS GUIDE, (formerly South Florida Living Magazine), Suite 300, 251 W. Hillsboro Blvd., Deerfield Beach FL 33442. (305)428-5602. Managing Editor: Dee Krams. Emphasizes real estate (new developments) and is directed to newcomers to South Florida; homebuyers. Bimonthly. Circ. 80,000. Accepts previously published material. Does not return original artwork after publication. Sample copy available.

© Steve Doty

Art director Candi Cohen commissioned freelance artist Steve Doty of Santa Rosa, California, to do this illustration for a story on city leadership in* Sonoma Business. *The piece, done in colored pencil and ink, conveys "the non-menacing strength in city leadership." Cohen, who purchased one-time rights, learned of Doty through word of mouth and says he "follows my directions and thinks for himself."

Cartoons: Send query letter with samples of style to be kept on file. Material not filed is returned by SASE. Reports within 1 month. Write for appointment to show portfolio. Buys first rights. Negotiates payment; pays on acceptance.
Illustrations: Buys "a few" illustrations/issue from freelancers. Works on assignment only. Send query letter with samples to be kept on file. Write for appointment to show portfolio. Prefers tear sheets or photographs as samples. Samples not filed are returned by SASE. Reports within 1 month. Buys first rights. Negotiates payment; pays on acceptance.

SOUTHERN GRAPHICS, Box 2028, 410 W. Verona St., Kissimmee FL 32742. (305)846-2800. Editor and Publisher: Ray Cody. Emphasizes news events and developments in the graphic arts industry. For commercial printing plant management in 14 southern states. Monthly. Circ. 10,000. Previously published work OK. Sample copy $1.25.
Cartoons: Buys cartoons on printing industry; single panel with gagline. Mail finished art. SASE. Reports in 4 weeks. Negotiates payment.
Illustrations: Send query letter with previously published work. Uses 4-color cover design. SASE. Reports in 4 weeks.

SOUTHERN MOTOR CARGO, Box 40169, Memphis TN 38104. Contact: Thomas R. Stone. For trucking management and maintenance personnel of private, contract and for-hire carriers in 16 southern states (Alabama, Arkansas, Delaware, Florida, Georgia, Kentucky, Louisana, Maryland, Mississippi, North Carolina, Oklahoma, South Carolina, Tennessee, Texas, Virginia and West Virginia) and the Disrict of Columbia. Special issues include "ATA Conventions," October; "Transportation Graduate Directory," February. Monthly. Circ. 56,000.
Cartoons: Buys various cartoons/issue on truck management situations. "Stay away from stereotyped 'truckin' on' theme." Mail roughs. Pays $20, b&w; on publication. SASE. Reports in 6 weeks.

***SOUTHWEST DIGEST**, 510 E. 23rd St., Lubbock TRX 79404. (806)762-3612. Co-Publisher-Managing Editor: Eddie P. Richardson. Newspaper emphasizing positive black images, and community building and rebuilding "primarily oriented to the black community and basically reflective of the black community, but serving all people." Weekly. Accepts previously published material. Original work returned after publication.
Cartoons: Number of cartoons purchased/issue from freelancers varies. Prefers economic development, community development, community pride and awareness, and black uplifting themes. Single, double or multi-panel with gagline; b&w line drawings. Send query letter with samples of style, roughs or finished cartoons to be kept on file. Write or call for appointment to show portfolio. Material not filed returned by SASE only if requested. Buys first, one-time, reprint, or all rights; or negotiates rights purchased. Pays on publication.
Illustrations: Send query letter with brochure or samples to be kept on file. Write or call for appointment to show portfolio which should include Photostats, tear sheets, photocopies, photographs, etc. as samples. Samples not filed returned by SASE only if requested. Reports only if interested. Negotiates rights purchased. Pays on publication.

SOYBEAN DIGEST, Box 41309, 777 Craig Rd., St. Louis MO 63141-1309. (314)432-1600. Editor: Gregg Hillyer. Concerns agricultural and ag-business, specifically soybean production and marketing. Audience: high-acreage soybean growers. Monthly except semi-monthly in February and March, bimonthly in June/July and August/September. Circ. 200,000. Previously published work OK. Original artwork returned after publication. Sample copy $3.
Cartoons and Illustrations: Buys maximum 6 cartoons/year and 3 illustrations/year on agriculture, soybean production and marketing. Send query letter or original art. SASE. Reports in 2-3 weeks. Buys all rights, but may reassign rights to artist after publication.

SPACE AND TIME, 4B, 138 W. 70th St., New York NY 10023-4432. Editor: Gordon Linzner. Emphasizes fantasy and science fiction stories. "Readers are sf/fantasy fans looking for an alternative to the newsstand magazines." Biannually. Circ. 450. Original artwork returned after publication. Sample copy $4.
Cartoons: Buys 1-2 cartoons/issue from freelancers. Considers sf/fantasy themes—any style. Prefers single panel with or without gagline; b&w line drawings. Send finished cartoons to be kept on file if accepted for publication. Material not filed is returned by SASE. Reports within 3 months. Buys first rights. Pays $2, b&w; on acceptance.
Illustrations: Buys 20-25 illustrations from freelancers. Assigns themes or styles illustrating specific stories. "We use all styles, but could use more representational material." Works on assignment only. Send query letter with brochure showing art style. Samples not filed are returned by SASE. Reports within 3 months. To show a portfolio, mail original/final art, Photostats and b&w. Buys first rights. Pays $2, b&w, inside; on acceptance.

SPACE WORLD MAGAZINE, Suite 203 W. 600 Maryland Ave. SW, Washington DC 20024. (202)484-1111. Editor: Tony Reichhardt. Feature magazine popularizing and advancing space exploration for the general public interested in all aspects of space program.
Needs: Works with 15-20 freelance artist/year. Uses for magazine illustration. "We are looking for original artwork on space themes, either conceptual or representing specific designs, events, etc."
First Contact & Terms: Send query letter with photographs to Kate McMains, editorial assistant. "Color prints are best." Samples not filed are returned by SASE. Reports back within 1 month. Pays for illustration by the project, $25-50. "We do not generally commission original art. These fees are for one-time reproduction of existing artwork. Considers rights purchased when establishing payment.
Tips: "We know there are a lot of talented 'space artists' out there. Give us a chance to showcase your work."

SPECTRUM STORIES, Box 58367, Louisville KY 40258. Editor: Walter Gammons. Emphasizes short stories, poems of science fiction, fantasy, experimental and horror and suspense; interviews, essays for a mostly well-educated professional adult audience. Quarterly. Circ. 2,500-3,000. Accepts previously published art only. Original artwork returned after publication. Sample copy $5.45; art guidelines for

SASE with 50¢ postage.
Cartoons: Buys 4 cartoons/issue from freelancers. Science fiction, science, high-tech, writing, publishing (small press angle), fantasy and horror (no gore) themes. Prefers single panel with gagline; b&w line drawings. Send query letter with samples of style or finished cartoons to be kept on file. Material not filed is returned by SASE only if requested. Reports within 2 months. Buys first rights. Pays $5-15, b&w; on publication.
Illustrations: Buys 12 illustrations/issue from freelancers. Prefers science fiction, fantasy, horror and experimental themes. Send query letter with resume, Photostats, slides or photographs to be kept on file. Samples not filed are returned by SASE only if requested. Reports within 2 months. Buys first rights. Pays $50-75, b&w and $75-100, color, cover; $10-25, b&w and $50, color, inside; on publication.
Tips: Include SASE with queries. Don't send samples you want returned. "We want samples to keep in our files."

SPITBALL, the Literary Baseball Magazine, 6224 Collegevue Pl., Cincinnati OH 45224. (513)541-4296. Editor: Mike Shannon. Magazine emphasizing baseball exclusively, for well-educated, literate baseball fans. Quarterly. Accepts previously published material. Returns original artwork after publication if the work is donated; does not return if purchases work. Sample copy $1; art guidelines for SASE with first-class postage.
Cartoons: "We have never used cartoons, but are open to using them in the future." Prefers single panel without gagline, b&w line drawings. Query with samples of style, roughs and finished cartoons. Samples not filed are returned by SASE. Reports back within 1 week. Negotiates rights purchased.
Illustrations: We need three types of art: cover work, illustration (for a story, essay or poem), and filler. All must be b&w ink. Sometimes we assign the cover piece on a particular subject; sometimes we just use a drawing we like. Interested artists should write to set out needs for future covers and specific illustration." Buys 3 or 4 illustration/issue. Send query letter with original b&w illustrations. Samples not filed are returned by SASE. Reports back within 1 week. To show a portfolio, mail appropriate materials. Negotiates rights purchased. Pays $10 minimum; on acceptance.

***SPLAT!**, Box 931389, Hollywood CA 90093. Editor: Tom Mason. Estab. 1987. "*SPLAT!* is a magazine of cartoon humor for people who like to laugh. Each issue features comics and cartoons on a variety of subjects—everyday life, science fiction, funny animals—by cartoonists from the United States, Canada, England, France, and Australia." Monthly. Circ. 20,000. Original artwork returned after publication. Sample copy $2. Art guidelines for SASE with first-class postage.
Cartoons: Send query letter with 2-3 published or unpublished humorous strips 1-8 pages in length. Samples are filed. Samples not filed are returned by SASE. Reports back within 2 weeks. Pays $50/page for a complete story. Pays on publication.

SPORTING CLASSICS, Box 1017, Camden SC 29290. (803)425-1003. Design Director: Duncan Grant. Magazine emphasizing outdoor sports such as hunting and fishing for "sophisticated, educated high-income, well-traveled sportsmen" who love art, decoys, collect guns, knives, etc. Circ. 85,000. Accepts previously published material. Original artwork returned after publication. Sample copy for SASE with 80¢ postage.
Illustrations: Uses 10-15 illustrations/issue. Works on assignment only. Prefers sporting, wildlife, outdoor, hunting and fishing themes. Send query letter with brochure showing art style or samples, tear sheets, Photostats, photocopies, slides and photographs. Reports only if interested. Write to schedule an appointment to show a portfolio, which should include color, tear sheets and photographs. Buys one-time rights. Pays $500, b&w and $1,200, color, cover; $50-250, b&w and $250-1,000, color, inside on publication.

SPORTS AFIELD MAGAZINE, 250 W. 55th St., New York NY 10019. (212)262-8839. Art Director: Gary Gretter. Magazine emphasizing outdoor activities—fishing, hunting and camping. Monthly. Circ. 600,000. Does not accept previously published material. Returns original artwork after publication.
Illustrations: Buys 2-3/issue. Works on assignment only. Send query letter with samples to be kept on file except for material not of interest. Prefers slides as samples. Samples not filed are returned by SASE. Call for appointment to show portfolio. Buys first rights or negotiates rights purchased. Pays $1,000 spread, color.

STARWIND, Box 98, Ripley OH 45167. Contact: Editor. Emphasizes science fiction, fantasy and nonfiction of scientific and technological interest. Quarterly. Circ. 2,500. Sample copy $3.50; art guidelines for SASE.
Cartoons: Buys 5-8 cartoons/issue from freelancers. Interested in science fiction and fantasy subjects. Format: single and multi panel b&w line drawings. Prefers finished cartoons. SASE. Reports in 6-8

weeks. Buys first North American serial rights. Pays on publication.
Illustrations: Uses 10-15 illustrations/issue. Sometimes uses humorous and cartoon-style illustrations depending on the type of work being published. Works on assignment only. Samples returned by SASE. Reports back on future assignment possibilities. Send resume or brochure and samples of style to be kept on file for future assignments. Illustrates stories rather extensively (normally an 8x11 and an interior illustration). Format: b&w line drawings (pen & ink and similar media). SASE. Reports in 6-8 weeks. Buys first North American rights. Pays for cover; on publication.
Tips: "We first of all look for work that falls into science fiction genre; if an artist has a feel for and appreciation of science fiction he/she is more likely to be able to meet our needs. We look to see that the artist can do well what he/she tried to do—for example, draw the human figure well. We are especially attracted to work that is clean and spare, not cluttered, and that has a finished, not sketchy quality."

STEREO REVIEW, 1515 Broadway, New York NY 10036. (212)719-6007. Art Director: Sue Llewellyn. Emphasizes audio technology, and classical and rock music. Monthly. Circ. 675,000.
Illustrations: Uses about 3-4 illustrations/issue. We are always looking for new and creative talent." Mostly 4-color art, any medium. Send samples of style or promotional cards. SASE. Pays by the project, $200 minimum. Buys one-time rights and negotiates any further use.
Tips: "Call for appointment or drop off any Thursday to show portfolio." Looks for "the ability to conceptualize a difficult idea and a clean expecution of that idea. Ideally, about 15-20 pieces is enough in a portfolio"

STERLING MAGAZINE, 355 Lexington Ave., New York NY 10017. Art Director: Larry Matthews. Magazine emphasizing sports, music and black romance for people interested in sports, ages 13-30; music, ages 13-17; black romance, ages 16-20. Monthly. Circ. 160,000. Original artwork returned after publication. Sample copy and art guidelines available.
Cartoons: Write for appointment to show a portfolio. Material not kept on file is returned by SASE. Buys all rights.
Illustrations: Send query letter with brochure showing art style or samples. Samples not filed are returned by SASE. Reports only if interested. Call or write to schedule an appointment to show a portfolio, which should include roughs, original/final art, final reproduction/product and color. Buys first or one-time rights. Pays $250, color, cover; on acceptance.

STICKERS & STUFF, Rm 1300, 10 Columbus Circle, New York NY 10019. (212)541-7300. Design Director: Altemus. Magazine for children 6-13. Quarterly. Circ. 200,000. Accepts previously published material. Returns original artwork after publication.
Illustrations: Buys 5-10 illustrations/issue. Works on assignment only. Prefers stylized, graphic, light styles. Send tear sheets. Samples not filed are returned by SASE. Does not report back. To show a portfolio, mail appropriate materials or call to schedule an appointment; portfolio should include tear sheets and Photostats. Buys first rights. Pays $300, b&w and $300, color, cover; $75, b&w and $100, color, inside; on publication.

***STOCK CAR RACING MAGAZINE**, Box 715, Ipswich MA 90138. Editor: Dick Berggren. For stock car racing, fans and competitors. Monthly. Circ. 120,000.
Cartoons: Uses 4 cartoons/issue; all from freelancers. Receives 4 cartoons from freelancers/week. Interested in cartoons pertaining to racing. Format: single or multipanel b&w line drawings with gag line. Prefers samples of style or finished cartoons. SASE. Reports in 2 weeks. Buys all rights. Pays $20-35 on publication.
Illustrations: Number of illustrations/issue varies. Format: b&w line drawings. Prefers finished art. SASE. Buys all rights. Pays on publication.

STONE COUNTRY, Box 132, Menemsha MA 02552. Editor-in-Chief: Judith Neeld. Art Editor: Pat McCormick. Submit to 69 Central Ave., Madison NJ 07940. For serious poets and poetry supporters. Published 2 times/year. Circ. 800. Previously published artwork OK. Sample copy $3.50; $2.50 for tear sheets and sample covers (postage included).
Illustrations: Uses 2 covers/year and 6-7 illustrations/issue. Receives 1 illustration/month from freelance artists. Must be camera-ready. Cover design should fit 5½x8½, "no lettering" inside drawings no larger than 3x4. Interested in b&w drawings only, no washes or pencil shading; to achieve shading, use fine b&w lines. Any style or theme; size is important. "We are interested in abstract as well as from-nature representational work. Rarely use the human form or face on a cover. Art students welcome." Send query letter with brochure showing art style or resume, tear sheets, Photostats and photocopies, "submit completed work directly to art editor." Reports in 6-8 weeks. "We don't view portfolios." Buys first North American serial rights. Cover: Pays $15, b&w; on publication. Inside: Pays 1 contributor's copy, b&w.

Tips: "Send original graphics directly to art editor with SASE. Or, to save both of us if the work isn't what we look for, order samples through general editor."

STONE IN AMERICA, 6902 N. High St., Worthington OH 43085. (614)885-2713. Managing Editor: Robert Moon. Journal of the American Monument Association; deals with design, marketing and sales of memorial stones. Circ. 2,600. Monthly. Reports in 4 weeks. Buys first rights. Pays on acceptance. Free sample copy.

***STONE SOUP, The Magazine by Children**, Box 83, Santa Cruz CA 95063. (408)426-5557. Editor: Gerry Mandel. Literary magazine emphasizing writing and art by children up to age 13. Features adventure, ethnic, experimental, fantasy, humorous and science fiction articles. "We publish writing and art by children up to age 13. We look for artwork that reveals that the artist is closely observing his or her world." Bimonthly. Circ. 9,000. Original artwork is sometimes returned after publication. Sample copies available. Art guidelines for SASE with first-class postage.
Illustrations: Buys 5 illustrations/issue from freelancers. Complete and detailed scenes from real life. Send query letter with Photostats, photocopies, slides and photographs. Samples are filed. Samples not filed are returned by SASE. Reports back within 2 months. Buys all rights. Pays $10, b&w; $10, color, inside; on acceptance.
Tips: "We accept artwork by children only, up to age 13."

THE SUN, 412 W. Rosemary, Chapel Hill NC 27514. (919)942-5282. Editor: Sy Safransky. Magazine of ideas. Monthly. Circ. 5,000. Accepts previously published material. Original artwork returned after publication. Sample copy $3. Art guidelines free for SASE with first-class postage.
Cartoons: Buys various cartoons/issue from freelancers. Send finished cartoons. Material not kept on file is returned by SASE. Reports within 1 month. Buys first rights. Pays $5 and up, b&w; plus copies and subscription.
Illustrations: Buys various illustrations/issue from freelancers. Works on assignment only. Send query letter with samples. Samples not filed are returned by SASE. Reports within 1 month. To show a portfolio, mail appropriate materials. Buys first rights. Pays $5 and up; plus copies and subscription. Pays on publication.

THE SUNDAY OREGONIAN'S NORTHWEST MAGAZINE, 1320 SW Broadway, Portland OR 97201. (503)221-8235. Graphic Coordinator: Kevin Murphy. Magazine emphasizing stories with Northwest orientation for aged 25-45 and upwardly mobile people. Weekly. Circ. 430,000. Original artwork returned after publication. Sample copy for SASE.
Illustrations: Buys 2 illustrations/issue from freelancers. Works on assignment only. Send query letter with brochure showing art style or resume and slides. Samples not filed are returned only if requested. Reports only if interested. Call or write to schedule an appointment to show a portfolio, which should include original/final art, color, photographs and slides. Buys first or one-time rights. Negotiates payment. Pays on publication.

SURFING MAGAZINE, 2720 Camino Capistrano, San Clemente CA 92672. Managing Art Director: Dave Vecker. Magazine emphasizing surfing. Monthly. Circ. 115,000. Original artwork returned after publication.
Illustrations: Buys 1 illustration/issue from freelancers. Works on assignment only. Send query letter with brochure showing art style or resume, tear sheets, slides and photographs. Samples not filed are returned by SASE. Reports within 3 weeks. Call or write to schedule an appointment to show a portfolio, which should include roughs, original/final art, final reproduction/product, color and photographs. Buys reprint rights. Pays on publication.

***SWIFTSURE**, 33 Chester Rd., Northwood, Middlesex HA6 1BG England. Editor: Martin Lock. Estab. 1985. Publishes comic books. Genres: adventure, fantasy and science fiction. Themes: outer space and social commentary. "*Swiftsure* is SF-based series/anthology title, aimed at comics readers who go beyond superhero comics." Bimonthly. Circ. 6,700. Original artwork returned after publication. Sample copy $1.
Illustrations: Uses three-tier page of 6 panels, vertical panels, horizontal panels, inset panels, borderless panels and circular panels. Uses freelance artists for inking, lettering, pencilling and covers. Send query letter with photocopies only. Samples are filed. Samples not filed are returned by a SAE (nonresidents include IRC). Reports back within 2 months. To show a portfolio, mail photocopies of original pencil art or inking reduced to 8½x11 of display pieces, action continuity, and lettering. Buys first rights. Payment is on profit-sharing basis, based on actual print order. Pays minimum $12/page for pencilling, $7/page for inking and $2-50 for lettering. Pays on publication.

***TEACHING AND COMPUTERS, SCHOLASTIC, INC.**, 730 Broadway, New York NY 10003. Art Editor: Shelley Laroche. Emphasizes teaching K-8th grade with computers for teachers and students. Monthly. Circ. 65,000. Accepts previously published material. Original artwork returned after publication. Sample copy and art guidelines available.
Cartoons: Buys 4 cartoons/issue from freelancers. Themes, style and format open. Send query letter with samples of styles to be kept on file; write for appointment to show portfolio or drop off portfolio. Material not filed is returned only if requested. Reports only if interested. Buys first rights or one-time rights depending on job. Payment open; pays on acceptance.
Illustrations: Buys 10-12 illustrations/issue from freelancers. Works on assignment only. Send query letter with brochure, resume, business card and samples to be kept on file; write for appointment to show portfolio. Prefers tear sheets or photographs as samples. Samples not filed are returned only if requested. Reports only if interested. Buys one-time rights. Payment open, b&w and color, inside; pays on acceptance.

TECHNOLOGY REVIEW, Massachusetts Institute of Technology, Cambridge MA 02139. (617)253-8255. Design Director: Nancy L. Cahners. Design Manager: Kathleen Sayre. Emphasizes technology and its implications. Published 8 times/year. Circ. 80,000. Accepts previously published material and simultaneous submissions. Original artwork returned after publication. Sample copy $3; art guidelines available.
Illustrations: Uses 10+ illustrations/issue; buys all from freelancers. Works on assignment only. Send query letter with brochure, resume, business card, samples and tear sheets to be kept on file. Prefers tear sheets or facsimile as samples. Samples not kept on file are returned by SASE. Reports only if interested. Call or write for appointment to show portfolio. Buys one-time rights. Pays on publication.

'TEEN, Petersen Publishing Co., 8490 Sunset Blvd., Los Angeles CA 90069. (213)854-2222. Art Director: Laurel Finnerty. Deals with self-development for girls 12-19. Circ. 1,000,000.
Illustrations: Buys 2-3 illustrations/issue for fiction, fashion and beauty sections. Contact only through artist's agent or send query letter with brochure showing art style or tear sheets, slides and photographs. Works on assignment only. Will see artists and photographers with finished and professional portfolios. Call to schedule an appointment to show a portfolio, which should include original/final art, final reproduction/product, color, tear sheets, photographs and b&w. Buys all rights. Pays $25-150, b&w and $150-250, color, inside; on acceptance. Other assignments are negotiable.
Tips: "Youth today are more involved and the keyword is *active*. Prefer youthful upbeat look. We're appealing to an audience that is bright, young and active."

TENNIS, 5520 Park Ave., Trumbull CT 06611. (203)373-7000. Contact: Art Director. For young, affluent tennis players. Monthly. Circ. 500,000.
Cartoons: Buys 3 cartoons/issue from freelancers. Receives 6 submissions/week from freelancers on tennis. Prefers finished cartoons, single panel. Reports in 2 weeks. Pays $75, b&w.
Illustrations: Buys 5 illustrations/issue from freelancers. Works on assignment only. Send query letter with tear sheets. To show a portfolio, mail appropriate materials or call to schedule an appointment; portfolio should include original/final art, final reproduction/product, color, tear sheets and photographs. Pays $400, color; on acceptance.
Tips: "There is a return to clean design, strong images, and purer color. I use illustrations whose work reflects these elements. They should first look through an issue of the magazine to make sure their style is appropriate for us."

***TENNIS BUYER'S GUIDE**,5520 Park Ave., Trumbull CT 06611. (203)373-7000. Executive Editor/Associate Publisher: Nick Romano. Art Director: Nancy Graham. Magazine emphasizing the tennis retailing industry. Bimonthly. Circ. 12,000.
Illustrations: Buys 4-6 illustrations/issue from freelancers. Works on assignment only. Soft goods oriented. Illustrations often used for conceptual pieces. Send query letter with brochure or tear sheets, slides and photographs. Reports back within 2 weeks. Call to schedule an appointment to show a portfolio, which should include: thumbnails, roughs, original/final art, tear sheets, final reproduction/product, color and b&w. Buys one-time reproduction rights on a work-for-hire basis. Pays $50-750; on acceptance.

***TEXAS ARCHITECT**, 1400 Norwood Tower, Austin TX 78701. Managing Editor: Charles Gallatin. Emphasizes architecture for architects, urban planners, developers, government officials, libraries. Bimonthly. Circ. 10,000. Returns original artwork after publication. Sample copy $3 plus 50¢ postage.
Illustrations: Works on assignment only. Send query letter with samples to be kept on file. Prefers Photostats as samples. Samples not filed are returned. Reports within 2 weeks. Buys first rights. Pays on publication.

THE TEXAS OBSERVER, 600 W. 28th, Austin TX 78705. (512)477-0746. Contact: Art Director. Emphasizes Texas political, social and literary topics. Biweekly. Circ. 12,000. Accepts previously published material. Returns original artwork after publication. Sample copy for SASE with 39¢ postage; art guidelines for SASE with 22¢ postage.
Illustrations: Buys 2 illustrations/issue from freelancers. "We only print black and white, so pen & ink is best, washes are fine." Send Photostats, tear sheets, photocopies, slides or photographs to be kept on file. Samples not filed are returned by SASE. Reports within 1 month. Write or call for appointment to show portfolio. Buys one-time rights. Pays $35 for b&w cover; $20, inside; on publication.

***TFR—THE FREELANCERS' REPORT**, Box 93, Poquonock CT 06064. (203)688-5496. Editor: Pat McDonald. Estab 1986. Monthly magazine emphasizing freelancing writers (all genres), illustrators and photographers. Circ. 200 at first issue Jan '87. Accepts previously published material. Returns original artwork to the artist after publication if requested. Sample copy for SASE with 56¢ postage.
Cartoons: Buys 3 cartoons/issue from freelancers. Buys 36 cartoons/year from freelancers. Prefers gag cartoons, caricatures and humorous illustrations. Prefers single panel, with gagline; b&w line drawings. Send finished cartoons. Samples not filed are returned by SASE only if requested by artist. Reports back within 60 days. Buys first rights or reprint rights. Pays $5-10 (½ fee for reprints).
Illustrations: Buys 3 illustrations/issue from freelancers. Buys 36 illustrations/year from freelancers. Prefers anything b&w which appeals to us and can be reproduced clearly by a quality photocopier. Send samples. Samples not filed are returned by SASE if requested. Reports back within 60 days. To show a portfolio, mail final reproduction/product, tear sheets, b&w and clear photocopies of original. Buys first rights or reprint rights. Pays $5-10 b&w; $30, cover; on publication.
Tips: "Contact us by letter with actual submission, clear photocopies suggested. Queries discouraged due to small overworked staff."

***THRESHOLD (Nomad Press)**, 10055 Vista Ct., Myersville MD 21773. (301)293-2829. Editor: Brian Clopper. Publishes comic books. Titles include "Threshold." Genres: adventure, fantasy, mystery, science fiction, horror and social parodies. Themes: outer space, future science, social commentary, alternative lifestyle, family situations and teenage exploits. "Threshold is an anthology book of various stories. Comics can be from any genre and can be ongoing or complete in one installment. The book will present three to four stories an issue. We plan to reach the direct sales more adult clientele." Quarterly. Original artwork returned after publication. Art guidelines available.
Illustrations: Uses three-tier page of 6 panels, vertical panels, horizontal panels, inset panels, borderless panels and double-page spreads. Uses freelance artists for inking, lettering, penciling and covers. Send query letter with resume and 3 pages of work. Samples are filed. Samples not filed are returned by SASE. Reports back within 1 month. Call or write to schedule an appointment to show a portfolio, which should include 3 pages of pencil or ink drawings one-and-one-half times up, 2 pages of action continuity; 2 photocopies of original pencil art or ink and 2 pages of lettering one-and-one-half times up with sound effects, titles and display lettering. Buys publishing rights only. Payment is a percentage of the profits/page, usually ½ percent/page penciled, $25-30/page average; on publication.
Tips: "The work should be of top quality and also should show intense knowledge of layout skills. A must for any comic book, the artist should have a thorough knowledge of pacing and storytelling as well. Many times the work isn't polished enough and many of the backgrounds are left empty, giving no sense of placement."

THRUST—Science Fiction & Fantasy Review, 8217 Langport Terrace, Gaithersburg MD 20877. Publisher/Editor: D. Douglas Fratz. Emphasizes science fiction and fantasy literature for highly knowledgeable science fiction professionals and well-read fans. Quarterly. Circ. 1,800. Accepts previously published material. Returns original artwork after publication. Sample copy $2.50. Art guidelines for SASE with first-class postage.
Cartoons: Buys 1-2/issue from freelance artists. Themes must be related to science fiction or fantasy. Prefers single panel; b&w line drawings. Send query letter with samples of style to be kept on file unless SASE included. Reports within 4 weeks. Buys one-time rights. Pays $2-4, b&w; on publication.
Illustrations: Buys 9-10/issue from freelance artists. Science fiction or fantasy themes only. Send query letter with tear sheets, Photostats or photocopies to be kept on file unless SASE included. Accepts any style. Samples not filed are returned by SASE. Reports within 4 weeks. To show a portfolio, mail appropriate materials, which should include original/final art, final reproduction/product, tear sheets and b&w. Buys one-time rights. Pays $25, b&w, cover; and $15/page, b&w, inside; on publication.

***TODAY'S FIREMAN**, Box 875108, Los Angeles CA 90087. Editor: Don Mack. Trade journal emphasizing the fire service. Features general interest, humor and technical articles. "Readers are firefighters—items should be of interest to the fire service." Quarterly. Circ. 10,000. Accepts previously published material. Original artwork is not returned after publication.

Cartoons: Prefers single panel with gagline; b&w line drawings. Send query letter with samples of style, roughs or finished cartoons. Reports back only if interested. Buys one-time rights. Pays $4.

TODAY'S POLICEMAN, Box 875108, Los Angeles CA 90087. Editor: Don Mack. For persons employed in and interested in police services. Semiannualy. Circ. 10,000.
Cartoons: Buys 6 cartoons/issue dealing with law enforcement and politics. Send finished art. SASE. Pays $2.50 for b&w.

TOURIST ATTRACTIONS AND PARKS, Suite 226, 401 N. Broad St., Philadelphia PA 19108. (215)925-9744. President: Scott Borowsky. Deals with arenas, attractions, fairgrounds, stadiums, concerts, theme and amusement parks. Published 6 times/year. Circ. 20,000. Also uses freelance artists for cover, layout and paste-up (each issue). Pays $7-8/hour for paste-up.
Illustrations: Buys 6/issue. Send query letter with resume and samples. SASE. Buys all rights. Cover: Pays $50 minimum, gray opaques; on publication. Inside: Buys gray opaques.

TQ (TEEN QUEST), (formerly Young Ambassador), Box 82808, Lincoln NE 68501. (402)474-4567. Art Director: Victoria Valentine. "Our main purpose is to help Christian teens live consistently for Christ, and to help them grow in their knowledge of the Bible and its principles for living." Monthly. Circ. 80,000. Original artwork returned after publication. Free sample copy.
Cartoons: Managing Editor: Nancy Brumbaugh Bayne. Buys 2-3 cartoons/issue from freelancers. Receives 4 submissions/week from freelancers. Interested in wholesome humor for teens; prefer cartoons with teens as main characters; single panel. Prefers to see finished cartoons. Reports in 3 weeks. Buys first rights on a work-for-hire basis.
Illustrations: Some illustrations purchased on assignment only. Submit slides or tear sheets with query letter. Pays $150 color.

TRADITION, 106 Navajo, Council Bluffs IA 51501. Editor-in-Chief/Art Director: Robert Everhart. "For players and listeners of traditional and country music. We are a small, nonprofit publication and will use whatever is sent to us. A first time gratis use is the best way to establish communication." Monthly. Circ. 2,000. Simultaneous submissions and previously published work OK. Buys one-time rights. Free sample copy.
Cartoons: Buys 1/issue on country music; single panel with gagline. Receives 10-15 cartoons/week from freelance artists. Mail roughs. Pays $5-15, b&w line drawings; on publication.
Illustrations: Buys 1/issue on country music. Query with resume and samples. SASE. Cover: Pays $5-15, b&w line drawings. Inside: Pays $5-15, b&w line drawings; on publication. Reports in 4 weeks.
Tips: "We'd like to see an emphasis on traditional country music."

TRAINING: THE MAGAZINE OF HUMAN RESOURCES DEVELOPMENT, 50 S. Ninth St., Minneapolis MN 55402. Editor: Jack Gordon. Art Director: Jodi Scharff. Covers "job-related training and education in business and industry, both theory and practice." Audience: "training directors, personnel managers, sales and data processing managers, general managers, etc." Monthly. Circ. 51,000. Especially needs cartoons on adult education on the job. Original artwork returned after publication "on request." Sample copy $3 plus 9x11 SASE.
Cartoons: Buys 2-4 cartoons/issue from freelancers. Prefers b&w drawings that reproduce well. Samples not filed are returned by SASE only if requested. Reports in 4 weeks. Buys reprint rights. Pays $25, b&w, on acceptance.
Illustrations: Buys 2-6 illustrations/issue from freelancers. Send query letter with photocopies or Photostats to be kept on file. Call (612)333-0471 or write art director for appointment to show portfolio. Samples not filed are returned only if requested and only by SASE. Reports within 4 weeks. Buys reprint rights. Pays $300 and up for color, cover; $75-200 for b&w, inside; $250 for color, inside; on acceptance.

TRAVEL & LEISURE, 1120 6th Ave., New York NY 10036. (212)382-5600. Design/Art Director: Bob Ciano. Associate Art Directors: Ken Kleppert and Joan Ferrell. Emphasizes travel, resorts, dining and entertainment. Monthly. Circ. 1,000,000. Original artwork returned after publication. Art guidelines for SASE.
Illustrations: Uses 1-15 illustrations/issue, all from freelancers. Interested in travel and leisure related themes. "Illustrators are selected by excellence and relevance to the subject." Works on assignment only. Provide business card to be kept on file for future assignment; samples returned by SASE. Reports in 1 week. Buys World serial rights. Pays a minimum of $150 inside b&w and $800-1,500 maximum, inside color; on publication.

TROPIC MAGAZINE, The Miami Herald, 1 Herald Plaza, Miami FL 33101. (305)376-3397. Art Director: Philip Brooker. Emphasizes general (local) interests for Sunday newspaper magazine readers. Weekly. Circ. 555,000. Original artwork returned after publication. Sample copy for with SASE; art guidelines available.
Illustrations: Buys 0-2 illustrations/issue from freelancers. Works on assignment only. Send query letter with slides to be kept on file. Reports within 2 weeks. Call for appointment to show portfolio. Pays $300, b&w and $400-500, color, cover; $100-400, b&w and $400-500, color, inside; on acceptance.

TRUE WEST, Box 2107, Stillwater OK 74076. Editor: John Joerschke. Emphasizes American western history from 1830 to 1910 for a primarily rural and suburban audience, middle-age and older, interested in Old West history, horses, cowboys, art, clothing, and all things western. Monthly. Circ. 90,000. Accepts previously published material and considers some simultaneous submissions. Original artwork returned after publication. Sample copy and art guidelines for SASE.
Illustrations: Buys 5-10 illustrations/issue from freelancers. "Inside illustrations are usually, but not always pen & ink line drawings; covers are western paintings." Send query letter with samples to be kept on file; "we return anything on request." "For inside illustrations, we want samples of artist's line drawings. For covers, we need to see full-color transparencies." Reports within 30 days. Call or write for appointment to show portfolio. Buys one-time rights. Pays $75-150, for color transparency for cover; $15-40, b&w, inside; on acceptance.

TURTLE MAGAZINE FOR PRESCHOOL KIDS, 1100 Waterway Blvd., Box 567, Indianapolis IN 46206. (317)636-8881. Art Director: Lawrence Simmons. Emphasizes health, nutrition, exercise and safety for children 2-5 years. Monthly except bimonthly February/March, April/May, June/July and August/September. Accepts previously published material and simultaneous submissions. Original artwork not returned after publication. Sample copy 75¢; art guidelines for SASE.
Illustrations: Buys 15-30 illustrations/issue from freelancers. Interested in "stylized, humorous, realistic and cartooned themes; also nature and health." Especially needs b&w and 2-color artwork for line or halftone reproduction; full-color text and cover art. Works on assignment only. Send query letter with resume, stats or good photocopies, slides and tear sheets to be kept on file. Samples not kept on file returned by SASE. Reports only if interested. Buys all rights. To show a portfolio, mail final reproduction/product, color, tear sheets, b&w and 2-color. Pays $225, 4-color, cover; $25-100, b&w and 2-color and $60-125, 4-color, inside; on publication.
Tips: "Be sure to send in appropriate material for the magazine (example: do not send *New Yorker* illustrations for a children's magazine for ages 2-5)."

TV GUIDE, Radnor PA 19088. Cartoon Editor: M.E. Bilisnansky. Emphasizes news, personalities and programs of television for a general audience. Weekly. Query. Reports in 2 weeks. Buys all rights. Pays on acceptance.
Cartoons: Buys about 35 cartoons/year on TV themes. Pays $200, single cartoon. Also uses cartoons for editorial features. Line drawings and halftones. Buys only single panel cartoons. No cartoon strips.

TWIN CITIES, 7831 East Bush Lake Rd., Minneapolis MN 55435. (612)835-6855. Art Director: Kathleen Timmerman. Magazine emphasizing lifestyle and general local interest for upscale, wealthy, well-educated, men and women. Monthly. Circ. 48,000. Original artwork returned after publication. Sample copy $3.
Illustrations: Buys 2-6 illustrations/issue from freelancers. Works on assignment only. Prefers original styles that illuminate the editorial theme. Send query letter with resume, tear sheets and photocopies. Samples not filed are returned by SASE. Reports only if interested. Call to schedule an appointment to show a portfolio, which should include roughs, original/final art, final reproduction/product, color, tear sheets, Photostats, photographs and b&w. Buys one-time rights. Pays for design by the hour, $25-40. Pays for illustration by the project. $150-600.
Tips: "I look for uniqueness of style and prefer to see published editorial work. I think our readership is quite sophisticated and the illustrators we choose must appeal to a target group."

U MAGAZINE, Box 1450, Downers Grove IL 60515. (312)964-5700. Art Director: Kathy Burrows. Emphasizes editing for students on the college campus for Christian college students. Monthly during school year (7 issues—October through April/May). Accepts simultaneous submissions. Original artwork returned after publication. Sample copy and art guidelines available.
Cartoons: Buys cartoons from freelancers. Send query letter with samples of style. Write for appointment to show portfolio. Material not kept on file is returned. Reports within 1 month. Buys one-time rights. Pays $50-100, b&w; on acceptance.
Illustrations: Buys illustrations from freelancers. Usually works on assignment. Send query letter

with samples. Write for appointment to show portfolio. Prefers photostats as samples. Samples not kept on file are returned. Reports within 4 weeks. Buys one-time rights. Pays $250, b&w and color, cover; $175, b&w, inside; on acceptance.

THE UNITED METHODIST PUBLISHING HOUSE, Publishing Division, 201 Box 801, Eighth Ave. S, Nashville TN 37202. Art Procurement Supervisor: David Dawson. Publishes 60 + magazines, and church and home leaflets for ages 1½ years and up. Uses 30-40 illustrations/publication. Assigns 500-1,000 jobs/year.
First Contact & Terms: Works with 25-50 freelance artists/year. Seeks "artists with editorial and publishing experience. Also seeks artists of ethnic background—Korean, Hispanic and black." Works on assignment only. Send brochure showing art style or slides, Photostats, photographs and tear sheets to be kept on file. Samples not filed are returned only if requested. Reports only if interested. Considers complexity of project, skill and experience of artist, project's budget and rights purchased when establishing payment. Buys all rights.
Magazine Covers: Pays by the project, negotiable $250 minimum for full-color.
Magazine Text Illustration: Pays by the project, $15-50 for spot illustrations, $70-150 for full color.
Tips: "The ability to render the human figure is important, good graphic design is helpful, other kinds of illustrations considered; how-to, game boards, maizes, etc. If you feel professionally competent in any of these areas please, respond."

THE UNSPEAKABLE VISIONS OF THE INDIVIDUAL, Box 439, California PA 15419. Editors-in-Chief: Arthur and Kit Knight. For people with a better-than-average education interested in "beat" literature. Annually. Circ. 2,000. Sample copy $3.50.
Illustrations: Uses 3-6 illustrations/issue. Number illustrations/issue bought from freelancers varies. Receives 1 submission/month from freelancers. Interested in "beat" related themes, such as writers Jack Kerouac, William S. Burroughs, Allen Ginsberg, Gary Snyder and Carolyn Cassady. Prefers to see finished art. SASE. "Work without SASE will be destroyed." Reports in 2 weeks-2 months. Buys first North American serial rights. Pays 2 contributor's copies, minimum; $10 maximum; on publication.
Tips: "See a sample copy."

USA TODAY, 99 W. Hawthorne Ave., Valley Stream NY 11580. (516)568-9191. Contact: Bob Rothenberg. For intellectual college graduates. Monthly. Circ. 235,000. Free sample copy.
Illustrations: Buys 70-80 illustrations/year on assigned themes. Uses only New York artists in the metropolitan area. Send query letter with samples. SASE. Reports in 1 week. Buys all rights. Cover: pays $200, color. Inside: Pays $25-75, b&w line drawings; on publication.

VEGETARIAN TIMES, Box 570, Oak Park IL 60303. (312)848-8120. Art Director: Gregory Chambers. Consumer food magazine with emphasis on fitness and health for readers 30-50, 75% women. Monthly. Circ. 100,000. Accepts previously published material. Original artwork returned after publication. Sample copy $2.
Illustrations: Buys 4 illustrations/issue from freelancers. Send query letter with samples showing art style. To show a portfolio, mail appropriate materials or call to schedule an appointment; portfolio should include roughs, original/final art, color, tear sheets, photographs and b&w. Pays $30-300, inside; on publication.
Tips: "I work primarily with food/health-related topics, and look for someone who is familiar with or sympathetic to vegetarianism and whole foods cuisine.

VENTURE, Box 150, Wheaton IL 60189. (312)665-0630. Art Director: Lawrence Libby. For boys 10-15. "We seek to promote consciousness, acceptance of and personal commitment to Jesus Christ." Published 6 times/year. Circ. 25,000. Simultaneous submissions and previously published work OK. Original artwork returned after publication. Sample copy $1.50 with large SASE; artists' guidelines with SASE.
Cartoons: Send to attention of cartoon editor. Uses 1-3 cartoons/issue; buys all from freelancers. Receives 2 submissions/week from freelancers, on nature, sports, school, camping, hiking; single panel with gagline. "Keep it clean." Prefers finished cartoons. SASE. Reports in 2-4 weeks. Buys first-time rights. Pays $20 minimum, b&w line drawings; on acceptance.
Illustrations: Contact art director. Uses 3 illustrations/issue; buys 2/issue from freelancers, on education, family life and camping; b&w only. Works on assignment only. Send business card, tear sheets and photocopies of samples to be kept on file for future assignments. Samples returned by SASE. Reports back on future assignment possibilities. SASE. Reports in 2 weeks. Buys first time rights. Pays $100-150 for inside use of b&w line drawings and washes; on publication.

© Ned Shaw

Acrylics and airbrush were used by Ned Shaw of Bloomington, Indiana, to render this illustration for an article on nut butters in* Vegetarian Times. *Shaw sold one-time rights for $150. Art director Greg Chambers says Shaw is "very good with developing an initial rough idea and adding his own sense of humor. He is very aware of deadlines and is always concerned that the art is prepared in such a way that it will reproduce well." Shaw had originally sent samples to Chambers with a recommendation.

VERDICT MAGAZINE, 124 Truxtun Ave., Bakersfield CA 93301. (805)325-7124. Editor: Steve Walsh. Emphasizes law for insurance defense lawyers. Circ. 5,000. Accepts previously published material. Original artwork returned after publication. Sample copy for SASE with $3 postage; art guidelines for SASE with first-class postage.

Cartoons: Buys 4 cartoons/issue from freelancers. Legal theme. Prefers single panel with gagline; b&w line drawings or b&w washes. Send finished cartoons to be kept on file. Material not filed is returned by SASE. Reports only if interested. Buys one-time rights or reprint rights. Write for appointment to show portfolio. Pays $5, b&w; on publication.

Illustrations: Buys 4 illustrations/issue from freelancers. Theme: legal. Send Photostats, tear sheets or photocopies to be kept on file. Samples not filed are returned by SASE. Reports only if interested. Write for appointment to show portfolio. Buys one-time rights or reprint rights. Pays $10, color, cover; $5, b&w, inside; on publication.

VICTIMOLOGY: AN INTERNATIONAL JOURNAL, 5535 Lee Hwy., Arlington VA 22207. (703)536-1750. Editor-in-Chief: Emilio Viano. For professionals, lawyers, criminologists, medical personnel and others helping child/spouse abuse programs, hotlines, rape crisis centers and other victim programs. "By 'victim,' we mean not only those victimized by crime but earthquakes, the environment, accidents, pollution and the state." Quarterly. Circ. 2,500. Send query letter with samples. SASE. Reports in 4 weeks. Buys all rights. Pays on publication. Sample copy $5. Write to be put on mailing list to receive periodical announcements.
Illustrations: Buys several illustrations/year on victimization. "We like to see illustrations on what is done in behalf of the victim." Pays $200, color, cover; $100, b&w. Pays $30, b&w, inside. Pays $50 for brochure work.

VIDEOGRAPHY, 50 W. 23rd St., New York NY 10010. (212)645-1000. Art Director: Justine Charles. Audience is video professionals. Monthly. Circ. 25,000 +. Original artwork returned after publication.
Cartoons: Number of cartoons used/issue varies. Themes vary. Prefers b&w line drawings. Send query letter with samples of style to be kept on file.
Illustrations: Number of illustrations used/issue varies. Send query letter with brochure showing art style or tear sheets, slides and photographs to be kept on file. Write to schedule an appointment to show a portfolio, which should include original/final art, final reproduction/product, color, tear sheets, Photostats, photographs and b&w. Pays on publication.
Tips: "There's a greater and greater sophistication in computer-generated graphics. We try to keep abreast on the latest techniques."

VIDEO REVIEW, 902 Broadway, New York NY 10010. (212)477-2200. Art Director: Bruce Cohen. Emphasizes home video for owners and prospective owners of home video equipment. Monthly. Circ. 475,000. Original artwork returned after publication.
Illustrations: Uses 1-2 illustrations/issue; buys all from freelancers. Prefers airbrush, line drawings, sculpture and color. Works on assignment only. Send samples of style. Samples not returned. Reports when an assignment is available. Call or write for appointment. Negotiates rights purchased.

***VIEWPOINT AQUARIUS**, Box 97, Camberley, Surrey GU15 2LH England. Tel. 0276-21312. Director: Rex Dutta. Emphasizes flying saucers, yoga, occult law, meditation. Monthly. Accepts previously published material. Original artwork not returned after publication. Sample copy $1.
Cartoons: Uses very few cartoons/issue. Prefers b&w line drawings. Send query letter; write for appointment to show portfolio. Reports only if interested. Pays on publication.
Illustrations: Uses very few illustrations/issue. Send query letter; write for appointment to show portfolio. Reports only if interested.

VIRGINIA BAR NEWS, Suite 1000, Ross Building, 801 East Main St., Richmond VA 23219. (804)786-2061. Coordinator of Public Information and Publications: Cathe Kervan. Magazine emphasizing legal profession for members of the bar throughout the state. Bimonthly. Circ. 20,000. Sample copy for SASE.
Illustrations: Buys various illustrations/issue from freelancers. Works on assignment only. Send query letter with resume, tear sheets, Photostats, photocopies and photographs. Samples not filed are returned only if requested. Reports within 1 month. Portfolio should include original/final art, photographs and b&w. Pays $150-200, b&w, cover; $25-75, b&w, inside; on publication.

VIRTUE MAGAZINE, Box 850, Sisters OR 97759. (503)549-8261. Art Director: Dennis Mortenson. Magazine aimed at Christian homemakers. The majority are ages 25-45, married, and have children living at home. Publishes 10 issues/year. Circ. 125,000. Accepts previously published material. Original artwork returned after publication. Sample copy $2 plus postage or SASE. Art guidelines for SASE with first-class stamp.
Cartoons: Buys 1-4 cartoons/issue from freelancers. Cartoons should involve family, children, homemaking, marriage or incidents in a woman's everyday life. They should be aimed at women. Prefers single panel with or without gagline; b&w line drawings or b&w washes. Send samples of style and finished cartoons. Samples not filed are returned by SASE. Reports within 5-10 days. Buys first rights. Pays $25-40, b&w.
Illustrations: Buys 4-6 illustrations/issue from freelancers. Works on assignment only. Send query letter with brochure showing art style or resume, tear sheets, Photostats, photocopies, slides or photographs. Prefers samples that can be filed. Samples not filed are returned by SASE. To show a portfolio, mail appropriate materials or call to schedule an appointment; portfolio should include original/final art and tear sheets. Buys first rights. Pays $50-125, b&w, and $100-250, color, inside; on publication.
Tips: "Artists should have knowledge of good leading lines, color and anatomy. We us mostly realistic art, though I'm leaning to 3-D and graphics/collage."

VISIONS, THE INTERNATIONAL MAGAZINE OF ILLUSTRATED POETRY, Black Buzzard Press, 4705 S. 8th Rd., Arlington VA 22204. Editors: Bradley R. Strahan, Ursula Gill and Shirley Sullivan. Emphasizes literature and the illustrative arts for "well educated, very literate audience, very much into art and poetry." Published 3 times/year. Circ. 650. Sometimes accepts previously published material under very special circumstances. Original artwork returned after publication only if requested. Sample copy $3 (latest issue $3.50); art guidelines for SASE.

Illustrations: Buys approximately 18/issue, 55 illustrations/year from freelancers. Works on assignment only. Representational to surrealistic and some cubism style. Send query letter with SASE and samples to be kept on file. Samples should clearly show artist's style and capability; no slides or originals. Samples not filed are returned by SASE. Reports within 2 months. Buys first rights. "For information on releases on artwork, please contact the editors at the above address." Pays by the project, in copies or up to $10.

Tips: "We don't follow trends. We publish imaginative, skillful artwork no matter what the style. We strongly recommend reviewing a recent issue before submitting work."

VOGUE, 350 Madison Ave., New York NY 10017. Art Director: Roger Schoening. Emphasizes fashion, health, beauty, culture and decorating for women. Write and send resume; will then review portfolio; works primarily with New York area artists. Leave photocopies for referral.

VOLKSWAGEN'S WORLD, Volkswagen of America, Troy MI 48099. (313)362-6770. Editor: Marlene Goldsmith. For Volkswagen owners. Quarterly. Circ. 300,000.

Cartoons: Seldom purchases cartoons unless the subject matter is particularly unique. Send query letter with samples. SASE. Reports in 6 weeks. Buys all rights. Pays $15 minimum, halftones and washes; on acceptance.

Illustrations: Send query letter with samples. SASE. Reports in 6 weeks. Buys all rights. Cover: pays $250 minimum, color. Inside: pays $15 minimum, b&w and color; on acceptance.

Tips: "We're happy to send sample issues to prospective contributors. It's the best way of seeing what our needs are."

***VORTEX COMICS INC.**, 92 Sumach St., Toronto, Ontario M5A 3S9 Canada. (416)363-0428. Publisher: Bill Marks. Publishes comic books. Genres: adventure, mystery, social parodies and "new ideas." Themes: social commentary and alternative lifestyles. "*Vortex* does not publish standard genre material. Emphasis in our line leans toward alternative material, with attention to excellence in all aspects of publication production and execution." Bimonthly. Circ. 30,000. Original artwork returned after publication. Sample copy $2. Art guidelines available.

Illustrations: Uses three-tier page of 6 panels, vertical panels and horizontal panels. Uses freelance artists for inking, lettering, pencilling, color work and covers. Send query letter with b&w photocopies, pencil and inks. Samples are filed. Samples not filed are returned if requested. Reports back within 2 months. To show a portfolio, mail 2 pages of pencil or ink drawings one-and-one-half times up and 2 pages of action continuity. Payment varies with project. Pays $30-150/page for pencilling and inking; on publication (30 days).

WASHINGTON FOOD DEALER MAGAZINE,Box 15300, 8288 Lake City Way NE, Seattle WA 98115-0030. Managing Editor/Advertising Director: Arden D. Gremmert. Emphasizes the food industry, particularly retail grocers (independents). Monthly. Circ. 4,300. Accepts previously published material. Does not return original artwork after publication. Sample copy $2.

Cartoons: Interested in cartoons on food industry trends with an editorial message. Prefers single panel with b&w line drawings. Send query letter with samples of style to be kept on file. Write for appointment to show Portfolio. Material not filed is returned only if requested. Reports only if interested. Negotiates rights purchased. Negotiates pay; pays on publication.

Illustrations: Buys 1-2 illustrations/issue from freelancers. Prefers food industry themes. Works on assignment only. Send query letter with resume and tear sheets to be kept on file. Write for appointment to show Portfolio. Samples not filed are returned by SASE. Reports only if interested. Pays for design by the hour, $30 minimum. Pays for illustrations by the project, $65 minimum. Negotiates rights purchased and payment. Pays on publication.

Tips: "Artists must be able to accurately convert written instructions into acceptable draft presentations. We need quick turnaround on extensive projects."

THE WASHINGTON MONTHLY, 1711 Connecticut Ave. NW, Washington DC 20009. (202)462-0128. Art Director: Kitry Krause. For journalists, government officials and general public interested in public affairs. "We examine government's failures and suggest solutions." Monthly. Circ. 30,000. Previously published and photocopied submissions OK.

Illustrations: Buys 20-40 illustrations/year on politics and government. Local artists preferred. Send

query letter with samples or arrange interview to show Portfolio. SASE. Reports in 4 weeks. Buys one-time rights. Pays $50-125, b&w line drawings and washes, inside; pay is negotiable for color-separated work; $100 minimum, b&w, cover; on publication.
Tips: "We need fast turn-around; artist should read articles before attempting work."

THE WASHINGTONIAN MAGAZINE, Suite 200, 1828 L St. NW, Washington DC 20036. (202)296-3600. Emphasizes politics, cultural events, personalities, entertainment and dining. About Washington, for Washingtonians. Monthly. Circ. 144,000. Simultaneous submissions and previously published work OK. Original artwork returned after publication if requested. No artists' guidelines available.
Cartoons: Buys 5 cartoons/issue from freelancers, on "sophisticated topics, urban life"; single and double panel with gagline. Uses b&w line drawings, gray opaques, b&w washes, and opaque watercolors. Prefers finished cartoons. Reports in 4-6 weeks. Buys one-time rights. Pays $50, b&w; on publication.
Illustrations: Design Director: Jan Drews. Uses 5 illustrations/issue; buys 3/issue from freelancers, on a variety of subjects. Works on assignment only. Uses b&w line drawings, gray opaques, b&w washes, color washes and opaque watercolor. Send resume, business card and tear sheets to be kept on file. Returns samples if requested. Does not report back on future assignment possibilities. Prefers to see Portfolio and samples of style. SASE. Reports in 1 week. Buys one-time rights. Pay is negotiable; on publication.

WATERFRONT MAGAZINE, Box 1579, Newport Beach CA 92663. Art Director: Jeffrey Fleming. Magazine emphasizing boating for Southern Californians who own a boat or like to go boating. Monthly. Circ. 38,000. Accepts previously published material. Original artwork returned after publication. Sample copy for SASE with $1.75 postage.
Cartoons: Buys 2 cartoons/year from freelancers. Prefers single panel without gagline; b&w line drawings. Send query letter with samples of style to be kept on file. Samples not filed are returned by SASE. Reports only if interested. Write to schedule an appointment to show a Portfolio. Negotiates rights purchased. Pays $75, b&w.
Illustrations: Buys 2 illustrations/issue from freelancers. Prefers boat-related themes (power or sail). Send query letter with resume, tear sheets, Photostats, photocopies, slides and photographs. Samples not filed are returned by SASE. Reports only if interested. To show a Portfolio, mail appropriate materials. Negotiates rights purchased. Pays by the project, $75-250.
Tips: Looks for "the ability to intelligently add detail to general illustration ideas, and for creative suggestions."

WATER SKI MAGAZINE, Box 2456, Winter Park Fl 32790. (305)628-4802. Publisher: Terry Snow. Send query letters to: Terry Temple, editor. Emphasizes water skiing for an audience generally 18-34 years old, 80% male, active, educated, affluent. Published 8 times/year. Circ. 72,000. Accepts previously published material and simultaneous submissions. Original artwork returned after publication. Query for guidelines.
Cartoons: Uses 1-4 cartoons/issue, buys all from freelancers. 90% assigned. Prefers single panel with gagline, color or b&w washes or b&w line drawings. Prefers to receive query letter with samples or roughs first, but will review finished work. Samples returned. Reports within 3 weeks. Negotiates rights purchased. Negotiates payment, usually $15-30, b&w; up to $300, color, depending on topic. Pays 30 days after publication.
Illustrations: Uses 10 illustrations/issue; buys 5 illustrations/issue from freelancers. Prefers strong lines in a realistic style. Works on assignment "most of the time." Send query letter with resume, samples and tear sheets to be kept on file. Samples returned by SASE if not kept on file. Reports within 3 weeks. May also submit Portfolio. Negotiates payment and rights purchased. Pays on publication.

WAVES, (Fine Canadian Writing), 79 Denham Dr., Richmond Hill, Ontario L4C 6H9 Canada. (416)889-6703. Editor: Bernice Lever. Emphasizes literature for readers of contemporary poetry and fiction. Published trianually. Circ. 1,100. Returns original artwork after publication. Sample copy for SASE (nonresidents include IRC). Art guidelines available.
Illustrations: Uses 3-15/issue. Themes and styles are open. "Art does not relate to the literature print-

The asterisk before a listing indicates that the listing is new in this edition. New markets are often the most receptive to freelance submissions.

ed. It can contrast or harmonize." Send query letter with samples to be kept on file for 6 months. Prefers Photostats or tear sheets as samples—high contrast line drawings. Samples not filed are returned by SASE (nonresidents include IRC). Reports within 1 month. Write for appointment to show Portfolio. Buys one-time North American rights. Pays $10, b&w, inside; and $25, b&w, or color cover; on publication.

WEBB CO., 1999 Shepard Rd., St. Paul MN 55116. Creative Director: Jerald Johnson.
Illustrations: Uses 1 illustration/issue from freelancer. Receives 1 submission/week from freelancers. Interested in themes for 10 agriculture magazines, 1 horticulture magazine, 1 home magazine, 1 snowmobile magazine, 13 consumer magazines. Buys business and general interest themes. Works on assignment only. Provide brochure, flyer, tear sheet and slides to be kept on file for future assignments. Prefers to see Portfolio and samples of style. Samples not kept on file are returned by SASE. Buys all rights on a work-for-hire basis and one-time publication rights. Pays $50-1,000, b&w or color; on acceptance.

WEIGHT WATCHERS MAGAZINE, 360 Lexington Ave., New York NY 10017. (212)370-0644. Art Director: Alan Richardson. Emphasizes food, health, fashion, beauty for the weight and beauty conscious, 25-45 years old. Monthly. Circ. 875,000. Original artwork returned after publication.
Illustrations: Uses 6 illustrations/issue. Works on assignment only. Send query letter with brochure to be kept on file. Reports only if interested. Portfolios seen by drop-off only. Buys one-time rights. Pays on acceptance.

THE WEIRDBOOK SAMPLER, Box 149, Amherst Branch, Buffalo NY 14226. Editor-in-Chief: W. Paul Ganley. An irregular companion publication to *Weirdbook* for those interested in fantasy, adventure and horror. Irregular publications. Circ. 200. Buys first or all rights. Sample copy $3.75.
Illustrations: Buys 10-20 illustrations/year. Interested in weird, macabre, supernatural and fantastic themes. "Illustrate scenes from famous weird writers like Bradbury, Lovecraft, Poe, etc." Mail art. Photocopies OK. Must be suited to photocopy. SASE. Reports within 3 months. Cover: pays $10, b&w. Inside: pays $5/page; on publication. *Currently overstocked*, inquire first.
Tips: "Plan to reduce art to 85% of actual size; column width of 4" or double column width of 8¼" 'intermediate sizes can be used.' Art that does not require half-toning preferred, particularly on interiors. Leave at least ¼" around interiors for cropping (⅜" on full page sizes). No pencil drawings or slides. Copies OK if suitable for reproduction. All due care will be used in handling, but send a reminder letter when you want them back (about 6 weeks after publication). B&w artwork only, no color."

WEST, 750 Ridder Park Dr., San Jose CA 95190. (408)920-5602. Editor: Jeffrey Klein. Art Director: Bambi Nicklen. General interest magazine for subscribers of the *San Jose Mercury News*. Circ. 307,000. Weekly. Free sample copy.
Illustrations: Buys 2-3/issue on all themes except erotica. Query with resume and samples or previously published work, or arrange interview to show Portfolio. Cover: pays up to $700, opaque watercolors, oils, acrylics or mixed media. Inside: pays $125-400, b&w line drawings, washes and gray opaques; $150-400, color washes, opaque watercolors, oils, acrylics or mixed media. Pays on acceptance.

WEST MICHIGAN MAGAZINE, 7 Ionia S.W., Grand Rapids MI 49503. Art Director: Rose Rosely. Magazine emphasizing people, places and issues related to West Michigan for upscale-higher than average incomes and education. Monthly. Circ. 22,000. Accepts previously published material. Original artwork returned after publication. Sample copy $2 with 98¢ postage.
Illustrations: Buys 1-3 illustrations/issue from freelancers. Works on assignment only. Send query letter with brochure showing art style. Samples not kept on file are returned by SASE. Reports only if interested. Call to schedule an appointment to show a Portfolio, which should include original/final art, final reproduction/product, color and b&w. Buys one-time rights. Pays by the project, $35-300. Pays on publication.

WESTERN OUTDOORS,3197-E Airport Loop Dr., Costa Mesa CA 92626. (714)546-4370. Art Director: Gayle Radestock. Emphasizes hunting and fishing and related activities in the western states; directed to men and women interested in pursuing these activities in the 11 contiguous western states plus Alaska, Hawaii, British Columbia and western Mexico. Published 10 times/year. Circ. 150,000. Returns original artwork after publication.
Illustrations: Works on assignment only. Send query letter with samples to be kept on file. Accepts photocopies as samples. Samples not filed are returned by SASE. Reports within 30 days. Write for appointment to show Portfolio. Buys first rights. Pays on acceptance.

WESTERN RV TRAVELER, 2019 Clement Ave., Alameda CA 94501. (415)865-7500. Creative Director: David Hebenstreit. 'RV magazine of the west'' for RV-owners and travel-oriented readers. Monthly. Circ. 100,000. Accepts previously published material. Original artwork returned after publication. Sample copy available.
Cartoons: Buys 1-5 cartoons/issue from freelancers. Prefers single panel with or without gagline; b&w line drawings or b&w washes. Send query letter with finished cartoons. Write to schedule an appointment to show a Portfolio. Material not kept on file is returned by SASE. Reports only if interested. Buys one-time rights. Pays $5, b&w.
Illustrations: Buys 5-10 illustrations/issue from freelancers. Prefers line drawings for newsprint publication. Send query letter with resume, tear sheets, Photostats, photocopies and photographs. Samples not filed are returned by SASE. Reports only if interested. Write to schedule an appointment to show a Portfolio, which should include original/final art, final reproduction/product, tear sheets, Photostats, photographs and three-dimensional work. Buys one-time rights. Pays $100, color, cover; $5, b&w, inside; on publication.

WESTERN SPORTSMAN, Box 737, Regina, Saskatchewan S4P 3A8 Canada. (306)352-8384. Editor-in-Chief: Rick Bates. For fishermen, hunters, campers and outdoorsmen. Bimonthly. Circ. 30,000. Original artwork returned after publication. Sample copy $3; artist's guidelines for SASE (nonresidents include IRC).
Cartoons: Buys 90 cartoons/year on the outdoors; single, double and multiple panel with gaglines. Send art or query with samples. SASE (nonresidents include IRC). Reports in 3 weeks. Buys first North American serial rights. Pays $20, b&w line drawings; on acceptance.
Illustrations: Buys 8 illustrations/year on the outdoors. Mail art or query with samples. SASE (nonresidents include IRC). Reports in 3 weeks. Buys first North American serial rights. Pays $50-200, b&w line drawings, inside; on acceptance.

WESTWAYS, Terminal Annex, Box 2890, Los Angeles CA 90051. (213)741-4760. Editor: Mary Ann Fisher. Production Manager: Vincent J. Corso. Art Director: Paul Miyamoto.For the people of the Western U.S. Emphasizes current and historical events, culture, art, travel and recreation. Monthly. Circ. 478,000.
Illustrations: Buys assigned themes on travel, history, and arts in the West. Send resume to be kept on file. Do not call. Buys first rights, based on decision of the editor. Cover: pays $400. Inside: pays $50-150, drawings; $150, 4-color illustrations. Pays on publication.

WHISKEY ISLAND MAGAZINE, University Center 7, Cleveland State University, Cleveland OH 44115. Editor: Katherine Murphy. For all writers; poetry, short fiction and drama. Published 2-3 times annually. Circ. 2,000. Photocopied submissions OK.
Illustrations: B&w photos and other graphics accepted; no limitation by theme. Send query letter with photocopies, photographs and b&w drawings. SASE. Reports in 12 weeks. To show a portfolio, mail thumbnails, roughs, original/final art, photographs and b&w. Payment is two contributor's copies; on publication.
Tips: "We look for something that goes with the realistic contemporary Midwestern voice we want the magazine to have."

***WHISPERING WIND MAGAZINE**, 8009 Wales St., New Orleans LA 70126. Editor: Jack B. Heriard. Magazine emphasizing American Indian crafts and culture. Features historical and how-to articles and ethnic and historical native American (Indian) essays. "Readership is 52% Indian, 49% 15-35 years of age." Bimonthly. Circ. 4,000. Accepts previously published material. Original artwork returned after publication if requested. Sample copy $2.50.
Cartoons: Uses 3 cartoons/year from freelancers. "Must be Indian-oriented—no stereotypes." Prefers single panel with gagline, b&w line drawings. Send query letter with roughs. Samples are returned by SASE. Reports back within 5 days. Negotiates rights purchased. No payment.
Illustrations: Works on assignment only. Prefers traditional style. Looks for "attention to detail, accuracy of subjects and clothing from an historical perspective. Avoid, stereotyping Indian clothing (all Indians wear war bonnets, etc.)." Send query letter with photocopies. Samples are returned by SASE. Reports back within 5 days. Negotiates rights purchased. No payment.

WHISPERS, 70 Highland Ave., Binghamton NY 13905. Editor-in-Chief/Art Director: Stuart David Schiff. For college-educated adults interested in literate fantasy, horror, art and fiction. Published 1-2 times/year. Circ. 3,000. Original artwork returned after publication. Sample copy $3.50.
Illustrations: Uses 10-20 illustrations/issue; buys 2-3/issue from freelancers. Receives 5-10 submis-

sions/week from freelancers. Interested in fantasy and horror. Send photocopied samples of finished art. SASE. Send flyer and tear sheets to be kept on file for future assignments. Reports in 30-60 days. Buys first North American serial rights. Pays $100-200, color, cover; $10-25, b&w, inside. Pays by arrangement to retain artwork after use.
Tips: Especially looks for "clean lines, originality and non-comic book appearance of human" in artwork.

WILSON LIBRARY BULLETIN, 950 University Ave., Bronx NY 10452. (212)588-8400. Editor: Milo Nelson. Emphasizes the issues and the practice of library science. Published 10 times/year. Circ. 25,000. Free sample copy.
Cartoons: Buys 2-3 cartoons/issue on education and library science; single panel with gagline. Mail finished art. SASE. Reports back only if interested. Buys first rights. Pays $100, b&w line drawings and washes; on acceptance.
Illustrations: Uses 1-2 illustrations/issue; buys all from freelancers. Works on assignment only. Send query letter, business card and samples to be kept on file. Reports back only if interested. Call for appointment to show portfolio. Buys first rights. Cover: pays $300, color washes. Inside: pays $100-200, b&w line drawings and washes; $20, spot drawings. Pays on publication.

WINDSOR THIS MONTH MAGAZINE, Box 1029, Station A, Windsor, Ontario N9A 6P4 Canada. (519)966-7411. Publisher: J.S. Woloschuk. Features Windsor-oriented issues, interviews, opinion, answers. Published 12 times/year. Circ. 24,000.
Illustrations: Buys 3/issue on assigned themes. Send query letter with samples. Include SAE (nonresidents include IRC). Reports in 1 week. Buys first North American serial rights. Negotiates pay, color and b&w; on publication.
Tips: "Send sample of published work."

WINES & VINES, 1800 Lincoln Ave., San Rafael CA 94901. (415)453-9700. Editor: Philip E. Hiaring. Emphasizes the grape and wine industry in North America for the trade—growers, winemakers, merchants. Monthly. Circ. 5,800. Accepts previously published material. Original artwork not returned after publication.
Cartoons: Buys approximately 3 cartoons/year. Prefers single panel with gagline; b&w line drawings. Send query letter with roughs to be kept on file. Material not kept on file is not returned. Reports within 1 month. Buys first rights. Pays $10.
Illustrations: Send query letter to be kept on file. Reports within 1 month. Buys first rights. Pays $50-100, color, cover; $15, b&w, inside. Pays on acceptance.

WINNING, 15115 S. 76 E. Ave., Bixby OK 74008. (918)366-4441. Executive Editor: André Hinds. Newspaper emphasizing contests, sweepstakes and lottery. Monthly. Circ. 250,000. Accepts previously published material after publication. Sample copy $2.
Cartoons: Buys 2-3 cartoons/issue from freelancers. Prefers contests, sweepstakes and lottery as themes. Prefers single, double or multiple panel, with or without gagline; b&w line drawings. Send samples of style to be kept on file. Material not kept on file is returned by SASE. Reports only if interested. Negotiates rights purchased.
Illustrations: Buys 2-3 illustrations/issue from freelancers. Send query letter with tear sheets. Samples not filed are returned by SASE. Does not report back.

***WIRE JOURNAL INTERNATIONAL**, 1570 Boston Post Rd., Guilford CT 06437. (203)453-2777. Contact: Art Director. Emphasizes the wire industry worldwide, members of Wire Association International, industry suppliers, manufacturers, research/developers, engineers, etc. Monthly. Circ. 12,500. Original artwork not returned after publication. Free sample copy and art guidelines.
Illustrations: Uses "no set number" of illustrations/issue; illustrations are "used infrequently." Works on assignment only. Provide samples, business card and tear sheets to be kept on file for possible future assignments. Call for appointment or submit portfolio. Reports "as soon as possible." Buys all rights. Pay is negotiable; on publication.
Tips: "Show practical artwork that relates to industrial needs and avoid bringing samples of surrealism art, for example. Also, show a better variety of techniques—and know something about who we are and the industry we serve."

WISCONSIN RESTAURATEUR, 122 W. Washington, Madison WI 53703. (608)251-3663. Editor: Jan LaRue. Emphasizes the restaurant industry. Readers are "restaurateurs, hospitals, schools, institutions, cafeterias, food service students, chefs, etc." Monthly. Circ. 3,600, except convention issue (March), 13,000. Original artwork returned after publication. Free sample copy; art guidelines for SASE. Especially needs cover material.

Cartoons: Buys 1 cartoon/issue from freelancer. Receives 5 cartoons/week from freelancers. "Uses much material pertaining to conventions, food shows, etc. Sanitation issue good. Cartoons about employees. No off-color material." Prefers b&w line drawings with gaglines. Send finished cartoons. SASE. Reports in 2 weeks. Buys first North American serial rights. Pays $8 on publication.
Illustrations: Uses 5 illustrations/issue; buys 1/issue from freelancer. Receives 1 illustration/week from freelance artists. Freelancers chosen "at random, depending on theme and articles featured for the month." Looks for "the unusual, pertaining to the food service industry. No offbeat or questionable material." Prefers b&w line drawings and washes for covers. Send brochure showing art style or resume to be kept on file for future assignments. Buys first North American serial rights. To show a portfolio, mail appropriate materials, which should include roughs, original/final art and b&w. Pays $25, b&w and $50, color, cover; $15, b&w, $20, color, inside; Pays on acceptance.
Tips: Trends within the field include "seafood, low-calorie beverages and more convenience foods." Changes within the magazine include "new cover design, and the use of more freelance material—pictures and illustrations. Study back issues."

WISCONSIN TRAILS, Box 5650, Madison WI 53705. (608)231-2444. Production Manager: Nancy Mead. Concerns travel, recreation, history, industry and personalities in Wisconsin. Published 6 times/year. Circ. 25,000. Previously published and photocopied submissions OK. Artists' guidelines for SASE.
Illustrations: Buys 6 illustrations/issue from freelancers. Receives less than 1 submission/week from freelancers. "Art work is done on assignment, to illustrate specific articles. All articles deal with Wisconsin. We allow artists considerable stylistic latitude." Send samples (photocopies OK) of style; indication of artist's favorite topics; name, address and phone number to be kept on file for future assignments. SASE. Reporting time varies. Buys one-time rights on a work-for-hire basis. Pays $25-300, inside; on publication.

THE WITTENBURG DOOR, 1224 Greenfield Dr., El Cajon CA 92021.(916)842-1301. Editor: Mike Yaconelli. For men and women, usually connected with the church. Bimonthly. Circ. 20,000.
Cartoons: Buys 2-3 cartoons/issue on assignment. Purchases 2-3 cartoons/month from freelance artists. "Very selective." Uses satire/humor on religious themes geared to evangelicals. Send query letter with original art. SASE. Reports in 3 months. Pays $50, b&w; on publication.
Tips: "Submit original art by mail—please don't send only a query letter. Humor should be biting, satirical, daring, subtle, 'off-the-wall,' or any combination of above."

WONDER TIME, 6401 The Paseo, Kansas City MO 64131. (816)333-7000. Editor: Evelyn Beals. "Story paper" emphasizing inspiration and character building material for first and second graders, 6-8 years old. Weekly. Circ. 40,000. Does not accept previously published material. Original artwork not returned to the artist after publication. Sample copy for SASE with 50¢ postage. Art guidelines available.
Illustrations: Buys 1/issue. Works on assignment only. Send query letter with tear sheets or photocopies to be kept on file. Reports only if interested. Buys all rights. Pays $40-70, color, cover; on acceptance.

WOODENBOAT, Box 78, Brooklin ME 04616. Editor: Jonathan A. Wilson. Executive Editor: Billy R. Sims. Contributing Editor: Peter H. Spectre. Managing Editor: Jennifer Buckley. Concerns designing, building, repairing, using and maintaining wooden boats. Bimonthly. Circ. 110,000. Previously published work OK. Sample copy $4.
Illustrations: Buys 48/year on wooden boats or related items. Send query letter with samples. SASE for return of material. Reports in 1-2 months. "We are always in need of high quality technical drawings. Rates vary, but usually $25-350. Buys first North American serial rights. Pays on publication.
Tips: "We work with several professionals on an assignment basis, but most of the illustrative material that we use in the magazine is submitted with a feature article. When we need additional material, however, we will try to contact a good freelancer in the appropriate geographic area."

WOODMEN OF THE WORLD, 1700 Farnam St., Omaha NE 68102. (402)342-1890. Editor-in-Chief: Leland A. Larson. For members of the Woodmen of the World Life Insurance Society and their families. Emphasizes Society activities, children's and women's interests and humor. Monthly. Circ. 470,000. Previously published work OK. Original artwork returned after publication, if arrangements are made. Free sample copy.
Cartoons: Buys 1-6 cartoons/issue from freelancers. Receives 10-50 submissions/week from freelancers. Especially needs cartoons. Interested in general interest subjects; single panel. Send finished cartoons. SASE. Reports in 2 weeks. Buys various rights. Pays $10, b&w line drawings, washes and halftones; on acceptance.

Illustrations: Uses 5-10 illustrations/year; buys 3-4/year from freelancers. Interested in lodge activities, seasonal, humorous and human interest themes. Works on assignment only. Send brochure showing art style or flyers to be kept on file. Prefers to see finished art. SASE. Reports in 2 weeks. Buys one-time rights. Payment varies according to job.
Tips: Especially looks for creative thinking, technique and quality when reviewing samples. Artists should avoid "one-track stylization; vary the media used and techniques, if possible."

WORDS, 1015 N. York Rd, Willow Grove PA 19090. (215)657-6300. Art Director: Nancy Okuniewski. Emphasizes information systems and word processing for word processing professionals, consultants, educators and manufacturers; male and female; 20-50 years of age. Bimonthly. Circ. over 18,000. Original artwork returned after publication. Sample copy for SASE.
Illustrations: Buys 1 illustration/issue from freelancers. Interested in "all styles" and "themes on editorial features of office automation." Works on assignment only. Send brochure with samples of style. Samples returned by SASE. Provide resume, business card and/or brochure to be kept on file for possible future assignments. Reports in 3 weeks. Call for appointment. Pays $50-300 inside, b&w line or wash; $300-500 for 4-color cover art; on publication.
Tips: "We're interested in a variety of styles and treatments. We're looking for clean, competent, modern and hi-tech looking graphics; simple, yet sophisticated. Present what you feel represents your best work (quality vs. quantity)."

WORKBENCH, Modern Handcraft, Inc., 4251 Pennsylvania, Kansas City MO 64111. Editor-in-Chief: Robert N. Hoffman. For woodworkers and do-it-yourself persons. Bimonthly. Circ. 870,000.
Cartoons: Buys 15 cartoons/year. Interested in woodworking and do-it-yourself themes; single panel with gagline. Submit art. SASE. Reports in 1 month. Buys all rights, but may reassign rights to artist after publication. Pays on acceptance. Pays $20 minimum, b&w line drawings.
Illustrations: Artists with experience in the area of technical drawings, especially house plans, exploded views of furniture construction, power tool and appliance cutaways, should write for free sample copy and artists' guidelines. Pays for illustration by the project, $100-1,500.

WRITER'S DIGEST, 1507 Dana Avenue, Cincinnati OH 45207. Art Director: Carol Buchanan. Assistant Editor: Bill Strickland (for cartoons). Emphasizes freelance writing for freelance writers. Monthly Circ. 200,000. Original artwork returned after publication. Sample copy $2.
Cartoons: Buys 3 cartoons/issue from freelancers. Theme: the writing life—cartoons that deal with writers and the trials of writing and selling their work. Also, writing from a historical standpoint (past works), language use and other literary themes. Prefers single panel with or without gagline. Send finished cartoons. Material returned by SASE. Reports within 1 month. Buys first rights or one-time rights. Pays $50-85, b&w; on acceptance.
Illustrations: Buys 4 illustrations/month from freelancers. Theme: the writing life (b&w line art primarily). Works on assignment only. Send brochure and nonreturnable samples to be kept on file. Accepts photocopies as samples. Write for appointment to show portfolio. Buys one-time rights. Pays $400, color, cover; $50-200, inside, b&w. Pays on acceptance.

WRITER'S YEARBOOK, 1507 Dana Ave., Cincinnati OH 45207. Submissions Editor: Bill Strickland. Emphasizes writing and marketing techniques, business topics for writers and writing opportunities for freelance writers and people trying to get started in writing. Annually. Original artwork returned with one copy of the issue in which it appears. Sample copy $3.95. Affiliated with *Writer's Digest*. Cartoons submitted to either publication are considered for both.
Cartoons: Uses 6-10 freelance cartoons/issue. "All cartoons must pertain to writing—its joys, agonies, quirks. All styles accepted, but high-quality art is a must." Prefers single panel, with or without gagline, b&w line drawings or washes. "Verticals are always considered, but horizontals—especially severe horizontals—are hard to come by." Send finished cartoons. Samples returned by SASE. Reports within 3 weeks. Buys first North American serial rights, one-time use. Pays $50 minimum, b&w. Pays on acceptance.
Tips: "A cluttery style does not appeal to us. Send finished, not rough art, with clearly typed gaglines. Cartoons without gaglines must be particularly well executed."

X-IT MAGAZINE, Box 102, Station C, St. John's, Newfoundland A1C 5H5 Canada. (709)753-8802. Editor: Ken J. Harvey. Emphasizes arts and entertainment for those interested in the visual and literary arts. Triannually. Circ. 3,000. Accepts previously published material. Original artwork returned after publication. Sample copy $3.
Cartoons: Buys 3-6 cartoons/issue from freelancers. Prefers contemporary, but open to wide area of styles. Accepts single, double or multi panel with or without gagline; b&w line drawings or washes. Send b&w samples of style or finished cartoons. Material returned by SAE (nonresidents include IRC)

only if requested. Reports within 3 weeks. Buys first rights or one-time rights. Write for appointment to show portfolio. Pays $15-150, b&w; on publication.
Illustrations: Buys 7-12 illustrations/issue from freelancers. Prefers contemporary, but open to many styles. Send query letter with brochure and tear sheets or photocopies. Samples returned by SAE (nonresidents include IRC) only if requested. Reports within 3 weeks. Buys first rights or one-time rights. Write for appointment to show portfolio. Pays $15-150, b&w, inside; on publication.

YACHTING, 5 River Rd., Box 1200, Cos Cob CT 06807. (203)629-8300. Editor: Ray Attaway. For top-level participants in boating in all its forms, power and sail. Monthly. Circ. 135,000. Art guidelines for SASE.
Illustrations: Buys 10 spot illustrations/year. Query. SASE. Reports in 2-3 weeks. Buys all rights. Pays $50, b&w, inside.

YACHTSMAN MAGAZINE, 2019 Clement Ave., Alameda CA 94501. (415)865-7500. Creative Director: David Hebenstreit. Tabloid emphasizing yachting and boating. Monthly. Circ. 50,000. Accepts previously published material. Original artwork returned after publication. Sample copy for SASE with 75¢ postage.
Cartoons: Buys 1-5 cartoons/issue from freelancers. Prefers boating or yachting themes. Prefers single, double or multiple panel with or without gagline; b&w line drawings or b&w washes. Send query letter with finished cartoons to be kept on file. Material not kept on file is returned by SASE. Does not report back. Write to schedule an appointment to show a portfolio. Buys one-time rights. Pays $5, b&w.
Illustrations: Buys 1-10 illustrations/issue from freelancers. Prefers yachting or boating themes. Send query letter with samples. Samples not filed are returned by SASE. Reports only if interested. Write to schedule an appointment to show a portfolio, which should include final reproductional/product. Buys one-time rights. Pays $100, b&w and $100, color.

YANKEE MAGAZINE, Main St., Dublin NH 03444. (603)563-8111. Design Editor: J. Porter. Regional magazine about New England. Monthly. Circ. 1 million. Accepts previously published material. Returns original artwork after publication. Sample copy $1.95.
Cartoons: Buys 4 cartoons/issue from freelancers. Cartoons must be "very funny and relative to New England lifestyle." Send query letter with samples of style to be kept on file. Material not filed is returned by SASE. Reports only if interested. Buys one-time rights. Pays $50 second rights, $100 first rights, b&w.
Illustrations: Buys various number/issue from freelancers. Send query letter with tear sheets, slides or photographs to be kept on file. Samples not filed are returned by SASE. Reports only if interested. Buys one-time rights. Pays $200-650, color, cover; $100-550 for b&w and $150-750 for color, inside; on acceptance.

YELLOW SILK: Journal of Erotic Arts, Box 6374, Albany CA 94706. (415)841-6500. Publisher: Lily Pond. Emphasizes erotic literature and arts for well educated, highly literate readership, generally personally involved in arts field. Quarterly. Circ. 12,000. Does not accept previously published material. Returns original artwork after publication. Sample copy $4.
Cartoons: Uses 0-3/issue. Prefers themes involving sexuality and/or human relationships. " 'All persuasions, no brutality' is editoral policy. Nothing tasteless." Accepts any cartoon format. Send query letter with finished cartoons or photocopies to be kept on file. Include phone number, name and address on each sample. Material not filed is returned by SASE with correct stamps, no meters. Reports only if SASE included. Buys first rights or reprint rights. Pays $15/page (4 panels) minimum plus 3 copies; on publication.
Illustrations: Uses 9-15/issue by one artist if possible. Considers "anything in the widest definitions of eroticism except brutality, bondage or S&M. Nothing tasteless. We're looking for work that is beautiful, artistically. No pornography. All sexual persuasions represented." Send photocopies, slides, Photostats, photographs or originals, "all sent at artist's risk" to be kept on file. Color and b&w examples in each submission are preferred. Include name, address and telephone number on all samples. Samples not filed returned by SASE. Reports within 8 weeks. To show a portfolio, mail original/final art, color, Photostats, photographs, b&w and slides. Buys first rights or reprint rights. Pays $50 minimum plus copies; on publication.
Tips: "See the magazine first. I'm using color every issue now and am not interested in work by amateurs, though more seem to feel 'anyone can get into this area' these days!"

Newspapers & Newsletters

Computers have revolutionized newspaper graphics, making them instantly available through satellite systems, phone lines and personal computers. This trend is changing the way newspapers convey information, emphasizing visual rather than verbal presentations. Larger newspapers were the frontrunners for using computerized typesetting and are now using the computer for production duties. Smaller publications are now investing in modern typesetting equipment but still rely on artists for graphics.

It's unlikely that computers will ever usurp the editorial cartoonist's place. Newspapers rely on the editorial cartoonist to tackle significant events and raise some political hackles. Since approximately 87% of daily readers pass through the editorial pages, the cartoon assumes a significant influence on public opinion. Most cartoons are drawn by staffers on dailies, but smaller weeklies are open to freelancers.

Since many of the publications in this section have specialized audiences, either by area of interest or geographic scope, your ability to understand the slant of a publication will be your greatest asset in making sales to these markets. We have listed daily, weekly, quarterly and semiannual publications. Newsletters can be consumer or trade, general or limited interest, large or small; medicine, psychology, softball, running, art and Ford Thunderbirds are just a few of their specialties.

The major needs of these publications are cartoons and illustrations, but if you reside nearby, don't overlook those that indicate they use freelance artists for advertising, layout, production work and peripheral services. Strong black-and-white work is most desirable here since few of these publications work in color. An understanding of reduction and the absorption quality of newsprint can help to produce work that will be useful to these markets.

For further information and other names and addresses, consult *Writer's Market 1988*, *The Newspaper and Allied Services Directory*, *Gale Directory of Publications* and *Editor & Publisher*. The Society of Newspaper Design publishes an annual which summarizes news and trends for the past year.

AMERICAN MEDICAL NEWS, 535 N. Dearborn St., Chicago IL 60610. (312)645-4441. Editor: Dick Walt. Emphasizes news and opinions on developments, legislation and business in medicine. For physicians. Weekly newspaper. Circ. 315,000. Original artwork not returned after publication. Free sample copy.

Cartoons: Contact: Sher Watts, assistant executive editor. Uses 1 cartoon/issue, all from freelancers. Receives "dozens" of submissions/week from freelancers. Interested in medical themes; single panel. Prefers to see finished cartoons. SASE. Reports in 4 weeks. Usually buys first North American rights. Pays up to $100, b&w; on acceptance.

Illustrations: Contact: Sher Watts, assistant executive editor. Number illustrations used/issue varies; number bought/issue from freelancers varies. Works on assignment only. Send query letter with brochure showing art style. Samples returned by SASE. "We don't look at many portfolios, but portfolio should include original/final art, color and tear sheets." Usually buys first North American rights. Payment varies; "we have paid as much as $600 for single illustration." Pays on acceptance.

Tips: "I will look at any cartoons. I usually work with artists only from the Chicago area, because we need to see them in person."

THE AMERICAN NEWSPAPER CARRIER, Box 15300, Winston-Salem NC 27113. Editor: Marilyn H. Rollins. A monthly newsletter for pre-teen and teenage newspaper carriers. Original artwork not returned after publication. Sample copy and art guidelines free for SASE.

Cartoons: Uses freelance and staff cartoons. Publishes 2-3 single panel and 1 multiple panel per issue. Prefers original b&w line drawings. Usually buys all rights. Pays $25 minimum on acceptance.
Illustrations: Buys 1-2 per issue, all freelance. Works on assignment only. Send query letter with tear sheets and photocopies to be kept on file. Samples not returned. Usually buys all rights. Pays $50 minimum on acceptance.

AMERICANS FOR LEGAL REFORM AND CITIZENS LEGAL MANUAL SERIES, Suite 300, Halt, 1319 F St. NW, Washington DC 20004. Creative Manager: Bob Schmitt. Tabloid emphasizing self help law, consumer education, and legal reform issues. Circ. 115,000. Accepts previously published material. Original artwork returned after publication.
Cartoons: Buys 1-2 cartoons/issue from freelancers. Prefers current legal reform issues as themes. Prefers single, double or multiple panel with or without gagline; b&w line drawings or b&w washes. Send query letter with samples of style to be kept on file. Write to schedule an appointment to show a portfolio. Samples not filed are not returned. Reports only if interested. Buys one-time rights, reprint rights or negotiates rights purchased. Negotiates payment.
Illustrations: Prefers legal reform issues as themes. Send query letter with resume, photocopies, halftones and photos. Samples not filed are not returned. Write to schedule an appointment to show a portfolio, which should include thumbnails, roughs, original/final art, final reproduction/product and b&w. Negotiates rights purchased. Negotiates payment. Pays on acceptance.

ANCHOR BAY BEACON, 51170 Washington, New Baltimore MI 48047. (313)725-4531. Executive Editor: Michael Eckert. Newspaper emphasizing local news for paid readership in one city, one village and three townships. Weekly. Circ. 8,000. Accepts previously published material. Original work returned after publication. Sample copy free for large manila SASE with 50¢ postage.
Cartoons: Number of cartoons purchased/issue from freelancers is open. No color. Send query letter with samples of style to be kept on file. Material filed returned only if requested. Reports only if interested. Buys reprint rights. Negotiates pay rate; pays on publication.
Illustrations: Works on assignment only. Send query letter to be kept on file. Write for appointment to show portfolio. Reports only if interested. Buys reprint rights. Negotiates pay rate; pays on publication.

***ANIMALS INTERNATIONAL**, Box 190, 29 Perkins St., Boston MA 02130. (617)522-7000. Regional Director: John Walsh. Quarterly newsletter. Emphasizes animal protection on an international level. "*Animals International* is an 11-15 page, illustrated newsletter that documents projects and issues that WSPA has been involved with during each quarter. It reaches approximately 63 countries and thousands of people around the world." Accepts previously published material. Returns original artwork after publication when requested. Sample copy available. Art guidelines available.
Cartoons: Send query letter with samples of style. Samples are filed. Samples not filed are returned only if requested. Reports back only if interested. Pays $30, b&w; $45, color; on acceptance.
Illustrations: Samples are filed. Samples not filed are returned if requested. Pays $30, b&w; $45, color.

APA MONITOR, American Psychological Association, 1200 17th St. NW, Washington DC 20036. (202)955-7690. Editor: Kathleen Fisher. Managing Editor: Laurie Denton. Monthly tabloid newspaper for psychologists and other behavioral scientists. 64-72 pages. Circ. 75,000.
Cartoons: Buys 1-2 cartoons/month from freelancers. Pays $50-100 b&w; on acceptance.
Illustrations: Buys 2-5 illustrations/month from freelancers. Uses 30 illustrations/year on current events and feature articles in behavioral sciences/mental health area. Washington area artists preferred. Works on assignment only. Reports back on future assignment possibilities. Query with resume, tear sheets and photocopies. Sample copy $3. SASE. To show a portfolio, mail appropriate materials or call to schedule an appointment; portfolio should include original/final art, final reproduction/product, photographs and b&w. Original artwork returned after publication, if requested. Buys first North American serial rights. Pays $200, b&w cover and inside; on publication.
Tips: "Be creative, think about topics relevant to psychology, and be willing to work at below-market rates in exchange for artistic freedom. I look for ability to develop simple, clean graphics to complement abstract, complex ideas."

***THE ART MARKETING LETTER**,2539 Post Rd., Darien CT 06820. (203)655-3798. Publisher: Amy Mongillo. Bimonthly newsletter for visual artists. Time articles written by and for artists with emphasis on marketing/sell artwork. Circ. 800. Accepts previously published material. Returns original artwork to the artists after publication. Sample copy $2.
Illustrations: Send resume and business card.

BALLS AND STRIKES NEWSPAPER, 2801 N.E. 50th St., Oklahoma City OK 73111. (405)424-5266. Communications Director: Bill Plummer III. Official publication of the amateur softball association.

Emphasizes amateur softball for "the more than 30 million people who play amateur softball; they come from all walks of life and hold varied jobs." Published 8 times/year. Circ. 250,000. Previously published material OK. Original work returned after publication. Free sample copy available.
Illustrations: Uses 2-4 illustrations/issue. No drug or alcohol themes. Works on assignment only. Send query letter with resume and business card to be kept on file. Samples returned. Reports in 3 days. Buys all rights. Pays on publication.

BALTIMORE SUN MAGAZINE, 501 N. Calvert St., Baltimore MD 21278. (301)332-6600. Editor: Susan Baer. Emphasizes general interest topics to the Maryland area; audience is families, educated. Weekly. Circ. 400,000. Accepts previously published material. Returns original art after publication. Sample copy free for SASE.
Illustrations: Uses 2 illustrations/issue; buys both from freelancers. Considers all styles. Works on assignment only. Send query letter with samples to be kept on file. Call or write for appointment to show portfolio. Prefers slides or tear sheets as samples. Material not filed is returned. Reports in 2-3 weeks. Negotiates rights purchased. Pays $200-300, color cover; $100, b&w, and $200, color, inside; on publication.
Tips: "Looking for a well-presented, consistent style. Common mistakes freelances make in presenting samples or portfolios is too many samples or too many styles—not one refined style."

BARTER COMMUNIQUE, Box 2527, Sarasota FL 33578. (813)349-3300. Art Director: Robert J. Murley. Concerns bartering; for radio, TV stations, newspapers, magazines, travel and ad agencies. Quarterly tabloid. Circ. 50,000.
Cartoons: Buys 5/issue on barter situations. Send roughs. Pays $5, b&w; on publication.
Illustrations: Query with samples. SASE. Reports in 2 weeks. Pays $5, b&w; on publication.
Tips: Looks for "uniqueness" in reviewing samples.

BIG BIRD,Box 2766, Cedar Rapids IA 52406. (319)364-6859. President: Bob Peterson. Bimonthly newsletter emphasizing 1967 through 1976 Ford Thunderbird automobiles. Publication of Thunderbirds of America. To members who own, restore and appreciate the Thunderbirds manufactured from 1967 through 1976. Circ. 500. Accepts previously published material. Returns original artwork to the artist after publication.
Illustrations: Prefers line art of 1967 through 1976 Thunderbirds. Send query letter with samples. Samples are filed. Samples not filed are returned by SASE. Reports back within 1 week. To show a portfolio, mail photostats. Negotiates rights purchased. Pays $25, b&w, cover or inside.; on acceptance.
Tips: "Our newsletter offers a showcase to artists who illustrate automobiles. An illustration published in our newsletter is viewed by potential buyers of originals and limited edition prints. The automobiles must the the Ford Thunderbird manufactured from 1967 through 1976."

BLACK VOICE NEWS, Box 581, Riverside CA 92502. (714)889-0506 or 682-6111. Contact: Hardy Brown, Jr. Newspaper emphasizing general topics for "the black community with various backgrounds, and Hispanics and whites who are in tune with that community." Weekly. Circ. 5,000. Sample copy free for SASE.
Cartoons: Prefers political, historic and topical themes. Accepts single, double or multiple panel with or without gagline; b&w line drawings. Send query letter with samples of style to be kept on file. Material not filed is returned by SASE. Reports back only if interested. Write for appointment to show portfolio. Buys one-time or reprint rights; pays on publication.
Illustrations: Send query letter with samples to be kept on file; write for appointment to show portfolio. Samples not filed are returned by SASE. Reports back only if interested. Buys one-time or reprint rights; pays on publication.

BOOKPLATES IN THE NEWS, Apt. F, 605 N. Stoneman Ave., Alhambra CA 91801. (213)283-1936. Director: Audrey Spencer Arellanes. Emphasizes bookplates for those who use bookplates whether individuals or institutions, those who collect them, artists who design them, art historians, genealogists, historians, antiquarian booktrade and others for tracing provenance of a volume; also publishes yearbook annually. Quarterly. Circ. 250. Original work returned after publication. Previously published material OK "on occasion, usually from foreign publications." Sample copy $5; art guidelines for SASE with 56¢ postage..
Illustrations: Illustrations are bookplates. "Appearance of work in our publications should produce requests for bookplate commissions." Send query letter and finished art. Reports in 3 weeks. No payment.
Tips: "We only publish bookplates, those marks of ownership used by individuals and institutions. Some artists and owners furnish 250 original prints of their bookplate to be tipped-in quarterly. Membership is international; this is reflected in artwork from around the world."

THE BOSTON PHOENIX, 120 Brookline Ave., Boston MA 02215. (617)536-5390. Design Director: Cleo Leontis. Weekly. Circ. 150,000. Original work returned after publication by SASE. Sample copy $3.50; send requests for sample copy to Circulation Department.
Illustrations: Uses 2-8 b&w illustrations/issue, occasional color; buys all from freelancers. On assignment only. Send samples of style (no originals) and resume to be kept on file for possible future assignments. Call for appointment. Reports in 6 weeks. Buys one-time rights. Pays on publication.

THE BOSTON REVIEW, 33 Harrison Ave., Boston MA 02111. (617)350-5353. Publisher: Margaret Ann Roth. Tabloid. Emphasizes arts and culture for persons of college age and older interested/involved in the arts, literature and related cultural and political topics. Bimonthly. Circ. 10,000. Accepts simultaneous submissions. Original artwork returned after publication. Sample copy $3.
Cartoons: Has not previously used cartoons, but will consider. "Must be b&w work, anything original, creative, inspiring." Send photocopies. Prefers single panel, b&w line drawings. Material not kept on file is returned by SASE. Reports only if interested. Negotiates rights purchased. Negotiates payment. Pays $60-100 b&w, inside; on publication.
Illustrations: Buys 2-4 illustrations/issue from freelancers. Themes and styles are open; b&w work only. Send query letter with resume and samples to be kept on file. Open to any type of sample. Samples not kept on file are returned by SASE. Reports only if interested. To show a portfolio, mail original/final art, final reproduction/product and tear sheets. Negotiates rights purchased. Negotiates pay for inside art. Pays on publication.

THE BREAD RAPPER, 2103 Noyes, Evanston IL 60201. Editor-in-Chief: Laurie Lawlor. Concerns banking services and involvement of bank with community; received with checking account statement. Photocopied submissions OK. Sample copy and artist's guidelines with SASE.
Cartoons: Buys 1 cartoon/issue on banking; single panel with gagline. No negative bank slants (bank robberies, etc.), please. Mail art. SASE. Reports within 8 weeks. Buys all rights. Pays $20 minimum, b&w line drawings and washes; on publication.

BUILDING BRIEFS, Dan Burch Associates, 2338 Frankfort Ave., Louisville KY 40206. (502)895-4881. Program Manager: Sharon Hildenbrandt. Newsletter. Emphasizes design/build and conventional methods of construction for commercial and industrial buildings, plus other topics such as landscaping, security, and energy-saving ideas. Directed to potential clients of a building contractor in the nonresidential market, company presidents, board members and managerial personnel who will construct or renovate their buildings. Bimonthly. Circ. 25,000+. Original artwork returned after publication. Sample copy available.
Cartoons: Buys 1 cartoon/issue from freelancers. Prefers themes related to construction; light humor, simple line art. Prefers single panel with gagline; b&w line drawings. Send query letter with finished cartoons to be kept on file. Material not kept on file is returned. Reports only if interested. Buys one-time rights. Pays $50, b&w; on publication.
Tips: "Spend a little time researching the commercial building industry. Talk to a building contractor. Two industry publications where more can be learned are *Metal Construction News* and *Metal Building Review*."

THE BURLINGTON LOOK, Burlington Industries, Box 21207, Greensboro NC 27420. (919)379-2339. Publications Editor: Flontina Miller. Tabloid. Emphasizes textiles and home furnishings for all domestic employees of Burlington Industries plus opinion leaders in the plant communities. Published 8 times/year. Circ. 52,000. Accepts previously published material and simultaneous submissions. Original artwork not returned after publication unless requested. Sample copy free for SASE.
Illustrations: Currently uses 1-2 illustrations/issue—"works with local artists mostly"; buys all from freelancers. Themes/styles vtextiles and home furnishings for all
domestic employees of Burlington Industries plus opinion leaders in the plant communities. Published 8 times/year. Circ. 52,000. Accepts previously published material and simultaneous submissions. Original artwork not returned after publication unless requested. Sample copy free for SASE.
Illustrations: Currently uses 1-2 illustrations/issue—"works with local artists mostly"; buys all from freelancers. Themes/styles vary depending on subject matter. Works on assignment only. Send query letter with resume, business card, samples and tear sheets to be kept on file. Prefers photostats or photographs as samples; "I'd rather not have original work for fear it may be damaged or get lost." Samples not kept on file are returned only if requested. Reports within 2 weeks. Negotiates rights purchased. Payment varies according to size and complexity; pays on acceptance.
Tips: "Looking for illustrators with the creativity to be able to illustrate and visually communicate various story concepts."

BY-LINES, Box 48, Ft. Smith AR 72902. Director Public Relations & Advertising: John T. Greer. Tabloid. Emphasizes business (trucking related) for employees of ABF Freight System, Inc. Monthly. Circ. 7,000. Accepts previously published material and simultaneous submissions. Original artwork returned after publication. Sends art guidelines only if specifically interested in artist's work.
Cartoons: Uses 1-2 cartoons/issue. Prefers single panel; b&w line drawings, b&w washes. Send query letter with samples of style to be kept on file. Material not kept on file is returned only if requested. Reports only if interested. Buys reprint rights. Write for appointment to show portfolio. Payment varies; pays on acceptance.
Illustrations: Number of illustrations used/issue varies. Works on assignment only. Send query letter with samples to be kept on file. Samples not kept on file are returned only if requested. Reports only if interested. Write for appointment to show portfolio. Buys reprint rights. Payment varies; pays on acceptance.

CALIFORNIA APPAREL NEWS, 945 S. Wall St., Los Angeles CA 90015. (213)626-0411. Art Director: Johnny Wentmiller. Emphasizes fashion for the trade. Weekly. Circ. 25,000. Returns originals after publication.
Illustrations: Buys 10 illustrations/issue from freelancers. Considers fashion illustration. Works on assignment only. Send query letter with brochure, resume, business card and samples to be kept on file. Call for appointment to show portfolio. Accepts photostats, tear sheets, photocopies, slides or photographs as samples. Samples not filed returned only if requested. Reports only if interested. Negotiates rights purchased. Pays on publication.

CARTOON WORLD, Box 30367, Lincoln NE 68503. (112)435-3191. Editor/Publisher: George Hartman. Newsletter "slanted to amateur and professional freelance cartoonists." Monthly. Circ. 300. Accepts previously published material. Returns original artwork after publication. Sample copy $5; art guidelines available.
Cartoons: Does not want individual cartoons; seeks articles on cartooning, illustrated with cartoons, that will benefit other cartoonists. Topics as how to cartoon, how to create ideas, cartoon business plans, hints and markets. Send query letter with originals only. Reports within 10 days. Material will not be returned nor considered for publication without return postage. To show a portfolio, mail appropriate materials, which should include final reproduction/product. Buys reprint rights. Pays $5/8 ½x11 page, on acceptance.
Tips: "I only use stuff that helps in some way any pro or amateur cartoonist or artist."

CHICAGO READER, Box 11101, Chicago IL 60611. (312)828-0350. Editor-in-Chief: Robert A. Roth. Cartoon/Illustration Editor: Robert E. McCamant. For young adults in lakefront neighborhoods interested in things to do in Chicago and feature stories on city life. Weekly. Circ. 129,000. Sample copy $2.
Cartoons: Buys 9 cartoons/issue on any topic; single, double and multi-panel. Pays $10 and up. "At present, we carry eight regular cartoon features, plus one or more irregularly-appearing ones. While we are not actively looking for more, we will consider anything, and find the space if the material warrants it." Send photocopies (no originals). Buys one-time rights; pays by 15th of month following publication.
Illustrations: Buys 3 illustrations/issue on assigned themes. Send photocopies or arrange interview to show portfolio. SASE. Buys one-time rights. Pays by 15th of month following publication. Cover and inside: Pays $120-220, b&w line drawings and washes.

THE CHRISTIAN SCIENCE MONITOR, 1 Norway St., Boston MA 02115. (617)450-2360. Design Director: Susan Ballenger Tyner. Newspaper emphasizing analytical reporting of current events; diverse features and news features for well-educated, well-informed readers in all fields—specifically politicians, educators, business people. Daily. Circ. 200,000. Original artwork returned after publication. Sample copy and art guidelines available.
Illustrations: Buys 1-2 illustrations/week from freelancers. Prefers editorial ("op-ed') conceptual themes; line, wash or scratchboard. Works on assignment only. Send samples to be filed. Samples should be 8½x11" photocopies; no originals. Samples not returned. Reports only if interested. Buys first rights. Pays $100-150, b&w; on publication.

THE CHRONICLE OF HIGHER EDUCATION, Suite 700, 1255 23rd St. NW, Washington DC 20037. (202)466-1035. Art Director: Peter Stafford. Emphasizes all aspects of higher education for college and university administrators, professors, students and staff. Weekly. Circ. 75,000. Sample copy available.
Cartoons: Uses approximately 30 cartoons/year. Prefers higher education related themes, i.e., sports, high cost of tuition, student loans, energy conservation on campus. Prefers single panel, with gagline; b&w line drawings or b&w washes. Send query letter with samples of style to be kept on file. Material

not kept on file is returned only if requested. Reports only if interested. Buys one-time rights. Pays on publication.
Illustrations: Buys 1 illustration/week from freelancers. Uses 1 illustration/issue; buys all from freelancers. Uses a variety of styles, depending on the tone of the story. Works on assignment only. Send query letter with photostats or good quality photocopy for line work; photographs or slides for halftone work, business card and tear sheets to be kept on file. Samples are returned only if requested. Reports only if interested. Buys one-time rights. Pays $100 and up depending on size, b&w, inside. Pays on publication.

***CITROEN CAR CLUB NEWSLETTER**,350 Hulbe Rd., Boise ID 83705. Editor: Karl Petersen. Emphasizing Citroen, Panhard and related cars, parts and international activities. Monthly. Circ. 1,200. Accepts previously published material. Original artwork returned after publication if requested. Art guidelines not available.
Cartoons: Send query letter with samples of style and finished cartoons. Samples are filed. Samples not filed are returned if requested. Reports back within 2 weeks. No payment.
Illustrations: Send query letter. Samples are filed. Samples not filed are returned if requested. Reports back within 2 weeks. Write to schedule an appointment to show a portfolio. No payment.
Tips "We have a limited forum of enthusiasts. We will give submissions international exposure at no cost to artist. We have done one-artist seven illustration duotone calendar, for example, for Kojiro Imamura, Japan."

CLEVELAND PLAIN DEALER, 1801 Superior Ave., Cleveland OH 44114. (216)344-4447. Contact: Graphics Editor. Newspaper. Emphasizes current events, features for metropolitan daily readership. Circ. 500,000. Accepts previously published material. Original artwork returned after publication if requested.
Illustrations: Rarely buys illustrations from freelancers. Preferred themes are any dealing with current affairs. Works on assignment only. Send query letter with resume, tear sheets, photostats, photocopies, slides and photographs to be kept on file. Samples not filed are returned only if requested. Reports only interested. To show a portfolio, mail tear sheets, photostats and b&w. Buys one-time rights. Pays $150, b&w, cover; $50, b&w, inside; on publication.
Tips: Likes to see *newspaper* or other editorial illustrations as samples. Prefers "working with local talent Needs fast turnaround. *No* cartoons!"

***COA REVIEW: THE NEWSLETTER ABOUT CHILDREN OF ALCOHOLICS**, Box 190, Rutherford NJ 07070. (201)460-7912. Managing Directors: Thomas W. Perrin or Janice A. Treggett. Bimonthly newsletter. Emphasizes children of alcoholics. Also covers co-dependency. "Articles appeal to the professional therapist and the lay person." Circ. 2,000. Sample copy $1.
Cartoons: "I have not been able to find any cartoonists as of yet." Prefers cartoons that lampoon psychologists or psychiatrists and the foibles of the client and aspects of his personality." Prefers single panel with gagline; b&w line drawings. Send roughs. Samples are filed. Samples not filed are returned. Reports back within 6 months. "If you don't hear from me after 6 months, forget it." Buys first rights. Pays $25, b&w; on publication.
Illustrations: Prefers pen & ink line drawings about alcoholic disorders. Works on assignment only. Send query letter with resume and samples. Samples are filed. Samples not filed are returned. Reports back within 6 months. To show a portfolio, mail tear sheets and photocopies. Buys first rights. Pays $75, b&w, cover. Pays on publication.
Tips: "Also interested in cover art for our catalog. We also publish books. If an artist can put together a catalog of his work, we will consider publishing a book."

THE COMDEX SHOW DAILY, (formerly the Official Comdex Show Daily), 300 1st Ave., Needham MA 02194. (617)449-6600. Tabloid. Emphasizes computers and computer-related products for attendees and exhibitors at the U.S. Comdex Shows. Seasonal: Fall, Spring. Circ. 40,000. Accepts previously published material. Original artwork returned after publication if requested. Sample copy free for SASE; art guidelines available.
Cartoons: Buys 50-100 cartoons/issue from freelancers; buys 300-400/year from freelancers. "Computer grahics used in cartoon illustration. Application ties in well as our newspaper is read by people in the computer industry." Wants anything related to computers, trade shows, Las Vegas or Atlanta. Prefers single panel with or without gagline; b&w line drawings. Send query letter with rough or finished cartoons to be kept on file. Material not filed is returned by SASE only if requested. Reports within several weeks. Buys one-time rights. Pays $18; on acceptance.
Illustrations: Themes: computers/trade shows/computer related products. Humorous and cartoon-style illustrations used once a year. Works on assignment only. Send query letter with tear sheets, photostats, photocopies, slides and photographs to be kept on file. Samples returned by SASE only if request-

ed. Reports within several weeks only if interested. Call or write to schedule an appointment to show a portfolio, which should include final reproduction/product, tear sheets and photostats. Buys one-time rights. Pays $50-100, b&w; on acceptance.

***COMMUNICATOR**, 5045 Wilshire Blvd., Los Angeles CA 90036. Manager, Sales Communications: Eric Gould. Newsletter. Emphasizes product marketing and sales for representative field sales panels and management. Monthly. Circ. 1,500. Accepts previously published material. Original artwork not returned after publication.
Cartoons: Uses 5-10 cartoons/issue. Prefers sales themes. Prefers single, double, or multiple panel, with or without gagline; b&w line drawings. Send query letter with roughs to be kept on file. Material not kept on file is returned. Material not copyrighted. Pays on acceptance.
Illustrations: Uses 15 illustrations/issue. Prefers product, food marketing, sales as themes. Send query letter with samples to be kept on file. Prefers photostats or photographs as samples. Samples not kept on file are returned. Reports within 10 days. Material not copyrighted. Pays on acceptance.

COMPUTERWORLD FOCUS, 375 Cochituate Rd., Framingham MA 01701. Art Director: Tom Monahan. Tabloid. Emphasizes news and products relating to the computer field. Monthly. Returns original artwork after publication.
Illustrations: Buys 2 illustrations/week. Themes depend on the storyline. Works on assignment only. Send query letter with brochure and photocopies or photostats to be kept on file. Reports back only if interested. Buys first rights. To show portfolio, mail appropriate materials or call to schedule an appointment; portfolio should include original/final art, final reproduction/product, color, photostats and b&w. Pays $200, b&w and $250-600 color, inside; on acceptance.

CONNECTICUT TRAVELER, 2276 Whitney Ave., Hamden CT 06518. (203)281-7505. Managing Director of Publications: Elke P. Martin. Newspaper. Estab. 1983. Emphasizes automobile travel, safety and maintenance, national and international travel and regional events (New England) for AAA members. Monthly. Circ. 155,000. Accepts previously published material. Returns original artwork after publication. Sample copy free for SASE; art guidelines available.
Cartoons: Buys 1 cartoon/issue from freelancers. Prefers single panel with gagline; b&w line drawings; b&w washes. Send query letter with samples of style to be kept on file. Reports within 2 weeks. Buys reprint rights or negotiates rights purchased. Pays on publication.

THE CONSTANTIAN, 123 Orr Rd., Pittsburgh PA 15241. (412)831-8750. Editor: Randall J. Dicks. "We (Constantian Society) are monarchists and royalists, interested in monarchy as a political system and royalty as persons and personalities." Bimonthly newsletter. Circ. 400. Previously published work OK. Sample copy for 39¢ and SASE; free artist's guidelines.
Cartoons: "We have not used many cartoons but we are certainly willing to consider them. We take our subject seriously, but there is room for a little humor. It is best to write us about the idea first and send samples." Send query letter with resume and samples. To show a portfolio, mail appropriate materials. SASE. Reports within 1 week. Buys various rights. Pays $5-10, b&w line drawings; on acceptance or publication.
Illustrations: "We use a lot of decorative drawings and work which relate to our subject matter (heraldic items of different nationalities, coats of arms, monograms, etc.)." We have a number of new projects in mind, and may need cover art and other illustrations for booklets or brochures. SASE. Reports within 1 week. Buys various rights. Pays $10 and up, b&w line drawings; on acceptance or publication.
Tips: "Now we are using a MacIntosh computer for our journal—it has new look and changes in format. Artists should have some understanding of our subject—monarchy and royalty."

CONSTRUCTION SUPERVISION & SAFETY LETTER, 24 Rope Ferry Rd., Waterford CT 06386. (203)442-4365. Editor: DeLoris Lidestri. Emphasizes construction supervision for supervisors who work with their crews. Covers bricklayers, carpenters, electricians, painters, plasterers, plumbers and building laborers. Semimonthly. Circ. 3,700. Original artwork not returned after publication. Free sample copy.
Cartoons: Uses 1-3 cartoons/issue which are done by freelancers. Receives 5-7 submissions/week from freelancers. Uses "situations that deal with supervision in construction. Cartoons that depict both men and women as workers and/or supervisors needed. No sexist material, please." Format: single panel, b&w line drawings with gagline. Prefers to see finished cartoons. SASE. Reports in 2 weeks. Buys all rights. Pays $10 on acceptance.
Tips: "Send cartoons that deal with supervision to me. But any to do with Construction safety send to Winifred Bonney, editor. CL has expanded from four pages to eight pages we have a four-page safety section now.

THE CRANSTON MIRROR, 250 Auburn St., Cranston RI 02910. Contact: Malcolm L. Daniels. Weekly newspaper. Circ. 10,000. Original artwork returned after publication. Prefers local artists. Also uses artists for layout, illustration, technical art, paste-up, lettering and retouching. Pays $175, booklet; $15-75, illustrations.

Cartoons: Uses 2 cartoons/issue; buys 1 or none/issue from freelancers. Receives 3-4 submissions/week from freelancers. Interested in local editorial subjects. Call for interview to show portfolio (except July and August). Prefers to see finished cartoons. Reports in 1 week. Pays $20, b&w.

Illustrations: Uses 2-4 illustrations/issue; buys 1-2/issue from freelancers. Send resume and photocopies to be kept on file for future assignments. Reports in 1 week. Call or write to schedule an appointment to show a portfolio, which should include original/final art and photostats. Pays $30-50, b&w, cover; $25, b&w, inside; on publication.

Tips: Especially looks for "unique idea, quality workmanship and regard to detail. Ideas, however, are paramount. Be neat. Have material ready and know what you want to say for a portfolio review."

CYCLE NEWS, Box 498, Long Beach CA 90801. (213)427-7433. Editor: Jack Mangus. For the motorcycle enthusiast. Weekly newspaper. Circ. 75,000. Previously published work OK. Returns originals to artist after publication. Sample copy available. Art guidelines not available.

Cartoons: Buys 0-2 cartoons/issue. Send query letter with finished cartoons and SASE. Reports back only if interested. Negotiates payment and rights purchased. Pays on publication.

Illustrations: Buys varying number of illustrations/issue. Works on assignment only. Send query letter with photocopies and SASE. Reports only if interested. Negotiates payment and rights purchased. Pays on publication.

DOLLARS & SENSE, 325 Pennsylvania Ave. SE, Washington DC 20003. (202)543-1300. Contact: Editor. For people interested in reducing taxes and government spending. 10 issues/year. Circ. 140,000. Previously published material and simultaneous submissions OK. Especially needs federal budget information. Original work not returned after publication. Free sample copy for SASE.

Cartoons: Uses 3 cartoons/issue; number bought from freelancers varies. Interested in political/taxation themes. Send finished cartoons. Samples returned by SASE. Reports within 2 weeks. Negotiates one-time and first rights. Payment varies; on publication.

Illustrations: Uses 4 illustrations/issue. Interested in political themes. Send finished art or samples of style. Samples returned by SASE. Reports within 2 weeks. Negotiates rights. Pays $60-150 cover, color washes; inside, payment varies; on publication.

Tips: "Either make the graphics very general in nature or send in very specific cartoons."

***THE ECO-HUMANE LETTER**, The International Ecology Society, 1471 Barclay St., St. Paul MN 55106-1405. (612)774-4971. Editor: R.J.F. Kramer. Periodic newsletter. Emphasizes animals/environment. Features "select article reprints, action alerts, general data for those interested in the protection of animals and nature." Circ. 6,000. Accepts previously published material. Sample copy free for SASE with first-class postage.

Cartoons: Prefers gag cartoons, editorial or political cartoons, caricatures and humorous illustrations. Prefers single panel, double panel, multi-panel with or without gagline; b&w line drawings and b&w washes. Prefers any size if readable. Send query leter with samples of style, roughs and finished cartoons. Samples are not filed. Samples are not returned. Reports back only if interested. Buys all rights. Pays $10, b&w; on publication.

Illustrations: Prefers line art. Send query letter or resume. Samples are not filed. Samples are not returned. Reports back only if interested. To show a portfolio, mail appropriate materials. Buys all rights. Pays $10, b&w, cover; $10, b&w, inside; on publication.

Tips: "Cover all bases. Volunteer for good causes."

EXPLORER,Box 302, Yonkers NY 10710-0302. (914)1406. President: William York. Bimonthly newsletter of IASP, a society of hundreds of space collectors, (stamps, covers and memorabilia). Circ. 1000. Accepts previously published material. Returns original artwork to the artists after publication, if requested. Sample copy available for SASE with 56¢ postage.

Cartoons: Prefers editorial cartoons. Prefers cartoons on recent space events including caricatures of astronauts. Prefers single panel with gaglines; small, ready to print without reducing. Send query letter with samples of style. Samples are not filed. "We will return anything we don't print and will return other work after we print it, if requested." Reports back within 2 weeks. Negotiates rights purchased. Pays $25 minimum. Pays on publication.

Illustration: Buys 6 illustrations/year from freelancers. Prefers line art, b&w only, no shades which do not copy well. Send query letter with samples. Samples are not filed. Samples not filed are returned by SASE. Reports back within 2 weeks. Call to schedule an appointment to show a portfolio or mail appropriate materials. Negotiates rights purchased. Pays $25 minimum b&w, cover or inside. Pays on publication.

Tips: "We need space editorial/cartoons, space designs for cachets and space cancels and diagrams of space events. A New York cartoonist is preferred, but not essential. Once published, we would use for cachets if appropriate. We have paid considerably above $25 minimum at times."

THE FOREMAN'S LETTER, 24 Rope Ferry Rd., Waterford CT 06386. Editor: Carl Thunberg. For industrial supervisors.
Cartoons: Usually uses 1 cartoon/issue; may buy up to 2/issue from freelancers. Receives 20 submissions/week from freelancers. Interested in "supervisor-worker relations; avoid sexism and other/discriminatory situations." Prefers single panel, finished cartoons. Send query letter with brochure showing art style. SASE. Reports in 1 week. To show a portfolio, mail photostats. Buys all rights. Pays $10-15; on acceptance.

FREEWAY, Box 632, Glen Ellyn IL 60138. (312)668-6000. Designer: Mardelle Ayers. Sunday School paper emphasizing Christian living for teenagers for high school and college age teens from a conservative, evangelical Christian upbringing. Published 4 quarters a year, 13 issues per quarter. Circ. 60,000. Accepts previously published material. Sample copy free for SASE with 22¢ postage.
Cartoons: Buys 4-5 cartoons/quarter. Prefers any style or theme that appeals to teens. Prefers commissioned artwork for specific articles; b&w line drawings or b&w washes. Send query letter with samples. Material not kept on file is returned by SASE. Reports within 4 weeks. Buys first rights. Pays $15-20, b&w.
Illustrations: Buys 1-3 illustrations/issue from freelancers. Works on assignment only. Prefers any theme or style appealing to teens. Send query letter with resume, photostats and photocopies. Samples not filed are returned by SASE if requested. Reports only if interested. To show a portfolio, mail photostats and b&w photos. Pays $15-150.
Tips: Looks for "good contrast and composition along with a contemporary look in technique."

THE GERMANTOWN COURIER, 162 W. Chelten Ave., Philadelphia PA 19144. (215)848-4300. Editor: Debbie Flood. Newspaper emphasizing neighborhood news in northwest Philadelphia; low to middle income. Weekly. Circ. 25,500. Original work returned after publication. Sample copy and art guidelines available.
Illustrations: Occasionally buys illustrations from freelancers. Uses illustrations to accompany news stories. Works on assignment only. Send query letter with resume and photocopies as samples. Samples not filed returned by SASE only if requested. Reports only if interested. Buys first rights or reprint rights. Pays $7.50 on publication.

THE GOODY MIRROR, 1000 W. Main St., Manchester GA 31816. (404)846-8481. Editor: Ward Garrett. Emphasizes employee communications for employees, production, supervision, management, stock holders. Quarterly. Circ. 5,000. Accepts previously published material and simultaneous submissions. Original artwork returned after publication. Sample copy for SASE.
Cartoons: Uses 1-2 cartoons/issue; buys all from freelancers. Prefers single panel with gagline; b&w line drawings. Send query letter with samples of style and roughs to be kept on file. Material not kept on file is returned only if requested. Reports within 3 weeks. Buys one-time rights. Pays $10, b&w. Pays on acceptance.
Illustrations: Uses 2 illustrations/issue; buys all from freelancers. Prefers themes illustrative of editorial thrusts—dollar breakdown, specific situations. Works on assignment only. Send query letter with photostats to be kept on file. Samples are returned by SASE if not kept on file. Reports within 3 weeks. Buys one-time rights. Payment depends on assignment. Pays on acceptance.

GUARDIAN,33 W. 17th ST., New York NY 10011. Photo/Graphics Editor: Anthony Parker. Independent radical newspaper with national and international news and cultural reviews for nonsectarian leftists and activists. Weekly. Circ. 20,000. Accepts previously published material. Original artwork returned by SASE after publication. Sample copy available; art guidelines free for SASE.
Cartoons: Buys 7 cartoons/issue from freelancers. Prefers b&w, pen & ink, scratch board; progressive themes. Prefers single, double or multiple panel; b&w line drawings. Send query letter with sample of style not larger than 8½x11" to be kept on file. Material not filed is returned by SASE. Reports only if interested. Write for appointment to show portfolio. Negotiates rights purchased. Pays $15, b&w; on publication.
Illustrations: Buys 3 illustrations/issue from freelancers. Themes: progressive politics, issues. Send query letter and photocopies not larger than 8½x11" to be kept on file. Samples not filed are returned by SASE. Reports only if interested. To show a portfolio, mail original/final art, tear sheets, photostats, photographs and b&w. Negotiates rights purchased. Pays $15, b&w, cover, inside; on publication.

HIGH COUNTRY NEWS, Box 1090, Paonia CO 81428. (303)527-4898. Editor: Betsy Marston. Emphasizes economic and environmental issues, Rocky Mountain regional pieces for national audience,

all ages, occupations. Biweekly. Circ. 4,500. Accepts previously published material and simultaneous submissions. Original artwork returned after publication if accompanied by postage.
Illustrations: Uses 5 illustrations/issue; buys 3 illustrations/issue from freelancers. Send query letter with samples and/or tear sheets to be kept on file. Prefers photocopies as samples. Samples not kept on file are returned by SASE. Reports within 1 month. Buys one-time rights. Pays after publication.

HIGH-TECH MANAGER'S BULLETIN, 24 Rope Ferry Rd., Waterford CT 06386. (203)442-4365. Contact: Editor. Emphasis is on the supervision of technicians in high technology industry. Semimonthly. Free sample copy.
Cartoons: Uses 1 cartoon/issue; buys from freelancer. Interested in non-sexist material which pokes fun at aspects of high technology production and supervision. "Send material after reading guidelines." Prefers single panel b&w line drawings with or without the gagline. SASE. Reports in 3-6 weeks. To show a portfolio, mail appropriate materials, which should include roughs. Buys all rights. Pays $10 for b&w; on acceptances.
Tips: "Read guidelines, know the field and study sample before submission."

JEWISH CURRENT EVENTS, 430 Keller Ave., Elmont NY 11003. Editor-in-Chief: Samuel Deutsch. Art Director: S. Askenazi. For Jewish audience. Biweekly. Previously published and simultaneous submissions OK.
Cartoons: Buys camera-ready art with Jewish content or flavor or adaptable for such; single, double and multiple panel. Submit art. SASE. Reports in 1 week. Pays $15-100 plus, b&w line drawings; on publication.

***JEWS FOR JESUS NEWSLETTER**, 60 Haight St., San Francisco CA 94102. Contact: Editor. Emphasizes Christian witness to Jews, evangelical Christian thought and humor to teach Christian truth for ministers and lay leaders who are evangelical, yet interested in Jews and Jewish customs. Monthly newsletter. Receives 6 cartoons and 12 illustrations/month from freelance artists. Simultaneous submissions OK. Original work not returned after publication. Free sample copy for SASE.
Illustrations: Uses 5-6 illustrations/issue; buys some from freelancers. Interested in religious humor. Send copies of finished art only. Samples returned by SASE. Reports in 6 weeks. Buys first rights or negotiates. Pays $25-100, cover and inside, color washes; $10-100 inside, b&w; on acceptance.
Tips: There is a trend toward "large evangelical magazines using more humor that helps us laugh at ourselves. Artists should show that they have an understanding of our beliefs and respect them."

THE JOURNAL, Addiction Research Foundation, 33 Russell St., Toronto, Ontario M5S 2S1 Canada. (416)595-6053. Editor: Anne MacLennan. Concerns drug and alcohol research, treatment, prevention and education. Monthly. Circ. 26,000. Free sample copy and guidelines.
Cartoons: Uses cartoons occasionally; buys 1/month from freelancers. Receives 1 submission/month from freelancers. Interested in "themes relating to alcohol and other drug use." Prefers finished cartoons. Pays from $30, 3x5 minimum cartoons; on publication.
Illustrations: Buys 1 illustration/month from freelancers. Send photocopies. Write to schedule an appointment to show a portfolio, which should include roughs and b&w. Pays $200 b&w, cover and inside; on publication.

THE JOURNAL NEWSPAPERS, The Journal, Springfield VA 22159. (703)750-8779. Entertainment Editor: Buzz McClain. Emphasizes daily news and features. Daily. Circ. 160,000. Accepts previously published material. Original artwork returned after publication.
Illustrations: Buys a few illustrations from freelancers. Works on assignment only. Send query letter with resume and tear sheets. Samples not filed are returned only if requested. Reports only if interested. Call to schedule an appointment to show a portfolio, which should include original/final art and tear sheets. Buys first rights. Pays on publication.

THE KERSHAW NEWS-ERA, 200 E. Marion, Box 398, Kershaw SC 29067. (803)475-6095. Co-owner/Editor: Jim McKeown Jr. Newspaper emphasizing general news including textile industry and agriculture; music, theatre and drama; hunting; and creative crafts. "We have a special edition TMC, Total Market Coverage, circ. 7,000." Weekly. Circ. 5,000. Accepts previously published material. Original work returned after publication. Sample copy free for SASE with 50¢ postage. Art guidelines free for SASE with 50¢ postage or postage required for return mailing.
Cartoons: Buys 2 cartoons/issue from freelancers. Prefers political and humorous themes appropriate for small town. Prefers multiple panel with gagline; b&w line drawings. Send query letter with samples of style to be kept on file. Material not filed returned by SASE. Reports only if interested. Buys reprint rights. Negotiates payment. Pays on publication.

LIGHTWAVE, the Journal of Fiber Optics, 235 Bear Hill Rd., Waltham MA 02154. (617)890-2700. Editor: Sharon Scully. Newspaper. Emphasizes fiber optics for communication and sensing for engineers. Monthly. Circ. 13,000. Sometimes accepts previously published material. Returns original artwork after publication on request. Sample copy $3.50 for paid subscribers; $4 nonsubscribers.
Cartoons: Considers b&w line drawings with or without gaglines. Send query letter with samples of style or roughs to be kept on file. Write for appointment to show portfolio. Material not filed returned by SASE. Reports only if interested. Buys first rights. Pays $100 for b&w; on acceptance.
Illustrations: Buys 2 illustrations/issue from freelancers. Prefers sketches of real people or objects. Send query letter with tear sheets or photocopies to be kept on file. Write for appointment to show portfolio. Samples not filed returned by SASE. Reports only if interested. Buys first rights. Pays $50-100 for b&w; on acceptance.

THE MANITOBA TEACHER, 191 Harcourt St., Winnipeg, Manitoba R3J 3H2 Canada. (204)888-7961. Editor: Mrs. Miep van Raalte. Emphasizes education for teachers and others in Manitoba. 4 issues/year between September and June. Circ. 16,900. Free sample copy and art guidelines.
Cartoons: Uses less than 2 cartoons/year relating to education in Manitoba. Prefers single panel, b&w line drawings with gagline. Send roughs and samples of style. SAE (nonresidents include IRC). Reports in 1 month.
Illustrations: Interested in b&w line drawings for inside. Send roughs and samples of style. SAE (nonresidents include IRC). Reports in 1 month.
Tips: Especially needs cartoons and illustrations related directly to the Manitoba scene. "Inquire before sending work."

MASS HIGH TECH, 755 Mt. Auburn St., Watertown MA 02172. (617)924-2422. Executive Editor: Alan R. Earls. Newspaper. Emphasizes high technology businesses, schools, etc., in greater Boston (Eastern Massachusetts) and New England area for programmers, engineers, managers and other technical professionals. Bimonthly. Circ. 36,000. Sample copy with $2 postage or money order.
Cartoons: Buys 1-2 cartoons/issue from freelancers. Prefers single panel. Send samples. Reports in 1 month. Buys all rights. Pays $25+ on publication.
Illustrations: Works on assignment only. Send query letter with brochure to be kept on file. Prefers photostats as samples. Samples not kept on file are returned by SASE only if requested. Reports only if interested. Material not copyrighted. Payment varies.

THE MIAMI HERALD, One Herald Plaza, Miami FL 33132. (305)376-3431. Director of Editorial Art and Design: Randy Stano. Daily newspaper. Circ. 475,000 daily, over 500,000 on Sunday. Accepts previously published material. Original artwork returned after publication. Sample copy available; plus job descriptions/specs are available.
Cartoons: Occasionally buys cartoons from freelancers. Material not filed is returned. Reports only if interested. Write or call for appointment to show portfolio. Buys one-time rights. Pays on acceptance.
Illustrations: Buys 1-6 illustrations/month from freelancers. Works on assignment only. Send resume, tear sheets and slides. Samples not filed are returned if requested. Reports only if interested. Call or write to schedule an appointment to show a portfolio, which should include final reproduction/product and tear sheets. Buys one-time or reprint rights. Pays $150-300 for b&w and $300-450 for color, cover. Pays on acceptance.
Tips: "Keep an open mind."

***MIAMI TODAY**, Box 1368, Miami FL 33101. (305)358-2663. Editor: Gloria B. Anderson. Weekly tabloid. Circ. 30,000. Accepts previously published material. Returns original artwork after publication. Sample copy free for SASE with $1.34 postage.
Cartoons: Occasionally buys cartoons from freelancers. Prefers business, real estate as themes. Prefers b&w line drawings and b&w washes. Send finished cartoons. Samples are not filed. Samples are returned by SASE. Reports back within weeks. Buys one-time and reprint rights. Pays $5-10, b&w; on publication.
Illustrations: Rarely buys illustrations from freelancers. Send query letter with brochure showing art style. Samples are returned by SASE. Reports back within weeks. Buys one-time and reprint rights. Pays $10, b&w.

MILKWEED CHRONICLE, Box 24303, Minneapolis MN 55424. (612)332-3192. Art Director: Rand Scholes. Emphasizes poetry and graphics with the conversation between the two for readers and writers of poetry, artists, and those interested in visuals. Consumer tabloid published 3 times/year. Circ. 5,000. Receives 3 cartoons and 2 illustrations/week from freelance artists. Previously pubilshed material OK but prefers original work. Original work returned after publication. Sample copy $4.

Illustrations: Uses 25-40 illustrations/issue; buys 10-30 from freelancers. Style is open, quantity, theme of page (poetry, essay, etc.) and issue. Provide finished art, samples of style and tear sheets to be kept on file for possible future assignments. Samples returned by SASE. "We try to answer queries and make decision at due times for each issue—every 4 months." Write for appointment or submit portfolio. Pays $20-100 cover, $10-50 inside, b&w line drawings and washes; on publication.

MILWAUKEE JOURNAL, Box 661, Milwaukee WI 53201. Managing Editor: Steve Hammah. Daily. Circ. 310,000.
Cartoons: Assistant Managing Editor/Features: Barbara Dembsky. Buys themes acceptable to family readership; single panel. Query with samples. SASE. Reports in 2 weeks. Buys one-time rights. Pays $15 minimum, washes.
Illustrations: Art Director: Vincent Catteruccia. Buys themes acceptable to family readership. Query with samples. SASE. Reports in 2 weeks. Buys all rights. Inside: Pays $10 minimum.
Tips: There is a trend toward "more graphics to accompany news stories."

NATIONAL ENQUIRER, Lantana FL 33464. Cartoon Editor: Michele L. Cooke. Weekly tabloid. Circ. 6,000,000. Previously published work OK if cartoonist owns rights.
Cartoons: Buys 450 cartoons/year on "all subjects the family reader can relate to, especially animal and husband-wife situations. Captionless cartoons have a better chance of selling here." Receives 2,000 cartoons/week from freelance artists, buys 8/week from freelancers. Especially needs Christmas cartoon spread (submit by August). Send query letter with original cartoons. Mail 8½x11" art. SASE. Reports in 2 weeks. "No portfolios, please." Buys first rights. Pays $300 maximum, b&w single panel; $40 every panel thereafter; pays on acceptance.
Tips: "Study 5-6 issues before submitting. Check captions for spelling. New submitters should send introductory letter. All cartoonists should include phone and social security number. Know your market. We have no use for political or off-color gags. Neatness counts and sloppy, stained artwork registers a negative reaction. Besides neatness, we also look for "correct spelling and punctuation on captions and in the body of the cartoon, accurate rendering of the subject (if the subject is a duck, make it look like a duck and not a goose, swan or chicken), and *most important* is visual impact! Prefers 8½x11" instead of 'halfs.' If submitting reprints, know *who* owns the rights."

THE NATIONAL LAW JOURNAL, Suite 900, 111 8th Ave., New York NY 10011. (212)741-8300. Art Director: Cynthia Currie. Tabloid emphasizing law for attorneys. Weekly. Circ. 38,000. Original artwork returned after publication. Sample copy $2.
Cartoons: Buys 1 cartoon/issue from freelancers. Prefers single panel; b&w line drawings. Send query letter with samples of style or finished cartoons. Material not filed is returned. Reports within 2 weeks. Buys one-time rights. Pays $100, b&w; on acceptance.
Illustrations: Buys 2 illustrations/month from freelancers. Works on assignment only. Send query letter with brochure to be kept on file. Samples returned only if requested. Reports within 2 weeks. Buys one-time rights. Pays $125-250, b&w, cover, inside; on acceptance.

NATIONAL LIBRARIAN, Box 586, Alma MI 48801. (517)463-7227. Editor: Peter Dollard. Emphasizes professional issues related to librarianship. Quarterly. Circ. 500. Original work returned after publication. Free sample copy and publication guidelines for SASE.
Cartoons: Uses single panel b&w line drawings with gagline. Send query letter with finished cartoons. Samples returned. Reports in 2-4 weeks. Material not copyrighted. Pays $25, b&w; on acceptance.
Illustrations: Uses 1-2 illustrations/issue. Send query letter with finished art. Reports in 2 weeks. Material not copyrighted. Pays $25; on acceptance.

NETWORK WORLD, 375 Cochituate Rd., Framingham MA 01701. (617)879-0700. Art Director: Dianne Barrett. Tabloid. Emphasizes news and features relating to the communications field. Weekly. Returns original artwork after publication. Sample copy free for SASE.
Illustrations: Number purchased/issue varies. Themes depend on the storyline. Works on assignment only. Send query letter with brochure and photocopies to be kept on file. Write for appointment to show portfolio. Reports only if interested. Buys first rights. Pays $175-200 for b&w and $225-400 for color, inside; on acceptance.

NEW ALASKAN, Rt. 1, Box 677, Ketchikan AK 99901. (907)247-2490. Editor: Bob Pickrell. Emphasizes Southeastern Alaska lifestyle, history and politics for general public in this area. Monthly. Circ. 6,000. Previously published material and simultaneous submissions OK. Original work returned after publication by SASE. Sample copy $1.50; art guidelines for SASE.
Cartoons: Uses 1 cartoon/issue; buys 1 from freelancers. Interested only in art with a Southeastern Alaska tie-in; single panel with or without gagline, b&w line drawings. Send roughs or samples of style.

© Marc Pacella

This pen-and-ink illustration was one of five drawn by illustrator Marc Pacella of South Orange, New Jersey, for the* National Law Journal. *The artwork accompanied an article focusing on the disappointments many full-time associates experience at law firms. Pacella found the journal through the* Artist's Market *and sent samples. He was paid $500 for one-time rights to the five illustrations. Art director Cynthia Currie finds Pacella "open to suggestion but also creative, with multiple visual interpretations for each concept."

Samples returned by SASE. Reports in 6 months. Negotiates rights purchased. Pays $25 up, b&w; on publication.

Illustrations: Uses 2 illustrations/issue; buys 1 from freelancers. Interested only in art with a Southeastern Alaska tie-in. "We prefer mss with illustrations except for cover art which can stand by itself." Works on assignment only. Provide business card and samples to be kept on file for possible future assignments. Samples returned by SASE. Reports in 6 months. Negotiates rights purchased and payment; on publication.

NEW ENGLAND RUNNING, Box 658, Brattleboro VT 05301. Contact: Editorial Department. Tabloid. Emphasizes New England running, primarily competitive. Monthly. Circ. 4,000. Original artwork returned after publication. Sample copy $2.

Cartoons: Uses 1 cartoon/issue; buys from freelancer. Prefers single panel, with gagline; b&w line drawings. Send query letter with samples of style to be kept on file. Material not kept on file is returned by SASE. Reports in 1 month. Buys one-time rights. Pays $10, b&w; on publication.

Illustrations: Uses 2 illustrations/year; buys all from freelancers. Send query letter with clippings and photocopies and tear sheets to be kept on file. Prefers clippings or photocopies as samples. Samples not kept on file are returned by SASE. Reports within 1 month. Buys one-time rights. Pays $10-20, b&w; on publication.

Tips: "We need simple cartoons done in bold, black lines for best reproduction."

***NEW ENGLAND SENIOR CITIZEN/SENIOR AMERICAN NEWS**,Prime National Publishing Corp., 470 Boston Post Rd., Weston MA 02193. Editor-in-Chief/Art Director: Ira Alterman. For men and women ages 60 and over who are interested in travel, retirement lifestyles and nostalgia. Monthly tabloid. Circ. 60,000. Previously published work OK. Sample copy 50¢.
Illustrations: Buys 1-4/issue. Query or mail samples. SASE. Reports in 6 months. Cover: Pays $10-50, b&w. Pays on publication.

THE NEW SOUTHERN LITERARY MESSENGER, 400 S. Laurel St., Richmond VA 23220. (804)780-1244. Editor: Charles Lohmann. Tabloid. Emphasizes poetry and short stories. Quarterly. Circ. 400. Accepts previously published material. Returns original artwork after publication. Sample copy $1. Art guidelines free for SASE with 32¢ postage.
Cartoons: Buys 3 or 4/issue. Prefers single, double or multiple panel with or without gagline; b&w line drawings. Send query letter to be kept on file. Write for appointment to show portfolio. Reports within 3 weeks. Purchases one-time reprint rights. Pays $5; on publication.
Tips: "Don't call or write unless you live in Richmond, VA. I only work personally, face-to-face with artists."

NEW YORK ANTIQUE ALMANAC, Box 335, Lawrence NY 11559. (516)371-3300. Editor: Carol Nadel. For art, antiques and nostalgia collectors/investors. Monthly tabloid. Circ. 52,000. Reports within 4-6 weeks. Previously published work OK. Original artwork returned after publication, if requested. Free sample copy.
Cartoons: Uses 1 cartoon/issue; buys 1/issue from freelancers. Receives 1 submission/week from freelancers. Interested in antiques, nostalgia and money. Prefers finished cartoons. SASE. Reports in 4 weeks. Buys all rights, but may reassign rights to artist after publication. Pays $5-20, b&w; on publication.
Illustrations: Buys 24/year on collecting and investing. Buys all rights, but may reassign rights to artist after publication. Pays $5 minimum, b&w; on publication.

NEWSDAY, 235 Pinelawn Rd., Melville NY 11050. (516)454-2303. Art Director: Warren Weilbacher. Daily newspaper. Circ. 500,000. Original artwork returned after publication. Sample copy and art guidelines available.
Illustrations: Buys 4-5 illustrations/week from freelancers. Send query letter with brochure showing art style. Samples not filed are returned. Reports only if interested. Call to schedule an appointment to show a portfolio, which should include original/final art, final reporduction/product, color, tear sheets, Photostats and b&w photos. Buys one-time rights. Pays $350 for b&w and $400 for color, cover; $100-250 for b&w; $150-300 for color, inside. Pays on publication.
Tips: "Let your portfolio talk for you."

NOVA PUBLISHING INC., Worcester Magazine, Centrumguide, Box 1000, Worcester MA 01614. (617)799-0511. Art Director: Mark Minter. Concerns central Massachusetts. Weekly and monthly newspapers. Circ. 50,000.
Illustrations: Buys on assigned themes. Send query letter with photocopies. To show a portfolio, mail final reproduction/product and tear sheets. Buys one-time rights. Cover: Pays $75-100, gray opaques, b&w line drawings and washes; $100, color. Inside: Pays $15-50, gray opaques, b&w line drawings and washes; on publication.
Tips: When reviewing a freelancers portfolio, looks for "graphic design projects and jobs, some illustrations in various media, typography (good with typed specing), clean mechanicals and 4-color experience." Common mistakes freelancers make in presenting samples or portfolios are "poor presentations, poorly typed resumes without cover letters, not enough examples of work in other medias and poor attitude and experience."

NURSINGWORLD JOURNAL, 470 Boston Post Rd., Weston MA 02193. (617)899-2702. Editor: Shirley Copithorne. Readers are "student and experienced nurses interested in keeping their skills current and seeking employment, trends in nursing, relocation or area hiring trends in nursing, reviews of nursing articles, feature stories." Specialty is health care publications. Monthly. Circ. 40,000. Sample copy $2.
Cartoons: Uses 1-3 cartoons/issue. Receives 25 submissions/month from freelancers. Interested in hospital or nursing themes. Prefers b&w line drawing with gagline. Send finished cartoons. SASE. Reports within 6 months. Buys one-time rights. Pays $5-10 for b&w; on publication.
Illustrations: Uses 3 illustrations/issue. Receives 10 submissions/month from freelancers. Interested in general illustrations that go along with editorial; usually people or nature. Works on assignment. "Freelancers call, send us samples, and we make a decision at that time if their style fits our paper. If it does, we keep their names on file, then contact them for assignments." Send roughs. SASE. Reports

within 6 months. Prefers b&w line drawings. Buys all rights on a work-for-hire basis. Pays $50-100 for b&w or color cover, $50 for inside b&w. Pays on publication.
Tips: Interested in seeing "any articles you're interested in. Submissions from editor's point of view."

NUTRITION HEALTH REVIEW, 171 Madison Ave., New York NY 10016. Features Editor: F.R. Rifkin. Tabloid. Emphasizes physical health, mental health, nutrition, food preparation and medicine. For a general audience. Quarterly. Circ. 165,000 paid. Accepts simultaneous submissions. Sample copy $2.
Cartoons: Uses 10 cartoons/issue. Prefers single panel with or without gagline; b&w line drawings. Send finished cartoons to be kept on file; samples returned by SASE if not purchased. Reports within 30 days. Buys first rights or all rights. Pays $15+, b&w; on acceptance.
Illustrations: Number illustrations varies/issue. Send samples to be kept on file; write for appointment to show portfolio. If samples are requested, prefers to see Photostats. Samples returned by SASE. Reports back. Buys first rights or all rights. Pays $200, b&w, cover and $25 for b&w inside; on acceptance.

OFFSHORE, New England's Boating Magazine, 220-9 Resevoir St., Needham MA 02194. (617)244-7520. Art Director: Dave Dauer. Tabloid emphasizing boating for New England boat owners. Monthly. Circ. 30,000. Accepts previously published material. Original artwork returned after publication. Sample copy for SASE with $1.15 postage.
Cartoons: Buys 2 cartoons/issue from freelancers. Prefers single panel; b&w line drawings. Send query letter with samples of style to be kept on file. Material not filed is returned by SASE. Reports within 1 week. Buys first rights. Pays $10-25, b&w; on acceptance.
Ilustrations: Buys 2 illustrations/issue from freelancers. Prefers hard line. Works on assignment only. Send Photostats or tear sheets to be kept on file. Samples not filed are returned by SASE. Reports within 1 week. Buys first rights. Pays $100-175, color, cover; $50-75, b&w, inside; on acceptance.

***ON THE MARK: THE NEWSLETTER FOR MARK HAMILL FANS**Box 5276, Orange CA 92613-5276. (714)538-1958. Editor/Publisher: Lisa E. Cowan. Quarterly newsletter emphasizing the acting career of Mark Hamill. This is a 6-page offset printed newsletter on the past and present career of actor Mark Hamill and Star Wars articles. Circ. 700. Accepts previously published material. Original artwork returned after publication. Sample copy free for SASE with 22¢ postage. Art guidelines free for SASE with 22¢ postage.
Cartoons: Buys 2-3 cartoons/year from freelancers. Prefers gag cartoons and humorous illustrations featuring Mark Hamill. Prefers single panel with gagline; b&w line drawings 3½x3½. Send query letter with samples of style. Samples are filed. Samples not filed are returned only if requested by artist. Reports back within 5 days. Buys one-time rights. Pays $10, b&w on acceptance.
Illustrations: Buys 1-2 illustrations/year from freelancers (usually get art free). Prefers line art. Works on assignment only. Send query letter with samples. Samples are filed. Samples not filed are returned if requested. Reports back within 5 days. To show a portfolio mail thumbnails, tear sheets and b&w. Buys one-time rights. Pays $10 b&w; on acceptance.
Tips: "We are mostly interested in quality line art of Mark Hamill in current roles. We mostly use assignment art."

THE PAPERWORKER, Box 1475, Nashville TN 37202. (615)834-8590. Editor/Director of Publications: Monte L. Byers. Emphasizes labor subjects for membership of industrial union. Monthly tabloid. Circ. 250,000. Accepts previously published material. Original artwork not returned after publication. Sample copy free for SASE with 20¢ postage.
Cartoons: Buys 1-5 cartoons/issue from freelancers. Considers labor and national issue themes. Prefers single panel with gagline; b&w line drawings. Send query letter with finished cartoons to be kept on file. Material not filed is returned by SASE only if requested. Reports within several weeks. Buys one-time rights. Pays variable rates for b&w and color; on publication.
Illustrations: Buys 1-3 illustrations/issue from freelancers. Themes/styles vary to accompany text. Works on assignment only. Send query letter with samples to be kept on file. Prefers tear sheets as samples. Samples returned only if requested. Reports within several weeks. Buys one-time rights. Pays variable rates for b&w and color, inside; on publication.

PERSONNEL ADVISORY BULLETIN, Bureau of Business Practice, 24 Rope Ferry Rd., Waterford CT 06386. Editor: Jill Peterson. For personnel managers and practitioners in smaller companies—white collar and industrial. Features interviewing and hiring, training, benefits, career development, promotion practices, counseling, record keeping, etc. Bimonthly newsletter. Original artwork not returned after publication. No previously published material or simultaneous submissions. Free sample copy.
Cartoons: Uses 1 cartoon/issue; buys 1/issue from freelancers. Receives 15-20 submissions/week

from freelancers. Buys 30/year on "personnel-oriented situations. Please, no sexist situations and male boss/dumb female secretary jokes." Prefers single panel. Mail finished art. SASE. Reports in 2 weeks. Buys all rights. Pays $15 for b&w line drawings. Pays on acceptance.
Tips: "We're trying to be more selective in choosing strictly personnel-oriented subject matter. Avoid anything smacking of sexism or other discriminatory attitudes. Don't overdo hiring-firing situations. Make captions *literate* and *funny*."

THE PLAIN DEALER MAGAZINE, 1801 Superior Ave., Cleveland OH 44114. (216)344-4578. Design Director: Gerard Sealy. Sunday color roto magazine supplement to *The Plain Dealer* newspaper. Broad-based, general audience. Weekly. Circ. 500,000. Original artwork returned after publication.
Cartoons: Uses 2-3 cartoons/issue; buys 1-2/issue from freelancers. Prefers single panel with or without gagline; b&w line drawings. Send finished cartoons. Material is returned by SASE. Reports only if interested. Buys one-time rights. Pays $50, b&w; on publication.
Illustrations: Buys 4-5 illustrations/issue; buys all from freelancers. All styles considered. Works on assignment basis only. Send query letter with brochure, business card and samples to be kept on file. No original art; all other types of samples considered. Reports only if interested. Call for appointment to show portfolio. Buys first rights. Pays $500 maximum, color, cover; $300 maximum, b&w, and $400 maximum, color, inside; on publication.

PRESS-ENTERPRISE, Box 792, Riverside CA 92502. (714)684-1200. Assistant Managing Editor/Features & Art: Sally Ann Maas. Daily newspaper in Southern California emphasizing general subjects. Circ. 147,000. Original artwork returned after publication.
Illustrations: Buys 1 editorial illustration/week from freelancers. Uses various themes and styles. Works on assignment only. Send query letter, resume and samples to be kept on file. Samples not filed are returned only if requested. Negotiates rights purchased. Write for appointment to show portfolio. Pays for illustration by the project, $35-150; on acceptance.
Tips: "Resume and samples absolute necessity." Looks for "ability to conceptualize editorially; the ability to draw well is not enough." A common mistake freelancers make is "not learning abut the publication before selecting portfolio pieces."

PUBLICATIONS CO., 1220 Maple Ave., Los Angeles CA 90015. Editor: Lucie Dubovik. Emphasizes general business for companies, service organizations, etc. and journalism in schools. Monthly. Accepts previously published material. Sample copy and art guidelines free for SASE.
Cartoons: Buys several cartoons/issue from freelancers. Prefers business, industry, factory, schools, and teen situations, plus seasonal material as themes. Prefers single panel with gagline; b&w line drawings. Send query letter with samples of style or finished cartoons. Material not filed is returned by SASE. Reports within 1 month. Buys reprint rights. Pays on acceptance.
Illustrations: Buys several illustrations/issue from freelancers. Prefers business, industry, factory, school and teen situations plus seasonal material as themes. Send query letter with original art. Samples not filed are returned by SASE. Reports within 1 month. Buys reprint rights. Pays on acceptance.

PUBLISHING CONCEPTS CORPORATION, Main St., Luttrell TN 37779. For a general audience with middle to upper incomes. Weekly. Circ. 60,190. Previously published material OK. Original artwork returned after publication. Free sample copy for SASE; art guidelines available. Receives 8 cartoons and 3 illustrations/week from freelance artists.
Cartoons: Uses 10 cartoons/issue; buys all from freelancers. Interested in general, national themes; single panel, b&w line drawings. Send finished cartoons. Samples returned by SASE. Reports in 1 week. Negotiates rights purchased. Pays $10-50, b&w; on acceptance.
Illustrations: Number of illustrations/issue varies. Will review all themes and styles for interest. Provide business card and samples to be kept on file for possible future assignments. Send samples of style. Samples returned by SASE. Reports in 1 week. Buys one-time rights. Pays $10-40 cover, b&w line drawings; on acceptance.
Tips: "We publish several publications and work submitted on a freelance basis may be considered for any one of several publications. Prices paid vary with quality of work, degree of interest at the time received or readership interest for the next two weeks."

ROLLING STONE, 745 5th Ave., New York NY 10151. (212)758-3800. Art Director: Derek Ungless. Coverage includes music, film, social issues, investigative reporting, books and new life styles. Biweekly, large format. Original artwork returned after publication.
Illustrations: Buys 1-2 illustrations/issue. Illustrations are assigned to particular editorial needs. Works on assignment only. Submit samples of style or drop off portfolio. Samples returned by SASE. Provide business card to be kept on file for future assignments. Reports as soon as possible. Buys one-time publication rights.

Close-up

Bill Ostendorf

Newspaper Graphics Editor
Bay Village, Ohio

Printer's ink runs through Bill Ostendorf's veins. "Newspapers are addicting," says the newspaper graphics editor. "Into each daily paper you put enough content to fill a novel. How can it get boring?"

Since newspapers are filled with current events, their content is never repetitive. But their layout can often make that morning yawn even wider. An editor is simply faced with filling pages with type, while a graphics editor must make those inches of type look interesting every day.

"A newspaper is a clearinghouse for a mass of information," says Ostendorf. "The design of newspapers is not as sophisticated as that of a magazine, where you can focus an appeal to a certain type of person. The priorities for a newspaper designer are to make a daily deadline, make the copy fit the space, make it communicate well and make it look good, in that order."

The duty of a newspaper's graphics editor—to integrate copy with visual elements—is even more important today than in the past. "The art department used to be a dumping ground called upon when editors needed to fill space, and newspapers relied on staged photos and pictures of accidents," says Ostendorf. Steady improvements began in design with the introduction of computerized typesetting systems, which set type more quickly and provided typographic flexibility. Speedy turnaround in the typesetting department meant more creative time at the layout desk; editors could afford to be more imaginative with layout and still meet deadlines.

In their increasing use of computers, graphics editors have not forgotten the importance of illustrators. In fact, the computer has encouraged more use of illustration. While photographs and graphics provide information, illustrations offer interpretation of articles and also provide visual surprises. Illustrations are particularly needed in the newspaper's Sunday feature sections, where work is assigned early in the week with a Wednesday deadline. "Freelancers must be able to work on a tight deadline," notes Ostendorf. "If you can meet deadlines and do editorial illustrations that help interpret a story, you're golden."

Ostendorf sees the newspaper field as a tremendous opportunity for artists. "Almost all newspapers are short-handed as far as artists and graphic designers are concerned." An artist's role at a newpaper can include graphics, illustration, page design, research and reporting. At a major daily, freelancers are generally used only for illustration; those skilled in page design or graphics might be eagerly received at their local paper.

Ostendorf warns artists that they can't expect perfection when working with a newspaper's tight deadlines. "One of the biggest problems at a newspaper is that you're never satisfied. You have to design and illustrate on the run. But it's a constant challenge to be creative."

—*Susan Conner*

SALESMANSHIP AND FOREMANSHIP AND EFFECTIVE EXECUTIVE, Dartnell Corporation, 4660 N. Ravenswood Ave., Chicago IL 60640. Art Director: G.C. Gormaly, Jr. Emphasizes salesmanship. Monthly. Previously published material OK.
Cartoons: Uses 1 cartoon/issue. Prefers single panel with or without gagline, b&w line drawings or b&w washes. Send query letter and samples of style. Samples returned. Reports in 1 month. Negotiates rights purchased. Pays $20-50, b&w; on acceptance.
Illustrations: Uses illustrations occasionally; seldom buys from freelancers. Send query letter and samples of style to be kept on file for possible future assignments. Samples not kept on file are returned. Reports in 2 months. Buys reprint rights. Pays $100-300 cover, $100-150 inside, b&w line or tone drawings; on acceptance.

***SAN FRANCISCO BAY GUARDIAN**, 2700 19th St., San Francisco CA 94110. (415)824-7660. Art Director: Kim Gale. For "a young, liberal, well-educated audience." Circ. 105,000. Weekly newspaper. SASE. Pays 60 days after publication. Reviews portfolios on Friday. Sets up appointment by phone.
Cartoons: "Almost all illustrations are assigned; we are, however, always looking for cartoons and strips that have a Bay Area theme. We pay, on the average, $35 per cartoon, which can be a one-shot deal or continuing." Query.
Illustrations: Buys assigned themes. Pays $40-150. Arrange interview to show portfolio.
Tips: "I am always looking for artwork for our cover done by *Bay Area* artists. Current trends include "the New Wave look which has affected all phases of graphics, type and design. The most sweeping change is in the use of typefaces which are mixed with absolute abandon and freedom. It's great!"

SANTA CRUZ SENTINEL, 207 Church St., Santa Cruz CA 95060. (408)423-4242. Entertainment Editor: Greg Beebe. Daily newspaper. Published Monday through Friday and Sunday. Circ. 35,000. Original artwork returned after publication. Sample copy and art guidelines available.
Illustrations: Buys 2 illustrations/month from freelancers. Works on assignment only. Send query letter with brochure showing art style or resume and tear sheets. Samples not filed are returned by SASE. Reports only if interested. To show a portfolio, mail appropriate materials or write to schedule an appointment; portfolio should include original/final art, final reproduction/product, color and tear sheets. Buys one-time rights. Pays $75 for b&w and $150 for color, cover; $50 for b&w, inside; on publication.
Tips: "Artists seem to be able to work quicker, without sacrificing quality. Keep trying."

SHOW BUSINESS, Suite 2900, 1501 Broadway, New York NY 10036. (212)354-7600, ext. 20. Assistant Publisher: Philip Anderson. Casting newspaper for investors, producers, directors, press people, agents, photographers, performing artists and models. Weekly. Circ. 36,000. Accepts previously published material. Art guidelines free for SASE with $1.37 postage.
Cartoons: Considers theatre or film themes. Prefers double panel. Send samples of style. Call for appointment to show portfolio. Material returned by SASE. Reports within 2 weeks. Negotiates rights purchased. Pays on publication.
Illustrations: Send query letter with samples. Call for appointment to show portfolio. Prefers photostats as samples. Samples are returned by SASE. Reports within 2 weeks. Negotiates rights purchased. Pays on publication.

***SKIERS ADVOCATE**, 7309 S. Ingalls Ct., Littleton CO 80123. (303)861-7669. Editor: Carolyn Martin. American Ski Association newsletter featuring general interest, how-to, humor, inspirational, interview/profile, personal experience, technical, travel articles and experimental, fantasy, adventure and humorous fiction. Quarterly. Accepts previously published material. Original artwork returned after publication. Sample copy available.
Illustrations: Send query letter with resume and tear sheets. To show a portfolio, call to schedule an appointment.

SKYDIVING, Box 1520, Deland FL 32721. (904)736-9779. Editor: Michael Truffer. Emphasizes skydiving for sport parachutists, worldwide dealers and equipment manufacturers. Monthly. Circ. 7,600.
Cartoons: Uses 1-2 cartoons/issue; buys 0-1 from freelancers. Receives 1-2 submissions/week from freelancers. Interested in themes relating to skydiving or aviation. Prefers single panel b&w line drawings with gagline. Send finished cartoons or samples of style. SASE. Reports in 1 week. Buys one-time rights. Pays $10 minimum for b&w; on publication.
Tips: Artists "must *know* parachuting; cartoons must be funny."

SOUTHERN JEWISH WEEKLY, Box 3297, Jacksonville FL 32206. (904)634-1812. Editor/Publisher: Isadore Moscovitz. Emphasizes human interest material and short stories. "The only Jewish newspaper covering all of Florida and the Southeast." Weekly. Circ. 28,500.
Illustrations: Buys 12 illustrations/year on Jewish themes that pertain to newspaper's articles. Send

query letter with resume and samples. Seasonal themes must arrive 2 weeks in advance of holiday. SASE. Reports in 1 week. Pays $10 minimum, b&w; on publication.
Tips: "Send samples of work along with resume to us two weeks or more in advance of Jewish holiday being featured."

SOUTHWEST DIGEST, 510 E. 23rd St., Lubbock TX 79404. (806)762-3612. Co-Publisher-Managing Editor: Eddie P. Richardson. Newspaper emphasizing positive black images, and community building and rebuilding "primarily oriented to the black community and basically reflective of the black community, but serving all people." Weekly. Accepts previously published material. Original work returned after publication.
Cartoons: Number of cartoons purchased/issue from freelancers varies. Prefers economic development, community development, community pride and awareness, and black uplifting themes. Single, double or multiple panel with gagline; b&w line drawings. Send query letter with samples of style, roughs or finished cartoons to be kept on file. Write or call for appointment to show portfolio. Material not filed returned by SASE only if requested. Buys first, one-time, reprint, or all rights; or negotiates rights purchased. Pays on publication.
Illustrations: Send query letter with brochure or samples to be kept on file. Write or call for appointment to show portfolio. Prefers photostats, tear sheets, photocopies, photographs, etc. as samples. Samples not filed returned by SASE only if requested. Reports only if interested. Negotiates rights purchased. Pays $5 minimum on publication.

SPARKS JOURNAL, Society of Wireless Pioneers, Box 530, Santa Rosa CA 95402. Editor: William A. Breniman. For radio-telegraph men who handle(d) communications with ships and at-shore stations; included are military, commercial, aeronautical and governmental communications personnel. "Since many have earned their living aboard ships as 'Sparks,' we like to bring a nautical flavor to our pages." Quarterly tabloid newspaper. Circ. 5,000 (members) plus some libraries and museums. Accepts previously published material "if it fits."
Cartoons: Buys 15-20 cartoons/issue. Send query letter with samples. To show a portfolio, mail appropriate materials, which should include b&w drawings. Pays $2-30 for b&w; on acceptance.
Illustrations: Uses illustrative headings for various articles. Buys 4-10 illustrations/issue. Send query letter with brochure showing art style or tear sheets and photocopies. Uses b&w only; no color. Include SASE. Buys reprint rights. Pays $25-100 for b&w, cover; $10-25 for b&w, inside; on acceptance.
Tips: "Those who have a love of the sea and things nautical, and are also versed in wireless telegraph or transmission via Hertzian waves (communications), would probably be able to furnish the type of material we use. We are a professional, nonprofit organization; we do not cater to the amateur radio (including CB) field. We also publish *The Skipper's Log* (quarterly tabloid, members only), *Port's O'Call* (biennial), *Sparks* (in series, annual), and a book-format almanac."

***SPORT SCENE: FOCUS ON YOUTH PROGRAMS**, 4985 Oak Garden Dr., Kernersville NC 27284. (919)784-4926. Director, Editor/Publisher: Jack Hutslar, PhD. Quarterly newsletter emphasizing children in sport and recreation, ages 12-13 and younger. For parents, youth and school coaches, teachers and program directors. Circ. 15,000. Accepts previously published material. Original artwork returned to the artist after publication. Sample copy free for SASE with 22¢ postage.
Cartoons: Prefers gag cartoons, caricatures and humorous illustrations. Prefers children, coaches, parents and referees, etc. as themes. Prefers single panel with or without gagline. Send query letter. Samples are filed. Reports back within 2 weeks.
Illustrations: Send query letter with brochure or business card. Samples are filed. Reports back within 2 weeks. Pays on publication.
Tips: Artists "can sell prints through sport scene." Artists also illustrate skill manuals for sports.

***MAXWELL SROGE PUBLISHING**, 731 N. Cascade Ave., Colorado Springs CO 80903. (303)633-5556. Associate Editor: Karen Pochert. Bi-weekly newsletters emphasizing catalog marketing, and direct marketing. There are three publications: 1) Non-Store Marketing Report (executives in mail order business); 2) Catalog Marketer (management in catalog marketing business); 3) Business-To-Business Catalog Marketer (management in business-to-business catalog marketing). We reach a healthy percentage of the 6,500 catalog marketers in the U.S. with each of our publications. Sample copy and art guidelines available.
Illustrations: Works on assignment only. Send query letter or resume. Samples are filed. Reports back only if interested. "We will call to schedule an appointment to show a portfolio, which should include, roughs, original/final art, tear sheets and final reproduction/product; on publication.
Tips: "We are primarily interested in paste-up artist to paste-up our three newsletters and to design and layout variable advertising and promotional materials.

THE STATE JOURNAL-REGISTER, 1 Copley Plaza, Box 219, Springfield IL 62705. (217)788-1477. Photography Editor: Elizabeth Novickas. Emphasizes news and features for the town and surrounding area. Daily. Circ. 75,000. Accepts previously published material and simultaneous submissions. Original artwork returned after publication. Sample copy and art guidelines free for SASE.
Illustrations: "Uses approximately 6-7 photographs/issue and occasionally graphs, charts, maps, artwork. We buy only some illustrations from freelancers, not all. Staff does some work." Works on assignment only. Send query letter with samples to be kept on file. Samples are returned if not kept on file. Negotiates rights purchased. Pays $100-200, b&w and color, cover. Pays $50-150, b&w and color, inside; on publication.

THE SUPERVISOR, Kemper Group, Long Grove IL 60049. (312)540-2094. Editor: Mary Puccinelli. Newsletter. Emphasizes industrial and fleet safety for supervisors responsible for industrial safety and/or fleet safety. Bimonthly. Circ. 50,000. Accepts simultaneous submissions. Original artwork not returned after publication. Sample copy free for SASE.
Cartoons: Uses 2 cartoons/issue; buys all from freelancers. Seeks "very funny cartoons;" can be "offbeat" but not offensive. Topics for the year are sent to prospective artists in June. Prefers single panel, with gagline; b&w line drawings. Send query letter with samples of style to be kept on file. Material not kept on file is returned by SASE. Reports within 1 month. Buys all rights. Payment varies; on acceptance.

SUPERVISOR'S BULLETIN, 24 Rope Ferry Rd., Waterford CT 06386. (203)739-0286. Editor: Bob Ellal. Emphasizes "manufacturing supervision for front-line supervision in the shop. Not office and non-union." Semimonthly. Free sample copy.
Cartoons: Uses 1-2 cartoons/issue; buys all from freelancers. Receives "a dozen or so/month." Interested in nonsexist material that represents the real world, women and minorities, and pokes fun at aspects of shop supervision: safety, productivity, motivation, discipline, etc. Prefers single panel b&w line drawings with or without gagline. Send roughs. SASE. Reports in 2 weeks. Buys all rights. Pays $10 for b&w; on acceptance.

***SWCP CATALYST**, (Self-Winding Clock Publications Catalyst), Box 7704, Long Beach CA 90807. (213)427-4202. Publisher: Dr. Bengt E. Honning. Emphasizes horology/clocks, the self-winding clock and other antique battery clocks for time standards department—USN, NASA, etc., Western Union, collectors, antique battery clock service. Bimonthly. Circ. 450. Accepts previously published material and simultaneous submissions. Original artwork returned after publication. Sample copy and art guidelines free for SASE.
Illustrations: Uses 3-4 illustrations/issue. Prefers horology themes. Send query letter with business card and samples. Prefers photocopies as samples; "dimensions of original if otherwise." Samples returned by SASE. Reports within 2 weeks. Original material not copyrighted.

TEENS TODAY, 6401 The Paseo, Kansas City MO 64131. (816)333-7000. Editor: Karen De Sollar. For junior and senior high school students who attend Church of the Nazarene. Weekly. Circ. 60,000. Original work not returned after publication. Free sample copy with SASE.
Illustrations: Uses 1-2 illustrations/issue; buys 1-2/issue from freelancers; all illustrations go with stories. Works on assignment only. Prefers to see resume, flyer and tear sheets to be kept on file. SASE. Reports in 6-8 weeks.

TELEBRIEFS, Illinois Bell Telephone Co., 225 W. Randolph, Chicago IL 60606. Contact: Editor. Monthly newsletter for telephone customers. Circ. 3,500,000. Mail art. SASE. Reports in 2 weeks. Photocopies OK. Original artwork not returned after publication. Free sample copy.
Cartoons: Uses 2 cartoons/issue, all from freelancers. Receives 8 submissions/month from freelancers. Cartoons "must be telephone company or telecommunications related." Single panel. "No ethnic humor. We reduce cartoons to 1¾x1¾ so we need few elements, drawn very boldly. Prefer strong visual with captions of 10 or fewer words." Prefers finished cartoons. SASE. Reports in 2 weeks. Buys all rights on a work-for-hire basis. Pays $40, line drawings with shading; on acceptance.
Illustrations: Buys 1 illustration/week from freelancers. Send photocopies. To show a portfolio, mail appropriate materials, which should include roughs, original/final art and photostats.
Tips: "Since break up of Bell System, Illinois Bell is no longer in the business of leasing, selling, or installing telephone equipment. Cartoons should mainly imply telephone usage, such as speaking on phone."

TOWERS CLUB, USA NEWSLETTER, Box 2038, Vancouver WA 98668. (206)574-3084. Chief Executive Officer: Jerry Buchanan. Emphasizes "anything that offers a new entrepreneurial opportunity, especially through mail order. The newsletter for 'Find a Need and Fill It' people." Readers are 80% male

with average age of 48 and income of $35,000. Monthly except August and December. Circ. 4,000. Previously published material and simultaneous submissions OK. Original work returned after publication by SASE. Sample copy $3.
Cartoons: Uses 1 cartoon/issue; buys all from freelancers. Interested in themes of selling how-to-do-it information, showing it as a profitable and honorable profession; single panel with gagline, b&w line drawings. Send finished cartoons. Samples returned by SASE. Reports in 1 week. Buys one-time rights. Pays $15-25, b&w; on publication.
Illustrations: Uses 5-7 illustrations/issue. Interested in realistic, illustrative art of typists, computers, small print shop operations, mail order, etc.; no comical themes. Especially needs line drawings of typists/writers/office workers, money, mail delivery, affluent people, intelligent and successful faces, etc. Send brochure showing art style. Provide samples to be kept on file for possible future assignments. Samples not kept on file are returned by SASE. Reports in 1 week. Buys one-time rights. Makes some permanent purchases. Negotiates payment depending on rights purchased; on acceptance.
Tips: "Newsletters are going more to using typesetting and artwork to brighten pages. Subscribe to our *Towers Club, USA* newsletter and study content and artwork used. Normally $60 per year, we will give discount to artists who show us a portfolio of their work. Our theme will lead them to much other business, as we are about creative self-publishing/marketing exclusively. Most cartoonists have little or no genuine sense of humor. I suggest they tie in with someone who does and split the fee. Illustrators should see several copies of the publication they hope to draw for before submitting their samples. It could save a lot of postage."

TRISTATE MAGAZINE, (formerly *Cincinnati Enquirer Sunday Magazine*), 617 Vine St., Cincinnati OH 45202. (513)721-2700. Editor: Alice Hornbaker. Art Director: Bill Parrish. Weekly. Circ. 500,000.
Illustrations: Uses 1-2 illustrations/issue on assigned themes. "We use, on occasion, unsolicited freelance art. We also will consider assignments after receiving a portfolio." Samples returned by SASE. Reports back on future assignment possibilities. Provide business card to be kept on file for future assignments. Prefers to see portfolio. SASE. Reporting time varies. Buys all rights on a work-for-hire basis. Pays $50-200 maximum, b&w line drawings and washes; $150-350 maximum, color illustrations and cover.

UNION ELECTRIC NEWS, Box 149, St. Louis MO 63166. Supervisor, Public Information: D.J. Walther. For employees and retirees. Semimonthly. Circ. 10,200. Previously published material and simultaneous submissions OK. Original work not returned after publication. Free sample copy and art guidelines for SASE.
Cartoons: Uses less than 1 cartoon/issue; buys all from freelancers. Interested in cartoons illustrative for article embellishment; b&w line drawings or washes. Send query letter with samples of style and resume. Samples returned by SASE. Reports in 2 weeks.
Illustrations: Uses 1 illustration/issue; buys all from freelancers. Works on assignment only. Interested in clean, current styles. Send query letter with resume and samples of style, prices and turn-around times. Provide resume, brochure, samples and tear sheets to be kept on file for possible future assignments. Samples not kept on file are returned by SASE. Reports in 2 weeks. Pays on acceptance.

UTILITY SUPERVISION, 24 Rope Ferry Rd., Waterford CT 06386. (203)442-4365. Editor: DeLoris Lidestri. Emphasizes utility system installation, maintenance and repair for front-line supervisors in the field (not plant or office). Semimonthly. Circ. 4,000. Free sample copy.
Cartoons: Uses 1 cartoon/issue; buys all from freelancers. Interested in non-sexist material which pokes fun at some of the problems of utility supervision and/or utility field work. Prefers single panel b&w line drawings with gagline. Send finished cartoons. SASE. Reports in 2 weeks. Buys all rights. Pays $15 for b&w on acceptance.

VELO-NEWS, Box 1257, Brattleboro VT 05301. Editor: Geoff Drake. Tabloid. Emphasizes bicycle racing for competitors, coaches, officials, enthusiasts. Published 18 times/year. Circ. 14,000. Accepts previously published material and simultaneous submissions. Original artwork returned after publication.
Cartoons: Uses cartoons irregularly; buys from freelancers. Prefers single panel, with gagline; b&w line drawings. Send query letter with samples of style to be kept on file. Material not kept on file is returned by SASE. Reports within 2 weeks. Buys one-time rights. Pays $15, b&w; on publication.

WAREHOUSING SUPERVISOR'S BULLETIN, 24 Rope Ferry Rd., Waterford CT 06386. (203)442-4365. Contact: Isabel Will-Becker. Emphasizes warehouse, shipping, traffic, material handling for front-line supervision. Semimonthly. Free sample copy.
Cartoons: Uses 1 cartoon/issue; buys from freelancer. Interested in non-sexist material which pokes fun at aspects of warehouse operations and supervision. Prefers single panel b&w line drawings with or

without gagline. SASE. Reports in 3-6 weeks. To show a portfolio, mail appropriate materials, which should include b&w. Buys all rights. Pays $15 for b&w on acceptance.
Tips: "I look for a developed, mature style of drawing. The gaglines are not very important to me."

WDS FORUM, 1507 Dana Rd., Cincinnati OH 45207. Editor: Ms. Kirk Polking. Sixteen-page quarterly newsletter emphasizing writing techniques and marketing for Writer's Digest School students. Circ. 13,000.
Cartoons: Needs work on "the joys and griefs of freelancing, that first check/rejection slip, trying to find time to write, postal problems, editor/author relations, etc." Send either finished art or roughs. SASE. Reports in 3 weeks. Pays $10, b&w.
Illustrations: "We might buy a few spot drawings, as fillers, of writer-related subject matter." SASE. Reports in 3 weeks. Send query letter with samples. Pays $5, each drawing; on acceptance. "Sorry our rates are so low but we carry no advertising and our newsletter is primarily a service to our students."

WESTART, Box 6868, Auburn CA 95604. Editor: Martha Garcia. Emphasizes art for practicing artists, teachers, students, craftsmen, collectors and art patrons. Biweekly. Circ. 6,500. Previously published material OK. Original work returned after publication; SASE required. Free sample copy for SASE; art guidelines available. Photographs, cartoons and illustrations used as works of art in connection with current West Coast exhibition.

***WESTERN CANADA OUTDOORS**, Box 430, North Battleford, Saskatchewan S9A 2Y5 Canada. (306)445-4401. Publisher: S. Nowakowski. For hunting, fishing and outdoor families. Bimonthly newspaper. Circ. 42,000. Previously published work OK. Free sample copy.
Cartoons: Uses 3 cartoons/issue, all by freelancers. Receives 0-1 submissions/week from freelancer. Interested in "an outdoor, conserving environment theme"; (nonresidents include SAE and International Reply Coupons). Reports in 1 month. Buys "once-rental" rights. Pays $5-10, halftones; on acceptance.
Illustrations: Uses 0-1 illustrations/issue, all from freelancers. Receives no submissions/week from freelancers. Interested in wildlife. Especially needs hunting and fishing related artwork; must have some interest for Western Canada. Prefers to see finished art. SASE (nonresidents include SAE and International Reply Coupons). Reports in 1 month. Buys "once-rental" rights. Pays on acceptance.

THE WESTERN PRODUCER, Box 2500, Saskatoon, Saskatchewan S7K 2C4 Canada. (306)665-3500. Managing Editor: Garry L. Fairbarn. For farm families in western Canada. Weekly. Circ. 140,000.
Cartoons: Receives 12/week from freelance artists. Uses only cartoons about rural life, computers, families. SAE (nonresidents include IRC). Reports in 3 weeks. Buys first Canadian rights. Pays $15, b&w line drawings; on acceptance.
Illustrations: Uses occasional theme logos and illustrations. Looks for "clarity, visual impact, accuracy." Pays by the project, $40-160.

THE WETUMPKA HERALD, 300 Green St., Box 29, Wetumpka AL 36092. (205)567-7811. Editor & Publisher: Ellen T. Harris. Newspaper emphasizing local news, sports, etc. (small town) for family audience. Weekly. Circ. 3,800. Accepts previously published material. Sample copy free for SASE with 25¢ postage. Art guidelines free for SASE with 50¢ postage.
Cartoons: Single-panel with gagline; b&w line drawings. Send samples of style to be kept on file "except for material we do not consider using in the future." Write for appointment to show portfolio. Material not filed not returned. Reports only if interested.
Illustrations: Buys 1 illustration/issue from freelancers. Send query letter with photocopies or tearsheets to be kept on file "except for material we do not consider using in future." Write for appointment to show portfolio. Samples not filed not returned. Reports only if interested. Pays on publication.

THE WINE SPECTATOR, Suite 2040, 601 Van Ness, San Francisco CA 94102. (415)673-2040. Production Manager: Karen Magnuson. Tabloid emphasizing wine for wine lovers—consumer and trade. Bimonthly. Circ. 65,000. Original artwork not returned after publication.
Cartoons: Buys 1/issue from freelance artists. Send samples of style to be kept on file. Write or call for appointment to show portfolio. Material not filed is not returned. Reports only if interested. Buys all rights. Pays $50, b&w.
Illustrations: Buys 2-3/issue from freelance artists. Works on assignment only. Send samples to be kept on file. Call for appointment to show portfolio. Prefers photostats or tear sheets as samples. Does not report back. Buys all rights. Pays $100-200, b&w, or $200-250, color cover; and $50-150, b&w or $150-200, color, inside; on publication.

WOMEN ARTISTS NEWS, Box 3304, Grand Central Station, New York NY 10163. (212)666-6990. Editor: Rena Hansen. For women in all the arts with focus on the visual arts fields. Circ. 5,000. SASE. Reports in 2 weeks. Photocopied submissions OK. Original artwork returned after publication. Pays on publication "when funds available." SASE (57¢) for sample copy. Also uses artists for layout and brochures. Needs photographs.
Cartoons: Uses 0-2 cartoons/issue. Receives 1 submission/week from freelancers. Contact feature editor. Accepts cartoons on art and artists; double panel. Send finished art. Reports in 2 weeks. Pays $0-5, b&w washes.
Illustrations: Uses 20-30 illustrations (photographs)/issue; buys 4/issue from freelancers. Receives 10 submissions/week from freelancers. Provide samples (roughs) or published work to be kept on file for future assignments. Reports in 2 weeks. Pays for design by the hour, $10. Buys all rights on a work-for-hire basis.

***WOMEN'S RIGHTS LAW REPORTER**, 15 Washington St., Newark NJ 07102. (201)648-5320. Contact: Grapics Coordinator. For lawyers, students and feminists; concerns law and feminism. Circ. 1,500. Quarterly. Pays on publication.
Illustrations: Uses illustrations occasionally. Send query letter with brochure showing art style and photographs. To show a portfolio, mail appropriate materials, which should include photographs and b&w. Pays on publciation.

***WOMEN WISE**, 38 S. Main St., Concord NH 03301. (603)225-2739. Contact: Editorial Committee. Quarterly tabloid. Emphasizes women's health and political issues. Features "updeated health information with a feminist analysis. Audience is primarily women." Circ. 3,000. Accepts previously published material. Returns original artwork after publication. Sample copy and art guidelines available.
Cartoons: Prefers editorial or political cartoons. Send query letter. Reports back only if interested, but will send back originals.
Illustrations: Prefers line drawings—women and health related. Send query letter with brochure showing art style or resume, business card and samples. Samples are filed. Samples not filed are returned. Reports back only if interested. Call or write to schedule an appointment to show a portfolio. Pays $15, b&w, cover; on publication. Pays in subscriptions for inside.

YOUNG AMERICAN, Box 12409, Portland OR 97212. (503)230-1895. Design Director: Richard Ferguson. Tabloid emphasizing fiction, fantasy, science, news and specialty subjects for children, 4-16 and family members. Twice monthly. Circ. 125,000. Accepts previously published material. Returns originals after publication. Sample copy SASE plus 50¢.
Cartoons: Buys 3-4/issue. "Themes should be relatable to children. We prefer realistic styles over free-style cartoons." Prefers single or multiple panel with gagline; b&w line drawings or b&w washes. Send finished cartoons to be kept on file. Material not filed returned by SASE. Reports only if interested. Buys reprint rights. Pays $5-10, b&w; on publication.
Illustrations: Buys 3-4/issue. Works on assignment only. Send brochure, business card, photostats, tear sheets, color slides or printed material to be kept on file. Samples not filed are returned by SASE. Reports only if interested. Call for appointment to show portfolio. Buys one-time rights. Pays $20-50, b&w, inside; $100 maximum, color, inside; on publication.

> ***"I am more impressed with the illustrator who has five excellent and consistent pieces in a portfolio than with the individual who shows 15 pieces showing inconsistent and various styles of mediocre to good work. I must know from their portfolios what I can expect to get on any assignment that I would give."***
>
> ***—Janet S. Taggart, Coronado Publishers***
> ***San Diego, California***

Performing Arts

Music, theatre, dance, opera—each of these performing arts categories seeks originality, dynamic design and strong imagery, but always with the goal of passing along information. Not only do artists literally set the stage for these groups, but they also provide visual exposure through promotional materials such as programs, brochures, flyers and invitations.

The needs of these groups vary according to their particular medium. Musical groups such as symphonies require artwork mainly for posters, programs and brochures. Similarly, ballet, opera and theatre companies require the talents of artists for promotional materials, but they also need scene designers and painters, costume designers and lighting specialists for their productions. "Performing arts," says Andrea Lammers of the Chicago City Ballet, "are beginning to see the need to market themselves as tangible products. This makes illustration and image extremely important."

It's best to work with a local performing arts group first to become acquainted with the demands of the field. If you find that you have an empathy for one category over another, perhaps a preference for dance rather than theatre, then focus your efforts in your area of preference.

As with any market area, research performing arts groups as much as possible before approaching them with your work. Some groups have only seasonal needs, such as summer theatres, so check to see if this information is listed and when the group's needs are heaviest. Residencies are also available, perfect for the artist seeking summer employment and a weekly salary.

For further names and information regarding performing arts, consult the *American Dance Directory*, *Dance Magazine*, the *Summer Theatre Directory*, *American Theatre Association Directory*, *Theatre Profiles*, the *Music Industry Directory*, *Musical America*, and the Central Opera Theatre's *Opera/Musical Theatre Companies and Workshops in the United States and Canada*.

***ACTORS THEATRE**, 28 W. 7th Pl., St. Paul MN 55102. Marketing Director (for graphics): Lori Anne Williams. Resident Designer (for designers): Nayna Ramey. "Actors Theatre is a resident professional theatre, with a commitment to cultural and educational advancement of legitimate theatre."
Needs: Works with freelance artists/year. Freelance art needed through the year. Works on assignment only. Uses freelance artists for advertising and brochure design, illustration and layout, set design, costume design, lighting and scenery.
First Contact & Terms: Send brochure or resume, tear sheets, Photostats and photocopies. Samples are filed. Samples not filed are returned by SASE. Reports back only if interested. Write to show a portfolio or mail final reproduction/product, tear sheets, Photostats, photographs and slides. Pays for design and illustration by the project; payment varies. Considers complexity of project, client's budget, turnaround time, skill and experience of artist, how work will be used and rights purchased. Negotiates rights purchased.
Tips: "Graphic artists need an understanding and appreciation of theatre. For set/light/costume design; relatively few design slots open each season."

ALASKA REPERTORY THEATRE, Suite 201, 705 W. 6th Ave., Anchorage AK 99501. (907)276-2327. Artistic Director: Andrew Traister. A LORT "B" House, producing 4 mainstage productions and a summer production every year.
Needs: Works with 10-20 freelance designers and craftspeople/year; needs heaviest September-April. Uses designers for costume design, lighting and scenery design.
First Contact & Terms: Send resume to be kept on file. Samples not returned. Reporting time "depends on show." Pays by the project, $700-2,200 average, for design.

***REYNALDO ALEJANDRO DANCE THEATER**, Suite 5-G W., 160 Bleecker St., New York NY 10012. (212)674-0673. Artistic Director: Ron Alejandro. Modern dance troupe inspired by Philippine traditions.

Needs: Works with 10 illustrators/year. Uses artists for advertising, costumes, direct mail brochures, flyers, posters and programs.

First Contact & Terms: Query with samples. SASE. Reports in 1 month. Works on assignment only. No samples returned. Reports back on future assignment possibilities. Provide business card and/or brochure to be kept on file for future assignments. Pays $30-50/job for illustration, design and lettering.

***ALLENBERRY PLAYHOUSE**, Boiling Springs PA 17007. (717)258-3211. Managing Director: Nelson Sheeley. 400 seat Equity summer stock theatre offering 10-12 productions, 2 of which are musicals; shows run 3-4 weeks.

Needs: Number of freelance artists used/year varies; needs heaviest during season, April-November. Uses artists for set and costume design, lighting and scenery. Especially needs scenic designer and costume designer.

First Contact & Terms: Send query letter with resume. Prefers slides as samples. Samples returned by SASE. Reports within 3 weeks. Provide material to be kept on file for possible future assignments. Pays scenic designers $250/week plus room; costumers $200/week plus room; assistant costumer $100/week plus room. Considers available budget when establishing payment.

Tips: "Be prepared to stay for entire season. Apply shortly after January 1."

ALLIANCE THEATRE COMPANY/ATLANTA CHILDREN'S THEATRE, 1280 Peachtree St. NE, Atlanta GA 30309. (404)898-1132. Marketing Director: Kim Resnik. Regional theatre company producing for adults and children.

Needs: Works with 2-3 freelance artists/year. Prefers experienced local artists. Uses artists for the design, illustration and layout of advertising and brochures plus poster design and illustration. Prefers "clean, modern, free strokes. But mostly, work that is appropriate to particular use."

First Contact & Terms: Send query letter with brochure showing art style or resume and tear sheets, photocopies and actual pieces. Samples not filed are returned by SASE. Reports only if interested. Write to schedule an appointment to show a portfolio, which should include thumbnails, roughs, final reproduction/product and photographs. Pays for design by the project, $50 minimum. Pays for illustration by the project, $50 minimum. Considers complexity of project, client's budget and skill and experience of artist.

Tips: "Do your home work on the pieces we do now. Know something of our company and design needs."

AMAS REPERTORY THEATRE, INC., 1 E. 104th St., New York NY 10029. (212)369-8000. Founder and Artistic Director: Rosetta LeNoire. Administrator & Business Manager: Gary Halcott. Administrator: Jerry Lapidus. A professional theatre. Programs include the creation of original musical theatre, classes for young people and adults, a senior citizens tour, workshops, etc.

Needs: Works with 8-12 freelance artists/year. Needs heaviest in fall, winter and spring (Sept.-June). Works on assignment only. Uses artists for brochure design, illustration and layout; poster design and illustration; program, set and costume design; lighting; and scenery.

First Contact & Terms: Send query letter with brochure showing art style or resume and samples to be kept on file. Reports back within 1 month. Call to schedule an appointment to show a portfolio. Pays for design by the project, $50-350 average. Considers how work will be used when establishing payment.

***AMERICAN FESTIVAL BALLET**, 217 North 10, Boise ID 83702. (208)343-0556. General Manager: Jack Alotto. Touring ballet company of 17 dancers with home seasons in Boise and Moscow, Idaho. Three productions per year: mixed repertoire, "The Nutcracker" and full-length classical ballet.

Needs: Works with 3-4 freelance artists/year. Freelance art needed throughout the year. Works with freelance artists on assignment only. Uses artists for advertising and brochure design and illustration, poster design, set design, costume design and scenery.

First Contact & Terms: Send query letter with brochure showing art style or resume, tear sheets, photocopies and slides. Samples are filed. Samples not filed are returned only if requested. Reports back within 1 month. Write to schedule a portfolio. Pays for design by the project, varies; has been $200-750. Considers complexity of project, skill and experience of artist, client's budget, how work will be used, turnaround time and rights purchased when establishing payment. Buys all rights; negotiates rights.

Tips: "Be thorough in sending material. Be reasonable in pricing."

***AMERICAN THEATRE DANCE CO., INC.**, Box 861, Coconut Grove FL 33233. (305)856-8825. Director: Diane Pariser. Promotion and management of dancers and musicians (bands and companies, other arts groups).

Needs: Works with 5 freelance artists/year. Freelance art needed through the year. Works on assignment only. Uses artists for advertising and brochure design, illustration and layout and poster design and illustration.
First Contact & Terms: Send query letter with brochure. Samples are filed. Reports back only if interested. Call to schedule an appointment to show a portfolio. Pays for design and illustration by the project, $100-350. Considers complexity of a project and available budget when establishing payment. Buys one-time rights, reprint rights or all rights.
Tips: Artists should have "some experience doing artwork for performers."

ARIZONA OPERA COMPANY, 3501 N. Mountain Ave., Tucson AZ 85719. (602)293-4336. General Director: Glynn Ross. "The only state-wide opera company in the United States, and the only opera company in Arizona, performing in both Tucson and Phoenix. It presents Grand Opera with professional artists, nationally recognized directors, full staging with elaborate costumes, lighting and so forth."
Needs: Works with 3-4 freelance artists/year. Experience is required. Works on assignments only. Needs heaviest October-March. Uses artists for advertising design, illustration and layout; poster design and illustration; brochure, set and costume design; lighting and scenery.
First Contact & Terms: Send query letter with resume to be kept on file. Material not filed returned by SASE. Considers complexity of project and how work will be used when establishing payment.

***ARIZONA THEATRE COMPANY**, Box 1631, Tucson AZ 85702. (602)884-8210. Director of Marketing/Public Relations: Gary Bacal. Nonprofit professional regional theatre.
Needs: Freelance art needed through the year. Works on assignment only. Uses artists for brochure illustration "relating to company's work on stage. Need show logos, sketches of playwrights etc."
First Contact & Terms: Send query letter with brochure or samples. Samples not filed are returned only if requested by artist. Call or write to schedule an appointment to show a portfolio. Pays for design by the project, $100 minimum. Pays for illustration by the project, $50 minimum. Buys all rights.

BACK ALLEY THEATRE, 15231 Burbank Blvd., Van Nuys CA 91411. (818)780-2240. Producer: Laura Zucker. Theatre company producing live theatre.
Needs: Prefers local artists. Uses artists for advertising and brochure design, illustration and layout; posters and set design.
First Contact & Terms: Send query letter with resume, tear sheets, slides and photographs. Samples not filed are returned by SASE. Reports only if interested. Write to schedule an appointment to show a portfolio, which should include roughs, tear sheets and photographs. Pays for design by the project, $100 minimum. Considers complexity of project and turnaround time when establishing payment.

BALLETACOMA, 508 6th Ave., Tacoma WA 98402. (206)272-9631. Administrative Director: Carlene Garner. Nonprofit regional ballet company composed of 30 dancers; performance season includes "The Nutcracker Ballet" and two other major productions.
Needs: Works with 3 freelance artists/year; needs heaviest in August-September, January, March. Uses artists for advertising, brochure and program design, illustration and layout; set and costume design; posters, lighting and scenery.
First Contact & Terms: Send query letter with brochure showing art style or resume, Photostats and photographs to be kept on file. Reports within 2 weeks. Call for appointment to show portfolio, which should include original/final art and Photostats. Pays for design and illustration by the project, $25-500 average. Considers complexity of project, available budget, skill and experience of artist and how work will be used when establishing payment."
Tips: "Art is usually the first impression one sees of an upcoming performance. Therefore the style and quality are vital to the production.

THE BATON ROUGE SYMPHONY ORCHESTRA, Box 103, Baton Rouge LA 70821. (504)344-8803. Publicist: Ruth Laney. Eighty-member professional symphony orchestra with fulltime resident music director/conductor. Fourteen regular-season concerts/year (October-May), an outdoor concert series, ensemble appearances, etc.; 2,500 subscribers.
Needs: Works with 1-2 freelance artists/year; needs heaviest in spring: design and produce brochure promoting fall season - 25,000 copies. Summer: design and produce 2 season program covers. Uses artists for advertising, brochure and program design, illustration and layout; posters, t-shirt and billboard design. "We look for extremely high quality, a certain level of sophistication, dramatic impact and an artist who can work well with our staff and who can project the image we want."
First Contact & Terms: Send query letter with brochure, resume, business card, Photostats and tear sheets to be kept on file. Call for appointment to show portfolio. Reports only if interested. Considers complexity of project, available budget, skill and experience of artist, how work will be used, turnaround time and rights purchased when establishing payment. "We prefer to establish a fee for the proj-

ect at hand. Our status as a nonprofit institution means we have a rather small budget, but we are willing to pay competitive prices for good work."

Tips: "We look for originality in design and concept and require technical accuracy. When submitting, submit treatments only and research thoroughly before including designs depicting musical instruments, instrumentation, period, etc."

BERKSHIRE PUBLIC THEATRE, INC., Box 860, 30 Union St., Pittsfield MA 01202. (413)445-4631. Director: Frank Bessell. Regional repertory theatre with an artistic and technical company of 100, an administrative staff of 15 and an audience of 30,000 yearly. "A year-round company performing classical and contemporary drama, musicals and cabarets, original works and children's theatre. Company of about 100—is ever expanding."

Needs: Works with 10 freelance artists/year. Needs are heaviest with the beginning of each production, an average of one/month. Uses artists for the design, illustration and layout of advertising and brochures, for poster design and illustration; set and costume design; lighting and scenery.

First Contact & Terms: Send query letter with resume and samples to be kept on file. Call or write to schedule an appointment to show a portfolio, which should include thumbnails, roughs, original/final art, final reproduction/product, color, tear sheets, Photostats, photographs, b&w or "anything that best represents you." Pays by the project for design and illustration; negotiates payment. "Sometimes barters exchanges in lieu of dollars."

Tips: Art must have "clean and sharp, meticulous detail, new and exciting, *not canned*." There is more use of warmer "pantone colors, more creative use of layout—as a result, there is more direct collaboration to fill our needs."

BETHUNE BALLET THEATRE, (formerly The Bethune Ballet), 3096 Lake Hollywood Dr., Hollywood CA 90068. (213)874-0481. Artistic Director: Zina Bethune. Ten member multi-media ballet company "incorporating visual technology (film, video, laser, animation and special effects) to enhance and expand the traditional theater of dance."

Needs: Works on assignment only. Uses artists for advertising, brochure, poster, program, set and costume design; lighting; scenery; film and video; special effects, i.e., lasers, image transference, etc.

First Contact & Terms: Send query letter with brochure, resume, business card and samples to be kept on file. Write for appointment to show portfolio. Prefers good representation of artist's work as samples. Samples not returned. Reports only if interested. Pays by the project, $50 minimum. Negotiates pay considering complexity of project, available budget, and skill and experience of artist.

Tips: Artists should use "the movement and sweep of dance to express a variety of concepts and images. As a dance company whose concept is a futuristic one, this helps us capture who and what we are." Research the company's needs before you attempt to sell to them.

***BOARSHEAD: MICHIGAN PUBLIC THEATER**, 425 S. Grand Ave., Lansing MI 48933. (517)484-7800. Director of Marketing and Public Relations: Timothy Sauers. Nonprofit equity regional theater with a season running from September-May. Seating capacity 250.

Needs: Needs heaviest in late summer or early winter. Uses artists for brochure design, illustration, layout; poster design.

First Contact & Terms: Send query letter with brochure showing art style or resume. Samples are filed. Samples not filed are returned by SASE if requested. Reports back within 1-2 weeks. Write to schedule an appointment to show a portfolio or mail roughs and final reproduction/product. Pays for design by the project, $50 minimum. Considers how work will be used when establishing payment. Negotiates rights purchased.

Tips: "Prefer single designs to be utilized for theater productions—advertising, programs, posters and brochure."

***BROOKLYN CENTER FOR THE PERFORMING ARTS AT BROOKLYN COLLEGE (BCBC)**, Box 163, Brooklyn NY 11210. (212)780-5291. Director of Communications: Marian Skokan. Two auditoriums used for music, dance and theatre. Assigns 5 jobs/year; local artists only. Query with samples. No work returned. Reports in 1 month.

Needs: Uses artists for illustration, design, layout and production of advertising, direct mail brochures, flyers and graphics. Pay determined by job.

BUFFALO PHILARMONIC ORCHESTRA, 71 Symphony Circle, Buffalo NY 14222. (716)885-0331. Marketing Director: Linda Schinelle. Assistant Marketing Director: Mary Rosenberry Stewart. Symphony orchestra presenting 150 musical concerts throughout western New York annually plus a state tour.

Needs: Works with 10 or more freelance artists/year. Uses artists for the design, illustration and layout of advertising and brochures plus window design, pack design, P-O-P displays, mechanicals, posters

and direct mail.
First Contact & Terms: Phone first, then send query letter with brochure showing art style. Samples not filed are returned only if requested. Reports back within 2 weeks. Call to schedule an appointment to show a portfolio, which should include original/final art and final reproduction/product. Pays for design by the project, $100-2,000. Considers complexity of project, skill and experience of artist and turnaround time when establishing payment.

***PAUL BUNYAN PLAYHOUSE**, Box 752, Bemidji MN 56601. (218)751-7270 (season); (218)751-9192 (off-season). Professional summer theatre with a 10-week season; "the oldest continuous running summer theater in the Midwest."
Needs: Works with 30 freelance artists in June-August. Uses artists for set and costume design, lighting and scenery.
First Contact & Terms: Artists must be in-residence during season. Artists are company members, hiring is done in March. Send query letter with brochure/flyer and resume. Samples returned by SASE. Reports in 4 weeks. Provide brochure/flyer, resume and business card to be kept on file for possible future assignments. Pays a salary for the season.

***CAPITAL REPERTORY COMPANY**, Box 399, Albany NY 12201-0399. (518)462-4531. Marketing Director: Hilde Schuster. Professional equity (Lort D) theatre.
Needs: Works with 1-6 freelance artists/year. Freelance needs are seasonal. Needs heaviest in fall and winter. Works on assignment only. Uses artists for advertising and brochure illustration. Prefers illustrations for individual plays to be used on self-mailers and in brochures.
First Contact & Terms: Send resume and tear sheets, Photostats and photocopies. Samples are filed. Samples not filed are returned if requested. Reports back only if interested. Call or write to show a portfolio, which should include b&w, tear sheets and Photostats. Pays for illustration by the project, $50-75. Considers complexity of project, skill and experience of artist and our budget. Negotiates rights purchased.

CASA MANANA MUSICALS INC., Box 9054, Ft. Worth TX 76107. (817)332-9319. General Producer/Manager: Bud Franks. Executive Director of Playhouse/Assistant Producer: Charles Ballinger. Theatrical company performing summer stock, children's theater and classics.
Needs: Assigns 8 jobs/year. Uses artists for costumes, promotional materials, sets and theatrical lighting.
First Contact & Terms: Query with resume. SASE. Reports within 2 weeks. Pay varies.

***CHARLESTON BALLET**, 213 Hoyer Bldg., Charleston WV 25301. (304)342-6541. Director/Choreographer: Andre Van Damme.
Needs: Works with 2-4 freelance artists/year. Needs heaviest in July-August. Works on assignment only. Uses artists for advertising, brochure and poster design, set design, costume design and scenery.
First Contact & Terms: Send a resume and tear sheets, photographs and slides. Samples are filed. Samples not filed are returned if requested. Reports back only if interested. Write to schedule an appointment to show a portfolio, which should include final reproduction/product, color and b&w. Pays for design and illustration by the project, $100 maximum. Considers how work will be used when establishing payment. Buys reprint rights.

THE CHARLESTON SYMPHONY ORCHESTRA, Box 2292, Charleston WV 25328. (304)342-0151. Director of Communications: Michael Fanning. Symphony orchestra "whose patrons represent a broad socio-economic spectrum of music lovers—from classical to pops."
Needs: Works with 1-2 freelance artists/year. Needs heaviest in January-February. Works on assignment only. Uses artists for advertising and brochure design and illustration; and poster illustration. Prefers "clean, contemporary lines with slight feel of elegance; however, not overstated."
First Contact & Terms: Send query letter with brochure, resume, business card and samples to be kept on file. Call for appointment to show portfolio. Samples not filed are returned. Reports only if interested. Payment negotiated; usually on a bidding process. Considers project's budget, skill and experience of the artist, and turnaround time when establishing payment.

***CHICAGO CITY BALLET**, 223 W. Erie St., Chicago IL 60610. (312)943-1315. Marketing Director: Andrea Lammers. "Classical ballet company based in Chicago; tours nationally. Features young talent and seasonal dance professionals. Affluent patrons and board members."
Needs: Works with 3 freelance artists/year. Freelance art needs are seasonal. Needs heaviest in fall and spring. Uses artists for advertising and brochure design, illustration and layout; poster design and illustration; set design.
First Contact & Terms: Send query letter with tear sheets, Photostats and photocopies. Samples are

Artist: Mark Schaming

Peter Kindlon, assistant marketing director of Capital Repertory Company in Albany, New York, bought all rights to this pen-and-ink illustration by Mark Schaming. The piece was used for promotional material, newspaper ads, postcards and in a newsletter. "It presents a picture of small-town industrialized America," says Kindlon. "The use of the moon and shooting star conveys a sense of dreams and possibilities." Kindlon says that Schaming, from Delmar, New York, is "always available for changes in his work so his illustrations convey the theatre's vision of what the play is all about."

filed. Samples not filed are returned only if requested. Reports back only if interested. Write to schedule an appointment to show a portfolio, which should include final reproduction/product, color, b&w, tear sheets, Photostats and photographs. Pays for design by the project, $25-1,000. Pays for illustration by the project, $100-300. Considers complexity of project and available budget. Buys one-time and reprint rights.

Tips: "We mostly use freelancers who donate their time and expertise, or else offer us a major discount in price since we are a not-for-profit organization. Our needs currently are concerned with creating a classical image which also conveys excitement/energy."

CHICAGO CITY THEATRE COMPANY, 3340 N. Clark St., Chicago IL 60657. (312)880-1002. Co-director: Joseph Ehrenberg. Performing arts organization including dance, training.

Needs: Works with 4-6 freelance artists/year; needs heaviest in late summer through spring. Uses artists for advertising, brochure and program design; set and costume design; posters and lighting. "We have logo and basic approach to advertising designs."

First Contact & Terms: Send brochure, resume and samples usually to be kept on file. "Samples might be thrown after observing" or returned by SASE if requested. Accepts any type of samples. Reports only if interested. Call or write for appointment to show portfolio. Pays for design by the project, $50-500 average. Considers complexity of project, available budget and rights purchased when establishing payment.

CHICAGO REPERTORY DANCE ENSEMBLE, 1016 N. Dearborn, Chicago IL 60610. (312)869-3149. Public Relations Director: Alice George. Repertory dance company performing modern, ballet and jazz styles.
Needs: Works with 30-50 freelance artists/year. Uses artists for the design, illustration and layout of advertising and brochures plus paste-up, posters, direct mail, postcards and newsletters. Prefers an innovative style with an artistic rather than business-like tone.
First Contact & Terms: Send query letter with brochure showing art style or resume and samples. Samples not filed are returned if accompanied by SASE. Reports only if interested. Call or write to schedule an appointment to show a portfolio. Payment is negotiable.
Tips: "Please call or write to establish our current schedule and needs. We are especially interested in artists who are eager to donate themselves (not materials) in return for enjoyable work. We are looking for stunning visual and theatrical effects."

***CIRCLE REPERTORY COMPANY**, 161 Avenue of the Americas, New York NY 10013. (212)691-3210. Marketing Director: Susan P. Conover.
Needs: Works with several freelance artists/year. Freelance art needs are seasonal. Needs heaviest in May and September. Works on assignment only. Uses artists for advertising and brochure design, illustration and layout; poster design and illustration.
First Contact & Terms: Send query letter with brochure showing art style or resume and samples. Samples are sometimes filed. Samples not filed are returned by SASE. Reports only if interested. Write to schedule an appointment to show a portfolio, which should include thumbnails, original/final art, final reproduction/product, color and b&w. Negotiates payment for design and illustration. Considers complexity of project, skill and experience of artist, client's budget, how work will be used, turnaround time and rights purchased when establishing payment. Negotiates rights purchased.
Tips: "Every season brings a new look to Circle Rep. The 'look' lasts for the entire season. Artists applying to Circle Rep should take into account all elements of a theatre season including subscription brochures, newsletters, single ticket ads and benefit invitations."

CITIARTS/THEATRE CONCORD, 1950 Parkside Dr., Concord CA 94519. (415)671-3065. Contact: Jim Jester. Visual Arts for public art competitions and display areas. Produces musicals, comedy, drama and ballet year round, primarily between September through July. Assigns 3-10 jobs/year.
Needs: Works with up to 4 illustrators and 4 designers/year. Works on assignment only. Uses artists for costume design, flyers, graphic/set design, posters, programs, theatrical lighting, Art in Public Places projects, and advertising and brochure design, illustration and layout.
First Contact & Terms: Query, then mail slides or photos. Samples returned by SASE. Reports back on future assignment possibilities. Call or write to schedule an appointment to show a portfolio, which should include thumbnails, roughs, original/final art, photographs and b&w.

***CIVIC BALLET CENTER AND DANCE ARTS**, 25 S. Sierra Madre Blvd., Pasadena CA 91107. (213)792-0873. Director: Elly Van Dijk. Home of the Pasadena Civic Ballet, Inc. a preprofessional ballet company, a nonprofit organization. Offers classes in classical ballet, modern, jazz, creative dance—all ages, all levels.
Needs: Works with about 15 freelance artists/year. Uses artists for brochure and program design, and posters.
First Contact & Terms: Los Angeles-area artists only; performing arts art experience necessary. Send query letter with resume to be kept on file. Reports only if interested and needed. Pays percentage basis with minimum guarantee. Considers skill and experience of artist when establishing payment.

THE CLEVELAND INSTITUTE OF MUSIC, 11021 East Blvd., Cleveland OH 44106. (216)791-5165. Public Relations Director: Jean Caldwell. Performing arts center and conservatory of music.
Needs: Assigns 40 jobs and buys 20 illustrations/year. Local artists only. Uses artists for illustration, layout and graphics for advertising, annual reports, bumper stickers, costumes, direct mail brochures, exhibits, flyers, graphics, posters, programs, record jackets and catalogs.
First Contact & Terms: Send query letter with brochure showing art style or tear sheets, Photostats and photocopies. SASE. Reports within 1 week. Call or write to schedule an appointment to show a portfolio, which should include thumbnails, roughs, original/final art, final reproduction/product, tear sheets and Photostats. Payment varies; on acceptance.

***CLEVELAND OPERA**, 1438 Euclid Ave., Cleveland OH 44115. Production Manager: Keith Nagy. Regional professional opera company, Proscenium stage 25'x52'.
Needs: Freelance art needs are seasonal. Needs heaviest in October-May. Works on assignment only. Uses artists for set design, costume design, lighting and scenery.
First Contact & Terms: Send a resume. Most samples are not filed. Samples not filed are returned. Reports back within 3 weeks. Write to show a portfolio. Pays for design by the project. Considers complexity of project, skill and experience of artist, show budget and turnaround time when establishing payment. Negotiates rights purchased.
Tips: "Keep resumes brief and up-to-date."

COCTEAU REPERTORY CO., 330 Bowery, New York NY 10012. (212)677-0060. Artistic Director: Eve Adamson. Performs 6 plays in rotating repertory with a resident company each year.
Needs: Works with 6-10 freelance artists/year. "We prefer classical repertory and/or European experience." Works on assignment only. Needs heaviest August-March. Uses artists for brochure, set and costume design; and lighting and scenery. "We prefer non-realistic designs, strong, central concepts."
First Contact & Terms: Send query letter with resume to be kept on file for 1 season. "We encourage artists to see our work before application." Samples accepted at interview only. Samples not filed are returned by SASE. Reports only if interested. Pays for design by the project, $200-300 average. Pays for illustration by the project, $150-650 average. Considers project's budget when establishing payment.

CONCORD PAVILION, Box 6166, Concord CA 94524. (415)671-3373. Programming Director: Lee Smith. Performing arts center; presents dance, rock, pop music, jazz, symphonies, sports and boat shows. Assigns 3-5 jobs/year.
Needs: Works with 1-2 illustrators and 1-2 designers/year; spring and summer only. Uses artists for advertising design/layout, billboards, bumper stickers, direct mail brochures, flyers, graphic design, posters, programs, set design, set/stage design painters, technical charts/illustrations and theatrical lighting design.
First Contact & Terms: Prefers local artists. Send photos, tear sheets or portfolio. SASE. Reports in 4 weeks. Works on assignment only. Samples returned by SASE. Provide resume, brochure and flyer to be kept on file for future assignments.

***CONNECTICUT GRAND OPERA**, 61 Atlantic St., Stamford CT 06901. (203)325-9570. General Manager: John Hiddlestone.
Needs: Works with 2-3 freelance artists/year. Freelance needs are seasonal. Needs heaviest in late summer; early fall. Uses artists for advertising design and layout, poster design and illustration.
First Contact & Terms: Send query letter with brochure showing art style. Samples are filed. Samples not filed are returned by SASE if requested. Reports back within 1 month. Write to schedule an appointment to show a portfolio, which should include original/final art and final reproduction/product. Pays for design by the project, $800-1,700. Pays for illustration by the project, $175-850. Considers complexity of project, client's budget and turnaround time when establishing payment.

CONNECTICUT OPERA, 226 Farmington Ave., Hartford CT 06105. (203)527-0713. Director of Communications: Ginny Ludwig. Sixth oldest professional opera company in the US. Main season is 2 performances each of 4 major productions, some in original language and some in English performed in Bushnell Hall. Also operates a resident touring company, which performs fully staged and costumed productions throughout New England and the East Coast.
Needs: Uses artists for advertising and brochure design, illustration and layout; program, set and costume design; and scenery.
First Contact & Terms: Send query letter with samples to be kept on file. "Send what is appropriate to designer style." Samples not kept on file are returned by SASE only if requested. Reports only if interested. Call or write for appointment to show portfolio. The fee depends on the project.
Tips: When reviewing an artist's work, looks for "originality and strong imagery whether it be graphic or illustrative; dynamic design rather than obscure. We are interested in strong graphic design that will help to market the product. Good design that doesn't translate into black-and-white newspaper ads is valueless."

CORTLAND REPERTORY THEATRE INC., Box 783, Cortland NY 13045. Resident summer theatre which produces 5 shows in summer. Assigns 5 jobs/summer.
Needs: Works with 5 designers/year; summers only. Uses designers for properties, sets, costume and lighting. Also uses artists for brochures (donation drive, subscription series) and flyer (early bird renewal).
First Contact & Terms: Query with resume in early winter. Works on assignment only. Pays $1,000-1,700 for 2 months work. Pays for design and illustrations by the project, $50-200 average. Considers

available budget, skill and experience of artist and rights purchased when establishing payment.
Tips: "Do volunteer work in the area of your interest. This way you keep your skills sharp, you learn, and it places you in front of people who may someday be able to hire you. I also find trading services an excellent means to opening job situations. More and more theatres are turning to professional artists for help in packaging, displays and advertising."

DALLAS THEATER CENTER, 3636 Turtle Creek Blvd., Dallas TX 75219. Contact: Public Relations Director. A professional resident theatre with 3 performing spaces—Frank LW Theater, Arts District Theatre and In The Basement (experimental theater). Performs variety of plays from classic to contemporary. Yearly attendance of 100,000.
Needs: Uses a varying number of freelance artists/year. Needs are heaviest in spring and fall although possibilities exist year-round for program and poster work. Uses freelance artists for advertising and brochure design, illustration and layout; poster and program design and illustration.
First Contact & Terms: Prefers local artists as "we often need work rather quickly." Works on assignment basis only. Send query letter with business card and samples to be kept on file. Prefers photocopies as samples. Samples not kept on file are returned only with an SASE. Reports only if interested. Write for appointment to show portfolio. Pays by the project for design; by the hour or by the project, for illustration. Considers complexity of project, project's budget, skill and experience of the artist, how work will be used, turnaround time and rights purchased when establishing payment.

DANCE KALEIDOSCOPE, 429 E. Vermont, Indianapolis IN 46202. (317)634-8484. Artistic Director: Cherri Jaffee. Professional modern dance repertory company which tours Indiana. The repertory comes largely from guest choreographers out of New York City.
Needs: Works with several freelance artists/year; needs heaviest in October, March and May. Uses artists for advertising, brochure, program, set and costume design; advertising, brochure and program layout; advertising illustration, posters, lighting and scenery. Prefers clean, bold style "that sells the product, not the graphics."
First Contact & Terms: Local artists only with previous experience in the arts "who enjoy the challenge of working within a limited budget. Artist must be willing to take direction from the board of directors." Send query letter with brochure, resume, business card, samples and tear sheets to be kept on file. Call for appointment to show portfolio. Samples not returned. Reports only if interested. Pays for design by the hour, $10-30 average; by the project, $50-100 average. Considers complexity of project, available budget, turnaround time and rights purchased when establishing payment.
Tips: "Artist must respect the company's need to use 'words' in some publications and not expect the art to carry the entire message."

***DANCEWORKS**, 1108 Boylston St., Boston MA 02215. (617)266-4661. Company Manager: Anne Trecker. Nonprofit professional dance training center and resident touring company. Under artistic direction of Susan Rose.
Needs: Works with 3 freelance artists/year; needs heaviest in fall and spring, some winter. Uses artists for brochure design, illustration and layout; costume design, posters, photography and lighting. Prefers graphics with a "good sense of architectural line, well representing our choreography."
First Contact & Terms: Send query letter with brochure, resume and samples to be kept on file. Prefers photographs and original work as samples. Pays for design and illustration by the project, $50-350 average. Considers complexity of project, available budget, and skill and experience of artist when establishing payment.

DAYTON BALLET, 140 N. Main St., Dayton OH 45402. (513)222-3661. Director/Choreographer: Stuart Sebastian. Ballet company of 17 professional dancers with a 22-member nonprofessional training company, board of trustees and Friends organization.
Needs: Works with 2-3 freelance artists/year. Uses artists for advertising, brochure, set and costume design; lighting and scenery.
First Contact & Terms: Send query letter with resume and samples. Samples returned. Reports within 3 weeks. Works on assignment only. Provide brochure/flyer and resume to be kept on file for possible future assignments. Pays by the project; negotiable.
Tips: "Line drawings are comic, romantic and flowing."

DENVER SYMPHONY ORCHESTRA, Suite 330, 910 Fifteenth St., Denver CO 80202.(303)572-1151. Marketing & Public Relations Director: John Wren. Professional 88-member symphony orchestra performing classical and pops concerts.
Needs: Works with "numerous" freelance artists/year. Works on assignment only. Uses artists for advertising, brochure and catalog design, illustration and layout; poster and program design and illustration.

First Contact & Terms: Send query letter with brochure, resume, Photostats, slides, photographs photocopies or tear sheets to be kept on file. Samples not filed are returned only if requested. Reports within 3 weeks. Call or write for appointment to show portfolio. Payment varies. Considers complexity of project, project's budget, skill and experience of the artist, how work will be used and turnaround time when establishing payment.

***DES MOINES BALLET ASSOCIATION, INC.**, 4333 Park Ave., Des Moines IA 50321. (515)282-3480. Artistic Director: Stephan Laurent. Ballet company of 18 professional members and school with Junior Company.
Needs: Uses artists for "all categories/in-kind services at present time."
First Contact & Terms: Send query letter. Samples are filed. Samples not filed are returned only if requested. Reports back within weeks. Write to schedule an appointment to show a portfolio.

***DIABLO VALLEY PHILHARMONIC**, 321 Golf Club Rd., Pleasant Hill CA 94523. (415)685-1230. Conductor: Fredric Johnson. Symphony orchestra.
Needs: Works with 1 freelance artist/year. Needs heaviest May-July. Uses artists for advertising and brochure design, illustration and layout; and program design and illustration. Prefers an "eloquent, classy" style.
First Contact & Terms: Send query letter with brochure and samples to be kept on file. Write for appointment to show portfolio. Samples not filed are not returned. Reports back only if interested. Pays for design and illustration by the project, $600 average. Considers complexity of project, project's budget and turnaround time when establishing payment.

DULUTH BALLET, The Depot, 506 W. Michigan St., Duluth MN 55802. (218)722-2314. Office Staff: Cathe Hauge-Hall. Artistic Director: Gernot Petzold. Managing Director: Diane Jacobs. Ballet company of 8 dancers with a repertoire ranging from modern/contemporary to classical dance styles.
Needs: Works with 3-4 freelance artists/year; needs heaviest approximately one month before summer, fall and winter concerts. Uses artists for advertising design, illustration and layout.
First Contact & Terms: Send query letter with brochure, resume, samples to be kept on file. Prefers photostats and photography as samples. Samples returned by SASE if not kept on file. Call or write for appointment to show portfolio. Pays for design by the project, $100-150 average. Pays for illustration by the project, $50-200 average. Considers complexity of project, available budget, skill and experience of artist, how work will be used, turnaround time and rights purchased when establishing payment.
Tips: "Make sure work is appropriate to our situation. Sometimes we receive material that has no application to what we are doing."

EMPIRE STATE INSTITUTE FOR THE PERFORMING ARTS (ESIPA at the EGG), Empire State Plaza, Albany NY 12223. (518)443-5222. Producing Director: Patricia B. Snyder. Professional resident theatre and performing arts center; 2 theatres 900, 450; usually 8 productions requiring designers each season.
Needs: Works with 30-40 artists/year. Works on assignment only. Uses artists for poster design and illustration, set and costume design, lighting and scenery.
First Contact & Terms: Send query letter and resume to be kept on file; do not send samples with first contact. Reports back only if interested. Write to schedule an appointment to show a portfolio. Pays for design; usually by the project, $1,000 average. Pays for illustration usually by the project, $500 average. Considers complexity of project, project's budget, skill and experience of the artist, and rights purchased when establishing payment.

***EUREKA THEATRE COMPANY**, 2730 16th St., San Francisco CA 94103. (415)558-9811. Marketing Director: John Spokes. This year Eureka Theater celebrates its fifteenth season. "We are an Equity Theatre with a $500,000 operating budget. We produce a 6-play subscription series running September through June and present new and commissioned works by emerging playwrights."
Needs: Works with 35 freelance artists/year. Freelance art needs are seasonal. Needs heaviest in August-May. Works on assignment only. Uses artists for advertising and brochure design, illustration and layout; poster design and illustration; set design; costume design; lighting and scenery. "Most designs are based in realism rather than abstraction. Designs must be variable."
First Contact & Terms: Send query letter with resume and tear sheets, photocopies and slides. Samples are filed. Samples not filed are returned only if requested. Reports back only if interested. Write to schedule an appointment to show a portfolio, which should include photographs, slides and transparencies. Pays for design and illustration by the project, $400 minimum. Considers skill and experience of artist when establishing payment. Work purchased outright.

FLAGSTAFF SYMPHONY ASSOCIATION, Box 122, Flagstaff AZ 86002. (602)774-4231. Manager: Harold Weller. The FSA is the "major musical arts organization in Northern Arizona, operating the Flagstaff Symphony Orchestra and sponsoring programs and concerts in addition to the orchestra's 15 concerts."

Needs: Works with 6 freelance artists/year. Needs heaviest in March and April. Local artists only. Works on assignment only. Uses artists for advertising, brochure and program design; newsletter layout and design (published quarterly).

First Contact & Terms: Send query letter with photocopies to be kept on file. Samples not filed are returned only if requested. Reports only if interested. Pays by individual arrangement. Considers project's budget when establishing payment.

***FORT WAYNE DANCE COLLECTIVE**, 1126 Broadway, Fort Wayne IN 46802. (219)424-6574. Artistic Director: Elizabeth Monnier.

Needs: Freelance art needed through the year. Uses artists for advertising and brochure design, illustration and layout; set design; costume design; lighting and scenery. Prefers "innovative, nontraditional" styles.

First Contact & Terms: Send query letter with brochure showing art style. Samples are filed. Samples not filed are returned by SASE if requested. Reports back only if interested. Pays for design and illustration by the project. Considers complexity of project and how work will be used when establishing payment.

***THE FULLER YOUNG PEOPLE'S THEATRE**, 3046 Aldrich Ave. S., Minneapolis MN 55408. (612)824-9576. Artistic Director: Stephen DiMenna. "Nonprofit professional theatre with three components: a production and touring program, a professional training institute for young artists and an artists-in-the-schools outreach program. Dedicated to the development of young emerging artists."

Needs: Works with 2-4 freelance artists/year. Freelance art needs are seasonal. Needs heaviest in September to May. Works on assignment only. Uses artists for brochure design, illustration and layout; poster design and illustration; set design; costume design; lighting and scenery. "Images that reflect many aspects of childhood and adolescence, reflecting the playful as well as the dark and spiritual."

First Contact & Terms: Send query letter with brochure showing art style or resume and samples. Samples are filed. Samples not filed are returned if requested. Reports back within 6 months. Call or write to schedule an appointment to show a portfolio, or mail thumbnails, roughs, final reproduction/product, color, photographs and slides. Pays for design by the project, $400-1,200. Pays for illustration by the project, $100-300. Considers complexity of project, client's budget, skill and experience of artist and grant monies available when establishing payment. Negotiates rights purchased.

Tips: "We work almost exclusively with visual artists for our theatrical designs. We do not use theatre or stage designers. Instead we like a young visual artists who may have never worked in the theatre before to bring his/her vision and tastes to our work. We don't need the artists to be well experienced in the theatre. "I look for images that reflect many aspects of childhood and adolescence, reflecting the playful as well as the dark and spiritual sides."

***GARLAND BALLET ASSOCIATION**, Banner Banc Building, Suite 210A, 800 W. Main St., Garland TX 75040. (214)272-1514. Treasurer: Melissa Crockett. "Speciality is classical ballet and company presently has 6 dancers. There are some social events connected with the ballet in addition to the regular season performances."

Needs: Works with 1-2 freelance artists/year. Freelance art needs are seasonal. Needs heaviest in spring. Works on assignment only. Uses artists for advertising and brochure illustration and poster illustation. Prefers "lyrical, romantic, and realistic art rather than modern or abstract with irritating color schemes."

First Contact & Terms: Send query letter with brochure showing art style. Samples are filed. Reports back within 2 weeks. Call to schedule an appointment to show a portfolio, which should include thumbnails, roughs, color, b&w and tear sheets. Pays for design by the project, $25-200. Pays for illustration by the hour, $25-200. Considers complexity of project, client's budget, how work will be used and rights purchased when establishing payment. Buys first rights an negotiates rights purchased.

GUS GIORDANO JAZZ DANCE CHICAGO, 614 Davis St., Evanston IL 60201. (312)866-6779. Coordinators: Peg and Nan Giordano. Jazz dance company consisting of 8-10 members.

Needs: Works with 2-3 freelance artists/year. Works on assignment only. Uses artists for advertising and costume design, lighting and scenery.

First Contact & Terms: Call for appointment. Samples returned by SASE. Reports within weeks. Send resume to be kept on file for possible future assignments. Negotiates payment.

GRAND RAPIDS SYMPHONY ORCHESTRA, 415 Exhibitors Bldg., Grand Rapids MI 49503. (616)454-9451. Marketing and Public Relations Director: Susan M. Schwartz. Executive Director: Peter W. Smith.
Needs: Uses artists for program covers, ads, fliers and posters.
First Contact & Terms: Contact Public Relations Director initially by letter or phone. "We will respond to all inquiries for work if a call is made first to the PR Director by the artist." Pay based on quality and intended use of the work; negotiates.

GROUP MOTION MULTI-MEDIA DANCE THEATER, 624 S. 4th St., Philadelphia PA 19147. (215)928-1495. Co-Directors: Brigitta Herrmann, Manfred Fishbeck. Group motion multi-media dance theatre specializing in modern and innovative dance. "We have a local audience and offer performances, a variety of classes for children and adults, and workshops."
Needs: Works with 12 freelance artists/year. Works on assignment only. Needs heaviest fall through spring. Uses artists for advertising, brochure and poster design; and lighting.
First Contact & Terms: Send query letter with samples to be kept on file; call or write for appointment to show portfolio. Reports only if interested. Pays for design and illustration by the project, $25 minimum. Considers complexity of project, project's budget, skill and experience of artist, and how work will be used when establishing payment.

THE GROUP THEATRE COMPANY, 3940 Brooklyn Ave. NE, Seattle WA 98105. (206)545-4969. Marketing Director: Victory Searle. Professional theatre promoting a full theatrical season using flyers, brochures and posters. Other events generate invitations, etc.
Needs: Works with 6 freelance artists/year. Prefers local artists only. Uses artists for advertising illustration, brochure design, illustration and layout, posters and annual reports.
First Contact & Terms: Send query letter with brochure showing art style or resume, tear sheets and photocopies. Samples not filed are returned by SASE. Reports only if interested. Call or write to schedule an appointment to show a portfolio, which should include thumbnails, roughs, final reproduction/product, color and tear sheets.
Tips: "We really negotiate each project. We are a non-profit organization. If you rigidly demand a top-of-the market fee, we're probably not for you."

HARTFORD BALLET, 226 Farmington Ave., Hartford CT 06105. (203)527-0713. Director of Communications: Ginny Ludwig. Nationally-recognized company under the artistic direction of Michael Uthoff, with a repertory in classical and contemporary ballet; mainstage performances include twelve local performances of the annual holiday "Nutcracker" and other repertory productions featuring world premieres and revivals.
Needs: Freelance artists needed for brochure and advertising design, particularly in the spring and fall. Designers also needed for costume, poster and scenic design, depending upon the needs of the current production.
First Contact & Terms: Send query letter and samples of work to be kept on file. Write for an appointment to show portfolio. If return of samples is requested, send SASE. Terms discussed before any work is contracted. Fees based upon project needs.
Tips: "We need a contemporary style with strong sales emphasis."

***HIP POCKET THEATRE**, 1627 Fairmont, Ft. Worth TX 76104. (817)927-2833. Design Coordinator: James Maynard. "Year-round producing theatre, specializing in original works. Utilize dance, mime, puppetry, media, music to enhance productions."
Needs: Works with 3-4 freelance artists/year. Freelance art needed throughout the year. Works on assignment only. Uses artists for advertising and brochure design and illustration; poster design and illustration; lighting and scenery. "Art reflects the particular show being advertised or designed, frequently a wide spectrum."
First Contact & Terms: Send query letter with brochure showing art style or resume and photocopies. Samples are filed. Samples not filed are returned by SASE if requested. Reports back within 2 weeks. Write to schedule an appointment to show a portfolio, or mail roughs, final reproduction/product and Photostats. Pays for design by the project, $50-300. Pays for illustration by the project, $25-200. Considers complexity of project, project's budget, turnaround time, skill and experience of artist and how work will be used when establishing payment. Negotiates rights purchased.
Tips: "Approach us with honesty, high imagination and energy."

***HONOLULU SYMPHONY**, Suite 1515, 1441 Kapiolani Blvd., Honolulu HI 96814. (808)537-6171. Director of Communications and Marketing: Henry Adams.
Needs: Assigns 30 jobs/year. Uses artists for direct mail, brochures, posters, programs, annual reports, newspaper ads and season promotions. "Graphic design should be bold, clean and careful."

First Contact & Terms: Local artists only. Query with previously published work. SASE. Reports within 2 weeks. Pays for design or illustration by the hour, $15-30 average; by the project, $100-250 average. Considers available budget, how work will be used and turnaround time when establishing payment.
Tips: "The local office of Ogilvy and Mather, Hawaii, has taken the Honolulu Symphony on as a public service account; therefore, freelance needs have been reduced."

HOUSTON GRAND OPERA, 510 Preston, Houston TX 77002. (713)546-0230. Contact: Peggy Read.
Needs: Works with 4-8 illustrators and 3-4 designers/year. Uses brochures, flyers, posters and newspapers.
First Contact & Terms: Send samples (designer: printed samples; illustrator: portfolio plus samples). Works on assignment only. Samples returned by SASE. Reports back on future assignment possibilities. Provide resume, business card, brochure, flyer, tear sheets and representative samples, if possible, to be kept on file for future assignments.
Tips: "As a nonprofit arts organization, we look for relationships with artists that can benefit the artists by associating with the Houston Grand Opera and can be economically feasible for us. Most of our artistic services are monetarily free, giving credit and a geat deal of exposure to artist."

HOUSTON SYMPHONY ORCHESTRA, 615 Louisiana St., Houston TX 77002. Manager/Publications: Nonprofit organization.
Needs: Works with 10-20 freelance artists/year. Prefers artists that are inexpensive and willing to take direction. Uses artists for advertising and brochure design, illustration and layout; posters, direct mail and annual reports.
First Contact & Terms: Send query letter with samples. Samples not filed are returned by SASE. Reports only if interested. Considers complexity of project, client's budget, skill and experience of artist, how work will be used and turnaround time when establishing payment.
Tips: "Artist must be willing to take strategy direction and be flexible through approval process."

INDIANAPOLIS BALLET THEATRE, 411 E. Michigan, Indianapolis IN 46204. (317)637-8979. Director of Marketing: Mary Bashaw. Ballet company with tours and residencies.
Needs: Works with 5 freelance artists/year. Uses artists for the design, illustration and layout of advertising and brochure plus calligraphy, paste-up, posters and direct mail.
First Contact & Terms: Send query letter with resume and samples. Samples not filed are returned only if requested. Reports back. To show a portfolio, mail appropriate materials or write to schedule an appointment; portfolio should include original/final art, color and photographs. Payment depends primarily on the nature of the job whether it's by the hour or by project. Considers complexity of project, client's budget, skill and experience of artist, how work will be used, turnaround time and rights purchased when establishing payment.
Tips: "Be flexible about deadlines, willingness to work with artistic staff and marketing on concept and final design."

INTAR-INTERNATIONAL ARTS RELATIONS, Box 788, New York NY 10109. (212)695-6135. Artistic Director: Max Ferra. Produces 1 stage reading/year and 2 playwriting labs/year.
Needs: Assigns 12-20 jobs/year; local artists only. Query with samples. Uses artists for set, costume, light design. Also flyers and posters. Pays for design by the project, $100-500 average. Pays for illustrations by the project, $100-300. Considers complexity of project, available budget, skill and experience of artist, how work will be used and turnaround time when establishing payment.
Tips: "We prefer designers of Hispanic background or empathy with our culture, but it's not a prerequisite. We are trying to produce only new works, not the classics. Hispanic-Americans are our number one consideration."

ROBERT IVEY BALLET COMPANY, 1632 Ashley Hall Rd., Charleston SC 29407. (803)556-1343. Artistic Director: Robert C. Ivey. Consists of two companies: The Senior Company—classically trained men and women chosen in open auditions providing educational outreach in schools, lecture-demonstrations for community organizations and joint performances with area arts groups; and The Charleston Youth Ballet, offering training to dancers age 9-13.
Needs: Works with 12 freelance artists/year; needs heaviest in spring and fall. Uses artists for advertising, brochure, program, set and costume design; posters, lighting and scenery.
First Contact & Terms: Send query letter with brochure showing art style. To show a portfolio, mail appropriate materials, which should include roughs, final reproduction/product, Photostats and photographs. Pays for design by the project, $300-500 average. Pays for illustration by the project, $500-800 average. "Poster illustrations and ad layouts change with each performance. Costume and set design

pays considerably more." Considers complexity of project and available budget when establishing payment.
Tips: Artists fail to consider "the budget of the organization when presenting specs. Also that total budget must cover many phases. Artwork should be able to be recycled for several ventures."

JOHNSTOWN SYMPHONY ORCHESTRA, 244 Walnut St., Johnstown PA 15901. General Manager: David Ball. Assigns 2-5 jobs/year.
Needs: Works with 1-2 illustrators/year in February. Needs design work in December and February. Uses artists for bumper stickers, direct mail brochures, flyers, graphics, posters, programs and record jackets. Pays $25-200/job for design.
First Contact & Terms: Send query letter with samples and resume. SASE. Reports within 1 week. Provide resume, brochure and flyer to be kept on file for future assignments.

***KNOXVILLE OPERA COMPANY**, Box 16, Knoxville TN 37901. Administrative Assistant: Marylaine H. Driese. Produces 3 operas per year, summer, fall, spring. Has working board of directors, 3 full-time staff and membership of approximately 400.
Needs: Works with 2-3 freelance artists/year. Freelance art needs are seasonal. Needs heaviest in January-February, June and September. Uses artist for advertising and brochure design, illustration and layout; poster design and illustration; set design; costume design; lighting and scenery.
First Contact & Terms: Send query letter with brochure showing art style or resume and samples. Samples are filed. Samples not filed are returned. Reports back within 6 weeks. To show a portfolio, mail thumbnails, roughs and color. Pays for design by the project, $150-450. Considers complexity of project, available budget, turnaround time and skill and experience of artist when establishing payment. Buys all rights.

***LA JOLLA PLAYHOUSE**, Box 12039, La Jolla CA 92039. (619)534-6760. Director of Marketing and Operations: Robert Friend. Professional resident theatre.
Needs: Works with 2-3 freelance artists/year. Freelance art needed throughout the year. Uses artists for advertising and brochure design, illustration and layout; catalog design, illustration and layout.
First Contact & Terms: Send query letter with resume and tear sheets, Photostats and photocopies. Samples are filed. Samples not filed are returned only if requested. Reports back only if interested. Write to schedule an appointment to show a portfolio, or mail final reproduction/product. Pays for design by the hour, $20 minimum and by the project. Pays for illustration by the hour and by the project. Considers complexity of project and client's budget when establishing payment.
Tips: "We look for unique and innovative work which reflects our artistic market."

MELANIE LAJOIE AND THE PYRAMID DANCE COMPANY, 199 Fairmont Ave., Worcester MA 01604. (617)756-3525 or 756-0110. Director/Featured Performer: Melanie Lajoie. Performs traditional ethnic dances of the Middle and Near East. Specializes in gypsy, peasant, religious ritual, tribal, harem, including dances of the sword, veils, and finger cymbals, from a variety of countries.
Needs: Works with 1 freelance artist/year. Uses artists for advertising, brochure, catalog and set design; advertising brochure and catalog layout; catalog illustration; posters, lighting and scenery. Prefers Middle Eastern (Oriental, Persian) Old World style.
First Contact & Terms: Local artists only; performing arts art experience necessary. Send query letter with brochure, resume, business card, photographs and Photostats to be kept on file. Samples returned by SASE only if requested. Reports within 1 month if interested. Pays for design by the project, $25-300 average. Considers complexity of project, available budget, skill and experience of artist, how work will be used and rights purchased when establishing payment.

MATTI LASCOE DANCE THEATRE CO., 1014-A Cabrillo Park Dr., Santa Ana CA 92701. (714)542-1463. Artistic Director: Matti Lascoe. Sixteen member Caribbean dance and music ensemble with drummers and the Trinidad Steel Drum Band. Concert is called "Caribbean Splash."
Needs: Works with 2 freelance artists/year; needs heaviest in September-November, January-May. Uses artists for advertising, brochure, set and costume design; lighting and scenery.
First Contact & Terms: Experienced artists only. Send resume, photographs and tear sheets to be kept on file. Write for artists' guidelines. Samples returned by SASE only if requested. Reports only if interested. Pays for design and illustration by the project. Considers available budget when establishing payment.

LE GROUPE DE LA PLACE ROYALE, 130 Sparks St., Ottawa, Ontario K1P 5B6 Canada. (613)235-1493. Director of Development: Rene Boucher. "Innovative, professional modern dance company with a 48-week season, 8 dancers, 1 artistic director, voice coach and an assistant artistic director. All choreography is original and there is voice, video and live musical accompaniment used in performance by the dancers. Use of original set and costume design by visual artists since 1966."

Needs: Works with 2-3 freelance artists/year. Uses artists for advertising, brochure and program design, illustration and layout; posters, lighting, holography, experimental video and film, photography and slide montage. Prefers to work with artists with at least a minimum exposure to modern dance. "Company normally has a very good idea of what it wants. It is then up to the artist to produce at least three variations on a given theme."

First Contact & Terms: Send query letter with brochure, resume and samples to be kept on file. "A letter will be sent if company is interested in artist's work. Will then ask about availability and request that an appointment be scheduled for an exchange with the artistic director and public relations officer." Prefers photographs, posters, flyers or slides if artwork is set or costume design, as samples. Samples returned by SASE only if requested. Reports within 2 weeks. Pays for design by the project, $200-1,000. "Maximum payment varies with scope of project and/or availability of funds." Considers complexity of project, available budget, skill and experience of artist, how work will be used and rights purchased when establishing payment.

Tips: "Approach should focus on movement and its visual expression." Looks for "innovative art or marketing concepts; knowledge of printing process, paper stock, etc.; awareness of costs."

***MANHATTAN THEATRE CLUB**, 453 W. 16th St., New York NY 10011. (212)645-5590. Director of Marketing/President: Helene Davis.

Needs: Freelance art needs are seasonal. Needs heaviest in spring and summer. Works on assignment only. Uses artists for brochure design, illustration and layout.

First Contact & Terms: Send query letter with brochure or resume, tear sheets, Photostats and photocopies. Write to schedule an appointment to show a portfolio. Pays for design by the hour, $10-15; by the project. Pays for illustration by the hour. Considers complexity of project, skill and experience of artist and "our own budget limitations" when establishing payment.

MARYLAND DANCE THEATER, Dance Dept., University of Maryland, College Park MD 20742. (301)454-3399. Artistic Directors: Larry and Anne Warren. Incorporated, nonprofit, modern dance repertory company in residence at the University of Maryland consisting of approximately 15 students, faculty and area artists. Performances are given in the Washington/Baltimore area and throughout the mid-Atlantic states.

Needs: Works with 3-4 freelance artists/year; needs heaviest in November-May. Works primarily with local artists. Uses artists for advertising, brochure and program design and layout; costume design, posters and lighting.

First Contact & Terms: Send query letter with description of past work. Call or write for appointment to show portfolio. Pays for design by the project, $25-300 average, maybe higher depending on project. Considers complexity of project, available budget, skill and experience of artist, how work will be used and turnaround time when establishing payment.

MID-WILLAMETTE BALLET ENSEMBLE, Box 55, Salem OR 97308. (503)363-1403. Director, Salem Ballet School: Elfie Stevenin, DMA-DEA. Dance company of 15 ensemble students performing locally for community events and traditional concerts.

Needs: Works with 3 artists for poster designs, photography, brochure design; all fund-raising through parent organization only. Needs heaviest in fall and spring. Local artists only—"for the most part, they are artists who have children enrolled in classes." Uses artists for brochure design, posters and photography.

First Contact & Terms: Send business card to be kept on file. Pays for design by the project. Considers available budget when establishing payment.

MILWAUKEE SYMPHONY ORCHESTRA, 212 W. Wisconsin Ave., Milwaukee WI 53203. (414)291-6010. Public Relations: Polly Scott.

Needs: Local artists only. Uses artists for advertising, flyers, graphics and posters.

First Contact & Terms: Query or arrange interview. SASE. Reports in 2 weeks. Pays for design by the project $100-300. Pays for illustration by the project, $50-200. Considers complexity of project, available budget and turnaround time when establishing payment. Also considers trade of symphony tickets for artwork.

Tips: "Find out my needs, ask for samples of our publications before coming to see me."

The asterisk before a listing indicates that the listing is new in this edition. New markets are often the most receptive to freelance submissions.

MINNESOTA JAZZ DANCE COMPANY, Zoe Sealy Dance Center, 1815 E. 38th St., Minneapolis MN 55407. (612)721-3031. Company and Studio Managers: Jim Streeer and Carol Stoutland. Dance company which "creates and presents jazz dance in its concert art form; collaborates with visual artists; educates audiences through lecture demonstrations and workshops throughout the US."
Needs: Works with 6 freelance artists/year. Uses artists for advertising, brochure and program design, illustration and layout; set and costume design, posters and lighting.
First Contact & Terms: Send query letter with brochure, resume, business card, original work and tear sheets to be kept on file. Call or write for appointment to show portfolio. Samples returned by SASE only if requested. Reports within 6 weeks. Pays for design and illustration by the hour, $5-40 average; by the project, $50-100 average; by the day, $25-50 average. Considers available budget, and skill and experience of artist when establishing payment.

MJT DANCE CO., Box 108, Watertown MA 02172. (617)482-0351. Director: Margie J. Topf. Modern dance troupe.
Needs: Assigns 2-10 jobs/year. Local artists only. Uses artists for advertising, bumper stickers, direct mail brochures, flyers, graphics, posters, programs, tickets, exhibits and lighting. Especially needs brochure design, layout, paste-up.
First Contact & Terms: Send query letter with resume or arrange interview. SASE. Reports within 2 weeks. Pays $5-10/hour.
Tips: "Video is becoming a major consideration in the performing arts. Be well-versed in many different art forms."

ELISA MONTE DANCE CO., 39 Great Jones St., New York NY 10012. (212)982-4264. Manager: Bernard Schmidt. Modern dance company "with strong international flavor."
Needs: Works with 2-3 freelance artists/year. Prefers local artists. Works on assignment only. Uses artists for advertising, brochure and catalog design, illustration and layout plus mechanicals, posters and direct mail.
First Contact & Terms: Send query letter with brochure showing art style or resume, photocopies or photographs. Samples not filed are returned by SASE only if requested by artist. Reports only if interested. Call or write to schedule an appointment to show a portfolio, which should include roughs, final reproduction/product, color and photographs. Pays for design by the project, $500 minimum. Considers complexity of project, skill and experience of artist and how work will be used when establishing payment.

NASHVILLE SYMPHONY ORCHESTRA, 208 23rd Ave. N., Nashville TN 37203. (615)329-3033. Contact: Pete Fosselman. Marketing and Public Relations Director: Debra Campagna. Regional symphony.
Needs: Works with 4 freelance artists/year. Works on assignment only. Uses artists for advertising and brochure design, illustration, and layout; poster and program design and illustration.
First Contact & Terms: Send query letter with brochure, business card and tear sheets to be kept on file. Call for appointment to show portfolio. Reports only if interested. "We determine a project's estimate." Considers complexity of project, project's budget, how work will be used and turnaround time when establishing payment. Looks for a "clean, simple design that makes an immediate visual statement—copy aside."

***NEW FEDERAL THEATRE**, 466 Grand St., New York NY 10002. Producer: Woodie King, Jr. "NFT has brought original, professionally-produced minority theatre to the audience for which it was initially designed—the multi-ethnic Lower East Side (Black, Hispanic, Jewish, Asian). Produces 5 shows per season, using union and non-union artists and technicians.
Needs: Freelance art needed through the year. Works on assignment only. Uses artists for advertising, brochure and poster design.
First Contact & Terms: Send resume. Samples are not filed. Reports back only if interested. Write to schedule an appointment to show a portfolio. Pays for design by the project. Considers project's budget when establishing payment. Buys all rights.

NEW JERSEY SHAKESPEARE FESTIVAL, Drew University, Madison NJ 07940. Artistic Director: Paul Barry. Contemporary and classical theatrical troupe. Assigns 3-6 jobs/year.
Needs: Works with 1 or 2 illustrators and 3 designers/year. Design work for costumes, sets, props and lighting is seasonal, May-December. Uses artists for advertising, costumes, designer-in-residence, direct mail brochures, exhibits, flyers, graphics, posters, programs, sets and theatrical lighting.
First Contact & Terms: Query with resume or arrange interview to show portfolio. SASE. Reports within 1 week. Interviews for designers are held in March and April. Provide resume to be kept on file for future assignments. Pays $1,000-1,200/show for set and costume design (large shows).

Tips: "Our season has expanded to 27 playing weeks." An artist's work should display an "understanding of historical period, good use of color, practicality and fit of costumes. Sets should show an ease to build, and to change from one show to another."

NEW MEXICO SYMPHONY ORCHESTRA, Box 769, Albuquerque NM 87103. (505)843-7657. Executive Administrator: William Weinrod. Regional orchestra based in Albuquerque but serving state of New Mexico. Performs 50-60 concerts/year and 150 school programs. Basic concert series currently consists of 18 subscription concerts. In addition there are pops concerts and "specials" which require graphic promotional materials.
Needs: Works with 3-4 freelance artists/year; needs heaviest in spring/fall. Prefers local artists with performing arts experience especially for layouts of ads and brochures. Uses artists for advertising, brochure and program design, illustration and layout; and posters.
First Contact & Terms: Send query letter with samples to be kept on file. Write for appointment to show portfolio. Prefers actual print samples. Samples returned only by request. Pays for design by the project, $100-2,500 average. Considers complexity of project and available budget when establishing payment.
Tips: "It is crucial that our designers understand our needs, our goals and most of all the budget crunches of the arts organization. Our designers give us good prices—lower than they give to their profits. Creativity in problem solving is also important."

NEW ORLEANS SYMPHONY ORCHESTRA, Suite 500, 212 Loyola Ave., New Orleans LA 70112. (504)524-0404. Contact: Marketing Director.
Needs: Works with 5 freelance artists/year. Uses artists for the design, illustration and layout of advertising, brochures and catalog plus window design, P-O-P displays, calligraphy, paste-up, mechanicals, posters and direct mail.
First Contact & Terms: Send query letter with resume and samples. Samples not filed are returned if requested. Reports back ASAP. Call to schedule an appointment to show a portfolio.

NEW PLAYWRIGHTS' THEATRE, 1742 Church St. NW, Washington DC 20036. (202)232-4527. Artistic Director: Peter Frisch; Assistant Artistic Director: Kate Bryer. New Playwrights' is an alternative theatre dedicated to the development of new American playwriting talent. It is an intimate theatre, seating only 125 people with over 1,000 season subscribers.
Needs: Works with 12 freelance artists/year. Works on assignment only. Needs heaviest September through June. Uses artists for brochure design, illustration and layout; poster design and illustration; set and costume design; lighting and scenery.
First Contact & Terms: Send query letter with slides, photographs, photocopies or tear sheets to be kept on file. Samples are not returned. Reports only if interested. Call or write for appointment to show portfolio. Pays by the project, $200-1,000 for design; $50-300 for illustration. Considers complexity of project, project's budget, skill and experience of artist, how work will be used and turnaround time when establishing payment.

NEW YORK CITY OPERA NATIONAL COMPANY, NY State Theater, Lincoln Center, New York NY 10023. (212)870-5635. Administrative Director: Nancy Kelly. Opera company founded in 1979 by Beverly Sills as a national touring company with the purpose of bringing opera to areas of the country without resident opera associations. Its primary function is to provide young singers an opportunity to gain performing experience; veteran singers use the tours to try new roles before singing them in New York.
Needs: Needs for freelance artists heaviest prior to tours in fall and winter. Uses artists for set and costume design. "Scenic and costume designers should be aware of the rigors of traveling productions and should think about portability and economics." Artists also used for graphics for marketing the current production.
First Contact & Terms: Previous experience is advisable; union memberships are required for set and costume design. Send query letter with resume to be kept on file. Reports only if interested. Pays for design by the project; "varies according to design; follows union rates." Considers complexity of project and available budget when establishing payment.
Tips: "The use of artists is tied specifically to whatever opera we may be performing in a given year. We generally tour in the January-April time period and hire artists one year ahead of each tour."

NEW YORK HARP ENSEMBLE, 140 W. End Ave., New York NY 10023. Director: Dr. Aristid von Wurtzler. Concert group which tours the U.S., Europe, Africa, South America, Australia and the Near and Far East.
Needs: Works with 1 designer/year, summer only. Local artists only. Works on assignment only. Uses artists for direct mail brochures, posters, programs and record cover layouts. Especially needs work for

brochures, posters and record covers.
First Contact & Terms: Submit samples (brochures, posters and record covers). Samples returned by SASE. Reports back on future assignment possibilities. Provide flyer to be kept on file for future assignments. Pays by the project for design and illustration. Considers available budget, and skill and experience of artist when establishing payment.

***OAKLAND ENSEMBLE THEATRE**, 1428 Alice St., Oakland CA 94612. (415)763-7774. Public Relations Director: Victoria Kirby. "Committed to producing insightful, engaging and substantive works of theatre particularly as they relate to pluralism in America's national life. Our frame of reference is Black."
Needs: Works with 2-3 freelance artists/year. Freelance art needs are seasonal. Needs heaviest in August-March. Works on assignment only. Uses artists for advertising and brochure design, illustration and layout; poster design and illustration; set design; costume design; lighting and scenery.
First Contact & Terms: Send query letter with brochure showing art style or resume and samples. Samples are filed. Samples not filed are returned by SASE only if requested. Reports back within 3 weeks. Write to schedule an appointment to show a portfolio. Pays for design by the hour, $25-35. Considers complexity of project, skill and experience of artist and available budget when establishing payment.

THE ODC/SAN FRANCISCO, 3153 17th St., San Francisco CA 94110. Dance company founded by Brenda Way in 1971 and based in San Francisco since 1976. Performs "a continuously evolving repertory of new dance works." Three choreographers draw from classically-based and modern dance technique, theater, music.
Needs: Works with approximately 16 freelance artists/year. Needs artist all year round, but most heavily in early spring and fall. Artist "must possess skills of resourcefulness and flexibility. We work with restricted budgets and specific artistic considerations." Uses artist for advertising, brochure, catalog, program and costume design; advertising and brochure layout, posters, scenery and photography. Style must be "clean and clear; a strong image that effectively communicates something distinctive about the nature of the dance company."
First Contact & Terms: Send query letter with brochure showing art style or resume and samples to be kept on file; do not call. "Since we work with limited budgets, I like to work closely with the artist in the concept and the carry-through of a project." Original work not necessary as samples. Will look at anything that fairly represents the quality of the artist's work. Samples returned by SASE if not kept on file. Reports within 2 weeks. Write for appointment to show portfolio. Pays for design by the project, $250-2,000. Considers complexity of project, available budget, and skill and experience of artist when establishing payment.

ODYSSEY THEATRE ENSEMBLE, 12111 Ohio Ave., West Los Angeles CA 90025. (213)826-1626. Production Manager: Lucy Pollak. Experimental theater troupe, specializing in live theatre in 3-theatre complex; equity waiver with 1,200 subscribers. Generally 20,000 audience members per year.
Needs: Uses artists for advertising and brochure design, illustration and layout; poster design and illustration, set and costume design, lighting, scenery, graphic and logo design for each play.
First Contact & Terms: Works with 20 artists. Send query letter with brochure showing art style or resume, tear sheets, photocopies, slides, photographs and "whatever is easy and inexpensive to send to indicate experience and style." SASE. Reports within 1 month. Call or write to schedule an appointment to show a portfolio, which should include roughs, final reproduction/product, Photostats and photographs. Pays $25-300 for design and illustration; negotiates payment. Considers complexity of project, budget, skill and experience of the artist, and previous work done on a volunteer basis for the theatre.
Tips: "We have expanded our facility to three 99-seat Equity-waiver performing spaces."

OLYMPIC BALLET THEATRE, Anderson Cultural Center, 700 Main St., Edmonds WA 98020. (206)774-7570. Director: John and Helen Wilkins. Ballet company with 20 dancers, approximately 100 members and a Board of Trustees of 20 which does a full-length "Nutcracker" Spring Showcase and tour, lecture-demo's and mini-performances.
Needs: Works with 2 freelance artists/year. Needs heaviest in fall, winter and spring. Uses freelance artists for advertising, brochure, catalog, poster and program design and illustration, set and costume design.
First Contact & Terms: Works on assignment only. Call or write for appointment to show portfolio. Pays by the project, $25-500 for design; $25-100 for illustration. Considers complexity of project and project's budget when establishing payment.

ONE ACT THEATRE COMPANY, 430 Mason St., San Francisco CA 94102. (415)421-5355. General Manager: Lauren Brown. Nonprofit theatre focusing on professional productions and one-act plays.

Needs: Works with 10 freelance artists/year. Local artists only. Uses artists for advertising and brochure illustration and layout; paste-up, mechanicals, posters, direct mail, program and season subscription brochure.
First Contact & Terms: Send query letter with resume, tear sheets and photocopies. Samples not filed are returned by SASE. Call to schedule an appointment to show a portfolio, which should include thumbnails and roughs. Pays for illustration by the project, $50-100. Considers available budget and turnaround time when establishing payment.
Tips: "Excellent starting exposure for Bay area artists making initial contacts for larger firms."

OPERA/COLUMBUS, 50 W. Broad St. Mezz., Columbus OH 43215. (614)461-8101. Audience Development Director: Richard Wickersham. Opera company with 11 full-time staff members, 43-member board of trustees and 3,200 series ticket subscribers.
Needs: Works primarily with advertising and graphic design agency. Prefers local experienced artists. Works on assignment only. Occasional needs include brochure illustration and layout, poster design, advertising design.
First Contact & Terms: Send query letter with brochure, resume and samples to be kept on file; write for appointment to show portfolio. Prefers slides, photos, renderings or tear sheets as samples; slides are not filed. Samples not filed are returned only if requested. Reports only if interested. Pays by the project. Considers complexity of project, available budget and turnaround time when establishing payment.

PARADISE AREA ARTS COUNCIL, (formerly Paradise Symphony Orchestra), 6686 Brook Way, Paradise CA 95969. (916)877-8360. President: Thomas E. Wilson. June art festival by various mediums. SASE. Reports within 1 month.
Needs: Prefers local artists. Needs heaviest in June and December. Works on assignment only. Uses artists for brochure design, poster design and costume design. Prefers "a smart, clean, exciting style."
First Contact & Terms: Send query letter with brochure showing art style. To show a portfolio, mail appropriate materials, which should include final reproduction/product and photographs.
Tips: "First-class promotional materials are necessary." Then is a "great need for excellent projection of the arts."

PENNSYLVANIA BALLET, 2525 Pennsylvania Ave., Philadelphia PA 19130. (215)636-4400. Marketing Director: Nancy E. Depke.
Needs: Works with about 12 freelance artists/year. Uses artists for advertising design and layout; brochure design, illustration and layout; paste-up, mechanicals, posters, direct mail and annual reports.
First Contact & Terms: Send resume, tear sheets, Photostats and photocopies. Samples not returned. Reports only if interested. Call to schedule an appointment to show a portfolio, which should include thumbnails, roughs, original/final art, final reproduction/product, color, tear sheets, Photostats and photographs. Pays for design by the hour. Considers complexity of project, available budget, and skill and experience of artist when establishing payment.

PENNSYLVANIA STAGE COMPANY, 837 Linden St., Allentown PA 18101. (215)434-6110. Producing Director: Gregory S. Hurst. "We are a LORT theatre, located 1½ hours from New York City devoted to a diverse repertory of new and old works from Shakespeare to the world premiere production of a new musical. Our house seats 274 people, and we currently have 6,000 subscribers."
Needs: Works with 10 freelance artists/year; "We need freelance designers for our season which runs from October-July." "Artists must be able to come to Allentown for design consultation and construction." Works on assignment only. Uses artists for set and costume design, lighting and scenery. "As a growing professional regional theatre, we have increased needs for graphic artists and photography for print materials (brochures, flyers), and particularly for our program magazine, *Callboard*, which is published eight times a year. "We would also be interested in theatre cartoons."
First Contact & Terms: Send query letter with resume. Prefers Photostats, slides, b&w photos, color washes, roughs as samples. Samples returned by SASE. Reports back whether to expect possible future assignments. Provide resume to be kept on file for possible future assignments. Pays by the project, $500-1,500 average, for design; $25-125 for print material. Considers complexity of project, available budget, and skill and experience of artist when establishing payment.
Tips: "We prefer that designers have extensive experience designing for professional theater."

RUDY PEREZ PERFORMANCE ENSEMBLE, Box 36614, Los Angeles CA 90036. (213)931-3604. Artistic Director: Rudy Perez. Performance art and experimental dance company, also known as the Rudy Perez Dance Theater, is a nonprofit organization dependent on funding from National Endowment for the Arts and the California Arts Council; corporate and private fundings; box office and bookings currently in the LA area.
Needs: "The work is mainly collaborations with visual artists and composers." Uses artists for publici-

ty before performances and updating press kits, brochures, etc.
First Contact & Terms: Send query letter with brochure and resume to be kept on file. Reports within 1 week. "Since we are a nonprofit organization we depend on in-kind services and/or negotiable fees."
Tips: Artists should have "an interest in dance and theatre."

***PHILADELPHIA DANCE CO. (Philadanco)**, 9 N. Preston St., Philadelphia PA 19104. (215)387-8200. Executive Director: Joan Myers Brown. Seventeen member dance company performing contemporary, neoclassic, jazz and modern works.
Needs: Works with 2-3 freelance artists/year. Freelance art needed throughout the year. Works on assignment only. Uses artists for advertising design and layout, brochure, poster and costume design and lighting and scenery.
First Contact & Terms: Send query letter with brochure showing art style. Samples are filed. Samples not filed are returned only if requested. Reports back within 25 days. Write to schedule an appointment to show a portfolio, which should include previous work samples. Pays for design and illustration by the hour, $100-1,000. Considers complexity of project and client's budget when establishing payment. Negotiates rights purchased.
Tips: "Philadanco is becoming more sophisticated in its printed matter and requires designs to reflect the maturity of the company. We look at past work with dancers/dance companies and at contemporary styles in photography and pen and ink."

***PHOENIX SYMPHONY ORCHESTRA**, 6328 N. 7th St., Phoenix AZ 85014. (602)264-4754. Marketing Coordinator: Holly Paulson.
Needs: Uses artists for advertising and brochure design, illustration and layout, product design, P-O-P displays, calligraphy, paste-up, mechanicals, posters, direct mail and programs.
First Contact & Terms: Send query letter with brochure showing art style or resume, tear sheets, Photostats, photocopies, slides and photographs. Samples not filed are returned only if requested. Reports only if interested. Write to schedule an appointment to show a portfolio, which should include thumbnails, roughs, original/final art, final reproduction/product, color, tear sheets, Photostats and photographs. Considers complexity of project, skill and experience of artist, how work will be used, turnaround time and rights purchased when establishing payment.

PIONEER PLAYHOUSE OF KENTUCKY, Danville KY 40422. (606)236-2747. Contact: Eben Henson. Regular summer stock theatre.
Needs: Works with 10 freelance artists/year; needs heaviest in summer. Uses artists for advertising, poster, set and costume design; lighting and scenery. Prefers artists willing to work in the nature of apprenticeship. Works on assignment only. Uses artists for the design, illustration and layout by advertising and brochures, the illustration and layout of catalogs, set design, costume design, lighting and scenery.
First Contact & Terms: Send query letter and material to be kept on file. Reports within 4 weeks. Call to schedule an appointment to show a portfolio. No payment of salary; apprenticeships provide room and board.
Tips: "For persons breaking into any form of the theatre, apprenticeship is necessary. First one must establish himself with a reputable theater in order to advance in the theatrical profession."

POSEY SCHOOL OF DANCE, INC., Box 254, Northport NY 11768. (516)757-2700. President: Elsa Posey. Private school/professional training in performing arts.
Needs: Works with 4 or more freelance artists/year; needs heaviest in spring and fall. Prefers regional artists willing to work within nonprofit performing arts budget. Works on assignment only. Uses artists for advertising and brochure design, illustration and layout; poster and program design and illustration, set and costume design, lighting and scenery. Also uses artists for a newsletter and for advertising copy. Interested in *appropriate* cartoons.
First Contact & Terms: Send query letter with resume, tear sheets, Photostats and photocopies. Samples returned by SASE. Reports within 4 weeks. To show a portfolio, mail tear sheets and Photostats. Pays for design, $10-200 average; for illustration, $10-50 average. Negotiates payment. Considers complexity of project, available budget, skill and experience of artist, how work will be used and rights purchased when establishing payment.
Tips: Artist must have "illustrative ability with understanding of dance, dancer's body and movement. Looking for honesty and a more personal approach."

PROJECT OPERA, INC., 160 Main St., Northampton MA 01060. (413)584-8811. Artistic Director: Richard R. Rescia. Stated productions of opera.
Needs: Needs heaviest in fall and spring. Uses artists for set and costume design, and scenery.
First Contact & Terms: "We use regional artists where possible." Send query letter with resume and

photocopies to be kept on file. Samples not filed are returned by SASE. Pays for design by the project. Considers complexity of project and project's budget when establishing payment.

RAPID CITY SYMPHONY ORCHESTRA, Box 8001, Rapid City SD 57709. (605)348-4676. Nonprofit organization.
Needs: Works with 3-4 freelance artists/year. Uses artists for advertising design, brochure design, calligraphy and direct mail.
First Contact & Terms: Send query letter with brochure showing art style. Samples not filed are returned only if requested. Reports only if interested. To show a portfolio, mail appropriate materials. Pays for design and illustration by the hour, $5-20. Considers complexity of project, skill and experience of artist, and how work will be used when establishing payment.

RENAISSANCE DANCE COMPANY OF DETROIT: Dances of Court and Country in Elizabethan England, (formerly Mme. Cadillac Dancers and Musicians), Apt. 903, 15 E. Kirby, Detroit MI 48202. (313)867-4030. Artistic Director: Harriet Berg.
Needs: Assigns 4 jobs/year. Uses artists for flyers, programs, announcements and ads.
First Contact & Terms: Send query letter. SASE. Negotiates pay.

***THE REPERTORY DANCE THEATRE (RDT)**, Box 8088, Salt Lake City UT 84108. General Manager: Nicole Guillemet. Ten-member modern dance company with national touring, home seasons in Salt Lake City and summer workshops.
Needs: Works with 2-3 freelance artists/year; needs heaviest in summer/fall. Uses artists for advertising and brochure design, illustration and layout; poster design and illustration.
First Contact & Terms: Prefers local artists. Send query letter with resume, brochure, tear sheets and samples to be kept on file. Prefers "any samples which best represent work;" samples should be dance or movement related. Samples returned by SASE if not kept on file. Reports within 2 weeks. Works on assignment only. Pays for design by the project, $50-500 average. Negotiates payment according to complexity of project and available budget.

***RITES AND REASON**, Brown University, Box 1148, Providence RI 02912. (401)863-4177. Managing Director: Alan Yaffe. Black performing arts organization.
Needs: Uses artists for all aspects of theater productions. Assigns 12 jobs/season.
First Contact & Terms: Query with resume. SASE. Negotiates pay.
Tips: "We are the professional theatre component of the Afro-American studies program at Brown University. Our original productions of drama, music and dance primarily concern the interpretation of black peoples' experiences in the New World. A multidisciplinary approach to research and performance is used by artists and scholars who work together in creation of new productions. An effort is made, through the performing arts, to bring members of the community to a forum where they are given the opportunity to confront scholars and artists, and to critique their work. The dialogues with the community direct subsequent scholarly research that often becomes the basis for other new productions."

ROCHESTER PHILHARMONIC ORCHESTRA, 108 East Ave., Rochester NY 14604. (716)454-2620. Director of Marketing: Nancy Calocerinos. Major orchestra performing 52 weeks/year, winter and summer seasons.
Needs: Works with 2 freelance artists/year. Needs heaviest between January and April. Local artists only, with at least three years' experience and a working knowledge of music. Works on assignment only. Uses artists for brochure, poster and program design.
First Contact & Terms: Send query letter with photocopies or tear sheets to be kept on file. Samples not filed are returned. Reports back only if interested. Pays for design by the project. Considers project's budget when establishing payment.

ROOSEVELT PARK AMPHITHEATRE, Middlesex County Department of Parks and Recreation, Box 661, New Brunswick NJ 08903. (201)548-2884. Producing Director: Ernest Albrecht. Musical theatre.
Needs: Works with 10 freelance artists/year; needs heaviest in spring through summer. Works on assignment only. Uses artists for set and costume design, lighting and scenery.
First Contact & Terms: Send query letter and resume. Prefers samples to be brought in person. Reports within 3 weeks. To show a portfolio, mail appropriate materials or write to schedule an appointment. Pays $1,500 average for design; salary.

SALT LAKE SYMPHONIC CHOIR, Box 45, Salt Lake City UT 84110. (801)466-8701. Contact: Manager. Assigns 5 jobs/year.
Needs: Works with 5 illustrators and 2 designers/year; fall only. Works on assignment. Uses artists for advertising, billboards, costumes, direct mail brochures, flyers, posters, programs, theatrical lighting

and record jackets.
First Contact & Terms: Mail resume, brochure and flyer to be kept on file. SASE. Negotiates pay by the project.

SAN FRANCISCO OPERA CENTER, War Memorial Opera House, San Francisco Opera, San Francisco CA 94102. (415)565-6435. Manager: Christine Bullin. Assistant to the Manager: Susan Lamb. SFOC is the umbrella organization for the affiliates of the San Francisco Opera.
Needs: Works with 3-4 freelance artists/year; needs heaviest in summer preparing for fall and spring seasons. Uses artists for advertising, brochure and program design, illustration and layout; set and costume design, posters, lighting, scenery, and PR and educational packets.
First Contact & Terms: Send query letter with brochure, resume and business card, Photostats, slides and photographs to be kept on file. Write for appointment to show portfolio. Reports only if interested. Pays for design and illustration by the project, $50-300 average. Considers available budget, how work will be used and rights purchased when establishing payment.

SAN JOSE SYMPHONY, Suite 200, 476 Park Ave., San Jose CA 95110. (408)287-7383. Director of Marketing/Public Relations: Gizella O'Neil.
Needs: Assigns 10-15 jobs/year. Local artists only. Uses artists for advertising, direct mail/developmental brochures, ticket sales material, flyers, posters, programs and educational materials.
First Contact & Terms: Send query letter with resume and samples. SASE. Reports within 1 month. Pays for design or illustration by the hour, $25 minimum; by the project, $275-500 average. Considers complexity of project, available budget and how work will be used when establishing payment.

SANTA BARBARA SYMPHONY, 214 E. Victoria St., Stanta Barbara CA 93101. (805)965-6596. Contact: Managing Director. Professional symphony orchestra, 78 members. Presents 6 matinee and 7 evening performances, October-May. Travels to outlying areas for repeats of subscription concerts and periodic run-out concerts; regular subscription concerts at the Arlington Theatre; internationally-renowned guest artists.
Needs: Works with 1-2 freelance artists/year; needs heaviest in early spring. Local artists only. Uses artists for advertising and brochure design, layout and illustration.
First Contact & Terms: Send query letter with brochure, resume and samples to be kept on file. Reports only if interested. Call for appointment to show portfolio, which should include final reproduction/product. Artists submit fee schedule. Considers complexity of project, available budget, how work will be used and personality—"willingness to listen to our needs and comply with them"—when establishing payment.

***THE SAVANNAH BALLET, INC.**, 2212 Lincoln St., Savannah GA 31401. (912)233-8492. Cultural and educational performing arts organization.
Needs: Works with 3 freelance artists/year; needs heaviest in September-April. Uses artists for advertising and brochure design, illustration and layout; poster and program design and illustration; set and costume design; lighting and scenery.
First Contact & Terms: Send query letter with resume and samples (tear sheets) to be kept on file for possible future assignments. Works on assignment only. Pays by the project for design and illustration.

***SEATTLE CHILDREN'S THEATRE**, 4649 Sunnyville Ave. N., Seattle WA 98103. (206)633-4591. Artistic Director: Linda Hartzell. "Provides professional theatre for young audiences and offers classes year-round for grades K-12. The mainstage serves approximately 80,000 patrons each year and the education programs enroll over 500 students each calendar year."
Needs: Works with 20 freelance artists/year. Freelance art needed throughout the year. Works on assignment only. Uses artists for advertising and brochure design, illustration and layout; poster design and illustration; set design; costume design; lighting and scenery.
First Contact & Terms: Send query letter with brochure showing art style or resume, tear sheets, Photostats, photocopies or slides. Samples are filed. Samples not filed are returned by SASE. Reports back only if interested. Write to schedule an appointment to show a portfolio, which should include final reproduction/product, color, b&w, tear sheets, Photostats, photographs or slides. Pays for design and illustration by the project, $50-400. Considers complexity of project, client's budget, turnaround time, skill and experience of artist and how work will be used when establishing payment. Negotiates rights purchased.
Tips: "SCT is a nonprofit arts organization and does not have a large budget for contracted work. We do, however, use artists regularly once they begin working for SCT so the workload can become overwhelming but consistent. March is the best time to approach SCT as this is when we are looking for and solidifying work. Write, don't call."

SEATTLE OPERA ASSOCIATION, 305 Harrison, Seattle WA 98109. (206)443-4700. Press and Public Relations Director: Jim Bailey. Opera company.
Needs: Works with 5-7 freelance artists/year; needs heaviest in winter and spring. Uses artists for flyer/brochure design and layout, and season/festival posters.
First Contact & Terms: Send query letter with brochure, business card, Photostats and photographs to be kept on file. Call for appointment to show portfolio. Samples returned by SASE if not kept on file. Pays $350/poster. Considers complexity of project, available budget and how work will be used when establishing payment.

***SHAW FESTIVAL THEATRE**, Box 774, Niagara-on-the Lake Ontario L0S 1J0 Canada. (416)468-2153. Director of Communications: Katherine Holmes. The Shaw Festival Theatre is the only professional theatre in North America devoted to the works of George Bernard Shaw and his contemporaries.
Needs: Works with 3 freelance artists/year. Freelance art needs are seasonal. Needs heaviest in October and February. Uses artists for advertising, brochure and poster design.
First Contact & Terms: Send query letter with brochure. Samples are filed. Samples not filed are returned only if requested. Reports only if interested. Write to show a portfolio, which should include original/final art, final reproduction/product, color and b&w. Payment is negotiated.
Tips: "Please contact the Shaw Festival in July-August (by mail) as our deadlines are early November."

SHAWNEE SUMMER THEATRE OF GREENE COUNTY, INC., Box 22, Bloomfield IN 47424. Producer: Tim Toothman. Resident production company offering 7 plays a year: serious, a musical, a mystery, comedies and 1 children's play.
Needs: Works with 25 freelance artists/year; only in late spring and summer. Uses artists for brochure illustration and layout, set and costume design, lighting and scenery.
First Contact & Terms: "Ours is a production company and all work is done by that company while in residence. All applicants must be willing to fill in as actors in large cast plays or musicals." Send query letter with resume and color photos or slides of sample works; "We also insist on some kind of photograph of the applicant, even if only a Polaroid." Samples returned by SASE. Pays by the week. Write to schedule an appointment to show a portfolio, which should include thumbnails, original/final art, final reproduction/product, color, photographs and b&w.
Tips: "The theatre manages an art gallery and artist's work could be hung for one of the weeks during productions. Also, photos of work, articles concerning work and exhibits, and a good strong resume are helpful."

SINGING BOYS OF PENNSYLVANIA, Box 110, State College, East Stroudsburg PA 18301, or Box 206, Wind Gap PA 18091. (717)421-6137 (business office) or (215)759-6002. Director: K. Bernard Schade. "Touring boychoir." Needs heaviest in fall and winter.
Needs: Local artists only. Works on assignment only. Uses artists for direct mail brochures, flyers, posters and record jackets; the design, illustration and layout of advertising and brochures; poster, set and costume design, lighting and scenery.
First Contact & Terms: Query. Pays for design by the project, $100-250.

***SOHO REP**, 80 Varick St., New York NY 10013. Artistic Director: Jerry Engelbach. "We are an equity showcase house, Tier IV, seating 100. We do original plays and revivals of theatrical, non-naturalists plays.
Needs: Freelance art needs are seasonal. Uses artists for poster design, set design, costume design, lighting and scenery.
First Contact & Terms: Send query letter with resume. Samples not filed are returned by SASE. Reports back only if interested. Write to schedule an appointment to show a portfolio. Pays for design by the project, $300 minimum.

***SOUTH CAROLINA BALLET THEATRE**,715 Harden St., Columbia SC 29205. (803-771-7228. Associate General Manager: Nancy Pope Stevens. Professional dance company specializing in jazz, modern, contemporary and classic ballet. "We have six full-time and four part-time dancers."
Needs: Works with 8-10 freelance artists/year. Freelance art needed throughout the year. Uses artists for advertising and brochure design illustration and layout, poster design and illustration, costume design, lighting and scenery. Prefers contemporary style.
First Contact & Terms: Send query letter with brochure. Samples not filed are returned by SASE. Reports back only if interested. Call to schedule an appointment to show a portfolio. Pays for design and illustration by the project, $50-500. Considers complexity of project, skill and experience of artist, client's budget, how work will be used and rights purchased when establishing payment. Negotiates rights purchased.
Tips: "Call. We'll give you more details. . .or send name and example of work. We'll hold work on file until needs arise.

***SOUTH PARK CONSERVATORY THEATRE**, Box 254, Bethel Park PA 15102. (412)831-8552. Contact: Executive Director. Theater offering 1 musical production or revue, 3 straight plays and 2 children's productions; seats 100 and is under Parks and Recreation Dept.
Needs: Works with 10 freelance artists/year; needs heaviest in May through August. Uses artists for advertising and brochure design, illustration and layout; poster, program, set and costume design; lighting and scenery.
First Contact & Terms: Send query letter with resume. Samples not returned. Reports in 3 weeks. Works on assignment only. Reports back whether to expect possible future assignments. Provide resume to be kept on file for possible future assignments. Pays for design and illustration by the project, $10-50 average. Considers complexity of project and available budget when establishing payment.

SOUTHWEST JAZZ BALLET COMPANY, Box 38233, Houston TX 77238. (713)694-6114. Contact: President. Professional touring ballet company; producers of "America in Concert."
Needs: Works with 5 freelance artists/year. Works on assignment only. Uses artists for advertising illustration, brochure illustration and layout; poster illustration, costume design and scenery.
First Contact & Terms: Send query letter with resume and "end product" to be kept on file. Reports within 1 month. Call or write to schedule an appointment to show a portfolio, which should include final reproduction/product. Considers complexity of project when establishing payment.
Tips: Looking for 40's Americana style.

SPRINGFIELD BALLET COMPANY, Box 561, Springfield IL 62705. (217)789-4229. Company Manager: Diana Lehmann. "Forty-member dance organization that presents an autumn divertissement program, featuring jazz, modern and classical dance; an annual 'Nutcracker'; a spring full-length fairytale ballet."
Needs: Works with 4-6 freelance artists/year; needs heaviest in October, February and August. Illinois artists given preference; performing arts experience necessary. Uses artists for advertising, brochure, program, set and costume design; brochure and program illustration, program layout, posters, lighting and scenery.
First Contact & Terms: Send query letter with brochure, resume and photos to be kept on file. Prefers photographs or slides plus letters of endorsement; recent work resume as samples. Samples returned only by request. Reports only if interested or if requested. Write for appointment to show portfolio which should include original/final art. Pays for design by the project. Considers complexity of project, available budget, skill and experience of artist and rights purchased when establishing payment.

SPRINGFIELD SYMPHONY ORCHESTRA, Box 5191, Springfield IL 62705. (217)522-2838. General Manager: Donald L. Andrews. Metropolitan symphony orchestra performing 20 concerts.
Needs: Works with 1 freelance artist/year. Uses artist for brochure and program design. Contact in April.
First Contact & Terms: Send "original brochure work and program cover for symphony concerts" and cost estimate to be kept on file. Reports only if interested. Pays by the project. Considers available budget when establishing payment.

***EDITH STEPHEN DANCE CONNECTION**, Studio 630A, 55 Bethume St., New York NY 10014. (212)989-2250. Administrator: E. Kapel. A dance/theatre company performing unique multi-media productions connecting dance, theatre, music, poetry, art, visuals and environmental sculpture.
Needs: Works with a varying number of freelance artists/year. Prefers avant-garde style art.
First Contact & Terms: Works on assignment only. Send query letter with resume to be kept on file.

MARK TAPER FORUM, 135 N. Grand Ave., Los Angeles CA 90012. (213)972-7259. Art Director: Kathleen Robin Lowry. In-house agency for the Mark Taper Forum of the Los Angeles Music Center. Provides advertising and posters for live theatre.
Needs: Works with 10 freelance artists/year. Prefers local artists only. Uses artists for the design and illustration of advertising, the illustration of brochures, paste-up and mechanicals. Prefers painterly styles, graphic b&w styles.
First Contact & Terms: Send brochure showing art style or tear sheets, Photostats and slides. Samples not filed are returned by SASE. Reports only if interested. Call or write to schedule an appointment to show a portfolio, which should include original/final art, final reproduction/product, color, b&w and tear sheets. Pays for illustration by the project, $300-1,000. Considers client's budget.

***THEATRE-BY-THE-SEA**, Moonstone Beach, Matunuck RI 02879. (401)789-0692. Producer: Tommy Brent. Summer theater. Musicals only. Proscenium stage with fly system. Assigns 9 jobs/year. Query with resume. SASE. Reports in 2 weeks.
Needs: "We have openings for scenic, lighting and costume designers and assistants in each department. We pay weekly salaries. Designers must execute their own work with a staff under them."

Close-up

Kathleen Robin-Lowry

Art Director
Mark Taper Forum
Los Angeles, California

The Mark Taper Forum is involved in so many projects that it keeps an inhouse design agency busy year-round. The 20-year-old nonprofit theatre is dedicated to producing provocative works by contemporary playwrights, and most of its productions are world premieres. The theatre presents six or seven plays per year on its main stage and another four per year on its auxiliary stage.

The Mark Taper Forum design agency is headed by art director Kathleen Robin-Lowry. She works with two staff designers and buys illustrations from freelance artists to produce posters, programs, brochures and newspaper advertisements. She also occasionally uses freelance artists for design and mechanical work on promotional material.

Robin-Lowry develops ideas for poster designs by talking to the artistic director, and there is usually input from the playwright, the set designer and the costume designer. After she has worked out a design and had it approved by the artistic director, she picks an illustrator who has the style she wants.

The illustrator is given a comp and reference material to work from. Usually the illustrator has about 10 days to do tissues and final art. The deadlines are tight even though there are a set number of plays scheduled in advance of the season. Schedules change because a play might not be ready, or a new "hot property" might be added. Except for reading the play and doing research, work on the promotional material doesn't usually start until the play goes into rehearsal.

"What's so hard about designing for the Taper is that the plays are usually premieres, and we're designing ahead of time for a play that sometimes they're rewriting up until opening night," Robin-Lowry explains. "If the focus of the play changes, the artist may have to change the illustration." That's why she appreciates artists who are flexible.

It is not important to Robin-Lowry whether an artist has experience in working for performing arts groups or not, but she requires experience in preparing printed art and experience in meeting deadlines.

Robin-Lowry looks at the portfolios of two or three illustrators a week. In a portfolio, she likes to see about 10 pieces of the artist's best work. She prefers printed pieces because they show that the artist is familiar with the printing process.

Most artists find being part of a larger collaboration one rewarding aspect of working for a performing arts group. Freelance artists who work for the Taper can see performances for free. And Robin-Lowry tries to get invitations for them to the opening-night party.

If you are a beginning freelance artist with hopes of doing illustrations for the theatre, Robin-Lowry offers this advice: "Don't get discouraged. Don't take criticism of your work personally. Get as much exposure as possible and work on your craft."

—Mary Tonnies

Artist: Joyce Kitchell

Robin-Lowry chose San Diego artist Joyce Kitchell to do this illustration for a poster after seeing her watercolor work in the LA Workbook. To create the image, Kitchell referred to black-and-white photos of the actors in street clothes, photos of the costumes and props, and swatches of fabric from the set. Once Kitchell completed the tissues, she and Robin-Lowry met at a restaurant halfway between Los Angeles and San Diego to discuss the final illustration. The theatre's staff designer, Jane Beard, worked closely with Robin-Lowry to develop the concept and choose the colors.

THEATRE OF YOUTH (TOY) CO. INC., 284 Franklin St., Buffalo NY 14202. (716)856-4410. Artistic Director: Meg Pantera. "Buffalo's only professional resident theatre company, performing a full season of children and adult plays at their residence; while also touring schools with productions and workshops." Assigns 5 full-time and 4-10 professional service jobs per year. Write.
Needs: Professional actors, set and costume designers, and graphic artists. Uses artists for brochure designs, flyers, marquees, posters. Pays $250-500 costume and set designs and per show publicity design.
Tips: "Small companies such as TOY are seeking well-rounded practitioners, as opposed to rigid specialists, with an emphasis on ensemble. Submit inquiries early in the year, January through March, so we can arrange personal interviews.

***THEATRE PLUS At The Lower St. Lawrence Centre For The Arts**,49 Front St., Toronto Ontario M5E 1B3 Canada. (716)869-1255. Director of Communications: Brenda Rooney.
Needs: Works with 5-10 freelance artists/year. Freelance art needs are seasonal; heavy in summer. Uses artist for advertising and brochure design, illustration and layout, poster design and illustration, set design, costume design, lighting and scenery.
First Contact & Terms: Send query letter with resume, tearsheets and photocopies. Samples are filed. Samples not filed are returned only if requested by artist. Considers skill and experience of artist when establishing payment.

UNIVERSITY OF ROCHESTER SUMMER THEATER, River Station, Box 30185, Rochester NY 14627. (716)275-4088 (Monday-Thursday). Managing Director: David Runzo. Semi-professional company offering 3 productions of classical and contemporary theatre each summer and a 4-hour college credit program.
Needs: Works with 6 freelance artists/year; needs heaviest in June, July, August. Artists must be able to teach area of concentration. Works on assignment only. Uses artists for set and costume design, lighting, scenery, as technical directors and stage manager. Also for brochures, programs and ads.
First Contact & Terms: Send query letter with resume, slides and b&w photos to be kept on file. Samples returned by SASE. Reports within 3 weeks. Call or write for appointment. Pays salary of $1,800-2,200 average for 11 weeks for design plus transportation and half room.

VICTORY GARDENS THEATER, 2257 N. Lincoln Ave., Chicago IL 60614. (312)549-5788. Managing Director: Marcelle McVay. "Subscriber-based not-for-profit professional theater, dedicated to the development of new works, and using Chicago talent."
Needs: Works with 10-20 freelance artists/year. Works with developing or experienced, local artists on assignment only. Uses artists for advertising, brochure, catalog and poster design and illustration; set, lighting and costume design.
First Contact & Terms: Send query letter with resume and tear sheets to be kept on file. Samples not filed are returned by SASE. Reports back only if interested. Pays for poster design by the project, $100-300 average; pays set, lighting and costume design according to U.S.A.A. Considers complexity of project, project's budget, skill and experience of the artist, and turnaround time when establishing payment.

WALNUT STREET THEATRE COMPANY, 9th and Walnut Sts., Philadelphia PA 19107. (215)574-3555. Promotions Manager: Leslie B. Goldstein. Theatre providing 5 major professional productions as part of a Subscription Series (19,000 + subscribers), a theatre school, a theatre camp for kids, co-productions, a Studio Theatre Season of five plays and a rental house.
Needs: Works with 2 freelance artists/year. Uses artists for brochure design, illustration and layout, posters, direct mail and annual reports.
First Contact & Terms: Send resume and samples. Samples not filed are returned by SASE. Reports within 6 weeks. Write to schedule an appointment to show a portfolio, which should include thumbnails, final reproduction/product, color and tear sheets. Considers complexity of project, available budget, skill and experience of artist, and how work will be used when establishing payment.
Tips: "We try to vary our style each season—something striking yet easily reproducible in many forms: brochures, posters, handbills and advertising."

***THE WILMA THEATER**, 2030 Sansom St., Philadelphia PA 19103. (215)963-0249. Marketing Director: Alexandra Kendrick. Professional regional theater presenting international, multi-media theater pieces, original adaptations and world premieres. 106 seats, 4 plays/year, 2,900 subscribers.
Needs: Works with 2 freelance artists/year. Freelance art needs are seasonal; heavy September-December. Works on assignment only. Uses artists for advertising design.
First Contact & Terms: Send query letter with brochure showing art style or tear sheets, Photostats and photocopies. Samples are filed. Reports back within weeks. Write to schedule an appointment to show a portfolio, which should include roughs, original/final art, final reproduction/product and b&w.

Pays for design by the project, $75-500; illustration by the project, $25-75. Consider complexity of project, client's budget, turnaround time and skill and experience of artist when establishing payment. Buys all rights.
Tips: "Our artistic directors maintain strict control over all public aspects of theater—understanding our style and the image we wish to project and working very closely with artistic directors is very important."

WISDOM BRIDGE THEATRE, 1559 W. Howard St., Chicago IL 60626. (312)743-0486. Contact: Executive Director. "We are a 196 theatre on Chicago's north side. We have a subscriber base of 9,500 and present an eclectic season of work. Our work tends to be socially and politically conscientious." Assigns 28-62 jobs/year.
Needs: Works with 3 illustrators and 15 designers/year. Works on assignment only. Uses artists for advertising, costumes, direct mail brochures, exhibits, flyers, graphics, posters, programs, sets, composition, sound design, and audiovisuals, technical art and lighting. Pays $500-1,500/job design of sets, lights and costumes. Pays $300-600/job, brochure design.
First Contact & Terms: Send query letter with resume and tear sheets, Photostats, photocopies, slides, photographs and technical drawings. Samples returned by SASE. Reports back on future assignment possibilities. Call or write to schedule an appointment to show a portfolio, which should include thumbnails, original/final art, final reproduction/product, color, tear sheets and photographs.
Tips: Prefers "a contemporary design embodying the latest in graphic trends."

ANNA WYMAN DANCE THEATRE, Box 86806, North Vancouver, British Columbia V7L 4L3 Canada. (604)984-3281. 18-member modern dance company.
Needs: Works with several freelance artists/year. Uses artists for advertising, brochure and program design, illustration and layout; set and costume design; poster design and illustration; lighting and scenery.
First Contact & Terms: All commercial artists are subject to portfolio review and recommendation/approval by Artistic Director Anna Wyman. Send query letter with brochure, resume, business card, tear sheets, Photostats, photocopies, slides and photographs to be kept on file. Samples not kept on file are returned only if requested. Reports within weeks. Portfolio should include thumbnails, roughs, original/final art, final reproduction/product, tear sheets, Photostats, photographs and b&w. Call or write for appointment to show portfolio. Pays by the project. Considers complexity of project and available budget when establishing payment.

ZIVILI/TO LIFE! Celebrating Yugoslavia in Dance and Song, 12 Clover Ct., Granville OH 43023. (614)855-7805. Executive Director: Melissa Pintar Obenauf. Professional dance company performing exclusively the dances and songs of Yugoslavia. Consists of 40 dancers, singers and musicians.
Needs: Works with 10 freelance artists/year; needs heaviest in fall and spring. Uses artists for advertising, brochure, program design, illustration and layout; posters and lighting.
First Contact & Terms: Send query letter with resume, business card and samples to be kept on file. Accepts "any type" of samples. Reports within 2 weeks. Negotiates pay. Considers complexity of project, available budget, skill and experience of artist and how work will be used when establishing payment.

"The collaboration between the visual artist and performing artist is becoming more central to the development of the work, its marketability and its fundability."

—D.L. King, ODC/San Francisco
San Francisco, California

Record Companies

Album cover design and illustration are the big drawing cards for freelance artists in this section, but don't overlook promotional materials and collaterals for assignments. The recording industry offers an opportunity for creativity, since most companies have no set theme for the artwork they seek but want the illustrator/designer to capture in an attention-getting manner the mood evoked by the music.

Artwork for album covers must be distinctive, provocative and appropriate to the performer and his music. Rock bands now have distinct visual styles, sharpened by their participation in videos. Gospel and country & western artists favor a more conservative image. Artwork for classical albums tends to be either representational or abstract, capturing the images of noted composers of the past or of historical genres.

Technological advances have increased the artistic needs of record companies. The most significant development in record album graphics is packaging for compact discs. Until this past year, the discs were marketed in 5"-square clear plastic boxes. Graphics were provided in a booklet, which was merely a reduction of the 12"-square album graphics. Now CD's are sold in a throw-away package measuring 12" long and 6" wide. As long as albums are sold in both formats, the artwork must be appropriate for both long-play record albums and CD boxes, resulting in a more vertical emphasis.

Creative directors at record companies are looking for a distinctive style that has a strong visual impact. If you wish to explore this market, study the current relationship of art and music on covers and promotional pieces by visiting record stores. Your sample package should include examples that reflect a strong graphic image that literally beckons a viewer. Personal appointments are a good idea, since creative directors prefer to develop a rapport with artists they hire. You don't have to live in one of the recording capitals to land the job, since most work is on assignment only. When negotiating a contract, remember to ask for a credit line on the album jacket and then, later, a number of samples for your portfolio. Skills such as layout and paste-up are useful to fill many production jobs at record companies.

The names and addresses of hundreds of record companies and affiliated services, such as design, artwork and promotions, are listed in the *Songwriter's Market 1988*, *Billboard International Buyer's Guide* and the *Music Industry Directory*.

***A&M RECORDS, INC.**, 1416 N. LaBrea Ave., Hollywood CA 90028. (213)469-2411. Vice President of Creative Services: Jeff Gold. Produces rock and roll, classical, disco, soul, pop, rhythm and blues, group and solo artists. Recent releases: "The Police—The Singles" by the Police and "Control" by Janet Jackson.

Needs: Works with visual artists. Works on assignment only. Uses artists for album cover and advertising design and illustration and posters.

First Contact & Terms: Send query letter with brochure or resume and tear sheets and slides. Samples are filed. Samples not filed are returned by SASE. Reports back only if interested. Call to schedule an appointment to show a portfolio, which should include final reproduction/product, color, b&w, tear sheets and photographs. Pays by the project. Considers complexity of project, available budget and how work will be used when establishing payment. Buys all rights.

***AIRWAVE INTERNATIONAL RECORDS & PUBLISHING**, 5th Floor, 6381 Hollywood Blvd., Hollywood CA 90028. Chairman: Terrence M. Brown. Produces rock and roll, disco/dance, soul, pop, and rhythm and blues; group and solo artists. Recent releases: "The Calling" by Ken Heaven and "I Don't Want Your Love" by Eleven Bells.

Needs: Produces 24 records/year; works with 12-24 recording artists/year. Works with 6-8 visual artists/year. Uses artists for album cover and advertising design and illustration, advertising layout and posters.
First Contact & Terms: "I would be willing to look at any work submitted for consideration." Send query letter with brochure, resume, Photostats, photographs, photocopies or tear sheets to be kept on file. Samples not filed are returned by SASE only if requested. Reports within 3 weeks. Call or write for appointment to show portfolio. Original artwork sometimes returned to artist. Pays by the project, $100-3,000 average. Considers complexity of project, available budget, turnaround time and rights purchased when establishing payment. "I negotiate the entire contract before deposit is made."

ALLEGIANCE RECORDS LTD. AND DISTRIBUTED LABELS, 1419 North LaBrea, Hollywood CA 90028. (213)851-8852. Director Creative Services: Dee Westlund.
First Contact & Terms: Send query letter with brochure showing art style or resume, tear sheets, Photostats and photographs. Samples not filed are returned by SASE, only if requested. Reports only if interested. Call to schedule an appointment to show a portfolio, which should include original/final art, final reproduction/product, color, tear sheets, Photostats, photographs and b&w. Pays for design by the project, $50-2,000. Pays for illustration by the project, $50-1,000.
Tips: "Need packaging ideas for compact discs. When showing a portfolio, try to be open and friendly. All art directors know you're scared and that your work is an extension of you; most of us don't bite unless you are obnoxious or have an attitude."

***AMERICAN MELODY RECORDS**,773 Hoop Pole Rd., Guilford CT 06437. (203)457-0881. President: Phil Rosenthal. Estab. 1985. Produces children's music. Recent releases: "Little Hands," by Jonathan Edwards; "Grandma's Patchwork Quilt," by John McCutcheon, Cathy Fink and others; and "Turkey in the Straw," by Phil Rosenthal.
Needs: Produces 3 soloists and 3 groups/year. Works with 2-3 visual artists/year. Works on assignment only. Uses freelance visual artists for album cover, brochure, catalog and advertising design and illustration.
First Contact & Terms: Send query letter with brochure showing art style or resume and samples. Samples are filed. Samples not filed are returned only if requested by artist. Reports back only if interested. Call to schedule an appointment to show a portfolio, which should include final reproduction/product. Pays by the project, $75. Considers complexity of project and rights purchased when establishing payment. Negotiates rights purchased.

***AMERICAN MUSIC CO./CUCA RECORD & CASSETTE MFG. CO.**, Box 8604, Madison WI 53708. Vice President, Marketing: Daniel W. Miller. Produces polka, rock and roll, soul, country/western and folk. Recent releases: "Mule Skinner Blues," by The Fenderment; and "Listen to Me," by Legend.
Needs: Produces 1-5 records/year. Uses artists for album cover design and illustrations; uses primarily caricatures and line drawings.
First Contact & Terms: Send query letter with business card and samples; may be kept on file. Prefers color slides as samples. Samples not filed are returned by SASE. Reports to the artist only if interested. Pays by the project, $25-100 average. Considers available budget when establishing payment. Purchases all rights.
Tips: Uses mostly "artists who are beginners."

AMERICAN MUSIC NETWORK, INC./SCARAMOUCHE RECORDS, Drawer 1967, Warner Robins GA 31099. (912)953-2800. President: Robert R. Kovach. Produces rock and roll, rhythm and blues, country/western, pop and gospel.
Needs: Produces 6 records/year; 50% of the album covers assigned to freelance designers. Works with 3 recording artists/year. Works with 2 visual artists/year. Assigns 5 freelance jobs/year. Works on assignment only. Uses artists for album cover design and illustration; brochure design, illustration and layout; advertising design, illustration and layout; and posters.
First Contact & Terms: Send query letter. Samples returned by SASE. Reports within 1 month. Original art returned. Pays by the project, $25-800 average. Considers complexity of project, available budget, skill and experience of artist and rights purchased when establishing payment. Negotiates rights purchased.

***AMETHYST GROUP**, 96 McGregor Downs, W. Cola SC 29169. (803)791-4137. Chairman: Jojo Mitchell. Produces rock and roll, disco, soul, rhythm and blues and solo artists. Recent releases: "Bad Damn Car" by Norwood and "Take it to the Floor" by Elijah Rock."
Needs: Produces 3 soloists and 5 groups/year. Uses artists for album cover and brochure design and direct mail packages.
First Contact & Terms: Send query letter with resume and samples. Samples are returned by SASE.

Close-up

Chuck Beeson

Art Director
A&M Records
Hollywood, California

If you wouldn't go to a rock concert dressed in a three-piece suit, would you solicit freelance graphic work at a record label with nothing but annual reports and stockholders magazines in your portfolio?

If your answer to this is a definite "no," then you would score some points in the office of Chuck Beeson, Senior Art Director and Director of Graphics at A&M Records in California.

"If your previous work is food-related or say, a corporate annual report, it shouldn't be brought to me," says Beeson, a 29-year veteran in the graphic arts business who's celebrating his twentieth year at A&M Records. "I'm not interested in anything unless it is entertainment-business-oriented. If you're interested in doing album covers but haven't done one yet, send me a fake, so I can see how you would approach such a job."

Perhaps the reason why the art director stresses this point so much is because art for the music business is vastly different from that of most other fields. A safe, standard layout would be demanded in an ad for vegetable oil, but an unusual, experimental or highly emotional design might be perfect for, say, the next techno-pop album cover.

"What might be junk art to someone else might be eclectic to us," he says. "A painting or a drawing might contain a nebulous feeling, but it's emotional. In the music business, we need something that represents the emotional side of life. Music is emotional, and therefore an album cover is emotional.

"So you see, experimental work is very important in our business," Beeson continues. "It might even be anti-art, but we try to do something totally unique. That's why even unpublished work is nice to see in someone's portfolio."

But be it unpublished, published, experimental or conventional, the portfolio itself is the most important part of an artist's presentation to an employer, according to Beeson. Next is education. Often, if an artist shows talent, but his skills are not quite adequate, Beeson will put a note in the returned portfolio suggesting that a few classes or a degree in graphic art might shape the person's talents into more marketable tools.

The Californian's own career is a paradigm of this marriage between work and education. After majoring in Advertising/Design at California State at Long Beach, Beeson served a hitch in the army and then landed a job at an ad agency. To further hone his skills when he got that job, he went to design school at night for two years. In his ninth year of working with ad agencies, he made the move to A&M, where he oversees art projects and hires freelance designers, illustrators, production artists and photographers.

"We are continually inundated by people wanting personal meetings to get jobs," Beeson says. "Unfortunately, that's impossible to do. There are not enough hours in the day to see that number of people. I try to schedule one or two portfolios three times a week. I ask the artists who telephone me to leave their samples at 11 a.m. and pick them up at 4 p.m. Between those hours, I can review the portfolio at my discretion."

Once hired by A&M, Beeson's freelancers work with materials such as watercolor, airbrush, collage, textures, chalk and spray cans to produce anything from marketing materials and press kits to posters and compact disc art to, of course, album covers.

Since the latter are the most displayed products of the art department, a lot of thought goes into making them appropriate companions to the music and musicians contained inside. "An album cover has to have emotional feeling," says the art director, "but because one man's ugly is another man's wonderful, you have to be constantly thinking about your audience. You have to ask yourself, 'Who am I trying to reach? What is that age group and taste level? Is it somewhat conservative? Hipper?'

"Most importantly, a good album cover has honesty," says Beeson. "The person or group you are doing has to be real. If the album art is not honest, when the musician goes on tour people will say, 'Hey, that's not the same person I saw on the cover.' "

—Betsy Schoellkopf

Designing and illustrating for record albums allow an artist a wider range of artistic expression than many other areas of graphic arts. For an album by Janet Jackson, designer Melanie Nissen uses color, typeface and a repeating geometric form to coordinate the album cover and the record sleeve.

Reports back within 3 weeks. Write to show a portfolio, which should include b&w and photographs. Pays by the project, $25 minimum. Considers available budget and rights purchased when establishing payment. Negotiates rights purchased.
Tips: "Be realistic and practical. Express talent not hype, be persistent."

***APON RECORD COMPANY, INC.**, Steinway Station, Box 3082, Long Island City NY 11103. (212)721-8599. President: Andre M. Poncic. Produces classical, folk and pop.
Needs: Produces 20 records/year. Works with 10 visual artists/year. Uses artists for album cover design and illustration, catalog illustration and layout, and posters.
First Contact & Terms: Works on assignment only. Send brochure and samples to be kept on file. Write for art guidelines. Samples not filed are returned by SASE. Reports to the artist within 60 days only if interested. Considers available budget when establishing payment. Purchases all rights.

***ARS NOVA MANAGEMENT**,Box 421268, San Francisco CA 94142-1268. (415)864-2800. Associate: Steven Scott. Estab. 1985. Produces rock and roll, soul, folk, pop, rhythm and blues, and solo artists. Recent releases: "Honolulu City Lights" by the Carpenters and "Voice on a Hotline" by Don Johnson.
Needs: Needs vary depending on projects; currently involved in several motion pictures.
First Contact & Terms: Send resume and samples. Samples are filed. Samples not filed are returned by SASE only if requested by artist. Reports back within 2-3 weeks. Pays by the project, $1,000-100,000. Considers complexity of project, skills and experience of artist, how work will be used and rights purchased when establishing payment. Buys first rights, one-time rights, reprint rights or all rights; negotiates rights purchased.
Tips: "Be as professional as possible when submitting material."

ARZEE RECORD COMPANY and ARCADE RECORD COMPANY, 3010 N. Front St., Philadelphia Pa 19133. (215)426-5682. President: Rex Zario. Produces rock and roll, country/western, and rhythm and blues. Recent releases: "Rock Around the Clock," by James E. Myers; "World Apart," by Ray Whitley; "Why Do I Cry Over You," by Bill Haley.
Needs: Produces 25 records/year. Works with 150 visual artists/year. Uses artists for brochure and catalog design; posters.
First Contact & Terms: Send query letter with brochure and tear sheets to be kept on file. Samples not kept on file are returned by SASE if requested. Reports within 6 weeks. Originals not returned after job's completion. Call for appointment to show portfolio. Buys all rights.

AUDIOFIDELITY ENTERPRISES, INC., 519 Capobianco Plaza, Rahway NJ 07065. (201)388-5000. Art Director: Ron Warwell. Producers of movie and music videos, cinema classics, compact discs, cassettes and records. Music catagories are classical, soul, country western, jazz, pop, educational, rhythm and blues, salsa, ethnic, and specialty, plus more. Recent releases: Charlie Parker's "Bird Symbols" and Willie Banks "The Legend."
Needs: Produces 100 records and cassettes/year by 30 groups and 20 soloists. Works with 10 freelance artists/year. "Super pros" only. Uses artists for album cover, catalog and advertising illustration, and posters.
First Contact & Terms: Send query letter with brochure showing art style or resume, tear sheets, Photostats, photocopies, slides, photographs and c-prints to be kept on file. Samples not kept on file are returned by SASE if requested. Reports only if interested. Call or write to schedule an appointment to show a portfolio, which should include original/final art, final reproduction/product, tear sheets, Photostats and photographs. Pays by the project, $500 maximum. Considers complexity of project, available budget, skill and experience of artist, how work will be used and rights purchased when establishing payment. Negotiates rights purchased.
Tips: "Artists should have a knowledge of *jazz*. We are specialists in producing the Great American Art form from the days of the Cotton Club to the present in audio and video formats. In the record industry, CDs and video are the hot items. Records are out—CDs in! Videos will service us in all areas of education, trade, sales and, of course, entertainment. Designs changes will relate to high-tech in the music and entertainment areas."

"There is an increasing need for more illustration in the marketing aspects of the record industry"

—Robert R. Kovach, American Music Network
Warner Robins, Georgia

CLIFF AYERS PRODUCTIONS, 830 Glastonbury Rd. #614, Nashville TN 37217-1708. Producer: Chris Ostermeyer. Produces rock and roll, country/western and pop; group and solo artists. Recent releases: "Talk Back Tremblin' Lips," by Ernie Ashworth; "As Long As We're Together," by John Melnick; and "Nobody's Perfect," by Marilyn Jeffries.
Needs: Produces 75 records/year. Works with 40 visual artists/year. Works on assignment only. Uses artists for album cover design and illustration, brochure design and layout and direct mail packages.
First Contact & Terms: Send resume and tear sheets to be kept on file. Samples are not returned. Reports only if interested. Original art returned at job's completion. Write for appointment to show portfolio. Pays by the project. Considers available budget when establishing payment. Buys first rights.

***AZRA INTERNATIONAL**, Box 459, Maywood CA 90270. (213)560-4223. Artist Development: D.T. Richards. Produces rock and roll and novelty records, by group and solo artists. Recent releases: "Salute the New Flag," by Mad Reign; "I Wanna Wrestle You," by Mad Matt; "And the Dead Shall Rise," by Ripper.
Needs: Produces 6 soloists and 6 groups/year. Uses artists for album cover design and illustration.
First Contact & Terms: Send query letter. Samples are filed. Samples not filed are returned by SASE. Reports back within 1 week. Call to show a portfolio. Pays by the project, $100 minimum. Considers how work will be used when establishing payment. Negotiates rights purchased.

***BERANDOL MUSIC LIMITED**, 110A Sackville St., Toronto, Ontario M5A 3E7 Canada. A&R Director: Tony T. Procewiat. Produces rock and roll, classical, disco and educational records. Recent releases: "Love Theme from Canada," by The Cosmic Orchestra; "The Magic Singing Animal Farm," by David Walden; "The Beastles Party Album," by the Beastles.
Needs: Produces 2 soloists and 2 groups/year. Works with 2 visual artists/year. Works on assignment only. Uses artists for album cover design and illustration, brochure design and illustration, direct mail packages and posters.
First Contact & Terms: Send query letter with brochure showing art style. Samples are filed. Reports back within 5 weeks. To show a portfolio, mail final reproduction/product. Pays by the project, $500-5,000. Considers skills and experience of artist and how work will be used when establishing payment. Buys all rights.

***BIG BEAR RECORDS**, 190 Monument Rd., Birmingham B16 8UU England. (021)454-7020. Managing Director: Jim Simpson. Produces soul, jazz, and rhythm and blues. Recent releases: "R&B Jam Session Series."
Needs: Produces 10 records/year. Works with 2 visual artists/year. Uses artists for album cover design and illustration.
First Contact & Terms: Works on assignment only. Send query letter with photographs or photocopies to be kept on file. Samples not filed are returned only by SAE (nonresidents include IRC). Negotiates payment. Considers complexity of project and how work will be used when establishing payment. Purchases all rights.

BLUE ISLAND GRAPHICS, Box 171265, San Diego CA 92117-0975. (619)576-9666. President: Bob Gilbert. Produces rock and roll, country/western and pop. "We are a new company and will be signing new artists this year. Even though we are new, we always are looking for talent."
Needs: Produces 10-15 records/year. Works on assignment only. Uses 3 visual artists/year. Uses artists for album cover, brochure and advertising illustration; brochure, catalog and advertising layout; brochure and advertising design.
First Contact & Terms: Send query letter with resume, Photostats, original work and tear sheets to be kept on file. SASE. Samples not kept on file are returned by SASE if requested. Reports within 1 month. Write for appointment to show portfolio. Originals not returned after job's completion. Pays by the hour, $10-15 average. Considers skill and experience of artist when establishing payment. Buys all rights.

BOLIVIA RECORDS CO., Box 1304, 1219 Kerlin Ave., Brewton AL 36427. (205)867-2228. Manager: Roy Edwards. Produces soul, country/western, pop, and rhythm and blues. Recent releases: "Was Young Love Born to Die," by Bobbie Roberson.
Needs: Produces 20 records/year; 40% of the album covers assigned to freelance designers and illustrators. Assigns 25 freelance jobs/year. Experienced artists only. Uses artists for album cover, brochure, poster, catalog and advertising design; album cover and catalog illustration; brochure and catalog layout; and direct mail packages. Prefers western scenes and color washes of landscapes as themes.
First Contact & Terms: Send query letter with brochure/flyer and samples or actual work. Samples returned by SASE. Works on assignment only. Reports back. Negotiates payment by the project. Buys all rights.
Tips: "Do good work and be dependable."

BOUQUET-ORCHID ENTERPRISES, Box 18284, Shreveport LA 71138. (318)686-7362. President: Bill Bohannon. Produces country, pop and contemporary gospel.
Needs: Produces 10 records/year; 5 of which have cover/jackets designed and illustrated by freelance artists. Uses artists for record album and brochure design.
First Contact & Terms: Send query letter with resume and samples. "I prefer a brief but concise overview of an artist's background and works showing the range of his talents." SASE. Reports within 2 weeks. Negotiates payment.

***BROADWAY/HOLLYWOOD PRODUCTIONS**, #107, 12720 Burbank Blvd., Hollywood CA 91607. Art Department: Jennifer Yeko. Produces film scores.
Needs: Prefers local artists only (Los Angeles, CA area). Must have extremely realistic color portrayals for movie posters. Send copy of non-returnable samples. We will refer you to producer of film company when appropriate. Works on assignment only. Uses artists for album cover, brochure and catalog design, illustration and layout, direct mail packages, advertising design and illustration and posters.
First Contact & Terms: Send resume, tear sheets, Photostats and photocopies. Samples are filed. Samples not filed are returned by SASE only if requested by artist. Reports back only if interested. "Do not contact us." Pays by the project. Considers complexity of project, available budget, skills and experience of artist, how work will be used, turnaround time and rights purchased when establishing payment. Buys all rights.
Tips: "Only the highest quality realistic-representational artists employed. Prefer artistic type of Star Wars posters. Others need not apply at this time."

***BRYDEN RECORD PRODUCTIONS**, Box 1508, Clackamas OR 97015. Contact: A&R Director. Estab. 1985. Produces rock and roll, new wave, blues, heavy metal, funk and reggae.
Needs: Produces 1 soloist and 1 group/year. Works with 3 visual artists/year. Uses artists for album cover design and illustration, brochure design, advertising design and illustration.
First Contact & Terms: Send query letter with brochure or tear sheets and photocopies. "Some samples are filed." Samples not filed are returned by SASE. Reports back within 3 months. Write to schedule an appointment to show a portfolio or mail thumbnails, roughs and photocopies. Pays by the project, $40-220. Considers available budget and how work will be used when establishing payment. Buys first rights or negotiates rights purchased.
Tips: Our topic themes are cars, sex, music, dance and global concerns.

***CALIFORNIA INTERNATIONAL RECORDS & VIDEO**, Box 2818, Newport Beach CA 92663. Produces rock and roll, and pop; solo artists. Recent releases: "Lets Put the Fun Back in Rock n' Roll," by Freddie Cannon & the Belmonts; "Child of Technology" and "Children Are the Future," by Joseph Nicoletti.
Needs: Produces 2-3 records/year; works with 1-2 recording artists/year. Uses artists for album cover design and illustration, catalog design, illustration and layout, advertising design and illustration, direct mail packages and posters.
First Contact & Terms: Works on assignment only. Send brochure, resume, business card and samples to be kept on file. Samples not filed are not returned. Reports only if interested. Original art sometimes returned. Pays by the project. Considers complexity of project, available budget, skill and experience of commercial artist, how work will be used, turnaround time and rights purchased when establishing payment. Negotiates rights purchased.

***CAPRICE RECORDS/DAWN PRODUCTIONS**, Suite 1, 621 Park City Center, Lancaster PA 17601. President: Joey Welz. Produces rock and roll, country/western, group and solo artists. Recent releases: "R&R Hall of Fame" and "Country Music Hall of Fame" by Joey Welz.
Needs: Produces 2 soloists and 2 groups/year. Works with 2 visual artists/year. Uses artists for album cover design.
First Contact & Terms: Send query letter with brochure or photocopies. Samples are filed. Samples not filed are not returned. Reports back only if interested. To show a portfolio, mail b&w, tear sheets and photographs. Pays by the project, percentage of record sales. Buys one-time rights.

***CARROLL ENTERPRISES**, Box 2385, Naransa FL 33032. (602)276-2039. President: Lawrence Carroll. Produces soul, and rhythm and blues. Recent releases: "Crossroads," by Bobby Barnes and "DJ Rap," by Poor Boy Rappers.
Needs: Produces 10 records/year. Works with 5 visual artists/year. Uses artists for cover design and illustration.
First Contact & Terms: Contact only through artist's representative with brochure, resume and photographs and albums to be kept on file. Samples not filed are returned by SASE. Original artwork returned to artist. Pays by the project or percentage basis. Considers available budget and skill and experience of commercial artist when establishing payment. Purchases one-time rights.

CELESTIAL SOUND PRODUCTIONS, 28 South Villas, London NW1 England. 41-01-405-9883. Managing Director: Ron Warren Ganderton. Produces rock and roll, classical, soul, country/western, jazz, pop, educational, and rhythm and blues; group and solo artists. Recent releases: "Starforce One," "Red Door," and "Once Bitten."
Needs: Works with "many" visual artists/year. Uses artists for album cover design and illustration; advertising and brochure design and illustrations, posters.
First Contact & Terms: Send query letter with brochure showing art style or resume, business card and photographs to be kept on file "for a reasonable time." Samples not filed are returned by SASE only if requested. Reports within 5 days. Call to schedule an appointment to show a portfolio, which should include roughs, color, photographs and b&w. Original artwork returned after job's completion. Pays by the project. Considers available budget, how work will be used and rights purchased when establishing payment. Buys all rights, reprint rights or negotiates rights purchased.
Tips: "We are searching for revolutionary developments and those who have ideas and inspirations to express in creative progress."

***CELTIC MUSIC AND RECORDS**,Box 3582, Hollywood CA 90028. (818)763-2028. President: Bob Davis. Produces rock and roll, country/western, pop, solo artists and inspirational. Recent releases: "American Memories," by Shamus M'Cool and "She Just Kept Comin Around" by Jerry Ray.
Needs: Uses artists for album cover design and illustration, direct mail packages, advertising illustration and posters.
First Contact & Terms: Send query letter. Reports back only if interested. Write to schedule an appointment to show a portfolio. Pays by the hour, $10 minimum. Considers skills and experience of artist when establishing payment. Buys one-time rights; negotiates rights purchased.
Tips: "Send a simple letter explaining your enclosed package."

CHAPMAN RECORDING STUDIOS, 228 W. 5th St., Kansas City MO 64105. (816)842-6854. Contact: Chuck Chapman. Produces rock and roll, soul, country, jazz, folk, pop, and rhythm and blues. Recent releases: "I Will Never Die" by Freddie Hart; "Phrogs, Pharaohs & Phorgiveness" by Paul Land & Ray Hildebrand.
Needs: Produces 25 records/year; 15 of which have cover/jackets designed and illustrated by freelance artists. Interested in record album design; no paintings.
First Contact & Terms: Send brochure or material that can be kept on file for future reference. Negotiates pay based on set fee/job.
Tips: "Original album jacket artwork has taken a jump within our operation."

***CLAY PIGEON INTERNATIONAL RECORDS**, Box 20346, Chicago IL 60620. (312)778-8760. Contact: Vito Beleska or Rudy Markus. Produces rock and roll, pop, New wave and avant-garde. Recent releases: "Automatic Vaudeville" by Vyto B. and "Tribe of Dolls," by The Band That Never Made It.
Needs: Produces 5 records/year; 3 of which have cover/jackets designed and illustrated by freelance artists. Uses artists for design and illustrations for LP jackets, brochures, 45 RPM picture sleeves and advertising. Interested in "anything good, especially newer concepts, unusually creative approaches, art that does more with less."
First Contact & Terms: Send query (do not phone) with resume or brochure and materials that can be kept on file for future reference. Prefers "whatever shows artist's work best" as samples; "simple, inexpensive presentation OK." Samples not returned except by special arrangement. Reports within 1 month or when assignment is available. Negotiates pay based on amount of creativity required and artist's previous experience/reputation.

***CONTEMPORARY RECORDING STUDIOS—CRS ARTISTS INC.**,724 Winchester Rd., Broomall, PA 19008. (215)544-5920. Artist Representative: Jack M. Shusterman. Produces classical and jazz records by group artists. "Open to new prospects."
Needs: Uses freelance visual artists for album cover and brochure design and illustration, catalog design, illustration and layout, direct mail packages, advertising design and illustration and posters.
First Contact & Terms: Send query letter with brochure showing art style or resume and tear sheets, Photostats and photocopies. Samples are filed. Samples not filed are returned by SASE. Reports back only if interested. Call to schedule an appointment to show a portfolio or mail original/final art. Pays by the project, $100-125. Considers complexity of project, available budget and turnaround time when establishing payment. Buys all rights.

***COSMOTONE RECORDS**, Box 71988, Los Angeles CA 90071-0988. Record Producer: Rafael Brom. Produces rock, disco, country/western, folk, pop, educational, group and solo artists. Recent releases: "Padre Pio" by Lord Hamilton and "No. 1" by R.B.
Needs: Produces 3 soloists and 1 group/year. Works with 4 visual artists/year. Prefers artists with 10 years of experience minimum. Works on assignment only. Uses artists for album cover and illustration,

brochure design and illustration, catalog design and illustration, catalog layout, direct mail packages, advertising design and illustration, posters and videos.
First Contact & Terms: Send query letter with resume, photocopies and slides. Samples not filed are not returned. Reports back only if interested. Pays by the project, $100 minimum. Considers complexity of project and skills and experience of artist when establishing payment. Buys all rights.

CREOLE RECORDS LTD., 91-93 High St., Harlesden, London NW10 England. (01)965-9223. General Manager: Steve Tantum. Produces dance, disco, soul and pop; group artists and solo artists. Recent releases: "I Want to Wake Up with You" by Bons Gardiner.
Needs: Produces 45 records/year. Produces 5 soloists and 4 groups/year. Works with 6 visual artists/year. Uses artists for album cover design and illustration, advertising design, illustration and layout and posters.
First Contact & Terms: Send resume and samples to be kept on file. Accepts any samples. Samples not filed are returned by SAE (nonresidents include IRC). Reports within 2 weeks. Write to schedule an appointment to show a portfolio, which should include roughs. Original art sometimes returned to artist. Payment varies. Considers complexity of project, available budget, skill and experience of commercial artist, how work will be used and rights purchased when establishing payment. Buys all rights.

CRYIN' IN THE STREETS RECORDS CORPORATION & AFFILIATES, Box 2544, Baton Rouge LA 70821. (504)924-6865. Director: Jimmy Angel/Ebb-Tide. Produces soul, country/western, jazz, pop, and rhythm and blues; group and solo artists. Recent releases: "Let 'Jesus' In," by The Mighty Serenades; "One More Lie," by Betsy Davidson; and "Ease My Mind," by George Perkins.
Needs: Produces fifteen 45's and 6 albums/year; works with 21-25 recording artists/year. Works with 100+ visual artists/year; averages 12 album covers/year. Uses artists for album cover design and illustration, brochure design and illustration, catalog layout, advertising illustration, direct mail packages, posters, video backdrops and production layouts. Acceptable art styles include cartoons and humorous and cartoon-style illustrations.
First Contact & Terms: Works with "professionals" only. Works on assignment only. Send query letter with resume and business card to be kept on file only if accepted. Send photocopies, photographs or tear sheets only when requested. Samples not filed are returned only by SASE. Reports within 30 days. Write for appointment to show portfolio. Original art returned to the artist. Pays by the project, $100-1,000 average. Considers complexity of project, available budget, skill and experience of commercial artist, how work will be used, turnaround time and rights purchased when establishing payment. Purchases all rights.

CURTISS UNIVERSAL RECORD MASTERS, Box 4740, Nashville TN 37216. (615)865-4740. Manager: S.D. Neal. Produces soul, country, jazz, folk, pop, rock and roll, and rhythm and blues. Recent releases by Dixie Dee & The Rhythm Rockers, and Ben Williams.
Needs: Produces 6 records/year; some of which have cover/jackets designed and illustrated by freelance artists. Works on assignment only. Uses artists for album cover and poster design.
First Contact & Terms: Send business card and samples to be kept on file. Submit portfolio for review. SASE. Reports within 3 weeks. Originals returned to artist after job's completion. Negotiates pay based on artist involved. Negotiates rights purchased.

DAWN PRODUCTIONS, Joey Welz Music Complex, 2338 Fruitville Pike, Lancaster PA 17601. President: Joey Welz. Produces country/western, New Wave, rock and pop music albums. Recent releases: "Rock and Roll Hall of Fame" and "Country Music Hall of Fame," by Joey Welz.
Needs: Produces 2 LPs and five 45s/year. Works with 3 groups and 3 soloists. Works with 2 visual artists/ year. Buys 1-3 illustrations/year. "Artists must be ready to go." Uses artists for album cover designs and illustrations. Especially needs stock jackets.
First Contact & Terms: Send brochure showing art style or tear sheets and photocopies. SASE. Reports only if interested. To show a portfolio, mail appropriate materials, which should include tear sheets, Photostats and photographs. Considers available budget, rights purchased and how work will be used when establishing payment; "percentage paid by label releasing product."
Tips: "Be creative and easy to work with on terms. Four-color is too expensive. We are looking for more economical covers. In the field, we see a lot of picture discs and stock backgrounds with overlay of photos."

DELMARK RECORDS, 4243 N. Lincoln, Chicago IL 60618. (312)528-8834. Art Director: Bob Koester. Produces blues and jazz. Recent releases: "All the Gin Is Gone" by Jimmy Forest.
Needs: Chicago area artists only. Produces 10-15 records/year; all of which have cover/jackets designed and illustrated by freelance artists. Works on assignment only. "Our records do not sell like hits, but remain in our catalog and active in the market for many years. We are therefore more interested in

clean designs that do not date rather than in flashy covers. Most of the artists who work for us are interested in the music we issue: jazz and blues. We are especially interested in artists who can arrive at interesting multi-color designs based on black and white photographs."
First Contact & Terms: Arrange interview to show portfolio (mixture of original and printed art). Samples returned by SASE. Reports back on future assignment possibilities. Send resume, tear sheet and samples to be kept on file for future assignments. Pays $50-300.

DESTINY RECORDS, Destiny Recording Studio, 31 Nassau Ave., Wilmington MA 01887. Contact: Larry Feeney. Produces rock and roll, disco, soul, country/western, jazz, folk, pop, and rhythm and blues; group and solo artists. Recent releases: "Decision," by Rude Awakening; "Prisoners," by Tinted Glass; "When You Thought I Had It," by True Desire; "Ritzi Anna," by Myron Skau.
Needs: Produces 6 records/year. Works with 3 visual artists/year. Uses artists for album cover design and illustration; brochure design, direct mail packages, advertising design and illustration and posters. "We're interested in futuristic forms." Especially needs "45 sleeves."
First Contact & Terms: Send query letter with nonreturnable color samples to be kept on file. Samples not filed are not returned. Write for appointment to show portfolio; do not call. Portfolio should include roughs, original/final art, color and photographs. Original art sometimes returned to the artist. Payment varies.

DUPUY RECORDS/PRODUCTIONS/PUBLISHING, INC., Suite 200, 10960 Ventura Blvd., Studio City CA 91604. Contact: Director. Produces rock and roll, soul, jazz, pop, rhythm and blues; group and solo artists. Recent releases: "Show Me The Way", "Livin' For Your Love", "Be There Tonight" and "She's My Lady" by Gordon Gilman.
Needs: Produces 3 or more records/year. Works with 6 visual artists/year. Local artists only with 5 years of experience or more. Works on assignment only. Uses artists for album covers, brochure, catalog and advertising design and illustration; posters.
First Contact & Terms: Send query letter with brochure showing art style. Samples not filed are returned by SASE. Reports only if interested. Call or write to schedule an appointment to show a portfolio, which should include roughs, original/final art, final reproduction/product, color, tear sheets, Photostats, photographs and b&w. Pays by the project. Considers skill and experience of artist when establishing payment.

***DYNACOM COMMUNICATIONS, INC.**, Box 702, Snowdon Station, Montreal, Quebec H3X 3X8 Canada. General Manager: D. Leonard. Produces rock and roll, disco, soul, country/western, jazz, folk, pop, educational, and rhythm and blues.
Needs: Produces 10 records/year. Uses artists for album cover design and illustration; brochure, catalog and advertising design, illustration and layout; direct mail packages and posters.
First Contact & Terms: Send query letter with brochure, resume, business card, Photostats, slides or photographs and tear sheets. Samples not returned. Works on assignment only. Considers complexity of project, available budget, skill and experience of artist, how work will be used, turnaround time and rights purchased when establishing payment. Negotiates rights purchased.

E.L.J. RECORD CO., 1344 Waldron, St. Louis MO 63130. (314)863-3605. President: Eddie Johnson. Produces rhythm and blues, rock and roll, jazz and pop music. Recent releases: "Morning Star," by Jimmy Jones; "Rock House Annie," by Ann Richardson; "Strange Feeling," by Eddie Johnson Trio; and "Wish I Was an Itty Bitty Girl," by the M&M Girls.
Needs: Produces 10 records/year by 4 groups and 4 soloists; all of which have cover/jackets designed and illustrated by freelance artists.
First Contact & Terms: Send query and samples. SASE. Reports within 6 weeks. To show a portfolio, mail appropriate materials, which should include photographs and tear sheets. Negotiates pay based on amount of creativity required and rights purchased.
Tips: "Send prices and sample designs of some of my material."

***EMPIRE RECORDS & TAPES**, 760 W. Sample Rd., Pompano Beach FL 33064. President: Josh Noland. Produces country/western, folk, pop and gospel records by group artists and solo artists. Recent releases: "Sand 'n My Shoes," by Touch of Grass; "Beyond My Fault," by Up Lifters and "Rhapsody in Blue," by Josh Noland.
Needs: Produces 5 soloists and 5 groups/year. Works with 1-2 visual artists/year. Prefers local artists, experience "not too important." Works on assignment only. Uses artists for album cover design and advertising design.
First Contact & Terms: Send query letter with brochure showing art style. Samples are filed. Samples not filed are not returned. Reports back only if interested. Write to schedule an appointment to show a portfolio, or mail color photographs and sample album covers. Payment varies. Considers complexity

of project and available budget when establishing payment. Negotiates rights purchased.
Tips: We are "looking for eye-catching album covers and photos for approximately 5 albums per year. We have a small budget with a wide range of subject matter. We use only local artists unless you can deal by mail."

***ENIGMA ENTERTAINMENT CORPORATION**,Box 2428, El Segundo CA 90245-2428. Art Director: Brian Ayuso. Produces rock and roll, jazz, pop, group artists and solo artists. Recent releases: "Especially For You" by Smithereens and "To Hell With The Devil" by Stryper.
Needs: Produces 3-4 soloists and 15-20 groups/year. Works with 10-15 visual artists/year. Prefers experienced artist only. Works on assignment only. Uses artists for album cover, catalog and advertising illustration.
First Contact & Terms: Send resume, tear sheets, Photostats and slides. Samples are filed. Samples not filed are returned by SASE. Reports back only if interested. Write to schedule an appointment to show a portfolio or mail color, b&w, tear sheets, Photostats and photographs. Pays by the project, $150 minimum. Considers complexity of project, available budget, skills and experience of artist and how work will be used and rights purchased when establishing payment.
Tips: "Be professional."

***ESPREE RECORDS/CASSETTES/VIDEOS**, Suite 1121, 1100 Glendon Ave., Los Angeles CA 90024. (213)824-3333. President: Joseph J. Kessler. Produces country/western, pop and educational. Recent releases: "A Head Start to A Better Memory" and "The Executive Memory Guide" by Hermine Hilton.
Needs: Freelance artists are used to provide a complete package that varies from recording to recording, but includes cover design and advertising.
First Contact & Terms: Send query letter with brochure showing art style. Samples are filed. Samples not filed are returned by SASE. Reports back only if interested. Pays by the project, $500-5,000. Considers available budget when establishing payment. Buys all rights.

***ESQUIRE RECORDS**, 185A Newmarket Rd., Norwich, Norfolk NR4 6AP England. 44-06-035-1139. Producer: Peter Newbrook. Produces jazz. Recent releases: " 'Scuse These Blues" by Quincy Jones and "Waxing the Winners" by the Melody Makers All Stars.
Needs: Produces 4-6 records/year. Works with 2 freelance artists/year. Uses artists for album cover design and illustration.
First Contact & Terms: Send query letter with Photostats or photographs to be kept on file. Reports only if interested. Works on assignment only. Originals returned to artist after job's completion. Negotiates pay rate. Considers available budget when establishing payment. Buys all rights.

***ETIQUETTE PRODUCTIONS**,#273, 2442 NW Market St., Seattle WA 98107. Art Director: Greg Butler. Produces rock and roll, soul, jazz, pop, rhythm and blues, group artists and solo artists. Recent releases: "Live Fanz Only" by The Sonics and "Hey La La Lee" by Kinetics.
Needs: Produces 2-3 soloists and 2-3 groups/year. Works with 2-3 visual artists/year. Works on assignment only. Uses artists for album cover design and illustration and posters.
First Contact & Terms: Send query letter with brochure or resume and tear sheets, Photostats and photocopies. Samples are filed. Samples not filed are returned by SASE or not returned. Reports back within 1 month. Write to schedule an appointment to show a portfolio. Pays by the project, $50 minimum. Considers complexity of project, available budget, skill and experience of artist, how work will be used, turnaround time and rights purchased when establishing payment. "We buy whatever rights are applicable to our needs."
Tips: "Send resume and samples—if we are interested, we will contact you."

EXECUTIVE RECORDS, 11 Shady Oak Trail, Charlotte NC 28210. (704)554-1162. Executive Director: Butch Kelly. Produces rock and roll, disco, soul, country/western, jazz, classical, gospel, pop, and rhythm and blues; group and solo artists. Recent releases include "Super Star" and "I Just Want Somebody to Love" by L.A. Star and "Show Me Love" by Jay Wylie.
Needs: Produces 9 records)year by 4 groups and 5 soloists. Works with 3 groups and 3 solo recording artists/year. Works with 2 visual artists/year. Seeks artists with 3 years experience. Works on assignment only. Uses artists for album cover design, advertising design and layout, and direct mail packages.
First Contact & Terms: Send query letter with brochure, resume and photographs to be kept on file. Samples not filed returned by SASE. Reports back only if interested. Original art sometimes returned to the artist. To show a portfolio, mail original/final art, color and photographs with SASE. Pays by the project, $25-100 average. Considers available budget, and skill and experience of commercial artist when establishing payment. Buys all rights.
Tips: "Just be original. We like to see more color. It's affected my use in a more positive way."

***FALCON PRODUCTIONS**, 3080 Lenworth Dr., Mississauga, Ontario L4X 2G1 Canada. (416)625-3865. Art Director: Rod Albrecht. Manager: Cliff Hunt. Produces rock and roll, pop, and rhythm and blues. Recent releases: "Affairs in Babylon" by Refugee; and "Call Billy" by Billy Durst.
Needs: Produces 3 records/year; works with 3 freelance artists/year. Works on assignment only. Uses artists and photographers for album cover design and illustration, advertising illustration and layout, and posters.
First Contact & Terms: Send resume, business card, Photostats, slides or photographs (of any 3-dimensional work). Call or write for appointment to show portfolio. Samples not filed are returned by SASE (nonresidents include IRC) only if requested. Reports within 30 days. Original work not returned after job's completion. Pays by the hour, $15-30 average. Considers complexity of project, available budget, how work will be used and rights purchased when establishing payment. Negotiates rights purchased.
Tips: Looks for artists who do not follow trends. "Originality is so difficult to achieve but so important to maintain."

***FATE RECORDS**,Box 273, Mill Valley CA 94942. (415)332-6363. PR & Distribution: Elaina Ashe. Produces rock and roll and country/western. Recent releases: "Bloodlines" and "Smoking the Dummy" by Terry Allen.
Needs: Uses artists for direct mail packages.
First Contact & Terms: Send query letter with brochure. Reports back only if interested. To show a portfolio, mail final reproduction/product. Pays by the project. Considers complexity of project and available budget when establishing payment. Negotiates rights purchased.

***FINER ARTS RECORDS/TRANSWORLD RECORDS**, Suite 115, 2170 S. Parker Rd., Denver CO 80231. President: R. Bernstein. Produces rock and roll, disco, soul, country/western, jazz, pop and rhythm and blues records by group and solo artists. Recent releases: "Israel Oh Israel," (a new Broadway musical); "Bonnie Delaney"; "Kaylen Wells," and "Leeona Miracle." New recording artists ready for release.
Needs: Produces 2-3 soloists and 2-3 groups/year. Uses artists for album cover design and illustration and posters.
First Contact & Terms: Send query letter with brochure showing art style or resume and tear sheets, Photostats and photocopies. Samples are filed. Samples not filed are returned only if requested. Reports back only if interested. Write to schedule an appointment to show a portfolio. Pays by the project, $500 minimum. Considers complexity of project, available budget and turnaround time when establishing payment. Buys all rights and negotiates rights purchased.

***FRECKLE RECORDS**, Pioneer Square, Box 4005, Seattle WA 98104. (206)682-3200. General Manager: Jack Burg. Produces folk and pop; group and solo artists. Recent release: "Back Stage" by Reilly & Maloney.
Needs: Produces 3 records/year. Uses artists for album cover design and illustration, brochure design and layout, advertising design and layout, and posters.
First Contact & Terms: Prefers local experienced artists. Works on assignment only. Send query letter with brochure, resume, business card and samples to be kept on file. Call or write for appointment to show portfolio. Samples not filed are returned by SASE. Reports only if interested. Pays by the project. Considers complexity of project, available budget, skill and experience of commercial artist, how work will be used, turnaround time and rights purchased when establishing payment. Negotiates rights purchased.

***FREDDIE RECORDS**, 6118 S. Padre Island Dr., Corpus Christi TX 78412. (512)992-8411. Contact: Production Manager. Produces Spanish records. Recent releases: "Little Joe" and "Ramon Ayala" by Freddie Martinez.
First Contact & Terms: Send query letter with brochure or samples. Samples not filed are not returned. Reports back only if interested.

***FRONTLINE RECORDS**, 2900 S. Bristol #C-106, Costa Mesa CA 92626. (714)751-2242. Creative/Art Director: Ed McTaggart. Estab. 1986. Produces rock and roll records by group and solo artists. Recent releases: "Detonation," by Bloodgood; "Fearful Symmetry," by DA and "Mad at the World," by Mad at the World.
Needs: Produces 5 soloists and 10 groups/year. Works with 8 visual artists/year. Prefers local (Orange County/LA County) artists. Will accept photo transparencies from out of state. Works on assignment only. Uses artists for album cover design and illustration, brochure design and illustration, catalog design, illustration and layout, direct mail packages, advertising design and illustration and posters.

First Contact & Terms: Send query letter with resume and tear sheets, Photostats, photocopies, slides and sample LP covers. Samples are filed. Reports back only if interested. Call to schedule an appointment to show a portfolio, which should include roughs, original/final art, final reproduction/product, color, b&w and photographs. Payment varies. Considers available budget, how work will be used and turnaround time when establishing payment. Buys one-time rights, all rights and negotiates rights purchased.
Tips: "I need artists that like creative challenges."

***GALLERY II RECORDS**,2301 W. 59th St., Los Angeles CA 90043. (213)294-7286. President: Johno Waller. Produces rock and roll, pop, soul, rhythm and blues, group and solo artists and gospel, rap, and salsa. Recent releases: "I'm Always Losing You" by Marsha Stewart and "Sexy Little Treat" by Percision.
First Contact & Terms: Send query letter with resume, tear sheets, photocopies, and slides. Samples are filed. Samples not filed are returned by SASE only if requested by artist. Reports back only if interested. Call or write to schedule an appointment to show a portfolio or mail original/final art final reproduction/product, color, b&w, tear sheets, Photostats, and photographs. Pays by the project. Considers complexity of project, available budget, skills and experience of artist, how work will be used, turnaround time and rights purchased. Buys first rights or all rights; negotiates rights purchased.
Tips: "If you're not serious and don't have a professional attitude, don't waste my time, and we won't waste your time."

GCS RECORDS, Suite 206, 1508 Harlem, Memphis TN 38114. (901)274-2726. Art Director: Reggie Ekridge. Produces disco, soul, pop, gospel, and rhythm and blues; group and solo artists. Recent releases: "Early Morning Man," by Cheryl Fox; "God is Coming Soon" by Stars of Nightingales.
Needs: Produces 20 records/year. Works with 3 visual artists/year. Prefers local artists. Uses artists for album cover design and illustration; brochure and advertising design and illustration; catalog design and layout; and direct mail packages. Especially needs album covers, catalog and brochure design.
First Contact & Terms: Send query letter with brochure showing art style, resume, tear sheets, Photostats, photocopies and photographs to be kept on file. Samples not filed are returned by SASE only if requested. Reports only if interested. To show a portfolio, mail final reproduction/product, color, tear sheets, Photostats and b&w. Payment negotiated/job. Considers complexity of project, available budget, how work will be used and rights purchased when establishing payment. Negotiates rights purchased.

***GLOBAL RECORDS, Bakersfield Records, Chris Music Publishing, Sara Lee Music Publishing**, 133 Arbutus Ave., Box 396, Mantistique MI 49854. Contact: Art Department. Produces soul, country/western, folk, rhythm and blues, and contemporary gospel; group artists. Recent releases "Diamonds & Pearls," by Paradons; Milestone Records and Tapes, K-Tel Albums and cassettes.
Needs: Produces 11 records/year. Works with 2 visual artists/year. Uses artists for advertising design, illustration and layout; also advertising design for other businesses.
First Contact & Terms: Prefers amateur artists. Works on assignment only. Send query letter with brochure to be kept on file. Prefers photographs or tear sheets as samples. Samples returned by SASE. Reports within 3 months. Original artwork not returned to artist. Negotiates payment by the project. Considers available budget when establishing payment. Purchases all rights.

***GORDON MUSIC COMPANY INC./PARIS RECORDS**, Box 2250, Canoga Park CA 91306. (818)883-8224. President: Jeff Gordon. Produces rock and roll, jazz, pop, group and solo artists. Recent releases: "Hold Me Tight" by Robert White and "Mr. D.J." by Concept.
Needs: Produces 1 soloist and 2 groups/year. Uses artists for album cover design and illustration and posters.
First Contact & Terms: Send query letter with brochure. Samples are filed. Samples not filed are not returned. Reports back within 1 month. Pays by the project. Considers complexity of project and available budget when establishing payment. Buys all rights; negotiates rights purchased.

GRANDVILLE RECORD CORP., Box 11960, Chicago IL 60611-0960. Art Director: Danielle Render.
Needs: Works with 10 freelance visual artists/year. Uses visual artists for album jackets and original logo designs.
First Contact & Terms: Send query letter with resume, tear sheets, Photostats and photocopies. Samples not filed are returned by SASE. Does not report back. To show a portfolio, mail roughs, original/final art, Photostats, photographs and b&w. Pays for design by the project, $150-250. Pays for illustration by the project, $100-200. Considers complexity of project, client's budget and rights purchased when establishing payment. Negotiates rights purchased.

HARD HAT RECORDS AND CASSETTE TAPES, 519 N. Halifax Ave., Daytona Beach FL 32018. (904)252-0381. Vice President, Sales/Promotion: Bobby Lee. Produces rock and roll, country/western, folk and educational; group and solo artists. Publishes high school/college marching band arrangements. Recent releases: "Sand in my Shoes & V-A-C-A-T-I-O-N" by the Hard Hatters; "Just a Piece of Paper," "Country Blues," "Can't Get Over Lovin' You," and "Only Lies" by the Blue Bandana Country Band.
Needs: Produces 12-30 records/year. Works with 2-3 visual artists/year. Works on assignment only. Uses artists for album cover design and illustration, advertising design and sheet music covers.
First Contact & Terms: Send query letter with brochure to be kept on file one year. Samples not filed are returned by SASE. Reports within 2 weeks. Write for appointment to show portfolio. Pays by the project. Considers complexity of project, available budget, skill and experience of artist, how work will be used, turnaround time and rights purchased when establishing payment. Purchases all rights.
Tips: "Video is playing a bigger part in the art market for record and tape companies. The market for this medium of musical entertainment has its own styles and needs."

HOLLYROCK RECORDS, Suite 170, 14116 E. Whittier Blvd., Whittier CA 90602. A&R Directors: Dave Paton, Bob Brown. Produces country/western, rock, progressive rock, folk, pop, and rhythm and blues; group and solo artists, also comedy acts.
Needs: Produces 10 records/year. Works with 4 visual artists/year.
First Contact & Terms: Send slides, Photostats, photographs, photocopies or tear sheets to be kept on file. Write for appointment to show portfolio. Reports within 4 weeks. Original art sometimes returned to the artist. Pay is negotiable. Considers complexity of project, available budget, skill and experience of artist, how work will be used, turnaround time and rights purchased when establishing payment. Buys first rights or all rights.

***HOMESTEAD RECORDS**,Box 25677, Chicago IL 60625. President: Tom Petreli. Produces rock and roll, classical, disco, soul, country/western, jazz, folk, pop, educational, rhythm and blues, group and solo artists, and Middle Eastern. Recent releases: "Arizonia" by Arizonia and "Sweetwater" by Sweetwater.
Needs: Produces 5-6 soloists and 15-20 groups/year. Works with 3-4 visual artists/year. Uses artists for album cover, brochure and catalog design, illustration and layout, direct mail packages, advertising design and illustration, posters and videos.
First Contact & Terms: Send query letter with photocopies and slides. Samples are filed. Samples not filed are returned by SASE only if requested by artist. Reports back only if interested. Write to schedule an appointment to show a portfolio or mail roughs, color, b&w, and photographs. Pays by the project, $200-600. Considers rights purchased when establishing payment. Buys all rights.

***HULA RECORDS, INC.**, Box 2135, Honolulu HA 96805. (808)847-4608. President: Donald P. McDiarmid III. Produces pop, educational, group and solo artists and Hawaiian records.
Needs: Produces 1-2 soloists and 3-4 groups/year. Works on assignment only. Uses artists for album cover design and illustration, brochure and catalog design, catalog layout, advertising design and posters.
First Contact & Terms: Send query letter with tear sheets and photocopies. Samples are filed. Samples not filed are returned only if requested. Reports back within 2 weeks. Write to schedule an appointment to show a portfolio. Pays by the project, $50-350. Considers available budget and rights purchased when establishing payment. Negotiates rights purchased.

***HYBRID RECORDS**,Box 333, Evanston IL 60204. (312)328-0400. Contact: Art Director. Produces all types of records. Recent releases: "Pick It, J.B." by Jethro Burns; "Digital Dulcimer" by Mark Nelson and "Home With the Armadillo" by Gary P. Nunn.
Needs: Works on assignment only. Uses freelance visual artists for album cover design and illustration, direct mail packages and posters.
First Contact & Terms: Send samples. Samples are not filed. Samples are returned by SASE. Reports back only if interested. To show a portfolio, mail photographs. Pays by the project, $40 minimum. Considers available budget when establishing payment. Buys all rights.

J & J MUSICAL ENTERPRISES, Suite 1103, 150 Fifth Ave., New York NY 10011. General Manager: Jeneane Claps.
Needs: Uses visual artists for record jackets/inserts.
First Contact & Terms: Send query letter with resume and tear sheets. Samples not filed are returned by SASE. Reports within 6 weeks. To show a portfolio, mail color, tear sheets and final reproduction/product. Pays for design by the project, $200 minimum. Pays for illustration by the project, $500 mini-

mum. Considers complexity of project, how work will be used and rights purchased when establishing payment. Buys all rights.
Tips: "Be as neat and organized as possible."

***JODY RECORDS**, 2557 E. First St., Brooklyn NY 11223. (718)339-8047. Contact: Art Director. Produces rock and roll, disco, soul, country/western, jazz and rhythm and blues. Recent releases: "I'll Never" by Inn the Mirror and "Pride and Joy" by Gloria Evans.
Needs: Works with 10 artists/year. Works on assignment only. Uses artists for album cover design and illustration, advertising illustration and posters.
First Contact & Terms: Send query letter with resume and samples. Samples not filed are returned by SASE. To show a portfolio, mail appropriate materials. Pays by the project, $200-500. Considers complexity of project, available budget and how work will be used when establishing payment. Buys all rights.

***K.A.M. EXECUTIVE RECORDS**,11 Shady Oak Trail, Charlotte NC 28210. (704)554-1162. Creative Director: Butch Kelly. Produces disco, soul, country/western, jazz, pop, rhythm and blues, group and solo artists. Recent releases: "M.C. Perpetrators" by Lady Crush & DJ Jazz and "Street Dancin" by Fresh Air.
Needs: Produces 4 soloists and 3 groups/year. Works with 1 visual artist/year. Prefers artists with 3 years of experience. Works on assignment only. Uses artists for album cover, brochure and catalog design, advertising design and illustration and posters.
First Contact & Terms: Send brochure or resume, tear sheets, Photostats, and photocopies. Samples are filed. Samples not filed are returned by SASE only if requested by artist. Reports back within 2 months or only if interested. Write to schedule an appointment to show a portfolio, which should include color, final reproduction/product, Photostats and photographs. Pays by the project, $50 minimum. Considers available budget, skills and experience of artist and rights purchased when establishing payment. Buys all rights; negotiates rights purchased.
Tips: "Be creative with new ideas."

***KENYON ENTERTAINMENT CORP.**, A#1, 8191 N.W. 91st. Terrace, Miami FL 33166. Contact: Joseph Stanzione. Produces Caribbean (reggae).
Needs: Produces 5-10 records/year.
First Contact & Terms: Works on assignment only. Send query letter with brochure and samples to be kept on file. Samples not filed are returned by SASE. Reports only if interested. Original art not returned to artist. Pays by the project. Considers how work will be used when establishing payment. Purchases all rights.

KIDERIAN RECORDS PRODUCTS, 4926 W. Gunnison, Chicago IL 60630. (312)764-1144. President: Raymond Peck. Produces rock and roll, classical, disco, soul, country/western, jazz, folk, pop, educational, rhythm and blues, and New Wave; group and solo artists. Recent releases: "Boyz," by Boy; "Creme Soda," by Creme Soda; and "Kiderian Sampler 2."
Needs: Produces 35-40 records/year; 100% of the album covers were assigned to freelance designers, 100% to freelance illustrators. Works with 8-14 visual artists/year. Half of all jobs/year require freelance artists. Works on assignment only. Uses artists for album cover design and illustration; posters; brochure design, illustration and layout; catalog design, illustration and layout; advertising design, illustration and layout; and direct mail packages. Accepts all styles.
First Contact & Terms: Send query letter with resume, photographs and slides to be kept on file. Samples not filed are returned by SASE. Original work returned to artist after job's completion. Pays by the project, $200-$450 average. Purchases all rights.

KIMBO EDUCATIONAL, 10 N. 3rd Ave., Long Branch NJ 07740. Production Coordinators: Amy Laufer and James Kimble. Educational record/cassette company. Produces 8 records and cassettes/year for schools, teacher supply stores and parents. Contents primarily early childhood physical fitness, although other materials are produced for all ages.
Needs: Works with 3 freelance artists/year. Local artists only. Works on assignment only. Uses artists for ads, catalog design, album covers and flyer designs. Artist must have experience in the preparation of album jackets.
First Contact & Terms: "It is very hard to do this type of material via mail." Write or call for appointment to show portfolio. Prefers photographs or actual samples of past work. Reports only if interested. Pays by the project. Album cover minimum $100; flyers, etc. lower minimum. Considers complexity of project and budget when establishing payment. Buys all rights.
Tips: "The jobs at Kimbo vary tremendously. We are an educational record company that produces ma-

terial from infant level to senior citizen level. Sometimes we need cute 'kid-like' illustrations and sometimes graphic design will suffice. A person experienced in preparing an album cover would certainly have an edge."

SID KLEINER MUSIC ENTERPRISES, 3701 25th Ave. SW, Naples FL 33964. Managing Director: Sid Kleiner. Produces folk, rock, jazz, middle of the road and country recordings, and nutritional, organic gardening and health audiovisuals. Recent releases: "In A Country Mood" by Sid Kleiner. Query. SASE. Reports within 4 weeks. Material copyrighted.
Needs: Uses artists for album design, type specifying and audiovisuals. Pays $50 minimum/job.

***KLW INTERNATIONAL INC.**, 408 Kathleen Ave., Cinnaminson NJ 08077. (604)786-8486. Executive Producer: Kevin L. Weakland. Produces rock and roll, soul, country/western, pop and rhythm and blues records by group artists and solo artists.
Needs: Produces 2 soloists and 2 groups/year. Works with 2 visual artists/year. Prefers artists with over 3 years of experience. Uses artists for album cover and brochure design, catalog design and layout, advertising design and posters.
First Contact & Terms: Send query letter with brochure showing art style or resume and tear sheets, Photostats, photocopies and slides. Samples are filed. Samples not filed are returned by SASE. Reports back within 1 week. Write to schedule an appointment to show a portfolio, which should include original/final art, final reproduction/product, color, tear sheets, Photostats and photographs. Pays by the hour, $10-17. Considers available budget, skill and experience of artist and rights purchased when establishing payment. Buys all rights.

***LARKSPUR MUSIC, BMI/LARKSPUR RECORDS**, Box 1001, Soquel CA 95073. A&R Director: Jon Hutchings. Produces rock and roll. Recent releases: "Heat From a Distant Fire" by Mars Wildfire and "She Lies" by Capco.
Needs: Produces 4-8 groups/year. Works with 4-8 visual artists/year. Uses artists for album cover design.
First Contact & Terms: Send query letter with brochure or resume and samples. Samples are filed. Samples not filed are returned by SASE only if requested. Reports back within 2 months. Write to schedule an appointment to show a portfolio. Pays by the project per commission. Considers complexity of project, available budget, skill and experience of artist, how work will be used, turnaround time and rights purchased when establishing payment. Buys one-time rights or negotiates rights purchased.

***LANA RECORDS/FUTURISTIC MARKETING**, Box 12444, Fresno CA 93777-2444. (209)442-3332. Director: Robby Roberson. Produces rock and roll, classical, disco, soul, country/western, jazz, folk, pop, educational, rhythm and blues, group and solo artists. Recent releases: "There" by Oh Lamour and "Has It All Ended" by Rick Holley.
Needs: Produces 5 soloists and 5 groups/year. Prefers at least 2 years of experience or past credits. Uses artists for album cover, brochure and catalog design and illustration, catalog layout, direct mail packages, advertising design and illustration and posters.
First Contact & Terms: Send query letter with resume and photocopies. Samples are filed. Samples not filed are returned by SASE. Reports back within 2 weeks. Write to schedule an appointment to show a portfolio or mail Photostats. Pays by the project, $50. Considers complexity of project and rights purchased when establishing payment. Buys all rights.
Tips: "Be honest about what you are capable of doing."

LEMATT MUSIC LTD./Pogo Records Ltd./Swoop Records/Grenouille Records/Zarg/R.T.F.M. Records-Check Records/Lee Music Ltd., % Stewart House, Hill Bottom Rd., Sands, IND, EST, Highwycombe, Buckinghamshire, 0494-36301/36401 England. Manager, Director: Ron Lee. Produces rock and roll, disco, country/western, pop, and rhythm and blues; group and solo artists. Recent releases "American Girl" by Hush; "Children Of The Night" by Nightmare; and "Phobias" by Orphan.
Needs: Produces 25 records/year; works with 12 groups and 6 soloists/year. Works with 1-2 visual artists/year. Works on assignment only. Uses a few cartoons and humorous and cartoon-style illustrations where applicable. Uses artists for album cover design and illustration; advertising design, illustration and layout; and posters.
First Contact & Terms: Send query letter with brochure, resume, business card, slides, photographs and videos to be kept on file. Samples not filed are returned by SASE (nonresidents send IRCs). Reports within 3 weeks. To show a portfolio, mail appropriate materials, which should include original/final art, final reproduction/product and photographs. Original artwork sometimes returned to artist. Considers complexity of project, available budget, skill and experience of artist, how work will be used and turnaround time when establishing payment.

***LITTLE RICHIE JOHNSON AGENCY**, Box 3, Belen NM 87002. (505)864-7442. Owner: Little Richie Johnson. Produces country/western records.
Needs: Produces 6-7 soloists/year. Works on assignment only. Uses artists for album cover design and advertising design.
First Contact & Terms: Send query letter with brochure showing art style or samples. Samples are not filed. Samples not filed are returned by SASE only if requested. Reports back only if interested. Writes to schedule an appointment to show a portfolio, or mail original/final art and final reproduction/product. Pays by the project, $500 minimum. Considers complexity of project and available budget when establishing payment. Negotiates rights purchased.

LOCONTO PRODUCTIONS, 7766 N.W. 44th St., Sunrise FL 33321. (305)741-7766. Executive Vice President: Phyllis Finney Loconto. Produces rock and roll, classical, disco, soul, country/western, jazz, folk, pop, educational, and rhythm and blues; group and solo artists. Recent releases: "Barber Shop Quartet," by Suntones; "Drama/Keyboard," by Irving Fields; and "Jamming-Country," by Bascom "Bill" Dillon.
Needs: Works with 10 visual artists/year. Works on assignment only. Uses artists for album cover design and illustration; brochure, catalog and advertising design, illustration and layout; direct mail packages; and posters.
First Contact & Terms: Send business card. Pays by the project. Considers available budget when establishing payment. Negotiates rights purchased.

LONGHORN RECORDS, Box 1995, Studio City CA 91604. (213)656-0574. Contact: Harvey Appell. Produces country/western and folk records by solo and group artists. Recent releases: "Country Music High" by River Road Boy; "Sheets of Fire" by Bobby Bonchers; and "Take Me Home" by the Mulligans.
Needs: Produces 12 records/year. Works with 2-3 visual artists/year. Works on assignment only. Uses artists for album cover design and illustration, brochure illustration, catalog design, illustration and layout and posters.
First Contact & Terms: Send query letter with brochure showing art style or slides, Photostats, photographs, photocopies or tear sheets. Call for appointment to show portfolio. Samples not filed are returned by SASE. Reports only if interested. To show a portfolio, mail appropriate materials or write to schedule an appointment; portfolio should include original/final art, final reproduction/product, photographs and b&w. Pays by the project. Considers available budget when establishing payment. Purchases all rights.

LUCIFER RECORDS, INC., Box 263, Brigantine NJ 08203. (609)266-2623. President: Ron Luciano. Produces pop, disco, and rock and roll.
Needs: Produces 2-12 records/year. Experienced artists only. Works on assignment only. Uses artists for album cover design; brochure design, illustration and layout; catalog design, direct mail packages, advertising layout design, illustration and posters.
First Contact & Terms: Send query letter with resume, business card, tear sheets, Photostats or photocopies. Reports only if interested. Original art sometimes returned to artist. Write to show a portfolio or mail tear sheets and Photostats. Pays by the project. Considers budget, how work will be used, rights purchased and the assignment when establishing payment. Negotiates pay and rights purchased.

LEE MAGID c/o GRASS ROOTS PRODUCTIONS, Box 532, Malibu CA 90265. (213)858-7282. President: Lee Magid. Produces jazz, rock, country, blues, instrumental, gospel, classical, folk, educational, pop and reggae; group and solo artists. Recent releases: "Hear Me Now," and "Again," by Ernie Andrews; "On The Streets Again," and "Live," by Rags Waldorf; and "Have Horns, Will Travel," by Russ Gary Big Band Express. Assigns 15 jobs/year.
Needs: Produces 15-20 records/year; works with 6 soloists and 6 groups/year. Local artists only. Works on assignment only. Uses artists for album cover design and illustration; brochure design, illustration and layout; catalog design, direct mail packages, posters and advertising illustration. Sometimes uses cartoons and humorous and cartoon-style illustrations depending on project.
First Contact & Terms: Send query letter with brochure, resume, and slides to be kept on file. SASE. Samples not filed are returned by SASE. Reports only if interested. Write for appointment to show portfolio. Pays by the project. Considers available budget when establishing payment. Buys all rights.
Tips: "It's important for the artist to work closely with the producer, to coincide the feeling of the album, rather than throwing a piece of art against the wrong sound." Artists shouldn't "get overly progressive. 'Commercial' is the name of the game."

MAJEGA RECORDS/PRODUCTIONS, 240 E. Radcliffe Dr., Claremont CA 91711. (714)624-0677. President: Gary K. Buckley. Produces country and pop records, audiovisual presentations; i.e., film-

strips, slide/sound sync and multimedia programs. Recent releases: "Steppin Out," by The Gospelmen; and "Sending a Copy Home," by Jody Barry; and "Sky's the Limit," by Michael Noll.
Needs: Produces about 6 records/year; 4 of which have covers/jackets designed and illustrated by freelance artists. Works on assignment only. Uses artists for album covers, ad illustrations, logo designs, cartoons, charts & graphs and other promotional materials.
First Contact & Terms: Send query letter with resume, brochure, flyer and samples (2-3 tear sheets of varied styles if possible) to be kept on file for future assignments. "Samples provided should be relevant to type of work requested." Samples returned by SASE. Reports back on future assignment possibilities. Negotiates pay according to complexity of project and available budget.
Tips: "Look at existing covers and be conscious of the style of music inside. This will illustrate what the industry is accepting and give the artist a solid base to start creating from."

***MASON RIDGE RECORDS**, Box 95841, Seattle WA 98145. (206)282-7860. A&R: Laurie Benezra. Estab. 1985. Produces classical and solo artists. Recent releases: "Time Alone" album by David Templeton.
Needs: Produces 1 soloist and 1 group/year. Works with 4 visual artists/year. Uses artists for album cover design and illustration, catalog layout and posters.
First Contact & Terms: Send query letter with tear sheets. Samples are filed. Samples not filed are returned only if requested. Reports back only if interested. Write to schedule an appointment to show a portfolio, which should include color, tear sheets and Photostats. Pays by the project. Considers available budget and skills and experience of artist when establishing payment. Buys all rights.
Tips: "We're a new company and extremely approachable."

***MASTER-TRAK ENTERPRISES**, 413 N. Parkerson Ave., Crowley LA 70526. (318)783-1601. General Manager: Mark Miller. Produces rock and roll, disco, soul, country/western, rhythm and blues, and Cajun French. Past clients: John Fogerty and Paul Simon.
Needs: Produces 15-20 records/year; 75% of the album covers were assigned to freelance designers, 25% to freelance illustrators. Uses artists for album cover design and illustration. Accepts various themes and styles.
First Contact & Terms: Send samples to be kept on file for possible future assignment; submit portfolio for review. Prefers variety of samples. Samples not returned. Reports within 5 weeks. Negotiates payment by the project. Considers available budget, and skill and experience of commercial artist when establishing payment. Buys one-time rights or negotiates.
Tips: There is a "present increase in use of artists. Would like to see sketches of phonographs. Submit work related to country, blues, rock and Cajun music."

MIRROR RECORDS INC; HOUSE OF GUITARS BLVD., 645 Titus Ave., Rochester NY 14617. (716)544-3500. Art Director: Armand Schaubroeck. Produces rock and roll, Heavy Metal, middle of the road and New Wave music. Recent releases: "Over the Rainbow," by Don Potter; "Here Are the Chesterfield Kings" and "I Shot My Guardian Angel," by Armand Schaubroeck Steals; "The Village Churchmice"; and "The Chesterfield"; "Stop," by the Kings.
Needs: Produces 4 records/year; all of which have cover/jackets designed and illustrated by freelance artists. Uses artists for catalogs, album covers, inner sleeves and advertising designs. "Always looking for new talent."
First Contact & Terms: Send query letter with brochure showing art style and samples. SASE. Reports within 1 month. Negotiates pay based on amount of creativity required, artist's previous experience, amount of time and artist expense.

MONTICANA RECORDS, Box 702, Snowdon Station, Montreal, Quebec H3X 3X8 Canada. General Manager: D. Leonard. Produces rock and roll, disco, soul, country/western, pop, educational and rhythm and blues.
Needs: Works with 4 freelance artists/year. Uses artists for album cover, brochure, catalog, advertising design; album cover, catalog, advertising illustration; brochure, catalog, advertising layout; and posters.
First Contact & Terms: Send query letter with brochure, resume, business card, Photostats, slides, photographs and tear sheets. Samples not returned. Reports only if interested. Originals not returned to artist after job's completion. Pays by the hour, $5-20 average; by the project, $75-300 average. Considers complexity of project, available budget and skill and experience of artist when establishing payment. Buys all rights.

MOTOWN RECORD CORP., Graphics Dept., 17th Floor, 6255 Sunset Blvd., Los Angeles CA 90028. (213)468-3500. Art Director: Johnny Lee. Produces rock and roll, soul, pop, and rhythm and blues. Recent releases: "Dancing on the Ceiling," by Lionel Richie; "The Return of Bruno" by Bruce

Willis; and "Skin on Skin," by Vanity.
Needs: Produces 50 records/year. Works with 30 freelance artists/year. Works on assignment. Uses artists for album cover, catalog and advertising design and illustration; catalog and advertising layout and posters.
First Contact & Terms: Send brochure, slides, photographs and tear sheets to be kept on file. Samples not kept on file returned by SASE. Reports only if interested. Write for appointment to show portfolio. Originals returned after job's completion. Pay depends on the project. Considers complexity of project, available budget and how work will be used when establishing payment. Buys one-time rights.

***M S B RECORDS, LTD.**2424 E. 12th St., Brooklyn NY 11235. (718)646-8969. President: Mark Berry. Produces rock and roll and pop dance. Recent releases "Love an Adventure" by Psuedo Echo and "Alisha" by Alisha.
Needs: Produces 2 soloists and 2 groups/year. Works with 2 visual artists/year. Uses artists for album cover and advertising design and logos.
First Contact & Terms: Send query letter with brochure. Samples are filed. Samples not filed are not returned. Reports back only if interested. Call to schedule an appointment to show a portfolio. Pays by the project, $500 minimum. Considers complexity of project and available budget when establishing payment. Negotiates rights purchased.

MUSIC AND ARTS PROGRAMS OF AMERICA, INC., Box 771, Berkeley CA 94701. (415)525-4583. Associate Producer: Mark Freeman. Estab. 1985. Record publisher. Produces record jacket graphics, catalog design and layout for wholesale, retail and mail order purchasers.
First Contact & Terms: Send resume and photocopies. Samples not filed are returned by SASE. Reports only if interested. Call or write to schedule an appointment to show a portfolio, which should include original/final art and final reproduction/product. Pays for design by the hour, $15 minimum. Pays for illustrations by the hour, $15 minimum. Considers complexity of project, client's budget and skill and experience of artist when establishing payment.
Tips: "This is a small nonprofit organization. We can offer national and international exposure plus an environment open to innovation and creativity. It is a good place for a talented but lesser-known artist to create published work."

MYSTIC OAK RECORDS, 1727 Elm St., Bethlehem PA 18017. (215)865-1083. Project Coordinator: Bill Byron. Produces rock and roll, classical, folk, pop, educational, New Wave and experimental. Recent releases: "Dreams," by Office Toys; "I Don't Lie," by the Polygraphs; and "Workin," by the Trendsetters.
Needs: Produces 10-20 records/year by 6 groups and 4 soloists. Works with 6-12 freelance artists/year. Uses artists for album cover, brochure, and advertising design and illustration; and posters.
First Contact & Terms: Send query letter with resume, slides, photographs and tear sheets to be kept on file. Prefers original work as samples. Reports only if interested. Returns original artwork after job's completion if requested. To show a portfolio, mail appropriate materials, which should include final reproduction/product, color, tear sheets and photographs. Pays by the project, $100-1,200 average. Considers complexity of project, available budget and how work will be used when establishing payment. Negotiates rights purchased.
Tips: Especially looks for a "developed style that can be used throughout a recording artist's career to identify and separate his work from others. Present a professional package." In the field, there is "more use of freelancers to minimize costs. Art is becoming more experimental and animated."

***NEAT RECORDS (D.W.E. LTD.)**, 71 High St. E, Wallsend NE28 7RJ England. A&R Director: Richard Denton. Produces rock and roll, and pop. Recent releases: "All For One," by Raven; and "At War with Satan," by Venom.
Needs: Produces 10 records/year. Works with 2-3 visual artists/year. Uses artists for album cover design and illustration, and posters.
First Contact & Terms: Send query letter with samples to be kept on file. Prefers examples of printed sleeves, not originals, as samples. Samples not filed are not returned. Reports only if interested. No originals returned to artist after job's completion. Negotiates fees. Considers complexity of project when establishing payment. Negotiates rights purchased.

***NEW DIXIE RECORDS**,Box 524, White House, TN 37188. (615)643-7721. President: Kenny Brent. Estab. 1986. Produces country/western records.
Needs: Works with 1-2 visual artists/year. Uses freelance artists for album cover design and illustration; flyers and posters.
First Contact & Terms: Send query letter with resume and samples. Samples are filed. Samples not

filed are not returned. Reports back within 7 days. Call or write to show a portfolio. Payment varies. Considers complexity of project, available budget and skills of artist when establishing payment for freelance work.

NEW ENGLAND ("HANK THE DRIFTER") HITS, Drawer 520, Stafford TX 77477. Produces country and western cassettes, albums, 45s and 8-track tapes.
Needs: Uses artists for record album and jacket design. Considers skill and experience of commercial artist when establishing payment. Send postage for reply and return of material.

NISE PRODUCTIONS INC., 413 Cooper St., Camden NJ 08102. (609)963-3190. General Manager: Sandy Perchetti. Head of A&R: Dan McKeown. Produces rock and roll, disco, soul, country/western, educational, and rhythm and blues; group and solo artists. A&R; also Production Offices for Power Up Records, distributed nationally by Sutra, New York NY.
Needs: Produces 20 records/year; works with 4 recording artists/year. Works with 2 visual artists/year. Uses artists for album cover design and illustration, brochure design, illustration and layout.
First Contact & Terms: Works on assignment only. Send query letter with samples to be kept on file. Write for appointment to show portfolio. Samples not filed are returned by SASE. Reports within 2 weeks. Pays by job. Considers available budget when establishing payment. Purchases all rights.

***ORANGE RECORDS**, Suite 1103, 150 Fifth Ave., New York NY 10011. Contact: Bruce E. Colfin. Produces rock and roll and rhythm and blues.
Needs: Produces 1 soloist and 2 groups/year. Works with 1-3 visual artists/year. Uses artists for album cover design and illustration.
First Contact & Terms: Send query letter with brochure or resume and samples. Samples are filed. Samples not filed are returned by SASE. Reports back within 3 weeks. Considers complexity of project, available budget, skills and experience of artist and rights purchased when establishing payment.

***ORBIT RECORDS**, Box 120675, Nashville TN 37212. (615)255-1068. Owner: Ray McGinnis. Produces rock and roll and country/western. Recent releases: "Rock-A-Bye Baby" by Sonny Martin; "It's So Easy" by Billy Burnett; and "Rainy Night in Georgia" by Kenny Wilson.
Needs: Produces 8 soloists and 2 groups/year. Works on assignment only. Uses artists for album cover design and illustration.
First Contact & Terms: Send query letter with resume and samples. Samples are filed. Samples not filed are returned by SASE only if requested. Reports back within 1 month only if interested. Write to show a portfolio or mail appropriate materials. Pays by the project. Considers complexity of project when establishing payment.

***ORIGINAL CAST RECORDS; BROADWAY/HOLLYWOOD VIDEO PRODUCTIONS**, Box 10051, Beverly Hills CA 90213. (213)761-2646. Executive Producer: Doris Chu. Produces educational and original cast musicals, children's shows, operettas, videotapes and movies. Recent releases: "Piano Bar," with Kelly Bishop, "Nefertiti," "Christy," by various artists.
Needs: Produces 10 records/year; all of which have cover/jackets designed and illustrated by freelance artists. Interested in musical poster art style, realistic styles, graphic designs, etc. Looking for artists with costume design, set design experience. Uses artists for record album design, insert designs, album illustrations and graphics, brochure design, video production design, print ad design and illustrations.
First Contact & Terms: Send brochure or materials that can be kept on file for future reference. SASE. Reports in 1 month or when assignment becomes available. Negotiates pay based on amount of creativity required and artist's previous experience/reputation "and also set fee/job of $1-75 for cover design and execution including paste-up; up to $150 for album cover front and back." Contact Doris Chu for information regarding internship of 6+ weeks.

***OUR GANG ENTERTAINMENT, INC.**, 33227 Lake Shore Blvd., Eastlake OH 44094. Art Director: Linda L. Lindeman. Produces rock and roll, jazz, pop, educational, rhythm and blues, exercise albums and promotional advertising discs. Recent releases: "All For You," by Link; "Dancersize," by Carol Hensel, and "Vintage Gold," collections of masters.
Needs: Produces 10 records/year. Assigns 50-75 freelance jobs/year. Uses artists for album cover, poster, brochure and advertising design and illustration; brochure and advertising layout, and direct mail packages. Theme depends on nature of the job; "we often use airbrush illustrations, line drawings of exercise positions and routines." Especially needs illustrations of human features and positions.
First Contact & Terms: Artist must show ability to produce. Send query letter with resume and samples; call or write for appointment, submit portfolio for review. Prefers Photostats, slides or originals as samples. Samples returned. Reports in 2 weeks. Works on assignment only. Provide resume and sam-

ples to be kept on file for possible future assignments. Original work not returned to artist after job's completion. Negotiates payment. Considers available budget and turnaround time when establishing payment. Buys all rights.
Tips: "We have a need for logo design; abstract and old fashioned designs are becoming a trend."

***PALACE RECORDS INC.**,2464 El Camino Real, Santa Clara CA 95051. (408)980-7257. President Michael Lindsay. Produces rock and roll, group and solo artists. "Shining Knight" by Graham Grace.
Needs: Produces 1 soloist and 3 groups/year. Works with 2-3 visual artists/year. Uses artists for album cover design and illustration and posters.
First Contact & Terms: Send query letter with brochure or photocopies. Samples are filed. Samples not filed are returned by SASE only if requested by artist. Reports back within 10 days only if interested. Call or write to schedule an appointment to show a portfolio, which should include final reproduction/product and photographs. Pays by the project, $300-2,000. Considers complexity of project, available budget, skills and experience of artist, how work will be used, turnaround time and rights purchased when establishing payment. Negotiates rights purchased.

***PARC RECORDS, INC.**, Box 547877, Orlando FL 32854-7877. (305)299-0077. Contact: Art Director. Produces rock and roll and pop records by group and solo artists. Recent releases: "Double Trouble Live," by Molly Hatchett.
Needs: Produces 3 soloists and 3 groups/year. Uses artists for album cover design and illustration, brochure design, direct mail packages, advertising design and illustration.
First Contact & Terms: Contact only through artist's agent. Reports back only if interested. Negotiates payment. Considers available budget when establishing payment.

***PENTAGRAM RECORDS**, Box 384, Holtsville NY 11742. (516)654-8459. A&R Director: Arthur Christopher. Produces rock and roll, soul, pop, educational and rhythm and blues records.
Needs: Produces 2 soloists and 5 groups/year. Works with 2 visual artists/year. Works on assignment only. Uses artists for album cover design and illustration and advertising design.
First Contact & Terms: Send query letter. Samples are not filed. Samples not filed are not returned. Reports back within 1 month only if interested. Write to schedule an appointment to show a portfolio. Pays by the hour, $20 minimum. Considers available budget when establishing payment. Buys first rights.
Tips: Artist "must write to see if we are accepting work—SASE postcard preferred."

***PINK STREET RECORDS, INC.**, Box 694, Highland Park IL 60035. (312)831-4162. Vice President: Charles Altholz. Estab. 1985. Produces rock and roll, disco, pop by group artists and solo artists. Recent releases: "Ten-28" and "E-Motion" by Ten-28; 'I Won't Sing in My Underwear" by Illicit.
Needs: Produces 3 soloists and 3 groups/year. Works with 2 visual artists/year. Works on assignment only. Uses artists for album cover design and illustration, direct mail packages, advertising design and illustration and posters.
First Contact & Terms: Send query letter with tear sheets. Samples are filed. Reports back within 3 weeks. Write to schedule an appointment to show a portfolio, which should include roughs, final reproduction/product, color and photographs. Pays by the hour, $50 minimum. Considers complexity of project, available budget, skills and experience of artist, how work will be used, turnaround time and rights purchased when establishing payment. Negotiates rights purchased.
Tips: Looks for "an understanding of promotion and advertising principles applied to make a clear, simple impact visually. Include hot, exciting finished work in your portfolio.

***PLANKTON RECORDS**, 236 Sebert Rd., Forest Gate, London E7 ONP England. (01)534-8500. Senior Partner: Simon Law. Produces rock and roll, rhythm and blues, group artists, solo artists, funk and gospel. Recent releases: "Never Surrender" by The Really Free Band; "Distance Grows" by Pete Ward and "Way Past Bedtime" by Solid Air.
Needs: Produces 2 soloists and 2 groups/year. Works with "in house artists" and 1 freelance artist/year. "We usually work with a freelance visual artist if he or she is connected with and sympathetic to the recording artist." Works on assignment only. Uses artists for album cover design and illustration.
First Contact & Terms: Send query letter with brochure. Samples not filed are returned by SASE and IRC's. Reports back within 2 months. Pays by the project, $75-150. Considers available budget when establishing payment. Buys reprint rights. "All the products that we release have a Christian bias, regardless of musical style. This should be borne in mind before making an approach."

POLKA TOWNE, 211 Post Ave., Westbury NY 11590. President: Teresa Zapolska. Produces polka records. Recent releases: "Dances of Poland," by Ted Maksymowicz Orchestra; "Jedzie Boat," by Frank Wojnarowski Orchestra; "Merry Christmas—Polish Carols," by Aria Choir; "I'm Proud To Be Polish"

and "We're The Girls" by Teresa Zapolska Orchestra; newest: "Live, Love, Laugh" Teresa Zapolska All Girl Orch. Plus One.
Needs: Works on assignment only. Uses freelance artists for album cover design and illustration; uses 4-color covers.
First Contact & Terms: Send query letter with pertinent samples to be kept on file for possible future assignments; "no Photostats." Samples must apply to the polka area only. Reply and samples returned by SASE. Reports within 6 weeks. To show a portfolio, mail final reproduction/product. Original work not returned to artist after job's completion. Negotiates flat fee. Buys all rights.

***PRESIDENT RECORDS LIMITED**, Broadmead House, 21 Panton St., London SW1Y 4DR England (01)839-4672. General Manager: David Kassner. Produces rock and roll, disco, soul, country/western, jazz, folk, pop, rhythm and blues, group artists and solo artists. Recent releases: "Automatic" by Jack Bruce; "Hometown Girls" by Denny Laine and "Crimes of Passion Soundtrack" by Rick Wakeman.
Needs: Produces variable amount of records/year. Works on assignment only. Uses artists for album cover, catalog and advertising design and posters.
First Contact & Terms: Send query letter with brochure. Samples are not filed. Samples not filed are returned by SASE only if requested. Reports back within 1 month. Call for an appointment to show a portfolio. Pays by the project; "subject to negotiation." Considers available budget, skills and experience of artist, turnaround time and rights purchased when establishing payment. Buys all rights.

***PUBLIC RECORDS**, #17B, 101 W. 79th, New York NY 10024. (212)724-0210. President: Walter Skallerup. Produces rock and roll, disco, soul, pop, rhythm and blues, group and solo artits and rap. Recent releases: "My Telephone" by Mikey D. & The L.A. Posse; "Extravagant Girls" by Symbolic Three; and "Concrete Island" by Cargo Cult.
Needs: Produces 3 soloists and 3 groups/year. Works with 2 visual artists/year. Works on assignment only. Uses artists for album cover design and illustration.
First Contact & Terms: Send query letter with resume and samples. Samples not filed are returned only if requested. Reports back only if interested. Call or write to show a portolio. Pays by the hour, $5 minimum. Considers complexity of project and available budget when establishing payment. Negotiates rights purchased.

R.E.F. RECORDING CO./FRICK MUSIC PUBLISHING CO., 404 Bluegrass Ave., Madison TN 37115. (615)865-6380. Contact: Bob Frick. Produces country/western and gospel. Recent releases: "I Love You In Jesus" and "Headin For Heaven" by Bob Scott Frick; "Unworthy" by Bob Myers.
Needs: Produces 10 records/year; works with 3 artists/year. Works on assignment only.
First Contact & Terms: Send resume and photocopies to be kept on file. Write for appointment to show portfolio. Samples not filed are returned by SASE. Reports within 10 days only if interested.

***RA-JO-RECORDS/ACE ADAMS MUSIC—BMI**, 100-19 Alcott Pl. 191, New York NY 10475. (212)379-2593. A&R Dept.: Adam Puertas. Recent releases: "Mr. Harvey" by Harvey Fouchia and "I'm So In Love Tonight" by the Heptones.
Needs: Produces soloists and groups. Works with artists. Works on assignment. Uses artists for album cover design and illustration, brochure design and posters.
First Contact & Terms: Send query letter with resume and tear sheets. Samples not filed are returned by SASE. Reports back within 3 weeks. Write to schedule an appointment to show a portfolio or mail color. Pays by the project, $1,000-5,000. Considers how work will be used when establishing payment. Negotiates rights purchased.

RANDALL PRODUCTIONS, Box 11960, Chicago IL 60611-0960. (312)561-0027. President/Director: Mary Freeman. Produces rock and roll, soul, country/western, pop, gospel, and rhythm and blues. Recent releases: "I Wanna Be With You," by Mickey Dee; "Why Do You Do Me Like You Do", by Emmett Beard (single), and "Someday You'll Be Runnin' To Me/Let Me Know, Let It Go" by Cabela/Schmitt.
Needs: Produces 10-12 records/year. Works with 5 freelance artists/year. Uses artists for album cover, brochure, catalog and advertising design; photography; video; and posters.
First Contact & Terms: Send query letter with brochure showing art style or original work and photographs to be kept on file. Samples not kept on file are returned by SASE if requested. Reports within 2 weeks. Pays by the project, $5-200 average. Considers complexity of project and available budget when establishing payment.
Tips: "We live in an age of identity, where the most liked are the least conservative."

RAVEN RECORDS, 1918 Wise Dr., Dothan AL 36303. (205)793-1329. President: Jerry Wise. Vice President: Steve Clayton. Produces rock and roll, soul, country/western, pop, and rhythm and blues.

Needs: Produces 5-10 records/year. Works with 2 freelance artists/year. "Most of our artists work on a speculation basis." Uses artists for album cover and brochure design.
First Contact & Terms: Send query letter with brochure and "a combination of original work and photographs" to be kept on file. Samples not kept on file returned by SASE. Reports within 30 days. Originals not returned to artist after job's completion. Call for appointment to show portfolio. Pays by the project, $25-500 average. Considers available budget, turnaround time and rights purchased when establishing payment. Buys all rights.

***RED BUS RECORDS (INT'L) LTD.**, Red Bus House, 48 Broadway Terrace, London NW1 England. 44-01-258-0324. Contact: Ellis Elias. Produces rock and roll, disco, soul, pop and rhythm and blues. Recent releases: "Changes," by Imagination; and "Brian Johnson," by Brian Johnson.
Needs: Produces 20 records/year. Works with 4 freelance artists/year. Uses artists for album cover and brochure design, and posters.
First Contact & Terms: Send samples to be kept on file. Prefers Photostats or photographs as samples. Samples not kept on file are returned by SASE. Reports within 21 days. Works on assignment only. Write for appointment to show portfolio. No originals returned to artist after job's completion. Pays by the project, $300 minimum. Considers complexity of project, and skill and experience of artist when establishing payment. Buys all rights.

***REDWOOD RECORDS**, 476 W. MacArthur Blvd., Oakland CA 94609. (415)428-9191. Advertising Manager: Shelly Lowe. Produces jazz, folk, pop, rhythm and blues and Latin American records by group and solo artists.
Needs: Prefers local artists and those with experience in music industry-related project. Works on assignment only. Uses freelance visual artists for album cover illustration, brochure and advertising design and illustration, catalog design, illustration and layout, direct mail packages and posters.
First Contact & Terms: Send query letter with brochure showing art style or resume and samples. Samples are filed. Samples not filed are returned by SASE only if requested by artist. Reports back within 2-3 weeks. Bring a portfolio to show original/final art in person. Negotiates payment. Considers available budget, skills and experience of artist, turnaround time and rights purchased when establishing payment. Buys all rights.

***RELATIVITY RECORDS**, 149-03 Guy R. Brewer Blvd., Jamaica NY 11434. (718)995-9200. Production Manager: Joe Leonard. Produces rock and roll, jazz, pop, solo artists and heavy metal. Recent releases: "Immaculate Deception" by Ludichrist and "Element of Light" by Robyn Hitchcock.
Needs: Works on assignment only. Uses artists for album cover, brochure, catalog design, illustration and layout, advertising design and illustration and posters.
First Contact & Terms: Send resume and color Photostats. Samples are not filed. Samples are not returned. Reports back only if interested. Call or write to show a portfolio, which should include final reproduction/product, color, b&w, tear sheets, Photostats and photographs. Pays by the project, $100-1,500. Considers complexity of project, available budget and rights purchased when establishing payment. Buys all rights.
Tips: "We seek creative young people with imagination."

***RELIX RECORDS**, Box 92, Brooklyn NY 11229. (718)258-0009. Vice President: Toni A. Brown. Produces rock and roll, country/western, folk, rhythm and blues, group and solo artists. Recent releases: "Vintage NRPS" by New Riders and "QUAH" by Jorma Kauknen.
Needs: Produces 2-5 solosists and 5-10 groups/year. Works with 305 visual artists/year. Works on assignment only. uses artists for album cover illustration, poster and *Relix Magazine* illustrations.
First Contact & Terms: Send query letter with Photostats. Samples are not filed. Samples are returned by SASE. Reports back only if interested. To show a portfolio, mail final reproduction/product, color, b&w and Photostats. Pays by the project, $15 minimum. Considers available budget and how work will be used when establishing payment. Negotiates rights purchased.
Tips: "Relix has a magazine as well as a record company. The magazine is likely to use much art (b&w especially). Specialty is '60s San Francisco/Grateful Dead."

REVONAH RECORDS, Box 217, Ferndale NY 12734. (914)292-5965. Contact: Paul Gerry. Produces country/western and bluegrass.
Needs: Produces 6-10 records/year. Works with 3-4 freelance artists/year. "Work must be of a professional grade." Works on assignment only. Uses artists for album cover design.
First Contact & Terms: Send query letter with slides or actual work to be kept on file. Samples not filed are returned by SASE. Reports within 1 month. Call or write for appointment to show portfolio. Return of original artwork after job's completion "can be negotiated." Pays by the project, $75-250 average. Considers complexity of project, available budget, skill and experience of artist, how work will be used, turnaround time and rights purchased when establishing payment. Buys all rights.

RHYTHMS PRODUCTIONS, Whitney Bldg., Box 34485, Los Angeles CA 90034. (213)836-4678. President: R.S. White. Record and book publisher for children's market.
Needs: Works on assignment only. Prefers California artists. Produces 12 records and cassettes/year; all of which have cover/jackets designed and illustrated by freelance artists. Works with 3 visual artists/year. Uses artists for catalog covers/illustrations, direct mail brochures, layout, magazine ads, multimedia kits, paste-up, album design and book illustration. Artists must have a style that appeals to children.
First Contact & Terms: Buys 3-4 designs/year. Send query letter with brochure, resume and samples. Accepts any type sample. SASE. Reports within 3 weeks. Buys all rights on a work-for-hire basis.

***RIPSAW RECORDS**, Suite 805, 4545 Connecticut Ave. NW, Washington DC 20008. (202)362-2286. President: Jonathan Strong. Produces rockabilly, rock and roll, and country/western. Recent releases: "Wanted: True Rock 'n' Roll" by Billy Hancock and "Two Sides" by Bobby Smith.
Needs: Produces 1-2 groups/year. Works with 1-4 visual artists/year. Works on assignment only. Uses artists for album cover design and illustration, posters and flyers.
First Contact & Terms: Send query letter with samples. Samples not filed are returned by SASE only. Reports back within 2-3 weeks if SASE included. Write to schedule an appointment to show a portfolio, which may include color, b&w and photographs. Payment varies. Considers complexity of project and available budget when establishing payment. Buys all rights.

ROBBINS RECORDS, INC., HC80, Box 5B, Leesville LA 71446. National Representative: Sheree Stephens. Produces country/western and religious. Recent releases: "Jesus Amazes Me," "Wait Till You See My Miracle Home," and "Since I've Had A Change of Heart" by Sheree Stephens.
Needs: Produces various number of records/year. Works with various number of freelance artists/year. Works on assignment only. Uses artists for album cover design and posters.
First Contact and Terms: Send brochure to be kept on file. Reports only if interested. Originals not returned to artist after job's completion. Write for appointment to show portfolio. Pays by the project. Considers skill and experience of artist, how work will be used and rights purchased when establishing payment. Buys all rights.

***ROCKLAND MUSIC, INC.**, 117 W. Rockland, Box 615, Libertyville IL 60048. (312)362-4060. Contact: Perry Johnson. Estab. 1985. Produces rock and roll, country/western, pop, educational and rhythm and blues records by group and solo artists. Recent releases: "This Feels Like Love to Me," by Sacha Distel; "Honeybear Rap," by Honeybears and "Hooper's Active Music for Children," by Bill Hooper.
Needs: Produces 10 soloists and 5 groups/year. Works with 3 visual artists/year. Uses artists for album cover design and illustration, brochure design and posters.
First Contact & Terms: Send query letter with brochure showing art style or resume and samples. Samples are filed. Samples not filed are returned by SASE only if requested. Reports back only if requested. Write to schedule an appointment to show a portfolio. Negotiates payment. Considers complexity of project, available budget, skills and experience of artist when establishing payment.
Tips: "Call or write first to see what our needs at the time are."

***SIRR RODD RECORD & PUBLISHING COMPANY**, Box 58116, Philadelphia PA 19102-8116. President: Rodney J. Keitt. Estab. 1985. Produces disco, soul, jazz, pop, rhythm and blues, group and solo artists. Recent releases: "Fashion & West Oak Lane Jam" by Klassy K and "The Essence of Love/Ghetto Jazz" by Rodney Jerome Keitt.
Needs: Produces 2 soloists and 3 groups/year. Works with 1 visual artist/year. Works on assignment only. Uses artists for album design and illustration, direct mail packages, advertising design and illustration and posters.
First Contact & Terms: Send query letter with resume, Photostats, photocopies and slides. Samples are filed. Samples not filed are not returned. Reports back within 2 months. Write to show a portfolio, which should include thumbnails, roughs, final reproduction/product, color, Photostats and photographs. Pays by the project, $100-3,500. Considers available budget, skills and experience of artist, how work will be used and rights purchased when establishing payment. Buys reprint rights or negotiates rights purchased.
Tips: "Treat every project as though it was a major project. Always request comments and criticism of your work."

The asterisk before a listing indicates that the listing is new in this edition. New markets are often the most receptive to freelance submissions.

SONIC WAVE RECORDS, c/o Kiderian Records, 4926 W. Gunnison, Chicago IL 60630. (312)764-1144. President: Tom Petreli. Produces rock and roll, rhythm and blues, and New Wave. Recent releases: "New Wave Sampler," by Tom Petreli.

Needs: Produces 5-10 records/year. Assigns all jobs/year to freelance artists. Uses artists for album cover, poster, brochure, catalog and advertising design; and direct mail packages. Prefers "outrageous" covers.

First Contact & Terms: Send resume, tear sheets, Photostats, slides. Reports within 1 month. Samples not kept on file are returned by SASE. Original work returned to artist after job's completion. Negotiates payment. Buys reprint rights.

***SOUNDS OF WINCHESTER**, Box 116-H, Berkley Springs WV 25411. (703)667-9379. Contact: Jim McCoy. Produces rock and roll, country/western and gospel. Recent releases: "Mr. Blue Grass," by Carroll County Ramblers; "Thank You Jesus," by Jubilee Travelers; "Going With Jesus," by Middleburg Harmonizers; and "The Outlaw," by Alvin Kesner.

Needs: Produces 18 records/year; 40% of the album covers were assigned to freelance designers. Assigns 3-4 freelance jobs/year. Uses artists for album cover and brochure design, and direct mail packages. Accepts "all types of scenes."

First Contact & Terms: Send material to be kept on file. Prefers original work as samples. Reports only if interested. Works on assignment only; reports back whether to expect possible future assignments. Provide brochure/flyer and samples to be kept on file for possible future assignments. Original work not returned to artist after job's completion. Pays by the project. Buys one-time rights.

***SPHEMUSATIONS**, 12 Northfield Rd., One House, Stowmarket Suffolk IP14 3HE England. 0449-613388. General Manager: James Butt. Produces classical, country/western, jazz and educational records. Recent releases: "Little Boy Dances," by G. Sudbury; "The Magic of Voice & Harp," by P. Scholomowitz and Andre Back and "P. Mendel: Route 56," by Paul Mendel.

Needs: Produces 6 soloists and 6 groups/year. Works with 1 visual artist/year. Works on assignment only. Uses artists for album cover design and illustration, brochure design and illustration, catalog design and layout, direct mail packages, advertising design and illustration and posters.

First Contact & Terms: Contact through artist's agent or send query letter with resume and tear sheets, Photostats and photocopies. Samples are filed. Samples not filed are returned only if requested. Reports back within 6 weeks. Write to show a portfolio, which should include final reproduction/product, color, b&w, Photostats and photographs. Pays for illustration by the proejct, $500-2,000. Considers complexity of project, available budget, skills and experience of artist, how work will be used, turnaround time and rights purchased when establishing payment. Buys reprint rights, all rights, or negotiates rights purchased.

Tips: Looks for "economy, simplicity and directness" in artwork for album covers.

STARCREST PRODUCTIONS, 209 Circ. Hills Dr., Grand Forks ND 58201. (701)772-6831. President: George Hastings. Produces country, pop and gospel music.

Needs: Produces 5 records/year; all of which have cover/jackets designed and illustrated by freelance artists. Uses artists for jacket and brochure design, and print ad illustrations.

First Contact & Terms: Send query letter and samples. SASE. Reports in 2 months. Negotiates pay based on amount of creativity required.

STARGARD RECORDS, Box 138, Boston MA 02101. (617)296-3327. Public Affairs: Karen Thompson. Estab. 1984. Produces disco, soul, jazz, pop, rhythm and blues, hiphop and reggae; group and solo artists. Recent releases: "Pipe Dreaming" by Tow Zone and "Run Me Down" by Joe Brown.

Needs: Produces 6 singles/year by 2 groups and 1 soloist. Works with 3 visual artists/year. Expects "reasonable rates and prompt service." Works on assignment only. Uses artists for album cover and advertising design and illustration.

First Contact & Terms: Send query letter with brochure showing art style or resume, Photostats and photographs. Samples not filed are returned only if requested. Reports only if interested. To show a portfolio, mail thumbnails. Pays by the hour, $15 minimum; payment by project and day varies. Considers complexity of project and available budget when establishing payment. Negotiates rights purchased.

***STARTIME RECORDS**, Fred Rice Productions, Inc., Box 643, La Quinta CA 92253. President: Fred Rice. Produces rock and roll, country/western, middle-of-the-road, novelty and educational records. Recent releases: "Rock & Roll Baby," "Shadow In The Door" and "Let's Take A Chance on Love Again" by Rob Carter.

Needs: Produces 4 records/year; works with 4 recording artists/year. "I would produce 12 records/year if I could find hit material." Works on assignment only. Works with 2-3 visual artists/year. Uses artists for album cover design and illustration, liner art, direct mail packages, advertising design, posters and

fan club merchandising.
First Contact & Terms: Send query letter with brochure showing art style or photographs, photocopies or tear sheets to be kept on file. Samples not filed are returned by SASE. Reports within 1 month. To show a portfolio, mail appropriate materials with SASE. Pays by the project, $250 minimum. Considers available budget when establishing payment. Buys all rights. Original art is not returned to the artist.
Tips: Especially seeks "art with a new look, and exciting, provocative concepts to match music. I'm looking for single hit record songs first, then artist to record them. Then comes artwork to package product. I do not know what kind of artwork is needed until song is recorded. Take a computer graphics design course. Examine current hit album graphics in record stores, but develop your own unique style and art technique. Be original! Take a course in video techniques and graphics."

SUSAN RECORDS, Box 4740, Nashville TN 37216. (615)865-4740. Manager: Susan Neal. Produces rock and roll, disco, soul, country/western, rock-a-billy, jazz, pop, and rhythm and blues; group and solo artists. Recent release: "That's It Baby," by Dixie Dee.
Needs: Produces 15 records/year. Uses artists for album cover design and illustration; brochure design, illustration and layout; catalog design, illustration and layout; advertising design and layout.
First Contact & Terms: Send brochure, business card, SASE and photographs to be kept on file unless return requested. Samples not filed are returned by SASE. Reports within 15 days. Original art returned to the artist. Write for appointment to show portfolio. Considers available budget and rights purchased when establishing payment. Negotiates rights purchased.

3 G'S INDUSTRIES INC., 5500 Troost, Kansas City MO 64110. (816)361-8455. General Manager: Eugene Gold. Produces disco, soul, country/western, and rhythm and blues; group and solo artists. Recent releases: "Magic," and "Doin' It After Hours," by Suspension; and "Bootie Cutie," by Robert Newsome.
Needs: Produces 4 records/year. Works with 5 visual artists/year. Works on assignment only. Uses artists for album cover and advertising design, illustration and layout; and direct mail packages.
First Contact & Terms: Send photographs to be kept on file; call for appointment to show portfolio. Samples not filed are returned by SASE. Reports only if interested. Original artwork not returned to artist. Negotiates payment by the project. Considers skill and experience of artist when establishing payment. Negotiates rights purchased.

TOM THUMB MUSIC, (division of Rhythms Productions), Box 34485, Los Angeles CA 90034. (213)836-4678. President: Ruth White. Record and book publisher for children's market.
Needs: Works on assignment only. Prefers local artists with cartooning talents and animation background. Uses artists for catalog covers/illustrations, direct mail brochures, layout, magazine ads, multimedia kits, paste-up, album design and book illustration. Artists must have a style that appeals to children.
First Contact & Terms: Buys 3-4 designs/year. Send query letter with brochure showing art style or resume and tear sheets and photocopies. Samples are filed. Samples not filed are returned by SASE. Reports within 3 weeks. Pays by the project. Considers complexity of project, available budget and rights purchased when establishing payment. Buys all rights on a work for hire basis.

***RIK TINORY PRODUCTIONS**, 180 Pond St., Box 311, Cohasset MA 02025. (617)383-9494. Artist Relations: Claire Babcock. Produces rock and roll, classical, country/western, jazz, folk, pop, educational, rhythm and blues, group and solo artists. Recent releases: "Here's To You, L.A.," by Rik Tinory and "Feeling Like I'm Wanted," by Jimmy Parker.
First Contact & Terms: Pays by the project. Considers how work will be used when establishing payment. Buys all rights.
Tips: "We do not accept unsolicited material. A phone call or letter describing what the artist's intentions are is necessary. Send a SASE."

TREND® RECORDS, Box 201, Smyrna GA 30081. (404)432-2454. President: Tom Hodges. Produces soul, country, pop, rhythm and blues, middle of the road music, jazz; will consider custom releases. Recent release: "The Deer Hunter," by Dave Compton.
Needs: Produces 4 records/year by 2 groups and 2 soloists. Freelance artists design and illustrate 1 cover/jacket per year.
First Contact & Terms: Send query letter with samples. Send brochure or samples that can be kept on file for future reference. SASE. Reports in 1-3 weeks. Negotiates pay based on amount of creativity required.

TURQUOISE RECORDS, HC-84, Box 1358, Whitesburg KY 41858. (606)633-0485. Director: Pat Martin. Estab. 1985. Produces folk and bluegrass records. Recent releases include "Traditional Music

of the Future" by No Strings Attached and "Thinking of Home" by Kentucky Ramblers.
Needs: Produces 4-6 records/year by 3-4 groups and 1-2 soloists. Works with 2-3 visual artists/year. Prefers regional artists. Works on assignment only. Uses artists for album cover, brochure, and catalog design and illustrations, and direct mail packages.
First Contact & Terms: Send query letter with tear sheets and photocopies. Samples not filed are returned by SASE. Reports within 3-4 weeks. To show a portfolio, mail roughs, final reproduction/product and tear sheets. Pays by the project, $50-250. Considers complexity of project, how work will be used and turnaround time when establishing payment. Buys all rights.

TYSCOT AND CIRCLE CITY RECORDS, 3532 N. Keystone Ave., Indianapolis IN 46218. (317)923-3343. President: Leonard Scott. Produces traditional and contemporary gospel. Recent releases: "Say You Believe," by Deliverance, "You Can Count On Me," by the Fords, "Glorious Day" by Derrick Brinkley.
Needs: Produces 10 records/year by 7 groups and 3 soloists. Works with 4 freelance artists/year. Works on assignment only. Uses artists for album cover, brochure, catalog and advertising design and illustration; direct mail packages and posters. Artists are used primarily for album cover design.
First Contact & Terms: Send query letter with brochure, resume, Photostats, slides, original work or photographs to be kept on file. Samples not kept on file are returned by SASE. Reports only if interested. Originals returned to artist after job's completion. Call for appointment to show portfolio. Pays by the project. Considers available budget when establishing payment. Negotiates rights purchased.
Tips: "We are open to all artists. We look for uniqueness and quality in an artist's work, whether the art portrays what is currently in the marketplace—whether the art is marketable."

ULTRAGROOVE/ORINDA RECORDS, Box 838, Orinda CA 94563. (415)254-7600. Executive Vice President: C.J. Black. Produces classical, jazz and pop records, about 3-6 albums per month.
First Contact & Terms: Send samples and tear sheets. Samples not filed are returned only if requested. Reports only if interested. To show a portfolio, mail appropriate materials. Buys all rights.

***UPSIDE RECORDS, INC.**, Suite 1109, 225 Lafayette St., New York NY 10012. (212)925-9599. President: Barry Feldman. Estab 1985. Produces rock and roll, soul, disco, jazz, pop, rhythm and blues, group and solo artists, and new age music. Recent releases: "Be My Power Station" by Che and Fats Comet and "Well, Well, Well" by the Wondertops.
Needs: Produces 3 soloists and 5 groups/year. Works with 5 visual artists/year. Designs should be based on New York City. Uses artists for album cover design and illustration, brochure design, catalog and advertising design, catalog layout and posters.
First Contact &Terms: Send brochure or resume and samples. Samples are filed. Samples not filed are returned by SASE only if requested by artist. Reports back only if interested. Call to schedule an appointment to show a portfolio. Pays by the project. Considers complexity of project, available budget and how work will be used when establishing payment. Negotiates rights purchased.
Tips: "Artists should be familiar with requirements of record industry work and have an interest and understanding of music."

***VELLA RECORDS INC.**, Box 1330, New York NY 10011. Chairman: David Vella. Estab. 1985. Produces rock and roll and disco; and 12" singles and EP's only. Recent releases: "Male Attraction" by Jahneen and "Madam Butterfly/Honcho" by David Vella.
Needs: Produces minimum of 3 soloists and 1-2 groups/year. Works with 3 artists/year. "I want to find more!" Prefers artists from New York, New Jersey or Connecticut only. "Personal contact is important. All work must be camera-ready." Uses artists for album and advertising design and illustration, posters, logo work and record labels.
First Contact & Terms: Send query letter with resume and tear sheets, Photostats and photocopies. Samples are filed. Samples not filed are returned by SASE. Reports back only if interested. "Portfolio reviewed after reviewing resume and samples; we will call." Pays by the project, $75 minimum. Considers complexity of project, available budget, turnaround time and rights purchased when establishing payment.
Tips: "Be yourself. No hype! Have vision and open-mindedness with a positive energy rate higher than experience. We look to develop on-going relationships with our artists."

VELVET PRODUCTION CO., 517 W. 57th St., Los Angeles CA 90037. (213)753-7893. Manager: Aaron Johnson. Produces soul, and rhythm and blues. Recent releases: "There Are Two Sides to Every Coin," by Arlene Bell; "I Ain't Jiving, Baby," by Chick Willis.
Needs: Produces 6 records/year. Works with 6 freelance artists/year. Experienced artists only. Works on assignment only. Uses artists for posters, album cover illustration, brochure design and catalog layout.

First Contact & Terms: Send query letter with brochure showing art style or resume, Photostats and photocopies to be kept on file. Samples not kept on file are returned by SASE. Reports only if interested. Original artwork is returned after job's completion. Write for appointment to show portfolio. Pays by the project, $50-200 average. Negotiates rights purchased.

***WESJAC RECORD ENTERPRISE**,129 W. Main St., Box 743, Lake City SC 29560. (803)394-3597. General Manager: W.R. Bragdton, Jr. Produces gospel. Recent releases: "Every Now and Then" by the Gospel Songbirds and "If Jesus Can't Fix It, Nobody Can" by the Gospel Creators.
Needs: Produces 3 records/year. Works with 1 freelance artist/year. Works on assignment only. Uses artists for album cover and advertising design; catalog layout; and posters.
First Contact & Terms: Send query letter with brochure or resume, tear sheets and photographs. Samples not returned. Reports within 3 months. Write for appointment to show portfolio, which should include roughs, original art, final reproduction/product, color, tear sheets and b&w. Original artwork is not returned after job's completion. Pays by the hour, $6-15 average; by the project, $100-200 average. Considers available budget and how work will be used when establishing payment. Buys all rights.

YATAHEY RECORDS, Box 31819, Dallas TX 75231. (214)750-0720. Art Director: C. Moran. Producer: Bart Barton. Produces country/western and gospel. Recent releases: "Catching Fire," by Angela Kaye; and "I Don't Want to Play the Cheatin' Game," by Brooks Brothers. Audie Henry LP "Gentleman", Audie Henry (singles) "Heaven Knows," "Sweet Salvation" (both top 10 Canada).
Needs: Produces 20 records/year. Uses artists for album cover and brochure design; advertising layout; and posters.
First Contact & Terms: Send query letter with business card, photographs and tear sheets to be kept on file. Samples not kept on file are returned by SASE. Reports only if interested. Original artwork is not returned after job's completion. Considers complexity of project, available budget, how work will be used and rights purchased when establishing payment. Buys all rights.

***Z-ZONE RECORDS**, Box 256577, Chicago IL 60625. President: George Peck. Estab. 1986. Produces rock and roll, classical, disco, soul, country/western, jazz, folk, pop, educational, rhythm and blues, group and solo artists. Recent releases: "Bambi" by Bambi & Z Zone and "George Peck" by George Peck.
Needs: Produces 4-5 soloists and 5-8 groups/year. Works with 1-2 visual artists/year. Uses artists for album cover, brochure and catalog design, illustration and layout, direct mail packages, advertising design and illustration and posters.
First Contact & Terms: Send query letter with photocopies and slides. Samples are filed. Samples not filed are returned by SASE only if requested by artists. Reports back only if interested. Write to schedule an appointment to show a portfolio or mail roughs, color, b&w, and photographs. Pays by the project, $400-650. Considers rights purchased when establishing payment. Buys all rights.

ZONDERVAN MUSIC GROUP, (formerly Singspiration Music Records), 365 Great Circle Rd., Nashville TN 37228. (615)742-6800. Contact: Greg Nicolson, Sue Gay or Connie Sneed. Produces religious records.
Needs: Produces 20 records/year; all have cover/jackets designed and illustrated by freelance artists. Works on assignment only. Uses artists for design and illustration of albums and jackets.
First Contact & Terms: Send query letter with photocopies of previous art to be kept on file. Reports within 2 weeks. SASE. Negotiates pay.
Tips: There is a trend toward "computer art and more airbrush; also more emphasis on lettering and type." When reviewing work looks for technique, style and up-to-date material—"no school assignment work if possible."

> ***"An effective album cover should give you something to think about, something relatable. It should have a universal vision and appeal."***
>
> ***—Jojo Mitchell, Amethyst Group West Cola, South Carolina***

Syndicates and Clip Art Firms

Syndicates and clip art firms serve as middlemen between artists and buyers. A syndicate sells cartoons and comic strips to newspapers and other outlets, and clip art firms furnish camera-ready cartoons, spot drawings and decorative art for use in newsletters, brochures and advertisements.

Syndicates seek cartoonists who can make the funny pages even funnier. Successful panels and strips are original, timely and have widespread appeal. Most syndicated cartoons have a strong central character. Jim Davis, creator of Garfield, says, "Long after readers have forgotten a gag, they remember the personality, the strength of the character." Those without a central character possess a strong theme or attitude, such as the bizarre personifications of Gary Larson's *The Far Side*.

Syndicates underwent significant changes last year. There were major acquisitions that strengthened the largest syndicates; King Features purchased Cowles and Hearst acquired News America Syndicate (now North America Syndicate). Syndicates are also affected by the dwindling number of daily newspapers. In the days when cities supported two newspapers, syndicate salesmen could play upon the intense rivalry between the two, either one not wanting a popular strip to slip away to the other to boost circulation. Now, there are only 11 cities that support two or more competitive newspapers (those with a circulation of over 100,000) and syndicates have to be more selective about the cartoons they promote. For example, Universal formerly introduced 15 or 16 new features a year, now it's nine or ten.

However, a tight market also means that syndicates are on the lookout for fresh, original material that they can heavily promote. To contact a syndicate, develop a sample package that contains a cover letter stating your background and the intent of the strip and also include at least four to six weeks of published work. If you're not published, build up your portfolio by cartooning for local papers, both dailies and weeklies. Syndicates look for artwork that is simple and straightforward. Most daily strips conform to the Standard Advertising Unit of 38.6 picas (panels are 19 picas wide). Consequently strips with too much detail become muddy when reduced. Your samples should be one-and-a-half times larger than the standard size of a daily strip. Send quality photocopies or Photostats, never originals.

Submissions go through a complicated screening process, being reviewed by a submissions editor, a comics editor, then an editorial committee. You may be offered a contract immediately, but you may still have months of developmental work ahead if the syndicate says it's interested but the strip needs a few changes. If you receive a rejection letter telling you to refine a few aspects and resubmit in a while, make sure you do so. When signing a contract, try to sell as few rights as possible.

Artists interested in approaching clip art firms should keep in mind that most firms are looking for art that appeals to a mass audience. Clip art firms usually purchase all rights for a flat fee and then send packets of camera-ready illustrations to firms that pay for the service. Syndicates, on the other hand, usually pay a flat fee or royalty, the amount depending on the number and circulation of the papers that buy the feature.

For more information, consult *Editor & Publisher Directory of Syndicated Services* for lists of syndicates and Susan Lane's *How to Make Money in Newspaper Syndication* (Newspaper Syndication Specialists) for an overview of the business.

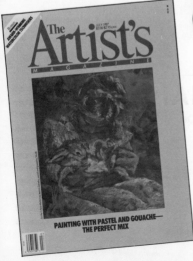

ADVENTURE FEATURE SYNDICATE, Suite 400, 329 Harvey Dr., Glendale CA 91206. (818)247-1721. Executive Editor: Orpha Harryman Barry. Syndicates to 200 newspaper and book publishers.
Needs: Buys from 20 freelance artists/year. Considers single, double and multi-panel cartoons. Prefers mystery, adventure and drama as themes. Also needs comic strips, and comic book and panel cartoonists. Works on assignment only.
First Contact & Terms: Send query letter with resume, Photostats and tear sheets to be kept on file. Samples not kept on file are returned by SASE. Reports within 30 days. Write for appointment to show portfolio. Pays 50% of gross income; on publication. Considers salability of artwork when establishing payment. Buys reprint rights; negotiates rights purchased.
Tips: "Comic strips need a four-week presentation package reduced to newspaper size."

***AMERICAN NEWSPAPER SYNDICATE**, 9 Woodrush Drive, Irvine CA 92714. (714) 559-8047. Executive Editor: Susan Smith. Syndicates to U.S. and Canadian medium and large-sized general interest and special interest newspapers.
Needs: Wants to syndicate 5 new cartoonists this year. Looking for comic strips, comic panels, editorial cartoons, illustrations, spot drawings, b&w and color. "We are particularly looking for humorous features that are fresh, contemporary and genuinely funny. We also will consider dramatic serial strip concepts that are unique and that have strong characters. We need features that can run daily and Sunday. Material should appeal to all ages, and can be on any subject."
First Contract & Terms: Send query letter with copies of 20 dailies. Samples not kept on file are returned by SASE. Please do *not* send original art. Reports within 3 weeks. Buys U.S. newspaper rights. Wants to sign contracts with cartoonists to produce material on a regular basis. Also looking for merchandising and licensing possibilities.
Tips: "We are willing to take on material that may be considered too unconventional by the other syndicates. Because of our understanding of the newspaper syndication market, we feel we can find a place for the previously unpublished cartoonists. We urge you to be fresh and original. Be yourself. Don't try to imitate other, well-known cartoonists. Develop three-dimensional characters in open-ended situations that will provide ample opportunities for comic possibilities. Ask yourself: do I *really like* these characters? Is this feature *really* funny? Would I want to read it every day? When you can honestly answer yes to these questions, you may have a feature that is a potential hit."

ARTISTS AND WRITERS SYNDICATE, 1034 National Press Building, Washington DC 20045. Vice President: David E. Steitz. Newspaper syndicate of comic features and new features serving daily and weekly publications world-wide. Buys from 2 freelance artists/year.
First Contact & Terms: Send query letter with resume and tear sheets, photocopies, and relevant newsprint background information. Samples not filed are returned by SASE. Reports within 15 days. To show a portfolio, mail tear sheets. Pays 50% of royalties or negotiates payment. Buys first rights.
Tips: "As a newspaper syndicate, we do not deal with one-time or occasional-use art. Keep submissions under six pages long and *include SASE*. Common mistakes freelancers make are: they send too many samples, write eager/overly assertive long letters and lack an understanding of how syndicates work."

***BLACK CONSCIENCE SYNDICATION, INC.**, 1 Hediger Dr., Wheatley Heights NY 11798. (516)491-7774. Director: Clyde R. Davis. Estab. 1987. Syndicate serving regional magazines, schools, daily newspapers and television.
Needs: Considers comic strips, gag cartoons, caricatures, editorial or political cartoons, illustrations and spot drawings. Prefers single, double or multi-panel cartoons. "All material must be of an importance to the Black community in America and the world." Especially needs material on gospel music and its history.
First Contact & Terms: Send query letter with resume, tear sheets and photocopies. Samples are filed. Samples not filed are returned by SASE only if requested by artist. Reports back within 2 weeks. Call to show a portfolio, which should include tear sheets. Pays 50% of gross income. Pays on publication. Considers client's preferences when establishing payment. Buys first rights.
Tips: "All material must be inspiring as well as informative. Our main search is for the truth."

B M ENTERPRISES, Box 421, Farrell PA 16121. President: William (Bill) Murray. Syndicates to 400 weekly newspapers, schools and national and regional magazines.
Needs: Buys from 12 freelance artists/year. Considers single, double and multiple panel cartoons; line and spot drawings; b&w. Prefers humorous themes. Also uses artists for advertising.
First Contact & Terms: Prefers published artists only; however, others may submit. Works on assignment only. Send query letter with resume and tear sheets to be kept on file. Write for artists' guidelines. Samples not kept on file are returned by SASE. Reports within 30 days. Write for appointment to show

portfolio. Pays for design by the hour, $10-50. Pays for illustration by the hour, $8-40. Pays on acceptance. Considers skill and experience of artist when establishing payment. Buys all rights.
Tips: "Submit only best work."

***CAROL BRYAN IMAGINES**, 1000 Byus Dr., Charleston WV 25311. Editor: Carol Bryan. Syndicates clip art for 3,000 public and school libraries. Sample issue $1.
Needs: Buys 6-15 illustrations/issue. Considers gag cartoons, illustrations and spot drawings. Prefers single panel b&w line drawings. Prefers library themes—"not negative towards library or stereotyped (example: showing a spinster librarian with glasses and bun)."
First Contact & Terms: Send query letter with tear sheets, photocopies and finished cartoons. Samples are filed. Samples not filed are returned by SASE. Reports back within 3 weeks. Pays flat fee, $10-25; on publication. Buys one-time or reprint rights.
Tips: "Seeing a sample issue is mandatory—we have a specific style and have been very successful with it. Your style may blend with our philosophy. Need great cartoons that libraries can publish in their newsletters."

CELEBRATION: A CREATIVE WORSHIP SERVICE, Box 414293, Kansas City MO 64141. (816)531-0538. Editorial Office, 11211 Monticello Ave., Silver Spring MD 20902. (301)649-4937. Editor: Bill Freburger. Clients: Churches, clergy and worship committees.
Needs: Assigns 60/year. Uses artists for spot and line drawings on religious themes.
First Contact & Terms: Query; out-of-town artists only. Reports within 1 week. No originals returned to artist at job's completion. Pays $35/illustration.

***CHURCH BULLETIN & NEWSLETTER RESOURCE**, Box 1149, Orange Park FL 32067-1149. (904)727-2745. Publisher: Wayne Hepburn. Clip art firm serving about 12,000 outlets, including churches, schools, associations and industry.
Needs: Buys 40-60 cartoons and 200-1,000 illustrations/year from freelance artists. Prefers illustrations and single panel cartoons with gagline and b&w art. Maximum size is 7x10 and must be reducible to 20% of size without losing detail. "We need very graphic material." Prefers religious or educational themes or corporate situations.
First Contact & Terms: Send photocopies. Samples are filed. Samples not filed are returned by SASE. Guidelines and catalog available for 9x12 SASE with 2 stamps. Reports back within 2 months. To show a portfolio, mail roughs and Photostats. Pays $8-40; on acceptance. Buys all rights.
Tips: "All our images are published as clip art to be reproduced by readers in their bulletins and newsletters for churches, schools, associations, etc."

CITY NEWS SERVICE, Box 39, Willow Springs MO 65793. (417)469-2423. President: Richard Weatherington. Editorial service providing editorial and graphic packages for magazines. Considers cartoons, caricature, tax and business subjects as themes; considers b&w line drawings and shading film.
Needs: Buys from 12 or more freelance artists/year.
First Contact & Terms: Send query letter with resume, tear sheets or photocopies. Samples should contain business subjects. Samples not filed are returned by SASE. Reports within 4-6 weeks. To show a portfolio, mail tear sheets or Photostats. Pays for illustration by the project, $25 minimum. "We may buy art outright or split percentage of sales." Considers complexity of project, skill and experience of artist, how work will be used and rights purchased when establishing payment.
Tips: "We have the markets for multiple sales of editorial support art. We need talented artists to supply specific projects. We will work with beginning artists."

CLASSIFIED INTERNATIONAL ADVERTISING SERVICES INC., 3211 N. 74th Ave., Hollywood FL 33024. Contact: Art & Research Director. Clip art service. Clients: auto dealers, real estate agencies and newspapers.
Needs: B&w line drawings, cartoons and limited photography.
First Contact & Terms: Mail samples only please. Samples returned by SASE. Reports only if interested. Works on assignment only. Pays by the project. Considers complexity of project, and skill and experience of artist when establishing payment.
Tips: "We provide work for classified departments of newspaper firms. We have three sections to our service: automotive, real estate and self-promotion. Our company provides our service to all parts of the country, so our needs range so as to provide for the variety of tastes in the field of art. We provide cartoons, illustrations and realism, depending on the particular idea we're trying to convey."

COMMUNITY AND SUBURBAN PRESS SERVICE, Box 639, Frankfort KY 40602. (502)223-1736. Editor/Publisher: Kennison Keene. Syndicates to 300 weekly, small daily and shopper publications throughout the USA, and 1,500 or more yearly.

Needs: Buys from 10 or more freelance artists/year. Considers double panel cartoons; illustrations and line drawings; b&w. Prefers humorous themes. Also uses artists for graduation and Christmas ads.
First Contact & Terms: Send samples. Write for artists' guidelines. Considers single panel cartoons. "Usually cartoon artists will submit 8 or 9 cartoons at a time, together with SASE." Samples not kept on file returned by SASE. Reports within 1 week. To show a portfolio, mail original/final art. "We pay $15/cartoon, if work is acceptable to us. Price to be negotiated on holiday greeting ads and graduation greeting ads." Pays on acceptance. Considers salability of artwork. Buys first rights.

COMMUNITY FEATURES, Dept. C, Box 1062, Berkeley CA 94701. Art Editor: B. Miller. Syndicates to 270 daily and weekly newspapers, shoppers, consumer magazines. Mails brochure of new syndicated offerings to 700+ newspapers. Guidelines $1 and #10 SASE. Specify "artists' guidelines."
Needs: Interested in professional quality b&w illustrations, spot drawings, line art, square single, double and multiple panel cartoons; illustrated educational panels, how-to, etc. Does not seek color. Looking for illustrators and editorial cartoonists for regular assignments.
First Contact & Terms: Send tear sheets, veloxes, PMTs or excellent photocopies (published and unpublished) that can be kept on file. Do not send art-boards. Reports within 3-6 weeks. Buys various rights. Purchases some one-shot. Will consider line-art on all topics listed in guidelines. Pays $20-500 flat rate for one-shot and occasional work; 50% commission for regularly appearing features. Pays on publication.
Tips: "We look for a bold, modern look. Submit very clear copies. Include SASE if return is desired. Often, freelancers go to too much trouble and expense in sending elaborate packages with long cover letters. The work always speaks for itself! Best to leave samples of your work on file with us and we will contact you as the need arises. (No art work is distributed to our clients without artist's written approval.) Pet peeve: misspelled captions!"

DYNAMIC GRAPHICS INC., 6000 N. Forest Park Dr., Peoria IL 61614-3592. (309)688-8800. Art Director: Frank Antal. Distributes to thousands of magazines, newspapers, agencies, industries and educational institutions.
Needs: Works with 30-40 artists/year. Illustrations, graphic design and elements; primarily b&w, but will consider some 2- and full-color. "We are currently seeking to contact established illustrators capable of handling b&w highly realistic illustration of contemporary people and situations."
First Contact & Terms: Submit portfolio. SASE. Reports within 1 month. Buys all rights. Negotiates payment. Pays on acceptance.
Tips: "Concentrate on mastering the basics in anatomy and figure illustration before settling into a 'personal' or 'interpretive' style!"

EDITOR'S CHOICE CLIP ART QUARTERLY, Box 529, Kitty Hawk NC 27979. (919)441-3141. Editor: Frances K. Ries. Clip art firm. Distributes quarterly to major corporations who publish employee newsletters or magazines.
Needs: Serious and humorous editorial illustrations, graphics, standing heads, etc. Works with 6-8 freelance aritsts/year. Prefers line illustrations in pen & ink, scratchboard, etc., or pencil illustration on textured board. Also buys graphic symbols. Work is related to business and industry, employee relations, health and wellness, physical fitness, family life, recreation, etc.
First Contact & Terms: Experienced illustrators and graphic designers only. Works on assignment only. Send query letter, resume and samples to be kept on file. Reports within 60 days. Prefers photocopies as samples. Samples returned by SASE if not kept on file. Original art not returned at job's completion. Buys all rights or negotiates limited use fee. Pays $30-100 for illustrations; negotiates payment amount, varies according to project. Pays on acceptance.
Tips: "Only accomplished illustrators will be considered. Amateurs need not apply. Send enough samples of variety of subjects and styles to show us what you can do."

***RICHARD R. FALK ASSOCIATES**, 1472 Broadway, New York NY 10036. President: R. Falk. Syndicates to regional magazines and daily newspapers.
Needs: Buys from 3-4 freelance artists/year. Works on assignment only. Considers caricatures, editorial or political cartoons and spot drawings. Prefers line drawings. Prefers theatrical, entertainment themes.
First Contact & Terms: "Only send simple flyers, throwaway illustrations." Reports back only if interested. Pays flat fee; $125-1,000. Pays on acceptance. Considers clients' preferences. Buys one-time rights.

FILLERS FOR PUBLICATIONS, 1220 Maple Ave., Los Angeles CA 90015. Editor-in-Chief: John Raydell. Managing Editor: Dean Bowie. Distributes to magazines and newspapers.
Needs: Buys 72 pieces/year. Considers single panel, current events, education, family life, retirement, factory and office themes.

Artist: Martha Perske

Clip artwork by Martha Perske of Darien, Connecticut, carries a Valentine's Day theme in Dynamic Graphic's clip art service. Perske, who sold all rights, used prismacolor black pencil to convey "the affection between children which we still feel as adults." Art Director Frank Antal comments that Perske "provides a fresh point of view for repetitive situations."

First Contact & Terms: Mail art. SASE. Reports in 2 weeks. Previously published and simultaneous submissions OK. Buys all rights, but may reassign rights to artist after publication. Originals only returned upon request. Pays $5-10, line drawings, on acceptance.

FOTO EXPRESSION, Box 681, Station "A"., Downsview Ontario M3M 3A9 Canada. (416)736-0119 or (416)665-8459. Director: M.J. Kubik. Serving 35 outlets.
Needs: Buys from 80 freelance artists/year. Considers single, double and multiple panel cartoons, illustrations, spot drawings, b&w and color.
First Contact & Terms: Send query letter with brochure showing art style or resume, tear sheets, slides and photographs. Samples not filed returned by SASE. Reports within one month. To show a portfolio, mail final reproduction/product, color, photographs and b&w. Artist receives percentage; on publication. Considers skill and experience of artist and rights purchased when establishing payment. Negotiates rights purchased.
Tips: "Quality and content are essential. Resume and samples must be accompanied by a SASE or, out of Canada, International Reply Coupon is required."

PAULA ROYCE GRAHAM, 2770 W. 5th St., Brooklyn NY 11224. (718)372-1920. Contact: Paula Royce Graham. Syndicates to newspapers and magazines.
Needs: Considers illustrations; b&w. Also uses artists for advertising and graphics.
First Contact & Terms: Send business card and tear sheets to be kept on file. Write for artists' guidelines. Samples returned by SASE only if requested. Reports within days. Write for appointment to show portfolio. Pay is negotiable; on publication. Considers skill and experience of artist, client's preferences and rights purchased when establishing payment. Buys all rights.

GRAPHIC ARTS COMMUNICATIONS, Box 421, Farrell PA 16121. (412)342-5300. President: Bill Murray. Syndicates to 200 newspapers and magazines. Buys 400 pieces/year.
Needs: Humor through youth and family themes for single panel, strips and multi-panel cartoons.

Needs ideas for anagrams, editorial cartoons and puzzles, and for new comic panel "Sugar & Spike."
First Contact & Terms: Query for guidelines. SASE. Reports within 4-6 weeks. No originals returned. Buys all rights. Pays 40% commission on acceptance.

GRAPHIC NEWS BUREAU, gabriel graphics. Box 38, Madison Square Station, New York NY 10010. (212)254-8863. Cable: NOLNOEL NY 5. Director: J.G. Bumberg. Custom syndications and promotions to customized lists, small dailies, suburbans and selected weeklies.
Needs: Buys from 4-6 freelance artists/year. Prefers artists within easy access. No dogmatic, regional or pornographic themes. Uses single panel cartoons, illustration, halftones in line conversions and line drawings.
First Contact & Terms: Send query letter only. Reports within 4-6 weeks. Returns original art after reproduction on request with SASE. Provide 3x5 card to be kept on file for possible future assignments. Negotiates rights purchased; on publication.

HISPANIC LINK NEWS SERVICE, 1420 N St. NW, Washington DC 20005. (202)234-0737. General Manager: Hector Ericksen-Mendoza. Syndicated column service to 200 newspapers and a newsletter serving 1,000 private subscribers, "movers and shakers in the Hispanic community in U.S., plus others interested in Hispanics."
Needs: Buys from 20 freelance artists/year. Considers single panel cartoons; b&w, pen & ink line drawings. Work should have a Hispanic angle; "most are editorial cartoons, some straight humor."
First Contact & Terms: Send query letter with resume and photocopies to be kept on file. Samples not filed returned by SASE. Reports within 3 weeks. Call for appointment to show portfolio or contact through artist's agent. Pays flat fee of $25 average; on acceptance. Considers clients' preferences when establishing payment. Buys reprint rights and negotiates rights purchased; "while we ask for reprint rights, we also allow the artist to sell later."
Tips: "While we accept work from all artists, we are particularly interested in helping Hispanic artists showcase their work. Cartoons should offer a Hispanic perspective on current events or a Hispanic view of life."

HOSPITAL PR GRAPHICS, Box 529, Kitty Hawk NC 27949. (919)441-3141. Editor: Frances K. Ries. Clip art firm. Distributes monthly to hospitals and other health care organizations.
Needs: Works wih 4-5 freelance artists/year (at present). Uses illustrations, line drawings, spot drawings and graphic symbols related to health care for use in brochures, folders, newsletters, etc. Prefers sensitive line illustrations, spot drawings and graphics related to hospitals, nurses, doctors, patients, technicians, medical apparatus. Also buys 12 cartoons/year maximum.
First Contact & Terms: Experienced illustrators only, preferably having hospital exposure or access to resource material. Works on assignment only. Send query letter, resume, Photostats or photocopies to be kept on file. Samples returned by SASE if not kept on file. Reports within 1 month. Original art not returned at job's completion. Buys all rights. Pays flat rate of $20-60 for illustrations; negotiates payment, varies according to project. Pays on acceptance.
Tips: "We are looking to establish a continuing relationship with at least 5-6 freelance graphic designers and illustrators. Illustration style should be serious, sensitive and somewhat idealized. Send enough samples to show the variety (if any) of styles you're capable of handling. Indicate the length of time it took to complete each illustration or graphic."

INTERPRESS OF LONDON AND NEW YORK, 400 Madison Ave., New York NY 10017. (212)832-2839. Editor/Publisher: Jeffrey Blyth. Syndicates to several dozen European magazines and newspapers.
Needs: Buys from 4-5 freelance artists/year. Prefers material which is universal in appeal; no "American only" material. Uses single and multi-panel cartoons.
First Contact & Terms: Send query letter and photographs; write for artists' guidelines. Samples not kept on file returned by SASE. Reports within 3 weeks. Purchases European rights. Pays 60% of net proceeds on publication.

***LANDMARK DESIGNS INC.**, Box 2832 Eugene OR 97401. (503)345-3429. Vice President: Richard McAlexander. Serves 80 outlets, such as daily newpapers, magazines, books.
Needs: Buys from 2 freelancers/year. Works on assignment only. Considers architectual renderings and illustrations. Prefers pen & ink. Prefers architecture, residential themes. Also needs artists for advertising.
First Contact & Terms: Send query letter with brochure or samples. Samples are filed. Samples not filed are returned by SASE. Reports back within 10 days only if interested. Write to show a portfolio or mail b&w and tear sheets. Pays for design by the project; 25% commission. Pays for illustration by the project, $40 minimum. Pays on acceptance. Considers skill and experience of artists when establishing payment. Buys all rights.

LOS ANGELES TIMES SYNDICATE, 218 S. Spring St., Los Angeles CA 90012. (213)237-7987. Comics Editor: David Seidman, (213)237-5198.
Needs: Comic strips, panel cartoons and editorial cartoons. "We prefer humor to dramatic continuity. We consider only cartoons that run 6 or 7 days/week." Cartoons may be of any size as long as they're to scale with cartoons running in newspapers. (Strips usually run approximately 6⁷⁄₁₆x2", panel cartoons 3⅛x4"; editorial cartoons vary.)
First Contact & Terms: Submit photocopies or Photostats of 24 dailies. Submitting Sunday cartoons is optional; if you choose to submit them, send at least four of them. Reports within 2 months. SASE. Syndicate buys all rights.
Tips: "Don't imitate cartoons that are already in the paper. Avoid linework or details that might bleed together, fade out or reproduce too small to see clearly. Keep sex, alcohol, violence and other potentially offensive subjects to a minimum. We hardly ever match artists with writers or vice versa. We prefer people or teams who can do the entire job of creating a feature."

***MAJOR NEWS SERVICE**, Box 41, New Brenen OH 45869. Vice President/Associate Editor: James R. Grilliot. Print Shop: Chris Diller. Syndicates to weekly newspapers and 4 national magazines.
Needs: Buys from 8 freelance artists/year. Considers single, double and multi-panel cartoons and illustrations. Prefers medicine, sports and outdoor themes.
First Contact & Terms: Send query letter with brochure and samples to be kept on file. Prefers Photostats as samples. Samples not kept on file are returned by SASE if requested. Reports only if interested. Works on assignment only. Artist receives flat rate; on acceptance. Considers saleability of artwork and rights purchased when establishing payment. Buys reprint rights.

***MCLEAN PROVIDENCE JOURNAL AND FAIRFAX HERALD**, Box 580, McLean VA 22101. Editor: David Dear. Syndicates to weekly newspapers.
Needs: Buys from 2 freelance artists/year. Prefers local or Virginia artists. Considers comic strips, gag cartoons, caricatures, editorial or political cartoons, illustrations and spot drawings. Prefers pen & ink with washes.
First Contact & Terms: Send query letter with brochure or resume and tear sheets. Samples are filed. Samples not filed are returned by SASE. Reports back only if interested. To show a portfolio, mail tear sheets. Pays flat fee; $5-90; on publication. Considers clients' preferences. Negotiates rights purchased.
Tips: "Best luck if they are local artists or if work has local theme or elements."

METRO CREATIVE GRAPHICS, INC., 33 W. 34th St., New York NY 10011. (800)223-1600. Contact: Andrew Shapiro. Clip art firm. Distributes to 6,000 daily and weekly paid and free circulation newspapers, schools, graphics and ad agencies and retail chains.
Needs: Buys from 50 freelance artists/year. Considers single panel cartoons; illustrations and line and spot drawings; b&w and color. Prefers all categories of themes associated with retail, classified, promotion and advertising. Also needs artists for special-interest tabloid section covers.
First Contact & Terms: Send query letter with brochure showing style or Photostats, photocopies, slides, photographs and tear sheets to be kept on file. Samples not kept on file returned by SASE. Reports only if interested. To show a portfolio, mail appropriate materials or call to schedule an appointment. Works on assignment only. Pays flat fee of $25-1,000; on acceptance. Considers skill and experience of artist, salability of artwork and clients' preferences when establishing payment.
Tips: "Metro provides steady work, lead time and prompt payment. All applicants are seriously considered. Don't rely on 1-2 samples to create interest. Show a variety of styles and special ability to draw people in realistic situations. If specialty is graphic design, think how you would use samples in advertising."

MINORITY FEATURES SYNDICATE, Box 421, Farrell PA 16121. (412)342-5300. Chairman of the Board: Bill Murray. Clip art firm serving approximately 500 outlets.
Needs: Buys from 600 freelance artists/year. Considers single, double and multi-panel cartoons; illustrations and spot drawings. Prefers b&w pen & ink line drawings with family themes. Also uses artists for advertising art. Also publishes comic books. Query first.
First Contact & Terms: Published artists only. Works on assignment only. Send query letter to be kept on file; write for artists' guidelines. Prefers photocopies as samples. Samples returned by SASE. Reports only if interested. Pay to artist is 50%; on acceptance. Considers rights purchased when establishing payment. Buys all rights.
Tips: "Submit only your best efforts."

NATIONAL NEWS BUREAU, 2019 Chancellor St., Philadelphia PA 19103. (215)569-0700. Editor: Harry Jay Katz. Syndicates to 1,000 outlets and publishes entertainment newspapers on a contract basis.
Needs: Buys from 500 freelance artists/year. Prefers entertainment themes. Uses single, double and

multiple panel cartoons, illustrations, line and spot drawings.
First Contact & Terms: Send samples and resume. Samples returned by SASE. Reports within 2 weeks. Returns original art after reproduction. Send resume and samples to be kept on file for future assignments. Negotiates rights purchased. Pays flat rate; $5-100 for each piece; on publication.

NEWSPAPER ENTERPRISE ASSOCIATION INC./UNITED FEATURE SYNDICATE, 200 Park Ave., New York NY 10166. Director of Comic Art: Sarah Gillespie. Syndicates to more than 1,500 newspapers.
Needs: Comic strip ideas, editorial cartoons and comic panels. Prefers pen & ink. Contact via mail. Send copies, not originals, and SASE for return. All submissions answered. If used in NEA Daily Service, pays flat fee. If used in syndicate division, 50% commission.
Tips: "We are looking for innovative comic features with interesting characters. There should be an idea behind your feature that allows it to be open-ended. Whatever the 'staging,' you need an on-going narrative structure. The market is very, very tight. We take 3 new strips a year and get over 3,000 submissions. Concentrate on character more than subject matter."

NORTH AMERICA SYNDICATE, (formerly News America Syndicate), 1703 Kaiser Ave., Irvine CA 92714. General Manager: John Killian. Syndicates to 2,500 daily and weekly newspapers around the world. Titles include "Andy Capp," "Mary Worth" and "Dennis the Menace."
Needs: Considers cartoon strips; single, double and multiple panel; illustrations, spot drawings, b&w and color. Must have strong main characters and theme. Prefers pen & ink and line drawings.
First Contact & Terms: Submit work (6-12 unpublished items) with cover letter. SASE. Reports within 2 months. Buys various rights. Write to schedule an appointment to show a portfolio, which should include original/final art and tear sheets. Pays royalties on publication. Free artists' guidelines.

NORTHWIND STUDIOS INTERNATIONAL, Box 295, Mobile Ave. #2, Camarillo CA 93010. (805)493-1661. Contact: John J. Tobin. Syndicates cartoons to 1,500 outlets of Christian magazines and Christian newspapers.
Needs: Buys from 8-10 freelance artists/year. Considers single panel cartoons. Prefers pen & ink line drawings with Christian themes only.
First Contact & Terms: Prefers experienced artists. Send resume or samples for consideration to be kept on file. Artists guidelines will be sent after review of resume and samples. Prefers photocopies as samples. Samples returned by SASE. Reports within 2 weeks. Pay artists $150-250; on acceptance. Considers skill and experience of artist, salability of artwork and rights purchased when establishing payment. Buys all rights.
Tips: "Northwind Studios International has a commitment of quality to all its subscribers, therefore we ask all artists who are applying for a position to be aware of these rules: 1) production of good wholesome, Christian cartoons; 2) no variations on our two characters; 3) maintain a 'Disney' style; 4) the ability to vary the widths of line; 5) willingness to rework. Because of this criteria it is necessary that we ask only qualified and talented Disney-style artists apply. The right artists will find a long term and pleasant relationship with our studio."

OCEANIC PRESS SERVICE, Box 6538, Buena Park CA 90622-6538. (714)527-5651. Manager: Nat Carlton. Syndicates to 300 magazines, newspapers and subscribers in 30 countries.
Needs: Buys several hundred pieces/year. Considers cartoon strips (single, double and multiple panel) and illustrations. Prefers camera ready material (tear sheets or clippings). Themes include published sex cartoons, family cartoons, inflation, juvenile activities and jacket covers for paperbacks (color transparencies). Especially needs juvenile activity drawings and unusual sports cartoons; also sex cartoons. "God, sex and action is still a good formula. Poke fun at established TV shows. Bad economy means people must do their own home, car and other repairs. How-to articles with b&w line drawings are needed. Magazines will buy less and have more features staff-written. Quality is needed. People like to read more about celebrities, but it has to have a special angle, not the usual biographic run-of-the-mill profile. Much will be TV related. I'd like to see a good cartoon book on Sherlock Holmes, on Hollywood, on leading TV shows."
First Contact & Terms: Send query letter with Photostats and samples of previously published work. Accepts tear sheets and clippings. SASE. Reports within 1 month. Pays on publication. Originals returned to artist, or put on auction. Guidelines $1 with SASE.
Tips: "The trend is definitely toward women's market: money saving topics, service features—how to do home repair—anything to fight inflation; also unusual cartoons about unusual happenings; unusual sports; and cartoons with sophisticated international settings, credit cards, air travel. We would like to receive more clippings for foreign reprints. Competition is keen—artists should strive for better quality submissions."

Close-up

David Seidman

Comics editor, Los Angeles Times Syndicate
Los Angeles, California

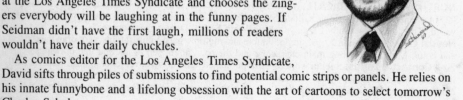

David Seidman doesn't need to stand in front of an audience to tickle some funny bones. He sits back in his chair at the Los Angeles Times Syndicate and chooses the zingers everybody will be laughing at in the funny pages. If Seidman didn't have the first laugh, millions of readers wouldn't have their daily chuckles.

As comics editor for the Los Angeles Times Syndicate, David sifts through piles of submissions to find potential comic strips or panels. He relies on his innate funnybone and a lifelong obsession with the art of cartoons to select tomorrow's Charles Schulz.

"I like to be surprised. Surprise and impact are the two qualities I look for. I want somebody who can make me laugh until I bust a gut." He likes syndicating such hard-hitters as editorial cartoonists Paul Conrad of the *Los Angeles Times* and Dan Wasserman of *The Boston Globe* because "their stuff grabs you; they hit home. After looking at their work, a reader goes to the office and says, 'Did you see that cartoon today?' Successful cartoonists," says Seidman, "are the guys who have the mind and the artistic skills to make you sit up and take notice. Those are the guys I'd give my pinky for."

Seidman knows a cartoonist's lot is not easy. He has tried to learn to draw, unsuccessfully. ("You could blackmail me with my drawing.") But he does understand the craft of cartooning. "I analyze both the writing and the drawing. When I read a comic strip that isn't funny, I sit down and analyze it—what's wrong with the gag line, are the wrong words used, does the situation fit the gag?"

The ability to make people laugh is an ephemeral quality, but there is a craft to it. "You have to know how to set up a gag. You can put in too much information or too little. Often a cartoonist will know his character's habits or method of speech so well that the cartoonist will assume the reader knows the character, also. You must set up the character before the gag."

Even though a cartoon can be well-crafted, it needs other qualities to succeed in syndication. It must have an original slant. "I've seen Garfield the Dog and Garfield the Chicken, and I don't want them." Also it must communicate to a wide audience; a cartoon based on violations of decency is not printed in family papers. For example, Seidman personally enjoys the humor of Gilbert Shelton, who creates the "Fabulous Furry Freak Brothers" for underground comics. Even though Shelton has a devoted cult following, his work would not translate to a syndicated strip because the material doesn't appeal to a mass audience. Also the artist does not produce work in quantity, and most syndicated cartoonists produce several cartoons a week.

After applying his own standards to a submission, Seidman shows it to his supervisor in a weekly development meeting. Occasionally he strikes gold. "I looked at one submission and it fractured me. Then, I asked myself, 'Am I just in the mood to laugh?' I brought the strip to the meeting and everyone fell apart laughing. We bought it." The strip was "The Quigmans," one of the syndicate's hits.

Seidman suggests that cartoonists should follow suit in asking other people their opinions. "Being a cartoonist is like being a stand-up comedian. You can't work in a closet. You have to go in front of an audience and see their reactions." Seidman suggests showing copies of the work to as many people as possible, especially people who don't know you. "Paying attention to what makes people laugh is the only way to improve."

Aspiring cartoonists must get in print, says Seidman. "Once you have skills you can acquire in a drawing class, get your work in print—in freebies at first, then work your way up to newsletters, weeklies and small dailies. Getting printed gives you a knowledge of print reproduction and provides material for your portfolio. It also gives you an idea of whether or not you're being noticed." Having honed your skills, Seidman suggests then sending your work to syndicates.

Most cartoonists who succeed, says Seidman, "are the ones who can't help but draw. They have a passion for cartooning and a need to communicate to people. Their strips are like a new baby to me. You love your relatives, but you rush to see the newborn."

—Susan Conner

"Our next speaker is . . . HEY! Who's that broad in the third row? MAMA! WOOO! WOOO!"

Seidman looks for cartoonists who have original ideas as well as the ability to make people laugh. He found both qualities in Buddy Hickerson, whose panel "The Quigmans" has become one of the syndicate's successes. Seidman, who reviews submissions initially, says Hickerson's work "fractured" him at first glance, then also received the editorial board's approval. Seidman suggests that cartoonists submit a series of panels or cartoon strips to a syndicate to show continuity of idea, character and style.

PRESS ASSOCIATES INC., 806 15th St. NW, Washington DC 20005. (202)638-0444. Contact: Art Editor. News service serving "hundreds" of trade union newspapers and magazines.
Needs: Buys from 10-15 freelance artists/year. Considers single panel cartoons; line drawings; b&w. Prefers humorous and workplace themes—manufacturing, office, retail, etc.
First Contact & Terms: Send query letter with original cartoons. Samples not kept on file returned by SASE only if requested. Pays flat rate of $7.50; on acceptance. Considers clients' preferences when establishing payment. Buys first or reprint rights.

PROFESSIONAL ADVISORY COUNSEL, INC., Suite A-10, 7701 Broadway, Oklahoma City OK 73116. President: Larry W. Beavers. Syndicate serving approximately 1,000 international outlets.
Needs: Buys from over 30 freelance artists/year. Considers illustrations and spot drawings, b&w and color. Prefers camera-ready artwork. Also uses artists for advertising. Considers any media.
First Contact & Terms: Works on assignment only. Send query letter with brochure, resume, business card and samples to be kept on file if interested. Samples not returned. Especially looks for "simplicity and fast-relating/assimilating potential." Reports only if interested. Write for appointment to show portfolio and for artists' guidelines. Pays flat fee, $10-100 average; on acceptance. Buys all rights.
Tips: "Make your contact quick, concise and to-the-point."

PUBLICATIONS CO., 1220 Maple Ave., Los Angeles CA 90015. (213)747-6541. Manager: John Raydell. Syndicates clip art to small newsletters. Buys 80 pages/year.
Needs: Buys full pages of 9-20 bits of art on the same subject, e.g., sports, office scenes, dancing, related objects, animals, cars, cowboys. Original can be on 8½x11" paper with 6x10" image area.
First Contact & Terms: Mail art. SASE. Reports in 3 weeks. Originals only returned to artist upon request. Pays $25-40/page.

***REPORTER, YOUR EDITORIAL ASSISTANT**, 1220 Maple Ave., Los Angeles CA 90015. (213)747-6542. Editor: George Dubow. Syndicates to newspapers and magazines from secondary level schools and colleges.
Needs: Considers single panel cartoons on teenage themes.
First Contact & Terms: Mail art. SASE. Reports in 2 weeks. Buys all rights. Originals returned to artist only upon request. Pays $5-10.

SINGER COMMUNICATIONS, INC., 3164 Tyler Ave., Anaheim CA 92801. (714)527-5650. Executive Vice President: Natalie Carlton. Syndicates to 300 magazines, newspapers, book publishers and poster firms; strips include *They Changed History*, and *How It Began*. Artists' guidelines $1.
Needs: Buys several thousand pieces/year. Considers cartoon strips; single, double and multiple panel; family, children, sex, juvenile activities and games themes; universal material on current topics. Especially needs business, outerspace and credit card cartoons of 3-4 panels. Prefers to buy reprints or clips of previously published material.
First Contact & Terms: Send query letter with tear sheets. "Prefer to see tear sheets or camera ready copy or clippings." SASE. Reports within 2-3 weeks. Returns originals to artist at job's completion if requested at time of submission with SASE. Licenses reprint or all rights; prefers foreign reprint rights. Pays 50% commission.
Tips: "Send us cartoons on subjects like inflation, taxes, sports or Christmas; we get thousands on sex. Everyone wants new ideas—not the same old characters, same old humor at the doctor or psychiatrist or at the bar. More sophistication is needed. Background is also needed—not just 2 people talking."

TEENAGE CORNER INC., 70-540 Gardenia Ct., Rancho Mirage CA 92270. President: David J. Lavin. Syndicates rights. Negotiates pay.
Needs: Spot drawings and illustrations.
First Contact & Terms: Send query letter. SASE. Reports within 1 week. Buys one-time and reprint rights. Negotiates commission. Pays on publication.

TRIBUNE MEDIA SERVICES, INC., 64 E. Concord St., Orlando FL 32801. (305)422-8181. Editor: Mike Argirion. Syndicate serving daily and Sunday newspapers.
Needs: Seeks comic strips and newspaper panels.
First Contact & Terms: Send query letter with resume and photocopies. Samples not filed are returned. Reports within 2-4 weeks.

UNITED CARTOONIST SYNDICATE, Box 7081, Corpus Christi TX 78415. (512)855-2480. President: Pedro R. Moreno. Syndicate serving South Africa outlets. Regular outlets vary from church newsletters to major newspapers or international comic syndicates.
Needs: Buys from 1-12 freelance artists/year. Consider single, double or multiple panel cartoons; b&w

or color on Sundays. Prefers (medium) line drawings of pen & ink with zip-a-tone (no washes). Prefers family entertainment (clean) as themes.
First Contact & Terms: Send query letter with $5 for guidelines. Samples not filed returned by SASE. Reports within 7 days. To show a portfolio, mail tear sheets, b&w and reduced newspaper page size. Pays 40% of gross income on publications. Considers saleability of artwork when establishing payment. Negotiates rights purchased.
Tips: "Before submitting your artwork, reduce your comic panel or comic strip in a newspaper page size. The amount of 2 to 48 comics are required for a good evaluation for possible syndication."

UNIVERSAL PRESS SYNDICATE, 4900 Main St., Kansas City MO 64112. Editorial Director: Lee Salem. Syndicate serving 2750 daily and weekly newspapers.
Needs: Comic strips and panels; text features. Considers single, double or multiple panel cartoons; b&w and color. Prefers photocopies of b&w, pen & ink, line drawings; other techniques are reviewed, but remember that this material will be published in newspapers.
First Contact & Terms: Reports within 4 weeks. To show a portfolio, mail Photostats. Buys syndication rights. Send query letter with resume and photocopies.
Tips: "A well-conceived comic strip with strong characters, good humor and a contemporary feel will almost always get a good response. Be original. Don't be afraid to try some new idea or technique. Don't be discouraged by rejection letters. Universal Press receives 100-150 comic submissions a week, and only takes on two or three a year, so keep plugging away. Talent has a way of rising to the top."

***WIDEWORLD ART STUDIOS**, Box 20056, St. Louis MO 63144. Director: John Ford. Syndicates to 30 regional magazines.
Needs: Buys from 12 freelance artists/year. Uses illustrations, line and spot drawings.
First Contact & Terms: Send Photostats or submit portfolio for review. Samples returned by SASE. Reports within 2 weeks. Returns original art after reproduction. Provide tear sheets to be kept on file for future assignments. Buys one-time rights. Negotiates payment. Pays on acceptance.

***WORLD MEDIA SYNDICATES**, 1299 E. Laguna Ave., Las Vegas NV 89109-1628. President: John R. Wardy. Syndicates to daily, weekly, monthly newpapers and magazines.
Needs: Prefers artists with a product suitable for syndication. No one-time submissions bought. Must have staying power for potential long-term syndication (comic strips, theme art). Considers comic strips, gag cartoons and editorial or political cartoons. "Open to all techniques and formats."
First Contact & Terms: Send query letter with tear sheets, Photostats and photocopies. Samples are filed. Samples not filed are returned by SASE. Reports back within 2 months. Write to schedule an appointment to show a portfolio or mail thumbnails, roughs, original/final art, final reproduction/product, color, b&w, tear sheets, Photostats and photographs. Pays 50% of gross income; on publication. Considers skill and experience of artist, saleability of art work and rights purchased when establishing payment. Negotiates rights purchased.
Tips: "Frankly, we do not currently handle comic strips or political cartoon syndication, but we are open to the possibility. Artists should keep our company's emphasis in mind before going to the time and expense of approaching us.

"Many freelancers do not represent themselves professionally. When someone seems like they're creative but not together, I get nervous that they won't be reliable. Reliability is as important as creativity when meeting a deadline."

***—Deborah Kuhfahl, Network Industries/Class Kid Ltd.
New York City***

Art Publishers and Distributors

Art publishers and distributors offer graphic designers and illustrators (and especially those artists who frequently cross the line between graphic and fine art) the opportunity to have their work reproduced and distributed. Sales of reproductions and prints offer the graphic artist creative freedom, repeat income and widespread exposure.

The services supplied by these firms vary. The publisher/printer handles only reproduction of works, leaving the actual distribution to the artist, while the publisher/distributor handles printing plus marketing. The distributor deals with the distribution and sales of works that have already been printed—either the artist has available editions or he is willing to have prints made at his own expense. There are also those publishers who seek artists skilled in printmaking to work exclusively with them to produce handpulled print editions.

Prints reproduced by photomechanical means (much like the illustrations reproduced in magazines) fall into three categories: limited edition prints, unlimited edition prints and posters. A limited edition involves a specific number of prints, say 250 or 500, and therefore commands a high retail price. There is a limit to the number of unlimited edition prints run in each edition, but there is *no* limit to the number of editions that can be run if the print is popular. Usually printed as unlimited editions, posters have evolved from an advertisement of an event or product into an affordable and collectible art form decorating homes and offices. They combine a decorative image with elements of type.

Publishers/distributors seek quality, saleable work with widespread appeal. An image must have good composition, reproduce well (have quality of line and good contrast) and appeal to a wide audience. Color plays a vital part, since print reproductions are often an integral factor in interior decoration. Subject matter is not as important as graphic content, but certain subjects will tend to sell better than others—children, florals, landscapes and Americana top the list. For continued sales, the subject treatment should lend itself to a series.

When contacting an art publisher, remember that you're a potential investment to him. Send a résumé listing galleries representing you and any other professional art credits. A proven record of accomplishment helps. Your sample package should include tear sheets or slides (transparencies or photographs will do) of your previously published or exhibited work. Label samples with information on size, medium and orientation (top, left, etc.). Be sure to include a SASE.

Know what services the firm is furnishing and what is expected of you before you sign a contract. Generally you are offered either a flat fee for reproduction rights, payment per piece or a royalty. You should retain the rights to reproduce the image in other media, while the publisher has the right to reproduce the image as an offset reproduction for a limited amount of time. Remember that you are allowing someone to make copies of your work; you should retain ownership of the original. The contract/agreement should also include the names and addresses of both parties, a description of the work, the size of the edition, payment and insurance terms, a copyright notice, guarantee of a credit line and the extent of promotion.

To keep current with this field, read *Decor* and *Art Business News*, monthly publications for the art dealer and framer. Also, the Pantone Color Institute publishes the monthly *Color News* that provides updates on color trends, which are so important to art publishers.

AA GRAPHICS, INC., 1200 N. 96th St., Seattle WA 98103. Art Director: Gail Gastfield. Publishes posters for a teenage market, minimum 5,000 run for department, record and poster stores, also discount drug stores. Artist's guidelines available. Send query letter with tear sheets, Photostats, photocopies, slides and photographs; then submit sketch or photo of art. SASE. Reports in 2 weeks. Usually pays royalties of 10¢ per poster sold and an advance of $500 against future royalties.
Acceptable Work: Prefers 7x11" sketches; full-size posters are 23x35".
Tips: "Become familiar with popular posters by looking at designs in poster racks in stores."

AARON ASHLEY INC., Room 1905, 230 5th Ave., New York NY 10001. (212)532-9227. Contact: Philip D. Ginsburg. Produces unlimited edition fine quality 4-color offset and hand-colored reproductions for distributors, manufacturers, jobbers, museums, schools and galleries. Publishes "many" new artists/year. Pays royalties or fee. Offers advance. Exclusive representation for unlimited editions. Written contract. Query, arrange interview or submit slides or photos. SASE. Reports immediately.
Needs: Unframed realistic and impressionistic paintings, especially marine, landscapes, sportings, florals, botanicals and Americana.

***ACM/AMERICAN PORTFOLIO**, Box 309, Englishtown NJ 07726. (201)577-0622. President: Marc Rosenbaum. Art publisher/distributor of original, signed and numbered lithographs. Clients: galleries. Works with 3 artists/year. Pays flat fee. Negotiates rights purchased. Requires exclusive representation of the artist. Provides insurance while work is at firm, promotion and a written contract. Send query letter with brochure. Samples not filed are returned. Reports back within 10 days. Call to schedule an appointment to show a portfolio, which should include transparencies and final reproduction/product.
Acceptable Work: Considers oil paintings, acrylic paintings and watercolor. Prefers realism and impresionism. Prefers individual works of art; maximum size 24x36'.

ALJON INTERNATIONAL, 1481 SW 32 Ave., Pompano Beach FL 33069. (305)971-0070. President: Ronald Dvoretz. Art distributor of watercolors, acrylic and oil paintings, enamels on copper and collages. Clients: galleries, furniture stores, home show people, interior designers and other wholesalers and jobbers. Distributes work for 18 domestic artists/year. Pays flat fee. Negotiates payment method; very often pays on weekly basis. Negotiates rights purchased. Requires exclusive representation. Provides insurance while work is at distributor, promotion and shipping to and from distributor. Send query letter with brochure, slides or photos of originals. Samples returned only if requested. Reports only if interested. Call or write for appointment to show portfolio.
Acceptable Work: Considers oil and acrylic paintings, watercolors, mixed media and enamels on copper. Especially likes large (4'x5' or larger) acrylic abstracts—can be college work.
Tips: "Disregard retail pricing and come equipped with adequate samples. We must know colors. Subject matter is not of utmost importance."

***AMERICAN GALLERY OF QUILT AND TEXTILE ART**, 7506 Soundview Dr., Gigttarbor WA 98335. (206)851-3965. Owner: Diane N. Wolf. Art distributor/gallery showing original textile art and paper casting. Clients: galleries, art consultants, interior designers, architects, corporate and residential. Distributes work for 50 artists/year. Pays on a consignment basis: 50%. Provides insurance while work is at firm, promotion, shipping from firm and a written contract.

***AMERICAN PRINT GALLERY**, 219 Steinwehr Ave., Gettysburg PA 17325. (717)334-6188. Owner: Ted Sutphen. Art publisher/art distributor/gallery. Publishes/distributes limited editions (maximum 250 prints), offset reproductions and bronzes. Clients: retail mail order, retail galleries and wholesale paint/frame shops. Publishes and distributes 3-5 artists/year and distributes. Works with 3-5 artists/year. Pays 15% royalties. Buys one-time rights. Provides in-transit insurance, insurance while work is at firm, promotion and shipping from firm. Send query letter with brochure or slides and transparencies. Samples are not filed. Samples not returned. Reports back within 1 week. Call or write to schedule an appointment to show a portfolio, which should include slides and transparencies.
Acceptable Work: Considers oil and acrylic paintings. Military themes only.

HERBERT ARNOT, INC., 250 W. 57th St., New York NY 10019. (212)245-8287. President: Peter Arnot. Art distributor of original oil paintings. Clients: galleries. Distributes work for 250 artists/year. Pays flat fee, $100-1,000 average. Provides promotion and shipping to and from distributor. Send query letter with brochure, resume, business card, slides, photographs or original work to be kept on file. Samples not filed are returned. Reports within 1 month. Call or write for appointment to show portfolio.
Acceptable Work: Considers oil and acrylic paintings. Has wide range of themes and styles—"mostly traditional/impressionistic, not modern."
Tips: "Professional quality, please."

ART BEATS, INC., 2435 S. Highland Dr., Salt Lake City UT 84106. (801)487-1588. President: Robert Gerrard. Vice President: Jill Gerrard. Art publisher and distributor of limited and unlimited editions and offset reproductions. Clients: gift shops, frame stores, department stores and galleries. Publishes 20 freelance artists/year. Distributes work for 50 artists/year. Pays royalty of 10%; negotiates payment method. Sometimes offers an advance. Prefers to buy all rights or first rights. Requires exclusive representation. Provides promotion, shipping from firm and written contract. Send query letter with brochure showing art style or tear sheets, slides and photographs to be kept on file. Samples not filed returned only if requested. Reports within 1 month. To show a portfolio, mail tear sheets, Photostats and photographs.
Acceptable Work: Considers oil and acrylic paintings, pastels, watercolors and mixed media; no b&w. Especially likes children's, country and floral themes, "but always interested in new things."

***ART DECOR DISTRIBUTORS**, Box 452, Worcester MA 01613. (617)987-2160. Owner: Stephen Dann. Art distributor of limited editions, offset reproductions and handpulled originals for galleries, contract framers, decorators, etc. Distributes work of 100 artists/year. Pays on consignment, 20% commission. Send query letter with photographs or slides. Samples are filed. Samples not filed are returned by SASE. Reports back only if interested.
Acceptable Work: Prefers impressionism, primitives, contemporary seascapes, clowns, florals. Maximum size 24x30".

ARTCHOLOGY, Box 1004, Redwood City CA 94064. (415)369-0126. President: Azucena Wells. Publisher/distributor of limited edition serigraphs and posters. Clients: art galleries, museums and interior designers.
Needs: Works with 5-7 artists/year. Pays $100-1,500; on acceptance. Buys all rights. Provides in-trust insurance and promotion.
First Contact & Terms: Send query letter with slides. Samples not filed are returned by SASE. Reports within 4-6 weeks. To show a portfolio, mail original/final art.
Acceptable Work: Considers line drawings and paintings no larger than 24x48". Considers rights purchased when establishing payment.
Tips: "We will consider all work in realism."

ART IMAGE INC., 1577 Barry Ave., Los Angeles CA 90025. (213)826-9000. President: Allan Fierstein. Publishes and produces unlimited editions and limited editions that are pencil signed and numbered by the artist. Also distributes etchings, serigraphs, lithographs and watercolor paintings. "Other work we publish and distribute includes handmade paper, cast paper, paper weavings and paper construction." All work sold to galleries, frame shops, framed picture manufacturers, interior decorators and auctioneers. Publishes 12-16 artists per year; distributes the work of 24 artists. Negotiates payment. Requires exclusive representation. Provides shipping and a written contract. Send query letter with brochure showing art style, tear sheets, slides and photographs. SASE. Reports within 1 week. To show a portfolio, mail appropriate materials or write to schedule an appointment; portfolio should include photographs.
Acceptable Work: "All subject matter and all media in pairs or series of companion pieces."
Tips: "We are publishing and distributing more and more subject matter from offset limited editions to etchings, serigraphs, lithographs and original watercolor paintings."

ART 101 LTD., 1401 Chattahoochee Ave. NW, Atlanta GA 30318. (404)351-9146. Creative Director: Jules Stine. Art publisher of unlimited editions. Clients: gift and card shops and department stores. Publishes 2-4 artists/year. Pays flat fee of $500-1,500 average. All work is "work for hire," fees negotiated. Buys all rights. Provides shipping to and from firm and written contract. Send query letter with brochure, resume and samples to be kept on file. Samples not filed are returned. Reports within 10 days. Call or write for appointment to show portfolio.
Acceptable Work: Posters combine extensive copy and specially selected type with strong graphic design. Illustrations are secondary to the copy and design.

ART RESOURCES INTERNATIONAL, LTD., 98 Commerce St., Stamford CT 06902-4506. (203)967-4545, (800)228-2989. Vice President: Robin E. Bonnist. Art publisher. Publishes unlimited edition offset lithographs. Clients: galleries, department stores, distributors, framers throughout the world. Publishes 100 freelance artists/year. Distributes work of 200 artists/year. Also uses artists for advertising layout and brochure illustration. Pays by royalty (5-10%), or flat fee of $250-1,000. Offers advance in some cases. Requires exclusive representation of the artist for prints/posters during period of contract. Provides in-transit insurance, insurance while work is at publisher, shipping to and from firm, promotion and a written contract. Artist owns original work. Send query letter with brochure, tear sheets, slides and photographs to be kept on file or returned if requested; prefers to see slides or transparencies

© Kirsten Leigh

Art Resources International published this decorative country print by Kirsten Leigh as one of a six-print series. Leigh, of Campbell Hall, New York, received 10% of gross sales from the Stamford, Connecticut, publisher who bought reprint rights. The artist originally queried with slides.

initially as samples, then reviews originals. Samples not kept on file returned by SASE. Reports within 1 month. Call or write for appointment to show portfolio, or mail appropriate materials, which should include transparencies, slides and photographs.
Acceptable Work: Considers oil and acrylic paintings, pastels, watercolors and mixed media. Prefers pairs or series, triptychs, diptychs.
Tips: "Please submit any and all ideas."

ART SOURCE, Unit 3, 210 Cochrane Dr., Markham, Toronto, Ontario L3R 8E6 Canada. (416)475-8181. Art publisher and distributor. Produces posters, offset reproductions, art cards, handpulled originals, and prints using offset, lithograph, screen and etching for galleries and department stores. Publishes 20-30 freelance artists/year; distributes the works of 20-30 artists/year. Negotiates payment method. Negotiates rights purchased. Provides insurance while work is at publisher, promotion and a written contract. Negotiates ownership of original art. Send query letter with brochure, resume, and tear sheets, slides and photographs to be kept on file. To show a portfolio, mail thumbnails, tear sheets, Photostats and photographs. Samples not kept on file returned by SASE if requested. Reports within 14 days.
Acceptable Work: Considers oil and acrylic paintings, pastels, watercolors, mixed media and photographs. Themes and styles open. Prefers pairs and series; unframed.
Tips: "Show us your work in its best possible way. We see you through what you show us." One of today's most popular mediums is the poster—"we publish many of them." Artists should be very sensitive to the needs of the markets where they are trying to sell their work.

ART SPECTRUM, division of Mitch Morse Gallery, Inc., 334 E. 59th St., New York NY 10022. (212)593-1812. President: Mitch Morse. Art publisher and distributor. Produces limited editions (maximum of 250 prints) and handpulled originals—all 'multi-original' editions of lithographs, etchings, collographs, serigraphs. Serves galleries, frame shops, hotels, interior designers, architects and corporate art specifiers. Publishes 8-10 freelance artists/year; distributes the works of 15-20 artists/year. Negotiates payment method. Offers advance. Negotiates rights purchased. Provides promotion and shipping. Artist owns original art. Send query letter with resume, slides and photographs to be kept on file. Call or write for appointment to show portfolio, which should include original/final art and photographs. Samples not kept on file are returned. Reports within 1 week.
Acceptable Work: Considers original fine art prints only. Offers "subjects primarily suitable for corporate offices. Not too literal; not too avant-garde." Prefers series; unframed (framed unacceptable); 30x40" maximum.
Tips: "Do not stop by without appointment. Do not come to an appointment with slides only—examples of actual work must be seen. No interest in reproductive (photo-mechanical) prints—originals only. Submit work that is "an improved version of an existing 'look' or something completely innovative."

Actively seeking additional artists who do original paintings on paper. Trends show that the "current demand for contemporary has not yet peaked in many parts of the country. The leading indicators in the New York City design market point to a strong resurgence of Old English."

***ART WAYS,** 4090 F Morena Blvd., San Diego CA 92117. (714)272-1264. Contact: Jo Dowell. Art publisher/distributor/gallery. Publishes limited edition prints, offset reproductions and handpulled originals. Clients: designers, distributors, wholesalers, galleries. Publishes 4 freelance artists/year. Payment method is negotiated; pays royalty of 3% or works on consignment (25% commission). Offers advance. Buys reprint rights. Provides promotion, shipping to publisher and a written contract. Send query letter with brochure, resume, business card and samples to be kept on file. Call or write for appointment to show portfolio. Must see original work by appointment. Samples not filed are returned by SASE only if requested. Reports within 3 months.
Acceptable Work: Considers watercolors and mixed media. Prefers Southwest, Impressionist, new and traditional styles. Prefers pairs or series; 40x50" maximum.
Tips: "Color is 90% to the designer market."

ARTHURIAN ART GALLERY, 5836 Lincoln Ave., Chicago IL 60053. Owner: Art Sahagian. Estab. 1985. Art distributor/gallery handling limited editions, handpulled originals, bronzes, watercolors, oil paintings and pastels. Works with 30-40 artists/year. Pays flat fee, $50-1,000 average. Rights purchased vary with work. Provides insurance while work is at firm, promotion and a written contract. Send query letter with brochure showing art style or resume, photocopies, slides and prices. Samples not filed returned by SASE. Reports within 30 days. To show a portfolio, mail appropriate materials or write to schedule an appointment. Portfolio should include original/final art, color, final reproduction/product and photographs. Considers complexity of project, client's budget, and skill and experience of artist when establishing payment.

ARTISTWORKS WHOLESALE INC., 32 S. Lansdowne Ave., Landsowne PA 19050. (215)626-7770. Contact: Michael Markowicz. Art publisher and art distributor of offset reproductions and handpulled originals. Clients: distributors, galleries, decorators and other retailers. Works with 2-4 freelance artists/year. Negotiates payment method. Advance depends on payment method. Negotiates rights purchased. Requires exclusive representation. Provides in-transit insurance, insurance while work is at firm, promotion, shipping to and from firm and written contract. Send query letter with resume, slides and photographs to be kept on file. To show a portfolio, mail appropriate materials, which should include original/final art, final reproduction/product and photographs. "We only review original work after first seeing slides." Samples not filed returned by SASE.
Acceptable Work: Considers oil and acrylic paintings, pastels and watercolors; serigraphs. Especially likes still life/landscapes.
Tips: "We are looking for very well-executed still lifes and landscapes. We are not looking for traditional pieces but would rather work with a contemporary look. We have also received many more submissions than we can possibly publish. Artists should realize that we can only publish a few of the best works submitted. Submit only if you have producing high-quality, contemporary art."

ATLANTIC GALLERY, 1055 Thomas Jefferson St. NW, Washington DC 20007. (202)337-2299. Director: Virginia Smith. Art publisher/distributor. Publishes signed prints using offset lithography and hand-colored, handpulled restrike engravings. Clients: retail galleries, department stores, decorators, large commercial accounts, and manufacturers. Publishes 3 freelance artists/year. Pays flat fee, $250-1,000 average. Offers advance. Buys one-time rights. Provides in-transit insurance, insurance while work is at publisher, promotion, shipping to and from publisher and a written contract. Negotiates ownership of original art. Send query letter with brochure, resume, slides, photographs and tear sheets to be kept on file. Samples not kept on file returned by SASE. Reports within 3 weeks. Call or write for appointment to show portfolio.
Acceptable Work: Considers oil and acrylic paintings, pastels and watercolors. Prefers traditional art.

BECOME A POSTER, (division of Photo Environments), 2021 Vista del Man Ave., Los Angeles CA 90068. (213)465-9947. President: Joan Yarfitz. Works on assignment only. Uses freelance artists for marketing and advertising, posters, brochures and collateral materials. Send query letter with brochure showing art style or samples. Samples not filed are returned by SASE if requested. Call or write to schedule an appointment to show a portfolio. Negotiates payment. Considers clients' preferences when establishing payment. Negotiates rights purchased.
Acceptable Work: Considers illustration, b&w, color and photograhy.

BERNARD PICTURE CO. INC., Box 4744, Stamford CT 06907. (203)357-7600. Vice President: Michael Katz. Designer: Rosemary Pellicone. Art publisher. Produces high quality reproductions using

offset lithography for galleries, picture framers, distributors, and manufacturers worldwide. Publishes over 300 freelance artists/year. Pays royalties to artist of 10%. Offers advance against royalties. Buys reprint rights. "Sometimes" requires exclusive representation of the artist. Provides in-transit insurance and insurance while work is at publisher and a written contract. Artist owns original art. Send query letter with samples. Prefers slides, photos as samples—"then original work." Samples returned. Reports within 2 weeks. Call or write for appointment to show portfolio.
Acceptable Work: Considers all media, including photography. Prefers series and sets; unframed.

***THE BRENTWOOD PORTFOLIO**, 100 Barrington Walk, Los Angeles CA 90049. (213)476-7310. President: Charles T. Moffitt. Art Publisher and gallery showing limited editions, offset reproductions and handpulled originals for galleries, designers and wholesalers. Publishes work of 10 artists/year and distributes the work of 20 artists/year. Payment method is negotiable. Offers an advance. Buys all rights. Requires exclusive representation. Provides promotion and a writen contract. Send query letter with brochure showing art style or slides and transparencies. Samples are not filed. Samples not filed are returned. Reports back within 1 week. To show a portfolio, mail color.
Acceptable Work: Considers oil paintings, acrylic paintings, pastels, watercolor, tempera and mixed media. Prefers contemporary, realism and impressionism. Prefers individual works of art.
Tips: "We are very selective."

C.R. FINE ARTS LTD., 249 A St., Boston MA 02210. (617)236-4225. President: Carol Robinson. Art publisher/distributor/gallery handling limited editions, sculptures and fine art posters. Clients: galleries, poster stores, department stores, decorators, art consultants. Publishes 5-6 artists/year; distributes work of 30 artists/year. Pays royalty (15-30%) or works on consignment (40% commission);pays a flat fee of $500; payment method is negotiated. Offers advance. Negotiates rights purchased. Provides in-transit insurance, insurance while work is at firm, promotion, shipping to and from firm and a written contract. Send query letter with resume and slides to be kept on file. Samples not filed returned by SASE only if requested. Reports within 3 weeks. Write for appointment to show portfolio.
Acceptable Work: Considers pastels, watercolors and mixed media; serigraphs, and stone or plate lithographs. Especially likes landscapes, seascapes, contemporary themes, beach scenes, animals, music themes, abstracts.
Tips: "We look for landscape artists who have a perspective an a depth of composition. Colors are important and a textural quality."

CANADIAN ART PRINTS INC., 736 Richards St., Vancouver, British Columbia V6B 3A4 Canada. (604)681-3485. President: Jasar Nassrin. Publishes limited edition handpulled originals and offset reproductions for galleries, card and gift shops, department stores, framers and museum shops. Publishes 40-50 artists/year. Send slides or photos. Reports within 5 weeks. Provides promotion, shipping from publisher and written contract. Pays royalties.
Acceptable Work: Considers paintings, pastels, watercolors, intaglio, stone lithographs and serigraphs by Canadian artists; series.

***CARIBBEAN ARTS, INC.**, 985 Westchester Pl., Los Angeles CA 90019. (213)732-4601. Director: Bernard Hoyes. Art publisher/distributor of limited and unlimited editons, offset reproductions and handpulled originals. Clients: galleries, stores, bookstores, corporations, art dealers and collectors. Works with 203 artists/year. Pays $50-1,200 flat fee; 15% royalties or on consignment (50% commission). Payment method is negotiated. Offers an advance. Purchases first rights or negotiates rights purchased. Provides in-transit insurance, insurance while work is at firm, promotion, shipping from firm and a written contract. Send query letter with brochure or resume and slides. Samples are filed. Samples not filed are returned only if requested. Reports back within 10 days. Call or write to schedule an appointment to show a portfolio, which should include original/final art.
Acceptable Work: Considers oil paintings, pastels and watercolor. Prefers original themes and primitivism. Prefers individual works of art. Maximum size 30x40".
Tips: "Do a lot of original work."

CARLA JEAN PUBLISHING, 2501 Monaco Dr., Oxnard CA 93035. Owner: Carla Bonny. Clients: galleries.
Needs: "Interested in artists that have potential for publishing limited editions." Send slides and photographs. Samples not filed are returned. Reports back within 2 weeks. To show a portfolio, mail photographs and slides. Considers saleability of artwork when establishing payment.
Acceptable Work: Prefers acrylics or watercolors. Presently publish an artist like Matisse . . . figurative.

***THE CHASEN PORTFOLIO**, 6 Sloan St., South Orange NJ 07079. (201)761-1966. President: Andrew Chasen. Art publisher/distributor of limited editions and handpulled originals for galleries, deco-

rators, designers, art consultants and corporate art buyers. Publishes work of 3 artists/year and distributes the work of 10-15 artists/year. Payment method is negotiated. Negotiates rights purchased. Requires exclusive representation. Provides in-transit insurance, insurance while work is at firm, promotion, shipping to your firm, shipping from your firm and a written contract. Send query letter with brochure or tear sheets, photographs and slides. Samples are filed. Samples not filed are returned by SASE only if requested. Reports back only if interested. Call or write to schedule an appointment to show a portfolio, which should include original/final art, final reproduction/product and color. Payment method is negotatied.
Acceptable Work: Considers oil paintings, acrylic paintings, pastels, watercolor, lithographs, serigraphs, etchings and mixed media. Prefers architecture, figurative, still life and impressionism. Prefers individual works of art, pairs and unframed series. Maximum size 40x60".

CHINA ARTS INTERNATIONAL TRADING CO., INC., 54 Mott St., New York NY 10013. (212)226-5094. Assistant Manager: Hall P. Tam. Art distributor and gallery handling unlimited editions. Clients: galleries and wholesale distributors. Works with 20 freelance artists/year. Negotiates payment method. Buys reprint rights or negotiates rights purchased. Provides promotion and shipping from firm. Send brochure and business card to be kept on file. Prefers original work as samples. Samples not filed returned by SASE. Reports within 1 month. Write for appointment to show portfolio.
Acceptable Work: Considers watercolors. Especially likes lady, flower and bird, and landscape themes. Handles oriental paintings only.
Tips: Low prices are an important consideration.

CIRRUS EDITIONS, 542 S. Alameda St., Los Angeles CA 90013. President: Jean R. Milant. Produces limited edition handpulled originals for museums, galleries and private collectors. Publishes 3-4 artists/year. Send slides of work. Prefers slides as samples. Samples returned by SASE.
Acceptable Work: Contemporary paintings and sculpture.

***CLASS PUBLICATIONS, INC.**, 237 Hamilton St., Hartford CT 06106. (203)522-9200. Vice President: Leo Smith. Art publisher of offset reproductions. Publishes work of 2-3 artists/year. Pays $500-1,500 flat fee. Offers an advance. Buys all rights. Provides promotion, shipping from firm and a written contract. Send query letter with brochure or slides and transparencies. Samples are not filed. Samples not filed are returned only if requested. Reports back only if interested. To show a portfolio, mail slides.
Acceptable Work: Considers oil paintings, acrylic paintings and airbrush. "Our posters are published on 100 lb. text, retailing for $4.50, for the college market. Artwork should be creative using strong colors with good detail. Common areas of humor are very much sought after. Examples of those areas include money, sex, married life, medicare." Prefers individual works of art.
Tips: "Take a look at the artwork. Does it have a broad market appeal? We look for artwork that will have the qualities of sophistication and mass appeal combined."

GREG COPELAND INC., 10-14 Courtland St., Paterson NJ 07503. (201)279-6166. President: Greg Copeland. Art publisher and distributor of limited editions, handpulled originals, editions of sculpture, cast paper, paintings and dimensional sculpture. Clients: designers, architects, galleries, commercial designers, department stores, galleries and designer showrooms. Publishes 10-15 freelance artists/year. Works with 25-40 artists/year. Pays in royalties of 5% or negotiates payment method. Negotiates rights purchased. Provides shipping to firm. Send query letter with samples; or call or write for appointment to show portfolio. Prefers original work as samples. Samples are returned. Reports within 10 days.
Acceptable Work: Considers pen & ink line drawings, acrylic paintings, pastels, watercolors, mixed media, dimensional sculpture and sculpture; serigraphs. Looks for "beauty-excitement." Especially likes still lifes; modern style.

***DANMAR PRODUCTIONS, INC.**, 7385 Ashcroft, Houston TX 77081. (713)774-3343. Vice President: Marlene Caress. Estab. 1985. Art publisher of limited and unlimited editions, offset reproductions and handpulled originals for galleries, designers and contract framers. Publishes work of 10-15 artists/year. Pays 10% royalties. Payment method is negotiated. Offers an advance. Negotiates rights purchased. Requires exclusive representation. Provides insurance while work is at firm, promotion, shipping from firm and a written contract. Send query letter with brochure or tear sheets, photographs, slides and transparencies. Samples not filed are returned by SASE. Reports back within 10 days. To show a portfolio, mail original/final art, tear sheets, slides, final reproduction/product and color.
Acceptable Work: Considers oil paintings, acrylic paintings, pastels, watercolor and mixed media.
Tips: "We are looking to work with talented people who maintain a professional attitude. Originality is important and color is critical in our industry. We welcome all new talent and offer a quick, honest appraisal."

***DESIGNART**, 2700 S. La Cienega Blvd., Los Angeles CA 90034. (213)870-0021. President: Carole Franklin. Art distributor of limited editions, offset reproductions and handpulled originals for designers, architects, art consultants and galleries. Distributes work of 200 artists/year. Payment method is negotiated. Buys one-time rights. Provides insurance while work is at firm and shipping from firm. Send query letter with brochure or resume, tear sheets, photographs and slides. Samples are filed. Samples not filed are returned only if requested. Reports back within 2 weeks. Call or write to schedule an appointment to show a portfolio, which should include original/final art.
Acceptable Work: Prefers contemporary, sculptural, 3-D, traditional and original themes. Prefers individual works of art, pairs and unframed series.

DONALD ART CO. INC., and division Impress-Graphics, 30 Commerce Rd., Stamford CT 06904-2102. (203)348-9494. Art Coordinator: Bob Roberts. Produces unlimited edition offset reproductions for wholesale picture frame manufacturers, and manufacturers using art in their end products, for premiums and promotions. Send query letter with resume and duplicate photos or slides. Exclusive area representation required. Provides in-transit insurance, insurance while work is at publisher, shipping, promotion and written contract. Samples returned by SASE. Negotiates rights purchased.
Acceptable Work: Publishes 150 artists/year. Considers all types of paintings; oil, acrylic, watercolor, pastels, mixed media. Also needs work suitable for gallery posters.
Tips: "We have developed our division, Impress Graphics, for the publication and distribution of gallery posters. We will also be entering into the limited edition field, with some limited edition subjects already available. Look at the market to see what type of artwork is selling."

EDELMAN FINE ARTS, LTD., Suite 1503, 1140 Broadway, New York NY 10001. (212)683-4266. Vice President: H. Heather Edelman. Art distributor of original oil paintings. "We now handle watercolors, lithographs, serigraphs and 'work on paper' as well as original oil paintings." Clients: galleries, interior designers and furniture stores. Distributes work for 150 artists/year. Pays $50-1,000 flat fee or works on consignment basis (20% commission). Buys all rights. Provides in-transit insurance, insurance while work is at firm, promotion, shipping from firm and written contract. Send query letter with brochure, resume, tear sheets, photographs and "a sample of work on paper or canvas" to be kept on file. Call or write for appointment to show portfolio or mail original/final art and photographs. Reports within 1 week.
Acceptable Work: Considers oil and acrylic paintings, watercolors and mixed media. Especially likes Old World and Impressionist themes or styles.
Tips: Portfolio should include originals and only best work.

***EDITIONS FINE ART**, 433 E. Broadway, Salt Lake City UT 84111. (801)531-0146. Partners: Ruby Reece and Tom Hacking. Art publisher/art distributor and printer of limited editions, offset reproductions and unlimited editions for galleries, department stores, collectors, interior designers, gift stores, frame shops and poster shops. Works with 50-60 artists/year. Payment method is negotiated. Negotiates rights purchased. Provides in-transit insurance, insurance while work is at firm, promotion, shipping from firm, a written contract and consultation on art production and handling of art production for artists. Send query letter with brochure or resume, tear sheets, photographs, slides and 4x5 transparencies. Samples are filed. Samples not filed are returned by SASE. Reports back within 1 month. Write or call to schedule an appointment to show a portfolio, which should include thumbnails, tear sheets, slides and 4x5 transparencies.
Acceptable Work: Considers pen & ink line drawings, oil paintings, acrylic paintings, pastels, watercolor, tempera and mixed media. Prefers wildlife, contemporary, original themes, abstract and designer themes. Prefers individual works of art, pairs and unframed series. Maximum size 26x40".
Tips: "Keep your presentation as professional looking as possible. Be willing to paint in colors, textures and mediums that are currently selling in the market."

ATELIER ETTINGER INCORPORATED, 155 Avenue of the Americas, New York NY 10013. (212)807-7607. President: Eleanor Ettinger. Flatbed Limited Edition Lithographic Studio. "All plates are hand drawn, and proofing is completed on our Charles Brand hand presses." The edition run is printed on one our our 12-ton, Voirin presses. . . classic flatbed lithographic presses hand built in France over 100 years ago. Atelier Ettinger is available for contract printing for individual artists, galleries and publishers. Provides insurance while work is on premises. Printed editions for established artists such as Agam, Warhol, Bearden, Neel, as well as emerging artists such as Johnson, Van Epps and Stavrinos. For printing estimate, send good slides or transparencies, finished paper size, and edition size required.

ELEANOR ETTINGER INCORPORATED, 155 Avenue of the Americas, New York NY 10013. (212)807-7607. President: Eleanor Ettinger. Established art publisher of limited edition lithographs,

Close-up

Eleanor Ettinger

Art publisher
New York City

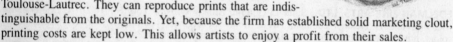

Art publishers offer quality printing and marketing exposure to artists. Eleanor Ettinger offers even more. Director of an art publishing firm and an atelier (an exclusive print workshop), Ettinger specializes in limited edition prints at affordable prices. The atelier is equipped with two flatbed presses that were originally used by master printmaker Toulouse-Lautrec. They can reproduce prints that are indistinguishable from the originals. Yet, because the firm has established solid marketing clout, printing costs are kept low. This allows artists to enjoy a profit from their sales.

Ettinger believes artists don't know enough about printmaking and are thus at a disadvantage when dealing with other publishers. "Artists are simply not knowledgeable about the many steps involved in printmaking. Thus, they're not equipped to ask the right questions when looking for a publisher who can supply all their needs." Ettinger's atelier is an open shop where artists are encouraged to ask questions about printmaking. Artists are assigned a master printer who works with them throughout the process of producing a print. Also, displayed on the walls of the atelier is a step-by-step photographic account of the process.

Ettinger recommends that artists who are looking for an art publisher first match their style to the publisher's specialty. Ettinger specializes in American realism. "Trends come and go, but we have found that a well-done realistic image has always been popular and appeals to a broad base of collectors." She looks for works which complement the images she already represents, with styles ranging from rustic to sophisticated but always American.

Ettinger also recommends artists find out as much as possible about the publisher's marketing efforts. "When talking to the publisher, find out how he would present your edition to galleries—if he has a direct sales representative who has developed reputable contacts. Ask how many galleries he is currently doing business with." Other important questions are: whether they provide promotional materials such as full-color brochures and if they attend national and international trade shows. These marketing tactics are the most effective means of promoting an artist. Ettinger always attends the international expos in New York and Los Angeles. She also arranges solo and group shows in galleries across the country.

While you must evaluate a publisher carefully, the publisher must also assess your potential. Most importantly, your work must be marketable. "Trying to determine what will be saleable is *the* most difficult task of being a publisher," says Ettinger. "If there were a surefire method of testing saleability, every edition would be sold out." She says publishers will often check with affiliated galleries to determine the artist's sales record; an established following will open even more sales opportunities to other galleries and collectors.

Publishers prefer to review slides for an initial look. "Slides are easier to mail, look at and handle," says Ettinger. If your work has potential, they will ask you to present a selection of original work. A good selling point, says Ettinger, is a series of images connected by a theme, such as paintings of the four seasons. "Galleries prefer to present more than one image by an artist. It shows that they are capable of creating a number of quality works, as opposed to just 'getting lucky' with one image. It makes selling a new artist's work much easier as well as providing an opportunity to collect an artist's work."

Publishing limited-edition prints seems to be a distant dream to many artists because publishers rely on established names for marketing purposes. Ettinger insists the dream is possible. "The best advice I can give is to keep submitting your work. As you grow and take on new directions, the same publisher who may have rejected your work may now be interested. You must, from the onset, be flexible and willing to work with a publisher to bring your work into the marketplace."

—Susan Conner

This painting by Vermont artist Audean Johnson was published as a limited edition of 275 pencil-signed and numbered lithographs and 25 artist proofs. Publisher Eleanor Ettinger specializes in American realism and looks for images that "mirror American society, its people, objects, places and culture."

limited edition sculpture, unique works (oils, watercolors, drawings, etc.). Currently distributes the work of 21 artists. All lithographs are printed on one of our Voirin presses, flat bed lithographic presses hand built in France over 100 years ago." Send query letter with visuals (slides, photographs, etc.). Reports within 7 days. Call for appointment to show portfolio.
Acceptable Work: Oils, watercolors, acrylic, pastels, mixed media, and pen and ink.
Tips: "Our focus for publication is towards the School of American Realism."

FAIRFAX PRINTS LTD., 4918 Delta River Dr., Lansing MI 48906. President: Gary Fairfax. General Manager: John Giuliani. Publishes limited and inexpensive unlimited edition offset reproductions for bookstores, gift shops, hobby shops, record stores, galleries and department stores. Publishes 1-2 artists/year. Send 4x6 or 3x5 prints. SASE. Reports within 4-6 weeks. Provides insurance while work is at publisher, promotion, shipping from publisher and written contract. Send query letter with brochure, slides and photographs. To show a portfolio, mail only 3x5 or 4x6 photographs. Buys poster rights only; sometimes negotiates rights; may also purchase originals. Pays royalties.
Acceptable Work: Subjects: wildlife and fantasy only. Realistic paintings (no photographic work) and sculpture on wildlife (primarily "big cats" and predatory birds), or fantasy/science fiction themes (though work can be quite stylized); series. Pays advance against 5-10% royalties.
Tips: Especially needs "science fiction fantasy, realistic or stylized (but no "primitive" styles or amateurish work!) and wildlife, realistic styles only (esp. "Big Cats" or "Predatory Birds"). Please submit only finished, *professional calibre* work. Send inexpensive 3x5 or 4x6 photos only—and include SASE if you wish work returned. *No* resumes/work experience needed."

FELIX ROSENSTIEL'S WIDOW & SON LTD., 33-35 Markham St., London SW3 England. 44-1-352-3551. Also New York office. Director: David A. Roe. Art publisher handling limited and unlimited editions, offset reproductions, hand coloured engravings and handpulled originals. Clients: galleries, department stores and wholesale picture manufactures. Publishes approximately 30-40 freelance artists/year. Pays $200-1,000 flat fee or 8% royalties. Buys all rights or negotiates rights purchased. Provides in-transit insurance, insurance while work is at firm, promotion, shipping from firm and a written contract. Send query letter with slides and photographs. Samples returned by SASE (nonresidents include IRC). Reports within 30 days.
Acceptable Work: Considers pen & ink line drawings, oils, acrylics, pastels, watercolors and mixed media; serigraphs and stone or plate lithographs, woodcuts, linocuts, etchings and engravings.
Tips: "Posters are declining."

***FINE ART DISTRIBUTORS**, 5954 Coca Cola Blvd., Columbus GA 31909. (404)563-9130. President: Wayne Bonner. Art publisher/distributor of limited and unlimited editions, offset reproductions and originals for art galleries, frame shops, gift shops, furniture stores, and interior designers/decorators. Publishes work of 4-5 artists/year and distributes the work of 35 artists/year. Pays 15% royalties and on consignment (50% commission of retail). Payment method is negotiated. Buys first rights. Negotiates rights purchased. Requires exclusive representation of the artist "we publish." Provides in-transit insurance, insurance while work is at firm, promotion, shipping from firm and a written contract. Send query letter with brochure or resume, tear sheets, Photostats, photographs, photocopies, slides or transparencies. Samples are not filed. Samples not filed are not returned. Reports back within 1 month only if interested. Call or write to schedule an appointment to show a portfolio, which should include final reproduction/product and color.
Acceptable Work: Considers acrylic paintings, pastels, watercolor, tempera and mixed media. Prefers contemporary, original themes and photorealistic works. Prefers individual works of art, pairs and unframed series. Maximum size 24x30".

FINE ART RESOURCES, INC., 2179 Queensburg Lane, Palatine IL 60074. President: Gerard V. Perez. Art publisher. Publishes limited editions of handpulled original prints for galleries. *Does not* publish reproductions. Publishes 80 freelance artists/year. Pays flat fee, $500-5,000 average. Offers advance. Negotiates rights purchased. Requires exclusive representation of the artist. Provides insurance while work is at publisher, promotion and a written contract. Plates or screens destroyed after printing. Send query letter with original work, slides, photographs and tear sheets. Samples returned by SASE. Reports within 10 days.
Acceptable Work: Considers "strictly original prints." Publishes representational style. Prefers individual works of art; unframed; 30x40" maximum.

RUSSELL A. FINK GALLERY, Box 250, 9843 Gunston Rd., Lorton VA 22079. (703)550-9699. Contact: Russell A. Fink. Art publisher/dealer. Publishes offset reproductions using five-color offset lithography for galleries, individuals, framers. Publishes 3 freelance artists/year. Pays royalties to artist or negotiates payment method. Negotiates rights purchased. Provides insurance while work is at publisher,

promotion and shipping from publisher. Negotiates ownership of original art. Send query letter with slides or photographs to be kept on file. Call or write for appointment to show portfolio. Samples returned if not kept on file.
Acceptable Work: Considers oil and acrylic paintings and watercolors. Prefers wildlife and sporting themes. Prefers individual works of art; unframed. "Submit photos or slides of at least near-professional quality. Include size, price, media and other pertinent data regarding the artwork. Also send personal resume and be courteous enough to include SASE for return of any material sent to me."
Tips: "Looks for composition, style and technique in samples. Also how the artist views his own art. Mistakes artists make are arrogance, overpricing, explaining their art and underrating the dealer."

FOXFIRE DIV., TOB, INC., 2730 N. Graham St., Charlotte NC 28206. Art Director: Larry O'Boyle. Series 500-750 outlets. "We sell lithographs, limited editions to frame shops, galleries and the like." Send query letter with resume and slides. Samples not filed are returned by SASE. Reports back within 10 days. To show a portfolio, mail appropriate materials, which should include slides. Artist receives flat fee; on acceptance. Considers saleability of artwork and rights purchased when establishing payment. Negotiates rights purchased.
Acceptable Work: Prefers watercolors/oils, with wildlife themes.

***FOXMAN'S OIL PAINTINGS LTD.**, 3350 Church, Skokie IL 60203. (312)679-3804. Secretary/Treasurer: Harold Lederman. Art distributor of limited and unlimited editions, oil paintings and watercolors for galleries, party plans and national chains. Publishes work of 4 artists/year and distributes work of 115 artists/year. Payment method is negotiated. Negotiates rights purchased. Requires exclusive representation. Provides promotion, shipping from firm and a written contract. Send query letter with resume, tear sheets, photographs and slides. Samples are not filed. Samples not filed are returned. Reports back within 2 weeks. Call to schedule an appointment to show a portfolio, which should include original/final art.
Acceptable Work: Considers oil paintings and pastels. Prefers simple themes, children, barns, countrysides and black art. Prefers individual works of art. Maximum size 24x36".

GALAXY OF GRAPHICS, LTD., 460 W. 34th St., New York NY 10001. (212)947-8989. President: Reid A. Fader. Art publisher of unlimited editions and offset reproductions. Clients: galleries, distributors and picture frame manufacturers. Publishes 25-50 freelance artists/year. Works with several hundred artists/year. Pays royalty of 10%. Offers advance. Buys all rights. Exclusive representation. Provides insurance while work is at firm, promotion, shipping from firm and written contract. Send photos or color slides or mail original/final art, final reproduction/product, color and photographs. Call or write for appointment to show portfolio. Samples are returned. Reports within a few days.
Acceptable Work: Any media. "Any currently popular and generally accepted theme welcomed."
Tips: "Traditional imagery is becoming very strong; posters are fading; diptychs and triptychs are still very good sellers. Pastels are *out*!"

GALLERY ENTERPRISES, 1881 Abington Rd. or 310 Bethlehem Plaza Mall, Bethlehem PA 18018. (215)868-1139. Contact: David Michael Donnangelo. Art publisher/distributor/gallery agents. Publishes limited edition offset reproductions and handpulled originals using etching; lithography and offset methods. Clients: galleries and volume art buyers. Publishes 2 freelance artists/year. Pays flat fee, $3,000 minimum. Negotiates rights purchased. Provides a written contract. Publishes own original art. Send resume and samples to be kept on file. To show a portfolio, mail appropriate materials. Prefers actual sample print as a representation. Samples are kept on file. Reports within 3 months.
Acceptable Work: Considers pen & ink drawings and etchings. All works considered but prefers traditional and wildlife themes. Especially needs abstract, corporate art for large works. Prefers series; 20x30" maximum.
Tips: Artists "must be able to produce original images in volume. Only interested in commercially-minded artists."

GEME ART INC., 209 W. 6th St., Vancouver WA 98660. (206)693-7772. Art Director: Merilee Will. Publishes fine art prints and reproductions in unlimited editions. Clients: galleries, department stores—the general art market. Works with 40-80 artists/year. Publishes the works of 15-20 artists; distributes 23-40. Payment is negotiated on a royalty basis. Normally purchases all rights. Provides promotion, shipping from publisher and a contract. Query with color slides or photos. SASE. Reports only if interested. Call or write for appointment to show portfolio. Simultaneous submissions OK.
Acceptable Work: Considers oils, acrylics, pastels, watercolor and mixed media. Themework is open.

GESTATION PERIOD, 1946 N. Fourth St., Columbus OH 43201. Operations Manager: Bob Richman. Art distributor of offset reproductions. "We do not publish." Clients: galleries, framers, college stores, gift stores, poster shops. Distributes 5-10 new artists/year "depending on what's available for our market." Payment method is negotiated. Generally offers an advance. Negotiates rights purchased. Generally does not require exclusive representation. Provides promotion packaging and shipping from firm. Send query letter with brochure and/or published samples to be kept on file. Samples not filed returned only if requested. Reports within 1 month.
Acceptable Work: Considers any medium including photography. Especially likes fine art/exhibition posters and humor.

***GETTYSBURG MILITARY ASSOC.**,Box 1117, Gettysburg PA 17325. (717)337-1000. Owner: Mary and Ted Sutphen. Art publisher/distributor. Publishes/distributes limited editions, offset reproductions and gold cast bronzes. Clients: retail mail order, retail galleries and wholesale art/frame shops. Publishes 3-5 artists/year and distributes the work of 3-5 artists/year. Pays 15% royalties. Buys one-time rights. Provides in-transit insurance, insurance while work is at firm, promotion and shipping from firm. Send query letter with brochure or slides and transparencies. Samples not returned. Reports back within 1 week. Call or write to schedule an appointment to show a portfolio, which should include slides and transparencies.
Acceptable Work: Considers oil and acrylic paintings. Military themes only.

GRAPHIC ORIGINALS INC., 153 W. 27th St., New York NY 10001. (212)807-6180. President: Martin Levine. Art publisher and dealer. Produces limited editions of etchings and silkscreens for galleries. Negotiates payment and rights purchased. Call for appointment. Send resume, photos or originals. Samples returned by SASE. Reports within 3 weeks.
Acceptable Work: Considers contemporary and realistic themes. Prefers unframed works; 24x30" maximum.

GRAPHICS INTERNATIONAL, Box 13292, Oakland CA 94661. (415)339-9310. Vice President: Rob R. Kral. Art publisher/distributor of limited and unlimited edition handpulled original etchings. Clients: galleries, frame shops, distributors and department stores. Number of artists worked with per year varies. Negotiates payment method. Buys all rights. Requires exclusive representation. Provides shipping from firm and a written contract. Send query letter with brochure, resume and samples to be kept on file. Accepts slides, photographs or original work as samples. Reports only if interested.
Acceptable Work: Considers pen & ink line drawings, watercolors and etchings. Especially likes traditional style.

***GREAT CANADIAN PRINT COMPANY LTD**, 404-63 Albert St., Winnipeg, Manitoba R3B 1G4 Canada. (204)942-7961. Officers: Gary Nerman and Allan Kiesler. Art publisher. Produces limited edition silkscreens for galleries, native craft stores. Publishes 15 freelance artists/year. "We publish only native (Indian) art with preference towards Canadian or Woodland. We will not look at queries from other sources and recommend that non-native artists not submit to us." Pays by royalty. Buys all rights. Requires exclusive representation of the artist. Provides a written contract. Send query letter with resume to be kept on file. If samples are requested, prefers to see original works, slides or photographs. Samples not kept on file returned only if requested. Reports within 4 weeks.
Acceptable Work: Prefers works on paper, any medium. Looks for "a unique style that still conforms to the parameters that make up native (Indian) art."

GREEN RIVER TRADING CO., Boston Corners Rd., RD2, Box 130, Millerton NY 12546. (518)789-3311. President: Art Kerber. Art publisher. Produces limited edition, signed and numbered prints of Western, wildlife and nautical art for galleries, wholesale and retail. Works with 3 freelance artists/year. Also uses artists for advertising, brochure and catalog design, illustration and layout.
First Contact & Terms: Works on assignment only. Send query letter with brochure, resume, business card, and tear sheets, slides and photographs to be kept on file. Samples not kept on file returned only if requested. Reports within 2 weeks. Write for appointment to show portfolio. Pays by the hour, $65 maximum; by the project, $200-2,000 average. Considers complexity of project, skill and experience of artist, turnaround time and rights purchased when establishing payment.
Tips: Artists must be willing "to take advice."

***GUILDHALL, INC.**, 2535 Weisenberger, Fort Worth TX 76107. (817)332-6733. President: John M. Thompson III. Art publisher/distributor of limited and unlimited editions, offset reproductions and handpulled originals for galleries, decorators, offices and department stores. Publishes work of 3 artists/year and distributes work of 6 artists/year. Pays $500-2,500 flat fee; 10-20% royalties. Payment method is negotiated. Negotiates rights purchased. Requires exclusive representation for contract artists. Pro-

vides insurance while work is at firm, promotion, shipping from firm and a written contract. Send query letter with resume, tear sheets, photographs, slides and 4x5 transparencies. Samples are not filed. Samples are returned only if requested. Reports back within 2 weeks. Call or write to schedule an appointment to show a portfolio, or mail thumbnails, tear sheets, slides, 4x5 transparencies, color and b&w.
Acceptable Work: Considers pen & ink drawings, oil paintings, acrylic paintings and watercolor. Prefers historical themes, westerns, abstract, equine and religious. Prefers individual works of art.

HADDAD'S FINE ARTS INC., Box 3016 C, Anaheim CA 92803. President: James Haddad. Produces limited and unlimited edition originals and offset reproductions for galleries, art stores, schools and libraries. Publishes 40-70 artists/year. Buys reproduction rights. Provides insurance while work is at publisher, shipping from publisher and written contract. Submit slides. SASE. Reports within 60 days.
Acceptable Work: Unframed individual works and pairs; all media.

ICART VENDOR GRAPHICS, 8568 Pico Blvd., Los Angeles CA 90035. (213)653-3190. Director: Sandy Verin. Art publisher/distributor/gallery. Produces limited and unlimited editions of offset reproductions and handpulled original prints for galleries, decorators, corporations, collectors. Publishes 3-5 freelance artists/year. Distributes 30-40 artists/year. Pays flat fee, $250-1,000; royalties (5-10%) or negotiates payment method. "We also distribute." Offers advance. Buys all rights. Usually requires exclusive representation of the artist. Provides insurance while work is at publisher. Negotiates ownership of original art. Send brochure, photographs, not slides. Samples returned by SASE. Reports within 1 month.
Acceptable Work: Considers oils, acrylics, watercolors and mixed media, also serigraphy and lithography. Likes airbrush. Prefers "turn-of-the-century through Art Deco period (1900s-1930s) styles." Prefers individual works of art, pairs, series; 30x40" maximum.
Tips: "Be original with your own ideas. Present clean, neat presentations in original or photographic form (no slides). Prefers Art Deco style or Art Nouveau. However, other work is certainly considered. No abstracts please."

IMPRESS GRAPHICS, 30 Commerce Rd., Stamford CT 06904. (203)348-9494. National Sales Manager: Bob Roberts. Provides for magazines, trade shows and mailings. Send query letter with resume, slides and photographs. Samples not filed returned by SASE. Reports within 2 weeks. To show a portfolio, mail photographs and slides (duplicates).
Acceptable Work: Considers photographs, airbrush and paintings.

ARTHUR A. KAPLAN CO. INC.,, 460 W. 34th St., New York NY 10001. (212)947-8989. National Sales Manager: Reid Fader. Art publisher of unlimited editions, offset reproduction, prints and posters. Clients: galleries, department stores and picture frame manufacturers. Publishes approximately 40 freelance artists/year. Works with 300+ artists/year. Pays a royalty of 5-10%. Offers advance. Buys all rights. Requires exclusive representation. Provides insurance while work is at firm, promotion, shipping from firm and a written contract. Send resume, tear sheets, slides, photographs and original art to be kept on file. Material not filed is returned. Reports within 2-3 weeks. To show a portfolio, mail appropriate materials or call to schedule an appointment. Portfolio should include original/final art, final reproduction/product, color, tear sheets and photographs.
Acceptable Work: Considers oils, acrylics, pastels, watercolors, mixed media, photography.
Tips: "We cater to a mass market and require fine quality art with decorative and appealing subject matter. Don't be afraid to submit work—we'll consider anything and everything."

KEY WEST GRAPHICS, INC., 232 S.E. 10th St., Fort Lauderdale FL 33301. (305)463-1150. President: Jennifer Roberts. Estab. 1985. Clients: galleries, interior design firms and private art dealers. Uses artists for illustrations and color. Send query letter with brochure showing art style or resume, tear sheets, slides and photographs. Samples not filed returned by SASE. Reports within 5 weeks. To show a portfolio, mail appropriate materials or write to schedule an appointment. Portfolio should include original/final art, color and tear sheets.
Acceptable Work: Considers saleability of artwork and rights purchased when establishing payment. Negotiates rights purchased. Considers pen & ink with washes and paintings and pastels. Prefers landscapes and figurative work as themes. Prefers oils and acrylics.

***MURRAY KLEIN ASSOCIATES INC.**, Box 741, 1983 Ladenburg Dr., Westbury NY 11590. (516)333-0516. President: Murray Klein. Publishes unlimited edition offset reproductions for art galleries, museums, colleges, and book and department stores. Publishes 4 artists/year. Query or arrange interview. Reports within 2-3 weeks. Provides promotion, shipping to publisher and written contract.
Acceptable Work: Impressionistic drawings, cartoons, paintings and watercolors including wildlife and flowers; series. Maximum size: 22x28". Pays $200 mimimum against 5-15% royalties. Also will work on consignment with commission arrangement. Offers advance.

DAVID LAWRENCE EDITIONS, Suite 38, 22541A Pacific Coast Hwy., Malibu CA 90265. (818)996-3509. President: David Lawrence. Art publisher/distributor handling limited and unlimited editions of offset reproductions. Clients: galleries and frame shops. Publishes 5-10 freelance artists and distributes work for 25 artists/year. Negotiates payment method and rights purchased. Requires exclusive representation. Provides promotion, shipping from firm and a written contract. Send a resume and "anything that gives a good representation of work" to be kept on file. Reports back only if interested. Call or write for appointment to show portfolio.
Acceptable Work: Considers all media for publication and distribution.

MARTIN LAWRENCE LIMITED EDITIONS, 16250 Stagg St., Van Nuys CA 91406. (818)988-0630. Art publisher. Publishes limited edition graphics, fine art posters and originals by internationally known, up-an-coming and new artists.
First Contact & Terms: Contact by mail only. Send good quality slides or photographs, pertinent biographical information and SASE. Exclusive representation required.
Acceptable Work: Prefers oils, acrylics, watercolors, serigraphs, lithographs and etchings.

***LAWRENCE UNLIMITED**, 8721 Darby Ave., Northridge CA 91328. (213)349-4120. Owner: Renee Anenberg. Distributes limited editions. Clients: designers. Distributes work of 10 artists/year. Payment method is negotiated. Negotiates rights purchased. Requires exclusive representation. Send query letter with tear sheets and photographs.
Acceptable Work: Considers watercolor. Prefers commercial—traditional and transitional. Prefers pairs and unframed series.

***LESLI ART, INC.**, 3715 Benedict Cyn. Ln., Sherman Oaks CA 91423. (818)986-6056. President: Stan Shevrin. Art publisher and artist agent handling offset reproductions and paintings for art galleries and the trade. Works with 20 artists/year. Payment method is negotiated. Offers an advance. Requires exclusive representation. Send query letter with photographs and slides. Samples not filed are returned by SASE. Reports back within 1 month. To show a portfolio, mail slides and color photographs.
Acceptable Work: Considers oil paintings, acrylic paintings, pastels, watercolor, tempera and mixed media. Prefers realism and impressionism—figures costumed, narrative content. Prefers individual works of art. Maximum size 36x48".

***LITHOS' Publishers and Distributors of Collector Prints**, Box 4591, St. Louis MO 63108. (314)367-2177. Publisher: Linda Thomas. Handles limited edition prints (maximum 1,000/edition). Clients: framers, galleries, interior designers and art collectors. Publishes 4-6 freelance artists/year; 6-10 artists/year; 8 artists/year. Pays negotiable royalty. Negotiates rights purchased. Provides insurance while work is at firm, promotion, shipping from firm and a written contract. Send query letter with resume, business card, slides and photographs to be kept on file. Reports back within 1 month. Write for appointment to show portfolio; or write for artists' guidelines.
Acceptable Work: Oil paintings, acrylic paintings, pastels and watercolors. Especially likes contemporary themes or styles.
Tips: "We are interested in never-before published images of black American subjects only. Artist should be prepared to give Lithos' exclusive publication rights for at least sixty months. Broad name recognition is not a prerequistion; good work is!"

***LITTLE CREATURES' COUNTRY ART**, 7385 N. Seneca Rd., Milwaukee WI 53217. President: Dianne Spector. Publishes open editions, offset reproductions for gift shops, department stores and country shops. "National sales distribution established." Publishes 1-2 freeelance artists/year. Payment method is negotiated. Send query letter with brochure showing art style or photocopies, slides, Photostats, photographs or transparencies. Samples are returned by SASE. Reports back within 1 month.
Acceptable Work: Considers oil painting, acrylic paintings, watercolor and mixed media. "Items with mass appeal; the folk art market for the upscale customer."
Tips: "Our customers are women aged 25-50, decorating their homes or purchasing affordable gifts. We publish the art, frame it and distribute it. Subjects should be warm and friendly but of high quality and with uniqueness of ideas."

***LONDON CONTEMPORARY ART, INC.**, 20526 N. Milwaukee, Deerfield IL 60015. (312)520-7779. President: Gerard Perez. Art publisher of handpulled original limited edition prints for art galleries. Publishes work of 60 artists/year. Pays 5% royalties. Buys all rights. Requires exclusive representation. Provides insurance while work is at firm. Send query letter with photographs. Samples are not filed. Samples are not returned. Reports back only if interested. To show a portfolio, mail color photos.
Acceptable Work: Any and all media. Prefers pointilism, impressionism and landscapes.

***MARCO DISTRIBUTORS**, 1412 S. Laredo, Aurora CO 80017. (303)752-4819. President: Mark Woodmansee. Art publisher and distributor of limited editions, handpulled originals, oil washes and oil on canvas. Clients: corporations, galleries and interior designers. Publishes 2 freelance artists/year. Distributes work for 10 artists/year. Pays royalty of 10-20%; on consignment basis; or negotiates payment method. Buys all rights or reprint rights or negotiates rights purchased. Requires exclusive representation. Provides promotion, shipping to and from firm and written contract. Send brochure and samples to be kept on file. Prefers photographs, tear sheets or original work as samples. Samples not filed are not returned. Reports back to artist. Call or write for appointment to show portfolio; or contact through artist's agent.
Acceptable work: Considers oil and acrylic paintings, pastels, watercolors and mixed media; serigraphs, stone lithographs, plate lithographs and woodcuts. Especially likes landscapes, some unique figures and impressionist style.
Tips: "Send photos of your work; follow with a call."

***DAVID MARSHALL**, Box 24635, St. Louis MO 63141. (314)423-1100. President: Marshall Gross. Art publisher/distributor/gallery handling and distributing sculpture, cast paper, silk screens, lithographs and sculpted paper. Clients: galleries, architects, designers and fine furniture stores. Distributes the work of 10-15 artists/year. Publishes/distributes the work of 25 artists/year. Pays flat fee of $15-50 for each item; royalties possible; payment method can be negotiated. Buys all rights. Provides insurance only while work is at firm, promotion and shipping from the firm. Send query letter with brochure showing art style or photographs. Samples are not filed. Samples not filed are returned only if requested by artist. Reports within 7 days. Call to schedule an appointment to show a portfolio, which should include roughs, slides and color photos.
Acceptable Work: Considers pastels, watercolor and castpaper. Prefers contemporary, original themes and primitivism. Prefers individual works and art and unframed series; 36x40 maximum.
Tips: "We prefer items that work with current home fashion color trends. Southwestern themes are needed; glass and mirror designs are given special consideration."

BRUCE MCGAW GRAPHICS, INC., 230 Fifth Ave., New York NY 10001. (212)679-7823. Acquisitions: Paul Liptak. Send query letter with brochure showing art style or resume, tear sheets, Photostats, photocopies, slides and photographs. Samples not filed returned by SASE. Reports within weeks. To show a portfolio, mail color, tear sheets and photographs. Considers skill and experience of artist, saleability of artwork, client's preferences and rights purchased when establishing contract.

***MEW ACQUISITION COMPANY, DBA Museum Editions West**, 9151 Exposition Dr., Los Angeles CA 90034. (213)204-6251. Owner: Grace Yu. Art publisher/distributor of limited and unlimited editions for galleries and museum chain stores. Publishes 5-10 artists/year and distributes the work of 10-20 artists/year. Works with 30-50 artists/year. Pays 2-3% royalties or 20-30% commission on consignment; payment method is negotiated. Buys reprint rights. Sometimes requires exclusive representation of the artist. Send query letter with brochure or slides. Samples are filed. Reports back only if interested. To show a portfolio, mail final reproduction/product.

MINOTAUR, # 221, 77 Mowat Ave., Toronto, Ontario M64 3E3 Canada. (416)530-1454. Contact: J. Kevin Kelleher. Art publisher/distributor of fine art and photography posters. Clients: galleries, framers, wholesale framers and gift shops. Works with 18 artists/year. Pays flat fee, royalty or negotiates method; "a combination of purchase of rights plus royalty." Offers advance. Buys first rights. Provides a written contract. Send query letter with business card, slides, photographs or tear sheets to be kept on file. Material not filed is returned. Reports within days. Write for appointment to show portfolio.
Acceptable Work: Considers pen & ink line drawings, oils, acrylics, pastels and watercolors; serigraphs and stone or plate lithographs. Accepts "almost any contemporary theme."

MITCH MORSE GALLERY INC., 334 E. 59th St., New York NY 10022. (212)593-1812. President: Mitch Morse. Art publisher and distributor. Produces limited edition handpulled originals for framers, galleries, interior designers, architects, hotels and better furniture stores. Publishes 8-10 artists/year; distributes the work of 15-20 artists/year. Negotiates payment. Offers advance. Provides promotion and shipping. Send query letter with resume, and slides and photographs. SASE. Reports within 1 week.
Acceptable Work: Unframed realistic, impressionistic and romantic paintings, lithographs, serigraphs and etchings; individual works; 4x6' maximum.
Tips: "There is continued emphasis on color as a major ingredient in the selection of art and greater interest in more traditional subject matter. Actively seeking additional artists who do original paintings on paper."

***THE NATURE COMPANY**, 750 Hearst Ave., Berkeley CA 94710. (415)524-9811. Product Development Director: Lon Murphy. Art publisher/distributor of unlimited editions. Publishes work of 8-14 artists/year. Pays $250-800 flat fee; royalties; 5% wholesale commission. Negotiates rights purchased. Provides in-transit insurance, insurance while work is at firm, promotion, shipping to your firm, shipping from firm and a written contract. Send query letter with brochure showing art style or tear sheets, Photostats, photographs, slides and transparencies. Samples are filed. Samples not filed are returned only if requested. Reports back within 2 months. To show a portfolio, mail roughs, Photostats, tear sheets, slides, transparencies, color and b&w.
Acceptable Work: Considers pen & ink line drawings, oil paintings, acrylic paintings, pastels, watercolor, tempera and mixed media. "Must be natural history subjects (i.e, plants, animals, landscapes). Avoid domesticated plants, animals, and people-made objects."

NEW DECO, INC., Suite A11, 10018 Spanish Isles Blvd., Boca Raton FL 33434. (305)482-6295. President: Brad Morris. Art publisher/distributor. Produces limited editions using offset lithography for galleries, also publishes/distributes unlimited editions. Publishes 1 freelance artist/year. Needs new designs for reproduction. Pays flat fee. Offers advance. Negotiates rights purchased. Provides promotion, shipping and a written contract. Negotiates ownership of original art. Send brochure, resume, and tear sheets, Photostats or photographs to be kept on file. Samples not kept on file are returned. Reports only if interested. Call or write for appointment to show portfolio, which should include tear sheets.
Acceptable Work: Prefers Art Deco, Art Nouveau themes and styles. Prefers individual works of art, pairs or series.

***NEW ENGLAND GRAPHIC IMAGES**, 5 Deer Brook Rd., Woodstock VT 05091. (802)672-3557. Publisher: J. Allmon. Estab. 1986. Art publisher of limited and open editions, offset reproductions and handpulled originals for galleries and interior designers. Works with 3-4 artists/year at present. Payment method is negotiated. Negotiates rights purchased. Provides a written contract. Send query letter with brochure showing art style or slides. Samples are filed. Samples not filed are returned. Reports back within 1 month. To show a portfolio, mail slides.
Acceptable Work: Considers oil paintings, acrylic paintings, watercolor and tempera. Prefers New England scenes.
Tips: "Don't send it unless it sells New England."

NEW YORK GRAPHIC SOCIETY, Box 1469, Greenwich CT 06836. (203)661-2400. Art & Production Manager: Caron Caswell. Art publisher/art distributor of offset reproductions, limited editions, posters and handpulled originals. Clients: galleries, frame shops, museums and foreign trade. Publishes 10 new freelance artists/year. Distributes work for 10 new artists/year. Pays flat fee or royalty of 1.2%. Offers advance. Buys all print reproduction rights. Provides in-transit insurance from firm to artist, insurance while work is at firm, promotion, shipping from firm and a written contract; provides insurance for art requested. Send query letter with slides or photographs. Write for artist's guidelines. All submissions returned to artists by SASE after review. Reports within 2 months.
Acceptable Work: Considers oils, acrylics, pastels, watercolors and mixed media; pencil drawings (colored). Distributes posters only. Publishes/distributes serigraphs, stone lithographs, plate lithographs and woodcuts.
Tips: "We publish a broad variety of styles and themes. However, we do not publish experimental, hard-edge, sexually explicit or suggestive material. Work that is by definition fine art and easy to live with, that is, which would be considered decorative, is what we look for."

NOKES BERRY GRAPHICS, LTD., (formerly Gourmet Grafiks, Inc.), 300 Montgomery St., Alexandria VA 22314. (703)683-4686. President: Mary Nokes Berry. Art publisher of offset reproductions. Clients: galleries, department stores, interior designers and independent stores. "When publishing freelance artists, negotiates payment method and rights purchased." Provides promotion and written contract. Send query letter with brochure, resume, business card and slides to be kept on file. Samples not filed returned only if requested. Reports within 1 month. Samples not filed returned only if requested. Write for appointment to show portfolio.
Acceptable Work: Considers oils, acrylics, pastels, watercolors, mixed media and photography for publication and distribution.
Tips: Especially looks for timely pieces-new graphic approaches, current subjects, colors and themes. And, of course, the rare "timeless" art that is acceptable always. A mistake artists make is "ignoring the trends of the times and the suggestions which will make their work reflect what people want in their homes. There's a balance between accepting an artist's work exactly as is and using modifications (interpretation) to make the work timely."

NORTH BEACH FINE ARTS, INC., 2565 Blackburn St., Clearwater FL 33575. President: James Cournoyer. Art publisher and art distributor handling limited editions of handpulled originals. Clients: galler-

ies, architects, interior designers and art consultants. Pays flat fee, $50-1,000; royalties, 50% or consignment, 50% commission. Negotiates rights purchased. Offers an advance. Requires exclusive representation. Provides insurance when work is at firm, promotion, written contract and markets expressly-select original handmade editions of a small number of contemporary artists. Send query letter with brochure, resume, tear sheets, Photostats, photocopies, slides and photographs to be kept on file. Accepts any sample showing reasonable reproduction. Samples returned by SASE only if requested. Reports within 1 month. To show a portfolio, mail original/final art, color, tear sheets, Photostats, photographs and b&w.
Acceptable Work: Considers pen & ink line drawings and mixed media; serigraphs, stone lithographs, plate lithographs, woodcuts and linocuts. Especially likes contemporary, unusual and original themes or styles.
Tips: Wants "original handpulled work by serious, experienced, career-oriented artists with a well developed and thought-out style. Unfortunately, 90% of submissions from *Artists Market* have been unprofessional hobbyists or else blatant plagiarism of an established artist's work. But the other 10% makes it worthwhile."

***OAKSPRINGS IMPRESSIONS**, 6840 Sir Francis Dr., Forest Knolls CA 94933. (415)488-0194. General Manager: Michael Pettit. Art publisher/distributor of limited and unlimited editions, offset reproductions and handpulled originals. Publishes work of 2 artists/year and distributes the work of 6 artists/year. Payment method is negotiated. Buys first rights, one-time rights and all rights. Negotiates rights purchased. Requires exclusive representation. Provides promotion, shipping from firm and a written contract. Send query letter with brochure or resume, tear sheets, photographs and slides. Samples are not filed. Samples are returned by SASE. Reports back within 1 month. To show a portfolio, mail slides and 4x5 transparencies.
Acceptable Work: Considers acrylic paintings, pastels, watercolor, tempera and mixed media. Prefers individual works of art, pairs and unframed series.

PETERSEN PRINTS, 6725 Sunset Blvd., Los Angeles CA 90028. Director: William L. Cooksey. Produces limited editions (maximum 950 prints) using offset lithography for galleries, department stores and publishes sporting merchandisers. Publishes 10-15 freelance artists/year. Buys all rights. Requires exclusive representation of the artist. Provides in-transit insurance, insurance while work is at publisher, promotion, shipping from publisher and a written contract. Artist owns original art. Send query letter with brochure, resume, slides or photographs to be kept on file. Samples not kept on file are returned by SASE. Reports within 3 weeks. Write for appointment to show portfolio.
Acceptable Work: Considers oil and acrylic paintings and watercolors. Prefers paintings of sporting subjects: game birds, waterfowl and game animals. Prefers individual works of art.

JUDITH L. POSNER & ASSOCIATES, INC., 207 N. Milwaukee St., Milwaukee WI 53202. (414)352-3097. President: Judith L. Posner. Art publisher/distributor/gallery. Produces limited and unlimited editions of offset reproductions and original serigraphs and lithographs. Publishes 100 freelance artists/year. Pays royalty or works on consignment (50% commission). Buys one-time rights. Sometimes requires exclusive representation of artist. Provides a written contract. Send resume and photographs, slides or transparencies. Samples not kept on file are returned. Reports within 10 days.
Acceptable Work: Considers all media. Prefers series. Specializes in contemporary themes.
Tips: "Have something very exciting and unusual to show."

***PRASADA PRESS, INC.**, 4303 Hamilton Ave., Cincinnati OH 45223. (513)542-0350. President: Janice R. Forberg. Publisher and contract printer for artists and publishers. Produces handpulled original lithographs as contract printing for selected artists and publishers. Clients are dealers, museums, publishers and artists. "The work is created in the studio at Prasada Press with technical help. The medium is lithography; all editions are handpulled; editions no larger than 50; work is on Bavarian limestone." Publishes up to 10 artists/year. Pays royalties of up to 50%. Negotiates rights purchased. Provides a written contract. Prasada Press as publisher owns the edition; negotiates percentage of sales to artist. Send resume with slides. Samples returned by SASE. Reports in 2 months. Write for appointment. Provide resume and slides to be kept on file for possible future assignments.
Acceptable Work: Work created in Prasada Studio on stones or plates.

PRESTIGE ART GALLERIES, INC., 3909 W. Howard St., Skokie IL 60076. (312)679-2555. President: Louis Schutz. Art publisher/dealer/gallery. Publishes limited editions and offset reproductions for retail professionals and galleries. Publishes 4 freelance artists/year. Works on consignment basis; firm charges 33% commission. Buys all rights or negotiates rights purchased. Provides insurance while work is at publisher, promotion and a written contract. Publisher owns original art. Send query letter with brochure, resume and slides to be kept on file. Samples returned by SASE. Reports only if interested.

Acceptable Work: Considers oil and acrylic paintings. Prefers realism, and mother and child themes. Prefers individual works of art; unframed; 30x40" maximum.

REECE GALLERIES INC., 24 West 57th St., New York NY 10019. (212)333-5830. Co-Directors: Shirley and Leon Reece. Art dealers and consultants to corporations and private collectors. Also distributes for other artists to galleries. Works with many freelance artists/year. Send query letter with resume, slides and photographs. Samples not filed returned by SASE. Reports within 14 days. Call to schedule an appointment to show a portfolio, which should include original/final art. Pays 50% of net proceeds.
Acceptable Work: Considers skill and experience of artist, saleability of artwork and clients' preferences when reviewing slides. Prefers urban, abstract landscapes, prints and other media.
Tips: Artist should have "technical skill that must be obvious in the media worked overall quality; no offset work."

SCAFA-TORNABENE ART PUBLISHING CO. INC., 100 Snake Hill Rd., West Nyack NY 10994. (914)358-7600. Co-owner: Claire Scafa. Produces unlimited edition offset reproductions for framers, galleries, museums, commercial art trade and manufacturers world-wide. Publishes 50-100 artists/year. Pays $200-350 flat fee for each accepted piece. Published artists (successful ones) can advance to royalty arrangements with advance against 5-10% royalty. Buys only reproduction rights (written contract). Artist maintains ownership of original art. Requires exclusive publication rights to all accepted work. Send query letter first; with slides or photos and then arrange interview. SASE. Reports in about 2 weeks.
Acceptable Work: Unframed decorative paintings, watercolors, posters, photos and drawings; usually pairs and series.
Tips: Always looking for something new and different. "Study the market first. See and learn from what stores and galleries display and sell. Try to originate in a genre, rather than copycat. Trends begin with the artist."

SOMERSET HOUSE PUBLISHING CORP., 10688 Haddington, Houston TX 77043. Contact: Lisa Ince. Clients: 5,000 retail art galleries. Publishes 15 artists/year. Payment method is negotiated. Send query letter with slides. Samples not filed returned. Reports within months. To show a portfolio, mail final reproduction/product and photographs. Considers salability of artwork when establishing payment. Buys first rights. Special interest: nautical/seascapes and wildlife themes.

STRICTLY LIMITED EDITIONS, 1258 2nd Ave., San Francisco CA 94122. Contact: Jacob F. Adler. Art publisher/distributor of limited edition handpulled originals. Clients: galleries. Works with 8-10 artists/year. Negotiates payment method and rights purchased. Provides promotion and a written contract. Send query letter with brochure and samples to be kept on file. Write for appointment to show portfolio. Prefers to review original work. Samples are returned only if requested. Reports back only if interested.
Acceptable Work: Considers original graphics; serigraphs and etchings. Especially likes a variety of styles in figurative art.
Tips: "Have patience!"

STUDIO HOUSE EDITIONS, 415 W. Superior, Chicago IL 60610. (312)751-0974. Director: Bill Sosin. Art publisher of offset reproductions. Clients: galleries. Publishes 7 freelance artists/year. Distributes 15 artists/year. Negotiates payment method and rights purchased. Provides promotion. Send query letter with brochure and slides to be kept on file. Samples not filed returned only if requested. Reports only if interested.
Acceptable Work: Photographs; stone lithographs and plate lithographs. Especially likes decor themes or styles.
Tips: "Send only high quality transparent duplicates of best work."

JOHN SZOKE GRAPHICS INC., 164 Mercer St., New York NY 10012. Director: John Szoke. Produces limited edition handpulled originals for galleries, museums and private collectors. Publishes 10-25 artists/year. Charges commission or negotiates royalties. Provides promotion and written contract. Arrange interview or submit slides. SASE. Reports within 1 week.

TELE GRAPHICS, 607 E. Walnut St., Pasadena CA 91101. President: Ron Rybak. Art publisher/art distributor handling limited editions, offset reproductions, unlimited editions and handpulled originals. Clients: galleries, picture framers, interior designers and regional distributors. Publishes 1-4 freelance artists/year. Distributes work for 25 artists/ year. Works with 35-40 artists/year. Negotiates payment method. Offers advance. Negotiates rights purchased. Requires exclusive representation. Provide promotion, shipping from your firm and a written contract. Send query letter with resume and samples. Samples not filed returned only if requested. Reports within 30 days. Call or write to schedule an ap-

pointment to show a portfolio, which should include original/final art. Pays for design by the project. Considers skill and experience of artist, and rights purchased when establishing payment.
Tips: "Be prepared to show as many varied examples of work as possible. We are not interested in seeing only 1 or 2 pieces."

***TOH-ATIN GALLERY**, 145 W. 9th St., Durango CO 81301. (303)247-8444. Vice President: Antonia Clark. Art publisher/distributor and gallery handling offset reproductions for galleries, gift shops, Indian art shops, interior design and decorators. Publishes work of 1-2 artists/year and distributes work of 10-12 artists/year. Payment method is negotiated. Negotiates rights purchased. Provides in-transit insurance, insurance while work is at firm and shipping from firm. Send query letter with brochure or resume, tear sheets, Photostats, photographs, slides and transparencies. Samples are filed. Samples not filed are returned by SASE. Reports within 2 months. Call or write to schedule an appointment to show a portfolio.
Acceptable Work: Considers oil paintings, acrylic paintings, pastels, watercolor and mixed media. Prefers Southwestern or Indian subjects. Prefers individual works of art. Maximum sixe 48x48".
Tips: "Send photos first—then call for an appointment. Don't use a company's toll-free lines to sell your images to them. If you have your own prints and want them marketed, price them reasonably."

***VOYAGEUR ART**, 2828 Anthony Ln. S, Minneapolis MN 55418. Executive Vice President: James Knuckey. Art publisher of limited editions, offset reproductions, unlimited editions and handpulled originals for galleries, frame shops, poster shops, department stores, retail catalog companies, corporations. Publishes the work of 15-20 freelance artists/year and distributes the work of 30 artists/year. Works with 30 artists/year. Payment method is negotiated. Offers an advance "in some instances." Negotiates rights purchased. Requires exclusive representation of the artist with exceptions. Provides in-transit insurance, insurance while work is at firm, promotion, shipping from your firm and a written contract. Send query letter with brochure or resume, tear sheets, photographs, slides or transparencies. Samples are filed. Samples not filed are returned only if requested. Reports back within 2 months. To show a portfolio, mail tear sheets, slides, transparencies and color.
Acceptable Work: Considers oil paintings, acrylic paintings, pastels, watercolor, tempera, scratch board and mixed media. Prefers traditional works with original themes, primitivism and photorealistic works. "Will consider all submissions."
Tips: "Apply only if you feel your work measures up with the best in your media. Send only your very best samples of your art. If you haven't painted at least 500 paintings, chances are you have not mastered your medium to the point that the art is publishable. Photos should be professionally done. Indicate why you feel your work will sell."

***WILD WINGS, INC.**, South Highway 61, Lake City MN 55041. (612)345-5355. Vice President: Byron G. Webster. Art publisher of offset reproductions. Clients: 24 Wild Wings galleries, 800 wholesale accounts. 2 million + mail order catalogs and brochures. Publishes/distributes the work of 140 artists/year. Payment method is negotiated. Provides insurance while work is at firm, promotion, shipping from firm, a written contract, five major shows a year, numerous local and regional shows at 24 galleries coast to coast and inclusion in 15-year annual original art catalog. Send query letter with brochure or resume, slides and 4x5 transparencies. Samples are not filed. Samples not filed are returned by SASE only if requested by artists. Reports back to the artist within 1 week. To show a portfolio, a freelance artist should: mail slides and 4x5" transparencies.
Acceptable Work: Considers oil and acrylic paintings and watercolor. Prefers wildlife and sporting art. Prefers: individual works of art. Maximum size of acceptable work: 36x48".
Tips: "Send slides or transparencies that show best current works. Preferably no duck stamp or conservation stamp entries. In addition, show and indicate earlier works to provide statement of growth to date. List prices realized for sales."

THE WINN CORPORATION, Box 80096, Seattle WA 98108. (206)763-9544. President: Larry Winn. Art publisher and distributor of limited editions, offset reproductions and handpulled originals. Clients: interior designers, art galleries, frame shops, architects, art consultants, corporations, hotels, etc. Publishes 10 freelance artists/year (prints). Distributes work for 120 artists/year (posters). Pays flat fee, $500-10,000; variable royalties; 50% commission; payment method is negotiated. Offers advance. Negotiates rights purchased. Requires exclusive representation. Provides in-transit insurance, insurance while work is at firm, promotion, shipping from firm and written contract. Send query letter with resume and slides. Slides returned by SASE. Reports within 1 month.
Acceptable Work: Considers pen & ink line drawings, oil and acrylic paintings, pastels, watercolors and mixed media; serigraphs, stone lithographs, plate lithographs, woodcuts and linocuts. Especially interested in "good design and contemporary imagery."
Tips: "I look for printmaking skills, versatility, design sense, and fresh look."

Appendix

The Business of Freelancing

As an artist, you are constantly applying your creative talents to your artwork. In order to succeed as a freelancer, you must also be creative in presenting yourself and your work to the marketplace, and you must be professional in handling the business details of freelancing. The ability to work effectively is more important now than ever because of the large number of freelance artists competing in the marketplace today; the competition is keen.

This section provides general guidelines to self-promotion, submitting your work and handling your business in a knowledgeable and professional manner.

The sample package

The first step in establishing yourself as a professional is the development of a sample package. From reading the listings in the *Artist's Market*, you have already determined where you want to sell your work. You have compiled a mailing list of names, addresses, phone numbers and contact people of your best prospects. You have also noted if the company wants to be contacted through the mail, by phone or through an agent and also what materials the art director likes to review. Now you're ready to make contact.

You'll either make contact through the mail or by phone. If calling, be pleasant and succinct. State your name and why you're calling. Keep in mind that the person at the other end of the phone is a stranger, too, and you are trying to find out as much about him as he is about you. You should follow up your call by mailing a sample.

Your initial contact through the mail will be your sample package. The main purpose of this package is to provide a concise overview of your talents. Since you know your budget, you know how ambitious you can be with your package. No matter what the size, make it visually exciting. A small coordinated brochure and résumé present a much better image than a sizable yet unimaginative package.

The contents of your promotional package can vary, but the basic components include: a cover letter, business card, samples and a self-addressed, stamped envelope (SASE). Optional materials are a brochure containing examples of your work (especially if the other samples are to be returned), a self-addressed, stamped reply card (with check-off responses to prompt action) and a résumé.

The cover letter personalizes your presentation; you're talking directly to someone about your best qualifications. What an art director wants to read is a one-page summary saying who you are, what you do, and how your work is suited to the firm. Write several versions of the letter to send to different markets. Include a request for an appointment to review your portfolio, either through the mail or in person. State that you will make a follow-up call, and be sure to do so. Remember to address the letter to a name, not a position.

A résumé lists your art-related experience, education and achievements. It spotlights your best features and your most outstanding achievements. List your professional special-

Use an up-to-date Market Directory!

1988 ARTIST'S MARKET

Order your 1989 Artist's Market NOW!

Don't let your *Artist's Market* turn old on you.

You may be reluctant to give up this copy of *Artist's Market.* After all, you would never discard an old friend.

But resist the urge to hold onto an old *Artist's Market!* Like your first portfolio or your favorite pair of jeans, the time will come when this copy of *Artist's Market* will have to be replaced.

In fact, if you're still using this *1988 Artist's Market* when the calendar reads 1989, your old friend isn't your best friend anymore. Many of the buyers listed here have moved or been promoted. Many of the addresses are now incorrect. Rates of pay have certainly changed, and even each buyer's art needs are changed from last year.

You can't afford to use an out-of-date book to plan your marketing efforts. But there's an easy way for you to stay current—order the *1989 Artist's Market.* All you have to do is complete the attached post card and return it with your payment or charge card information. Best of all, we'll send you the 1989 edition at the 1988 price—just $18.95. The *1989 Artist's Market* will be published and ready for shipment in September 1988.

Make sure you have the most current marketing information—order the new edition of *Artist's Market* now.

(See other side for more books for graphic art professionals)

To order, drop this postpaid card in the mail.

☐ YES! I want the most current edition of *Artist's Market.* Please send me the 1989 edition at the 1988 price—$18.95* (NOTE: *1989 Artist's Market* will be ready for shipment in September 1988.) #10003

☐ Also send me:

_____(30009) How to Draw & Sell Comic Strips, $18.95* (available NOW)

_____(7666) How to Draw & Sell Cartoons, $15.95* (available NOW)

_____(30005) The Complete Guide to Greeting Card Design & Illustration, $24.95* (available December 1987)

***Plus postage & handling: $2.00 for one book, 50¢ for each additional book. Ohio residents add 5½% sales tax.**

☐ Payment enclosed (Slip this card and your payment into an envelope.)

☐ Charge my: ☐ Visa ☐ MasterCard

Account #_____________________ Exp. Date __________

Signature _____________________

Name_____________________

Address_____________________

City_____________ State_____________ Zip_____________

(This offer expires August 1, 1989.)

Writer's Digest Books
1507 Dana Avenue
Cincinnati, OH 45207

2477

More books for graphic art professionals

NEW! How to Draw & Sell Comic Strips
by Alan McKenzie
McKenzie uses 180 color illustrations to show you step by step how to create both gag and story strips for newspapers and comic books. He also includes detailed advice on how to promote, copyright, and sell your comics.
144 pages/180 color illus./$18.95

How to Draw & Sell Cartoons
by Ross Thomson & Bill Hewison
Turn caricatures into checks and cartoons into cash with this complete guide (amply illustrated with the work of the world's leading cartoonists) to creating and selling all types of cartoons—political satire, visual jokes, and comic strips. A seller's guide tells you how to prepare cartoons for submission, match style to publication, and get your work published.
160 pages/32 color, 170 one & two color illus./$15.95

NEW! The Complete Guide to Greeting Card Design & Illustration
by Eva Szela
This former Hallmark design manager shows you how to create, execute, and sell designs for every greeting card style and subject using a wide variety of media and techniques.
160 pages/150 color, 54 b&w illus./$24.95

Use coupon on other side to order today!

NO POSTAGE
NECESSARY
IF MAILED
IN THE
UNITED STATES

BUSINESS REPLY MAIL

FIRST CLASS PERMIT NO. 17 CINCINNATI, OHIO

POSTAGE WILL BE PAID BY ADDRESSEE

Writer's Digest Books

1507 Dana Avenue
Cincinnati, Ohio 45207-9988

ties, such as medical illustration or airbrush work. Include both freelance and staff work that applies to the market you're contacting. Remember to list achievements in reverse chronological order.

A brochure can be a multi-purpose folder, a one-page flyer or a multi-purpose booklet. Used in your promotional package, it should provide a brief synopsis of your talents, plus a few striking examples of your work. It should never be larger than 8½x11" so it can fit easily into an art director's files. If it is to be your *only* mailing piece, it must be comprehensive in scope; it must then supply all the necessary information about your skills and successes.

A business card can be a calling card, an addendum to your package or a leave-behind after an interview. It should list your name, phone number and address plus a mention of your specialty. Use simple, clear type and standard dimensions (2x3½").

Samples are your visual candy. Samples, whether they are tear sheets, Photostats, slides, photocopies or photographs, are visual statements that best convey your style and technique. Select only the most appropriate and only the best. Many art directors claim they judge you by the worst piece they see. Gear your samples to the specific needs of the market you're approaching.

Establish a visual unity to your presentation. Each printed piece should be topped by your letterhead, which in a graphic way summarizes your specialty. Notice in the accompanying examples how the artists coordinate their mailing pieces through the use of an appropriate logo and consistent typography. Throughout the whole package, remember to use the same paper stock, typeface and color scheme to unify the graphic presentation.

Types of samples

Art directors most commonly request to see transparencies, photographs, Photostats, photocopies and tear sheets. Black-and-white work lends itself to photocopies and Photostats (produced by a photographic process utilizing paper negatives). Color work is best depicted by either photographs or transparencies (a transparency is a positive image on a translucent film base; a slide is a 35mm transparency in a mount). Transparencies reproduce a greater range of tones than any other method of printing and can be made in varying sizes (2¼x2¼", 4x5" and 8x10"). Tear sheets, which are examples of published work "torn" from a publication, can bolster your professional image and give an art director a notion of how your work appears in print. Tear sheets should be laminated to prevent tearing and folding.

Label everything. With photographs, Photostats, and photocopies, use the back to list your name, address and phone number (a pre-printed label hurries this process); arrows indicating which way is up; the size of the original; and, if submitting several, mark each "1 of 5 photographs" or "2 of 5 Photostats". These numbers may also refer to a separate information sheet which gives details of the project. If you send one, add "See info sheet" under the number.

Slides are labelled in similar fashion. On the "front" (image is correct when held up to a light), list your name, size of original work, medium, number and arrows indicating the top. If your slides are accompanied by an info sheet, indicate reference to it on the slides. Your full name, address and phone number may be printed on the reverse side.

Portfolio

You've been able to get your foot into the door with your first submission of self-promotional materials and samples. You've called to request an appointment to show your portfolio to the art director, either through the mail or in person, and he has agreed. Now is the chance to display to him the creative and professional artist you really are.

The overall appearance of the portfolio affects your professional presentation. A neat, organized three-ring binder is going to create a better impression than a bulky, time-worn leather case. The most popular portfolios are simulated leather with puncture-proof sides that allow the use of loose samples. The size of the portfolio should be dictated by the size of your

New York City illustrator Andy Lackow knows the importance of self-promotion. He developed a campaign carefully coordinated by style, typeface and message. Lackow spent over a month developing the effective logo, which is used on self-promotional pieces such as his business card (bottom left); his ad in the* Creative Black Book *(bottom right) and in the* RSVP *talent directory; and also on his stationery, address stickers and invoices. "I designed it [the logo] carefully knowing its importance in helping establish my name and image in the field." Lackow also uses his talent directory ads as mailers and drop-off pieces. He bought a mailing list (names and addresses) of 2,500 art directors in New York, Chicago and Los Angeles and sent them the calendar mailer.

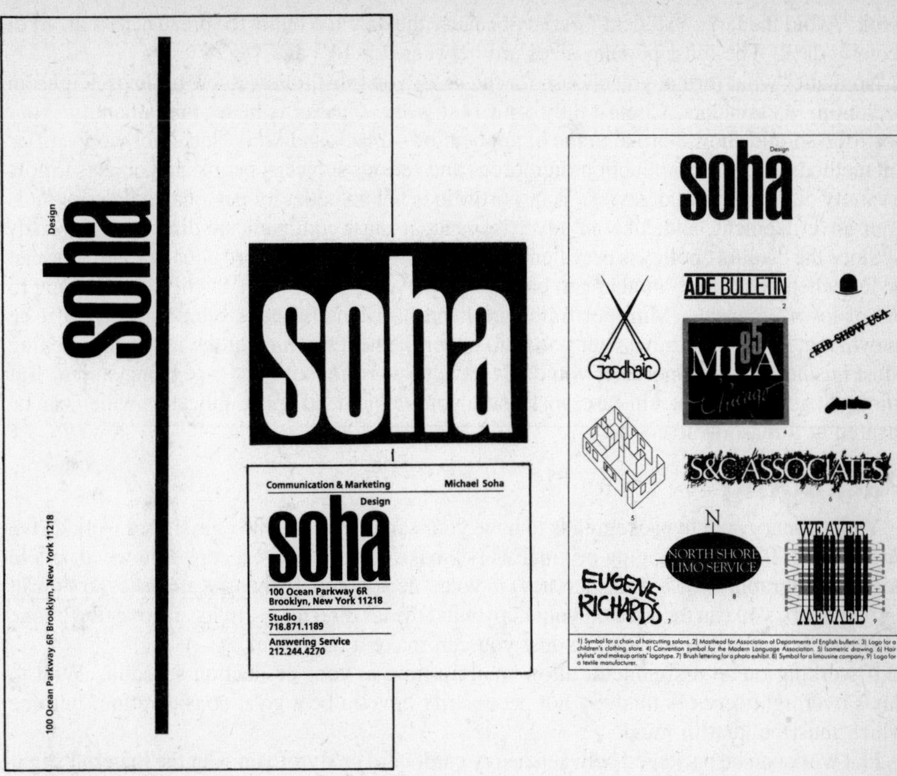

Design
soha

Job #
Project:
☐ Production Schedule
☐ Job Specifications

29 Greene Street New York, New York 10013 212.431.8442

Client:

Printing Instructions

Quantity:
Trim Size:
Fold:
Colors:
Stock:
Halftones:

Special Instructions:

Miscellaneous:

Delivery Date:
Estimate:

☐ For reproduction purposes only.
☐ Artwork cannot be altered or retouched.

Printer

Delivery Instructions

Billing Instructions

Return Mechanical and Artwork to:

Designer Michael Soha of New York City used his own artistic talents to promote himself through the creation of a distinctive design for his logo. "Like most designers, I have had many logos. This one took a year to develop. I wanted something that was professional, simple, flexible and easy to use." With this simple design, he achieves variety by printing his materials on eight different colors of paper. "I can color code projects and also have some variety." Note how his logo works with other logos in his RSVP ad (top right).

work. Avoid the large "student" variety because they are too bulky to spread across an art director's desk. The most popular sizes are between 11x14" and 18x24".

No matter what format you choose for the case, you must follow a few basic principles in presenting its contents. Choose only your best work. Quality is better than quantity. Your portfolio should show a broad range of application—black-and-white and color work, different methods of print reproduction, humorous and serious subjects, people and objects. Show a variety of jobs but not of styles. Your portfolio is not an outlet for personal expression; it is your advertisement, and, like an advertisement, it must communicate directly and swiftly.

Since the drop-off policy is prevalent, have at least two or three portfolios at hand. One can be left when necessary, another can be used on personal calls, while the third can be sent to out-of-town prospects. Mini-portfolios are handy for simultaneous submissions. Let it be known that you will retrieve your portfolio either the next morning or the following evening. Most businesses are honorable; you don't have to worry about your case being stolen. But things do get lost, so, just in case, make sure you've included only duplicates, which can be insured at a reasonable cost.

Packaging

Your primary goal in packaging is to have your samples, portfolio or assigned work arrive undamaged. Before packaging original work, make sure you have a copy (photostat, photocopy, photograph, slide or transparency) in your file at home. If changes are necessary on an assigned job, you can then see on your copy what the art director is discussing over the phone. Most importantly, if your work is lost you can make a duplicate.

If working on an assignment, allow mailing time in your production schedule. With today's overnight services this will not necessarily have to be a great consideration, but one which must be kept in mind.

Flat work can be packaged between heavy cardboard or styrofoam. Cut the material slightly larger than the piece of flatwork and tape it closed. It is wise to include your business card or a piece of paper with your name and address on it on the outside of this packaging material in case the outer wrapper becomes separated from the inner packing. The work at least can then be returned to you.

The outer wrapping, depending on package size and quality of inner wrapping, may be a manila envelope, a foam-padded envelope, a "bubble" envelope (one with plastic "bubbles" lining the inside), or brown wrapping paper. Use reinforced tape for closures. Make sure one side is clearly addressed.

Check the various types of envelopes and packaging materials available at your local art supply, photography or stationery stores. Don't miss the opportunity to buy in bulk quantities if you are going to be doing a lot of mailing. The price is always lower.

Mailing

Become familiar with the types of mailing available. Your local post office has an information number for your questions and will be glad to provide you with the information you need. Keep in mind that postal rates will be changing this year.

The U.S. Post Office mail classifications with which you will be most concerned are First Class and Fourth Class, more commonly called parcel post.

First Class mail is the type used every day for letters, etc. If the piece you are mailing is not the usual letter size, make sure to mark it First Class. Fourth Class is used for packages weighing 1-70 pounds and not more than 108 inches in length and girth combined.

The greatest disadvantage to using these classes of mail is that you cannot be guaranteed when the package/letter will arrive. If time is important to you, consider the special services the post office offers, such as, Priority Mail, Express Mail Next Day Service, and Special Delivery.

Certified mail includes a mailing receipt and provides a record of delivery at the addressee's post office. This type of mail is handled like ordinary mail, but you can request a return receipt on certain types of mail as your proof of delivery.

The post office offers insurance for a nominal cost.

United Parcel Service (UPS) will accept packages up to 70 pounds in weight and 108" length and girth combined. Cost is determined by weight, size and destination of the package and automatically includes insurance up to $100. You can purchase additional insurance.

UPS does have wrapping restrictions. Packages must be in heavy corrugated cardboard, with no string or paper on the outside, and be sealed with reinforced tape. UPS cannot guarantee how long it will take a package to arrive at its destination, but will track lost packages. It also offers Two-Day Blue Label Air Service to any destination in the U.S., and Next Day Service in specific zip code zones. Check locally to see if Next Day Service is available for your package. There is an additional charge for these services and for package pickup.

Today there is a growing number of airfreight services which make overnight delivery common. Check to see which ones are available in your area, but some of the more familiar names are Emery, Purolator and Federal Express. These firms offer varying rates according to weight of the package and urgency.

If you will be airfreighting large numbers of works or portfolios, it is advisable to set up an account. Most have priority service which offers overnight delivery direct to the client, or regular service which is delivery within two days. Some companies offer both an airfreight service and a ground courier service. The advantages of airfreight are the guaranteed delivery time and efficiency in tracking missing packages. The cost reflects these added services.

Greyhound Bus Lines and some commercial airlines also offer same-day or overnight package delivery. Check locally for rates and restrictions.

Copyright

A copyright gives the creator the right to control the usage of his work. Copyright protection prevents unauthorized use, copying, selling or other infringements on your work of art. The copyright law gives you the right to print, reprint and copy the work, and so to sell or distribute copies of the work.

The minute you finish a piece of artwork, you own the copyright, whether you put a copyright notice on it or not. The copyright notice is a *c* with a circle around it (©), followed by the year, date and your name or an abbreviation by which your name can be recognized. You can place the copyright notice on any accessible place, such as the back of a framed piece, but the front is preferable for graphic art. Definitely have your copyright notice on any work you are submitting to a noncopyrighted publication. Under the current law it is still best to protect yourself by placing a copyright notice on your work as soon as it is created. As this book goes to press, an amendment to the Copyright Law is being considered which would eliminate the need for copyright notice. The anticipated changes may take effect sometime in 1988.

Your work is also copyrighted whether you register it or not. You do not have to register your work with the U.S. Copyright Office until an infringement takes place. However, if you want to collect damages and attorney's fees, you have to register it within three months of publication. To register your work, write to the U.S. Copyright Office, Library of Congress, Washington, DC 20559. You will be asked to complete the appropriate forms (Form VA is for material in the Visual Arts) and send them with the required fee ($10 per individual published piece or for a group of unpublished pieces) and copies or photos of your work. You will receive a certificate of registration which offers you more indepth protection than the copyright notice alone, if you anticipate legal problems. You can also write and request the Copyright Information Kit, which explains copyright in more detail.

Protection for copyrights obtained after 1978 lasts for the life of the artist plus 50 years; those obtained before 1978 last for 28 years, or 56 years if renewed, or a maximum of 75 years depending on when they were renewed.

There are two exceptions to owning the copyright to a work from the moment of its creation. They are when you create work as part of your fulltime employment for someone else or when you agree to "work-for-hire," i.e. you're working for a client as if you are a fulltime employee. Then you own neither the copyright nor any of the reproduction rights to your work. Opposition by artists to work-for-hire is growing nationwide. Contact your state art council, national art organizations, and state and federal legislators to determine what legislation is being considered to change work-for-hire.

Remember that the copyright and ownership of the art are two separate entities. Selling the copyright does not transfer ownership of the piece to the client unless it is specified in a contract. Nor does selling the physical artwork transfer any rights of copyright to the purchaser.

To receive a free guideline on copyright regulations and procedures for cartoons and comic strips, write for Circular R44, Information & Publication Section LM-455, U.S. Copyright Office, Library of Congress, Washington, DC 20559.

An Artist's Handbook on Copyright is available for $6.95 (price includes postage and handling) from the Georgia Volunteer Lawyers for the Arts, Inc., Plaza Level 16, 42 Spring St., SW, Atlanta GA 30302.

Reproduction rights

Your copyright is a "bundle" of rights. As creator you possess all rights, and therefore you can sell your work as many times and ways as you see fit. When someone buys "rights" to your work, they are buying the right to reproduce your work for a certain duration of time. Unless all rights are purchased, the artwork will be *temporarily* given to the client in order to make reproductions; the artwork must be returned unless otherwise specified. Once the buyer has used the rights he purchased, he has no further claim to your work. If he wants to use it a second or third time, he must pay additional fees for that privilege.

If you sell first reproduction rights, you are giving the art buyer the right to reproduce your work once and be the first to use it. You cannot sell first rights to two buyers—each cannot be "first." This differs from one-time rights, which give one art buyer the right to reproduce your work once, but he does not have to be first. When you sell all reproduction rights, you are essentially allowing the buyer to reproduce the work as many times and in any way he wishes.

The more rights you sell to one client, the more money you should receive. Negotiate this upfront with the art buyer *before* an agreement is signed. Try to ascertain how the work will be used so that you will not relinquish too many rights. For example, a publisher may ask for all rights but may actually only need First North American serial rights, (first rights covering publication in the United States and Canada). Your immediate compensation may be less, but once he has published it, you can sell the use of the artwork to other buyers which you could not do if the publisher owned all rights.

Contact the Graphic Artists Guild (30 E. 20th St., New York NY 10003) or other professional organizations for guidance in the areas of copyright and contracts. For further information, consult the *Legal Guide for the Visual Artist* by Tad Crawford (Madison Square Press), *Selling Your Graphic Design & Illustration* (St. Martin's Press), and *The Graphic Artists Guild Handbook: Pricing and Ethical Guidelines*, available from the Graphic Artists Guild.

Recordkeeping

The IRS doesn't rely on an art critic to assess your professional status. It examines your business records. Recordkeeping is usually considered a drudgery by artists, yet it is an essential part of your business. A freelancer is an independent businessperson and, like any other entrepreneur, must be accountable for financial statements.

In your records, you must keep detailed accounts of sales and expenses plus proofs of these transactions. Your records do not have to be an elaborate setup of ledgers. A relatively simple form of bookkeeping is the single-entry system. With this system, records of income or *accounts receivable* (money paid or owed you for work you have created) and *accounts payable* (expenses for supplies, studio rent, overhead expenses) are shown on the same page. Whenever you receive income or pay for expenses, either by check or cash, an entry is made on the journal page. Under accounts receivable, set aside areas for listing each project completed; the date it was completed; to whom it was delivered; the delivery date; the price of the job; the amount you received; the date you received it and any further remarks you think are necessary, such as rights sold. The accounts payable section should include entries for work supplies purchased, the quantity, the cost, the date of the bill, the amount you paid, the date you paid it and any further remarks necessary.

Begin to develop standard business practices. Save all bills and receipts. Ask for a receipt with every purchase. If you're entertaining a client at a business dinner, ask the waiter or cashier for a receipt. Keep a record of the date, place, cost, business relationship and the purpose of the meeting. Don't forget to record driving expenses. Even if you are not sure in some cases if a particular expense qualifies as a business-related tax deduction, obtain a receipt or bill. A tax advisor can clarify it for you later, and it is always better to be safe than sorry.

If possible, keep a separate checking account for business expenses. Cancelled checks not only help keep accurate records but serve as evidence if a payment is challenged.

If your business is very complex, you can have books set up for you by an accountant and continue the recordkeeping yourself. Retain your business records for at least four years.

Developing a file for each job is a good way to keep track of expenses. Drop in all related receipts and you can then determine if your fee was sufficient to cover these expenses and give you a profit. When preparing an invoice, you will have all pertinent material in one place. By placing a copy of the invoice in the job file as well as records of payment, you can keep track of billing.

Income tax

Knowing what income you must report and what deductions you can claim are the two most important factors in computing your taxes. To know these factors, you must first determine whether you are a professional or a hobbyist. You must prove you are a professional in order to claim business-related deductions which reduce the amount of taxable income you have to report.

Some of the factors which set you apart as a professional are: conducting your activity in a business-like manner (such as keeping accurate records, having business cards and keeping a business checking account); your expertise and training; the time you devote to your work and if you have no other substantial source of income, and your history of income or losses. In the past, a professional had to show two out of three years of profit. Now, under the Tax Reform Act of 1986, you must show a profit for three out of five years to attain a professional status.

As a professional who is the owner of an unincorporated business, you must report business expenses and income on Schedule C of Form 1040, Profit (or Loss) from Business or Profession. The Reform Act has eliminated or limits the deductibility of many items that were previously allowed. Only 80 percent of your business meals, entertainment, tips, cover charges, parking and related expenses are deductible. Home office expenses are now deductible to the extent of net income from self-employment. Income averaging, which helped taxpayers with income that fluctuated widely from year to year, has been abolished. That also goes for the 10-percent credit for purchases of business equipment. Estimated tax payments must now be at least 90 percent of your current tax liability. The IRS's *Publication 553* (Highlights) covers the details (such as what items are 80% deductible) entailed in the Reform Act.

Depending on the complexity of your business and tax expertise, you may want to have a professional tax advisor to consult with or to complete your tax form. Most IRS offices have walk-in centers open year-round and offer over 90 free IRS publications containing tax information to help in preparation of your return. The booklet that comes with your tax return forms contains names and addresses of Forms Distribution Centers by region where you can write for further information. The U.S. Small Business Administration offers seminars on taxes, and arts organizations hold many workshops covering business management, often including detailed tax information. Inquire at your arts council, local arts organization or a nearby college/university to see if a workshop is scheduled.

You will be asked to provide your Social Security number or your Employer Identification number (if you are a business) to the person/firm for whom you are doing a freelance project. This information is now necessary in order to make payments.

Home office deduction

A home office deduction allows you to claim a business portion of the expenses incurred for the upkeep and running of your entire home. You may deduct business expenses that apply to a part of your home only if that part is used exclusively on a regular basis as your principal place of business at which you meet or deal with clients, or a separate structure used in your trade or business that is not attached to your residence. Your office must be a space devoted only to your artwork and its business activity.

The taxpayer with more than one business can claim a principal place of business for each and claim a deduction for the studio at home. The factors considered by the IRS are the amount of income produced, the amount of time spent there and the nature of the facility. In some areas of the country, a studio can even share the same space with a nonbusiness use if a clearly defined area is used exclusively for business.

When a studio is part of the principal residence, deductions are possible on an appropriate portion of mortgage interest, property taxes, rent, repair and utility bills, and depreciation.

There are two ways to determine what percentage of your home is used for business purposes. If the rooms in the house are approximately the same size, divide the number of rooms used as your office into the total number of rooms in your house. If your rooms differ in size, divide the square footage of your business area into the total square footage of your house.

Consult a tax advisor to be certain you meet all of the requirements before attempting to take this deduction since its requirements and interpretations frequently change.

Sales tax

Check regarding your state's regulations on sales tax. Some states claim that "creativity" and a service rendered cannot be taxed while others view it as a product you are selling and therefore taxable. Be certain you understand the sales tax laws to avoid being held liable for uncollected money at tax time. Write to your state auditor for sales tax information.

On your federal tax form, remember that sales taxes may no longer be deducted.

Artist's Resource List

The section introductions in this directory recommend the following additional reading material and/or names and addresses of art buyers. Most are available either in a library or bookstore or from the publisher. To insure accurate names and addresses, use copies of these resources that are no older than a year.

AIA Journal
The American Institute of Architects, 457 Madison Ave., New York NY 10022

Advertising Age
740 Rush St., Chicago IL 60611

Adweek
A/S/M Communications, Inc., 49 E. 21st St., New York NY 10010

American Art Directory
R.R. Bowker Company, 245 W. 17th St., New York NY 10011

American Showcase
American Showcase, Inc., 724 Fifth Ave., New York NY 10019

American Theatre Association Directory
6th floor, 1010 Wisconsin Ave. NW, Washington DC 20007

Architectural Digest
Knapp Communications Corp., 5900 Wilshire Blvd., Los Angeles CA 90036

Architectural Record
McGraw-Hill Inc., 1221 Avenue of the Americas, New York NY 10020

The Art and Craft of Greeting Cards
(by Susan Evarts), North Light Publishing, 1507 Dana Ave., Cincinnati OH 45207

Art Business News
Myers Publishing Co., 60 Ridgeway Plaza, Stamford CT 06905

Art Directors Annual
Art Directors Club, 250 Park Ave. S., New York NY 10003

Audio Video Market Place
R.R. Bowker Company, 245 W. 17th St., New York NY 10011

Barron's Profiles of American Colleges
Barron's Educational Series, Inc., 113 Crossways Park Dr., Woodbury NY 11797

Better Homes & Gardens
Meredith Corporation, 1716 Locust St., Des Moines IA 50336

Billboard International Buyer's Guide
Affiliated Publications, 1515 Broadway, New York NY 10035

Books In Print
(vol. 4), R.R. Bowker Company, 245 W. 17th St., New York NY 10011

Cartoon World
Box 30367, Lincoln, NE 68503

Chicago Creative Directory
333 N. Michigan Ave., Chicago IL 60601

Collector's Mart
WEB Publications, Inc., 15100 W. Kellogg, Wichita KS 67235

Comparative Guide to American Colleges
Harper & Row, 10 E. 53rd St., New York NY 10022

Creative Black Book
Creative Black Book, 401 Park Ave. S., New York NY 10016

Creative Source
Wilcord Publications Ltd., Suite 200, 206 Laird Dr., Toronto Ontario M4G 3W5

Dancemagazine
Dance Magazine Inc., 33 W. 60th St., New York NY 10036

Decor
Source List, Commerce Publishing Co., 408 Olive St., St. Louis MO 63102

The Design Directory
Wefler & Associates, Inc., Box 1591, Evanston IL 60204

Designing Greeting Cards and Paper Products
(by Ron Lister), Prentice-Hall, Inc., Englewood Cliffs NJ 07632

Directory of Directories
Gale Research Co., Book Tower, Detroit MI 48226

Editor & Publisher
The Editor & Publisher Co. Inc., 11 W. 19th St., New York NY 10011

Editor & Publisher's Syndicate Directory
The Editor & Publisher Co. Inc., 11 W. 19th St., New York NY 10011

Encyclopedia of Associations
Gale Research Co., Book Tower, Detroit MI 48226

Gebbie Press All-In-One-Directory
Gebbie Press, Box 1000, New Paltz NY 12561

Gifts and Decorative Accessories
Geyer-McAllister Publications, 51 Madison Ave., New York NY 10010. (Buyer's guide and December issue)

Graphic Artists Guild Directory
Graphic Artists Guild, 30 E. 20th St., New York NY 10003

Graphic Artists Guild Handbook: Pricing & Ethical Guidelines
Robert Silver Associates, 95 Madison Ave., New York NY 10016

Greetings Magazine
MacKay Publishing Corp., 309 Fifth Ave., New York NY 10016

Homesewing Trade News
Homesewing Trade News, Inc., 330 Sunrise Hwy., Box 286, Rockville Centre NY 11571

House and Garden
The Conde Nast Publications, Inc., Conde Nast Bldg., 350 Madison Ave., New York NY 10017

House Beautiful
Hearst Corporation, 1700 Broadway, New York NY 10019

How to Make Money in Newspaper Syndication
(by Susan Lane), Newspaper Syndication Specialists, Suite 326, Box 19654, Irvine, CA 92720

Interior Design
475 Park Ave. S., New York NY 10016

Internal Publications Directory
National Research Bureau, Suite 1150, 310 S. Michigan Ave., Chicago IL 60604

International Directory of Little Magazines and Small Presses
Dustbooks, Box 100, Paradise CA 95969

Legal Guide for the Visual Artist
E.P. Dutton, Two Park Ave., New York NY 10016

Literary Market Place
R.R. Bowker Company, 245 W. 17th St., New York NY 10011

Madison Avenue Handbook
Peter Glenn Publications, 17 E. 48th St., New York NY 10017

Magazine Industry Market Place
R.R. Bowker Company, 245 E. 17th St., New York NY 10011

Medical Marketing & Media
CPS Communications, Inc., Suite 215, 7200 W. Camino Real, Boca Raton FL 33431. December issue

Musical America Directory
Clasical Artists International, Suite 901, 1995 Broadway, New York NY 10023

The Newsletter Directory
Gale Research Co., Suite 300, 8800 Hwy. 7, Minneapolis MN 55426

O'Dwyer's Directory of Public Relations Firms
J.R. O'Dwyer Company, Inc., 271 Madison Ave., New York NY 10016

Plate World
Plate World Inc., 9200 N. Maryland Ave., Niles IL 60648

ProFile
Archimedia, Box 4403, Topeka KS 66604

Publishers Weekly
205 W. 42nd St., New York NY 10017

Selling Your Graphic Design & Illustration
St. Martin's Press, 175 Fifth Ave., New York NY 10010

Songwriter's Market
Writer's Digest Books, 1507 Dana Ave. Cincinnati OH 45207

Standard Directory of Advertising Agencies
National Register Publishing Co., Inc., 3004 Glenview Rd., Wilmette IL 60091

Standard Periodical Directory
Oxbridge Communications, Inc., Room 301, 150 Fifth Ave., New York NY 10011

Standard Rate and Data Service
3004 Glenview Rd., Wilmette IL 60091. (Consumer magazine volume)

Summer Theatre Directory
Leo Shull Publications, 1501 Broadway, New York NY 10036

Theatre Profiles
Theatre Communications Group, Inc., 355 Lexington Ave., New York NY 10017

Thomas Register of Manufacturers
Thomas Publishing Co., 1 Penn Plaza, New York NY 10001

Ulrich's International Periodicals Directory
R.R. Bowker Company, 245 W. 17th St., New York NY 10011

Visual Merchandising & Store Design
Signs of the Times Publishing Company, 407 Gilbert Ave., Cincinnati OH 45202

W
Fairchild Publications, 7 E. 12th St., New York NY 10003

Women's Wear Daily
Fairchild Publications, 7 E. 12th St., New York NY 10003

The Work Book
Scott & Daughters Publishing, #204, 1545 Wilcox Ave., Los Angeles CA 90028

Working Press of the Nation
National Research Bureau, Suite 1150, 310 S. Michigan Ave., Chicago IL 60604

Writer's Market
Writer's Digest Books, 1507 Dana Ave., Cincinnati OH 45207

Glossary

Acceptance (payment on). The artist is paid for his work as soon as the buyer decides to use it.
Airbrush. Small pencil-shaped pressure gun used to spray ink, paint or dyes to obtain graduated tonal effects.
Architectural delineator. An illustrator who sketches preliminary ideas for a presentation to a client.
ASAP. Abbreviation for as soon as possible.
Ben-day. An artificial process of shading line illustrations, named after its inventor.
Biennially. Once every two years.
Bimonthly. Once every two months.
Biweekly. Once every two weeks.
Bleed. Area of a plate or print that extends (bleeds off) beyond the edge of trimmed sheet.
Buy-out. The sale of all reproduction rights, and sometimes the original work, by the artist; also subcontracted portions of a job resold at a cost or profit to the end client by the artist.
Calligraphy. The art of fine handwriting.
Camera-ready. Art that is completely prepared for copy camera platemaking.
Cel art. Artwork applied to plastic film, especially used in animation; also an abbreviation for artwork on celluloid.
Cibachrome. Trade mark for a full color positive print made from a transparency.
Collaterals. Accompanying or auxiliary pieces, especially in advertising.
Collotype. A screenless, flat, printing process in which plates are coated with gelatin, exposed to continuous-tone negatives and printed on lithographic presses.
Color separation. Photographic process of separating any multi-color image into its primary component parts (cyan, magenta, yellow and black) for printing.
Commission. 1. Percentage of retail price taken by a sponsor/salesman on artwork sold. 2. Assignment given to an artist.
Compact disc. A small disc, about 4.7'' in diameter, which contains digitized music that is incorporated as miscroscopic pits in the aluminum base. Also called digital audio discs.
Comprehensive. Complete sketch of layout showing how a finished illustration will look when printed; also called a comp.
Direct-mail package. Sales or promotional material that is distributed by mail. Usually consists of an outer envelope, a cover letter, brochure or flyer, SASE, and postpaid reply card, or order form with business reply envelope.
Edition. The total number of prints published of one piece of art.
Elhi. Abbreviation for elementary/high school.
Etching. A print made by the intaglio process, creating a design in the surface of a metal or other plate with a needle and using a mordant to bite out the design.
Gouache. Opaque watercolor with definite, appreciable film thickness and an actual paint layer.
Gagline. The words printed, usually directly beneath, a cartoon; also called a caption.
Halftone. Reproduction of a continuous tone illustration with the image formed by dots produced by a camera lens screen.
IRC. International Reply Coupon; purchased at the post office to enclose with artwork sent to a foreign buyer to cover his postage cost when replying.
Keyline. Identification, through signs and symbols, of the positions of illustrations and copy for the printer.
Kill fee. Portion of the agreed-upon price the artist receives for a job that was assigned, started, but then canceled.
Layout. Arrangement of photographs, illustrations, text and headlines for printed material.
Light table. Table with a light source beneath a glass top; especially useful in transferring art by tracing.
Line drawing. Illustration done with pencil or ink using no wash or other shading.
Lithography. Printing process based on a design made with a greasy substance on a limestone slab or metal plate and chemically treated so image areas take ink and non-image areas repel ink; during printing, non-image areas are kept wet with water.
Logotype. Name or design of a company or product used as a trademark on letterheads, direct mail packages, in advertising, etc., to establish visual identity; also called logo.
Mechanicals. Paste-up or preparation of work for printing.
Ms, mss. Abbreviation for manuscript(s).

Offset. Printing process in which a flat printing plate is treated to be ink-receptive in image areas and ink-repellent in non-image areas. Ink is transferred from the printing plate to a rubber plate, and then to the paper.
Overlay. Transparent cover over copy, where instructions, corrections or color location directions are given.
Panel. In cartooning, refers to the number of boxed-in illustrations, i.e. single panel, double panel or multi-panel.
Paste-up. Procedure involving coating the backside of art, type, photostats, etc., with rubber cement or wax and adhering them in their proper positions to the mechanical board. The boards are then used as finished art by the printer.
Perspective. The ability to see objects in relation to their relative positions and distance, and depict the volume and spatial relationships on paper.
Photostat. Black-and-white copies produced by an inexpensive photographic process using paper negatives; only line values are held with accuracy. Also called stat.
Pin registration. The use of highly accurate holes and special pins on copy, film, plates and presses to insure proper positioning and alignment of colors.
PMT. Photostat produced without a negative, somewhat like the Polaroid process.
P-O-P. Point-of-purchase; a display device or structure located with the product in or at the retail outlet to advertise or hold the product to increase sales.
Publication (payment on). The artist is paid for his work when it is published.
Query. Letter of inquiry to an editor or buyer eliciting his interest in a work you want to do or sell.
Rendering. A drawn representation of a building, interior, etc., in perspective.
Roughs. Preliminary sketches or drawings.
Royalty. An agreed percentage paid by the publisher to the artist for each copy of his work sold.
SASE. Abbreviation for self-addressed, stamped envelope.
Semiannual. Once every six months.
Semimonthly. Once every two weeks.
Semiweekly. Twice a week.
Serigraph. Silkscreen; stencil method of printing involving a stencil adhered to a fine mesh cloth and stretched tightly over a wooden frame. Paint is forced through the holes of the screen not blocked by the stencil.
Simultaneous submissions. Submission of the same artwork to more than one potential buyer at the same time.
Speculation. Creating artwork with no assurance that the buyer will purchase it or reimburse expenses in any way, as opposed to creating artwork on assignment.
Spot drawing. Small illustration used to decorate or enhance a page of type, or to serve as a column ending.
Storyboard. Series of panels which illustrates a progressive sequence of graphics and story copy for a TV commercial, film or filmstrip. Serves as a guide for the eventual finished product.
Tabloid. Publication where an ordinary newspaper page is turned sideways.
Tear sheet. Published page containing an artist's illustration, cartoon, design or photograph.
Template. Plastic stencil containing various sizes of commonly used shapes, symbols or letters which can be traced one at a time.
Thumbnail. A rough layout in miniature.
Transparency. A photographic positive film such as a color slide.
Type spec. Type specification; determination of the size and style of type to be used in a layout.
UPS. Universal Postal Union, a coupon for return of first-class surface letters.
Velox. Photoprint of a continuous tone subject that has been transformed into line art by means of a halftone screen.
Video. General category comprised of videocassettes and videotapes.
Wash. Thin application of transparent color, or watercolor black, for a pastel or gray tonal effect.

Index

B

Boston Magazine 337
Boston Phoenix, The 462
Boston Review, The 462
Bosustow Video 29
Both Sides Now 337
Bouquet-Orchid Enterprises 516
Bow & Arrow Magazine 338
Bowhunter 338
Bowlers Journal 338
Bowling Digest 338
Bowling Green University Popular Press 200
Bowyer Associates, Inc. 130
Bozell Jacobs Kenyon & Eckhardt 95

N

Q

R

S

W

X Y Z